Glencoe

Mathematics

for Business and Personal Finance

COVER: Blend Images/Getty Images

MHEonline.com

Send inquiries to:
McGraw-Hill Education
8787 Orion Place
Columbus, OH 43240

ISBN: 978-0-02-140096-6
MHID: 0-02-140096-2

Printed in the United States of America

1 2 3 4 5 6 7 8 9 DOW 22 21 20 19 18 17 16 15

Authors

Walter H. Lange is a professor of mathematics at the University of Toledo in the College of Arts & Sciences.

Temoleon G. Rousos is a professor emeritus of mathematics at the University of Toledo in the College of Arts & Sciences.

Glencoe/McGraw-Hill Business and Career Education Industry Advisory Board

Educational Reviewers

We wish to acknowledge the contributions of the following reviewers:

Carol K. Bartz
Beach High School
Beach, ND

Stephanie Bennett
Stillwater High School
Lafayette, LA

Sarah Britton
Sullivan High School
Sullivan, IL

Mrs. Ann Cheman
Seneca Valley Senior High School
Harmony, PA

Christopher S. Cheske
Two Rivers High School
Two Rivers, WI

Dianne Cole
Valley Charter High School
Modesto, CA

Linda Dills
Chaparral High School
Anthony, KS

Debbra Finney
Valley Charter High School
Modesto, CA

Ms. Jackie Floetke
Wilson Creek High School
Wilson Creek, WA

Mr. John Gard
Lakeworth High School
Lake Worth, FL

Mr. Jeff Gatlin
Woodland Park High School
Woodland Park, CO

Louanna Goodrich
Eastern Howard School Corporation
Greentown, IN

Jim Keefe
Aurora Central High School
Aurora, CO

Cindy Kemp
Henry Foss High School
Tacoma, WA

Jeff Koenig
Stanley-Boyd High School
Stanley, WI

Renee Marchese
Craig High School
Janesville, WI

Andrea Martin
Business Teacher
Easton, MD

Mrs. Kristi Mayo
Manzanola Jr/Sr High School
Manzanola, CO

James A. Michaelian
School of International Business
San Diego, CA

Todd Otake
Laupahoehoe High and
Elementary School
Laupahoehoe, HI

Lisa Perry
Blair-Taylor High School
Blair, WI

Paula Prior
Chilton I.S.D.
Chilton, TX

Mr. Davlon J. Rost
Kaplan High School
Kaplan, LA

Linda C. Roybal
Two Rivers High School
Ogden, UT

Kim Saville
Compass High School
Grandview, WA

Cheryl A. Stanley
Jackson Heights High School
Holton, KS

Katherine Tomasek
East Hartford High School
East Hartford, CT

Gayle E. Topp
Homestead High School
Fort Wayne, IN

Theresa Twaddle
Avon High School
Avon, IL

Joyce Walsh-Portillo
Broward Community College
Davie, FL

Kathy Whiting
Glenwood Springs High School
Glenwood Springs, CO

UNIT  Basic Math Skills: Workshops 2

UNIT 2 Managing Your Money 92

Purestock/SuperStock

UNIT 3 Managing Your Expenses 250

UNIT 4 Making Financial Decisions 336

OJO Images/SuperStock

UNIT 6 Managing Business Finances 626

CHAPTER 17 Services 628

CHAPTER 18 Accounting 656

CHAPTER 19 Financial Management 704

Your Reference Files 738

SKILLS FILE

APPLICATIONS FILE

Basic Math Skills: Workshops

Explore the Photo

Self Exploration
The first step in finding a career is thinking about your own interests, skills, likes, and dislikes. *What are your work-related interests?*

The Big Picture

Dream Jobs

The figure below shows some of the most desirable employers in the United States.

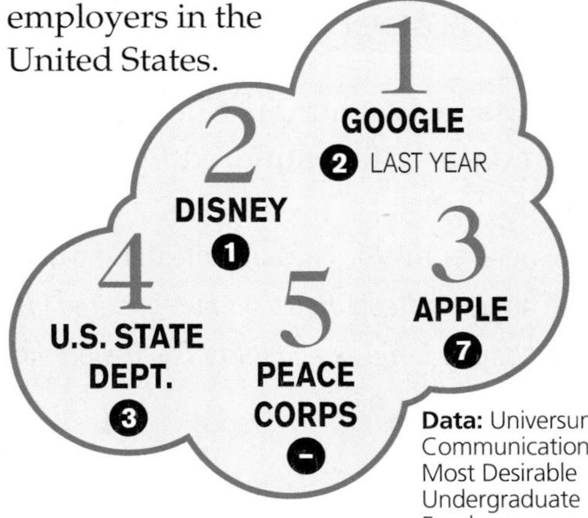

Data: Universum Communications, Most Desirable Undergraduate Employer survey

Go to **connectED.mcgraw-hill.com** for the Unit 1 WebQuest activity. You will complete a self-evaluation and discover your work-related interests, talents, and values.

Thematic Project Preview

Career Exploration

When it comes to the world of work, the possibilities are endless. With every new technology that changes how we work, play, and communicate, new career opportunities are created. With so many choices available to you, it is never too soon to start exploring your options. What will bring you the most satisfaction in your career? This Unit Thematic Project will help you take the first steps in finding the right career.

Pre-Project Checklist

As you read this unit, use this checklist to prepare for the unit project:

- ✓ Think about your unique skills, interests, and values.
- ✓ Interview people who work in a career field that you find intriguing.
- ✓ Summarize the advantages and challenges each career choice presents to you.

WORKSHOP 1

Writing and Reading Numbers

Need Help? Go to...
Skill 1: Numbers, p. SK1–SK2

Writing Numbers The number system you use is based on *tens* and has ten digits that you use to write the numbers. Use the ten digits 1, 2, 3, 4, 5, 6, 7, 8, 9, and 0 and a decimal point to write any number.

EXAMPLE 1

Write the following using digits:

a. Twenty-one
b. Fifteen thousand four hundred fifty-six
c. Forty-six and thirty-five hundredths

Read the number and write it.

a. Read the number *twenty-one* but write it using digits as **21.**
b. Read the number *fifteen thousand four hundred fifty-six* but write it as **15,456.**
c. Read the number *forty-six and thirty-five hundredths* but write it as **46.35.**

Place Value You read numbers from *left to right.* However, you usually learn the names of the place values from *right to left.* The place-value chart shows the place of each digit in the number 5,647,210.392. A decimal point separates the whole numbers (to the left of the decimal point) and the decimal numbers (to the right of the decimal point). The place-value chart can help you write numbers. The whole-number part is separated into groups of three digits with a comma. The name of each group is used to read the number.

Figure W1.1

Millions		Thousands			Hundreds				Decimals		
Ten Millions	Millions	Hundred Thousands	Ten Thousands	Thousands	Hundreds	Tens	Ones	Decimal	Tenths	Hundredths	Thousandths
	5	6	4	7	2	1	0	.	3	9	2
					← Whole Numbers				Decimals →		

EXAMPLE 2

Give the place value for each of the following:

a. The digit 5 **b.** The digit 7 **c.** The digit 3 **d.** The digit 9

Find the place value for the given digit.

a. The digit 5 is in the **millions place.**
b. The digit 7 is in the **thousands place.**
c. The digit 3 is in the **tenths place.**
d. The digit 9 is in the **hundredths place.**

Reading and Writing Whole Numbers and Decimals Here are some ways to read and write numbers:

	Whole Numbers	Decimals
Standard Form	5,647,210	0.392
Word Form	five million six hundred forty-seven thousand two hundred ten	three hundred ninety-two thousandths
Short Word Form	5 million, 647 thousand, 210	392 thousandths
Expanded Form	5,000,000 + 600,000 + 40,000 + 7,000 + 200 + 10	0.3 + 0.09 + 0.002
***Point* Form**	five six four seven two one zero point	zero point three nine two

[Note: The point form is used when you proofread a business document and want to stress the placement of the "decimal point."]

Concept CHECK

Complete the problems. Check your answers in the back of the book. On a separate piece of paper, fill in the blank.

1. Read the number *twenty-four thousand three hundred sixty-six* but write it as ___________.
2. Read the number *four hundred thirty-six and seven hundred eighty-five thousandths* but write it as ___________.
3. (Refer to Figure W1.1 for this question.) The digit 2 is in the _________ place and the _________ place.
4. Write 5 thousand, 456 and 68 hundredths in standard form, word form, and point form.
5. Write 50 + 6 + 0.8 + 0.01 + 0.007 in standard form, word form, and point form.
6. Write $875.48 in word form.

Practice

Use the number 98,045,132.706 to fill in the blanks.

7. The digit 8 is in the _________ place.
8. The digit 1 is in the _________ place.

Write each number in word form and short form.

9. 543,698
10. 45,987,159.9

Write each number in standard form and word form.

11. 654 thousand, 321
12. five six point nine nine

Write each number in expanded form.

13. 4,678
14. 98,438

WORKSHOPS

WORKSHOP 2

Rounding Numbers

Need Help? Go to...
Skill 2: Rounding Numbers, p. SK3

Place Value The place-value chart shows the value of each digit in the number 5,647,210.392. Place value is used in rounding numbers. If the digit to the right of the place value you want to round is 5 or more, round up by adding 1 to the number in the place value and then change all the digits to the right of the place value to zeros. If the number is 4 or less, round down by changing all the numbers to the right of the place value to zeros.

Figure 2.1

Millions		Thousands			Hundreds				Decimals		
Ten Millions	Millions	Hundred Thousands	Ten Thousands	Thousands	Hundreds	Tens	Ones	Decimal	Tenths	Hundredths	Thousandths
	5	6	4	7	2	1	0	.	3	9	2
					← Whole Numbers				Decimals →		

EXAMPLE 1

Round 7,862 to the nearest hundred.

Step 1: Find the digit in the hundreds place. 7,<u>8</u>62

Step 2: Read the number to the right of the digit in the hundreds place. If the digit is five or more then you'll want to round up. 7,8<u>6</u>2

Step 3: Add 1 to the hundreds place.
Change the digits to the right to zeros. 7,<u>9</u>00

EXAMPLE 2

Round 0.637 to the nearest tenth.

Step 1: Find the digit in the tenths place. 0.<u>6</u>37

Step 2: Read the number to the right of the digit in the tenths place. If the digit is four or less, then you'll want to round down. 0.6<u>3</u>7

Step 3: Do not change the tenths digit.
Drop the digits to the right. 0.<u>6</u>

Complete the problems. Check your answers in the back of the book.
Round 5,693.251 to the place value given.

1. thousands **2.** tenths **3.** hundreds **4.** ones

Rounding to the Nearest Place Value Dollar and cents amounts are often rounded to the nearest cent, or the hundredths place. Begin with the digit in the hundredths place.

EXAMPLE 3

Round to the nearest cent.

Step 1: Find the digit in the hundredths place. $112.4<u>1</u>7

Step 2: Read the number to the right of the digit in the hundredths place. If the number is five or more, then you'll want to round up. $112.41<u>7</u>

Step 3: Round up the hundredths digit. Do not change the tenths digit. **$112.42**

Complete the problems. Check your answers in the back of the book.
Round to the nearest cent.

5. $21.277 **6.** $967.461 **7.** $138.7836 **8.** $647.555

Practice

Round 15,748,516 to the place value given.

9. millions **10.** ten millions **11.** thousands
12. hundreds **13.** ten thousands **14.** hundred thousands

15. Amy Cole records the attendance data for the sporting events at the Glass Bowl. Round each number to the amount indicated.

	Football Game	Number	Nearest Thousand	Nearest Hundred	Nearest Ten
a.	Austin Peavey	18,971			
b.	Bowling Green	25,687			
c.	Ohio University	20,119			
d.	Western Michigan	24,567			
e.	Central Michigan	19,424			

WORKSHOPS

WORKSHOP 3

Comparing Numbers

Need Help? Go to...
Skill 1: Numbers, p. SK1–SK2

Finding the Greater Number To compare numbers to see which one is greater, first find out if one of the numbers has more digits to the left of the decimal point. For example, 100 is greater than 99.62 because 100 has three digits to the left of the decimal point and 99.62 has only two. If both numbers have the same number of digits to the left of the decimal point, compare each digit, beginning at the left. One way is to write the value of each digit.

EXAMPLE 1

Compare 5,972 and 5,983. Which number is greater?

Step 1: Break down the numbers.

5,972 = 5,000 + 900 + 70 + 2
5,983 = 5,000 + 900 + 80 + 3

Step 2: Compare the numbers that you have broken down.

5,972 = 5,000 + 900 + 70 + 2
5,983 = 5,000 + 900 + 80 + 3
same same 80 is greater than 70

Therefore, **5,983 is greater than 5,972.**

Complete the problems. Check your answers in the back of the book. Which number is greater?

1. 8,891 or 8,889

2. 7,521 or 7,520

Comparing Decimals When you are comparing decimals, you may have to write zeros to the right of the decimal point so that the numbers being compared have the same number of decimal places.

EXAMPLE 2

Compare 5.17 and 5.149 (without writing the value of each digit). Which number is greater?

Step 1: Compare numbers by looking at the numbers to the right of the decimal. — 5.17 and 5.149

Step 2: Write in a 0 next to the 7. — 5.17<u>0</u>

Step 3: Decide which number is greater. — 5.170 and 5.149
7 is greater than 4,
so **5.170 is greater than 5.149**.

Complete the problems. Check your answers in the back of the book.
Which number is greater?

3. 284.4 or 284.396

4. 0.06 or 0.006

WORKSHOPS

Practice

Which number is greater?

5. 26 or 29

6. 4,201 or 4,210

7. 2.65 or 2.56

8. 0.696 or 0.695

9. 0.4 or 0.04

10. 0.1 or 0.9

11. 0.03 or 0.003

12. 2.234 or 2.244

Write the numbers in order from least to greatest.

13. 1.37, 1.36, 1.39

14. 5.11, 5.09, 5.10

15. 7.18, 7.38, 7.58

16. 5.86, 5.95, 5.81

17. 40.004, 40.04, 40.4

18. 121.012, 121.021, 121.210

19. 365.15, 365.51, 365.490

20. 0.1234, 0.1342, 0.1423

21. Janet Swick works part-time shelving books in the school library. Arrange the following library call numbers from least to greatest.

a. Science: 513.12, 519.03, 532.626, 571.113, 587.41

b. Literature: 94.79, 32.615, 11.7, 67.192, 34.9

c. Religion: 46.94, 18.7, 15.04, 71.21, 26.311

d. Language: 22.5, 67.21, 48.275, 38.9, 93.047

22. Janet Swick is filing a set of books. Between which two books would she file the book with the given call number?

a. Call number of book to shelve is 874.192.

Filed books: 872.41, 873.15, 877.142, 879.190.

b. Call number of book to shelve is 332.75.

Filed books are: 309.8, 311.75, 332.075, 332.749, 333.54.

WORKSHOPS

WORKSHOP 4

Adding Decimals

Need Help? Go to...
Skill 5: Adding Decimals, p. SK6

Write in Vertical Form When adding decimals, write the addition problem in vertical form. Be sure to line up the decimal points. Write a decimal point in the answer directly below the decimal points in the problem. Then add as you would whole numbers.

EXAMPLE 1

20.99 + 32.07 + 18.04

Step 1: Line up decimals.

$$\begin{array}{r} 20.99 \\ 32.07 \\ 18.04 \end{array}$$

Step 2: Add.

$$\begin{array}{r} 20.99 \\ 32.07 \\ +\,18.04 \\ \hline \mathbf{71.10} \end{array}$$

EXAMPLE 2

48.26 + 193.47 + 2.77

Step 1: Line up decimals.

$$\begin{array}{r} 48.26 \\ 193.47 \\ 2.77 \end{array}$$

Step 2: Add.

$$\begin{array}{r} 48.26 \\ 193.47 \\ +\quad 2.77 \\ \hline \mathbf{244.50} \end{array}$$

Concept CHECK

Complete the problems. Check your answers in the back of the book.

1. 34.33 + 12.34 + 24.21 =

2. 56.42 + 39.65 + 82.37 =

3. 72.52 + 52.12 + 98.22 =

4. 93.35 + 67.88 + 22.53 =

When to Add Zeros When adding amounts with different numbers of decimal places, adding zeros in the empty decimal places will help you keep track of your places. Put a decimal point in any whole number included in the problem.

EXAMPLE 3

86.583 + 957.26 + 3 + 98.5

Step 1: Line up decimals.

$$\begin{array}{r} 86.583 \\ 957.26 \\ 3. \\ 98.5 \end{array}$$

Step 2: Write zeros.

$$\begin{array}{r} 86.583 \\ 957.260 \\ 3.000 \\ 98.500 \end{array}$$

Step 3: Add.

$$\begin{array}{r} 86.583 \\ 957.260 \\ 3.000 \\ +\quad 98.500 \\ \hline \mathbf{1{,}145.343} \end{array}$$

Dollar Signs Adding amounts of money is just like adding decimals. The decimal point separates the dollars and cents. Remember to put a dollar sign in the total.

Concept CHECK

Complete the problems. Check your answers in the back of the book.

5. 87.23 + 235.12 + 43.125 =

6. 597.2 + 62.3 + 623.342 =

7. $521.12 + $23.12 + $53.12 =

8. $235.12 + $256.72 + $88 =

Practice

9. 82.22 + 51.27

10. 83.41 + 8.62

11. 862.82 + 8.94

12. 362.22 + 431.93

13. 82.637 + 92.727

14. 92.627 + 76.522

15. 9.235 + 4.847

16. 9.252 + 6.257

17. 58.62, 84.51 + 58.25

18. 84.87, 55.22 + 87.94

19. 9.8551, 9.9908 + 2.555

20. 15.854, 84.265 + 55.842

21. 513.8, 2.584 + 84.85

22. 254.65, 25.847 + 8.4

23. 9.847, 87.8 + 552

24. 25.658, 157.65 + 6.892

25. 5.894, 526.8 + 596.2

26. 5621.8, 23.453 + 125.2

27. 56.21, 8.958 + 126.8

28. 0.58, 526 + 56.8954

29. 17.47 + 34.71 + 56.78 + 15.07

30. 0.17 + 17.94 + 13 + 147.7

31. 14.6 + 19.314 + 4.17 + 264.5176

32. 4.917 + 6 + 4.37 + 15.971

33. $1.98 + $71.49 + $0.49 + $50

34. $7.79 + $0.89 + $412.37 + $7

35. $71.84 + $2.79 + $143.54 + $71

36. $7.98 + $4.14 + $71.84 + $0.47

WORKSHOPS

WORKSHOP 5

Subtracting Decimals

Need Help? Go to...

Skill 6: Subtracting Decimals, p. SK7

Aligning the Decimals When you are subtracting decimals, write the subtraction problem in vertical form. Be sure to line up the decimal points. Write a decimal point in the answer directly below the decimal points in the problem. Then subtract as you would with whole numbers.

EXAMPLE 1

Subtract 85.29 − 34.72.

Step 1: Line up decimals.

```
85.29
34.72
```

Step 2: Subtract.

```
  85.29
− 34.72
  50.57
```

Writing Zeros as Place Holders When subtracting amounts with different numbers of decimal places, you may want to write zeros in the empty decimal places. Put a decimal point in any whole number included in the problem.

EXAMPLE 2

Subtract 838.5 − 39.248.

Step 1: Put in zeros. 838.5<u>00</u>

Step 2: Subtract.

```
  838.500
−  39.248
  799.252
```

Concept CHECK

Complete the problems. Check your answers in the back of the book.

1. 87.86 − 34.25 =
2. 125.9 − 87.6 =
3. 675.4 − 65.32 =
4. 76.76 − 8 =

Practice

5. 94.7 − 31.4
6. 98.6 − 88.5
7. 19.87 − 8.54
8. 7.93 − 2.03
9. 49.64 − 10.34
10. 96.13 − 12.37
11. 38.065 − 33.426
12. 68.111 − 9.648

13. $99.85 − 32.16

14. $75.67 − 28.30

15. $953.22 − 287.32

16. $506.37 − 243.70

17. $347. − 82.97

18. $275. − 85.12

19. $55,553.65 − 38,872.58

20. $47,005.45 − 3,257.64

21. 335.4 − 217.9

22. 148.1 − 132.5

23. 5.21 − 0.71

24. $434.66 − $51.43

25. $3,479.31 − $2,616.16

26. $6,000 − $4,333.83

27. You work as a cashier in a restaurant. Compute the correct change for each of the following orders.

	Customer's Order	Customer Gives You	Change
a.	$ 6.94	$ 7.00	
b.	9.12	10.00	
c.	16.97	17.00	
d.	3.42	5.42	
e.	5.01	5.01	
f.	23.11	25.00	
g.	41.97	42.07	
h.	27.42	30.00	
i.	20.13	21.13	
j.	150.84	151.00	

28. The marketing department for Jackson Sporting Goods Company prepared a comparison sheet that shows sales projections and actual sales for ten products. Find the difference between the projected sales and the actual sales by subtracting actual sales from projected sales.

	Jackson Sporting Goods Company			
	Product	**Sales Projections**	**Actual Sales**	**Difference**
a.	Electric motors	$ 3,000.00	$ 2,749.67	
b.	Fishing tackle	32,000.00	31,897.40	
c.	Wilderness boots	6,500.00	5,607.15	
d.	Boat moccasin	950.00	571.28	
e.	Campware sets	400.00	339.67	
f.	Geodesic dome tent	6,400.00	5,379.58	
g.	Backpacking tent	2,500.00	1,999.40	

WORKSHOPS

WORKSHOP 6

Multiplying Decimals

Need Help? Go to...

Skill 8: Multiplying Decimals, p. SK9

Line Up Like Whole Numbers When multiplying decimals, multiply as if the decimal numbers were whole numbers. Then count the total number of decimal places to the right of the decimals in the factors. This number will be the number of decimal places in the product.

EXAMPLE 1

Multiply as if whole numbers, then count the total number of decimal places to put in the product.

18.1 ← factor		Multiply.	**18.1** ←	1 decimal place
× 0.35 ← factor			**× 0.35** ←	+ 2 decimal places
905			**905**	
543			**543**	
6335 ← product			**6.335** ←	3 decimal places

When to Write Zeros If the product does not have enough digits to place the decimal in the correct position, you will need to write in zeros. Start at the right of the product in counting the decimal places and write zeros at the left.

EXAMPLE 2

0.72	Count the decimal places, and write zeros at the left.	**0.72** ←	2 decimal places
× 0.03		**× 0.03** ←	+ 2 decimal places
216		**0.0216** ←	4 decimal places

Concept CHECK

Complete the problems. Check your answers in the back of the book.

1. 24.7 × 0.33

2. 41.8 × 2.14

3. 0.78 × 0.11

4. 0.74 × 0.08

When to Round the Answer When you are multiplying amounts of money, you will want to round the answer off to the nearest cent. Remember to put a dollar sign in the answer.

WORKSHOPS

EXAMPLE 3

$\$3.35 \times 4.5$ = 15075

Round to the nearest cent. Put the dollar sign in the answer.

$$\begin{array}{rl} \$3.35 & \leftarrow \text{2 places} \\ \times\ 4.5 & \leftarrow +\text{1 place} \\ \hline 15.075 & \leftarrow \text{3 places} \end{array}$$

$\$3.35 \times 4.5 = \$15.075$

$= \$15.08$ **(rounded to the nearest cent)**

Moving the Decimal Point When multiplying by 10, 100, or 1,000, count the number of zeros and then move the decimal point to the right the same number of spaces.

EXAMPLE 4

a. 6.7×10 **b.** 5.24×100

Count the number of zeros. Move the decimal point accordingly.

a. $6.7 \times 10 = 6.7 = \mathbf{67}$ 10 has 1 zero; move decimal 1 place.

b. $5.24 \times 100 = 5.24 = \mathbf{524}$ 100 has 2 zeros; move decimal 2 places.

Concept CHECK

Complete the problems. Check your answers in the back of the book.

5. $\$4.15 \times 8.5$ **6.** 71.4×10 **7.** 41.861×100

Practice

8. 41.3×0.2 **9.** 78.4×0.3 **10.** 84.8×0.25 **11.** 51.7×0.72

12. 97.8×0.31 **13.** 51.7×0.67 **14.** 0.41×0.02 **15.** 0.74×0.08

16. 0.51×0.06 **17.** $\$5.15 \times 85$ **18.** $\$5.85 \times 3.5$ **19.** $\$3.35 \times 7.6$

Multiply by 10. **20.** 31.7 **21.** 5.71

Multiply by 100. **22.** 32.85 **23.** 41.786

Multiply by 1,000. **24.** 72.716 **25.** 7.1956

Multiply by 10,000. **26.** 6.9178 **27.** 3.42876

WORKSHOPS

WORKSHOP 7

Dividing Decimals

Need Help? Go to...
- Skill 9: Dividing (Fractional Remainder), p. SK10
- Skill 10: Dividing (Decimal Remainder), p. SK11
- Skill 11: Dividing Decimals, p. SK12

Dividing Decimals When you are dividing decimals, it is important to keep these steps in mind:

1. Check if there is a decimal point in the divisor. If there is, move the decimal point to the right to make the divisor a whole number.
2. Move the decimal point in the dividend to the right the same number of places you moved the decimal point in the divisor.
3. Write the decimal point in the quotient directly above the decimal point in the dividend.
4. Divide as with whole numbers.

$$\text{divisor} \rightarrow 3\overline{)693} \leftarrow \text{dividend}, \quad 231 \leftarrow \text{quotient}$$

EXAMPLE 1

23.78 ÷ 5.8 or $5.8\overline{)23.78}$

Divide. $5.8\overline{)23.78}$

```
      4.1
 58)237.8
   -232
      58
     -58
```

Adding Zeros to Decimal Point Add zeros to the right of the decimal point in the dividend if needed.

EXAMPLE 2

0.147 ÷ 0.42 or $0.42\overline{)0.147}$

Divide. $0.42\overline{)0.147}$

```
      0.35
  42)14.70    (zero added)
    -126
      210
     -210
```

Concept CHECK

Complete the problems. Check your answers in the back of the book.

1. 35.96 ÷ 5.8
2. $12.9\overline{)55.341}$
3. $0.052\overline{)1.872}$

Dividend as Amount of Money When the dividend is an amount of money, remember to place the dollar sign in the quotient and round the answer to the nearest cent.

EXAMPLE 3

$47.56 ÷ 24

Divide. $24\overline{)\$47.560}$ = 1.981 or **$1.98** (rounded to nearest cent)

Dividing by 10, 100, or 1,000 When dividing by 10, 100, or 1,000, count the number of zeros in 10, 100, or 1,000 and move the decimal point to the left the same number of places.

EXAMPLE 4

9.3 ÷ 10

Divide. 9.3 ÷ 10 = 09.3 = **0.93** (10 has 1 zero. Move decimal 1 place.)

EXAMPLE 5

742.64 ÷ 100

Divide. 742.64 ÷ 100 = 742.64 (100 has 2 zeros. Move decimal 2 places.)

= **7.4264**

EXAMPLE 6

13,436.1 ÷ 1,000

Divide. 13,436.1 ÷ 1,000 = 13436.1 (1,000 has 3 zeros. Move decimal 3 places.)

= **13.4361**

Concept CHECK

Complete the problems. Check your answers in the back of the book.

4. $16.32 ÷ 12 **5.** 7.9 ÷ 10 **6.** 138.9 ÷ 100 **7.** 9,862.8 ÷ 1,000

Practice

Divide. Round answers to the nearest tenths.

8. $5.3\overline{)9.54}$ **9.** $3.2\overline{)11.2}$ **10.** $2.6\overline{)24.18}$

Divide. Round answers to the nearest hundredths.

11. $4.3\overline{)7.871}$ **12.** $5.9\overline{)5.343}$ **13.** $7.36\overline{)88.34}$

Divide by 10.

14. 9.3 **15.** 14.42 **16.** 726.81

Divide by 100.

17. 429.8 **18.** 133.39 **19.** 8,462.65

Divide by 1,000.

20. 5,896.9 **21.** 321.29 **22.** 22.098

Divide by 10,000.

23. 63,652.18 **24.** 3,879.19 **25.** 415.49

WORKSHOP 8

Multiplying Fractions

Need Help? Go to...
Skill 20: Multiplying Fractions/Mixed Numbers, p. SK21

Method to Multiplication When multiplying fractions, first multiply the numerators and then multiply the denominators. The product of the numerators is placed over the product of the denominators to give the answer in the form of a fraction.

EXAMPLE 1

$\frac{2}{3} \times \frac{4}{5}$ Multiply. $\frac{2}{3} \times \frac{4}{5} = \frac{8}{15}$ ← product of numerators / ← product of denominators

A Whole Number's Denominator When multiplying a fraction and a whole number, note that every whole number has a denominator of 1.

EXAMPLE 2

$\frac{4}{5} \times 300$ Multiply. $\frac{4}{5} \times 300 = \frac{4}{5} \times \frac{300}{1} = \frac{1200}{5} = 240$

Complete the problems. Check your answers in the back of the book. Multiply.

1. $\frac{3}{4} \times \frac{5}{8}$ **2.** $\frac{7}{8} \times \frac{3}{8}$ **3.** $\frac{2}{3} \times 600$

Simplifying Fractions It is customary business practice to reduce all fractions to lowest terms. Reducing a fraction to lowest term is also called *simplifying the fraction.* To simplify a fraction, you can use prime factorization and then cancel the common factors. To review, prime factorization is a composite number (a whole number that has more than two factors, such as 4, 6, 8, and 9) that is expressed as a product of prime factors (a whole number that has exactly two factors, 1 and itself). For example, the prime factorization of 63 is as follows:

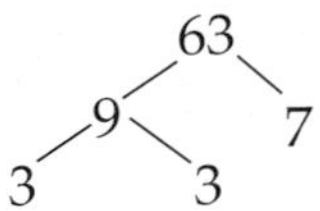

EXAMPLE 3

$\frac{5}{6} \times \frac{3}{7}$ Multiply. Write the product in simplest form.

$$\frac{5}{6} \times \frac{3}{7} = \frac{5 \times \cancel{3}}{2 \times \cancel{3} \times 7} = \frac{5}{14}$$

Complete the problems. Check your answers in the back of the book.
Multiply.

4. $\frac{3}{4} \times \frac{5}{9}$ **5.** $\frac{2}{15} \times \frac{5}{8}$ **6.** $\frac{5}{6} \times 180$

WORKSHOPS

Multiplying Mixed Numbers When multiplying mixed numbers, first change the mixed number to an improper fraction and then multiply and simplify.

EXAMPLE 4

$2\frac{1}{2} \times 4$

$1\frac{4}{5} \times 2\frac{2}{9}$

$3\frac{1}{2} \times 2\frac{1}{3}$

Multiply the mixed numbers.

$2\frac{1}{2} \times 4 = \frac{5}{2} \times \frac{4}{1} = \mathbf{10}$

$1\frac{4}{5} \times 2\frac{2}{9} = \frac{9}{5} \times \frac{20}{9} = \frac{20}{5} = \mathbf{4}$

$3\frac{1}{2} \times 2\frac{1}{3} = \frac{7}{2} \times \frac{7}{3} = \frac{49}{6} = \mathbf{8\frac{1}{6}}$

Concept CHECK

Complete the problems. Check your answers in the back of the book.
Multiply and simplify.

7. $4\frac{1}{2} \times 8$ **8.** $3\frac{3}{5} \times 2\frac{2}{9}$ **9.** $4\frac{1}{2} \times 3\frac{1}{3}$

Practice

Multiply and simplify.

10. $\frac{3}{4} \times \frac{7}{8}$ **11.** $\frac{7}{5} \times \frac{3}{8}$ **12.** $\frac{3}{11} \times \frac{7}{2}$

13. $\frac{9}{10} \times \frac{3}{5}$ **14.** $\frac{5}{8} \times 80$ **15.** $\frac{3}{4} \times 20$

16. $\frac{3}{5} \times 300$ **17.** $\frac{2}{3} \times 660$ **18.** $\frac{7}{8} \times 248$

19. $\frac{9}{10} \times \frac{5}{3}$ **20.** $\frac{9}{12} \times \frac{3}{15}$ **21.** $\frac{12}{35} \times \frac{21}{30}$

22. $5\frac{3}{4} \times 288$ **23.** $8\frac{1}{2} \times 3\frac{1}{4}$ **24.** $6\frac{3}{4} \times 2\frac{2}{3}$

25. $12\frac{1}{2} \times 4\frac{3}{4}$ **26.** $12\frac{3}{4} \times 8\frac{2}{3}$ **27.** $27\frac{1}{5} \times 8\frac{3}{4}$

WORKSHOPS

WORKSHOP 9

Dividing Fractions

Need Help? Go to...
Skill 21: Dividing Fractions/Mixed Numbers, p. SK22

Finding the Reciprocal Dividing fractions involves finding the reciprocal of the divisor. The reciprocal of a fraction is found by interchanging the numerator and the denominator.

EXAMPLE 1

a. $\frac{2}{3}$ **b.** $\frac{5}{8}$

c. 4 **d.** $1\frac{3}{4}$

Find the reciprocal.

a. $\frac{2}{3} \times \frac{3}{2}$ $\frac{3}{2}$ **is the reciprocal**

b. $\frac{5}{8} \times \frac{8}{5}$ $\frac{8}{5}$ **is the reciprocal**

c. $\frac{4}{1} \times \frac{1}{4}$ $\frac{1}{4}$ **is the reciprocal**

d. $1\frac{3}{4} = \frac{7}{4} \times \frac{4}{7}$ $\frac{4}{7}$ **is the reciprocal**

Concept CHECK

Complete the problems. Check your answers in the back of the book. Write the reciprocal for each number.

1. $\frac{5}{3}$ **2.** $\frac{7}{8}$

3. 10 **4.** $2\frac{1}{2}$

Changing the Divisor to Its Reciprocal To divide fractions, first change the divisor to its reciprocal, multiply the resulting fraction, and simplify.

EXAMPLE 2

a. $\frac{3}{4} \div \frac{1}{2}$ **b.** $\frac{8}{5} \div \frac{4}{3}$

c. $\frac{2}{3} \div 6$ **d.** $4\frac{1}{2} \div 1\frac{3}{4}$

Divide.

a. $\frac{3}{4} \div \frac{1}{2} = \frac{3}{4} \times \frac{2}{1} = \frac{6}{4} = \mathbf{1\frac{1}{2}}$

b. $\frac{8}{5} \div \frac{4}{3} = \frac{8}{5} \times \frac{3}{4} = \frac{24}{20} = 1\frac{4}{20} = \mathbf{1\frac{1}{5}}$

c. $\frac{2}{3} \div 6 = \frac{2}{3} \times \frac{1}{6} = \frac{2}{18} = \mathbf{\frac{1}{9}}$

d. $4\frac{1}{2} \div 1\frac{3}{4} = \frac{9}{2} \div \frac{7}{4} = \frac{9}{2} \times \frac{4}{7} = \frac{36}{14} = \mathbf{2\frac{4}{7}}$

Complete the problems. Check your answers in the back of the book. Divide and simplify.

5. $\frac{5}{8} \div \frac{3}{4}$

6. $\frac{9}{16} \div \frac{3}{2}$

7. $\frac{4}{5} \div 2$

8. $8\frac{1}{3} \div 1\frac{2}{3}$

WORKSHOPS

Practice

Write the reciprocal.

9. $\frac{3}{4}$

10. $\frac{5}{8}$

11. $\frac{3}{16}$

12. $\frac{21}{2}$

13. $\frac{1}{10}$

14. 9

15. 15

16. 7

17. $1\frac{1}{2}$

Divide and simplify.

18. $\frac{3}{5} \div \frac{2}{3}$

19. $\frac{1}{3} \div \frac{8}{7}$

20. $\frac{9}{16} \div \frac{1}{4}$

21. $\frac{7}{8} \div \frac{1}{3}$

22. $7 \div \frac{7}{6}$

23. $12 \div \frac{3}{4}$

24. $\frac{5}{8} \div 2$

25. $\frac{7}{16} \div 8$

26. $1\frac{7}{8} \div \frac{3}{4}$

27. $6\frac{2}{3} \div \frac{5}{3}$

28. $15\frac{1}{2} \div 1\frac{1}{2}$

29. $12\frac{7}{8} \div 1\frac{5}{8}$

30. It takes $1\frac{1}{4}$ ounces of oatmeal to make 1 serving. How many servings are contained in a 16-ounce box?

31. You work in a bulk food store. How many $\frac{1}{4}$ pound bags of redskin peanuts can you package from a $24\frac{1}{2}$ pound box?

32. How many pieces of wire, each $12\frac{1}{2}$ feet long, can an electrician cut from a 100-foot coil?

33. A quart of milk is equal to $\frac{1}{4}$ of a gallon. How many quarts of milk are in $\frac{7}{8}$ of a gallon?

WORKSHOPS

WORKSHOP 10

Adding Fractions

Need Help? Go to...

- Skill 15: Adding Fractions, Like Denominators, p. SK16
- Skill 16: Adding Fractions, Unlike Denominators, p. SK17

Fractions with a Common Denominator To add fractions which have a common denominator, the numerators are summed and the sum is placed over the common denominator.

EXAMPLE 1

$\frac{3}{8} + \frac{1}{8} + \frac{5}{8}$

Find the sum. $\frac{3}{8} + \frac{1}{8} + \frac{5}{8} = \frac{(3 + 1 + 5)}{8} = \frac{9}{8}$ or $1\frac{1}{8}$

Concept CHECK

Complete the problems. Check your answers in the back of the book.

1. $\frac{2}{3} + \frac{1}{3} =$

2. $\frac{11}{18} + \frac{5}{18} + \frac{7}{18} =$

3. $\frac{5}{7} + \frac{1}{7} + \frac{2}{7} + \frac{6}{7} =$

4. $\frac{4}{9} + \frac{2}{9} + \frac{1}{9} + \frac{5}{9} =$

Fractions without a Common Denominator To add fractions which do not have common denominators, each fraction is expressed in terms of the least common denominator, the numerators are then summed, and the sum is placed over the least common denominator.

EXAMPLE 2

$\frac{3}{4} + \frac{5}{6} + \frac{1}{2}$

Find the sum.

To add fractions without a common denominator, first find the least common denominator. This is the lowest number that can be evenly divided by each denominator. To find the least common denominator, find the prime factors of the denominators 4, 6, and 2. Write the denominator 4 as 2×2, the denominator 6 as 2×3, and the denominator 2 as 2×1. The least common denominator must contain two factors of 2 and one factor of 3. Therefore, the least common denominator is $2 \times 2 \times 3$ or 12.

$$\frac{3}{4} + \frac{5}{6} + \frac{1}{2} = \frac{(3 \times 3)}{(3 \times 4)} + \frac{(2 \times 5)}{(2 \times 6)} + \frac{(6 \times 1)}{(6 \times 2)} = \frac{9}{12} + \frac{10}{12} + \frac{6}{12} = \frac{25}{12} \text{ or } 2\frac{1}{12}$$

Concept CHECK

Complete the problems. Check your answers in the back of the book.

5. $\frac{1}{2} + \frac{1}{4} + \frac{3}{8} =$

6. $\frac{1}{3} + \frac{5}{6} + \frac{2}{3} =$

7. $\frac{2}{5} + \frac{2}{3} + \frac{7}{10} =$

8. $\frac{3}{4} + \frac{2}{5} + \frac{1}{6} =$

Practice

9. $\frac{2}{3}+\frac{4}{5}=$

10. $\frac{1}{2}+\frac{3}{4}=$

11. $\frac{5}{6}+\frac{2}{9}=$

12. $\frac{1}{2}+\frac{1}{4}+\frac{1}{3}=$

13. $\frac{5}{7}+\frac{2}{3}+\frac{1}{6}=$

14. $\frac{5}{8}+\frac{5}{12}+\frac{5}{18}=$

15. $\frac{8}{11}+\frac{3}{4}=$

16. $\frac{5}{8}+\frac{3}{5}=$

17. $\frac{5}{7}+\frac{2}{9}=$

18. $\frac{3}{5}+\frac{2}{3}+\frac{4}{7}=$

19. $\frac{7}{8}+\frac{2}{5}+\frac{1}{3}=$

20. $\frac{3}{4}+\frac{3}{11}+\frac{2}{3}=$

21. $\frac{3}{5}+\frac{2}{15}+\frac{1}{3}=$

22. $\frac{3}{8}+\frac{1}{4}+\frac{1}{2}=$

23. $\frac{3}{4}+\frac{5}{6}+\frac{7}{12}=$

24. $\frac{2}{5}+\frac{1}{3}+\frac{7}{10}=$

25. $\frac{5}{8}+\frac{1}{6}+\frac{11}{12}=$

26. $\frac{1}{2}+\frac{1}{3}+\frac{1}{5}=$

27. $\frac{3}{4}+\frac{5}{9}+\frac{5}{6}=$

28. $\frac{3}{4}+\frac{4}{5}+\frac{5}{6}=$

29. $\frac{8}{11}+\frac{2}{3}+\frac{3}{22}=$

30. $\frac{1}{2}+\frac{1}{3}+\frac{1}{4}+\frac{1}{5}+\frac{1}{6}=$

31. $\frac{3}{7}+\frac{5}{6}+\frac{2}{3}+\frac{1}{2}+\frac{3}{4}=$

32. Tom, Kwasi, and Juan purchased a large pizza to share. If Tom ate $\frac{1}{3}$ of the pizza, Kwasi ate $\frac{1}{4}$ of the pizza, and Juan ate $\frac{1}{6}$ of the pizza, what fractional part of the pizza was eaten?

33. On the Jones farm, a large cylindrical container is used to catch rain water. If $\frac{1}{2}$ of the container was filled in one rainfall, $\frac{4}{5}$ of the container was filled in a second rainfall, and $\frac{7}{10}$ of the container was filled in a third rainfall, how many containers were filled in the three rainfalls?

34. Zeno started to walk from his home to work. After walking $\frac{1}{2}$ of the way he got tired and stopped for a rest. He then walked $\frac{1}{4}$ of the way and rested again. After walking $\frac{1}{8}$ of the way, he rested again. After walking $\frac{1}{16}$ of the way, he rested again. How far towards his place of work had he walked?

35. A nickel is $\frac{1}{20}$ of a dollar. A dime is $\frac{1}{10}$ of a dollar and a quarter is $\frac{1}{4}$ of a dollar, while a fifty cent piece is $\frac{1}{2}$ of a dollar. If you had a nickel, a dime, a quarter, and a fifty cent piece, what fractional part of a dollar would you have?

36. John spent $\frac{1}{4}$ of his life as a boy growing up, $\frac{1}{6}$ of his life in college, and $\frac{1}{2}$ of his life as a teacher before he retired. What fractional part of his life did he spend before he retired?

37. Luis Delgado owns $\frac{2}{5}$ of the Terrytown Restaurant. His brother, Juan, owns $\frac{1}{3}$ and his daughter Angel owns $\frac{1}{4}$. What fractional part of the restaurant do the Delgados own?

38. About $\frac{11}{12}$ of a golf course is fairways, $\frac{1}{18}$ greens, and the rest tees. What fractional part of the golf course is fairways and greens?

WORKSHOPS

WORKSHOP 11

Subtracting Fractions

Need Help? Go to...
- Skill 17: Subtracting Fractions, Like Denominators, p. SK18
- Skill 18: Subtracting Fractions, Unlike Denominators, p. SK19
- Skill 19: Subtracting Mixed Numbers, Borrowing, p. SK20

Fractions with a Common Denominator To subtract fractions which have a common denominator, the numerators are subtracted and the difference is placed over the common denominator.

EXAMPLE 1

$\frac{7}{8} - \frac{3}{8}$

Find the difference between the fractions.

$\frac{7}{8} - \frac{3}{8} = \frac{4}{8}$, which simplifies to $\frac{1}{2}$

Concept CHECK

Complete the problems. Check your answers in the back of the book.

1. $\frac{3}{4} - \frac{1}{4} =$ **2.** $\frac{5}{6} - \frac{1}{6} =$ **3.** $\frac{12}{17} - \frac{1}{17} =$ **4.** $\frac{13}{29} - \frac{11}{29} =$

Fractions without a Common Denominator To subtract fractions which do not have common denominators, each fraction is expressed in terms of the least common denominator, the numerators are then subtracted, and the difference is placed over the least common denominator.

EXAMPLE 2

$\frac{5}{6} - \frac{1}{4}$

Find the difference between fractions without a common denominator.

To find the least common denominator, write the prime factors of the denominators 6 and 4 ($6 = 2 \times 3$ and $4 = 2 \times 2$). The least common denominator must contain two factors of 2 and one factor of 3. Therefore, the least common denominator is $2 \times 2 \times 3$ or 12.

$$\frac{5}{6} - \frac{1}{4} = \frac{(5 \times 2)}{(6 \times 2)} - \frac{(1 \times 3)}{(4 \times 3)} = \frac{10}{12} - \frac{3}{12} = \frac{7}{12}$$

Concept CHECK

Complete the problems. Check your answers in the back of the book.

5. $\frac{3}{4} - \frac{1}{2} =$ **6.** $\frac{5}{8} - \frac{1}{6} =$ **7.** $\frac{5}{12} - \frac{3}{10} =$ 8. $\frac{5}{6} - \frac{7}{20} =$

Subtracting Mixed Fractions To subtract mixed numbers it is sometimes necessary to borrow one from the whole number in the minuend and convert it to a fraction. Here's an example to review minuend and subtrahend:

$$\begin{array}{r} 500 \\ -\ 30 \\ \hline 470 \end{array} \begin{array}{l} \longleftarrow \text{minuend} \\ \longleftarrow \text{subtrahend} \\ \\ \end{array}$$

This is necessary when the fraction in the minuend is less than the fraction in the subtrahend. This can be determined after the fractions have been converted to the least common denominator.

EXAMPLE 3

$4\frac{3}{8} - 2\frac{5}{8}$

Find the difference by subtracting mixed fractions.

Borrow 1 from the whole number 4 in the minuend. Next, add 1 to the fraction $\frac{3}{8}$ in the minuend. Change 1 to $\frac{8}{8}$ and add it to the fraction in the minuend. Then subtract: $3\frac{11}{8} - 2\frac{5}{8}$.

$4\frac{3}{8} - 2\frac{5}{8} = [(3 + 1) + \frac{3}{8}] - 2\frac{5}{8} = [3 + (1 + \frac{3}{8})] - 2\frac{5}{8} =$
$[3 + (\frac{8}{8} + \frac{3}{8})] - 2\frac{5}{8} = 3\frac{11}{8} - 2\frac{5}{8} = 1\frac{6}{8}$ or $1\frac{3}{4}$

Concept CHECK

Complete the problems. Check your answers in the back of the book.

9. $5\frac{6}{7} - 2\frac{3}{7} =$ **10.** $7\frac{2}{3} - 3\frac{1}{6} =$ **11.** $12\frac{3}{8} - 4\frac{3}{4} =$ **12.** $1 - \frac{15}{16} =$

Practice

13. $\frac{11}{12} - \frac{7}{12} =$ **14.** $\frac{7}{9} - \frac{2}{9} =$ **15.** $\frac{14}{17} - \frac{3}{17} =$ **16.** $\frac{3}{4} - \frac{1}{2} =$

17. $\frac{5}{8} - \frac{5}{12} =$ **18.** $\frac{5}{6} - \frac{2}{15} =$ **19.** $\frac{7}{8} - \frac{2}{3} =$ **20.** $\frac{4}{5} - \frac{1}{4} =$

21. $\frac{5}{7} - \frac{2}{9} =$ **22.** $\frac{1}{2} - \frac{3}{10} =$ **23.** $\frac{9}{10} - \frac{7}{15} =$ **24.** $\frac{7}{12} - \frac{5}{18} =$

25. $3\frac{2}{3} - 1\frac{1}{4} =$ **26.** $7\frac{5}{6} - 2\frac{7}{10} =$ **27.** $23\frac{4}{5} - 16\frac{1}{2} =$ **28.** $8\frac{1}{5} - 3\frac{1}{3} =$

29. Alice ran $\frac{7}{8}$ of the way home while Meredith ran $\frac{5}{6}$ of the way home. What fractional part more of the distance home did Alice run?

30. Juan got $\frac{3}{4}$ of the problems correct on the last test. Julio got $\frac{5}{8}$ of the problems correct on the last test. What fractional part more of the test questions did Juan get correct than Julio?

31. Megan completed $\frac{1}{6}$ of the church quilt while Samanthia completed $\frac{1}{4}$. What fractional part more of the church quilt did Samanthia complete than Megan?

32. If $2\frac{1}{2}$ inches of rain fell on Monday and $1\frac{3}{4}$ inches of rain fell on Tuesday, how much more rain fell on Monday?

33. Akili had a quarter and a dime. Recall that a quarter is $\frac{1}{4}$ of a dollar and a dime is $\frac{1}{10}$ of a dollar. Duhon had a dime and a nickel. Recall that a nickel is $\frac{1}{20}$ of a dollar. What fractional part more of a dollar did Akili have than Duhon had?

WORKSHOPS

WORKSHOP 12

Comparing Fractions

Fractions with a Common Denominator To compare fractions having common denominators, simply compare their numerators. The fraction having the smaller numerator is the smaller fraction.

EXAMPLE 1

$\frac{5}{7}$ **and** $\frac{4}{7}$

Compare these fractions $\quad \frac{4}{7} < \frac{5}{7}$ because $4 < 5$

Concept CHECK

Complete the problems. Check your answers in the back of the book.

1. Compare $\frac{5}{8}$ and $\frac{7}{8}$.

2. Compare $\frac{11}{12}$ and $\frac{7}{12}$.

3. Compare $\frac{2}{3}$ and $\frac{1}{3}$.

4. Compare $\frac{49}{50}$ and $\frac{41}{50}$.

Fractions without a Common Denominator To compare fractions having different denominators, one approach is to get a common denominator and then compare numerators.

EXAMPLE 2

Compare the fractions without a common denominator.

$\frac{7}{11}$ **and** $\frac{13}{21}$

Step 1: One way to compare two fractions with unlike denominators is to multiply the numerator and the denominator of each fraction you are comparing by 1. However, write the value of 1 as a fraction using the denominator of the other fraction.

$\frac{7}{11}$ and $\frac{13}{21} \qquad \frac{7}{11} \times \frac{21}{21} = \mathbf{\frac{147}{231}} \qquad \frac{13}{21} \times \frac{11}{11} = \mathbf{\frac{143}{231}}$

Step 2: Change the fractions to equivalent form.

Since $\frac{21}{21}$ is equal to 1 and $\frac{11}{11}$ is equal to 1, you're not changing the value of $\frac{7}{11}$ or $\frac{13}{21}$. However, you are changing the fractions to their equivalent forms. That means the fractions now have a common denominator so you can easily compare them.

$\frac{143}{231} < \frac{147}{231}$ because $143 < 147$

Remember that $\frac{7}{11} = \frac{147}{231}$ and $\frac{13}{21} = \frac{143}{231}$ so $\mathbf{\frac{13}{21} < \frac{7}{11}}$

Complete the problems. Check your answers in the back of the book. Compare fractions.

5. $\frac{5}{6}$ and $\frac{7}{8}$ **6.** $\frac{7}{12}$ and $\frac{5}{9}$ **7.** $\frac{3}{7}$ and $\frac{7}{15}$ **8.** $\frac{45}{47}$ and $\frac{89}{93}$

9. $\frac{8}{11}$ and $\frac{15}{19}$ **10.** $\frac{1}{23}$ and $\frac{2}{45}$ **11.** $\frac{5}{13}$ and $\frac{9}{25}$ **12.** $\frac{147}{347}$ and $\frac{440}{1,039}$

WORKSHOPS

Practice

Compare the following fractions.

13. $\frac{4}{5}$ and $\frac{3}{5}$ **14.** $\frac{8}{13}$ and $\frac{10}{13}$ **15.** $\frac{347}{498}$ and $\frac{299}{498}$ **16.** $\frac{1}{4}$ and $\frac{1}{5}$

17. $\frac{5}{8}$ and $\frac{11}{18}$ **18.** $\frac{4}{9}$ and $\frac{7}{12}$ **19.** $\frac{43}{45}$ and $\frac{22}{23}$ **20.** $\frac{91}{97}$ and $\frac{45}{49}$

21. $\frac{14}{19}$ and $\frac{27}{37}$ **22.** $\frac{7}{15}$ and $\frac{15}{31}$ **23.** $\frac{23}{25}$ and $\frac{45}{49}$ **24.** $\frac{57}{59}$ and $\frac{115}{119}$

25. $\frac{3}{11}$ and $\frac{7}{23}$ **26.** $\frac{5}{34}$ and $\frac{9}{67}$ **27.** $\frac{12}{17}$ and $\frac{26}{37}$ **28.** $\frac{132}{235}$ and $\frac{260}{463}$

29. The Clothing Hut advertised $\frac{1}{3}$ off its summer clearance items while Apparel Outlet advertised $\frac{1}{4}$ off. Which store was taking the most off?

30. The newspaper reported that on the "big board," where 1.24 billion shares were traded, 1,366 stocks fell and 1,788 rose. On the NASDAQ, where 1.76 billion shares were traded, 1,587 fell and 2,068 rose. Comparing the fractions of stocks that fell to stocks that rose, which market had the largest fraction?

31. The newspaper reported that the Dow Jones Industrials have had a low of 8,062 and a high of 11,350. The Dow Jones Transportation index has had a low of 1,942 and a high of 3,157. Comparing the fraction of low to high for the year, did the Dow Jones Industrials or the Dow Jones Transportation index have the largest fraction?

32. The Tampa Bay Buccaneers completed 18 passes out of 40 attempts. The Chicago Bears completed 14 out of 29. Which team had the greatest fractional part of attempted passes completed?

33. Data from a recent *Waste News* indicates that Chicago, Illinois was generating 2,146,321 tons of waste per year, and of that amount, 378,954 tons was paper. Los Angeles, on the other hand, was generating approximately 664,045 tons of waste per year, and of that amount, 160,366 tons was paper. Which city had the greater ratio of paper to waste?

WORKSHOPS

Need Help? Go to...

Skill 14: Changing Fractions/Decimals, p. SK15

WORKSHOP 13

Fraction to Decimal, Decimal to Percent

Fraction as Decimal Any fraction can be renamed as a decimal and any decimal can be renamed as a fraction. To rename a fraction as a decimal, use division. Think of the fraction bar in the fraction as meaning "divide by." For example, $\frac{5}{8}$ means "5 divided by 8." After the 5, you will write a decimal point and as many zeros as are needed. Then divide by 8. If a fraction does not divide out evenly, divide to one more decimal place than you are rounding to.

EXAMPLE 1

Change $\frac{5}{6}$ to a decimal rounded to the nearest thousandth. (Divide to the ten thousandths place.)

Change the fraction to a decimal and then round the decimal to the nearest thousandths place.

$\frac{5}{6} \longrightarrow 6\overline{)5.0000}$ 0.8333 = 0.833 (rounded)

Concept CHECK

Complete the problems. Check your answers in the back of the book. Change the fractions to decimals. Round to the nearest thousandth. (Divide to the ten thousandths place.)

1. $\frac{3}{7}$ **2.** $\frac{7}{8}$

Renaming a Decimal as a Fraction To rename a decimal as a fraction, name the place value of the digit at the far right. This is the denominator of the fraction. Note that the number of zeros in the denominator is the same as the number of places to the right of the decimal point. The fraction should always be written in lowest terms.

EXAMPLE 2

a. 0.79 **b.** 0.003 **c.** 4.625

Change each decimal to a fraction.

a. $0.79 = \frac{79}{100}$ (9 is in the hundredths place, so the denominator is 100.)

b. $0.003 = \frac{3}{1{,}000}$ (3 is in the thousandths place, so the denominator is 1,000.)

c. $4.625 = \frac{4{,}625}{1{,}000} = 4\frac{7}{8}$

Concept CHECK

Complete the problems. Check your answers in the back of the book. Change the decimals to fractions reduced to lowest terms.

3. 0.4 **4.** 7.82

Writing a Percent as a Decimal Percent is an abbreviation of the Latin words *per centum,* meaning "by the hundred." So percent means "divide by 100." A percent can be written as a decimal. To change a percent to a decimal, first write the percent as a fraction with a denominator of 100, then divide by 100.

When dividing by 100, you can just move the decimal point two places to the left. So when you write a percent as a decimal, you are moving the decimal point two places to the left and dropping the percent sign (%). If necessary, use zero as a placeholder.

EXAMPLE 3

Change each percent to a decimal. **a. 42%** **b. 19.4%**

Change each percent to a decimal.

a. $42\% = \frac{42}{100} = \mathbf{0.42}$ **b.** $19.4\% = \frac{19.4}{100} = \mathbf{0.194}$

Concept CHECK

Complete the problems. Check your answers in the back of the book. Change the percents to decimals.

5. 37.5% **6.** 9%

Writing a Decimal as a Percent To write a decimal as a percent, move the decimal point two places to the right and add a percent sign (%).

EXAMPLE 4

a. 0.42 **b. 0.005**

Change the decimals to percents. **a.** 0.42 = 0.42 = **42%**

Move decimal 2 places. Add % sign. **b.** 0.005 = 0.005 = **0.5%**

Complete the problems. Check your answers in the back of the book. Change the decimals to percents.

7. 0.85 **8.** 0.07 **9.** 0.3 **10.** 1.55

Practice

Change the fractions to decimals. Round to the nearest thousandth.

11. $\frac{13}{50}$ **12.** $\frac{1}{2}$ **13.** $\frac{8}{9}$

Change the fractions to decimals. Round to the nearest hundredth.

14. $\frac{4}{5}$ **15.** $\frac{5}{9}$ **16.** $\frac{1}{3}$

Change the decimals to fractions reduced to lowest terms.

17. 0.375 **18.** 0.05 **19.** 14.35

Write as decimals. **20.** 34% **21.** 817% **22.** 1.1%

Write as percents. **23.** 0.35 **24.** 0.016 **25.** 4.125

WORKSHOPS

WORKSHOP 14

Finding a Percentage

Need Help? Go to...
Skill 30: Finding the Percentage, p. SK31

Finding a Percentage Finding a percentage means finding a percent of a number. To find a percent of a number, change the percent to a decimal and then multiply it by the number.

EXAMPLE 1

What number is 20% of 95?

Write it out as an equation.

Let *n* stand for the unknown number.

$n = 20\% \times 95$ (In mathematics, *of* means "times" and *is* means "equals.")

$n = 0.20 \times 95$ (Change the percent to a decimal. Multiply.)

$n =$ **19**

Write the answer. **20% of 95 is 19.**

Concept CHECK

Complete the problems. Check your answers in the back of the book. Find the percentage in Problems 1–4.

1. 40% of 70

2. 25% of 120

3. 5% of 30

4. 145% of 200

EXAMPLE 2

The delivery charge is 7% of the selling price of $140.00. Find the delivery charge.

Write it out as an equation.

Let *n* stand for the unknown number.

$n = 7\% \times \$140$

$n = 0.07 \times \$140$

$n =$ **$9.80**

The delivery charge is $9.80.

EXAMPLE 3

A student had 85% correct out of 60 questions. How many answers were correct?

Write it out as an equation.

Let n stand for the unknown number.

$n = 85\% \times 60$

$n = 0.85 \times 60$

$n = \mathbf{51}$

There were 51 correct answers.

Complete the problems. Check your answers in the back of the book.

5. The discount is 35% of the selling price of $70. Find the discount.
6. Your share of the crop of beans is 60% of the total. Find your share if the total is 95 tons.

Practice

Find the percentage.

7. 20% of 54
8. 40% of 216
9. 42% of 335
10. 75% of 815
11. 32% of 315
12. 8% of 50
13. 4% of 95
14. 6% of 48

Round answers to the nearest cent.

15. 5.5% of $60
16. 6% of $70
17. 7.75% of $30
18. 6.5% of $420
19. 7.5% of $160
20. 4.25% of $470
21. 8.25% of $76
22. 4.5% of $36
23. When installing a sub-floor using 1-inch by 8-inch boards laid diagonally, 18% is allowed for waste. How many board feet will be wasted out of 1,350 board feet?
24. An electrical repair shop charges 37% of the cost of a new motor for rewinding the motor. If the motor costs $375 new, how much would the rewinding cost be?

WORKSHOP 15

Negative Numbers—Adding and Subtracting

Signed Numbers Positive and negative numbers are often referred to as *signed numbers.* When adding signed numbers that have the same sign, add the two numbers and attach the same sign as the numbers being added.

EXAMPLE 1

a. $4 + 2$ **b.** $-5 + (23)$ **c.** $(-7.2) + (-4.5)$ **d.** $-\frac{1}{2} + (-\frac{3}{2})$

Add the numbers.

a. $4 + 2 = 6$ **b.** $25 + (-3) = -8$

c. $(-7.2) + (-4.5) = -11.7$ **d.** $-\frac{1}{2} + (-\frac{3}{2}) = -\frac{4}{2} = -2$

Concept CHECK

Complete the problems. Check your answers in the back of the book.

1. $6 + 10$ **2.** $-8 + (-4)$ **3.** $-12 + (-5.5)$ **4.** $-\frac{4}{5} + (-\frac{3}{5})$

Absolute Value When adding signed numbers with different signs, you need to know the *absolute value* of the numbers. The absolute value of a number is its distance from zero on the number line. The symbol for absolute value is: $|\ |$

EXAMPLE 2

What is the absolute value of -2?

Find the absolute value.

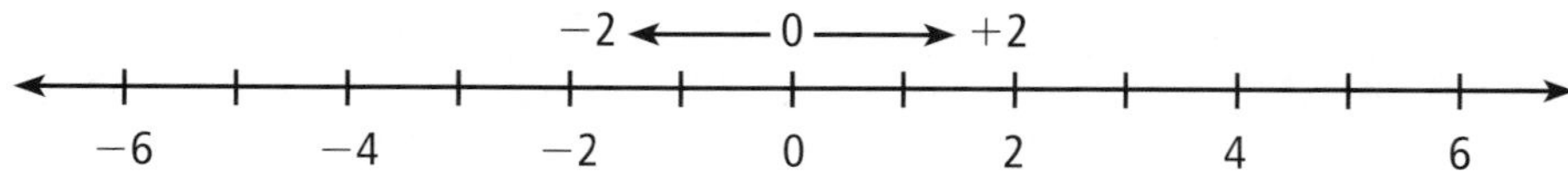

(Note: -2 is 2 units from zero on the number line.) Thus, $|-2|$ is 2.

Concept CHECK

Complete the problems. Check your answers in the back of the book. What is the absolute value of the following?

5. -4 **6.** -15 **7.** $+4$

Finding the Difference between Absolute Values When you are adding two signed numbers with different signs, find the difference between the absolute values of the numbers. Give the answer the same sign as the number with the larger absolute value.

EXAMPLE 3

Add.

a. $-12 + 6$ **b.** $-7 + 15$

Add.

a.	$-12 + 6$	← The signs are different. →	**b.** $-7 + 15$
	$\lvert -12 \rvert = 12$	← Find the absolute value. →	$\lvert -7 \rvert = 7$
	$12 - 6 = 6$	← Subtract the smaller number from the larger number. →	$15 - 7 = 8$
	$-12 + 6 = \mathbf{-6}$	← Attach the sign of the number with the larger absolute value. →	$-7 + 15 = \mathbf{8}$

Concept CHECK

Complete the problems. Check your answers in the back of the book.

8. $-21 + 8$ **9.** $-23.5 + 21.2$ **10.** $15 + (-$45)

Opposite of a Signed Number Subtracting signed numbers is based on knowing the opposite of a signed number. The opposite of -3 is $+3$ and the opposite of $+8$ is -8. To subtract signed numbers change the subtraction symbol to addition and add the opposite of the number being subtracted.

EXAMPLE 4

Subtract.

a. $-5 - 7$ **b.** $-3 - (-9)$

Subtract.

a.	$-5 - (+7)$	Change the subtraction sign to addition and find the opposite of $+7$ (it is -7) and -9 (it is $+9$).	**b.** $-3 - (-9)$
	$-5 + (-7)$		$-3 + 9$
	$-5 + (-7) = \mathbf{-12}$	← Follow the rules of addition. →	$-3 + 9 = \mathbf{6}$

Concept CHECK

Complete the problems. Check your answers in the back of the book.

11. $10 - 12$ **12.** $8 - 15$ **13.** $-12 - (-3)$ **14.** $9 - (-3)$

Practice

15. $-3 + (-8)$ **16.** $-8 + 3$ **17.** $-3 + (-4)$ **18.** $-12 + (-4)$

19. $-15 + (-15)$ **20.** $18 + (-18)$ **21.** $6 + (-4)$ **22.** $8 + (-5)$

23. $4 + (-8)$ **24.** $-7 + (-5)$ **25.** $16 + (-9)$ **26.** $-12 + 8$

27. The record high temperature of 134°F was recorded in Death Valley, California, in 1913. The record low was −80°F at Prospect Creek, Alaska, in 1971. What is the difference between the highest and lowest temperatures?

28. At 2:00 AM, a plant worker found that a dial was reading 12.0. At 3:00 AM, she found that the reading had changed to −3.0. Find the difference between these two readings.

WORKSHOPS

WORKSHOP 16

Average (Mean)

Need Help? Go to...
Application Q: Mean, p. AP12

Finding the Average The average, or mean, is a single number used to represent a group of numbers. The average of two or more numbers is the sum of the numbers divided by the number of items added.

EXAMPLE 1

Find the average of 7, 9, 4, 6, and 4.

Find the average.

$$\frac{7 + 9 + 4 + 6 + 4}{5} = \frac{30}{5} = \mathbf{6}$$

(Add to find the total. Divide by the number of items.)

EXAMPLE 2

Find the average of 693, 367, 528, and 626.

Find the average.

$$\frac{693 + 367 + 528 + 626}{4} = \frac{2{,}214}{4} = \mathbf{553.5}$$

EXAMPLE 3

Find the average of 5.7, 6.3, 4.2, 5.8, and 3.4.

Find the average. Round to the nearest tenth.

$$\frac{5.7 + 6.3 + 4.2 + 5.8 + 3.4}{5} = \frac{2.54}{5} = \mathbf{5.08 \text{ or } 5.1}$$

EXAMPLE 4

Find the average of $17, $24, $38, $23, $19, and $26.

Find the average. Round to the nearest dollar.

$$\frac{\$17 + \$24 + \$38 + \$23 + \$19 + \$26}{6} = \frac{\$147}{6} = \mathbf{\$24.5 \text{ or } \$25}$$

Concept CHECK

Complete the problems. Check your answers in the back of the book. Find the average for each set of numbers. Round to the nearest cent.

1. 3, 6, 2, 5, 8, 6

2. 3.2, 1.8, 6.5, 8.1, 5.9

3. 134, 126, 130

4. $25, $37, $49, $53, $42, $42

Practice

Find the average for each group.

5. 7, 8, 9, 12, 14

6. 4, 6, 10, 12, 8

7. 70, 85, 90, 75

8. 44, 86, 35, 95

9. 197, 108, 115

10. 225, 432, 321

11. 776, 709, 754, 733

12. 526, 387, 431, 388

13. 2.4, 3.5, 4.7, 2.9, 8.4

14. 6.8, 5.6, 3.4, 2.5, 4.7

15. 1.4, 2.5, 4.8, 3.7, 2.0, 3.9

16. 8.1, 5.3, 3.6, 7.9, 4.6, 3.2

17. \$14, \$12, \$16, \$14, \$15

18. \$64, \$38, \$92, \$51, \$65

Find the average for each group. Round to the amount indicated.

19. 7.8, 6.3, 8.3, 4.9, 7.7, 6.9, 5.1 (nearest tenth)

20. 9.2, 7.6, 8.2, 5.9, 9.5, 7.8 (nearest tenth)

21. 31.7, 33.9, 36.1, 33.8 (nearest tenth)

22. 4.37, 3.74, 4.90, 5.74 (nearest hundredth)

23. 34.87, 42.90, 46.21, 36.34, 39.89 (nearest hundredth)

24. \$37.50, \$44.50, \$39.65, \$34.25, \$15.61, \$11.22 (nearest cent)

25. Ben Agars had bowling scores of 175, 132, and 142. What was his average?

26. Latoya Miller recorded her pulse rate on four occasions as follows: 68, 85, 77, and 82. What was her average pulse rate?

27. Rachel Kelley's tips from being a bellhop were \$4.00, \$2.00, \$3.50, \$1.00, \$4.00, \$2.00, \$1.00, and \$3.00. What was her average tip?

28. During a 6-day period in June, you earned an average of \$25 a day for mowing lawns. What were your total earnings?

29. Last year, Andre Barsotti's telephone bills averaged \$35.45 a month. What was his total bill for the year?

30. Hung Lee had an average grade of 92 on his first 4 business math tests. He had a 95 and a 98 on the next two tests. What was his average grade for the 6 tests?

31. Carlita Cruz recorded her math test scores this quarter. What was her average?

Test Number	1	2	3	4	5	6	7	8
Score	87	75	98	95	82	77	78	88

32. What does she need on the next test to have an average of 86?

33. If there are a total of ten 100-point tests for the quarter, is it possible for her to raise her average to 90?

WORKSHOPS

WORKSHOPS

WORKSHOP 17

Elapsed Time

Need Help? Go to...
Application F: Elapsed Time (Hours), p. AP5

Calculating Elapsed Time To find elapsed time, subtract the earlier time from the later time.

EXAMPLE 1

Find the elapsed time for someone who worked from:

a. 2:15 PM to 10:30 PM **b. 6:45 AM to 12:56 PM**

Subtract.

a. 10:30
− 2:15
8:15 or 8 hours, 15 minutes; written as **8 h:15 min**

b. 12:56
− 6:45
6:11 or 6 hours, 11 minutes; written as **6 h:11 min**

Concept CHECK

Complete the problems. Check your answers in the back of the book. Find the elapsed time for a person who worked from:

1. 9:15 AM to 11:15 AM
2. 8:30 AM to 11:50 AM
3. 1:45 PM to 8:50 PM
4. 3:10 PM to 11:15 PM

You cannot subtract 45 minutes from 30 minutes unless you borrow an hour and add it to the 30 minutes. Remember that 1 hour = 60 minutes.

EXAMPLE 2

Find the elapsed time from 1:45 PM to 8:30 PM

Subtract and add.

8:30	=	7:30 + :60	=	7:90 borrowed 1 hour
− 1:45	=	−1:45	=	−1:45
				6:45 or **6 h:45 min**

Concept CHECK

Complete the problems. Check your answers in the back of the book. Find the elapsed time for a person who worked from:

5. 8:45 AM to 12:30 PM
6. 2:50 PM to 10:20 PM
7. 9:25 AM to 11:10 AM
8. 1:25 PM to 11:15 PM

To find elapsed time when the time period spans 1:00 o'clock, add 12 hours to the later time before subtracting.

EXAMPLE 3

Find the elapsed time from 10:20 AM to 3:30 PM

Subtract and add.

$$\begin{array}{rcl} 3{:}30 & = & (12+3)+{:}30 & = & 15{:}30 \\ \underline{-\,10{:}20} & = & \underline{-10{:}20\qquad} & = & \underline{-10{:}20} \\ & & & & 5{:}10 \end{array}$$

5:10 or **5 h:10 min**

Concept CHECK

Complete the problems. Check your answers in the back of the book. Find the elapsed time for a person who worked from:

9. 8:30 AM to 4:30 PM

10. 9:15 AM to 5:30 PM

11. 7:45 AM to 4:00 PM

12. 9:25 PM to 6:15 AM

Practice

Find the elapsed time for a person who worked from:

13. 4:30 PM to 11:45 PM

14. 6:30 AM to 11:45 AM

15. 4:15 PM to 10:10 PM

16. 7:43 AM to 10:40 AM

17. 8:00 AM to 4:30 PM

18. 9:15 AM to 6:25 PM

Find the elapsed time.

19. From 7:35 AM to 11:28 AM

20. From 2:50 AM to 11:05 AM

21. From 6:20 PM to 11:05 PM

22. From 1:37 AM to 9:28 AM

23. Samaki Watson worked from 9:45 AM to 6:12 PM How long did he work?

24. Helene Angell took a bus that left Detroit at 9:25 AM and arrived in Chicago at 3:20 PM How long was the trip? (Disregard time zones.)

25. Tom Henry started mowing his lawn at 10:45 AM and finished at 3:15 PM If he took one hour off for lunch, how much time did he spend mowing his lawn?

26. Boyson's opened at 7:00 AM on Sunday, December 23 and did not close until 6:00 PM on Monday, December 24. How many hours straight did Boyson's stay open?

27. Ashilla Grant started her actuarial exam at 9:45 AM and worked on it for $6\frac{1}{2}$ hours. What time did she finish?

WORKSHOPS

WORKSHOP 18

Business Data Analysis: Reading Tables and Charts

Need Help? Go to...
Application C: Tables and Charts, p. AP3

Reading a Table To read a table or chart, find the column containing one of the pieces of information you have. Look across the row containing the other piece of information. Read down the column and across the row. You will find the information you need where the column and row cross.

EXAMPLE 1

Any fraction of a pound over the weight shown takes the next higher rate. What is the cost to ship a 10-lb package to Rate Group 4? (Use Figure W18.1.)

Figure W18.1

Table 1b: Postal Rates

Weight Not Over (lb)	Rate Groups							
	1	2	3	4	5	6	7	8
0.5	$28.50	$ 28.75	$ 37.00	$ 75.00	$ 38.00	$ 38.00	$ 37.00	$ 52.00
1.0	41.00	42.50	49.00	93.00	58.00	55.00	47.00	65.00
2.0	44.50	47.50	56.00	107.75	65.75	63.45	54.20	80.90
3.0	48.00	52.50	63.00	122.50	73.50	71.90	61.60	96.80
4.0	51.50	57.50	70.00	137.25	81.25	80.35	68.60	112.70
5.0	55.00	62.50	77.00	152.00	89.00	88.80	75.80	128.60
6.0	58.50	67.50	84.00	166.75	96.75	97.25	83.00	144.50
7.0	62.00	72.50	91.00	181.50	104.50	105.70	90.20	160.40
8.0	65.50	77.50	98.00	196.25	112.25	114.15	97.40	176.30
9.0	69.00	82.50	105.00	211.00	120.00	122.60	104.60	192.20
10.0	72.50	87.50	112.00	225.75	127.75	131.05	111.80	208.10
11.0	75.35	90.65	116.30	237.00	132.65	137.45	116.05	218.10
12.0	78.20	93.80	120.60	248.25	137.55	143.85	120.30	228.10
13.0	81.05	96.95	124.90	259.50	142.45	150.25	124.55	238.10
14.0	83.90	100.10	129.20	270.75	147.35	156.65	128.80	248.10
15.0	86.75	103.25	133.50	282.00	152.25	163.05	133.05	258.10

Source: USPS International Postal Rates and Fees Publication 51

Step 1: Find the Rate Group 4 column.

Step 2: Find the 10-lb row.

Step 3: Read across the 10-lb row to the Rate Group 4 column. The cost is $225.75.

Concept CHECK

Complete the problems. Check your answers in the back of the book. Find the cost to ship each package to the indicated Rate Group in Figure W18.1.

1. 1 lb, Rate Group 1

2. 1 lb, Rate Group 7

3. 10 lb, Rate Group 6

4. 13.2 lb, Rate Group 3

Classifying an Item To classify an item, find the row that contains the known data. Then read the classification from the head of the column.

Figure W18.2

Size Chart—Men's Sizes									
Suits and Sport Coats Sizes 36 to 46 Order by chest size. Be sure waist will fit comfortably.	Order Size	36	37	38	39	40	42	44	46
	If chest is (inches)	35–36	36–37	37–38	38–39	39–40	41–42	43–44	45–46
	And waist is (inches)	28–31	29–32	30–33	31–34	32–35	34–37	36–39	38–41
Jackets Sizes 36 to 46 Order by chest size.	Order Size	36	38	40	42	44	46		
	If chest is (inches)	$34\frac{1}{2}$–36	$36\frac{1}{2}$–38	$38\frac{1}{2}$–40	$40\frac{1}{2}$–42	$42\frac{1}{2}$–44	$44\frac{1}{2}$–46		

EXAMPLE 2

What size suit should a man with a 41-inch chest order?

Step 1: Find the Suits and Sport Coats section.

Step 2: Find the row "if chest is (inches)."

Step 3: Read across the row to 41-42.

Step 4: Read the number at the head of the column (42).

A man with a 41-inch chest should order a size 42 suit.

Concept CHECK

Complete the problems. Check your answers in the back of the book. Determine what size garment should be ordered.

5. Suit, chest size 38 inches

6. Jacket, chest size 41 inches

Practice

Use Figure W18.1 to find the cost to ship each package to the indicated Rate Group.

7. 6 lb, Rate Group 5
8. 2 lb, Rate Group 2
9. 11 lb, Rate Group 5
10. 9 lb, Rate Group 8
11. 12 lb, Rate Group 3
12. 9 lb, Rate Group 1
13. 6.5 lb, Rate Group 4
14. 9.75 lb, Rate Group 6
15. 11.2 lb, Rate Group 7
16. 2.6 lb, Rate Group 2
17. 1.35 lb, Rate Group 4
18. 0.75 lb, Rate Group 8

Use Figure W18.1 to determine the maximum weight a package can weigh.

	Shipping to Rate Group	Shipping Cost	Maximum Weight
19. a.	1	$ 78.20	
b.	2	52.50	
c.	3	116.3	
d.	4	166.75	
e.	5	142.45	
f.	6	38.00	

Use Figure W18.2 to determine what size garment should be ordered.

	Chest Size (inches)	Waist Size (inches)	Suit Order Size	Jacket Order Size
20. a.	37	30		
b.	42	35		
c.	45	39		
d.	36	32		
e.	40	35		
f.	38	34		

21. What size of suit should a man with a 36-inch chest and a 31-inch waist order?

22. What size of suit should a man with a 39-inch chest and a 33-inch waist order?

WORKSHOP 19

Business Data Analysis: Reading Graphs

Need Help? Go to...
- Application M: Reading Bar Graphs, p. AP8
- Application N: Reading Line Graphs, pp. AP9–AP10

Visual Reading Many mathematical applications are related to graphs. There are many different types of graphs including bar graphs, pie charts, and line graphs. Being able to analyze the information contained within a graph helps to make deductions and to interpret data. Because there are many different parts to a graph, identifying each part can help to answer questions related to the graph.

EXAMPLE

Answer the questions about the graph.

a. What type of graph is shown?
b. What is the title of the graph?
c. What does the vertical axis represent?
d. In what year did the most thefts occur?
e. Did more thefts occur in Year I or Year J?

Figure W19.1

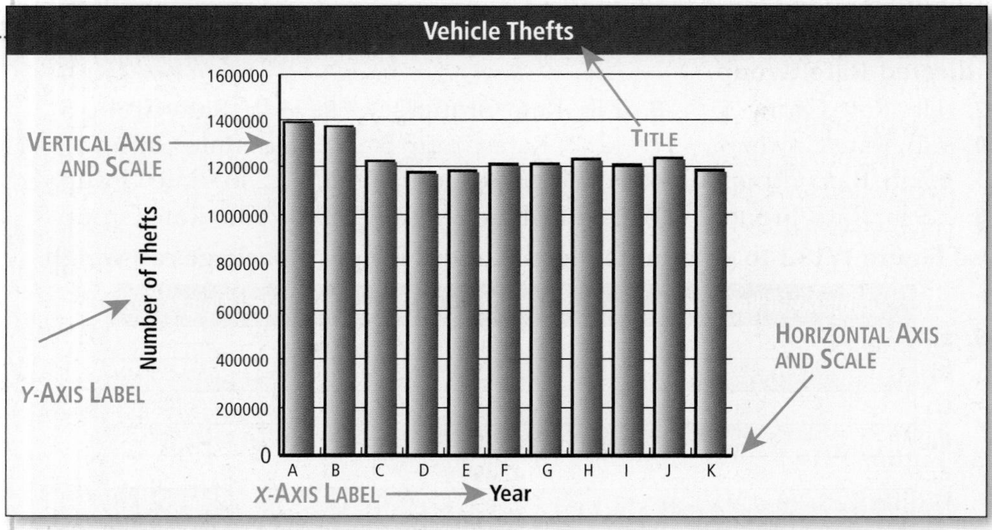

Read and follow the directions.

a. A **bar graph** is shown. **(It displays data and compares facts in a vertical or horizontal format.)**

b. The title of the graph is **Vehicle Thefts.**

c. The vertical axis represents the **number of thefts committed.**

d. Most of the thefts occurred in **Year A. (This is determined by looking at the bar that is the tallest.)**

e. Just by looking at the graph, it is difficult to determine in which year more thefts occurred. (The scale is so large that a small difference in numbers is difficult to distinguish.)

Complete the problems. Check your answers in the back of the book. Answer the questions about Figure W19.1.

1. What year had about 1,400,000 thefts?
2. Which two years had about the same number of thefts?
3. About how many thefts occurred in 2006?

Practice

Use Figure W19.2 to answer Problems 4–6.

4. What was the top Initial Public Offering (IPO) stock?
5. What two IPOs had about the same performance?
6. If the total revenue generated by the IPOs was $20 million, how much was generated by MF Global?

Figure W19.2

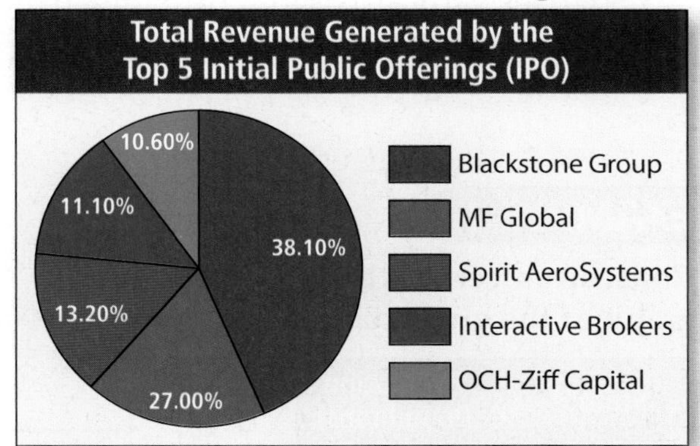

Source: http://www.ipohome.com/marketwatch/performance.asp?sort=offer&order=DESC

Use Figure W19.3 for Problems 7–10.

7. Which industry employed the most people?
8. In which industry were there about 16 million people employed?
9. Which industry had about 13 million people employed?
10. Estimate the number of Manufacturing employees.

Figure W19.3

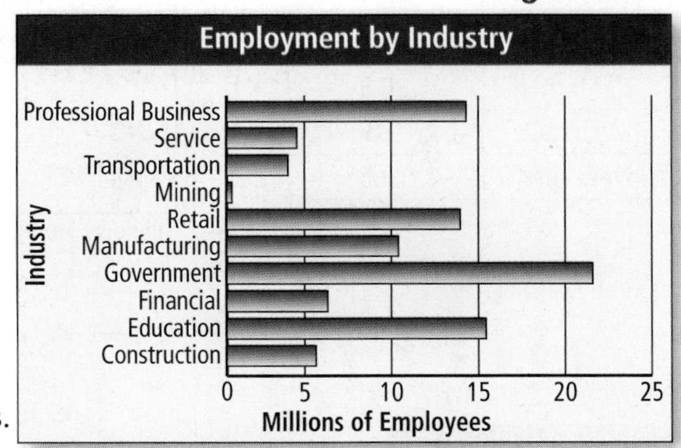

Source: http://www.bls.gov/iag/iaghome.htm

Use Figure W19-4 for Problems 11–16.

11. Which year had the lowest stock price?
12. Estimate the lowest stock price.
13. What year showed the highest stock price?
14. Estimate the highest stock price.
15. Estimate how much the stock declined in price from Year H to Year J.
16. Estimate the stock price in Year A.

Figure W19.4

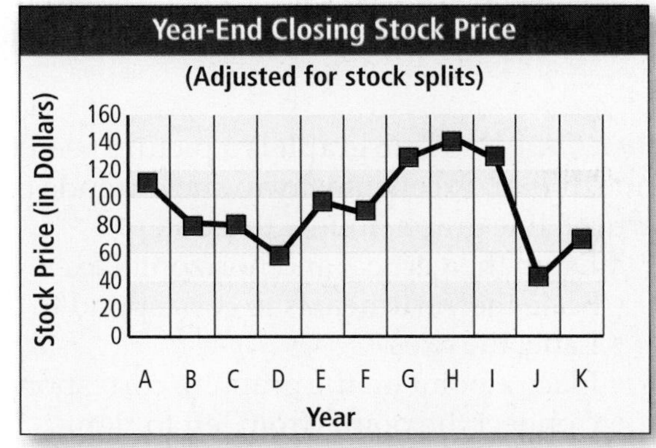

WORKSHOP 20

Business Data Analysis: Constructing Graphs

Need Help? Go to...
Application M: Reading Bar Graphs, p. AP8
Application N: Reading Line Graphs, pp. AP9–AP10

Bar Graph A **bar graph** is a picture that displays and compares numerical facts in the form of vertical or horizontal bars. To construct a vertical bar graph, follow these steps:

- Draw the vertical y-axis and the horizontal x-axis.
- Scale the vertical axis to correspond to the given data. Draw one bar to represent each quantity.
- Label each bar and the vertical and horizontal axes and title the graph.

EXAMPLE 1

Construct a vertical bar graph of the given data.

State	Population (in millions)
Illinois	12.8
Florida	19.5
Texas	26.4
California	38.3
Michigan	9.8
New York	19.6

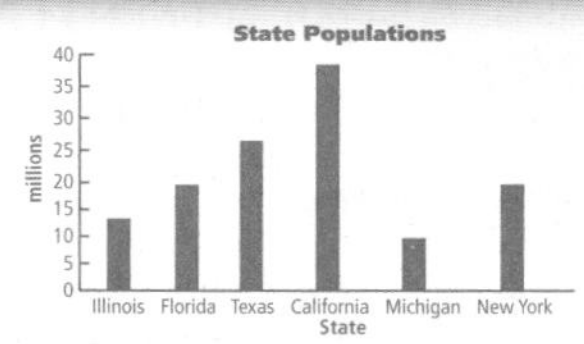

Construct a vertical bar graph.

a. Draw vertical and horizontal axes.
b. Scale the vertical axis.

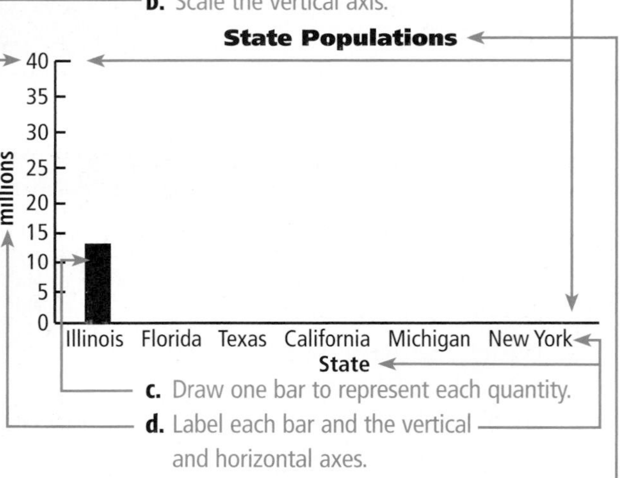

c. Draw one bar to represent each quantity.
d. Label each bar and the vertical and horizontal axes.
e. Title the graph.

Concept CHECK

Complete the problem. Check your answer in the back of the book.

1. Complete construction of the vertical bar graph started in Example 1.

Line Graph A **line graph** is a picture used to compare data over a period of time. It is an excellent way to show trends (increases or decreases). To construct a line graph, follow these steps:

- Draw the vertical and horizontal axes.
- Scale the vertical axis to correspond to the given data.
- Label the axes.
- Place a point on the graph to correspond to each item of data.
- Connect the points from left to right.
- Title the graph.

EXAMPLE 2

Construct a line graph of the given data.

Computer Classes	
Year	**Enrollment**
A	30
B	38
C	60
D	90
E	100

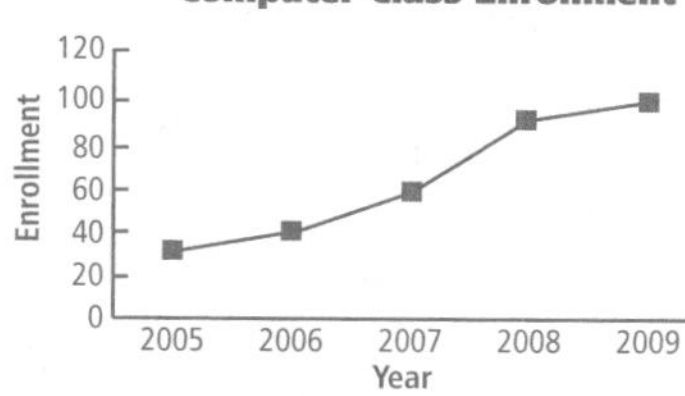

Construct a line graph.

a. Draw vertical and horizontal axes.

b. Scale the vertical axis.

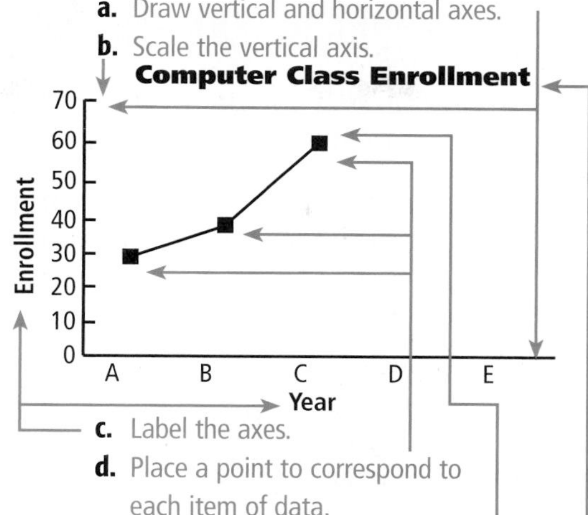

c. Label the axes.

d. Place a point to correspond to each item of data.

e. Connect the points from left to right.

f. Title the line graph.

Concept CHECK

Complete the problem. Check your answer in the back of the book.

2. Complete construction of the line graph started in Example 2.

Practice

For Problems 3 and 4, construct vertical bar graphs of the given data.

3.

World Population	
Country	**Millions of People**
Brazil	202
China	1,355
India	1,236
Indonesia	253
Russia	142
United States	318

4.

Department Store Sales	
Department	**Total Sales in Thousands**
Children's clothing	$145
Housewares	$ 82
Women's clothing	$120
Men's clothing	$112
Appliances	$ 75
Dishes	$130

For Problems 5 and 6, construct line graphs for the given data.

5.

Trade with Advanced Technology	
Month	**Millions of Dollars**
January	18.4
February	18.1
March	20.6
April	16.6
May	17.2
June	17.7
July	15.0
August	15.7
September	14.8
October	15.7
November	14.9

6.

Coffee Prices	
Month	**Colombian Mild**
January	$106
February	$104
March	$100
April	$ 99
May	$100
June	$107
July	$106
August	$108
September	$113
October	$116
November	$120
December	$122

WORKSHOPS

WORKSHOP 21

Units of Measurement

Dimensional Analysis Below are the abbreviations and conversions for units of measure in the U.S. Customary System.

Length	Volume	Weight
12 inches (in) = 1 foot (ft)	2 cups (c) = 1 pint (pt)	16 ounces (oz) = 1 pound (lb)
3 feet (ft) = 1 yard (yd)	2 pt = 1 quart (qt)	2,000 lb = 1 ton (t)
5,280 ft = 1 mile (mi)	4 qt = 1 gallon (gal)	

Below are the symbols and conversions for units of measure in the metric system.

Length	Volume
1,000 millimeters (mm) = 1 meter (m)	1,000 milliliters (mL) = 1 liter (L)
100 centimeters (cm) = 1 m	**Mass**
1,000 m = 1 kilometer (km)	1,000 grams (g) = 1 kilogram (kg)

To convert from one unit of measure to another, use the conversion lists above. When converting to a smaller unit, multiply.

EXAMPLE 1

Convert 6 feet to inches.

Convert. (Note: Use 12 in = 1 ft) $6 \times 12 = 72$ **6 ft = 72 in**

EXAMPLE 2

Convert 2 meters to centimeters.

Convert. (Note: Use 100 cm = 1 m) $2 \times 100 = 200$ **2 m = 200 cm**

EXAMPLE 3

Convert 12 pints to quarts. (When converting to a larger unit, divide.)

Convert. (Note: Use 2 pt = 1 qt) $12 \div 2 = 6$ **12 pt = 6 qt**

EXAMPLE 4

Convert 8,400 grams to kilograms.

Convert. (Note: Use 1,000 g = 1 kg) $8{,}400 \div 1{,}000 = 8.4$ **8,400 g = 8.4 kg**

Concept CHECK

Complete the problems. Check your answers in the back of the book.
Convert.

1. 9 ft to inches

2. 0.15 L to milliliters

3. 24 ft to yards

4. 350 cm to meters

Practice

Do the following conversions.

5. 9 yd to feet
6. 14 gal to quarts
7. 7 lb to ounces
8. 3 ft to inches
9. 6 lb to ounces
10. 4 L to milliliters
11. 3.8 km to meters
12. 16 pt to cups
13. 3.2 kg to grams
14. 96 in to yards
15. 9 qt to gallons
16. 42 oz to pounds
17. 14 qt to gallons
18. 33 oz to pounds
19. 2,000 g to kilograms
20. 90 cm to meters
21. 3,300 mL to liters
22. 450 cm to meters
23. 72.1 kg to grams
24. 3.4 L to milliliters
25. 723 g to kilograms
26. 11.316 mL to liters
27. 18 cm to millimeters
28. 383.2 cm to meters
29. 1 yd 4 in to inches
30. 4 ft 2 in to inches
31. 5 qt 1 pt to pints
32. 3 lb 7 oz to ounces
33. 2 gal 2 qt to quarts
34. 2 yd 2 ft 2 in to inches

35. How many quarts will a 5-gallon plastic bag hold?

36. How many milliliters will a 1-liter bottle hold?

37. How many cups of coffee does a 2-quart coffee pot hold?

38. How many cups of hot chocolate will a 2-gallon thermos jug hold?

39. How many inches long is a $6\frac{2}{3}$-yard roll of aluminium foil?

40. Cottage cheese is sold in 1-pint containers. How many pints must be bought to have enough for a recipe that calls for 5 cups?

41. James Hartman knows that his jogging stride is about 1 meter long. The jogging track he uses is 3.9 kilometers long. How many strides does it take him to go around the track once?

42. The cafeteria receives 32 cases of milk each day. Each case contains 24 half-pint cartons. How many gallons of milk are received each day?

43. A soft drink is sold in 355 milliliter cans. How many liters are in a six-pack?

44. Enrique Diaz, a pastry chef, baked a walnut cake weighing 2.4 kilograms. How many 75-gram servings can be cut from the cake?

45. Lakita Moore ordered baseboard moulding for the rooms of a new house. Moore needs to complete this chart to determine the total number of feet of moulding needed. How much moulding is needed?

	Length	Width	2 Lengths	+	2 Widths	=	Perimeter
	12 ft	9 ft	24 ft	+	18 ft	=	42 ft
a.	10 ft	8 ft	20 ft	+	16 ft	=	
b.	18 ft	24 ft		+		=	
c.	10 ft 6 in	9 ft 4 in		+		=	
d.	11 ft 3 in	7 ft 8 in		+		=	
e.	11 ft 4 in	13 ft 2 in		+		=	
f.	17 ft 8 in	12 ft 9 in		+		=	
g.	8 ft 5 in	7 ft 9 in		+		=	
h.						**Total**	

WORKSHOP 22

Metric System

Basic Unit of Measuring The basic unit for measuring length in the metric system is the *meter* (m). The basic unit of capacity is the *liter* (L) and the basic unit of mass is the *gram* (g).

All metric measurements use the same prefix(es). Look at **Figure W22.1** for the prefix abbreviations and the length. The prefix of each unit of length tells you how that unit is related to the meter.

Figure W22.1

Units of Measurement		
1 **kilo**meter (k)	=	1,000 meters
1 **hecto**meter (h)	=	100 meters
1 **deka**meter (da)	=	10 meters
1 **deci**meter (d)	=	0.1 meter
1 **centi**meter (c)	=	0.01 meter
1 **milli**meter (m)	=	0.001 meter

Converting Units The procedure for converting from one metric unit to another can be accomplished by moving the decimal point of the original unit to the right or left. It is the same as multiplying or dividing by a power of 10. Here are some steps to take when converting units:

Step 1: Locate the original metric unit on the chart below.

Step 2: Count the number of jumps to the new desired unit.

Step 3: Move the decimal point of the original unit as many places as jumps in the same left or right direction.

Figure W22.2

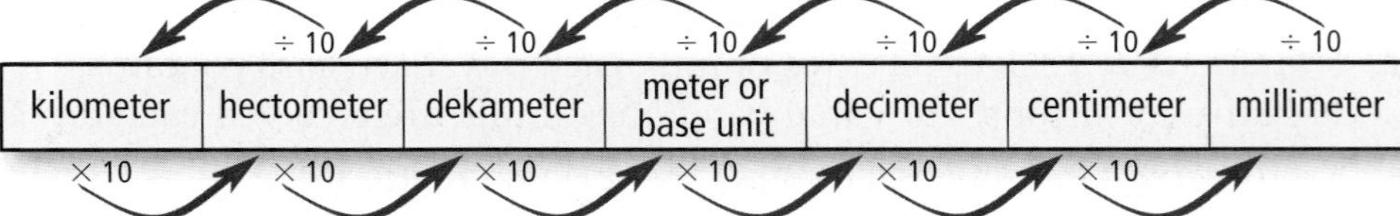

EXAMPLE 1

A shipping crate is 2.5 meters long. How many centimeters is this?

Convert units. Locate the original unit. [It is 2 jumps to the right to go from meters (base unit) to centimeters.]

Figure W22.3

kilo	hecto	deka	base unit	deci	centi	milli

Move the decimal point right 2 places. **2.5 m = 250 cm**

Concept CHECK

Complete the problems. Check your answers in the back of the book.

1. 2.8 m = ________ cm

2. 0.15 m = ________ dm

3. 261 cm = ________ m

4. 3,260 m = ________ km

EXAMPLE 2

How many liters are in a 2,000 mL plastic bottle?

Convert units. Locate the original unit, which is milliliters. (It is three jumps to the left to go from milliliters to liters—base unit.)

Figure W22.4

kilo	hecto	deka	base unit	deci	centi	milli

Move the decimal point left three places.

2,000 mL = 2.000 L = 2 L

Concept CHECK

Complete the problems. Check your answers in the back of the book.

5. 2,500 mL = ___ L

6. 980 cm = ___ hm

7. 3.87 L = ___ mL

8. 2.0 kg = ___ g

Practice

Complete the table. Each row should contain equivalent measures.

	Kilo	Hecto	Deka	Base Unit	Deci	Centi	Milli
9.	9	a.	b.	c.	d.	e.	f.
10.	a.	4	b.	c.	d.	e.	f.
11.	a.	b.	20	c.	d.	e.	f.
12.	a.	b.	c.	d.	5,000	e.	f.
13.	a.	b.	c.	d.	e.	3,300	f.
14.	a.	b.	c.	d.	e.	f.	1,200,000

15. 2 m = ___ cm

16. 400 cm = ___ mm

17. 200 cm = ___ dm

18. 80 mm = ___ m

19. 4,000 m = ___ km

20. 3 L = ___ mL

21. 250 mL = ___ L

22. 0.6 L = ___ mL

23. 0.5 L = ___ mL

24. 5 kg = ___ g

25. 10,000 g = ___ kg

26. 8.27 kg = ___ g

27. 0.038 kg = ___ mg

28. 18.2 g = ___ mg

29. 736 g = ___ kg

30. 6 dm = ___ mm

31. 50 cm = ___ dm

32. 2,500 mm = ___ cm

33. 800 m = ___ hm

34. 400 cm = ___ km

35. 32 km = ___ m

36. 8 m = ___ dam

37. 3.21 g = ___ hg

38. 2.854 g = ___ cg

39. A package of cereal weighs 3.17 kilograms. How many grams does it weigh?

40. A can of chili weighs 425 grams. How many kilograms does it weigh?

41. A roll of aluminum foil measures 76.2 meters long by 304 millimeters wide. What is the length in millimeters? What is the width in meters?

42. Sandwich bags measure 16.51 centimeters by 14.92 centimeters. What are the dimensions in millimeters?

43. A bag of flour weighs 2,270 grams. How many kilograms does it weigh?

WORKSHOPS

WORKSHOP 23

Conversion of International Currency–Rates of Exchange

Currency Exchange Rate An *exchange rate* is established between the national currencies to facilitate international travel and international trade. This exchange rate, as published daily in *The Wall Street Journal*, is based on the U.S. dollar. It changes frequently. A partial table is given below.

Figure W23.1

Currency Exchange Rates		
Country	**U.S. Dollar Equivalent**	**Currency per U.S. Dollar**
Australia (dollar)	0.8764	1.1410
Bahrain (dinar)	2.6560	0.3765
Brazil (real)	0.5575	1.7937
Britain (pound)	2.0550	0.4866
Canada (dollar)	1.0306	0.9703
China (renminbi)	0.1349	7.4120
Denmark (krone)	0.1951	5.1256
Eurodollar	1.4539	0.6878
India (rupee)	0.02548	39.246
Israel (shekel)	0.2520	3.9683
Japan (yen)	0.009118	109.67
Mexico (peso)	0.09141	10.9397
Russia (ruble)	0.04066	24.594
Sweden (krona)	0.1567	6.3816
Venezuela (bolivar)	0.000466	2145.92

U.S. Dollars to Foreign Currency To exchange U.S. dollars to foreign currency, you need to multiply the number of U.S. dollars by the currency per U.S. dollars from **Figure W23.1.** Or it looks like:

U.S. Dollar to Foreign Currency = U.S. Dollar × Currency per U.S. Dollar

EXAMPLE 1

A businessperson is traveling to the Far East and needs to exchange U.S. dollars to Japanese yen and Chinese renminbi. Exchange: $5,000 to Japanese yen.

Exchange.

U.S. Dollar × Currency per U.S. Dollar

$5,000 × 109.67 yen per U.S. dollar = **548,350 yen**

$5,000 × 7.4120 renminbi per U.S. dollar = **37,060 renminbi**

Complete the problems. Check your answers in the back of the book.

1. Exchange $500 to Bahraini dinars.
2. Exchange $4,500 to Mexican pesos.

Foreign Currency to Foreign Currency To exchange from one foreign currency to another foreign currency, exchange to U.S. dollars and then exchange the U.S. dollars to the other foreign currency. It looks like…

U.S. Dollars to Foreign Currency = Foreign Currency × U.S. Dollar Equivalent

EXAMPLE 2

Exchange 500 Swedish krona to euros.

Step 1: Exchange Swedish krona to U.S. dollars.

Foreign Currency × U.S. Dollar Equivalent

500 × 0.1567 U.S. dollars per krona = $78.35

Step 2: Exchange U.S. dollars to euros.

$78.35 × 0.6878 euros per U.S. dollars = 53.88913 euros,

therefore, **500 Swedish krona = 53.89 euros**

Concept CHECK

Complete the problems. Check your answers in the back of the book.

3. Exchange 560 Canadian dollars to Australian dollars.
4. Exchange 6,000 Israeli shekels to Indian rupees.

Practice

5. Exchange $12,750 to Brazilian real.
6. Exchange $375 to Danish kroner.
7. Exchange 15,800 euros to U.S. dollars.
8. Exchange 498 Australian dollars to U.S. dollars.
9. Exchange 500 Swedish krona to Venezuelan bolivares.
10. Exchange 45,750 Chinese renminbi to Japanese yen.
11. At an auction held in London, an antique box sold for 1,150 British pounds. How much is that in U.S. dollars?
12. A sandwich in Cleveland, Ohio, sold for $4.95. The same sandwich, at the same price, would sell for how many rubles in Russia?
13. A large bar of orange/olive oil soap sold for 6 euros. How much is that in U.S. dollars?
14. The *International Herald Tribune* sold for 1.5 euros in Frankfurt, Germany. At the given rate of exchange, how much would it sell for in British pounds?

WORKSHOPS

WORKSHOP 24

Estimation: Rounding

Estimating an Answer Estimation is one method to determine the reasonableness of an answer. Rounding is often used to estimate an answer. First, round the numbers to the highest place value. Then perform the indicated computation. If all the numbers do not have the same place value, round the numbers to the highest place value of the smaller number and estimate the answer.

EXAMPLE 1

Estimate 76.761 − 39.302.

Estimate.

76.761	(round to)	80
−39.302	(round to)	−40
		40

(By computation it is 37.459.)

EXAMPLE 2

Estimate 23.79 ÷ 6.1.

Estimate.

$6.1\overline{)23.79}$ (round to) $\quad \overset{4}{6\overline{)24}}$ By computation it is 3.9.)

Concept CHECK

Complete the problems. Check your answers in the back of the book. First round the numbers to the highest place value, estimate the answer, then perform the computation.

1. 43.986 − 27.491

2. 41.8474 ÷ 7.1

EXAMPLE 3

Estimate $2\frac{3}{4} \times 8\frac{1}{4}$.

Round, estimate the answer, then perform the computation.

Round $2\frac{3}{4}$ to 3 and $8\frac{1}{4}$ to 8. Then $3 \times 8 = 24$, so the answer is **about 24.**

(By computation it is $22\frac{11}{16}$.)

EXAMPLE 4

Estimate 33% of $62.

Round, estimate the answer, then perform the computation.

Round 33% to $\frac{1}{3}$ and $62 to $60.

Then $\frac{1}{3} \times \$60 = \$20$, so the answer is **about $20.**

(By computation it is $20.46.)

Concept CHECK

Complete the problems. Check your answers in the back of the book. First round the numbers to the highest place value, estimate the answer, then perform the computation.

3. $5\frac{1}{8} \times 4\frac{2}{3}$

4. 63.91×9.83

Practice

Round and estimate, then perform the indicated computation.

5. $5{,}965 + 1{,}824$

6. $7.791 + 2.151$

7. $15.86 - 13.72$

8. $\$72.75 - \$6.47$

9. 9.34×7.92

10. $\$28.40 \times 5.20$

11. $48.518 \div 6.8$

12. $57.723 \div 21.3$

13. $2\frac{3}{4} \times 1\frac{1}{2}$

14. $12\frac{1}{2} \times 2\frac{3}{5}$

15. $\frac{1}{4} \times 12\frac{1}{2}$

16. 31% of 18

17. 70% of $49.95

18. 27% of $12

19. 52% of 160

20. You purchase items for $39.45, $17.55, and $32.53. Estimate the total, then calculate.

21. Forty-two people charter a bus for $788. Estimate the amount each person pays, then calculate.

22. A living room measures $16\frac{1}{4}$ feet by $12\frac{1}{2}$ feet. Estimate the area in square feet, then calculate.

23. Blue jeans are on sale for 33% off the regular price of $35.95. Estimate the savings, then calculate.

WORKSHOP 25

Estimation: Front End

Adding Front-End Digits Estimation is a very valuable tool in business mathematics. It can be used as a quick method of checking the reasonableness of a calculation or when an exact answer is not needed. It is important to know how to estimate. One way to estimate a sum is to add the front-end digits.

EXAMPLE 1

6,477
2,142
+ 1,321

Estimate.

6,477	⟶	6
2,142	⟶	2
+ 1,321	⟶	+ 1
		9 or about 9,000

(By computation it is 9,940.)

EXAMPLE 2

\$8.60
3.19
+ 0.65

Estimate.

\$8.60	⟶	8
3.19	⟶	3
+ 0.65	⟶	+ 0
		11

(By computation it is \$12.44.)

Concept CHECK

Complete the problems. Check your answers in the back of the book. Estimate by adding the front-end digits. Perform the computations.

1.	**2.**	**3.**	**4.**
389	475	\$1,215	101.25
467	810	876	217.65
15	36	4,932	341.50
+ 240	+ 310	+ 315	+ 211.35

Finding a Closer Estimate Each estimate in the examples above is less than the correct sum. A closer estimate can be found by adjusting the sum of the front-end digits.

EXAMPLE 3

```
  567
  335
  124
+  84
```

Step 1: Seek a closer estimation. Look at a cluster of numbers. Decide if the two together add up to about 100.

```
  5|67|
  3|35|
  1|24|
+  |84|
```

Cluster adds up to about 100.
So, 100 + 100 = 200.

Step 2: Round and add up the front-end numbers.

```
  |5|67
  |3|35
  |1|24
 +   84
    900
```

Step 3: Add up the estimations in steps above.

900 + 200 = **1,100** (By computation it is 1,110.)

Concept CHECK

Complete the problems. Check your answers in the back of the book. Estimate by first adding the front-end digits and then by adjusting the sum of the front-end digits. Perform the computations.

5.	6.	7.	8.
335	127	359	825.19
660	259	286	367.42
74	85	924	598.15
+126	+535	+331	+791.85

Practice

Estimate by adding the front-end digits. Perform the computations.

9.	10.	11.	12.
5,623	$3.45	4,427	7,178
221	1.49	3,274	4,298
9,879	9.72	+ 1,245	+ 5,370
+ 1,061	+ 0.35		

Estimate by adjusting the sum of the front-end digits. Perform the computations.

13.	14.	15.	16.
285	$39.37	$15.95	$340.05
315	7.49	54.20	21.65
544	23.75	12.57	47.32
+ 361	+ 4.35	+ 21.54	+ 53.79

17. Estimate first, then calculate the total attendance for six home soccer games: 3,187, 2,234, 2,108, 3,421, 6,790, and 3,907.

18. Estimate first, then calculate the cost of these grocery items: tissues $1.29, coffee $6.99, orange juice $1.45, T-bone steak $6.79, oatmeal $1.99, cocoa mix $2.89, and a jar of salad dressing $1.99.

WORKSHOPS

WORKSHOP 26

Estimation: Compatible Numbers

Arriving at a Reasonable Estimate By changing the numbers in a problem to numbers that can be computed easily, you can arrive at a reasonable estimate. These are called *compatible numbers.*

EXAMPLE 1

36,414 ÷ 9

Estimate.

$$36{,}414 \div 9 \longrightarrow 9\overline{)36{,}000} = 4{,}000$$

The estimate is easy since 36,000 is close to 36,414 and is compatible with 9. The answer is **about 4,000**. (By computation it is 4,046.)

EXAMPLE 2

798 ÷ 42

Estimate.

$$798 \div 42 \longrightarrow 40\overline{)800} = 20$$

The estimate is easy since 800 is close to 798 and 40 is close to 42. Eight hundred and 40 are compatible. The answer is **about 20**. (By computation it is 19.)

Concept CHECK

Complete the problems. Check your answers in the back of the book. Estimate and then divide.

1. 661.74 ÷ 82 **2.** 8,763.3 ÷ 321 **3.** 47.6 ÷ 5.1 **4.** 329.95 ÷ 6

EXAMPLE 3

$\frac{1}{3} \times 8\frac{3}{4}$

Estimate. $\frac{1}{3} \times 8\frac{3}{4} \longrightarrow \frac{1}{3} \times 9 = 3$

The estimate is easy since 9 is close to $8\frac{3}{4}$ and is compatible with $\frac{1}{3}$. The answer is **about 3.** (By computation it is $2\frac{11}{12}$.)

EXAMPLE 4

25.5% of $420

Estimate. 25.5% of \$420 $\longrightarrow \frac{1}{4} \times 400 = 100$

The estimate is easy since 25.5 percent is about $\frac{1}{4}$, \$420 is about 400, and 400 and $\frac{1}{4}$ are compatible. The answer is **about $100**. (By computation it is $107.10.)

Complete the problems. Check your answers in the back of the book. Estimate using compatible numbers, then perform the computations.

5. $\frac{1}{4}$ of $12\frac{1}{8}$ **6.** $\frac{5}{8} \times 30.6$ **7.** 35% × \$926 **8.** 27% × \$820

WORKSHOPS

Practice

Estimate using compatible numbers, then perform the computations.

9. 8,824 ÷ 8 **10.** 4,879 ÷ 7 **11.** 6,095 ÷ 5

12. 642 ÷ 6 **13.** 896 ÷ 32 **14.** 24,564 ÷ 575

15. 8,766.63 ÷ 81 **16.** \$6,447.6 ÷ 7.2 **17.** $\frac{1}{2} \times 8\frac{1}{2}$

18. $\frac{5}{7} \times 44\frac{1}{2}$ **19.** 50% of \$430 **20.** 65% of \$75

21. Delbert Rowell drove his tractor-trailer rig 84,572.5 miles in 6 months. Estimate how many miles he drove each month.

22. Anna Nethery earned \$47,500 this year as a stock analyst. Estimate how much she earns each month.

23. A walking path is $20\frac{1}{2}$ miles long. You walk $\frac{1}{3}$ of the path by noon. Estimate the distance walked.

24. Harriet Murdock saves 33 percent of her paycheck each week. Last week, her check was for \$247.95. Estimate the amount saved.

25. During the high school state basketball finals, 75 percent of the 22,000 tickets were sold. Estimate how many tickets were not sold.

26. The hotel-motel tax in Pittsburgh is 9.5 percent of the price of a room. If a room costs \$112.50 per night, estimate the tax for 3 nights.

27. Fred Eskelsejah was hired as the bookkeeper at an annual salary of \$36,300. Estimate his monthly salary.

28. Cassius Russell learned at the job interview that he would be paid an annual salary of \$24,600 as account executive. Estimate his monthly salary.

29. Anitra Gatling took a job as a bookkeeper at an annual salary of \$25,200. Estimate her weekly salary.

30. Linda Jackson took a job at a manufacturing outlet. She earns \$350 a week. Estimate her daily income if she works 5 days a week. Calculate her annual salary.

31. Jianguo Wang is hired for a data entry position earning \$8.50 per hour. Estimate his annual salary if he works 40 hours a week.

32. Suppose you take a job as an office clerk earning \$13.85 per hour. Estimate your weekly salary if you work 40 hours a week.

33. Gonzalo Carlos purchased a cordless telephone that had a regular price of \$71.50. If he received 25 percent off, estimate how much he saved.

WORKSHOP 27

Estimation: Clustering

Estimation by clustering is another way of projecting what an answer will be. When the numbers to be added are close to the same quantity, the sum can be found by clustering.

EXAMPLE 1

\$4.85 + 5.15 + 4.89 + 5.17

Step 1: Estimate.

```
  $4.85
   5.15
   4.89
 + 5.17
```

All cluster around \$5.00

Step 2: Calculate.
\$5.00 × 4 = **\$20**
(Approximately)
(By computation it is \$20.06.)

EXAMPLE 2

\$15.95 + 16.50 + 15.75 + 7.95

Step 1: Estimate.

```
  $15.95
   16.50
   15.75
 +  7.95
```

\$15.95, 16.50, 15.75: Cluster around \$16.00
7.95: Clusters around \$8.00

Step 2: Calculate.
\$16 × 3 = \$48
\$48 + 8 = **\$56**
(Approximately)
(By computation it is \$56.15.)

Concept CHECK

Complete the problems. Check your answers in the back of the book. Estimate the sums by clustering, then compute the sums.

1.
```
  563
  598
  559
 +612
```

2.
```
  $27.95
   31.42
   30.25
 + 29.47
```

3.
```
  $1.59
   1.79
   2.21
 + 0.75
```

Practice

Estimate the sums by clustering. Compute the actual amount.

4.
```
  763
  781
  773
 +810
```

5.
```
  525
  496
  512
 +530
```

6.
```
  $53.39
   55.24
   49.26
 + 49.97
```

7.
```
  $36.20
   39.67
   41.78
 + 43.59
```

8.
```
  88,026
  91,521
  87,842
 +94,819
```

9.
```
  7.95
  7.87
  8.13
  8.25
 +3.67
```

10. 16.05
15.95
15.50
15.50
+5.50

11. $2.29
2.39
2.25
2.40
+ 8.95

12. $25.95
26.30
25.70
37.95
+ 38.50

13. School supplies costing $6.95, $7.25, $7.45, $6.65, and $6.79.

14. Groceries costing $2.89, $3.15, $3.29, $2.67, $3.25, and $3.35.

15. Work clothes costing $25.95, $23.95, $26.50, $39.95, and $41.25.

16. School supplies costing $1.09, $0.99, $0.89, $2.29, $1.99, and $2.15.

17. Clothes costing: shirt $17.95, shoes $39.95, six pairs of socks $18.25, tie $16.95, and belt $16.95.

18. Cordell Brown drove the miles indicated: Monday 367, Tuesday 390, Wednesday 405, Thursday 386, Friday 402, and Saturday 396. Estimate first, then calculate the total miles for the week.

19. Jane Flanagan had the following sales: first quarter $52,900, second quarter $88,900, third quarter $91,980, and fourth quarter $89,830. Estimate first, then calculate the total sales for the year.

20. Juan Perez had the following long-distance phone charges: $6.15, $2.15, $5.98, $1.81, $5.87, $1.89, and $11.71. Estimate first, then calculate the total long-distance charges.

21. During an extended stay at the Union Square Hotel, Stacy Anderson had these dry cleaning charges: $29.90, $15.90, $7.95, $24.75, $15.90, $15.90, and $12.50. Estimate and then calculate the total.

22. Shandel Williams used a calculator to solve the following problems. If she entered each number properly into the calculator, her answers should be correct. Estimate each answer and decide if Williams's answers are correct.

	Problem	Her Answer on Calculator	Your Estimate	Is She Right? Yes/No
a.	672 + 703 + 725 + 130	2,230.00		
b.	$9.80 + $9.95 + $10.35 + $10.01	40.11		
c.	1.23 + 1.95 + 7.8 + 7.6 + 8.4	24.98		
d.	82 + 75 + 79 + 34 + 29 + 32	299.00		
e.	44.20 + 44.51 + 30.07 + 29.35	148.13		
f.	625.1 + 615.2 + 12.35 + 10.75	1,263.40		
g.	9.89 + 2.9 + 9.49 + 3.1 + 2.75	24.73		
h.	12,341 + 25,452 + 13,021 + 12,981	61,231.00		

WORKSHOP 28

Scientific Notation

The Power of Numbers On most calculators, when you multiply 123,456 times 987,654, the product is displayed as 1.219318122 11. The number displayed is written in *scientific notation* and is interpreted as 1.219318122 times 10^{11} and is equal to 121,931,181,220 or one hundred twenty-one billion nine hundred thirty-one million one hundred eighty-one thousand two hundred twenty. Extremely large or extremely small numbers are often written in scientific notation and are examples of the elegance of concise mathematical notation.

Numbers written in scientific notation will be expressed as the product of a number equal to or greater than one and less than ten (1.219…) and a power of ten (10^{11}). Changing a number written in scientific notation to standard form requires moving the decimal point. If the exponent on ten is positive, move the decimal point that many places to the right; if the exponent on ten is negative, move the decimal point that many places to the left.

EXAMPLE 1

Write these numbers in standard notation and using words.

a. 1.1234×10^{7} **b.** 4.56789×10^{10} **c.** $8.123456789 \times 10^{12}$

d. 1.8765×10^{-5} **e.** 2.987×10^{-10}

Write the numbers in standard notation and using words.

a. 11,234,000 or eleven million two hundred thirty-four thousand

b. 45,678,900,000 or forty-five billion six hundred seventy-eight million nine hundred thousand

c. 8,123,456,789,000 or eight trillion one hundred twenty-three billion four hundred fifty-six million seven hundred eighty-nine thousand

d. 0.000018765 or eighteen thousand seven hundred sixty-five billionths

e. 0.0000000002987 or two thousand nine hundred eighty-seven ten trillionths

Concept CHECK

Complete the problems. Check your answers in the back of the book. Write these numbers in standard notation and using words.

1. 1.375×10^{6} **2.** 3.8642×10^{8} **3.** 7.123×10^{2} **4.** 4.7945×10^{-7}

Counting the Placement of the Decimal Point To write numbers that appear in standard notation in scientific notation, count how many places the decimal point must be moved to get a number larger than one but less than ten, that is the exponent on ten. If the decimal point is moved to the left, the exponent is positive. If the decimal point is moved to the right, the exponent is negative.

EXAMPLE 2

Write these numbers in scientific notation.

a. **12,632** **b.** **\$12.6 million** **c.** **0.000000571**

d. **Two hundred forty-one million five hundred six thousand three hundred seventy-nine**

e. **Ninety-three millionths**

Write the numbers in scientific notation.

a. 1.2632×10^4

b. $\$12,600,000 = \$1.26 \times 10^7$

c. 5.71×10^{-7}

d. $241,506,379 = 2.41506379 \times 10^8$

e. $0.000093 = 9.3 \times 10^{-5}$

Complete the problems. Check your answers in the back of the book.
Write these numbers in scientific notation.

5. 93,000,000

6. 0.0000000386

7. Seven million two hundred sixteen

8. Four thousand twenty-one ten thousandths

Practice

For Problems 9–14, write the numbers in standard notation and using words.

9. 7.391×10^5

10. 3.51096×10^8

11. 8.71×10^{-4}

12. 6.200841×10^7

13. 2.92651×10^{11}

14. 1.82×10^{-6}

In Problems 15–20, write the numbers in scientific notation.

15. 12,620,380

16. 4,390,487,285,302

17. 0.0000286

18. 0.00000000000182

19. 4.75 million

20. 4.75 millionths

21. Beneath the tundra of Alaska's North Slope is a vast reservoir of natural gas, estimated at 2.6×10^{12} cubic feet. Write this number in standard notation and using words.

22. A health care company announced a need to increase the present monthly premium of some 2.47×10^5 senior citizens. Write this number in standard notation and using words.

23. During a recent water shortage, residents of Marin County, California, reduced their daily consumption of water to 1.04×10^7 gallons. Write this number in standard notation and using words.

24. Edward's Food Warehouse had baby food in the 220 gram size for \$0.32. That is a unit price of $\$1.45 \times 10^{-3}$ per gram. Write this number in standard notation and using words.

25. Early in January, the currency exchange rate for one Indonesian rupiah was equivalent to 9.6×10^{-5} U. S. dollars. Write this number in standard notation and using words.

26. A finance company had earnings of \$53,091,000 before income taxes for the third quarter. Write this number in scientific notation.

27. Many life insurance companies set an annual level of sales for each of their underwriters. The goal set for Anne Lopez was \$2 million. Write this number in scientific notation.

WORKSHOP 29

Problem-Solving Strategy: Using the Four-Step Method

A Step-by-Step Procedure The problem-solving process consists of several interrelated actions. The steps to some problems are obvious and require very little effort. Others require a step-by-step procedure. Using a procedure such as the four-step method should help you to solve word problems.

THE FOUR-STEP METHOD

Step 1: Understand — What is the problem? What is given? What are you asked to do?

Step 2: Plan — What do you need to do to solve the problem? Choose a problem-solving strategy.

Step 3: Work — Carry out the plan. Do any necessary calculations.

Step 4: Check — Check your answer. Is it reasonable? Did you answer the question?

EXAMPLE 1

A small office building is being remodeled. It will take 3 plumbers 7 days to install all the pipes. Each plumber works 8 hours a day at $35 per hour. How much will it cost to hire the plumbers?

Step 1: Given — 3 plumbers, 7 days, 8 hours, $35 per hour

Find — The cost per day for 1 plumber.
The cost per day for 3 plumbers.
The cost of 3 plumbers for 7 days.

Step 2: Plan — Find the cost per day for 1 plumber, then multiply by the number of plumbers, and then multiply by the number of days.

Step 3: Work — 8 hrs per day × $35 per hr = $280 per day for 1 plumber
3 plumbers × $280 per day for 1 plumber = $840 per day for 3 plumbers
7 days × $840 per day for 3 plumbers = $5,880 for 3 plumbers for 7 days

It will cost $5,880 for 3 plumbers for 7 days.

EXAMPLE 2

One hundred twenty-eight players entered the U. S. Open Men's Singles Tennis Tournament in Flushing Meadows, New York, held over the Labor Day weekend. How many tennis matches must be played in order to determine a winner if it's a single elimination tournament? (Single elimination means that if you lose one match you are eliminated from the tournament.)

Step 1: Given — One hundred twenty-eight players entered in the tournament. Every player but the winner must lose one match.

Find — How many matches must be played to determine a winner.

Step 2: Plan — Find out how many matches must be played for every player but one (the winner) to lose a match.

Step 3: Work — If there are 128 players and every player but one must lose a match, then 128 – 1 would be the answer.

There must be 127 matches played.

Complete the problem. Check your answer in the back of the book.

1. It takes 2 finish carpenters 8 days to do the work. Each finish carpenter earns $37.50 per hour and works 7 hours per day. How much will it cost to hire the finish carpenters?

Practice

Identify the plan, work, and answer for each problem.

2. Calvina Miller makes a car payment of $214.50 every month. Her car loan is for 5 years. How much will she pay in 5 years?
3. Teresa Gonzalez and Alan Carillo spent a total of $215.75 on their prom date. Dinner cost $75.87. How much did everything else cost the couple?
4. Elaine Wong purchased 2 sweaters at $24.99 each, a belt for $14.49, slacks for $19.79, shoes for $54.49, and 5 pairs of socks at $3.99 a pair. How much did Wong spend?
5. A builder is building 5 new homes. It will take 4 electricians 2 days to wire each home. The electricians work 8 hours per day and earn $37.45 per hour. How much will it cost to pay the electricians?
6. A builder is building 5 new homes. Each home has a foyer measuring 9 feet by 18 feet. Laminate flooring for each foyer costs $26.91 per square yard. What is the cost of the laminate floors for the foyers in all 5 homes?
7. Chantel Monroe charges $3.75 per page for typing rough drafts and an additional $0.50 per page for changes and deletions. A manuscript had 212 pages, of which 147 pages had changes and deletions. What was the total cost of typing the manuscript?
8. Max Schulmann is paying $13.35 per week for a HD television. The total cost was $694.20. How long will it take Max to pay for the HD television?
9. Karen Johnson rode her 27" bicycle to the store and back. The store is 1 mile from Johnson's home. Approximately how many rotations did Johnson's bicycle wheels make in going to the store and back? (Hint: The circumference of a circle is approximately 3.14 times the diameter.)
10. Ben Cornell and Tom Ingulli drove to Chicago—a distance of 510 miles. Their car gets 23 miles per gallon of gasoline. Gasoline costs them $4.09 per gallon. How much did they spend for gasoline on their trip?
11. Sita Rahim drove due north for 3 hours at 46 miles per hour. From the same spot, Yasmina Young drove due south for 2 hours at 43 miles per hour. How far apart were they after their trip?
12. Lincoln Norris bought 3 boxes of cereal at $3.79 each, a roll of paper towels for $1.78, and 2 pounds of margarine at $1.28 a pound. How much change would Norris get back from $20.00 if there was no sales tax?

WORKSHOP 30

Problem-Solving Strategy: Identifying Information

Reading the Problem Carefully Before you begin to solve an application problem, a word problem, or a story problem, first read the problem carefully and answer these questions:

- What are you asked to find?
- What facts are given?
- Are enough facts given? Do you need more information than the problem provides?

Some problems provide more information than is needed to solve the problem. Others cannot be solved without additional information. Identifying what is wanted, what is given, and what is needed allows you to organize the information and plan your solution.

EXAMPLE 1

Laneshia James earns $27.25 per hour. She is married and claims 2 withholding allowances. Last week she worked 40 hours at the regular rate and 4 hours at the weekend rate. She is 28 years old. Find her gross pay last week.

Identify information.

1. What you are asked to find: Laneshia James's gross pay last week.
2. Facts given: She earns $27.25 per hour.
   - 40 hours worked at regular rate.
   - 4 hours worked at weekend rate.
3. Facts needed: Weekend rate.

This problem cannot be solved.

EXAMPLE 2

John Skaggs runs 6 miles every day. How many miles does Skaggs run in a week?

Identify information.

1. What you are asked to find: Number of miles ran in 1 week.
2. Facts given: Runs 6 miles every day.
3. Facts needed: None.

This problem can be solved. Multiply the miles ran per day (6) by the number of days in a week (7). **The answer is 42 miles.**

Concept CHECK

Complete the problem. Check your answer in the back of the book.

1. Tonia Walsh bought a new car with a $2,000 down payment and monthly payments of $274.50. How much did Walsh pay, in total, for her new car?

Practice

Identify the wanted, given, and needed information. If enough information is given, solve the problem.

2. The Camp Store is having a sale on camping equipment. It has two-person tents for $79.49, cookstoves for $27.45, and cooking sets for $24.79. How much does a lantern and a tent cost?
3. The D & J Fruit Farm pays pickers $0.50 per pound to pick blueberries. The berries are packed in pint baskets and sold to grocery stores for $1.15 per pint. How many pint baskets are needed for 300 pounds of berries?
4. Manuel Munoz paid $84 each way to fly round-trip from Detroit to Pittsburgh. Bob Tucker paid $139 for the round-trip fare. Who paid more? How much more?
5. Edith Fairmont paid $226 for 3 tickets to a stage play. She paid for the tickets with three $100 bills. How much change did she receive?
6. Find the cost of 3 tablecloths, each 68 inches long and 52 inches wide. Each tablecloth costs $21.95.
7. Adam Larson paid for 2 watermelons with a $10 bill. He received $2.10 in change. What did the watermelons cost per pound?
8. Food for the party cost $44.95. Party supplies cost $17.48. Jayla Drake and her friends have agreed to share the total cost of food and supplies equally. How much will each pay?
9. Ajou Hart is 6 feet 2 inches tall and weighs 195 pounds. He grew 3 inches in the past year. How tall was Hart one year ago?
10. Tamara Williams has finished 25 of the 30 mathematics problems on her test. It is now 11:50 A.M. The 1-hour test started at 11:00 a.m. What is the average number of minutes she can spend on each of the remaining problems?
11. A tennis racket and a can of balls cost a total of $159.89. What is the cost of the tennis racket?
12. A bottle of cider costs $1.95. The cider costs $0.95 more than the bottle. How much does the cider cost?
13. Richard Anderson sells magazine subscriptions and receives a weekly salary of $145. He also receives a $3 bonus for each subscription that he sells. Last week his gross pay was $202. How many subscriptions did Anderson sell last week?
14. In shopping for the latest recording of her favorite artist, Alejandra Ramos found that the cost of the DVD was $19.20 more than the cost of the cassette tape, and the cost of the cassette tape was $4.84 less than the cost of the compact disc. How much less was the cost of the compact disc than the DVD?
15. Bob Jackson swims every Monday, Wednesday, and Friday morning at the senior center. He swims 18 lengths in 15 minutes. Each length is 75 feet long. To the nearest mile per hour, how fast is he swimming?
16. Assume you are driving on a two-mile circular racetrack. For the first half of the track, you average 30 miles per hour. What speed must you maintain for the second half of the racetrack to average 60 miles per hour?

WORKSHOPS

WORKSHOP 31

Problem-Solving Strategy: Multiple Operations

Prioritizing Operations Some problems require several operations to solve. After deciding which operations to use, you must decide the correct order in which to perform them.

EXAMPLE 1

The cash price of a used sedan is $18,750. Arthur Dennis cannot pay cash, so he is making a down payment of $2,750 and 60 monthly payments of $325 each. How much more does it cost to buy the vehicle this way?

Step 1: Given — Cash price of $18,750
$2,750 down + 60 payments of $325 each

Step 2: Multiply — To get total of payments
60 × $325 = $19,500

Step 3: Add — $2,750 to total of payments
$2,750 + $19,500 = $22,250

Step 4: Subtract — Total payments from cash price of car
$22,250 – $18,750 = $3,500

It costs $3,500 more to buy the car this way. (In this example, the order of operations is very important; that is, to first multiply, then add, then subtract.)

Concept CHECK

Complete the problems. Check your answers in the back of the book.

1. Sami Kemal spent $7.95, $15.20, and $12.47 on entertainment. His entertainment budget is $50.00. How much is left in his entertainment budget?
2. Donna Preski works 8 hours a day, 5 days a week. So far this year she has worked 680 hours. How many weeks has she worked?

EXAMPLE 2

Nancy Paris bought 3 notebooks costing $3.98 each. She gave the cashier a $20 bill. How much change did she receive if there was no sales tax?

Step 1: Given — Bought 3 notebooks at $3.98 each.
No sales tax. Gave cashier $20.00

Step 2: Multiply — To get total cost
3 × $3.98 = $11.94

Step 3: Subtract — To find change
$20.00 – $11.94 = $8.06

Nancy received $8.06 in change.

Complete the problems. Check your answers in the back of the book.

3. The band boosters sell cider and doughnuts at home football games. Last week they sold 318 cups of cider at $0.75 per cup and 12 dozen doughnuts at $1.25 per doughnut. What were the total sales?
4. Maria Fernandez paid monthly electric bills of $51.72, $47.75, and $53.21. Her electric budget is $150.00 for 3 months. Is she over or under her budget? By how much is she over or under?

WORKSHOPS

Practice

Complete the problems.

5. Victor Haddad sold 8 pumpkins for $2.75 each, 9 for $2.00 each, 24 for $1.50 each, and 15 for $1.00 each. He receives $0.35 for each pumpkin sold plus a $10.00 bonus if his sales total $75.00 or more. How much did he receive?
6. Xavier Zermeno worked through 174 pages of a 408-page computer training manual. It took him 2 days to work through the remaining pages. If he worked through the same number of pages each day, how many pages did he work through each day?
7. Hoshi Sato worked 40 hours at $9.75 per hour. He worked 5 hours at $11.00 an hour. How much money did Sato earn?
8. The Parkers spent $142.78, $145.91, and $141.15 in 3 visits to the grocery store. Their food budget is $450.00. How much money do they have left to spend for food?
9. The temperature in the production department is 21° C at 12 noon. If the temperature increases 1.5° C every hour, what will the temperature be at 5 PM?
10. Flora Sturgeon walks 4 miles round-trip 3 times a week to work. How far will she walk in 1 year?
11. John Piotrowski assembled a total of 642 circuit boards in 3 days of work. During the first 2 days, he assembled 211 and 208 circuit boards, respectively. How many did he assemble the last day?
12. In a one-month sales contest, Ernie Johnkovich earned 4 two-point certificates, 2 three-point certificates, and 6 one-point certificates. How many points did he earn for the month?
13. Seventeen hundred tickets costing $5 each were sold for a scholarship fund-raiser. One prize of $2,000, 3 prizes of $1,000, and 5 prizes of $250 were given away. How much money did the scholarship fund-raiser make?
14. Pepe Garza, sales leader for the past month, earned 47 one-point certificates. If he earned a total of 68 points, how many three-point certificates did he earn?
15. DeBorah Miles bought 3 t-shirts for $7.50 each and a sweatshirt for $22.95. How much change did she receive from a $50 bill?
16. Adahy Catolst saved $212. After he earned an additional $124, he spent $149 for a small color TV, $35 for a rugby shirt, and $79 for a pair of sneakers. How much money did Catolst have left?

WORKSHOP 32

Problem-Solving Strategy: Using Estimation

Checking the Reasonableness of an Answer An important part of problem solving is determining the reasonableness of an answer. Checking an answer does not mean that you must recalculate it. Quite often, it is sufficient simply to determine if your answer is reasonable. Estimation can be used to help determine if you made an error in your measurements or calculations. Some problems may ask for just an estimate.

EXAMPLE 1

Three cans of juice cost $2.37, six cans of soda cost $2.40, and six peaches cost $1.98. About how much will it cost for one of each item?

Use estimation.

$2.37 ÷ 3 is about	$0.80
$2.40 ÷ 6 is about	$0.40
$1.98 ÷ 6 is about	$0.33
Total is about	**$1.53**

Concept CHECK

Complete the problems. Check your answers in the back of the book.

1. Tom Lucas estimated the cost of 10 gallons of gas at $3.93 a gallon to be $393. Is his estimate reasonable? If not, what error did he make?

EXAMPLE 2

Sandra Kaselman used her calculator to find 25% of $198.50 for a total of $4,962.50. Is her answer reasonable? What error did she make?

Step 1: Check the reasonableness of the answer.

Her answer is not reasonable because 25% is equal to $\frac{1}{4}$, and $\frac{1}{4}$ of $198.50 is about $50.

Step 2: What error did she make?

It looks as if she multiplied by 25, not 0.25 which is the decimal for 25%.

Concept CHECK

Complete the problems. Check your answers in the back of the book.

2. Harold Roberts needs 36 inches of frame moulding that costs $5.99 a foot. Harold estimated that the moulding would cost $216. **(a)** Is his answer reasonable? **(b)** If not, what error did he make?

Practice

Determine the reasonableness of the estimate. If it is not reasonable, state what error was made.

	Problem	Estimate	Reasonable	Error (if any)
3.	20% of $496.98	$ 100	a.	b.
4.	5 gallons of gas at $4.29 per gallon	200	a.	b.
5.	$14,203.00 ÷ 200	700	a.	b.
6.	98.7 × 516	50,000	a.	b.
7.	Tip of 15% on $19.47	3	a.	b.
8.	Sales tax of 5% on $1,014.74	5	a.	b.
9.	$15.00 per sq yd carpeting for 2′ × 5′ area	150	a.	b.
10.	$49.79 − $19.49	70	a.	b.

11. Ursula VanMeer bought 100 shares of stock at $18 per share. One year later, she sold all her shares at $23 per share. About how much did she make on her stock?

12. A new minivan costs $24,897. About how much would 4 minivans cost?

13. If the sales tax rate is 6.5%, about how much sales tax will be due on a $24,897 minivan?

14. A 10% down payment is required to finance the purchase of a $24,897 minivan and you estimate the down payment to be $248.97. **(a)** Is the answer reasonable? **(b)** If not, what error was made?

15. Emil Wauseka is buying a used car with a total purchase price including interest of $14,987. He plans to make a $3,000 down payment and to finance the rest for 5 years. About how much will his monthly payments be?

16. Cheng Siau Yian purchased 6 dozen cupcakes for the 25 children attending a birthday party. All the cupcakes were eaten. About how many cupcakes did each child eat?

17. Clayton Burrington purchased the following school supplies on sale: a $2.79 notebook for $1.99, a $1.49 ballpoint pen for $0.99, a $1.99 pack of notebook paper for $0.99, and a $3.49 automatic pencil for $2.79. Clayton estimated the total savings to be $7.00. **(a)** Is the answer reasonable? **(b)** If not, what error was made?

18. It is about 1,300 feet around the bicycle test track. How many times must you ride around the track to ride about 1 mile?

19. Fruit baskets contain 6 apples, 4 oranges, and 2 grapefruits. If you have 148 apples, 121 oranges, and 64 grapefruits, about how many fruit baskets can you make?

WORKSHOPS

WORKSHOP 33

Problem-Solving Strategy: Constructing a Table

Constructing a table can be a good way of solving some problems. By organizing the data into a table, it is easier to identify the information that you need. A table is useful in classifying information.

EXAMPLE 1

Meredith McCall is a car salesperson. For each new car she sells, she earns 10 bonus points; for each used car she sells, she earns 5 bonus points. She earned 125 bonus points by selling 16 cars last week. How many of each type of car did she sell?

Construct a table in order to evaluate the possibilities.

Figure W33.1

	New Cars	Used Cars	Total Points	
Start at 16 and 0 →	16	0	160 ←	$(16 \times 10) + (0) = 160 + 0$
	15	1	155 ←	$(15 \times 10) + (1 \times 5) = 150 + 5$
Too high; try a lower combination →	14	2	150 ←	$(14 \times 10) + (2 \times 5) = 140 + 10$
	9	7	125 ←	$(9 \times 10) + (7 \times 5) = 90 + 35$

McCall sold 9 new cars and 7 used cars.

Concept CHECK

Complete the problems. Check your answers in the back of the book.

1. A total of 11 vehicles consisting of unicycles (1 wheel) and bicycles (2 wheels) went by. Eighteen wheels were counted. How many of each were there?

Number of Bikes		Number of Wheels		Total Number of Wheels
Unicycles	Bicycles	Unicycles	Bicycles	
1	10	1	20	21
2	9	2	18	20
3	8	3	16	19
4	7	4	14	18

EXAMPLE 2

Tomas Flores has a total of 20 coins consisting of dimes and quarters. The total value of the coins is $4.70. How many of each coin does he have?

Construct a table in order to evaluate the possibilities.

Figure W33.2

Number of		Value of		Total Value
Quarters	Dimes	Quarters	Dimes	
20	0	$5.00	$0.00	$5.00
19	1	4.75	0.10	4.85
18	2	4.50	0.20	4.70

Flores has 18 quarters and 2 dimes.

Complete the problem. Check your answer in the back of the book.

2. Lieutenant Sampson is a recruitment officer for the Marines. For each high school graduate he recruits, he gets 5 points; for each college graduate, 11 points. He earned 100 points last week by recruiting 14 high school and college graduates. How many of each did he recruit?

Practice

3. Nine cycles were produced using 21 wheels. How many bicycles and tricycles were produced?
4. A bank charges a monthly service fee of $5.00 plus $0.25 per check. The bank is changing its policy to a $6 service charge and $0.15 per check. You may save money with the new system. How many checks must you write each month in order to save money?
5. Wanda Cross has a total of 40 coins consisting of nickels and quarters with a total value of $6. How many of each coin does she have?
6. The Theatre Club sold a total of 415 tickets. The adult tickets cost $5 and the children's tickets cost $3. If $1,615 was collected, how many adult tickets were sold?
7. There are 56 stools in the storeroom. Some stools have 3 legs and some have 4 legs. If there are 193 legs, how many 4-legged stools are in the storeroom?
8. How many different ways can you make change for a quarter?
9. Cambria Davis has exactly 20 dimes, 20 nickels, and 20 pennies. Find all the ways Davis can choose 22 coins whose total value is $1 if she must use at least 1 coin of each type.
10. Frank DeGeorge has $0.69 in coins. Bob White asked DeGeorge for change for a half-dollar. DeGeorge tried to make change but found that he didn't have the coins to do so. What coins did DeGeorge have if each coin was less than a half-dollar?
11. Christina Carranza was playing darts. She threw six darts, all of which hit the target shown in **Figure W33.3**. Which of the following scores could be hers: 2, 19, 58, 28, 33, or 37?

Figure W33.3

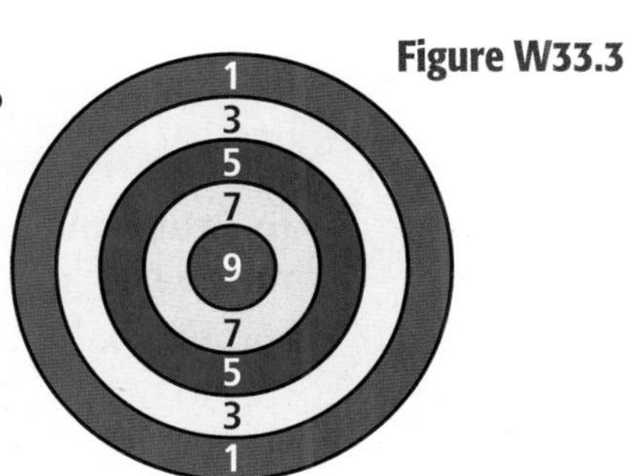

WORKSHOP 34

Problem-Solving Strategy: Looking for a Pattern

Organizing the Information Some problems can be solved more easily if the information is first organized into a list or table. Then the list or table can be examined to see if a pattern exists. A pattern may not "jump out" at you, but you may be able to discover a pattern after manipulating the information.

EXAMPLE 1

Marie Arteshaw has 15 coins consisting of dimes and quarters. The total value of the coins is $2.55. How many of each coin does she have?

Calculate the number of coins given.

Given: Fifteen coins consisting of dimes and quarters.
The table displays different combinations of dimes and quarters with the total number of coins equaling 15.

Number of Dimes	15	14	13	12	11	
Number of Quarters	0	1	2	3	4	Look for
Total Value	$1.50	$1.65	$1.80	$1.95	$2.10	← a pattern

You could continue the table, but it is easier if you see the pattern. Each time you take away a dime and add a quarter, the total value increases by $0.15. The difference between $2.55 and $1.50 is $1.05 and $1.05 ÷ $0.15 = 7. Therefore, subtract 7 from 15 and conclude that **there are 8 dimes and 7 quarters.** The total value of 7 quarters and 8 dimes is

$(7 \times \$0.25) + (8 \times \$0.10) = \$1.75 + \$0.80 = \$2.55$

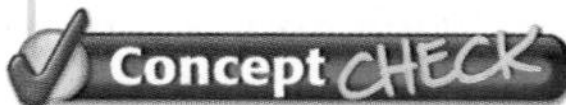

Complete the problems. Check your answers in the back of the book. Write the next three numbers for the established pattern.

1. 1, 3, 9, 27, . . .

2. 2, 4, 7, 11, . . .

Practice

In Problems 3–10, look for a pattern and then write the next three numbers.

3. 10, 16, 22, 28, . . .

4. 2, 4, 8, 16, . . .

5. 30, 27, 24, 21, . . .

6. 8, 4, 2, 1, . . .

7. 1, 4, 9, 16, . . .

8. 2, 3, 5, 9, 17, 33, . . .

9. 1, 4, 13, 40, 121, 364, . . .

10. 1, 1, 2, 3, 5, 8, 13, . . .

11. Sy Mah has 20 coins consisting of dimes and quarters. Their total value is $3.80. How many of each coin does Mah have?

12. Alicia Sanchez had 185 tickets to the school play. Adult tickets sold for $4 each and children's tickets sold for $2 each. The total value was $594. How many of each ticket did she sell?

13. **(Refer to Figure W34.1.)** Three-sided numbers, such as 3, are so named because dots can be used to form a triangle with an equal number of dots on each side. What three-sided number has 12 dots on a side?

Figure W34.1

Three-Sided Numbers

3 6 9 12

14. On the first day of school, your teacher agrees to allow 1 minute of "fun" at the end of the first day, 2 minutes on the second day, 4 minutes on the third day, 8 minutes on the fourth day, and so on. How much time will you have for "fun" at the end of 10 days?

15. At 9 AM there were 7 students in the computer room. At 9:30 AM 2 students left and at 10 AM 1 student arrived. At 10:30 AM 2 students left and at 11 AM 1 student arrived. This pattern continued with 2 students leaving at half past the hour and 1 student arriving on each hour. At what time did the computer room first become empty?

16. Keshawn and Derrick Kinsman were responsible for total lawn care of the factory grounds. The first week Keshawn mowed half the lawn. The next week, he mowed two-thirds as much as he had the first week. The third week, he mowed three-fourths as much as he had the second week, and so on. The tenth week, he mowed ten-elevenths as much as he mowed the ninth week. How much of the lawn did Keshawn mow the tenth week?

17. There are 2 rectangular storage rooms whose sides are whole numbers and whose area and perimeter are the same number. What are their dimensions?

18. A 5-pound bag of lawn food sells for $3.25 and a 3-pound bag sells for $2.29. You need 17 pounds of lawn food. What is the least amount you can pay and buy at least 17 pounds?

19. When it is 12 o'clock, the hands on the face of the clock overlap. How many more times will the hands overlap as the clock runs until it is again 12 o'clock? (Count the second time it is 12 o'clock but not the first.)

20. Before the U.S. Supreme Court opens each year all 9 justices shake hands with each other. How many handshakes are involved in this ceremony?

WORKSHOPS

WORKSHOP 35

Problem-Solving Strategy: Using Guess and Check

One way to solve a problem is by using guess and check, or trial and error. Guessing at a solution does not mean making a blind guess in the hopes that it is correct. It means making an informed guess and then checking it against the conditions stated in the problem to determine if it is correct or how to make a better guess. The process is repeated until the correct answer is found.

EXAMPLE 1

You need 80 sandwich buns. You can buy 8 for $2.09 or 12 for $2.59. What do you buy to obtain at least 80 sandwich buns at the lowest cost?

Guess and check until you find the lowest cost. Keep your information organized by using a table.

Figure W35.1

Number			Cost		
12/pkg	8/pkg	Total Buns	12/pkg	8/pkg	Total Cost
7	0	84	(7 × $2.59) +	(0× $2.09)	$18.13
6	1	80	(6 × 2.59) +	(1 × 2.09)	17.63
5	3	84	(5 × 2.59) +	(3 × 2.09)	19.22
4	4	80	(4 × 2.59) +	(4 × 2.09)	18.72
3	6	84	(3 × 2.59) +	(6 × 2.09)	20.31
2	7	80	(2 × 2.59) +	(7 × 2.09)	19.81
1	9	84	(1 × 2.59) +	(9 × 2.09)	21.40
0	10	80	(0 × 2.59) +	(10 × 2.09)	20.90

Six packages of 12 sandwich buns and one package of 8 sandwich buns cost $17.63, the least amount, and result in 80 sandwich buns.

EXAMPLE 2

The factory building is 4 times as old as the equipment in the factory. Three years from now, the factory building will be 3 times as old as the equipment in the factory. How old is the equipment?

Guess and check to find the answer. Keep your information organized by using a table.

Figure W35.2

Current Age		Three Years from Now		
Guess Equipment Age	Building (4 × Equipment Age)	Equipment	Building (Current Age + 3)	Check
7	28	10	28 + 3 = 31	Does 10 × 3 = 31? (No)
8	32	11	32 + 3 = 35	Does 11 × 3 = 35? (No)
6	24	9	24 + 3 = 27	Does 9 × 3 = 27? **(Yes)**

The equipment is now 6 years old.

Complete the problem. Check your answer in the back of the book.

1. The product of 3 consecutive whole numbers is 504. What are the numbers?

Practice

2. The hypothetical planet Tetriad only has creatures with 3 legs (triads) or 4 legs (tetrads). Astronauts Peter North and Sally Clark could not bear to look at these ugly creatures, so they kept their eyes on the ground. On their first day on Tetriad, they counted 81 legs as 22 creatures walked by. How many Triads and Tetrads did they meet?
3. It costs $0.50 to mail a postcard to Canada and $0.60 to mail a one ounce letter to Canada. Ahmad Checkers wrote to 21 friends and spent $12.00 for postage. How many letters and how many postcards did he write?
4. Chantel McDale earns $12 per hour Monday through Friday and $18 per hour on weekends. One week, she worked 49 hours and earned $654. How many hours did she work on the weekend?

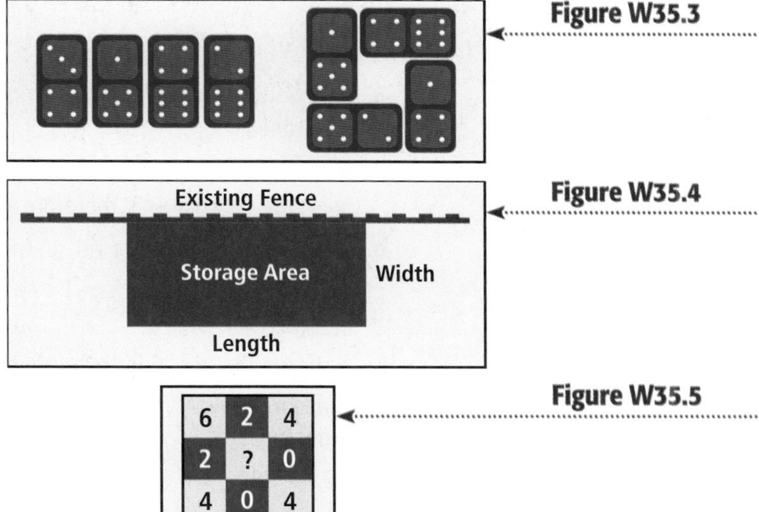

Figure W35.3

Figure W35.4

Figure W35.5

5. Arrange the 4 dominoes to the right into a domino donut so that all sides equal the same sum (not necessarily the same sum as that of the example at the right).
6. Ti Sun wants to fence off a storage area for surplus lumber. She has 96 meters of new fencing to put along an existing fence. What are the dimensions that will give Sun the largest storage area?
7. In the square at the right, a rule applies from top to bottom and from left to right. Find the rule and figure out the missing number.
8. Batteries come in packs of 3 or 4. If your class needs 30 batteries, how many different ways are there of buying exactly 30 batteries? Which combination do you think would be the cheapest?
9. The ages of three delivery vans total 22 years. The green van is the oldest and is 10 years old. The blue van is 6 years younger than the green van. The third delivery van is white. What are the ages of the vans?
10. The product of 3 consecutive whole numbers is 120. What are the numbers?
11. Make a sum of 1,000 using some eights and some plus signs.
12. Allison McCardle gave the counter person at Pizza Town a $20 bill for her large one-topping pizza. If the change she received was one-third the cost of the pizza, what did the pizza cost?
13. At the MetroPark Annual Bike Ride there were 486 participants. Most rode bicycles but there were some that rode tricycles. If there were 1,080 wheels in all, how many bicycles were there? How many tricycles?

WORKSHOP 36

Problem-Solving Strategy: Using Simple Algebraic Operations

Previously you practiced writing and solving some basic equations. In this Workshop you will apply the same technique to additional applications. Remember that equations are solved by applying simple algebraic operations, which are the inverse—or opposite—of the operations indicated, to both sides of the equation.

EXAMPLE 1

Solve these equations:

a. $x - 3 = 18$ **b.** $y + 6 = 27$ **c.** $12z = 48$

d. $\frac{a}{7} = 5$ **e.** $3b - 5 = 13$ **f.** $\frac{c}{5} + 3 = 7$

Use simple algebraic operations.

a. Since subtraction is indicated, do the inverse of the operation by adding 3 to both sides:

$x - 3 = 18$

$x - 3 + 3 = 18 + 3$, therefore $\mathbf{x = 21}$

b. Since addition is indicated, do the inverse of the operation by subtracting 6 from both sides:

$y + 6 = 27$

$y + 6 - 6 = 27 - 6$, therefore $\mathbf{y = 21}$

c. Since multiplication is indicated, do the inverse of the operation by dividing both sides by 12:

$12z = 48$

$\frac{12z}{12} = \frac{48}{12}$, therefore $\mathbf{z = 4}$

d. Since division is indicated, do the inverse of the operation by multiplying both sides by 7:

$\frac{a}{7} = 5$

$(\frac{a}{7}) \times 7 = 5 \times 7$, therefore $\mathbf{a = 35}$

e. Since both subtraction and multiplication are indicated, do the inverse in the reverse order of operations.

$3b - 5 = 13$

Add 5 to both sides: $3b - 5 + 5 = 13 + 5$, therefore $3b = 18$

Divide both sides by 3: $\frac{3b}{3} = \frac{18}{3}$, therefore $\mathbf{b = 6}$

f. Since both addition and division are indicated, do the inverse in the reverse order of operations.

$\frac{c}{5} + 3 = 7$

Subtract 3 from both sides: $\frac{c}{5} + 3 - 3 = 7 - 3$, therefore $\frac{c}{5} = 4$

Multiply both sides by 5: $\frac{c}{5} \times 5 = 4 \times 5$, therefore $\mathbf{c = 20}$

Complete the problems. Check your answers in the back of the book.

1. Solve these equations:
   a. $6m - 4 = 26$ b. $\frac{n}{3} + 12 = 15$ c. $\frac{2p}{5} - 9 = 3$

WORKSHOPS

Practice

Solve the equations in Problems 2–7.

2. $5r - 6 = 29$
3. $\frac{s}{5} + 3 = 6$
4. $\frac{2t}{7} - 4 = 6$
5. $7u + 12 = 75$
6. $\frac{v}{11} - 4 = 3$
7. $\frac{5w}{8} + 31 = 36$
8. You're thinking of a number, such that, if you add 9 to the product of that number and 5, then the sum will be 49. What number are you thinking of?
9. Julio Montoya earns $16.80 per hour for a 40-hour work week. How much more per week would Montoya earn if he received a 10 percent increase in his hourly rate?
10. Alicia McKey has a plot of land that has a perimeter of 1,490 feet. If the length is 5 feet more than the width:
    a. What is the width of the plot of land?
    b. What is the length of the plot of land?
    c. What is the area of the plot of land?
11. The Drama Club sold $1,345 worth of tickets for their production of *Oliver.* Adult tickets sold for $6.75 per ticket, while children's tickets sold for $3.50. If there were 245 tickets sold in all, how many adult tickets were sold?
12. Krio Packaging Corporation averaged 158 units per day for Monday through Thursday. How many units would have to be produced on Friday for Krio to average 165 units per day for Monday through Friday?
13. Malcolm Freddy starts out on a 100-mile bicycle ride at 9:00 AM, averaging 12 miles per hour. At 11:00 AM, Justin Garret starts out on the same route, averaging 18 miles per hour. At what time would Garret catch up with Freddy?
14. You are thinking of a number, such that, if you subtract 3 from the product of that number and 7, and then divide that difference by 13, and then double that quotient and add 30, you will end up with 50. What number are you thinking of?
15. Robert is thinking that his father is 7 years more than twice his own age, and his grandfather is 4 years less than twice his father's age. If Robert's grandfather is 70 years of age, how old is Robert?

WORKSHOPS

WORKSHOP 37

Problem-Solving Strategy: Working Backward

Problems that involve a sequence of events or actions can sometimes be solved by working backward. If the final result of the problem is given, start your solution with that result and work backward to arrive at the beginning conditions of the problem.

EXAMPLE 1

Each year a delivery van is worth $\frac{3}{4}$ of its value from the previous year. A van is now worth $9,000. What was its value last year?

Step 1: Work backward. What is the van worth now?

$9,000

Step 2: How does last year's value relate to this year's value?

$\frac{3}{4}$ of last year's value = this year's value

$$\frac{3}{4}x = \$9{,}000$$

Step 3: Solve.

$x = \$9{,}000 \div \frac{3}{4}$

$x = \mathbf{\$12{,}000}$

The van was worth $12,000 last year.

EXAMPLE 2

Central Bakery baked some cookies and put $\frac{1}{2}$ of them away for the next day. Then Central Bakery divided the remaining cookies evenly among its 3 sales outlets so that each outlet received 40 dozen. How many cookies did Central Bakery bake?

Work backward.

Each of the 3 sales outlets received 40 dozen cookies. Thus, Central Bakery divided a total of 120 dozen cookies. The 120 dozen cookies represent one half of what was baked; therefore, **they baked 240 dozen cookies.**

Concept CHECK

Complete the problem. Check your answer in the back of the book.

1. A water lily doubles itself in size each day. It takes 30 days from the time the original plant is placed in a pond until the surface of the pond is completely covered with lilies. How long does it take for the pond to be half covered?

Practice

2. Cab Company charges a flat fee of \$3.75 plus \$0.30 for every $\frac{1}{4}$ mile driven. Dick Lewis paid a driver a total of \$7.95 for a trip from the airport to his office. How many miles did he travel?
3. A recipe for 24 medium-sized pancakes requires 2 eggs. Eggs are sold in cartons of 12 eggs. You plan to serve 240 people an average of 3 pancakes each. How many cartons of eggs are needed?
4. Two barrels—A and B—contain unspecified amounts of cider, with A containing more than B. From A, pour into B as much cider as B already contains. Then from B, pour into A as much cider as A now contains. Finally, pour from A into B as much cider as B presently has. Both barrels now contain 80 litres of cider. How many liters of cider were in each barrel at the start of the process?
5. Your company issued you a car that is now worth \$12,000. An article states that each year this car is worth 80 percent of its previous year's value. What was the value of this car last year when you got it?
6. Tiffany Cole starts at point A and enters a fun house. She pays \$2 to get in and loses half of the money in her possession while she is in the fun house. She then pays \$1 when she exits at B. She goes to the next entrance (C), pays \$2 to get in, loses half of her money, and pays \$1 to exit at D. This is repeated until she exits at H and gives her last \$1 to get out. How much money did she start with?

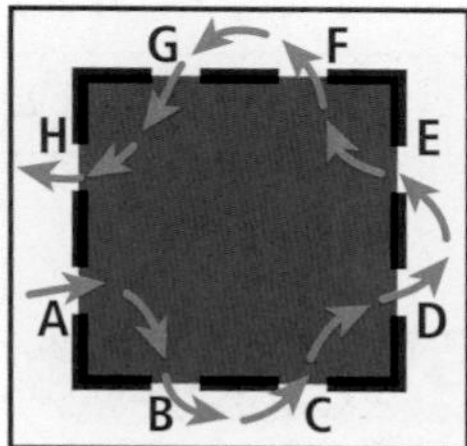

Figure W37.1

7. Wixey Bakery baked some cookies in their new solar powered oven. Stores No. 1, No. 2, No. 3, and No. 4 sold a total of 4 dozen cookies each. The remainder were put in storage. Later, another dozen cookies were sold and $\frac{1}{3}$ of what was left was sent to stores No. 5 and No. 6. Those two stores sold 2 dozen cookies each and had 9 dozen left between them. How many cookies did Wixey Bakery bake?
8. Sixty-four players are entered in the company single elimination horseshoe competition. How many matches must be played to determine the winner?
9. In **Figure W37.2,** if you were to continue the number pattern until you got to the star, what number would you put in the star's square?

Figure W37.2

10. Three girls played a game in which 2 of them won and 1 lost on each play. The girl who lost had to double the points that each winner had at that time by subtracting from her own points. The girls played the game 3 times, each winning twice and losing once. At the end of the 3 plays, each girl had 40 points. How many points did each girl have to start?
11. Sixty-five teams are selected for a single-elimination tournament. How many games must be played to determine a champion?
12. In **Problem 11,** if it were a double elimination tournament, how many games would have to be played to determine a champion?

WORKSHOPS

WORKSHOP 38

Problem-Solving Strategy: Writing an Equation

A word problem can be translated into an equation that is solved by performing the same mathematical operation (adding, subtracting, multiplying, or dividing) to both sides. Solving the equation then leads to the solution of the problem. To set up the equation, look for words in the problem that suggest which of the four mathematical operations to use.

Words	Symbol	Mathematical Operation
The total, how many in all, the sum, plus	+	Addition
The difference, how much more, how much smaller, minus	−	Subtraction
The total for a number of equal items, the product	×	Multiplication
The number left over, the quotient	÷	Division

EXAMPLE 1

In 40 hours at your regular rate of pay plus 5 hours of double time (twice your regular rate of pay), you earn $625. What is your regular rate of pay?

Step 1: Use the letter x to stand for your regular rate of pay.

Step 2: Write and solve an equation.

$40x + 5(2x) = 625$

$40x + 10x = 625$ Multiply $5 \times 2x$

$50x = 625$ Combine like terms

$x = \mathbf{12.50}$ Divide both sides by 50.

Regular rate of pay is $12.50

EXAMPLE 2

A rectangle with a perimeter of 48 mm is 20 mm long. What is the width of the rectangle?

Write an equation. (Let w equal the width of the rectangle.)

$w + 20 + w + 20 = 48$

$2w + 40 = 48$ (Subtract 40 from both sides.)

$2w = 8$ (Divide both sides by 2.)

$w =$ **4 mm wide**

The width of the rectangle is 4 mm

Complete the problems. Check your answers in the back of the book.

1. The sum of 2 consecutive numbers is 23. What is the smaller number?

Practice

2. One brand of computer scanner can read 74 documents per hour while a second scanner can read 92 documents per hour. How many hours will it take for both scanners together to read 747 documents?
3. A bottle and a cork cost $1.10. The bottle costs $1.00 more than the cork. How much does each cost?
4. A robotic delivery unit travels 54 meters in traveling completely around the edge of a rectangular mailroom. If the rectangle is twice as long as it is wide, how long is each side?
5. A football field is 100 yards long and has a distance around of 308 yards. How wide is it?
6. Kotori and Lenmana Tewamina make monthly payments of $727.20 on their $80,000.00 mortgage. They will have paid $138,160.00 in interest when their mortgage is paid off. For how many years is their mortgage?
7. Edith Harris had gross pay of $624.86 last week. She earns $12.85 per hour plus a 3% commission on all sales. She knows she worked 40 hours last week, but can not remember her total sales. What were her total sales?
8. Regina Herrera earns $17.60 per hour plus double time for all hours over 40 per week. How much did Herrera earn for working 46 hours last week?
9. Wilson Davis has 3 Guernsey cows and 2 Holstein cows that give as much milk in 4 days as 2 Guernsey and 4 Holstein cows give in 3 days. Which kind of cow is the better milk producer: the Guernsey or the Holstein?
10. The Karis Tool & Die Company building is 5 times as old as the equipment. The building was 24 years old when the equipment was purchased. How old is the equipment?
11. The sum of 3 consecutive odd numbers is 27. What are the 3 numbers?
12. Universal stock sells for $17 a share. ABC Stock Brokers charges a flat fee of $40 for every transaction. How many shares could you buy for $730?
13. Write an equation expressing the relationship between A and B given in **Figure W38.1.** What would B equal when A is 40?

A	1	2	3	4	5	...
B	1	4	7	10	13	...

Figure W38.1

14. In Problem 13, write an equation for A in terms of B. What would A equal when B is 253?
15. Harry, Jerry, and Darrel have a combined weight of 599 pounds. Jerry weighs 13 pounds more than Harry, while Harry weighs 5 pounds more than Darrel. How much does each man weigh?

WORKSHOPS

WORKSHOP 39

Problem-Solving Strategy: Linear Combinations

There are many applications which result in two equations with two unknowns that need to be solved. Such systems are identified as linear combinations and are solved, algebraically, in this method:

Eliminate one of the variables by adding or subtracting the two equations. Then solve the resulting equation in one unknown. Substitute the solution into one of the original equations to find the value of the other variable.

EXAMPLE 1

At the starting point of the 30 k Cycle Run there were a total of 50 cycles. Some were tricycles (3 wheels) while most were bicycles (2 wheels). The equipment counted just the wheels and found a total of 107 wheels. How many bicycles were there? How many tricycles were there?

Step 1: Identify the unknowns.

Let $B =$ the number of Bicycles ($2B$ wheels)

Let $T =$ the number of Tricycles ($3T$ wheels)

Step 2: Write the equations.

$B + T = 50$

$2B + 3T = 107$

Multiply the first equation by 3 $\quad 3B + 3T = 150$

Subtract the second equation from the first $\quad \underline{2B + 3T = 107}$

$B = \mathbf{43}$

Now substitute 43 for B in the first equation: $\quad 43 + T = 50$

Therefore $T = \mathbf{7}$

There were 43 bicycles and 7 tricycles.

Concept CHECK

Complete the problem. Check your answers in the back of the book.

1. The length of a rectangle is twice the width and the perimeter of the rectangle is 42 feet. After finding the width and the length, find the area of the rectangle.

Practice

Solve the system of equations in Problems 2–7.

2. $4c + 3d = 43$
   $5c - 2d = 25$

3. $2g + 7f = 23$
$2g - f = 15$

4. $3m + 2n = 66$
$2m - 3n = 31$

5. $12p + 5q = 63$
$9p + 7q = 57$

6. $2r - 3s = 4$
$3r - 2s = 21$

7. $5v - 4w = 189$
$2v + 5w = 201$

8. When astronauts Antoine Weber and Rachel Sun landed on the hypothetical planet Trifour they found the inhabitants had either 3 or 4 extremities. Weber could not look at the inhabitants' faces so he just counted their extremities. He counted 173 extremities. Sun, on the other hand, could not look at their extremities so she just counted faces. She counted 51 faces. How many inhabitants had 3 extremities? How many were there that had 4 extremities?

9. On Friday the corner newsstand sold 5 more copies of *The New York Times* than it did copies of *The Washington Post.* If the newsstand sold 59 copies of *The New York Times* and *The Washington Post* combined, how many of each was sold?

10. If there are twice as many girls as boys in fourth period English and there are 33 students in all, how many girls are in fourth period English? How many boys?

11. General Auto Sales had sales totaling \$1,900,500 during the first quarter compared to sales totaling \$2,446,500 during the second quarter. During the second quarter, General Auto sold half as many of their \$21,500 model and twice the number of their \$28,500 model in the second quarter compared to the first quarter. How many of each model did General Auto sell in the first quarter? How many of each model in the second quarter?

12. John North has a paper route of 73 daily customers and 46 Sunday customers. North earns \$0.25 more for each Sunday paper he delivers compared to the Monday through Saturday deliveries. If he earns \$84.10 per week, how much does he earn from each daily delivery, and how much does he earn from the Sunday delivery?

WORKSHOP 40

Problem-Solving Strategy: Drawing a Sketch

Some word problems, particularly those that involve lengths, widths, and dimensions, can be simplified if you draw a sketch. Sketches and diagrams can also help you keep track of information in multi-step problems.

EXAMPLE 1

A 30-cm piece of pipe is cut into 3 pieces. The second piece is 2 cm longer than the first piece, and the third piece is 2 cm shorter than the first piece. How long is each piece?

Draw a sketch.

Figure W40.1

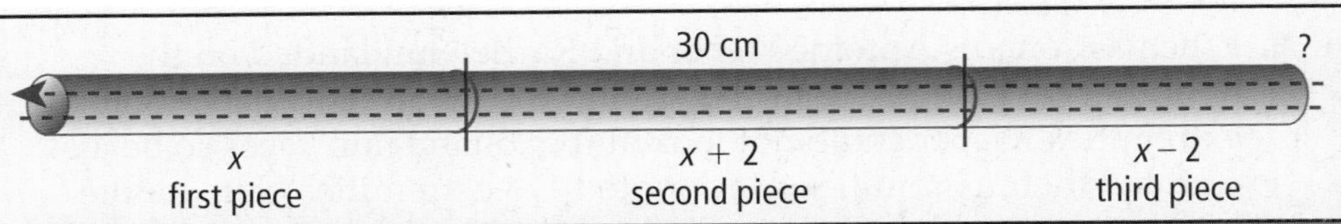

$$x + (x + 2) + (x - 2) = 30$$
$$3x = 30$$
$$x = \textbf{10 cm}$$ (Length of first piece is 10 cm.)
$$x + 2 = \textbf{12 cm}$$ (Length of second piece is 12 cm.)
$$x - 2 = \textbf{8 cm}$$ (Length of third piece is 8 cm.)

EXAMPLE 2

A 2-volume set of classics is bound in $\frac{1}{4}$-inch covers. The text in each volume is 3 inches thick. The 2 volumes are side by side on the shelf. A bookworm travels from inside the front cover of Volume I to the inside back cover of Volume II. How far does the bookworm travel?

Draw a sketch.

Figure W40.2

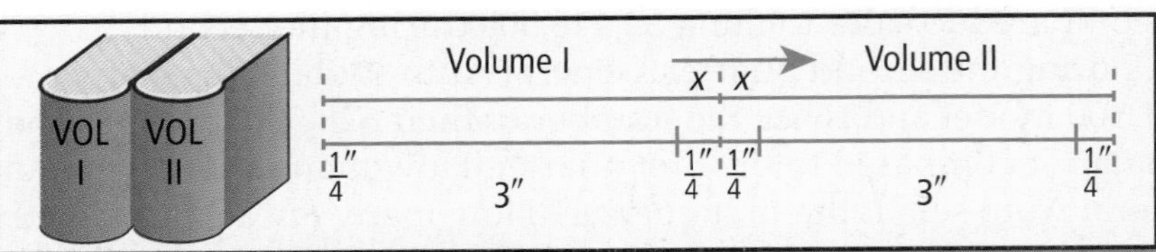

Bookworm travels: $\frac{1}{4}'' + \frac{1}{4}'' = \frac{1}{2}''$

The bookworm travels $\frac{1}{2}$ inch from inside the front cover of Volume I to inside the back cover of Volume II.

Concept CHECK

Complete the problems. Check your answers in the back of the book.

1. Suppose the bookworm in Example 2 travels from the inside back cover of Volume I to exit out on the front cover of Volume II. How far does the bookworm travel?

2. Use an 18-inch, 10-inch, and 7-inch length of board to mark off a length of 15 inches.

Practice

3. Tom Khoury leaves his house and jogs 8 blocks west, 5 blocks south, 3 blocks east, 9 blocks north, 6 blocks east, 12 blocks south, 3 blocks west, and then stops to rest. Where is he in relation to his house?
4. Mariko Fujiwara bicycles to work. She travels 3 miles north of her house, turns right and bikes 2 miles, turns left and bikes 3 miles, and turns left and bikes 5 miles. At this point, where is she in relation to her home?
5. The rectangular area allotted to the shoe department of a store has a perimeter of 96 feet. The length of the rectangle is 8 feet longer than the width. What is the width of the rectangle?
6. A barn has dimensions of 50 feet by 60 feet. A cow is tethered to 1 corner of the barn with a 60-foot rope. The cow always stays outside the barn. How many square feet of grazing land can the cow reach?
7. A 60-foot piece of fencing is cut into 3 pieces. The second piece is 3 feet longer than the first piece, and the third piece is 9 feet longer than the first piece. Find the lengths of the pieces.
8. Assuming that each corner must be tacked, what is the least number of tacks that you need to display eight 8-inch by 10-inch photographs?
9. Making identical cuts, a lumberjack can saw a log into 4 pieces in 12 minutes. How long would it take to cut a log of the same size and shape into 8 pieces?
10. Master Chemical Company has containers with capacities of 4 liters, 7 liters, and 10 liters. How could you use these containers to measure exactly 1 liter?
11. Three book volumes are arranged as shown. The thickness of each cover is 0.2 cm. The text in each volume is 3 cm thick. What is the distance from the first page of Volume I to the last page of Volume III?

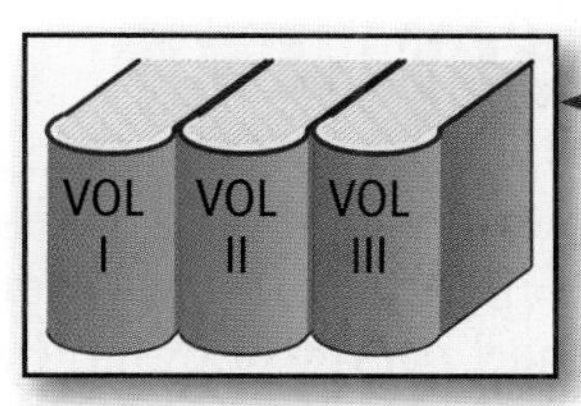

Figure W40.3

12. A dog is on a 12-foot leash that is tied to the corner of a 10-foot by 15-foot shed. The dog always stays outside the shed. How many square feet of ground can the dog reach?
13. Ohio Airlines is to provide service between cities as shown on the map. The airline employed 5 new people to sit in the control tower at each of the 5 cities. The people are Carol, Connie, Clare, Charles, and Cedric. The 2 people in the cities with connecting routes will be talking to each other a great deal, so it would be helpful if these people were friends. The pairs of friends are: Charles Connie, Carol Cedric, Charles Carol, Clare Cedric, and Carol Clare. Place the 5 people in the 5 cities so that the ones in connecting cities are friends.

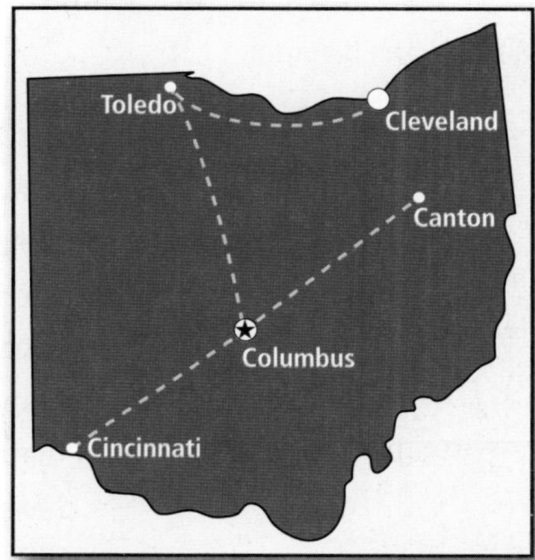

Figure W40.4

WORKSHOP 41

Problem-Solving Strategy: Making a Venn Diagram

Some problems can be solved with a diagram. Making a diagram can be an effective way of showing the information in a problem. In this workshop, you will use diagrams called Venn diagrams. They can be used to show the relationship among several groups of people, animals, or objects.

EXAMPLE 1

Figure W41.1

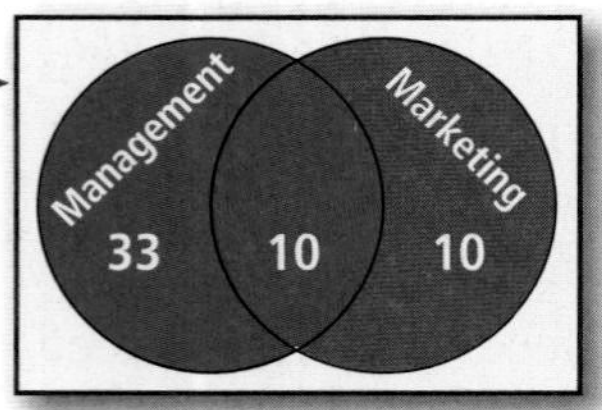

Of 53 employees surveyed, 43 have degrees in management, 20 have degrees in marketing, and 10 in both. How many have degrees in marketing but not management? Make a Venn diagram. Draw two intersecting circles—one for management and one for marketing. Work out from the middle region.

Step 1:	Fill in the number in both classes.	10
Step 2:	Fill in the remaining number in management.	$43 - 10 = 33$
Step 3:	Fill in the remaining number in marketing.	$20 - 10 = 10$
Step 4:	Add the numbers.	$33 + 10 + 10 = 53$

Ten employees have degrees in marketing but not management.

EXAMPLE 2

Two hundred people returning from a trip to Europe were asked which countries they had visited. One hundred forty-eight had been to England, 116 had been to France, and 96 had been to Spain. Eighty-two had been to England and France, 71 had been to France and Spain, 56 had been to England and Spain, and 44 had visited all 3 countries.

a. How many had visited France but not England or Spain?

b. How many had not visited any of these 3 countries?

Make a Venn diagram.

Figure W41.2

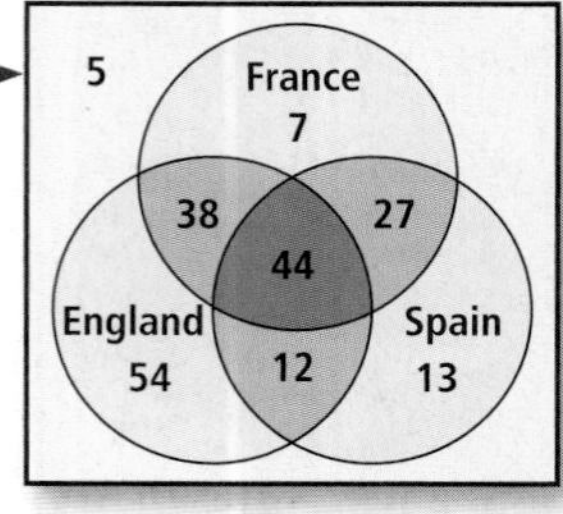

a. Follow the procedures:

- Draw a Venn diagram as shown.
- Forty-four visited all 3 countries.
- Twelve visited England and Spain only. $(56 - 44)$
- Twenty-seven visited France and Spain only. $(71 - 44)$
- Thirty-eight visited England and France only. $(82 - 44)$
- Thirteen visited Spain only. $[96 - (12 + 44 + 27)]$
- Seven visited France only. $[116 - (38 + 44 + 27)]$
- Fifty-four visited England only. $[148 - (38 + 44 + 12)]$

Seven people visited France only.

b. $[200 - (54 + 7 + 13 + 38 + 27 + 12 + 44)] = 200 - 195 = 5$

Five people did not visit any of the 3 countries.

Complete the problems. Check your answers in the back of the book.

1. Of 12 classmates, 6 went to the game, 7 went to the dance, and 4 went to both. How many went to neither?

WORKSHOPS

Practice

2. There are 197 delegates in the International Trade Association. Eighty-five of them speak Spanish, 74 speak French, and 15 speak both French and Spanish.
   a. How many speak Spanish but not French?
   b. How many speak French but not Spanish?
   c. How many speak neither French nor Spanish?

3. A survey of 150 people revealed that 121 people watch the early evening TV news, 64 watch the noon news, and 47 watch both. How many do not watch either one?

4. A survey of 120 college junior business students produced these results: 40 read a national newspaper, 48 read the local paper, 70 read the campus paper, 25 read a national newspaper and the local paper, 28 read the local paper and the campus paper, 21 read the campus paper and a national newspaper, and 18 read all three papers.
   a. How many do not read any of the papers?
   b. How many read a national newspaper and the local paper but not the campus paper?

5. Of 20 students eating at a local deli, 14 ordered salad, 10 ordered soup, and 4 ordered both salad and soup. How many did not order either?

6. One hundred employees were asked which sports they play. Fifty play football, 48 play basketball, 54 play baseball, 24 play both football and basketball, 22 play both basketball and baseball, 25 play both football and baseball, and 14 play all 3 sports.
   a. How many play basketball only?
   b. How many play football and baseball but not basketball?
   c. How many play none of the 3 sports?

7. In a marketing survey, 500 people were asked their 2 favorite colors. Red was chosen by 380, blue by 292, and 10 chose neither red nor blue.
   a. How many like both colors?
   b. How many like red but not blue?

WORKSHOP 42

Problem-Solving Strategy: Using Simpler Numbers

To solve a problem, you may find it helpful to restate the problem in a different way. A difficult problem can be restated as a simpler problem and become easier to solve. Or a problem may involve a series of simpler problems that will lead to the solution of the original problem. Sometimes solving a similar problem with smaller or easier numbers will help.

EXAMPLE 1

The National Football League playoffs start with twelve teams. The playoffs are a single elimination tournament. Single elimination means that you are eliminated from the playoffs if you lose a game. How many games will have to be played to determine the Super Bowl Champion? (Hint: A similar problem was encountered in the "Working Backward" workshop.)

Restate the problem.

Given that it is a single elimination tournament, every team (but the champion) will have to lose one game. Since 11 teams will have to lose 1 game, 11 games will have to be played. **Eleven games will have to be played to determine the Super Bowl Champion.**

EXAMPLE 2

A 27-inch bicycle wheel makes 100 revolutions per minute. A stone stuck in the treads will travel how many feet in 1 hour?

Restate the problem to follow a series of simpler problems.

a. How many inches will the stone travel in 1 revolution?
$C = 3.14d$ or 3.14×27 inches $=$ 84.78 inches

b. How many inches will the stone travel in 1 minute?
100 rpm $=$ 84.78 inches per revolution $=$ 8,478 inches

c. How many inches will the stone travel in 1 hour?
8,478 inches per minute $=$ 60 minutes per hour $=$ 508,680 inches

d. How many feet will the stone travel in 1 hour?
508,680 inches $\div$ 12 inches per foot $=$ 42,390 feet
The stone will travel 42,390 feet in one hour.

Concept CHECK

Complete the problem. Check your answer in the back of the book.

1. A 27-inch bicycle wheel makes 100 revolutions per minute. A stone stuck in the treads will travel how many *miles* in 1 hour? (Round the answer to the nearest mile.)

Practice

2. Your automobile's gas mileage is 27.5 miles per gallon. Last month your automobile was driven 1,595 miles and a gallon of gasoline cost \$3.95. What did it cost to buy gasoline for your automobile last month?

3. (Note that $1 + 3 = 4$, $1 + 3 + 5 = 9$, and $1 + 3 + 5 + 7 = 16$)
What is the sum of the first 25 odd numbers?

4. Vanna Burzinski works in the stockroom at Keynote Auto Supply. Burzinski always stacks crates using the triangular pattern shown. The top row always has 1 crate. Each row always has 2 fewer crates than the row before it.

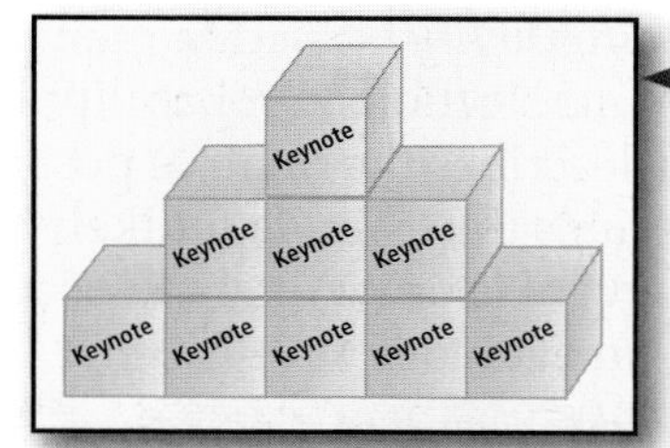

Figure W42.1

a. How many crates are in a stack that has 20 rows?
b. How many crates are in a stack if the bottom row has 29 crates?

5. Tabathia Russell is having a party. The first time the doorbell rings, 3 guests arrive. Each time the doorbell rings after that, a group arrives with 2 more guests than the preceding group.
a. How many guests arrive on the seventh ring?
b. If the doorbell rings ten times, how many guests came to the party?

6. The Baron Collier High School Shootout is a 48 team double elimination basketball tournament. Double elimination means that a team is out of the tournament if it loses two games.
a. How many games will have to be played to determine a winner?
b. Why are there two possible answers?

7. A train traveling at 60 miles per hour takes 4 seconds to enter a tunnel and another 50 seconds to pass completely through the tunnel.
a. What is the length of the train in feet?
b. What is the length of the tunnel in feet?

8. There are 32 teams in the National Football League. To conduct their annual draft, teams in each city must have a direct telephone line to each of the other teams.
a. How many direct telephone lines must be installed to accomplish this?
b. How many direct telephone lines must be installed if the league expands to 36 teams?

9. Grandpa Moyer wanted to leave his 17 horses to his 3 grandsons. Rick was to get $\frac{1}{2}$ of the horses, Mike was to get $\frac{1}{3}$, and Peter was to get $\frac{1}{9}$. How could he accomplish this?

10. Two cyclists start toward each other from points 25 miles apart. Cyclist No. 1 travels 15 mph, while Cyclist No. 2 travels 10 mph. A trained bird leaves the shoulder of Cyclist No. 1 and travels to the shoulder of Cyclist No. 2 and back and forth until the cyclists meet. If the bird flies at 40 mph, how far will the bird fly?

11. Chairs ready for shipment at the Northern Chair factory come down a ramp in single file. Inspector Edgerran Will checks every third chair, beginning with the third. Inspector Julio Lopez checks every fifth chair, beginning with the fifth. If 98 chairs came down the ramp while both inspectors were working on Monday, how many of these chairs were not checked by either of these two inspectors?

WORKSHOP 43

Business Data Analysis: Probability

Probability is used in many areas, including marketing, finance, insurance, and elections. Probability is a value between zero and one, inclusive, that describes the relative possibility an event will occur. A value close to 0 indicates the event is unlikely to occur and a value close to 1.0 indicates that the event is quite likely to occur. The formula for computing the probability of an event is:

$$\text{Probability of an event} = \frac{\text{Number of favorable outcomes}}{\text{Total number of possible outcomes}}$$

Some additional probability observations are:

The probability of an event A *and* an event B, occurring is:

$$P(A \text{ and } B) = P(A) \times P(B)$$

The probability of an event A *or* an event B, occurring is:

$$P(A \text{ or } B) = P(A) + P(B) - P(A \text{ and } B)$$

EXAMPLE 1

The Used Car Store has the inventory shown. If one car is selected at random, what is the probability that it would be red?

Used Car Store Inventory	
Color	**Number**
Silver	17
Red	14
Blue	9
Green	8
Beige	1
White	1
Total	50

Find the probability of selecting a red car.

$$P(\text{Red car}) = \frac{\text{Total number of red cars}}{\text{Total number of cars}} = \frac{14}{50} = 0.28$$

$$= 28\%$$

There is a 28% chance that a red car will be selected at random from the lot.

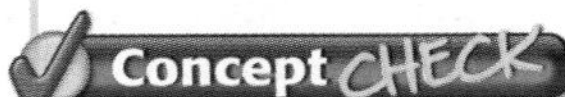

Complete the problems. Check your answers in the back of the book. For Problems 1 and 2 use the "Used Car Lot" from Example 1.

1. What is the probability that a car selected at random would be blue?
2. What is the probability that a car selected at random would be green or red?

EXAMPLE 2

A standard deck of 52 cards has four suits (clubs, diamonds, hearts, and spades) with thirteen cards per suit (Ace, 2, 3, 4, 5, 6, 7, 8, 9, 10, jack, queen, and king).

a. If one card is selected, what is the probability that it is a heart?
b. If one card is selected, what is the probability that it is an Ace?
c. If one card is selected, what is the probability that it is a club or a heart?
d. If one card is selected, what is the probability that it is the King of diamonds?

Step 1: a. Find the probability of selecting a heart. $P(\text{Heart}) = \frac{13 \text{ hearts}}{52 \text{ cards}} = \frac{1}{4} = 0.25$ or 25% chance of selecting a heart.

Step 2: b. Find the probability of selecting an ace. $P(\text{Ace}) = \frac{4 \text{ Aces}}{52 \text{ cards}} = \frac{1}{13} = 0.0769$ = 7.7% chance of selecting an ace.

Step 3: c. Find the probability of selecting a club or a heart

$P(\text{Club or Heart}) = P(\text{Club}) + P(\text{Heart}) - P(\text{Club and Heart}) = \frac{1}{4} + \frac{1}{4} - 0 = \frac{1}{2} = 0.5 = 50\%$

P(Club and Heart) = 0 because a card cannot be both a club and a heart. If it is impossible for both events to occur at the same time, the events are said to be "mutually exclusive".

Step 4: d. Find the probability of selecting a king and a diamond.

$P(\text{King and Diamond}) = P(\text{King}) \times P(\text{Diamond}) = \frac{4}{52} \times \frac{13}{52} = \frac{1}{52} = 0.0192 = 1.9\%$

Concept CHECK

Complete the problems. Check your answers in the back of the book. For Problems 3 and 4 use a standard deck of cards as described in Example 2.

3. If one card is selected, what is the probability that it is a 2?

4. If one card is selected, what is the probability that it is a 5 or a club?

Practice

5. A picnic cooler contains 60 cans of soda covered by ice. If one can is selected at random from the cooler, find the probability that the soda selected is: **(a)** root beer, **(b)** cola or orange soda; **(c)** ginger ale and root beer.

Picnic Cooler Contents

Type	Number
Cola	24
Orange	12
Ginger Ale	12
Root Beer	12
Total	60

6. A TV remote has keys for channels 0 through 9. If you select one key at random:

a. What is the probability that you press channel 7?

b. What is the probability that you press a key for an odd number?

c. What is the probability that you press a key for a number less than 8?

7. Each individual letter of the word "mathematics" is placed on a piece of paper, and all 11 pieces of paper are placed in a hat. If one letter is selected at random from the hat, find the probability that:

a. the letter "m" is selected.

b. the letter "a" is not selected.

c. a vowel is selected.

d. the letter "t" or "h" is selected.

e. the letter "o" is selected.

f. the letter "u" is not selected.

8. Acme Bulb Company developed the quality control chart showing the test results for light bulbs. If one of these light bulbs is selected at random, find the probability that the light bulb is: **(a)** Good; **(b)** Good, given that it is 60 watts; **(c)** defective, given that it is not 30 watts

Light Bulb Test Results

Wattage	Good	Defective	Total
30	75	20	95
60	125	10	135
100	110	15	125
Total	310	45	355

UNIT 1 Thematic Project

Career Exploration

This project asks you to explore two careers that reflect your personal work interests.

Your Project Assignment

✓ Choose two careers that interest you.

✓ Use the Internet and the library to research each career's responsibilities, education requirements, salary and benefits, and advancement opportunities.

✓ Interview at least two people in your community who work in one of your chosen career fields.

✓ Use word processing software to write a report on the two careers you researched.

✓ Create a 3–5 minute presentation.

Career Exploration

REQUIREMENTS	CAREER 1	CAREER 2
Job Responsibilities		
Education Requirements		
Salary		
Benefits		
Advancement Opportunities		

Skills Preview

A successful career search depends on your skills. This project may require you to use the following:

Academic Skills reading and writing

Basic Skills speaking, listening, thinking, problem-solving, and interpersonal skills

Technology Skills word-processing, keyboarding, presentation, and Internet skills

Math Online Go to connectED.mcgraw-hill.com to download a spreadsheet application for the unit project.

Bananastock/AGE Fotostock

Project Steps

Step 1 Do Your Research

- Think of two careers that suit your talents, interest, and values.
- Use the Internet or library resources to research both careers. Determine the responsibilities, education requirements, salary and benefits, and advancement opportunities for both.
- Visit the Web site of the U.S. Department of Labor Bureau of Labor Statistics to look up the occupational outlook for both careers.

Step 2 Explore Your Community

Interview two people in your community who work in either field of interest to you. Ask them about their day-to-day responsibilities, work environment, and background. What led them to their current position?

Step 3 Brainstorm

- Consider your personal interests, skills, likes, and dislikes. Now that you know more about your two chosen careers, do they seem like a good fit for you?
- Do you have a hobby or extracurricular interest that could become a full-time career someday?
- Think about what you can do now to develop your skills and confidence.

Step 4 Develop Your Presentation

Prepare a report of your findings using the following tools, if available:

- Use a word-processing program to write a 2-page report.
  - ✓ Describe your interests, talents, and work values, and explain how the two careers might present a good fit for you.
  - ✓ Use spreadsheet software or the downloadable spreadsheet to report your findings on the two careers you researched.
  - ✓ Summarize the advantages and challenges you would face in each position.
  - ✓ Make recommendations to your fellow students on how they can enhance their skills and confidence while in school.
- Using presentation software, create a 4-slide presentation describing a "day in the life" for both careers.
- Print your completed report to present to your class.

Academic and Career Portfolio

Add this report to your Academic and Career Portfolio.

Step 5 Evaluate

Go to **connectED.mcgraw-hill.com** to download an evaluation rubric.

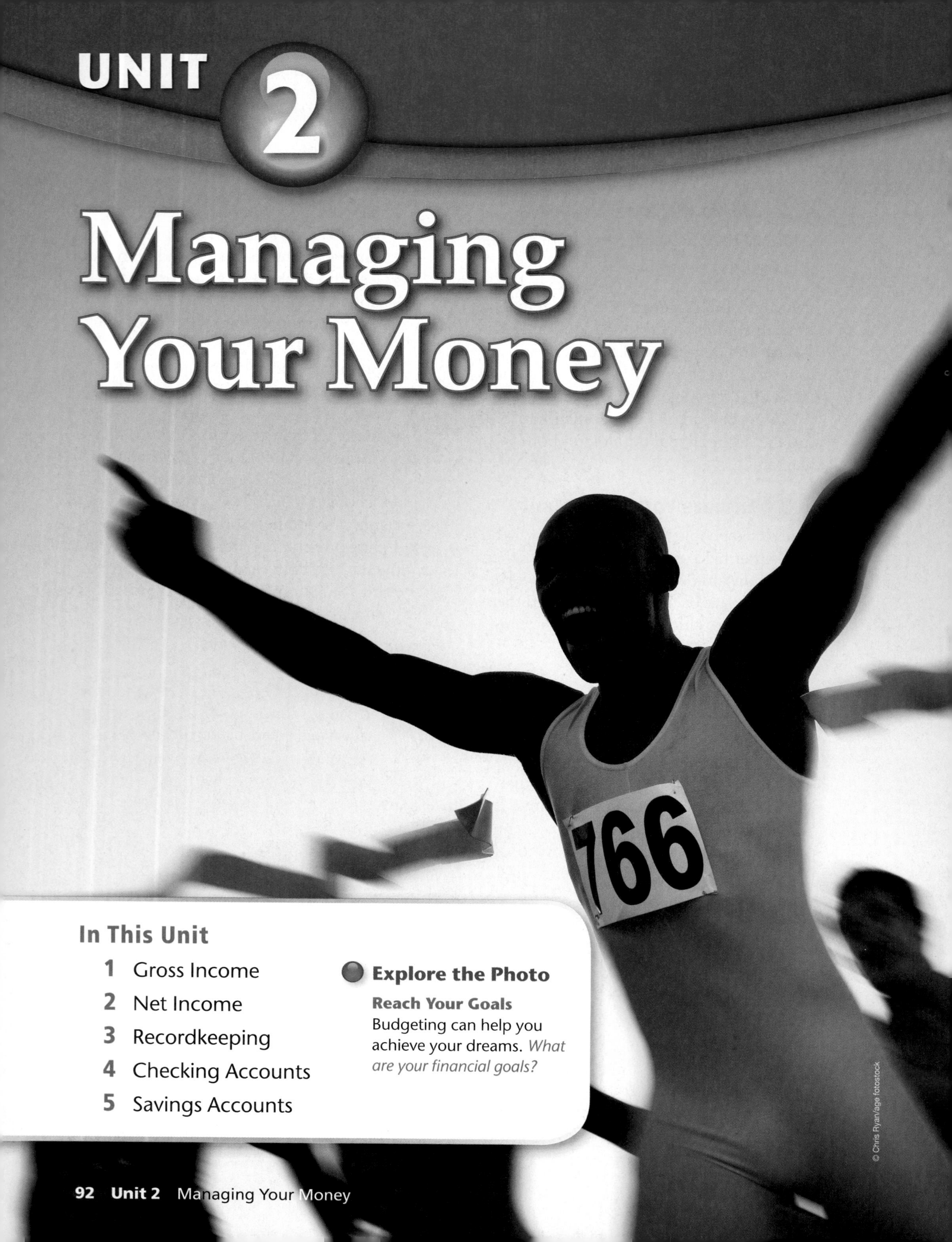

UNIT 2

Managing Your Money

In This Unit

1 Gross Income
2 Net Income
3 Recordkeeping
4 Checking Accounts
5 Savings Accounts

Explore the Photo

Reach Your Goals
Budgeting can help you achieve your dreams. *What are your financial goals?*

© Chris Ryan/age fotostock

The Big Picture

Marathons

The table below shows the largest marathons in the United States based on number of finishers.

Marathon	Number of finishers
1. ING New York City Marathon	37,866
2. LaSalle Bank Chicago Marathon	33,635
3. Honolulu Marathon	24,573
4. Marine Corps Marathon (D.C.)	20,910
5. City of Los Angeles Marathon	20,333
6. Boston Marathon	19,682
7. Rock 'n' Roll Marathon (CA)	15,759
8. Walt Disney World Marathon (FL)	10,311
9. Twin Cities Marathon (MN)	8,196
10. Portland Marathon (OR)	7,724

Go to **connectED.mcgraw-hill.com** for the Unit 2 WebQuest activity on marathon tourism.

Thematic Project Preview

Budget for Success

Do you want to own a home? Travel around the world? A budget can help you reach the finish line. You will set short- and long-term financial goals to meet your wants and needs. After you complete the Unit Thematic Project, you will have the information you need to prepare a personal budget to help you meet your financial goal.

Pre-Project Checklist

As you read this unit, use this checklist to prepare for the unit project:

- ✓ List general categories in which to identify how you spend your money.
- ✓ Differentiate between gross pay and net pay.
- ✓ Keep accurate financial records.
- ✓ Compare interest rates on savings accounts.
- ✓ Identify the steps in the budgeting process.

CHAPTER 1 Gross Income

Big Idea

Whether you work as a salesperson or as an airline pilot, you may need to know how to calculate your straight-time pay, overtime pay, total pay, salary, and commission in order to determine your gross pay.

Explore the Photo

Your Reward for Hard Work

Your paycheck should reflect your gross income. *Why is it important to know how to calculate your gross income?*

Ask AN EXPERT

Inflation and Income

Q: My grandfather said that in the 1950s he could afford a new house and car on a gross income of $12,000 a year. Why does $12,000 not buy as much today?

A: The purchasing power of an amount of money decreases because of inflation. Inflation is a general rise in prices. The government uses the consumer price index (CPI) to keep track of changes in the prices of goods and services used by households. The CPI is important for the economy because it helps measure if workers' pay is rising fast enough to keep up with inflation. When offered a job, consider asking if the employer gives annual "cost of living" raises. These raises are meant to protect workers from inflation.

English Language Arts/Writing Write a short essay about the lifestyle changes you would make if inflation increased suddenly while your pay remained the same.

GET READY for the Chapter

Math Online

To take the Online Readiness Quiz, go to connectED.mcgraw-hill.com.

Chapter 1 Gross Income

Reading Guide

Before You Read

Connect Have you ever received a paycheck? Was the pay what you expected?

Main Idea

When you work and get paid, it is important to know how to calculate your gross income.

Graphic Organizer

Before you read this chapter, draw a diagram like the one below. As you read, note seven formulas to calculate pay.

Formulas to Calculate Pay
1.
2.
3.
4.
5.
6.
7.

Math Online Go to connectED.mcgraw-hill.com to download this graphic organizer.

Content Vocabulary

You will learn these key terms in this chapter.

- hourly rate
- straight-time pay
- gross income
- overtime pay
- time and a half
- double time
- weekly time card
- piecework
- salary
- commission
- commission rate
- straight commission
- graduated commission

Academic Vocabulary

You will see these words in your reading and on your tests.

- calculate
- rate
- compute
- candidate
- fixed
- service
- incentive

You can find vocabulary definitions in the **Content Vocabulary** Glossary and the **Academic Vocabulary** Glossary in the back of the book.

Straight-Time Pay

Lesson Objective

Calculate straight-time pay.

Content Vocabulary

- hourly rate
- straight-time pay
- gross income

GET READY for the Lesson

Why is it important for you to understand the information on your paychecks?

Vince Bana works for a custom furniture shop. He did not pay much attention to the information on his paychecks until he realized that the raise he had been given was not being calculated correctly. He contacted the payroll clerk, who corrected the error.

Design Pics/Darren Greenwood

As You Read

Question What are the benefits of being paid an hourly rate?

Straight-Time Pay Some jobs pay you a fixed amount of money for each hour you work. This is the **hourly rate**. For example, you might receive $7.50 an hour from the local cinema to sell tickets and work at the concession stand. The $7.50 is the hourly rate the cinema pays you. The manager has scheduled you to work 15 hours a week. Use the number of hours worked to **calculate** your **straight-time pay**, or the total amount of money you earn for a pay period at the regular hourly rate.

The formula for calculating straight-time pay is:

Straight-Time Pay = Hourly Rate × Hours Worked

The total amount you are paid during a pay period is often called **gross income**, *gross pay*, or the *gross amount*. It consists of the total amount you earned, no matter how your pay was calculated.

Need Help? Go to...

- **Workshop 2:** Rounding Numbers, p. 6
- **Workshop 6:** Multiplying Decimals, p. 14
- **Skill 2:** Rounding Numbers, p. SK3
- **Skill 8:** Multiplying Decimals, p. SK9
- **Skill 14:** Changing Fractions/Decimals, p. SK15
- **Application A:** Formulas, p. AP1

EXAMPLE 1

Shawna Nguyen is a mail clerk at an advertising firm. She earns $12.00 per hour. This week she worked $39\frac{1}{2}$ hours. What is her straight-time pay for the week?

Find the straight-time pay.

Hourly Rate × Hours Worked

$12.00 × 39.5 = **$474.00**

Concept CHECK

Find the straight-time pay. Check your answers in the back of the book.

1. $7.60 per hour × 40 hours
2. $7.90 per hour × 37 hours

Need Help? Go to...

- **Workshop 29:** Using the Four-Step Method, p. 60
- **Workshop 38:** Writing an Equation, p. 78

EXAMPLE 2 Algebra

Ralph Masales is an accounting clerk. He earns \$14.40 per hour. How many hours per week must he work if he wants to earn approximately \$550.00 per week?

Find the straight-time pay.

Let h represent the hours.

Straight time pay = Hourly Rate × Hours Worked

To solve for h, divide both sides of the equation by \$14.40.

$$\$550.00 = \$14.40 \times h$$

$$\frac{\$550.00}{\$14.40} = \frac{\$14.40h}{\$14.40}$$

$$38.19 = h$$

Ralph will have to work about 38.25 hours (nearest quarter hour).

Study Tip

Is It Reasonable?
Always check to be sure that your answer is reasonable. If the answer seems unreasonable, solve the problem again.

Concept CHECK

Find the straight-time pay. Round to the nearest quarter hour. Check your answers in the back of the book.

3. Bobby Hsu is an office manager at a weekly newspaper. He earns \$22.50 per hour. How many hours per week does Bobby work if he earns \$522.00 per week?
4. Lauren Rodriguez earns \$8.35 per hour as a swimming instructor. How many hours per week must she work if she wants to earn approximately \$190.00 per week?

Lesson Practice

Find the straight-time pay.

	Employee	Regular Hourly Rate	×	Hours Worked	=	Straight-Time Pay
5.	Wright, S.	\$ 8.00	×	36	=	\$
6.	Ivanovich, E.	7.50	×	18	=	
7.	Levitt, R.	16.20	×	30	=	
8.	Maguire, M.	10.25	×	24.5	=	
9.	Reyes, A.	14.525	×	31.125	=	
10.	Vadola, G.	26.675	×	25.625	=	
11.	Gershwin, A.	b	×	37.5	=	\$937.50
12.	Mercer, D.	17.50	×	b	=	\$630.00
13.	Leon, J.	26.567	×	b	=	\$664.175
14.	Chung, C.	b	×	40	=	\$390.20

15. You earn \$8.50 per hour and work 30 hours this week. What is your straight-time pay?
16. A mobile auto-detailing company pays you \$12.75 per hour. Last summer you worked 35.25 hours a week. What was your total straight-time pay for one week?

Construction Worker
Construction workers use math to measure and cut lumber, plan stairways, and calculate window dimensions.
Why should construction workers have a solid understanding of mathematics?

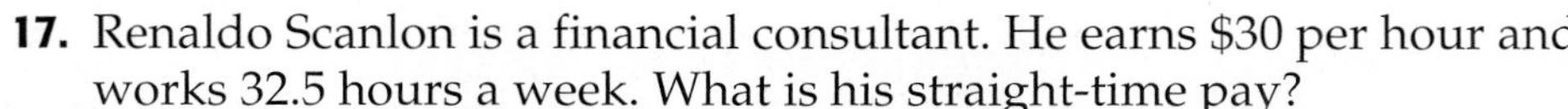

17. Renaldo Scanlon is a financial consultant. He earns $30 per hour and works 32.5 hours a week. What is his straight-time pay?

18. Marian Abelt tests video games. She earns $8.125 per hour. Last week she worked 35.50 hours. What was her straight-time pay?

19. Sylvia O'Keefe builds sets for independent movies and plays. She earns $15.80 per hour. Last week she worked 34 hours. What was her straight-time pay for last week?

20. Madison Tanaka has a part-time job as a cashier at a shoe store. She earns $8.32 per hour and works 20 hours each week. What is her straight-time pay for one week?

21. Polly Brennan earns $8.62 per hour for playing guitar at Kaldi's coffee shop. She works 12.5 hours a week. What is the musician's straight-time pay?

22. Dominic Marzetti is a fish and game warden at Natural Bridge State Park. He works 38 hours per week and earns $20.85 per hour. What is his straight-time pay each week?

23. Don Moline, a construction worker, earns $18.25 per hour. He worked his regular 36 hours last week. He also worked 15 hours at a part-time job building decks at $13.00 per hour. What is Don's total straight-time pay for both jobs?

H.O.T. Problems

24. ALGEBRA Elaine Mellon earns $17.80 per hour as an electronic billing specialist for a legal clinic. How many hours per week must she work if she wants to earn approximately $675.00 per week?

25. CHALLENGE PROBLEM Ellen O'Brien earns $23.68 per hour as an assistant aircraft mechanic at a local airport. How many hours per week must she work if she wants to earn approximately $900.00 per week?

Spiral Review

Write the fractions as decimals. (Skill 14)

26. $\frac{1}{4}$ **27.** $\frac{1}{2}$ **28.** $\frac{3}{4}$

Multiply the numbers. Round the answers to the nearest cent. (Skill 8)

29. $4.50 × 30.25 **30.** $8.30 × 3.25 **31.** $14.50 × 32.5

Round to the nearest ten. (Skill 2)

32. 22 **33.** 138 **34.** 8

GET READY for the Next Lesson

PREREQUISITE SKILL Adding Decimals (Skill 5)

Add.

35. $35.90 + 8.64

36. $106.75 + 27.30

37. $13.675 + 0.125 + 74.08

38. $135.00 + 205.00

39. $270.00 + 165.75 + 25.50

Comstock/SuperStock

LESSON 1.2 Overtime Pay

Lesson Objective
Calculate straight-time, overtime, and total pay.

Content Vocabulary
- overtime pay
- time and a half
- double time

GET READY for the Lesson

Why do employers pay a higher rate for overtime work?

Jake Norris works at the local library. He works a regular 40-hour workweek shelving books at the library. His salary is $10 per hour, and he makes $15 an hour when he works on Saturdays. Sometimes he would rather be out with his friends on Saturday, but he likes the extra pay.

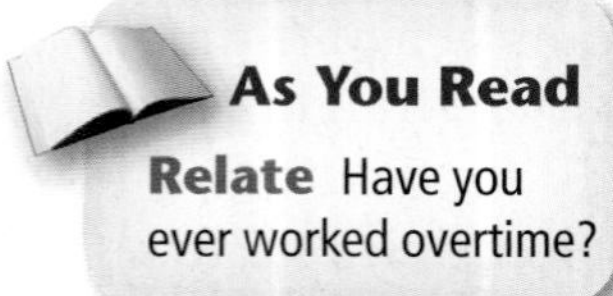

As You Read

Relate Have you ever worked overtime?

Overtime Pay When you work more than the regular number of hours, you may earn **overtime pay**. The overtime rate, called **time and a half**, is usually $1\frac{1}{2}$ times your hourly rate. You may receive an overtime pay rate of **double time**, or twice your regular hourly rate. Employers often pay double time for Sundays and holidays. To calculate your overtime pay, remember this:

Overtime Pay = Overtime Rate × Overtime Hours Worked

Total Pay = Straight-Time Pay + Overtime Pay

Need Help? Go to...
- **Workshop 4:** Adding Decimals, p. 10
- **Skill 5:** Adding Decimals, p. SK6
- **Application A:** Formulas, p. AP1

EXAMPLE 1

Alan Moore is paid $8.20 an hour for a regular 40-hour week as a restaurant host. His overtime rate is $1\frac{1}{2}$ times his regular hourly rate. This week he worked his regular 40 hours plus 10 hours of overtime. What is his total pay?

Step 1: Find the straight-time pay.

Hourly Rate × Regular Hours Worked
$8.20 × 40 = $328.00 straight-time pay

Step 2: Find the overtime pay.

Overtime Rate × Overtime Hours Worked
($1\frac{1}{2}$ × $8.20) × 10 = $123.00 overtime pay

Step 3: Find the total pay.

Straight-Time Pay + Overtime Pay
$328.00 + $123.00 = **$451.00 total pay**

Concept CHECK

Find the total pay. Check your answers in the back of the book.

1. Josie Perez makes $9.00 an hour. She worked 40 regular hours and 6 hours at time and a half.
2. Ed Lange makes $11.50 an hour. This week he worked 36 regular hours and 7 hours at time and a half.

Need Help? Go to...

- Workshop 29: Using the Four-Step Method, p. 60
- Workshop 38: Writing an Equation, p. 78

EXAMPLE 2 Algebra

Jessica Cooper is a receptionist at a hotel and conference center. She is paid $12.50 an hour for a regular 40-hour week. Her overtime pay is $1\frac{1}{2}$ times her regular hourly rate. This past week Jessica earned $612.50 in total pay. How many hours of overtime did she work?

Step 1: Use the total pay formula:

Total Pay = Straight-Time Pay + Overtime Pay

Step 2: Let h = the number of hours of overtime she worked.

Step 3: Substitute in the formula the values we know and solve for h.

Total Pay = Straight-Time Pay + Overtime Pay

Do the multiplication →
$$\$612.50 = (\$12.50 \times 40) + [(\$12.50 \times 1.5) \times h]$$

$$\$612.50 = \$500.00 + \$18.75h$$

Subtract $500.00 from each side of the equation →
$$\$612.50 - \$500.00 = \$500.00 + \$18.75h - \$500.00$$

Divide both sides of the equation by $18.75 →
$$\frac{\$112.50}{\$18.75} = \frac{\$18.75h}{\$18.75}$$

$$6 = h$$

Jessica worked 6 hours of overtime this past week.

Concept CHECK

Complete the problems. Check your answers in the back of the book.

3. Corey Murphy earns $11.80 an hour for a regular 40-hour week at the pet store. His overtime pay is $1\frac{1}{2}$ times his regular hourly rate. Last week Corey earned $613.60 in total pay. How many hours of overtime did he work?

4. Western Deli pays its couriers straight time for 36 hours per week and double time for any hours more than 36 worked. Last week Kevin Alvarez worked a total of 42 hours and had total pay of $545.28. What is his straight-time pay?

Lesson Practice

Study Tip

Formulas
When using a formula to solve a problem, remember to perform any computations within parentheses first.

Find the (a) straight-time pay, (b) overtime pay, and (c) total pay.

	Hourly Pay (for 40-hour week)	Straight-Time Pay	Overtime Rate	Overtime Hours	Overtime Pay	Total Pay
5.	$16.20	a. $	$1\frac{1}{2}$	8	b. $	c. $
6.	10.25	a.	$1\frac{1}{2}$	5	b.	c.
7.	14.525	a.	$1\frac{1}{2}$	4	b.	c.
8.	26.675	a.	2	8	b.	c.
9.	10.20	a.	2	13	b.	c.
10.	32.25	a.	$1\frac{1}{2}$	6.25	b.	c.

11. Dorothy Katz, a computer programmer, earns a regular hourly rate of $32.25 and time and a half when she works overtime. In a typical week, she works 40 regular hours and 12 hours overtime. Find Dorothy's **(a)** straight-time pay, **(b)** overtime pay, and **(c)** total pay.

Did You Know?

Airbus A380 **The world's largest passenger plane, the Airbus A380, is over 239 feet long. The A380 has a wingspan of over 261 feet, can carry up to 555 passengers, and reach a top speed of 652 miles per hour.**

12. Steven Kellogg, a jet airplane mechanic, works at an hourly rate of \$36 and earns time and a half if he works any overtime. Last week he worked 37 hours plus 8 hours overtime. What are his **(a)** straight-time pay, **(b)** overtime pay, and **(c)** total pay?

13. Rick Haskins is paid \$18 an hour as a pastry chef for a regular 35-hour week. His overtime rate is 1.5 times his regular hourly rate. This week he worked his regular 35 hours plus 8 hours of overtime. What is Rick's total pay?

14. As a case worker, Bonnie Armstrong earns \$13.47 an hour plus time and a half for weekend work. Last week she worked her regular 40 hours plus 8 hours of overtime on the weekend. What was her total pay for the week?

15. George Keller, a small-engine mechanic, earns a regular hourly rate of \$15.68. For overtime, he earns time and a half on Saturdays and double time on Sundays. This week he worked his regular 40 hours plus 8 hours on Saturday and 7 hours on Sunday. What is George's total pay for the week?

H.O.T. Problems

16. ALGEBRA Denise Cho is a broadcast technician and earns \$17.00 an hour with time and a half for overtime. Last week she worked 40 hours plus overtime. If her total pay was \$839.38, how many overtime hours did Denise work?

17. CHALLENGE PROBLEM Ken Santos is a tour guide at an art museum and earns \$11 an hour with time and a half for overtime. Last week he worked 40 hours plus overtime. If his total pay was \$506, how many overtime hours did Ken work?

Spiral Review

Use multiplication to solve Problems 18–21. (Skills 8, 14)

18. $(1\frac{1}{2} \times \$8.40) \times 7$

19. $(2 \times \$18.40) \times 12$

20. $(1\frac{1}{4} \times \$9.60) \times 9$

21. $(1.5 \times \$12.50) \times 8$

22. You earn \$7.25 per hour and work 30 hours this week delivering groceries. What is your straight-time pay? (Lesson 1.1)

23. A local pet care center pays you \$8 per hour to walk dogs. Last summer you worked 36.75 hours a week. What was your total weekly straight-time pay for one week? (Lesson 1.1)

GET READY for the Next Lesson

PREREQUISITE SKILL **Elapsed Time (Hours)** (Application F)

Find the elapsed time.

24. From 9:00 AM to 11:15 AM

25. From 9:00 PM to 11:15 AM

26. From 9:30 AM to 1:15 PM

27. From 10:55 AM to 11:15 AM

28. From 6:00 PM to 12:00 noon

29. From 11:18 AM to 5:05 PM

Ingram Publishing/SuperStock

LESSON 1.3

Weekly Time Card

Lesson Objective
Calculate the total hours on a weekly time card.

Content Vocabulary
- weekly time card

GET READY for the Lesson

Why is it important to accurately record your hours at work?

Hilary Dunlop-Brown makes $9.75 an hour helping customers at a bicycle rental shop. She kept track of her hours every day this week, and now she wants to know her gross income.

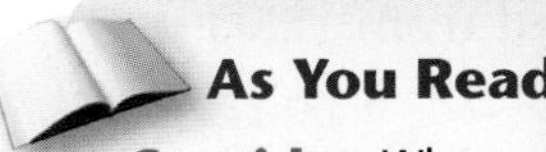

As You Read

Consider What should you do if you forget to clock in or clock out?

Time Cards At your job at the cinema, you are required to keep track of your hours on a **weekly time card**. This is a daily record of the time you report to work and the time you depart. You **compute** the hours you worked each day. At the end of the week, you add the number of daily hours to find the total number of hours worked. If you do not work an entire hour, round your time to the nearest quarter of an hour.

To compute the number of hours worked in a week:

Total Hours = Sum of Daily Hours

Need Help? Go to...
- **Workshop 10:** Adding Fractions, p. 22
- **Workshop 17:** Elapsed Time, p. 36
- **Skill 2:** Rounding Numbers, p. SK3
- **Skill 16:** Adding Fractions, Unlike Denominators, p. SK17
- **Application E:** Rounding Time: Nearest Quarter Hour, p. AP5
- **Application F:** Elapsed Time (Hours), p. AP5

EXAMPLE

Gail Stough is required to keep a weekly time card. Based on the time card in **Figure 1.1,** what is the number of her **(a)** daily hours worked on September 18 and **(b)** total hours for the week?

Figure 1.1

Employee Time Card

Employee Name: Gail Stough Department: Customer Service

	DATE	IN	OUT	IN	OUT	HOURS
Sun.						
Mon.	9/15	8:15 AM	12:15 PM	1:00 PM	5:00 PM	8
Tue.	9/16	8:30 AM	12:05 PM	12:35 PM	5:20 PM	$8\frac{1}{4}$
Wed.	9/17	8:28 AM	12:05 PM	12:30 PM	4:30 PM	$7\frac{1}{2}$
Thur.	9/18	8:15 AM	1:45 PM	2:15 PM	4:59 PM	$8\frac{1}{4}$
Fri.	9/19	8:30 AM	12:20 PM	12:50 PM	5:00 PM	8
Sat.						
Employee Signature: Gail Stough					TOTAL HOURS	40

Step 1: Find the hours worked on September 18.

A. Time between 8:15 AM and 1:45 PM

When the start time is prior to 1:00 and the end time is 1:00 or later, add 12:00 to the end time.

(1:45 + 12:00) − 8:15
13:45 − 8:15 = 5h:30min

Continued on next page

B. Time between 2:15 PM and 4:59 PM

4:59 − 2:15 = 2h:44min

5h:30min + 2h:44min = 7h:74min = 8h:14min

(Round to the nearest quarter hour) = $8\frac{1}{4}$ **hours**

Step 2: Find the total hours for the week.

Sum of daily hours

$8 + 8\frac{1}{4} + 7\frac{1}{2} + 8\frac{1}{4} + 8$

$8 + 8\frac{1}{4} + 7\frac{1}{2} + 8\frac{1}{4} + 8 = 39 + \frac{4}{4} =$ **40 total hours**

Concept CHECK

Find the total number of hours for each person. Check your answers in the back of the book.

1. Reggie Blanco worked from 8:00 AM to 10:45 AM and from 12:15 PM to 4:15 PM.
2. Ruth Anderson worked from 7:30 AM to 11:55 AM and from 1:00 PM to 4:50 PM.

Study Tip

Check Your Work

Always check your work after finding an answer. If $39 + \frac{4}{4} = 40$, does $40 - \frac{4}{4} = 39$?

Lesson Practice

Eddie Irwin works in the data processing department at the local medical center. He is required to keep a weekly time card. Use the information in **Figure 1.2** to calculate the number of hours worked for **(a)** each day and **(b)** the week.

Figure 1.2

Employee Time Card — **Needham Medical Center**

Employee Name: Eddie Irwin — Department: Data Processing

		DATE	IN	OUT	IN	OUT	TOTAL
	Sun.						
3.	Mon.	12/13	8:15 AM	12:00 PM	12:30 PM	4:30 PM	
4.	Tue.	12/14	8:30 AM	12:30 PM	1:10 PM	5:10 PM	
5.	Wed.	12/15	8:35 AM	12:50 PM	1:30 PM	5:00 PM	
6.	Thur.	12/16	8:15 AM	12:10 PM	12:45 PM	4:20 PM	
7.	Fri.	12/17	8:25 AM	1:15 PM	1:50 PM	5:30 PM	
	Sat.						
8.	Employee Signature: Eddie Irwin					TOTAL HOURS	

9. Eddie Irwin is paid \$17.25 per hour for a regular 37-hour week. His overtime rate is $1\frac{1}{2}$ times his regular hourly rate. Use his time card (see **Figure 1.2**) to find his total pay for the week.
10. Using Eddie Irwin's time card (see **Figure 1.2**), find his total pay for the week if his overtime rate is 2 times his regular hourly rate of \$17.25 per hour for a regular 37-hour week.

Did You Know?

Coney Island **In 1895, Sea Lion Park opened on Coney Island in Brooklyn, New York. It was the first permanent amusement park in North America.**

11. Gail Stough is a customer service representative at an amusement park and earns \$8.40 per hour. Use her time card (see **Figure 1.1** on page 103) to find her total pay for the week.

12. You work from 7:00 AM to 11:00 AM and from 12:00 noon to 4:00 PM. You do not work overtime. Your hourly rate is \$7.50. Use the table below to find the hours worked and the total pay for the week.

Employee Time Card

	DATE	IN	OUT	IN	OUT	HOURS
Sun.						
Mon.	—	7:00 AM	11:00 AM	12:00 PM	4:04 PM	a.
Tue.	—	7:05 AM	11:10 AM	11:55 PM	3:59 PM	b.
Wed.	—	7:01 AM	10:59 AM	12:05 PM	3:58 PM	c.
Thur.	—	6:59 AM	10:55 AM	12:01 PM	4:03 PM	d.
Fri.	—	6:55 AM	11:01 AM	12:02 PM	3:49 PM	e.
					TOTAL HOURS	f.

13. In **Problem 12,** you worked the following weekend hours:

	DATE	IN	OUT	IN	OUT	HOURS
Sat.	—	7:00 AM	11:30 AM	12:00 PM	4:00 PM	
Sun.	—	8:15 AM	11:45 AM	12:15 PM	4:30 PM	

If you are paid time and a half for Saturday and double time for Sunday, **(a)** what is your overtime pay for the weekend? **(b)** What is your total pay if you include the hours worked Monday through Friday in Problem 12?

14. CHALLENGE PROBLEM Maurice Andrews earns \$8.40 per hour bussing tables at Joey's Café. He works until 10:00 PM each night when the café closes. If he works 5 days a week and his total pay for the week is \$294.00, what time does he come in each day?

Spiral Review

Add. (Skill 16)

15. $\frac{1}{4} + \frac{1}{4} + \frac{1}{2}$

16. $\frac{3}{4} + \frac{1}{8}$

Round to the nearest quarter hour. (Application E, Skill 2)

17. 8:09 **18.** 7:47 **19.** 11:55

20. Maria Krisp, a licensed physical therapist assistant, earns an hourly rate of \$18.40 and time and a half if she works any overtime. Last week she worked 38 hours plus 6 hours overtime. What is Maria's **(a)** straight-time pay, **(b)** overtime pay, and **(c)** total pay? (Lesson 1.2)

GET READY for the Next Lesson

PREREQUISITE SKILL **Multiplying Decimals** (Skill 8)

Multiply.

21. $\begin{array}{r}\$0.36\\ \times\ 65\\ \hline\end{array}$

22. $\begin{array}{r}\$4.70\\ \times\ 76\\ \hline\end{array}$

23. $\begin{array}{r}\$0.07\\ \times\ 4{,}660\\ \hline\end{array}$

LESSON 1.4

Piecework

Lesson Objective

Compute total pay on a piecework basis.

Content Vocabulary

- piecework

GET READY for the Lesson

Have you ever been paid per item?

Josh had a job collecting signatures for a friend's mother who wanted to run for mayor. The **candidate** told him he could either earn $8.00 per hour, or work on a piecework basis for $0.80 per signature.

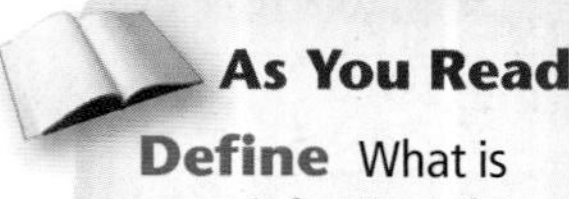

As You Read

Define What is your definition of piecework?

Piecework Some jobs pay you on a **piecework** basis. A worker receives a specified amount of money for each item of work completed. To calculate this, use this formula:

Total Pay = Rate per Item × Number of Items Produced

For example, if your soccer team had a car wash, received $20 per vehicle, and washed 40 vehicles, you earned $800.
$800 = $20 (rate per vehicle) × 40 (number of vehicles).

Need Help? Go to...

- **Workshop 6:** Multiplying Decimals, p. 14
- **Skill 8:** Multiplying Decimals, p. SK9
- **Application A:** Formulas, p. AP1

EXAMPLE 1

Ramon Hernandez silk-screens prints for a local artist who pays $4 for each print he completes. Last week he silk-screened 75 prints. This week he completed 71. What is his pay each week?

Find the total pay.

	Rate per Item	×	Number Produced	=	Total Pay
Last Week	$4	×	75	=	$300
This Week	4	×	71	=	284

Concept CHECK

Find the total pay. Check your answers in the back of the book.

1. $3.20 per item, 140 items produced
2. $0.15 per item, 1,494 items produced

Need Help? Go to...

- **Workshop 29:** Using the Four-Step Method, p. 60
- **Workshop 6:** Multiplying Decimals, p. 14

EXAMPLE 2 Algebra

The Sunscreen Company, LLC, sells and installs window film for automobiles. Sara Miller manages one Sunscreen shop. She reports that during the past week, her shop applied window film to 19 autos. It charges $179.99 for a four-door sedan and $149.99 for a two-door coupe. Sara reports that $3,209.81 in total receipts had been collected. In that week, how many **(a)** four-door sedans and **(b)** two-door coupes had been serviced?

Step 1: Let s = Number of four-door sedans serviced.
Let $(19 - s)$ = Number of two-door coupes serviced.

Step 2: Write an equation to identify the total of each type serviced.

The value of the four-door sales added to the value of the two-door sales equals the total receipts.

Step 3: Solve the equation

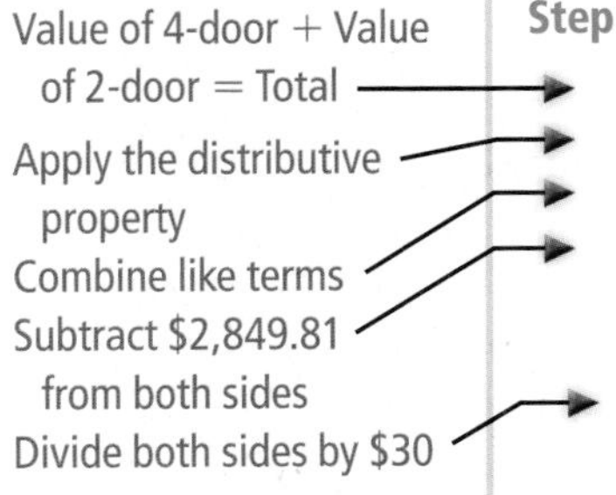

$$\$179.99s + \$149.99(19 - s) = \$3{,}209.81$$
$$\$179.99s + \$2{,}849.81 - \$149.99s = \$3{,}209.81$$
$$\$30.00s + \$2{,}849.81 = \$3{,}209.81$$
$$\$30.00s + \$2{,}849.81 - \$2{,}849.81 = \$3{,}209.81 - \$2{,}849.81$$
$$\$30.00s = \$360.00$$
$$\frac{\$30.00s}{\$30.00} = \frac{\$360.00}{\$30.00}$$
$$s = 12$$

The company installed window film on 12 four-door sedans and 7 two-door coupes.

Reading Math +−÷=

Grouping Symbols

Grouping symbols include parentheses ( ), brackets [ ], and fraction bars, as in $\frac{6+2}{4}$, which means $(6 + 2) \div 4$.

Concept CHECK

Complete the problems. Check your answers in the back of the book.

3. Copy Center charges 8¢ a page for machine-fed copies and 20¢ per page for hand-fed copies. If Logan Kaminski's bill for 80 copies of his movie script is $13.00, how many copies of each type were made?
4. Mary Tuttle owns a carpet-cleaning business. She charges $67.95 for a two-bedroom house and $82.25 for a three-bedroom house. Last month the company had gross receipts of $4,413.00 for cleaning carpet in 8 more three-bedroom houses than two-bedroom houses. How many of each type did the company clean?

Lesson Practice

Complete the table.

	Worker	Rate per Item	×	Number of Items	=	Total Pay
5.	Montgomery, Hal	$ 1.45	×	340	=	$
6.	Dressler, Ginger	0.06	×	4,234	=	
7.	Danielli, Ella	0.19	×	719	=	
8.	Koop, Evan	15.625	×	326	=	
9.	Dawson, Ted	658.55	×	*a*	=	$71,781.95
10.	Orlov, Irina	*a*	×	15	=	$32,179.95

11. Anthony Harris earns $0.50 per hamper of heirloom tomatoes. One day he picked 43 hampers-worth. What was his total pay that day?
12. Your aunt and uncle ask you to hang pictures in their home. They offer to pay you $3.50 per picture. What is your total pay if you hang 15 pictures?
13. Lee Wu writes 48 résumés for $35 each. What is her pay?
14. Craig Rose is an over-the-road truck driver. If he is paid $0.54 per mile, what is Craig's total pay for the day he drove 527 miles?

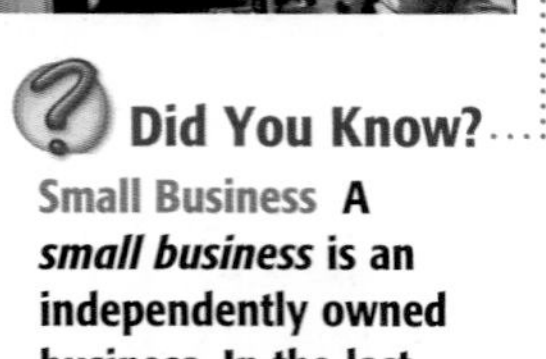

Did You Know?

Small Business A ***small business*** is an independently owned business. In the last decade, the Small Business Administration has helped almost 435,000 small businesses obtain more than $94.6 billion in loans.

15. Landon Elliott fumigates rooms and charges $21.95 per room. On Monday, he fumigated 3 rooms in one house, 2 in another, and 4 in a third. Find his total charges.

16. Paul James is a chrome plater at a local plant. If he plates 300 items or more, he is paid $1.25 each. For less than 300 items, he is paid $0.75 each. What is his total pay if he plates 321 items on Wednesday and 154 items on Thursday?

17. Audrey Lorenz assembles gift baskets for a florist. The owner pays her $0.45 per small basket and $0.75 per large basket. On Tuesday, she assembled 288 small baskets and 72 large ones. What is her total pay?

18. Karen Sullivan delivers newspapers for the *Tribune Dispatch.* She receives 18.2 cents per paper, 6 days a week (for the daily paper), and 70 cents for the Sunday paper. She delivers 124 daily papers each day and 151 Sunday papers each week. What is her total pay?

19. Charlene Levington operates an oil change and tune-up service. She charges $33.95 per oil change. Tune-up is $72.50 for a four-cylinder engine, $82.50 for a six-cylinder engine, and $92.50 for an eight-cylinder engine. What are the charges for a week in which Charlene's facility did 35 oil changes and tuned 5 four-cylinder engines, 7 six-cylinder engines, and 2 eight-cylinder engines?

20. **ALGEBRA** Wing Ko replaces watch bands. He is paid $24.60 per band. How many bands must he replace to earn at least $122.50 per day?

21. **CHALLENGE PROBLEM** Lindsay Bedford works at the baseball cap shop. She is paid $6.50 per hour plus $0.45 for each cap she embroiders. How many caps must she embroider to earn at least $85 in an 8-hour day?

Spiral Review

Multiply the numbers. Round the answers to the nearest cent. (Skill 8)

22. $0.23 × 89

23. $1.10 × 240

24. $0.06 × 4,192

25. $0.06 × 906

26. You are scheduled to work from 7:00 AM to 11:00 AM and from 12:00 noon to 3:30 PM Monday through Friday at the local television station. Your hourly rate is $8.55. What is your pay for the week? (Lesson 1.3)

27. You earn $9.35 per hour and work 32 hours week at an advertisement agency. What is your straight-time pay? (Lesson 1.1)

GET READY for the Next Lesson

PREREQUISITE SKILL Rounding Decimals to the Nearest Hundredth (Skill 2)

Round to the nearest hundredth.

28. 35,987.642

29. 0.0125

30. 283.8549

31. 1.005

32. 0.123

33. 49.667

LESSON 1.5

Salary

Lesson Objective
Determine salary per pay period.

Content Vocabulary
- salary

GET READY for the Lesson

What is the difference between being paid once or twice a month?

Chelsea Patterson teaches photography at a community college. She earns an annual salary of $50,000. Her classes start in September and end in June, and she has a two-month summer break. She can choose to be paid monthly or bimonthly.

As You Read

Relate How could the number of times you are paid each year affect your budgeting plans?

Salary Many employees are paid a **salary**. A salary is a **fixed** amount of money that you earn on a regular basis. Your salary may be paid weekly, biweekly, semimonthly, or monthly. Your annual salary is the total salary you earn during a year. There are 52 weekly, 26 biweekly, 24 semimonthly, and 12 monthly pay periods per year.

$$\text{Salary per Pay Period} = \frac{\text{Annual Salary}}{\text{Number of Pay Periods per Year}}$$

Need Help? Go to...
- **Workshop 7:** Dividing Decimals, p. 16
- **Skill 11:** Dividing Decimals, p. SK12
- **Application K:** Chronological Expressions, p. AP7

EXAMPLE 1

Tom Costello is a Web site designer. His annual salary is $67,400. What is Tom's monthly salary? What is his weekly salary?

Find the salary per pay period.

Step 1: Use the salary per pay period formula.

$$\text{Salary per Pay Period} = \frac{\text{Annual Salary}}{\text{Number of Pay Periods per Year}}$$

Step 2: Substitute into the formula to find salary per month.

$$\text{Salary per Month} = \frac{\$67{,}400}{12} = \mathbf{\$5{,}616.67}$$

Step 3: Substitute into the formula to find the salary per week.

$$\text{Salary per Week} = \frac{\$67{,}400}{52} = \mathbf{\$1{,}296.15}$$

67400 ÷ 52 = 1296.153846

Concept CHECK

Complete the problems. Check your answers in the back of the book.

1. Sam Gerber earns $42,900 per year. Find his biweekly salary.
2. Brenda Ortiz earns $18,200 per year. Find her semimonthly salary.

Need Help? Go to...
- **Skill 11:** Dividing Decimals, p. SK12
- **Application K:** Chronological Expressions, p. AP7

EXAMPLE 2 Algebra

Your current job as a wedding planner pays a monthly gross salary of \$2,560. You are offered a new position as an event planner at a children's museum that pays \$12.60 per hour with time and a half per hour for all hours over 40 per week. How many hours of overtime per week would you need to work to earn the same amount as your current job?

Step 1: Let h represent the number of overtime hours needed.

Step 2: Write an equation to show the relationship between your hourly wages, your overtime pay and your weekly pay. Let h represent the overtime hours.

Hourly wages + Overtime pay = Weekly pay

$$(12.60 \times 40) + (1.5 \times 12.60 \times h) = \frac{(2{,}560 \times 12)}{52}$$

Step 3: Solve the equation

Perform the multiplication and division →
$$(12.60 \times 40) + (1.5 \times 12.60 \times h) = \frac{(2{,}560 \times 12)}{52}$$

Collect like terms →
$$504 + 18.9h = 509.77$$

Subtract 504 from both sides →
$$504 + 18.9h - 504 = 509.77 - 504$$

Divide both sides by 18.9 →
$$18.9h = 86.77$$

$$h = \frac{86.77}{18.9} = 4.59 = \mathbf{4.75}$$

You would need to work 4.75 hours of overtime.

GRAPHING CALCULATOR LAB

Use Lists to Solve Problems

You have two different job offers. Job 1 has a starting salary of \$36,000 with a potential pay raise of 3.5% per year. Job 2 has a starting salary of \$34,500 with a potential pay raise of 4.5% per year.

L1	L2	L3 2
0	36000	34500
1	37260	36053
2	38564	37675
3	39914	39370
4	41311	41142
5	42757	42993
6	44253	44928

L2 ="36000*1.035^

Think and Discuss

1. Use the LIST feature to determine the projected annual salary for Job 1 and Job 2 for the first six years.
   - Press the STAT key, select 1:Edit.
   - In L1 enter the numbers, 0, 1, 2, 3, 4, 5, 6.
   - In the L2 formula bar, enter the formula for calculating the yearly salary for Job 1 as follows:

 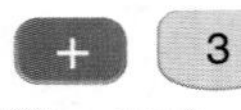        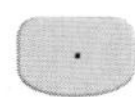    

In the L3 formula bar, enter the formula for calculating the yearly salary for Job 2.

2. For what years is Job 1 the best offer?
3. In what year does the salary for Job 2 surpass that for Job 1?
4. Suppose Job 1 renegotiates and offers a starting salary of \$37,000. In what year will the salary for Job 2 exceed that for Job 1?
5. Under what conditions should you accept the second job?
6. West Coast Supplies is offering a starting salary of \$43,250 and a pay raise of 2% per year. Eastern Heritage is offering \$44,275 with a pay raise of 1.5% per year. Determine what the salaries will be in year 3, 5 and 8. If you are planning to relocate and change jobs in 6 years, which is the better job offer?

Complete the problem. Check your answer in the back of the book.

3. Mark Adler earned $1,650 per month as an assistant technician at a recording studio. His new job pays $9.80 per hour with time and a half for all hours over 36 per week. How many hours of overtime per week will he need to work to earn the same amount per week as his current job?

Mark Dierker/McGraw-Hill Education

Lesson Practice

Did You Know?

Hybrid Ahead **Hybrid cars have a small, fuel-efficient gas engine combined with an electric motor. The batteries that power the electric motor are automatically recharged as the car is driven.**

4. Brad Hamilton's annual salary as an accounting clerk is $32,500. What is his weekly salary?

5 Kylie Matsumoto is a set designer. Her annual salary is $45,320. What is Kylie's semimonthly salary?

6. Alia Valbuena earns $68,400 per year as an automotive engineer. **(a)** What is her monthly salary? **(b)** What is her weekly salary?

7. Ethan van Doran is a physical therapist. His biweekly salary is $3,985. **(a)** What is his annual salary? **(b)** What is his monthly salary?

8. Savannah Bryan is a career coach. Her biweekly salary is $3,010. What is Savannah's annual salary?

9. Zachary Meyers is a forensic scientist. His monthly salary is $4,397. What is Zachary's annual salary?

H.O.T. Problems

10. **ALGEBRA** André Iverson was paid a biweekly salary of $1,230 as an assistant exterminator. Now he is paid on a semimonthly basis. What is André's semimonthly salary?

Spiral Review

Divide the numbers and then round to the nearest hundredth. (Skill 11)

11. $14,290 ÷ 50

12. 41.62 ÷ 8.6

13. 191.3 ÷ 14.7

14. Diego Rollins is paid $10.20 an hour for a regular 40-hour week at the driving range. His overtime rate is $1\frac{1}{2}$ times his regular hourly rate. This week he worked his regular 40 hours plus 8 hours of overtime. What is Diego's total pay? (Lesson 1.2)

GET READY for the Next Lesson

PREREQUISITE SKILL **Writing Percents as Decimals** (Skill 28)

Write as a decimal.

15. 135%

16. 14.2%

17. 0.5%

18. 2.25%

19. 0.123%

20. 105.6%

LESSON 1.6

Commission

Lesson Objective
Calculate straight commission and determine gross pay.

Content Vocabulary
- commission
- commission rate
- straight commission

GET READY for the Lesson

What are the risks in being paid on commission?

Kayla Johnson's first job is selling condos at a new development. She can choose to be paid either an annual salary or a commission based on the number of condos she sells.

As You Read

Compare What is the difference between being paid a salary and being paid on commission?

Commission If you are outgoing and friendly, you may want to be a salesperson. You might work in retail, selling furniture or cars, or you might sell plumbing supplies. Often the pay for a sales position is based on **commission**. This is an amount of money that you are paid for selling a product or **service**.

Commission works in two ways. First, you might work on a **commission rate**. This is either a specified amount of money paid for each sale or a percent of the total value of your sales. If the commission is the only pay you receive, you work on **straight commission**. The formula for calculating straight commission is:

Straight Commission = Total Sales × Commission Rate

Need Help? Go to...
- Workshop 2: Rounding Numbers, p. 6
- Workshop 14: Finding a Percentage, p. 30
- Skill 2: Rounding Numbers, p. SK3
- Skill 30: Finding the Percentage, p. SK31
- Application A: Formulas, p. AP1

EXAMPLE 1

Bob Morales sells commercial real estate at a $7\frac{1}{2}\%$ straight commission. Last week his sales totaled \$290,000. What was his commission?

Find the straight commission.

Straight Commission	=	Total Sales	×	Commission Rate
		\$290,000	×	$7\frac{1}{2}\%$
\$21,750	=	\$290,000	×	0.075

Concept CHECK

Find the straight commission. Check your answers in the back of the book.

1. \$9,400 × 8% commission rate
2. \$143,400 × 5.5% commission rate

Minimum Salary Instead of working only on commission, you might be guaranteed a minimum weekly or monthly salary. In some cases, the commission you earn during a week or month is compared with your minimum salary and your gross pay is the higher of the two amounts. In other cases, you might be paid a base salary and earn commission in addition to this base salary.

Glow Images

Need Help? Go to...

- Workshop 3: Comparing Numbers, p. 8
- Workshop 6: Multiplying Decimals, p. 14

EXAMPLE 2 Algebra

Marcia Stein sells ergonomic chairs at The Office Center. She is guaranteed a minimum salary of $1,850 per month plus commission of 6.25% of her total sales. What are Marcia's total sales for a month in which her gross pay was $3,890?

Step 1: Let s = Total sales for the month.

Step 2: Write an equation to show the relationship for her total pay.

Total = Minimum Salary + Commission

Step 3: Solve the equation

$$\$3{,}890 = \$1{,}850 + 6.25\%s$$

Subtract $1,850 from both sides →

$$\$3{,}890 - \$1{,}850 = \$1{,}850 + 6.25\%s - \$1{,}850$$

$$\$2{,}040 = 0.0625s$$

To solve for s, divide both sides by 0.0625 →

$$\frac{\$2{,}040}{0.0625} = \frac{0.0625s}{0.0625}$$

$$\mathbf{\$32{,}640} = s$$

Marcia's total sales for the month are $32,640.

Reading Math +−÷=

Finding the Commission

Think of commission as a percentage of sales. To find a commission, change the percent to a decimal and then multiply it by the sales amount.

Concept CHECK

Complete the problems. Check your answers in the back of the book.

3. Isaiah Copeland sells tennis equipment. He is guaranteed a minimum salary of $1,500 per month plus 5.75% of his total sales. What are Isaiah's total sales for a month in which his gross pay was $2,075?

4. Harold Pope is a ticket broker. He is guaranteed a minimum weekly salary of $650 or 5% of his total sales, whichever is higher. What are his total sales for a week in which his gross pay was $725?

Lesson Practice

Find the commission.

	Sales Position	Total Sales	×	Straight Commission Rate	=	Commission
5.	Real estate	$198,000	×	8%	=	$
6.	Computers	18,100	×	2	=	
7.	Major appliances	9,598	×	6	=	
8.	Clothing	1,311	×	9	=	
9.	Computer supplies	929	×	15	=	
10.	Siding contract	*b*	×	12	=	$ 690.48
11.	Auto	68,417	×	*b*	=	$2,052.51

These salespeople are paid a minimum monthly salary or commission, whichever is greater. Find the (a) monthly commission and (b) gross pay.

	Salesperson	Minimum Monthly Salary	Total Monthly Sales	×	Commission Rate	=	Monthly Commission	Gross Pay
12.	Moser, Isabel	$2,100	$28,000	×	8.0%	=	a.	b.
13.	Zinn, Paolo	1,600	23,000	×	6.5	=	a.	b.
14.	Schwartz, Byron	3,140	31,000	×	9.25	=	a.	b.
15.	Flores, Yvette	850	10,000	×	3.5	=	a.	b.
16.	Barksdale, DeWanda	3,410	29,100	×	12.1	=	a.	b.

Did You Know?

Harrods of London

Harrods department store is almost a city within a city. The massive London store covers 4.5 acres and generates 70% of its electricity from its own generators. Its famous facade is lit by 12,000 light bulbs, 300 of which are changed each day.

17. Roger Tong earns 3% commission on sales of $9,500 as an electrical supplies wholesaler. What is his commission?

18. Sam Taylor earns $6\frac{1}{2}$% commission on sales of $4,226 as an advertising agent. What is his commission?

19. Some jobs pay a commission plus a bonus at the end of the year. The bonus may be a percent of the salesperson's total commission. Madelyn Carr is a sales representative for a luxury home builder. She receives 7% commission on all sales. At the end of the year, she receives a bonus of 5% of her commission. **(a)** What is her gross pay for a year in which she had sales totaling $412,454? **(b)** What would Madelyn's gross pay be if her sales were $316,250?

H.O.T. Problems

20. ALGEBRA Lou Harris is guaranteed a minimum $275 weekly salary plus $5\frac{1}{4}$% of his total sales. What are his total sales for a week in which his gross pay was $700?

21. ALGEBRA Caitlin Grasso is a salesperson in the kitchen and bath department at Morris Supplies, Inc. She is guaranteed a minimum salary of $200 per week plus 5.5% of her total sales. What are her total sales for a week in which her gross pay was $560?

Spiral Review

Write each as a decimal. (Skill 14)

22. $5\frac{1}{2}$ **23.** $6\frac{3}{4}$ **24.** $9\frac{1}{4}$

Find the percentage of each and round to the nearest cent if necessary. (Skill 30)

25. 4% of $1,250 **26.** $8\frac{1}{2}$% of $4,300 **27.** $7\frac{1}{4}$% of $8,200

28. 9.2% of $3,600 **29.** 7.3% of $120 **30.** 8.92% of $1,380

31. Tate Kelly is a teacher whose biweekly salary is $2,231.23. What are his gross **(a)** annual and **(b)** monthly salaries? (Lesson 1.5)

32. You earn $8.25 per hour and work 34 hours this week. What is your straight-time gross pay? (Lesson 1.1)

GET READY for the Next Lesson

PREREQUISITE SKILL Finding the Percentage (Skill 30)

Find the percentage of each.

33. 5.75% of $6,000 **34.** 0.5% of 60

35. $16\frac{2}{3}$% of $3,000 **36.** $\frac{1}{4}$% of 25

LESSON 1.7

Graduated Commission

Lesson Objective
Compute total graduated commission.

Content Vocabulary
- graduated commission

GET READY for the Lesson

Why do you think some employers offer graduated commission?

To motivate Kayla Johnson to sell more condominiums, her boss set up a new plan. Now Kayla can earn at a higher rate as she sells more.

As You Read

Describe What is your definition of the word *incentive*?

Graduated Commission Your commission rate may increase as your sales increase. A **graduated commission** offers a different rate of commission for each of several levels of sales. It provides an extra **incentive** to sell more. The general formula is:

Total Graduated Commission = Sum of Commissions for All Levels of Sales

Need Help? Go to...
- Skill 5: Adding Decimals, p. SK6
- Skill 28: Writing Percents as Decimals, p. SK29
- Skill 30: Finding the Percentage, p. SK31
- Application A: Formulas, p. AP1

EXAMPLE 1

Irene Gomaz sells appliances at Twin City Sales. She receives a graduated commission as shown. Irene's sales for the past month totaled $9,840. What was her commission for the month?

Commission Percent	Level of Sales
4%	First $1,000
6	Next 2,000
8	Over 3,000

Find the sum of commissions for all levels of sales.

	Sales	× Commission Rate	
First $1,000:	$1,000	× 4%	= $ 40.00
Next $2,000:	$2,000	× 6%	= 120.00
Over $3,000:	($9,840 − $3,000)	× 8%	=
	$6,840	× 8%	= 547.20
		Total Graduated Commission	= **$707.20**

Concept CHECK

Complete the problems. Check your answers in the back of the book.

1. Sal Espinosa makes a 10% commission on the first $5,000 of sales and 15% on any sales over $5,000. Find his total graduated commission on $15,000 in sales.
2. Jenitha Forrest makes a 5% commission on the first $2,000 of sales she makes and 8% on any sales over $2,000. Find her total graduated commission on $7,740 in sales.

Need Help? Go to...

- Workshop 3: Comparing Numbers, p. 8
- Workshop 6: Multiplying Decimals, p. 14

EXAMPLE 2 Algebra

Mike Turino is paid weekly and earns a 4% straight commission on sales of $5,000 or less and 5% on sales in excess of $5,000. One week Mike's total graduated commission was $362. What were his total sales for that week?

Step 1: Let s = His total sales for the week.

Step 2: Write an equation for his total graduated commision.

Total Graduated Commission = Commission on first $5,000 + Commission on sales over $5,000

Step 3: Solve for s.

Apply distributive property → $\$362 = (0.04 \times \$5{,}000) + [0.05(s - \$5{,}000)]$

Combine like terms → $\$362 = \$200 + 0.05s - \$250$

$\$362 = 0.05s - \$50$

Add $50 to both sides → $\$412 = 0.05s$

Divide both sides by 0.05 → $\frac{\$412}{0.05} = \frac{0.05s}{0.05s}$

$\$8{,}240 = s$

Mike's total sales for the week must have been $8,240 to have a total graduated commission of $362.

Concept CHECK

Complete the problems. Check your answers in the back of the book.

3. Dabney Washington is paid a weekly commission of 3.5% on sales of $7,500 or less and 5.5% on sales in excess of $7,500. Last week Dabney's commission was $822.40. What was the total of her sales for the week?
4. Nate Belloir earns a weekly commission of 2.5% on sales of $75,000 or less and 3.0% on sales in excess of $75,000. One week Nate's commission was $2,135. What was the total of his sales for that week?

Study Tip

Rounding the Answer
When you multiply amounts of money, round the answer to the nearest cent. Remember to put a dollar sign in the answer.

Lesson Practice

Use the following commission schedule to find the total graduated commission in Problems 5–8.

	Sales Amount	5% on First $5,000	8% on Next $10,000	10% on sales Over $15,000	Total Commission
5.	$ 4,000	a.	b.	c.	d.
6.	8,000	a.	b.	c.	d.
7.	18,000	a.	b.	c.	d.
8.	27,500	a.	b.	c.	d.

9. Mary Robertson sells tires at a large car service center. She earns 10% commission on the first $1,000, 15% on the next $2,000, and 20% on sales of more than $3,000. Last week she sold $3,400 worth of tires. What was her total commission?
10. Jean Gray earns a graduated commission of 4% on her first $2,000 of sales and 8% on all sales over $2,000. Jean's sales for the past week totaled $3,925. What was her commission for the week?

11. Charles Beaudry sells computer hardware for a computer manufacturer. He is paid 4% commission on the first $8,000 of sales, 6% on the next $10,000, and $8\frac{1}{2}$% on sales over $18,000. What is his commission on $24,550 in sales?

12. Tunisia Buehrer sells musical instruments and equipment at Let It Rock in the mall. She earns a commission of 5% on the first $6,000, $7\frac{1}{2}$% on the next $6,000, and 10% on sales over $12,000. Her total sales for the month are $14,640. What is Tunisia's total commission?

Did You Know?

Dubai The Dubai Mall in Dubai, United Arab Emirates, covers more than 12 million square feet and has 10 to15 individual smaller malls built inside it. Once completed, the mall will be the largest in the world with more than 1,000 shops, an Olympic-sized ice-skating rink, and a waterfall.

13. Blake Brown demonstrates cookware at the National Food Fair. He is paid $7.00 each for the first 10 demonstrations in one day and $8.50 for each demonstration over 10. What is his commission if Blake makes 12 demonstrations in one day?

14. Some sales positions pay a commission only if sales exceed a sales quota. The salesperson is rewarded only for having sales beyond an expected amount. Joyce Doyle is a sales trainee. She is paid $1,550 per month plus a commission of 7.5% on all sales of more than a $20,000 monthly quota. What is Joyce's total pay for a month in which her sales totaled $22,650?

15. **ALGEBRA** Adnan Hassan earned 5% commission as a sales trainee. After promotion to a sales associate, he earned 8% commission. His year-end report showed $673,874 in total sales and $45,006.52 in commission. What did his sales total as **(a)** a sales trainee and **(b)** a sales associate?

16. **CHALLENGE PROBLEM** Marie Stefanski sells outdoor grills. She knows she earns 10% commission on the first $10,000 and 12% on the next $15,000. She does not remember the rate on the sales of more than $25,000. Her total sales for the month are $30,000, and her total commission is $3,550. What is her rate of commission for the sales over $25,000?

17. **WRITING IN MATH** Use the information you have learned in this lesson to write your own graduated commission word problem.

Spiral Review

Write each as a decimal. (Skill 28)

18. $5\frac{1}{2}$% 19. $10\frac{1}{4}$% 20. 15%

Find the percentage of each. (Skill 30)

21. $5\frac{1}{4}$% of $2,000 22. 7% of $4,560

23. $15\frac{1}{2}$% of $3,500 24. 3.75% of $1,500

25. Morgan DuBois was just hired as a chemical engineer for Hobart Company. Her starting salary is $60,985 per year. What are her **(a)** monthly salary and **(b)** weekly salary? (Lesson 1.5)

26. Carissa Jackson is paid $15 for each bicycle that she assembles. Last week she assembled 12 bicycles. What was her total pay? (Lesson 1.4)

GET READY for the Next Lesson

PREREQUISITE SKILL Numbers (Skill 1)

Give the place and value of the underlined digit.

27. 2,5<u>2</u>9.00 28. 345.<u>8</u>3 29. 0.42<u>5</u>5

30. <u>5</u>2,800 31. 62.4<u>2</u> 32. 107,<u>0</u>50

CHAPTER 1 Review and Assessment

AFTER YOU READ

Chapter SUMMARY

When you work and get paid, it is important to know how to compute your gross income. In this chapter, you have learned to calculate your straight-time pay, figure out your overtime and total pay, calculate your total hours on a weekly time card, compute your total pay on a piecework basis, determine your salary per pay period, calculate your straight commission, and compute your total graduated commission.

Vocabulary Check

1. On a sheet of paper, use each of these terms in a sentence.

Content Vocabulary

- hourly rate (p. 97)
- straight-time pay (p. 97)
- gross income (p. 97)
- overtime pay (p. 100)
- time and a half (p. 100)
- double time (p. 100)
- weekly time card (p. 103)
- piecework (p. 106)
- salary (p. 109)
- commission (p. 112)
- commission rate (p. 112)
- straight commission (p. 112)
- graduated commission (p. 115)

Academic Vocabulary

- calculate (p. 97)
- rate (p. 100)
- compute (p. 103)
- candidate (p. 106)
- fixed (p. 109)
- service (p. 112)
- incentive (p. 115)

Concept Check

2. Define *hourly rate*.
3. Give the formula for figuring straight-time pay.
4. How do you become eligible for overtime pay?
5. Give the formula for figuring double time.
6. Why do some employers require weekly time cards?
7. Define *piecework*.
8. Differentiate between straight-time pay and salary.
9. Define *commission*.
10. Give the formula for determining straight commission.
11. Give the formula for determining your total graduated commission.
12. **CRITICAL THINKING** Would you like to work in a job that may require you to work overtime? Why or why not? Write a paragraph explaining your choice.
13. **CRITICAL THINKING** Brainstorm the skills and personality traits a salesperson should possess. Are you interested in working for commission? Why or why not?

Lesson-by-Lesson Review

1.1 Straight-Time Pay (pp. 97–99)

Calculate the straight-time pay.

Rita Carlson works at a coffee house. She earns $8.75 per hour. Last week she worked 28 hours. What was her straight-time pay?

Find the straight-time pay: Hourly Rate × Hours Worked

$8.75 × 28 hours = **$245 straight-time pay**

Review Exercises

Find the straight-time pay.

14. $6.55 per hour, 40 hours worked
15. $8.96 per hour, 36 hours worked
16. $12.85 per hour, 19.5 hours worked
17. $8.755 per hour, 38.925 hours worked
18. Ed Gregory is a surveying technician earning $12.97 per hour. He worked 39 hours last week. What is his pay for the week?
19. **ALGEBRA** Ron Mason is a laborer. He earns $15.40 per hour. How many hours per week must he work if he wants to earn approximately $450.00 per week?

1.2 Overtime Pay (pp. 100–102)

Figure out straight-time, overtime, and total pay.

Tiffany Newman earns $9.50 per hour for 40 hours and time and a half for overtime as a clerk for a circuit judge. If she worked 5 hours overtime, what is her total pay?

Step 1: Find the straight-time pay.
Hourly Rate × Regular Hours Worked
$9.50 × 40 = $380.00 straight-time pay

Step 2: Find the overtime pay.
Overtime Rate × Overtime Hours Worked
(1.5 × $9.50) × 5 = $71.25 overtime pay

Step 3: Find the total pay.
Straight-Time Pay + Overtime Pay
$380.00 + $71.25 = **$451.25 total pay**

Review Exercises

Find the total pay.

20. $8.20 per hour for 40 hours and time and a half for 7 hours.
21. $9.65 per hour for 40 hours and time and a half for 5 hours.
22. Cameron Benson is a dental assistant. He earns $11.17 per hour and time and a half for overtime. Last week he worked 40 hours plus 7 hours of overtime.
23. As a zookeeper, Frank Horton earns $15.35 an hour plus time and a half for weekend work. Last week Frank worked 40 hours plus 16 hours of overtime on the weekend.
24. **ALGEBRA** Martha earns $16.50 an hour for a regular 40 hour week. Her overtime pay is $1\frac{1}{2}$ times her regular hourly rate. This past week Martha earned $948.75 in total pay. How many hours of overtime did she work this past week?

Lesson-by-Lesson Review (continued)

1.3 Weekly Time Card (pp. 103–105)

Compute the total hours on a weekly time card.
Terry Bartlett worked from 7:00 AM to 10:45 AM and from 12:30 PM to 3:15 PM at a chocolate shop. Find the total hours.

Calculate the total hours: Total Hours = Sum of Daily Hours

10:45 − 7:00 = 3h:45min

3:15 − 12:30 = 2h:45min

3h:45min + 2h:45min = 5h:90min = **6h:30min**

Review Exercises

John Kim works in a hospital gift shop. Use his time card to find his total hours worked each day and his total hours for the week. Round off the total hours each day to the nearest quarter hour.

	Employee Time Card Central Arkansas Hospital						
	Employee Name: John Kim Department: Gift Shop						
		DATE	IN	OUT	IN	OUT	TOTAL
25.	Mon.	9/1	6:45 AM	11:30 AM	12:00 PM	3:45 PM	
26.	Tue.	9/2	7:00 AM	11:30 AM	12:00 PM	3:45 PM	
27.	Wed.	9/3	6:56 AM	11:45 AM	12:30 PM	4:00 PM	
28.	Thur.	9/4	6:45 AM	12:50 PM	1:50 PM	3:00 PM	
29.	Fri.	9/5	7:10 AM	11:30 AM	12:30 PM	4:25 PM	
30.	TOTAL HOURS						
	Employee Signature: *John Kim*						

31. **ALGEBRA** Don Swifter earns $9.75 per hour as a clerk. He starts work Monday through Friday morning at 8:00 AM. He takes a one-half hour lunch break every day. If he finishes work at 3:30 PM Monday through Thursday, how late must he work on Friday to have total pay of $360.75 for the week?

1.4 Piecework (pp. 106–108)

Compute the total pay on a piecework basis.
Vidia Roswell earns $2.57 per printer that she boxes for shipment. Yesterday, she boxed 85 printers. What was her total pay?

Find the total pay: Rate per Item × Number of Items Produced

$2.57 × 85 = **$218.45 total pay**

Review Exercises

Compute the total pay on a piecework basis.

32. $3.05 per item, 136 items produced
33. $2.38 per item, 85 items produced
34. Roger Levingold works in a motorcycle shop. He is paid to set up new motorcycles when they arrive from the factory. He is also responsible for test riding each one. His boss pays him $125 per motorcycle and another $18 per test ride. Last week he set up 11 motorcycles and test rode 9 of them. What was his total pay?

Lesson-by-Lesson Review (continued)

35. Vicki Giddeon delivers flowers every Valentine's Day. She earns \$3.50 to deliver a small arrangement, \$4.50 to deliver a medium arrangement, and \$6.05 to deliver a large arrangement. Last year, she delivered 68 small arrangements, 15 medium arrangements, and 23 large arrangements. What was her total pay for the day?

36. **ALGEBRA** Dakota Shilah works for Arizona Bath Company as a repairman. He earns \$12.00 for each fiberglass bathroom sink and \$59 for each fiberglass tub enclosure he repairs. Last week he repaired a total of 23 items. Dakota's pay for the week was \$652. How many of each type of repair did he make?

1.5 Salary (pp. 109–111)

Compute the salary per pay period.
Richard Martin is a network administrator for a large law firm. His annual salary is \$65,590. What is his monthly salary? What is his weekly salary?

Find the salary per pay period.

Annual Salary	÷	Number of Pay Periods per Year		
\$65,590	÷	12	=	**\$5,465.83 monthly salary**
\$65,590	÷	52	=	**\$1,261.35 weekly salary**

Review Exercises

Determine the salary per pay period.

37. Surveyor: Annual \$48,950; weekly.

38. Law Clerk: Annual \$36,980; biweekly.

39. Pharmacist: Annual \$86,660; semimonthly.

40. Pilot: Annual \$136,800; monthly.

41. The educational television service at Brooke Green State University advertised for a development officer at a minimum salary of \$40,663. What is the monthly salary?

42. Schnider National Trucking stated in a "Help Wanted" advertisement that an experienced driver could earn \$930 per week. How much is the annual salary?

43. **ALGEBRA** Assume that your current job pays a monthly gross salary of \$3,780. You are offered a new position that pays \$18.50 per hour with $1\frac{1}{2}$ per hour for all hours over 44 per week. How many hours of overtime per week would you need to work to earn approximately the same amount per week as your current job?

1.6 Commission (pp. 112–114)

Calculate the straight commission and determine the gross pay.
Bonnie Heisey sells clothing. Her commission rate is 7.5%. Last month her sales were \$10,875. What was her commission?

Find the commission.

Total Sales	×	Commission Rate		
\$10,875	×	7.5%	=	\$815.625 = **\$815.63 commission**

Lesson-by-Lesson Review (continued)

Review Exercises

Compute the straight commission.

44. $7,600 total sales, 4% commission rate.

45. $122,360 total sales, $6\frac{1}{4}$% commission rate.

Compute the straight commission and gross pay (the gross pay is whichever is higher: the minimum salary or the straight commission).

46. Minimum weekly salary is $185. Rate of commission is 6.5%. Weekly sales are $3,790.

47. Minimum weekly salary is $250. Rate of commission is 5.65%. Weekly sales are $1,515.

48. Suzie Clarke sells real estate at a 7% straight commission. What is her commission on the sale of a $98,000 home?

49. Walt Watson sells snowmobiles, dirt bikes, and ATVs at a commission of 18%. Last week his sales totaled $26,348. What is his commission?

50. **ALGEBRA** Celine McCaw sells jewelry. She is guaranteed a minimum salary of $1,950 per month plus commission of 6.75% of her total sales. How much in total sales does she need in order to have a gross pay for the month of $4,190?

1.7 Graduated Commission (pp. 115–117)

Compute the total graduated commission.

Carl Brock earns a commission rate of 6% for the first $6,500 in sales and 9% on sales over $6,500. Find the total graduated commission on sales of $10,500.

Find the graduated commission. Multiply and add.

Total Graduated Commission = Sum of Commissions for All Levels of Sales

$6,500 × 0.06 = $390

($10,500 − $6,500) × 0.09 = $360

$390 + $360 = **$750 total graduated commission**

Review Exercises

Compute the graduated commission.

51. Commission: 25% on the first $1,900; 27% on the next $1,000; 30% on sales over $2,900. Total sales equal $3,500. What is the total commission?

52. Commission: 5% on the first $4,000; $6\frac{1}{2}$% on the next $6,000; 11% on sales over $10,000. Total sales equal $12,360. What is the total commission?

53. Tom Avido is a roofing material sales representative. He receives a graduated commission of 5% on the first $5,000 of sales, 6.5% on the next $15,000, and 7% on sales over $20,000. What is his commission on $23,458 in sales?

54. Connie Hamm demonstrates microwave ovens. She earns $5.00 per demonstration for the first 10 demonstrations and $6.00 for each demonstration over 10. For every microwave sold, she earns $10.55. What is Connie's commission on a day in which she makes 12 demonstrations and 4 sales?

55. Dennis Hampton earns a straight commission of 7% on sales of $5,000 or less and 9% on sales in excess of $5,000. One week Dennis had a gross pay of $578. What were his total sales for that week?

Practice Test

Record your answers on a sheet of paper.

1. Joe Mathis works as a pianist in a local restaurant. He makes $8.50 an hour. He was able to work 45 hours last week. How much money did he make that week?
2. Ballet teacher Monica Lawry earns time and a half for the number of hours she works over 40. One week she worked 48 hours. If her base pay is $9.00, how much did she earn that week?

For Problems 3–5, use the Employee Time Card below for lifeguard Gwen Ramirez. Note: Gwen takes a 1-hour lunch break each day.

	In	Out	In	Out
Sun.	7:00 AM	11:00 AM	12:00 PM	4:00 PM
Mon.	7:10 AM	11:30 AM	12:30 PM	4:30 PM
Tue.	7:05 AM	11:10 AM	12:00 PM	3:55 PM
Wed	7:00 AM	12:00 PM	1:10 PM	4:10 PM
Thur.	8:00 AM	1:00 PM	1:30 PM	4:30 PM
Fri.	6:00 AM	11:00 AM	12:00 PM	?

3. How many hours did Gwen Ramirez work on Sunday?
   A 9 hours **B** 8 hours
   C 7 hours and 15 minutes **D** 9 hours and 5 minutes
4. If Gwen worked a total of 9 hours on Friday, what time would she leave at the end of the day?
   A 4:00 PM **B** 3:00 PM
   C 8:00 PM **D** 4:00 AM
5. Look at the Employee Time Card for Gwen Ramirez. If Gwen's hourly wage is $12.00 how much money did she make on Tuesday?
   A $84.00 **B** $64.00
   C $84.50 **D** $96.00
6. Max Quimby picks raspberries for his grandmother every Tuesday during the summer. She pays him $0.75 per quart. If he were able to pick 93 quarts, how much would he be paid?
7. Julianne Kelly makes $450 per week as an assistant in the human resources department of a large office. What is her annual salary?
8. Jermaine Samson earns $6\frac{1}{2}\%$ commission on sales of $5,600 selling flat screen TVs. What is his commission?
9. Susan Nicholson sells home furnishings. She is paid an 8% commission on the first $2,000-worth of sales, 10% on the next $2,500, and 15% on all sales over $4,500. What is her commission on $4,910-worth of sales?
10. Tyrone Jeffries is the supervisor at a water park. His annual salary is $34,540. What is his monthly salary?
11. Rebecca Harper's boss pays her time and a half for overtime work at the comic book store. If her regular wage is $8.50, what is Rebecca paid for overtime work?
12. **ALGEBRA** Martha Owens is paid $14.50 per hour for a regular forty-hour work week. Her overtime pay is one-and-one-half times her regular hourly rate. This past week Martha earned $754.00 in total pay. How many hours of overtime did Martha work this past week?
13. Round to the nearest hundredth: $25,625 ÷ 16.5
14. Write as a decimal: $4\frac{1}{4}$
15. Round to the nearest cent: $3\frac{1}{2}\%$ of $1,275

PART 1 Multiple Choice

Record your answers on the answer sheet provided by your teacher or on a sheet of paper.

1. Alyssa Sheridan earned $465.60 for a week of work at a bakery. She worked a total of 40 hours. What is her hourly wage?
   A $8.65 **B** $9.50
   C $10.55 **D** $11.64

2. Jose Escalante worked at the skateboard shop for 40 hours at his regular wage of $7.50. He then worked for 8 hours at his overtime wage of time and a half. What is the total amount Jose earned?
   A $90.00 **B** $390.00
   C $300.00 **D** $180.00

3. Avery Gould is a tailor. He is paid $7.50 for each pair of jeans he hems. How much would he be paid for 12 pairs of jeans?
   A $84.00 **B** $72.50
   C $90.00 **D** $63.50

4. Samara Park gets $0.25 for each pound of apricots she dries. How much will she be paid if she dries 16.4 pounds?
   A $16.00 **B** $4.10
   C $8.20 **D** $6.00

5. If Brenda Reardon's yearly salary as a skiing instructor is $43,550 what is her biweekly salary?
   A $1,888.76 **B** $1,550.00
   C $2,125.50 **D** $1,675.00

6. If Sarah Hsu earns a $60,840 annual salary, what is her weekly salary?
   A $1,216.80 **B** $2,340.00
   C $2,535.00 **D** $1,170.00

TEST-TAKING TIP

New Vocabulary When you study for a test, spend the time needed to memorize the meanings of new vocabulary words and special terms.

7. Nick Jones is a satellite radio sales representative. He receives 7% commission on all sales. If the total sales for the year were $345,000, what would his commission be?
   A $24,150 **B** $36,550
   C $32,000 **D** $28,677

8. Anna Drew sells custom cabinets and doors. She receives a 15% commission on the doors she sells and a 7% commission for each cabinet. What would her total commission be if she sold $5,200-worth of cabinets and $760-worth of doors?
   A $112 **B** $230
   C $478 **D** $542

PART 2 Short Response/Griddable

9. Roberto Alvarez is a teaching assistant. He earns $11.40 per hour. He is allowed to work flexible hours. He was only able to work 32.25 hours last week. How much money did he earn?

10. Martha McKenzie sells advertising for a local TV station. She earns 15% on the first $5,000 in sales, 25% on the next $1,000, and 30% on all sales over $6,000. If she were to sell $15,000-worth of advertising, what would her commission be?

PART 3 Extended Response

Show your work.

11. **ALGEBRA** Greg Bonner delivers plants for a local nursery. He earns $8.25 an hour plus 3% commission on the total price of his deliveries. If Greg worked for 6 hours on Saturday and earned a total of $58.50 that day, what was the total price of the plants he delivered?

Building Academic Skills

Mathematics

You work 6-hour shifts at the marina for $8.00 an hour. How many days do you need to work in order to save $2,000 to buy a used jet ski?

English Language Arts/Writing

Make a list of your top three dream jobs. List the skills required to succeed at each job. Which skills appear the most often?

Social Studies/Government

Incomes vary regionally, and the U.S. Census Bureau tracks this information, by state and by size of family. One of the key statistics tracked is the median family income. (If you take the highest number and the lowest number in a group, the median will be the one that falls directly in the middle.) Find the U.S. Census Bureau Web site. Then locate the median family income for a 4-person family in your state.

Building Real-World Skills

Ethics in Action

Your Résumé Imagine that a new animation and special effects studio has opened an office in your town. You have some experience working in an office, and you are interested when you see an advertisement for a position in the studio's accounting department. You would like to work for them as an accounting clerk, but you are afraid you do not have the right qualifications. A friend suggests that you change or "pad" your résumé by adding experiences you really do not have. She also says you should list a certification you have not obtained.

Discuss and Write:

a. As a class, discuss the possible effects of padding your résumé. For example, how might you feel during the interview? What might happen if you were hired based on false information in your résumé?

b. Write a paragraph suggesting an alternative solution.

21st Century Workplace

Time Management Juggling school, work, sports, hobbies, and other activities can be a challenge. Learning to manage your time as a student can help you prepare for the real world. Prioritizing is a vital aspect of an efficient workplace.

Research and Write:

a. Make a list of your daily activities, identify the relative importance of your activities, then arrange them in order of importance, or priority.

b. Present your priority list to the class, explaining how you will manage your time.

CHAPTER 2 Net Income

Big Idea

When you earn a paycheck, it is important to know how to compute the deductions from your gross pay.

Explore the Photo

Take-Home Pay
The deductions taken out of your paycheck help support schools, roads, national parks, and more. *Why do you think you have to pay taxes?*

Ask AN EXPERT

Taxes and Donations

Q: I gave a tax-deductible, $50 donation to help a nonprofit animal rescue shelter, but I am not sure what "tax-deductible" means. What is the benefit of this donation?

A: Many nonprofit groups that perform public services are exempt from, or do not have to pay, federal taxes. Donations are tax deductible to encourage people to give to these groups. You can deduct, or subtract, a percentage of a tax-deductible donation from your total taxable income. Your donation benefits the public and reduces the amount you pay in taxes. When you make a tax-deductible donation, ask for a receipt, and keep it with your records so you may include it with your tax return.

English Language Arts/Writing Make a list of charities or nonprofit organizations to which you would be interested in making a donation.

GET READY for the Chapter

Math Online

To take the Online Readiness Quiz, go to connectED.mcgraw-hill.com.

Chapter 2 Net Income

Reading Guide

Before You Read

Predict How does *net income* differ from *gross income*?

Main Idea

Whether you earn a salary, are paid hourly, or work on commission, you will have deductions taken from your gross income. Deductions may include federal income taxes, Social Security and Medicare taxes, state taxes, local taxes, medical insurance premiums, union dues, and retirement account contributions.

Graphic Organizer

Before you read this chapter, draw a diagram like the one below. As you read, list three deductions.

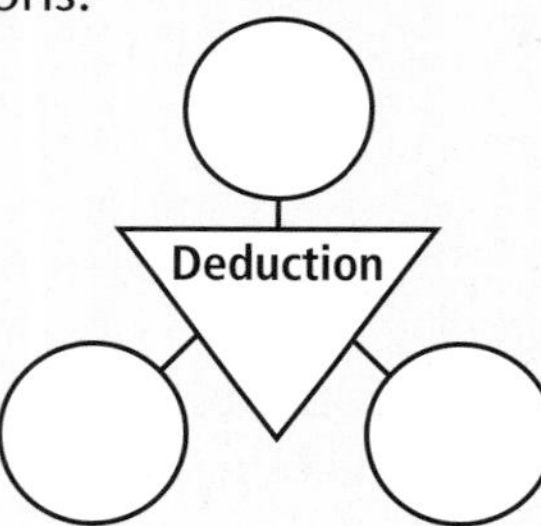

Math Online Go to **connectED.mcgraw-hill.com** to download this graphic organizer.

Content Vocabulary

You will learn these key terms in this chapter.

- federal income tax
- withholding allowance
- exemption
- graduated income tax
- Social Security
- Medicare
- group insurance
- net pay

Academic Vocabulary

You will see these words in your reading and on your tests. Make sure you know their meanings.

- claim
- percent
- income
- require
- medical
- community

You can find vocabulary definitions in the **Content Vocabulary** Glossary and the **Academic Vocabulary** Glossary in the back of the book.

LESSON 2.1

Federal Income Tax

Lesson Objective

Determine the amount withheld for federal income tax.

Content Vocabulary

- federal income tax
- withholding allowance

GET READY for the Lesson

If you have ever received a paycheck, was the amount what you expected?

Jack Myers was surprised to see that his employer had deducted approximately 19% from his gross income.

July 20, 20 – –
Dave's Drilling and Equipment
10406 Overlook
Kentville, MI 99909
Pay to: Jack Myers $510.43
Five hundred ten ------------------DOLLARS 43/100 CENTS
Memo: weekly pay Signature: *Dave Davey*

As You Read

Summarize What is the difference between gross income and net income?

Federal Income Tax Federal taxes provide money to pay for federal government agencies and services. The law requires employers to withhold a certain amount of your pay for **federal income tax** (FIT). The Internal Revenue Service (IRS) provides employers with tables that show how much money to withhold. The amount withheld depends on your income, marital status, and **withholding allowances**. You may **claim** one allowance for yourself and if you are married, one allowance for your spouse. You may claim additional allowances for any others you support.

Need Help? Go to...
- Skill 1: Numbers, p. SK1
- Application C: Tables and Charts, p. AP3

EXAMPLE 1

Carla Good is an actuary. Her gross pay for this week is $425.88. She is married and claims 2 allowances for herself and her husband. What amount will Carla's employer withhold from her pay for FIT? (Use *Married Persons Weekly Payroll* table on pages A4–A5.)

Step 1: Find the income range from the table. (It is at least $420 but less than $430.)

Step 2: Find the column for 2 allowances.

Step 3: The amount of federal income tax to be withheld is $14.00.

Concept CHECK

Find the federal income tax withheld each week using the *Weekly Payroll* tables (see pages A2–A5). Check your answers in the back of the book.

1. Dan Caine, a welder, is married, claims 1 allowance, and earns $390.50.
2. Angie Kim, an executive assistant, is single, claims 2 allowances, and earns $435.95.

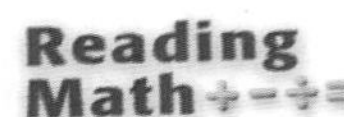

Charts and Tables

Read and understand titles and headings for columns and rows before you analyze the data in a chart or table.

Percentage Method Some companies use a percentage method instead of the tax tables to compute the income tax withheld. With the percentage method, you use taxable wages to find the withholding amount. Taxable wages depend on the number of allowances you claim. Use **Figure 2.1** to find the amount withheld for a single employee paid weekly. Each weekly allowance is $63.46.

Allowance Amount = Number of Allowances × $63.46
Taxable Wage = Gross Pay − Allowance Amount
Amount withheld for FIT = Use the Taxable Wage and the table below to compute.

Figure 2.1

Percentage Method of Withholding – Single Person		
Each weekly allowance is 63.46.		
Weekly Taxable Wage		The amount of income tax to withhold is:
Over	But not over	
$ 51.00	$ 195.00	$ 0.00 plus (10% of the excess over $51.00)
195.00	645.00	14.40 plus (15% of the excess over 195.00)
645.00	1,482.00	81.90 plus (25% of the excess over 645.00)

EXAMPLE 2

Lance Hart's gross pay for this week is $393.23. He is a carpenter's apprentice, is single, and claims 2 allowances. Using the percentage method of withholding, what amount will Lance's employer withhold from his pay for federal income tax?

Step 1: Find the allowance amount.

Allowance Amount = Number of Allowances × $63.46
$126.92 = 2 × $63.46

Step 2: Find the taxable wage.

Taxable Wage = Gross Pay − Allowance Amount
$266.31 = $393.23 − $126.92

Step 3: Find the amount withheld for FIT using the table.

a. Find the taxable wage in the row over $195 but not over $645.00.

b. Find the amount of income tax withheld by:

Tax Withheld for FIT = **$14.40** plus 15% of the excess over $195.00
= $14.40 + [0.15 × ($266.31 − $195.00)]
= $14.40 + (0.15 × $71.31)
$25.10 = $14.40 + $10.70

Concept CHECK

Use the percentage method of withholding to find the amount of federal income tax withheld each week. Check your answers in the back of the book.

3. Deb Boon is single, claims 2 allowances, and earns $293.23.

4. Mitch Watt is single, claims 4 allowances, and earns $587.94.

Lesson Practice

Use the Single Persons Weekly Payroll and Married Persons Weekly Payroll tables on pages A2–A5 to find the federal income tax withheld.

5. Carrie Burnside is single, earns $350.15 weekly, and claims 1 allowance.
6. Ray Barbee, a radio announcer, is single, earns $300.74 weekly, and claims 2 allowances.
7. Stephen Jensen, a pharmacist, is married, earns $369.23 weekly, and claims 2 allowances.
8. Lisa Steamer is married, earns $290.34 weekly as a receptionist, and claims no allowances.
9. Catherine Hall, a restaurant hostess, earns $208.35 a week. She is single and claims 2 allowances.
10. Veterinarian Ike Stone earns $925.32 a week. He is single and claims 1 allowance.
11. Doug Smalley, a meteorologist, is married and earns $1,304.30 a week. He claims 2 allowances.
12. Kristen Martinez, a dentist, is married, earns $1,352.75 a week, and claims 1 allowance.

Did You Know?

First Federal Income Tax **The federal income tax has not always existed in the United States. President Abraham Lincoln signed the first federal income tax into law in 1861. In 1862, Congress passed a two-tier rate, taxing incomes from $600 to $10,000 at 3%, and incomes from $10,000 to $50,000 at 5%.**

Use the percentage method to calculate the (a) allowance amount, (b) taxable wage, and (c) amount withheld for federal income tax.

13. Bob Mound, a theater director, is single, earns $792.02 each week, and claims 1 allowance.
14. Charlene Kirkwood manages a gift shop. She is single, earns $1,243.49 each week, and claims 3 allowances.

15. **CHALLENGE PROBLEM** Alan Tako works as a box office manager and has gross pay this week of $593.23. He is single and claims 2 allowances. Using the percentage method of withholding, what amount will Alan's employer withhold for federal income tax? Compare the amount withheld using the tax table on pages A2–A3.

Spiral Review

Find the percent. (Skill 30)

16. 228% × $52
17. 26.5% × $656
18. $\frac{1}{4}$% × $621
19. Alice McGuiness sells printers at Office Express. She receives a graduated commission of 5% on her first $4,000 and 8% on all sales over $4,000. Her sales total was $6,980 this past week. What is her commission for the week? (Lesson 1.7)
20. Marta Kellogg, a health care worker, has an hourly pay rate of $15.40 and earns time and a half if she works any overtime. Last week she worked 37 hours plus 5 hours overtime. What is her total pay? (Lesson 1.2)

GET READY for the Next Lesson

PREREQUISITE SKILL Subtracting Decimals (Skill 6)

Subtract.

21. $2,459.00 – $1,200.00
22. 487.38 – 34.08
23. $3,389.95 – $2,400.80
24. 4,567.67 – 2,345.86
25. $10,023.73 – $603.72
26. $73,731.10 – $5,420.93

LESSON 2.2

State Income Tax

Lesson Objective

Compute state taxes on a straight percent basis.

Content Vocabulary

- exemption

GET READY for the Lesson

How are the taxes you pay used?

Heidi Winston was surprised to see how much was taken from her earnings to pay taxes. She remembered from history classes that U.S. citizens' taxes support government at three levels—federal, state, and local.

As You Read

Recognize Have you ever paid state income taxes?

State Income Tax Most states require employers to withhold a certain amount of pay for income tax. In some states, the tax withheld is a **percent** of taxable wages. Your taxable wages depend on **exemptions**, or withholding allowances, which allow for supporting yourself, your spouse, and others in your family who are your dependents.

Taxable Wages = Annual Gross Pay − Exemptions

State Income Tax = Taxable Wages × Tax Rate

Need Help? Go to...

Skill 1: Numbers, p. SK1

Application C: Tables and Charts, p. AP3

EXAMPLE 1

Tony Raymond's gross pay as a landscape designer is $44,750 a year. The state income tax rate is 3% of taxable wages. He takes an exemption for himself and 1 exemption for his child. How much does Tony's employer withhold yearly from his gross earnings for state income tax? (Use the Exemptions table in **Figure 2.2** to find the annual state income tax withheld.)

Figure 2.2

Exemptions	
Single	$2,000
Married	4,000
Each Dependent	2,000

Step 1: Find the taxable wages.

Annual Gross Pay − Exemptions

$44,750 − ($2,000 + $2,000)

$44,750 − $4,000 = $40,750 taxable wages

Step 2: Find the annual tax withheld.

Taxable Wages × Tax Rate

$40,750.00 × 3% = **$1,222.50 annual state income tax withheld**

Concept CHECK

Use Figure 2.2 to find the amount withheld annually for state tax. Check your answers in the back of the book.

1. Gross pay: $23,760
Married with 3 dependents
State income tax rate: 4%

2. Gross pay: $43,300
Single with 1 dependent
State income tax rate: 5%

David Planchet

EXAMPLE 2 Algebra

Andrea McReedy is a dispatcher for a local trucking company. She earns \$52,600 per year. She is married and pays \$2,430 in state income tax per year. She claims no other dependents. What is the state income tax rate for her state? (See **Figure 2.2**)

Step 1: Let r = State income tax rate for Andrea's state.

Step 2: Use the formula for State Income Tax, substituting for Taxable Wages and solve for r.

$$\text{State Income Tax} = (\text{Taxable Wages} - \text{Exemptions}) \times \text{Tax Rate}$$

$$\$2{,}430 = (\$52{,}600 - \$4{,}000) \times r$$

Combine like terms →

$$\$2{,}430 = \$48{,}600r$$

Divide both sides by \$48,600 →

$$\frac{\$2{,}430}{\$48{,}600} = \frac{\$48{,}600r}{\$48{,}600}$$

$$\mathbf{0.05} = r$$

The state income tax rate for Andrea's state is 5.0%.

Reading Math +−÷=

Equations
Read equations as you would read a sentence. The *equals* sign is the verb.

Concept CHECK

Using Figure 2.2, complete the following problems. Check your answers in the back of the book.

3. Bela Deere is an audiologist. She is married and claims 3 dependents. The state income tax rate is 4%. If her employer withholds \$3,040 for state income tax annually, find her annual salary.

4. Anton Louis is a junior partner in an accounting firm. He is single and has an annual salary of \$63,400. If the state income tax rate is 4.5% and his company withholds \$2,493 annually for state income tax, how many exemptions does Anton claim? Each exemption is \$2,000.

Lesson Practice

Complete the formula to find the tax withheld.

	Gross Pay	−	Exemptions	=	Taxable Wage	×	Tax Rate	=	Tax Withheld
5.	\$ 7,000	−	\$4,000	=	**a.** \$	×	2%	=	**b.** \$
6.	78,000	−	6,000	=	**a.**	×	6.25	=	**b.**
7.	32,000	−	8,000	=	**a.**	×	5	=	**b.**
8.	12,500	−	2,000	=	**a.**	×	3.5	=	**b.**
9.	135,000	−	2,000	=	**a.**	×	**b.**	=	\$4,655.00
10.	64,550	−	6,000	=	**a.**	×	**b.**	=	\$3,586.19

Film/Video Editor
After a film is shot and processed, film and video editors study footage, select the best shots, and assemble them in the most effective way. Non-linear editing is based on timelines, so editors use timecode to shape the tone and mood of the story.
How do editors use math in creating their work?

Use the Exemption amounts in Figure 2.2 on page 132 to find the (a) amount for exemptions and (b) annual state income taxes.

11. Jeff Falls, a heating system salesman, is single with 3 dependents. He earns $57,900 annually, and his state's tax rate is 3%.

12. Sara Moon is a video editor who earns $63,840 annually. She is married, has 2 dependents, and her state tax rate is 4%.

13. Rick Delgado earns $43,500 annually as an automobile mechanic. He is married but has no dependents. The state tax rate is 4.6%.

14. Julie Bookwalter is single, claims 1 dependent, and earns $32,300 annually. The state tax rate is 2.5%.

For Problems 15–17, determine the amount withheld yearly for state income tax. Use the exemption amounts in Figure 2.2 on page 132.

15. Wayne Anthony earns $36,200 annually. He is married and supports 2 children. The state tax rate in his state is 4% of taxable income.

16. Erica Matthews is married and earns $54,730 per year as a grant writer. Her state's tax rate is 3.5% of taxable income.

17. Dale Ivers is a physical therapist. He earns $59,830 a year and is single with no dependents. The state income tax rate is 5% of taxable income.

Use the *Married Persons Weekly Payroll* table on pages A4–A5 for federal withholding taxes.

18. CHALLENGE PROBLEM David Chow earns $42,000 a year. He is paid weekly. He is married, has no dependents, and claims 2 withholding allowances for federal income tax purposes. The state tax rate is 2% of taxable income. How much does his employer withhold annually from David's gross pay for state and federal income taxes combined?

19. ALGEBRA Drew Swanson is an insurance appraiser who earns $48,650 a year. He is married with no dependents. He pays $1,786 in state income taxes. What is the state income tax rate?

20. ALGEBRA Harry Parsons' annual salary is $112,600. He pays $4,424 in state taxes annually based on a state tax rate of 4%. What is Harry's marital status, and how many dependents does he claim?

Spiral Review

Subtract. (Skill 6)

21. 83.17 − 56.19 **22.** 43 − 17.24 **23.** 65.2 − 34.309

24. Kit Burns, a bookstore clerk, is single, earns $450.15 weekly, and claims 2 allowances. What is the FIT withheld? (Lesson 2.1)

25. Steve Calabrese, a delivery service driver, is married, earns $382.24 weekly, and claims 2 allowances. What is the FIT withheld? (Lesson 2.1)

GET READY for the Next Lesson

PREREQUISITE SKILL Dividing Decimals (Skill 11)

Divide. Round answers to the nearest hundredth.

26. 12,500.00 ÷ 25.00 **27.** 144.48 ÷ 12 **28.** 236.50 ÷ 45

29. 34,984.88 ÷ 52 **30.** 24 ÷ 1.34 **31.** 1.95 ÷ 7.25

LESSON 2.3

Graduated State Income Tax

Lesson Objective

Determine state taxes on a graduated income tax basis.

Content Vocabulary

- graduated income tax

GET READY for the Lesson

Do you think everyone should pay the same tax rate? Why or why not?

When Skyler Montrose reviewed her paycheck, she realized that her state income tax was based on a percentage of her income. She wondered whether other states used the same basis or different methods.

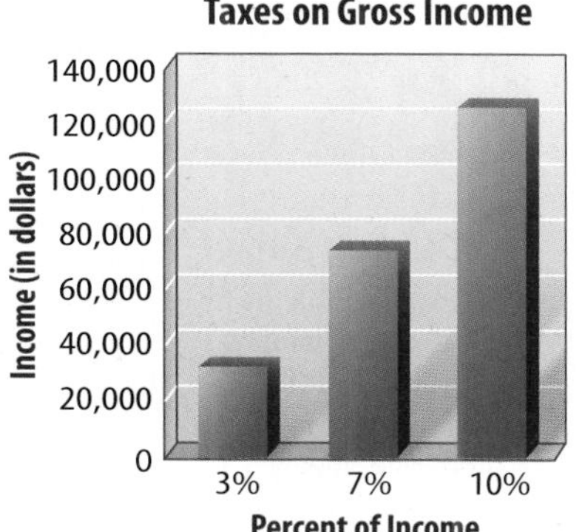

As You Read

Describe What is graduated income tax?

Graduated Income Tax Some states have a **graduated income tax**, which is a system that increases the tax rate at different levels of **income**. This tax sets a different rate for each of several levels of income. The tax rate increases as income increases. The tax rate on low incomes is usually 1% to 3%. The tax rate on high incomes may be as much as 10%.

$$\text{Tax Withheld per Pay Period} = \frac{\text{Annual Tax Withheld}}{\text{Number of Pay Periods per Year}}$$

Need Help? Go to...

- **Workshop 4:** Adding Decimals, p. 10
- **Workshop 7:** Dividing Decimals, p. 16
- **Application K:** Chronological Expressions, p. AP7

EXAMPLE

Figure 2.3

State Tax	
Taxable Wages	**Tax Rate**
First $1,000	1.5%
Next 2,000	3.0%
Next 2,000	4.5%
Over 5,000	5.0%
Exemptions	
Single	$2,000
Married	4,000
Each Dependent	2,000

Louise Main's annual salary as a police officer is $34,500. She receives her pay semimonthly, or twice a month. Her exemptions total $2,000. Use **Figure 2.3** to determine how much her employer deducts for state income tax from each of her semimonthly paychecks.

Step 1: Find the taxable wages.

Annual Gross Pay − Exemptions

$34,500.00 − $2,000.00 = $32,500.00

Step 2: Find the annual state tax withheld.

a. First $1,000: 1.5% of $1,000.00 = $15.00

b. Next 2,000: 3.0% of 2,000.00 = 60.00

c. Next 2,000: 4.5% of 2,000.00 = 90.00

d. Over 5,000: 5.0% of (32,500.00 − 5,000.00) = 5.0% of 27,500.00 = $1,375.00

Total **$1,540.00**

Step 3: Find the tax withheld per pay period.

$$\text{Tax Withheld per Pay Period} = \frac{\text{Annual Tax Withheld}}{\text{Number of Pay Periods per Year}} = \frac{\$1{,}540}{24} = \$64.166 = \mathbf{\$64.17}$$

Use the graduated income tax rates and exemption amounts in Figure 2.3 on page 135 to find the tax withheld per pay period. Check your answers in the back of the book.

1. Eddie Black is single and receives his pay biweekly, or every 2 weeks. His annual salary as a tailor for Whyte and Broom is $21,350.
2. Lydia Robins' annual salary from Dresler & Everhard is $67,500. She is married, has one dependent, and is paid monthly.

Did You Know?

State Income Tax Rates
Tax rates vary widely from state to state. California, Hawaii, Iowa, Maine, New Jersey, North Carolina, Oregon, and Vermont have top rates of 8% or higher. Alaska, Florida, Nevada, South Dakota, Texas, Washington, and Wyoming do not have a personal income tax.

Lesson Practice

Find the tax withheld for Problems 3 and 4.

3. Tobi Vail, an aesthetician, has an annual gross pay of $18,200. Her exemptions total $1,500. The state tax on the first $3,000 is 1.5% and on amounts over $3,000 is 3%.
4. Carl Brownstein is a golf course groundskeeper whose annual gross pay is $45,500. He has exemptions of $3,000. The state tax on the first $2,500 is 1.5% and 3% on amounts over $2,500.

Use Figure 2.3 on page 135 for tax rates and exemptions.

5. Leslie Chan's annual gross pay as a dance company treasurer is $54,400. He is single and receives his pay on a monthly basis. How much does the dance company withhold from his wages monthly for state tax?
6. Anita Munoz, a medical transcriber, earns an annual gross pay of $45,520. She is married with 2 dependents. How much does her employer withhold from her biweekly paycheck for state income tax?

7. **CHALLENGE** Gabriel Harris earns an annual salary of $156,000 as CFO of TechMedia, Inc. He is married and claims three dependents. TechMedia recently converted from a weekly pay plan to a monthly pay plan. How much more will Gabriel have deducted from his monthly pay than from his weekly pay for state income tax?

Spiral Review

Divide. Round answers to the nearest hundredth. (Skill 11)

8. 327 ÷ 73 **9.** 67.632 ÷ 3.3 **10.** 223.46 ÷ 0.25

11. Rebecca Lyne's gross pay as a personal trainer is $55,800 a year. The state income tax rate is 3% of taxable wages. Rebecca takes a married exemption. How much is withheld from Rebecca's yearly gross earnings for state income tax? (Lesson 2.2)
12. Zachary Tylar earns $7\frac{1}{2}$% commission on sales of $4,255. What is his commission? (Lesson 1.6)

GET READY for the Next Lesson

PREREQUISITE SKILL Rounding Numbers (Skill 2)

Round to the place value shown.

Nearest tenth:	Nearest hundredth:	Nearest thousandth:
13. 0.73	**15.** 4.653	**17.** 0.5674
14. $12.46	**16.** $45.955	**18.** 35.1349

LESSON 2.4

Social Security and Medicare Taxes

Lesson Objective

Compute the amount withheld for Social Security and Medicare taxes.

Content Vocabulary

- Social Security
- Medicare

As You Read

Explain How does the government use Social Security and Medicare taxes?

GET READY for the Lesson

Why does the United States have programs such as Social Security and Medicare?

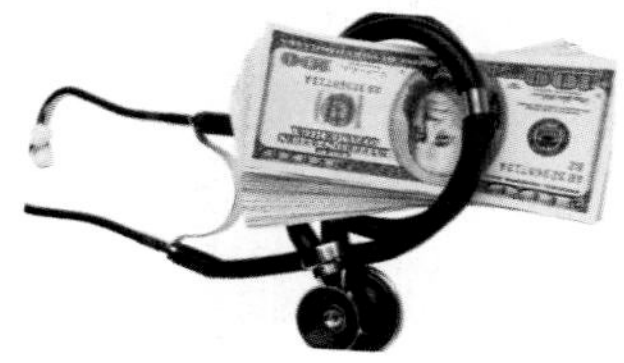

Charles Marks is thankful for Social Security and Medicare benefits. Medicare helps to pay his grandmother's medical bills.

Social Security and Medicare Taxes The Federal Insurance Contributions Act (FICA) **requires** employers to deduct a percent of your income as taxes for **Social Security** to pay for retirement and disability benefits and **Medicare**, which provides medical insurance. The Social Security tax rate is 6.2% and is paid on the first $97,500 of income. The Medicare tax rate is 1.45%, with no limit on your earnings. The employer must contribute an amount that equals your contribution. The federal government uses Social Security to pay for retirement and disability benefits, and Medicare provides health insurance for those 65 and older.

Tax Withheld = Gross Pay × Tax Rate

Need Help? Go to...

Skill 1: Numbers, p. SK1

Application C: Tables and Charts, p. AP3

Study Tip

Use the Index

Refer to the index at the back of this book to locate and read more about things you are interested in or have questions about. The index is arranged in alphabetical order by topic.

EXAMPLE

Riley Henderson's gross biweekly pay as a manufacturing parts inspector is $728. His earnings to date for the year total $26,208. What amount does his employer deduct from his pay this pay period for Social Security taxes? What are his Medicare taxes? What is the total deduction? His earnings to date are less than $97,500.

Step 1: Find the Social Security tax amount withheld.

Gross Pay × Tax Rate

728.00 × 6.2% = $45.136 = **$45.14 Social Security tax**

Step 2: Find the Medicare tax withheld.

Gross Pay × Tax Rate

728.00 × 1.45% = $10.556 = **$10.56 Medicare tax**

Step 3: Find the total deduction.

Social Security Tax + Medicare Tax

$45.14 + $10.56 = **$55.70 total deduction**

Concept CHECK

Find the amount withheld for Social Security and Medicare, and total deductions. Check your answers in the back of the book.

1. Monthly salary: $3,100
Earnings to date: $15,500

2. Weekly salary: $350
Earnings to date: $16,800

Lesson Practice

For Problems 3–6, use the Social Security tax rate of 6.2% and Medicare tax rate of 1.45% to determine each tax and the total deduction.

	Gross Pay	Soc. Sec. Tax Withheld	Medicare Tax Withheld	Total Deduction
3.	$ 125.00	a. $	b. $	c. $
4.	432.00	a.	b.	c.
5.	241.00	a.	b.	c.
6.	1,562.00	a.	b.	c.

Use the Social Security tax rate of 6.2% of the first $97,500 and Medicare tax rate of 1.45% on all income when solving the following problems.

7. Shelly Kelso's gross pay this month is $6,223. Her earnings to date for this year are $23,631. How much does her employer deduct from her paycheck this month for **(a)** Social Security and **(b)** Medicare?

8. Oliver Gelfand earns $45,440 a year as a basketball coach and receives his pay on a semimonthly basis. How much does the school deduct per pay period for **(a)** Social Security tax and **(b)** Medicare tax? **(c)** What is the total monthly deduction?

Changing Tastes in Toys

Children are increasingly giving up traditional toys for high-tech gadgets. Manufacturers are responding by designing high-tech toys, such as robots and robot kits. At a recent American International Toy Fair, at least 75% of the toys introduced contained some sort of microchip.

Use the *Married Persons Weekly Payroll* table on pages A4–A5 for federal withholding taxes.

9. Thomas Schmitt is a designer for Hull Toys. He is married, earns $526 weekly, and claims no allowances. His gross pay to date this year totals $9,912. **(a)** How much does the company deduct from his paycheck this week for federal income, Social Security, and Medicare taxes? **(b)** What is the total deduction amount?

10. Jorge Powell is married and claims 2 allowances. **(a)** How much does the company withhold from his weekly paycheck of $550 for the last week of December for federal income, Social Security, and Medicare taxes? **(b)** What is the total deduction amount?

11. **CHALLENGE PROBLEM** A dental practice hired Stacey Pearl on January 2 as an orthodontist. She earns a $98,000 salary paid monthly. **(a)** How much are her December deductions for Social Security and Medicare? **(b)** What is the total deduction amount?

Spiral Review

Round to the nearest ten. (Skill 2)

12. 216 **13.** 624.83 **14.** 8,990.97

15. Georgia Braun has an annual gross pay of $55,500. Her exemptions total $3,000. The state tax rate is 1.5% on the first $2,500 and 3% on any amount over $2,500. What is the amount of her annual state tax? (Lesson 2.3)

16. Timothy Harquist is a photographer for a modeling agency. His biweekly salary is $2,115.25. What are his annual and monthly salaries? (Lesson 1.5)

GET READY for the Next Lesson

PREREQUISITE SKILL **Finding the Percentage** (Skill 30)

Find the percentage.

17. 5% of $20,000 **18.** 44.5% of $9,500 **19.** 6.25% of $10.34

20. 80% of $80.00 **21.** 97.45% of $13,454 **22.** 23.5% of $23.50

LESSON 2.5

Group Health Insurance

Lesson Objective
Calculate the deduction for group insurance.

Content Vocabulary
- group insurance

GET READY for the Lesson

Why do you think employers contribute to the cost of health insurance?

Both Jack Myers and his employer pay a part of the cost of health insurance for Jack's family. His share of the cost is deducted from each paycheck. Jack pays 30% of the cost, and his employer pays 70%.

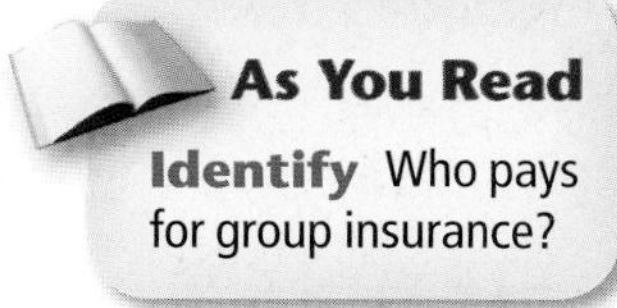

As You Read
Identify Who pays for group insurance?

Group Insurance Premium Many businesses offer group insurance plans to their employees. **Group insurance** costs less to purchase than individual insurance. Businesses often pay part of the insurance cost, or premium, and the employee pays the remaining amount.

Employee's Share = Annual Amount × Employee's Percent

The employee's amount is usually deducted each pay period.

$$\text{Deduction per Pay Period} = \frac{\text{Total Annual Amount Paid by Employee}}{\text{Number of Pay Periods per Year}}$$

Need Help? Go to...
- Workshop 5: Subtracting Decimals, p. 12
- Workshop 7: Dividing Decimals, p. 16
- Workshop 14: Finding the Percentage, p. 30
- Application A: Formulas, p. AP1

EXAMPLE 1

Nadine McClure is a carpenter for Ozark Construction Company. She has family **medical** coverage through Ozark's group medical plan. The annual cost of Nadine's family membership is $9,800. The company pays 75% of the cost. How much does she have deducted from her biweekly paycheck for medical insurance?

Step 1: Find the percent the employee pays.

100% − Percent Company Pays
100% − 75% = 25% Percent employee pays

Step 2: Find the total amount the employee pays.

Annual Amount × Employee's Percent
$9,800 × 25% = $2,450 total employee pays

Step 3: Find the deduction per pay period.

$$\text{Deduction per Pay Period} = \frac{\text{Total Annual Amount Paid by Employee}}{\text{Number of Pay Periods per Year}} = \frac{\$2{,}450}{26} = \mathbf{\$94.23}$$

Concept CHECK

Find the deduction per pay period. Check your answers in the back of the book.

1. Annual cost of insurance: $6,570; employer pays 70%; 12 pay periods
2. Annual cost of insurance: $12,000; employer pays 80%; 52 pay periods

EXAMPLE 2 Algebra

Kim Choi pays $115.80 per month for her group medical coverage. Her employer pays 55% of the cost. How much is the annual premium for Kim's health insurance?

Step 1: Find the percent that the employee pays.

100% − Percent Company Pays

100% − 55% = **45%** percent employee pays

Step 2: Let a = Annual Premium for Kim's Health Insurance

Step 3: Write and solve an equation for the deduction per pay period.

$$\frac{\text{Employee's Percent} \times \text{Annual Premium}}{\text{Number of Pay Periods per Year}} = \text{Deduction per Pay Period}$$

$$\frac{0.45 \times a}{12} = \$115.80$$

Multiply both sides by 12 →

$$0.45a = \$1{,}389.60$$

Divide both sides by 0.45 →

$$\frac{0.45a}{0.45} = \frac{\$1{,}389.60}{0.45}$$

$$a = \mathbf{\$3{,}088.00}$$

The annual premium for Kim's health insurance is $3,088.

Complete the problems. Check your answers in the back of the book.

3. Lars Olsen authorized a deduction of $163.75 from his monthly pay for group health insurance. His employer pays 45% of the cost. What is the annual premium amount for his group health insurance?
4. Rhonda Martin has $215.25 deducted from her semimonthly pay for group health insurance. Rocky Mountain Auto Parts, her employer, pays 60% of the cost. What is the annual premium amount for Rhonda's group health insurance?

Lesson Practice

Did You Know?

Honeybee Populations

Only a small percentage of the world's estimated 30,000 bee species produces honey. A typical colony includes 50,000–60,000 workers, 500–1,000 drones (fertile males), and a single queen bee.

5. Marge Torelli is a pilot. Her annual group insurance costs $4,400, and her company pays 80% of the cost. How much of the cost does Marge pay monthly?
6. Max Fischer is a beekeeper. His annual group insurance costs $11,700. His employer pays 60% of the cost. How much does Max pay semimonthly for it?
7. Royce Bernstein's group medical insurance coverage costs $5,480 a year. His employer pays 65% of the cost. What is the amount of the deduction each month from his paycheck for medical insurance?
8. Kathy Parker, who plans conferences and parties for a resort, earns $342.22 weekly. Her group medical insurance costs $4,650.00 a year, and the company pays 70% of the costs. How much does she have deducted weekly from her paycheck for medical insurance?

Photo by Stephen Ausmus, USDA-ARS

9. Lawrence Butler is a manager for Sound Pharmaceuticals. His family medical coverage is through the group medical plan that Sound provides for its employees. The annual cost of Lawrence's family coverage is $12,312. The company pays 60% of the cost. How much does he pay weekly for medical insurance?

10. Carmelita Delp is a social worker. The annual cost of Carmelita's family health insurance is $10,019.40. The company pays 66% of the cost. How much does she pay weekly for medical insurance?

11. ALGEBRA Mickey Doren's group medical insurance coverage costs $94.50 semimonthly. His employer pays 65% of the cost. How much is the annual premium?

12. CHALLENGE PROBLEM Mary Jo Holt has medical, dental, and vision insurance coverage through her employer, a newspaper. Annual coverage costs are medical, $6,478.16; dental, $598.00; and vision, $254.24. The newspaper pays 60% of the medical, 55% of the dental, and 50% of the vision coverage. What total amount does she have deducted weekly from her paycheck for this coverage?

13. ALGEBRA Linda West, a dental lab technician, pays three times as much for dental insurance as she does for vision insurance and three times as much for health insurance as for vision and dental combined. Linda's employer pays 40% of the cost for all three. If the total annual premium for all three is $9,360, how much will Linda pay biweekly for **(a)** vision, **(b)** dental, and **(c)** health insurance?

Reading Math +−÷=

Division

Read the line separating the numerator from the denominator in a fraction just like the symbol ÷. Both 1/5 and 1 ÷ 5 are read "1 *divided by* 5."

Spiral Review

Find the percentage. (Skill 30)

14. 5% of 340 **15.** 98% of 742 **16.** 5¼% of 56

17. Sheila Kerr, a magazine editor, receives a monthly gross pay of $5,922. Her earnings to date this year total $47,376. Using the Social Security tax rate of 6.2% of the first $97,500 and the Medicare tax rate of 1.45%, how much does Sheila have deducted from her paycheck this month for **(a)** Social Security and **(b)** Medicare? (Lesson 2.4)

18. Wallis Rainwater earns $37,200 annually. He is married and claims 2 children as dependents. His state's tax rate is 4% of taxable income. What is the amount for state income tax if his exemptions are $4,000 for a married person and $2,000 for each dependent? (Lesson 2.2)

GET READY for the Next Lesson

PREREQUISITE SKILL **Subtracting Decimals** (Skill 6)

Subtract.

19. 475.85 − 45.00

20. $12.00 − $0.62

21. $13,450.67 − $876.50 − $12.45

22. 3,546 − 289 − 43

23. $444.44 − $33.33 − $2.22

24. $12,561.72 − $408.89 − $11.38 − $4.20

LESSON 2.6

Statement of Earnings

Lesson Objective
Calculate net pay per pay period.

Content Vocabulary
- net pay

GET READY for the Lesson

Why should you save for retirement?

Ember Rigsby just started her first job as a golf instructor. She has $45 deducted each pay period for her retirement account. Ember is saving money now so she can enjoy her retirement later.

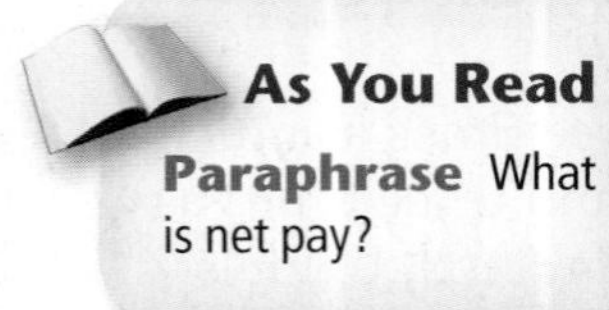

As You Read

Paraphrase What is net pay?

Net Pay You may have additional deductions taken from your gross pay for union dues, contributions to **community** funds, savings plans, and retirement account contributions. The earnings statement attached to your paycheck lists all of your deductions, your gross pay, and your net pay for the pay period. **Net pay** is the amount of money you have left after your employer subtracts all tax withholdings and personal deductions from your gross pay. It is sometimes called *net income* or *take-home pay.*

Net Pay = Gross Pay − Total Deductions

Need Help? Go to...
- Skill 5: Adding Decimals, p. SK6
- Skill 6: Subtracting Decimals, p. SK7
- Application A: Formulas, p. AP1

EXAMPLE 1

Angela Moore's gross weekly salary is $600.00. She is married and claims 3 allowances. The Social Security tax is 6.2% of the first $97,500.00. The Medicare tax is 1.45% of gross pay. The state tax is 1.5% of gross pay. Each week she has $28.40 deducted for medical insurance and $5.00 for charity. Is Angela's earnings statement correct?

Dept	Employee		Check Number		Gross Pay		Net Pay
15	Angela Moore		1501		$600.00		$485.70
Tax Deductions					Other Deductions		
FIT	SS	Medicare	State	Local	Medical	Union Dues	Others
26.00	37.20	8.70	9.00		28.40		5.00

Step 1: Find the total deductions.

a.	Federal withholding: (from table above)		$26.00
b.	Social Security: 6.2% of 600.00	=	37.20
c.	Medicare: 1.45% of 600.00	=	8.70
d.	State tax: 1.5% of 600.00	=	9.00
e.	Medical insurance		28.40
f.	Charity	+	5.00
	Total		**$114.30**

Step 2: Find the net pay.

Gross Pay − Total Deductions
$600.00 − $114.30 = **$485.70 net pay**

Her statement is correct.

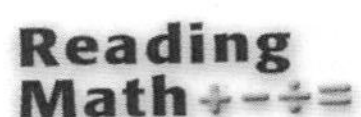

Multiplication

In a mathematical expression, "of" means "times." The expression "5% of 340" is the same as 5% *times* 340.

Complete the problems. Check your answers in the back of the book.

1. Ron King is a single airline ticket agent who claims 1 allowance. His gross weekly salary is $320.00. Each week he has deducted federal, Social Security, and Medicare taxes; $26.20 for medical insurance; 1.5% state tax; and $25.00 for the credit union.

Find the total deductions and net pay.

Deductions		Amount
Federal Tax	(from table on page 142)	**a.**
Social Security	6.20% of 320 =	**b.**
Medicare	1.45% of $320 =	**c.**
State Tax	1.50% of $320 =	**d.**
Medical Insurance		**e.**
Credit Union		**f.**
Total		**g.**

2. Briana Ralph, a pastry chef, is married and claims 2 allowances. Her gross weekly salary is $450.00. Each week she has the company deduct federal, Social Security, and Medicare taxes; $21.20 for medical insurance; and $5.00 for savings. She pays no state taxes. What is her net pay?

EXAMPLE 2 Algebra

The deductions from Esther Stein's monthly pay are federal income tax (FIT) of $98, state income tax (SIT) of 3.5% of gross, city income tax (CIT) of 1.5% of gross, Social Security, and Medicare. Her monthly net pay is $4,147.21. Find Esther's monthly gross pay.

Step 1: Let m = Esther's monthly gross pay.

Step 2: Use the net pay formula and solve for m.

Net Pay = Gross Pay − (FIT + SIT + CIT + Social Security + Medicare)

$\$4{,}147.21 = m - [\$98.00 + (0.035m) + (0.015m) + (0.062m) + (0.0145m)]$

Combine like terms → $\$4{,}147.21 = m - (\$98.00 + 0.1265m)$

Distributive property → $\$4{,}147.21 = m - \$98.00 - 0.1265m$

Combine like terms; add $98 to both sides → $\$4{,}245.21 = 0.8735m$

Divide both sides by 0.8735 → $\mathbf{\$4{,}860} = m$

Esther's monthly gross pay is $4,860.

Concept CHECK

Find the weekly gross pay. Check your answer in the back of the book.

3. John Pelson's weekly net pay is $972.11. His weekly deductions are $185.00 for FIT; 5% of gross for SIT; 2% of gross for CIT; Social Security and Medicare; $64.00 for health insurance; and $25.00 for charity.

Lesson Practice

Find the deductions and the net pay. Social Security is 6.2% of the first $97,500. Medicare is 1.45% of all income. Use the tax tables on pages A2–A5 for federal tax. For Problems 4–8, the state tax is 2% of gross pay, and the local tax is 1.5% of gross pay.

4. Terence Hall is single and claims 1 allowance.

Dept	Employee	Check Number	Gross Pay	Net Pay			
23	Terence Hall	463	$598.00	f.			
FIT	**SS**	**Medicare**	**State**	**Local**	**Medical**	**Union Dues**	**Others**
a.	b.	c.	d.	e.	$15.50	$14.00	$6.00

Did You Know?

Single adults According to the U.S. Census Bureau, the country has more than 89.8 million single adults today. The Bureau reports that 60% of single adults have never been married, 25% are divorced, and 15% are widowed. The percentage of single-person households has doubled since 1960.

5. Julia DeFoe, an interior decorator for Custom Design, is married and claims 1 allowance. Each week she pays $38 for medical insurance, $18 for union dues, and $20 for a stock option plan.

Dept	Employee	Check Number	Gross Pay	Net Pay			
CUDI	Julia DeFoe	1574	$425.00	f.			
FIT	**SS**	**Medicare**	**State**	**Local**	**Medical**	**Union Dues**	**Others**
a.	b.	c.	d.	e.	$38.00	$18.00	$20.00

6. Jeri Lammers, a part-time teller at Second State Bank, is married and claims 3 allowances.

Dept	Employee	Check Number	Gross Pay	Net Pay			
448	Jeri Lammers	3205	$735.00	f.			
FIT	**SS**	**Medicare**	**State**	**Local**	**Medical**	**Union Dues**	**Others**
a.	b.	c.	d.	e.	$32.00	—	—

7. Orville Staples is a painter who earns $30,000.00 a year. He is single and claims 3 allowances. Weekly deductions include $34.50 for medical insurance and union dues of $15.00.

Dept	Employee	Check Number	Gross Pay	Net Pay			
	Orville Staples	235	a.	i.			
FIT	**SS**	**Medicare**	**State**	**Local**	**Medical**	**Union Dues**	**Others**
b.	c.	d.	e.	f.	g.	h.	0.00

8. Lynn Golding is employed as a payroll supervisor and earns $18 per hour. This pay period she worked 40 hours. She is married and claims 6 allowances. The state tax is 3.0% of gross earnings, and the local tax is 1.5% of gross earnings. Lynn pays $35 for medical insurance and $17 in union dues.

Dept	Employee	Check Number	Gross Pay	Net Pay			
PAYR	Lynn Golding	355-5887-01	a.	i.			
FIT	**SS**	**Medicare**	**State**	**Local**	**Medical**	**Union Dues**	**Others**
b.	c.	d.	e.	f.	g.	h.	0.00

9. **CHALLENGE PROBLEM** Claude Johnson, a purchasing agent, earns \$14.60 an hour with time and a half for working more than 40 hours a week. He is married and claims 4 allowances. The state tax is 25% of the federal tax. The local tax is 2.5% of gross pay. Medical insurance costs \$8,540.00 a year, and his company pays 75% of its cost. Claude has a credit union deduction of \$80.00 a week. What is his net pay for a week in which he worked 48 hours?

10. **ALGEBRA** Laura Russo lost her earnings statement from Siler's Lawn and Garden. She recalls paying \$43.00 in federal income taxes and knows she deposited \$306.36 in her checking account. Each week she had deductions for Social Security and Medicare taxes; \$22.35 for medical insurance; 1.5% state tax; 1.5% local tax; and \$25.00 for the credit union. What is her gross weekly pay?

11. **ALGEBRA** Hollis Porter is the chef at Chez Paulina. He was studying his pay stub when he noted that his FIT was three times his SIT and his SIT was the same as his health insurance premium. His Social Security and Medicare deductions were the usual 6.2% and 1.45% of gross, respectively. If Hollis's monthly gross pay was \$4,800 and his monthly net pay was \$3,232.80, find the monthly deductions for FIT, SIT, and his health insurance premium.

Spiral Review

Add.

12. $125.231 + 1.008 + 42.112$ **13.** $16.3 + 2 + 43.432$ **14.** $321.9 + 6.157 + 33.45$

15. Robert Key's group medical insurance coverage costs \$6,480 a year. His employer, Covington Arts Center, pays 65% of the cost. What is his monthly paycheck deduction for medical insurance? (Lesson 2.5)

16. Amy Langston, the volunteer services coordinator at Jackson Memorial, has an annual gross pay of \$45,600. Her exemptions total \$4,000. The state tax rate is 1.5% on the first \$2,500 and 3% on any amount over \$2,500. What is her annual state tax? (Lesson 2.3)

17. Rae Jing is paid \$0.18 for every telemarketing phone call she makes. If a call results in a sale, she receives a bonus of an additional \$1.80 for that call. One day Rae made 220 phone calls, and 22 of them resulted in a sale. What was her total pay for that day? (Lesson 1.4)

GET READY for the Next Lesson

PREREQUISITE SKILL **Finding the Mean** (Application Q)

Find the mean for each group.

18. 13, 76, 55, 43, 24, 35
19. 189, 206, 176, 149, 215
20. 2,116; 1,889; 2,205; 1,794
21. 3.65, 4.55, 6.05, 2.97, 3.65, 4.3
22. \$17, 225; \$55,400; \$34,950; \$22,560; \$45,830

CHAPTER 2 Review and Assessment

AFTER YOU READ

Chapter SUMMARY

Net pay is the amount you have left after subtracting all tax withholdings and personal deductions from your gross pay. Deductions may include federal income tax, state taxes on a straight percent basis, state taxes on a graduated income tax basis, Social Security and Medicare taxes, a group health insurance premium, and various personal deductions.

Vocabulary Check

1. On a sheet of paper, use each of these terms in a sentence.

Content Vocabulary

- federal income tax (p. 129)
- withholding allowance (p. 129)
- exemption (p. 132)
- graduated income tax (p. 135)
- Social Security (p. 137)
- Medicare (p. 137)
- group insurance (p. 139)
- net pay (p. 142)

Academic Vocabulary

- claim (p. 129)
- percent (p. 132)
- income (p. 135)
- require (p. 137)
- medical (p. 139)
- community (p. 142)

Concept Check

2. Differentiate between gross pay and net pay.
3. List the factors that determine the amount withheld for federal income tax.
4. Give the formula for determining taxable wages.
5. Give the formula for determining state income tax on a straight percent basis.
6. Differentiate between computing taxes on a graduated income tax basis and on a straight percent basis.
7. Summarize how the government uses Social Security and Medicare.
8. Give the formula for computing a deduction for group health insurance.
9. Give the formula for calculating net pay.
10. **CRITICAL THINKING** Why is it important to account for taxes and personal deductions from gross pay when you make a budget? Write a paragraph explaining your answer.

Lesson-by-Lesson Review

2.1 Federal Income Tax (pp. 129–131)

Use the *Married Persons Weekly Payroll* and *Single Persons Weekly Payroll* tables on pages A2–A5 to find the amount withheld for federal income taxes.
Will Stevenson, a chemist who is married and claims 2 allowances, earns $600.50 a week. How much does he have withheld from his weekly paycheck for federal income tax?

Step 1: Find the income range from the Married Persons table.

Step 2: Find the column for 2 allowances.

Step 3: Amount to be withheld is **$33.00**.

Some companies use a percentage method instead of the tax tables to compute the income tax withheld. Use **Figure 2.1** on page 130 to find the amount withheld for a single employee. Each weekly allowance is $63.46.

Step 1: Find the allowance amount.

Step 2: Find the taxable wage.

Step 3: Find the amount withheld for the employee using the table.

Review Exercises

Use these exercises to review and prepare for the chapter test.

11. Maggie Brown, a customer service representative at Kelly's Floral Designs, is single, earns $455 weekly, and claims 2 allowances. What is the amount of federal income tax withheld?

12. Larry Gold's gross pay for this week as a stock clerk for Hensley's is $375.15. He is single and claims 2 allowances. Using the percentage method of withholding, what is his withholding for federal income tax?

13. Cynthia Markova, the bookkeeper at Falls Supply, has gross pay this week of $555.72. She is single and claims 3 allowances. Using the percentage method of withholding, what is her withholding for federal income tax?

14. **ALGEBRA** Angie Simon is a single Palmetto County deputy sheriff. She has $103.92 in federal income tax withheld from her weekly salary. Her weekly salary exceeds $645.00. She claims 2 withholding allowances. The county computes her federal income tax using the percentage method. Use **Figure 2.1** on page 130 to determine Angie's weekly salary.

2.2 State Income Tax (pp. 132–134)

Compute the state taxes on a straight percent basis.
Mila Rossi earns $68,000 a year as a researcher. The state income tax rate is 2.6% of taxable income. Her exemptions total $3,700. How much does her employer withhold from Mila's gross pay for state income tax for the year?

Step 1: Find the taxable wages.

Annual Gross Pay − Exemptions
$68,000.00 − $3,700 = $64,300.00

Step 2: Find the annual tax withheld.

Taxable Wages × Tax Rate
$64,300.00 × $0.026 = **1,671.80 annual tax withheld**

Lesson-by-Lesson Review (continued)

Review Exercises

Find the state tax withheld using the following figures:

Exemptions	
Single	$1,500
Married	3,000
Each Dependent	1,500

15. Chris Butcher earns $21,423 per year as a forestry technician. His exemptions include himself, his wife, and their son. The state tax rate in his state is 4.5% of taxable income.

16. Missy Kimble earns $42,000 per year. She is single. Her state tax rate is 2%.

17. Rita Lo earns $59,000. She is married with 2 dependents. Her state tax rate is 3%.

18. **ALGEBRA** Al Masters earns $32,500 as a medical lab technician. He is single with 1 dependent. His annual state income tax is $1,475. What is his state income tax rate?

2.3 Graduated State Income Tax (pp. 135–136)

Determine the state taxes on a graduated income tax basis.

Hugh Cooper earns an annual salary of $32,540 paid monthly. His exemptions total $2,400. What amount is deducted each pay period for state income tax?

Step 1: Find the taxable wages.

Taxable Wages = Annual Gross Pay − Exemptions

$30,140 = $32,540 − $2,400

Step 2: Find the annual tax withheld. Base your calculations on the state's graduated income tax rate.

a. First $1,000:	1.5% of $1,000	=	$15
b. Next 2,000:	3.0% of 2,000	=	60
c. Next 2,000:	4.5% of 2,000	=	90
d. Over 5,000:	5.0% of (30,140 − 5,000)	=	1,257
	Total		$1,422

Step 3: Find how much is deducted per pay period.

Deducted per pay period = $1,422 ÷ 12 = **$118.50**

Review Exercises

Find the state tax withheld per pay period using the exemptions and tax rates below:

State Tax		
Taxable Wages	**Tax Rate**	**Exemptions**
First $1,000	1.5%	Single $2,000
Next 2,000	3.0	Married 4,000
Next 2,000	4.5	Each Dependent 2,000
Over 5,000	5.0	

19. Maurice Jordan's annual salary as a motorcycle mechanic is $18,750 paid in 26 pay periods. He is married.

20. Jo Ha is single and earns $24,400 paid in 24 pay periods.

21. Emil Martin is the manager of Brio Restaurant and earns a $30,000 annual salary. He receives his pay weekly, is married, and claims 1 exemption. What is the deduction each pay period from his paycheck for state income tax?

Lesson-by-Lesson Review (continued)

2.4 Social Security and Medicare Taxes (pp. 137–138)

Compute the amount withheld for Social Security and Medicare taxes.
Denny Carter earns $255.20 a week. His pay to date this year totals $10,718.40. The Social Security tax rate is 6.2% of the first $97,500.00 earned. The Medicare tax is 1.45% of gross pay. How much are his paycheck deductions this week for Social Security and Medicare tax?

Step 1: Find the Social Security tax withheld.
Gross Pay × Tax Rate
$255.20 × 6.2% = **$15.82 Social Security tax**

Step 2: Find the Medicare tax withheld.
Gross Pay × Tax Rate
$255.20 × 1.45% = **$3.70 Medicare tax**

Review Exercises

Find the Social Security (6.2% up to $97,500) and Medicare (1.45%) taxes withheld for each pay period.

		Annual Gross Pay	Pay Periods per Year	Social Security	Medicare
22.	J. Otto	$76,432	12	a. $	b. $
23.	G. Hernandez	43,902	26	a.	b.
24.	A. Toms	20,235	24	a.	b.

2.5 Group Health Insurance (pp. 139–141)

Calculate the deduction for group insurance.
Kendra Alvarez earns $1,110 a week. Her medical insurance costs $5,500 a year. Her company pays 65% of its cost. How much are her paycheck deductions each week for medical insurance?

Step 1: Find the percent paid by employee.
100% − Percent Company Pays
100% − 65% = 35%

Step 2: Find the total amount paid by the employee.
Annual Amount × Employee's Percent
$5500 × 0.35 = $1925

Step 3: Find the deduction per pay period.
Total Amount Paid ÷ Number of Pay Periods
$1925 ÷ 52 = $37.0192 = **$37.02 deducted**

Review Exercises

Find the deduction per pay period.

25. Cassandra Matthews, a software designer, has insurance whose premium is $6,800 a year. Her employer pays 75%. She receives her pay in 24 pay periods.
26. Kelly Bell, the senior ski instructor at Snow Slopes, has a $15,000 annual cost of insurance, and her employer pays 60% of it. She has 52 pay periods.
27. **ALGEBRA** Mike Haus has $215.26 deducted from his monthly pay for group health insurance. His employer pays 65% of the cost. What is the annual premium?

Lesson-by-Lesson Review (continued)

2.6 Statement of Earnings (pp. 142–145)

Calculate the net pay per pay period.

Tonya Lombardo, a Department of Social Services case worker, is married and claims 2 allowances. She earns $432.75 a week. The Social Security tax rate is 6.2% of the first $97,500.00 earned. The Medicare tax rate is 1.45% of gross. The state tax is $10.82 a week. She has weekly deductions of $35.00 for medical insurance and $30.00 for a savings account. Use the table on pages A4–A5 to find Tonya's federal tax withheld. What is her net pay for a week?

Step 1: Find the total deductions.

Federal Withholding (from table)			$15.00
Social Security:	6.2% of $432.75	=	26.83
Medicare:	1.45% of 432.75	=	6.27
State Tax			10.82
Medical Insurance			35.00
Savings Account			+ 30.00
Total Deductions			**$123.92**

Step 2: Find the net pay.

Weekly Income − Deductions
$432.75 − $123.92 = **$308.83 net pay**

Review Exercises

Find the deductions and the net pay.

Social Security is 6.2% of the first 97,500. Medicare is 1.45% of all income. Use the tax tables on pages A2–A5 for federal tax. The state tax is 2% of gross pay and the local tax is 1.5% of gross pay.

28. Don Chapman works at the library, is single, and has 1 allowance.

General Check Information					
Dept	Employee	Check #	Week Ending	Gross Pay	Net Pay
23	Chapman, D	432	3/5/20--	$640.00	f.

Tax and Personal Information							
FIT	SS	Medicare	State	Local	Medical	Union Dues	Others
a.	b.	c.	d.	e.	30.00	—	—

29. ALGEBRA Melba Westover, a stock analyst at Tweed & Snell, receives her pay monthly, and her deductions are FIT of $112, SIT of 3.5% of gross, CIT of 2.5% of gross, and Social Security and Medicare taxes. She knows her monthly net pay is $5,161.28. Find Melba's monthly gross pay.

Practice Test

Record your answer on a sheet of paper.

Use the federal tax tables on pp. A2–A5 to answer Questions 1 and 2.

1. Madison Finn, single, makes $540.75 a week as the first violinist for the Grove Park Philharmonic. If she claims 1 allowance, what is the tax amount withheld?
   A $58 **B** $57
   C $67 **D** $38

2. If Erica Morrison, a machine operator at Stanley Foundry, makes $513.66 a week and has $33 in FIT withheld, how many allowances has she claimed?
   A 0 **B** 1
   C 2 **D** 3

3. What are Julio Dempsey's taxable wages as a data-entry operator if his withholding allowances total $1,500 and his annual gross pay is $23,400?
   A $21,900 **B** $23,400
   C $24,900 **D** $24,400

4. How much tax is withheld from $45,580 if the tax rate is 4%?
   A $2,300.10 **B** $1,855.50
   C $3,500.40 **D** $1,823.20

Use the state income tax table below to answer Question 5.

Exemptions	
Single	$2,000
Married	4,000
Each Dependent	2,000

5. **ALGEBRA** Alistair Julius earns $47,800 a year working for a delivery service. He is single and pays $2,152.60 in state income tax each year. He claims no dependents. What is the tax rate of Alistair's state?
   A 4.5% **B** 4.7%
   C 3.9% **D** 5.0%

6. Lily Friedman's gross pay is $350.00 per pay period. The Medicare tax rate is 1.45%. How much Medicare tax does Lily pay per pay period?
   A $15.08 **B** $5.08
   C $4.20 **D** $21.70

Use the state income tax table below to answer Question 7.

Percentage Method of Withholding – Single Person		
Each weekly allowance is $63.46.		
Weekly Taxable Wage		The amount of income tax to withhold is:
Over	But not over	
$ 51.00	$ 195.00	$0.00 plus (10% of the excess over 51.00)
195.00	645.00	14.40 plus (15% of the excess over 195.00)
645.00	1,482.00	81.90 plus (25% of the excess over 645.00)

7. Terry Harrison is single and works for the Dade County animal control department. He claims no allowances, and his employer computes federal tax using the percentage method. Dade County withholds $85.80 in federal income tax from his weekly salary, which exceeds $645.00. What is Terry's weekly salary?
   A $680.80 **B** $595.75
   C $665.15 **D** $660.60

8. If Manny Long's wages as a fork lift operator are $520.75, he is single, he claims 3 allowances, what amount is deducted for federal taxes? Use the federal tax table on pp. A2–A5.

9. Amber Holloway's gross pay is $45,700 a year. The income tax rate is 4%, and she takes $2,000 in exemptions. What is her withholding for the year?

10. Jackie Douglas is an airline mechanic. Her company pays 40% of the $3,500 annual cost of group health insurance. How much does she pay for it monthly?

11. $0.45 \times \$6,800$

12. $\$5,600 \div 24$

13. $(\$78,000 - \$5,580) \times 3$

Standardized Test Practice

Cumulative, Chapters 1–2

PART 1 Multiple Choice

Record your answers on the answer sheet provided by your teacher or on a sheet of paper.

1. Patty Randall's insurance costs $3,400. If Elgin Power, her employer, pays 40%, how much does Patty pay?

A $3,000 **B** $600
C $3,040 **D** $2,040

Use the table below to answer Question 2.

If the wages are—		And the number of withholding allowances claimed is—				
At least	But less than	0	1	2	3	4
		The amount of income tax to be withheld is—				
500	$510	$61	$51	$41	$32	$22
510	520	62	53	43	33	23
520	530	64	54	44	35	25
530	540	65	56	46	36	26
540	550	67	57	47	38	28

2. Using the preceding table, how much does Charles Ferraro's employer withhold from his wages of $525 as a city park employee if he claims 2 allowances?

A $44 **B** $54
C $46 **D** $64

3. Marty Keith's annual salary is $56,000 as a computer-aided designer. If the state tax rate is 4%, what does he pay yearly in state taxes?

A $3,240 **B** $2,240
C $4,000 **D** $4,220

TEST-TAKING TIP

Multiple Steps Multistep problems require you to do several different tasks. First write down all information given and determine what steps to take to solve the problem.

4. Clare Wahl's annual gross pay as an account manager is $54,000. If the graduated state tax rate is 1% for the first $1,000, 3% for the next $3,000, and 5 percent for amounts over $4,000, what amount is the deduction for state taxes?

A $2,500 **B** $3,000
C $2,000 **D** $2,600

5. Dane Cotter's gross biweekly pay as a receptionist is $560. If the Social Security tax rate is 5.4% and the Medicare tax rate is 2.3%, what is the total amount of deductions from his pay for Social Security and Medicare?

A $30.24 **B** $12.88
C $43.12 **D** $43.88

6. Chad Palmer's gross weekly salary as a logger is $630. He pays 6.2% Social Security tax, 1.45% Medicare tax, and $14.20 for health insurance. What is Chad's monthly net pay?

A $2,459.60 **B** $2,313.02
C $2,520 **D** $2,505.80

PART 2 Short Response/Griddable

7. Carol Ryan is a pet groomer whose yearly gross pay is $14,600. She does not claim any allowances, and the state tax rate is 3.5%. How much does she pay in state taxes each month?

PART 3 Extended Response

Show your work.

8. Samantha Hewitt is a nutritionist. Her weekly salary is $420.00. Of that amount, 6.2% goes to Social Security taxes and 1.45% to Medicare taxes. She pays $10.23 for health coverage and donates $5.00 to charity. What is her net pay amount?

Building Academic Skills

Mathematics

Your employer has encouraged you to participate in your company's retirement savings plan. Not only will you be saving for the future, but your federal income taxes will be lower. You will not have to pay taxes on money you save until you withdraw it. Calculate your taxes if your tax rate is 15%, your adjusted gross income is $37,522 after allowances, and you contribute 6% of that adjusted gross income to a tax-deferred retirement savings plan.

English Language Arts/Writing

Imagine that you work for a corporation's Human Resources department. One of your jobs is to explain the company's benefits plan to new employees. Develop a short presentation explaining why it is important to begin saving for retirement early in your career. Make a list of points to convince new, young employees to join your company's tax-deferred retirement plan.

Social Studies/Government

President Franklin D. Roosevelt started Social Security during the Great Depression of the 1930s. It was a major change in how government was involved in the lives of U.S. citizens. Go to the Social Security Administration Web site. Click on "About Us," and then read the history of the Social Security program. Make a time line that shows how government has become involved in retirement income.

Building Real-World Skills

Ethics in Action

Confidentiality Imagine that you are a store manager for a coffeehouse chain and have access to your store's accounting records. A close friend is opening her own coffeehouse. She wants you to share some of your store's records, such as sales and payroll costs, to better plan her business.

Discuss and Write:

a. Discuss the possible negative consequences of sharing confidential financial information. Why is confidentiality important?

b. Write a paragraph explaining some ethical ways you could help your friend.

21st Century Workplace

Payroll Cards Approximately 25 million people in the United States have no bank account. Instead of paying employees without an account by check, some employers use payroll cards. The employee can withdraw funds by using the card at specified locations worldwide or as a debit card.

Research and Write:

a. Visit the Web site of Consumers Union and search for information on "payroll cards."

b. Where do you think people who do not have bank accounts cash payroll checks?

Recordkeeping

Big Idea

Recordkeeping will allow you to manage your money so you can prepare for tax season and plan for the future.

Explore the Photo

Budget for Fun
Purchasing concert tickets, buying electronics, and dining out can become expensive. *Why should you budget for entertainment?*

Purestock/SuperStock

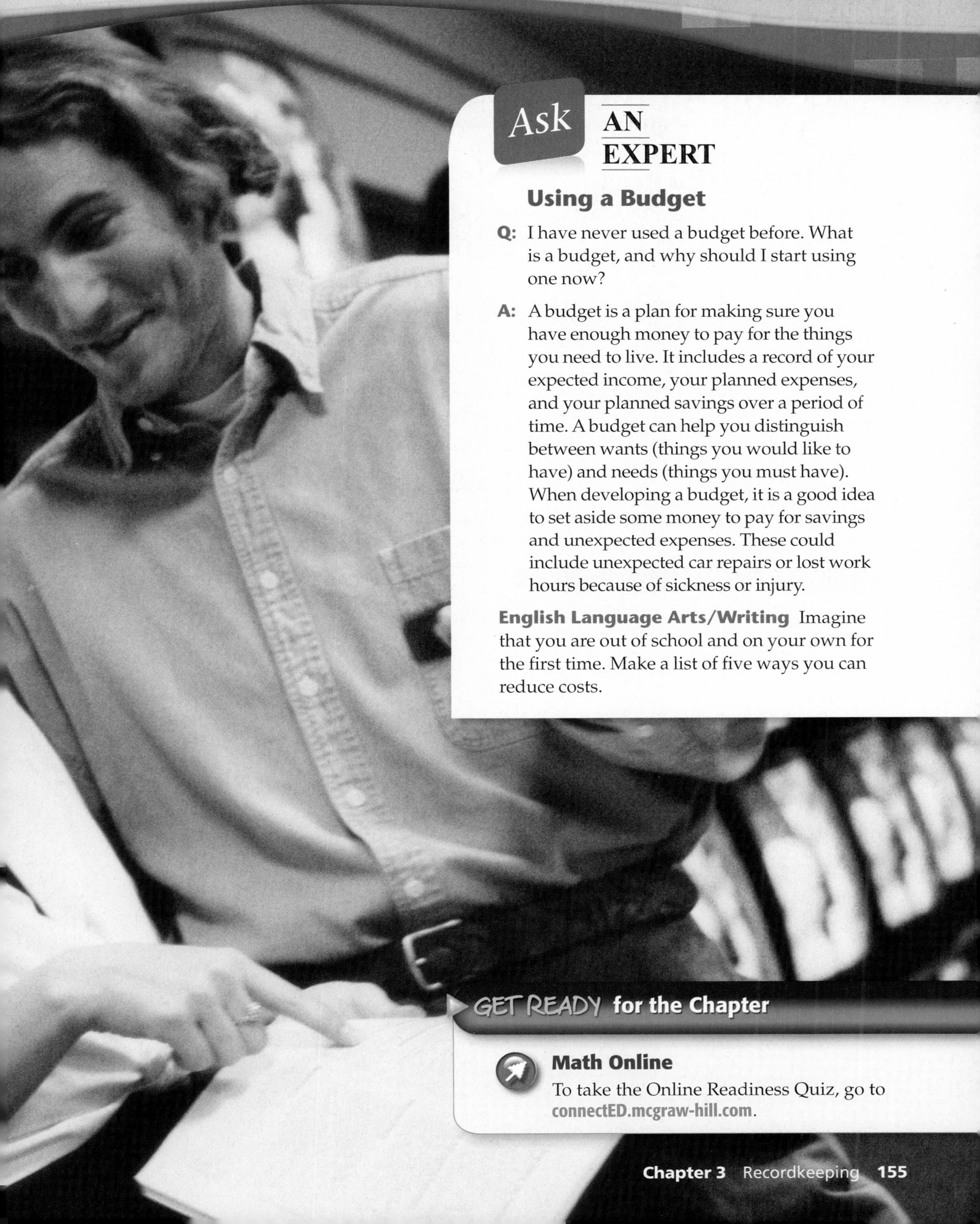

Ask AN EXPERT

Using a Budget

Q: I have never used a budget before. What is a budget, and why should I start using one now?

A: A budget is a plan for making sure you have enough money to pay for the things you need to live. It includes a record of your expected income, your planned expenses, and your planned savings over a period of time. A budget can help you distinguish between wants (things you would like to have) and needs (things you must have). When developing a budget, it is a good idea to set aside some money to pay for savings and unexpected expenses. These could include unexpected car repairs or lost work hours because of sickness or injury.

English Language Arts/Writing Imagine that you are out of school and on your own for the first time. Make a list of five ways you can reduce costs.

GET READY for the Chapter

Math Online

To take the Online Readiness Quiz, go to **connectED.mcgraw-hill.com**.

Chapter 3 Recordkeeping

Reading Guide

Before You Read

Predict What do you think you will learn from your budget?

Main Idea

A budget is a recordkeeping process that helps individuals, families, businesses and governments to make wise financial decisions. With a budget, you compare how much money you are spending with how much money you are earning.

Graphic Organizer

Before you read this chapter, draw a diagram like the one below. As you read, list examples of monthly and annual expenses.

Expenses	
Monthly	Annual

Math Online Go to **connectED.mcgraw-hill.com** to download this graphic organizer.

Content Vocabulary

You will learn these key terms in this chapter.

- recordkeeping
- expenditures
- budget sheet
- living expenses
- budget
- fixed expenses
- annual expense
- expense summary
- emergency fund

Academic Vocabulary

You will see these words in your reading and on your tests.

- device
- vary
- vehicle

You can find vocabulary definitions in the **Content Vocabulary** Glossary and the **Academic Vocabulary** Glossary in the back of the book.

LESSON 3.1

Average Monthly Expenditures

Lesson Objective
Compute the average monthly expenditure.

Content Vocabulary
- recordkeeping
- expenditures
- budget sheet
- living expenses
- budget

GET READY for the Lesson

Do you think both businesses and individuals should keep track of financial records? Why or why not?

Susan Tan owns a clothing boutique. She tracks her company's monthly expenses with computer software. She files her receipts, invoices, and bills. Susan also uses this information when she prepares her company's tax returns.

As You Read

Identify List your monthly expenditures.

Recordkeeping You might write things down in order to remember them tomorrow morning or next week. Think of utilizing this same memory **device** and applying it to your money. **Recordkeeping** is a way for you to manage your money. It involves keeping track of items you spend money on, or your **expenditures**, during a period of time. The tool you use is a **budget sheet** on which you record your expenses, usually on a monthly basis. By budgeting, you can find out how you have spent your money and how much money you need for **living expenses**. These include amounts for food, utility bills, and pocket money. Record your expenditures on a notepad or computer spreadsheet on the day you make them. At the end of the day, you will have a record of what you have spent. Then at the end of the month, group them and total them. Then you can calculate your average monthly expenditure.

$$\text{Average Monthly Expenditure} = \frac{\text{Sum of Monthly Expenditures}}{\text{Number of Months}}$$

With this information, you can make a **budget**, which is a plan for using money in a way that best meets your wants and needs.

Need Help? Go to...
- Workshop 4: Adding Decimals, p. 10
- Skill 11: Dividing Decimals, p. SK12
- Application A: Formulas, p. AP1
- Application Q: Mean, p. AP12

EXAMPLE 1

Selena and Trent Miller keep records of their expenditures. See **Figure 3.1** on page 158. They want to know how much they spend each month (on the average) for various categories. Here are their records for three months. What is their average monthly electric bill?

Compute the average monthly expenditure.

$$\frac{\text{Sum of Monthly Expenditures}}{\text{Number of Months}} = \frac{\$121.47 + \$153.56 + \$125.88}{3}$$

$$= \frac{\$400.91}{3}$$

$$= \textbf{\$133.64 average monthly electric bill}$$

Figure 3.1

July		August		September	
Mortgage Loan	$ 675.00	Mortgage Loan	$ 675.00	Mortgage Loan	$ 675.00
Groceries	275.00	Electricity	153.56	Electricity	125.88
Electricity	121.47	Restaurants	119.30	Airplane ticket	352.00
Dentist	143.50	Movies	29.50	Doctor Copay	25.00
Phone/Internet	37.85	Phone/Internet	47.29	Phone/Internet	37.85
Gasoline	118.60	Groceries	319.00	Gasoline	96.74
Water/Sewer	41.45	Gasoline	123.36	Groceries	285.92
Credit Card(s)	121.74	Water/Sewer Bill	89.94	Football Game	66.00
Baseball Game	52.50	Credit Card(s)	298.65	Credit Card(s)	171.28
Gift	45.00	Gift	85.95	Water/Sewer	56.66
Clothing	151.56	Dry Cleaning	26.88	Home Repair	96.45
Car Loan	278.50	Car Loan	278.50	Car Loan	278.50
Car Repair	126.36	Home Repair	275.68	Fuel Oil	198.31
Total	$2,188.53	Total	$2,522.61	Total	$2,465.59

Reading Math + − ÷ =

Average
The word *average* means the result obtained by totaling a number of quantities and then dividing by the number of quantities that were totaled.

Use Figure 3.1 to compute the average monthly expenditure for the following. Check your answers in the back of the book.

1. Credit Card(s) **2.** Groceries **3.** Home repairs

EXAMPLE 2 Algebra

Need Help? Go to...
- **Workshop 16:** Average, p. 34
- **Workshop 36:** Using Simple Algebraic Operations, p. 74
- **Skill 5:** Adding Decimals, p. SK6
- **Application A:** Formulas, p. AP1

Rudy Timmons had a $287.80 average monthly expenditure for groceries during the first quarter of this year. He spent $312.56 in April and $235.40 in May. How much can Rudy spend in June to have the same average as in the first quarter?

Step 1: Let j = The amount Rudy spent for groceries in June.

Step 2: Write an equation using the average expenditure formula and solve.

$$\text{Average Monthly Expenditure} = \frac{\$312.56 + \$235.40 + j}{3} = \$287.80$$

Multiply both sides by 3.

$$3\left(\frac{\$312.56 + \$235.40 + j}{3}\right) = 3(\$287.80)$$

$$\$547.96 + j = \$863.40.$$

Subtract $547.96 from both sides

$$j = \mathbf{\$315.44}$$

Rudy can spend $315.44 for groceries in June.

Concept CHECK

Complete the problem. Check your answer in the back of the book.

4. Your average monthly expenditure for gasoline during the first quarter was $167.70. You spent $147.20 in April and $172.90 in May. How much can you spend in June to have the same average as in the first quarter?

Financial Planner
Financial planners use math to help their clients understand how to make wise financial decisions, such as saving for retirement. **How can planning help you have a comfortable retirement?**

Lesson Practice

Find the average monthly expenditure.

	May	June	July	Aug	Sept	Total	Average
5.	$ 640.00	$ 710.00	$ 700.00	$ 685.00	$ 705.00	a. $	b. $
6.	1,178.50	1,091.80	1,207.70	1,187.80	1,245.90	a.	b.
7.	1,789.75	1,741.36	1,707.85	1,751.63	1,811.75	a.	b.
8.	2,311.75	2,210.91	2,371.85	2,553.67	2,412.91	a.	b.
9.	112.11	97.13	106.45	121.85	a.	b.	$ 109.09
10.	23,687.12	19,871.03	20,056.90	24,510.30	a.	b.	$21,603.52

Use the records of monthly expenditures for Selena and Trent Miller in Figure 3.1 to answer the following questions.

11. What do the Millers pay each month to repay their mortgage loan?

12. Can you determine how much they save each month? Why or why not?

13. What is the Millers' average monthly expenditure for the telephone?

14. Transportation costs include car payments and costs for gasoline, repairs, and so on. What is their average monthly expenditure for transportation costs?

H.O.T. Problems

15. CHALLENGE PROBLEM Household expenses include amounts for electric bills, water and sewer bills, telephone and Internet charges, home repairs, and home fuel oil bills. What is the Millers' average monthly expenditure for all of those household expenses combined?

16. ALGEBRA The Trevor family pays its home insurance premium quarterly. After the family made some improvements on the home, their home insurance premium went up by $65.80 for the fourth quarter. If the average quarterly home insurance premium after the increase was $163.35, what was the quarterly premium before the increase?

Spiral Review

Add. (Workshop 4)

17. $716.45 + $820.97 **18.** $21.63 + $22.71 + $24.95

19. Use the Social Security tax rate of 6.2% and Medicare tax rate of 1.45% on all income to solve this problem. Sheena Carston is paid monthly. Her gross pay this month is $5,102. How much is deducted from her paycheck this month for Social Security? How much is deducted for Medicare? (Lesson 2.4)

GET READY for the Next Lesson

PREREQUISITE SKILL Dividing Decimals (Skill 11)

Divide

20. $767 ÷ 13.01 **21.** $435.78 ÷ 24.35 **22.** $16,919.43 ÷ 52.67

23. $12,401 ÷ 12.12 **24.** $2,398 ÷ 475.12 **25.** $467,985 ÷ 12.05

LESSON 3.2

Preparing a Budget Sheet

Lesson Objective
Use records of past expenditures to prepare a monthly budget sheet.

Content Vocabulary
- fixed expenses
- annual expenses

GET READY for the Lesson

Do you have a monthly budget?

David Beran is not sure where all of his money goes. David's friend suggests that he make a monthly budget.

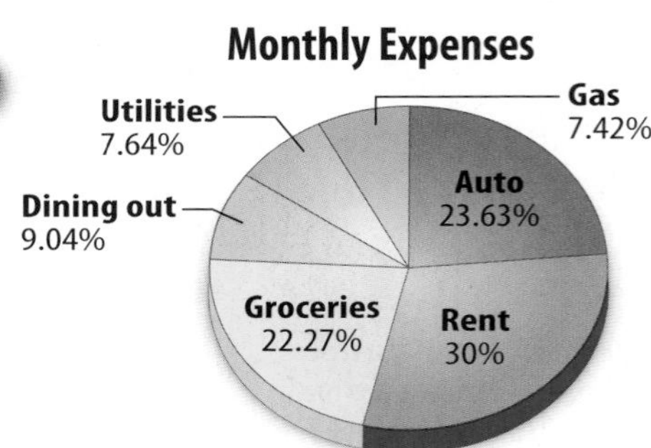

As You Read
Identify How do you compute total monthly expenses?

Monthly Expenses You can use records of your past expenditures to prepare a budget sheet outlining your total monthly expenses. You will want to calculate your living expenses. These include amounts for food, utility bills, and pocket money. They will **vary** from month to month. Other expenses, such as rent, are more fixed. These are called **fixed expenses** because they *do not* vary from one month to the next. Also remember to consider any **annual expenses**, such as real estate taxes, which occur only once a year.

$$\text{Total Monthly Expenses} = \text{Monthly Living Expenses} + \text{Monthly Fixed Expenses} + \text{Monthly Share of Annual Expenses}$$

$$\text{Monthly Share of Annual Expenses} = \frac{\text{Annual Expenses}}{12}$$

Need Help? Go to...
- **Skill 3:** Adding Numbers, p. SK4
- **Skill 5:** Adding Decimals, p. SK6
- **Skill 11:** Dividing Decimals, p. SK12
- **Application A:** Formulas, p. AP1

EXAMPLE

The Millers use records of their past expenditures to complete the budget sheet in **Figure 3.2**. After calculating their monthly share of annual expenses, find their total monthly expenses.

Step 1: Find the monthly share of annual expenses.

$$\text{Monthly Share of Annual Expenses} = \frac{\$3{,}759.00}{12} = \mathbf{\$313.25}$$

Step 2: Find the total monthly expenses.

$$= \text{Monthly Living Expenses} + \text{Monthly Fixed Expenses} + \text{Monthly Share of Annual Expenses}$$

$$= \$1{,}089.00 + \$1{,}078.00 + \$313.25$$

$$= \mathbf{\$2{,}480.25 \text{ total monthly expenses}}$$

Study Tip

Reading Word Problems
Read questions carefully. Be certain that you understand what they ask.

Concept CHECK

Calculate the monthly share of annual expenses and find the total monthly expenses. Check your answers in the back of the book.

1. Annual, $4,200; Living, $670; Fixed, $800
2. Annual, $3,494.04; Living, $475.75; fixed, $679.65

Figure 3.2

A Money Manager for Selena and Trent Miller		Date 10/1/20—	
Monthly Living Expenses		**Monthly Fixed Expenses**	
Food/Groceries	$ 275.00	Rent/Mortgage Loan	$ 675.00
Household Expenses		Car Loan	278.00
Electricity	70.00	Savings	125.00
Heating	65.00	**Total**	**$1,078.00**
Phone/Internet/Cable	95.00	**Annual Expenses**	
Water	12.00	Life Insurance	$ 575.00
		Home/Renter's Insurance	840.00
Transportation		Car Insurance	475.00
Gasoline/Oil	115.00	Real Estate/Property Taxes	1,215.00
Parking		Car Registration	54.00
Tolls		Charitable Contributions	600.00
Personal Spending		**Total**	**$3,759.00**
Clothing	70.00	**Monthly Share (Divide by 12)**	**$ 313.25**
Credit Card(s)	110.00	**Monthly Balance Sheet**	
Newspaper, Gifts, etc.	45.00	Net Income (Total Budget)	$
Pocket Money	57.00		
Entertainment		Living Expenses	1,089.00
Movie/Theater	35.00	Fixed Expenses	1,078.00
Sporting Events	65.00	Annual Expenses	313.25
Dining Out	75.00	**Total Monthly Expenses**	$ ______
Total	**$1,089.00**	**Balance**	$ ______

GRAPHING CALCULATOR LAB

Summing a List

Using Figure 3.2, enter the Monthly Living Expenses in L1 and the Monthly Fixed Expenses in L2.

Press STAT ENTER and input the values.

Return to the home screen by pressing 2nd MODE

To sum L1, press:

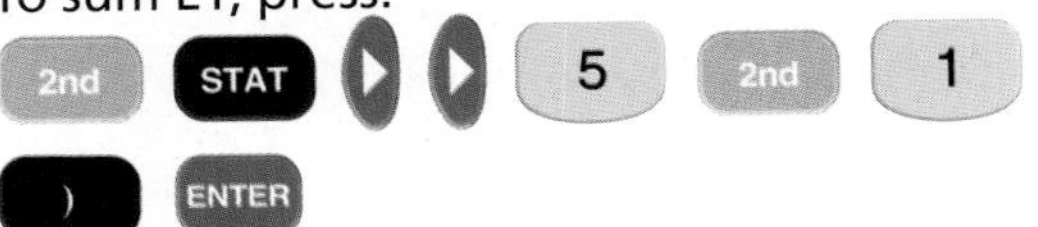

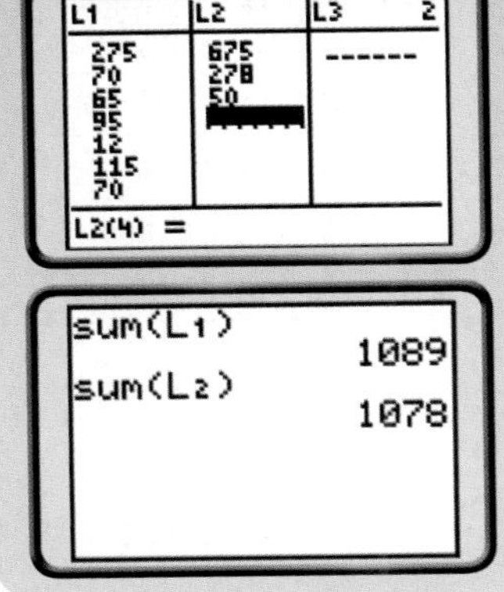

Think and Discuss

1. Describe the display of the first calculator screen.
2. Describe what is displayed on the second calculator screen.
3. Use the graphing calculator to enter the Annual Expenses in L3 and then find the sum.
4. Suppose that home insurance increases to $925 and real estate taxes increase to $1,315. What is the new sum of the Annual Expenses?
5. How does using the sum feature with a List make changing a value and calculating the new sum easier?

Lesson Practice

Diana Pender is a landscaper. Her husband, Paul, is a radio sportscaster. They completed the budget sheet shown in **Figure 3.3** using records of their past expenditures. Use the budget sheet to answer the following questions.

Figure 3.3

A Money Manager for Diana and Paul Pender		Date 4/10/20—	
Monthly Living Expenses		**Monthly Fixed Expenses**	
Food/Groceries	$290.00	Rent/Mortgage Loan	$ 625.00
Household Expenses		Car Loan	
Electricity	45.00	Installment Loans	
Heating	50.00	Appliances	
Phone/Cell	65.00	Furniture	125.00
Water	24.50	Regular Savings	200.00
Garbage/Sewer		Emergency Fund	50.00
Cable TV	95.00	**Total**	$______
Other ______		**Annual Expenses**	
Transportation		Life Insurance	$ 840.00
Gasoline/Oil	85.00	Home/Renter's Insurance	
Parking	45.00	Car Insurance	750.00
Tolls	25.00	Real Estate/Property Taxes	
Commuting		Car Registration	52.00
Other ______		Charitable Contributions	100.00
Personal Spending		Other ______	
Clothing	60.00	**Total**	$______
Credit Card(s)	50.00	**Monthly Share (Divide by 12)**	$______
Newspaper, Gifts, etc.	20.00	**Monthly Balance Sheet**	
Pocket Money	60.00	Net Income (Total Budget)	$2,600.00
Entertainment			
Movie/Theater	20.00	Living Expenses	
Sporting Events	65.00	Fixed Expenses	
Recreation	22.00	Annual Expenses	$______
Dining Out	140.00	**Total Monthly Expenses**	$______
Total	$______	**Balance**	$______

Did You Know?

Worldwide Gas Prices
U.S. gasoline prices seem high, but consumers in other nations pay much more. In some Western European countries, gas costs well over $5 per gallon. The lowest prices tend to be in leading oil-producing countries. For example, gas in Venezuela costs less than 25 cents per gallon.

3. How much are the Penders' total monthly living expenses?
4. What is the total of their monthly fixed expenses?
5. What is the total of their annual expenses?
6. What must they set aside each month for annual expenses?
7. What are their total monthly expenses?
8. Do the Penders live within their monthly net income?
9. What individual expenses would the Penders find difficult to cut back?

H.O.T. Problems

10. **WRITING IN MATH** A *want* is something for which you have a strong desire. A *need* is a physical or psychological requirement for well-being. Refer to **Figure 3.3**. Categorize the Penders' expenditures as either wants or needs.
11. **CHALLENGE PROBLEM** What percent of the Penders' total monthly net income are the monthly living expenses and fixed expenses? What is the monthly share of annual expenses? Total your three percents and analyze the result.

Spiral Review

Add. (Skill 5)

12. $75 + $45 + $53 + $68
13. $475.80 + $519.20 + $647.80

Divide and round to the nearest cent. (Skill 10)

14. $241 ÷ 4
15. $1,642.80 ÷ 3
16. Find the average monthly expenditure: January, $882; February, $924; March, $943. (Lesson 3.1)
17. Melanie Cavell's annual medical insurance costs $7,400. Her company pays 80% of the cost. How much does Melanie pay semimonthly? (Lesson 2.5)

GET READY for the Next Lesson

PREREQUISITE SKILL Subtracting Decimals (Skill 6)

Subtract.

18. $12,500.00 – $25.00
19. $144.48 – $132.89
20. $236.50 – $44.45
21. $984,088 – $98,967.52
22. $24,567.00 – $1.34
23. $1,958.96 – $67.25

Big Cheese Photo/SuperStock

LESSON 3.3

Using a Budget

Lesson Objective
Compare the amount budgeted to actual expenditures.

Content Vocabulary
- expense summary
- emergency fund

Have you ever been surprised by an unexpected expense?

Mark Simpson tried out for basketball at school and made the team. He planned to pay the sports participation fee from money he had saved working in the summer. However, he had not realized that he would also have to buy his uniform.

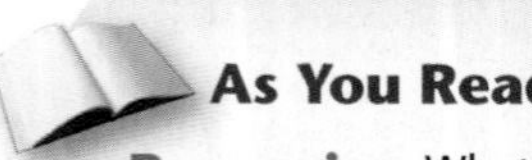

As You Read

Recognize What are some examples of unexpected expenses?

Expense Summary Once you have completed a budget sheet outlining your past expenditures, you can use it to plan for future spending. You may want to prepare a monthly **expense summary**. This report compares the amounts that you have spent to the amounts that you have budgeted. When you draft a budget, you should include an **emergency fund**. This is extra money set aside to be used for unpredictable expenses, such as medical bills and **vehicle** repairs.

Need Help? Go to...
- **Workshop 3:** Comparing Numbers, p. 8
- **Workshop 5:** Subtracting Decimals, p. 12
- **Skill 1:** Numbers, p. SK1
- **Skill 6:** Subtracting Decimals, p. SK7

EXAMPLE

Frank and Minnie Zorn have always kept accurate records of their expenditures. At the end of March, they prepared an expense summary. They had planned to spend $340 on groceries but actually spent $361.85. How much more or less did they spend on groceries than they had budgeted?

Step 1: Compare.

Is the amount spent more or less than the amount budgeted?

Is $361.85 more or less than $340.00?

Step 2: Find the difference.

$361.85 − $340.00 = **$21.85 more than the amount budgeted**

Concept CHECK

Complete the problems to find how much more or less the amount spent is than the amount budgeted. Check your answers in the back of the book.

1. Zoe and Douglas Hamilton budgeted $167.80 and spent $158.90.
2. Millie Bradley budgeted $647.50 and spent $671.92.

Hero/Corbis/Glow Images

Lesson Practice

Figure 3.4

Expense Summary for Paul and Diana Pender for the Month of July 20—			
Expenses	**Amount Budgeted**	**Amount Spent**	**Difference**
Food/Groceries	$ 290.00	$ 302.60	a. $
Household Expenses			
Electricity	45.00	44.35	b.
Heating	80.00	0.00	c.
Cell Phone	35.00	35.00	d.
Water	24.50	31.70	e.
Cable/Internet	95.00	95.00	f.
Transportation			
Gasoline/Oil	85.00	101.70	g.
Parking/Tolls	70.00	50.00	h.
Personal			
Clothing	60.00	31.75	i.
Credit Card(s)	50.00	60.00	j.
Pocket Money	80.00	93.75	k.
Entertainment			
Movies/Theater	20.00	35.00	l.
Sporting Events	65.00	32.00	m.
Recreation	22.00	63.80	n.
Dining Out	140.00	158.40	o.
Fixed			
Rent/Mortgage	625.00	625.00	p.
Furniture	125.00	125.00	q.
Savings	250.00	150.00	r.
Contributions	8.33	8.33	s.

Did You Know?

International Cell Phone Use **At one time, the United States was the world leader in per capita cell phone subscribers. In the 21st century, however, cell phone use has grown dramatically in Western Europe. Experts predict the region will soon have more cellular subscriptions than people.**

For problems 3 to 10, use the Penders' expense summary in Figure 3.4 to answer the following questions.

3. Determine for all categories how much more or less the amount spent is than the amount budgeted.
4. Which expenses for the month had a negative variance (were more than the amount budgeted)?
5. How much more or less did the Penders spend for all fixed expenses than the amount budgeted?
6. How much more or less did the Penders budget for transportation costs than they spent on transportation?
7. Which personal expenses did the Penders spend more on than they had budgeted?

Need Help? Go to...

- Skill 1: Numbers, p. SK1
- Application C: Tables and Charts, p. AP3
- Workshop 38: Problem Solving Strategies: Writing an Equation, p. 78

8. How much more or less were their total personal expenditures for the month than the amount budgeted?

9. How much more or less were their total entertainment expenditures for the month than the amount budgeted?

10. How much more or less were the Penders' total expenditures for the month of July than the amount they had budgeted?

11. Your total monthly expenditure will vary from month to month. During the winter months, your home heating bills may push your total monthly expenditure over the amount budgeted. In some months, spending will be less. Name some other factors that might affect your spending for specific months.

12. WRITING IN MATH Some expenditures depend on your choice or judgment. This is often referred to as *discretionary expenses*. Write a paragraph that explains what individual discretionary expenses you would consider easier to cut than others.

13. WRITING IN MATH Do you think everyone should have a budget and track monthly his or her expenditures? Write a paragraph explaining why or why not.

Spiral Review

Identify which number is higher. (Skill 1)

14. \$174.85 or \$159.94

15. \$35 or \$37.19

Reading Math

Subtraction

Terms such as *less than* and *difference* indicate that subtraction is the operation you need to use.

Subtract. (Skill 6)

16. \$47.50 – \$43.86

17. \$171.84 – \$165.00

18. Connie Thorsen has annual gross pay of \$32,000 and exemptions totaling \$4,000. If the state tax rate is 3%, how much state tax is withheld from her salary weekly? (Lesson 2.2)

19. Steve Davis earns a 6% commission on sales of \$3,714. What is his commission? (Lesson 1.6)

GET READY for the Next Lesson

PREREQUISITE SKILL Adding Decimals (Skill 5)

20. 0.78 + 0.567

21. \$1.46 + \$12.23

22. 4.067 + 73.1023

23. \$5.89 + \$0.95

24. 43.604 + 72.603

25. \$63.879 + \$556.090

CHAPTER 3

Review and Assessment

AFTER YOU READ

Chapter SUMMARY

Wise money management requires keeping track of the money you spend. This includes using records of past expenditures to prepare a monthly budget sheet and computing average monthly expenditure. Then compare the amount budgeted to actual expenditures.

Vocabulary Check

1. On a sheet of paper, use each of these terms in a sentence.

Content Vocabulary

- recordkeeping (p. 157)
- expenditures (p. 157)
- budget sheet (p. 157)
- living expenses (p. 157)
- budget (p. 157)
- fixed expenses (p. 160)
- annual expenses (p. 160)
- expense summary (p. 164)
- emergency fund (p. 164)

Academic Vocabulary

- device (p. 157)
- vary (p. 160)
- vehicle (p. 164)

Concept Check

2. Explain the purpose of a budget.
3. List your current living expenses.
4. Give the formula for computing average monthly expenditure.
5. Differentiate between living expenses, fixed expenses, and annual expenses.
6. Explain the purpose of an expense summary.
7. List common fixed expenses and annual expenses.
8. Explain the difference between amount budgeted and actual expenditures.
9. **CRITICAL THINKING** Explain the purpose of having an emergency fund in your budget.

Lesson-by-Lesson Review

3.1 Average Monthly Expenditures (pp. 157–159)

Compute the average monthly expenditure.
Dewan Burris keeps records of his living expenses. Total monthly expenses for January, February, and March were $1,341.29, $1,438.77, and $1,399.11, respectively. What was his average monthly expenditure?

Compute the average monthly expenditure.

$$\text{Average Monthly Expenditure} = \frac{\text{Sum of Monthly Expenditures}}{\text{Number of Months}}$$

$$\frac{\$1{,}341.29 + \$1{,}438.77 + \$1{,}399.11}{3} = \mathbf{\$1{,}393.06}$$

Review Exercises

Find the average monthly expenditure.

10. Sabrina West has been keeping track of her parents' living expenses. The total monthly expenses for June, July, August, and September were $2,334.09, $2,567.33, $3,451.96, and $1,988.78, respectively.
11. The recent electric bills for the Cox family were as follows: September, $87.55; October, $97.34; November, $100.44; and December, $156.88.
12. Charlotte Grady's average monthly expenditure for groceries the first quarter this year was $297.80. She spent $212.56 in April and $435.40 in May. How much can she spend in June to have the same average as she did in the first quarter?

3.2 Preparing a Budget Sheet (pp. 160–163)

Use records of past expenditures to prepare a monthly budget sheet.
Use the budget sheet in Figure 3.5 to answer the following questions.

Step 1: Find the total monthly expenses.
Monthly Living Expenses + Monthly Fixed Expenses + Monthly Share of Annual Expenses

Step 2: Find the total of Kevin Berstein's monthly living expenses.
Add all items in first column under Monthly Living Expenses.
Total = $1,433.00

Step 3: Find the total of his monthly fixed expenses.
Add.
$1,160.00 + $235.00 + $200.00 + $150.00 = $1,745.00 monthly fixed expenses

Step 4: Find the total of his annual expenses.
Add.
$875.00 + $960.00 + $995.00 + $674.00 + $76.75 + $120.00 = $3,700.75 total annual expenses

Lesson-by-Lesson Review (continued)

Step 5: Find the total amount he must set aside each month for his annual expenses.
Divide.
$$\frac{\$3{,}700.75}{12} = \$308.40 \text{ set aside monthly}$$

Step 6: Find the total of his monthly expenses.
Add
$1,433.00 + $1,745.00 + $308.40 = $3,486.40 total monthly expenses

Step 7: Find whether Kevin lives within his monthly net income.
Subtract.
$3,650.00 − $3,486.40 = $163.60; yes

Step 8: Find the individual expenses that would be difficult for Kevin to cut.
Analyze.
All annual expenses, mortgage, car loan, electricity, and heating fuel would be difficult to cut. He could cut his charitable contributions and some monthly living expenses.

Figure 3.5

A Money Manager for Kevin Berstein		For the Month of October 20--	
Monthly Living Expenses		**Monthly Fixed Expenses**	
Food/Groceries	$ 350.61	Rent/Mortgage Loan	$ 1,160.00
Household Expenses		Car Loan	235.00
Electricity	89.68	Regular Savings	200.00
Heating	67.82	Emergency Fund	150.00
Phone	45.72	**Total**	**$1,745.00**
Water	11.00	**Annual Expenses**	
Cable TV	79.95	Life Insurance	$ 875.00
Transportation		Home/Renter's Insurance	960.00
Gasoline/Oil	95.80	Car Insurance	995.00
Parking	70.50	Real Estate/Property Taxes	674.00
Tolls	18.00	Car Registration	76.75
Commuting	60.00	Charitable Contributions	120.00
Miscellaneous	24.88	**Total**	**$3,700.75**
Personal Spending		**Monthly Share (Divide by 12)**	$ 308.40
Clothing	98.24	**Monthly Balance Sheet**	
Credit Card(s)	155.00	Net Income (Total Budget)	**$3,650.00**
Newspaper	20.12		
Pocket Money	115.00	Living Expenses	**1,433.00**
Entertainment		Fixed Expenses	**1,745.00**
Movie/Theater	55.00	Annual Expenses	**308.40**
Dining Out	75.68	**Total Monthly Expenses**	**$3,486.40**
Total	**$1,433.00**	**Balance**	**$ 163.60**

Lesson-by-Lesson Review (continued)

Review Exercises

Use the budget sheet in Figure 3.6 for Leslie Wang to answer the following questions.

13. What are Leslie's total monthly living expenses?

14. What are her total monthly fixed expenses?

15. What must Leslie set aside each month for annual expenses?

16. What is her total monthly expenditure?

17. Is Leslie able to live within her monthly net income of $2,350?

Figure 3.6

A Money Manager for ___Leslie Wang___		For the Month of February 20--	
Monthly Living Expenses		**Monthly Fixed Expenses**	
Food/Groceries	$230.65	Rent/Mortgage Loan	$ 660.00
Household Expenses		Car Loan	185.00
Electricity	75.67	Regular Savings	100.00
Heating	34.55	Emergency Fund	50.00
Phone	38.76	**Total**	$_______
Water	12.30	**Annual Expenses**	
Cable TV	88.00	Life Insurance	$ 675.00
Transportation		Home/Renter's Insurance	360.00
Gasoline/Oil	152.33	Car Insurance	895.00
Parking	60.00	Car Registration	56.75
Personal Spending		Charitable Contributions	100.00
Clothing	58.00	**Total**	$_______
Credit Card(s)	128.00	**Monthly Share (Divide by 12)**	$_______
Newspaper	45.34	**Monthly Balance Sheet**	
Pocket Money	85.00	Net Income (Total Budget)	$ 2,350.00
Entertainment			
Movie/Theater	45.00	Living Expenses	$_______
Sporting Events	65.00	Fixed Expenses	$_______
Recreation	32.00	Annual Expenses	$_______
Dining Out	135.70	**Total Monthly Expenses**	$_______
Total	$_____	**Balance**	$_______

Lesson-by-Lesson Review (continued)

3.3 Using a Budget (pp. 164–166)

Compare the amount budgeted to actual expenditures.
Oscar and Angela Vasquez kept accurate records of their expenditures. Compare the amount budgeted to the amount spent. (You will find the rest of the example and accompanying problems on page 172.)

Expenses	Amount Budgeted	Actual Amount Spent
Food/Groceries	$235.00	$261.38
Household		
Electric	48.48	51.29
Phone	65.90	59.88
Heating	46.77	60.10
Water	12.30	12.30
Garbage/Sewer	21.90	19.85
Security	19.95	21.95
Transportation		
Gasoline	68.00	87.00
Parking/Misc.	75.00	60.80
Personal Spending		
Clothing	125.00	73.89
Credit Card(s)	50.00	50.00
Newspapers/Gifts	45.00	39.85
Pocket Money	60.00	75.12
Entertainment		
Movies/Theater	30.00	22.50
Sports Events	35.00	38.00
Dining Out	75.00	82.35
Fixed		
Rent/Mortgage Loan	859.00	859.00
Car Loan	185.23	185.23
Savings	125.00	125.00
Life/Home/Car Insurance	186.50	186.50
Real Estate/Property Taxes	93.45	93.45
Car Registration	5.41	0.00
Contributions	40.00	40.00

Lesson-by-Lesson Review (continued)

Step 1: Find expenses for the month that were more than the amount Oscar and Angela budgeted.

Think critically. Compare and contrast.

Expenses: Food, Electric, Heating, Security, Gasoline, Pocket Money, Sports Events, and Dining Out.

Step 2: Find by how much more or less than the amount budgeted for the month's household expenses did Oscar and Angela spend.

Find the amounts. Compare.

Household expenses budgeted = \$215.30

Actual household expenses = \$225.37

Find the difference.

\$225.37 − \$215.30 = \$10.07

They spent more than the amount budgeted by \$10.07.

Review Exercises

18. Which transportation expense was more than the amount budgeted?
19. How much more or less did Oscar and Angela spend for personal expenses than they budgeted?
20. Were their total entertainment expenditures for the month more or less than the amount budgeted?
21. Were there any monthly fixed expenses for which Oscar and Angela spent less than the amount budgeted?
22. Which personal spending expense was more than the amount budgeted?
23. How much more or less did Oscar and Angela spend for fixed expenses than they budgeted? Explain the discrepancy.
24. Were their transportation expenditures for the month more or less than the amount budgeted?
25. Were there any entertainment expenses for which Oscar and Angela spent less than the amount budgeted?
26. What was the Vasquez's total expenditure for the month? By how much was this amount more or less than the amount they had budgeted?

Practice Test

Record your answers on a sheet of paper.

Use the following table to answer Problems 1–3.

Expenditures for the Month of June		
Expenses	**Amount Budgeted**	**Actual Amount Spent**
Food	$180.00	$150.50
Utilities	223.75	245.85
Entertainment	120.00	150.00
Rent	585.00	585.00

1. Which category is on budget?
A utilities **B** food and entertainment
C rent **D** rent and food

2. Which category is over budget?
A entertainment **B** rent and utilities
C food **D** entertainment and utilities

3. How much more or less was spent on food during June?
A $30.00 more **B** $30.00 less
C $29.50 more **D** $29.50 less

4. Cliff Alsworth spent $369.75 for utilities in April, $330.90 for utilities in May, and $297.00 for utilities in June. What was Cliff's average monthly expenditure for utilities for those three months?
A $330.90 **B** $332.55
C $997.65 **D** $327.80

5. How much should Tabatha Lange budget monthly for insurance that costs $956.89 for the entire year?
A $79.74 **B** $159.48
C $350.40 **D** $956.89

6. How much over budget would Jonah Mason be if he spends $650.75 for something that he had budgeted at $485.00?
A $650.75 **B** $165.75
C $1,135.75 **D** $485.00

7. If Amelia Townsend spent $5,695 over 3 months, what is her average monthly expenditure?
A $1,898.33 **B** $17,085.00
C $2,000.00 **D** $1,993.06

8. If Thad Reed's average monthly expenditure for 4 months is $2,303.50, what is the total of his expenditures for that period?
A $575.85 **B** $9,214.00
C $12,545.50 **D** $685.75

9. If Peter Gower paid $650 for rent monthly for an entire year, how much should he budget for rent each month?
A $108.33 **B** $54.17
C $7,800 **D** $650

10. When Sao Welna bundled his phone, Internet, and cable service, his monthly charge went from $145.84 to $99.99. How much will Sao save in a year with this new service compared to his old service?
A $1,199.88 **B** $1,750.08
C $550.20 **D** $45.85

11. How much should Teddy Perkins budget monthly for an annual expenditure that costs $614.66?

12. 12 × $680.75

13. $5,980 ÷ 12

14. ($4,568.95 + $568) ÷ 6

15. $675 − $555

16. $93,100 ÷ ($2,310 + $630)

17. ($420 + $6,700 + $2,233) ÷ 12

Standardized Test Practice

Cumulative, Chapters 1–3

PART 1 Multiple Choice

Record your answers on the answer sheet provided by your teacher or on a sheet of paper.

1. Janice Martinelli's insurance costs $1,245 a year. How much should she budget for insurance each month?
   A $1,245 **B** $103.75
   C $107.35 **D** $240.55

If the wages are—		And the number of withholding allowances claimed is—				
At least	But less than	0	1	2	3	4
		The amount of income tax to be withheld is—				
$500	$510	$61	$51	$41	$32	$22
510	520	62	53	43	33	23
520	530	64	54	44	35	25
530	540	65	56	46	36	26
540	550	67	57	47	38	28

2. Using the table above, how much is withheld from Norris Houston's wages of $505 if no allowances are claimed?
   A $44 **B** $61
   C $46 **D** $64

3. Marcus Hatfield earns an annual salary of $43,500 working for a natural history museum. He is single, and his exemptions total $2,000. He pays $954.50 in state taxes each year. What is the tax rate for his state?
   A 2.19% **B** 2.30%
   C 4.77% **D** 3.05%

TEST-TAKING TIP

Reading Comprehension Do not read the passage first when completing reading comprehension questions; start by reading the questions first.

4. Cecelia Nutt's weekly pay is $420. If the state tax rate is 5.4%, how much is deducted for state taxes each week?
   A $250.55 **B** $54.00
   C $22.68 **D** $122.68

5. Bart Rice budgeted $285.75 each month for utilities. His utility bills this month were $130.50 for electric, and $240.50 for gas. How much over budget is he?
   A $341.00 **B** $85.25
   C $75.85 **D** $65.00

6. Belinda Weedman's company pays 70% of her health insurance premiums. If she pays $60 a month, what is the total cost of her insurance each month?
   A $200 **B** $600
   C $130 **D** $140

PART 2 Short Response/Griddable

7. Clarice Sloan is a shift supervisor for Ace Tomato Inc. She is paid monthly with FIT deductions of $102, SIT of 3.2% of gross, and CIT of 1.8% of gross. Her monthly net pay is $3,804.33. What is her monthly gross pay?

PART 3 Extended Response

Show your work.

8. For 6 consecutive months, Tyrone Donnelly maintained a record of what he spent each month on food and groceries. He spent $302 the first month, $287 each for the next two months, $292 for the next month, $297 for the next month, and $287 for the last month. **(a)** Based on those expenditures, how much should Tyrone budget monthly for food and groceries? **(b)** Give one suggestion for cutting grocery costs.

Building Academic Skills

Mathematics

To go on a school trip, you need to save $850. You baby-sit about 7 hours each week for $10 per hour. You spend about $50 a week on variable expenses. Your monthly fixed expenses are $55. Write a short paragraph describing one way you can save $850 in 6 months.

English Language Arts/Writing

Think about the reasons that you might want to save money. Do you have a short-term goal for savings, such as a school trip or music downloads? Do you have long-term goals, such as a car, college expenses, or your own apartment? Write a list of reasons for including savings in your budget.

Science

Many careers may involve paying attention to patterns. Careers in biology may involve working with DNA. DNA is made up of four molecules: Adenine (A), Guanine (G), Cytosine (C), and Thymine (T). These molecules line up across from each other, much like a zipper: A always lines up across from T, and G always lines up across from C. For example:

```
Strand 1:  A C G T C A G G T
           | | | | | | | | |
Strand 2:  T G C A G T C C A
```

You are given the following strand of DNA. Can you figure out the second strand?

```
Strand 1:  A G C T A C
           | | | | | |
Strand 2:  ? ? ? ? ? ?
```

Fancy Collection/SuperStock

Building Real-World Skills

Career WISE

Bookkeeper While accountants design and maintain the overall system of record-keeping that runs a business, the bookkeeper is charged with the day-to-day maintenance of that system — managing the checkbooks, updating customer payments, disbursing cash to vendors and employees, and providing statements to the accountant. They must stay up to date on changes in bookkeeping, accounting, and tax.

Research and Share:

a. Find the Web site of the American Institute of Professional Bookkeepers, and find the name of their certification program. Visit the Web site of the U.S. Department of Labor's Bureau of Labor Statistics, and locate the median salary for a bookkeeper.

b. What is the name of the AIPB's certification program? What is the median salary for a bookkeeper?

Tech TRENDS

Direct Deposit For many employees, the days of getting a paycheck and taking it to the bank are long gone. Many employers use direct deposit by which they place a worker's pay directly into her or his bank account. To set up direct deposit, the worker usually has to provide his or her bank account number and the bank's routing number to the employer. The worker may supply the employer with a voided check or deposit slip. With this, the payroll clerk is able to deposit money into the worker's account.

Discuss and Write:

a. Discuss with a partner why you think businesses are willing to offer direct deposit to employees.

b. List three benefits direct deposit offers to workers. Would you like to have direct deposit? Why or why not?

Checking Accounts

Big Idea

A checking account enables you to spend money without having to carry cash.

Explore the Photo

Check It Out

When you receive a paycheck, you may want to have a checking account. *Do you have a checking account?*

Purestock/SuperStock

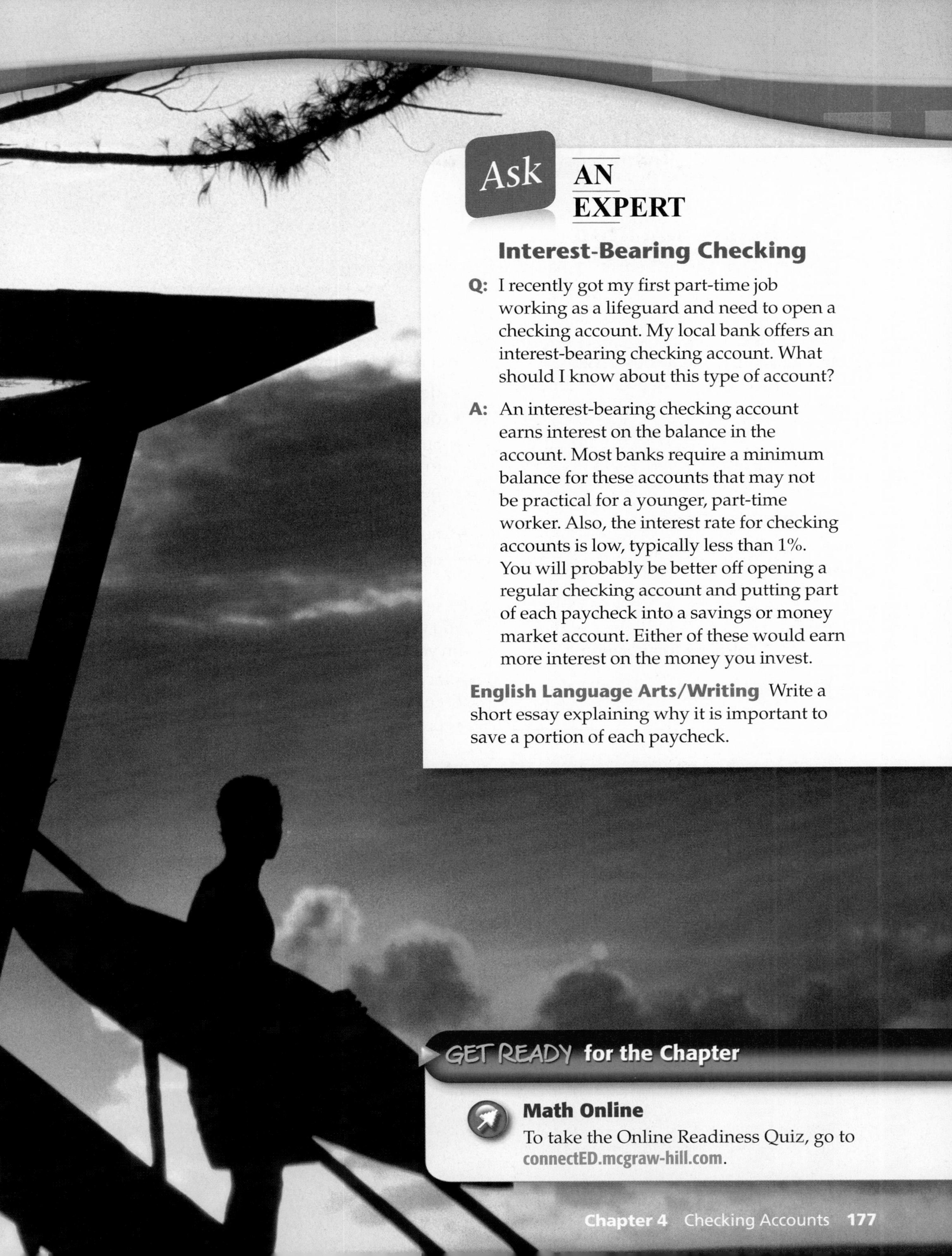

Ask AN EXPERT

Interest-Bearing Checking

Q: I recently got my first part-time job working as a lifeguard and need to open a checking account. My local bank offers an interest-bearing checking account. What should I know about this type of account?

A: An interest-bearing checking account earns interest on the balance in the account. Most banks require a minimum balance for these accounts that may not be practical for a younger, part-time worker. Also, the interest rate for checking accounts is low, typically less than 1%. You will probably be better off opening a regular checking account and putting part of each paycheck into a savings or money market account. Either of these would earn more interest on the money you invest.

English Language Arts/Writing Write a short essay explaining why it is important to save a portion of each paycheck.

GET READY for the Chapter

Math Online
To take the Online Readiness Quiz, go to **connectED.mcgraw-hill.com**.

Chapter 4 Checking Accounts

Reading Guide

Before You Read

Predict What are the benefits of having a checking account?

Main Idea

Most individuals and all businesses use checking accounts for depositing currency and checks and for writing checks to pay expenses. A checking account is a safe place to hold money, and its records provide information for tracking expenses.

Graphic Organizer

Before you read this chapter, draw a diagram like the one below. As you read, write the formula for calculating total deposit.

Calculate Total Deposit

Total deposit = (+   +   ) − ______

Math Online Go to connectED.mcgraw-hill.com to download this graphic organizer.

Content Vocabulary

You will learn these key terms in this chapter.

- deposit
- direct deposit
- automated teller machine (ATM)
- personal identification number (PIN)
- checking account
- check
- check register
- balance
- bank statement
- service charge
- reconcile
- online banking

Academic Vocabulary

You will see these words in your reading and on your tests.

- access
- currency
- previous
- transfer
- coincide
- monitor

You can find vocabulary definitions in the **Content Vocabulary** Glossary and the **Academic Vocabulary** Glossary in the back of the book.

Deposits

Lesson Objective
Compute the total checking account deposit.

Content Vocabulary
- deposit
- direct deposit
- automated teller machine (ATM)
- personal identification number (PIN)

GET READY for the Lesson

How do you think most people receive their pay from their employer?

Leslie Doyle has her employer deposit her paycheck directly into her checking account at the bank. She finds this more convenient than having to go to the bank to deposit a paper check.

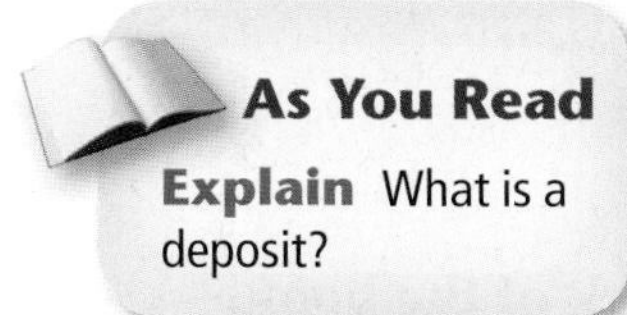

As You Read

Explain What is a deposit?

Depositing Money A **deposit** consists of checks, currency, or coins put into a bank account. The phrase "For Deposit Only" and the account number should be written on the back of the check. This ensures the check cannot be cashed by someone else if it is lost or stolen. Your employer can also make a **direct deposit** of your check. This is a deposit electronically transferred from your employer's checking account to your checking account.

Another way to make a deposit is to use an **automated teller machine (ATM)**, which performs basic banking functions (such as handling check deposits or issuing cash withdrawals). To use an ATM, you will need an ATM card and a **personal identification number (PIN)**. The card allows you to **access** your bank account and deposit your check into the machine.

Business owners should always deposit all of the money received in order to establish what accountants call a "money trail." They should always deposit all of the money received—currency, coin, and checks—and then separately withdraw cash for the business.

Total Deposit = (Currency + Coins + Checks) − Cash Received

Need Help? Go to...
- Skill 5: Adding Decimals, p. SK6
- Skill 6: Subtracting Decimals, p. SK7

EXAMPLE 1

Manuel Romeo is making a deposit to his checking account. He has checks for $435.20, $271.19, and $327.96. His cash consists of 15 one-dollar bills, 7 five-dollar bills, 3 ten-dollar bills, 24 quarters, 5 dimes, 15 nickels, and 14 pennies. He also withdraws $75.00 in cash. What is his total deposit? See **Figure 4.1** on p. 180 for his deposit slip.

Continued on next page

Compute the total deposit

$$\text{Currency Deposit} = \$15.00 + (\$7.00 \times \$5.00) + (\$3.00 \times \$10.00)$$
$$= \$15.00 + \$35.00 + \$30.00$$
$$= \$80.00$$
$$\text{Coins Deposit} = (24 \times \$0.25) + (5 \times \$0.10) + (15 \times \$0.05) + \$0.14$$
$$= \$6.00 + \$0.50 + \$0.75 + \$0.14 = \$7.39$$
$$\text{Total Deposit} = (\$80.00 + \$7.39 + \$435.20 + \$271.19 + \$327.96) - \$75.00$$
$$= \$1{,}121.74 - \$75.00 = \mathbf{\$1{,}046.74}$$

Figure 4.1

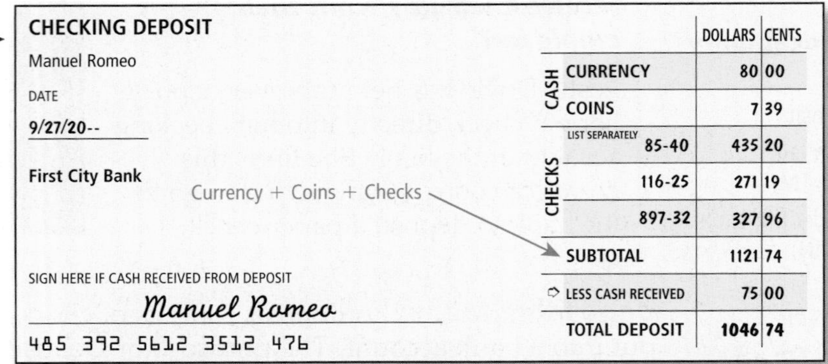

CHECKING DEPOSIT

Manuel Romeo

DATE 9/27/20--

First City Bank

SIGN HERE IF CASH RECEIVED FROM DEPOSIT Manuel Romeo

485 392 5612 3512 476

		DOLLARS	CENTS
CASH	CURRENCY	80	00
	COINS	7	39
CHECKS (LIST SEPARATELY)	85-40	435	20
	116-25	271	19
	897-32	327	96
	SUBTOTAL	1121	74
	LESS CASH RECEIVED	75	00
	TOTAL DEPOSIT	1046	74

Concept CHECK

Find the total deposit. Check your answers in the back of the book.

1. Emily Anderson's deposit includes two checks: \$231.09 and \$987.67; cash: 9 one-dollar bills, 9 five-dollar bills, 8 ten-dollar bills, 14 quarters, 25 dimes, 18 nickels, and 64 pennies. She received \$40.00 cash from the total amount.
2. Jacob Thomas had a deposit of two checks: \$341.79 and \$17.96; cash: 35 one-dollar bills, 17 five-dollar bills, 44 ten-dollar bills, 54 quarters, 36 dimes, 32 nickels, and 21 pennies.

Need Help? Go to...

Workshop 38: Problem-Solving Strategies: Writing an Equation, p. 78

EXAMPLE 2 Algebra

Hannah Stewart makes a deposit at an ATM and walks away with the \$100 in cash she received and the receipt for the \$986 total deposit she made. She remembers that the checks deposited totaled twice the amount of currency she had deposited. She did not deposit any coins. What amount in currency did she deposit? What amount in checks did she deposit?

Step 1: Let d = Amount she deposited in currency.

$2d$ = Amount she deposited in checks

Step 2: Use the total deposit formula and solve for d.

$$\text{Total Deposit} = (\text{Currency} + \text{Checks}) - \text{Cash Received}$$
$$\$986 = (d + 2d) - \$100$$

Add \$100 to both sides and combine like terms →
$$\$1{,}086 = 3d$$

Divide both sides by 3 →
$$\$362 = d$$

Hannah deposited \$362 in currency.

She deposited 2(\$362) = \$724 in checks.

Complete these problems. Check your answers in the back of the book.

3. Joshua Quick made a deposit to his checking account and received $50 in cash. His deposit slip shows a total deposit of $90. If Joshua deposited checks worth six times the value of the coins he deposited, how much did he deposit in **(a)** coins and **(b)** checks?
4. Larry McCoy deposited three checks to his checking account. He remembers that one of the checks was twice the amount of the smallest check and the largest check was equal in amount to the sum of the other two. If Larry received $50 in cash and had a total deposit of $355, what was the amount of each of the three checks?

Electronics Engineer

Electronics engineers design and test many items, including global positioning systems (GPS). These are popular for use in automobiles to help drivers from getting lost. **What kind of mathematics might someone use to measure signal trajectories from GPS satellites?**

Lesson Practice

Find the total deposit for Problems 5 through 19.

	Currency			Coins						
	Tens	**Fives**	**Ones**	**Half Dollars**	**Quarters**	**Dimes**	**Nickels**	**Pennies**	**Checks**	**Total**
5.	12	11	8	11	18				$ 96.23	$
6.	32	9	15	9	32				6.51	
7.	40	54	23	40	56	21	45	63	874.56	
8.	75	32	74	15	13	86	70	85	123.65	
9.	8	7	0	13	9	11	27	0	347.98	
10.	11	13	9	7	5	6	13	37	134.97	
11.	10	12	6	0	7	8	2	0	43.44	
12.	1	16	7	3	12	17	13	5	168.14	
13.	67	3	4	13	11	3	7	31	777.50	
14.	133	19	27	34	62	319	99	154	123.19	

15. Jess Norton stopped at an ATM location to deposit 2 one hundred-dollar bills and checks for $474.85 and $321.15. He received $50.00 in cash.
16. Olive Baker, Spirit club treasurer, deposits the club's receipts. She has 4 checks for $10.00 each, 12 for $7.50, and cash consisting of six 20-dollar bills, five 10-dollar bills, and 18 one-dollar bills.
17. Cyndi Winer deposits three checks for $425.22, $883.99, and $57.05. She also deposits cash of 45 one-dollar bills, 15 five-dollar bills, and 12 ten-dollar bills. The change deposited includes 28 quarters, 16 dimes, 19 nickels, and 65 pennies. She would like to receive $60.00 in cash.
18. Elias Rubio deposits three checks for $598.20, $2,274.26, and $3,248.79. His cash consists of 75 one-dollar bills, 78 five-dollar bills, 33 ten-dollar bills, 80 quarters, 32 dimes, 95 nickels, and 5 pennies. He would like to receive $40.00 in cash.

Reading Math

Dollars and Cents

Dollars and cents can be written in decimal form, such as \$4.20. Cents can also be expressed as fractions of 100, such as $\frac{20}{100}$.

19. Sarah Kelly deposits four checks for \$901.20, \$3760.26, \$655.79, and \$252.00. Her cash consists of 30 one-dollar bills, 2 two-dollar bills, 16 five-dollar bills, 119 ten-dollar bills, 6 quarters, 11 dimes, 37 nickels, and 9 pennies. She would like to receive \$325.00 in cash.

20. **ALGEBRA** Martha O'Brien made a deposit to her checking account at an ATM and received \$75 in cash. The checks deposited totaled \$50 less than twice the currency amount, and the total deposit was \$25 more than the check amount. Determine the amounts Martha deposited in checks and in currency as well as the total deposit.
21. **ALGEBRA** Ahmad Conan deposited 60 quarters, 53 dimes, 44 nickels, and 50 pennies into his checking account. The total of the checks he deposited equaled \$17 less than twice his total deposit. If Ahmad received 2 twenty-dollar bills in cash, what was his total deposit?
22. **CHALLENGE PROBLEM** You are a bank teller, and your cash drawer contains checks for \$1,548.62, \$321.05, \$87.65, \$245.10, \$100.00, \$32.22, \$12.32, \$9.90, \$4,598.00, \$765.09, and \$468.21. You have cash consisting of 12 one hundred-dollar bills, 11 fifty-dollar bills, 31 twenty-dollar bills, 17 ten-dollar bills, 45 five-dollar bills, and 36 one-dollar bills. Coins consist of 5 one-dollar pieces, 28 half dollars, 11 quarters, 22 dimes, 7 nickels, and 32 pennies. What is the total value of the drawer?
23. **WRITING IN MATH** Write a sentence that explains why a small business owner should not deposit checks, cash, and coins totaling \$55 and then receive \$55 in cash in the same transaction.

Spiral Review

Subtract. (Skill 6)

24. \$734.40 − \$75.00
25. \$619.20 − \$40.00
26. \$718.32 − \$65.00
27. Matthew Thompson's group medical insurance coverage costs \$6,340 a year. The company pays 65% of the cost. What amount does his employer deduct from his paycheck for medical insurance each month? (Lesson 2.5)
28. Find the **(a)** monthly share of annual expenses and **(b)** total monthly expenses: Annual, \$3,900; Living, \$770; Fixed, \$900. (Lesson 3.2)

GET READY for the Next Lesson

PREREQUISITE SKILL Numbers (Skill 1)

Write as numerals.

29. Twenty-three and $\frac{10}{100}$
30. Four hundred and $\frac{48}{100}$

Write in word form, with cents expressed as a fraction of a dollar.

31. \$3.45
32. \$475.86
33. \$86.66

LESSON 4.2

The Check-Writing Process

Lesson Objective
Write a check.

Content Vocabulary
- checking account
- check

GET READY for the Lesson

Do you have a checkbook?

When Kirby Dahl opened a checking account, he purchased a box of checks for paying bills.

As You Read

Connect Have you ever written a check?

Writing a Check When you open a **checking account** at a bank, you deposit checks and **currency** into the account. Then you can write checks on this account. A **check** is a paper document directing a bank to deduct money from your checking account and make a payment. Your account must contain as much money as the amount of the check you are writing so that you do not *overdraw* your account. If you overdraw, your account does not have enough funds to pay a check you wrote. A returned check is sometimes called an *overdraft*. To write checks, you need to be able to write dollar amounts in word form with the decimal portion expressed as a fraction.

Need Help? Go to...
Skill 1: Numbers, p. SK1
Workshop 1: Writing and Reading Numbers, p. 4

EXAMPLE 1

Write the amounts in word form or as a numeral.

a. $65.29 in word form is *sixty-five and* $\frac{29}{100}$ *dollars.*

b. *Twenty-three and* $\frac{42}{100}$ *dollars* as a numeral is $23.42.

Concept CHECK

Write each of the following in word form or as a numeral. Check your answers in the back of the book.

1. $26.55

2. *Thirty and* $\frac{20}{100}$ *dollars*

EXAMPLE 2

Margaret Miller is buying a gift at The Department Store on March 23, 20--. The cost of the gift is $45.78, and she pays by check. (See **Figure 4.2** on page 184.) How should she write the check?

Step 1: Write the date. (All writing should be in *pen*.)

Step 2: Write the name of the person or organization to whom payment will be made.

Step 3: Write the amount of the check as a numeral.

Step 4: Write the amount of the check in words with cents as a fraction of a dollar.

Step 5: Make a notation on the memo line to indicate the check's purpose.

Step 6: Sign the check.

Continued on next page

Figure 4.2

Margaret C. Miller — Date March 2, 20-- — 202 — 6-32/1

Pay to the order of Department Store — $ 45.78

Forty-five and 78/100 Dollars

First City Bank

Memo Kendra's Birthday — *Margaret C. Miller*

531 876 5220 2795 202

Concept CHECK

Complete the problems. Check your answers in the back of the book.

Manuel Romeo is buying a drill press at Harry's Hardware (see **Figure 4.3**). The cost is \$165.52. He is going to write a check. Answer the following questions about the check:

Figure 4.3

Manuel Romeo — Date ______ — 555 — 32-568/231

Pay to the order of Harry's Hardware — $ 165.52

______ Dollars

First City Bank

Memo ______ ______

565 851 2541 5867 555

3. To whom is the check payable?
4. How do you write the amount in word form?
5. What should be put in the memo portion?
6. Who signs the check?

Did You Know?

Home Improvement

Fixing up homes is a big business in the United States. Home improvement product sales total more than \$300 billion, according to most recent statistics. Experts say the kitchen and a room addition top the list, followed by landscaping.

Lesson Practice

Write each amount in word form as it would appear on a check.

7. \$40.40
8. \$703.00
9. \$63.74
10. \$201.09
11. \$1,327.17
12. \$47,983.39

Write each of the following as a numeral.

13. Two hundred twenty-one and $\frac{33}{100}$ dollars
14. Fifty-nine and $\frac{00}{100}$ dollars
15. One hundred and $\frac{01}{100}$ dollars
16. Eight hundred ninety-one thousand four hundred thirty-three and $\frac{89}{100}$ dollars

For Problems 17 and 18, use Figure 4.4a.

17. Jim Liebert is paying for a home repair bill in the amount of \$247.25 by check. Did he write the amount of the check as both a numeral and words correctly?
18. What is the check number Jim used to pay for his home repair bill?

Figure 4.4a

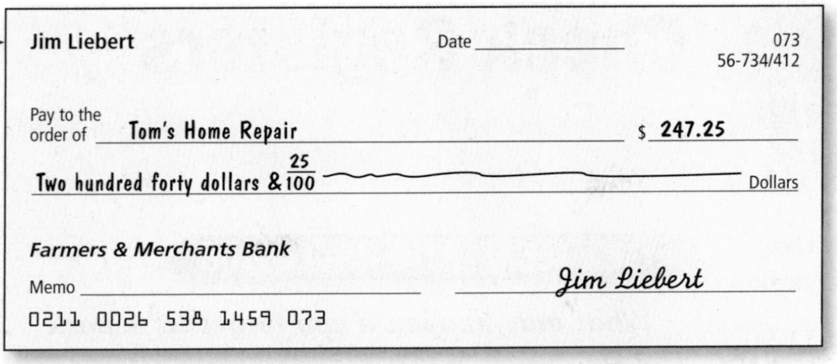

Jim Liebert Date ________ 073
56-734/412

Pay to the order of Tom's Home Repair $ 247.25

Two hundred forty dollars & 25/100 ———— Dollars

Farmers & Merchants Bank

Memo ________ *Jim Liebert*

0211 0026 538 1459 073

For Problems 19 and 20, use Figure 4.4b.

Figure 4.4b

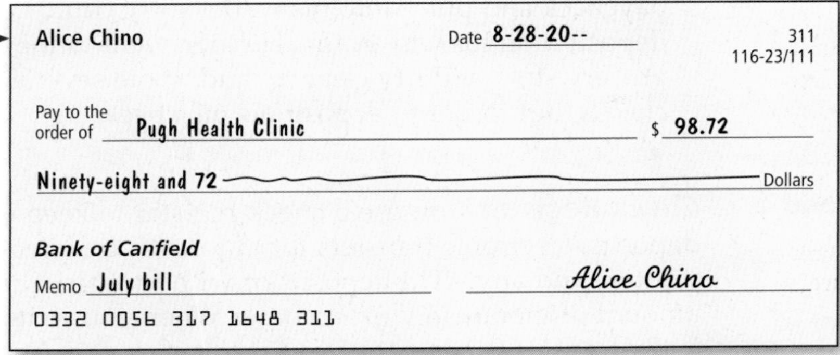

Alice Chino Date 8-28-20-- 311
116-23/111

Pay to the order of Pugh Health Clinic $ 98.72

Ninety-eight and 72 ———— Dollars

Bank of Canfield

Memo July bill *Alice Chino*

0332 0056 317 1648 311

19. Alice Chino wrote check No. 311 to Pugh Health Clinic for $98.72. Did she write the amount in words correctly? If not, write them correctly.

20. For what purpose did Alice write the check to Pugh Health Clinic?

For Problems 21 and 22, the amounts were written in word form incorrectly. Write each amount (a) as a numeral and (b) as the correct word form.

21. CHALLENGE PROBLEM *Twenty-four thousand and five hundred forty-five dollars and 43 cents.*

22. CHALLENGE PROBLEM *Nineteen million and seventeen thousand and three hundred nine dollars and 5¢.*

Spiral Review

Adding decimals. (Skill 5)

23. $456.07 + $2,000.09 + $3.52 **24.** $10,258.45 + $987.35 + $6,937.30

25. Olivia Robinson earns $12 per hour for a regular 38-hour week. Her overtime rate is 1.5 times her regular hourly rate. This week she worked her regular 38 hours plus 6 hours of overtime. What is her total pay? (Lesson 1.2)

GET READY for the Next Lesson

PREREQUISITE SKILL **Adding Decimals** (Skill 5)

Add.

26. 500.00 + 5.063 **27.** $4.48 + $13.28 **28.** 36.56 + 4.4

29. $9,323.66 + $967.52 **30.** $56.73 + $734.28 **31.** $978.96 + $7.58

LESSON 4.3

Check Registers

Lesson Objective
Calculate the balance in a check register.

Content Vocabulary
- check register
- balance

GET READY for the Lesson

What may happen if you forget to deposit a check?

Oliver Monroe, an office assistant, received his paycheck and put it into his wallet so he could deposit it on his way home. He then went to the grocery store and dry cleaners and wrote several checks, but forgot to deposit his paycheck.

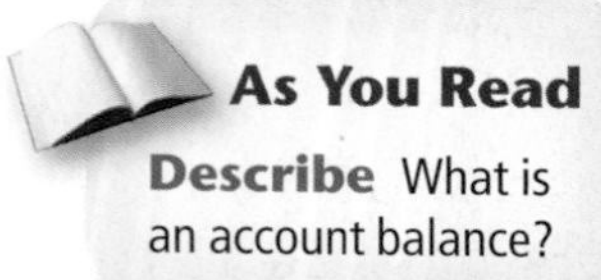

As You Read
Describe What is an account balance?

Check Register You use a **check register** to keep a record of your deposits, electronic transfers (or automatic transfers), checks you have written, and any ATM deposits or withdrawals. The **balance** is the amount of money in your account. When you write a check or electronically transfer funds out of your account, you subtract the amount from the **previous** balance. When you make a deposit, you add the amount of the deposit to the previous balance.

New Balance = Previous Balance − Check Amount − Automatic Transfers

New Balance = Previous Balance + Deposit Amount

EXAMPLE

See **Figure 4.5** for Margaret Miller's checking account. It had a balance of \$313.54. She wrote a check for \$45.78 on March 2. The bank made an automatic transfer (AT) of \$52.55 on March 5 to pay her phone bill. She made a deposit of \$240.32 on March 10. What is the new balance in Margaret's account?

Step 1: Calculate the new balance.

Figure 4.5

Trans. Type or Check No.	Date	Description of Transaction	Payment/ Debit (−)		✔	Deposit/ Credit (+)		Balance	
Previous Balance − Check Amount − Automatic Transfer						Balance Brought Forward		**313**	**54**
202	3/2	Department Store	45	78				267	76
AT	3/5	TransNation Phone	52	55				215	21
	3/10	Deposit				240	32	455	53
						Previous Balance + Deposit Amount			

Step 2: New Balance = Previous Balance − Check Amount − Automatic Transfers
\$215.21 = \$313.54 − \$45.78 − \$52.55

Step 3: New Balance = Previous Balance + Deposit Amount
\$455.53 = \$215.21 + \$240.32

OJO Images/SuperStock

Reading Math +−÷=

Bank Statements
The word *deposit* on bank statements indicates addition. The word *withdrawal* indicates subtraction.

Complete the problems. Check your answers in the back of the book.

1.

Balance	$625.39
Deposit	+ 875.80
Deposit	+ 14.27
Balance	
Amount of Check	− 953.24
Amount of Check	− 74.96
Balance	

2.

Balance	$7,357.87
Amount of Check	− 132.75
AT	− 6,544.55
Balance	
Deposit	+ 138.84
Balance	

SPREADSHEET APPLICATION

Check Registers

Part of the spreadsheet is shown below. Enter the check number, date, description, payment or deposit. The spreadsheet automatically calculates the balance.

Math Online Go to **connectED.mcgraw-hill.com** to download a spreadsheet application for this activity.

Check No.	Date	Description	Payment	Deposit	Balance
		Balance as of 3/1			

Enter the following data:
Balance as of 3/1 $250.23
Deposit on 3/4 of $1,234.78
Check 701 on 3/6 to Pettisville Grain in the amount of $134.48
Check 702 on 3/8 to Thomas Woodson for $125.00
Check 703 on 3/9 to Warsaw Schools for $30.00
Check 704 on 3/12 to Robinson, DDS for $15.25
Deposit on 3/15 of $1,234.78

Think and Discuss

1. What is the balance in the account after the deposit on 3/4?
2. What is the balance in the account after writing check 703?
3. What is the balance after the last deposit?

Lesson Practice

Find the new balance after each check or deposit.

	Check Register							
	Payment/ Debit (−)		✔	Deposit/ Credit (+)		Balance	
	Balance Brought Forward →					448	35
3.	46	92					
4.				216	84		
5.	251	55					

For Problems 6 and 7, determine the new balance.

6. Your balance was $89.75 on May 23. Your May 30 deposit was $156.90. On June 1, you wrote a $34.79 check and withdrew $50.00 from an ATM.
7. On April 4, your balance was $131.02. You wrote a check for $31.28 on April 9 and one for $45.92 on April 14. You deposited your $215.48 paycheck on April 15.
8. Mac Valent deposited his paycheck for $209.81. The check register below shows his transactions since opening his account. What is his balance after each transaction?

Did You Know?

Auto Repair Costs Doing your own repairs on your automobile can save you hundreds of dollars each year on maintenance. Labor is usually the most expensive part of an auto repair bill. Most shops charge between $60 and $90 per hour for labor.

Trans. Type or Check No.	Date	Description of Transaction	Payment/ Debit (−)		✔	Deposit/ Credit (+)		Balance	
			Balance Brought Forward →					209	81
101	8/12	Electric Cooperative	47	15				a.	
102	8/18	Sharp's Groceries	53	03				b.	
103	8/20	Gimble's Auto Repair	107	30				c.	

9. Ashley Martinez's checkbook balance was $149.21 on October 5. The check register below shows her transactions since then. What is her balance after each transaction?

Trans. Type or Check No.	Date	Description of Transaction	Payment/ Debit (−)		✔	Deposit/ Credit (+)		Balance	
			Balance Brought Forward →					149	21
571	10/6	Pettisville Flowers	45	79				a.	
	10/9	Deposit				213	80	b.	
572	10/10	Donald's Bookstore	16	94				c.	
AT	10/19	Langley Phone Co.	75	25				d.	

10. **CHALLENGE PROBLEM** Christopher Little's checking account has a beginning balance of $576.34. He wrote two checks. The first one was for $123.90. He forgot to record the second check. His current balance is $235.78. What was the amount of the second check?
11. **CHALLENGE PROBLEM** Alexis Weber wrote a check for $57.15. In her check register, she switched the first two digits and wrote $75.15. What amount should she add or subtract to correct her check register?

Spiral Review

Add or subtract. (Skill 5 and Skill 6)

12. $414.85 + $265.50
13. $845.96 + $400.00
14. $192.78 + $112.50
15. $579.23 − $212.60
16. $347.89 − $99.92
17. $3,427.80 − $635.60
18. Find Lindsay Remson's total deposit for two checks of $112.54 and $453.24 and cash of 3 one-dollar bills, 4 five-dollar bills, 7 ten-dollar bills, 15 quarters, 12 dimes, 34 nickels, and 64 pennies. Less $10.00 cash received. (Lesson 4.2)

GET READY for the Next Lesson

PREREQUISITE SKILL **Subtracting Decimals** (Skill 6)

19. 10.93 − 6.50
20. $4.29 − $0.73
21. 6.53 − 6.471

Fancy/SuperStock

LESSON 4.4

Bank Statements

Lesson Objective
Calculate the current balance on a checking account bank statement.

Content Vocabulary
- bank statement
- service charge

Why is it important to read your bank statements?

Sarah Hall's health club automatically deducts her monthly club membership fee from her checking account. She noticed on a recent bank statement that she had been charged twice for this fee. Sarah contacted the health club and they fixed the problem.

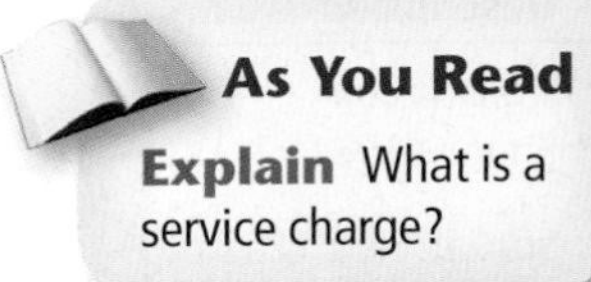

As You Read

Explain What is a service charge?

Bank Statement Your bank may send you a monthly **bank statement** for your checking account. It lists all activity in your account since your last statement including your checks that the bank has cleared and recorded. It also reports any automatic **transfers**, ATM transactions, and deposits that the bank has recorded. Instead of sending a statement by mail, the bank may send it through its Internet connection. The bank might add a **service charge**, a charge for services it rendered, to your statement. Other terms for service charge are *basic monthly charge, fee, new charge/fees, basic fee, service fee,* and *basic charge*. A service charge can be composed of individual fees for services such as making ATM withdrawals from a bank not in your bank's network and paying bills automatically.

Your account balance is determined by the formula:

$$\text{Present Balance} = \text{Previous Balance} + \text{Deposits} - \text{Withdrawals} - \text{Service Charges} + \text{Interest}$$

Need Help? Go to...
- **Workshop 4:** Adding Decimals, p. 10
- **Workshop 5:** Subtracting Decimals, p. 12
- **Skill 5:** Adding Decimals, p. SK6
- **Skill 6:** Subtracting Decimals, p. SK7

EXAMPLE 1

Margaret Miller received her bank statement for March. (See **Figure 4.6** on p. 190.) She checks the statement. Verify her present balance.

Calculate the balance in the account.

$$\text{Total Deposits} = \$240.32 + \$673.08 = \$913.40$$

$$\text{Total Withdrawals} = \$45.78 + \$137.42 + \$275.81 + \$52.55 + \$42.98 = \$554.54$$

$$\text{Balance} = \text{Previous Balance} + \text{Deposits} - \text{Withdrawals} - \text{Service Charges} + \text{Interest}$$

$$= \$313.54 + \$913.40 - \$554.54$$

$$= \mathbf{\$672.40}$$

Continued on next page

Figure 4.6

First City Bank — **Monthly Statement**

Margaret Miller
175 LaPlas Court
San Diego, California

Statement Period	Account Number
3/2 through 3/31	87652

3/1	Previous Balance	313.54
	2 Deposits	913.40
	5 Withdrawals	554.54
	Service Charge	
	Interest Earned	
4/1	Present Balance	672.40

CHECKS

Check	Date	Amount	Check	Date	Amount	Check	Date	Amount
202	3/2	45.78	203	3/12	137.42	204	3/19	275.81

DEPOSITS/CREDITS			PAYMENTS/DEBITS		
Date	Amount	Description	Date	Amount	Description
3/10	240.32	Deposit	3/5	52.55	TransNation Phone 11564
3/15	673.08	Appliance Corp. Payroll 25760	3/28	42.98	So. Cal. Elec. 11020

DAILY BALANCE

Daily Balance		Daily Balance		Daily Balance		Daily Balance	
3/1	313.54	3/5	215.21	3/12	318.11	3/19	715.38
3/2	267.76	3/10	455.53	3/15	991.19	3/28	672.40

Concept CHECK

Complete the problems. Check your answers in the back of the book.

	Previous Balance	+	Deposits	−	Withdrawals	−	Service Charges	+	Interest	=	Present Balance
1.	$290.00	+ +	$120.00 150.00	− −	$140.00 110.00	−	$2.70	+	$0.25	=	
2.	965.15	+ + +	125.54 175.98 30.20	− −	265.32 210.03	−	2.30	+	0.00	=	

Need Help? Go to...

Workshop 36: Problem Solving Strategies: Using Simple Algebraic Operations, p. 74

EXAMPLE 2 Algebra

Toby Allen received his bank statement in the mail and checked it to verify his pay increase. His employer deposits his monthly pay directly into his account. The previous month's pay was $4,176.80. Toby's account activity showed a $397.90 previous balance, checks of $3,876.90, ATM withdrawals of $200.00, and a service charge of $4.50. If Toby's new balance is $618.30, what increase in pay was direct deposited?

Let x = Increase in Toby's monthly pay direct deposited

Balance = Previous Balance + Deposits − Withdrawals − Service Charges + Interest

$\$618.30 = \$397.90 + (\$4{,}176.80 + x) - \$3{,}876.90 - \$200.00 - \$4.50$

Combine like terms. → $\$618.30 = 493.30 + x$

Subtract $493.30 from both sides. → $\$125.00 = x$

$125.00 in increased pay is direct deposited to Toby's checking account.

Reading Math +−÷=

Credits and Debits

The word *credit* implies that addition is involved. The word *debit* implies subtraction.

Concept CHECK

Complete the problem. Check your answer in the back of the book.

3. Juanita and Luis Rodriguez expected the automatic withdrawal of their fuel oil bill to be more than last month's bill of $259.85 but did not know by how much. The activity on their account showed a previous balance of $528.76, checks processed of $416.79, an automatic deposit of $400.00, and interest earned of $3.56. If their new balance was $228.58, by how much did this month's fuel oil bill exceed last month's bill?

Lesson Practice

Find the present balance for Problems 4–11.

	Previous Balance	Deposits	Withdrawals	Service Charge	Interest	Present Balance
4.	$ 40.10	$ 200.00	$ 190.00	$2.34	$ 0.00	
5.	487.67	430.75	598.17	0.00	1.38	
6.	768.89	77.76	450.00	2.50	1.27	
7.	1,200	515.65	605.13	5.00	0.00	
8.	3,079	489.41	799.99	0.00	6.26	
9.	7,345	310.25	119.00 1,768.89	4.25	11.26	
10.	1,949.07	4,201.00 750.90	319.80 289.34	4.15	0.00	
11.	9,421.99	7,509.23 1,412.46 256.40	1,397.86 1,209.32	5.60	12.47	

12. See below for a portion of Elizabeth Hallett's bank statement. Her previous balance was $271.31. What is her present balance?

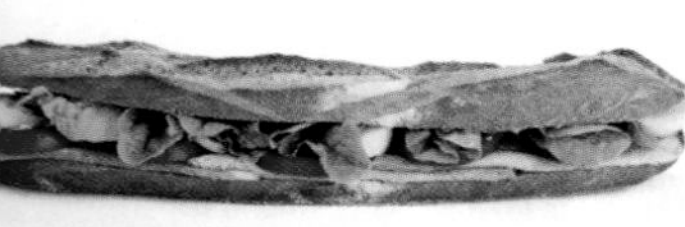

CHECKS								
Check	Date	Amount	Check	Date	Amount	Check	Date	Amount
304	6/11	19.45	305	6/15	21.02	307	6/30	95.98

DEPOSITS/CREDITS			PAYMENTS/DEBITS		
Date	Amount	Description	Date	Amount	Description
6/12	115.90	Deli Payroll 11002	6/26	25.85	Crestview Gas 11564
6/19	115.90	Deli Payroll 11012	6/28	2.00	Service Charge
6/26	345.85	Deposit			

Did You Know?

Vietnamese Deli **The word *deli* usually brings to mind pastrami and roast beef sandwiches. But a growing number of Americans prefer *bánh mì*, a Vietnamese baguette filled with thinly sliced vegetables and meat or tofu. Most Vietnamese delis sell *bánh mì* for no more than $2 to $3 per sandwich.**

13. **ALGEBRA** Adam Bassett wants to know the amount by which his service charge has increased before he receives his bank statement. In the past, the service charge has been $5.00. His previous balance was $619.83. He had $398.50 in deposits, $471.63 in withdrawals, and $2.50 in interest earned. If his present balance is $540.70, by what amount did his service charge increase?

14. **ALGEBRA** When Isabella Young received her bank statement, she noticed that her present balance was the same as her previous balance. Her deposits were $\frac{1}{2}$ her present balance, her withdrawals were $\frac{1}{3}$ her present balance, and her auto payments were $\frac{1}{4}$ her present balance. Her direct deposit was $\frac{1}{10}$ her present balance. The account had a $9.29 service charge but no interest. What is Isabella's present balance?

15. **ALGEBRA** Eli Wong noticed his present balance was three times his previous balance. His withdrawals were 95% of his previous balance, and his deposits were $1.60 less than his present balance. The interest posted to his account equaled 0.5% of his previous balance. If the service charge on his account was $5.00, what is Eli's present balance?

Spiral Review

Add or Subtract. (Skill 5 and Skill 6)

16. $346.50 + $215.50 + $35.97 **17.** $543.07 + $172.40 + $351.23

18. $915.87 – $748.42 **19.** $684.31 – $83.49

20. Wilma Adams had a balance of $412.57 in her checking account. She wrote a check for $25.36 on April 2. The bank made an automatic transfer (AT) of $55.75 on April 8 to pay her phone bill. She made a deposit of $250.45 on April 17. What is Wilma's new balance? (Lesson 4.3)

GET READY for the Next Lesson

PREREQUISITE SKILL **Subtracting Decimals** (Skill 6)

Subtract.

21. $5.83 – $4.32 **22.** $13.98 – $2.38 **23.** $35.07 – $21.93

24. $23,095.76 – $8,059.65 **25.** $9,786.99 – $7,687.09 **26.** $8,777.93 – $5,940.34

LESSON 4.5

Bank Statement Reconciliation

Lesson Objective

Reconcile a check register with a bank account statement.

Content Vocabulary

- reconcile

GET READY for the Lesson

What do you think might happen if you forget to record bank charges?

Kelly Lansbury frequently forgets to record the monthly service charges for his checking account in his check register. Kelly paid $151.49 for a surfboard, but it was $9 more than his checking account balance. This error caused him to overdraw his account.

As You Read

Summarize What does it mean to reconcile a bank statement?

Reconciling a Bank Statement When you receive your bank statement, you **reconcile** or compare it with your check register to be sure they **coincide** or agree. You may find some deposits or outstanding checks in your register that are not listed on the statement. This happens because the bank had not posted (recorded, processed, or cleared) them by the statement date. It is important for you to keep your bank account records accurate and up to date. You do not want to write a check for more money than you have in your account. If you do, you will overdraw the account and will be charged a penalty.

When comparing the check register with the bank statement the formula is:

Adjusted Balance = Statement Balance − Outstanding Checks, Payments, and/or Debits + Outstanding Deposits

Need Help? Go to...

- **Skill 5:** Adding decimals, p. SK6
- **Skill 6:** Subtracting decimals, p. SK7
- **Application A:** Formulas, p. AP1

EXAMPLE 1

Your statement balance is $598.67. You have an outstanding check for $125.44 and an outstanding debit of $235.42. You also have an outstanding deposit of $231.98. What is your adjusted balance?

Calculate the adjusted balance *(AB)*.

AB = Statement Balance − Outstanding Checks, Payments, or Debits + Outstanding Deposits

= $598.67 − ($125.44 + $235.42) + $231.98

= $598.67 − $360.86 + $231.98

= **$469.79**

Concept CHECK

Find the adjusted balance. Check your answers in the back of the book.

1. Statement balance $ 374.47
Outstanding checks −238.98
Outstanding deposits +140.00

2. Statement balance $ 772.33
Outstanding checks −283.75
Outstanding deposits +427.75

EXAMPLE 2

Margaret Miller's check register balance is $2,261.50. She compares her statement and check register. For each check and deposit listed on her statement, she places a check mark (√) next to the information in her register. She indicates that the bank paid her $0.86 in interest. Margaret finds these outstanding checks and deposits:

Check 525: $341.50 Check 527: $266.25 Deposit: $709.75

How does Margaret reconcile her statement?

Reconcile the balance.

She uses the reconciliation form on the back of her bank statement (see **Figure 4.7**) to reconcile her account.

Figure 4.7

Reconciliation Statement				
Check Register Balance	$2,261.50	**Statement Balance**		$2,160.36
Service Charges		Outstanding Checks/ Payments/Debits		
		Check 525	$341.50	
Interest	+0.86	Check 527	266.25	
		(Total outstanding checks/payments/debits)		−607.75
		Outstanding Deposits/ Credits		
		Deposit	709.75	+709.75
New Balance	$2,262.36	**Adjusted Balance**		$2,262.36

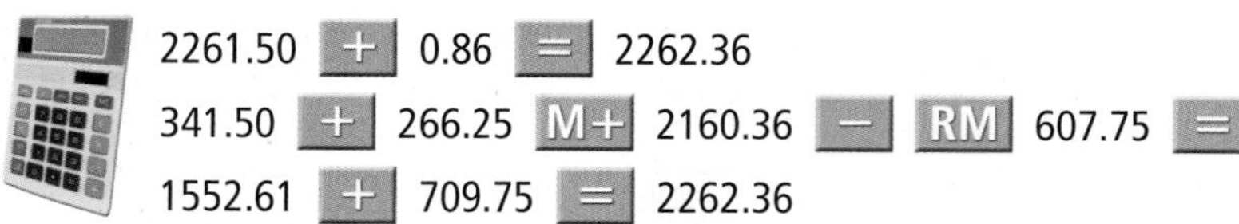

2261.50 [+] 0.86 [=] 2262.36

341.50 [+] 266.25 [M+] 2160.36 [−] [RM] 607.75 [=]

1552.61 [+] 709.75 [=] 2262.36

Concept CHECK

Complete the problem. Check your answer in the back of the book.

3. Joseph Lee's check register balance is $8,754.33. He compares his statement with his check register. He notes that the bank paid him $2.86 in interest and deducted a $1.20 service charge for bill payment. He finds these outstanding checks and deposits:

Check 845: $751.75 Check 847: $2,455.89 Deposit: $805.14.

Reconcile the statement in Figure 4.8 by filling in the information at the letters.

Figure 4.8

Reconciliation Statement				
Check Register Balance	$8,754.33	**Statement Balance**		$11,158.49
Service Charges	a.	Outstanding Checks/ Payments/Debits		
		Check 845	$ 751.75	
Interest	b.	Check 847	2,455.89	
		(Total outstanding checks/payments/debits)		d.
		Outstanding Deposits/ Credits		
		Deposit	805.14	e.
New Balance	c.	**Adjusted Balance**		f.

Did You Know?

Digital Home Phones Many U.S. households are canceling their land line telephone service and subscribing to digital phone service from cable companies.

Lesson Practice

Complete the table. Do the register and statement balances agree?

	Check Register Balance	Interest	Service Charge/ Fees	New Balance	Statement Balance	Outstanding Checks	Outstanding Deposits	Adjusted Balance
4.	$ 147.60	$ 0.00	$4.70	a.	$ 388.29	$345.39	$ 100.00	b.
5.	505.85	0.00	9.80	a.	507.21	132.90	121.74	b.

6. David Cassadore received his bank statement and canceled checks for the period ending November 20. He compared the check register (**Figure 4.9a**) with the canceled checks and deposits listed on the statement (**Figure 4.9b**). Then he placed a check mark next to the items processed. He reconciled the bank statement (**Figure 4.9c**).

(a) What total amount does David have in outstanding checks?

(b) What total amount does he have in outstanding deposits?

(c) What is his adjusted balance?

(d) What is his new check register balance?

(e) Do the register and adjusted balances agree?

Figure 4.9a

Trans. Type or Check No.	Date	Description of Transaction	Payment/ Debit (−)	✔	Deposit/ Credit (+)	Balance
			Balance Brought Forward →			389 49
047	11/03	Country Pride	47 29			342 20
	11/04	Deposit			400 00	742 20
048	11/09	General Telephone Co.	37 35			704 85
	11/15	Cash	50 00			654 85
	11/20	Deposit			191 37	846 22
049	11/20	Consumer Power Co.	44 89			801 33

Figure 4.9b

Sky Bank			Monthly Statement
David Cassadore 255 West Ash Red Lodge, Montana		**Statement Period** 10/20 through 11/20	**Account Number** 83-30283
	10/20	Previous Balance	389.49
		1 Deposit	400.00
		3 Withdrawals	134.64
		Service Charge	6.50
		Interest Earned	
	11/20	Present Balance	648.35

CHECKS

Check	Date	Amount	Check	Date	Amount	Check	Date	Amount
047	11/3	47.29	048	11/09	37.35			

DEPOSITS/CREDITS			PAYMENTS/DEBITS		
Date	**Amount**	**Description**	**Date**	**Amount**	**Description**
11/04	400.00	Deposit	11/15	50.00	ATM Cash

DAILY BALANCE

Daily Balance		Daily Balance		Daily Balance		Daily Balance	
10/20	389.49	11/04	742.20	11/15	654.85		
11/30	342.20	11/09	704.85	11/20	648.35		

Reading Math +-÷=

Banking

In banking, the word *transaction* refers to a process that has either deposited or withdrawn money, requiring addition or subtraction.

Figure 4.9c

Reconciliation Statement				
Check Register Balance	$801.33	**Statement Balance**		$648.35
Service Charges	6.50	Outstanding Checks/ Payments/Debits		
		Check 049	$ 44.89	
Interest	0.00			
		(Total outstanding checks/payments/debits)		a.
		Outstanding Deposits/ Credits		
		Deposit	191.37	b.
New Balance	d.	**Adjusted Balance**		c.

Spiral Review

Subtract. (Skill 6)

7. $412.30 − $1.25 **8.** $219.63 − $2.50 **9.** $96.78 − $3.00

10. Keith Mitchell had a previous balance of $542.34. He made deposits totaling $321.90, wrote checks totaling $533.12, and had a service charge of $5.00 and no interest. What is Keith's new balance? (Lesson 4.4)

GET READY for the Next Lesson

PREREQUISITE SKILL **Adding Decimals** (Skill 5)

Add.

11. $0.72 + $10.82 **12.** $5.78 + $30.03

13. $24.97 + $45.17 **14.** $689.77 + $356.04

15. $8,966.45 + $2,345.13 **16.** $16,454.67 + $12,785.33

LESSON 4.6

Online Banking

Lesson Objective

Compute online banking charges and update the check register.

Content Vocabulary

- online banking

GET READY for the Lesson

Do you bank online? Why or why not?

Liz Macon used to forget to record checking account transactions in her check register. Online banking allows her to keep track of her transactions.

As You Read

Identify What services does online banking offer?

Internet Banking It is 1 AM, and you need to **monitor** your bank account. You can do this by using **online banking**, or Internet banking. It allows you to bank from anywhere. Internet banking is very popular because all you need is an electronic connection to the Internet to view your account, pay bills, and transfer money around the clock (24/7).

When you bank online, you need to maintain a record of your activities in your check register. One feature of online banking is that you can download your current transactions and put the information into a computer program (such as an Excel® spreadsheet, Microsoft® Money, or Quicken®) that will contain a check register.

You may be charged for these services. See **Figure 4.10** for some online service charges.

Once you have logged onto your account at the online bank, you can:

Figure 4.10

Online Banking Service	Service Charge
Basic Monthly Charge	$ 6.95
Bill Payment—first 5 N/C	0.50
Printed Statement	4.00
Replace Lost Card	5.00
Overdraft	25.00
International Wire Transfer	20.00
ATM Transaction Charges	
Local Network	N/C
Regional Network	1.00
National Network	2.00
Out-of-Network	3.00
Cash Advance—2.00% of Amt.	$10.00 Max

- transfer funds from checking to savings or savings to checking,
- make loan payments from checking to loan accounts,
- make payments to third parties (such as utility companies),
- get information about account balances, previous deposits, previous withdrawals, and loan balances.

Remember that:

Total Service Charge = Basic Monthly Charge + Bill Payments + Statement + ATM Service Charge + Cash Advance Service Charge

Need Help? Go to...
- Workshop 18: Reading Tables and Charts, p. 38
- Workshop 30: Problem-Solving Strategy: Identifying Information, p. 62
- Application A: Formulas, p. AP1

EXAMPLE 1

Alyssa Perez uses online banking for her business, Alyssa's Personal Shopping. She pays the service charge and 7 bills, and she requests a printed statement. She also has ATM transactions, including 1 out of network, and a cash advance of $400. What is her total service charge including fees for the month?

Add the service charge fees.

Total Service Charge		Basic Monthly Charge		Bill Payments		Statement		ATM Service Charge		Cash Advance Service Charge
	=	$6.95	+	$0.50(7 − 5)	+	$4.00	+	$3.00	+	(2% × $400)
$22.95	=	6.95	+	1.00	+	4.00	+	3.00	+	8.00

The Total Service Charge is $22.95.

GRAPHING CALCULATOR LAB

Using the Math Solver

EQUATION SOLVER
eqn:0=X+2X−100−9
86

Many graphing calculators have a solver feature that can be used to solve an equation. The equation must first be written so that 0 is on one side.

The equation in **Example 2** is: 986 = (*d* + 2*d*) − 100

It can be rewritten as: 0 = *d* + 2*d* − 100 − 986

Press: MATH 0 then ^ CLEAR if you do not see **eqn:0=**.

To enter the equation press:

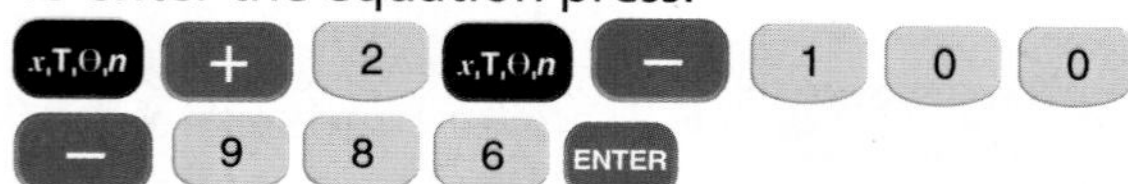

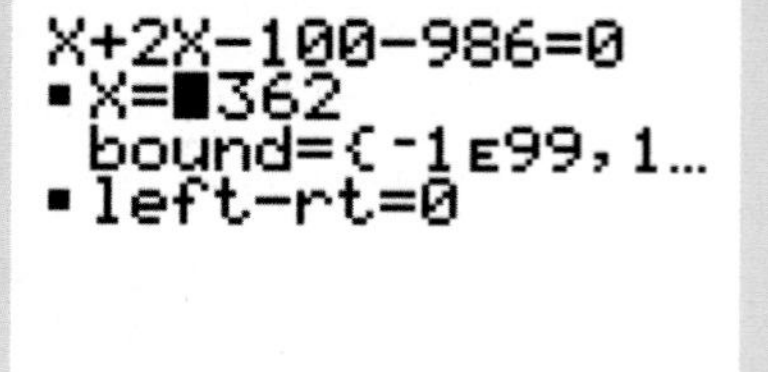

Make sure the cursor appears on the line containing ***x*** =.

Leave bound at the default setting.

Then press ALPHA ENTER to solve.

The solution is 362.

Think and Discuss

1. Describe the display of the first calculator screen.
2. Use the graphing calculator to solve $12x - 4 - 2x - 5x - 11 = 0$
3. Use the graphing calculator to solve $7(2w - 5) = 21$
4. Rhonda Rhobards makes a deposit at an ATM and receives $150 in cash and the receipt for the $774.00 total deposit. She remembers that the checks deposited totaled twice the currency she deposited. She did not deposit any coins. How much in currency did she deposit? How much in checks did she deposit?

Use Figure 4.10 on page 197 to compute the total service charge in the following problems. Check your answers in the back of the book.

1. Alan Booker's service charges: basic charge, 8 bills paid, a lost card replacement, and four ATM transactions, 2 national and 2 out-of-network.
2. Cindy Parker's service charges: the basic charge, 6 bills paid, 1 overdraft, 3 regional ATM transactions, and a $500 advance.

EXAMPLE 2

On March 15, Alyssa Perez goes online and downloads the transactions shown in **Figure 4.11**. She does this so she can put them on her spreadsheet where she keeps a check register (see **Figure 4.12** on page 200). Note the transactions since her last logon.

Figure 4.11

Date	Amount		Check Number	Description
03/06/20—	$ 400.00			ATM Withdrawal
03/06/20—	2.00			ATM National Network Fee
03/15/20—	1,661.57	+		Payee/Description: AT Deposit Memo: Computer Inc. EDI payment 0555
03/15/20—	0.50			Memo: Service Charge (bill pmt. fee)
03/15/20—	0.50			Memo: Service Charge (bill pmt. fee)
03/15/20—	3,341.29			Credit Card to 004:555-555 Online Pmt.
03/15/20—	100.00			Findlay Youth Pmt to 009:W555 Online Pmt.
03/15/20—	30.55		1289	Check Memo: Food Town
03/15/20—	153.39			AT Withdrawal Memo: Insurance 031202

Reading Math +−÷=

Service Charge
A service charge results in a subtraction.

Update the check register.

Compute the new balance.

Alyssa had check number 1288 entered and started with a balance of $2,895.90 − $59.46 = $2,836.44. She subtracted the $400.00 ATM withdrawal and the $2.00 service charge for the ATM fee. Then she added the payroll check and subtracted the other items.

Continued on next page

Figure 4.12

Trans. Type or Check No.	Date	Description of Transaction	Payment Debit (–)		√	Deposit/or Credit (+)		Balance	
						Balance Brought Forward→		**2,895**	**90**
1288	3/12	Fabric Store	59	46				2,836	44
ATM	3/6	ATM withdrawal	400	00				2,436	44
ATM	3/6	Service Charge (ATM fee)	2	00				2,434	44
AT	3/15	Computer Inc. Payroll				1,661	57	4,096	01
Online	3/15	Service Charge (bill pmt. fee)	0	50				4,095	51
Online	3/15	Service Charge (bill pmt. fee)	0	50				4,095	01
Online	3/15	Credit Card Pmt.	3,341	29				753	72
Online	3/15	Findlay Youth Pmt.	100	00				653	72
1289	3/15	Food Town	30	55				623	17
AT	3/15	Insurance Company	153	39				469	78

Complete the problem. Check your answer in the back of the book.

3. On April 1, Alyssa Perez (from **Example 2**) had the online transactions shown in **Figure 4.13**. Note that the balance brought forward is $871.78.

Figure 4.13

Date	Amount		Check Number	Description
04/01/20—	1,661.57	+		Payee/Description: AT Deposit Memo: Computer Inc. EDI Pmt. 0555
04/01/20—	0.50			Memo: Service Charge (bill pmt. fee)
04/01/20—	38.49			Wireless Store to 003:4555-555 Online Pmt.
04/01/20—	14.07		1290	Check Memo: Office Supply
04/01/20—	86.95			Payee/Description: AT Withdrawal Memo: Gas OH Serv Pmt. 031202

Complete the check register in Figure 4.14 for these transactions.

Figure 4.14

Trans. Type or Check No.	Date	Description of Transaction	Payment Debit (–)		√	Deposit/or Credit (+)		Balance	
						Balance Brought Forward→		**871**	**78**
AT	4/1	Payroll				a.		b.	
Online	4/1	Service Charge (bill pmt. fee)	c.					d.	
Online	4/1	Wireless Service	e.					f.	
1290	4/1	Office Supplies	g.					h.	
AT	4/1	State Street Gas Comp.	i.					j.	

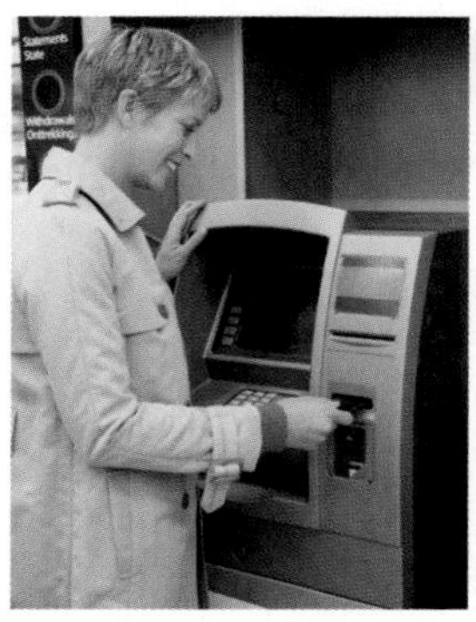

Did You Know?

The First ATM **John Shepherd-Barron of Great Britain invented the electronic automated teller machine (ATM). Barclays Bank installed the first one in London, England, on June 27, 1967.**

Onoky/SuperStock

Lesson Practice

Use Figure 4.10 on page 197 to determine the total of the service charge.

4. Sally Hudson's service charges: basic charge, 9 bills paid, lost card replacement, and 6 ATM transactions, 3 national and 3 out of network.

5. Service charges for Gary Baxter's account were the basic charge, 8 bills paid, 1 overdraft, $450 cash advance, and 3 regional ATM transactions.

6. See George Kirkland's end-of-month bank statement in **Figure 4.15.** Notice that the last activity is at the top of the list. *Start at the bottom of the list* and calculate the balance for each date shown.

Figure 4.15

National City—Online Banking				
Account: Checking 555-561-663				**ACTIVITY**
Date	**Amount**		**Check**	**Description**
04/01/20—	**d.**			**Balance**
04/01/20—	$ 6.95			Service Charge (online banking fee)
03/31-Mar	78.94		5174	
03/31/20—	25.00		5172	
03/31/20—	321.20			Debit Card, Karl's Dept. Store, point-of-sale purchase
03/31/20—	172.73		5167	
03/31/20—	24.95		5170	
03/31/20—	252.70		5161	
03/31/20—	147.80			AT—American Electric Power
03/31/20—	**c.**			**Balance**
03/20/20—	150.00			ATM Withdrawal
03/20/20—	2.00			ATM National Network Chg.
03/20/20—	0.50			Service Charge (bill pmt. fee) No. 8
03/20/20—	1,095.73			Household Credit Online payment. 200-55-5555
03/20/20—	65.32		5165	
03/20/20—	495.72		5166	
03/20/20—	**b.**			**Balance**
03/19/20—	2,458.50	+		AT—Payroll MSNBC Inc.
03/19/20—	45.62			Debit Card, Joe's Pizza, point-of-sale purchase
03/19/20—	0.50			Service Charge (bill pmt. fee) No. 7
03/19/20—	365.89			Commercial Truck Plate, Online Pmt.
03/19/20—	**a.**			**Balance**
03/10/20—	0.50			Service Charge (bill pmt. fee) Fee No. 6
03/10/20—	468.52			Credit Card Pmt.
03/10/20—	300.00			ATM Withdrawal
03/10/20—	3.00			Service Charge (ATM out-of-network fee)
03/01-Mar	2,365.99			**Balance**

7. On June 15, Benton Andrews uses First USA online banking and downloads these transactions so he can put them on his spreadsheet where he keeps his check register. Use **Figure 4.16a** to complete the check register for the transactions on **Figure 4.16b**.

H.O.T. Problems

Figure 4.16a

Date	Amount		Check Number	Description
06/01/20—	6.95			Online Banking Basic Charge
06/05/20—	250.00			ATM Withdrawal
06/12/20—	5,850.00	+		AT Deposit Memo: Transfer from Savings acct. 066555
06/15/20—	0.50			Memo: Service Charge (bill pmt. fee) No. 6
06/15/20—	0.50			Memo: Service Charge (bill pmt. fee) No. 7
06/15/20—	557.86			Credit Card To 008-555-555 Online Pmt.
06/15/20—	35.00			Fair Board Trophy to 002:W6555 Online Pmt.
06/15/20—	85.55		789	Check Memo: Food
06/15/20—	853.39			AT Withdrawal Memo: Real Estate Taxes

Figure 4.16b

Check Register								
Trans. Type or Check No.	Date	Description of Transaction	Payment Debit (–)		√	Deposit/or Credit (+)	Balance	
		Balance Brought Forward ⟶					1,574	99
Bank Charge	6/1	Online Basic Charge	a.					b.
ATM	6/5	ATM Withdrawal	c.					d.
AT	6/15	Transfer from Savings				e.		f.
Online	6/15	Service Charge (bill pmt. fee)	g.					h.
Online	6/15	Service Charge (bill pmt. fee)	i.					j.
Online	6/15	Credit Card Pmt.	k.				l.	
Online	15-June	Fair Board Trophy	m.				n.	
789	15-June	Food	o.				p.	
AT	15-June	Real Estate Taxes	q.				r.	

Spiral Review

Add or Subtract. (Skill 5 and Skill 6)

8. \$9,887.89 – \$23.61
9. \$16,246.64 – \$887.35
10. \$568.35 + \$98.23
11. \$89,564.89 + \$85.21
12. Your checking account had a \$124.56 balance on June 3. You deposited \$123.67 on June 12. Then you wrote a \$75.59 check on June 15 and had an \$80.00 ATM withdrawal on June 19. What is your new balance? (Lesson 4.3)
13. Randy Fleming earns 6.25% commission on sales of \$7,500. What is her commission? (Lesson 1.6)

GET READY for the Next Lesson

PREREQUISITE SKILL Subtracting Decimals (Skill 6)

14. \$345.57 – \$125.39
15. \$45.57 – \$42.63
16. \$60.60 – \$7.89
17. \$357.80 – \$22.77
18. \$24,687.99 – \$5,467
19. \$86,300.63 – \$8,544.01

CHAPTER 4 Review and Assessment

AFTER YOU READ

Chapter SUMMARY

A checking account is a safe and convenient place to hold money. Its records give you information to track your expenses. Using a checking account includes knowing how to compute the total of a deposit and write a check. You must also calculate the balance in a check register and the present balance on a checking account bank statement. The final steps are to reconcile a check register with a bank account statement, compute online banking charges, and update the check register.

Vocabulary Check

1. On a sheet of paper, use each of these terms in a sentence.

Content Vocabulary

- deposit (p. 179)
- direct deposit (p. 179)
- automated teller machine (ATM) (p. 179)
- personal identification number (PIN) (p. 179)
- checking account (p. 183)
- check (p. 183)
- check register (p. 186)
- balance (p. 186)
- bank statement (p. 189)
- service charge (p. 189)
- reconcile (p. 193)
- online banking (p. 197)

Academic Vocabulary

- access (p. 179)
- currency (p. 183)
- previous (p. 186)
- transfer (p. 189)
- coincide (p. 193)
- monitor (p. 197)

Concept Check

2. List benefits of having a checking account.
3. Give the formula for determining the total amount of a bank deposit.
4. What is direct deposit?
5. Give the formula for calculating the present balance of a checking account.
6. What is the purpose of a check register?
7. What is a bank statement?
8. Summarize the steps in reconciling a check register with a bank account statement.
9. List advantages of online banking.
10. List possible online banking service charges.
11. CRITICAL THINKING What are the benefits of using direct deposit?

Lesson-by-Lesson Review

4.1 Deposits (pp. 179–182)

Compute the total checking account deposit.

Robin Jenkins deposited currency totaling $119.00 and coins totaling $12.36. She also deposited a check for $532.19. What was the total amount of her deposit?

Compute the total checking account deposit.

(Currency + Coins + Checks) − Cash Received =

$119.00 + $12.36 + $532.19 = **$663.55 total deposit**

Review Exercises

12. Nicholas Roberts has two checks, one for $256.00 and the other for $194.55. He wants to deposit the checks and receive 3 ten-dollar bills, 7 one-dollar bills, 8 quarters, and 3 dimes. What is his total deposit amount?

13. **ALGEBRA** Debbie Turner makes a deposit at an ATM and receives $75.00 in cash and a receipt for the $872.25 total deposit. She remembers that the checks deposited totaled twice the currency she deposited. She did not deposit any coins. What amount in currency did she deposit? What amount in checks did she deposit?

4.2 The Check-Writing Process (pp. 183–185)

Write a check.

Write $403.98 in words, as it would appear on a check: Four hundred three and $\frac{98}{100}$ dollars

Review Exercises

Write each amount in word form as it would appear on a check. Some amounts might require that the cents be expressed as a fraction of a dollar.

14. $845.00
15. $54.33
16. $13,586.16
17. $387.21
18. Carla Phillips wrote a $57.02 check to Archer's Grocery Store. Write the check's amount with cents expressed as a fraction of a dollar.

4.3 Check Registers (pp. 186–188)

Calculate the balance in a check register.

Harrison Campbell's checkbook balance was $376.22 on June 25. His check register that follows shows the transactions since then. What was his balance after each transaction?

Check Register

Trans. Type or Check No.	Date	Description of Transaction	Payment Debit (–)		√	Deposit/or Credit (+)		Balance	
		Balance Brought Forward →						376	22
234	6/27	ABC Cable TV	34	12				a.	
235	6/28	Hills Water Company	15	77				b.	
	6/28	Deposit				776	50	c.	
236	6/29	Carolina Apt.	540	00				d.	

Calculate the balance.

New Balance = Previous Balance − Check Amount − Automatic Transfers

New Balance = Previous Balance + Deposit Amount

Lesson-by-Lesson Review (continued)

Review Exercises

Find the new balance in each problem.

19. Your balance on May 20 was $189.75, and you made a $112.45 deposit on May 22. On May 29, you wrote a $75.68 check, and on June 1, you made an ATM withdrawal of $50.00.

20. Your balance was $226.45 on April 14. You wrote two checks, one on April 19 for $45.97 and the second on April 24 for $62.14. Then you had an AT paycheck deposit for $312.47 on April 25.

4.4 Bank Statements (pp. 189–192)

Calculate the current balance on a checking account bank statement.
Kippen Edwards received his checking account statement for July. His previous balance was $966.51. What is his present balance?

Calculate the new balance:

Previous Balance + Deposits Recorded – Checks Paid – Service Charges + Interest

Checks and Other Charges			Deposits and Credits		Balance
Date	Number	Amount	Date	Amount	
7/06	213	$ 712.90	7/08	$ 112.54	$
7/14	214	34.29	7/15	459.96	
			Interest	1.29	
Service Charge		5.60	Deposit	572.50	

$966.51 + ($112.54 + $459.96) – ($712.90 + $34.29) – $5.60 + $1.29

= $966.51 + $572.50 – $747.19 – $5.60 + $1.29

= **$787.51 present balance**

Review Exercises

21. Grace Collins received her checking account statement for March. Her previous balance was $851.97. What is her present balance?

Checks and Other Charges			Deposits and Credits		Balance
Date	Number	Amount	Date	Amount	
3/17	333	$ 34.55	3/18	$259.00	$
3/18	334	123.44	3/20	102.00	
3/22	335	210.00	3/21	50.00	
Service Charge		3.45			

22. ALGEBRA Tom Eckhart received his bank statement and wanted to verify his pay increase. His previous month's pay was $3,076.60. His account activity showed a previous balance of $597.90, processed checks of $2,696.90, ATM withdrawals of $300, and a service charge of $5.50. If Tom's new balance is $818.30, what increase in pay was direct deposited?

Lesson-by-Lesson Review (continued)

4.5 Bank Statement Reconciliation (pp. 193–196)

Reconcile a check register with a bank account statement.

Calculate the adjusted balance.

Statement Balance − Outstanding Checks + Outstanding Deposits

a. $4,562.74
b. $4,562.74
c. $358.17
d. $358.17

Check Register Balance	$4,561.20	$357.99
Interest	6.59	2.33
Service Charge	5.05	2.15
New Balance	a.	c.
Statement Balance	3,987.00	476.35
Outstanding Checks	75.74	435.18
Outstanding Deposits	651.48	317.00
Adjusted Balance	b.	d.

Review Exercises

Complete the table. Do the register balance and the adjusted balances agree?

	Check Register Balance	Interest	Service Charge	New Balance	Statement Balance	Outstanding Checks	Outstanding Deposits	Adjusted Balance
23.	$ 176.55	$ 0.00	$4.34	a. $	$ 79.21	$ 27.50	$ 120.50	b. $
24.	525.79	0.00	5.05	a.	752.45	232.33	0.00	b.
25.	1,254.62	3.70	5.95	a.	2,140.11	1,287.74	400.00	b.

4.6 Online Banking (pp. 197–202)

Compute online banking charges and update the check register.
You use online banking. Last month you had a basic service charge of $7.50. Service charges included 8 fees at $0.50 each, and a $4.00 fee for a printed statement, $3.00 out-of-network ATM fee, and a cash advance fee of 2% of $300. What are the total service charges?

Add the service charge fees.

Basic Service Charge	+	Bill Payments	+	Statement	+	ATM Service Charge Fee	+	Cash Advance Service Charge Fee	=	Total Service Charge
$7.50	+	(8 × $0.50)	+	$4.00	+	$3.00	+	(0.02 × $300)		
= $7.50	+	$4.00	+	$4.00	+	$3.00	+	$6.00	=	**$24.50 total service charge**

Review Exercises

26. Lauren Woods had a basic service charge of $6.95. Individual service charges included 7 fees at $0.50 each, a $5.00 lost card replacement fee, $4.00 out-of-network ATM fee, and a cash advance fee of 2% of $200. What was the total service charge?

27. Roger Sand banks online. Last month he had a basic service charge of $7.95. Service charges included 6 fees at $0.70 each, a $25.00 overdraft fee, a $2.00 regional network ATM fee, and a cash advance fee of 2.5% of $400. What was the total service charge?

Practice Test

Record your answer on another sheet of paper.

1. Corina Juarez made a deposit to her checking account and received $80 in cash. The deposit totaled $832. She did not deposit any coins. The checks she deposited totaled 3 times the currency she deposited. How much did she deposit in checks?
   A $228 **B** $684
   C $912 **D** $752

2. If you deposited a check for $456.89 at an ATM that has a $4.50 service charge fee for all transactions, what was the total amount deposited?
   A $452.39 **B** $456.89
   C $461.39 **D** $460.50

3. What is the total of a deposit for $324.75, 15 pennies, 8 nickels, 5 dimes, and 3 quarters?
   A $325.15 **B** $326.45
   C $325.95 **D** $326.55

4. What amount of money do you have if you have 5 pennies, 13 nickels, 14 dimes, 2 quarters, and one 5-dollar bill?
   A $2.60 **B** $5.75
   C $7.60 **D** $7.65

5. Which of the following does *not* have to appear on a check?
   A Date
   B Dollar amount of check
   C Social Security number
   D Name of person to whom payment will be made

6. If Amy Morris had $6,756.02 in her checking account and wrote a check for $543.88, what amount was left in her account?
   A $7,489.14 **B** $7,299.90
   C $6,212.14 **D** $6,312.16

7. Caitlyn Bailey had $4,765.58 in her checking account. If she wrote three checks totaling $867.23 and was charged a $2.45 service, what amount was left in the account?
   A $3,898.35 **B** $3,895.90
   C $4,763.13 **D** $3,965.54

8. Juan Torres had $899.58 in his bank account and made a $12.85 deposit. What amount was in the account after the deposit?
   A $914.68 **B** $872.85
   C $886.73 **D** $912.43

9. Taylor Cook has her monthly pay deposited directly to her checking account. She recently received a pay increase and wanted to determine the increase amount. Her previous month's pay was $2,350.75. The checking account shows a previous balance of $1,012.84, checks processed totaling $741.68, ATM withdrawals of $120, and a service charge of $2.75. Taylor's new balance is $2,614.26. What was the increase in pay deposited?

10. What amount did Kayla Morgan withdraw from her account if she wrote 4 checks of $54.68, $685.45, $93.93, and $76.54?

11. Clare Belk withdrew $43.00 from her bank account that had $1,029.93 in it. What amount did she have left?

12. $36.59 + $54.69

13. $6,459 – $2,123.94

14. $340.45 – $45.00 – $68.59 + $2.45

15. $10,987 – $1,234.56

16. $9,856.87 + $5,765.01 – $459.12

17. $3,456.54 – $42.63 – $2.67 – $1,457.89

Standardized Test Practice

Cumulative, Chapters 1–4

PART 1 Multiple Choice

Record your answers on the answer sheet provided by your teacher or on a sheet of paper.

1. Jen Murphy's average monthly expenditure for groceries was $169.40 for the first quarter this year. In April, she spent $201.35, and in May, she spent $158.10. How much can she spend in June and maintain the average of the first quarter?
   A $160.61 **B** $123.45
   C $148.75 **D** $153.81

2. Marcia Richardson's bank charges a $0.15 service charge fee each time she writes a check. What amount will the bank withdraw if she writes 5 checks totaling $485.96?
   A $488.72 **B** $0.75
   C $486.71 **D** $496.71

3. If the Medicare tax rate is 5.4%, what is the amount deducted from a $561.98 paycheck?
   A $5.40 **B** $30.35
   C $40.85 **D** $20.15

4. Sam Howard's bank charges a $1.23 fee for every check more than 10 that he writes. What amount does the bank withdraw from his account if he writes 18 checks totaling $754.89?
   A $22.14 **B** $9.84
   C $764.73 **D** $777.03

5. If Sophia Cox budgeted $340.00 for utilities and the actual cost was $405.54, how much over or under budget is she?
   A $65.54 under budget **B** $69.54 over budget
   C $69.54 under budget **D** $65.54 over budget

TEST-TAKING TIP

For multiple choice questions, read all of the choices carefully before you select an answer.

6. Bill Peterson's bank account had $1,428.74 in it. What amount did it have after he wrote a check for $24.54, got $60.00 at the ATM, and wrote another check for $75.88?
   A $1,268.32 **B** $160.42
   C $1,589.16 **D** $1,628.23

PART 2 Short Response/Griddable

7. Anna Ward wrote three checks for $45.50 each. If she started with $666.90 in her account, what amount was left?

Exemptions	
Single	$2,000
Married	4,000
Each Dependent	2,000

8. Jaime Greer is the assistant principal at a high school earning an annual salary of $58,980. He is married, claims 2 dependents, and pays $2,549 in state income tax per year. What is the state income tax rate for his state? Use the table above.

9. Sally Lybrand's annual medical insurances costs $9,500. Her company pays 82% of the cost. How much does Sally pay monthly?

PART 3 Extended Response

Show your work.

10. Do you think everyone should use online banking? Why or why not?

Building Academic Skills

Mathematics

You just received your checking account statement that says you have a balance of $3,744.27 in your account. You know that checks written for $401.32, $147.98, and $76.88 have not yet cleared the account. The $1,024.00 deposit you made yesterday has not yet been posted either. What is your adjusted balance?

English Language Arts/Writing

You plan to open a checking account. You are interested in its online banking services. Prepare a list of questions. Visit Web sites of local or regional banks to find the answers to your questions. Create a spreadsheet to compare and contrast different financial institutions and their services.

Social Studies/Government

Check Clearing for the 21st Century Act, or Check 21, is a federal law that lets banks handle checks electronically. It is supposed to make check processing and clearing faster, more efficient, and less expensive. Under this law, you receive a picture of the front and back of your checks from your bank instead of the actual canceled checks. Use library and online sources to find out more about Check 21. Who do you think benefits the most from this change? The least?

Digital Vision/Alamy

Building Real-World Skills

Career WISE

Bank Teller As the person who handles money and deals directly with customers, a teller is one of the most important people in a bank. This job includes accepting cash for deposit, printing receipts, answering questions about balances, and sometimes helping customers open new accounts.

Research and Share:

a. Visit the Web site of the U.S. Department of Labor's Bureau of Labor Statistics and obtain information about the career of bank teller.
b. What level of education is required to be a bank teller? What is the median income?

Tech TRENDS

Checking Account Software One of the most popular computer applications is personal finance software, which can track checking account balances. Often, the on-screen program looks just like a checkbook register. The user simply types in the name of the business or individual paid with each check, the amount, and the date. The software can also remember what the next check number should be, which can alert you to a missing check.

Research and Write:

a. Using the Internet, find the names of two popular personal finance software packages.
b. What are some of the benefits of tracking your checking account on a computer? What do you think disadvantages could be?

CHAPTER 5 Savings Accounts

Big Idea

You will learn how to manage deposits and withdrawals to your savings account, the power of compound interest, and how savings accounts earn money for you.

Exactostock/SuperStock

Explore the Photo

Planning Ahead
Saving money is an important part of financial freedom and responsibility. *What are the advantages of having a savings account?*

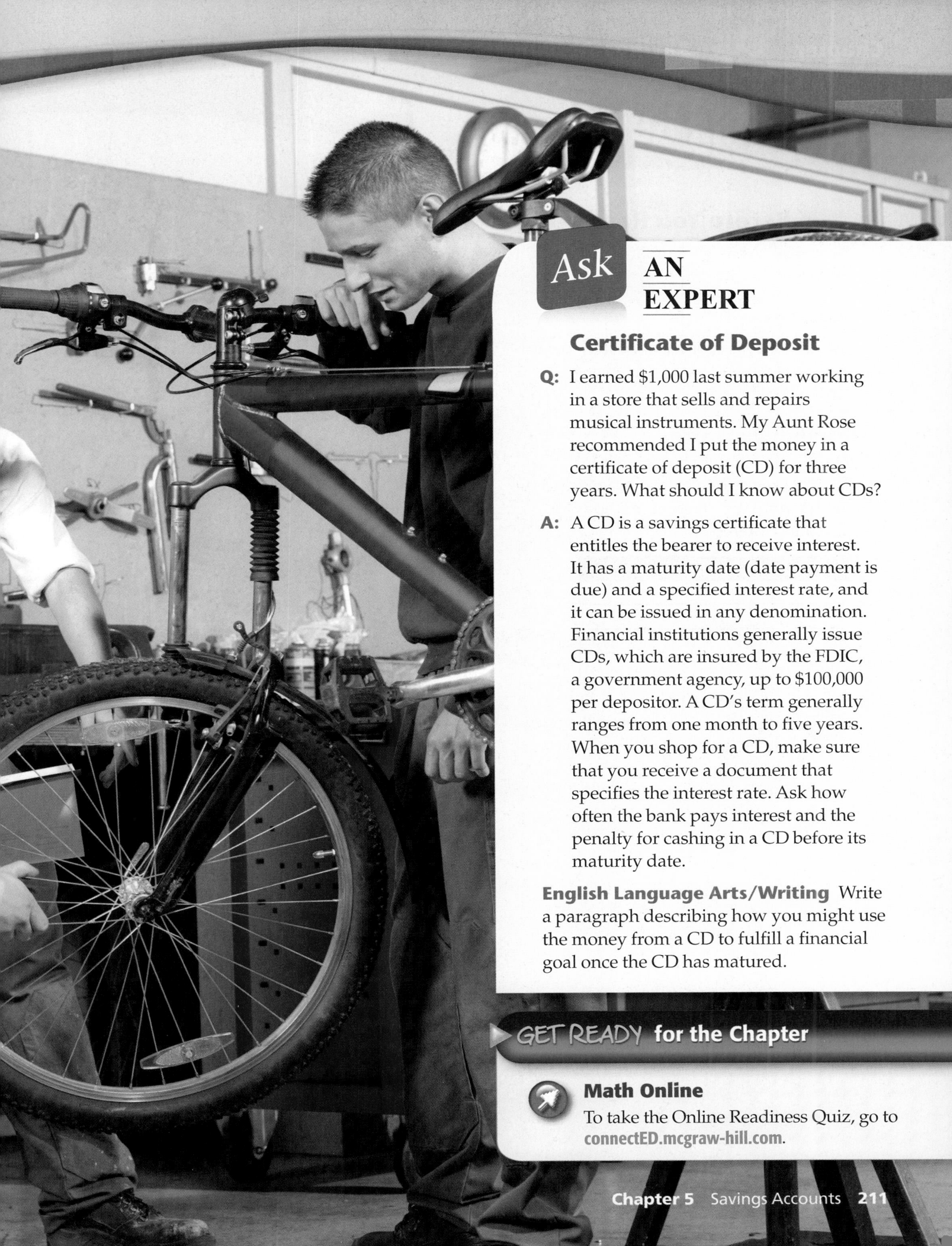

Ask AN EXPERT

Certificate of Deposit

Q: I earned $1,000 last summer working in a store that sells and repairs musical instruments. My Aunt Rose recommended I put the money in a certificate of deposit (CD) for three years. What should I know about CDs?

A: A CD is a savings certificate that entitles the bearer to receive interest. It has a maturity date (date payment is due) and a specified interest rate, and it can be issued in any denomination. Financial institutions generally issue CDs, which are insured by the FDIC, a government agency, up to $100,000 per depositor. A CD's term generally ranges from one month to five years. When you shop for a CD, make sure that you receive a document that specifies the interest rate. Ask how often the bank pays interest and the penalty for cashing in a CD before its maturity date.

English Language Arts/Writing Write a paragraph describing how you might use the money from a CD to fulfill a financial goal once the CD has matured.

GET READY for the Chapter

Math Online

To take the Online Readiness Quiz, go to **connectED.mcgraw-hill.com**.

Chapter 5 Savings Accounts

Reading Guide

Before You Read

Describe What are your financial goals? How can saving help you meet them?

Main Idea

Saving money is an important step toward meeting goals and living a financially responsible life.

Graphic Organizer

Before you read this chapter, draw a diagram like the one below. As you read the chapter, note the different methods for calculating interest.

Methods for Calculating Interest

Math Online Go to connectED.mcgraw-hill.com to download this graphic organizer.

Content Vocabulary

You will learn these key terms in this chapter.

- savings account
- deposit
- withdrawal
- account statement
- interest
- simple interest
- principal
- annual interest rate
- compound interest
- compound interest table
- daily compounding
- annuity
- ordinary annuity
- annuity due

Academic Vocabulary

You will see these words in your reading and on your tests.

- specific
- portion
- status
- method
- period
- utilize
- potential
- interval

You can find vocabulary definitions in the **Content Vocabulary** Glossary and the **Academic Vocabulary** Glossary in the back of the book.

LESSON 5.1

Deposits

Lesson Objective
Complete a savings account deposit slip and compute the total deposit.

Content Vocabulary
- savings account
- deposit

GET READY for the Lesson

What are your savings goals?

Carlton Reed deposits money into his savings account every month. He would like to go to the Super Bowl next year.

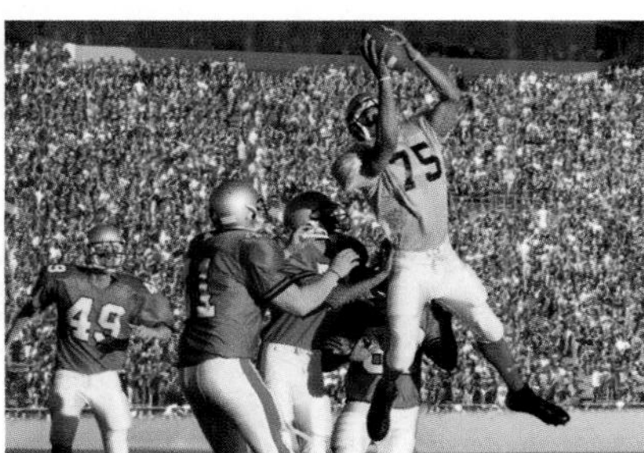

As You Read
Identify Do you have a savings account?

Opening a Savings Account To open a **savings account**, which is a **specific** kind of bank account that earns interest, you must make a deposit. A **deposit** is the money you put in the bank, savings and loan, credit union, or brokerage firm. You can make a deposit at an ATM machine, in person, by direct deposit, or by electronic transfer. There are several ways to transfer funds; evaluate what is right for you. Each time you make a deposit, it is added to your account's balance. To make a deposit in person, you fill out a savings account deposit slip to record currency, coins, and checks that you are depositing. If you want to receive cash back, subtract the amount from the subtotal to find the total deposit amount.

Total Deposit = (Currency + Coins + Checks) − Cash Received

EXAMPLE 1

Robert Cassidy wants to deposit the following into his savings account: 28 one-dollar bills, 8 five-dollar bills, 24 quarters, 35 dimes, 90 pennies, a check for $29.34, and a check for $124.19. He wants to receive a $50.00 bill in cash. How much will he deposit? See **Figure 5.1.**

Figure 5.1

SAVINGS DEPOSIT

Date March 11, 20--

Account Number 0113014

Name Robert Cassidy

SIGN HERE IF CASH RECEIVED FROM DEPOSIT

Robert Cassidy

Currency + Coins + Checks → SUBTOTAL

		DOLLARS	CENTS
CASH	CURRENCY	68	00
	COINS	10	40
CHECKS	LIST SEPARATELY 14-6	29	34
	35-165	124	19
	SUBTOTAL	231	93
	LESS CASH RECEIVED	50	00
	TOTAL DEPOSIT	181	93

Step 1: Compute the amount of currency and coins in the deposit.

The currency deposit: $28.00 + (8 × $5.00) = $28.00 + $40.00 = **$68.00**

The coins deposit: (24 × $0.25) + (35 × $0.10) + $0.90 = $6.00 + $3.50 + $0.90 = **$10.40**

Step 2: Total Deposit = (Currency + Coins + Checks) − Cash Received

$181.93 = $68.00 + $10.40 + $29.34 + $124.19 − $50.00

Find the total deposit. Check your answers in the back of the book.

1. Checks: \$63.21, \$37.79, and \$15.50; cash: 24 one-dollar bills, 11 ten-dollar bills, 20 quarters, 22 dimes, and 40 pennies; less \$20.00 as cash received.
2. Checks: \$152.54 and \$147.46; cash: 54 one-dollar bills, 12 five-dollar bills, 6 ten-dollar bills, 35 quarters, 18 dimes, 40 nickels, and 75 pennies; less \$50.00 as cash received.

Need Help? Go to...
Workshop 36: Problem Solving Strategies: Using Simple Algebraic Operations, p. 74

EXAMPLE 2 Algebra

George Pappas deposited one check into his savings account for \$629.75, one check for \$398.00, and a third check, the amount of which he cannot remember. His total deposit was for \$1,227.51 after he received \$150.00 in cash. What was the amount of the third check deposited?

Let x = The amount of the third check deposited

Total Deposit = Checks − Cash Received

$\$1,227.51 = (\$629.75 + \$398.00 + x) - \$150.00$

Combine like terms → $\$1,227.51 = \$877.75 + x$

Subtract \$877.75 from both sides → $\mathbf{\$349.76} = x$

Concept CHECK

Complete the problem. Check your answer in the back of the book.

3. Natalie Albert deposited checks totaling \$1,735.97 into her savings account. She withdrew \$100.00 while depositing some coins. If her total deposit was \$1,668.71, how much did Natalie deposit in coins?

Real World CAREER

Marketing Manager
Selling T-shirts and other items at concerts is a form of marketing. Marketing managers use it to increase public awareness of their clients. **What products or entertainers have you seen marketed on T-shirts?**

MIXA/Glow Images

Lesson Practice

For Problems 4–10, find the total deposit.

4. Checks: \$152.54 and \$147.46; cash: 54 one-dollar bills, 12 five-dollar bills, and 6 ten-dollar bills; less \$20.00 as cash received.
5. Checks: \$32.96, \$121.03, and \$24.70; cash: 22 one-dollar bills, 5 ten-dollar bills, and \$15.21 in coins; less \$20.00 cash received.
6. Ryan Massey wants to deposit the following into his savings account: 28 ten-dollar bills, 9 five-dollar bills, 20 quarters, 85 dimes, 32 pennies, and three checks for \$654.24, \$100.00, and \$458.92. He wants to receive \$50.00 in cash.
7. Jonathan Rodero operates a booth selling T-shirts during concerts. Following each event, he makes a deposit to his savings account. Today he has checks: \$40.00, \$50.00, and \$35.00; cash and coins: 8 fifty-dollar bills, 12 twenty-dollar bills, 12 ten-dollar bills, 8 five-dollar bills, 22 one-dollar bills, 48 quarters, 19 dimes, 22 nickels, and 52 pennies; less \$100.00 in cash.

Reading Math

Just Checking
If there is a discrepancy between the amount in numbers and the amount in words on a check, the bank will use the number in words.

8. James Augustine wants to deposit the following into his savings account: 12 one-dollar bills, 4 five-dollar bills, 10 quarters, 12 dimes, 40 pennies, a check for $132.51, and a check for $32.12. He wants to receive 2 twenty-dollar bills in cash. How much will he deposit?
9. Phyllis Truitt wants to deposit the following into her savings account: 3 one-hundred dollar bills, 15 twenty-dollar bills, 15 five-dollar bills, and four checks for $25.32, $120.00, $96.66, and $1,425.00. She wants to receive 10 one-dollar bills in cash.
10. Ella Bell operates a company that buys and sells tickets to sporting events. She deposits the day's receipts into her savings account. In bills, she had 52 one hundreds, 21 fifties, 19 tens, 71 fives, and 63 ones. Change included 6 one-dollar coins, 60 fifty-cent pieces, 32 quarters, 121 dimes, and 165 pennies. She also deposited checks for $29.44, $125.65, and $45.94. She wants to receive 5 two-dollar bills in cash.

11. **ALGEBRA** Nancy and Curtis Eckard deposited one check for $416.32, a second one for $509.85, and a third check into a brokerage account. They also deposited $72.00 in currency and $41.50 in coins. If they withdrew $150.00 in cash and their total deposit was $1,209.22, what was the amount of their third check?
12. **CHALLENGE PROBLEM** Winona Carlson owns a sports memorabilia store. She deposits her sales income directly into a savings account. Her deposit in bills today consists of 5 one hundreds, 8 fifties, 25 twenties, 22 fives, 8 twos, and 19 ones. The deposit includes 18 half-dollars, 42 quarters, 36 dimes, 28 nickels, and one check for $40.00. She wants to receive starting cash for the next day as follows: 3 twenties, 3 tens, a five, and 5 ones. How much was the total deposit?
13. **ALGEBRA** Angel Rivera deposits his paycheck directly into his account every week. He received a raise of $16.15 per week in his last pay period. If he withdrew $100.00 in cash and had a total deposit of $641.85, what was Angel's weekly pay before the raise?

Spiral Review

Add or Subtract. (Skill 5 and Skill 6)

14. $98.93 − $20.00
15. $173.79 + $45.93
16. $687.28 − $75.00
17. Tamara Clinton uses online banking. Last month, she had a basic charge of $5.95, 8 service fees at $0.50 each, and a $5.00 fee to replace a lost card. Tamara also had a cash advance fee of 2% of $300.00. What is the total amount of fees? (Lesson 4.6)
18. Your straight-time pay is $15.21 an hour for 40 hours; last month you worked an aditional 12 hours at time and a half. What was your total pay? (Lesson 1.2)

GET READY for the Next Lesson

PREREQUISITE SKILL Numbers (Skill 1)

Write the numeral.

19. Nineteen and $\frac{15}{100}$
20. Forty-five and $\frac{38}{100}$

Write in word form with cents expressed as a fraction of a dollar.

21. $98.40
22. $11.23
23. $29.29

LESSON 5.2

Withdrawals

Lesson Objective
Fill out a savings account withdrawal slip.

Content Vocabulary
- withdrawal

GET READY for the Lesson

How can you access the money in your savings account?

Danh Trang decided to buy a home entertainment center using money from his savings account. He went to the credit union and withdrew money from the account.

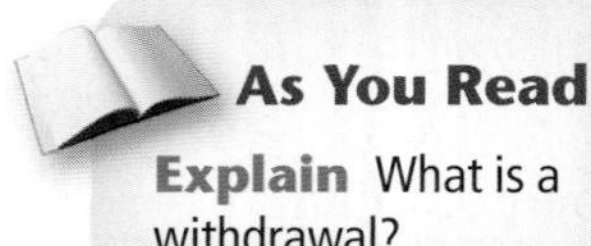

As You Read

Explain What is a withdrawal?

Making a Withdrawal When you make a **withdrawal**, you are taking money out of your bank account. Your withdrawal is subtracted from the account's balance. When making a withdrawal from a savings account, you fill out a withdrawal slip. On it, you need to write dollar amounts in *word form* with the decimal **portion** as a fraction. (You learned the same process in Chapter 4 Checking Accounts.) If the amount in word form does not match the amount in numeral form, the financial institution honors the word form.

Need Help? Go to...

- **Workshop 1:** Writing and Reading Numbers, p. 4
- **Application C:** Tables and Charts, p. AP3

EXAMPLE 1

Write each of the following as words or a numeral.

a. Write \$45.00 in word form.
b. Write \$355.34 in word form.
c. Write Twenty-five and $\frac{50}{100}$ dollars as a numeral.
d. Write Three thousand ninety-nine and $\frac{22}{100}$ dollars as a numeral.

Write the amounts in word form or as numerals.

a. \$45.00 in word form is **forty-five and $\frac{00}{100}$ dollars.**
b. \$355.34 in word form is **three hundred fifty-five and $\frac{34}{100}$ dollars.**
c. Twenty-five and $\frac{50}{100}$ dollars as a numeral is **\$25.50.**
d. Three thousand ninety-nine and $\frac{22}{100}$ dollars as a numeral is **\$3,099.22**

Concept CHECK

Write each of the following as words or a numeral. Check your answers in the back of the book.

1. \$60.00
2. \$280.50
3. Ninety-eight and $\frac{75}{100}$ dollars
4. Six thousand five hundred eighty-six and $\frac{95}{100}$ dollars

william casey/Alamy

EXAMPLE 2

Dalton Rhodes would like to withdraw $45 from his savings account. His account number is 0113014. How should he fill out the withdrawal slip? See **Figure 5.2.** (*Note:* To prevent someone from altering your withdrawal slip, you always start writing out the amount at the far left.)

Figure 5.2

State Bank — **Savings Withdrawal**

DATE	ACCOUNT NUMBER	AMOUNT
November 14, 20--	0113014	$45.00

NOT NEGOTIABLE—TO BE USED ONLY AT COUNTER OF THIS BANK BY DEPOSITOR PERSONALLY

Forty-five and $\frac{00}{100}$ ———————— DOLLARS

NAME (SIGNATURE) *Dalton Rhodes*

ADDRESS 18 Laurel Lane, Bridgetown, CT 05120

Step 1: Write the date of withdrawal.

Step 2: Write the savings account number.

Step 3: Write the amount withdrawn in words with cents expressed as a fraction of a dollar. (Note that you start at the far left.)

Step 4: Write the amount withdrawn as a numeral.

Step 5: Sign the withdrawal slip.

Concept CHECK

Complete the problem. Check your answer in the back of the book.

5. Tyrone Shumpert would like to withdraw $150 from his savings account. Use the withdrawal slip in **Figure 5.3** to answer the following:

Figure 5.3

University Bank — **Savings Withdrawal**

DATE	ACCOUNT NUMBER	AMOUNT
January 10, 20--	559821	$150.00

NOT NEGOTIABLE—TO BE USED ONLY AT COUNTER OF THIS BANK BY DEPOSITOR PERSONALLY

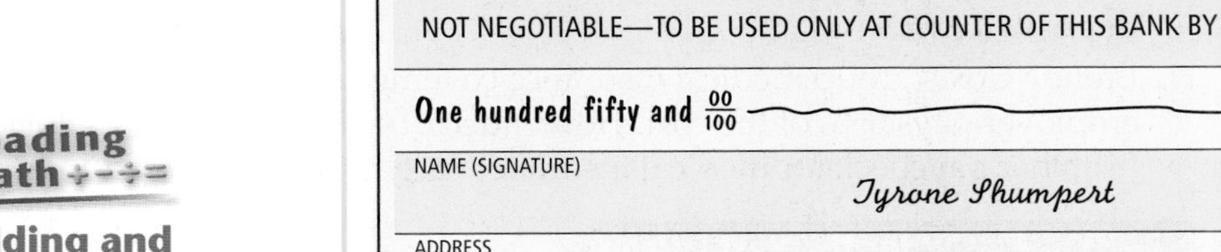

One hundred fifty and $\frac{00}{100}$ ———————— DOLLARS

NAME (SIGNATURE) *Tyrone Shumpert*

ADDRESS 5532 Hilltop Court, Lake Havasu City, AZ 86403

a. What is the date of withdrawal?

b. What is the savings account number?

c. Is the amount withdrawn correctly written in word form?

d. Who signed the withdrawal slip?

Reading Math +−÷=

Adding and Subtracting
When you read a bank statement, note that a deposit indicates that money was added. A withdrawal indicates that money was subtracted.

Did You Know?

Commemorative Stamps
In 1893, Congress criticized Postmaster General John Wanamaker's idea to make a special stamp celebrating the 400th anniversary of Christopher Columbus's journey to the new world. Today, commemorative stamps provide a major source of revenue for the U.S. Postal Service.

Lesson Practice

Write each amount in word form as it would appear on a withdrawal slip.

6. \$68.74 **7.** \$406.00 **8.** \$137.51

Write each amount as a numeral.

9. Seventy-four and $\frac{10}{100}$ dollars

10. Seven thousand five hundred eighty-five and $\frac{00}{100}$ dollars

For Problems 11–15, write the (a) account number, (b) amount as a numeral for the withdrawal slip, and (c) amount in words.

11. Galen Bogart's savings account number is 81-0-174927. He fills out a savings withdrawal slip for \$318.29 to purchase a gift.

12. Nina Coleman has been saving for a trip abroad. Her travel agent has arranged a trip to Europe that will cost \$2,460. Nina withdraws the amount from her savings account whose number is 13-122-541.

13. Dylan Bashier has been saving to buy a commemorative stamp for his stamp collection. He fills out a savings withdrawal slip for \$76.70. His account number is 06-029-175.

14.

Farmer's Mercantile		
Date	Savings Acct. No.	
5/19/20--	17594179	\$831.95
Pay to Myself or to Home Finance Co.		
Dollars		
And Charge to the above Numbered Account		
Sign Here *Calvin Gordon*		
Withdrawal		

15.

Farmer's Mercantile		
Date	Savings Acct. No.	
1/12/20--	16010368	\$374.28
Pay to Myself or to Odessa French		
Dollars		
And Charge to the above Numbered Account		
Sign Here *Odessa French*		
Withdrawal		

H.O.T. Problems

16. WRITING IN MATH Explain what a bank would do if you wrote \$17.98 in the numeral space and *Seventeen and* $\frac{88}{100}$ in the word form space on a check.

Spiral Review

Multiply or divide. (Skill 8 and Skill 10)

17. \$23.45 × 6 **18.** \$2,315.94 ÷ 11 **19.** \$54.72 × 3.25

20. Amy Gomez made a deposit of three checks for \$84.21, \$27.47, and \$12.79. Cash included 24 one-dollar bills, 8 ten-dollar bills, 15 quarters, 12 dimes, and 9 pennies, less \$20.00 in cash received. Find the total deposit. (Lesson 5.1)

21. Brenda Cox's group medical insurance coverage costs \$7,480 a year. Her employer pays 65% of the cost. How much does her employer deduct from her paycheck for medical insurance each month? (Lesson 2.5)

GET READY for the Next Lesson

PREREQUISITE SKILL Subtracting Decimals (Skill 6)

Subtract.

22. \$8,500.00 − \$125.00 **23.** \$44.58 − \$32.68 **24.** \$86.54 − \$14.42

25. \$94,328 − \$9,997.32 **26.** \$28,567.73 − \$1,234.56 **27.** \$988.96 − \$827.25

LESSON 5.3

Account Statements

Lesson Objective
Compute the new balance of a savings account statement.

Content Vocabulary
- account statement

GET READY for the Lesson

Why might you want to keep track of the daily events in your life?

Tak Jerrod likes to keep a day planner in which he records his meetings, deadlines, and family events. He also lists his goals for each week and indicates whether he has met them.

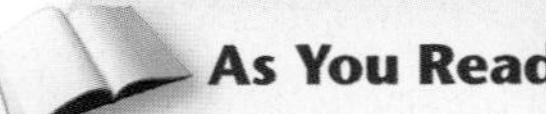

As You Read

Summarize What information does an account statement show?

Account Statements When you have a savings account, your bank may mail or make available on the Internet a monthly or quarterly account statement. The bank's **account statement** shows the **status** of your account. This includes all deposits to, withdrawals from, and interest earned and credited to your savings account. Many financial institutions are encouraging their patrons to go paperless and check the status of their account online.

New Balance = Previous Balance + Interest + Deposits − Withdrawals

EXAMPLE 1

Lauren Yamaguchi receives her savings account statement quarterly (see **Figure 5.4**). After checking to be sure all transactions have been recorded correctly, she checks the calculations. What is the balance in her account on July 1?

Figure 5.4

Savings Account Statement

Name		Beginning Date	4/01/20--
Lauren Yamaguchi		Ending Date	7/01/20--
Account Number	5891235	Interest Earned This Period	4.11

Date	Withdrawal	Deposit	Interest	Balance
4/01				274.50
4/15		250.00		524.50
5/11		125.00		649.50
6/10	100.00			549.50
7/01			4.11	553.61
7/01		80.00		633.61

Find the new balance.

New Balance = Previous Balance + Interest + Deposits − Withdrawals

= \$274.50 + \$4.11 + (\$250 + \$125 + \$80) − \$100.00

= **\$633.61**

274.5 [+] 4.11 [+] 250 [+] 125 [+] 80 [−] 100 [=] 633.61

Find the new balance. Check your answers in the back of the book.

1. The previous balance in Rolf Lutzger's account is $700.00; activities in it include interest, $1.50; deposits, $100.00 and $250.00; withdrawals, $80.00 and $110.00.
2. Crissy Leon's account statement showed previous balance, $6,756.21; interest, $28.15; deposits, $12,350.22, $3,210.57, and $3,209.87; withdrawals, $175.00 and $2,900.00.

Need Help? Go to...
Workshop 38: Problem Solving Strategies: Writing an Equation, p. 78

EXAMPLE 2 Algebra

Allison McKnight reviewed her account statement and wanted to verify that the interest amount was correct. Her new balance was $17,015.97 and her previous balance had been $14,761.93. She had deposited $2,386.20 and withdrawn $200.00. Find the interest earned on Allison's savings account.

Let i = The interest earned on Allison's savings account

New Balance = Previous Balance + Interest + Deposits − Withdrawals

$17,015.97 = $14,761.93 + i + $2,386.20 − $200.00

Combine like terms. → $17,015.97 = $16,948.13 + i

Subtract $16,948.13 from both sides. → **$67.84** = i

Concept CHECK

Complete the problem. Check your answer in the back of the book.

3. Hideo Tomita wanted to verify that the amount of his savings account withdrawals was correct. His new balance was $7,680.08, and his previous balance had been $7,147.50. In addition, his savings account had earned $32.58 in interest, and he had made deposits totaling $1,000.00. How much had he withdrawn?

Study Tip

Comfort

Find a comfortable and quiet place to study with good lighting and few distractions.

Lesson Practice

Find the new balance.

	Previous Balance	+	Interest	+	Deposits	−	Withdrawals	=	New Balance
4.	$ 400.00	+	$1.90	+	$ 50.00	−	$150.00	=	
5.	485.00	+	1.95	+	125.00	−	200.00	=	
6.	674.00	+	1.22	+	160.00	−	190.00	=	
7.	7,381.19	+	9.64	+	231.43	−	180.00	=	

8. Judi Imhoff's previous balance was $717.52. She received $4.36 in interest and had $125.00 and $276.95 in deposits and $90.00 in withdrawals. What is her new balance?

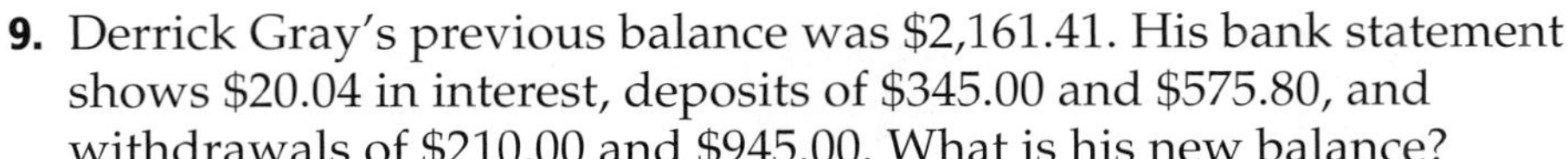

Did You Know?

History of Interest **For centuries, the rulers of England considered the practice of charging interest for loans immoral. In the early 16th century, King Henry VIII allowed interest to be charged at a fixed rate.**

9. Derrick Gray's previous balance was $2,161.41. His bank statement shows $20.04 in interest, deposits of $345.00 and $575.80, and withdrawals of $210.00 and $945.00. What is his new balance?

10. Sara Averett's previous savings account balance was $74,561.49 with $1,017.98 in interest, deposits of $918.37 and $944.56, and withdrawals of $959.40 and $14,391.47. What is her new balance?

11. Lars Torvall received his savings account statement (see **Figure 5.5**). Fill in the missing information on his statement.

Figure 5.5

Savings Account Statement				
Name: Lars Torvall		**Beginning Date**	01/15/20 --	
		Ending Date	07/15/20 --	
Account Number	12-36-5000	**Total Interest this period**	f.	
Date	**Withdrawals**	**Deposits**	**Interest**	**Balance**
15-Jan				$503.27
28-Jan		$ 45.00	$0.90	549.17
3-Feb		80.40	0.45	630.02
15-Feb			1.04	631.06
15-Mar			2.42	633.48
10-Apr	$400.00		2.26	235.74
15-Apr			0.16	a.
1-May		335.60	0.52	b.
15-May			1.10	c.
15-Jun			2.43	d.
15-Jul			2.37	e.

12. ALGEBRA Shirley Cohen wants to verify her deposit to her savings account. Her new balance is $2,675.08, the previous balance was $2,176.49, interest earned was $8.74, and withdrawals totaled $275.00. Find the amount she deposited to her savings account.

Spiral Review

Add or subtract. (Skill 5 and Skill 6)

13. $450.00 + $9.50 + $40.00

14. $426.30 + $278.41 + $342.91

15. $7,942.70 – $3,453.80

16. $16,865.95 – $14,991.39

17. Charlotte Franklin earns $18.75 per hour. She worked her regular 38 hours last week. What is her straight-time pay? (Lesson 1.1)

18. Dean Willis earns $315.75 per week. The Social Security tax rate is 6.2% and Medicare tax is 1.45% of gross pay. How much is the deduction from his pay check for Social Security and Medicare? (Lesson 2.4)

GET READY for the Next Lesson

PREREQUISITE SKILL **Writing Percents as Decimals** (Skill 28)

Write the percents as decimals.

19. 25%
20. 5%
21. 1.24%
22. 123%
23. 603%
24. 0.03%

LESSON 5.4

Simple Interest

Lesson Objective
Calculate simple interest and the amount.

Content Vocabulary
- interest
- simple interest
- principal
- annual interest rate

GET READY for the Lesson

Why should you start saving now for the future?

Chris Gupta's uncle gave him a surprise wedding gift. When Chris was born, Uncle Bill deposited $5,000 in a savings account. Over time, the amount earned interest and grew. When Chris received the gift 30 years later, he realized he could use it as part of his down payment on the condo he and his wife wanted.

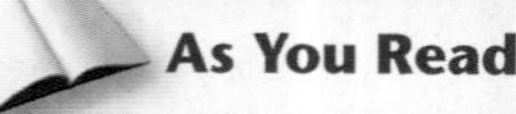

As You Read

Identify What three factors affect simple interest?

Calculating Simple Interest When you deposit money into a savings account, you are permitting the bank to use the money. The bank pays **interest**, the amount of money paid for the use of a lender's money. The most common **method** for calculating interest is the **simple interest** formula. This is the interest paid on the original **principal**, the amount of money earning interest. Simple interest is based on three factors: the principal; **annual interest rate** (the percent of the principal earned as interest in one year); and the amount of time for which the principal is borrowed or invested.

To compute interest, use the formula:

Interest = Principal × Rate × Time or $I = prt$

Note that this formula expresses the rate as percent and the time in years or a fraction of a year. If the interest is computed and then deposited into the account, you have a new quantity called the amount.

Amount = Principal + Interest, or $A = P + I$

Need Help? Go to...
- Workshop 6: Multiplying Decimals, p. 14
- Workshop 13: Fraction to Decimal, Decimal to Percent, p. 28

EXAMPLE 1

Joyce Tyler deposits $9,000 in an account that pays an annual 5.5% interest rate. Determine the simple interest and the amount in the account for **(a)** 3 years, **(b)** 3 months, and **(c)** 3 days.

Step 1: Find the interest amount at 5.5% for the given time periods:

Interest = Principal × Rate × Time

Step 2: Find the amount in the account:

Amount = Principal + Interest

Purestock/SuperStock

(a) Interest for 3 years

$I = \$9,000 \times 5.5\% \times 3 =$ **\$1,485** and $A = \$9,000 + \$1,485 =$ **\$10,485**

(b) Interest for 3 months

Note: 3 months is $\frac{3}{12}$ of a year. → $I = \$9,000.00 \times 5.5\% \times \frac{3}{12}$

$I = \$9,000.00 \times 0.055 \times 0.25 =$ **\$123.75** and $A = \$9,000.00 + \$123.75 =$ **\$9,123.75**

(c) Interest for 3 days

Note: 3 days is $\frac{3}{365}$ of a year. → $I = \$9,000.00 \times 5.5\% \times \frac{3}{365}$

$I = \$9,000.00 \times 0.055 \times 3 \div 365 = \$4.06849 =$ **\$4.07** and
$A = \$9,000.00 + \$4.07 =$ **\$9,004.07**

Need Help? Go to...
Application A: Formulas, p. AP1

Concept CHECK

Determine the interest and the amount for the indicated time. Check your answers in the back of the book.

1. Principal: \$4,000 at 6% for **(a)** 4 years, **(b)** 4 months, and **(c)** 4 days.
2. Principal: \$6,580 at 6.5% for **(a)** 10 years, **(b)** 10 months, and **(c)** 10 days.

EXAMPLE 2 Algebra

Martin Ellis earned \$150.00 in simple interest in 8 months at an annual interest rate of 6%. How much money did he invest?

Let p = the principal

$I = prt$

$\$150 = p \times (6\%) \times \frac{8}{12}$

Substitute what is known → $\$150 = p \times (0.06) \times \frac{8}{12}$

Multiply: $0.06 \times 8 \div 12$ → $\$150 = 0.04p$

Divide both sides by 0.04 → $p =$ **\$3,750**

Concept CHECK

Complete the problems. Check your answers in the back of the book.

3. Brenna O'Connor earned \$120 in simple interest in 9 months at an annual interest rate of 8%. How much money did she invest?
4. What annual simple interest rate must Hosea Sokolski earn to have \$80,000 increase to \$90,000 in two years?

Reading Math

Mixed Numbers

A mixed number is a number consisting of an integer and a fraction less than 1. The fraction has a numerator less than its denominator, a proper fraction.

Lesson Practice

Determine the interest and the amount.

	Principal	Rate	Time	Interest	Amount
5.	$ 720.00	6.00%	5 years	a. $	b. $
6.	720.00	6.00	5 months	a.	b.
7.	720.00	6.00	5 days	a.	b.
8.	5,892.15	6.875	15 months	a.	b.
9.	26,968.44	3.459	91 days	a.	b.

Did You Know?

Return to Sender Each year the Internal Revenue Service is unable to deliver thousands of tax refund checks because recipients have moved to unknown addresses. In one recent year, the IRS owed an average of $871 to more than 84,000 taxpayers who could not be found.

10. Tyrell Otis deposited his IRS refund check for $760 at 5% and made no other deposits or withdrawals. How much simple interest did his money earn in 3 months? What is the final amount in the account?

11. Sydney Dukes-Miller deposited $2,430 at 6.75%. She made no other deposits or withdrawals. How much simple interest did she earn in 65 days? What is the amount in the account?

H.O.T. Problems

12. ALGEBRA Megan Dunstall wants to know how many months it would take for $15,000.00 to earn $618.75 at $5\frac{1}{2}$% simple interest.

13. ALGEBRA What amount of money must Kurt Blixen invest at 4.75% to have it earn $10,000 in 90 days?

14. ALGEBRA If Mia Wong invests $73,000 at $7\frac{1}{2}$% annual simple interest on March 1, when will her investment be worth $75,760?

15. CHALLENGE PROBLEM On March 1, Tessa Obato deposited a check for $9,364.85 in a savings account at State Bank. The account pays 4% interest calculated on a daily basis. Five days later, on March 6, she withdrew $1,000.00. On March 18, 12 days later, she withdrew $2,000.00. On March 28, 10 days later, she withdrew another $2,000.00. Three days later, on March 31, the bank computed interest. How much simple interest did her money earn?

Spiral Review

Change the fractions and mixed numbers to decimals. (Skill 14)

16. $\frac{1}{2}$ **17.** $\frac{1}{4}$ **18.** $5\frac{1}{2}$ **19.** $6\frac{1}{4}$

20. Gary and Vi Sargento's average monthly expenditure for groceries in the first quarter of this year was $322.18. In April, they spent $372.15, and in May, they spent $295.16. How much can they spend in June and have the same average as the first quarter? (Lesson 3.1)

21. Beth Irwin is a computer programmer. Her annual salary is $72,400. What are her **(a)** monthly salary and **(b)** weekly salary? (Lesson 1.5)

GET READY for the Next Lesson

PREREQUISITE SKILL Finding the Percentage (Skill 30)

Find the percentage.

22. 965 × 5% **23.** $1,248 × 65%

24. $603 × 1.24% **25.** 123% × 251

26. $393 × 63% **27.** $5,893 × 0.03%

LESSON 5.5

Compound Interest

Lesson Objective
Determine the compound interest and the amount.

Content Vocabulary
- compound interest

GET READY for the Lesson

Should you have a savings account even if you are in high school? Why or why not?

Personal Banker Rachael Gleason helped Aisha Wilson open her savings account. Rachael tells Aisha about the time value of money—the longer she keeps her money in the account, the more money she will make.

As You Read
Summarize What is compound interest?

Computing Compound Interest Interest that you earn in a savings account during an interest **period** is added to your account. Your new balance is used for calculating the interest for the next interest period, the interest period after that, and so on.

Compound interest earns interest not only on the original principal but also on the interest earned during previous interest periods, earning interest on interest. Adding interest to an initial principal, thus forming a new and larger principal in the next period, is the procedure for computing compound interest.

The first step in computing compound interest is to use this formula:

Amount = Principal + Interest

Again, the amount is the balance in the account at the end of an interest period. When you have the amount, you do a series of simple interest computations. To find the compound interest, you find the difference between the amount in the account and the original principal. The formula is:

Compound Interest = Amount − Original Principal

Need Help? Go to...
- **Skill 14:** Changing Fractions/Decimals, p. SK15
- **Skill 28:** Writing Percents as Decimals, p. SK29
- **Skill 30:** Finding the Percentage, p. SK31
- **Application K:** Chronological Expressions, p. AP7

EXAMPLE

Jamal Washington deposited $1,000 in a savings account that earns 6% interest compounded quarterly. He made no other deposits or withdrawals. What was the amount in the account at the end of one year? How much is the compound interest?

Step 1: Calculate the interest and the amount for each quarter.

Interest = Principal × Rate × Time

Amount = Principal + Interest

Step 2: Calculate the compound interest

Amount − Original Principal

$1,061.37 − $1,000 = **$61.37 compound interest**

Continued on next page

Original Principal					$1,000.00
Interest for First Quarter	$\$1,000.00 \times 6\% \times \frac{1}{4} =$	$15.000	=	+	15.00
Amount at End of First Quarter	1,000.00 + $15.00 =				1,015.00
Interest for Second Quarter	$\$1,015.00 \times 6\% \times \frac{1}{4} =$	15.225	=	+	15.23
Amount at End of Second Quarter	1,015.00 + $15.23 =				1,030.23
Interest for Third Quarter	$\$1,030.23 \times 6\% \times \frac{1}{4} =$	15.453	=	+	15.45
Amount at End of Third Quarter	1,030.23 + $15.45 =				1,045.68
Interest for Fourth Quarter	$\$1,045.68 \times 6\% \times \frac{1}{4} =$	**15.685**	=	+	15.69
Amount at End of Fourth Quarter	1,045.68 + $15.69 =				**$1,061.37**

Study Tip

Flash Cards

When you study for a test, use flash cards on which you have written important ideas, definitions, and formulas. Make sure that you shuffle them each time you review them.

Concept CHECK

Complete the problems. Check your answers in the back of the book.

1. Liz Reynolds deposited $2,000 into a savings account that pays 8% compounded quarterly. Complete the table to compute the amount in the account after 1 year.

Original Principal					$2,000
Interest for First Quarter	$\$2,000 \times 8\% \times \frac{1}{4} =$	$40	=	+	$ 40
Amount at End of First Quarter	2,000 + 40 =				a.
Interest for Second Quarter	$2,040 \times 8 \times \frac{1}{4} =$	b.	=	+	c.
Amount at End of Second Quarter					d.
Interest for Third Quarter		e.	=	+	f.
Amount at End of Third Quarter					g.
Interest for Fourth Quarter		h.	=	+	i.
Amount at End of Fourth Quarter					j.

2. Calculate the compound interest.

Lesson Practice

	Principal	Annual Interest Rate	Interest Period	First Period Interest	Amount	Second Period Interest	Amount
3.	$ 900.00	6%	Quarterly	$13.50	$913.50	a. $	b. $
4.	400.00	6%	Monthly	2.00	402.00	a.	b.
5.	2,360.00	$4\frac{1}{2}\%$	Semi-annually	53.10	a.	b.	c.
6.	18,260.00	2.5%	Quarterly	a.	b.	c.	d.
7.	27,721.00	9.513%	Annually	a.	b.	c.	d.
8.	45,687.23	7.555%	Monthly	a.	b.	c.	d.

Did You Know?

Credit Unions **The international credit union system extends to 92 countries with more than 150,000,000 members worldwide. More than 43% of U.S. banking customers belong to a credit union.**

For the period indicated, calculate (a) the amount and (b) the compound interest.

9. Alicia Martin's savings account has a principal of $1,200. It earns 6% interest compounded quarterly for two quarters.
10. Aubrey Daniel's savings account has a principal of $5,725. It earns 4% interest compounded quarterly for 3 years.
11. The principal of Angelo Carrera's savings account is $9,855. It earns 6% interest compounded quarterly for two quarters.
12. Milo Simpson deposited $860 in a new regular savings account that earns 5.5% interest compounded semiannually for 1 year.
13. Jana Lacey deposited $4,860 in a new credit union savings account on the first day of the quarter. The principal earns 4% interest compounded quarterly for 6 months.
14. Mariel and Sam Trent's savings account had a balance of $9,544 on May 1. The account earns interest at a rate of 5.25% compounded monthly until the end of August.
15. Ernie Brody had $3,620 on deposit at Savings Bank on July 1. The money earns interest at a rate of 6.5% compounded quarterly until April 1 of the following year.

H.O.T. Problems

16. **CHALLENGE PROBLEM** Kaitlyn and Jamie Watson opened a savings account with a $2,000 deposit on January 1. The account pays interest at 6% compounded semiannually. On July 1, they deposited another $2,000. What is the amount of **(a)** their account on July 1, **(b)** the account one year later on January 1, and **(c)** the compound interest?
17. **CHALLENGE PROBLEM** A $10,000 investment earned interest at 4.5% compounded quarterly for 1 year and 5.5% compounded quarterly for the next year. What is the amount in the account at the end of 2 years?

Spiral Review

Write the percents as decimals. (Skill 28)

18. $5\frac{1}{4}\%$ **19.** $8\frac{1}{2}\%$ **20.** $5\frac{3}{4}\%$

21. Min Kurata deposited $875 for 3 months at 4% and made no other deposits or withdrawals. How much simple interest did his money earn? What is the amount in the account? (Lesson 5.4)
22. Rachel van Dressler earns 3% commission on all sales. What was her total sales amount if she earns a commission of $365? (Lesson 1.6)

GET READY for the Next Lesson

PREREQUISITE SKILL **Dividing Decimals** (Skill 11)

Convert the percent to a decimal and then divide.

23. 5% ÷ 5 **24.** 15% ÷ 3 **25.** 3.24% ÷ 6 **26.** 1.8% ÷ 6
27. 2.1% ÷ 4 **28.** 7.1% ÷ 7 **29.** 17% ÷ 9 **30.** 16.25% ÷ 4

LESSON 5.6 Compound Interest Tables

Lesson Objective

Find compound interest using a table and the compound interest formula.

Content Vocabulary

- compound interest table

GET READY for the Lesson

How does compound interest help build towards your financial goals?

Holly Dunn found it difficult to project the compound interest and new balance on her savings account. After she learned that she could use a compound interest table, she found the task much easier.

As You Read

Explain Why might you want to use a compound interest table?

Using a Compound Interest Table To compute compound interest quickly, you can use a **compound interest table**, which shows the amount of $1.00 for many interest rates and interest periods. To **utilize** the table, you must know the *total number of interest periods* and the *interest rate per period.* You use these formulas:

Amount = Original Principal × Amount of $1.00

Compound Interest = Amount − Original Principal

Need Help? Go to...

- Workshop 7: Dividing Decimals, p. 16
- Workshop 6: Multiplying Decimals, p. 14
- Application C: Tables and Charts, p. AP3

EXAMPLE 1

State Bank pays 6% interest compounded quarterly on regular savings accounts. Marta Carmona deposited $3,000 for 2 years. She made no other deposits or withdrawals. How much interest did Marta earn during the 2 years? (*Note:* Use the *Compound Interest—Amount of $1.00* table on page A11 to solve this problem.)

Step 1: Find the total number of interest periods.

Total Number of Interest Periods = Periods per Year × Number of Years

8 = 4 quarters per year × 2 years

Step 2: Find the interest rate per period.

$$\frac{\text{Annual Rate}}{\text{Number of Periods per Year}}$$

$$\frac{6\%}{4} = 1.5\%$$

Step 3: Find the amount of $1.00 for 8 periods at 1.5% per period using the Compound Interest—Amount of $1.00 table on page A11.

Read across the top to the 1.5% column and read down to the $n = 8$ row: Value = 1.12649

Step 4: Find the amount.

Original Principal × Amount of $1.00

$3,000.00 × 1.12649 = $3,379.47

Step 5: Find the compound interest.

Amount − Original Principal

$3,379.47 − $3,000.00 = **$379.47 compound interest**

Ingram Publishing/age Fotostock

Find the amount and compound interest using the *Compound Interest—Amount of $1.00* table on page A11. Check your answers in the back of the book.

1. Ed Cure invested $2,000 at 5.5% interest compounded quarterly for 2 years.
2. Louisa Foster invested $4,500 at 3% interest compounded semiannually for 2 years.

Need Help? Go to...

Application B: More Formulas, p. AP2

EXAMPLE 2 Algebra

If you have a calculator with a y^x key, you can compute compound interest and the amount by using this formula:

$A = P(1.00 + r)^n$

Where A = Amount, called the Future Value (FV)

P = Principal, called the Present Value (PV)

$r = \text{Rate per period} = \dfrac{\text{Annual Interest Rate}}{\text{Number of Periods Per Year}}$

n = Number of periods = Number of years × Number of periods per year

Elliot Frazier deposited $10,000 (present value) into a savings account paying 6% annual interest compounded monthly. What amount (future value) will he have in his account after 5 years? How much compound interest will he have earned?

Step 1: Rate per period: $r = \dfrac{6\%}{12} = \dfrac{0.06}{12} = \mathbf{0.005}$

Step 2: Number of periods: $n = 5 \times 12 = 60$

Step 3: Substitute into the formula:

$A = P(1.00 + r)^n$

$A = \$10{,}000\ (1.00 + 0.005)^{60}$

$A = \$10{,}000\ (1.005)^{60}$

$A = \$10{,}000\ (1.348850153)$

$A = \$13{,}488.50153 = \$13{,}488.50$

Step 4: Find the compound interest.

Amount	−	Original Principal		
$13,488.50	−	$10,000.00	=	**$3,488.50 compound interest**

Study Tip

Taking Notes

Date your notes. Rewrite them after class during study time. Add titles and subtitles for easy referencing when you prepare for a test later.

Concept CHECK

Complete the problems. Check your answers in the back of the book.

3. How much compound interest will $50,000 have earned in 10 years at 6.4% annual interest compounded quarterly?
4. Margie Spencer wants to have $100,000 in her savings account in 20 years. If her account pays 6.6% annual interest compounded semiannually, how much must Margie deposit into her account now to meet her goal?

SPREADSHEET APPLICATION

Compound Interest

You can use a spreadsheet like the partial one below to demonstrate the power of compounding. You will need to enter the name, principal, rate, periods per year, and number of years. The spreadsheet will automatically calculate the amount in the account and the interest earned.

Math Online Go to connectED.mcgraw-hill.com to download an evaluation rubric.

	A	B	C	D	E	F	G	H
1								
2		Name	Principal	Rate	Period per Year	Years	Amount	Interest
3	1							

Think and Discuss

1. Suppose that June Williams deposited $10,000 into a savings account paying 6% annual interest compounded monthly. What amount will be in the account after 1 year?
2. Suppose that June's interest is compounded quarterly instead of monthly. Determine the amount in the account after 5 years. What columns did you change?
3. Larry Kincaid deposited $2,000 into a savings account paying 5% annual interest compounded quarterly. What amount will be in the account after **(a)** 1 year, **(b)** 5 years, and **(c)** 10 years?

Lesson Practice

Use the *Compound Interest—Amount of $1.00* table on page A11 to solve Problems 5 to 10. Round your answers to the nearest cent.

		Annual Interest Rate	Compounded	Rate per Period	Total Time	Total Number of Periods	Amount	Compound Interest
5.	$ 900.00	5.50	Quarterly	**a.** $	2 years	**b.**	**c.** $	**d.** $
6.	640.00	6.00	Semiannually	**a.**	4 years	**b.**	**c.**	**d.**
7.	1,340.00	5.00	Quarterly	**a.**	3 years	**b.**	**c.**	**d.**
8.	6,231.40	5.75	Semiannually	**a.**	5 years	**b.**	**c.**	**d.**
9.	3,871.67	12.00	Monthly	**a.**	4 years	**b.**	**c.**	**d.**
10.	9,000.00	18.00	Monthly	**a.**	2 years	**b.**	**c.**	**d.**

Manhattan In 1626, Peter Minuit, a director of the Dutch West India Trading Company, bought the island of Manhattan for 60 guilders (about $24) worth of beads and trinkets. If he had instead invested that $24 at 8% interest, compounded annually for 374 years (1626–2000), his investment would have grown to $76 trillion.

11. Bobbie Jean Byrd deposited $900 in a savings plan with her credit union. The credit union savings plan pays 6% interest compounded quarterly. If she makes no other deposits or withdrawals, how much interest will her money earn in $2\frac{1}{2}$ years?
12. National Credit Union pays 6.25% interest compounded semiannually on special notice savings accounts. Jessie McKenzie deposits $3,438.70 in a savings account for 2 years. At the end of 2 years, she deposits $5,000.00 in the account. How much is in the account at the end of 5 more years?
13. University Bank pays 5% interest compounded quarterly on regular savings accounts and Rosemont Savings Bank pays 5.5% compounded semiannually. Vasily and Oxana Cherchenko had $4,000 to invest for 4 years. Based on the interest to be earned, which bank offers the better investment?

14. **ALGEBRA** If you deposit $25,000 now at 6.5% compounded quarterly, how much will you have in 30 years?
15. **ALGEBRA** Tony Peyton, age 20, would like to have $1,000,000 by the time he is 65 years of age. If Tony could earn 6.9% annual interest compounded monthly, how much must he invest now to have $1,000,000 by the time he is 65?
16. **CHALLENGE PROBLEM** Winnie Bracken opened a savings account at Dallas Trust Bank on March 1. It pays 4% interest compounded quarterly. She opened her account with an initial deposit of $10,000. She made $1,000 deposits at the end of each quarter. How much is in the account at the end of 6 quarters?

Spiral Review

Convert the percent to a decimal and then divide. (Skill 28)

17. 7% ÷ 4 18. 8.5% ÷ 2 19. 3.5% ÷ 4

20. Your checking account balance on May 15 is $124.25. You deposit $223.56 on May 20, write a check for $89.56, and withdraw $80.00 from an ATM on May 25. What is your current balance? (Lesson 4.3)
21. Matthew Westhoven deposited $925 in a new regular savings account that earns 5.5% interest compounded semiannually for 1 year. What is the compound interest? (Lesson 5.5)

GET READY for the Next Lesson

PREREQUISITE SKILL **Rounding Numbers** (Skill 2)

Multiply. Round the answer to the nearest hundredth.

22. 2,504 × 0.0457 23. 55 × 2.435 24. 1.249 × 232
25. 0.758 × 6 26. 6 × 45.193 27. 0.269 × 12.35

LESSON 5.7

Daily Compounding

Lesson Objective
Calculate the interest for daily compounding.

Content Vocabulary
- daily compounding

GET READY for the Lesson

Would you rather have a savings account that compounds interest annually, monthly, or daily? Why?

Etwaun Bryant came up with a good way to understand the concept of compounding. He compared it to the way pushing on a car's gas pedal makes the car go faster and faster. When a bank adds interest to a savings account daily and recalculates the amount, the total in the account grows.

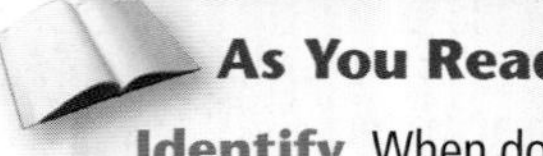

As You Read

Identify When does an account with daily compounding begin earning interest?

Daily Compounding The more often banks compound interest, the more **potential** you have to earn more interest. Many banks offer savings accounts with **daily compounding**. When they compound interest daily, it is computed each day and added to the account balance. The account will earn interest from the day of deposit to the day of withdrawal. You can use a table to calculate the amount and the interest for daily compounding.

We used these formulas in previous sections:

Amount = Original Principal × Amount of $1.00

Compound Interest = Amount − Original Principal

Need Help? Go to...
- Workshop 6: Multiplying Decimals, p. 14
- Workshop 17: Elapsed Time, p. 36
- Skill 8: Multiplying Decimals, p. SK9
- Application G: Elapsed Time (days), p. AP6

EXAMPLE 1

Suppose you deposit $8,000 in an account that pays 5.5% interest compounded daily. How much interest will you earn in 31 days?

Step 1: Find the amount of $1.00 for 31 days using **Figure 5.6.**
Amount = 1.00468

Figure 5.6

Amount of $1.00 at 5.5%			
Compounded Daily (365 Day-Year)			
Day	Amount	Day	Amount
21	1.00316	31	1.00468
22	1.00331	32	1.00483
23	1.00347	33	1.00498
24	1.00362	34	1.00513
25	1.00377	35	1.00528

Step 2: Find the amount.

Amount	=	Original Principal	×	Amount of $1.00
$8,037.44	=	$8,000	×	1.00468

Step 3: Find the compound interest.

Compound Interest	=	Amount	–	Original Principal
$37.44	=	$8,037.44	–	$8,000.00

Concept CHECK

Find the (a) amount and (b) compound interest. Check your answers in the back of the book.

1. Ramona Oden deposited $6,000 at 5.5% interest compounded daily for 25 days.
2. Chuck Lange deposited $6,000 at 5.5% interest compounded daily for 31 days.

Need Help? Go to...
Workshop 17: Elapsed Time, p. 36

EXAMPLE 2

On May 31, Deloris Caudill deposited $1,000 in a savings account that pays 5.5% interest compounded daily. On July 1, how much interest had the principal in her account earned?

Step 1: Find the number of days from May 31 to July 1. Use the *Elapsed Time* table on page A10.

July 1 is day 182. May 31 is day 151.
Number of Days = 182 – 151 = 31 days

Step 2: Find the amount of $1.00 for 31 days using the *Compounded Interest—Amount of $1.00 at 5.5%, Compounded Daily (365-Day Year)* table on page A10.

Amount = $1.00468

Step 3: Find the amount.

Amount	=	Original Principal	×	Amount of $1.00
$1,004.68	=	$1,000	×	$1.00468

Step 4: Find the compound interest.

Compound Interest Principal	=	Amount	–	Original Principal
$4.68	=	$1,004.68	–	$1,000.00

Concept CHECK

Determine how much interest the principal in each account had earned. Check your answers in the back of the book.

3. On March 3, Raul Avila deposited $10,000 in a savings account that pays 5.5% interest compounded daily until June 21.
4. On March 26, Samuel Griffin deposited $20,000 in a savings account that pays 5.5% interest compounded daily until July 24.

Lesson Practice

Use the *Amount of $1.00 at 5.5%, Compounded Daily (365-Day Year)* table on page A10 to solve. Round the answers to the nearest cent.

	Principal	Number of Days	Amount	Compound Interest
5.	$80,000	25	a. $	b. $
6.	3,800	90	a.	b.
7.	15,321	May 5 to Sept. 12	a.	b.
8.	10,500	Aug. 2 to Dec. 20	a.	b.

Did You Know?

Piggy Bank **The origin of the piggy bank actually has nothing to do with pigs. More than 500 years ago, people often threw spare coins into pots made of pygg, an inexpensive clay. Over the centuries, "pygg bank" became "piggy bank."**

9. On June 10, Bertha Wooten deposited $8,241.78 in a savings account that pays 5.5% interest compounded daily. How much interest will the money earn in 31 days?

10. Alexandra Efland has a savings account that earns 5.5% interest compounded daily. On May 5, the amount in the account was $28,214.35. How much interest will the money earn in the next 90 days?

11. On April 11, George Jimerson had $6,521.37 in his savings account. The account pays 5.5% interest compounded daily. How much interest will the money earn by June 30?

12. On August 23, Carlito Rosselini had $1,432.19 in his savings account at Camden Savings and Trust. The account earns 5.5% interest compounded daily. What will be the amount in his savings account when he closes it on October 1?

H.O.T. Problems

13. CHALLENGE PROBLEM Debra Gondry's savings account showed a $904.31 balance on March 1. The same day, she deposited $375.00 to the account. She also deposited $500.00 on April 1 and May 1. The bank pays interest at a rate of 5.5% compounded daily. What will be the amount in her account on May 29?

14. CHALLENGE PROBLEM Use the compound interest formula from Lesson 5.6 to find the interest on $20,000 at 7.3% compounded daily from June 15 to October 15.

Spiral Review

Multiply and round to the nearest hundredth. (Skill 2 and Skill 7)

15. $4,000 × 1.02131 **16.** $9,000 × 1.00135

17. Lila Koepke's savings account with $700 pays 6% interest compounded quarterly. If she makes no deposits or withdrawals, how much interest will the account earn in $2\frac{1}{2}$ years? (Lesson 5.6)

18. ALGEBRA Tendo Mutema pays $199.50 per month for group medical insurance. His employer pays 65% of the cost. How much is the annual premium? (Lesson 2.5)

GET READY for the Next Lesson

PREREQUISITE SKILL **Multiplying Decimals** (Skill 8)

Multiply.

19. 22 × 3.323 **20.** 1.2 × 183 **21.** 6.03 × 10.23

22. 91 × 48.9 **23.** 7.5432 × 62 **24.** 0.614 × 1.988

LESSON 5.8

Annuities

Lesson Objective

Compute the future value of an ordinary annuity and an annuity due.

Content Vocabulary

- annuity
- ordinary annuity
- annuity due

GET READY for the Lesson

When is the right time to plan for your retirement years?

Lana and Mario Ruiz were concerned about their retirement. The couple began working with an advisor who could help them decide how much they should be saving and how to choose among different savings options.

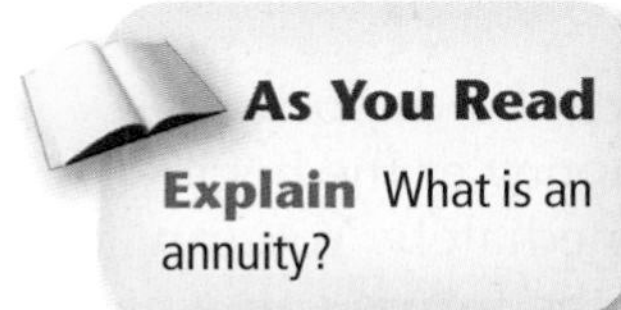

As You Read

Explain What is an annuity?

Investing in Annuities Financial advisors recommend that their clients make regular deposits in a savings plan, such as an Individual Retirement Account (IRA). An account into which someone deposits an equal amount of money at equal periods or equal **intervals** of time is an **annuity**. There are two categories of annuities:

1. **Ordinary annuity** occurs when equal deposits are made at the *end* of each interest period.
2. **Annuity Due** occurs when you make regular deposits at the *beginning* of the interest period. The money immediately starts earning interest because it is deposited at the beginning of the interest period.

The *future value* of an annuity is the amount of money in the annuity account at the *end* of a specific period of time. To compute the future value of an ordinary annuity, follow the steps in **Example 1** using this formula:

Future Value = Amount of Deposit × Future Value of $1.00

To compute the total interest, use this formula:

Total Interest = Future Value − Total of all Deposits

(Throughout this section, you must refer to a *value* found in the table: *Future Value of an Ordinary Annuity for $1.00 per Period* on page A12.)

Need Help? Go to...

- **Workshop 18:** Reading Tables and Charts, p. 38
- **Workshop 6:** Multiplying Decimals, p. 14
- Skill 8: Multiplying Decimals, p. SK9
- **Application C:** Tables and Charts (days), p. AP3

EXAMPLE 1

Phil Larrick deposits $500 in an ordinary annuity at the end of each quarter. The account earns 6% interest compounded quarterly. What is the future value of the account in 2 years? How much interest has it earned?

Step 1: Find the total number of periods.

Total Number of Periods = Periods per Year × Number of Years = $(4 \times 2) = 8$

Step 2: Find the interest rate per period.

$$\text{Interest Rate per Period} = \frac{\text{Annual Rate}}{\text{Number of Periods per Year}} = \frac{6\%}{4} = 1.5\%$$

Continued on next page

Step 3: Find the future value of \$1.00 for 8 periods at 1.5 % per period using the value found in the table: *Future Value of an Ordinary Annuity for \$1.00 per Period* on page A12.
Look down the 1.50% column to the $n = 8$ row. The value = 8.43284

Step 4: Find the future value.
Amount of Deposit × Future Value of \$1.00
\$500 × 8.43284 = \$4,216.42 future value

Step 5: Find the total interest.
Future Value − Total of all Deposits
\$4,216.42 − (8 × \$500)
\$4,216.42 − \$4,000 = **\$216.42 total interest**

Determine (a) the future value of each account and (b) the total interest amount earned. Check your answers in the back of the book.

1. Roy Drennan deposited \$5,000 into an ordinary annuity after each quarter for 3 years at 6% interest compounded quarterly.

Annuity Due An annuity due occurs when you have regular deposits at the beginning of the period. Because you deposit the money at the beginning of the interest period, it starts earning interest immediately. You can find the future value of an annuity due by multiplying the future value of an ordinary annuity by 1 plus the rate per period:

Future Value of an Annuity Due = Future Value of an Ordinary Annuity × (1 + Rate per Period)

EXAMPLE 2

Suppose that Phil Larrick (from **Example 1**) had made \$500 deposits in an annuity due at the beginning of each quarter in an account earning 6% interest compounded quarterly. What is the future value of the account in 2 years? How much interest will it have earned?

Step 1: You know from **Example 1** that the future value of the ordinary annuity is \$4,216.42.

Step 2: You also know that the rate per period is 1.5% or 0.015.

Step 3: Calculate the future value of an annuity due.
Future Value of an Ordinary Annuity × (1.00 + Rate per Period)
FV of an Annuity Due = \$4,216.42 × (1.00 + 0.015)
= \$4,216.42 × 1.015
= \$4,279.6663 = **\$4,279.67**

Step 4: Find the total interest.
Total Interest = Future Value − Total of All Deposits
= \$4,279.67 − (8 × \$500)
= \$4,279.67 − \$4,000 = **\$279.67**

Concept CHECK

Calculate the (a) future value of the annuity due and (b) total interest earned. Check your answers in the back of the book.

2. See Lesson 5.8 Concept Check problem 1. Recalculate assuming that Roy Drennan deposited \$5,000 in an annuity due at the beginning of each quarter for 3 years at 6% compounded quarterly.

Need Help? Go to...

Application B: More Formulas, p. AP2

EXAMPLE 3 Algebra

You can compute the future value (FV) of an ordinary annuity by using this formula:

$$FV = \frac{AD[(\$1.00 + r)^n - \$1.00]}{r}$$

Where FV = Future Value of the Ordinary Annuity

AD = Amount Deposited Each Period

r = Interest Rate per Period = $\frac{\text{Annual Interest Rate}}{\text{Number of Periods per Year}}$

n = Number of Periods = (Number of Years × Number of Periods per Year)

Diane Tennet deposits $500 in an ordinary annuity at the end of each month in an account earning 6% interest compounded monthly. What is the future value of the annuity in 15 years? How much interest will Diane have earned in the 15 years?

Step 1: Rate per period: $r = \frac{6\%}{12} = \frac{0.06}{12} = 0.005$

Step 2: Number of periods: $n = 15 \times 12 = 180$

Step 3: Substitute into the formula:

$$FV = \frac{AD[(1.00 + r)^n - 1.00]}{r}$$

$$FV = \frac{\$500[(1.00 + 0.005)^{180} - 1.00]}{0.005}$$

$$FV = \frac{\$500[(1.005)^{180} - 1.00]}{0.005}$$

$$FV = \frac{\$500[2.454093562) - 1.00]}{0.005}$$

$$FV = \frac{\$500[1.454093562]}{.005} = \frac{\$727.0467811}{0.005}$$

$$= \$145{,}409.3562 = \mathbf{\$145{,}409.36}$$

Step 4: Calculate the interest

Future Value − Total Deposit

$145,409.36 − [(12 × 15)($500)]

$145,409.36 − [(180)($500)]

$145,409.36 − $90,000 = **$55,409.36 interest**

Per Period

If the word *per* is included in a math problem, such as "per day" or "per period," you need to multiply or divide.

Concept CHECK

Complete the problems. Check your answers in the back of the book.

3. Alex Bundt saves $500 at the end of every quarter in an ordinary annuity earning 6.2% interest compounded quarterly. How much will Alex have saved in 20 years? How much interest will he have earned?
4. Tina Hinojosa wants to have $1,000,000 by the time she is 62. She is 16. If she can earn 6.5% interest compounded daily in an ordinary annuity, how much would she have to save every day?

Lesson Practice

Use the table *Future Value of an Ordinary Annuity for $1.00 per Period* on page A12 to solve the following problems.

	Deposit	Rate	Compounded	Years	Number of Periods	Rate per Period	Table Value	FV of Ordinary Annuity	Interest Earned	FV of Annuity Due
5.	$5,000	6.00%	Quarterly	2	a.	b.%	c.$	d.$	e.$	f.$
6.	800	4.00	Semiannually	6	a.	b.	c.	d.	e.	f.
7.	2,000	4.00	Annually	10	a.	b.	c.	d.	e.	f.
8.	1,000	6.00	Monthly	3	a.	b.	c.	d.	e.	f.

Did You Know?

Retirement Age Retirees used to receive full Social Security benefits starting on their 65th birthday. Longer life spans today mean the retirement age is gradually going up. Retirees born in 1960 or later will have to wait until at least their 67th birthday to receive full benefits.

For Problems 9 and 10, find: (a) future value and (b) total interest earned.

9. Regina Aguirre deposits $2,000 into an ordinary annuity after each 6-month period for 4 years. The account pays 6% interest compounded semiannually.

10. Vernon Taber deposits $600 into an ordinary annuity after each quarter for 4 years. The account pays 4% interest compounded quarterly.

11. Kimi Skuban deposits $2,000 at the beginning of each year into an Individual Retirement Account at Boise Bank. The account pays 7% compounded annually. How much will be in the account in 25 years?

12. Richard and Elaine McCormick would like to have $20,000 in 5 years to make a down payment on a home. They decide to save $350 at the beginning of each month for the next 4 years. The money is in an account that pays 6% compounded monthly. How much will they need to save in the fifth year?

13. ALGEBRA Norm Kandel puts $3,500 into his IRA, an ordinary annuity, at the end of every year. If he earns 5.762% interest compounded annually, how much will he have after 25 years? How much interest will he have earned?

14. ALGEBRA When Alice Dill and Donald Nash married, they set a goal of having $1,000,000 on their 50th wedding anniversary. If they could earn 6.6% interest compounded monthly in an ordinary annuity, how much would they have to save monthly to reach their goal?

Spiral Review

Multiply (Skill 8)

15. $3,698 × 4.12161 **16.** $1,100 × 5.10101 **17.** $1,587 × 6.07550

18. Gina Basco worked from 8:00 to 10:45 and from 11:15 to 3:45. Find the total number of hours she worked. (Lesson 1.3)

GET READY for the Next Lesson

PREREQUISITE SKILL Finding the Percentage (Skill 30)

Find the percentage. Round to the nearest cent.

19. 5% of 342 **20.** 15% of 30 **21.** 24% of $192 **22.** 5.75% of $132

CHAPTER 5 Review and Assessment

AFTER YOU READ

Chapter SUMMARY

Saving money is an important step in accomplishing goals and living a financially responsible life. Savings account holders should know how to manage deposits and withdrawals to their savings account and compute the new balance on the account statement. They should also know how to calculate simple and compound interest and compute the future value of an ordinary annuity and an annuity due.

Vocabulary Check

1. On a sheet of paper, use each of these terms in a sentence.

Content Vocabulary

- savings account (p. 213)
- deposit (p. 213)
- withdrawal (p. 216)
- account statement (p. 219)
- interest (p. 222)
- simple interest (p. 222)
- principal (p. 222)
- annual interest rate (p. 222)
- compound interest (p. 225)
- compound interest table (p. 228)
- daily compounding (p. 232)
- annuity (p. 235)
- ordinary annuity (p. 235)
- annuity due (p. 235)

Academic Vocabulary

- specific (p. 213)
- portion (p. 216)
- status (p. 219)
- method (p. 222)
- period (p. 225)
- utilize (p. 228)
- potential (p. 232)
- interval (p. 235)

Concept Check

2. List three ways to make a deposit.
3. Give the formula for calculating the total amount of a deposit.
4. Give the formula for determining simple interest.
5. List factors that affect the amount of interest earned.
6. Define *principal* as it relates to a savings account.
7. Explain the difference between compound interest and simple interest.
8. Give the formula for finding the amount of compound interest.
9. Differentiate between an ordinary annuity and an annuity due.
10. Define *future value of an annuity.*
11. **CRITICAL THINKING** Explain why money grows faster with compound interest than with simple interest.

Lesson-by-Lesson Review

5.1 Deposits (pp. 213–215)

Complete a savings account deposit slip and compute the total deposit.
Freddie Enberg has 34 one-dollar bills in currency, $8.74 in coins, and a check for $102.35 to deposit into his savings account. He wants to receive a $10 bill in cash.

How much will he deposit?

Compute the total deposit: Total Deposit = (Currency + Coins + Checks) − Cash Received

$135.09 = ($34.00 + $8.74 + $102.35) − $10.00

Review Exercises

Find the subtotal and total deposit.

	Deposits	Subtotal	Less Cash Received	Total Deposit
12.	$ 38.90 34.28 21.01	a. $	$ 0.00	b. $
13.	$184.66 54.76 96.44	a. $	$ 50.98	b. $

14. **ALGEBRA** Annalise Kamal deposited into her savings account one check for $536.78, another for $195.00, and a third check. Her total deposit was for $1,146.23 after she received $125.00 in cash. What was the amount of the third check deposited?

5.2 Withdrawals (pp. 216–218)

Fill out a savings account withdrawal slip.
Serita Escobar would like to withdraw $85.34 from her savings account. Her account number is 00-170-14. Write the **(a)** account number, **(b)** amount as a numeral, and **(c)** amount in words.

Review Exercises

Write each amount in words.

15. $21.44

16. $396.00

For Problems 17–19, write the (a) account number, (b) amount as a numeral, and (c) amount in words.

17.

Farmer's Mercantile

Date	Savings Acct. No.	
11/8/20--	06029175	$76.60

Pay to Myself or to Damone Bashier

Dollars

And Charge to the above Numbered Account

Sign Here *Damone Bashier*

Withdrawal

18. Murphie Wallace has been saving to buy a big-screen TV. The total purchase price is $2,359.04. She fills out a withdrawal slip for the amount. Her savings account number is 8642-00-908.

19. Harry Birdsong withdraws $985.40 using a withdrawal slip. His savings account number is 045-8996.

Lesson-by-Lesson Review (continued)

5.3 Account Statements (pp. 219–221)

Compute the new balance of a savings account statement.
Your savings account statement shows a previous balance of $543.92 and $1.23 in interest. You made deposits of $100.00, $50.00, and $300.86. You had withdrawals of $35.46 and $128.44. What is your new balance?

Compute the new balance.

New Balance = Previous Balance + Interest + Deposits − Withdrawals

$832.11 = $543.92 + $1.23 + ($100.00 + $50.00 + $300.86) − ($35.46 + $128.44)

Review Exercises

20. What is the new balance if the previous balance was $650.25, interest was $4.02, the deposit was $125.44, and the withdrawal was $50.00?

21. Sergio Monteleone's savings account statement showed a previous balance of $234.95 and interest of $1.06. The statement also showed deposits of $123.42 and $50.66 and withdrawals of $323.09. What is his new balance?

22. **ALGEBRA** Lee Sun's savings account statement shows a present balance of $13,508.79 and a previous balance of $21,395.65. The statement also shows deposits of $498.88 and $98.10 and withdrawals of $8,498.23. What interest amount did she earn?

5.4 Simple Interest (pp. 222–224)

Calculate simple interest and the amount.
Your principal is $800. The annual rate of interest is 5.5%. What is the interest after 6 months?

Find the interest at $5\frac{1}{2}$%.

Interest = Principal × Rate × Time

Interest = $800.00 × $5\frac{1}{2}$% × $\frac{6}{12}$

$22.00 = $800.00 × 0.055 × 0.5

Review Exercises

23. $328.00 invested at 5% for 3 years

24. $635.85 invested at 7% for 6 months

25. $175.00 invested at 8% for 90 days

26. Craig Deloy's bank computes 4.25% interest on a daily basis. In one period, he had $1,250 in the account for 20 days. He deposited $450 and left it in the account for 10 days. Then he withdrew $300, and the balance earned interest for 8 days. How much interest did he earn in the period? What is the amount in the account?

27. **ALGEBRA** Tron Nguyen earned $110 in simple interest in 9 months at an annual interest rate of 8%. What was the amount of money he invested?

28. **ALGEBRA** What annual simple interest rate would Danae Jefferson have to earn to make $70,000 grow into $80,000 in two years?

Lesson-by-Lesson Review (continued)

5.5 Compound Interest (pp. 225–227)

Determine the compound interest and the amount.

Pat Villas deposited \$3,000 into a savings account that earns 4% interest compounded quarterly. She made no deposits or withdrawals. What is the amount in the account at the end of the second quarter?

Find the interest amount for each quarter.

Interest Amount = 1st Quarter Principal × Rate × Time
\$30.00 interest per quarter = \$3,000.00 × 4% × $\frac{1}{4}$

Total Amount in Account = Principal + Interest
\$3,030.00 total account amount = \$3,000.00 + \$30.00
2nd quarter \$3,030.00 × 4% × $\frac{1}{4}$ = \$30.30 interest amount 2nd quarter

Total Amount after 2nd Quarter = Principal + Interest
\$3,060.30 = \$3,030.00 + \$30.30

Review Exercises

	Principal	Annual Interest Rate	Interest Period	First Period Interest	Amount	Second Period Interest	Amount
29.	\$1,200.00	6.0%	Quarterly	a. \$	b. \$	c. \$	d. \$
30.	3,500.00	5.5%	Monthly	a.	b.	c.	d.

31. Piers Nardo deposited \$350 into a new regular savings account that earns 6.5% interest compounded semiannually. He made no other deposits or withdrawals. What amount was in his account at the end of 1 year?

5.6 Compound Interest Tables (pp. 228–231)

Find compound interest using a table and the compound interest formula.

First Central Bank pays 6% interest compounded quarterly on regular savings accounts. Jay Shaw made a single deposit of \$6,500 for 3 years. He made no other deposits or withdrawals.

Step 1: Find the total interest periods: Periods per Year × Number of Years
4 quarters per year × 3 years = 12 total interest periods

Step 2: Find the interest rate per period.

$$\frac{\text{Annual Rate}}{\text{Number of Periods per Year}} = \frac{6\%}{4} = 1.5\%$$

Step 3: Find the amount of \$1.00 for 12 periods at 1.5% per period using the *Compound Interest—Amount of \$1.00* table on page A11.
Amount of \$1.00 = 1.19562

Step 4: Find the amount: Original Principal × Amount of \$1.00
\$6,500 × 1.19562 = \$7,771.53

Step 5: Find the compound interest: Amount − Original Principal
\$7,771.53 − \$6,500 = **\$1271.53 compound interest**

Lesson-by-Lesson Review (continued)

Review Exercises

Use *Compound Interest—Amount of $1.00* table on page A11 to solve. Round answers to the nearest cent.

	Principal	Annual Interest Rate	Interest Periods per Year	Total Time	Amount	Compound Interest
32.	$1,200.00	6.0%	Semiannually	1 year	a. $	b. $
33.	750.00	5.5	Quarterly	3 years	a.	b.
34.	1,230.00	5.0	Quarterly	2 years	a.	b.

35. Kathy Cole deposited $875 in a savings plan with her credit union. The credit union savings plan pays $5\frac{1}{2}$% interest compounded semiannually. If she makes no other deposits or withdrawals, how much interest will her money earn in 2 years?

36. **ALGEBRA** What will Bradley Hudepohl's $50,000 (present value) be worth in 10 years (future value) at 7.5% annual interest compounded quarterly? How much compound interest will the $50,000 have earned?

5.7 Daily Compounding (pp. 232–234)

Calculate the interest for daily compounding.
You deposit $4,500 into an account that pays 5.5% interest compounded daily. How much interest will you earn in 30 days?

Step 1: Find the amount of $1.00 using the *Amount of $1.00 at 5.5% Compounded Daily (365-Day Year)* table on page A10 for 30 days.
Amount of $1.00 = 1.00452

Step 2: Find the amount.
Original Principal × Amount of $1.00
$4,500 × 1.00452 = $4,520.34

Step 3: Find the compound interest.
Amount − Original Principal
$4,520.34 − $4,500 = **$20.34 compound interest**

Review Exercises

Use the *Amount of $1.00 at 5.5% Compounded Daily (365-Day Year)* table on page A10 to solve. Round answers to the nearest cent.

	Principal	Number of Days	Amount	Compound Interest
37.	$120,000.00	30	a. $	b. $
38.	8,500.00	40	a.	b.
39.	1,730.00	60	a.	b.

40. On June 30, Ed Klempel deposited $1,500 into a savings account that pays 5.5% interest compounded daily. On August 1, how much interest had his account earned on the principal?

Lesson-by-Lesson Review (continued)

5.8 Annuities (pp. 235–238)

Compute the future value of an ordinary annuity and an annuity due.
Suppose that you deposited $750 into an ordinary annuity at the end of each quarter in an account earning 6% interest compounded quarterly. What is the future value of the account in 3 years? Suppose instead that it had been an annuity due. What is the future value of the account in 3 years?

Step 1: Find the total number of periods.

Number of Periods = Periods per Year × Number of Years = 4 × 3 = 12

Step 2: Find the interest rate per period.

$$\frac{\text{Annual Rate}}{\text{Number of Periods per Year}} = \frac{6\%}{4} = 1.5\% \text{ interest rate per period}$$

Step 3: Find the future value of $1.00 for 12 periods at 1.5% from the *Future Value of an Ordinary Annuity for $1.00 per Period* table on page A12.
Look down the 1.50% column to the $n = 12$ row. The value = 13.04121

Step 4: Find the future value of an ordinary annuity.

Amount of Deposit × Future Value of $1.00
$750.00 × 13.04121
= **$9,780.91 FV of an Ordinary Annuity**

Step 5: Find the future value of an annuity due.

$9,780.91 × ($1.00 + 0.015)
$9,780.91 × 1.015 = $9,927.624
= **$9,927.62 Future Value**

Review Exercises

Use the *Future Value of an Ordinary Annuity for $1.00 per Period* table on page A12 to solve the following.

	End of Period Deposit	Compounded	Rate	Years	Rate per Period	Number of Periods	Amount of $1.00	Future Value of Ordinary Annuity
41.	$3,000	Quarterly	4%	2	a. %	b.	c. $	d. $
42.	2,500	Quarterly	8	3	a.	b.	c.	d.

43. Ozzie Foster deposits $2,000 at the end of each year (Ordinary annuity) into an Individual Retirement Account at Boise Bank. The account pays 7% compounded annually. **(a)** How much will be in the account in 25 years? **(b)** If Ozzie had deposited the $2,000 at the beginning of each year (Annuity due), how much would be in the account in 25 years?

44. Bertie Frye saves $500 at the end of every quarter in an ordinary annuity earning 7.2% interest compounded quarterly. What is the amount of **(a)** his savings in 20 years and **(b)** interest will he have earned? If Bertie had saved the $500 at the beginning of each quarter in an annuity due, what would **(c)** the amount of his savings be in 20 years and **(d)** how much interest would he have earned?

Practice Test

Record your answer on a separate sheet of paper.

1. If you deposit a check for $43.95 and $12.39 in cash, what is the total deposit amount?
   A $58.43 **B** $12.39
   C $56.34 **D** $43.95

2. **ALGEBRA** Allen Barry deposited checks totaling $1,584.19 into his savings account. He withdrew $96.00 while depositing some loose change. Allen's total deposit was $1,530.24. How much did he deposit in loose change?
   A $42.05 **B** $39.75
   C $11.25 **D** $30.50

3. What is thirty-three and $\frac{09}{100}$ dollars written as a numeral?
   A $92.33 **B** $33.192
   C $125.00 **D** $33.09

4. If your checking account's balance is $3,678.89 and you withdraw $1,514, what is the remaining balance?
   A $2,164.89 **B** $5,192.89
   C $2,614.89 **D** $3,678.89

5. What is 93% of 10.93?
   A 10.1649 **B** 10.00
   C 0.93 **D** 11.865

6. **ALGEBRA** Vito Melvin's bank account has a balance of $9,685.06. The previous balance was $6,955.01. Vito made a deposit of $2,815.85 and withdrew $100.00. How much did he earn in interest?
   A $18.40 **B** $56.50
   C $14.20 **D** $29.90

7. How much interest will Lashana Burrows earn on $875.00 after 3 months if the annual interest rate is $5\frac{1}{2}$%
   A $5.85 **B** $12.03
   C $887.03 **D** $34.05

8. If the original principal of Jimmy Christensen's account balance today is $3,450.00, the balance after 2 years is $3,485.95, and he made no other deposits, how much interest did he earn?
   A $123.95 **B** $34.95
   C $3,485.95 **D** $35.95

9. **ALGEBRA** Rebecca Wright earned $115 in simple interest for 8 months at an annual interest rate of 5%. How much money did she invest?

10. If $1.00 at 5.5% interest compounded daily has a value of $1.00513 after 34 days, how much interest would June Akin's account have earned on $5,000.00 after 34 days?

11. Yanni Crable deposits $122.00 in an ordinary annuity at the end of every quarter. The annuity earns 6% interest compounded quarterly. After 4 quarters, the value of $1.00 with this interest rate is $4.0909. What is the future value of the annuity after 1 year?

12. 54% of 212

13. $12,967 ÷ 111

14. $12.47 × 0.56

15. 3.519 ÷ 23

16. $0.85 × $43.98

17. 420% of $3,636

Standardized Test Practice

Cumulative, Chapters 1–5

PART 1 Multiple Choice

Record your answers on the answer sheet provided by your teacher or on a sheet of paper.

1. What is Mickey Voelker's straight-time pay if he works 34 hours and his hourly rate is $8.75?
   A $2,363.50 **B** $297.50
   C $200.85 **D** $220.15

2. **ALGEBRA** What is the interest rate of Claire Englebert's account that started the year with $5,678.00 and ended it with $5,990.29?
   A 5.65% **B** 5%
   C 5.5% **D** 4.5%

3. Joe Carpenter's car insurance premium costs $985.50 every 6 months. How much should he budget for this monthly?
   A $124.15 **B** $103.75
   C $164.25 **D** $82.25

4. Shannon Jenks deposits $600 in an ordinary annuity at the end of each month earning 6% interest compounded monthly. What is the value of the annuity in 10 years?
   A $72,000.00 **B** $98,327.61
   C $89,756.34 **D** $95,687.23

5. **ALGEBRA** Lati Duell made a deposit to his checking account and received $43 in cash. The deposit totaled $952. The checks he deposited totaled 4 times the currency deposited. How much in currency did he deposit?
   A $199 **B** $796
   C $227 **D** $410

6. Using the following table, how much is withheld from wages of $545 if the person claims 4 allowances?
   A $67 **B** $38
   C $28 **D** $26

If the wages are—		And the number of withholding allowances claimed is—				
At least	But less than	0	1	2	3	4
		The amount of income tax to be withheld is—				
$500	$510	$61	$51	$41	$32	$22
510	520	62	53	43	33	23
520	530	64	54	44	35	25
530	540	65	56	46	36	26
540	550	67	57	47	38	28

TEST-TAKING TIP

Arrive Having Eaten Eat breakfast or a light snack before a test. Food will give you energy and help you focus.

PART 2 Short Response/Griddable

7. **ALGEBRA** Timon Steiner's average monthly expenditure for gasoline in the second quarter of this year was $142.48. In July he spent $165.20, and in August he spent $139.95. How much can he spend in September and maintain the second quarter average?

8. Jen Dodson deposits $372 in a savings account that pays an annual interest rate of 5.25%. If she makes no other deposits, how much will she have after 3 months?

PART 3 Extended Response

Show your work.

9. Jerrod and Shelia Mooney have monthly living expenses of $755.00, monthly fixed expenses of $1,345.95, and annual expenses of $5,210.64. What is their monthly share of annual expenses? What is their total monthly expense?

Building Academic Skills

Mathematics

Cameron Estevez puts $1,000 into a CD that pays 5.5% interest compounded daily for 4 years (48 months). What would his account balance be at the end of the period?

English Language Arts/Writing

An asset's *liquidity* relates to how easy it is to convert that asset into cash. Checking and savings accounts are very liquid. You can use them to buy just about any other asset. A house is a less liquid asset. You have to sell it or take out a loan against its value before you can buy other assets. Order this list of assets from most to least liquid: stocks and bonds, new car, single-family house, checking account, power tools, certificates of deposit, office condo complex, and clothing.

Social Studies/Economics

Interest on savings and checking accounts varies widely. Go to an Internet search engine such as Google and type in "history of interest rates." Find out what has happened to interest rates in the last 100 years. Write a brief report on the subject. Discuss how interest rates relate to the liquidity of assets.

Building Real-World Skills

Career WISE

Physical Therapist Assistant Under the direction and supervision of a physical therapist, a physical therapist assistant provides many aspects of patient treatment, such as exercises, massages, and electrical stimulation. The physical therapist assistant records the patient's responses to treatment and reports the outcome to the physical therapist.

Research and Share:

Locate the following and then answer the question.

a. Using the Internet, locate the Web site for the American Physical Therapy Association to learn more about careers in physical therapy. How many APTA certified physical therapist assistant programs are currently available?

b. As a class, make a list of the various programs available.

Tech TRENDS

Online Bank Statements Banks typically send a bank statement at the end of each month to every person who has an account. This statement shows all of the activity that took place in that account during the month. More and more banks are encouraging customers to use online bank statements to reduce printing and postage costs. Customers can log on to the bank's Web site and see all of the information that would have been mailed to them.

Research and Write:

Answer the following questions.

a. If a bank has 25,000 customers, how much money could it save on postage in a year if half of those customers switched to online bank statements?

b. What are some of the benefits of using online bank statements for your bank accounts?

UNIT 2 Thematic Project

Building a Budget

In this project you will use what you learned to create a personal budget to help you meet your financial goals.

Your Project Assignment

- ✓ Choose a job that interests you.
- ✓ Investigate rent, utilities, transportation, and grocery costs in your community.
- ✓ Learn about effective decision making for building a budget.
- ✓ Use the spreadsheet application to plan your budget.
- ✓ Create a 3–5 minute presentation.

A Money Manager for ______________________ **Date** ____________

MONTHLY LIVING EXPENSES		MONTHLY FIXED EXPENSES	
Food/Grocery Bill	$	Rent/Mortgage Payment	$
Household Expenses		Car Payment	$
Electricity	$	Other Installments	
Gas	$	Appliances	$
Telephone	$	Furniture	$
Water	$	Regular Savings	$
Garbage/Sewer Fee	$	Emergency Fund	$
Other ________	$	**TOTAL**	$
________	$	ANNUAL EXPENSES	

Skills Preview

Your success in creating a realistic budget will depend on your skills. Some skills you might use include:

Academic Skills reading, writing, and mathematics

Basic Skills speaking, listening, thinking, problem-solving, and interpersonal skills

Technology Skills word-processing, keyboarding, spreadsheet, and Internet skills

Math Online Go to **connectED.mcgraw-hill.com** to download a spreadsheet application for the unit project.

Greg Vote/Corbis

Project Steps

Step 1 Brainstorm

- List several careers that interest you. Choose one.
- Brainstorm monthly living expenses, monthly fixed expenses, and annual expenses. Include rent, utilities, transportation, and groceries.

Step 2 Research

- Use the Internet and/or local newspapers to search for job openings in your chosen career.
- Research the cost of monthly living expenses, monthly fixed expenses, and annual expenses in your community.

Step 3 Explore Your Community

Interview two adults in your community about the decision-making process they use when developing a personal budget. Ask them how they prioritize expenses and to share any tips they might have for sticking to their budgets.

Step 4 Create Your Budget

- Calculate your monthly net income. Assume your annual gross pay is $40,000, you are unmarried, are paid monthly, and have no exemptions. Use the tax tables on pages A2–A5.
- Use the spreadsheet application to determine your monthly budget.
- Adjust personal spending, entertainment, and other expenses as needed to live within your monthly net income.
- Develop a pie chart showing your monthly expenses.

Academic and Career Portfolio

Add this report to your Academic and Career Portfolio.

Step 5 Develop Your Presentation

- Use a word-processing program to write a one-page report.
  - ✓ List the job you chose and explain why.
  - ✓ Summarize your conversations about a budget.
  - ✓ Describe any adjustments you might have made to personal spending, entertainment, and other expenses.
  - ✓ Share your thoughts or observations about the experience of preparing a budget.
- Create a 3–5 slide presentation to share with your class. Include your pie chart.
- Print your completed Monthly Manager or include it in your presentation.

Step 6 Evaluate Your Presentation

Math Online Go to connectED.mcgraw-hill.com to download an evaluation rubric.

UNIT 3

Managing Your Expenses

In This Unit

Explore the Photo

Tax Season
When you earn an income, you also must file a tax return. *How can you plan ahead for tax season?*

Radius Images / Alamy

The Big Picture

You may be able to reduce your property tax by challenging your assessment. The image below shows how few people take advantage of this opportunity.

2%	33%
Homeowners who challenge their assessments*	Challengers who win their appeals*

*Estimated

Data: National Taxpayers Union

Go to **connectED.mcgraw-hill.com** for the Unit 2 WebQuest activity about resources and education for taxpayers.

Thematic Project Preview

Doing Your Taxes

You are probably familiar with sales tax on purchases. What you may not know is that income is taxed, too. When you make an income, the law requires you to prepare an income tax return. Every year it is due by April 15, and you send it to the Internal Revenue Service (IRS). After completing this Unit Thematic Project, you will be familiar with and prepared to file the 1040EZ income tax return.

Pre-Project Checklist

As you read this unit, use this checklist to prepare for the unit project:

- ✓ Understand federal income tax.
- ✓ Practice reading a tax table.
- ✓ Familiarize yourself with 1040EZ and W-2 forms.
- ✓ Identify resources in your community and online for taxpayers.

Cash Purchases

Big Idea

Use all product information, not just the selling price or unit price, to make good buying decisions.

Juice Images/age fotostock

Explore the Photo

The Real Cost

When you save to make a big purchase, be sure to consider the sales tax you will have to pay. *Have you ever paid sales tax?*

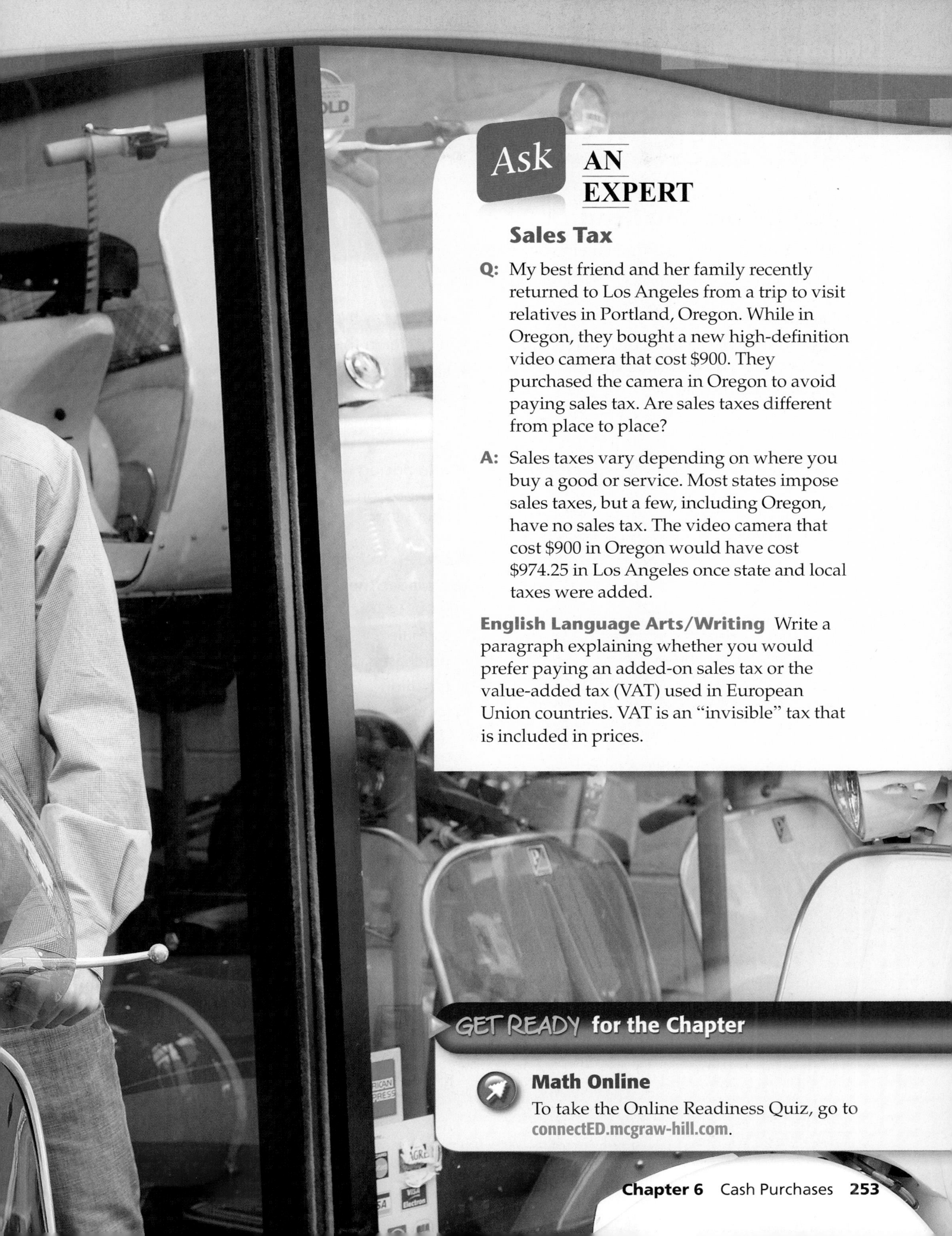

Ask AN EXPERT

Sales Tax

Q: My best friend and her family recently returned to Los Angeles from a trip to visit relatives in Portland, Oregon. While in Oregon, they bought a new high-definition video camera that cost $900. They purchased the camera in Oregon to avoid paying sales tax. Are sales taxes different from place to place?

A: Sales taxes vary depending on where you buy a good or service. Most states impose sales taxes, but a few, including Oregon, have no sales tax. The video camera that cost $900 in Oregon would have cost $974.25 in Los Angeles once state and local taxes were added.

English Language Arts/Writing Write a paragraph explaining whether you would prefer paying an added-on sales tax or the value-added tax (VAT) used in European Union countries. VAT is an "invisible" tax that is included in prices.

GET READY for the Chapter

Math Online

To take the Online Readiness Quiz, go to **connectED.mcgraw-hill.com**.

Reading Guide

Before You Read

Relate What is the sales tax rate in your state?

Main Idea

Knowing how to calculate the final selling price will help you to decide whether or not a purchase is prudent.

Graphic Organizer

Before you read this chapter, draw a diagram like the one below. As you read, note three strategies for making good purchase decisions.

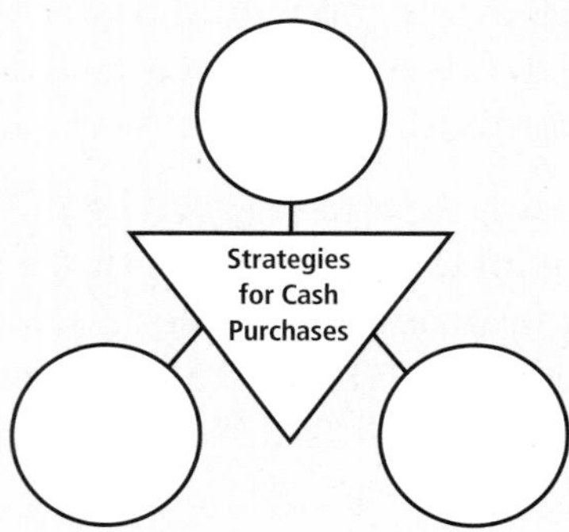

 **Math Online** Go to connectED.mcgraw-hill.com to download this graphic organizer.

Content Vocabulary

You will learn these key terms in this chapter.

- sales tax
- sales receipt
- total purchase price
- unit pricing
- comparison shopping
- coupons
- rebates
- markdown
- markdown rate
- sale price

Academic Vocabulary

You will see these words in your reading and on your tests.

- formula
- purchase
- technique
- factor
- incentive
- promote
- capable

You can find vocabulary definitions in the **Content Vocabulary** Glossary and the **Academic Vocabulary** Glossary in the back of the book.

Sales Tax

Lesson Objective
Compute sales tax.

Content Vocabulary
- sales tax

GET READY for the Lesson

Why do you think you have to pay sales tax?

When Tim Hall purchased a new video game, he was surprised that he had to pay sales tax. He lives in Florida, where the sales tax rate is 6%.

As You Read

Identify What are some items on which you have paid sales tax?

Sales Tax You just purchased a computer game at the electronics store. When you purchased it, you might have paid a state or local tax. A tax on the selling price of an item or service you purchase is a **sales tax**. The sales tax rate is usually expressed as a percent and varies from state to state. Many states that have a state sales tax permit county and city governments to add an additional tax to the state sales tax.

To calculate the sales tax, use this **formula**:

Sales Tax = Total Selling Price × Sales Tax Rate

Need Help? Go to...
- Workshop 14: Finding a Percentage, p. 30
- Workshop 2: Rounding Numbers, p. 6
- Skill 30: Finding the Percentage, p. SK31
- Skill 2: Rounding Numbers, p. SK3

EXAMPLE

Harley Watson bought a cell phone for \$199.95 and a phone case for \$19.95. What is the total sales tax if Harley lives in Austin, Texas, where the state tax is 6.25% and the combined local city and county tax is 2.00%?

Step 1: Calculate the total selling price.

Total Selling Price = \$199.95 + \$19.95
= \$219.90

Step 2: Calculate the sales tax

Sales Tax = Total Selling Price × Sales Tax Rate
= \$219.90 × (6.25% + 2.00%)
= \$219.90 × 0.0825
= **\$18.14175 or \$18.14**

Concept CHECK

Calculate the sales tax. Check your answers in the back of the book.

1. Sandy Zuppa bought an outboard motor for a total selling price of \$420 in Maine, which has a 7% sales tax rate.
2. Savannah Tyson purchased a vacation for a total selling price of \$2,520. The Florida sales tax rate is 6%, and the Gainesville sales tax rate is 1.25%.

Lawyer
Lawyers must have strong mathematical, reasoning, and communication skills for working with clients, collaborating with colleagues, writing legal documents, and appearing in court. **When do lawyers work with numbers?**

Lesson Practice

Calculate the (a) total tax rate and (b) sales tax.

	Item	Total Selling Price	State Tax Rate	City Tax Rate	Total Tax Rate	Sales Tax
3.	Clothing	$ 81.39	3.00%	0.00%	a. %	b. $
4.	Cell Phone	159.95	5.00	0.00	a.	b.
5.	MP3 Player	195.55	4.00	2.00	a.	b.
6.	Computer	1,599.75	4.88	1.50	a.	b.
7.	Take-Out	49.85	8.13	2.50	a.	b.
8.	Pickup Truck	38,562.42	6.50	1.25	a.	b.

9. Ivana Nagy's purchases include a $39.95 blanket, a $24.95 miniblind, an adjustable screen for $15.95, and a 12-foot, eight-outlet power strip for $9.49. The purchases were made in Massachusetts, where the tax rate is 5%. What are the **(a)** sales tax and **(b)** total selling price?

10. Clarissa Byrne purchased a $399.99 electronic organizer, $78.94 in office supplies, and a $98.95 office chair for work. What is the **(a)** total selling price and **(b)** total sales tax if Clarissa lives in New Orleans, Louisiana, where the state tax is 4% and the city tax is 4%?

11. Jenny Tarver purchases a $1,599.99 treadmill, a $49.99 pair of walking shoes, a $79.99 leather handbag, 6 pairs of socks at $8.99 per pair, and 2 pairs of running shorts at $19.99 each at the County Store in Bay Shore, New York. The state sales tax rate is 4%, the county rate is 4.25%, and the city transportation tax rate is 0.25%. What is the sales tax on her purchases?

12. CHALLENGE PROBLEM You purchase 4 boxes of cereal at 2 for $2.33, 8 cans of mushrooms at $1.02 per can, 12 rolls of paper towels at $0.79 per roll, 2 bags of cat litter at $2.99 each, 2 coffee mugs at $7.99 each, and 2 containers of laundry detergent at 2 for $12.50. Your state's sales tax is 6.25%, the local tax is 1.10%, and the foodstuffs are tax exempt. What is your sales tax?

Spiral Review

Round to the nearest hundredth (also known as cent). (Skill 2)

13. $34.125 **14.** $279.5429 **15.** $357.346

16. ALGEBRA Zeb Ellis saves $500 in the back of every quarter in an ordinary annuity earning 5.8% interest compounded quarterly. How much will he have saved in 10 years? How much interest will he have earned? (Lesson 5.8)

17. Andrea Tremblay is paid $9.20 an hour for a regular 40-hour week. Her overtime rate is $1\frac{1}{2}$ times her regular hourly rate. This week she worked her regular 40 hours plus 10 hours of overtime. What is her total pay? (Lesson 1.2)

GET READY for the Next Lesson

PREREQUISITE SKILL Multiplying Decimals (Skill 8)

Multiply.

18. 34.5×2.6 **19.** 0.45×5.78 **20.** 19.43×2.5 **21.** $\$12.40 \times 2.1$

Aaron Roeth Photography

LESSON 6.2

Total Purchase Price

Lesson Objective
Calculate the total purchase price.

Content Vocabulary
- sales receipt
- total purchase price

GET READY for the Lesson

How do the sales taxes you pay get to the proper government agencies?

Like other merchants, Carlson's Media acts as an agent for collecting taxes. The bookkeeper calculates the amount of taxes Carlson's collected during each period and, along with the proper forms, sends the taxes to federal, state, and local governments.

As You Read

Identify What is included in an item's total purchase price?

Total Purchase Price Most stores give you a **sales receipt** as proof of **purchase**. The sales receipt may be a handwritten sales slip or cash register tape. The receipt shows the selling price of each item or service you purchased, the total selling price of all items purchased, any sales tax, and the total purchase amount. Note that the tax is computed using the combined state, county, and city tax rates.

The **total purchase price** equals the total selling price plus the sales tax. The formula is:

Sales Tax = Total Selling Price × Sales Tax Rate

Total Purchase Price = Total Selling Price + Sales Tax

Need Help? Go to...
- **Skill 8:** Multiplying Decimals, p. SK9
- **Skill 5:** Adding Decimals, p. SK6
- **Application A:** Formulas, p. AP1

EXAMPLE 1

Mike Krause owns a tree-trimming company. He purchases the items listed on the sales receipt **(Figure 6.1)**. Mike checks the information on the receipt. The sales tax rate is 5%. What is the total purchase price?

Figure 6.1

Verl's Saw Shop

Quantity	Description	Price	Amount
1	Chain saw	$539.95	$539.95
12	Chain saw bar oil	4.95	59.40
2	Safety chaps	69.95	139.90
2	Safety helmet	45.95	91.90
	TOTAL SELLING PRICE →	Subtotal	$831.15
		Sales Tax 5%	41.56
	TOTAL PURCHASE PRICE →	Total	$872.71

(Labels: NUMBER PURCHASED → Quantity; PRICE PER ITEM → Price; TOTAL PRICE → Amount)

Step 1: Find the total selling price.

$539.95 + $59.40 + $139.90 + $91.90 = $831.15 total selling price

Step 2: Find the sales tax.

Sales Tax = Total Selling Price × Sales Tax Rate

$41.56 = $831.15 × 0.05

Continued on next page

Corbis/SuperStock

Step 3: Find the total purchase price.

Total Purchase Price = Total Selling Price + Sales Tax

$872.71 = $831.15 + $41.56

Complete the problem. Check your answer in the back of the book.

1. Wesley Novak bought 2 two-way radios for $59.99 each, 2 surge protectors at $19.99 each, a wireless printer router for $79.98, and 3 color ink cartridges at $34.99 each. What is the total purchase price if he lives in West Virginia, where the sales tax rate is 6%?

Need Help? Go to...

Workshop 38: Problem Solving Strategies: Writing an Equation, p. 78

EXAMPLE 2 Algebra

Rennie Gaston purchased a bathing suit from the clearance rack and gave the clerk $20.00. He received $3.98 in change. If the sales tax rate was 7%, find the total selling price.

Step 1: Total purchase price = Cash Given − Change

$16.02 = $20.00 − $3.98

Step 2: Let s = Total selling price of the bathing suit

Step 3: Total Purchase Price = Total Selling Price + Sales Tax

$16.02 = s + $(0.07 \times s)$

Combine like terms → $16.02 = $1.00s$ + $0.07s$

Divide both sides by 1.07. → $16.02 = $1.07s$

$14.97 = s

The total selling price for the bathing suit was $14.97.

Study Tip

Reviewing

It is best to review lesson material right after class when it is still fresh in your memory.

Concept CHECK

Complete the problem. Check your answer in the back of the book.

2. Alonzo and Catalyn Diaz paid a total of $23,289.26 for their new automobile. If the sales tax rate in their community is 6.5%, what was the total selling price of the Diaz's new automobile?

Lesson Practice

Find the (a) total tax rate, (b) sales tax, and (c) total purchase price.

	Item	Total Selling Price	State Tax Rate	City Tax Rate	Total Tax Rate	Sales Tax	Total Purchase Price
3.	Laptop	$ 949.99	4.00%	0.00%	a. %	b. $	c. $
4.	Hiking Boots	159.95	5.00	0.00	a.	b.	c.
5.	DVD Player	195.55	5.50	1.00	a.	b.	c.
6.	Plasma TV	1,999.99	6.25	1.25	a.	b.	c.
7.	Play Tickets	49.85	8.13	2.50	a.	b.	c.
8.	Van	28,365.57	6.50	1.25	a.	b.	c.

Lesson Practice

For Problems 9–13, determine the (a) total selling price, (b) sales tax, and (c) total purchase price.

9. Goldie Esparza buys 4 paper lanterns at $14.95 each, 2 piñatas for $19.95, and 2 strings of white lights at $19.99 each. The sales tax rate is 4%.

10. Norma Engel buys an inflatable canoe for $194.94, 2 paddles for $44.95, and 9 energy bars at $0.89 each. The sales tax rate is 5.5%.

11. Nicole Burley purchases 6 quarts of motor oil at $1.79 per quart, 8 spark plugs at 4 for $7.99, 2 wiper blades at $13.99 each, 4 packs of polishing rags at 2 for $3.99, a can of polish for $7.55, and an oil filter for $5.99 in Cleveland, Ohio, where the sales tax rate is 7.5%.

12. Ralph Chang purchases a scanner for $85.85, 12 boxes of toner at $14.55 each, 24 ballpoint pens at $1.14 each, 2 boxes of memo pads at $4.19 a box, 12 report covers at $2.89 each, and an extension cord for $25.95 at Ned's Office Store in Los Angeles. The sales tax rate is 8.25%.

13. Gavin Franks purchases a digital camera for $599.99, a tripod for $59.97, a camera accessory kit for $89.99, a printer for $84.99, 4 photo printer cartridges at $44.99 each, 2 black ink cartridges at $19.99 each, 4 packs of premium grade photo paper at 2 for $39.99, and 4 photo writing pens at 2 for $2.39. The sales tax rate is 6.4 %.

Did You Know?

The First Digital Camera
Steven Sasson, an engineer for the Eastman Kodak Company, made the first prototype of a digital camera in 1975. The camera weighed 8 pounds and produced black-and-white pictures with .01 megapixel resolution, one-thousandth the capability of the 10-megapixel cameras commercially available today.

14. ALGEBRA Mi Lynn Sato gave the sales clerk a $50 bill and a $5 bill and received $2.40 in change. If the sales tax rate in her community was 5.25%, what was the item's total selling price?

15. ALGEBRA Elaine and Abraham Martz have homes in Florida and Ohio. They realize that they could save $1,154.13 in sales tax on their new luxury automobile if they purchase it in their Florida community, where the sales tax rate is 4.75%, rather than in their Ohio community, where the sales tax rate is 7.5%. The auto's total selling price is the same in Florida and Ohio. What is the total purchase price of their auto if they purchase it in Florida?

Spiral Review

Multiply. (Skill 8)

16. 7.4×9.2 **17.** 15.6×9.142 **18.** 0.91×0.004

19. Meg Harrington's savings account has a principal of $1,200 and earns 6% interest compounded quarterly for 2 quarters. Calculate the compound interest amount. (Lesson 5.5)

GET READY for the Next Lesson

PREREQUISITE SKILL **Rounding Numbers** (Skill 2)

Round to the nearest hundredth.

20. 6.873 **21.** 59.8655

Round to the nearest tenth.

22. 44.45 **23.** $984.08

Round to the nearest whole number.

24. 25.886 **25.** $24.59

LESSON 6.3

Unit Pricing

Lesson Objective
Determine the unit price.

Content Vocabulary
- unit pricing

GET READY for the Lesson

Many items come in different sizes. What do you consider when deciding which size to buy?

Cat food comes in many different flavors and sizes. Kendra Hester chooses based on price, nutritional value, and flavor.

Image Source/Getty Images

As You Read
Recall Have you ever made a purchase based on unit pricing?

Unit Pricing Grocery stores often give the unit price for their products. **Unit pricing** is a **technique** that allows shoppers to compare the prices of various items. Use this information to determine which size of a product is the best buy based on price.

The unit price formula is:

$$\text{Unit Price} = \frac{\text{Price of Item}}{\text{Measure or Count}}$$

Figure 6.2

Paper Plates	
55 plates ← COUNT PER PACKAGE	
PRICE PER UNIT → $0.02 per plate	$1.10 ← PRICE PER PACKAGE
Unit Price ↑ UNIT OF MEASURE	Your Price

Need Help? Go to...
- Workshop 7: Dividing Decimals, p. 16
- Workshop 2: Rounding Numbers, p. 6
- Application A: Formulas, p. AP1

EXAMPLE

Shane Ladd purchased a 64-ounce container of orange juice for $3.49, a 2-liter bottle of bleach for $1.99, and a dozen ears of sweet corn for $3.50. What is the unit price of each item to the nearest tenth of a cent?

Find the unit price: $\text{Unit Price} = \frac{\text{Price of Item}}{\text{Measure or Count}}$

$$\text{Orange juice} = \frac{\$3.49}{64\text{ oz}} = \$0.0545\text{ per ounce} = \mathbf{\$0.055\text{ per ounce}}$$

$$\text{Bleach} = \frac{\$1.99}{2\text{ liter}} = \mathbf{\$0.995\text{ per liter}}$$

$$\text{Corn} = \frac{\$3.50}{12\text{ ears}} = \$0.2916\text{ per ear} = \mathbf{\$0.292\text{ per ear}}$$

Concept CHECK

Find the unit price to the nearest tenth of a cent. Check your answers in the back of the book.

1. A 4.5-pound chicken costs $5.25.
2. A 20-count package of plastic storage bags costs $2.29.

Study Tip

Self Test
Test yourself or have someone else test you on the material to find out what your weak and strong areas are. Use review questions in the back of the chapter.

Lesson Practice

Calculate the unit price of the items to the nearest tenth of a cent.

	Item	Price	Measure/Count	Unit Price
3.	Batteries	$ 2.89	4 pack	$
4.	Frozen Pie	2.89	15.4 oz	
5.	Dog Food	40.99	38 lbs	
6.	Magic Markers	2.19	8 count	
7.	Chain Link Fence	34.88	50 ft	
8.	Olive Oil	8.99	18.5 oz	

For Problems 9–14, find the unit price of each item to the nearest tenth of a cent.

9. Brooke Sudbury purchases 4 tires for her car for $339.16.

10. Latona Hitchens purchases 25 hanging file folders for $6.99.

11. Market Foods sells 24 cans of soda for $6.79, a 128-ounce bottle of detergent for $2.89, a 13.8-ounce can of peanuts for $2.59, and a cooked 1.75-pound chicken half for $2.65.

12. Campellini's sells 2 packs of 6-pack 24-ounce bottles of sports drink for $10.50. What is the price per **(a)** bottle and **(b)** ounce?

13. Maggie Ryan is pricing materials for a deck project. She notes that deck boards are sold in standard lengths by the foot as follows: 6 feet for $5.88, 8 feet for $8.79, 10 feet for $10.68, 12 feet for $13.43, 14 feet for $15.65, 16 feet for $17.88, 18 feet for $20.99, and 20 feet for $24.99. What is the price per foot for each length?

14. Henry Levin is buying first aid supplies for a midsummer camping trip. He purchases sunscreen that costs $2.97 for 0.5 ounce, antibacterial ointment that costs $3.34 for 28.35 grams, a box of 34 bandages for $4.25, and a 0.75-ounce tube of lip balm for $2.29. What is the unit price for each item?

15. WRITING IN MATH Explain in a paragraph why in **Problem 14** the unit price for the sunscreen and the lip balm was more than the selling price.

Spiral Review

Divide. Round answers to the nearest cent. (Skill 2)

16. $190.50 ÷ 76 **17.** $13.40 ÷ 2.9 **18.** $27.218 ÷ 7.6

19. ALGEBRA Alicia Waterson makes a deposit at an ATM and receives $50 in cash. The receipt for her total deposit shows $793. The checks deposited totaled twice the currency deposited. She did not deposit any coins. How much in currency did she deposit? (Lesson 4.1)

GET READY for the Next Lesson

PREREQUISITE SKILL **Dividing Decimals** (Skill 11)

Divide.

20. 0.565 ÷ 5 **21.** $12.23 ÷ $0.43 **22.** 473.123 ÷ 5.55

LESSON 6.4

Comparison Shopping

Lesson Objective

Find the best buy based on unit price.

Content Vocabulary

- comparison shopping

GET READY for the Lesson

Have you ever comparison shopped?

Larry O'Rourke wanted to take piano lessons. A local music school offered packages of 5 lessons for $100, 10 for $180, and 20 for $320.

As You Read

Identify What kinds of products do you buy based on comparing prices?

Comparison Shopping You compare the unit prices of products so you can decide which size to buy. If price is the only **factor** to consider, the package with the lowest unit price is the best buy. When you are **comparison shopping**, or comparing prices to find the best value, you should consider factors other than the lowest unit price. For example, if the largest size product is the best buy per unit, consider whether or not you will use it all before it spoils.

Some stores have a shelf tag that shows the unit price in cents. To change the dollar amount to cents, multiply by 100.

Need Help? Go to...

- Skill 11: Dividing Decimals, p. SK12
- Skill 1: Numbers, p. SK1
- Application A: Formulas, p. AP1

EXAMPLE 1

Tolliver's Groceries sells ranch salad dressing in three sizes. The price of a 16-ounce bottle is $3.49, of a 20-ounce bottle is $4.69, and of a 36-ounce bottle is $6.19. Based on price alone, which package is the best buy?

Step 1: Find the unit price for each item: Unit Price $= \frac{\text{Item Price}}{\text{Measure or Count}}$

16 oz package: $\frac{\$3.49}{16} = \$0.21812 \times 100 = \mathbf{21.81¢ \text{ per oz}}$

20 oz package: $\frac{\$4.69}{20} = \$0.2345 \times 100 = \mathbf{23.45¢ \text{ per oz}}$

36 oz package: $\frac{\$6.19}{36} = \$0.17194 \times 100 = \mathbf{17.19¢ \text{ per oz}}$

Step 2: Find the best buy.

Compare: 21.81¢, 23.45¢, and 17.19¢

The lowest price per ounce is the 36-ounce size; thus, it is the best buy.

Concept CHECK

Find the better buy. Check your answers in the back of the book.

1. Facial tissues: 75-count box for $1.49; 184-count box for $2.89.
2. Granola cereal: 14-ounce box for $2.50; 20-ounce box for $3.58.

Need Help? Go to...

Workshop 38: Problem Solving Strategies: Writing an Equation, p. 78

EXAMPLE 2 Algebra

Justin Sanders computed the unit price of a 2-liter bottle of a soft drink and found it to be $0.005 more per ounce than the unit price on a 12-pack of 12-ounce cans of the same soft drink. If the 2-liter bottle costs $1.19 less than the cost of the 12-pack of 12-ounce cans, find the cost of a 2-liter bottle and the cost of the 12-pack of 12-ounce cans. (Note that 2 liters are equivalent to 67.6 fluid ounces.)

Step 1: Let x = Cost of a 2-liter bottle (67.6 fluid ounces)

$x + 1.19$ = Cost of a 12-pack of 12-ounce cans (144 fluid ounces)

Step 2: Write an equation for unit prices and solve for x.

Unit price of a 2-liter bottle = Unit price of a 12-pack of 12-ounce cans + $0.005

$$\frac{x}{67.6} = \frac{(x + \$1.19)}{144} + \$0.005$$

Multiply both sides to clear fractions →

$$(67.6)(144)\frac{x}{67.6} = (67.6)(144)\frac{(x + \$1.19)}{144} + (67.6)(144)(\$0.005)$$

Apply the distributive property →

$$144x = (67.6)(x + \$1.19) + \$48.672$$

Combine like terms and subtract 67.6x from both →

$$144x = 67.6x + \$80.444 + \$48.672$$

Divide both sides by 76.4 →

$$76.4x = \$129.116$$

$$x = \$1.69$$

The 2-liter bottle costs $1.69, and the 12 pack of 12-ounce cans costs $1.69 + $1.19, or $2.88.

SPREADSHEET APPLICATION

Comparison Shopping

You can use a spreadsheet to help determine the unit cost of an item. Part of the spreadsheet is shown below. Enter the name of the item, size, and cost. The unit cost will automatically be calculated for you.

Math Online Go to connectED.mcgraw-hill.com to download a spreadsheet application for this activity.

	A	B	C	D
1	Item	Size	Cost	Unit Cost
2				

Kitty litter: 40-pound bag; $5.99
Tooth paste: 6.4 ounces for $1.00
Dinner plates: 32-count package for $5.99
Baking mix: 20 ounces for $1.00
Liquid soap: 36 ounces for $7.00
Diapers: 56-count package for $5.88
Paper towels: 8 rolls for $5.19
Salad dressing: 16 ounces for $1.99
Canned pineapple: 15 ounces for $1.00
Batteries: 16 for $11.00
Allergy medicine: 30-count box for $19.49
Charcoal: 18 pounds for $7.99

Think and Discuss

1. What is the unit cost for each item?
2. Suppose that you have a 50¢ off coupon for the salad dressing. What is the unit cost after you use the coupon?

Complete the problem. Check your answer in the back of the book.

3. The unit price on a 100-pound container of swimming pool chlorine is $0.06 per pound less than the unit price on a 75-pound container. If the 100-pound container costs $55.50 more than the 75-pound container, find the cost of each.

Reading Math

Word Problems
In word problems, the sentence that tells you what you are asked to find will contain key words or phrases such as *find, how much,* or *what.*

Lesson Practice

For Problems 4–10, calculate the unit price to the nearest tenth of a cent, and determine the better or best buy based on price alone.

4. Note cards: **(a)** one pack of 100 for $5.33 or **(b)** one pack of 300 for $14.84.

5. Paper clips: **(a)** one box of 100 for $0.38 or **(b)** one five-pack of 100 each for $1.27.

6. Jeff Bardo wants to purchase chocolates. The price of a 2-ounce box is $1.10, of a 16-ounce box is $8.98, and of a 32-ounce box is $17.98.

7. Ella Kruse is shopping for a bottle of vegetable oil, which is sold as follows: 16 ounces for $2.06, 48 ounces for $4.29, 64 ounces for $5.79, and 128 ounces for $8.89.

8. Theo Berken wants to purchase some batteries. The cost of a 6-pack is $5.97, an 8-pack is $7.97, and a carton of 4 4-packs is $9.97.

9. Kenny Chapen's favorite microwave burritos sell in a 3-pack for $1.25, an 8 pack for $2.60, and a 28 pack for $7.79.

10. Chen Wu is buying potato chips. The following sizes are for sale: 1.5 ounce, $0.65; 5.75 ounce, $1.30; and a 2-pack of the 5.75 ounce size, $2.45.

11. CHALLENGE PROBLEM Ricardo Price wants to purchase laundry detergent. Double-strength detergent costs $7.11 for a 50-ounce box that will wash 26 loads, $9.99 for a 100-ounce box that will wash 64 loads, and $20.29 for a 150-ounce box that will wash 96 loads. Regular-strength detergent costs $9.99 for a 200-ounce box that will wash 64 loads. Calculate the price **(a)** per ounce and **(b)** per load, and then **(c)** determine the best buy.

12. ALGEBRA Sherri Cole found that the 12-ounce can of frozen orange juice sells for $0.16 less than the 16-ounce can, which is $0.68 less than the 24-ounce can. If the unit price of the 24-ounce can is $0.005 less than the unit price of the 12-ounce can, which of the three is the best buy based on the lowest unit price?

Spiral Review

Divide. Round answers to the nearest cent. (Skill 11)

13. $2.30 ÷ 49.16 **14.** $0.250 ÷ 18.5 **15.** $0.006 ÷ 0.8703

16. ALGEBRA Cheyenne Bennett earned $72 in simple interest in 9 months at an annual interest rate of 8%. How much money did she invest? (Lesson 5.4)

GET READY for the Next Lesson

PREREQUISITE SKILL Subtracting Decimals (Skill 6)

Subtract.

17. $3.85 − $0.37 **18.** $1.86 − $0.94 **19.** 26.99 − 24.34

20. $6.74 − $5.89 **21.** $9.54 − $3.34 **22.** $12,012.69 − $4,206.96

LESSON 6.5

Coupons and Rebates

Lesson Objective

Calculate an item's final price after using a coupon or receiving a rebate.

Content Vocabulary

- coupons
- rebates

As You Read

Recall Have you ever mailed in a rebate form?

GET READY for the Lesson

Why do you think manufacturers use coupons or rebates for a new product?

Rory Willis usually buys Angelo brand pizza, but she has a coupon for a pizza from a new company. She decides to take a chance and purchases the new brand.

Coupons and Rebates Many manufacturers, stores, and service establishments offer customers discounts through **coupons** and **rebates**, or refunds. Each special discount is an **incentive** for customers to purchase a particular item because they will save money (paper coupon) or get money back (rebate). Manufacturer or store coupons are redeemed at the time of purchase. To obtain a manufacturer's rebate, the consumer must mail in a rebate form along with the sales slip and the Universal Product Code (UPC) label from the item purchased.

The final price of an item is determined by the formula:

Final Price = Total Selling Price − Total Savings

Need Help? Go to...

- Workshop 5: Subtracting Decimals, p. 12
- Skill 6: Subtracting Decimals, p. SK7

EXAMPLE

Gil Austen purchased a 12-speed bicycle for \$249, and his brother Daniel purchased a 21-speed bicycle for \$349. Each had a coupon for \$25 off one bicycle. What is the final price of the two bicycles?

Find the final price.

Final Price	=	Total Selling Price	−	Total Savings
	=	(\$249 + \$349)	−	(2 × \$25)
\$548	=	\$598	−	\$50

Concept CHECK

Determine the final price. Check your answers in the back of the book.

1. Makayla Barnes bought a 40-ounce box of pancake mix for \$4.79 and used a \$0.75 coupon.
2. Kim Ross bought a box of tea for \$3.59 and used a \$0.65 coupon.
3. Chris Lowe bought a 32-ounce jar of jam costing \$3.69 and a 28-ounce jar of peanut butter costing \$3.79. He used a \$0.95 coupon that was valid only if he purchased both items.
4. Pat Sears bought 2 boxes of oatmeal that cost \$4.19 each and used a \$1.00 coupon for purchasing 2 boxes.

Lesson Practice

For Problems 5–13, find the final price paid.

	Item	Total Selling Price	Coupon	Final Price
5.	Bleach	$ 3.95	$0.50	$
6.	Oil change	22.99	3.00	
7.	Book	29.99	5.00 buy 2	

8. Audrey Patterson purchased a chicken sandwich for $4.59 and a $1.79 drink. She used a $0.50 store coupon when she paid.

9. Gabe Noll purchased a razor for $9.99, a refill pack of razor blades for the regular price of $12.99, shaving cream for $2.99, and lotion for $5.55. He had a $4.00 coupon for the razor, a $0.75 coupon for the shaving cream, and a $2.00 manufacturer's rebate form for the refill.

10. Jonnie Marker has a coupon for $1.00 off a jar of bean dip if he buys 2 bags of corn chips. He purchased 2 bags of chips for $3.99 per bag and a jar of bean dip for $2.79.

Did You Know?

How Popcorn Pops

How does a kernel of corn turn into a piece of popcorn? It is a physical reaction: When the kernel heats to between 460 and 500 degrees Fahrenheit, pressure causes the starch inside the kernel to puff up, exploding the shell and creating a white, fluffy solid.

11. Faith Hughes purchased 3 gallons of paint at $29.99 per gallon, a paint pan for $6.99, paint roller for $6.95, 4 roller covers for $1.95 each, 3 paint brushes for $8.99 each, and a stepladder for $119.00. She has a $3.00 coupon for each gallon of paint, a $0.50 coupon for each roller cover, and a $25.00 manufacturer's rebate form for the ladder.

12. Mikail Rasmussen purchased 2 gallons of ice cream for $4.99 each, 2 bags of popcorn for $1.88 each, 3 pounds of strawberries at $1.98 per pound, 4 packs of sliced cheese at 2 for $4.00, and 3 cartons of orange juice at 2 for $5.00. He had a coupon for $10.00 off if his purchases totaled $25.00.

13. Additional memory for your computer sells for $109.99 with a $10.00 mail-in rebate. What is the final price after the rebate if an envelope costs $0.35 and a "forever" postage stamp costs $0.41?

H.O.T. Problems

14. CHALLENGE PROBLEM You and your friends are planning a Final Four party, and you are in charge of purchasing the sodas. You can buy a 6 pack of 8-ounce bottles for $4.79 with a $1.00 off coupon, a 6 pack of 8-ounce cans for $2.69 with no coupon, a 12 pack of 8-ounce cans for $4.49 with no coupon, or an 8 pack of 12-ounce bottles for $3.79 with a $0.75 off coupon. Sodas are subject to a 6% beverage tax. Based on the unit price per ounce, what size is the best buy?

Spiral Review

Subtract. (Skill 6)

15. $1.65 − $0.35 **16.** $11.65 − $3.00 **17.** $1.79 − $0.25

18. ALGEBRA Misty Gonzalez receives her paycheck weekly. She earns a straight commission of 4% on sales of $5,000 or less and 5% on sales in excess of $5,000. One week Misty had a gross pay of $462. What was that week's total sales amount? (Lesson 1.7)

GET READY for the Next Lesson

PREREQUISITE SKILL Finding the Percentage (Skill 30)

19. 23% of 216 **20.** 20% of $54.60 **21.** 0.005% of 180

LESSON 6.6

Markdown

Lesson Objective
Find the dollar amount of the markdown.

Content Vocabulary
- markdown
- markdown rate

GET READY for the Lesson

Why do you think merchants put goods on sale?

While Kumar Davis was shopping for a birthday present for his sister, he noticed a display with fleece pullover hoodies below the sign "Final Markdowns." It was such a good deal that he bought two.

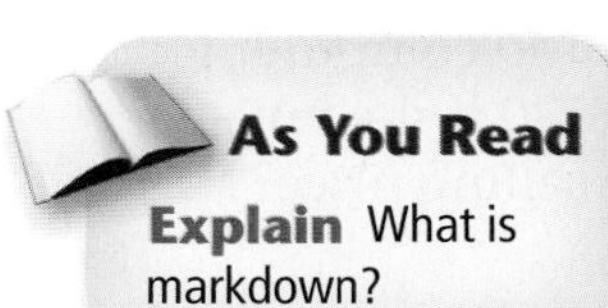

As You Read
Explain What is markdown?

Markdown Stores often **promote** products at sale prices, which are lower than their regular selling prices. The **markdown**, or *discount*, is the amount of money that you save by purchasing a product at the sale price. The markdown could be a dollar amount or a **markdown rate**, which is a percent of the regular selling price, such as 20% off. Two formulas determine the markdown:

Markdown = Regular Selling Price – Sale Price

Markdown = Regular Selling Price × Markdown Rate

Need Help? Go to...
- **Workshop 5:** Subtracting Decimals, p. 12
- **Application A:** Formulas, p. AP1

EXAMPLE 1

Nora Ishino purchased a camcorder at a sale price of $499.99. The regular selling price was $549.99. She also purchased a flat screen TV at 30% off the regular price of $1,499. What was the markdown?

Step 1: Find the markdown on the camcorder.

Markdown	=	Regular Selling Price	–	Sale Price
$50.00	=	$549.99	–	$499.99

Step 2: Find the markdown on the flat screen TV.

Markdown	=	Regular Selling Price	–	Markdown Rate
$449.70	=	$1,499.00	–	$30%

Concept CHECK

Find the markdown. Check your answers in the back of the book.

1. Shirts Are Us has a clearance on overstocked merchandise. A long-sleeve V-neck top that usually sells for $36 is on sale for $23.
2. Outerwear coats and jackets are on sale. A leather jacket is on sale for 40% off the regular selling price of $219.99.

Need Help? Go to...

Workshop 38: Problem Solving Strategies: Writing an Equation, p. 78

EXAMPLE 2 Algebra

Nels Johanssen noticed an advertisement that said "Save $75.00 on Chamber three-piece luggage sets, this week only. All Chamber three-piece luggage sets marked down 30%." What is the regular selling price of a Chamber three-piece luggage set?

Let r = Regular selling price of a Chamber three-piece luggage set

Markdown = Regular Selling Price × Markdown Rate

$\$75.00 = r \times 30\%$

$\$75.00 = 0.30r$

Divide both sides by 0.30 → $r = \$250.00$

The regular selling price of a Chamber three-piece luggage set is $250.00.

Concept CHECK

Complete the problem. Check your answer in the back of the book.

3. Cassie Marino is interested in purchasing a new laptop computer for school. It has a markdown of 18%. She could save $120 if she buys the computer while it is on sale. What is its regular selling price?

Reading Math +−÷=

Markdown Rate

A problem asking for the markdown rate is asking for a percent.

Lesson Practice

For Problems 4–11, determine the total markdown.

	Item	Regular Selling Price	−	Sale Price	Markdown Rate	=	Markdown
4.	Grill	$169.99	−	$99.99	—	=	$
5.	T-Shirt	16.99	−	11.99	—	=	
6.	Purse	65.95	−	—	30%	=	
7.	Golf Clubs	499.00	−	—	20	=	

8. Kaylee Bryant purchased tax software that regularly sells for $74.95 but is on sale for $59.95.

9. Jordan Alexander bought an all-in-one printer that regularly sells for $249.99 at the markdown rate of 32%.

10. Angie Sigler purchases a video game console set that regularly sells for $59.95 and is on sale for $44.95. She also buys 2 DVDs for $13.95 each that were regularly priced at $15.95.

11. The lumber company regularly sells a sheet of cedar paneling for $98.50. Jud Stassi purchases 4 sheets of the paneling on sale for $88.95 a sheet. He also purchases 2 tubes of adhesive for $2.95, marked down from $3.59.

12. Instant oatmeal regularly sells for $3.67 a box. Oatmeal is now 2 for $5.00. How much can Norris Russell save by purchasing 2 boxes?

13. Printer Paper Store normally sells laser paper for $9.99 per ream. It has a special: 1 ream free with a purchase of 2. If you buy 2 reams and get 1 free, what is your **(a)** cost per ream and **(b)** markdown per ream?

14. Office Products has a box of 500 envelopes on sale for $12.99 (with a list price of $44.00). If you buy 4 boxes, what is the total markdown?

Did You Know?

Product Placement

Some manufacturers and advertisers pay a fee for brand products to be prominently displayed in a movie or TV show. Companies such as Aéropostale, Apple, BMW, Coca-Cola, Converse, Nike, and Range Rover often pay for product placement.

15. Mattress & Furniture sells a queen two-piece bedroom set for $1,100.00. The sale price is $559.95 with a bonus discount of $60.00 by purchasing during a midwinter clearance sale. What is the total markdown?

16. John Custer wants a pair of name brand sneakers he saw on his favorite TV show. At the store, he discovers items that were already marked down 30% to a clearance rack are now marked "50% off the lowest marked price." The sneakers were originally $129.80. What is the final sale price?

17. Annie's marks down clearance items based on how long they have been in the sale section. Items in the sale section for 7 days or less are marked down 20%; items in the section for 8 to 14 days are marked down 30%; items there 15 to 21 days are marked down 40%; and items in the sale section for over 21 days are marked down 50%. You see a cashmere sweater that was originally priced at $149.00. It was moved to the sale section on March 7. How much more could you save if you wait until March 22 rather than March 11 to purchase the sweater?

H.O.T. Problems

18. CHALLENGE PROBLEM Filmore's has a sale on men's clothing. The store will take an extra 50% off its dress shirts on clearance for a total savings of 60% to 65%. Shirts that were originally $29.50 to $45.00 will have a final cost of $11.06 to $16.88. Is the total savings 60% to 65%?

19. ALGEBRA The sidewalk sale is over. Dorie Sparrow, assistant manager of The Clothes Horse, Inc., must mark all clearance rack dresses back to their regular selling price. She had marked all of them down 70%. What regular selling price does Dorie put on a dress that had been marked down to $104.98?

20. ALGEBRA Cerron's had portable speakers for laptops, MP3s, and iPods marked down 60% during a closeout sale. The speakers have surround sound effect and bass boost, can fold for storage, and include an AC adapter and a storage bag. If a certain speaker offers a $30.00 savings, what is its regular selling price?

21. ALGEBRA During its Door-Buster Sale from 7 AM to 1 PM on Saturday, Martin's Men's Store has marked down men's designer tees 35%. At 1 PM, Mark Hays must reprice the tees to their regular selling price. What is the regular selling price of a tee that is marked down to $6.99?

Spiral Review

Subtract. (Skill 6)

22. 401.44 − 98.25 **23.** 79.7 − 9.924 **24.** 5.6 − 4.6301

25. Bethany Myers bought a printer for $99.95 and a printer cartridge for $39.95. What is the total sales tax if the state tax is 7.25% and the county tax rate is 1.75%? (Lesson 6.1)

26. ALGEBRA Nathan Kim deposited $5,000 into a savings account paying 6% annual interest compounded monthly. What amount (future value) will be in the account after 3 years? How much compound interest will Nathan's account have earned? (Lesson 5.6)

GET READY for the Next Lesson

PREREQUISITE SKILL Subtracting Decimals (Skill 6)

27. 71.254 − 13.9358 **28.** $1.86 − $0.73 **29.** 4.9627 − 3.672

30. $88.93 − $10.06 **31.** 4,591.06 − 682.836 **32.** 36,591.866 − 2,419.83

LESSON 6.7

Sale Price

Lesson Objective
Compute the sale price when the markdown rate is known.

Content Vocabulary
- sale price

GET READY for the Lesson

What are some ways merchants mark sale prices on goods?

Gabrielle Wells was shopping for an outdoor grill. She found one marked $140 on sale. Another store had a $175 grill marked down 20%. The final price was the same, so she bought the grill on sale for $140 because it came with BBQ tongs.

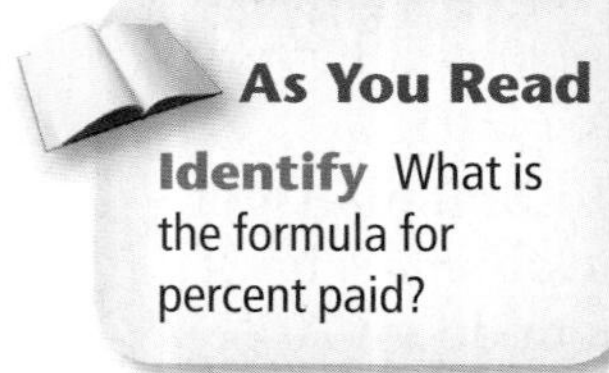

As You Read

Identify What is the formula for percent paid?

Sale Price Some stores advertise the amount of markdown and the regular selling price. They may also indicate that the item's price is a stated percent off the regular price. If you know the markdown, you can calculate the **sale price** as follows:

Sale Price = Regular Selling Price − Markdown

If you know the markdown rate or percent, you will then be **capable** of determining the percent paid. When you receive 25% off the selling price of an item, you pay 75% of the item's regular selling price. The regular selling price is 100%.

The *percent paid,* then, is 100% minus the percent off. You can calculate the percent paid as follows:

Percent Paid = 100% − Percent Off

When you know the percent paid, you can calculate the sale price with this formula:

Sale Price = Percent Paid × Regular Selling Price

Need Help? Go to...
- **Workshop 14:** Finding a Percentage, p. 30
- **Workshop 5:** Subtracting Decimals, p. 12
- **Application A:** Formulas, p. AP1

EXAMPLE 1

Debralee Medford has a 25% off coupon and is purchasing a watch that has a regular price of $125.00. What is the watch's sale price? What is the sale price using the percent paid method?

Step 1: Find the markdown.

Regular Selling Price × Markdown Rate
$125.00 × 25% = $31.25 markdown

Step 2: Find the sale price.

Regular Selling Price − Markdown
$125.00 − $31.25 = **$93.75 sale price**

Step 3: Find the percent paid.

100% − Percent Off =
100% − 25% = 75%

Ken Karp/McGraw-Hill Education

Step 4: Find the sale price (using percent paid method).

Percent Paid × Regular Selling Price

75% × $125.00 = **$93.75 sale price**

Concept CHECK

Find the sale price using the (a) percent off and (b) percent paid methods. Check your answers in the back of the book.

1. The regular selling price of a pair of men's jeans is $37.99. The markdown rate is 20%.
2. The regular selling price of a computer desk is $329.99. The markdown rate is 30%.

Need Help? Go to...

Workshop 38: Problem-Solving Strategies: Writing an Equation, p. 78

EXAMPLE 2 Algebra

Talley's marked down a new 19-inch widescreen flat panel monitor 30% if a customer purchased it with a desktop computer. The monitor's sale price was $199.00. What would be its regular selling price if it was purchased alone?

Let x = Regular selling price of the monitor if purchased alone.

Sale Price = Regular Selling Price − (Markdown Rate × Regular Selling Price)

$199.00 = $x - 30\%x$

$199.00 = $1.00x - 0.30x$

Combine like terms. → $199.00 = $0.70x$

Divide both sides by 0.70. → x = **$284.2857** or **$284.29**

Complete this problem. Check your answer in the back of the book.

3. For its back-to school sale, Freda's Books marked down its entire stock of classic novels 60% from 4 PM to 6 PM on Saturday only. Their sale price during this time is $12.99. What will the regular selling price be after 6 PM?

Reading Math +−÷=

Comprehension
To check your comprehension of a new idea, ask yourself if you could explain it to a classmate. If you could, you are ready to move to other concepts.

Lesson Practice

For Problems 4–7, determine the sale price using the (a) percent off and (b) percent paid methods.

4. Frank Choi bought a rechargeable lantern that regularly sells for $29.99 when its markdown rate was 30%.
5. Jenna Ford purchased a compact stereo that regularly sells for $229.99 at a markdown rate of 53%.
6. Jules Girard bought 1 gallon of paint at a 33% markdown. Its regular price is $39.99.
7. Mary West's new carpet sweeper regularly sells for $239.99, but it had a 25% markdown.

Did You Know?

Sugary Cereals According to a Canadian study, some brands of breakfast cereals contain as much sugar as candy bars. For example, the amount of sugar in a serving of Kellogg's Fruit Loops is equal to a dark chocolate Kit Kat bar.

8. Shoe Store has marked down men's work and outdoor boots 25% during its spring sale. What is the sale price of a pair of boots with a regular price of $149.99?
9. During an August back-to-school sale, the campus sundry shop marked down its cereal by 30%. Boxes of cereal were regularly priced at $5.95 each. What was the sale price?
10. G&G Applicances marked down a 25.5-cubic foot side-by-side refrigerator that regularly sells for $2,498.00 12% during a May sale. A set of kitchen cabinets that regularly sell for $1,499.50 is on sale at 15% off. For each, what are the **(a)** total markdown amount and **(b)** sale price?
11. Office Products has a box of 250 binder clips on sale for $9.99. The list price is $10.99. If you buy 4 boxes, what are the **(a)** sale price, **(b)** amount you save, and **(c)** total purchase price if the sales tax is 6.75%?
12. Pizza Shack discounts the regular selling price on the purchase of 3 or more pizzas by 15%. What is the sale price on the purchase of 3 pizzas that regularly sell for $9.75, $15.75, and $19.75?

13. **CHALLENGE PROBLEM** Danny's Department Store advertises savings of 45% to 51% off women's fall collections. Items with original prices of $44.00 to $152.00 are now $14.95 to $76.00. Use the percent paid to determine whether this advertisement is correct.
14. **ALGEBRA** Computers.com, Inc. has name brand all-in-one printers that print, copy, scan, and fax on sale at a 35% markdown. The price includes free shipping and handling. Tommy Woodruff purchased a printer for $97.49. What is this printer's regular selling price?
15. **ALGEBRA** On the first Tuesday of every month, Roth's gives seniors a 15% markdown on everything they purchase including sales merchandise. On the first Tuesday of this month, Jack Graham, a senior, purchased a three-piece suit marked down 40%. If he paid a total of $152.79, including a 7% sales tax, what was the suit's regular selling price?
16. **ALGEBRA** The Clearance Rack advertised an additional 70% off already marked down prices. Bea Cole picked out a pair of boot-cut jeans that had been marked down 40%. If she paid $9.56 including 6.25% sales tax, what was the regular selling price of the jeans before the markdowns and the sales tax?

Spiral Review

Subtract. (Skill 6)

17. 471.814 − 389.008 **18.** 37 − 26.321 **19.** 0.016 − 0.0019

20. Jay Owens purchased a small canoe that sells for $399.95 in Texas where the state sales tax is 6.25%, county tax is 1.5%, and city sales tax is 0.5%. What is the total sales tax amount? (Lesson 6.1)
21. **ALGEBRA** Copy Center charges $0.09 a page for machine-fed copies and $0.22 per page for all other copies. The French Club paid $12.65 for 90 copies. How many copies of each type did it make? (Lesson 1.4)

GET READY for the Next Lesson

PREREQUISITE SKILL Adding Decimals (Skill 5)

Add.

22. 0.752 + 2.631 **23.** $10.18 + $9.19 **24.** 869.91485 + 12.245

25. 385.92 + 31.475 **26.** $93.72 + $73.94 **27.** $1,349.75 + $576.89

Sean Justice/Corbis

CHAPTER 6

Review and Assessment

AFTER YOU READ

Chapter SUMMARY

Consumers base good buying decisions on all product information, not just the selling price or unit price. To make good buying decisions, you should know how to determine the best buy based on unit price. You also need to compute the sales tax and total purchase price. In addition, you should be able to calculate the final price after using a coupon or receiving a rebate from a manufacturer. You also should know how to find a markdown's dollar amount and compute the sale price when you know the markdown rate.

Vocabulary Check

1. On a sheet of paper, use each of these terms in a sentence.

Content Vocabulary

- sales tax (p. 255)
- sales receipt (p. 257)
- total purchase price (p. 257)
- unit pricing (p. 260)
- comparison shopping (p. 262)
- coupons (p. 265)
- rebates (p. 265)
- markdown (p. 267)
- markdown rate (p. 267)
- sale price (p. 270)

Academic Vocabulary

- formula (p. 255)
- purchase (p. 257)
- technique (p. 260)
- factor (p. 262)
- incentive (p. 265)
- promote (p. 267)
- capable (p. 270)

Concept Check

2. What is sales tax?
3. Give the formula for calculating sales tax.
4. What information does the sales receipt include?
5. What is the formula for computing total purchase price?
6. Explain the purpose of unit pricing.
7. Differentiate between a coupon and a rebate.
8. Define *markdown*.
9. Give the formula for finding the sale price.
10. CRITICAL THINKING List factors other than price that may affect purchasing decisions.

Lesson-by-Lesson Review

6.1 Sales Tax (pp. 255–256)

Compute the sales tax.
Jeffrey Gibson bought a backpack that had a $49.50 selling price. What is the sales tax on his purchase if he lives in Florida where the general sales tax rate is 6%?

Find the sales tax.

Sales Tax = Total Selling Price × Sales Tax Rate
= $49.50 × 0.06
= **$ 2.97**

Review Exercises

Compute the sales tax.

11. Reba Gomez bought an airline ticket whose selling price is $654.34 and sales tax rate is 5%.
12. Paige Westbrook bought a computer, printer, scanner, fax machine, and stands for a total selling price of $1,238.45; the sales tax rate was 8.5%.
13. Jessica Wing purchased a baseball cap with a selling price $12.84 and a 7.25% sales tax rate.
14. Kio Yu was planning a family camping trip. He purchased a tent for $199.98, a lantern for $39.50, and an outdoor stove for $59.95. He lives in South Carolina, where the sales tax is 6%.
15. Madeline Poulin is purchasing a new skateboard for $75.99, skate shoes for $45.99, and a set of wrist guards for $15.99. She lives in California, which has a state sales tax of 6.25% and city tax of 1.45%.

6.2 Total Purchase Price (pp. 257–259)

Calculate the total purchase price.
Anderson's Country Store in Ohio advertised wool blankets for $36.99. What is the sales tax if the Ohio rate is 5.5%? What is the total purchase price?

Step 1: Find the sales tax.

Sales Tax = Total Selling Price × Sales Tax Rate
= $36.99 × 0.055
= **$ 2.03**

Step 2: Find the total purchase price.

Total Purchase Price = Total Selling Price + Sales Tax
= $36.99 + $2.03
= **$39.02**

Review Exercises

Determine the total purchase price.

16. Gene DeWitt purchased a paper shredder for $99.95 and a case of computer paper for $24.95 in Champaign, Illinois, where the sales tax rate is 7.75%.
17. Avery Johnson purchased cat food for $9.99, cat litter for $13.99, and flea powder for $5.33 in Louisville, Kentucky, where the sales tax rate is 6.0%.

Lesson-by-Lesson Review (continued)

18. Marsha Harrington purchased a ski jacket for $149.95, a snowboard for $350.00, and a hat for $12.75 in Houston, Texas. The sales tax rate is 8.25%.

19. Dana Holley purchased a dozen votive candles for 58¢ each. She lives in San Francisco, which has the highest tax rate in California—8.5%. What is the total purchase price, including sales tax?

20. Luke Freeman is purchasing 4 MP3 players at $249 for raffle prizes. What is the total purchase price, including sales tax, if he purchased them in New York City where the state sales tax is 4% and the city and county taxes total an additional 4.25%?

21. **ALGEBRA** Miriam Perdue purchased a short-sleeve top from the clearance rack and gave the clerk $20.00. She received $6.98 in change. Miriam lives in Niagara Falls, New York, where the sales tax rate is 8%. Find the total selling price.

22. **ALGEBRA** Les Webb purchased some tennis shoes at a store in Mobile, Alabama. The clerk gave him $38.58 in change from $100.00. The sales tax rate in Alabama is 4%. What was the total selling price of the shoes?

6.3 Unit Pricing (pp. 260–261)

Determine the unit price.

Bret Franco purchased a 64-ounce bottle of shampoo for $3.99. What is the unit price of the shampoo (to the nearest tenth of a cent)?

Find the unit price.

$$\text{Unit Price} = \frac{\text{Price per Item}}{\text{Measure or Count}}$$

$$\frac{\$3.99}{64 \text{ ounces}} = \$0.062343 = \$0.0623 = \mathbf{6.2¢\ per\ ounce}$$

Review Exercises

Determine the unit price. Round answers to the nearest tenth of a cent if necessary.

23. Kimberly Stevens bought a 2-liter bottle of weed killer for $12.50.
24. Michelle Tucker takes a multivitamin tablet each morning. She purchased a 500-tablet bottle at the drugstore for $11.58.
25. Connor Drosick loves pretzels and takes a bag to work each day. He recently purchased a 32-ounce bag for $1.99.
26. Carmen Rutger recently purchased 15 1-liter bottles of water for $6.44.

Lesson-by-Lesson Review (continued)

6.4 Comparison Shopping (pp. 262–264)

Find the best buy based on unit price alone.
Cody's Market sells pickles in two sizes. The price of a 16-ounce jar is $2.49. The price of a 32-ounce jar is $3.15.

Step 1: Find the unit price for each item.

$$\text{Unit Price} = \frac{\text{Price per Item}}{\text{Measure or Count}}$$

16-ounce jar: $\frac{\$2.49}{16 \text{ ounces}} = \$0.155625$ or 15.56¢ per ounce

32-ounce jar: $\frac{\$3.15}{32 \text{ ounces}} = \$0.09843$ or 9.84¢ per ounce

Step 2: Find the better buy.

The 32-ounce jar is the better buy.

Review Exercises

Based on price alone, which would you buy?

27. Quick Shop sells a box of 7.5-ounce size crackers for $2.50 and a 10.5-ounce size for $3.29.

28. Grant's sells three different boxes of envelopes: A box of 50 sells for $2.49, a box of 100 envelopes costs $4.99, and a box of 500 envelopes costs $10.99.

29. Jungle Jerry's sells a small box of 30 animal crackers for $12.69 and a large box of 96, for $23.49.

30. At Lollie's, an 8-ounce jar of jam costs $1.09 and a 12-ounce jar costs $1.69.

31. Evan Crawford teaches family and consumer science. For this week's comparison shopping activity, one student reported different prices for sweet peas: 10-ounce package, $1.09; 14-ounce package, $1.79; and 16-ounce package, $2.29.

32. **ALGEBRA** Juana Moreno computed the unit price on a 32-ounce container of yogurt and found it to be $0.002 more per ounce than the unit price on 6 8-ounce containers of the same yogurt. If the 32-ounce container costs $1.33 less than the cost of 6 8-ounce containers, find the cost of a 32-ounce container and the cost of 6 8-ounce containers.

Lesson-by-Lesson Review (continued)

6.5 Coupons and Rebates (pp. 265–266)

Calculate the final price after using a coupon or receiving a rebate.
Barbara Henry purchased a pair of sun glasses for $24.99. She had a coupon for 25% off. What was the final price?

Find the final price.

Final Price	=	Total Selling Price	−	Total Savings		
	=	$24.99	−	(25% × 24.99)		
	=	$24.99	−	$6.25	=	**$18.74**

Review Exercises

Compute the final price.

33. Marlo Boyd purchased a bottle of ketchup costing $1.98 with a $0.75 coupon.
34. Lynn Marek bought dog food that sells for $15.97 with a $1.25 coupon.
35. Carlos Ruiz purchased a water pitcher for $19.99. What is the price after he receives the $2.50 manufacturer's rebate?
36. As Peder Bauer entered his favorite sporting goods store, he received a coupon for $15.00 off any item over $100.00 in the store. He decided to purchase a tennis racket that was selling for $125.98.
37. Chloe Kellerman purchased a complete computer system for $1,436.88 and received a manufacturer's rebate for $55.00.
38. Richmond High School purchased 90 graphing calculators for $118 each. The school received a manufacturer's rebate of $10 per calculator.

6.6 Markdown (pp. 267–269)

Find the dollar amount of the markdown.
Maura Britt purchased a dress coat on sale for $149.95. The regular selling price is $249.50. What was the markdown?

Find the markdown.

Regular Selling Price	−	Sale Price		
$249.50	−	$149.95	=	**$99.55 markdown**

Review Exercises

Determine the markdown.

39. A pillow costs $34.99 and is on sale for $29.69.
40. A floor lamp costs $95.59 and is on sale at 40% off.
41. Isaiah Segel purchased a pair of golf shoes for $69.99. The regular selling price is $89.00.
42. Shelly Mason purchased a mountain bike for 35% off the regular price of $899.
43. Wendy Kenton purchased a new stereo system for 25% off the regular price of $499.

Lesson-by-Lesson Review (continued)

44. Lenny Jaworski is a general manager of a large department store chain. This week he has decided to offer 33% off any item in the store. Find the total markdown for the following items: wool pants, $65.95; leather shoes, $126.50; and straw purses, $19.95.

45. **ALGEBRA** Elisa Carsten noticed this advertisement: "This week only: Save $125.00 on all mattress sets. All sets marked down 25%." What is the regular selling price of a mattress set?

6.7 Sale Price (pp. 270–272)

Compute the sale price when the markdown rate is known.
Lee Ogawa has a coupon for 30% off and is purchasing a 12-cup coffee maker that has a $79.99 regular price. What will he pay for the coffee maker?

Step 1: Find the markdown.

Regular Selling Price × Markdown Rate

$79.99 × 30% = $23.997 = $24.00 markdown

Step 2: Find the sale price.

Regular Selling Price − Markdown

$79.99 − $24.00 = **$55.99 sale price**

Review Exercises

Determine the sale price for Problems 46–50.

46. Dean's is selling football equipment at 25% off the regular $349.75 selling price.
47. Lois Fargo bought a new subcompact car at 8.5% off the $23,450.00 regular selling price.
48. Lyndon's is selling a 15-foot trampoline at 30% off its $599 regular selling price.
49. If the regular selling price of a silk scarf is $49 and the markdown rate is 38%, what is its sale price using the percent paid method?
50. **ALGEBRA** Hubbard's marked down a new dresser 20% when purchased with a mirror. The dresser's sale price was $650. What was the regular selling price of the dresser when purchased alone?

Practice Test

Record your answers on a sheet of paper.

1. If the sales tax rate is 3.0% , what is the purchase price of a $12.00 shirt?
   A $15.00 **B** $11.64
   C $12.30 **D** $12.36

2. If the sales tax rate in Wapakoneta, Ohio, is 5.5%, how much sales tax does the purchase of a $34 carrying case include?
   A $35.88 **B** $1.87
   C $5.50 **D** $17.50

3. What is the total purchase price of a $13.65 lamp if the sales tax rate is 6.2%?
   A $14.50 **B** $19.85
   C $15.84 **D** $14.27

4. If 12 oranges cost $4.20, how much does 1 orange cost?
   A $0.42 **B** $0.12
   C $0.35 **D** $0.70

5. **ALGEBRA** A new HDTV was marked down 20% when sold with a DVR. The TV's sale price was $1,752. What would the HDTV's regular selling price be if a customer purchased it alone?
   A $2,010.00 **B** $2,500.80
   C $1,995.60 **D** $2,190.00

6. Shea O'Malley has a coupon for $0.35 off a $2.89 box of labels. What will the labels cost if the coupon is used?
   A $2.54 **B** $2.34
   C $3.35 **D** $2.35

7. What is the markdown if a $35 dress sells for $26?
   A $11 **B** $9
   C $12 **D** $26

8. **ALGEBRA** Diego's Subs is offering $0.75 off its foot-long meatball sub. If this represents a 20% markdown, what is the sub's regular selling price?
   A $3.25 **B** $4.25
   C $2.75 **D** $3.75

9. **ALGEBRA** Susie Kovacs purchased a DVD from the discount bin and gave the clerk a 20-dollar bill. The clerk gave Julia $9.89 in change. The sales tax rate where she purchased the DVD was 7.5%. What was the DVD's total selling price?

10. Mason Witt bought a 12-ounce bottle of mango juice for $1.12. What was the unit price per ounce?

11. A laptop computer costs $2,799.99 and has a $150 mail-in rebate. What is its cost after the rebate if the envelope and stamp cost a total of $0.55?

12. A leading brand of toothpaste is available in four sizes: 6.4 ounces for $3.99; 4.2 ounces for $2.99; 4.0 ounces for $2.49; and a travel size of 0.85 ounces for $0.99. Based on unit price, what size is the best buy?

13. Martha's Clothing is having its semiannual clearance sale and is marking down all sale clothing an additional 60%. Their line of designer jeans had previously been marked down 30%. The pair that Betty Clark wants to purchase had originally been priced at $119.50. What final sale price will Betty pay if she purchases that pair?

14. 24% of $1,680.75

15. $4,680 ÷ 12.2

16. $132.45 – $43.62

17. $2,300.89 + $23.23

18. 0.0025% of $1,321.00

19. 391.67 × 31.2

PART 1 Multiple Choice

Record your answers on the answer sheet provided by your teacher or on a sheet of paper.

1. Use this table to solve the question. Jan Zima earns $35,650 a year working for an electronics supplier. He is single with no dependents and pays $1,749.80 in state income tax each year. What is his state's tax rate?

Exemptions	
Single	$2,000
Married	$4,000
Each Dependent	$2,000

   A 5.2% **B** 4.9%
   C 2.3% **D** 4.0%

2. Danni Gould earns $45,580 a year. How much tax does her employer withhold if the tax rate is 4%?
   A $2,300.10 **B** $1,855.50
   C $3,500.40 **D** $1,823.20

3. What is Caroline Salcedo's total deposit of a check for $524.75, 5 dimes, 8 nickels, 5 quarters, and 5 pennies?
   A $525.15 **B** $526.45
   C $526.95 **D** $526.55

4. Donna DeWine bought a bicycle for $185.99 that had a mail-in rebate of 20%. What was her cost?
   A $165.99 **B** $148.79
   C $137.19 **D** $122.68

5. Cole Robertson purchased a bag of peanuts priced at $1.55 with a sales tax rate of 3.3%. What was the purchase price?
   A $0.08 **B** $1.60
   C $0.05 **D** $1.63

6. **ALGEBRA** Wan Taru's average monthly spending on entertainment for the first quarter this year was $175.45. In April, he spent $205.90, and in May, he spent $150.40. How much can he spend in June and have the same average as in the first quarter?
   A $149.15 **B** $169.70
   C $156.50 **D** $170.05

PART 2 Short Response/Griddable

7. Alphonse Martel purchased sunscreen for $8.99 at a discount store that had a sales tax rate of 5.75%. How much did he pay in tax?

8. **ALGEBRA** Julio Rossi's bank account has a $6,785.58 balance. The previous balance was $5,905.68. After he deposited $931 and withdrew $60, how much did he earn in interest?

PART 3 Extended Response

Show your work.

9. Ari and Selena Panglos deposited $2,000 into a joint savings account that earns interest at an annual rate of 5.5%, compounded semiannually. They made no other deposits or withdrawals. "We have earned $110 on our money so far," Ari said to Selena after six months. She said, "Think again, Ari. It will take us almost another six months to earn that much." Write a sentence explaining who is correct, and suggest why Ari or Selena made the mistake. Then calculate the interest they have earned after six months.

TEST-TAKING TIP

Read the Directions Never assume you know what the directions say. For example, some questions might have more than one correct answer.

Building Academic Skills

Mathematics

A new store in the mall prices all clothing at $17.95. Anya Sendak has a coupon for $25.00 off $100.00 before tax. How many items would Anya have to buy to spend at least $100.00? What would her final bill be if she used the coupon?

English Language Arts/Writing

Write a poem, song, rap, pamphlet, or paragraph about the advantages and disadvantages of buying something as soon as it goes on sale.

Social Studies/Government

Sales taxes are examples of usage taxes. Unlike income taxes that everyone who works has to pay, the amount of sales tax you pay depends on the amount of goods and services you buy. Write a one page position paper on one of the following topics:

- Sales Taxes Are Fairer Than Income Taxes
- Income Taxes Are Fairer Than Sales Taxes

Building Real-World Skills

Career WISE

Product Designer Every product you see on store shelves begins as an idea. Product designers take ideas from start to finish by working with artists, engineers, and manufacturing specialists. One recent *BusinessWeek* Best Product Design Award winner was the Intel Mobile Clinical Assistant.

Research and Share:

a. Using the Internet, locate the most recent winners of the *BusinessWeek* Best Product Design awards.

b. What was the Gold Medal winner for last year's award? What does the item do?

21st Century Workplace

Special Savings Programs Many employers offer savings programs to help employees save for end-of-year purchases. The employee makes regular, automatic withdrawals from each paycheck to a company-managed savings account. The employee can withdraw the total amount at the end of the year.

Discuss and Write:

a. As a class, discuss why some people set aside money for the end of the year.

b. Write a list of items for which you would like to save.

Juice Images/Alamy

CHAPTER 7 Charge Accounts and Credit Cards

Big Idea

Banks use several methods to compute finance charges on charge account and credit card balances.

Explore the Photo

Buy Now, Pay Later Many people make purchases using credit cards. *Why might you want to buy something using a credit card instead of cash?*

Ask AN EXPERT

"Good" and "Bad" Debt

Q: Are certain kinds of debt better than others, and how do I avoid having problems with debt?

A: Financial advisors consider things such as real-estate and college loans to be "good" debt because they are investments for the future. Also, in many cases the borrower can deduct interest on real-estate and college loans from income tax. Advisors consider unpaid credit card balances "bad" debt because finance charges greatly increase the amount you are actually paying for goods purchased using the card. Any kind of debt can become a problem, however, if you cannot afford to pay your bills.

English Language Arts/Writing Imagine that you are just out of school and living on your own. Make a list of purchases you might make, including both everyday goods and more expensive items. Then indicate which purchases are best to put on a credit card instead of paying cash.

GET READY for the Chapter

Math Online

To take the Online Readiness Quiz, go to **connectED.mcgraw-hill.com**.

Chapter 7 Charge Accounts and Credit Cards

Reading Guide

Before You Read

Connect Have you ever purchased something by borrowing money from someone, or by paying in installments?

Main Idea

If you need to make a purchase, perhaps in an emergency, using a credit card to make the purchase allows you the flexibility to "buy now and pay later."

Graphic Organizer

Before you read this chapter, draw a diagram like the one below. As you read, keep track of advantages and disadvantages of using credit cards.

Using Credit Cards	
Advantages	Disadvantages

Math Online Go to connectED.mcgraw-hill.com to download this graphic organizer.

Content Vocabulary

You will learn these key terms in this chapter.

- credit card
- charge account
- account statement
- finance charge
- unpaid-balance method
- average-daily-balance method

Academic Vocabulary

You will see these words in your reading and on your tests.

- acquire
- compute
- fee

You can find vocabulary definitions in the **Content Vocabulary** Glossary and the **Academic Vocabulary** Glossary in the back of the book.

LESSON 7.1

Account Statements

Lesson Objective
Calculate the new balance on a charge account.

Content Vocabulary
- credit card
- charge account
- account statement
- finance charge

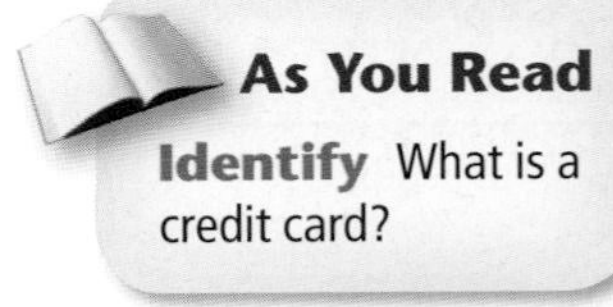
As You Read
Identify What is a credit card?

GET READY for the Lesson

Have you ever used a credit card?

Rebecca Holmes used her credit card to pay for having her car towed. Now she is using her credit card to rent a car to drive until her car has been repaired.

Credit and Charge Accounts A popular method of purchasing goods is to use a **credit card**, which is a card authorizing purchases on credit. Banks issue credit cards to allow the cardholder to **acquire** goods and services on demand. Consumers can use the cards at many different places for charges, cash advances, and to make balance transfers.

Another type of credit account is a **charge account**, which is an existing line of credit at the business that issued it. The customer can use it to charge purchases made only at that store.

Offering credit to customers generally results in more sales for a business. However, businesses must pay a certain percent of a sale to the bank issuing the credit card and accounts may not be paid.

If you have a credit or charge card, you receive a monthly **account statement** that lists all of the items you purchased and other transactions. The statement shows all activity in the account during a one-month period. Many credit card companies allow you to review your statement online and make payments by electronic transfer of funds.

Your account statement indicates your previous balance, finance charge, total of purchases, any payments and credits, and new balance. If you did not pay your previous bill in full, the credit card or charge account company adds a **finance charge.** This is interest that the company charges to a credit account for not paying the total amount owed by the due date. The summary line on the account statement uses this formula to determine your new balance:

$$\text{New Balance} = \text{Previous Balance} + \text{Finance Charge} + \text{New Purchases} - (\text{Payments} + \text{Credits})$$

Need Help? Go to...
- **Workshop 4:** Adding Decimals, p. 10
- **Workshop 5:** Subtracting Decimals, p. 12
- **Application A:** Formulas, p. AP1

EXAMPLE

See **Figure 7.1** on page 286 for Marina Palmer's charge account statement. What is her new balance?

Find the new balance.

$$\text{New Balance} = \text{Previous Balance} + \text{Finance Charge} + \text{New Purchases} - (\text{Payments} + \text{Credits})$$

$$= (\$332.64 + \$5.64 + \$173.03) - (\$50.00 + \$31.94)$$

$$\mathbf{\$429.37} = \$511.31 - \$81.94$$

Marina's new balance is $429.37.

Continued on next page

Figure 7.1

D&L Department Store						

MAIL THIS PORTION WITH PAYMENT TO P.O. BOX 1027

Marina Palmer
1234 Main St.
Toledo, OH 43605

(IF ADDRESS IS INCORRECT, PLEASE CHECK BOX AND CORRECT ON REVERSE SIDE)

ACCOUNT NUMBER 101-04076
NEW BALANCE
TOTAL MINIMUM AMOUNT NOW DUE $43.00
SEND PAYMENT TO REACH US BY 10/30/20--

DATE	DEPT. NO.	DESCRIPTION	PURCHASES	CREDITS	PAYMENTS	ITEM NO.
09/07	162	SPORTSWEAR		$23.42		0-06-18005
09/10	363	SPORTSWEAR	$108.63			0-07-20015
09/17		PAYMENT—THANK YOU			$50.00	0-06-47023
09/19	214	JR SPORTSWEAR		8.52		0-07-45005
09/19	53	HOUSEWARES	19.53			0-07-45006
09/27	34	COSMETICS	25.62			0-07-64004
09/29	1	LINENS-TOWELS	19.25			0-07-70012

Bill Closing Date	Previous Balance	Finance Charge	Total Purchases This Month	Credits	Payment	New Balance
9/30	$332.64	$5.64	$173.03	$31.94	$50.00	$429.37

Paying the new balance in full within 25 days of the bill closing date avoids having a finance charge added next month. If the company adds a finance charge, it computes the charge on the average daily balance of $375.72 by applying the monthly periodic rate. The *periodic rate* is the interest percentage the company charges for a specific period.
SUBJECT TO A MINIMUM FINANCE CHARGE OF $.50. **NOTICE:** SEE REVERSE SIDE FOR IMPORTANT INFORMATION.

MARINA'S ACCOUNT NUMBER

CREDIT FOR ITEMS RETURNED

$50.00 PAYMENT TOWARD LAST MONTH'S BILL

LAST DATE TRANSACTIONS WERE PROCESSED

AMOUNT MARINA OWED LAST MONTH

AMOUNT MARINA NOW OWES

Concept CHECK

Find the new balance. Check your answers in the back of the book.

	Previous Balance	+	Finance Charge	+	New Purchases	−	(Payments + Credits)	=	New Balance
1.	$600.00	+	$7.50	+	$90.00	−	$100.00	=	
2.	278.75	+	4.18	+	35.85	−	48.00	=	

Lesson Practice

For Problems 3–12, determine the new balance.

	Billing Date	Previous Balance	Finance Charge	New Purchases	Payments & Credits	New Balance
3.	08/15	$ 600.00	$ 9.00	$140.00	$100.00	
4.	01/22	410.75	7.20	175.00	150.00	
5.	03/01	450.95	6.75	39.95	160.00	
6.	09/04	233.23	2.33	40.36	133.23	
7.	06/15	675.19	—	416.34	675.19	
8.	08/01	2,494.21	43.65	137.25	450.00	

9. Andre Moore's charge card account has a previous balance of $1,787.29. Moore made a $200 payment. The new purchases include $47.97, $49.28, $83.21, and $75.63 with a finance charge of $11.81 and a credit of $45.89.

Atmospheric Scientist
Atmospheric scientists, such as meteorologists and climatologists, provide weather forecasts and study environmental concerns. **Name other types of scientists.**

10. Alice Nako's monthly credit card statement has a previous balance of $307.85. It shows Alice's $40.00 payment. This month's new purchases were $9.50 and $41.75. The account posted a $23.75 credit, and the finance charge is $4.62.
11. The previous monthly balance on Barney Laurent's charge card is $144.79. He made a payment of $144.79 and had charges of $125.22, $23.22, and $33.65. There is no finance charge.
12. Amber Cho's monthly statement for her credit card shows a $529.78 previous balance, her $85.00 payment, a $7.95 finance charge, and credits of $49.45 and $39.22. This month's new purchases are $277.32 and $38.20.
13. Mario Azaria received the charge account statement partially shown below. Find his **(a)** payments and credits, **(b)** new purchases, and **(c)** new balance.

Dept.	Description	Charges	Payment/ Credit	Date	Ref. #
109	Garden Shop	$ 42.75		1/25	6004
85	Menswear	145.98		1/25	7018
	PAYMENT		$74.40	2/01	8014
71	Appliances		35.50	2/02	3113
Billing Date: 2/16					
Previous Balance	**Payments & Credits**	**Unpaid Balance**	**Finance Charge**	**New Purchases**	**New Balance**
$285.92	a.	—	$4.29	b.	c.

14. **CHALLENGE PROBLEM** Chester Boles reviewed his credit card's monthly statement. It shows a $2,376.10 previous balance and this month's new purchases of $875.22, $65.75, $45.22, and $21.23. It also shows a $875.22 credit and a $45.30 finance charge. He also made the minimum payment of 2.5% of the previous balance. What is the new balance?

Study Tip
Main Idea
As you read through your study materials, list the main ideas to write your own summary of the material.

Spiral Review

Add. (Skill 5)

15. $532.75 + $45.90 + $38.90 + $16.55
16. $44.29 + $324.60 + $8.65 + $27.50
17. Chan Hee Wu purchased a bicycle for $259.99 and a helmet for $62.99. The sales tax rate is 8.25%. What is the total purchase price? (Lesson 6.2)
18. **ALGEBRA** Angelina Cisneros earns $15.60 per hour. How many hours per week must she work if she wants to earn approximately $550.00 per week? (Lesson 1.1)

GET READY for the Next Lesson

PREREQUISITE SKILL **Finding the Percentage** (Skill 30)

19. 3% of 96
20. 8% of 60
21. 10% of 46.8
22. 4.5% of 840

LESSON 7.2

Finance Charge: Unpaid-Balance Method

Lesson Objective
Compute the finance charge by using the unpaid-balance method.

Content Vocabulary
- unpaid-balance method

GET READY for the Lesson

What are the advantages of shopping online?

Ken Harper likes to shop online. He recently downloaded a new album and purchased a cell phone that he found at a good price on the Internet. He used his credit card to pay for his purchases.

As You Read
Explain What is the finance charge based on when using the unpaid-balance method?

Determining the Finance Charge A credit card company or a charge account at a store may utilize the **unpaid-balance method** to **compute** finance charges. This method computes the finance charge based on the portion of the previous balance you have not paid. The formula is:

Unpaid Balance = Previous Balance − (Payments + Credits)

Finance Charge = Unpaid Balance × Periodic Rate

New Balance = Unpaid Balance + Finance Charge + New Purchases

Need Help? Go to...
- **Workshop 14:** Finding a Percentage, p. 30
- **Skill 30:** Finding the Percentage, p. SK31
- **Application A:** Formulas, p. AP1

EXAMPLE 1

See **Figure 7.2** for the summary portion of Lucille Sherman's charge account statement. She had a previous balance of $132.40, made a $40.00 payment and purchased an item for $79.55. The monthly finance charge is computed at 1.5% of the unpaid balance. Determine the **(a)** unpaid balance, **(b)** finance charge, and **(c)** new balance.

Figure 7.2

Charge Account Statement

88	PAYMENT / Thank You		40.00		
Billing Date: 2/16					
Previous Balance	**Payments & Credits**	**Unpaid Balance**	**Finance Charge**	**New Purchases**	**New Balance**
$132.40	$40.00	a.	b.	$79.55	c.

Step 1: Find the unpaid balance.

Unpaid Balance = Previous Balance − (Payments + Credits)
$92.40 = $132.40 − $40.00

Step 2: Find the finance charge.

Finance Charge = Unpaid Balance × Periodic Rate
$1.386 or **$1.39** = $92.40 × 1.5%

Step 3: Find the new balance.

New Balance = Unpaid Balance + Finance Charge + New Purchases
$173.34 = $92.40 + $1.39 + $79.55

Complete problems 1 and 2 by finding (a) the unpaid balance, (b) the finance charge, and (c) the new balance. (The periodic rate is 1.5%.) Check your answers in the back of the book.

	(Previous Balance	− Payments & Credits	= Unpaid Balance)	+ Finance Charge	+ New Purchases	= New Balance
1.	\$600	\$100	a.	b.	\$70	c.
2.	220	150	a.	b.	95	c.

Need Help? Go to...

- **Workshop 38:** Problem Solving Strategies: Writing an Equation, p. 78
- **Application C:** Tables and Charts, p. AP3

EXAMPLE 2 Algebra

Roy Nelson's charge account uses the unpaid-balance method to compute the finance charge at a monthly periodic rate of 1.75%. During the month, he charged \$156.89, made a \$200.00 payment, and had a \$9.90 finance charge. Find his **(a)** unpaid balance, **(b)** previous balance, and **(c)** new balance.

Step 1: Let a = Roy Nelson's unpaid balance

Finance Charge = Unpaid Balance × Periodic Rate

$$\$9.90 = a \times 1.75\%$$

Divide both sides by 0.0175

$$\frac{\$9.90}{0.0175} = \frac{a \times 0.0175}{0.0175}$$

$$\mathbf{\$565.714} = a$$

Roy's unpaid balance is \$565.71.

Step 2: Let b = Roy's previous balance

Unpaid Balance = Previous Balance − (Payments + Credits)

$$\$565.71 = b - \$200.00$$

Add \$200.00 to both sides

$$\mathbf{\$765.71} = b$$

His previous balance was \$765.71.

Step 3: New Balance = Unpaid Balance + Finance Charge + New Purchases

$$\mathbf{\$732.50} = \$565.71 + \$9.90 + \$156.89$$

The new balance is \$732.50.

Reading Math +−÷=

Portion

A *portion* is a part of a whole. If a problem uses *portion*, it refers to something that has been divided into two or more parts or among two or more things.

Complete the problems. Check your answers in the back of the book.

3. Omar Tariq has a credit card that uses the unpaid-balance method to compute the finance charge. His monthly periodic rate is 2.4%. During this past billing cycle, he charged a total of \$256.28 and made payments totaling \$350.00. If he has a finance charge of \$18.28, find his **(a)** unpaid balance, **(b)** previous balance, and **(c)** new balance.
4. Jordan Amodeo's charge account statement shows a previous balance of \$284.86, payments of \$100.00, and a finance charge of \$3.51. To the nearest hundreth percent, what monthly periodic rate is he being charged?

Lesson Practice

For Problems 5–7, use a periodic rate of 1.5% and the unpaid-balance method to compute the (a) unpaid balance, (b) finance charge, and (c) new balance.

	(Previous Balance	−	Payments & Credits	=	Unpaid Balance)	+	Finance Charge	+	New Purchases	+	New Balance
5.	(350.00	−	75.00	=	a.)	+	b.	+	90.00	+	c.
6.	(125.50	−	45.50	=	a.)	+	b.	+	42.50	+	c.
7.	(437.50	−	57.50	=	a.)	+	b.	+	222.50	+	c.

Did You Know?

Consumers and Credit The typical U.S. consumer has 13 credit obligations, four of which are installment loans and nine of which are credit cards; and has never been more than 30 days late paying a bill.

For Problems 8–12, find the new balance.

8. Previous balance: $1,280; payment: $200; new purchases: $52 and $48; periodic rate: 1.6%.

9. Previous balance: $1,221.35; payment: $300; new purchases: $25.90 and $18.53; periodic rate: 1.75%.

10. A portion of Alvin Lombardi's charge account statement follows. The finance charge is computed at 2% of the unpaid balance.

Previous Balance	Payments & Credits	Unpaid Balance	Finance Charge	New Purchases	New Balance
$419.29	$45.00	a.	b.	$79.31	c.

11. A portion of Vanessa Buell's charge account statement follows. The finance charge is 1.25% of the unpaid balance.

Previous Balance	Payments & Credits	Unpaid Balance	Finance Charge	New Purchases	New Balance
$556.71	$147.55	a.	b.	$21.64	c.

12. Kwami Endabe's charge account uses the unpaid-balance method. The periodic rate is 1.85%. The previous balance is $478.68. He had payments of $150 and $60 and an $89.95 credit. He has new purchases of $38.50, $65.74, and $125.61.

13. ALGEBRA Cody Ray's credit card company uses the unpaid-balance method and charges a monthly periodic rate of 1.8%. His finance charge was $17.54, he made $376.90 in new purchases, and a $250.00 payment. Find **(a)** his unpaid balance, **(b)** previous balance, and **(c)** new balance.

Spiral Review

Add or subtract. (Skill 5, 6)

14. $425.10 + $38.75 + $29.51 + $4.22 **15.** $499.24 − $88.31

16. The regular selling price of a popcorn popper is $53.99. The markdown rate is 45%. What is the selling price? (Lesson 6.7)

GET READY for the Next Lesson

PREREQUISITE SKILL **Dividing Decimals** (Skill 11)

17. 7.8 ÷ 24 **18.** 597 ÷ 15 **19.** 4,215 ÷ 75

LESSON 7.3

Finance Charge: Average-Daily-Balance Method

Lesson Objective

Compute the finance charge based on the average-daily-balance method–new purchases included.

Content Vocabulary

- average-daily-balance method

GET READY for the Lesson

What are the advantages and disadvantages of using credit cards?

Kinnori Yamada is glad he did some research before applying for a credit card. By comparing the annual percentage rate that different banks charge, he was able to get a low one. His card also offered low fees in comparison to others he had investigated.

	APR	Fees
Credit card #1	18%	Annual fee: $10
Credit card #2	14.5%	Annual fee: $5
Credit card #3	16%	No annual fee

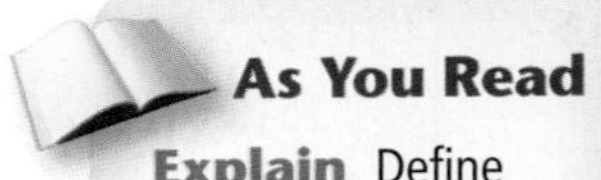

As You Read

Explain Define new purchases included in your own words.

Determining Finance Charge When New Purchases Are Included

Most companies granting credit compute the finance charge using the **average-daily-balance method**–*new purchases included. New purchases included* means that the company adds any new purchase to the balance at the end of each day. In other words, the daily balance equals the previous day's balance plus new purchases minus the payments and credits. Credit card companies also charge a late **fee** if they do not receive payment by the due date.

The first step in calculating the average daily balance–new purchases included is to determine the balance for each day in the billing period and then use the following formula to find the average daily balance for the billing period.

$$\text{Average Daily Balance} = \frac{\text{Sum of Daily Balances}}{\text{Number of Days}}$$

The next step is to calculate the finance charge and the new balance. Use these formulas:

$$\text{Finance Charge} = \text{Average Daily Balance} \times \text{Periodic Rate}$$

$$\text{New Balance} = \text{Unpaid Balance} + \text{Finance Charge} + \text{New Purchases}$$

Need Help? Go to...

- Skill 8: Multiplying Decimals, p. SK9
- Skill 11: Dividing Decimals, p. SK12
- Application G: Elapsed Time (Days), p. AP6

EXAMPLE 1

Sierra Warren has a charge account with a company that computes the finance charge using the average daily balance–new purchases included. She checks to be sure the average daily balance is correct. See **Figure 7.3** on p. 292 for part of her statement.

Figure 7.3

Reference	Posting Date	Description	Purchases & Advances	Payments & Credits
1-32734	12/10	Housewares	$25.85	
2-44998	12/20	PAYMENT		$70.00
Billing Period	**Previous Balance**	**Periodic Rate**	**Average Daily Balance**	**Finance Charge**
12/1–12/31	$125.80	2%	$117.05	$2.34
Payments & Credits	**Purchases & Advances**	**New Balance**	**Minimum Payment**	**Payment Due**
$70.00	$25.85	$83.99	$20.00	1/21

Step 1: Find the sum of daily balances.

Dates	Payment	Purchases	End-of-Day Balance	×	Number of Days	Sum of Balances
12/1–12/9			$125.80	×	9	$1,132.20
12/10		$25.85	151.65	×	1	151.65
12/11–12/19			151.65	×	9	1,364.85
12/20	$70.00		81.65	×	1	81.65
12/21–12/31			81.65	×	11	898.15
			TOTAL		31	**$3,628.50**

Step 2: Find the average daily balance.

$$\text{Average Daily Balance} = \frac{\text{Sum of Daily Balances}}{\text{Number of Days}} = \frac{\$3{,}628.50}{31} = \$117.048 = \mathbf{\$117.05}$$

Sierra's average daily balance was $117.05.

Concept CHECK

Find the average daily balance including new purchases. Check your answers in the back of the book.

	Dates	Payment	Purchase	End-of-Day Balance	×	Number of Days	Sum of Balances
1.	9/9–9/15			$500	×	7	a.
2.	9/16		$100	600	×	1	a.
3.	9/17–9/21			a.	×	5	b.
4.	9/22	$150		a.	×	b.	c.
5.	9/23–10/8			a.	×	b.	c.
6.				TOTAL		a.	b.
	Sum of Daily Balances	÷	Number of Days		=	Average Daily Balance	
7.	a.	÷	b.		=	c.	

Need Help? Go to...

Workshop 38: Problem Solving Strategies: Writing an Equation, p. 78

EXAMPLE 2

Sierra Warren (from **Example 1**) checks the finance charge and the new balance. The finance charge is computed at 2% of the average daily balance. What is her new balance?

Step 1: Find the finance charge.

Finance Charge = Average Daily Balance × Periodic Rate

\$2.341 or \$2.34 = \$117.05 × 2%

Step 2: Find the unpaid balance.

Unpaid Balance = Previous Balance − (Payments + Credits)

\$55.80 = \$125.80 − \$70.00

Step 3: Find the new purchases.

New purchases totaled \$25.85.

Step 4: Find the new balance.

New Balance = Unpaid Balance + Finance Charge + New Purchases

\$83.99 = \$55.80 + \$2.34 + \$25.85

Her new balance is \$83.99.

Concept CHECK

Complete the problems by using the information in Concept Check Problems 1–7 to find the following if the finance charge is computed at 1.5% of the average daily balance. Check your answers in the back of the book.

8. The finance charge. **9.** The unpaid balance. **10.** The new balance.

EXAMPLE 3 Algebra

Vana Dodd's credit card finance charge is based on the average-daily-balance method–new purchases included. Her monthly periodic rate is 2.3%, and her finance charge for the past billing cycle was \$29.00. Find her average daily balance.

Let a = Vana's average daily balance

Finance Charge = Average Daily Balance × Periodic Rate

\$29.00 = $a \times 2.3\%$

Divide both sides by 0.023 → **\$1,260.869** = a

Vana's average daily balance was \$1,260.87.

Concept CHECK

Complete the problem. Check your answer in the back of the book.

11. Seth Dixon has a credit card with a monthly periodic rate of 1.95%. The finance charge is computed using the average-daily-balance method–new purchases included. If his credit card statement shows a finance charge of \$32.76 for the last billing cycle, find his average daily balance.

Reading Math +−÷=

Dates

The hyphen between two dates such as 12/1-12/31 can be read as "through."

Lesson Practice

Find the average daily balance, with new purchases included.

	Dates	Payment	Purchase	End-of-Day Balance	×	Number of Days	Sum of Balances
12.	9/6–9/17			$600	×	a.	b.
13.	9/18		$140	740	×	a.	b.
14.	9/19–9/24			a.	×	b.	c.
15.	9/25	$120		a.	×	b.	c.
16.	9/26–10/5			a.	×	b.	c.
17.				TOTAL		a.	b.

	Sum of Daily Balances	÷	Number of Days	=	Average Daily Balance
18.	a.	÷	b.	=	c.

Did You Know?
Credit in the United States Early American merchants offered credit because some customers could not afford to pay cash. Sears Roebuck Company and General Motors once resisted credit, but later gave in to consumer demand.

19. Edie Bertelli received her statement from a department store. (See below.) Find the **(a)** average daily balance–new purchases included, **(b)** finance charge, and **(c)** new balance.

Reference	Posting Date	Transaction Date	Description	Purchases & Advances	Payments & Credits
1027485	4/11		PAYMENT		$40.00
4500298	4/15	4/01	Menswear	$39.95	
5473390	4/23	4/21	Housewares	15.99	
1374655	4/25		PAYMENT		50.00

Billing Period	Previous Balance	Periodic Rate	Average Daily Balance	Finance Charge
4/1–4/30	$175.00	1.2%	a.	b.

Payments & Credits	Purchases & Advances	New Balance	Minimum Payment	Payment Due
$90.00	$55.94	c.	$25.00	5/25

20. CHALLENGE PROBLEM Refer to Problem 19. Calculate the average daily balance and the finance charge if **(a)** both payments are made on April 2 and **(b)** both payments are made on April 25.

21. ALGEBRA Leah Horowitz's credit card uses the average-daily-balance method–new purchases included. Her finance charge this past billing cycle was $25.95, and her average daily balance was $998.08. Find her monthly periodic rate to the nearest tenth of a percent.

Spiral Review

Multiply or divide. Round to nearest hundredth. (Skill 7, 8)

22. 7 × 145 **23.** 31 × 56.23 **24.** 1,608.75 ÷ 30 **25.** 1,329.89 ÷ 31

26. On Friday, you worked from 7:15 AM to 11:30 AM and then from 12:15 PM to 4:45 PM. How many hours did you work? (Lesson 1.3)

GET READY for the Next Lesson

PREREQUISITE SKILL **Writing Percents as Decimals** (Skill 28)
Write the percents as decimals.

27. 34% **28.** 6% **29.** 86.4% **30.** 5.6%

Review and Assessment

AFTER YOU READ
Chapter SUMMARY

Having a credit card or charge account gives the account holder the option to buy now and pay later. Responsible use of credit cards and charge accounts involves knowing how to calculate the new balance on a charge account, find the finance charge by using the unpaid-balance method, and compute the finance charge based on the average-daily-balance method–new purchases included.

Vocabulary Check

1. On a sheet of paper, use each of these terms in a sentence.

Content Vocabulary

- credit card (p. 285)
- charge account (p. 285)
- account statement (p. 285)
- finance charge (p. 285)
- unpaid-balance method (p. 288)
- average-daily-balance method (p. 291)

Academic Vocabulary

- acquire (p. 285)
- compute (p. 288)
- fee (p. 291)

Concept Check

2. Differentiate between a credit card and a charge account.
3. What is a finance charge?
4. Summarize how the finance charge is computed using the unpaid-balance method.
5. Summarize what "new purchases included" means in relation to finance charges.
6. Give the formula for determining the average daily balance.
7. CRITICAL THINKING Make two lists, one of advantages and one of disadvantages, of using a credit card to make purchases.
8. CRITICAL THINKING Name the advantages and disadvantages of offering customers charge accounts.

Lesson-by-Lesson Review

7.1 Account Statements (pp. 285–287)

Calculate the new balance in a charge account.
Your monthly statement shows a $504.33 previous balance, a $50.00 payment, new purchases of $12.35 and $39.54, and a $5.67 finance charge. What is the new balance?

Find the new balance.

New Balance = Previous Balance + Finance Charge + New Purchases − (Payments + Credits)
$511.89 = $504.33 + $5.67 + $12.35 + $39.54 − $50.00

Review Exercises

What is the new balance for the credit card statement whose data are in the following table?

	Billing Date	Previous Balance	Finance Charge	New Purchases	Payments & Credits	New Balance
9.	9/27	$ 306.55	$ 6.75	$ 209.54	$175.00	
10.	6/29	985.66	9.06	1,239.44	300.00	
11.	5/25	121.09	2.35	219.30	53.00	
12.	6/15	1,239.92	18.56	500.00	895.00	

7.2 Finance Charge: Unpaid-Balance Method (pp. 288–290)

Compute the finance charge by using the unpaid-balance method.
Aldo Weigant has a charge account at Robert's Bike Shop, which uses the unpaid-balance method to compute finance charges. The periodic rate is 1.25%. Aldo's previous balance was $569.32, and he had payments and credits of $150.00. If he had new purchases of $97.50, find his **(a)** unpaid balance, **(b)** finance charges, and **(c)** new balance.

Step 1: Find the unpaid balance.

Unpaid Balance = Previous Balance − (Payments + Credits)
$419.32 = $569.32 − $150.00

Step 2: Find the finance charge.

Finance Charge = Unpaid Balance × Periodic Rate
$5.2415 or **$5.24** = $419.32 × 1.25%

Step 3: Find the new balance.

New Balance = Unpaid Balance + Finance Charge + New Purchases
$522.06 = $419.32 + $5.24 + $97.50

Review Exercises

13. Denise Robb's account statement shows a $210.94 unpaid balance. With a periodic rate of 1.85%,what is the finance charge? She had new purchases of $341.22. What is the new balance?

14. Frederick Kluth's account statement shows a $75.06 unpaid balance. What is the finance charge if the periodic rate is 2%? He had $432.11 of new purchases. What is the new balance?

Lesson-by-Lesson Review (continued)

15. **ALGEBRA** Marty Vance's charge account uses the unpaid-balance method to compute the finance charge at a monthly periodic rate of 1.75%. During the month, she charged \$276.15, made a payment of \$175.00, and had a finance charge of \$8.52. Find her **(a)** unpaid balance, **(b)** previous balance, and **(c)** new balance.

7.3 Finance Charge: Average-Daily-Balance Method (pp. 291–294)

Compute the finance charge based on the average-daily-balance method–new purchases included.

Fred Choi has a department store charge account on which the store charges a finance charge using the average-daily-balance method–new purchases included. What is his **(a)** average daily balance, **(b)** finance charge, **(c)** unpaid balance, and **(d)** new balance?

Reference	Posting Date	Transaction Date	Description	Purchases & Advances	Payments & Credits
3809018	11/10	11/8	Fine art	\$125.44	
3809117	11/20	11/15	PAYMENT		\$200.00

Billing Period	Previous Balance	Periodic Rate	Average Daily Balance	Finance Charge
11/04–12/03	\$623.11	1.25%	a.	b.

Payments & Credits	Purchases & Advances	New Balance	Minimum Payment	Payment Due
\$200.00	\$125.44	c.	\$20.00	12/20

Step 1: Find the sum of the daily balances.

Dates	Payment	Purchase	End-of-Day Balance	Number of Days	Sum of Balances
11/04–11/09			\$623.11	6	\$ 3,738.66
11/10		\$125.44	748.55	1	748.55
11/11–11/19			748.55	9	6,736.95
11/20	\$200.00		548.55	1	548.55
11/21–12/3			548.55	13	7,131.15
			TOTAL	30	**\$18,903.86**

Step 2: Find the average daily balance.

Average Daily Balance = Sum of Daily Balances ÷ Number of Days

\$630.13 = \$18,903.86 ÷ 30

Step 3: Find the finance charge.

\$7.88 = \$630.13 × 1.25%

Continued on next page

Lesson-by-Lesson Review (continued)

Step 4: Find the unpaid balance.

Unpaid Balance = Previous Balance − (Payments + Credits)

\$423.11 = \$623.11 − \$200.00

Step 5: Find the new balance.

New Balance = Unpaid Balance + Finance Charge + New Purchases

\$556.43 = \$423.11 + \$7.88 + \$125.44

Review Exercises

16. Niles Hunt received this information on the statement from his bank. Find the **(a)** average daily balance–new purchases included, **(b)** finance charge, and **(c)** new balance.

Reference	Posting Date	Transaction Date	Description	Purchases & Advances	Payments & Credits
1238090	2/5	2/3	Home repairs	\$ 75.66	
2789433	2/10	2/8	PAYMENT		\$100.00
3459811	2/17	2/15	Discount store	198.33	
4334681	2/27	2/24	PAYMENT		50.00

Billing Period	Previous Balance	Periodic Rate	Average Daily Balance	Finance Charge
2/01–2/28	\$36.54	2.1%	a.	b.

Payments & Credits	Purchases & Advances	New Balance	Minimum Payment	Payment Due
\$150.00	\$273.99	c.	\$10.00	3/15

17. Fern Lewis received the following information on her account statement from a department store. Use the average-daily-balance method–new purchases included to find the **(a)** finance charge and **(b)** new balance.

Reference	Posting Date	Transaction Date	Description	Purchases & Advances	Payments & Credits
2034599	3/2		PAYMENT		\$35.00
2034766	3/11	3/8	Housewares	\$123.96	
2040009	3/20	3/12	Shoes	56.49	
2040065	3/25		PAYMENT		50.00

Billing Period	Previous Balance	Periodic Rate	Average Daily Balance	Finance Charge
3/1–3/31	\$200.34	2%	a.	b.

Payments & Credits	Purchases & Advances	New Balance	Minimum Payment	Payment Due
\$85.00	\$180.45	c.	\$25.00	4/30

18. ALGEBRA Dane Bryant's credit card company computes the finance charge using the average-daily-balance method–new purchases included. The monthly periodic rate is 2.3%, and the finance charge for the past billing cycle was \$23.76. Find the average daily balance.

Practice Test

Record your answer on a sheet of paper.

1. What is the average of 12, 43, 51, 62?
   A 32 **B** 51
   C 42 **D** 36

2. If the sum of the daily balances of a credit card totals $3,865.50 over 30 days, what is the average daily balance?
   A $238.85 **B** $128.85
   C $218.58 **D** $175.96

3. What is 23.6% of 4,585?
   A 1,541.44 **B** 1,345.983
   C 1,254.30 **D** 1,082.06

4. If Colin Hardaway's finance charge is computed at 2% of $4,586, what is its dollar amount?
   A $91.72 **B** $45.86
   C $86.54 **D** $110.70

5. If Lana Fodor paid $825.80 on a $3,169.78 credit card balance, what is the new balance?
   A $2,343.98 **B** $3,995.58
   C $3,087.02 **D** $2,546.98

6. If Scott Hoff has a balance of $429.50 on a credit card that charges a finance charge computed at 2.5%, what is the new balance? Round your answer to the nearest cent.
   A $432.00 **B** $486.98
   C $440.24 **D** $455.35

7. Piper Rothermel's credit card has a $926.42 balance. She makes a $223.50 payment. What is the new balance?
   A $1,149.92 **B** $702.92
   C $685.90 **D** $782.43

8. If Rocky Massimo's credit card has a $1,329.64 balance and he charged $528.44 in new purchases, what is the new balance?
   A $1,972.32 **B** $1,867.45
   C $896.45 **D** $1,858.08

9. Your credit card has a $2,142.62 balance. You charge $475.95. What is the new balance?

10. Rhonda Harmon's credit card statement showed an $839.78 balance. Since then, she has made a $110.50 payment and purchases totaling $143.75. What is Rhonda's new balance?

11. **ALGEBRA** Mary Morgan has a credit card that uses the unpaid-balance method to compute the finance charge. Her monthly periodic rate is 1.8%. During the past billing cycle, her previous balance was $426 and she made purchases totaling $100. If she had $48 in returns and her new balance was $383, what amount did she make in payments?

12. Alice Rayburn has a charge card from National Bank which uses the unpaid-balance method of computing finance charges. The periodic rate is 1.95%. Alice's previous balance is $1485.23. She made the minimum payment of 2% of the previous balance. She returned a pair of tennis shoes and a jacket for a credit of $68.63 and $117.47. She has new purchases of $49.50, $65.32 and $45.10 for gasoline. She had restaurant charges of $15.89, $20.22 and $52.54. Her final charge was $156.32 for auto repairs. Calculate the new balance.

13. Tony Albert's credit card finance charge is based on the average-daily-balance method with new purchases included. His monthly periodic rate is 2.25% and his finance charge for the past billing cycle was $12.60. Find his average daily balance.

14. $293.43 ÷ 93.2

15. 0.46 × (35.82 − 3.68)

16. 92.54% of 12,639

Standardized Test Practice

Cumulative, Chapters 1–7

PART 1 Multiple Choice

Record your answers on the answer sheet provided by your teacher or on a sheet of paper.

1. Ricky Shu earns a regular hourly rate of $10.50. How much would he earn in 5 days if he worked 5 hours a day?
   A $262.50 **B** $252.60
   C $315.00 **D** $52.50

2. Sasha Abbott earns $62,550.00 in taxable income each year. The tax rate is 3.6%, and she takes zero deductions. How much tax does her employer withhold each year?
   A $2,380.50 **B** $2,251.80
   C $2,500.40 **D** $1,823.20

3. What is the average daily balance of Eli Tucci's credit card if the sum of the daily balances is $5,376.50 for 31 days? Round to the nearest cent.
   A $425.43 **B** $226.58
   C $127.95 **D** $173.44

4. Charlene Perotta's annual fixed expenses total $5,256.96. How much should she budget for the monthly share of annual expenses?
   A $565.39 **B** $448.79
   C $438.08 **D** $550.12

5. Tom Shaley's credit card company adds a finance charge of 4.5% on any unpaid balance on his credit card. If his unpaid balance totals $1,963.33, what will his finance charge be?
   A $49.35 **B** $89.75
   C $45.00 **D** $88.35

6. What is the amount withdrawn from Alana Karhan's checking account if she writes 5 checks for $32.85 each?
   A $164.25 **B** $532.85
   C $275.65 **D** $166.80

TEST-TAKING TIP

Key Terms Identify key terms to find the main idea of the question.

PART 2 Short Response/Griddable

7. Ben Stamos received a credit of $52.80 on his credit card. If the account balance was $438.45 before the credit, what is the new balance?

8. Jada Kirby liked to jump on her trampoline after school. She was on it for 35 minutes on Monday, 45 minutes on Tuesday, 20 minutes on Thursday, and 59 minutes on Friday. What is the average time she spent on the trampoline?

9. Tara Lopez's charge account uses the unpaid-balance method of computing the finance charge. Her monthly periodic rate is 2.0%. If Tara had a previous balance of $1262.00 and a finance charge of $15.24, find the amount of her payment.

PART 3 Extended Response

Show your work.

10. What is Rene Dubois' average daily balance on his credit card if the sum of the daily balances equaled $591.85 over 29 days? Round your answer to the nearest cent.

11. Kai-Ning Huang's credit card account had a $424.56 balance. She made a payment of $130.50 and received a credit of $45.99 for a pair of shorts she returned. What is her new balance if she made no other purchases?

12. Explain how you would convert 41.9% to a decimal, and then show the result.

Building Academic Skills

Mathematics

Rupa Nagpur receives the following statement from her credit card company:

Trans Date	Post Date	Transaction Descriptions	Charges	Payments
01/07	01/08	Mike's Photo	207.33	
01/07	01/08	Brewster Cable TV Auto Payment	127.45	
01/14	01/15	Empress Wok	38.87	
01/22	01/23	Office Supplies Inc.	77.24	
01/27	01/28	Phone Store, Inc.	312.76	
01/31	01/31	Payment—Thank you	25.00	

If Rupa pays only the $25.00 minimum payment on January 31, how much will her bill be next month if she purchases nothing more on her credit card? The company's finance charge is 18% annually. It calculates the monthly finance charges based on the average-daily-balance method–new purchases included from the transaction date.

English Language Arts/Writing

A $5 finance charge on your credit card bill may not seem like much. However, if you pay only the minimum due every month and continue to make purchases, the finance charges can add up to a significant amount of money. Discuss why it is important to handle credit in a responsible manner from the beginning. How do you think your use (or misuse) of credit now can affect you in the future?

Social Studies/Economics

Your credit has to do with your history of bill payment. It includes how much you owe, to whom you owe it, and whether you have made payments on time. This information is the basis for determining your credit score, which determines the interest rate you will pay on loans.

Use online sources to research credit scores and their use. Write a short report that discusses how a system of credit scoring increases fairness in the granting of credit. For example, how does credit scoring help eliminate racial or cultural bias?

Building Real-World Skills

Ethics in Action

Company Credit Card You are an assistant at a recording studio. The owner hands you a company credit card and asks you to buy snacks for the musicians' lounge. When you get to the store, you are hungry and want to buy lunch. You consider using the company card.

Discuss and Write:

a. Discuss the ethical responsibilities of a person who is entrusted with the use of a company credit card.

b. Write a short essay about alternatives to using the company credit card in this manner.

Tech TRENDS

Paying Off Credit Debt Carrying credit card debt can lead to financial problems. If you are carrying more debt than you can handle, you can use online planning tools to determine how to pay off the debt as quickly as possible.

Research and Write:

a. Use the Internet to locate the credit card payoff calculator at Bankrate. Using this calculator, compute how long it would take to pay off a $5,000 debt at 13% interest with a monthly payment of $200.

b. How much should you pay monthly to eliminate a $5,000 debt in 12 months?

CHAPTER 8 Loans

Big Idea

In this chapter, you will investigate loans, loan payments, interest payments, and how to compare the costs of taking out a loan.

Explore the Photo

Student Loans
Someday you might want to earn a college degree, buy a car, or purchase a home. A loan can help you reach those goals. *Why might you consider obtaining a loan?*

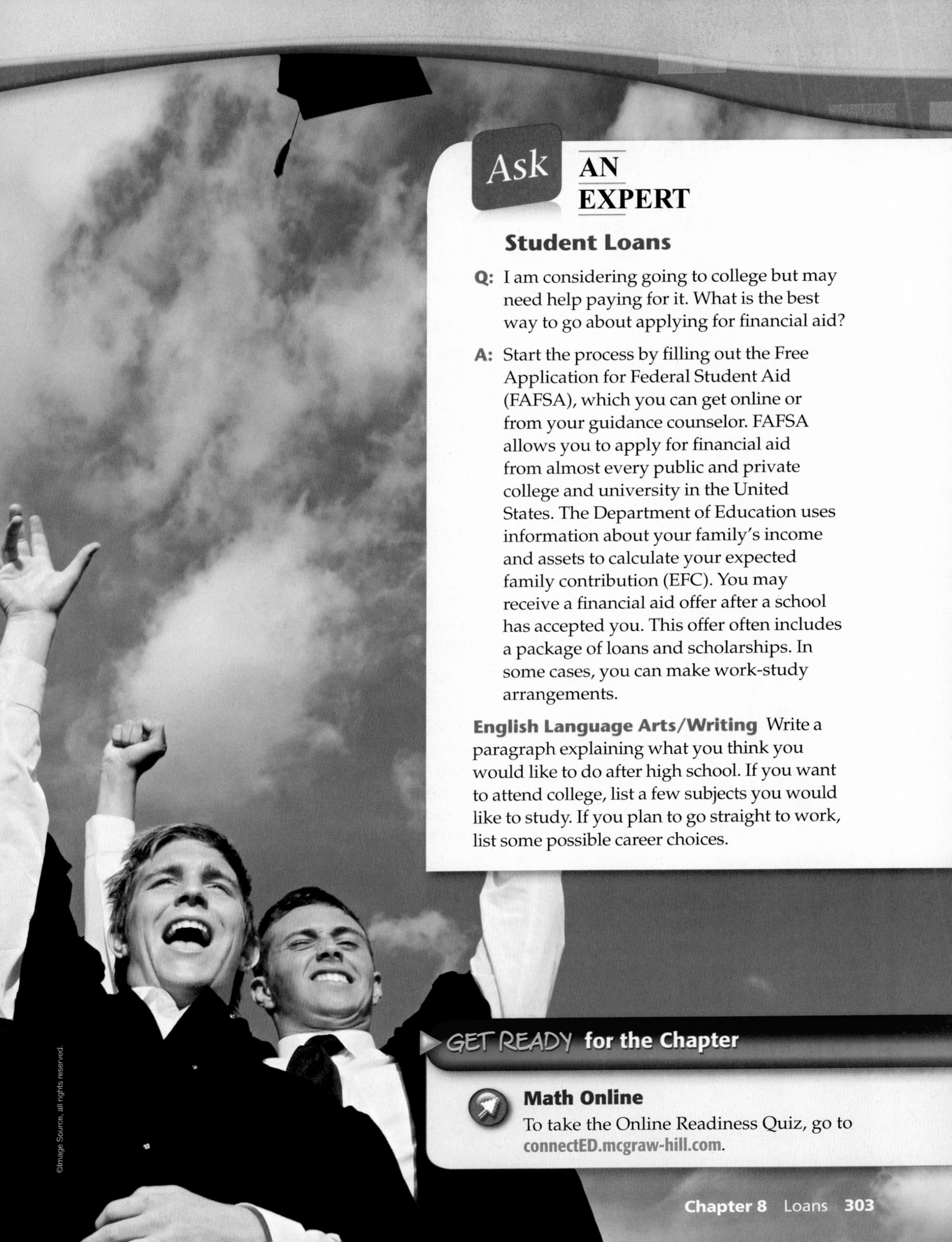

Ask AN EXPERT

Student Loans

Q: I am considering going to college but may need help paying for it. What is the best way to go about applying for financial aid?

A: Start the process by filling out the Free Application for Federal Student Aid (FAFSA), which you can get online or from your guidance counselor. FAFSA allows you to apply for financial aid from almost every public and private college and university in the United States. The Department of Education uses information about your family's income and assets to calculate your expected family contribution (EFC). You may receive a financial aid offer after a school has accepted you. This offer often includes a package of loans and scholarships. In some cases, you can make work-study arrangements.

English Language Arts/Writing Write a paragraph explaining what you think you would like to do after high school. If you want to attend college, list a few subjects you would like to study. If you plan to go straight to work, list some possible career choices.

GET READY for the Chapter

Math Online

To take the Online Readiness Quiz, go to **connectED.mcgraw-hill.com**.

Chapter  Loans

Reading Guide

Before You Read

Identify Have you ever taken out a loan?

Main Idea

Someday you may want to borrow money for a student loan or to buy a car or purchase a home. Taking out a loan is a common way to borrow the money now and repay it later or over a period of time.

Graphic Organizer

Before you read this chapter, draw a diagram like the one below. As you read, compare and contrast the two types of loans.

Compare and Contrast

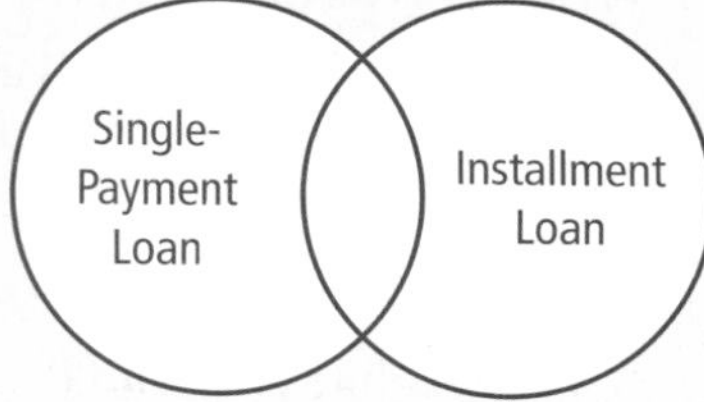

Math Online Go to **connectED.mcgraw-hill.com** to download this graphic organizer.

Content Vocabulary

You will learn these key terms in this chapter.

- single-payment loan
- promissory note
- maturity value
- term
- ordinary interest
- exact interest
- installment loan
- down payment
- amount financed
- annual percentage rate
- repayment schedule
- final payment

Academic Vocabulary

You will see these words in your reading and on your tests.

- principal
- specify
- index
- allocate
- motive
- financed

You can find vocabulary definitions in the **Content Vocabulary** Glossary and the **Academic Vocabulary** Glossary in the back of the book.

LESSON 8.1

Single-Payment Loans

Lesson Objective
Compute the maturity value and interest rate of a single-payment loan.

Content Vocabulary
- single-payment loan
- promissory note
- maturity value
- term
- ordinary interest
- exact interest

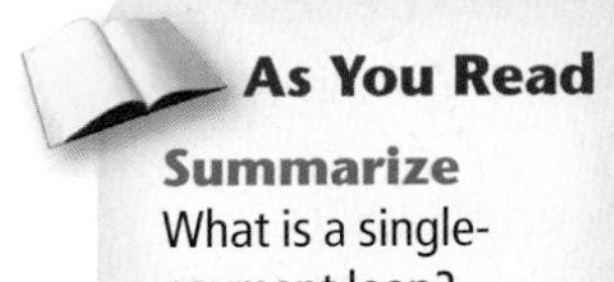

Summarize
What is a single-payment loan?

GET READY for the Lesson

If you had a dream for starting a business, how would you finance it?

Hailey Hannigan always dreamed of opening a ballet studio. She taught ballet at a local studio for several years in order to save money, but when the time was right, she took out a loan to open her own business.

Single-Payment Loans A **single-payment loan** is a loan that you repay with one payment after a specified period of time. A business may be short of funds and need to borrow money to meet its payroll or pay for inventory and supplies. The business owner could sign a promissory note with its financial institution. A **promissory note** is a written promise to pay a certain sum of money on a specific date in the future. The **maturity value** of the loan is the total amount you must repay. It includes both the principal and the interest owed. Remember from Chapter 5 that **principal** is the amount borrowed.

A loan's **term** is the amount of time for which the loan is granted. For example, a single-payment loan may be granted for a number of years, months, or days. When the term is a specific number of days, the lending agency may calculate interest in one of two ways:

1. **Ordinary interest** is based on a 360-day year.
2. **Exact interest** is based on a 365-day year.

The following formulas are used:

$$\text{Interest} = \text{Principal} \times \text{Rate} \times \text{Time}$$

$$\text{Ordinary Interest} = \text{Principal} \times \text{Rate} \times \frac{\text{Time}}{360}$$

$$\text{Exact Interest} = \text{Principal} \times \text{Rate} \times \frac{\text{Time}}{365}$$

$$\text{Maturity Value} = \text{Principal} + \text{Interest}$$

Need Help? Go to...
- Workshop 13: Fractions to Decimals, Decimals to Percents, p. 28
- Skill 28: Writing Percents as Decimals, p. SK29
- Application J: Fractional Parts of a Year, p. AP7

EXAMPLE 1

Anita Sloane's bank granted her a single-payment loan of $7,200 for 91 days to pay for new merchandise for her candle shop. Determine the maturity value of the loan if the rate is **(a)** 6% ordinary interest or **(b)** 6% exact interest.

Continued on next page

Step 1: Find the ordinary interest owed.

$$\text{Ordinary Interest} = \text{Principal} \times \text{Rate} \times \frac{\text{Time}}{360}$$

$$\$109.20 = \$7{,}200.00 \times 0.06 \times \frac{91}{360}$$

Step 2: Find the maturity value with ordinary interest.

$$\text{Maturity Value} = \text{Principal} + \text{Interest}$$

$$\mathbf{\$7{,}309.20} = \$7{,}200.00 + \$109.20$$

Step 3: Find the exact interest owed.

$$\text{Principal} \times \text{Rate} \times \frac{\text{Time}}{365}$$

$$\$7{,}200.00 \times 0.06 \times \frac{91}{365} = \$107.704 = \$107.70 \text{ Exact Interest}$$

Step 4: Find the maturity value with exact interest.

$$\text{Maturity Value} = \text{Principal} + \text{Interest}$$

$$\mathbf{\$7{,}307.70} = \$7{,}200.00 + \$107.70$$

Study Tip

Timing

Study when you are feeling well rested and alert. Avoid staying up late to study.

Compute the (a) interest and (b) maturity value for each loan. Check your answers in the back of the book.

1. Parker Logan purchased a new surfboard costing $600 and financed it at 9% ordinary interest for 90 days.
2. Holmes Ostendorf added a tack room to his barn costing $4,850 financed at 7% exact interest for 120 days.

EXAMPLE 2 Algebra

Claudia Valdez took out a single-payment loan for $1,500.00 at 7.8% ordinary interest to pay her federal income tax bill. If the loan's maturity value is $1,529.25, when would Claudia have to pay back the loan if she took it out on March 1?

Step 1: Find the interest

Maturity Value = Principal + Interest *or* Interest = Maturity Value – Principal

Interest = $1,529.25 – $1,500.00 = $29.25

Step 2: Find the time of the loan in days, *t*.

$$\text{Ordinary Interest} = \text{Principal} \times \text{Rate} \times \frac{t}{360}$$

$$\$29.25 = \$1{,}500.00 \times 0.078 \times \frac{t}{360}$$

Multiply both sides by 360 → $\$10{,}530 = \$117t$

Divide both sides by $117 → $\mathbf{90} = t$

Claudia would have to pay back the loan in 90 days.

Step 3: Find the due date. Use the *Elapsed Time Table* on page A10. March 1 is day 60 + 90 days = day 150, which is May 30.

Complete the problem. Check your answer in the back of the book.

3. How long would it take a construction loan for $548,048 to earn interest of $50,000 at 9% exact interest?

Lesson Practice

Computer Software Engineer

As computer usage increases, the need grows for workers who can design, build, test, and maintain the software that individuals and businesses use.

What other careers require strong problem-solving and analytical skills?

For Problems 4–7, calculate the interest and maturity value.

	Purpose	Principal	Interest Rates		Term (Days)	Interest	Maturity Value
			Ordinary	Exact			
4.	Drum Set	$ 900.00	4%	—	45	a. $	b. $
5.	Used Car	1,960.00	—	6%	30	a.	b.
6.	Used Dirt Bike	4,800.00	10	—	123	a.	b.
7.	School Tuition for Twins	9,675.00	—	9	275	a.	b.

For Problems 8 and 9, determine the (a) interest owed and (b) maturity value.

8. Sari Tagore obtains a $1,000 loan to purchase a laser printer. Her interest rate is 7% ordinary interest for 108 days.

9. Helio DaSilva obtains a loan to buy a piano for $8,400. His interest rate is 12% exact interest for 146 days.

10. Jolene Kendrick borrowed $24,000 for new computers for her software production company. Her bank granted her a single-payment loan of $24,000 for 144 days. Determine the maturity value of the loan if the rate is 9% **(a)** ordinary interest or **(b)** exact interest.

11. **ALGEBRA** Suppose that your bank has a minimum loan charge of $48 when you borrow at 6% ordinary interest for 90 days. What principal borrowed will result in a $48 interest charge?

12. **ALGEBRA** On April 14, Mikos Souvakis borrowed $100,000 to remodel his restaurant kitchen with a single-payment loan at 10.5% ordinary interest. If his loan's maturity value was $104,375, when does Mikos have to pay it back?

13. **ALGEBRA** Arianna North borrowed $12,500 to purchase a new cello and agreed to pay back $13,250 in 270 days. What exact interest rate was she paying? (Round your answer to the nearest tenth of a percent.)

Spiral Review

Reduce the fractions to lowest terms. (Skill 12)

14. $\frac{40}{60}$ **15.** $\frac{180}{360}$ **16.** $\frac{90}{360}$

17. **ALGEBRA** Hubert Crum is interested in a color television marked down 40%. Its sale price is $329.00. What was the television's regular selling price? (Lesson 6.7)

18. You have a $45,500 annual gross income and exemptions totaling $3,000. If the state tax is 1.5% on the first $2,500 and 3% on amounts over $2,500, what is your annual income tax obligation? (Lesson 2.3)

GET READY for the Next Lesson

PREREQUISITE SKILL Rounding Numbers (Skill 2)

Round to the nearest cent.

19. $45.1745 **20.** $1,345.265 **21.** $51.3093

22. $681.455 **23.** $5,001.013 **24.** $725.765

LESSON 8.2

Installment Loans—Amount Financed

Lesson Objective
Calculate the down payment and the amount financed on an installment loan.

Content Vocabulary
- installment loan
- down payment
- amount financed

GET READY for the Lesson

If you were interested in starting a small business, what would it be?

Kerry Holland decided to turn his experience in doing yard work for his parents into a business. His first clients were neighbors. Soon he had so much business that he had to purchase equipment and hire a friend to help him.

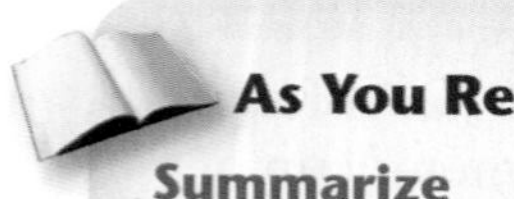

As You Read
Summarize
What is a down payment?

Installment Loans You could apply for an installment loan to finance the purchase of a new or used vehicle, such as a car, truck, or motorcycle. You repay an **installment loan** in equal payments over a **specified** period of time. Usually when you purchase an item with an installment loan, you must make a down payment. The **down payment** is a portion of the cash price of the item you are purchasing before financing the rest on credit. It could be a dollar amount or a percent of the cash price. The **amount financed** is the portion of the cash price that you owe after making the down payment. The formulas to calculate the amount financed are:

Amount Financed = Cash Price − Down Payment

Down Payment = Cash Price × Percent

Need Help? Go to...
- **Workshop 14:** Finding a Percentage, p. 30
- **Workshop 13:** Fractions to Decimals, Decimals to Percents, p. 28
- **Workshop 2:** Rounding Numbers, p. 6
- **Application A:** Formulas, p. AP1

EXAMPLE 1

Trudy Quintero is buying gym equipment for $1,399. She makes a $199 down payment and finances the remainder. How much does she finance?

Find the amount financed.

Cash Price − Down Payment

$1,399 − $199 = **$1,200 amount financed**

Trudy financed $1,200.

Concept CHECK

Complete the problems by determining the amount financed. Check your answers in the back of the book.

1. Melina Vardalos purchased season concert tickets for $1,999.99. The down payment is $199.99.
2. Bertellini Dentistry purchased new equipment for $3,950. The down payment is $150.

Equivalents
"Twenty percent" can be written in many different ways: 20%, 0.2, $\frac{20}{100}$, $\frac{2}{10}$, $\frac{1}{5}$.

EXAMPLE 2

Roslyn Clay purchased a previously owned piano for $1,140 using the store's installment credit plan. She made a 20% down payment and financed the remaining amount. What amount did she finance?

Step 1: Find the 20% down payment.

Down Payment = $1,140 × 20% = $228

Roslyn made a $228 down payment.

Step 2: Find the amount financed.

Amount Financed = Cash Price − Down Payment

$912 = $1,140 − $228

She financed $912.

1140 M+ × 20 % 228 M− RM 912

Find the (a) down payment and (b) amount financed. Check your answers in the back of the book.

3. Antonio Reyes purchased an antique chest for a $1,360 cash price. He made a 20% down payment.

4. Maya DiNardo purchased a diamond bracelet for $1,725. The down payment was 30%.

Lesson Practice

	Item	Cash Price	Down Payment (Cash)	Down Payment (Percent)	Down Payment (in Dollars)	Amount Financed
5.	Camcorder	$ 640	$ 120	—	a. $	b. $
6.	Family Vacation	4,860	1,400	—	a.	b.
7.	Used Truck	9,774	1,500	—	a.	b.
8.	Dining Room Set	3,600	—	40%	a.	b.
9.	Office Equipment	9,480	—	15	a.	b.
10.	Cruise Tickets	5,364	—	25	a.	b.

For problems 11–14, find the amount financed.

11. Owen Hawkins purchased carpentry equipment for $1,265 with a $100 down payment.

12. Audrey Copeland purchased a used car for $14,470 with a $3,000 down payment.

13. Austin Powell purchased a television for $2,200 with a $500 down payment.

14. Meghan Barnes purchased photography equipment for $4,100 with a $1,000 down payment.

For problems 15–19, find the (a) down payment and (b) amount financed.

15. Laurenz Huber financed the purchase of an $8,371.39 snowmobile with a 15% down payment.

16. Bailey Ruffin bought a new motorcycle for $18,936.50 and made a 30% down payment.

17. Devin Gallagher purchased home entertainment equipment for $4,020.19 using the store's credit plan. He made a 20% down payment.

18. Linda Cusak purchased a $279.50 DVD player/stereo for her car. Using the store's credit plan, she made a $50.00 down payment.

Did You Know?

Finland Vacation Time

Workers in Finland know that if they feel stressed out by their job, they will not have to wait long to take some time off to relax. Finnish labor laws mandate at least 30 paid vacation days each year plus up to 14 paid holidays.

19. Ernst Hoffmann took a $2,876 trip to visit relatives in Europe. He financed it through State Bank. He made a 25% down payment and financed the remaining amount on an installment plan.

20. Amy and Cliff Rice plan to buy 2 hang gliders. They want to finance part of the cost but no more than $9,000. The cost of the gliders is $12,000. Will a 25% down payment be enough?

H.O.T. Problems

21. CHALLENGE PROBLEM Ardella Haubert purchased a sofa for $1,156.50, a love seat for $877.50, 2 recliner chairs at $588.75 each, 2 end tables at $177.50 each, 2 lamps at $125.77 each, and a framed print for $169.91. She lives in Ohio and pays a 6.5% sales tax. If she made a down payment of 20% and financed the remaining amount using the store's installment plan, what amount did she finance?

22. CHALLENGE PROBLEM Chase Delucca wants to purchase a convertible costing $14,590. He will finance it with an installment loan from the bank but plans to finance no more than $10,000. What percent of a down payment does he need?

Spiral Review

Round to the nearest cent. (Skill 2)

23. $49.9638

24. $178.3813

25. $413.995

26. Diego Chavez has a charge account with a previous $112.34 balance, a $3.55 finance charge, new purchases of $87.50 and $115.60, a $100.00 payment, and a $25.00 credit. What is the new balance? (Lesson 7.1)

27. Find the amount of federal income tax withheld each week for Sebastian Daniels, who is single, claims 2 allowances, and earns $437.95. (Lesson 2.1)

GET READY for the Next Lesson

PREREQUISITE SKILL Subtracting Decimals (Skill 6)

Subtract.

28. 10.29 – 4.07

29. 44.69 – 2.34

30. 653 – 12.95

31. 3,519.00 – 280.29

32. 2,439.23 – 203.39

33. 5,189.24 – 902.05

ThinkStock/SuperStock

LESSON 8.3 Installment Loans—Monthly Payment & Finance Charge

Lesson Objective

Calculate the monthly payment, total amount repaid, and finance charge on an installment loan.

Content Vocabulary

- annual percentage rate (APR)

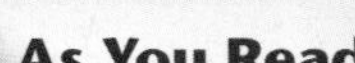

GET READY for the Lesson

Why is it important to have a good credit score?

Jenny Foster is a science major in college. She knows she wants to open her own biotechnology company someday and that she may have to take out a loan, so she is working hard to make sure she has a good credit score. Jenny keeps a low balance on her credit cards and pays her student loans and credit card bills on time.

As You Read

Explain What factors affect the amount of each monthly loan payment?

Installment Loans When you obtain an installment loan, you must pay finance charges for the use of the money. You repay the loan with equal monthly payments over a specified period of time. Part of each payment pays the interest on the loan's unpaid balance. The remaining part of the payment is used to reduce the balance of the loan principal.

The amount of each monthly payment depends on the amount financed, the number of payments, and the annual percentage rate. The **annual percentage rate (APR)** is an **index** showing the cost of borrowing money on a yearly basis, expressed as a percent. You will need to refer to the *Monthly Payment on an Installment Loan of $100* table on page A13 for a table value to calculate related amounts.

The following formulas are used:

$$\text{Monthly Payment} = \frac{\text{Amount of Loan}}{\$100} \times \text{Monthly Payment for a \$100 Loan}$$

$$\text{Total Amount Repaid} = \text{Number of Payments} \times \text{Monthly Payment}$$

$$\text{Finance Charge} = \text{Total Amount Repaid} - \text{Amount Financed}$$

Need Help? Go to...

- **Workshop 6:** Multiplying Decimals, p. 14
- **Workshop 5:** Subtracting Decimals, p. 12
- **Workshop 18:** Reading Tables and Charts, p. 38
- **Application C:** Tables and Charts, p. AP3

EXAMPLE 1

Blake and Jacqueline Toepfer are purchasing a $1,399.99 side-by-side refrigerator with an installment loan that has an APR of 12%. The store financing requires a 10% down payment and 12 monthly payments. What is the finance charge?

Step 1: Find the amount financed.

Amount Financed = Selling Price − Down Payment

$1,399.99 − (0.10 × $1,399.99)

$1,399.99 − $140.00 = $1,259.99

Step 2: Find the monthly payment. (Refer to the *Monthly Payment on an Installment Loan of $100* table on page A13 for a table value)

$$\frac{\text{Amount of Loan}}{\$100} \times \text{Monthly Payment for a \$100 Loan}$$

$$\frac{\$1{,}259.99}{\$100} \times \$8.88 = \$111.887 = \$111.89 \text{ Monthly Payment}$$

Continued on next page

Step 3: Find the total amount repaid.

Total Amount Repaid = Number of Payments × Monthly Payment

$1,342.68 = 12 × $111.89

Step 4: Find the finance charge.

Finance Charge = Total Amount Repaid − Amount Financed

$82.69 = $1,342.68 − $1,259.99

Complete the problem. Check your answer in the back of the book.

1. Ingrid Nilsen purchased a $4,000 gazebo for her garden. The down payment is 20%, and the installment loan has an APR of 10% for 36 months. Find the **(a)** down payment, **(b)** amount financed, **(c)** monthly payment, **(d)** total amount repaid, and **(e)** finance charge.

Need Help? Go to...
Application A: Formulas, p. AP1

EXAMPLE 2 Algebra

Compute the monthly payment on an installment loan using this formula:

$$\text{Monthly Payment} = \frac{pr(1.00+r)^n}{(1.00+r)^n - 1.00}$$

Where p = Principal or the amount of the loan.

r = Rate per payment (APR divided by number of payments per year)

n = Number of payments required to pay off the loan.

Solving problems with the formula requires the use of a y^x key on your calculator.

Harry Mills obtained a $4,500 installment loan at an APR of 9%. He must repay the loan in 24 months. Find the **(a)** monthly payment using the formula, then **(b)** total amount repaid, and **(c)** finance charge.

Step 1: First, $r = \frac{9\%}{12} = \frac{0.09}{12} = 0.0075$ and $n = 24$

Step 2: Then, substitute into the monthly payment (mp) formula:

$$mp = \frac{pr(1.00+r)^n}{(1.00+r)^n-1.00}$$

$$= \frac{4500(0.0075)(1.00+0.0075)^{24}}{(1+0.0075)^{24}-1.00}$$

$$= \frac{33.75(1.196413529)}{1.196413529-1.00}$$

$$= \frac{40.37895662}{0.196413529}$$

$mp = \$205.58134 = \mathbf{\$205.58}$

Harry's monthly payment will be $205.58.

[If you worked this problem using the table on p. A13, you would get a monthly payment of ($\frac{\$4,500}{\$100}$ *× $4.57), or $205.65. The difference is due to rounding in the table.]*

Step 3: Find the total amount repaid.

24 × $205.58 = **$4,933.92**

Step 4: Find the finance charge.

$4,933.92 − $4,500.00 = **$433.92**

Complete the problem. Check your answer in the back of the book.

2. Lisa McCorkle purchased her new $45,000 automobile with a $5,000 down payment and financed the rest with an installment loan for 72 months at an annual percentage rate of 6%. Find Lisa's **(a)** monthly payment, **(b)** total amount repaid, and **(c)** finance charge.

GRAPHING CALCULATOR LAB

Monthly Payments

Suppose that you obtained an installment loan of $5,600 for college expenses. The annual percentage rate is 8%. You must repay the loan in 24 months. What is the finance charge?
To determine the monthly payment, you need to access the TMV Solver from the CALC FINANCE menu.

```
N=24
I%=8
PV=5600
PMT=■251.59552
FV=0
P/Y=12
C/Y=12
PMT:END BEGIN
```

Step 1: From the home screen, press

Enter: N = 24 (24 month)
I% = 8%
PV = Present Value (amount borrowed)
FV = 0
P/Y = 12 and C/Y = 12

To determine the payment, place your cursor on PMT and press

The payment is $251.60 per month. It appears as a negative number because this is the amount to be paid.

To determine the finance charge, follow these steps:

Answers will be slightly different than those found using the tables in the text due to rounding.

Think and Discuss

1. Describe the display of the first calculator screen.
2. Describe the display of the second calculator screen.
3. What is the total finance charge?
4. Determine the monthly payment and total finance charge on a $15,000 loan for 5 years at 7% interest.
5. You are thinking about buying a new computer. You can afford a monthly payment of $120 for the next 2 years. If the interest rate is 9%, what is the highest priced computer you can afford? (*Hint:* Substitute the information you are given.)

Lesson Practice

For Problems 3–6, use the *Monthly Payment on an Installment Loan of $100* table on page A13 to solve the following.

	Purpose	APR	Term (Months)	Table Value	Amount Financed	Monthly Payment	Total Repaid	Finance Charge
3.	Skis	10%	6	a. $	$1,000	b. $	c. $	d. $
4.	Vacation	12%	18	a.	2,000	b.	c.	d.
5.	All-Terrain Vehicle	8%	24	a.	5,600	b.	c.	d.
6.	Swimming Pool	9%	30	a.	9,900	b.	c.	d.

For Problems 7 and 8, determine the (a) monthly payment and (b) finance charge.

7. Hazel Basanez obtains an installment loan of $2,000 for a boat trailer. The loan requires 12 monthly payments and has an 8% APR.

8. Brian Rehr obtains an installment loan of $1,250 to buy a canoe. The loan requires 24 monthly payments and has an APR of 10%.

For Problems 9–12, determine the (a) down payment, (b) amount of the loan, (c) monthly payment, and (d) finance charge.

9. Jason Wagoner obtains an installment loan to buy a $12,000 hot air balloon. His down payment is 25%, and the APR is 9% for 36 months.

10. Shelby Lenz obtains an installment loan to purchase a small plane for $20,000. Her down payment is 20%, and the APR is 12% for 30 months.

11. James Agnew obtains a loan for $16,000 to purchase a used pickup truck. His down payment is 25% and the APR is 10% for 24 months.

12. Shelly Lemony obtains an equipment loan for $120,000. Her down payment is 20% and the APR is 8% for 12 months.

13. Patrick Worachek obtains an installment loan of $6,400 to buy a professional digital camera and lenses. The APR is 12%. The loan is to be repaid in 36 monthly payments. What is the finance charge?

14. Jill Paa obtained a $1,450 installment loan to pay for a new laptop computer for her class work. She agreed to repay the loan in 18 monthly payments at an APR of 8%. What is the finance charge?

15. Herb and Marci Jordan obtained an installment loan that has a 10% APR to purchase a dishwasher that sells for $699.95. They agree to make a down payment of 20% and to make 12 monthly payments. What is the finance charge?

16. Adolfo LaRosa obtained an installment loan of $6,800 to help pay his college tuition. Student loans do not require a down payment. He obtained the loan from a local bank and agreed to repay the loan in 24 monthly payments at an 18% APR. What is the finance charge?

17. Andrew and Ruth Bacon would like to obtain an installment loan of $1,850 to repaint their home. They can get the loan at an APR of **(a)** 8% for 24 months or **(b)** 11% for 18 months. Which loan has the lower finance charge?

Did You Know?

Help for Developing Nations **In 2006, Muhammad Yunus and the Grameen Bank he founded won the Nobel Peace Prize for his work on "microcredit." He has made loans as small as $27 to help people, mostly women in developing countries, to start their own businesses.**

18. Lola Segal needs to take out an installment loan of $1,200 to pay for auto repairs. Walton Savings and Loan will lend her the money at 9% for 12 months. Horton Finance Company will lend her the money at 12% for 24 months. How much will she save by taking the loan with the lower finance charge?
19. Lucy and Don Pflum need an installment loan of $12,900 to remodel their hair salon. City Loan will lend the money at 10% for 24 months. Economy Line Finance Company will lend the money at 9% for 30 months. Which loan costs less? How much will they save by taking the loan that costs less?
20. Mark Sutton needs an installment loan of $24,500 for home remodeling. He can obtain a loan at an APR of 11%. How much could Mark save in finance charges if he took out the loan for 54 months instead of 60 months? Why might he not do this?
21. Alice Miller obtains a $100,000 installment loan at an APR of 9% for 36 months. How much could Alice save in finance charges if she had been able to find the loan at an APR of 8% rather than 9%?

H.O.T. Problems

22. **ALGEBRA** Ian and May Conte obtained an installment loan of $3,500 to furnish an apartment. The APR is 7.2% for 12 monthly payments. Find the finance charge.
23. **ALGEBRA** Miyoshi Yee borrowed $8,500 to purchase an organ on which to compose her music. She obtained an installment loan for 36 months at an APR of 8.4%. Find her **(a)** monthly payment, **(b)** total payback, and **(c)** finance charge.
24. **ALGEBRA** Jocelyn Tiller purchased a new fishing boat for $37,500. After a 20% down payment, she financed the rest with an installment loan for 40 months at a 9.6% APR. Find her finance charge.

Spiral Review

Multiply. (Skill 30 and Skill 20) **Round to the nearest thousandth.**

25. $4{,}000.00 \div 100.00 \times 3.33$
26. $1{,}240.00 \div 250.00 \times 5.09$
27. Troy York bought a leather jacket on sale for 35% off the regular selling price of $199.99. What was the amount of markdown? (Lesson 6.6)
28. You have gross pay this month of $622.30 and total earnings to date of $28,221.00. Use the Social Security tax rate of 6.2% of the first $97,500.00 and Medicare tax rate of 1.45%. How much is deducted from your paycheck this month for Social Security and Medicare? (Lesson 2.4)

GET READY for the Next Lesson

PREREQUISITE SKILL **Finding the Percentage** (Skill 30)

Find the percentage.

29. $325 \times 45\%$
30. $865 \times 23\%$
31. $310 \times 12\%$
32. $1{,}721 \times 39\%$
33. $4{,}758 \times 58\%$
34. $1{,}023 \times 63\%$

LESSON 8.4

Installment Loans—Monthly Payment Allocation

Lesson Objective

Calculate the payment to interest, payment to principal, and new balance.

Content Vocabulary

- repayment schedule

GET READY for the Lesson

If you needed to take a loan, what factors other than loan rates would you look for?

Freddie Perez wanted to obtain a loan to pay for classes required to become an ASE certified automotive technician. State Bank and CAA Credit Union were offering the same terms for the loan. Freddie decided to take the State Bank loan because he had his checking account there and because State Bank offered online banking.

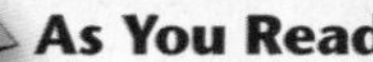

As You Read

Explain How do you allocate installment loan payments?

Allocation of Payment on Installment Loans As you learned in Lesson 8.3, an installment loan is repaid in equal monthly payments. Part of each payment is **allocated** to pay the interest on the unpaid balance of the loan, and the remaining part is used to reduce the balance. The interest is calculated each month on the unpaid balance using the simple interest formula. The amount of principal that you owe *decreases* with each monthly payment. The formulas follow:

Interest = Principal × Rate × Time

Payment to Principal = Monthly Payment – Interest

New Principal = Previous Principal – Payment to Principal

A **repayment schedule** shows the distribution of interest and principal over the life of a loan. The repayment schedule in **Figure 8.1** shows the interest and principal on an $1,800 installment loan for 6 months at 8%.

Figure 8.1

Repayment Schedule for a $1,800 Loan at 8.0% for 6 Months				
Payment Number	Monthly Payment	Amount for Interest	Amount for Principal	Balance $1,800.00
1	$307.08	$12.00	$295.08	$1,504.92
2	307.08	10.03	297.05	1,207.87
3	307.08	8.05	299.03	908.85
4	307.08	6.06	301.02	607.82
5	307.08	4.05	303.03	304.80
6	307.08	2.03	305.05	–0.25

Note that the last payment could be $306.83 to zero out the loan.

EXAMPLE 1

Melinda and Xavier Garza obtained a loan for a used pickup truck. See the loan of $1,800 at 8% for 6 months in the repayment schedule in **Figure 8.1.** Show the calculation for the first payment. What are the **(a)** interest, **(b)** payment to principal, and **(c)** new principal after they make the first payment?

Need Help? Go to...

- **Workshop 5:** Subtracting Decimals, p. 12
- **Workshop 6:** Multiplying Decimals, p. 14
- **Workshop 14:** Finding a Percentage, p. 30
- **Application A:** Formulas, p. AP1

Step 1: Find the interest.

Interest = Principal × Rate × Time

$12 = $1,800.00 × 8% × $\frac{1}{12}$

Step 2: Find the payment to principal.

Payment to Principal = Monthly Payment − Interest

$295.08 = $307.08 − $12.00

Step 3: Find the new principal.

New Principal = Previous Principal − Payment to Principal

$1,504.92 = $1,800.00 − $295.08

Concept CHECK

Complete these problems. Check your answers in the back of the book. Regarding the loan for the Garzas from **Example 1,** compute the second month values for:

1. The interest. **2.** The payment to principal. **3.** The new balance.

EXAMPLE 2

Anton Grindenko obtained a $6,000.00 loan to update his café's kitchen equipment at 8% for 36 months. The monthly payment is $187.80. The balance of the loan after 20 payments is $2,849.08. What is the interest for the first payment? What is the interest for the 21st payment? Why is the interest so much different for the two payments?

Step 1: Find the interest for the first payment.

Interest for First Payment = Principal × Rate × Time

$40.00 = $6,000.00 × 8% × $\frac{1}{12}$

Anton pays $40.00 interest in the first payment.

Step 2: Find the interest for the 21st payment.

Interest for 21st Payment = Principal × Rate × Time

$18.99 = $2,849.08 × 8% × $\frac{1}{12}$

Anton pays $18.99 interest in the 21st payment.

The interest in the 21st payment is reduced by more than half because the principal on which the interest is calculated for the first payment is much higher than the principal on which the interest for the 21st payment is calculated.

Concept CHECK

Complete this problem. Check your answers in the back of the book.

4. You take out an $8,000 loan on a new motorcycle at 12% for 24 months. The monthly payment is $376.80. The balance of the loan after 15 payments is $3,222.44. What is the interest for the **(a)** first payment and **(b)** 16th payment?

Lesson Practice

For Problems 5–7, determine the missing amounts in the following table.

	Purpose	Loan Balance	Interest Rate	Monthly Payment	Amount for Interest	Amount for Principal	New Principal
5.	Stereo System	$1,200	12%	$106.56	$12.00	$94.56	a.
6.	Riding Mower	3,460	10%	207.95	a.	b.	c.
7.	Pool Cabana	7,200	9%	329.04	a.	b.	c.

Did You Know?

Bono's African Campaign U2's vocalist, Bono, has had many successes in his career, but his biggest recent achievement was not musical. Bono took part in a campaign for African prosperity. As a result, the world's richest nations agreed to cancel $40 billion in debts owed by 18 impoverished nations, mostly in Africa.

For Problems 8–14, complete the repayment schedule for a $2,400 loan at 12% for 12 months.

Repayment Schedule for a $2,400 Loan at 12% for 12 Months

	Payment Number	Monthly Payment	Amount for Interest	Amount for Principal	New Principal
	1	$213.12	$24.00	$189.12	$2,210.88
	2	213.12	22.11	191.01	2,019.87
	3	213.12	20.20	192.92	1,826.95
	4	213.12	18.27	194.85	1,632.10
	5	213.12	16.32	196.80	1,435.30
8.	6	213.12	14.35	198.77	a.
9.	7	213.12	12.37	a.	b.
10.	8	213.12	a.	b.	c.
11.	9	213.12	a.	b.	c.
12.	10	213.12	a.	b.	c.
13.	11	213.12	a.	b.	c.
14.	12	a.	b.	c.	d.

15. CHALLENGE PROBLEM Complete the last line of the preceding repayment schedule and adjust the 12th payment, which is the last, to make the principal balance zero.

Spiral Review

Find the percent. (Skill 30)

16. 12% of 5,000 **17.** 22% of 1,282.15 **18.** 6% of 340.80

19. Your bank granted you a single-payment loan of $3,200 for 91 days at 8% ordinary interest. What is the loan's maturity value? (Lesson 8.1)

20. An outboard motor is on sale in Chicago, Illinois, for $1,235. The state tax is 6.25%, and the city tax is 1.35%. What is the total sales tax amount? (Lesson 6.1)

GET READY for the Next Lesson

PREREQUISITE SKILL Multiplying Decimals (Skill 8)

Multiply.

21. 9.19×0.35 **22.** 4.24×3.29 **23.** $1,023 \times 6.03$ **24.** 207×7.22

LESSON 8.5

Paying Off Installment Loans

Lesson Objective

Compute the final payment when paying off an installment loan.

Content Vocabulary

- final payment

If you want to continue your education after high school, how would you pay the related costs?

Frank Sutton decided to go to college. He completed the Free Application for Federal Student Aid (FAFSA) form and applied for scholarships. Frank also saved money from summer jobs to help pay for books.

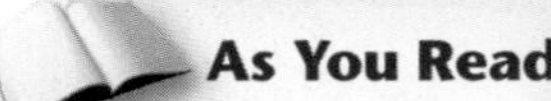

As You Read

Identify What is included in a final loan payment?

Determining the Final Payment When you have an installment loan, you pay interest on the unpaid balance. You might have a simple interest installment loan for a car and sell the car before the end of the loan term. If so, you pay only the previous balance plus the current month's interest. This is known as the **final payment**. Note that there may be a penalty for paying off a loan early.

One **motive** to pay off a loan before the end of the term is to pay less interest. The amount of interest saved depends on the total payback minus the sum of the previous payments and the final payment. You will need to use three formulas:

Interest = Principal × Rate × Time

Final Payment = Previous Balance + Current Month's Interest

Interest Saved = Total Payback – (Sum of Previous Payments + Final Payment)

Need Help? Go to...

- Workshop 4: Adding Decimals, p. 10
- Workshop 5: Subtracting Decimals, p. 12
- Workshop 6: Multiplying Decimals, p. 14
- Workshop 14: Finding a Percentage, p. 30

EXAMPLE 1

See **Figure 8.2** for the first 3 months of the repayment schedule for Darlene and Hayden Grant's home repair loan of $1,800 at 12% interest for 6 months. What is the final payment if they pay the loan off with the fourth payment?

Figure 8.2

Repayment Schedule for a $1,800 Loan at 12.0% for 6 Months				
Payment Number	Monthly Payment	Amount for Interest	Amount for Principal	Balance $1,800.00
1	$310.50	$18.00	$292.50	1,507.50
2	310.50	15.08	295.42	1,212.08
3	310.50	12.12	298.38	913.70

Step 1: Find the previous balance.

Read the repayment schedule for the balance after the third payment. It is $913.70.

Continued on next page

Step 2: Find the interest for the fourth month.

Principal × Rate × Time

$\$913.70 \times 12\% \times \frac{1}{12} = \$9.137 = \$9.14$ Interest (fourth month)

Step 3: Find the final payment.

Final Payment = Previous Balance + Current Month's Interest

$922.84 = $913.70 + $9.14

Brackets [ ] When solving an equation with brackets, do the math in the brackets first.

Complete this problem. Check your answer in the back of the book.

1. You plan to finance the purchase of a $1,200.00 electric scooter with a 12-month loan at 12% interest with a balance of $816.04 after the fourth payment. What is the final payment amount if you pay off the loan with the fifth payment?

EXAMPLE 2

How much would the Grants in **Example 1** save by paying off the loan early?

Find the interest saved.

Interest Saved = Total Payback − (Sum of Previous Payments + Final Payment)

= (6 × $310.50) − [(3 × $310.50) + $922.84]

= $1,863.00 − [$931.50 + $922.84]

$8.66 = $1,863.00 − $1,854.34

They saved $8.66.

Complete this problem. Check your answer in the back of the book.

2. In Problem 1, you had a 12-month loan of $1,200.00 at 12% interest to purchase an electric scooter. The balance after the fourth payment of $106.56 is $816.04. How much do you save by paying off the loan with the fifth payment?

Lesson Practice

Find the interest and the final payment.

	Purpose	Interest Rate	Previous Balance	Interest	Final Payment
3.	High-Speed Color Copier	12%	$4,800.00	**a.** $	**b.** $
4.	Computer Maintenance Contract	8%	3,000.00	**a.**	**b.**
5.	Miscellaneous Software	10%	1,460.80	**a.**	**b.**
6.	Computer Server System	9%	3,987.60	**a.**	**b.**
7.	Multipurpose Scanner	11%	3,265.87	**a.**	**b.**

8. Willard Hudson paid for a shipment of bicycles with a $6,000 installment loan at 10% interest for 24 months. His monthly payment is $276.60. After 4 payments, the balance is $5,082.21. He pays off the loan when the next payment is due. What is the amount of **(a)** interest, **(b)** final payment, and **(c)** savings if Willard pays off the loan with the fifth payment?

9. Lillian Hartwick paid for tuition at a summer management institute with an installment loan of $3,600 at 8% for 12 months with a $313.20 monthly payment. After 6 payments, the balance was $1,835.62. She paid off the loan with the next payment. What is the amount of **(a)** interest, **(b)** final payment, and **(c)** savings by paying the loan off early?

Did You Know?

Hatching New Businesses
The National Business Incubation Association (NBIA) is the world's leading organization advancing business incubation and entrepreneurship. Business incubation is a support process that accelerates the successful development of start-up businesses.

10. Jean-Claude DuBose will be best man at his friend's wedding. To pay for plane fare, gifts, and other expenses, he took an $1,800 installment loan. The loan is for 12 months at 8% interest with a $156.60 monthly payment. After 8 months, the balance is $615.87, and he pays off the loan when the next payment is due. What is the amount of final payment? How much does he save by paying the loan off early?

H.O.T. Problems

11. **CHALLENGE PROBLEM** Dennis and Gail Schultz are looking over the repayment schedule for their $5,500 loan for lake house remodeling at 15% interest for 42 months with a monthly payment of $168.85. They note that the balance after payment 18 is $3,493.39, after 24 is $2,718.43, and after 30 is $1,883.50. How much would they save by paying off the loan early at payment **(a)** 19, **(b)** 25, or **(c)** 31?

Spiral Review

Multiply. (Skill 8)

12. $5,489 \times 0.15$
13. $2,729 \times 0.22$
14. $9,032 \times 0.18$
15. What is the finance charge on a $1,499.99 purchase requiring 10% down and 12 monthly payments on an installment loan that has an APR of 12%? (Lesson 8.3)
16. **ALGEBRA** Your pay as a lifeguard is $14.50 an hour for a regular 40-hour week. Your overtime rate is $1\frac{1}{2}$ times your regular hourly rate. During this past week, you earned $712.50 in total pay. How many hours of overtime did you work in that week? (Lesson 1.2)

GET READY for the Next Lesson

PREREQUISITE SKILL Dividing (Decimal Remainder) (Skill 10)

Divide. Round answers to the nearest hundredth.

17. $430 \div 91$
18. $1,328 \div 65$
19. $4,517 \div 33$
20. $222 \div 77$
21. $3,612 \div 53$
22. $2,462 \div 47$

LESSON 8.6

Determining the APR

Lesson Objective
Determine the annual percentage rate of a loan using a table and a formula.

GET READY for the Lesson

Why should you compare the cost related to different loans?

Ben Jackson would like to attend culinary school. He researches several loan options and compares the offers.

As You Read
Describe Why should you know a loan's APR?

Determining the APR You should know that a lender who gives you an installment loan must tell you the annual percentage rate (APR). If you know the number of monthly payments and the finance charge per $100 of the amount **financed**, you can determine the loan's APR. You can use a table such as **Figure 8.3** to find the APR. With this information, you can compare the cost related to different loans.

Figure 8.3

Annual Percentage Rate for Monthly Payment Plans

	Annual Percentage Rate										
	10.00%	10.25%	10.50%	10.75%	11.00%	11.25%	11.50%	11.75%	12.00%	12.25%	12.50%
Term	**Finance Charge per $100 of Amount Financed**										
6	$ 2.94	$ 3.01	$ 3.08	$ 3.16	$ 3.23	$ 3.31	$ 3.38	$ 3.45	$ 3.53	$ 3.60	$ 3.68
12	5.50	5.64	5.78	5.92	6.06	6.20	6.34	6.48	6.62	6.76	6.90
18	8.10	8.31	8.52	8.73	8.93	9.14	9.35	9.56	9.77	9.98	10.19
24	10.75	11.02	11.30	11.58	11.86	12.14	12.42	12.70	12.98	13.26	13.54

Note: An expanded table can be found in the Appendix on pages A8–A9.

To use the *Annual Percentage Rate for Monthly Payment Plans* table, you need to know the finance charge per $100 of the amount financed. You will need this formula:

$$\text{Finance Charge per \$100} = \$100.00 \times \frac{\text{Finance Charge}}{\text{Amount Financed}}$$

Need Help? Go to...
- Skill 11: Dividing Decimals, p. SK12
- Skill 2: Rounding Numbers, p. SK3

EXAMPLE 1

Paul Norris obtained a $1,500.00 installment loan to buy a racing bicycle. The finance charge is $146.25, and he will repay the loan in 18 monthly payments. What is the APR?

Step 1: Find the finance charge per $100.

$$\text{Finance Charge per \$100} = \$100.00 \times \frac{\text{Finance Charge}}{\text{Amount Financed}}$$

$$= \$100.00 \times \frac{\$146.25}{\$1{,}500.00}$$

$$\$9.75 = \$100.00 \times 0.0975$$

For every $100 he borrows, Paul will pay a $9.75 finance charge.

Tim Pannell/Corbis

Study Tip

Be Prepared
Having all of your notes, textbooks, and study guides in front of you when you study will help you easily answer questions that arise.

Step 2: Find the APR. (Refer to **Figure 8.3**, the *Annual Percentage Rate for Monthly Payment Plans* table.)

In the row for 18 payments, find the number closest to \$9.75. It is \$9.77. Read the APR at the top of the column. **APR is 12.00%.**

Concept CHECK

Complete this problem by finding the (a) finance charge per \$100 and (b) APR. Check your answers in the back of the book.

1. Francesa Santorelli took a 6-month loan of \$800 to buy art supplies. The finance charge is \$24.64.

Need Help? Go to...
Application B: More Formulas, p. AP2

EXAMPLE 2 Algebra

You can compute the APR on an installment loan by using this formula:

$$\text{APR} = \frac{mf(95n+9)}{(12n)(n+1)(4a+f)}$$

Where m = Number of payments per year
f = Finance charge
n = Number of scheduled payments
a = Amount financed

After he repaid his first loan, Paul Norris (**Example 1**) obtained another \$1,500 installment loan to buy a kayak. The finance charge is \$146.25. He agreed to repay the loan in 18 monthly payments. To the nearest hundredth of a percent, what is the annual percentage rate?

$$\text{APR} = \frac{12\times\$146.25[(95\times18)+9]}{(12\times18)(18+1)[(4\times\$1{,}500)+\$146.25]}$$

$$= \frac{\$1{,}755(1{,}719)}{216(19)(\$6{,}146.25)}$$

$$= \frac{\$3{,}016{,}845}{\$25{,}224{,}210} = 0.119601 = \mathbf{11.96\%}$$

The APR is 11.96%.

Note that the APR in **Example 1** was 12.00%. The difference is due to rounding in the table.

Concept CHECK

Find the APR using the formula. Check your answer in the back of the book.

2. Crissy Moreau took out an installment loan to pay for her new car. She borrowed \$22,500.00 for 40 months with a \$6,743.25 finance charge. Find her APR (to the nearest hundredth of a percent).

Lesson Practice

Complete the table. Using the *Annual Percentage Rate for Monthly Payment Plans* table on pages A8–A9, find the finance charge per $100 and the APR.

	Finance Charge	Amount Financed	Finance Charge per $100	Number of Payments	Annual Percentage Rate
3.	$ 33.10	$1,000	a.	6	b.
4.	159.36	2,400	a.	24	b.
5.	108.00	3,000	a.	18	b.
6.	691.74	5,400	a.	36	b.

For Problems 7–11, determine the APR.

7. Melissa Costouras obtains a $3,000 loan for darkroom equipment. She makes six monthly payments of $511.18.

8. Jeff Stapleton acquired a $1,995 installment loan to pay for a new laptop computer. He will repay the loan in 12 monthly payments of $174.70.

9. Oneta Correy wants to obtain an installment loan of $9,900.00 to purchase a used truck. The bank has agreed to a loan for 24 months at $439.89 per month.

10. Helen Olson needs an installment loan of $999.00. She must repay the loan in 24 months. The monthly payment is $44.96.

11. Jorge Alonzo obtained an installment loan for $3,500.00 to finance his new invention. The bank requires a down payment of 20% and 36 monthly payments of $85.18 each.

Did You Know?

The First Portable Computer The Osborne 1 is generally recognized as the world's first portable computer. Introduced in 1981, the Osborne 1 weighed 24.5 pounds and had a 5-inch monitor and a minuscule 64K of memory. Its original retail price was $1,795.

H.O.T. Problems

12. ALGEBRA Malik and Brianna Gray took out an installment loan to pay for their new car. They borrowed $25,000.00 for 72 months with a finance charge of $10,500.00. To the nearest hundredth of a percent, what is their APR?

13. ALGEBRA Four friends were comparing installment loans. They each planned to borrow $850. Adam Carter wanted to make one monthly payment of $900. Betsy Dunn preferred to make 900 monthly payments of $1 each. More realistically, Chris Evans decided to make 18 monthly payments of $50 each. Darcy Fogel chose to make 30 monthly payments of $30 each. To the nearest hundredth of a percent, find the APR for each. You can use the table or the formula for Chris and Darcy. (*Hint:* In the formula, $m = 12$ even with only one monthly payment.) Why is there such a difference in the respective APRs?

Spiral Review

Divide. Round answers to the nearest hundredth. (Skill 10 and Skill 11)

14. 510 ÷ 17 **15.** 1,060 ÷ 24 **16.** 2,642 ÷ 47

17. Is an 8-ounce can of fruit for $1.19 or a 64-ounce can for $5.87 the better buy? (Lesson 6.4)

GET READY for the Next Lesson

PREREQUISITE SKILL Adding Decimals (Skill 5)

18. 65.32 + 21.34 + 32.33 **19.** 4,263.01 + 59.42 + 4.13 + 27.15

20. 93.4 + 73.8 + 1,995.9 **21.** 44.5 + 357.8 + 38.3 + 306.5

CHAPTER 8 Review and Assessment

AFTER YOU READ

Chapter SUMMARY

You may want to consider a number of factors when thinking about taking out a loan. You may want to compute the maturity value and interest rate of a single-payment loan. On installment loans, you may want to determine the amount financed and compute the monthly payment, total amount repaid, finance charge, the payment to interest, payment to principal, and the new balance. You may also want to know how to compute the final payment of an installment loan and use a table to find the annual percentage rate of a loan.

Vocabulary Check

1. On a sheet of paper, use each of these terms in a sentence.

Content Vocabulary

- single-payment loan (p. 305)
- promissory note (p. 305)
- maturity value (p. 305)
- term (p. 305)
- ordinary interest (p. 305)
- exact interest (p. 305)
- installment loan (p. 308)
- down payment (p. 308)
- amount financed (p. 308)
- annual percentage rate (p. 311)
- repayment schedule (p. 316)
- final payment (p. 319)

Academic Vocabulary

- principal (p. 305)
- specify (p. 308)
- index (p. 311)
- allocate (p. 316)
- motive (p. 319)
- financed (p. 322)

Concept Check

2. Describe a single-payment loan.
3. What two factors make up the maturity value of a single-payment loan?
4. What is an installment loan?
5. Give the formula for amount financed.
6. What is the formula for total amount repaid?
7. Summarize the information found on a repayment schedule.
8. Locate the formula for final payment.
9. List two factors you need in order to determine APR.
10. **CRITICAL THINKING** Give one motive for paying off a loan early.

Lesson-by-Lesson Review

8.1 Single-Payment Loans (pp. 305–307)

Compute the maturity value and interest rate of a single-payment loan.
Jaime Tavare's bank granted him a $3,500 single-payment loan for 80 days at 11% ordinary interest so he could make payroll. What is the loan's maturity value?

Step 1: Find the ordinary interest.

Ordinary Interest = Principal × Rate × Time

$$\$85.56 = \$3{,}500.00 \times 11\% \times \frac{80}{360}$$

Step 2: Find the maturity value.

Maturity Value = Principal + Interest Owed

$3,585.56 = $3,500 + $85.56

Review Exercises

11. Dontice Thomas obtained a single-payment loan of $21,400 to purchase a diamond necklace and bracelet set. She agreed to repay the loan in 120 days at an ordinary interest rate of 8.5%. What is the maturity value of her loan?

12. Jodi Pelfrey obtained a single-payment loan of $1,600 to buy a pedigreed dog. She agrees to repay the loan in 120 days at an ordinary interest rate of 7.5%. What is the maturity value of her loan?

13. **ALGEBRA** Birgit Dohr took out an $1,800 single-payment loan at 8.2% ordinary interest. She used it to purchase transportation, lodging, and tickets to the national figure skating championship on March 9. If the loan's maturity value was $1,825.01, when would she have to pay it back?

8.2 Installment Loans–Amount Financed (pp. 308–310)

Calculate the down payment and amount financed on an installment loan.
Katie Burns is buying a new guitar for $635.88. She made a 15% down payment and will finance the remainder. How much did she finance?

Step 1: Find the down payment.

Down Payment = Cash Price × Percent

$95.38 = $635.88 × 15%

Step 2: Find the amount financed.

Amount Financed = Cash Price – Down Payment

$540.50 = $635.88 – $95.38

Review Exercises

	Purpose	Cash Price	Down Payment (Cash)	Down Payment (Percent)	Down Payment (in Dollars)	Amount Financed
14.	Treadmill	$ 789	$300	—	a. $	b. $
15.	Symphony Season Tickets	4,500	—	25%	a.	b.

Lesson-by-Lesson Review (continued)

16. Madelyn Cramer purchased a desk for her home office for $587.33. Using the store's installment plan, she made a $147.00 down payment. What amount did she finance?

17. Levi Hempke wants to buy a car costing $21,000. He will finance the purchase with an installment loan from the bank, but he would like to finance no more than $14,280. What percent of the car's total cost should his down payment be?

18. Tyler Ferguson had a pond added to his backyard. He financed its total cost of $1,189 and made a down payment of 25%. What amount did he finance?

8.3 Installment Loans—Monthly Payment & Finance Charge (pp. 311–315)

Calculate the (a) monthly payment, (b) total amount repaid, and (c) finance charge on an installment loan.

Kelsey Berger obtained a $2,200 installment loan to finance her trip to a family reunion. The annual percentage rate is 10%. She must repay the loan in 24 months. What is the finance charge?

Step 1: Find the monthly payment. (Refer to the *Monthly Payment on an Installment Loan of $100* table on page A13.)

$$\text{Monthly Payment } (mp) = \frac{\text{Amount of Loan}}{\$100} \times \text{Monthly Payment for a \$100 Loan}$$

$$\$101.42 = \frac{\$2{,}200.00}{\$100.00} \times \$4.61$$

Step 2: Find the total amount repaid.

Total Amount Repaid = Number of Payments × Monthly Payment

$2,434.08 = 24 × $101.42

Step 3: Find the finance charge.

Finance Charge = Total Amount Repaid − Amount Financed

$234.08 = $2,434.08 − $2,200.00

Review Exercises

For these problems, refer to the *Monthly Payment on an Installment Loan of $100* table on page A13.

19. Jesse Procter obtained an installment loan of $3,500 to have some storm-damaged trees in his yard removed. The APR is 12%, and the loan is to be repaid in 30 months. What is the finance charge?

20. Etienne and Corinne Bertrand purchased a new living room set at Allied Furniture Store for $2,896.00. They agreed to make a 20% down payment and to finance the remainder for 12 monthly payments. The APR is 8%. What is the finance charge?

21. Laura and Dwayne Knight purchased a new riding lawn mower for $7,500. They agreed to make a 25% down payment and to finance the remainder with 12 monthly payments. The APR is 9%. What is the finance charge?

22. Henrietta Burke obtained a $3,200 installment loan for a marble floor in her foyer. The annual percentage rate is 9%. She must repay the loan in 24 months. Find the **(a)** monthly payment using the formula, **(b)** total amount repaid, and **(c)** finance charge.

Lesson-by-Lesson Review (continued)

8.4 Installment Loans—Monthly Payment Allocation (pp. 316–318)

Calculate the payment to interest, payment to principal, and the new balance.
Francisco Ortega obtained a 1-year loan of $2,800.00 to buy a new gas grill. Interest is 8%. The monthly payment was $243.60. For the first payment, what was the amount of **(a)** interest, **(b)** payment to principal, and **(c)** new principal?

Step 1: Find the interest.

Interest = Principal × Rate × Time

$18.67 = $2,800.00 × 8% × $\frac{1}{12}$

a. Interest was $18.67.

Step 2: Find the payment to principal.

Payment to Principal = Monthly Payment − Interest

$224.93 = $243.60 − $18.67

b. His payment to principal was $224.93.

Step 3: Find the new principal.

New Principal = Previous Principal − Payment to Principal

$2,575.07 = $2,800.00 − $224.93

c. Francisco's new principal was $2,575.07.

Review Exercises

	Purpose	Loan Balance	Interest Rate	Monthly Payment	Amount for Interest	Amount for Principal	New Principal
23.	Kentucky Derby Trip	$3,900	12%	$303.55	a. $	b. $	c. $
24.	Pearl and Ruby Necklace	1,800	9%	114.48	a.	b.	c.
25.	Pro Tennis Lessons	1,300	8%	105.43	a.	b.	c.
26.	Antique Chair	2,600	10%	189.45	a.	b.	c.

27. To go on an African safari, Don Stone obtained an $8,500 installment loan at 14% for 42 months. The loan's balance after 26 payments is $3,733.55. What is the interest for payment 27?

28. Daniela Nanz obtained a $2,500 loan at 12.5% to buy porch furniture. The monthly payment is $118.23. What is the amount of the **(a)** interest for the first payment, **(b)** payment to principal, and **(c)** new principal?

29. Demarrio Kibbe obtained a loan for a new deck. The loan is for $4,500 at 10%. The monthly payment is $270.45. What is the amount of the **(a)** interest for the first payment, **(b)** payment to principal, and **(c)** new principal?

30. Emma Jarmel obtained a $6,000 loan at 10% for home improvements. The monthly payment is $276.60. What is the amount of the **(a)** interest for the first payment, **(b)** payment to principal, and **(c)** new principal?

Lesson-by-Lesson Review (continued)

8.5 Paying Off Installment Loans (pp. 319–321)

Compute the final payment when paying off an installment loan.
You have a 6-month loan of $1,000.00 at 10% with a balance of $338.89 after the fourth payment. What is the final payment if you pay off the loan with the fifth payment?

Step 1: Find the previous balance.

= $338.89

Step 2: Find the interest for the fifth month.

Fifth Month Interest = Principal × Rate × Time

$\$2.82 = \$338.89 \times 10\% \times \frac{1}{12}$

Interest for the fifth monthly payment is $2.82.

Step 3: Find the final payment.

Final Payment = Previous Balance + Current Month's Interest

$341.71 = $338.89 + $2.82

Your final payment is $341.71.

Review Exercises

	Purpose	Interest Rate	Previous Balance	Interest	Final Payment
31.	Camper	10%	$3,600.00	a. $	b. $
32.	Water Scooter	8	2,400.00	a.	b.
33.	ATV	12	4,860.80	a.	b.
34.	Pontoon Boat	6	2,984.50	a.	b.
35.	Billiard Table	12	1,824.25	a.	b.
36.	Air Conditioner	10	1,200.00	a.	b.
37.	Television	8	1,499.00	a.	b.
38.	Camcorder	6	1,050.00	a.	b.

39. John Marks has a loan at 10% interest for $33,825 for 96 months. The monthly payment is $512.90. The balance after payment number 70 is $12,397.86. What is the final payment if the loan is paid off with payment number 71?

40. In problem 39, how much would John save by paying off the loan with payment number 71?

41. Nancy Parker has a $12,000 simple-interest installment loan at 12% for 36 months. The monthly payment is $398.52. The balance after the sixth payment is $10,286.53. **(a)** What is the final payment if the loan is paid off with the seventh payment? **(b)** How much will Nancy save by paying off the loan with payment number seven?

Lesson-by-Lesson Review (continued)

8.6 Determining the APR (pp. 322–324)

Determine the annual percentage rate of a loan using a table and a formula.
Uma Hartmann obtained a $900.00 installment loan to pay for brochures to advertise her new business. The finance charge is $13.14, and she must repay the loan in 6 months. What is the annual percentage rate?

Step 1: Find the finance charge per $100.

$$\text{Finance Charge per \$100} = \$100 \times \frac{\text{Finance Charge}}{\text{Amount Financed}}$$

$$= \$100 \times \frac{\$13.14}{\$900}$$

$$\mathbf{\$1.46} = \$100 \times 0.0146$$

The finance charge per $100 is $1.46.

Step 2: Find the APR. (Refer to the *Annual Percentage Rate for Monthly Payment Plans* table on pages A8–A9.)
In the row for 6 payments, find the number closest to $1.46. It is $1.46. Read the APR at the top of the column. **The APR is 5.00%.**

Review Exercises

For Problems 42–45, refer to the *Annual Percentage Rate for Monthly Payment Plans* table on pages A8–A9.

	Purpose	Finance Charge	Amount Financed	Finance Charge per $100	Number of Payments	Annual Percentage Rate
42.	Storage Cabinets	$ 45.20	$2,000	a. $	6	b. %
43.	Security Files	84.24	3,600	a.	12	b.
44.	Oak Conference Table	160.00	2,500	a.	18	b.
45.	Intercom System	81.00	4,500	a.	18	b.

46. ALGEBRA Liam Elliott obtained a $1,700 installment loan to pay for an invisible fence for his dog. The finance charge is $154.25. He agreed to repay the loan in 18 monthly payments. Use the APR formula to determine the annual percentage rate. Round the answer to the nearest hundredth of a percent.

47. ALGEBRA Tynetta Mafundo obtained an installment loan of $3,600.00 to buy a sculpture from the local art gallery. The finance charge is $126.18. She agreed to repay the loan in 18 monthly payments. Use the APR formula to determine the annual percentage rate. Round the answer to the nearest hundredth of a percent.

48. Tom North obtained a $12,000 installment loan to purchase a used truck. The loan was for 36 months at 12% with a monthly payment of $398.52. Find the APR.

Practice Test

Record your answer on another sheet of paper.

1. What is the maturity value of a single-payment loan of $650 given for 80 days at 15% exact interest?
   A $685.39 **B** $671.37
   C $652.37 **D** $670.36

2. Marcus Gardner is buying a new computer for $1,299.50. He made a 12% down payment. How much money did he put down?
   A $155.94 **B** $120.00
   C $212.84 **D** $420.50

3. Jenna Cox bought a home gym for $1,299.50. If she made a 15% down payment, how much would she finance?
   A $989.60 **B** $1,149.56
   C $1,284.50 **D** $1,104.58

4. You take a $4,500 loan to pay for a trip to the Amazon rainforest to photograph wild animals. If the loan's interest rate is 8% for 1 year, what is the interest for the first payment?
   A $12.58 **B** $26.00
   C $30.00 **D** $80.99

5. Vincent Falcone has a 6-month loan of $1,500.00 at 12% with a balance of $435.85 after the fourth payment. What is the final payment if the loan is paid off with the fifth payment?
   A $438.20 **B** $440.29
   C $440.21 **D** $441.28

6. Harold Stephens found a home theater surround-sound system on sale for $1,585.99 cash or $155.16 per month for 12 months. What is the finance charge if he pays monthly?
   A $122.83 **B** $22.00
   C $275.93 **D** $1,310.06

7. Kim-Ly Vanh's bank granted her a single-payment loan of $2,580 for 90 days at 12% ordinary interest. What is the amount of interest?
   A $127.44 **B** $77.40
   C $87.54 **D** $98.12

8. If you wanted to make an 8% down payment on a $3,585 loan to buy cashmere sweaters for your boutique, how much money would you need?
   A $94.68 **B** $72.85
   C $186.73 **D** $286.80

9. Steve Elroy needs an installment loan of $1,900. He must repay the loan at $169.00 a month for 12 months. What is the APR?

10. Carla Payne obtained a $3,500.00 loan at 8.5% for 1 year. If the monthly payments were $285.55, what would the interest amount be in the first payment?

11. Samantha Beese took a loan of $2,800 at 8% for 1 year. Her monthly payment was $233.50. For the first monthly payment, what is the payment to the principal?

12. Stu Walton's bank gave him a single-payment loan of $4,300 for 120 days at 14% ordinary interest. What is the maturity value of the loan?

13. How long would it take for a home-improvement loan for $22,800 to earn interest of $608.00 at 8% ordinary interest?

14. William Meller has a 180-day loan from his bank to pay for a new swimming pool. His loan's maturity value is $30,640 and he is paying 10% exact interest. How much did he borrow?

15. 40% of 592

16. 4,192 × 7%

17. $\$856 \times 12\% \times \frac{30}{360}$

18. 21 ÷ 210.00 × 4.44

19. 3,582.60 − 13.21

20. $\$7{,}300 \times 10\% \times \frac{90}{365}$

Standardized Test Practice

Cumulative, Chapters 1–8

PART 1 Multiple Choice

Record your answers on the answer sheet provided by your teacher or on a sheet of paper.

1. Dakota Lane purchased a car stereo for $279.99. If he made a 35% down payment, how much did he finance?
   A $189.99 **B** $244.99
   C $181.99 **D** $98.99

2. Margaret Papal's bank charges a $0.35 service fee for each check she writes. How much will the bank withdraw from her account if she writes 8 checks totaling $815.60?
   A $815.25 **B** $817.25
   C $818.40 **D** $815.95

3. How much would a $15.99 book cost if your state's sales tax is 5.65%?
   A $18.45 **B** $16.89
   C $20.64 **D** $16.35

4. Whitney Snyder ate 17 jellybeans on Monday, 32 on Tuesday, 11 on Wednesday, 24 on Thursday, and 53 on Friday. What was the average number of jellybeans she ate?
   A 22.14 **B** 31.5
   C 27.4 **D** 28.5

5. Thalia Cassavetes earns $32,500.89 annually. If she gives 8.5% to charity, how much will she have left?
   A $22,543.75 **B** $31,700.89
   C $24,100.91 **D** $29,738.31

6. Ingmar Knudsen has $5,289.76 in his checking account. How much would he have if he deposited 2 checks for $95.87 each and withdrew $65.00?
   A $5,416.50 **B** $5,481.50
   C $5,321.50 **D** $5,659.50

TEST-TAKING TIP

Seating When choosing your seat for a test, be sure to find one where you'll be comfortable.

PART 2 Short Response/Griddable

7. Joel Bradley purchased a new cooler for his florist shop for $4,500. He wants to finance it with an installment loan from his bank. If he wants to finance only $2,800, what percent of the total cost should his down payment be?

8. Stacy Ferris moved to Orlando, Florida. She left $236.66 in a bank account in Streamwood, Illinois, where she used to live. The account's interest rate is 3.5%. If she does not make any withdrawals or deposits, what amount would be in the account after one year?

9. If $10,000 was worth $11,000 in 480 days, what ordinary interest rate was being earned?

10. Nathaniel Barnes obtained a single-payment loan of $1,200 to purchase a computer. He agreed to repay the loan in 120 days at an ordinary interest rate of 7%. What is the maturity value of his loan?

PART 3 Extended Response

Show your work.

11. How can you budget for yearly fixed expenses on a monthly basis?

12. Explain how you would find the average of 20, 54, 65, 31, 86, and 45. Then show the result.

13. What is the difference between ordinary interest and exact interest when calculating the interest owed?

14. Jim Ayers delivers artwork. He earns $10 an hour plus 3% commission on the total price of deliveries. If he worked for 7 hours on Monday and earned $98.50 that day, what was the total price of the artwork he delivered?

Building Academic Skills

Mathematics

A person's debt-payments-to-income ratio tells lenders whether he or she is a good candidate for a loan. Generally, a person's monthly debt payments should be no more than 36% of his or her monthly income. Calculate the debt-to-income ratio for someone with monthly take-home pay of $2,250, a car payment of $336, and a college loan payment of $163. Would a bank be interested in giving him or her a mortgage loan? Why or why not?

English Language Arts/Writing

Entrepreneurs often use loans to start a business or to buy the materials necessary to create a product. Write a paragraph about one way you could use a loan to implement a business idea. What kind of business or product do you think would be successful? Consider what you would need to purchase and how much money you think you would need.

Social Studies/Government

The five Cs of credit—character, capacity, capital, collateral, and credit history—are factors that banks and credit card companies use to determine whether you should receive credit and how much. Use the Internet to research the five Cs of credit and write a short assessment of your current creditworthiness.

Blend images / Superstock

Building Real-World Skills

Tech TRENDS

Finding the Best Loan Banks and lenders are more competitive than ever, and smart consumers can use this to their advantage when shopping for a loan. Many sites on the Internet let users easily compare interest rates and terms, and some actually have lenders bidding on the loan, trying to get the customer.

Research and Discuss:

a. Using the Internet, search for "loan comparisons" and "loan finder." What are some of the popular services that make it easy to shop for loans?

b. As a class, make a list of the different services available. Discuss how loan comparison services can help consumers. What factors do you think are important to consider when shopping for a loan?

Ethics in Action

Inflating Credentials To make extra spending money, you charge a small fee to help friends write their résumés. One friend supplies information about her education and work history that you find unlikely, based on what you know about her. When you ask, she claims all of the information is true. You figure you are just doing a job and that it is her résumé, not yours.

Discuss and Write:

a. As a class or in groups, discuss why it is risky for job applicants to inflate their credentials on their résumés. What are some potential consequences of doing so?

b. Would you help your friend write her résumé? Write a paragraph detailing why or why not.

UNIT 3 Thematic Project

Doing Your Taxes

Project Assignment

In this project you will use a W-2 form to prepare a 1040EZ income tax return. A W-2 tells you how much you earned, and how much employers withheld to pay taxes. Every year that you receive income, you will receive multiple copies of your W-2. When you file your taxes, one copy goes with each federal, state, and local income tax return. One copy is for your personal records.

Your Project Assignment

- ✓ Get organized. Collect the necessary documents to fill out the 1040EZ form.
- ✓ Complete the 1040EZ income tax return following the Project Steps.
- ✓ Find your tax liability using tax tables.

Form **1040EZ**

Department of the Treasury – Internal Revenue Service
Income Tax Return for Single and Joint Filers With No Dependents
OMB No. 1545-0074

Label (See page 8.)
Use the IRS label. Otherwise, please print or type.
LABEL HERE

Your first name and initial | Last name | Your social security number

If a joint return, spouse's first name and initial | Last name | Spouse's social security number

Home address (number and street). If you have a P.O. box, see page 9. | Apt. no.

▲ You must enter your SSN(s) above. ▲

City, town or post office, state, and ZIP code. If you have a foreign address, see page9.

Presidential Election Campaign (page 9)
Checking a box below will not change your tax or refund.
Check here if you, or your spouse if a joint return, want $3 to go to this fund . . . . ▶ ☐ **You** ☐ **Spouse**

Income
Attach Form(s) W–2 here.

1 Wages, salaries, and tips. This should be shown in box 1 of your Form(s) W–2. Attach you Form(s) W–2. **1**

2 Taxable interest. If the total is over $1,500, you cannot use Form 1040EZ. **2**

Skills Preview

To fill out the 1040EZ income tax return, you must use your skills. Some skills you might use include:

Academic Skills reading, writing, and mathematics
Basic Skills thinking and problem-solving stills
Technology Skills Internet skills

Rachel Frank/Fancy Photography/Alamy

Project Steps

Step 1 Get Organized

- Each year employers send a Wage and Tax Statement called a W-2 to their employees. Keep them organized.
- Obtain a copy of the 1040EZ income tax return and a W-2 form.

Step 2 Explore Your Community

Interview two employed individuals in your community. How do they prepare their income tax returns? Ask them for advice on keeping your financial records organized.

Step 3 Complete Your 1040EZ

- Fill out the 1040EZ form. Assume $10.66 savings interest and no unemployment compensation.
  - ✓ Fill out lines 1–3.
  - ✓ Add the amounts on lines 1–3 to find the adjusted gross income. Write this sum on line 4.
- Assume that you will be claimed as a dependent. Check "Yes" on line 5 and complete the following:
  - ✓ Complete the "Worksheet for Dependents Who Checked 'Yes' on line 5" section.
  - ✓ On line A, enter the amount from line 1.
  - ✓ On line C, enter the larger of the two amounts listed in lines A and B.
  - ✓ For line D, enter the maximum standard deduction.
  - ✓ Compare the amounts on lines C and D. Enter the smaller of the two amounts here and on line 5.
- Next, subtract line 5 from line 4 and write the difference on line 6. This is your taxable income.
- Refer to the W-2 to find the amount of income already withheld.
  - ✓ What amount will go on line 7?
  - ✓ For line 8, assume that you did not receive the earned income tax credit.
  - ✓ Add lines 7 and 8 for line 9.
- For line 10 of a 1040EZ return, you will determine your tax liability. This is the amount you are obligated to pay in federal income tax. It depends on your filing status, the exemptions you claim, and your taxable income. Refer to the tax tables found online and to line 6 on the 1040EZ.
- Sign your tax return.

Step 4 Evaluate Your Presentation

Go to **connectED.mcgraw-hill.com** to download an evaluation rubric.

Academic and Career Portfolio

Add this report to your Academic and Career Portfolio.

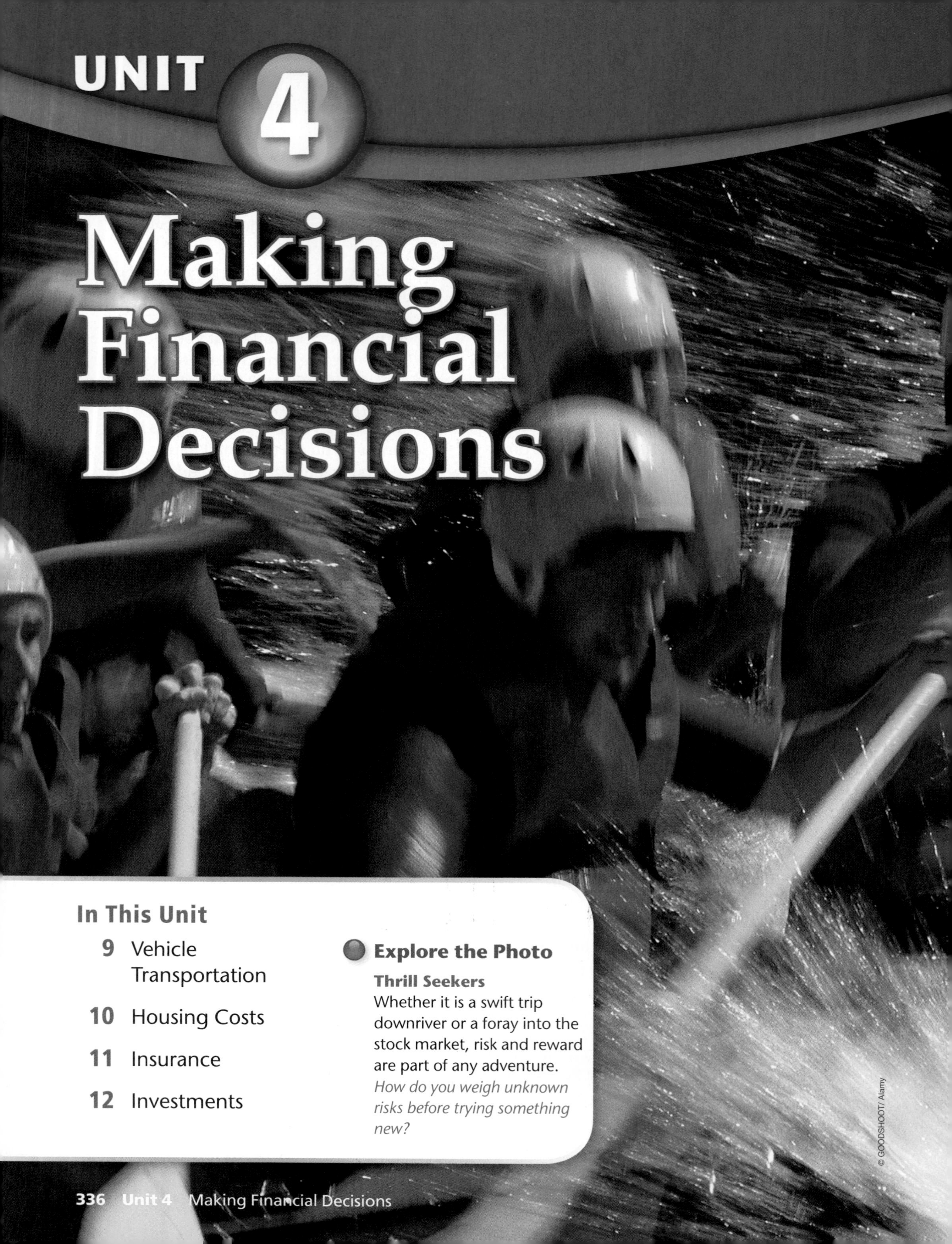

UNIT 4

Making Financial Decisions

In This Unit

Explore the Photo

Thrill Seekers

Whether it is a swift trip downriver or a foray into the stock market, risk and reward are part of any adventure. *How do you weigh unknown risks before trying something new?*

The Big Picture

Does it pay to invest in collectibles? The image below shows the price paid for some historic home run baseballs.

*Date of home run

Data: Michael Barnes, Barnes Sports Group; ESPN

Go to **connectED.mcgraw-hill.com** for the Unit 4 WebQuest activity about the investment possibilities in collectibles.

Thematic Project Preview

Picking Stocks

If you invest in a company's stock and that company does well, you may reap considerable returns on your investment. On the other hand, if you invest in a company that performs poorly, you may lose a substantial amount. What is your tolerance for making risky investments? After completing this Unit Thematic Project, you will be better equipped to consider your own investment options.

Pre-Project Checklist

As you read this unit, use this checklist to prepare for the unit project:

- ✓ Understand how to determine the cost of a stock and how to calculate profits and loss on stocks.
- ✓ Visit the Companies Channel at *BusinessWeek's* Web site and practice reading a stock table.
- ✓ Discover resources in the newspaper and online for tracking stock performance.

Chapter 9 Vehicle Transportation

Big Idea

The cost of a vehicle includes the total of the cost to buy, lease, or rent it plus the cost to operate it, such as charges for insurance and maintenance.

Explore the Photo

The Open Road

A vehicle can be a symbol of freedom, but it requires responsibility. *What responsibilities come along with owning and operating a vehicle?*

Ask AN EXPERT

Vehicle Insurance Rates

Q: My classmate James just got his own car and was surprised to learn how much insurance costs. What can he do to lower his insurance rates?

A: Statistics have shown men under 25 years of age to be more likely than other people to drive unsafely and have accidents. Their automobile insurance rates are higher because insurance companies consider them a high risk. Young drivers can lower their insurance costs by shopping around for the best rates, driving used vehicles, getting good grades, and taking defensive driving courses.

English Language Arts/Writing Write a paragraph explaining why you do or do not need to own your own vehicle (if you already own one, describe how you use it). Consider the cost of fuel, where you live, your schedule, and your lifestyle. Could you bicycle, walk, or use public transportation?

GET READY for the Chapter

Math Online

To take the Online Readiness Quiz, go to **connectED.mcgraw-hill.com**.

Reading Guide

Before You Read

Describe What factors would influence your decision when purchasing a vehicle?

Main Idea

One of the first major purchases people make is a vehicle. The purchase involves making many decisions, such as new versus used, lease versus purchase, payments versus full payment, and type of insurance coverage. Determining the cost of operating a vehicle is also an important factor in acquiring one.

Graphic Organizer

Before you read this chapter, draw a diagram like the one you see below. As you read, compare the related costs of owning a vehicle, leasing a vehicle, and renting a vehicle.

Buying Costs	Leasing Costs	Renting Costs

Math Online Go to **connectED.mcgraw-hill.com** to download this graphic organizer.

Content Vocabulary

You will learn these content vocabulary terms in this chapter.

- sticker price
- base price
- options
- destination charge
- dealer's cost
- used-vehicle guide
- liability insurance
- collision insurance
- comprehensive insurance
- deductible clause
- annual premium
- variable costs
- fixed costs
- depreciation
- lease
- closed-end lease
- open-end lease
- rent

Academic Vocabulary

You will see these words in your reading and on your tests.

- display
- consumer
- published
- injury
- media
- license
- plus

You can find vocabulary definitions in the **Content Vocabulary** Glossary and the **Academic Vocabulary** Glossary in the back of the book.

LESSON 9.1

Purchasing a New Vehicle

Lesson Objective
Compute the sticker price of a new vehicle.

Content Vocabulary
- sticker price
- base price
- options
- destination charge

When can you generally get the best price on new vehicles?

Sandy Lim is planning to buy a new car in the fall. Many manufacturers are eager to sell the past year's models in the fall to make way for new ones.

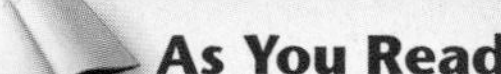

Identify What is the sticker price?

Computing the Sticker Price Laws require vehicle manufacturers to **display** a buyer's guide sticker on a new vehicle's window that shows the price. The **sticker price** includes three charges.

The **base price**, sometimes referred to as the *manufacturer's suggested retail price* (MSRP), is the price of the engine, chassis (that is, the vehicle's frame), and any other standard equipment for a particular model. **Options** are extra equipment for convenience, safety, or appearance, such as a sunroof, air conditioning, and tinted glass, not included in the base price. The **destination charge** is the cost of shipping the vehicle from the factory to the dealer.

Therefore, the sticker price is the total of the base price, options, and destination charge.

Sticker Price = Base Price + Options + Destination Charge

Some dealers add other charges such as a dealer preparation ("prep") charge for servicing the vehicle before delivering it to the consumer as well as various other delivery, processing, and handling fees such as a title fee.

Need Help? Go to...
- **Workshop 4:** Adding Decimals, p. 10
- **Skill 5:** Adding Decimals, p. SK6

EXAMPLE 1

Scott Oliver is shopping for a sports car. See **Figure 9.1** for a portion of the sticker for a convertible. What is this vehicle's sticker price?

Figure 9.1

Zephyr Convertible	
Base Price	$30,665
Optional Equipment	
5-Speed Automatic Transmission	665
Polished Aluminum Wheels	925
Interior Upgrade	460
Destination Charge	745

Continued on next page

Step 1: Find the options price.

$665 + $925 + $460 = $2,050 options price

Step 2: Find the sticker price.

Base Price + Options + Destination Charge

$30,665 + $2,050 + $745 = **$33,460 sticker price**

Study Tip

Organizing Information

When you organize information in a chart, make sure you label the columns and rows accurately.

Concept CHECK

Find the sticker price. Check your answers in the back of the book.

1. River City Autos has a pickup truck for sale. Its base price is $22,225. Prices for available options are 6-speed transmission, $2,908; cruise control, $240; trailer towing package, $230; and power windows, $738. Its destination charge is $900.
2. Coble Downtown is selling a sport coupe hybrid at a base price of $24,990. Options are the convenience package, $1,300; sunroof, $850; and sunroof wind deflector, $100. Destination charge is $625.

Need Help? Go to...

- **Workshop 38:** Problem-Solving Strategy: Writing an Equation, p. 78
- **Application C:** Tables and Charts, p. AP3

EXAMPLE 2 Algebra

Anna and Luke Shore are purchasing a new sport utility vehicle (SUV) with an MSRP of $25,525.00 including the delivery, processing, and handling fee. The Driver Convenience Package, which includes mounted radio controls and power seats, costs five times the amount of the Appearance Package, which includes body side molding and chrome inserts. The SUV's total cost is $29,137.41, including a 6.75% sales tax. What is the cost of the Appearance Package and the Driver Convenience Package?

Let x = Cost of appearance package

Let $5x$ = Cost of convenience package

Total Cost = Base Price + Destination Charge + Appearance Pkg. + Convenience Pkg. + Tax

$29,137.41 = ($25,525.00 + x + $5x$) + 6.75%($25,525.00 + x + $5x$)

Combine like terms → $29,137.41 = ($25,525.00 + $6x$) + 0.0675($25,525.00 + $6x$)

Apply the distributive property → $29,137.41 = $25,525.00 + $6x$ + $1,722.9375 + $0.405x$

Combine like terms → $29,137.41 = $27,247.9375 + $6.405x$

Subract $27,247.9375 from both sides → $1,889.4725 = $6.405x$

Divide both sides by 6.405 → **$295** = x

The Appearance Package costs $295.

The Driver Convenience Package costs 5 × $295 = $1,475.

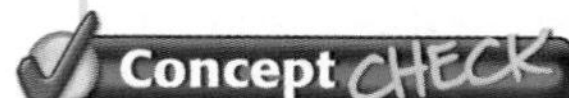

Concept CHECK

Complete the problem. Check your answer in the back of the book.

3. Nayan Patel purchases a compact vehicle with an MSRP of $17,980.00, including the destination charge and title fee. He selects a 6-way power front passenger seat, which costs 10 times the amount of remote keyless entry. The total cost of the compact vehicle, including a 7% sales tax, is $19,591.70. Find the cost of the power front passenger seat and the remote keyless entry.

Automotive Electronics Installer
Installers ensure that valuable vehicle electronic devices are properly set up and function correctly. **Why do installers need to understand units of measurement?**

Lesson Practice

Find the sticker price.

	Base Price	Options	Destination Charge	Sticker Price
4.	$19,900	$2,400	$350	$
5.	21,540	1,260	345	
6.	32,654	4,865	338	
7.	49,842	3,861	425	

8. Dalton Slade is interested in an SUV that has a $31,145 base price. Factory-installed options include folding rear seat, $325; front leather trim split bench seat, $425; sport package, $690; tow package, $650; engine block heater, $85; and optional 4-wheel drive, $950. The destination charge from its assembly plant in Michigan is $852. What is this SUV's sticker price?

9. Andy Tedesco is interested in buying a small pickup with a base price of $31,100. It has these options: stereo/CD player/navigation system, $1,445; power sunroof, $850; security package, $640; aluminum wheels, $545; tubular side steps, $525; heated front seats, $250; trailer tow group, $525; pearlcoat paint, $225; and all-terrain tires, $100. Its destination charge is $645. Determine its sticker price.

10. Devin and Marlika Randolph are shopping for a new minivan with all-wheel drive. Its base price is $25,535. The options are a touch-screen DVD/TV at $650, satellite navigation system at $225, a heavy-duty engine cooling system at $354, a trailer-tow package at $568, and a keyless entry system at $332. The destination charge is $850. What is the minivan's sticker price?

11. ALGEBRA Betty Richard's new luxury sedan has a $43,895.60 MSRP including title and processing fees. The navigation system cost twice as much as the upgraded sound system, which included AM/FM stereo with CD/MP3 player, and 9 speakers. Including the 6.5% sales tax, the total cost of her new auto was $48,346.31. Find the cost of the upgraded sound system and the navigation system.

Spiral Review

Add. (Skill 3)

12. 8,850 + 995 + 660 + 242 **13.** 6,770 + 1,217 + 648 + 344 + 85

14. Penny Banks purchased a new washer and dryer for $1,526.39. She used the store's credit plan and made a 25% down payment. How much did she finance? (Lesson 8.2)

15. Determine the future value of $4,000 deposited into an ordinary annuity after each quarter for 3 years at 6% interest compounded quarterly. (Lesson 5.8)

GET READY for the Next Lesson

PREREQUISITE SKILL Finding the Percentage (Skill 30)

Find the percentage.

16. 8% of 649 **17.** 78% of 454 **18.** 19% of 936

LESSON 9.2

Dealer's Cost

Lesson Objective
Calculate the dealer's cost of a new vehicle.

Content Vocabulary
- dealer's cost

GET READY for the Lesson

Why do you pay more than the dealer does when you buy a car?

Serena Gamble just bought a new car. She realized that the dealer paid less than the sticker price.

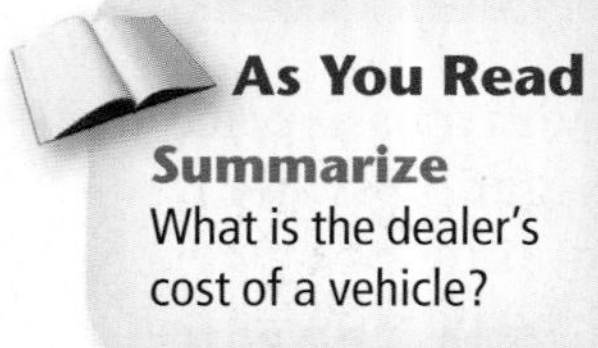

As You Read

Summarize
What is the dealer's cost of a vehicle?

Calculating Dealer's Cost In Lesson 9.1, you learned that vehicle dealers place a "sticker price" on a new vehicle. In order to make a profit the dealer pays less than the sticker price for both the basic vehicle and the options. Internet sites show the sticker price and the invoice price or dealer's cost of a vehicle. **Consumer** magazines often report the **dealer's cost** as a percent of the base price plus a percent of the options price plus the destination charge. You may save money when purchasing a new vehicle by making an offer that is higher than the estimated dealer's cost but lower than the sticker price. Keep this in mind as you work through this section. Use this formula to calculate the dealer's cost.

Dealer's Cost = Percent of Base Price + Percent of Options Price + Destination Charge

Need Help? Go to...
- **Workshop 14:** Finding a Percentage, p. 30
- **Skill 30:** Finding the Percentage, p. SK31

EXAMPLE 1

The pickup truck sticker shows a base price of $41,036.00, with options totaling $2,425.00 and a destination charge of $850.00. *Consumer Reports* shows the dealer cost as 87.7% of the base price and 90.2% of the options. What is the dealer's cost?

Step 1: Find the percent of base price.

$41,036.00 × 87.7% = $35,988.57

Step 2: Find the percent of options price.

$2,425.00 × 90.2% = $2,187.35

Step 3: Find the dealer's cost.

Percent of Base Price	+	Percent of Options Price	+	Destination Charge		
$35,988.57	+	$2,187.35	+	$850.00	=	**$39,025.92 dealer's cost**

Concept CHECK

Complete the problem. Check your answer in the back of the book.

1. At Lakeland Autos, the dealer's cost on an SUV is 88% of the $53,105 base price and 90% of the $1,785 options price plus a $640 destination charge. Find the dealer's cost for the SUV.

Need Help? Go to...

Workshop 36: Problem Solving Strategy: Using Simple Algebraic Operations, p. 74

EXAMPLE 2 Algebra

Abbie Williamson checked the Internet to find the dealer's cost of the domestic hybrid sedan she wanted to purchase. She found that the dealer's base cost was $21,971.90 and the dealer's cost for options was $2,459.60. The dealer would pass the $298.00 destination charge on to the consumer. If the percent of the dealer's cost is 82% and of dealer's cost of options is 86%, find the car's sticker price.

Step 1: Let b = Base price of the car

Dealer's Cost = Base Price × Dealer's Percent

$21,971.90 = b × 82%

Divide both sides by 0.82 → **$26,795.00 = b**

Step 2: Let s = Price of the options

Dealer's Options Cost = Total Options × Dealer's Percent

$2,459.60 = s × 86%

Divide both sides by 0.86 → **$2,860.00 = s**

Step 3: Find the sticker price.

Sticker Price = Base Price + Options + Destination Charge

$26,795.00 + $2,860.00 + $298.00 = **$29,953.00 sticker price**

Reading Math +−÷=

Percents with Decimals

In a percent with a decimal, the digit to the right of the decimal point stands for a fraction of 1%. Think of 87.7% as 87% plus another $\frac{7}{10}$ of a percent.

Concept CHECK

Complete the problem. Check your answer in the back of the book.

2. Omar and Zina Aboud found that the dealer's cost of the base price was $16,558.16 and the dealer's options cost was $611.60. The consumer paid the $475.00 destination charge. If the percent of the dealer's cost is 92% and the percent of dealer's options cost is 88%, find the car's sticker price.

Lesson Practice

For Problems 3–8, calculate the dealer's cost.

	Base Price	×	Dealer's Percent	+	Option Price	×	Dealer's Percent	+	Destination Charge	=	Dealer's Cost
3.	$25,800	×	85.0%	+	$2,200	×	88.0%	+	$660		
4.	36,890	×	87.0	+	5,680	×	91.0	+	980		
5.	48,990	×	91.5	+	1,200	×	85.0	+	770		

6. Gretchen Utley is considering the purchase of a station wagon. Its base price is $37,125, options total is $2,975, and destination charge is $870. The dealer's costs are 93% of base price and 91% of options price.

7. Lonnie Burrows is purchasing a sedan with a $29,375 base price, $4,200 options total, and $840 destination charge. The dealer's costs are 91.7% of base price and 83.3% of options price.

8. Elliott Sutor is considering a truck with a $23,855 base price, $2,856 options total, and a $910 destination charge. The dealer's costs are 90.5% of the base price and 87% of the options price.

9. Jace Fontana is looking at a new sedan with a $27,680 base price, $2,495 options total, and a $680 destination charge. The dealer's costs are 92.5% of the base price and 88.3% of the options price. What are the car's **(a)** total sticker price and **(b)** dealer's cost?

Did You Know?

SUV Prices Recent reports show that the most expensive SUV in the U.S. market is the Mercedes-Benz G55 AMG that has a price of $112,727. A fully-loaded edition of this vehicle includes heated seats and steering wheel, hands-free communication system, DVD-based navigation system, digital surround sound, and satellite radio.

10. Poloma Caetano is considering the purchase of a large SUV. She sees one with a $38,988 base price, $3,275 options total, and $735 destination charge. She estimates the dealer's costs as 88% of the base price and 80% of the options price. If Poloma offers the dealer $250 above the estimated dealer's cost, what is her offer?

11. Deanne Baldwin offered an automobile dealer $150 over the estimated dealer's cost on a car with a base price of $24,495 and options total $1,600. The dealer's costs were 89.7% of the base price and 81.0% of the options. The destination charge was $720. What was her offer?

H.O.T. Problems

12. **CHALLENGE PROBLEM** Evander King is ordering a luxury convertible. The base price is $81,975. Options include satellite radio, $475; keyless entry, $555; navigation system, $1,250; and custom paint, $983. The destination charge is $890. The dealer's costs are 90% of the base price and 88% of the options price. The dealer will sell Evander the car for $200 more than the dealer's cost plus a 6% sales tax. What is the total cost of the convertible, including tax?

13. **ALGEBRA** Joe Dooley checked the Internet to find the dealer's cost of a new truck. He found that the dealer's costs were $14,772.60 of base price and $833.00 of options price. The destination charge was $250.00. If the dealer's costs are 87% of base price and 85% of options, find the truck's sticker price.

14. **ALGEBRA** Di Lanier has her eye on a four-door sedan in the dealer's showroom. She checks the Internet to find that the dealer's costs are $19,972.58 base price, and options are moon roof wind deflector, $84.00; emergency aid package, $117.60; and floor mats, $147.00. The destination charge is $598.00. The dealer's cost of base price is 82% and of options is 84%. If Di pays the sticker price plus a 6% sales tax, what is her cost?

Spiral Review

Find the percent. (Skill 30)

15. 15% of 980   16. 22% of 756   17. 78% of 3,440

18. **ALGEBRA** Todd Hess found an ad this week stating "Save $125.00 on area rugs. All 10' by 12' area rugs marked down 35%." What is a 10' by 12' area rug's regular selling price? (Lesson 6.6)

19. Sara Lucas is a lifeguard. She earns $8.25 per hour. This week she worked $37\frac{1}{2}$ hours. What is her straight-time pay for the week? (Lesson 1.1)

GET READY for the Next Lesson

PREREQUISITE SKILL Subtracting Whole Numbers (Skill 4)

Subtract.

20. 4,850 − 561   21. 6,334 − 3,140   22. 4,445 − 1,729

LESSON 9.3

Purchasing a Used Vehicle

Lesson Objective
Calculate the average retail price or wholesale price of a used vehicle.

Content Vocabulary
- used-vehicle guide

GET READY for the Lesson

Why do you think people buy used vehicles?

A buyer's guide gives information about a used car's warranty, if any, and some of the major mechanical and electrical problems it has.

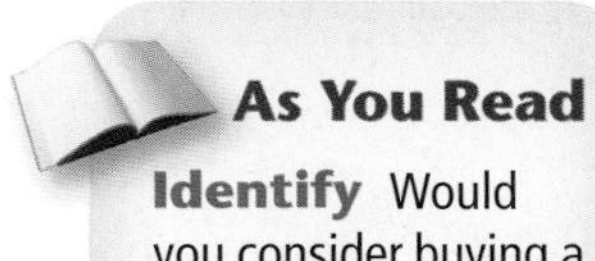

As You Read

Identify Would you consider buying a used vehicle?

Purchasing a Used Vehicle Dealers must display a buyer's guide sticker in the window of a used vehicle for sale. Dealers usually advertise used vehicles for prices that are higher than they expect you to pay. A **used-vehicle guide** gives the average prices for used vehicles. The National Automobile Dealers Association (NADA) and Vehicle Market Research (VMR) guides **published** monthly give the average prices for vehicles purchased from dealers during the previous month. Information from Web sites such as Kelley Blue Book and Edmunds can help you decide how much to pay for a used vehicle.

A merchant makes a *retail* sale directly to the customer. Merchants buy at a *wholesale* price. Calculate the average retail price of a used vehicle using this formula:

Average Retail Price = Average Retail Value + Additional Options − Options Deductions − Mileage Deduction

Need Help? Go to...
- Workshop 4: Adding Decimals, p. 10
- Workshop 5: Subtracting Decimals, p. 12
- Application C: Tables and Charts, p. AP3

EXAMPLE 1

Caryn Demaline wants to purchase a 4-year-old Palomino V8 four-door sedan advertised for $16,450. It has a DVD player, power mirrors, and a power sunroof but no air conditioning. It has been driven 51,760 miles. Use the data in **Figure 9.2** on page 348 to find the average retail price Caryn should keep in mind when she makes an offer for the vehicle.

Find the average retail price.

Average Retail Price = Average Retail Value + Additional Options − Options Deductions − Mileage Deductions

$16,675 + ($540 + 250 + 475) − $850 − $675 =

$16,675 + $1,265 − $850 − $675 = **$16,415 average retail value**

Caryn needs to remember the $16,450 asking price and the $16,415 average retail price.

540 [+] 250 [+] 475 [M+] 1265 16675 [+] [RM] 1265 [−] 850 [−] 675 [=] 16415

Dave Moyer.

Figure 9.2

Palomino Four-Year-Old Sedan	Average Retail Value	Average Wholesale Value
V6 Four-Door	$15,500	$13,100
V8 Four-Door	16,675	13,270
Adjustments for Retail or Wholesale		**Mileage Deduction**
Deduct w/o Air Conditioning	$850	40,001–50,000 $175
Deduct Manual Transmission	650	50,001–60,000 $675
Add DVD Player	540	60,001–70,000 $1,225
Add Power Mirrors	250	70,001–80,000 $1,775
Add Leather Seats	240	80,001–90,000 $2,025
Add Front Bucket Seats	220	90,001–100,000 $2,200
Add Power Sunroof	475	More than 100,001 $2,200 + $150 per 10,000
Add Aluminum Wheels	120	

Study Tip

Checking Answers

If answers to examples and exercises are available in a book, always check them as soon as you are satisfied with your answer. Immediate feedback helps you learn.

Concept CHECK

Use Figure 9.2 to complete the problem. Check your answer in the back of the book.

1. Find the average retail price for a 4-year old V6 four-door sedan with air conditioning, power mirrors, leather seats, power sunroof, and aluminum wheels. It has been driven 42,510 miles.

EXAMPLE 2

Using **Figure 9.2,** find the average wholesale price for a 4-year-old V8 four-door that has no air conditioning but does have a DVD player and a power sunroof. It has 63,580 miles.

Average Wholesale Price = Average Wholesale Value + Additional Options − Options Deductions − Mileage Deductions

$13,270 + ($540 + 475) − $850 − $1,225

$13,270 + $1,015 − $850 − $1,225 = **$12,210 average wholesale price**

Concept CHECK

Use Figure 9.2 to complete problems 2 and 3. Check your answers in the back of the book.

2. Find the average wholesale price for a used V6 four-door sedan with air conditioning, leather seats, front bucket seats, power sunroof, and aluminum wheels. It has 75,500 miles.
3. Jacob North wants to buy a four-year-old Palomino sedan. His friend has a V8 four-door that he will sell Jacob at wholesale. The car has a manual transmission, a DVD player, leather seats, a power sunroof and 53,480 miles. Premier Certified Pre-Owned Autos has a V6 four-door that is being sold at retail. That car has power mirrors, front bucket seats, aluminum wheels, and 73,840 miles. It does not have air conditioning. Which car will cost Jacob less and how much less?

Lesson Practice

For Problems 4–8, use Figure 9.2 to find the average retail value and the average retail price.

	Model	Average Retail Value	A/C	DVD Player	Power Mirror	Leather Seats	Bucket Seats	Power Sunroof	Mileage	Average Retail Price
4.	V6 four-dr	**a.** $	Yes	No	Yes	No	Yes	No	35,000	**b.** $
5.	V6 four-dr	**a.**	No	No	No	Yes	No	Yes	58,400	**b.**
6.	V8 four-dr	**a.**	Yes	Yes	Yes	Yes	No	Yes	80,255	**b.**

Did You Know?
Loudest Car Stereos
Wayne Harris won the 1985 "Thunder on Wheels" competition with a 1960 Cadillac hearse equipped with four 12-inch woofers, seven amplifiers, and 23 speakers, all monitored and activated by a computer.

7. Monica Rizzo wants to buy a 4-year-old V6 four-door sedan that has 52,686 miles. It has manual transmission, a DVD player, leather seats, front bucket seats, and power sunroof but no air conditioning.

8. Kurt Sorensen is looking at a 4-year-old V8 four-door sedan that has 80,575 miles. It also has a DVD player, power mirrors, leather seats, front bucket seats, and a power sunroof.

9. Use **Figure 9.2** to calculate the average wholesale price for Kordell Henson's 4-year-old V6 four-door sedan. It has 126,540 miles, manual transmission, leather seats, a DVD player, power sunroof, aluminum wheels, and bucket seats.

10. CHALLENGE PROBLEM Yen Luong owns a used pickup truck that she wants to sell. A used-vehicle guide shows that its average retail value is $17,600. She adds $1,700 for 4-wheel drive, $475 for an entertainment system, $800 for a special trim package, and $225 for power locks. She also adds $125 for a sliding rear window, $325 for a towing package, $250 for power windows, and $3,125 for a diesel engine. She deducts $675 for having a manual transmission. She adds $450 for having less than the expected mileage. What is the average retail price of Yen's vehicle?

Spiral Review

Subtract. (Skill 4)

11. 8,450 − 475 **12.** 3,890 − 2,530 **13.** 2,205 − 225

14. Find Randall Kramer's average monthly expenditure if his expenses were: October, $1,423; November, $1,164; December, $1,987. (Lesson 3.1)

15. Your checking account balance is $226.34 on June 4. You write a $15.28 check on June 9 and a $61.80 check on June 14. On June 15, you deposit your $228.23 paycheck. What is your checking account balance then? (Lesson 4.3)

GET READY for the Next Lesson

PREREQUISITE SKILL Multiplying Decimals (Skill 8)

Multiply.

16. 2.46×5.93 **17.** 7.33×8.50 **18.** 44.8×56.1

19. 270.76×27.06 **20.** 10.73×6.72 **21.** 93.10×94.04

LESSON 9.4

Vehicle Insurance

Lesson Objective
Use tables to compute the annual premium for vehicle insurance.

Content Vocabulary
- liability insurance
- collision insurance
- comprehensive insurance
- deductible clause
- annual premium

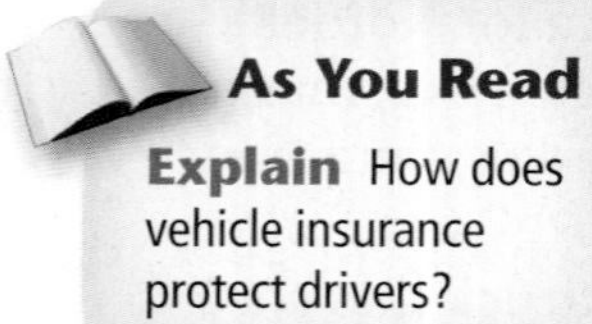

As You Read
Explain How does vehicle insurance protect drivers?

GET READY for the Lesson

Why does a car owner need insurance?

Judy Watson's car hit another car. She was glad she had good insurance when she found out how much the repairs would cost.

Buying Vehicle Insurance If your vehicle is involved in an accident, it can cause bodily **injury** to the people involved, property damage to other vehicles or property, such as light poles, and collision damage to your vehicle. Vehicle owners carry insurance to cover the costs associated with an accident.

Liability insurance coverage provides financial protection to the policyholder against claims for bodily injury and property damage as a result of an accident. The combined coverage is often listed as 100/300/50. The 100/300 refers to the bodily injury coverage and means:

The insurance company will pay up to **$100,000** to any *one person injured.*	→ 100/300 ←	The insurance company pays up to **$300,000** if *more than one* person is injured.

The *50* refers to a property damage limit of $50,000.

In addition to liability insurance, you also will need to consider carrying two other types of insurance on your vehicle. **Collision insurance** pays for damage to the insured vehicle caused by a collision with another motor vehicle or an object such as a telephone pole. **Comprehensive insurance** pays for damage to the insured vehicle from losses due to fire, vandalism, theft, and just about any cause other than a collision.

Both collision and comprehensive insurance may have a **deductible clause**. This is a clause in an insurance policy that requires the insured to pay a certain amount to cover repairs before the insurance company pays. For example, if your insurance policy states that you have a $500-deductible clause, this means that you pay the first $500 of the repair bill. If your total repair bill is $4,400, you have to pay $500 and the insurance company pays the remaining amount ($3,900 in this example).

The annual *base premium* determines the cost of your vehicle insurance. It involves three factors:

- the amount of insurance you carry,
- how old your vehicle is, and
- the insurance-rating group depending on the size and value of your vehicle.

RubberBall/age fotostock.

The **annual premium** is the amount you pay each year for insurance coverage. These factors determine your annual premium:

1. The cost of the *annual base premium,* which depends on the amount and type of coverage you carry.
2. The *driver-rating factor,* which depends on your age, marital status, number of miles you drive each week, whether you drive a long distance to work, and if you use your vehicle for pleasure or business.

If several people drive your vehicle, the insurance company uses the highest driver-rating factor among them to determine the annual premium. Insurance companies use tables to determine your basic premium. You use these two formulas to determine the annual premium:

$$\text{Annual Base Premium} = \text{Liability Premium} + \text{Collision Premium} + \text{Comprehensive Premium}$$

$$\text{Annual Premium} = \text{Annual Base Premium} \times \text{Driver-Rating Factor}$$

EXAMPLE

Della Welch is the principal operator of her vehicle. Her driver-rating factor is 2.20. Her insurance includes 50/100 bodily injury and $50,000 property damage. Her vehicle is in age group A and insurance-rating group 13 (or A, 13). She has $50-deductible comprehensive and $50-deductible collision insurance. What is her annual base premium? What is her annual premium? Use **Figure 9.3** to find insurance rates.

Figure 9.3

Annual Liability Premium

Property Damage Limits	Bodily Injury Limits					
	25/50	25/100	50/100	100/200	100/300	300/300
$ 25,000	$299	$319	$309	$365	$374	$416
50,000	307	326	344	374	383	425
100,000	464	338	357	386	394	437

Collision and Comprehensive Premium

Coverage	Age Group	Insurance Rating Group					
		10	11	12	13	14	15
Collision $50 Deductible	A	$236	$257	$279	$300	$322	$343
	B	224	243	264	284	305	325
	C	213	233	253	272	291	310
	D	203	222	240	259	277	296
Comprehensive $50 Deductible	A	$80	$86	$99	$113	$127	$142
	B	68	82	94	107	121	134
	C	65	77	90	102	115	129
	D	62	73	86	97	110	122

Continued on next page

Step 1: Find the annual base premium.

Liability Premium + Collision Premium + Comprehensive Premium

$344 + $300 + $113 = **$757 annual basic premium**

Step 2: Find the annual premium.

Base Premium × Driver-Rating Factor

$757.00 × 2.20 = **$1,665.40 annual premium**

344 + 300 + 113 = 757 × 2.2 = 1665.40

Use Figure 9.3 on page 351 to find the (a) annual base premium and (b) annual premium. Check your answers in the back of the book.

1. Fran Nader's insurance covers bodily injury 25/100 and $100,000 property damage. It has a $50-deductible comprehensive and a $50-deductible collision. Her car is in age group C and insurance-rating group 10 (or C, 10), and her driver-rating factor is 1.50.

Words for Time Periods
Remember that *annual* means "once yearly."

Lesson Practice

For Problems 2–10, determine the (a) annual base premium and (b) the annual premium. Use Figure 9.3 on page 351 for insurance premiums. All policies have a $50 deductible for both comprehensive and collision.

2. Pierce Keenan has a 1.30 driver-rating factor and his car is in age group A and insurance-rating group 14. The coverage he wants is 50/100 bodily injury and $25,000 for property damage.
3. Danielle Cecil's driver-rating factor is 1.60 and her car is in age group D and insurance-rating group 12. She wants 100/300 bodily injury and $50,000 property damage coverage.
4. Marcy Kirkpatrick uses her vehicle primarily for pleasure. She has 100/200 bodily injury and $25,000 property damage coverage. Because of her excellent driving record, her driver-rating factor is 1.00. Her vehicle is classified as D, 14.
5. Jill Wilson uses her vehicle primarily for pleasure. She has 100/300 bodily injury, and $50,000 property damage coverage. Because of her excellent driving record, her driver-rating factor is 1.00. Her vehicle is classified as A, 14.
6. Samuel Haskins uses his minivan primarily for his delivery business. He has 100/300 bodily injury, and $100,000 property damage coverage. Because of his business use, his driver-rating factor is 3.55. His vehicle is classified A, 15.
7. Ruby Mason uses her sports car mainly for pleasure. She has 100/200 bodily injury, and $100,000 property damage coverage. Her driver-rating factor is 2.65 and her sports car is classified as B, 15.

8. Deon Hanson uses his silver minivan primarily for business. He has 300/300 bodily injury and $100,000 property damage coverage. Because of his business use, his driver-rating factor is 3.35. His vehicle is classified B, 15.

9. Magdalena Castillo uses her SUV mainly for pleasure. She has 100/300 bodily injury and $50,000 property damage coverage. Her driver-rating factor is 2.15, and her SUV is classified as C, 15.

10. Carl Adams uses his minivan to deliver office supplies. He has 100/200 bodily injury and $50,000 property damage coverage. Because of the business use of his van, his driver-rating factor is 3.10. His van is classified as D, 14.

Did You Know?
Favorite Vehicle Colors
According to a recent survey, silver was the most popular automobile color in North America for five years in a row, covering 26% of vehicles.

H.O.T. Problems

11. **CHALLENGE PROBLEM** Ned Bishop delivers firewood to retail outlets in his truck. His driver-rating factor is 3.15. His insurance coverage includes 25/100 bodily injury and $25,000 property damage. He has $50-deductible comprehensive and $50-deductible collision. His truck is in age group D and insurance-rating group 10. Calculate his annual **(a)** base premium and **(b)** premium and then **(c)** his annual premium if he gets a 20% discount by increasing his deductible to $200.

12. **CHALLENGE PROBLEM** Pamela Kruse drives to and from work in her red sports car. Her driver-rating factor is 4.85. Her insurance coverage includes 100/200 bodily injury and $100,000 property damage. She has $50-deductible comprehensive and $50-deductible collision coverage. Her car is in age group A and insurance-rating group 13. How much more will her annual premium be if she increases the liability coverage to 300/300/100?

Spiral Review

Multiply. (Skill 8)

13. 1.25 × 79.90 **14.** 2.40 × 360 **15.** 3.90 × 67.70

16. Ona Scully's charge account statement showed a previous balance of $523.94, a finance charge of $8.96, new purchases of $154.21, $34.28, and $75.21, a credit of $45.16, and a $250.00 payment. What is her new balance? (Lesson 7.1)

17. **ALGEBRA** Matthew Epstein sells appliances. He receives weekly pay on a straight commission of 5% on sales up to $5,000 and 6% on sales over $5,000. One week Matthew had a gross pay of $652. What was his sales total for that week? (Lesson 1.7)

GET READY for the Next Lesson

PREREQUISITE SKILL Dividing (Decimal Remainder) (Skill 10)

Divide. Round answers to the nearest hundredth.

18. 751 ÷ 305
19. 846 ÷ 120
20. 688 ÷ 321
21. 5,489 ÷ 294
22. 776 ÷ 492
23. 963 ÷ 3,500

Operating and Maintaining a Vehicle

Lesson Objective
Compute the total cost per mile of operating and maintaining a vehicle.

Content Vocabulary
- variable costs
- fixed costs
- depreciation

As You Read
Summarize
What is the difference between variable and fixed costs?

GET READY for the Lesson

If you could buy a new vehicle today, how long would you want to keep it?

Sam and Kate Hines often drive their SUV to soccer games out of town. They keep their vehicle in good condition to avoid problems while traveling long distances.

moodboard/Alamy

Operating and Maintaining Your Vehicle Although the **media** focuses a significant amount of attention on gasoline prices, operating and maintaining a vehicle involves numerous costs. They can be classified as variable costs and fixed costs. **Variable costs** increase as the number of miles driven increase. They include the cost of gasoline, oil, filters, tires, and repairs. **Fixed costs** remain about the same regardless of how many miles you drive. They include insurance, registration fees, loan interest, and depreciation. **Depreciation** is the decrease in the value of your vehicle from one year to the next because of its age and condition. You can compute the depreciation using this formula:

$$\text{Depreciation} = \frac{\text{Purchase Price} - \text{Today's Value}}{\text{Number of Years Owned}}$$

You use the cost per mile of operating a vehicle to compare the costs of driving various vehicles. Calculate the cost per mile as follows:

$$\text{Cost per Mile} = \frac{\text{Annual Variable Cost} + \text{Annual Fixed Cost}}{\text{Number of Miles}}$$

Need Help? Go to...
Workshop 7: Dividing Decimals, p. 16
Skill 2: Rounding Numbers, p. SK3

EXAMPLE 1

Chantal Jones purchased a new two-door coupe for $24,590 two years ago. She drove 14,322 miles last year and kept a record of all auto expenses. She estimates the vehicle's present value at $19,219. Calculate her **(a)** depreciation, **(b)** total variable costs, **(c)** total fixed costs, and **(d)** cost per mile to operate her vehicle last year.

Variable Costs		Fixed Costs	
Gasoline	$1,576.24	Insurance	$985.00
Oil Changes	71.85	License/registration	125.63
Maintenance	154.36	Loan Interest	380.30
Cleaning, tolls and Parking	322.65	Depreciation	a.
Total	b. $	**Total**	c. $

Study Tip

Working with Numbers

When performing paper and pencil calculations with numbers representing money, make sure you align them by place value to ensure accuracy.

Step 1: Compute the annual depreciation

$$\text{Annual Depreciation} = \frac{\text{Purchase Price} - \text{Today's Value}}{\text{Number of Years Owned}}$$

$$= \frac{\$24{,}590.00 - \$19{,}219.00}{2} = \frac{\$5{,}371.00}{2}$$

$$= \mathbf{\$2{,}685.50}$$

Step 2: Total Variable Costs = $1,576.24 + 71.85 + 154.36 + 322.65 = $2,125.10

Step 3: Total Fixed Costs = $985 + 125.63 + 380.30 + 2,685.50 = $4,176.43

Step 4: Compute the Cost per Mile

$$\text{Cost per Mile} = \frac{\text{Annual Variable Cost} + \text{Annual Fixed Cost}}{\text{Number of Miles}}$$

$$= \frac{\$2{,}125.10 + \$4{,}176.43}{14{,}322.00} = \frac{\$6{,}301.53}{14{,}322.00} = \$0.43999$$

$$= \mathbf{\$0.44}$$

Concept CHECK

Complete the problem. Check your answer in the back of the book.

1. DeeDee Farrar purchased a new car 3 years ago for $33,500.00. Its current value estimate is $19,900.00. Annual variable costs this year were $995.60. The cost of insurance this year was $2,350.00, registration was $132.50, and loan interest totaled $1,080.00. She drove 13,540 miles this year. Compute the **(a)** depreciation, **(b)** annual fixed costs, and **(c)** cost per mile.

Need Help? Go to...
Workshop 38: Problem-Solving Strategy: Writing an Equation, p. 78

EXAMPLE 2 Algebra

Tiffany East estimates that she will drive 15,000 miles during the year and will have $2,400.00 in annual fixed costs. If her goal is to have a cost per mile of $0.30 or less for her compact car, what is the maximum annual variable cost she can have?

Let x = Annual variable cost

$$\text{Cost per Mile} = \frac{\text{Annual Variable Cost} + \text{Annual Fixed Cost}}{\text{Number of Miles}}$$

$$\$0.30 = \frac{x + \$2{,}400}{15{,}000}$$

Multiply both sides by 15,000 →

$$4{,}500 = x + \$2{,}400$$

Subtract $2,400 from both sides →

$$\mathbf{\$2{,}100} = x$$

Tiffany must have annual variable costs of $2,100 or less.

Concept CHECK

Complete the problem. Check your answer in the back of the book.

2. Anwar Mabak incurs $2,818.00 in annual fixed costs to operate his car. He estimates that he will drive 22,500 miles during the year. What are his annual variable costs if his cost per mile is $0.32?

Lesson Practice

For Problems 3–7, determine (a) the total annual cost and (b) the cost per mile to the nearest cent.

	Annual Variable Costs		Annual Fixed Costs		Total Annual Cost	Miles Driven	Cost per Mile
3.	$1,000.00	+	$1,250.00	=	**a.** $	6,000	**b.** $
4.	4,530.00	+	3,750.00	=	**a.**	15,000	**b.**

Did You Know?

Fuel Economy **Which of the tips for conserving fuel actually work? According to one testing team, the best ways to stretch your gasoline dollars include not accelerating aggressively (31% average fuel savings) and avoiding idling for more than one minute (19%).**

5. Jamar Burr drove 9,500 miles in his car last year. The total of fixed costs was $1,215 and of variable costs was $1,985.

6. Liz Nolan drove 34,500 miles last year. The total of fixed costs was $9,916 and of variable costs was $4,897.

7. Nina Karas purchased a used car 3 years ago for $11,425.00. Its current value is $6,897.00. Annual variable costs this year are gasoline, $2,524.90; oil and filters, $145.21; new battery, $65.45; and transmission repair $981.33. This year insurance cost $1,546.00, registration was $114.95, and loan interest totaled $457.88. Nina drove 19,214 miles this year. Compute the **(a)** depreciation, **(b)** annual costs, and **(c)** cost per mile.

8. Last year Carlito Olmstead drove 142,400 miles in the delivery van that he purchased 2 years ago for $22,565.00. It is now worth $10,320.00. His variable costs this year were gasoline $28,365.21, oil and filters $598.10, 2 sets of tires $897.60, battery $85.95, and maintenance $1,256.54. His insurance cost $2,884.26, registration was $159.65, and loan interest was $658.93. What was the cost per mile for him to operate his van?

9. CHALLENGE PROBLEM John Baker is considering two cars. The first is a new four-door, 2.3 liter, 4-cylinder gas engine sedan for $21,735.00. The gas engine sedan gets 21 miles per gallon (mpg) in city driving and 31 in highway driving. The other is a new four-door, 2.3 liter, 4-cylinder gas/electric hybrid sedan for $27,040.00. Its mpg is 33 in city and 34 in highway driving. John drives about 15,000 miles per year equally divided between city driving and highway driving. He decides to buy the hybrid. If he can buy gas for $4.08 per gallon, how long would it take for his gas savings to match the price difference?

10. ALGEBRA Rachel Kauffman drove her SUV 17,600 miles last year. If her cost per mile was $0.47 and her annual variable costs were $48.00 more than her annual fixed costs, find her **(a)** annual variable costs and **(b)** annual fixed costs.

Spiral Review

Round to the nearest hundredth. (Skill 2)

11. 21.751 **12.** 4.3981 **13.** 0.3179

14. Taylor Hardy deposited $980 for 6 months at 5%. She made no other deposits or withdrawals; **(a)** how much simple interest did her money earn and **(b)** what was the amount in the account? (Lesson 5.4)

GET READY for the Next Lesson

PREREQUISITE SKILL Multiplying Decimals (Skill 8)

15. 34.66×9 **16.** 25.19×2 **17.** 56.18×4 **18.** 65.92×5

LESSON 9.6

Leasing a Vehicle

Lesson Objective
Calculate the total cost of leasing a vehicle.

Content Vocabulary
- lease
- closed-end lease
- open-end lease

GET READY for the Lesson

Would you consider changing your driving habits to drive fewer miles?

Fizzah Hopkins had become aware of the numerous short trips she made to the grocery, drug, and convenience stores. She decided to plan ahead so that she could make fewer trips and lower her mileage.

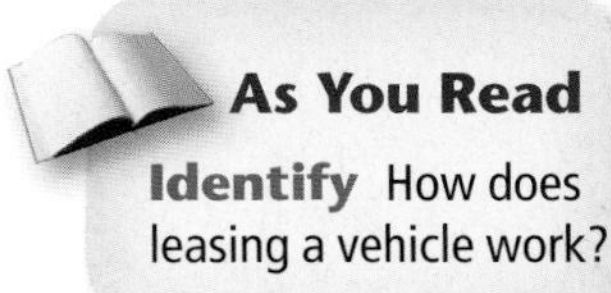

As You Read
Identify How does leasing a vehicle work?

Leasing a Vehicle Rather than purchase a vehicle, you might want to lease one. When you **lease** a vehicle, you make monthly payments to the leasing company, the dealer, or the bank for two to five years. You do not own the vehicle but are essentially renting it. At the end of the lease, you may either return the vehicle to the leasing company or purchase it.

The most common lease is a **closed-end lease**, which is a contract that allows you to use a vehicle for a set time period by making a specified number of payments. You return it owing nothing unless it is damaged beyond fair wear and tear or exceeds a mileage limit. If you damage the vehicle or exceed the mileage limit, then you owe money to the leasing company.

Another type of lease is an **open-end lease**. It is also a contract allowing you to use a vehicle for a set time period by making a specified number of payments. At lease end, you can buy it for its residual value. The residual value is the vehicle's expected value at the end of the lease period and is often established at the lease signing. With either the closed-end lease or the open-end lease, you must pay all monthly payments, a security deposit, a title fee, and a **license** fee.

You calculate the total cost of the lease using this formula:

$$\text{Total Lease Cost} = \left(\text{Number of Payments} \times \text{Amount of Payment}\right) + \text{Deposit} + \text{Title Fee} + \text{License Fee}$$

Need Help? Go to...
Workshop 38: Problem-Solving Strategy: Writing an Equation, p. 78

EXAMPLE 1

Edwin Reid leases a pickup truck to use in his lawn care business. He pays a \$2,000 deposit, \$450 per month for 36 months, and an \$80 title fee and a \$240 license fee. What is his total lease cost?

Find the total lease cost.

$$\left(\text{Number of Payments} \times \text{Amount of Payment}\right) + \text{Deposit} + \text{Title Fee} + \text{License Fee} + \text{Tax [when applicable]}$$

$$(36 \times \$450) + \$2{,}000 + \$80 + \$240$$

$$\$16{,}200 + \$2{,}000 + \$80 + \$240 = \textbf{\$18,520 total lease cost}$$

Concept CHECK

Find the total lease cost. Check your answers in the back of the book.

1. Cara Green leased a convertible by making a \$3,000.00 deposit and paying \$349.00 per month for 36 months, an \$80.00 title fee, and a \$112.86 license fee.
2. Haru Ito leased a sedan by depositing \$1,500.00 and paying \$450.00 per month for 39 months, a \$145.00 title fee, and a \$99.95 license fee.

EXAMPLE 2 Algebra

William Tracey is leasing a midsize four-door sports sedan. The \$1,999.00 due at signing includes title and fees. His monthly lease payment is \$169.00 plus 6% sales tax. The leasing company allows 10,500 miles per year with a \$0.15 per mile overage charge. If the total lease cost is \$6,298.36, for how many months does the lease last?

Let n = Number of months the lease will last

Total Lease Cost = (Number of Payments × Amount of Payment) + Deposit + Title Fee + License Fee + Tax

\$6,298.36 = n ×[\$169.00 + (\$169.00 × 6%)] + \$1,999.00

Multiply and combine like terms → \$6,298.36 = \$179.14n + \$1,999

Subtract \$1,999 from both sides → \$4,299.36 = \$179.14n

Divide both sides by \$179.14 → 24 = n

William's lease is for 24 months.

Study Tip

Problem Solving

When preparing to solve a word problem, list the information from the problem that you will need to solve it.

Concept CHECK

Complete the problem. Check your answer in the back of the book.

3. Dantelle Moss considers leasing a sports coupe with a \$4,324.00 deposit due at signing. Each monthly payment is \$589.00 plus 7% sales tax. Dantelle would be responsible for \$0.30 per mile more than 10,000 miles driven per year. If the total lease cost is \$34,575.04, for how many months does the lease run?

Lesson Practice

For Problems 4–9, find the (a) total amount of payments and (b) total lease cost.

	(Number of Payments	×	Amount of Payment	=	Total Amount of Payments)	+	Deposit	+	Title Fee	+	License Fee	=	Total Lease Cost
4.	24	×	\$219	=	a. \$	+	\$1,419	+	\$ 80	+	\$ 65	=	b. \$
5.	48	×	299	=	a.	+	\$ 749	+	\$ 95	+	\$ 28	=	b.
6.	54	×	589	=	a.	+	\$1,860	+	120	+	\$126	=	b.
7.	60	×	345	=	a.	+	\$2,450	+	140	+	\$ 98	=	b.

Did You Know?

Leasing Popularity

According to a recent survey, leases account for 20% of all U.S. vehicles, including 75% of luxury vehicles.

8. Kirk Ryder agreed to a deposit of $475 and 48 payments of $475 to lease a luxury car. He paid the $65 title fee and $85 license fee.
9. Suzi Doohan leased an SUV by making a $2,295.00 deposit and agreeing to 39 payments of $421.38. She also paid the $160.00 title fee and $271.00 license fee.
10. Teneshia Clayton has an open-end lease for an SUV that she uses for her fabric store. The lease costs $421.38 a month for 48 months. She paid a $2,500.00 deposit, an $85 title fee, and a $235.00 license fee. At the end of the lease, she can buy the vehicle for its $15,446.00 residual value. What is the total **(a)** to lease and **(b)** to buy the vehicle?
11. Nikolai Rakov leases a vehicle for $399.00 a month for 48 months. He pays a deposit of $1,225.00, an $85.00 title fee, and a $160.00 license fee. The lease stipulates a $0.20 per mile charge for all miles more than 60,000 driven. If he drives the vehicle 68,515 miles, what is the total cost of leasing the vehicle?

H.O.T. Problems

12. **CHALLENGE PROBLEM** Alicia Hanover can lease a sedan for $454.95 a month for 48 months. She must pay a $250.00 deposit, a $75.00 title fee, and a $120.00 license fee. After 48 months, the sedan will be worth $4,117.00. Alternately, she can purchase the vehicle for $478.96 a month for 48 months plus a $978.00 down payment and the same title and license fees. Is it less expensive to purchase it as described or at the end of the open-end lease?
13. **ALGEBRA** For its year-end model clearance sale, a new auto dealership is offering a 2-year lease with $1,999.00 due at signing, which includes all taxes, title, and fees. The lessee is responsible for $0.12 per mile more than 12,000 miles driven per year and must have approved credit. If the total lease cost is $6,775.00, how much is the monthly lease payment?

Spiral Review

Multiply. (Skill 8)

14. 33.190×5 15. 29.95×4 16. 7×54.65

17. Len and Pat Mayfield are purchasing a swimming pool with an installment loan that has a 12% APR. The pool sells for $1,899.99. The store financing requires a 10% down payment and 12 monthly payments. What is the finance charge? (Lesson 8.3)
18. Stephanie Lamden purchases two dozen binders at $1.79 per binder, 8 packages of pens at $2.49 per package, and 4 packages of highlighters at $3.99 per package in Cleveland, Ohio, where the sales tax rate is 7.5%. What is the total purchase price? (Lesson 6.2)

GET READY for the Next Lesson

PREREQUISITE SKILL Adding Decimals (Skill 5)

Add.

19. $71.25 + 4.33 + 67.5$
20. $132.45 + 51.78 + 96.01 + 182.43$
21. $4.57 + 5.29 + 141.82 + 3.11$
22. $53.4 + 27.68 + 90.06 + 19.97$

Fancy/SuperStock

LESSON 9.7 Renting a Vehicle

Lesson Objective

Calculate the cost to rent a vehicle and the cost per mile to drive a rented vehicle.

Content Vocabulary

- rent

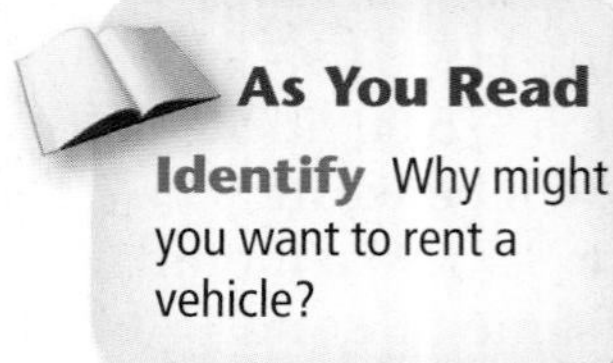

As You Read

Identify Why might you want to rent a vehicle?

GET READY for the Lesson

Would you consider purchasing a hybrid vehicle? Why or why not?

Robin Grady recently rented a hybrid car while on a business trip. She was very pleased with its operation and is thinking about purchasing one.

Renting a Vehicle From time to time, you may need to **rent** a vehicle, which means to use a vehicle by agreeing to pay a set fee. Some vehicle rental agencies charge a daily rate **plus** a per-mile rate. Others charge a daily rate with no mileage fee. In either case, you pay for the gasoline used.

You might also have to pay a collision damage waiver (CDW) fee on a rented vehicle. It requires you to pay a fee so that the rental company waives its right to recover from you losses for any physical damage that you cause. Use this formula to determine how much you are paying to rent per mile:

$$\text{Cost per Mile} = \frac{\text{Total Cost}}{\text{Number of Miles}}$$

EXAMPLE

Joe Wozniak rented a standard SUV in Cleveland for 3 days at \$49.95 per day plus \$0.20 per mile. He purchased the collision waiver for \$24.99 per day. Joe drove 468 miles and paid \$66.70 for gasoline. What is the: **(a)** total cost to rent the SUV, **(b)** cost per mile to rent the SUV?

Step 1: Find the total cost.

$$\text{Daily cost} + \text{Mileage cost} + \text{Collision waiver} + \text{Gasoline cost}$$
$$(\$49.95 \times 3) + (\$0.20 \times 468) + (\$24.99 \times 3) + \$66.70$$
$$= \$149.85 + \$93.60 + \$74.97 + \$66.70 = \mathbf{\$385.12}$$

total cost

Step 2: Find the cost per mile.

$$\text{Cost per Mile} = \frac{\text{Total Cost}}{\text{Number of Miles}} = \frac{\$385.12}{468} = \$0.8229 = \mathbf{\$0.82}$$

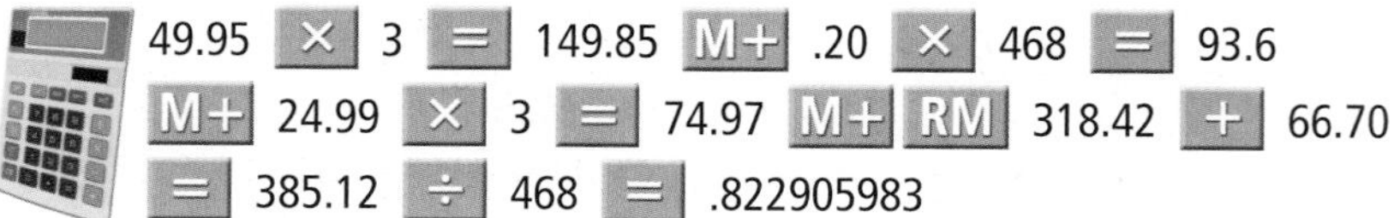

49.95 × 3 = 149.85 M+ .20 × 468 = 93.6 M+ 24.99 × 3 = 74.97 M+ RM 318.42 + 66.70 = 385.12 ÷ 468 = .822905983

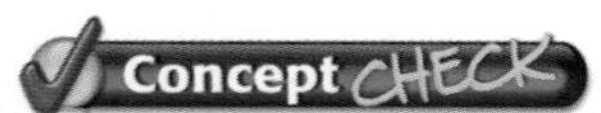

Calculate the (a) total cost and (b) cost per mile. Check your answers in the back of the book.

1. Winona Perry rents a car for $30.00 a day for 4 days plus $0.22 per mile and does not need CDW. She drives 430 miles and spends $59.90 on gasoline.
2. Wilson Swartz rents a car for 5 days at $51.29 a day and has unlimited miles. Wilson drives 198 miles and spends $29.90 on gasoline. The CDW fee is $15.50 per day.

GRAPHING CALCULATOR LAB

Graphing Functions

You are moving from an apartment to a house and are planning to rent a 24-foot moving truck. You have two options.

Rent-a-Truck charges $39.95 plus $0.79 per mile.
Tom's Rentals charges $49.95 plus $0.59 per mile.
For what number of miles is the price the same?

Step 1: Write an equation to represent each company.

Rent a Truck: $39.95 + 0.79x$
Tom's Rentals: $49.95 + 0.59x$

Step 2: Enter each equation into the calculator:

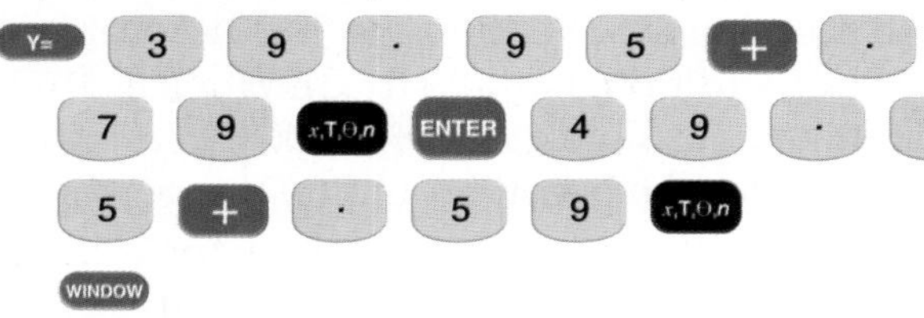

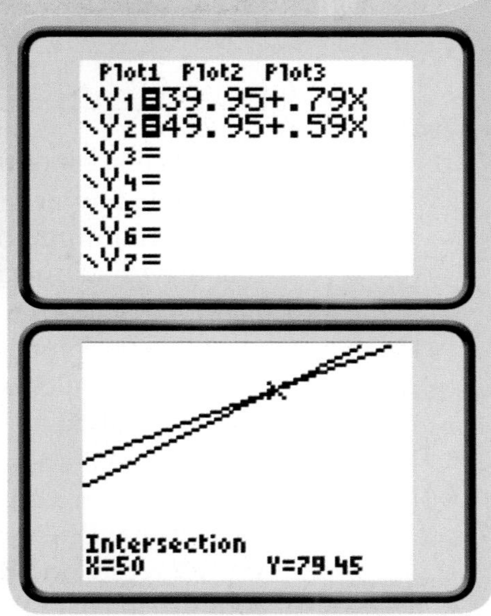

WINDOW

Set the viewing window to [0, 100, 5, 0, 100, 5]

Step 3: Graph each equation: GRAPH

Step 4: To determine the number of miles when the price is the same, find the point of intersection. Press:

Think and Discuss

1. Describe the display of the first calculator screen.
2. Describe the display of the second calculator screen.
3. For what number of miles is the price the same? What is the cost?
4. Which company is the better deal if you only drive the moving van 40 miles? Explain.
5. For how many miles is Tom's Rentals a better deal for a 16 foot truck? Explain.
   - Rent-a-Truck charges $25.95 plus $0.79 per mile.
   - Tom's Rentals charges $39.95 plus $0.59 per mile.

Reading Math

Reading Lines In a fraction, a horizontal line indicates division. In a stacked addition, subtraction, or multiplication problem, the sum, difference, or product is written below the line.

Lesson Practice

For Problems, 3–5 find the (a) total cost and (b) cost per mile.

	(Total Daily Cost	+	Total Mileage Cost	+	Gasoline Cost	=	Total Cost)	÷	Miles Driven	=	Cost per Mile
3.	($ 21.00	+	$94.00	+	$73.89	=	a. $)	÷	500	=	b. $
4.	(79.95	+	74.40	+	74.53	=	a.)	÷	620	=	b.
5.	(102.60	+	63.55	+	75.67	=	a.)	÷	420	=	b.

For Problems 6–10, find the (a) total cost and (b) cost per mile.

	(Rental Cost	+	Gasoline Cost	=	Total Cost)	÷	Miles Driven	=	Cost per Mile
6.	($ 66.50	+	$40.39	=	a. $)	÷	240	=	b. $
7.	(96.00	+	45.98	=	a.)	÷	300	=	b.
8.	(154.75	+	78.27	=	a.)	÷	476	=	b.

9. Ranjini Sangwar rents a compact car for 2 days in Chicago for $32.95 a day with unlimited miles. She also pays a CDW fee of $21.50 per day. She drives 70 miles each day and pays $18.39 for gasoline.

10. Jacinto Corado rented a minivan for 4 days in Tampa, Florida, for $88.00 a day plus $0.20 a mile for all miles over 200. He drove 75, 120, 85, and 140 miles on the days rented. He paid a CDW fee of $18.50 per day and $61.83 for gasoline.

11. You rent an 8-passenger van for a week to transport 8 people to a convention in a city 1,240 miles away. The rate is $399.00 a week with 1,500 free miles and $0.25 per additional mile. The CDW fee is $165.00 for the week, and the estimated gasoline cost is $600.00. Determine the round-trip cost **(a)** for total rental, **(b)** per mile, and **(c)** per person.

12. CHALLENGE PROBLEM Candy Lowell needs a moving truck for 2 days. She can rent a 14-foot panel truck for $50.00 a day plus $1.20 a mile or an 18-foot truck for $60.00 a day plus $1.30 a mile. She expects to make 4 trips in the 14-foot truck or 3 trips in the larger truck. She estimates gasoline would cost $49.00 for the small truck and $60.00 for the large truck. It is 60 miles round trip to her new home. How much would it cost per mile to rent each truck? Which size truck should she rent?

Spiral Review

Divide. Round answers to the nearest hundredth. (Skill 11)

13. 762.20 ÷ 32 **14.** 684.26 ÷ 42.2 **15.** 502.00 ÷ 361.9

16. You have a 12-month loan of $1,100.00 at 8% interest with a $724.23 balance after the fourth payment. What is the final payment if you pay off the loan with the fifth payment? (Lesson 8.5)

GET READY for the Next Lesson

PREREQUISITE SKILL Subtracting Whole Numbers (Skill 4)

Subtract.

17. 56,955 – 4,242 **18.** 47,627 – 5,632 **19.** 71,853 – 19,712

CHAPTER 9

Review and Assessment

AFTER YOU READ

Chapter SUMMARY

To own, lease, or rent a vehicle involves numerous costs. As a potential buyer, you should know how to compute the sticker price and the dealer's cost of a new vehicle and the average retail price of a used vehicle. You also should be able to determine the total operating and maintenance cost per mile and the total cost and cost per mile of leasing. You can use tables to compute the vehicle's annual premium for insurance.

Vocabulary Check

1. On a sheet of paper, use each of these terms in a sentence.

Content Vocabulary

- sticker price (p. 341)
- base price (p. 341)
- options (p. 341)
- destination charge (p. 341)
- dealer's cost (p. 344)
- used-vehicle guide (p. 347)
- liability insurance (p. 350)
- collision insurance (p. 350)
- comprehensive insurance (p. 350)
- deductible clause (p. 350)
- annual premium (p. 351)
- variable costs (p. 354)
- fixed costs (p. 354)
- depreciation (p. 354)
- lease (p. 357)
- closed-end lease (p. 357)
- open-end lease (p. 357)
- rent (p. 360)

Academic Vocabulary

- display (p. 341)
- consumer (p. 344)
- published (p. 347)
- injury (p. 350)
- media (p. 354)
- license (p. 357)
- plus (p. 360)

Concept Check

2. What does the sticker price include?
3. Give the formula for calculating the dealer's cost of a vehicle.
4. What types of claims does liability insurance cover?
5. What does collision insurance cover?
6. What is a deductible?
7. List the two factors that determine a vehicle's annual insurance premium.
8. Differentiate between variable and fixed costs.
9. What is depreciation?
10. Differentiate between a closed-end lease and an open-end lease.
11. CRITICAL THINKING List two sources for information on the value of used vehicles.

Lesson-by-Lesson Review

9.1 Purchasing a New Vehicle (pp. 341–343)

Compute the sticker price of a new vehicle.
Trevon Darling wants to buy a new car. He has been looking at one with an $18,705.00 base price and is interested in several options totaling $4,326.54. The destination charge is $654.00. Find the sticker price.

Find the sticker price: Sticker Price = Base Price + Options + Destination Charge
$23,685.54 = $18,705.00 + $4,326.54 + $654.00

Review Exercises

Find the sticker price.

	Base Price	Options	Destination Charge	Sticker Price
12.	$21,500	$1,750	$450	$
13.	22,430	2,390	340	
14.	25,400	3,244	458	
15.	31,000	4,459	654	

16. Howie Caldwell wants to purchase a sports car that has a $27,495 base price. He chooses three options, a satellite radio for $600, 4-speed automatic transmission at $1,495, and sunroof for $455. The destination charge is $775.

17. ALGEBRA Beth Hazelton purchased a compact vehicle with an $18,240.00 MSRP including the delivery and title fee. She selected a leather interior, which cost 5 times the upgraded stereo system. If the total cost of the vehicle, including a 7% sales tax, was $21,365.20, find the cost of the **(a)** stereo system and **(b)** leather interior.

9.2 Dealer's Cost (pp. 344–346)

Calculate the dealer's cost of a new vehicle.
Travis Whitcomb wants to purchase a new car with a $25,000 base price and options totaling $2,190. The destination charge is $643. He read in a consumer magazine article that the dealer's cost for the car is about 91% of the base price and 87.5% of the options price. What should he estimate as the dealer's cost?

Step 1: Find the percent of the base price.
$25,000.00 × 91.0% = $22,750.00 base price

Step 2: Find the percent of the options price.
$2,190.00 × 87.5% = $1,916.25 options price

Step 3: Find the dealer's cost.
Percent of Base Price + Percent of Options Price + Destination Charge
$22,750.00 + $1,916.25 + $643.00 = **$25,309.25 dealer's cost**

Lesson-by-Lesson Review (continued)

Review Exercises

Find the dealer's cost.

	(Base Price × Dealer's Percent)	+	(Options Price × Dealer's Percent)	+	Destination Charge	=	Dealer's Cost
18.	$16,500 × 90%	+	$3,500 × 85%	+	$450	=	$
19.	21,600 × 88	+	2,300 × 91	+	562	=	
20.	31,500 × 92	+	4,500 × 86	+	782	=	
21.	42,000 × 86	+	3,400 × 81	+	754	=	

22. ALGEBRA Talia Spears checked the Internet to find the dealer's cost of a sedan. The dealer's cost of the base price was $18,321.50 and of the options price was $3,218.40. The dealer passed the $498.00 destination charge on to the consumer. If the dealer's percent of the base price is 87% and of the options is 92%, find the sedan's sticker price.

9.3 Purchasing a Used Vehicle (pp. 347–349)

Calculate the average retail or wholesale price of a used vehicle.

Phylicia Van Pelt is interested in a V-6 coupe with 85,000 miles. A used vehicle guide listed its average retail value at $13,490 and recommends subtracting $540 if the mileage exceeds 30,000. The car has air conditioning, power seats, and a power sunroof, which total $1,020. What is this used vehicle's average retail price?

Find the average retail price.

Average Retail Price	+	Additional Options	−	Options Deductions	−	Mileage Deduction		
$13,490	+	$1,020	−	$0	−	$540	=	**$13,970 average retail price**

Review Exercises

23. Rick Takei has a 4-wheel drive vehicle whose average retail value is $15,857. A used vehicle guide adds $60 for heated outside mirrors, $250 for rear and side air bags, $175 for cruise control, and $100 for remote keyless entry. It suggests deducting $750 for excessive mileage. What is the average retail price?

24. Peg Alcott owns a compact car and wants to know its average wholesale price. An Internet guide lists $2,600 as the average retail value. She adds $100 for power windows and $50 for a tilt steering wheel and deducts $600 for no air conditioning. What is the car's average wholesale price?

25. You are interested in purchasing a 2-year-old sedan with a $16,667 average retail value. You want to add a power sunroof for $543, a satellite radio system for $196, and a remote engine start for $115. If you deduct $225 for excessive mileage, what is the average retail price?

26. Bellamy Previously Owned Vehicles has a 5-year-old luxury vehicle with a $17,800 average retail value. Add $450 for a tilt steering wheel and $400 for a surround-sound speaker system. Deduct $660 for excessive mileage. What is the average retail price?

Lesson-by-Lesson Review (continued)

9.4 Vehicle Insurance (pp. 350–353)

Use Figure 9.3 on page 351 to compute the annual premium for vehicle insurance in the following problem.

Sheryl deLuca has a 2.10 driver-rating factor. Her vehicle is in age group C and insurance-rating group 12 (C, 12). Her insurance includes 100/200 bodily injury and $25,000 property damage. Her insurance deductible is $50 each for comprehensive and collision. What are her **(a)** annual basic premium and **(b)** annual premium?

Step 1: Find the annual basic premium.

Annual Basic Premium = Liability Premium + Collision Premium + Comprehensive Premium

$365.00 + $253.00 + $90 = **$708.00 annual basic premium**

Step 2: Find the annual premium.

Annual Premium = Basic Premium × Driver-Rating Factor

$708.00 × 2.10 = **$1,486.80 annual premium**

Review Exercises

Use Figure 9.3 on page 351 to solve these problems.

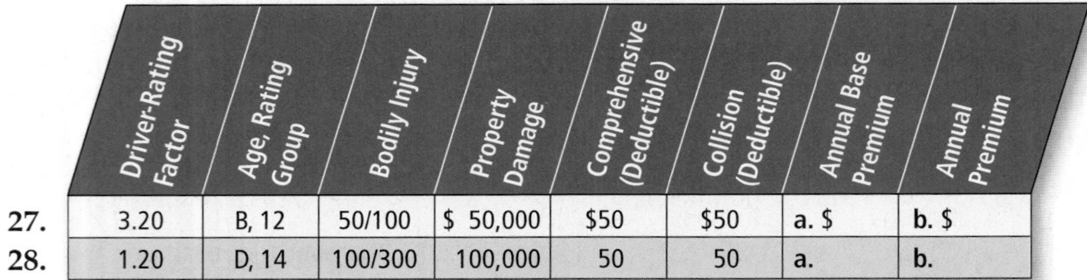

	Driver-Rating Factor	Age, Rating Group	Bodily Injury	Property Damage	Comprehensive (Deductible)	Collision (Deductible)	Annual Base Premium	Annual Premium
27.	3.20	B, 12	50/100	$ 50,000	$50	$50	**a.** $	**b.** $
28.	1.20	D, 14	100/300	100,000	50	50	**a.**	**b.**

29. Data for Skyler Higgins are driver-rating factor, 1.45 and age and rating group, B, 11. Insurance coverage is 50/100 bodily injury, $50,000 property damage, and $50 deductible each for comprehensive and collision. What are the **(a)** annual basic premium and **(b)** annual premium?

30. Raven Sandler uses her car to drive to and from work. Her driver-rating factor is 3.85. Her insurance coverage includes 100/300 bodily injury and $100,000 property damage. Her car is in age group A and insurance-rating group 14. What are her **(a)** annual basic premium and **(b)** annual premium?

Lesson-by-Lesson Review (continued)

9.5 Operating and Maintaining a Vehicle (pp. 354–356)

Compute the total cost per mile of operating and maintaining a vehicle.
Jackson McCoy purchased a used car a year ago. He drove 8,564 miles during the year and kept a record of all of his expenses. He calculated the annual variable cost to be $1,342.90. His annual fixed costs were $905.44. Find the cost per mile.

Find the cost per mile.

$$\text{Cost per Mile} = \frac{\text{Annual Variable Cost} + \text{Annual Fixed Cost}}{\text{Number of Miles}}$$

$$\text{Cost per Mile} = \frac{\$1{,}342.90 + \$905.44}{8{,}564} = \frac{\$2.248.34}{8{,}564} = 0.2625 = \mathbf{\$0.26}$$

Review Exercises

For Problems 31–33, find the (a) total annual cost and (b) cost per mile.

	Annual Variable Cost	Annual Fixed Cost	Total Annual Cost	Miles Driven	Cost per Mile
31.	$1,300.00	$3,287.33	a. $	9,500	b. $
32.	1,549.98	1,200.31	a.	11,500	b.
33.	1,139.45	2,300.88	a.	14,546	b.

34. Two years ago Ernest Dorsey purchased a used sport coupe for $8,000.00 that is now worth $6,000.00. Last year he drove it 13,569 miles and kept a record of all expenses. His variable costs were gasoline, $1,589.56; oil changes, $245.98; and repairs, $548.11. His fixed costs were insurance, $1,105.32 and license, $85.00. What was the cost per mile?

35. ALGEBRA Leann Wolfe estimates that she will drive 14,000 miles during the year and will have $2,200.00 in annual fixed costs. If her goal is to have a cost per mile of $0.31 or less for her compact car, what is the maximum annual variable cost she can have?

9.6 Leasing a Vehicle (pp. 357–359)

Calculate the total cost of leasing a vehicle.
Ursula Schoenfeld is leasing a vehicle and pays $403.50 per month for 48 months. Her deposit was $1,600.00. She paid a $75.00 title fee and a $55.00 license fee. What is her total lease cost?

Find the total lease cost.

$$\left(\text{Number of Payments} \times \text{Amount of Payment}\right) + \text{Deposit} + \text{Title Fee} + \text{License Fee} + \text{Tax (if applicable)}$$

$$(48 \times \$403.50) + \$1{,}600.00 + \$75.00 + \$55.00 = \mathbf{\$21{,}098.00 \text{ total lease cost}}$$

Lesson-by-Lesson Review (continued)

Review Exercises

Find the total of payments and the total lease cost.

	(Number of Payments	×	Amount of Payment	=	Total of Payments)	+	Deposit	+	Title Fee	+	License Fee	=	Total Lease Cost
36.	(24	×	$289	=	a. $)	+	$ 660	+	$50	+	$85	=	b. $
37.	(24	×	508	=	a.)	+	590	+	25	+	79	=	b.
38.	(30	×	216	=	a.)	+	1,240	+	75	+	55	=	b.
39.	(36	×	385	=	a.)	+	1,500	+	95	+	89	=	b.

40. **ALGEBRA** Jamarcus Holifield is thinking about leasing a four-door sports sedan. The $1,599.00 due at signing includes title and fees. His monthly lease payment will be $189.00 plus 6% sales tax, and he must have approved credit. If the total lease cost is $8,811.24, for how many months does the lease last?

9.7 Renting a Vehicle (pp. 360–362)

For a rental vehicle, calculate the cost of renting and the cost per mile. Last weekend Wheels & Deals had a rental car special on sedans for $26.51 per day plus $0.25 per mile. If Daisy Fitzgerald rented one for 3 days, drove 865 miles, and paid $86.50 for gas, what was the total cost **(a)** to rent the sedan and **(b)** per mile?

Step 1: Find the total cost.

$$(26.51 \times 3) + (\$0.25 \times 865) + 86.50$$
$$79.53 + 216.25 + 86.50 = \mathbf{\$382.28\ total\ cost}$$

Step 2: Find the cost per mile.

$$\text{Cost per Mile} = \frac{\$382.28}{865} = \$0.4419 = \mathbf{\$0.44}$$

Review Exercises

Find the cost per mile to the nearest cent.

	(Total Daily Cost	+	Total Mileage Cost	+	Gasoline Cost	=	Total Cost)	÷	Miles Driven	=	Cost per Mile
41.	($ 45.95	+	$91.25	+	$32.54	=	a. $)	÷	365	=	b. $
42.	(110.00	+	86.50	+	91.13	=	a.)	÷	865	=	b.

For Problems 43 and 44, determine the (a) total cost of renting the vehicle and (b) cost per mile.

43. Sarah Leo rented an economy car for 5 days for $22.93 per day with unlimited mileage. She drove 750 miles and paid $77.58 for gas.

44. Dallas Palmeri rented an SUV with 150 free miles and $0.25 each additional mile for $62.93 per day. Dallas rented the vehicle for 5 days, drove 428 miles, and paid $63.13 for gas.

Practice Test

Record your answer on a sheet of paper.

1. If Violet Atkins is purchasing a car whose base price is $15,499 with no options and $589 destination charge, what is its sticker price?
   A $16,288 **B** $14,910
   C $15,499 **D** $16,088

2. **ALGEBRA** Emily Kohl's new SUV has a $56,450.80 base MSRP including delivery and title fees but excluding the upgraded navigation system. Including 6.5% sales tax, the total cost of the SUV was $61,085.27. What was the cost of the upgraded navigation system?
   A $4,634.47 **B** $906.26
   C $1,186.00 **D** $869.86

Used Vehicle	Average Retail Value	Average Wholesale Value
V6 Four-Door	$14,088	$13,068
V8 Four-Door	15,710	13,868
Deduct w/o Air-Conditioning	850	725
Add Power Seats	125	100
Add Aluminum Wheels	150	125

3. Using the preceding table, determine the average retail price of a used V6 four-door car with aluminum wheels but no air conditioning.
   A $13,388 **B** $15,088
   C $13,088 **D** $14,388

4. Simeon Roseberg has a 3.4 driver-rating factor. If his car's basic insurance premium is $768.00, what is his annual premium?
   A $1,536.00 **B** $2,582.30
   C $2,611.20 **D** $225.88

5. **ALGEBRA** Jake Duffy drove 12,568 miles in his car last year. His fixed costs totaled $1,485.00, and his variable costs totaled $2,015.75. What was his cost per mile?
   A $0.44 **B** $0.29
   C $0.31 **D** $0.28

6. If you pay $315 per month for 36 months to lease a car and made an initial deposit of $3,500, what additional information would you need to determine the total lease cost?
   A the title and license fee amounts **B** just the title fee amount
   C just the license fee amount **D** nothing; the total lease cost is $14,840

7. Catrice Jarrell rented a car for $35.50 a day. The mileage charge was $0.19 for every mile more than 250 driven. If she had the car for 4 days and drove 230 miles, what was her total cost?
   A $185.70 **B** $142.00
   C $145.80 **D** $172.93

8. What is the sticker price of a car with a base price of $21,550, $2,430 of options, and a $573 destination charge?
   A $27,583 **B** $22,123
   C $23,980 **D** $24,553

9. **ALGEBRA** Rosie Bates bought a new car with a $24,014.89 sticker price. If the basic price was $18,675 and the destination charge was $672, what was the price of the options?

10. Amir Najjar did research on the Internet to find the dealer's cost of a new car he wanted to purchase. He found that the dealer's cost of the base price was $15,455.40 and cost of the options was $585.00. The dealer will pass the $675 destination charge on to the consumer. If the dealer's cost is 85% of the base and 82% of the options, what is the car's sticker price?

Standardized Test Practice

Cumulative, Chapters 1–9

PART 1 Multiple Choice

Record your answers on the answer sheet provided by your teacher or on a sheet of paper.

1. Dave Finney leases a vehicle for $245.50 for 36 months. The deposit is $575.00, and the title and license fees total $105.00. What is the total lease cost?
   A $9,518.00 **B** $10,546.00
   C $9,815.00 **D** $11,213.00
2. Charmaine Birney's bank account had a $5,294.58 balance. After she deposited a check for $338.54 and a $50 bill, what is the new balance?
   A $6,020.02 **B** $5,658.12
   C $5,683.12 **D** $5,863.33
3. How much tax is withheld from Luanne Potter's yearly salary of $145,580 if the tax rate is 3.8%?
   A $6,792.04 **B** $4,581.34
   C $3,572.24 **D** $5,532.04
4. Ning Park's car had a $24,875.65 sticker price. She bought $3,692.84 worth of options and paid the $682.00 destination charge. What was her car's base price?
   A $29,250.89 **B** $20,500.81
   C $27,886.49 **D** $25,557.65
5. What sale price does Joe Buckley pay for a $185.99 MP3 player if it is discounted 15%?
   A $168.50 **B** $200.95
   C $170.99 **D** $158.09
6. Paulie Mateja purchased a digital camera for $699.99. The store charged 4.65% sales tax. What was the camera's total purchase price?
   A $703.64 **B** $732.54
   C $753.64 **D** $767.54

TEST-TAKING TIP

Review When you complete a test, make sure you have answered all questions and marked your answer sheet correctly.

PART 2 Short Response/Griddable

7. Tany Crow has annual fixed expenses that total $4,683. What should she budget for her monthly share of annual expenses?
8. Bobbie Dirksen's bank granted her a single-payment loan of $8,575 for 90 days at 13% exact interest. What is the loan's maturity value?
9. Dru Lindsay drove his car 12,842 miles last year. The total of variable costs was $3,822.54 and of fixed costs was $2,184.00. What was the cost per mile to operate his car last year? Round to the nearest hundredth.

PART 3 Extended Response

Show your work.

10. Explain how you would determine a new car's sticker price.
11. How would you determine the unit price of a jellybean if a bag of 500 costs $3.99?
12. How do you calculate a loan's maturity value?
13. $14,819.55 + $3,903 + $582.53
14. $6,539 + $597.85 – $139.20
15. 86.4% of $98,361.25
16. $5,368.55 + $918 + $551.68 + $1,462
17. $585.65 × 4.2
18. $692.65 ÷ 12,485

Building Academic Skills

Mathematics

Driving comes with many financial obligations—gasoline, insurance, and maintenance. Assume you are considering buying, leasing, or renting a car. Use Internet or library sources to research the related costs. Construct a bar graph comparing the related costs of owning, leasing, and renting a car.

English Language Arts/Writing

If you are a good driver, you may save money by increasing the deductible of your auto insurance. Your insurance premiums will go down. If you have a high deductible, the insurance company will not have to pay for most of your repairs. Use Internet or library sources to find how the cost of auto insurance varies with deductible amounts. Write a short report on your findings.

Science

Auto insurance is more expensive for teens because studies show that they are easily distracted. Talking on cell phones while driving, for example, reduces reaction time. Slower reaction times lead to more accidents, which lead to higher insurance rates. Use Internet or library sources to research the effects of cell phone use on reaction times. Write a brief report on your findings to present to your class or to submit to your school newspaper.

Building Real-World Skills

Career WISE

Automotive Retail Salesperson Manufacturers usually sell their vehicles to consumers through automobile dealers. Dealers may sell new or used vehicles. Automotive retail salespeople are the first to greet customers on the lot. They must have good mathematics, communication, and negotiation skills and like working with people. Most dealers require salespeople to have their high school diploma. Physical fitness is important because automotive retail sales requires long hours and long periods of standing and working outdoors. Salespeople are typically paid on commission.

Research and Write:

a. Visit the Web site of the Bureau of Labor Statistics and locate the entry on automobile dealers. Determine the job outlook and earnings potential for automotive retail salespeople.

b. Would you like to work in retail sales? Write a one-page report describing why or why not. Include the job outlook and average median hourly earnings for automotive retail salespeople.

21st Century Workplace

Plugging into Your Vehicle As more people use their PDAs, cell phones, and MP3 players on the go, more cars are being equipped to handle them. Newer models of luxury cars often include built-in chargers and connections for these gadgets, making it easy, for instance, to listen to music from an MP3 player on the car stereo.

Research and Write:

a. Using the Internet, search for the phrase "PDA car accessories." What are the most popular ways to mount a PDA in a car?

b. Research MP3 players and cars on the Internet. Name three auto manufacturers that have added MP3 player interfaces as features on their automobiles.

CHAPTER 10 Housing Costs

Big Idea

Owning a home involves several costs, such as costs for a mortgage, insurance, and maintenance.

Explore the Photo

House Hunting
Finding your own place is exciting, but it is also a big responsibility. *What are some costs associated with renting or buying a home?*

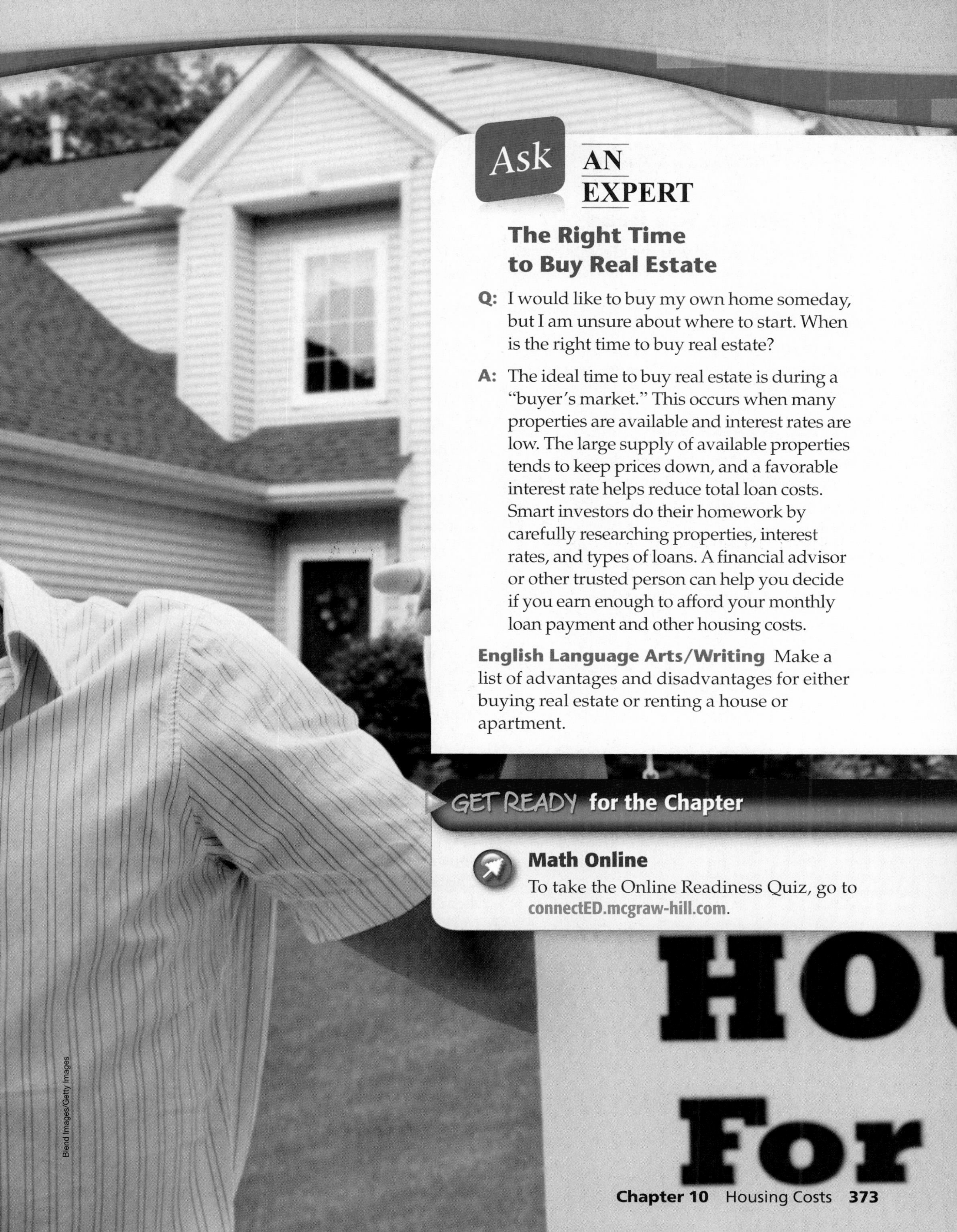

Blend Images/Getty Images

Ask AN EXPERT

The Right Time to Buy Real Estate

Q: I would like to buy my own home someday, but I am unsure about where to start. When is the right time to buy real estate?

A: The ideal time to buy real estate is during a "buyer's market." This occurs when many properties are available and interest rates are low. The large supply of available properties tends to keep prices down, and a favorable interest rate helps reduce total loan costs. Smart investors do their homework by carefully researching properties, interest rates, and types of loans. A financial advisor or other trusted person can help you decide if you earn enough to afford your monthly loan payment and other housing costs.

English Language Arts/Writing Make a list of advantages and disadvantages for either buying real estate or renting a house or apartment.

GET READY for the Chapter

Math Online
To take the Online Readiness Quiz, go to **connectED.mcgraw-hill.com**.

Chapter 10 Housing Costs

Reading Guide

Before You Read

Connect How will you decide whether to rent or to purchase a home?

Main Idea

One of the most expensive purchases that people make is a home. Owners incur many related costs.

Graphic Organizer

Before you read this chapter, draw a diagram like the one below. As you read, list the costs associated with purchasing a home.

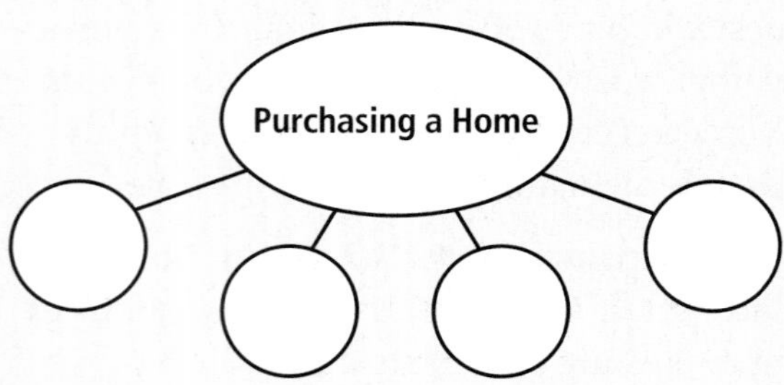

Math Online Go to connectED.mcgraw-hill.com to download this graphic organizer.

Content Vocabulary

You will learn these key terms in this chapter.

- mortgage loan
- closing costs
- real estate taxes
- assessed value
- tax rate
- market value
- rate of assessment
- homeowners insurance
- property damage coverage
- personal liability coverage
- medical coverage
- loss-of-use coverage
- replacement value
- premium
- fire protection class
- utility costs
- security deposit

Academic Vocabulary

You will see these words in your reading and on your tests.

- secure
- fluctuate
- documents
- obtain
- assessed
- recover
- affects
- sustain
- termination

You can find vocabulary definitions in the **Content Vocabulary** Glossary and the **Academic Vocabulary** Glossary in the back of the book.

LESSON 10.1

Mortgage Loans

Lesson Objective

Compute the mortgage loan amount.

Content Vocabulary

- mortgage loan

How will you pay for your first home?

Harold Armon has been saving 10% of his income since he started working. He must take out a mortgage to purchase a condominium, but he has cash for the down payment.

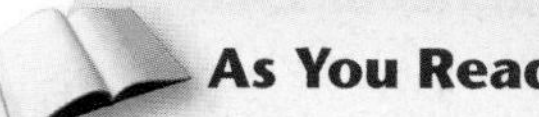

Identify How do you find the mortgage loan amount?

Securing a Mortgage Loan When you secure a **mortgage loan**, which is a long-term loan extended to someone to buy property, first you will make a down payment. Generally, the down payment is between 10% and 40% of the selling price, although many first-time homeowners put down as little as 5%.

You **secure** the remaining portion of the selling price with a mortgage loan from a lender, such as a bank, S&L association, credit union, or mortgage company. The mortgage gives the lender the right to seize and sell the property if you fail to make the payments. Owners usually repay the mortgage loan with interest in equal monthly payments. The mortgage loan amount is calculated with this formula:

Mortgage Loan Amount = Selling Price − Down Payment

Need Help? Go to...

- **Workshop 14:** Finding a Percentage, p. 30
- **Skill 6:** Subtracting Decimals, p. SK7

EXAMPLE

Jessica and Kirk Cramer are considering the purchase of a new home for $140,000. They must make a 15% down payment. What is the amount of the mortgage loan needed to finance the purchase?

Step 1: Find the down payment.

$140,000 × 15% = $21,000

Step 2: Find the mortgage loan amount.

Mortgage Loan Amount = Selling Price − Down Payment

$119,000 = $140,000 − $21,000

Concept CHECK

Find the (a) down payment and (b) amount of the mortgage. Check your answers in the back of the book.

1. Tom and Sally Becker are considering the purchase of a home that sells for $280,000. The down payment is 20%.
2. Bart and Kyle Kilpatrick want to buy a home selling for $242,500. The down payment is 30%.

Real World CAREER

Veterinarian
The field of veterinary medicine involves more than checking the health of pets. Some veterinarians specialize in large or exotic animals. Others research diseases carried by animals. **What other careers can you think of that have various areas of specialization?**

Lesson Practice

For Problems 3–8, determine the amount of the (a) down payment and (b) mortgage loan.

	Buyer	Selling Price	Percent of Down Payment	Amount of Down Payment	Mortgage Loan Amount
3.	Sumi Ganet	$187,000	20%	a. $	b. $
4.	Carla Gonzalez	262,500	25	a.	b.
5.	Albert Nash	398,800	25	a.	b.
6.	Dario Valencia	856,000	40	a.	b.

7. David and Peggy Chin purchased a town home priced at $177,400 and made a 20% down payment.
8. Alvira and Barry Gomez purchased a home priced at $280,000. They put down 40%.
9. Rita and Alfred Johnson offered $185,000 for a home that had been priced at $190,000. The Johnsons and the seller agreed on a $186,500 selling price. What is the amount of the mortgage loan if they make a 20% down payment?
10. Grant and Caroline Mackey have purchased a duplex for a selling price of $278,800. They plan to use the rental income from one part of the duplex to help meet the mortgage payments. What is the amount of the mortgage loan that requires a 30% down payment?

11. **WRITING IN MATH** Write a brief paragraph about the amount of the down payment required in order to be approved for a mortgage. Why do you think lenders require a down payment?
12. **CHALLENGE PROBLEM** Dan and Sue Willingham have saved $14,000 for a down payment on their future home. Their bank has informed them that the minimum down payment required to obtain a mortgage loan is 20%. What is the most that they can spend for a home and expect to receive bank approval for their loan?

Spiral Review

Subtract. (Skill 4)

13. 40,000 − 8,400 **14.** 94,000 − 18,000 **15.** 180,000 − 36,000

16. **ALGEBRA** The markdown on a jet ski was 25%. If its sale price was $3,150, what was its regular selling price? (Lesson 6.7)

GET READY for the Next Lesson

PREREQUISITE SKILL Multiplying Decimals (Skill 8)

Multiply.

17. 42 × 12.8 **18.** 63 × 314.33
19. 6.03 × 1,023 **20.** 3,406 × 21.9
21. 289.34 × 11 **22.** 56.3 × 90

LESSON 10.2

Monthly Payment and Total Interest

Lesson Objective

Use a table or formula to determine the monthly payment, the total amount paid, and the total interest charged.

GET READY for the Lesson

What are some things other than costs that you should consider before purchasing a home?

Kwami and Enid Tavares thought about purchasing a home. When Kwami took a new job that required him to travel out of town several days a week, they decided that yard work and maintenance would be too much responsibility for them.

As You Read

Identify Why is it wise to "shop around" when looking for a lender?

Determining the Monthly Payment and Total Interest Lenders that make mortgage loans charge interest. This is the money the borrower pays for the use of the lender's money. The interest rate will **fluctuate** from lender to lender, so it pays to "shop around." If you know the annual interest rate, the amount of the loan, and the length of the loan, you can use a table to find the monthly payment. When you know the monthly payment, you can determine the total amount paid and total interest charged.

See **Figure 10.1** for the Monthly Payment for a $1,000 Loan at various rates and periods of time.

Figure 10.1

Monthly Payment for a $1,000 Loan*

Interest Rate	Length of Loan in Years		
	20	25	30
5.00%	$6.60	$5.85	$5.37
5.50	6.88	6.14	5.68
6.00	7.16	6.44	6.00
6.50	7.46	6.75	6.32
7.00	7.75	7.07	6.65
7.50	8.06	7.39	6.99
8.00	8.36	7.72	7.34
8.50	8.68	8.05	7.69
9.00	9.00	8.39	8.05

*See the Appendix on page A13 for an expanded form.

The formula to determine the monthly payment is:

$$\text{Monthly Payment} = \frac{\text{Amount of Mortgage}}{1{,}000} \times \text{Monthly Payment for \$1,000 Loan}$$

When you know the monthly payment, you can calculate the total amount paid over the life of the loan using this formula:

Amount Paid = Monthly Payment × Number of Payments

You can calculate the total interest paid over the life of the loan using this formula:

Total Interest Charged = Amount Paid − Amount of Mortgage

Need Help? Go to...
Workshop 6: Multiplying Decimals, p. 14
Workshop 5: Subtracting Decimals, p. 12

EXAMPLE 1

Carol and Adam Burke have applied for a $280,000 mortgage loan at a 9% annual interest rate. The loan is for 30 years, and the Burkes will pay it in equal monthly payments that include interest. What is the total amount of interest charged?

Step 1: Find the monthly payment.

(Refer to **Figure 10.1** for the *Monthly Payment for a $1,000 Loan* table on page 377.)

The value for 9% and 30 years is $8.05.

$$\frac{\text{Amount of Mortgage}}{1{,}000} \times \text{Monthly Payment for \$1,000 Loan}$$

$$\frac{\$280{,}000}{\$1{,}000} \times \$8.05 = \$2{,}254.00 \text{ monthly payment}$$

Step 2: Find the amount paid.

Monthly Payment × Number of Payments

$2,254.00 × (12 months × 30 years)

$2,254.00 × 360 = $811,440.00 amount paid

Step 3: Find the total interest charged.

Total Interest Charged = Amount Paid − Amount of Mortgage

$811,440.00 − $280,000.00 = **$531,440.00**

280000 ÷ 1000 × 8.05 = 2254 × 12 × 30 = 811440

− 280000 = 531440

Concept CHECK

Use the *Monthly Payment for a $1,000 Loan* table in Figure 10.1 on page 377. Check your answer in the back of the book.

1. Find Cameron Bond's **(a)** monthly payment, **(b)** amount paid, and **(c)** interest charged for a $390,000 mortgage loan at a 5% annual interest rate for 20 years.

Monthly Payment Formula Another way to determine the monthly payment is to use the Monthly Payment Formula introduced in Lesson 8.1, Installment Loans—Monthly Payment and Finance Charge. You can compute the monthly payment on a mortgage loan using this formula:

$$\text{Monthly Payment} = \frac{pr(1+r)^n}{(1+r)^n - 1}$$

Where p = Principal, or the amount of the mortgage

r = Rate per payment, that is, the mortgage rate divided 12.

n = Number of payments required to pay off the loan, that is, the number of years multiplied by 12.

The use of the formula requires a calculator with a y^x key. The formula enables you to determine the monthly payment for numerous mortgage rates and terms.

Need Help? Go to...
Application B: More Formulas, p. AP2

EXAMPLE 2 Algebra

Carol and Adam Burke have applied for a $280,000 mortgage loan at a 9% annual interest rate. The loan is for a period of 30 years, and they will pay it in equal monthly payments that include interest. Find the **(a)** monthly payment, **(b)** amount paid, and **(c)** total interest charged.

First, $r = \frac{9\%}{12} = 0.0075$ and $n = 30 \times 12 = 360$

Then, substitute into the formula:

$$\text{Monthly Payment} = \frac{pr(1+r)^n}{(1+r)^n-1} = \frac{\$280{,}000(0.0075)(1+.0075)^{360}}{(1+.0075)^{360}-1}$$

$$= \frac{\$2{,}100(14.73057612)}{14.73057612-1} = \frac{\$30{,}934.20986}{13.73057612} = \mathbf{\$2{,}252.943328}$$

The Burkes' monthly payment is $2,252.94.

The amount paid is $2,252.94 × 360 = $811,058.40.

The total interest charged is $811,058.40 – $280,000 = $531,058.40.

Note that the difference in monthly payment between **Example 1** ($2,254) and **Example 2** ($2,252.94) occurs because of rounding the table value from 8.046226170 to 8.05.

Concept CHECK

Complete the problem. Check your answer in the back of the book.

2. Ramin and Akbar Habil obtained a $98,000 mortgage loan at an annual interest rate of 6.24%. The loan is for a period of 22 years, and the Habils will pay it in equal monthly payments that include interest. Find the **(a)** monthly payment, **(b)** amount paid, and **(c)** total interest charged.

Reading Math

Annual and Monthly

Annual means *yearly.* If you know the amount of interest owed annually, divide by 12, the number of months, to find the monthly payment.

Lesson Practice

Use the *Monthly Payment for a $1,000 Loan* table in Figure 10.1 on page 377 to solve Problems 3–6.

	Mortgage	Years	Rate	Payment	Amount Paid	Total Interest
3.	$ 70,000	25	8.00%	a. $	b. $	c. $
4.	95,000	30	6.00%	a.	b.	c.
5.	225,000	20	8.00%	a.	b.	c.
6.	395,000	30	5.50%	a.	b.	c.

Did You Know?

Word Roots **The word *mortgage* dates from around the year 1390. Its origin is the 13th century Old French term *mort gaige,* or "dead pledge." The term refers to a deal that expires when a debt is fully paid or when payment fails.**

For Problems 7–10, find the (a) monthly payment, (b) total amount paid, and (c) total interest charged.

7. Charles and Sandy Compton: $80,000 mortgage at 6.5% for 25 years.

8. Abigail and Curtis Siebert: $270,000 mortgage at 7% for 20 years.

9. Ivan and Vicki Egan have obtained a $160,000 mortgage loan at an annual interest rate of 7.5% for 20 years.

10. Pierre Bolton has reached an agreed-upon selling price of $197,000 for a new home. He plans to make a 30% down payment and finance the rest at 6% for 20 years.

11. Ellen and Tim Hinojosa reached an agreed-upon price of $140,000 for the purchase of a house. They made a 10% down payment and had two options for financing the remaining amount: at 5.5% for 25 years or at 6% for 20 years. Which mortgage results in a higher amount of interest paid and by how much?

12. ALGEBRA Allison Higgins applied for a $320,000 mortgage loan at an annual interest rate of 6.00%. The loan is for 25 years and will be paid in equal monthly payments that include interest. **(a)** What is the monthly payment using **Figure 10.1** on page 377? **(b)** What is the monthly payment using the formula?

13. CHALLENGE PROBLEM How much can you save in total interest by making a $75,000 down payment rather than a $50,000 down payment on a $495,000 home financed at 6% for 30 years?

14. ALGEBRA Eva and Irving Cole just took out a $132,500 mortgage loan at an annual interest rate of 5.97%. The loan is for a period of 33 years, and the Coles will pay it in equal monthly payments that include interest. Find the **(a)** monthly payment, **(b)** amount paid, and **(c)** total interest charged.

15. ALGEBRA Nadia Turner offered 5% less than the $198,900 asking price for a new home. The owners accepted her offer and, with a 20% down payment, she obtained a 6.3% mortgage. How much could Nadia save in total interest if she took a 23-year mortgage rather than a 26-year mortgage? Why might she not take a 23-year mortgage?

Spiral Review

Multiply. (Skill 8)

16. 24×120.50 **17.** 36×431.20 **18.** 12×832.40

19. Fran Sullivan wants to buy a truck with a $25,955 base price, options totaling $3,246, and a destination charge of $710. If the dealer's cost is 90.5% of the base price and 87% of the options, what is the dealer's cost for the truck? (Lesson 9.2)

GET READY for the Next Lesson

PREREQUISITE SKILL **Finding the Percentage** (Skill 30)

Find the percentage.

20. 20% of 1,405 **21.** 45% of 6,321

22. 3.4% of 340 **23.** 55% of 2,438

24. 75% of 29,544 **25.** 0.04% of 214,568

LESSON 10.3

Closing Costs

Lesson Objective
Calculate the total closing costs.

Content Vocabulary
- closing costs

GET READY for the Lesson

Who makes money when you buy a home?

Ramie and Neal Goldstein just purchased their first home. The sale involved many people—the seller, inspector, real estate agent, the mortgage bank, and the lawyer.

As You Read
Summarize What is a closing?

Computing Closing Costs When you purchase a home, you may have a closing. The closing is usually a meeting attended by the buyer, the seller, their lawyers, the mortgage lender, and the real estate agent. At the meeting, buyer and seller sign a number of **documents** to formalize the mortgage, distribute funds, and transfer ownership of the home to the buyer. **Closing costs** may include fees for the property survey, loan application, document preparation, and points. See **Figure 10.2** for common closing costs. One point is 1.0% of the loan amount. Other fees may also be a percent of the amount of the loan. The total closing costs are determined using the formula:

Total Closing Costs = Sum of the Various Closing Fees

Need Help? Go to...
- **Skill 30:** Finding the Percentage, p. SK31
- **Skill 3:** Adding Whole Numbers, p. SK4

EXAMPLE

State Bank has approved a mortgage loan for Trisha and Brice Hallett at an annual interest rate of 8% for 25 years. The home's selling price was $125,000. They need a 20% down payment. State Bank will allow them to finance the closing costs as part of the mortgage. Their closing costs are shown in **Figure 10.2**. What are the total closing costs? What is the actual amount financed with the mortgage?

Figure 10.2

Closing Costs	
Application Fee	$252
Borrower's Credit Check	65
Points	2.00% of Mortgage
Appraisal Fee	$325
Title Search	212
Title Insurance	410
Inspection	350
Attorney Fee	450
Documentation Stamp	0.30% of Mortgage
Processing Fee	1.10% of Mortgage

Continued on next page

Step 1: Find the down payment.

Down Payment = $125,000 × 20% = $25,000

Step 2: Find the mortgage amount.

Mortgage Amount = $125,000 – $25,000 = $100,000

Step 3: Calculate the various fee amounts.

Points = 2.00% × $100,000 = $2,000

Documentation stamp = 0.30% × $100,000 = $300

Processing fee = 1.10% × $100,000 = $1,100

Step 4: Find the sum of the various closing fees.

$252 + $65 + $2,000 + $325 + $212 + $410 + $350 + $450 + $300 + $1,100 = **$5,464**

Step 5: Find the actual amount financed.

Amount Financed = Amount of Mortgage + Total Closing Costs

$105,464 = $100,000 + $5,464

The total closing cost is $5,464 and the total amount financed is $105,464.

Complete the problem. Check your answer in the back of the book.

1. USA Mortgage has approved a mortgage loan for Kyung Ja and Hideo Hakola at a 7.5% annual interest rate for 15 years. The home has a $100,000 selling price. They need a 10% down payment. USA Mortgage will allow them to finance the closing costs as part of the mortgage. Use **Figure 10.2** on page 381 to find the total closing costs. What actual amount did they finance with the mortgage?

Study Tip

Estimate, Calculate, Check

Develop the habit of estimating, calculating, and checking the answer to each problem you solve.

Lesson Practice

For Problems 2–8, use the closing costs in Figure 10.2 on page 381 to calculate the (a) total closing costs and (b) total amount of the mortgage if the closing costs are financed.

2. Jeremy Roberts purchases a condo with a mortgage loan of $50,000.
3. Vincent and Sue Helmsley buy a home with a mortgage loan of $120,000.
4. Christi Schrock purchases a home with a mortgage loan of $271,000.
5. Jack and Dina King purchase a home with a mortgage loan of $420,000.
6. Lateefah and Eric Lewis have obtained a mortgage loan at a 5.5% annual interest rate for 25 years. The home's selling price is $175,000, and they need a 20% down payment. The bank will allow them to finance the closing costs as part of the mortgage. What is the actual amount they financed with the mortgage?
7. Barry and Kate Ellerson have agreed to purchase a house for $96,500. Universal Savings and Loan Association is willing to lend the money at 6% for 25 years, provided they can make a $10,000 down payment. What is the mortgage total if they finance the closing costs?

8. Clark and Lindsay Banks have agreed to purchase a home for $225,000. They made a down payment of 15%. They have obtained a mortgage loan at a 6.5% annual interest rate for 25 years. What is the mortgage total if they finance the closing costs?

9. Chris and Beth Micelli made a $235,000 offer for the purchase of a new home, which was accepted. They made a 30% down payment and financed the rest. Using the closing cost table below, find the mortgage total if they include the closing costs in the mortgage amount.

Closing Costs	
Application Fee	$450
Borrower's Credit Check	$100
Points	1.50% of mortgage
Appraisal Fee	$350
Title Search	$250
Title Insurance	1.00% of mortgage
Inspection	$500
Attorney Fee	$650
Documentation Stamp	0.30% of mortgage
Processing Fee	2.40% of mortgage

10. **CHALLENGE** Rene and Jefferson Franklin want to purchase a $560,000 home. They plan to make a 25% down payment and finance the remaining amount through Peabody Savings Association. Peabody has these closing costs: application fee, $325; credit report, $90; appraisal report, $555; title insurance, $490; survey and photographs, $325; recording fee, $65; legal fees, $780; and first 6 months of property taxes, $1,789. If the seller agreed to pay 50% of the closing costs, how much money will the Franklins need to secure the loan, including the down payment?

Spiral Review

Find the percent. (Skill 30)

11. 7% of 252,000
12. 2.4% of 78,000
13. 0.3% of 92,000
14. If your annual expenses are $7,000, your monthly living expenses are $870, and your monthly fixed expenses are $987, find your monthly share of annual expenses and your total monthly expenses. (Lesson 3.2)
15. Riccardo Frierson deposits $1,200 in a savings account. The account pays a 3.5% annual interest rate. He makes no other deposits or withdrawals. How much simple interest does his account earn in 6 months? (Lesson 5.4)

GET READY for the Next Lesson

PREREQUISITE SKILL Subtracting Decimals (Skill 6)

Subtract.

16. 25 − 0.14
17. 23,101 − 24.04
18. 13,124 − 34.24
19. 672 − 1.023
20. 76.854 − 33
21. 19,514 − 701.65

LESSON 10.4

Allocation of the Monthly Payment

Lesson Objective
Compute the allocation of the monthly payment to principal and interest and the new principal.

GET READY for the Lesson

How long do you think you will live in your first home?

Sang and Kim-Ly Vanh have purchased a home. They chose a 25-year loan period rather than 20 or 30 years. They will pay their mortgage on a monthly basis.

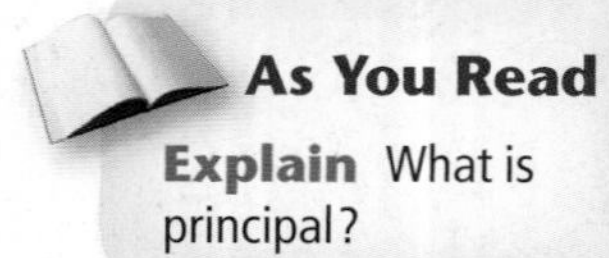

As You Read
Explain What is principal?

Allocation of the Monthly Payment Most people **obtain** a loan to finance their mortgage and repay the loan in equal monthly payments. Each payment includes an amount for interest and an amount for the loan's principal. The amount of interest is calculated using the simple interest formula:

Interest = Principal × Rate × Time

The interest is deducted from the payment and the remaining amount is used to reduce the principal resulting in a new principal or balance. The amount of principal that you owe decreases with each payment that you make. See **Figure 10.3** for the interest and principal paid in the first 4 months on a $280,000 mortgage loan at 8% for 30 years.

Figure 10.3

$280,000 Mortgage Loan at 8% for 30 Years				
Payment Number	Monthly Payment	Amount for Interest	Amount for Principal	Balance
				$280,000.00
1	$2,055.20	$1,866.67	$188.53	279,811.47
2	2,055.20	1,865.41	189.79	279,621.68
3	2,055.20	1,864.14	191.06	279,430.62
4	2,055.20	1,862.87	192.33	$279,238.29

You need the following formulas to complete a repayment schedule:

Interest = Principal × Rate × Time

Payment to Principal = Monthly Payment − Interest

New Principal = Previous Balance − Payment to Principal

Need Help? Go to...
Workshop 5: Subtracting Decimals, p. 12
Workshop 6: Multiplying Decimals, p. 14

EXAMPLE 1

Rod and Carey Finn obtained a 30-year, $280,000.00 mortgage loan from State Bank and Trust. The interest rate is 8%. Their monthly payment is $2,055.20. For the first payment, what is the amount of **(a)** interest, **(b)** payment to principal, and **(c)** new principal?

Step 1: Find the interest.

Principal × Rate × Time

$280,000.00 × 8% × $\frac{1}{12}$ = **$1,866.67 interest**

Step 2: Find the payment to principal.

Monthly Payment − Interest

$2,055.20 − $1,866.67 = **$188.53 payment to principal**

Step 3: Find the new principal.

Previous Balance − Payment to Principal

$280,000.00 − $188.53 = **$279,811.47 new principal**

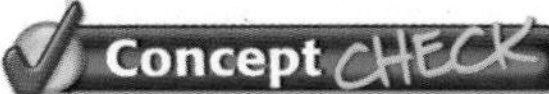

Complete the problems. Check your answers in the back of the book.

In **Example 1,** Step 3, the new principal is $279,811.47. For the second payment, show the work to find:

1. The interest on $279,811.47.
2. The payment to principal.
3. The new balance.

EXAMPLE 2

The amount of principal that you owe decreases with each payment that you make. See **Figure 10.4** for the interest and principal paid for payments 325, 326, and 327 on an original $280,000 mortgage loan. For payment number 328, what are the **(a)** interest, **(b)** payment to principal, and **(c)** new principal?

Figure 10.4

$280,000 Mortgage Loan at 8% for 30 Years				
Payment Number	Monthly Payment	Amount for Interest	Amount for Principal	Balance $64,811.95
325	$2,055.20	$432.08	$1,623.12	63,188.83
326	2,055.20	421.26	1,633.94	61,554.89
327	2,055.20	410.37	1,644.83	59,910.06

Step 1: Find the interest.

Principal × Rate × Time

$59,910.06 × 8% × $\frac{1}{12}$ = **$399.40 interest**

Step 2: Find the payment to principal.

Monthly Payment − Interest

$2,055.20 − $399.40 = **$1,655.80 payment to principal**

Step 3: Find the new principal or balance.

Previous Balance − Payment to Principal

$59,910.06 − $1,655.80 = **$58,254.26 new principal**

Complete the problems. Check your answers in the back of the book.

In **Example 2**, the new principal is $58,254.26. For payment 329, find:

4. The interest on $58,254.26.

5. The payment to principal.

6. The new principal.

SPREADSHEET APPLICATION

Allocation of Monthly Payment

You can use a spreadsheet like the partial one below to allocate a mortgage loan payment to principal and interest. In the input area (not shown), you will enter the property's selling price, the down payment amount or percent (optional), the interest rate, and the number of years. The monthly payment, the amount to interest, amount to principal and new balance are computed automatically.

Math Online Go to **connectED.mcgraw-hill.com** to download a spreadsheet application for this activity.

	A	B	C	D	E
1	Payment Number	Monthly Payment	Amount to Interest	Amount to Principal	Balance
2	1		$	$	$
3	2		$	$	$

Think and Discuss

1. The Richardsons bought a house for $150,000 and made a $30,000 down payment. They borrowed the remainder at 7.25% for 30 years.
   (a) What is their monthly payment?
   (b) What is the amount of their first payment to interest?
   (c) What is the amount of their first payment to principal?
   (d) What is the new principal?
2. What is the balance after the second payment?
3. How many months does it take before at least half the payment is going toward the principal?

Lesson Practice

For problems 7–14, for the first monthly payment, compute the (a) interest, (b) amount for principal, and (c) new principal.

	Mortgage Amount	Interest Rate	1st Monthly Payment	Amount for Interest	Amount for Principal	New Principal
7.	$170,000	6.0%	$1,020.00	a. $	b. $	c. $
8.	260,000	5.5	1,476.80	a.	b.	c.
9.	120,000	6.5	1,045.20	a.	b.	c.
10.	225,000	7.0	1,437.75	a.	b.	c.

Did You Know?

Sweat Equity ***Sweat equity*** **refers to the amount of money owners save by doing necessary work on the home themselves. For example, painting your house yourself instead of spending $4,000 for a professional painter is equivalent to keeping an extra $4,000 in the bank.**

11. Lois Isbel buys a "fixer-upper" house. She obtains a $46,000.00 mortgage loan with a 5% interest rate. Her monthly payment is $269.10.

12. Patrick Yunus obtained a $284,000.00 mortgage with a 6% interest rate to buy a condo. His monthly payment is $2,033.44.

13. Matthew Hansen bought a home for which he obtained a $538,600.00 mortgage loan at a 5.5% interest rate. His monthly payment is $2,779.18.

14. Dee Pollen bought a condo that has a $98,000.00 mortgage loan with a 7.5% interest rate. Her monthly payment is $686.00.

15. Jill Barkley obtained a 25-year, $460,000.00 mortgage loan from University Savings and Loan Association with 6% interest rate. The monthly payment is $2,962.40. For the first payment, find the **(a)** interest, **(b)** payment to principal, and **(c)** new balance.

16. Norman Foster obtained a 30-year, $180,000 mortgage loan from American Savings and Loan Association. The interest rate is 7%. Using the Monthly Payment for a $1,000 Loan table in **Figure 10.1** on page 377, find the **(a)** monthly payment, **(b)** interest for the first payment, **(c)** payment to principal, and **(d)** new balance.

H.O.T. Problems

17. CHALLENGE PROBLEM Amelia McGuire obtained a 20-year, $236,000.00 mortgage loan. The interest rate is 6.5%. Her monthly payment is $1,760.56. Calculate the missing amounts in repayment schedule in the table below.

$236,000 Mortgage Loan at 8% for 20 Years				
Payment Number	Monthly Payment	Amount for Interest	Amount for Principal	Balance
				$34,416.45
220	$1,760.56	$ 186.42	$ 1,574.14	32,842.31
221	1,760.56	a.	b.	c.
222	1,760.56	d.	e.	f.

Spiral Review

Subtract. (Skill 6)

18. 48,000 − 29.46 **19.** 78,902 − 22.98 **20.** 18,185 − 45.11

21. Gloria and Jeff Dunne have reached an agreed-upon price of $225,000 to purchase a home. They plan to make a 30% down payment and finance the rest at 6% for 25 years. What is the monthly payment? (Lesson 10.2)

22. ALGEBRA Silvia Eisner purchases a DVD, a paperback novel, and a magazine. She gives the clerk a $50.00 bill and receives $11.58 in change. If the sales tax rate is 10.1%, find the total price of the sale. (Lesson 6.2)

GET READY for the Next Lesson

PREREQUISITE SKILL Multiplying Decimals (Skill 8)

Multiply.

23. 7.2 × 154.8 **24.** 44.2 × 31.93

25. 151.5 × 23.8 **26.** 36.585 × 971.2

27. 71.34 × 485.13 **28.** 75.3 × 7.53

LESSON 10.5

Real Estate Taxes

Lesson Objective

Calculate the assessed value and real estate taxes for a home.

Content Vocabulary

- real estate taxes
- assessed value
- tax rate
- market value
- rate of assessment

As You Read

Identify What is a real estate tax?

GET READY for the Lesson

Why do local governments sometimes need to increase property taxes?

Ursula Wilkes read about the property tax increase the City of Hampton was seeking. Since Hampton had grown in the last ten years, the newer sections of town needed fire stations and the schools were overcrowded.

Computing Your Real Estate Taxes When you own a home, you will have to pay city or county **real estate taxes**. The government uses the money collected to pay for roads, parks, schools, government offices, and other services. The amount of real estate tax that you pay in one year depends on:

The **assessed value** of your property. This is the dollar value a tax assessor assigns to a property for taxation purposes.The **tax rate** on property is sometimes expressed in mills per dollar of the property's assessed value. A mill is 0.001. A tax rate of 80 mills is $80 per $1,000 of **assessed** value. When working with mills, it is often convenient to express them in dollars by dividing by 1,000.

You can calculate the assessed value by multiplying **market value** (the price to buy or sell the property) by the **rate of assessment**, a percent of the property's market value that is taxed. The municipality employs an assessor to determine the market value. The rate of assessment is a percent of the market value. The assessed value is computed using the formula:

Assessed Value = Market Value × Rate of Assessment

The real estate tax is calculated using this formula:

Real Estate Tax = Tax Rate × Assessed Value

EXAMPLE 1

The Madison County tax assessor determined that the market value of Courtland Farm is $340,000.00. The rate of assessment in the county is 40% of market value, and the tax rate is 50.73 mills. Calculate the **(a)** assessed value, **(b)** tax rate as a decimal, and **(c)** real estate tax.

Step 1: Find the assessed value.

Assessed Value = Market Value × Rate of Assessment

$136,000.00 = $340,000 × 40%

Westend61/Glow Images

Step 2: Express the tax rate as a decimal.

$$\text{Tax Rate as a Decimal} = \frac{50.73}{1{,}000} = \mathbf{0.05073}$$

Step 3: Find the real estate tax.

Real Estate Tax = Tax Rate × Assessed Value

\$6,899.28 = 0.05073 × \$136,000.00

Concept CHECK

The tax rate for Problems 1–3 is 65.50 mills, market value is \$70,000.00, and rate of assessment is 40%. After finding the following, check your answers in the back of the book:

1. The assessed value.
2. The tax rate as a decimal.
3. The real estate tax.

Need Help? Go to...
Workshop 38: Problem-Solving Strategies: Writing an Equation, p. 78

EXAMPLE 2 Algebra

Gilberto and Cristina Espinosa pay \$3,188.16 in annual property taxes. The rate of assessment for their tax district is 45%, and their tax rate is 46 mills. What is their property's market value?

Let m = Market value of the Espinosa property.

Market Value = Tax Rate × Assessed Value

$$\$3{,}188.16 = \frac{46}{1{,}000} \times (m \times 45\%)$$

Convert tax rate to decimal → $\$3{,}188.16 = 0.046 \times m \times 0.45$

Multiply → $\$3{,}188.16 = 0.0207m$

Divide both sides by 0.0207 → $\mathbf{\$154{,}017.39} = m$

The market value of the Espinosa property is \$154,017.39

Concept CHECK

Complete the problem. Check your answer in the back of the book.

4. Peter and Kay Thibault pay annual real estate taxes of \$3,270.00. The tax rate in their tax district is 62 mills and the rate of assessment is 54%. What is the Thibault property's market value?
5. John Stringham pays \$4,650.00 in annual real estate tax. The tax rate in his district is 57 mills and the rate of assessment is 37%. What is John's property's value?

Lesson Practice

For Problems 6 and 7, calculate the (a) assessed value, (b) tax rate as a decimal, and (c) real estate tax.

6. Jevon Noda's home has a market value of \$72,000, the rate of assessment is 30%, and the tax rate is 85.50 mills.
7. The Simms' condominium has a \$159,800 market value. The rate of assessment is 40%, and the tax rate is 46.23 mills.

Did You Know?

Walt Disney World Walt Disney decided to build a new version of his California resort, Disneyland, because only 2% of Disneyland's visitors came from the East Coast. Walt Disney World opened in 1971, five years after Disney's death, on 27,400 acres of former swampland near Orlando, Florida.

8. Brenda Roth's home is located in Columbus, Ohio, where the rate of assessment is 35% of market value. The tax rate is $59.56 per $1,000.00 of assessed value. If her home has a market value of $392,000.00, what are its **(a)** assessed value and **(b)** property tax?

9. The rate of assessment in Foster, Rhode Island, is 50%, and the tax rate is $11.29 per $1,000 of assessed value. What is the real estate tax on a piece of property that has a market value of $236,000.00?

10. Ajani Zeta's home is located in Baton Rouge, Louisiana, where the rate of assessment is 10% of market value. The tax rate is 94.523 mills. His home has a market value of $480,000. **(a)** What is its assessed value? **(b)** What is the property tax?

11. The rate of assessment in Manchester, New Hampshire, is 100%. The tax rate is $16.85 per $1,000.00 of assessed value. What is the real estate tax on a piece of property that has a market value of $186,000.00?

12. Gina Jasinski lives in Orlando, Florida, in a home with a $124,600 market value. The rate of assessment is 40%, and her tax rate is 19.126 mills. She receives her tax bill in early November. She can get a discount on her taxes if she pays the bill prior to the due date. The discount is 4% if paid in November, 3% if paid in December, 2% if paid in January, and 1% if paid in February. Calculate her tax payment for each of the four discount periods.

H.O.T. Problems

13. CHALLENGE PROBLEM Jose and Trudy Engstrom, who live in Dallas, Texas, own a home that has a $246,000 market value. The rate of assessment is 80% of the market value. The tax rate in mills is composed of city, 7.292; school, 11.7264; county, 2.18935; and community college, 0.081. What are the **(a)** annual real estate tax for each entity and **(b)** total tax?

14. ALGEBRA Toby and Betty Combs pay $8,719.38 in annual property taxes. Their home has a market value of $361,800.00 with a tax rate of 48.2 mills. What is the rate of assessment in their tax district?

Spiral Review

Multiply. (Skill 8)

15. 37.3×78.4 **16.** 13.18×9.42 **17.** 13.3×4.37

18. Anna Kissling obtained a single-payment loan of $4,600 for 181 days from her bank. Determine the maturity value of the loan if the rate is **(a)** 9% ordinary interest and **(b)** 9% exact interest. (Lesson 8.1)

GET READY for the Next Lesson

PREREQUISITE SKILL Finding the Percentage (Skill 30)

Find the percentage.

19. $65 × 25% **20.** $12,831 × 52%

21. $823 × 21.4% **22.** 23% × $25,711

23. $33,333 × 4.3% **24.** $44,893 × 3.4%

LESSON 10.6

Homeowners Insurance

Lesson Objective

Determine the amount of coverage for homeowners insurance.

Content Vocabulary

- homeowners insurance
- property damage coverage
- personal liability coverage
- medical coverage
- loss-of-use coverage
- replacement value

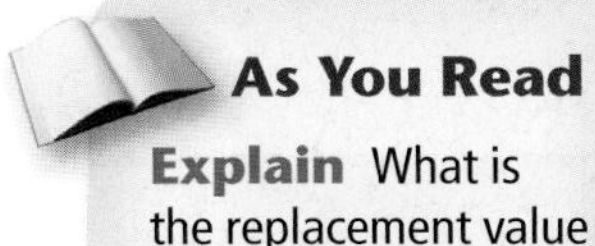

As You Read

Explain What is the replacement value of a home?

GET READY for the Lesson

Why would you need to insure your home?

A forest fire destroyed Randy and Connie Silver's home. They managed to save some family mementoes and important papers but lost everything else. They were overwhelmed by the expense of rebuilding their home.

Homeowners Insurance When you are a homeowner, you will need to buy **homeowners insurance** to provide financial protection against various losses. Basic coverage included in a homeowners insurance policy includes four kinds of coverage:

Property damage coverage pays for damage to the home and personal property such as computers, furniture, and clothing. Fire, windstorm, rain, lightning, and so on may cause the damage. The homeowner must purchase special coverage for damage caused by flooding. **Personal liability coverage** protects you as a homeowner if someone alleges that your negligence caused her or him bodily injury or property damage. For example, if a neighbor falls off the deck of your house and breaks a leg, personal liability will protect you from financial losses. **Medical coverage** pays for medical expenses for nonfamily members accidently injured on your property. It does not matter who is at fault. **Loss-of-use coverage** pays for the expenses for living away from home while your damaged home is being repaired.

To **recover** full payment for any loss up to the amount of the policy, you must insure your home for at least 80% of its replacement value. **Replacement value** is the amount required to reconstruct your home if it is destroyed. To calculate the minimum amount of coverage, use the formula:

Amount of Coverage on Home = Replacement Value × Insured Percent

Figure 10.5

Coverage	Percent Covered
Garage and other structures	10%
Loss of use	20%
Personal property	50%

Insurance companies use the amount of coverage on your home to calculate the amount of coverage you receive on a detached garage, personal property, and for loss of use.

To calculate the amount of coverage for each type of protection, use the formula:

Amount of Coverage = Amount of Coverage on Home × Percent Covered

moodboard/Corbis

Study Tip

Write Your Own Questions
Write and solve your own word problems as you study. Use the practice problems in the book as models.

EXAMPLE

Joy and Ron Amodeo estimate the replacement value of their home at $194,000. They have insured the home for 80% of its replacement value. According to the preceding guidelines and using **Figure 10.5** on page 391, what is the amount of coverage on the Amodeos' personal property?

Step 1: Find the amount of coverage on the home.

Replacement Value × Insured Percent

$194,000 × 80% = $155,200 coverage on home

Step 2: Find the amount of coverage on personal property.

Amount of Coverage on Home × Percent Covered

$155,200 × 50% = **$77,600 coverage on personal property**

Concept CHECK

Complete the problems. Check your answers in the back of the book.

Assume that Tilda and Nolan Wendt insure their home for 90% of its replacement value of $320,000, or $288,000. Using the percents from **Figure 10.5** on page 391, find the coverage for the following.

1. Personal property **2.** Loss of use **3.** Garage

Lesson Practice

For Problems 4–8, use Figure 10.5 on page 391 for the percent of coverage to determine the (a) amount of insurance on the home, (b) amount of coverage for the garage, (c) amount of coverage for loss of use, and (d) amount of coverage for personal property.

4. Replacement value: $270,000; coverage: 80%.

5. Replacement value: $405,000; coverage: 100%.

6. Replacement value: $538,500; coverage: 90%.

7. Replacement value: $324,000; coverage: 90%.

8. Replacement value: $324,000; coverage: 80%.

9. WRITING Write a brief paragraph that compares the answers for Problem 7 to those for Problem 8.

Spiral Review

Find the percent. (Skill 30)

10. 10% of 90,000 **11.** 80% of 30,000 **12.** 75% of 140,000

13. ALGEBRA Amber Hawke estimates that she will drive 12,000 miles during the year and will have $2,200 in annual vehicle-related fixed costs. If her goal is to have a cost per mile of $0.36 or less for her compact car, what is the maximum annual variable cost she can have? (Lesson 9.5)

GET READY for the Next Lesson

PREREQUISITE SKILL Finding the Percentage (Skill 30)

Find the percentage.

14. 60% of 24,000 **15.** 55% of 13,400 **16.** 94% of 45,300

LESSON 10.7

Homeowners Insurance Premium

Lesson Objective
Calculate the annual homeowners insurance premium.

Content Vocabulary
- premium
- fire protection class

GET READY for the Lesson

How much does it cost to insure a home?

Ashley and Tim Huggins are buying their first home, and they want to make sure that they purchase adequate insurance coverage. They meet with several insurance agents.

Glow Images

As You Read

Summarize
What is a premium?

Homeowners Insurance Premium The important considerations when buying a home, as they say in real estate, are location, location, location. Your location even **affects** your homeowners policy **premium**—the amount you must pay for insurance coverage. Also, the type of house (brick, masonry, veneer, or wood frame) and the amount of coverage affect your premium. The insurance company will assign your home a number that reflects how fire resistant it is and how close you are to a water source. This number is called your **fire protection class**.

Figure 10.6

Homeowners Insurance Premiums

Amount of Insurance Coverage	Annual Premiums for a Typical Homeowners Policy									
	Brick/Masonry Veneer Fire Protection Class					Wood Frame Fire Protection Class				
	1–6	7–8	9	10	11	1–6	7–8	9	10	11
$ 80,000	$ 301	$ 310	$ 410	$ 429	$ 493	$ 321	$ 331	$ 429	$ 454	$ 519
90,000	335	345	456	480	551	361	370	480	504	580
100,000	373	384	509	533	613	400	411	533	561	644
120,000	443	455	605	635	730	476	489	635	668	768
150,000	574	589	781	821	944	616	633	821	865	993
200,000	770	791	1,051	1,105	1,271	828	850	1,105	1,164	1,338
250,000	921	943	1,201	1,276	1,459	975	998	1,276	1,358	1,554
300,000	1,099	1,126	1,434	1,523	1,743	1,164	1,191	1,523	1,619	1,854
400,000	1,276	1,306	1,664	1,766	2,021	1,334	1,381	1,766	1,880	2,154
500,000	1,636	1,675	2,134	2,265	2,593	1,731	1,773	2,265	2,411	2,761

EXAMPLE

The replacement value of Marcia Syke's home is $150,000, and she has insured it for 80% of its replacement value. The home is of wood-frame construction and has been rated in fire protection class 4. What is the amount of **(a)** coverage and **(b)** annual premium?

Step 1: Find the amount of coverage.

Replacement Value of Home × Insured Percent of Replacement Value

$150,000 × 80% = **$120,000 coverage**

Continued on next page

Step 2: Find the annual premium. (See **Figure 10.6** on page 393.)

Find the column, Wood Frame.

Find the Fire Protection Class 1–6 column.

Find the Amount of Insurance Coverage row with 120,000.

Follow across the row and down the column to where 120,000 and 1–6 meet.

= **$476 annual premium**

Concept CHECK

Find the (a) amount of coverage and (b) annual insurance premium using Figure 10.6 on page 393. Check your answer in the back of the book.

1. The replacement cost of Jalese Chiara's brick home is $200,000. It is insured at 75% of its replacement value. The home is in fire protection class 11.

Lesson Practice

For Problems 2 and 3, find (a) the amount of coverage and (b) the annual insurance premium. Use Figure 10.6 on page 393.

2. The Campbells own a $150,000 wood-frame house. It is in fire protection class 8, and they insured it for 100% of its replacement value.

3. Kuen Yee owns a $400,000 brick home in fire protection class 11 that is insured for 75% of its replacement value.

4. The Quicks own a brick home that has a replacement value of $375,000. They purchased a homeowners policy for 80% of its replacement value. They live in an area rated fire protection class 9. **(a)** What is the annual policy premium? **(b)** What would the annual policy premium be if they were in class 11?

5. CHALLENGE PROBLEM Gary Penn owns a $150,000 brick home. He insures it for 100% of its replacement value. His rate of assessment is 35%, his tax rate is 51.58 mills, and his fire protection is rated class 6. He has a $120,000.00 mortgage at 8% for 20 years. How much is the monthly payment for the **(a)** mortgage, **(b)** real estate taxes, **(c)** insurance, and **(d)** total monthly payment?

Spiral Review

Round to the nearest thousandth. (Skill 2)

6. 0.1245 **7.** 7.21973 **8.** 456.25478

9. ALGEBRA Donald Houston can save $55 on a new microwave if he buys it on sale. The store has marked down the microwave 45%. What is its regular price? (Lesson 6.6)

GET READY for the Next Lesson

PREREQUISITE SKILL Adding Decimals (Skill 5)

Add.

10. 28.4 + 73.2 + 221.88 **11.** 98.34 + 17.626 **12.** 191.34 + 58.177 + 2.03

LESSON 10.8

Other Housing Costs

Lesson Objective

Compute the total housing cost and compare it with suggested guidelines.

Content Vocabulary

- utility costs

GET READY for the Lesson

What are some simple steps you can take to reduce your use of energy and save money?

Amy and Lloyd Devereux have been investigating ways to burn less fossil fuel to create energy. They are considering a wind turbine and solar panels.

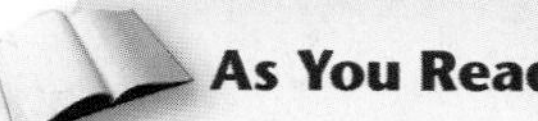

As You Read

Identify Name several home improvements you might want to make.

Computing Other Housing Costs In addition to your monthly mortgage payment, real estate taxes, and insurance payment, you will **sustain** expenses for utilities, maintenance, home improvements, and so on. **Utility costs** may include charges for electricity, gas, water, telephone, cell phone, cable TV, Internet service, and heating fuel.

Many budget studies and lenders recommend that your total monthly housing cost be less than 35% of your monthly gross pay.

EXAMPLE

Figure 10.7

Housing Expenses for May	
Mortgage Payment	$698.24
Insurance	26.50
Real Estate Taxes	157.08
Electricity	65.90
Heating Fuel	64.20
Telephone	66.26
Water	28.90
Cell Phone	59.95
Internet/Cable TV	95.89
Loan Payment	50.00
Repair Storm Door	78.36

Sue and Paul Kwan have a combined monthly gross pay of $3,820. See **Figure 10.7** for the list of their expenses for May. Were their May housing costs within the 35% guideline?

Step 1: Find the total monthly cost.

Sum of expenses: = $1,391.28 total monthly cost

Step 2: Find the recommended maximum.

$3,820 × 35% = $1,337 recommended maximum

Step 3: Compare. Is the total monthly cost less than the recommended maximum?

Is $1,391.28 less than $1,337.00?

No, the Kwans are not within the guideline.

Concept CHECK

Complete the problems. Check your answers in the back of the book.

Determine whether the Kwans in the above **Example** would be within the 35% guideline if they had a gross pay of:

1. $3,950 **2.** $4,000

Did You Know?

Satellite Coin Toss

Although he was thousands of miles away in Washington, D.C., President Ronald Reagan participated in the pregame coin toss for Super Bowl XIX by way of satellite television link. San Francisco defeated Miami 38–16 in the game played in Palo Alto, California, on January 20, 1985.

Lesson Practice

Monthly Expenses for April	
Mortgage Payment	$644.00
Insurance	40.83
Real Estate Taxes	228.33
Electricity	166.24
Heating Fuel	178.26
Telephone	69.61
Water & Sewer	55.50
Cell Phone	69.99
Satellite TV Service	85.99
Home Equity Loan	75.00
Miscellaneous Repairs	89.65
Total	$

3. Dan Hosteler's monthly gross pay is $5,100. Find the total expenses for April. Was Dan within the 35% guideline?

Housing Expenses for January	
Mortgage Payment	$885.50
Insurance	19.75
Real Estate Taxes	282.33
Home Equity Loan	32.40
Electricity	275.90
Heating (gas)	243.80
Internet & Phone Bundle	68.75
Water & Sewer	42.75
Satellite TV Service	51.00
Total	$

4. Joan Ryder's monthly gross pay is $5,525. Find the total expenses for January. Was Joan within the 35% guideline?

Condo Expenses for March	
Mortgage Payment	$533.50
Insurance–Liability and Contents	35.55
Home Equity Loan	132.40
Electricity	158.66
Heating (gas)	243.80
Internet & Phone Bundle	68.75
Water & Sewer	65.30
Satellite TV Service	51.00
Total	$

5. Frank and Yvette Shelby have a condo. The monthly gross income for Frank is $1,860 and for Yvette is $1,900. Find the total expenses for March. Are their housing costs within the 35% guideline for their combined income?

6. Fara Pinkston recorded her housing expenses for the month of August: mortgage payment, $347.90; insurance, $52.00; taxes, $184.00; electricity, $64.40; phone service, $33.50; fuel, $38.25; water, $27.44; and repairs, $179.87. Her monthly gross pay is $2,150. What is her total monthly cost? Is it within the 35% recommendation?

Annual Home Expenses	
Water/Sewer Charges	$ 352.66
Electricity	1,194.00
Phone Service	655.92
Water Heater Replacement	590.34
Window Repairs	580.10
New Furnace/AC	6,458.90
Internet & Phone Bundle	1,198.80
Gutter Replacements	2,560.00
New Lawn Mower	579.20
Total	$

7. David and Helen Voss have a combined monthly gross income of $5,750.00. Their records show that for last year, they paid $10,789.20 in mortgage payments, $581.00 for insurance premiums, and $2,685.00 in real estate taxes. In addition, they had the annual home expenses listed to the left. What was their average monthly housing cost for last year? Was it within the 35% recommendation?

For Problem 8, use Figure 10.1 on page 377 to find the loan payment and Figure 10.6 on page 393 to find the insurance premium.

8. **CHALLENGE PROBLEM** Molly and Chris Spaulding purchased a brick house for $150,000. They made a 20% down payment and financed the remaining amount at 8% for 30 years. The real estate tax rate is 71.57 mills, and the rate of assessment is 40%. They have a homeowners insurance policy for the purchase price of the house. The fire protection is rated class 9. For the month of August, they recorded the following housing expenses: electricity, $69.20; phone, $44.85; cable, $39.95; water, $18.80; and $74.65 to repair a door. They have a combined monthly gross income of $5,400. Find the monthly **(a)** mortgage payment, and **(b)** insurance premium, **(c)** taxes, and **(d)** the total housing cost for August. Are they within the 35% recommendation?

Spiral Review

Which number is higher? (Skill 1)

9. 2,109.8 or 2,107.9
10. 7,484.08 or 74,846.50

11. **ALGEBRA** Wade Torres is leasing a domestic midsize sedan. The $1,599.00 due at signing includes title and fees. His monthly lease payment will be $159.00 plus 6% sales tax. If the total lease cost is $7,666.44, for how many months does the lease last? (Lesson 9.6)

GET READY for the Next Lesson

PREREQUISITE SKILL Adding Whole Numbers (Skill 3)

Add.

12. $78 + $195 + $692
13. $675 + $834 + $297
14. $965 + $1,055 + $2,430
15. $728 + $692 + $111 + $4,376
16. $59 + $77 + $461 + $7,954
17. $794 + $1,429 + $3,680 + $5,291

Renting or Owning a Home

Lesson Objective
Calculate the average monthly cost of renting a home, and compare the total costs of renting to the total costs of owning a home.

Content Vocabulary
- security deposit

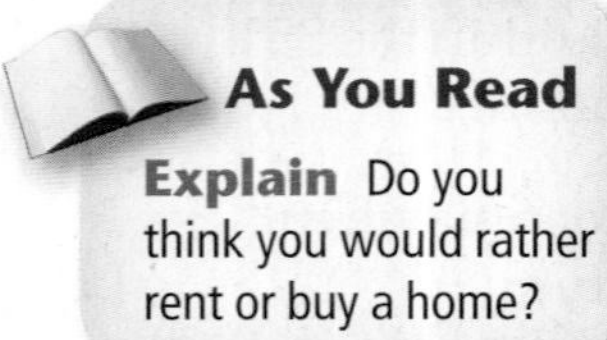

Explain Do you think you would rather rent or buy a home?

GET READY for the Lesson

How will you decide whether to rent or to buy a home?

Marcel and Lorraine East are searching for their first home. They have to decide whether to rent or to buy a home.

Renting or Owning a Home Many people rent homes, condominiums, apartments, or manufactured homes. Some of them rent because they either cannot afford to purchase a home or do not want the responsibilities that go with homeownership. One advantage of renting includes not having to make the down payment that ownership requires. Another is not having to worry about major unplanned housing expenses, such as roof repairs, broken appliances, and leaking pipes. Renters also have more flexibility than owners—they do not have to sell before moving.

Some renting disadvantages are that renters, unlike homeowners, do not receive federal income tax benefits such as mortgage interest and property tax deductions. Renters do not build up any equity in the house or apartment they are renting. In addition, most renters pay a one-time **security deposit** plus the first month's rent when they sign a lease. The security deposit may be used to pay for cleaning the apartment at **termination** of the rental agreement. It may also be used to change the locks or repair damage to the rental unit.

Compare Costs The cost of renting includes such items as the monthly rent, premiums on renter's insurance, loss of interest on the security deposit, and utilities. As the cost of living increases, monthly rent payments may increase just as an owner's real estate taxes may rise.

One disadvantage for home buyers involves the closing costs they must pay. Another is the loss of interest they could be making if their down payment were in a savings account. The tax savings may offset some of the lost interest. A home may appreciate (increase) in value or depreciate (decrease) in value depending on market conditions. The monthly mortgage payment will stay the same for the life of the loan if the interest rate is fixed. With an adjustable rate, the mortgage payment may increase or decrease depending on the interest rate at the time of the adjustment.

You cannot easily compare the costs of renting an apartment to buying a home. You can, however, compare the costs of renting versus buying similar homes. You calculate the total annual cost by adding all expenses for the year. You determine the average monthly cost by dividing the total annual cost by the number of months (12).

$$\text{Average Monthly Cost} = \frac{\text{Total Annual Cost}}{\text{Number of Months}}$$

Alan Schein/Alamy

Need Help? Go to...

- Skill 3: Adding Whole Numbers, p. SK4
- Workshop 7: Dividing Decimals, p. 16

EXAMPLE 1

Mike Cheng plans to rent an apartment for $675 a month. The security deposit is one month's rent. He estimates that annual expenses will be as shown in **Figure 10.8.** What is his average monthly cost?

Figure 10.8

Annual Rental Expenses	
Rent ($675 × 12) =	$8,100.00
Loss of Interest	28.00
Renters Insurance	320.00
Electricity	1,280.00
Heating (gas)	1,500.00
Telephone/Internet/Cable TV	1,255.00
Cell Phone	848.00

Step 1: Find the total yearly cost.

$8,100 + $28 + $320 + $1,280 + $1,500 + $1,255 + $848 = $13,331

Step 2: Find the average monthly cost.

$$\frac{\text{Total Annual Cost}}{\text{Number of Months}} = \frac{\$13{,}331.00}{12} = \$1{,}110.916 = \mathbf{\$1{,}110.92}$$

Concept CHECK

Calculate the average monthly cost of renting (e). Check your answers in the back of the book.

1. Joe and Allison Zurski

Annual Rental Expenses	
Rent: $820 × 12 =	**a.** $
Loss of Interest	42
Renters Insurance	280
Electricity	360
Heating (gas)	1,600
Telephone: $40 × 12	**b.**
Cell Phone: $44 × 12	**c.**
Cable TV: $60 × 12	**d.**

2. Tasha Rollins

Annual Rental Expenses	
Rent: $480 × 12 =	**a.** $
Loss of Interest	25.00
Renters Insurance	175.00
Electricity	400.00
Heating (gas)	960.00
Satellite TV: $53 × 12	**b.**
Cell Phone: $44 × 12	**c.**
Trash pickup: $8 × 12	**d.**

Reading Math +−÷=

Multiple Questions

Sometimes math problems contain more than one question. To answer them correctly, read carefully to understand all of the questions and the answers you need to provide.

EXAMPLE 2

Margaret Fairchild currently rents a home and has the expenses shown in **Figure 10.9.** She is considering buying a similar house with a $21,000 down payment. She estimates her housing and rental expenses as shown in **Figure 10.9**. Is it less expensive for Margaret to buy or rent a home? What is the difference?

Step 1: Find the annual cost of renting.

$10,500 + $45 + $380 + $720 + $1,800 + $480 + $528 + $720 = $15,173 annual renting cost

Step 2: Find the annual homeownership cost.

($6,000 + $2,200 + $975 + $1,200 + $2,140 + $636 + $528 + $1,200 + $570) − $725 = $14,724 annual homeownership cost

Step 3: Find the difference.

$15,173 − $14,724 = **$449 less for owning than renting.**

Figure 10.9

Annual Rental Expenses	
Rent: $875 × 12 =	$10,500
Loss of Interest	45
Renters Insurance	380
Electricity	720
Heating (gas)	1,800
Telephone: $40 × 12	480
Cell Phone: $44 × 12	528
Cable TV: $60 × 12	720
	$15,173

Annual Homeowner Expenses	
Mortgage Payment: $500 × 12 =	$ 6,000
Property Taxes	2,200
Homeowner Insurance	975
Electricity	1,200
Heating (gas)	2,140
Satellite TV: $53 × 12	636
Cell Phone: $44 × 12	528
Maintenance	1,200
Lost Interest	570
Tax Savings	(725)
	$14,724

Concept CHECK

Complete Figure 10.10. Compare the expenses that Art and Megan Fowler would incur renting versus the cost of owning a home. Check your answers in the back of the book.

3. Is it less expensive for Art and Megan Fowler to buy or rent a home? Find the difference.

Figure 10.10

Annual Rental Expenses	
Rent: $775 × 12 =	**a.** $
Loss of Interest	40
Renters Insurance	400
Electricity	860
Heating (gas)	1,800
Telephone: $50 × 12	**b.**
Cell Phone: $55 × 12	**c.**
Cable TV: $65 × 12	**d.**
Total	**e.** $

Annual Homeowner Expenses	
Mortgage Payment	$5,500
Property Taxes	2,380
Homeowner Insurance	1,150
Electricity	1,440
Heating (gas)	2,800
Satellite TV: $53 × 12	**f.**
Cell Phone: $44 × 12	**g.**
Maintenance	960
Lost Interest	670
Tax Savings	(1,225)
Total	**h.** $

Lesson Practice

For Problems 4–9, calculate the (a) total annual cost and (b) average monthly cost.

	Own/ Rent	Monthly Payment	Annual Property Taxes	Annual Insurance	Annual Repairs	Annual Utilities	Total Annual Cost	Average Monthly Cost
4.	Own	$ 660.00	$1,900	$660	$1,540	$2,840	a. $	b. $
5.	Rent	450.00	0	350	0	2,160	a.	b.
6.	Rent	1,450.00	0	720	0	3,200	a.	b.
7.	Own	738.80	2,000	651	650	2,210	a.	b.

8. Wilfred and Fiona Lowell plan to rent an apartment for $475 a month. The security deposit is one month's rent. They estimate that annual expenses will be insurance, $220; utilities, $1,789; and lost interest, $20.

9. Cara and Nels Ashcroft are buying a $225,000.00 home. Their annual housing expenses are mortgage payments, $14,169.60; real estate taxes, $4,832.00; annual insurance premium, $1,276.00; maintenance, $1,200.00; utilities, $2,415.00; cable TV, $792.00; and trash pickup, $180.00. The lost interest on the down payment is $1,200.00, and the tax savings is $1,500.00.

10. Tony Quinn rents a condominium for $620 a month. He pays a $75 monthly fee for all maintenance work. His annual expenses are: insurance, $234; lost interest, $32; and utility bills, $2,280. What is his average monthly expense?

11. Daniel and Angie Callan are buying a $480,000 home. Their annual housing expenses are: mortgage payments, $38,304; real estate taxes, $9,240; annual insurance premium, $1,766; maintenance (for example, plumbing repairs, painting, insulation), $1,275; and utilities (heating, electricity, telephone, and so on), $4,600. The lost interest on the down payment is $4,800, and the tax savings is $6,400. What is the Callans' average monthly expense?

12. Morris and Rose Benedetto are buying a $180,000 home. Their annual housing expenses are: mortgage payments, $13,200; real estate taxes, $4,200; annual insurance premium, $961; maintenance (plumbing repairs, painting, insulation), $1,629; and utilities (heating, electric, telephone), $4,246. The lost interest on the down payment is $1,440, and the tax savings is $1,650. What is their average monthly expense?

13. Sharon Wilson rents an apartment $930 a month. She has these annual expenses: electricity, $1,464; gas, $1,320; phone/cable, $1,224; insurance, $300; and lost interest, $32.55. What are **(a)** the annual expenses, and **(b)** the average monthly expenses?

14. Carrington Alvarez rents an apartment for $1,100 a month. She has these annual expenses: electricity, $960; gas, $1,010; phone/cable/Internet, $1,900; insurance, $375; and lost interest, $47. What are **(a)** the annual expenses, and **(b)** the average monthly expenses?

Did You Know?

Garbage Barge For two months, a barge carrying 3,186 tons of trash from Long Island, New York, sailed the Atlantic Ocean and Gulf of Mexico, unable to find a port where it would be allowed to dump its cargo. Finally, after 6,000 miles, it unloaded the garbage—back in New York.

Figure 10.11

Annual Rental Expenses	
Rent: $750 × 12 =	**a.** $
Loss of Interest	41
Renters Insurance	289
Electricity	1,560
Heating (gas)	1,800
Telephone: $50 × 12	**b.**
Cell Phone: $55 × 12	**c.**
Cable TV: $65 × 12	**d.**
Total	**e.** $

Annual Homeowner Expenses	
Mortgage Payment	$6,100
Property Taxes	2,100
Homeowner Insurance	374
Electricity	1,980
Heating (gas)	1,800
Satellite TV: $53 × 12	**f.**
Cell Phone: $44 × 12	**g.**
Maintenance	890
Lost Interest	680
Tax Savings	(850)
Total	**h.** $

15. Compare Geneva Amend's expenses for renting versus owning a home in **Figure 10.11.** Is it less expensive for her to buy or to rent a home, and what is the difference?

16. CHALLENGE PROBLEM Cyril DeBoer puts $25,000 down on a $175,000 home. Annual expenses would be mortgage payment, $10,800; property taxes, $3,400; insurance, $850; electricity, $1,220; heat, $980; water, $270; and maintenance, $1,260. Monthly expenses would be cell phone, $54 and cable, $85. He would lose $1,125 interest on his down payment and closing costs but would save $850 on income taxes. Cyril could rent a similar home for $1,100 a month with a one-month security deposit plus a $150 pet deposit. His annual expenses would be renters insurance, $420; electricity, $1,560; propane gas, $1,160; and lost interest, $54. His monthly expenses would be cell phone, $54 and cable, $85. Determine **(a)** whether it would be less expensive for Cyril to buy or to rent a home and **(b)** the difference.

Spiral Review

Add. (Skill 15)

17. $12\frac{3}{8} + 4\frac{3}{8}$ **18.** $7\frac{5}{6} + 4\frac{1}{2}$ **19.** $16\frac{5}{8} + 9\frac{1}{24}$

20. Douglas Aikin drove 13,000 miles in his car last year. His variable costs totaled $2,860, and his fixed costs totaled $2,936. What was the cost per mile for him to operate his car? (Lesson 9.5)

21. LaMyra Jeffcoat wants to buy a house selling for $109,000. The down payment is 20%. Find the **(a)** down payment and **(b)** amount of the mortgage. (Lesson 10.1)

GET READY for the Next Lesson

PREREQUISITE SKILL Finding the Percentage (Skill 30)

Find the percentage.

22. What percent of $80 is $16? **23.** What percent of $210 is $63?

24. What percent of $75 is $60? **25.** What percent of $85 is $38.25?

26. What percent of $235 is $148.05? **27.** What percent of $37.50 is $15.75?

CHAPTER 10 Review and Assessment

AFTER YOU READ
Chapter SUMMARY

Many costs come along with owning a home. It is useful to know how to compute the mortgage loan amount, monthly payment, total amount paid, total interest charged, and total closing costs. You can determine the allocation of the monthly payment toward principal and interest, and find the new principal. It is also useful to be able to calculate the assessed value and the real estate taxes, and determine the amount of coverage for homeowners insurance and the insurance premium. You can compute the total housing cost and compare it with suggested guidelines, and calculate the average cost of renting a dwelling and compare the total costs of renting versus owning a home.

Vocabulary Check

1. On a sheet of paper, use each of these terms in a sentence.

Content Vocabulary

- mortgage loan (p. 375)
- closing costs (p. 381)
- real estate taxes (p. 388)
- assessed value (p. 388)
- tax rate (p. 388)
- market value (p. 388)
- rate of assessment (p. 388)
- homeowners insurance (p. 391)
- property damage coverage (p. 391)
- personal liability coverage (p. 391)
- medical coverage (p. 391)
- loss-of-use coverage (p. 391)
- replacement value (p. 391)
- premium (p. 393)
- fire protection class (p. 393)
- utility costs (p. 395)
- security deposit (p. 398)

Academic Vocabulary

- secure (p. 375)
- fluctuate (p. 377)
- documents (p. 381)
- obtain (p. 384)
- assessed (p. 388)
- recover (p. 391)
- affects (p. 393)
- sustain (p. 395)
- termination (p. 398)

Concept Check

2. What is a mortgage?
3. Give the formula to determine the monthly payment.
4. List two closing costs.
5. How is the monthly payment on a loan allocated?
6. What is the assessed value of a property?
7. Give the formula for calculating real estate tax.
8. What does personal liability coverage protect homeowners from?
9. Name one factor that affects a homeowners insurance premium.
10. List three utility costs.
11. **CRITICAL THINKING** Explain the purpose of property damage coverage.

Lesson-by-Lesson Review

10.1 Mortgage Loans (pp. 375–376)

Compute the mortgage loan amount.

Desiree Ramsey is considering the purchase of a new condominium for $95,500. She must make a 20% down payment. What amount of mortgage loan does she need to finance the purchase?

Step 1: Find the down payment.

$95,500 × 20% = $19,100 down payment

Step 2: Find the mortgage loan amount.

Selling Price − Down Payment

$95,500 − $19,100 = **$76,400 mortgage loan amount**

Review Exercises

Find the (a) down payment and (b) mortgage loan amount.

	Selling Price	Down Payment	Down Payment	Mortgage Loan Amount
12.	$132,600	25.0%	a. $	b. $
13.	87,500	15.0%	a.	b.
14.	306,200	17.5%	a.	b.
15.	198,000	12.5%	a.	b.

16. The Windens have purchased their first home at a selling price of $110,900. What is the amount of the mortgage loan if they made a 30% down payment?

10.2 Monthly Payment and Total Interest (pp. 377–380)

Use a table or formula to determine the (a) monthly payment, (b) total amount paid, and (c) total interest charged.

Dee and Cissy White have applied for a $125,500 mortgage loan at an annual interest rate of 6%. The loan is for 25 years, and they will pay it in equal monthly payments that include interest. What is the total amount of interest on the loan?

Step 1: Find the monthly payment. (Refer to **Figure 10.1** on page 377.)

$$\frac{\text{Amount of Mortgage}}{\$1{,}000} \times \text{Monthly Payment for \$1,000 for a \$1,000 Loan}$$

$$\frac{\$125{,}500}{\$1{,}000} \times \$6.44 = \$808.22 \text{ monthly payment}$$

Step 2: Find the amount paid.

Monthly Payment × Number of Payments

$808.22 × (12 months × 25 years)

$808.22 × 300 = $242,466.00 amount paid

Step 3: Find the total interest charged.

Amount Paid − Amount of Mortgage

$242,466 − $125,500 = **$116,966 total interest charged**

Lesson-by-Lesson Review (continued)

Review Exercises

Use Figure 10.1 on page 377 to find the (a) monthly payment, (b) total amount paid, and (c) total interest charged.

	Mortgage Amount	Years	Rate	Monthly Payment	Total Amount Paid	Total Interest Charged
17.	$ 75,500	25	5.5%	a. $	b. $	c. $
18.	83,900	20	6.0	a.	b.	c.
19.	123,900	25	6.5	a.	b.	c.
20.	156,000	30	7.5	a.	b.	c.

21. **ALGEBRA** Kim and Sarah Carson applied for a $120,000 mortgage loan at an 8.25% annual interest rate. The loan is for 30 years, and the Carsons will repay it in equal monthly payments that include interest. Find the **(a)** monthly payment using the formula, **(b)** amount paid, and **(c)** total interest charged.

10.3 Closing Costs (pp. 381–383)

Calculate the total closing costs.

Shannon and Glenn Taylor have secured a $150,000 loan. They will finance the closing costs shown as part of the mortgage. What is the total of **(a)** their closing costs and **(b)** the actual amount financed with the mortgage?

Step 1: Find the closing costs. (Refer to **Figure 10.12**)

Closing Costs = $252 + $65 + ($150,000 × 2.0%) + $325 + $212 + $410 + $350 + $450 + ($150,000 × 0.30%) + ($150,000 × 1.10%) = **$7,164**

Step 2: Find the actual amount financed.

Amount of Mortgage + Closing Costs

$150,000 + $7,164 = **$157,164 actual amount financed**

Figure 10.12

Closing Costs	
Application Fee	$252
Credit Check	65
Points	2.00% of mortgage
Appraisal Fee	$325
Title Search	212
Title Insurance	410
Inspection	350
Attorney Fee	450
Documentation Stamp	0.30% of mortgage
Processing Fee	1.10% of mortgage

Review Exercises

Use the list of closing costs in Figure 10.12 for Problems 22–25 to determine the total closing costs.

22. Sung and Mu Lee obtain a mortgage loan of $245,600.
23. Greg and Kaye Meiers obtain a mortgage loan of $97,500.
24. Dave and Judy Levin obtain a mortgage loan of $128,300.
25. Rochelle St. James obtains a mortgage loan of $88,000.

Lesson-by-Lesson Review (continued)

10.4 Allocation of the Monthly Payment (pp. 384–387)

Compute (a) the allocation of the monthly payment toward principal and interest and (b) the new principal.

Rowena Tinley obtains a 30-year, $90,000 mortgage from State Bank. The interest rate is 7.5%, and her monthly payment is $629.10. For the first payment, what is the amount of **(a)** interest, **(b)** payment to principal, and **(c)** new principal?

Step 1: Find the interest.

Principal × Rate × Time

$90,000.00 × 7.5% × $\frac{1}{12}$ = **$562.50 interest**

Step 2: Find the payment to principal.

Monthly Payment − Interest

$629.10 − $562.50 = **$66.60 payment to principal**

Step 3: Find the new principal.

Previous Balance − Payment to Principal

$90,000.00 − $66.60 = **$89,933.40 new principal**

Review Exercises

Find the (a) amount for interest, (b) amount for principal, and (c) new principal.

	Mortgage Amount	Interest Rate	First Monthly Payment	Amount for Interest	Amount for Principal	New Principal
26.	$ 60,000	7.0%	$399.00	a. $	b. $	c. $
27.	130,000	5.5	738.40	a.	b.	c.
28.	145,500	6.0	873.00	a.	b.	c.
29.	159,900	5.0	858.66	a.	b.	c.

10.5 Real Estate Taxes (pp. 388–390)

Calculate the assessed value and real estate taxes for a home.

The Orange County tax assessor states that the Marvin Hotel's market value is $950,000. The rate of assessment in Orange County is 55% of market value, and the tax rate is 34.50 mills. What is the real estate tax on the Marvin Hotel?

Step 1: Find the assessed value.

Market Value × Rate of Assessment

$950,000 × 55% = $522,500 assessed value

Step 2: Express the tax rate as a decimal.

Tax Rate as a Decimal = $\frac{34.50}{1,000}$ = 0.0345

Step 3: Find the real estate tax.

Tax Rate × Assessed Value

0.0345 × $522,500.00 = **$18,026.25 real estate tax**

Lesson-by-Lesson Review (continued)

Review Exercises

30. The tax rate is 54.5 mills, the market value is $95,000, and the rate of assessment is 45%. Find the **(a)** assessed value, **(b)** tax rate as a decimal, and **(c)** real estate tax.

31. Sun Ri Pak's home is in a town that has an assessment rate of 30% of market value. The tax rate is $43.46 per $1,000 of assessed value. His home has a market value of $229,500. Determine the **(a)** assessed value and **(b)** property tax.

32. Harvey and Marie Levan own a home with a $542,000 market value. The assessment rate is 60%, and the tax rate is 24.31 mills. What is the annual real estate tax?

33. Steve and Shelia Hitt's home in a retirement community has a market value of $87,400. The assessment rate is 50%, and the tax rate is $30.45 per $1,000 of assessed value. What is their yearly real estate tax?

34. **ALGEBRA** Debra and Charles Winston pay $4,318.26 in annual property taxes. The assessment rate for their tax district is 35%, and their tax rate is 42 mills. What is their property's market value?

10.6 Homeowners Insurance (pp. 391–392)

Determine the amount of coverage for homeowners insurance using Figure 10.5 on page 391 to answer the problems in this section.

The replacement value of Todd and Melissa Dewey's home is $86,500. They have insured it for 80% of the replacement value. What is the amount of coverage on the Deweys' personal property?

Step 1: Find the amount of coverage on the home.

Replacement Value × Insured Percent

$86,500 × 80% = **$69,200 amount of coverage on the home**

Step 2: Find the personal property coverage.

Amount of Coverage on Home × Percent Covered

$69,200 × 50% = **$34,600 personal property coverage**

Review Exercises

Find the (a) amount of coverage and (b) amount of insurance.

	Replacement Value	Percent Covered	Amount of Coverage	Amount of Insurance for:
35.	$124,500	90%	a. $	b. Personal Property
36.	65,000	75%	a.	b. Loss of Use
37.	250,000	85%	a.	b. Garage
38.	87,000	80%	a.	b. Loss of Use

Lesson-by-Lesson Review (continued)

10.7 Homeowners Insurance Premium (pp. 393–394)

Calculate the annual homeowner's insurance premium.

The Cunninghams have insured their wood-frame house for 80% of its $150,000 replacement value. It is located in fire protection class 10. What is the amount of **(a)** coverage and **(b)** annual premium? (Use **Figure 10.6** on page 393 to answer the problem.)

Step 1: Find the amount of coverage.

Amount of Coverage = Replacement Value of Home × Insured Percent of Replacement Value

= $150,000 × 80% = **$120,000 coverage on home**

Step 2: Find the annual premium. (See **Figure 10.6** on page 393.)

Follow across the row and down the column to where 120,000 and wood-frame class 10 meet. **The premium is $668.**

Review Exercises

Complete the following table. Use Figure 10.6 on page 393 to answer the problems.

	Type of Construction	Replacement Value	Percent Covered	Fire Protection Class	Amount of Coverage	Annual Premium
39.	Brick	$100,000	80%	5	a. $	b. $
40.	Brick	100,000	90%	11	a.	b.
41.	Brick	120,000	75%	11	a.	b.
42.	Wood frame	120,000	100%	8	a.	b.
43.	Wood frame	200,000	75%	10	a.	b.
44.	Wood frame	300,000	100%	11	a.	b.

45. The Bhatias own a wood-frame home in an area rated fire protection class 6. Their two-family home has a replacement value of $300,000 and is insured for 100% of its replacement value. What is **(a)** the amount of coverage, and **(b)** the annual insurance premium?

46. Steve and Linda Patroulis own a brick home that has a replacement value of $500,000. They purchased a homeowners policy for 80% of the home's replacement value. They live in an area rated fire protection class 8. **(a)** What is their annual policy premium? **(b)** What would the premium be if they were in class 11?

47. Gary Gainsvoort owns a brick home with a replacement value of $500,000. He purchased a homeowners policy for 80% of the home's replacement value. He lives in an area with a fire protection class of 10. **(a)** What is his annual policy premium? **(b)** What would the premium be if he was in a fire protection class of 11?

Lesson-by-Lesson Review (continued)

10.8 Other Housing Costs (pp. 395–397)

Compute the total housing cost and compare it with the 35% guideline.
Peter and Lucy Cole have a combined monthly gross pay of $2,550. They keep a record of their monthly housing expenses. **Figure 10.13** lists the April expenses. Were their housing costs for April within the guideline?

Figure 10.13

Housing Expenses for April	
Rent Payment	$886.50
Renters Insurance	36.00
Heating (gas)	54.00
Electricity	108.20
Telephone Service	35.50

Step 1: Find the total monthly cost.

Total Monthly Cost = $886.50 + $36.00 + $54.00 + $108.20 + $35.50 = **$1,120.20**

Step 2: Find the recommended maximum.

Recommended Maximum = $2,550.00 × 35% = $892.50

Step 3: Compare. Is the total monthly cost less than the recommended maximum?

The Coles are not within the guideline because $1,120.20 is not less than $892.50.

Review Exercises

For Problems 48–51, determine the 35% recommended maximum for monthly housing costs.

48. Gross pay of $2,540

49. Gross pay of $3,298

50. Gross pay of $1,298 and $1,060

51. Gross pay of $2,440 and $3,056

52. Fredricka Paliski's monthly expenses were: mortgage payment, $547.90; insurance, $52.00; taxes, $184.00; electricity, $64.40; phone, $53.50; heating, $138.25; water, $27.44; and repairs, $179.87. Her monthly gross pay is $2,750. **(a)** What is her total monthly cost? **(b)** Is it within the 35% recommendation?

53. Yolanda and Josha Spezzano have a combined monthly gross income of $5,000.00. Last year they paid $11,841.20 in mortgage payments, $681.00 for insurance premiums, and $2,896.32 in real estate taxes. They had these monthly expenses: $58.30 for cell phone, $115.50 for electricity, $99.60 for telephone, Internet, cable bundle service, $146.00 for gas heat, and $56.60 for water. **(a)** What was their average monthly housing cost for last year? **(b)** Was it within the 35% recommendation?

54. Melvin Hayashi's monthly expenses for December were: $548.36 for mortgage payment, $29.50 for insurance premium, $122.50 for real estate taxes, $46.75 for refrigerator installment payment, $104.70 for electricity, $115.60 for telephone, Internet, and cable, $315.75 for home heating oil, and $21.80 for water. His monthly take-home pay is $4,500.00. What is his total monthly housing cost? Is it within the FHA recommendation?

Lesson-by-Lesson Review (continued)

10.9 Renting or Owning a Home (pp. 398–402)

Calculate the average monthly cost of renting a home, and compare the total costs of renting with the total costs of owning a home.

Vanessa Ardella plans to rent an apartment for $600 a month. The security deposit is one month's rent. She estimates that annual expenses will be as shown in **Figure 10.14.**

Figure 10.14

Annual Rental Expenses	
Rent: $600 × 12 =	$7,200
Loss of Interest	36
Renters Insurance	240
Electricity	420
Heating (gas)	1,560
Telephone	440
Cell Phone	436
Cable Vision	480

What is Vanessa's average monthly cost of renting the apartment?

Step 1: Find the total yearly cost.

Total Yearly Cost = $7,200 + $36 + $240 + $420 + $1,560 + $440 + $436 + $480 = $10,812

Step 2: Find the average monthly cost.

$$\text{Average Monthly Cost} = \frac{\text{Total Annual Cost}}{\text{Number of Months}} = \frac{\$10{,}812}{12} = \mathbf{\$901}$$

Vanessa's average monthly cost of renting the apartment is $901.

55. Complete the tables. Then compare the expenses of renting to those of owning a home.

Annual Rental Expenses	
Rent: $675 × 12 =	a. $
Loss of Interest	42
Renters Insurance	460
Electricity	960
Heating (gas)	1,600
Telephone: $55 × 12	b.
Cell Phone: $50 × 12	c.
Internet & Cable TV: $65 × 12	d.
Total	e. $

Annual Homeowner Expenses	
Mortgage Payment	$5,500
Property Taxes	2,280
Homeowner Insurance	1,164
Electricity	960
Heating (gas)	1,600
Satellite TV: $53 × 12	f.
Cell Phone: $44 × 12	g.
Maintenance	1,080
Lost Interest	660
Tax Savings	(1,120)
Total	h. $

56. Find the average monthly cost for the rental expenses and for the homeowner expenses.

Practice Test

Record your answer on a sheet of paper.

1. The selling price of the home Chuck Hill is buying is $135,000. He must make a 15% down payment. How much will he finance?
   A $133,500 **B** $135,000
   C $114,750 **D** $120,000
2. A townhouse's market value is $163,000. Rate of assessment is 36%. Tax rate is $75 per $1,000. What is the annual real estate tax?
   A $4,401 **B** $4,000
   C $401 **D** $5,868
3. Selling price: $276,000. Down payment: 25%. Terms: 8% for 15 years. What is the total interest charged?
   A $145,925.00 **B** $69,000.60
   C $149,205.60 **D** $194,205.00
4. What is the interest for Martha Sinclair's first monthly payment of a 30-year mortgage loan for $85,000 with a 9% interest rate?
   A $637.50 **B** $592.00
   C $620.50 **D** $578.00
5. The market value of Jake Ciccion's home is $110,450, and the assessment rate is 35% of market value. What is his home's assessed value?
   A $38,657.50 **B** $149,107.50
   C $42,548.75 **D** $37,420.55
6. The replacement value of Rebecca Gillian's home is $132,000; she has 80% covered by insurance. What is the dollar amount covered by her insurance?
   A $122,440 **B** $132,000
   C $105,600 **D** $106,500
7. Danny Pintero's home cost $210,430. If the federal government program for flood damage insurance covers only $95,906.08, what percent of the total value does this represent?
   A 36.2% **B** 45.6%
   C 56.4% **D** 65.0%
8. Ernie Kuchar's monthly gross pay is $2,420. His monthly housing costs total $1,145. What percent of his gross pay does this equal?
   A 46.2% **B** 48.3%
   C 49.2% **D** 47.3%
9. Max Roach rents an apartment for $750 a month. His security deposit is one month's rent. His annual expenses are $3,075 for water and power utilities, $875 for phone service, $420 for cable, and $15 in lost interest on his security deposit. What is his average monthly rental cost?
   A $1,177.92 **B** $1,115.42
   C $1,176.67 **D** $1,006.25
10. **ALGEBRA** Ray Kwan saved $14,500 for a down payment on a home. His bank requires a minimum down payment of 20% to qualify for a loan. What is the most he could spend on a home and still receive a loan?
11. Kim Bataglino applied for a 30-year, $95,000.00 mortgage loan. She would repay the loan in equal monthly payments. The interest rate would make the monthly payment on a $1,000.00 loan equal $6.32. What is the total amount she will pay on her $95,000.00 loan?
12. Barb Quinn owns a home with a $245,500.00 market value. It is in an area where the rate of assessment is 42% of market value. If the tax rate were $59.96 per $1,000.00, what would she pay in property tax?
13. 48.9% of 512
14. $4,392.44 + $31 + $0.87
15. $385 ÷ $2.52
16. 568 × 3.041
17. $865,090 × 0.73
18. 0.385 × 9.735

PART 1 Multiple Choice

Record your answers on the answer sheet provided by your teacher or on a sheet of paper.

1. What is Heather Witt's straight-time pay if she works 30 hours at an hourly rate of $8.75?

A $463.55 **B** $262.50
C $300.50 **D** $230.75

2. Bernie Vance's bank account had a balance of $6,435.96. He deposited a check for $837.59. Find the new balance.

A $7,345.65 **B** $5,598.37
C $7,273.55 **D** $8,737.68

3. Shannon Ho obtained a single payment loan of $5,678 for 90 days. If the exact interest rate were 12%, what would the loan's maturity value be?

A $5,848.34 **B** $6,010.00
C $5,846.01 **D** $5,980.71

4. Sam Dodd's house has an assessed value of $136,000. What is the real estate tax if the tax rate is 29.65 mills?

A $3,432.20 **B** $4,032.40
C $7,852.75 **D** $5,052.80

5. What is the purchase price of a $1,280.99 laptop that Jeri Walker bought in an area with a 5.75% sales tax rate?

A $1,354.65 **B** $1,554.55
C $1,857.55 **D** $2,016.05

6. What is the sticker price of a car with a base price of $19,865, $1,850 of options, and a $347 destination charge?

A $20,894 **B** $21,355
C $22,062 **D** $26,412

PART 2 Short Response/Griddable

7. Sherri Wessner bought a home with a $102,500 selling price. If she put down 20%, how much did she finance?

8. Hand lotion is tested by 1,000 people and 5.8% said they would buy it. The estimated market size is 2,800,000. The company estimates that each person would buy the lotion 6– times a year. Find the annual sales potential.

9. Alejandro Marco's group medical insurance coverage costs $6,880 a year. The company pays 65% of the cost. How much does he pay each month for medical insurance?

10. Jimmy Duffy purchased a 34.5-ounce can of coffee for $2.99. What is its unit price?

11. Robert Allen's credit card company uses the average-daily-balance method with new purchases included. His monthly periodic rate is 2.5% and last billing cycle's finance charge was $15.64. Find his average daily balance.

12. How long would it take for a home-improvement loan for $20,000 to earn interest of $500 at 8% ordinary interest?

13. Andrew Shepard drove his car 12,500 miles last year. The total of variable costs was $3,800.54 and of fixed costs was $2,230.00. What was the cost per mile to operate his car last year? Round to the nearest hundredth.

PART 3 Extended Response

Show your work.

14. Explain how you would find the assessed value of a $98,000 home.

15. What equation would you use to determine the new balance of a bank account?

16. Using the 35% guideline, what is the maximum amount for housing expenses if the owner's gross pay is $2,586?

TEST-TAKING TIP

Review Be sure to carefully review all of your answers, double-checking your figures for accuracy.

Building Academic Skills

Mathematics

Sometimes people with good credit can buy a home without making a down payment. This is called a *100% mortgage.* Suppose that you want to buy a house with a $100,000 asking price. You have two mortgage loan options. One is a 30-year, 100% mortgage loan of $100,000 at 6.35% interest. The other is a conventional loan of $80,000 at 6.25% that requires a $20,000 down payment. What would the monthly payments for each loan be?

English Language Arts/Writing

Choosing whether to buy or to rent a home depends on such factors as your current lifestyle, job expectations, and income. Why might a married couple in their late 20s with a baby due in five months be interested in buying a house? What type of housing would most attract a 21-year-old single person just beginning his or her career? Write a paragraph explaining your opinions about these individuals' housing priorities and the advantages and disadvantages of buying or renting for each.

Social Studies/Economics

People may buy houses at high prices, thinking the houses will continue to rise in value. However, if the value of the homes fall, homeowners may end up "upside-down" in their loan. This means that the value of their homes is less than the mortgage on it. Go to the Internet, newspaper, or magazine sources to find out more about current housing market conditions. Write a short article summarizing what you learn.

Building Real-World Skills

Ethics in Action

Reporting Tips At your job waiting tables, you earn much of your income from cash tips. The law requires servers to report their full tip amounts for tax purposes. However, your coworkers tell you that they report only the tips they received from credit card transactions. They say cash tips are "under the table," so it is okay to underreport, and they encourage you to do the same.

Discuss and Write:

a. Discuss what might happen if everyone avoided paying taxes because they thought they could get away with it.
b. Write a paragraph about the consequences of underreporting tips and other forms of income.

21st Century Workplace

Telecommuting The Internet has made it possible for more people to work away from their office—that is, to telecommute. With an Internet connection and a computer, workers can accomplish in the comfort of their own home all of the things they normally would at their employer's office. Many employers now offer this as an extra benefit to attract the best employees.

Research and Share:

a. Research technologies companies can use to stay in touch with remote workers.
b. Share the results of your research with your class, then, as a class or with a partner, discuss the benefits and drawbacks of telecommuting.

Insurance

Big Idea

You will focus on finding the cost of health insurance and life insurance premiums and the amount the patient pays for medical care.

Explore the Photo

Peace of Mind
Insurance can give you financial security and peace of mind, especially in case of unexpected expenses. *When do people use insurance?*

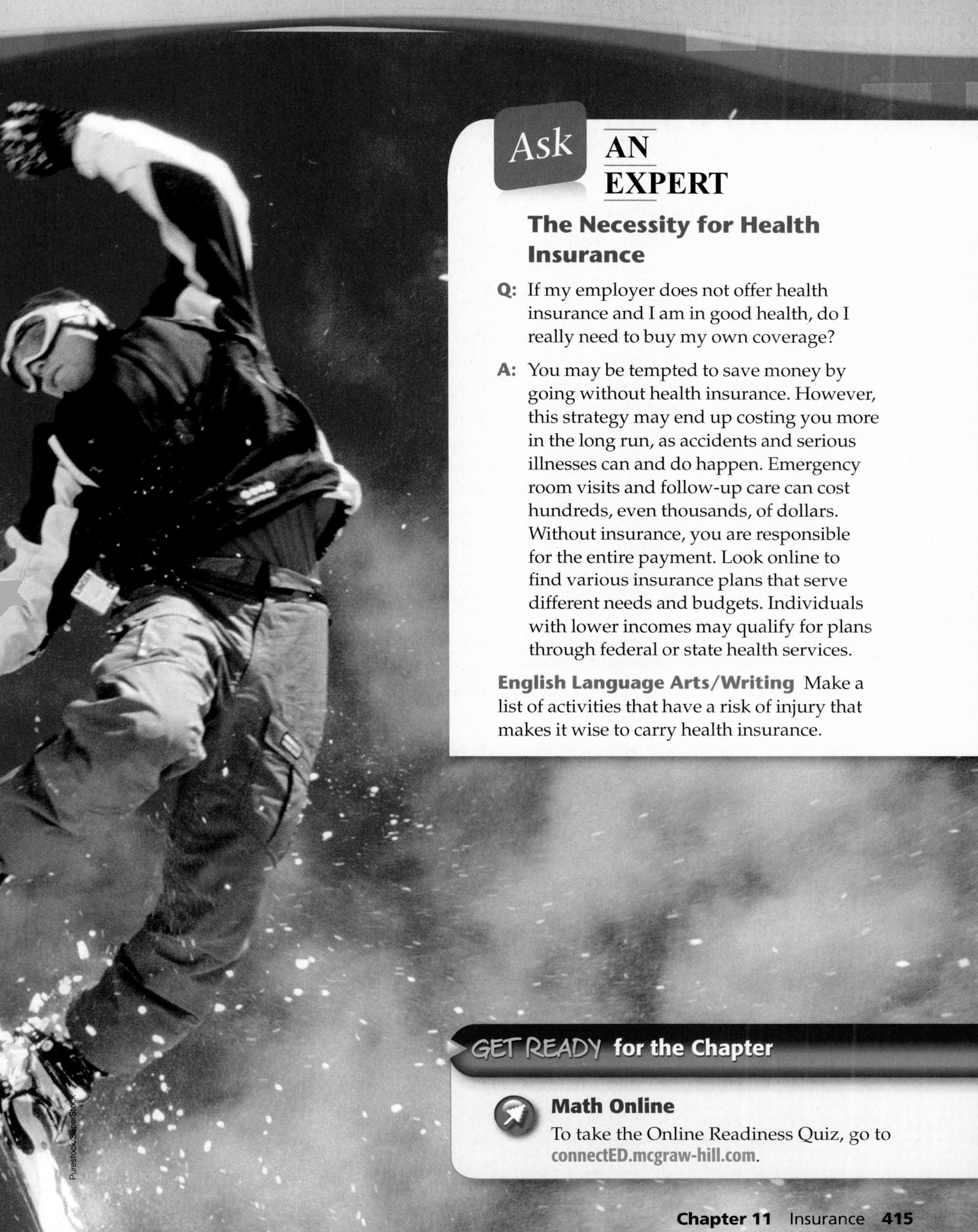

Ask AN EXPERT

The Necessity for Health Insurance

Q: If my employer does not offer health insurance and I am in good health, do I really need to buy my own coverage?

A: You may be tempted to save money by going without health insurance. However, this strategy may end up costing you more in the long run, as accidents and serious illnesses can and do happen. Emergency room visits and follow-up care can cost hundreds, even thousands, of dollars. Without insurance, you are responsible for the entire payment. Look online to find various insurance plans that serve different needs and budgets. Individuals with lower incomes may qualify for plans through federal or state health services.

English Language Arts/Writing Make a list of activities that have a risk of injury that makes it wise to carry health insurance.

GET READY for the Chapter

Math Online

To take the Online Readiness Quiz, go to **connectED.mcgraw-hill.com**.

Reading Guide

Before You Read

Identify Do you know how medical bills are paid?

Main Idea

Health and life insurance protect you and your dependents against financial loss in case of illness or death. Knowing what type of insurance policy you need or want can help you make a wise choice in purchasing coverage for you and your family.

Graphic Organizer

Before you read this chapter, draw a diagram like the one below. As you read, keep track of the different kinds of health and life insurance coverage, and note the benefits of each.

Insurance Coverage	Benefits

Math Online Go to **connectED.mcgraw-hill.com** to download this graphic organizer.

Content Vocabulary

You will learn these key terms in this chapter.

- health insurance
- traditional plan
- preferred provider organization (PPO)
- health maintenance organization (HMO)
- deductible
- co-insurance
- co-payment
- life insurance
- term life insurance
- beneficiary
- whole life insurance
- cash value
- limited payment policy
- universal life insurance

Academic Vocabulary

You will see these words in your reading and on your tests.

- comprehensive
- annual
- classic
- duration

You can find vocabulary definitions in the **Content Vocabulary** Glossary and the **Academic Vocabulary** Glossary in the back of the book.

Health Insurance Premiums

Lesson Objective

Compute health insurance premiums.

Content Vocabulary

- health insurance
- traditional plan
- preferred provider organization (PPO)
- health maintenance organization (HMO)

GET READY for the Lesson

Do young, healthy people really need health insurance?

André Batista regularly plays basketball with his friends. Last week, he hurt his ankle and had to go to the hospital. André wondered how much the treatment would cost.

As You Read

Identify What is the purpose of health insurance?

Determining Health Insurance Premiums An accident or illness could take away your income, deplete your savings, and leave you in debt. Just as important as vehicle insurance is **health insurance**. It protects *you* against overwhelming medical expenses.

Many types of health care coverage plans exist. We will focus on just three group health insurance plans: a **traditional plan**, a **preferred provider organization** (PPO), and a **health maintenance organization** (HMO).

A traditional plan offers health care coverage where the health care provider is paid a predetermined dollar amount for the service given. You may use any health care provider.

A PPO is a group of selected health care providers who offer **comprehensive** services at preset reimbursement levels. You are required to use these "network" providers (that is, a selected group of doctors) unless you are willing to pay additional costs to non-network providers.

An HMO is a prepaid health plan in which care providers contract with (or are) employees of the HMO. You may select a "primary care" physician and agree to receive all non-specialist and non-emergency services from that physician. The physician may refer you to a specialist (an obstetrician, a psychiatrist, or a cardiologist, for example).

Often the employer pays 75% to 80% of the premiums and the employee pays the remaining 20% to 25% in the form of a payroll deduction. The health insurance premium you pay is determined by the following formulas:

Employee's Percent = 100% − Employer's Percent

Employee's Contribution = Total Premium × Employee's Percent

EXAMPLE

Sean Derricotte has a family membership in a group medical insurance program. The annual premium is $11,880. Sean's employer pays 80% of the total cost. His contribution is deducted monthly from his paycheck. What is Sean's annual contribution? What is his monthly deduction?

Continued on next page

Need Help? Go to...

- **Workshop 7:** Dividing Decimals, p. 16
- **Skill 30:** Finding the Percentage, p. SK31
- **Application K:** Chronological Expressions, p. AP7

Step 1: Find the employee's percent.

100% − 80% = 20% employee's percent

Step 2: Find the employee's annual contribution.

Total Premium × Employee's Percent

$11,880.00 × 20% = **$2,376.00 employee's annual contribution**

Step 3: Find the employee's monthly deduction.

$$\frac{\text{Employee's Contribution}}{12}$$

$$\frac{\$2,376.00}{12} = \textbf{\$198.00 employee's monthly deduction}$$

100 [−] 80 [=] 20

11880 [×] 20 [%] 2376 [÷] 12 [=] 198

Concept CHECK

Complete the problems. Find the (a) employee's total annual contribution and (b) employee's monthly deduction. Check your answers in the back of the book.

1. Dorsey Williams has a single plan. His PPO annual premium is $4,325. His employer pays 65%.
2. Rubina Shaw has a family plan. Her HMO annual premium is $11,473. Her employer pays 73%.

Real World CAREER

Clinical Laboratory Technologist

Technologists play a crucial role in fighting diseases. They perform complex tests to detect microorganisms, test chemical reactions, and match blood samples for transfusions. **As a class, brainstorm careers in the medical field.**

Lesson Practice

For Problems 3–7, find the (a) employee's percent, (b) employee's contribution, and (c) monthly premium.

	Insurance Plan	Annual Premium	Employer's Percent	Employee's Percent	Employee's Contribution	Monthly Premium
3.	Single PPO	$ 4,980	60%	a.	b.	c.
4.	Single HMO	$ 4,368	80%	a.	b.	c.
5.	Family Trad.	$10,666	75%	a.	b.	c.
6.	Family HMO	$12,540	85%	a.	b.	c.
7.	Family PPO	$14,600	75%	a.	b.	c.

8. Sing-Chi Chow has a single plan. The PPO annual premium is $12,436. The employer pays 85% of the cost. **(a)** How much does Sing-Chi pay annually? **(b)** How much is deducted from his weekly paycheck?
9. Lance Alpern has a single plan. The HMO annual premium is $9,255. His employer pays 70% of the cost. **(a)** How much does Lance pay annually? **(b)** How much is deducted from his weekly paycheck?
10. Darrell Morris has a family plan. The HMO annual premium is $12,240. The employer pays 90% of the cost. **(a)** How much is Darrell's annual contribution? **(b)** How much is his semimonthly deduction?

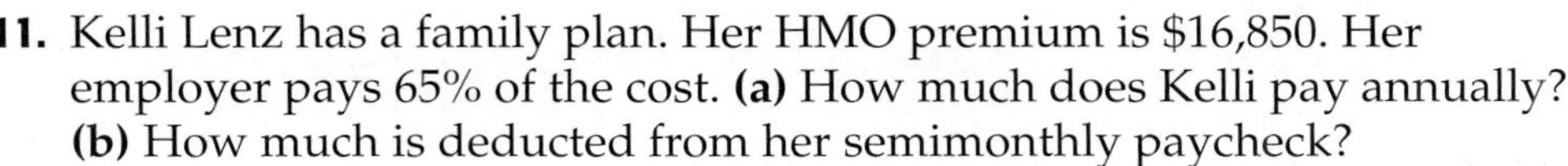

11. Kelli Lenz has a family plan. Her HMO premium is $16,850. Her employer pays 65% of the cost. **(a)** How much does Kelli pay annually? **(b)** How much is deducted from her semimonthly paycheck?

Study Tip

Read Twice
The first time you read through a lesson, look for the main ideas. Look for details on the second time through.

12. Luisa Hernandez has a family membership in her company's traditional group medical insurance program. The total cost is $12,988 annually and the employer pays 75% of the total cost. She also pays the optional annual dental premium of $980 and the optional vision premium of $324. Her contribution is deducted biweekly from her paycheck. **(a)** How much is her total annual contribution? **(b)** How much is her biweekly deduction?

13. Boris Heban is single and pays into an HMO. The total cost is $8,190 annually, and the employer pays 90% of the total cost. Boris also pays 50% of the optional annual dental premium of $662 and 50% of the optional annual vision premium of $288. How much is deducted each week from his paycheck?

14. Rachel and Dustin Lutts are self-employed photographers. They pay 100% of the PPO insurance premium of $12,640 annually. They also have a dental plan that costs $866 annually and a vision plan that costs $444 annually. The premiums are paid quarterly. How much do they pay each quarter?

15. **CHALLENGE PROBLEM** Placido Lucero is retired and covered by Medicare Parts A & B. His retirement plan covers 75% of his Medicare HMO annual premium of $4,200. His retirement plan also covers 50% of his wife's Medicare HMO annual premium of $4,200. Also, Placido has a dependent grandchild whose HMO annual premium of $3,600 is 40% covered by his retirement plan. What is the monthly amount deducted from Placido's retirement check for health care?

Spiral Review

Find the percent. (Skill 30)

16. What percent of $60 is $3?
17. What percent of $150 is $60?
18. What percent of $475 is $95?
19. What percent of $210.00 is $73.50?
20. **ALGEBRA** The Westmarks expected the automatic withdrawal of their natural gas bill to be more than last month's bill of $154.65 but did not know by how much. Their account showed a previous balance of $445.28, cleared checks totaling $316.79, an automatic deposit of $300, and interest earned of $2.56. If the Westmarks' new balance was $228.58, by how much did this month's natural gas bill exceed last month's bill? (Lesson 4.4)

GET READY for the Next Lesson

PREREQUISITE SKILL Subtracting Whole Numbers (Skill 4)

Subtract.

21. 642 − 195	**22.** 2,692 − 867
23. 33,579 − 19,668	**24.** 213,535 − 187,950
25. 678,876 − 39,691	**26.** 967,852 − 753,918

LESSON 11.2 Health Insurance Benefits

Lesson Objective

Calculate the amount the patient pays for health care.

Content Vocabulary

- deductible
- co-insurance
- co-payment

GET READY for the Lesson

How might exercising regularly lower medical costs?

Jason Olsen's employer encourages employees to exercise by offering a 50% discount off membership to a local gym. For the employer, this expense saves money over time because healthy employees are less likely to have expensive hospital visits.

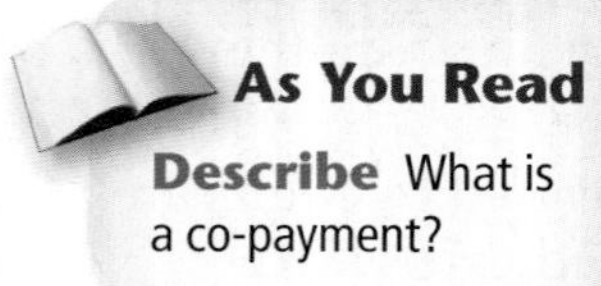

As You Read

Describe What is a co-payment?

Health Insurance Benefits Just because you have health insurance does not mean all medical procedures are covered. In fact, the insurance plan and the state you live in determine the services provided. For example, you might have difficulty securing health insurance to cover weight loss and pre-existing conditions such as congenital heart disease.

Many health insurance policies have an **annual deductible**, which is the amount of money you must pay each year before your insurance company starts paying. Some health care services also have a **co-payment** clause or a **co-insurance** clause. This requires you to pay either a set amount or a certain percent of medical expenses, including prescription drugs.

For example, you might have a $10 co-payment for visiting the doctor regardless of the type of service provided. A 20% co-insurance clause means your insurance company pays 80% of the cost and you pay 20% of the cost. The following formula is used to calculate the amount the patient pays:

$$\text{Amount Paid by Patient} = \text{Deductible} + \text{Co-payments} + \text{Co-insurance Amount} + \text{Hospital Charges}$$

Need Help? Go to...

- **Skill 4:** Subtracting Whole Numbers, p. SK5
- **Skill 30:** Finding the Percentage, p. SK31

EXAMPLE

Brooke Kolodie is single and has a health insurance plan with the benefits shown in **Figure 11.1**. After meeting her $1,000 deductible, her recent network health care costs include co-payments for 8 physician visits and 9 specialist visits. Following hospital surgery, she made co-payments for 12 physical therapy visits at $85 each and she had 4 co-payments at her local pharmacy, for 3 generic drugs and 1 brand-name drug. Her hospital admission charge was $200 and her hospital bill was $34,560. What amount did she pay?

Continued on next page

Step 1: Find the deductible.

The deductible is $1,000.

Step 2: Find the cost of the co-payments.

Physician + Specialist + Physical Therapy + Pharmacy

$(20 \times 8) + (30 \times 9) + (85 \times 20\% \times 12) + [(3 \times 10) + 20] =$

$160 + 270 + 204 + 50 = \$684$

Step 3: Find the hospital co-insurance charges. (Note: The patient pays 10% of the hospital charge and 100% of the admission charge.)

$(34{,}560 \times 10\%) + 200 = \$3{,}456 + 200 = \$3{,}656$

Step 4: Find the total amount paid by patient.

Deductible + Co-payments + Co-insurance Amount + Hospital Charges

$1{,}000 + 684 + 3{,}656 =$ **$5,340 total paid**

Figure 11.1

Health Care Benefits Schedule			
		Network	Non-Network*
Annual Deductible	Single	$1,000	$1,500
	Family	$3,000	$4,500
Hospital Charges	—	10% **	30% **
Co-insurance/ Co-payments	Physician visit	$ 20	$ 30
	Specialist visit	$ 30	$ 40
	Physical Therapy	20% **	30% **
Retail Pharmacy	Generic	$ 10	
	Brand-Name	$ 20	
Mail-Order Pharmacy (90 day supply)	Generic	$ 25	
	Brand-Name	$ 50	
	Emergency Room-ER	$ 100	$ 100
	Ambulance	$ 100	$ 100

*Non-Network refers to a health care provider who does not have a contract with the health plan administrator.
**Percent of total cost that you must pay.

Concept CHECK

Using Figure 11.1, complete the problems. Check your answers in the back of the book.

1. Determine your network plan costs with the following co-payments: 7 physician visits, 2 specialist visits, 12 physical therapy appointments at $90 each. You also have the following pharmacy charges: 2 local generic drugs, 1 local brand-name drug, 3 mail-order generic drugs and 1 mail-order brand-name drug. You have no hospital charges and no deductible.
2. Determine a family's network plan costs with the following co-payments: 22 physician visits, 12 specialist visits, 15 physical therapy appointments at $80 each, and 1 emergency room visit plus ambulance fee. The family also had the following pharmacy charges: 9 local generic drugs, 4 local brand-name drugs, 6 mail-order generic drugs, and 2 mail-order brand-name drugs. There was also a hospital charge of $9,260. The family already met its annual deductible.

SPREADSHEET APPLICATION

Health Insurance Benefits

You can use a spreadsheet like the partial one below to determine your total health care charges. You will enter the number of visits or cost for network or non-network care, and the spreadsheet will calculate the total cost.

Math Online Go to connectED.mcgraw-hill.com to download the spreadsheet application.

	A	B	C	D	E	F	G	H
1	Health Care Benefits Schedule							
2			Network	No. of visits cost	Subtotal	Non-Network*	No. of visits cost	Subtotal
3	Annual Deductible	Single	$1,000		0.00	$1,500		$0

Think and Discuss

1. Determine a family's network plan costs. The family had the following co-payments: 24 physician visits, 8 specialist visits, 25 physical therapy appointments at $90 each, and 2 emergency room visits. There were also these pharmacy charges: 7 local generic drugs, 2 local brand-name drugs, 5 mail-order generic drugs, and 1 mail-order brand-name drug. There is also a hospital charge of $19,260. Hint: In cell E13 enter: *=25*90*
2. How much would they have saved if they had purchased all generic instead of brand-name drugs?
3. Determine the Weston family's non-network costs. They had the following co-payments: 5 physician visits, 2 specialist visits, 10 physical therapy appointments at $75 each, and 1 emergency room visit. They also had the following pharmacy charges: 2 local generic, 2 local brand name drugs, 3 mail order generic, and 1 mail order brand name. There is also a hospital charge of $8,113. Hint: In the physical therapy cell, enter: *=10*75*
4. How much would the Weston family have saved if they had used the network plan?

Lesson Practice

For Problems 3–10, find the (a) co-payments, (b) co-insurance, and (c) total paid by insured.

	Deductible Amount	Number of Co-payments at $10.00 Each	Amount of the Co-payments	Amount Subject to Co-insurance	Insured Co-insurance Rate	Amount of Co-insurance	Total Paid by Insured
3.	$3,000	25	a.	$12,000	20%	b.	c.
4.	$2,000	40	a.	$34,600	30%	b.	c.
5.	$3,500	52	a.	$16,980	15%	b.	c.
6.	$6,000	32	a.	$66,540	10%	b.	c.
7.	$5,000	30	a.	$45,000	15%	b.	c.
8.	$2,500	50	a.	$25,000	25%	b.	c.
9.	$4,000	35	a.	$37,500	20%	b.	c.
10.	$4,500	25	a.	$22,500	30%	b.	c.

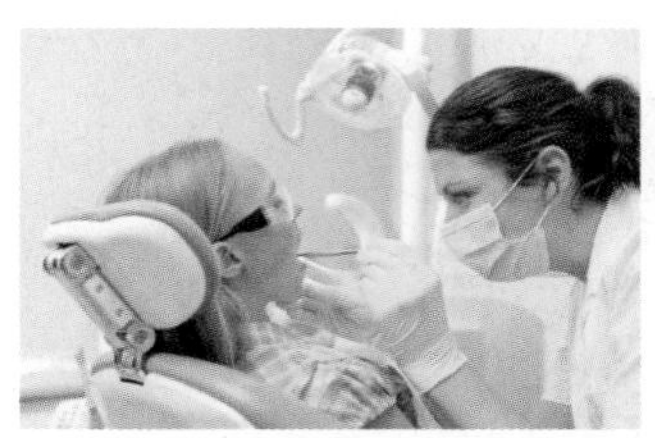

For Problems 11 and 12, find the (a) deductible, (b) co-payment amount, (c) hospital charges, and (d) total paid by the insured. (Use Figure 11.1 on page 421.)

11. Sofia Carbondale has a network single plan. After meeting her annual deductible, she had these co-payments: 18 physician visits, 15 specialist visits, and 15 physical therapy visits at $90 each. Sofia also had 1 emergency room visit and a hospital charge of $24,560.

Did You Know?
Neolithic Dentistry
Scientists using an electron microscope to study 9,000-year-old teeth from a graveyard in present-day Pakistan found evidence of dental work. The research indicates that a drill made of flint heads was "surprisingly effective" at removing rotting dental tissue, and that the technique was used for about 1,500 years.

12. After meeting the family's deductible, Jacobi Duarte had the following family, non-network medical bills: 22 physician visits, 12 specialist visits, 25 physical therapy appointments at $95 each, 8 generic local drug prescriptions, and 4 mail-in prescriptions for 3 generic drugs and 1 brand-name drug. Hospital charges totaled $55,600 plus an emergency room visit.

13. Tom Buell is single and has a health insurance plan with the benefits shown in **Figure 11.1** on page 421. After meeting his annual deductible, his recent network health care costs include co-payments for 4 physician visits and 5 specialist visits. He made co-payments for 4 non-network physical therapy visits at $125 each. He had 3 co-payments at his local pharmacy, for one generic and 2 brand-name drugs. His hospital admission charge was $150 and his hospital bill was $18,750. What amount did he pay?

14. Emily Ward is married and has a non-network family health insurance plan with the benefits shown in **Figure 11.1** on page 421. Her recent non-network health care costs include 5 physician visits and 2 specialist visits. She made co-payments for 6 physical therapy visits at $110 each. Emily had one ambulance trip to the emergency room and a subsequent hospital bill of $14,680. Emily has no deductible. What amount did she pay?

15. CHALLENGE PROBLEM Wanda Orsini broke her leg playing basketball. She has the family network insurance plan with the benefits shown in **Figure 11.1** on page 421. After meeting her annual deductible, her health care costs include co-payments for 9 physician visits, 12 orthopedic bone specialist visits, and hospital costs of $52,940. She had 40 physical therapy visits at $60 each. Wanda's hospital admission charge was $200. There was an ER charge and an ambulance charge. She also had 8 generic local drug prescriptions and 4 mail-in prescriptions for 2 generic drugs and 2 brand-name drugs. Find her total charges.

Spiral Review

Subtract. (Skill 4)

16. 978 – 865 **17.** 77,521 – 66,842 **18.** 997,341 – 942,876

19. ALGEBRA Rob Glover's group medical coverage costs $178.45 per month. His employer pays 65% of the cost. How much is the annual premium for Rob's health insurance? (Lesson 2.5)

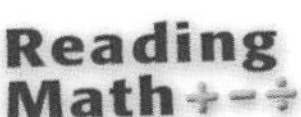

Read With Pen and Paper
When a word problem contains a lot of information, such as problem 15, read it several times. Make a list of the key information you need to solve.

GET READY for the Next Lesson

PREREQUISITE SKILL **Dividing Decimals** (Skill 11)

Divide. Round answers to the nearest thousandth.

20. 72.84 ÷ 2.41 **21.** 23.97 ÷ 5.942 **22.** 42.158 ÷ 7.66

23. 186.4 ÷ 55.726 **24.** 646.9 ÷ 19.547 **25.** 238.007 ÷ 84.593

LESSON 11.3 Term Life Insurance

Lesson Objective
Utilize tables to compute the annual premium for term life insurance.

Content Vocabulary
- life insurance
- term life insurance
- beneficiary

GET READY for the Lesson

Why should young adults have life insurance?

Dylan Hughes once thought he had no need for life insurance. But when his first child was born, Dylan worried about how his family would get by if something were to happen to him.

As You Read

Explain What is life insurance?

Term Life Insurance When the main source of income of a family dies, what happens financially? For a family with children, it is the **classic** case of financial setback. **Life insurance**, however, can soften the financial blow. This is financial protection for the family in case the main source of income dies.

Term life insurance is the least expensive form of life insurance that you can purchase. You buy term life insurance for a specified term, such as five years, or to a specified age. Unless you renew your policy at the end of each term, the insurance coverage ends.

The annual premium depends on your age at the time you buy the policy and the number of *units.* One unit of insurance has a face value of $1,000. The annual premium for term life insurance usually increases with each new term.

The annual premium is computed using the following formula:

Annual Premium = Number of Units Purchased × Premium per $1,000

The person whose name is on the policy chooses a **beneficiary**. The beneficiary will receive the *face value* of the policy. The face value is the amount of insurance coverage that you buy.

Figure 11.2 shows the premiums per $1,000 for a 5-year term policy. The rates are lower for females because statistically they have a longer life expectancy.

Need Help? Go to...
- **Skill 11:** Dividing Decimals, p. SK12
- **Skill 8:** Multiplying Decimals, p. SK9
- **Application C:** Tables and Charts, p. AP3

EXAMPLE 1

Kenny Calloway is 30 years old. He wants to purchase a $50,000, 5-year term life insurance policy. What is his annual premium?

Step 1: Find the number of units purchased.

$$\frac{50{,}000}{1{,}000} = 50 \text{ units purchased}$$

Step 2: Find the premium per $1,000.

Refer to **Figure 11.2**. Read the table.

Male, age 30 = $3.21

Step 3: Find the annual premium.

Number of Units Purchased × Premium per $1,000

50 × $3.21 = **$160.50 annual premium**

Lisette Le Bon/Purestock/SuperStock

Figure 11.2

Annual Premiums per $1,000 of Life Insurance: 5-Year Term*		
Age	Male	Female
18–30	$ 3.21	$ 2.77
35	$ 3.51	$ 2.98
40	$ 4.25	$ 3.47
45	$ 5.42	$ 4.60
50	$ 7.59	$ 6.27
55	$11.45	$ 8.58
60	$17.19	$12.62
*Minimum amount is $50,000		

Reading Math +−÷=

Charts

When you look at a chart, think about the story it tells. **Figure 11.2** gives three factors to consider when determining a premium: age, gender, and the amount of life insurance purchased.

Concept CHECK

Use Figure 11.2 to complete the problems. Check your answers in the back of the book.

Find the annual premium for a 5-year term policy.

1. An eighteen-year-old female purchases a $50,000, 5-year term policy. What is the annual premium?
2. A forty-five-year-old male purchases a $60,000, 5-year term policy. What is the annual premium?

EXAMPLE 2

Maria Rita Gomez purchased an $80,000, 5-year term policy at age 30. She will be 35 years old this year. What will the annual premium be at age 35? What was the annual premium at age 30? How much is the increase? What is the percent increase?

Step 1: Find the number of units purchased.

$\frac{80,000}{1,000} = 80$ units purchased

Step 2: Find premium at age 35.

$80 \times 2.98 =$ **$238.40 annual premium at 35**

Step 3: Find premium at age 30.

$80 \times 2.77 =$ **$221.60 annual premium at 30**

Step 4: Find the increase.

238.40 − $221.60 = **$16.80 increase**

Step 5: Find the percent increase.

$\frac{\text{Increase}}{\text{Original Amount}} = \frac{16.80}{221.60} = 0.075812 =$ **7.6% increase**

Concept CHECK

Use Figure 11.2 to find the percent increase in premiums. Check your answer in the back of the book.

3. At age 40, Julie Johnson purchases a $60,000, 5-year term policy. She is now 45 years old.
4. Harold McDonough at age 55 purchases a $100,000, 5-year term policy. He is now 60 years old.

Lesson Practice

For Problems 5–14, determine (a) number of units, (b) annual premium per $1,000, and (c) annual premium. Use Figure 11.2 on page 425.

	Insured	Age	Coverage	Number of Units	Annual Premium per $1,000	Annual Premium
5.	Lianna Torrez	20	$ 60,000	a.	b.	c.
6.	John O'Neill	45	$ 85,000	a.	b.	c.
7.	Kate Owens	35	$ 95,000	a.	b.	c.
8.	Debra Green	50	$200,000	a.	b.	c.

Did You Know?

Women and Life Insurance A historic law passed by New York in 1840 gave women equal protection to men concerning life-insurance policies. Before then, no U.S. woman could have her own policy, and in the case of a husband's death his creditors were entitled to funds before his wife and children.

For Problems 9 and 10, determine the annual premium.

9. Joni Hauck wants to purchase a $65,000, 5-year term life insurance policy. She is 25 years old.

10. Paul Barojas wants to purchase a $105,000, 5-year term life insurance policy. He is 25 years old.

For Problems 11 and 12, determine the percent increase in the premium.

11. Phil Davis purchased a $75,000, 5-year term life insurance policy when he was 40. Now he is 45.

12. Marica Deerfoot purchased a $120,000, 5-year term life insurance policy when she was 55. Now she is 60.

13. Peter and Edith Lichtner have a child. Peter is a 30-year old career counselor, and Edith is a 25-year old child psychologist. Both want to purchase $80,000, 5-year term life insurance policies. What is Edith's annual premium? What is Peter's annual premium?

14. CHALLENGE PROBLEM Sam and Kolleen Hastings have two children. Sam was 30 years old when he first purchased a $125,000, 5-year term life insurance policy. He is now 35 years old and decides to increase the policy to $200,000.

(a) What is his new annual premium?
(b) What is his new monthly premium?
(c) What total amount did he pay during the previous 5-year term?
(d) What total amount will he pay for the next 5-year term?

Spiral Review

Multiply or Divide. Round answers to the nearest thousandth. (Skill 8)

15. $76.26 \div 0.14$ **16.** $1.025 \div 0.05$ **17.** 34.362×100 **18.** 0.95×0.16

19. ALGEBRA Your current job pays a monthly gross salary of $1,860. You are offered a new position that pays $9.60 per hour with time and a half for all hours over 40 per week. How many hours of overtime per week would you need to work to earn the same amount per week as in your current job? (Lesson 1.5)

GET READY for the Next Lesson

PREREQUISITE SKILL **Multiplying Decimals** (Skill 8)

Multiply. Round answers to the nearest hundredth.

20. 1.43×0.57 **21.** 0.072×6.42 **22.** 5.31×0.213

23. 21.93×0.72 **24.** 3.045×0.04 **25.** 6.751×1.51

LESSON 11.4

Other Types of Life Insurance

Lesson Objective

Apply tables to data to compute the annual premiums for three types of life insurance.

Content Vocabulary

- whole life insurance
- cash value
- limited payment policy
- universal life insurance

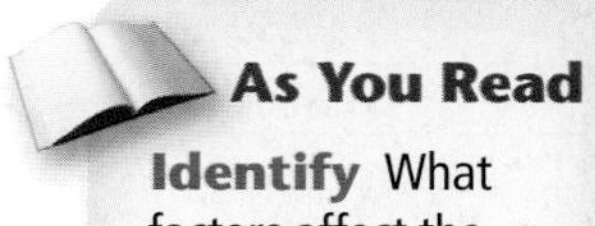

As You Read

Identify What factors affect the amount of the premium?

GET READY for the Lesson

How does risk affect insurance?

Marlon Fuentes is healthy and his family has no history of disease. However, he drives a race car for a living.

Life Insurance Policies **Whole life insurance**, also known as permanent insurance, offers financial protection for your entire life. You pay a specific premium for the entire **duration** of the policy. When you die, the insurance company pays your beneficiary a declared sum. The amount of the premium depends on your age, the condition of your health and your smoking habits at the time when you purchase the policy. Some insurance companies require a physical examination by a physician to see if you qualify for a policy.

A whole life insurance policy provides your beneficiary financial coverage, and it can also be used as an investment. In addition to the face value that your beneficiary will receive, whole life insurance has a **cash value** and *loan value.* The cash value is the amount of money you will receive if you cancel your policy. Think of whole life insurance as both a death benefit and a savings account. You can borrow money on the policy and then pay interest on the loan. The insurance company will lend you the same amount as the cash value, if you request it.

Insurance companies offer many different types of whole life insurance policies. Two common ones are a **limited payment policy** and **universal life insurance**. A limited payment policy offers lifetime protection. You pay premiums only for a limited number of years or until you reach a certain age, such as a "paid up at age 65" policy. Universal life insurance is a combination of a life insurance policy and a savings plan. The policy covers you for your entire life. Part of your premium goes into an investment account that grows and earns interest. You are able to borrow or withdraw your cash value. Annual premiums are calculated using the following formula:

Annual Premium = Number of Units Purchased × Premium per $1,000

Need Help? Go to...

- **Skill 11:** Dividing Decimals, p. SK12
- **Skill 8:** Multiplying Decimals, p. SK9
- **Application C:** Tables and Charts, p. AP3

EXAMPLE 1

Phyllis Saul is 25 years old. She wants to purchase a whole life policy with a face value of $125,000. What is her annual premium?

Step 1: Find the number of units purchased.

$$\frac{125{,}000}{1{,}000} = 125 \text{ units purchased}$$

Continued on next page

Step 2: Find the premium per $1,000. (Refer to **Figure 11.3.**)
Whole Life, Female, Age 25 = $7.50

Step 3: Find the annual premium.
Number of Units Purchased × Premium per $1,000
125 × 7.50 = **$937.50 annual premium**

Figure 11.3

Age	Annual Premiums per $1,000 of Life Insurance				Monthly Premium
	Paid Up at Age 65		Whole Life		$50,000 Universal Life
	Male	Female	Male	Female	Male or Female
20	$11.75	$ 9.75	$ 8.00	$ 6.25	$ 19.00
25	$13.75	$11.50	$ 9.50	$ 7.50	$ 24.00
30	$17.00	$14.50	$11.75	$ 9.25	$ 29.00
35	$21.50	$18.00	$15.00	$11.50	$ 37.50
40	$29.75	$25.00	$19.50	$14.50	$ 52.00
45	$39.50	$32.50	$25.50	$18.75	$ 69.50
50	$56.25	$45.75	$34.00	$24.25	$ 93.50
55			$46.50	$32.25	$126.00

Concept CHECK

Find the annual premium. Check your answers in the back of the book.

1. A 30-year-old male obtains a $70,000 whole life policy.
2. A 40-old female obtains a limited payment policy until age 65 of $90,000.

Figure 11.4

Optional Payment Plans		
Percent of Annual Premium		
Semi-annual Premiums	=	50.5%
Quarterly Premiums	=	25.5%
Monthly Premiums	=	8.5%

Payment Plans Many insurance companies will allow you to make smaller payments several times a year, rather than one annual payment. A small fee is charged to cover the additional expense of collecting and handling the payments. Many companies use the guidelines shown in **Figure 11.4.**

Reading Math ÷−÷=

Glossary and Index
Use the glossary in the back of the book to check the definition of important terms. Use the index to cross check other references to the term.

EXAMPLE 2

Suppose Phyllis Saul (from **Example 1**) wants to pay the $937.50 annual premium monthly. What are her monthly payments? How much can she save in one year by paying the premium annually?

Step 1: Find the monthly premium. (Note: Refer to **Figure 11.4** for percent of monthly premium.)
Annual Premium × 8.5%
$937.50 × 0.085 = $79.6875 = **$79.69** monthly premium

Step 2: Find how much she can save.

(12 × $79.69) – $937.50 =

$956.28 – $937.50 = **$18.78 amount saved**

Concept CHECK

Determine how much can be saved by paying annually. (Refer to Figure 11.3 and Figure 11.4.) Check your answers in the back of the book.

3. A 20-year-old male has a $100,000 whole life policy paid monthly.

4. A 40-year-old female has a $150,000 paid up at age 65 policy that she pays quarterly.

Did You Know?

Staying in Shape **Studies conducted by scientists from the National Institute on Aging suggest that a healthy diet and exercise can combat obesity, which may increase life expectancy.**

Lesson Practice

Use Figure 11.3 and Figure 11.4 to solve.

	Type	Gender	Age	Face Value	Number of Units	Cost per $1,000	Annual Premium	Monthly Premium
5.	Whole Life	Female	20	$ 50,000	a.	b.	c.	d.
6.	Paid at 65	Male	30	$120,000	a.	b.	c.	d.
7.	Paid at 65	Female	35	$200,000	a.	b.	c.	d.
8.	Whole Life	Male	45	$200,000	a.	b.	c.	d.

9. Forty-year old Ann Gosik's policy is a "whole life" for $50,000. **(a)** What is her annual premium? **(b)** What is her semi-annual premium?

10. James Dolby, 20 years old, has a $50,000 policy that is "paid up at age 65." **(a)** What is his annual premium? **(b)** What is his quarterly premium?

11. Robert and Lucy Dubbs each purchase a $100,000 whole life insurance policy. Both are 25 years of age. What are their total annual premiums? How much more is Robert Dubbs's annual premium than his wife's?

12. **CHALLENGE** Leona Sowinski purchased a $50,000 universal life insurance policy at the age of 20. What is her annual premium? If Leona pays $150 a month, how much is she saving annually?

Spiral Review

Multiply or Divide. Round answers to the nearest hundredth. (Skill 8, 11)

13. 18.4 ÷ 0.032 **14.** 0.31 × 0.84 **15.** 7.81 × 8.1

16. **ALGEBRA** Double Impressions charges 9¢ a page for machine fed copies and 21¢ per page for copies that are placed by hand on the copy machine. If your bill for 120 copies is $19.44, how many copies of each type were made? (Lesson 1.4)

GET READY for the Next Lesson

PREREQUISITE SKILL **Rounding Numbers** (Skill 2)

Round to the nearest ten.

17. 84 **18.** 15 **19.** 221 **20.** 336

Purestock/SuperStock

CHAPTER 11 Review and Assessment

AFTER YOU READ

Chapter SUMMARY

Health and life insurance protect you and your dependents against financial loss in case of illness, injury, or death. Making a wise choice in purchasing coverage includes knowing how to compute the health insurance premiums and the amount the patient pays for health care. It is also useful to know how to utilize tables to compute the annual premium for term life insurance and apply tables to data to compute the annual premiums for various types of life insurance.

Vocabulary Check

1. On a sheet of paper, use each of these terms in a sentence.

Content Vocabulary

- health insurance (p. 417)
- traditional plan (p. 417)
- preferred provider organization (PPO) (p. 417)
- health maintenance organization (HMO) (p. 417)
- deductible (p. 420)
- co-insurance (p. 420)
- co-payment (p. 420)
- life insurance (p. 424)
- term life insurance (p. 424)
- beneficiary (p. 424)
- whole life insurance (p. 427)
- cash value (p. 427)
- limited payment policy (p. 427)
- universal life insurance (p. 427)

Academic Vocabulary

- comprehensive (p. 417)
- annual (p. 420)
- classic (p. 424)
- duration (p. 427)

Concept Check

2. List three types of health insurance plans.
3. Explain how a traditional health care plan works.
4. Summarize the meaning of *annual deductible.*
5. Identify the formula for calculating the amount the patient pays.
6. What is a beneficiary?
7. Differentiate between term life insurance and whole life insurance.
8. List two types of whole life insurance policies.
9. **CRITICAL THINKING** Explain why it is important to have health and life insurance.

Lesson-by-Lesson Review

11.1 Health Insurance Premiums (pp. 417–419)

Compute health insurance premiums.

Pedro Martinez is employed by the Wise and Wonderful Gift Corporation. He has a family plan with a traditional group medical insurance program. The annual premium is $8,540. Pedro's employer pays 90% of the total cost. Pedro's contribution is deducted monthly from his paycheck. What is his annual contribution? What is his monthly deduction?

Step 1: Find the employee's percent.

100% − Employer's Percent

100% − 90% = 10% employee's percent

Step 2: Find the employee's annual contribution.

Total Premium × Employee's Percent

$8,540 × 10% = **$854 employee's contribution**

Step 3: Find the employee's monthly deduction.

$$\frac{\text{Employee's Contribution}}{12}$$

$$\frac{\$854}{12} = \textbf{\$71.17 employee's monthly deduction}$$

Review Exercises

Complete the table below.

	Insurance Plan	Annual Premium	Employer's Percent	Employee's Percent	Employee's Contribution	Monthly Premium
10.	Single PPO	$ 3,006	65%	a.	b.	c.
11.	Family PPO	$ 3,259	50%	a.	b.	c.
12.	Family Trad.	$ 5,832	75%	a.	b.	c.
13.	Family PPO	$15,600	90%	a.	b.	c.
14.	Single HMO	$ 2,560	85%	a.	b.	c.
15.	Family HMO	$13,650	70%	a.	b.	c.

16. Brandon Alverez is single and pays into an HMO. The total cost is $9,370 annually, and the employer pays 90% of the total cost. He also pays 50% of the optional annual dental premium of $782 and 50% of the optional annual vision premium of $275. How much is deducted each week from his paycheck?

17. Chi and An Pham are self-employed writers. They pay 100% of the PPO insurance premium of $13,120 annually. They also have a dental plan that costs $975 annually and a vision plan that costs $432 annually. The premiums are paid quarterly. How much do they pay each quarter?

Lesson-by-Lesson Review (continued)

11.2 Health Insurance Benefits (pp. 420–423)

Calculate the amount the patient pays for health care. Use Figure 11.1 on page 421 to solve the example and problems.

Tawney Manuel is single and has a health insurance plan with the benefits shown in **Figure 11.1**. After meeting her annual deductible, her recent network health care costs include co-payments for 4 physician visits and 6 specialist visits. She also had 8 physical therapy appointments at $105 each. What was the total amount she paid?

Step 1: Find the deductible.

The deductible is $1,000.

Step 2: Find the cost of co-payments.

Physician + Specialist + Physical Therapy

($20 × 4) + ($30 × 6) + ($105 × 8 × 20%) = $428 cost of co-payments

Step 3: Find the total amount paid by patient.

Deductible + Co-payments + Co-insurance Amount + Hospital Charges

$1,000 + $428 + 0 + 0 = **$1,428 total amount paid**

Review Exercises

Complete the table below.

	Deductible Amount	Number of Co-payments at $20.00 Each	Amount of the Co-payments	Amount Subject to Co-insurance	Insured Co-insurance Rate	Amount of Co-insurance	Total Paid by Insured
18.	$1,000	15	a.	$15,000	20%	b.	c.
19.	$3,000	25	a.	$10,000	30%	b.	c.
20.	$2,000	45	a.	$25,000	10%	b.	c.
21.	$1,000	56	a.	$12,000	30%	b.	c.
22.	$1,500	41	a.	$35,000	20%	b.	c.
23.	$5,000	35	a.	$55,000	20%	b.	c.

Use Figure 11.1, *Health Care Benefits Schedule*, on page 421, for the following problems:

24. Donald Westhoven is single. After meeting his annual deductible, he had the following non-network plan costs: co-payments: 7 physician visits, and 2 specialist visits. He also had the following pharmacy charges: 3 local generic drugs, 2 local brand-name drugs, 10 mail-order generic drugs, and 1 mail-order brand-name drug. There is also a hospital charge of $2,575. What amount did he pay?

25. Determine a family's network plan costs, with the following co-payments: 35 physician visits, 10 specialist visits, 8 physical therapy appointments at $80 each, and 2 emergency room visits. They also had the following pharmacy charges: 10 local generic drugs, 5 local brand-name drugs, 7 mail-order generic drugs, and 1 mail-order brand-name drug. There is also a hospital charge of $12,260. The family has no deductible.

Lesson-by-Lesson Review (continued)

11.3 Term Life Insurance (pp. 424–426)

Utilize tables to compute the annual premium for term life insurance.
Yamid Haad purchased a 5-year term life insurance policy. It provides $100,000 coverage. He is 35 years old. What is his annual premium?

Step 1: Find the number of units purchased.

$$\frac{100{,}000}{1{,}000} = 100 \text{ units purchased}$$

Step 2: Find the premium per $1,000. (Refer to **Figure 11.2** on page 425.)

Male, age 35 = $3.51 premium per $1,000

Step 3: Find the annual premium.

Number of Units Purchased × Premium per $1,000

100 × 3.5 = **$351 annual premium**

Review Exercises

Use Figure 11.2 on page 425 to answer the following:

	Insured	Age	Coverage	Number of Units	Annual Premium per $1,000	Annual Premium
26.	Cesar Martinez (M)	25	$ 50,000	a.	b.	c.
27.	Rose McNerney (F)	30	$ 75,000	a.	b.	c.
28.	David Rotunno (M)	45	$ 80,000	a.	b.	c.
29.	Erin McCamie (F)	55	$100,000	a.	b.	c.
30.	Terrie Creek (F)	60	$200,000	a.	b.	c.
31.	John Kim (M)	40	$500,000	a.	b.	c.

32. Paul Lopez has a 5-year term life insurance policy with $125,000 coverage. He is 50 years old. What is his annual premium?
33. Alexis Finley is 35 years old and has a $150,000, 5-year term life insurance policy. **(a)** What is her annual premium for the $150,000 policy? **(b)** What would it be if she increases the policy to $200,000? **(c)** What would her monthly premium be for the $200,000 policy?

For Problems 34 and 35, determine the percent increase in the premium.

34. Rogelio Lugo purchased a $95,000, 5-year term life insurance policy when he was 40. Now he is 45.
35. Shani Tang purchased a $150,000, 5-year term life insurance policy when she was 55. Now she is 60.

Lesson-by-Lesson Review (continued)

11.4 Other Types of Life Insurance (pp. 427–429)

Apply tables to data to compute the annual premiums for three types of life insurance.

Gretchen Kuhn is 30 years old. She wants to purchase a whole life insurance policy valued at \$150,000. What is her annual premium?

Step 1: Find the number of units purchased.

$$\frac{\$150{,}000}{\$1{,}000} = 150 \text{ units purchased}$$

Step 2: Find the premium per \$1,000. (Refer to **Figure 11.3** on page 428.)

Female, age 30 = \$9.25

Step 3: Find the annual premium.

Number of Units Purchased × Premium per \$1,000

150 × \$9.25 = **\$1,387.50 annual premium**

Review Exercises

Use Figure 11.3 and Figure 11.4 on page 428 to solve the following problems.

	Type	Gender	Age	Face Value	Number of Units	Cost per \$1,000	Annual Premium	Monthly Premium
36.	Paid at 65	Male	20	\$ 50,000	a.	b.	c.	d.
37.	Whole Life	Female	40	125,000	a.	b.	c.	d.
38.	Paid at 65	Male	25	150,000	a.	b.	c.	d.
39.	Whole Life	Male	55	50,000	a.	b.	c.	d.

40. Emilio Ramos is 35 years old and wants to purchase a \$50,000 life insurance policy. He is considering a universal life insurance policy. **(a)** What is his annual premium? **(b)** What is his monthly premium?

41. Sam and Rita Duncan each purchase a \$100,000 whole life insurance policy. Both are 30 years of age. **(a)** What are their total annual premiums? **(b)** How much more is Sam's annual premium than his wife's?

42. Thirty-five-year-old May Clark purchases a \$250,000 "paid up at age 65" life insurance policy. She pays the premium quarterly. How much more would Mary pay quarterly if she had waited until she was 40 years of age to purchase the insurance?

43. Fifty-year-old Toby Watts purchases a \$500,000 whole life policy. How much more per year would Toby pay if he paid the premium monthly rather than semi-annually?

Practice Test

Record your answers on a sheet of paper.

1. Jessica Lopez's employer pays 80% of her medical insurance. If the annual premium is $6,854 what is Jessica's cost?
   A $1,975.40 **B** $5,483.20
   C $1,370.80 **D** $2,456.95

2. Susan Grant has a co-payment of $12.50 every time she sees a doctor. How much would she pay for 13 doctor visits?
   A $242.00 **B** $162.50
   C $128.50 **D** $175.00

Use the table below to answer questions 3–5.

Annual Premium per $1,000		
Age	Male	Female
18–30	$2.47	$2.13
35	$2.70	$2.29
40	$3.27	$2.67

3. Jean Hernandez is a 20-year-old female who has a $75,000 life insurance policy. What is her annual premium?
   A $200.25 **B** $245.25
   C $185.25 **D** $159.75

4. Ms. Hernandez (in question 3) has the option of paying her annual premium on a quarterly basis. To do this she would pay 25.5% of the annual premium every three months. How much would she pay every three months?
   A $40.74 **B** $45.86
   C $68.54 **D** $70.70

5. How much would Ms. Hernandez (in questions 3 and 4) save if she paid the premium annually rather than quarterly?
   A $3.21 **B** $5.65
   C $3.85 **D** $9.85

6. Miguel Diamonds is 25 years old. He wants to purchase a $50,000, 5-year term life insurance policy. The annual premium is $2.47 per $1,000. What is his annual premium?

7. Joe Hatchum's employer pays 80% of a $7,534 health insurance premium. How much does Joe pay?
   A $2,687.00 **B** $1,506.80
   C $1,857.50 **D** $2,310.20

8. For a trip to the hospital, Evan Appleton paid $1,656 in hospital charges, a $750 insurance deductible, and a $457 co-payment. What was his total bill?
   A $1,656 **B** $2,406
   C $2,113 **D** $2,863

9. Alicia Ward is 30 years old. She wants to buy a whole life policy valued at $185,000. The annual premium per $1,000 is $9.25. What is her annual premium?

10. Tim Belby is a member of a group medical insurance program. His employer pays 80% of the annual premium. The annual premium is $5,739. How much does Tim pay each month for his health insurance?

11. Ronaldo Munz has a $12.50 co-pay each time he visits a doctor. He also pays $65 for every home visit done by a nurse. He saw a doctor 13 times last year and had a nurse come to his home 6 times. What did he pay for these services?

12. $267.85 + $44.67 + $13.88

13. 0.55 × 38.50 + 55.78

14. 852.008 ÷ 43.1

15. $54.78 – $31.99 + $76.82

16. 893.774 × 22.32 + 73.93

17. 860 × 14.2%

PART 1 Multiple Choice

Record your answers on the answer sheet provided by your teacher or on a sheet of paper.

1. Amez McLaughlin cashed a $65.75 check from an account that had a balance of $4,023. What is the new balance?
   A $3,957.25 **B** $4,088.75
   C $3,965.25 **D** $4,057.25

2. A $125.00 mp3 player is discounted 35%. What is the discounted selling price?
   A $43.75 **B** $81.25
   C $90.00 **D** $98.55

3. Danni Gold budgets $258.75 each month for annual fixed expenses. What are her total annual fixed expenses?
   A $1,950.00 **B** $3,005.25
   C $2,580.75 **D** $3,105.00

4. A mortgage loan for $85,000 has an interest rate of 8%. What is the interest for the first monthly payment?
   A $578.50 **B** $585.76
   C $566.67 **D** $560.72

5. The annual premium for Jim Canton's health insurance is $7,680. His employer pays 75% of that. How much does Joe pay?
   A $1,680.00 **B** $1,980.00
   C $2,130.00 **D** $1,920.00

6. Marcus Riggs rented a car for 3 days at $42.95 per day. If he drove a total of 537 miles, what was his cost per mile? Round your answer to the nearest cent.
   A $0.24 **B** $0.57
   C $0.65 **D** $0.80

TEST-TAKING TIP

Multiple Choice When taking multiple-choice tests, be sure to read the entire question before you look at the answer choices.

PART 2 Short Response/Griddable

7. **ALGEBRA** Bob Stefanakus received a tax statement showing that his house has an assessed value of $53,700. The rate of assessment in his area is 30%. What is the market value of his house?

8. Jodi Mao leased a vehicle. She pays $355.99 per month for 48 months. She had to make a $1,575 deposit, pay a $73 title fee, and pay a $42 license fee. What is her total lease cost?

PART 3 Extended Response

Show your work.

9. How do you calculate how much you will contribute, each paycheck, to health insurance if you are paid monthly?

10. At your local grocery store coffee is sold in several different sizes. Each size is priced differently. How can you determine which coffee is the best buy?

11. Amber Holub earns $23,875 a year working part-time in an accounting office. Her personal exemptions total $1,800. The state income tax rate is 2.8% of taxable income. How would you determine her taxable wages? How much is withheld from Amber's gross pay for state income tax for the year?

12. How do you find the mortgage loan amount?

Building Academic Skills

Mathematics

One of your friends, who is self-employed, started buying individual health insurance 11 years ago at a cost of $579 per quarter. Now, the quarterly premium is $1,107. The policy has a $2,500 deductible and a $25 co-payment. Calculate the annual premiums 11 years ago and today, and the percent increase over the period.

English Language Arts/Writing

You may have seen TV commercials about Web sites where you can get quotes from insurance companies. Use an Internet search engine in your classroom or school library to find Web sites of life insurance companies. Obtain at least three quotes for a term life insurance policy. Create a chart showing the three different quotes.

Science/Health

Risk relates to prediction and probability. In determining the insurance premium you pay, insurance companies use their experience in risk assessment. That is why the younger you are when you start buying life insurance, the lower your premiums usually are. Generally, the younger you are, the lower your health risk. Think about a job that you might like to have. What are some risks associated with that job? How likely are those risks to occur? Write a paragraph on your personal risk assessment of that job.

DreamPictures/Pam Ostrow/Blend Images LLC

Building Real-World Skills

Career WISE

Certified Payroll Professional (CPP)

CPP is one of two certifications offered by the American Payroll Association. A CPP must have at least three years of experience in payroll administration, payroll production, or payroll accounting. A CPP also must pass an exam demonstrating skills in dealing with employee issues such as taxes, benefits, regulatory requirements, and auditing.

Research and Write:

a. Locate the Web site of the American Payroll Association (APA). Download the "CPP Knowledge, Skills, and Abilities" guidelines.

b. What other certification does the APA offer, and how does it differ from the CPP? Put your results in a table.

21st Century Workplace

Hunting for Life Insurance Bargains Online

Just a few years ago, most life insurance was purchased through a sales agent. Today, many people buy their life insurance online, usually through one of the many Web sites that "shop around" to find the best rate. Customers type in personal information—such as age, health, job, and whether or not they smoke—and the sites return estimated premiums from several different insurance providers.

Research and Write:

a. Use the Internet to locate Web sites that provide life insurance rate quotes. Create a spreadsheet to organize your findings.

b. Write a paragraph describing the benefits and drawbacks to shopping for and buying life insurance online.

CHAPTER 12 Investments

Big Idea

By investing and diversifying your portfolio, you can make your money work for you.

Aurora Images/SuperStock

Explore the Photo

Planning for the Future

How you spend and invest your money can have an impact on your lifestyle at a later time. *What might you want to start saving for in the near future?*

Ask AN EXPERT

"Green" Mutual Funds

Q: I want to make investments someday. I also want to do my part to help the environment. How can I avoid investing in companies that pollute?

A: "Green" mutual funds have become popular with eco-minded investors. Green fund managers use investor money to buy stock in companies that meet environmental requirements. You can learn more about green mutual funds at your local library. Standard & Poor's publishes *Industry Surveys,* which analyzes more than 50 different industries. Standard & Poor's also publishes *Investment Survey,* which gives data on more than 1,700 stocks, and a weekly investment advice newsletter called *The Outlook.* Web sites such as *BusinessWeek's* Web site can be useful sources for industry updates.

English Language Arts/Writing When deciding to invest in a mutual fund, how important is the fund's financial performance compared to the environmental practices of the companies in the fund? Write a paragraph explaining your answer.

GET READY for the Chapter

Math Online
To take the Online Readiness Quiz, go to connectED.mcgraw-hill.com.

Chapter 12 Investments

Reading Guide

Before You Read

Identify Have you ever had to save to buy something? Why plan ahead?

Main Idea

Achieving your goal of saving for college, a home, or a new car will happen faster if you invest your money.

Graphic Organizer

Use a chart like the one below to write two or three sentences describing each of the following: certificate of deposit, stock, mutual fund, bond, and real estate.

Investment	Notes

Math Online Go to **connectED.mcgraw-hill.com** to download this graphic organizer.

Content Vocabulary

You will learn these key terms in this chapter.

- certificate of deposit (CD)
- annual percentage yield (APY)
- stocks
- stock certificate
- profit
- loss
- dividend
- mutual fund
- net asset value (NAV)
- loading charge
- bonds
- rental property
- rent
- individual retirement account (IRA)
- Roth IRA
- required minimum distribution (RMD)

Academic Vocabulary

You will see these words in your reading and on your tests.

- invest
- compounding
- quoted
- initial
- proceeds
- accumulate
- matures
- alternative
- distribution

You can find vocabulary definitions in the **Content Vocabulary** Glossary and the **Academic Vocabulary** Glossary in the back of the book.

LESSON 12.1

Certificates of Deposit

Lesson Objective
Use tables or a formula to compute interest on certificates of deposit.

Content Vocabulary
- certificate of deposit (CD)

GET READY for the Lesson

What are some ways to plan for the future?

When planning a vacation, John Robins invests some of his savings in a certificate of deposit. The money will earn interest so that he will have extra funds for his trip.

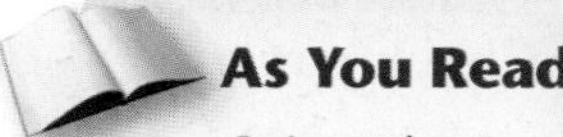

As You Read
Explain What is one advantage of investing in a CD instead of in a savings account?

Certificate of Deposit One way to **invest** your money is to purchase a **certificate of deposit** (CD), which earns interest at a higher rate than a regular savings account. You buy CDs for specific amounts, such as $500 or $1,000, and you must leave the money on deposit for a specified time (ranging from three months to 30 years). You are penalized for early withdrawal. Most CDs earn interest compounded daily, monthly, or quarterly. Although banks use computers to calculate interest earned, you can use the *Amount of $1.00 Invested—Daily, Monthly, and Quarterly Compounding* table on page A14 or the compound interest formula in Lesson 5.6 page 229. Use these formulas:

Amount = Original Principal × Amount of $1.00

Compound Interest = Amount − Original Principal

Study Tip
Calculators
Keep a calculator handy when studying math. Learn to use the memory keys. The M+ key means "add to memory." The RM key means "Recall Memory." Use them when you want to remember a number and use it again later in a calculation that has several steps.

EXAMPLE 1

Ching-Hsia Chan invests $5,000 in a 1-year CD that earns interest at an annual rate of 4% compounded monthly. Use the *Amount of $1.00 Invested—Daily, Monthly, and Quarterly Compounding* table on page A14 to determine the interest earned.

Step 1: Find the amount.

Original Principal × Amount of $1.00

Monthly: $5,000 × 1.040742 = $5,203.71

Step 2: Find the compound interest.

Amount − Original Principal

$5,203.71 − $5,000 = **$203.71 interest earned**

Concept CHECK

Complete the problem. Check your answer in the back of the book.

1. Helen Angel invests $7,500 in 2-year CD that pays 6% compounded quarterly. What is the amount of interest that Helen would earn?

Need Help? Go to...

Application A: Formulas, p. AP1

Real World CAREER

Surveyor
Surveyors use special equipment to establish property boundaries before new houses are built. They measure more than land; they also measure water boundaries and define airspace for airports. **What types of measurements might surveyors make?**

EXAMPLE 2 Algebra

Compute the interest earned on the CD in **Example 1** using the compound interest formula from Lesson 5.6.

$A = P(1.00 + r)^n$

Step 1: Find the rate per period and the number of periods.

$r = \frac{4\%}{12} = \frac{0.04}{12} = 0.00333333$ and $n = 1 \times 12 = 12$

Step 2: Substitute into the formula to find the amount.

$A = P(1.00 + r)^n$

$A = \$5,000(1 + 0.00333333)^{12}$

$A = \$5,000(1.040741543)$

$A = \$5,203.707714 = \$5,203.71$

Step 3: Interest = $5,203.71 – $5,000 = **$203.71**

Concept CHECK

Complete the problems to find the amount of interest. Check your answers in the back of the book.

2. A $10,000 CD at 4.50% for 4 years compounded quarterly using the table.

3. A $10,000 CD at 4.50% for 10 years compounded quarterly using the formula.

Lesson Practice

Use the *Amount of $1.00 Invested—Daily, Monthly, and Quarterly Compounding* table on page A14 to complete Problems 4–7.

	Annual Rate	Interest Period	Original Principal	Amount per $1.00	Amount	Interest Earned
4.	5.00%	1 year quarterly	$ 4,500	a.	b.	c.
5.	3.50%	4 years daily	$ 18,000	a.	b.	c.
6.	4.75%	4 years monthly	$ 9,000	a.	b.	c.
7.	4.25%	1 year quarterly	$140,000	a.	b.	c.

8. Elliot Chambers invests $30,000 in a 1-year CD that earns interest at an annual rate of 3.75% compounded monthly. **(a)** What is the amount of the CD at maturity? **(b)** What is the interest earned?

9. Emily Gast deposits $50,000 in a 4-year CD that earns interest at an annual rate of 5.25% compounded daily. **(a)** Find the amount of the CD in 4-years. **(b)** Find the interest earned in 4-years.

10. Janet Spurlock can invest $25,000 at 5.25% in a 1-year CD compounded quarterly or a 1-year CD compounded daily. **(a)** What is the amount of the CD at maturity for each rate? **(b)** What is the difference in the interest earned?

11. Clifford and Hazel Ida can purchase a 4-year CD for $10,000 at 4.5% compounded daily or compounded monthly. **(a)** What is the amount of the CD at each rate at maturity? **(b)** What is the difference in the interest earned?

12. National Trust advertises a 1-year certificate of deposit at 4.00% compounded daily with a minimum deposit of $10,000. First National offers a 1-year certificate of deposit at 4.25% compounded quarterly with no minimum deposit. John Culbert has $20,000 to invest. **(a)** Which bank should he choose? **(b)** How much more would he earn on his $20,000 by choosing that bank?

13. Marsha Johnson has $50,000 to invest in a 4-year CD. Fifth Central Bank offers 4.50% compounded monthly, while American National offers 4.50% compounded daily. However, Fifth Central is giving a toaster to anyone who opens a CD. What will the toaster cost Marsha if she goes with Fifth Central?

14. The LaGelleys have $25,000 that they want to invest in a certificate of deposit. Granite Trust offers a 4-year certificate of deposit that earns interest at 3.50% compounded quarterly. Hancock Cooperative Bank offers a 4-year certificate that earns interest at 3.25% compounded daily. **(a)** Which CD earns more interest? **(b)** By how much?

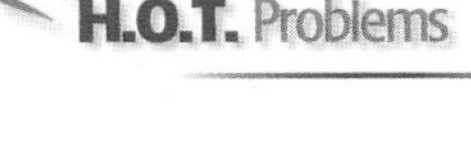

15. **ALGEBRA** Kati Sweigart invests $100,000 in a 4 year CD at 6.75% compounded monthly. **(a)** Find amount and interest using tables. **(b)** Find amount and interest using the formula.

16. **ALGEBRA** Tammy Smith deposits $5,000 in First Internet Bank's 5-year CD, which pays 5.22% compounded monthly. **(a)** How much will she have in the account at the end of 5 years? **(b)** How much interest did she earn?

17. **ALGEBRA** Mali and Den Hayashi deposit $19,756 in a 1-year CD with Countrywide Bank, which pays 5.49% compounded daily (365-day year). **(a)** How much will the Hayashis have in their account after one year? **(b)** How much interest will they have earned?

Spiral Review

Round to the nearest ten. (Skill 2)

18. 78 **19.** 144 **20.** 3,045

21. Mary Johnston has a single PPO plan with an annual premium of $9,225. Her employer pays 85% of the cost. **(a)** How much does Mary pay annually? **(b)** How much is deducted from her monthly paycheck? (Lesson 11.1)

GET READY for the Next Lesson

PREREQUISITE SKILL Writing Decimals as Percents (Skill 26)

Write each as a percent. Round to the nearest hundredth.

22. 0.06245 **23.** 0.08545 **24.** 1.58642

25. 1.07629 **26.** 4.0 **27.** 2.7368

LESSON 12.2

Annual Percentage Yield

Lesson Objective

Determine the annual percentage yield.

Content Vocabulary

- annual percentage yield (APY)

GET READY for the Lesson

Do you need a lot of money to start investing?

Bryan Price lives on a tight budget. He knows that the earlier he starts investing, the more interest he can earn for the future. Bryan researched investment types and learned that some require only a small amount of money to start.

FreeNet Checking Account

Account Balance	APY	Interest Rate
Introductory yield[3]	6.01%	5.84%
$100,000 and up	5.01%	4.89%
$50,000 –$99,999	4.15%	4.07%
$25,000 –$49,999	3.65%	3.59%
$10,000 –$24,999	3.45%	3.39%
$9,999 or less	3.41%	3.35%

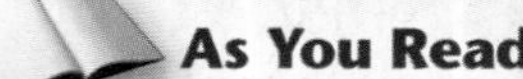
As You Read

Identify Which is the better investment: a high or low APY?

Determining the Annual Percentage Yield The **annual percentage yield (APY)** is also called the *effective annual yield*. Financial institutions advertise not only their annual interest rates, but also the annual percentage yield (APY) on certificates of deposit and savings accounts. The APY is the rate of return on your investment for a one-year period. The APY is your index to investing your money. The higher the APY, the better the investment.

In the real world when you walk into a bank you will see the term "Annual Percentage Yield (APY)" used in connection with savings account rates.

You will find that as the frequency of **compounding** increases, the APY also increases. To calcuate the annual percentage yield on an investment, you need this formula:

$$\text{Annual Percentage Yield} = \frac{\text{Interest for 1 Year}}{\text{Principal}}$$

EXAMPLE 1

Randall Raye invests $5,000 in a certificate of deposit for 3 years. The certificate earns interest at an annual rate of 5.25% compounded quarterly. What is the annual percentage yield to the nearest thousandth of a percent?

Step 1: Find the amount for 1 year. (Refer to the *Amount of $1.00 Invested—Daily, Monthly, and Quarterly Compounding* table on page A14.)

Amount = Original Principal × Amount of $1.00

$5,267.72 = $5,000.00 × 1.053543

Step 2: Find the compound interest.

Compound Interest = Amount − Original Principal

$267.72 = $5,267.72 − $5,000.00

Step 3: Find the annual percentage yield.

$$\frac{\text{Interest for 1 Year}}{\text{Principal}} = \frac{\$267.72}{\$5{,}000.00} = \mathbf{0.053544 \text{ or } 5.354\%}$$

Complete the problems to find the annual percentage yield. Check your answers in the back of the book. (Refer to the *Amount of $1.00 Invested-Daily, Monthly, and Quarterly Compounding* table on page A14.)

1. National Bank offers a $10,000 certificate of deposit at 5.75% compounded monthly.
2. Lancaster Savings offers a $25,000 certificate of deposit at 5% compounded quarterly.

EXAMPLE 2

Galeno Villarreal can invest $10,000.00 at either 4.75% compounded daily for 4 years or 5% compounded quarterly for 4 years. Based on the annual percentage yield, which is the better investment?

Step 1: Find the interest for 1 year and the annual yield for both investments.

Daily: ($10,000.00 × 1.048643) − $10,000.00

$10,486.43 − $10,000.00 = $486.43

$$\text{Yield} = \frac{486.43}{\$10{,}000.00} = 0.048643 \text{ or } 4.864\%$$

Quarterly: ($10,000.00 × 1.050945) − $10,000.00

$10,509.45 − $10,000.00 = $509.45

$$\text{Yield} = \frac{509.45}{\$10{,}000.00} = 0.050945 \text{ or } 5.095\%$$

Step 2: Compare the two.

The better investment is the 5% compounded quarterly; it yields 5.095% which is greater than the 4.864% yield.

Reading Math +−÷=

Decimal Place Value

The first place to the right of the decimal point is tenths. Hundredths, thousandths, and ten-thousandths follow to the right. When rounding to the nearest thousandth, look first at the digit to its right in the ten-thousandths place. If it is 5 or greater, round up. If it is less than 5, round down.

Concept CHECK

Complete the problems. Check your answers in the back of the book.

Luisa Hernandez wants to invest $20,000. Which 4-year investment is the best deal?

3. Compounded daily at 3.5% or compounded monthly at 3.75%.
4. Compounded quarterly at 4.5% or compounded monthly at 4.25%.

Lesson Practice

For Problems 5–8, use the *Amount of $1.00 Invested—Daily, Monthly, and Quarterly Compounding* table on page A14.

	Annual Rate	Interest Period	Original Principal	Amount per $1.00	Amount	Interest Earned	Annual percentage yield
5.	3.50%	1 year quarterly	$6,000	a.	b.	c.	d.
6.	4.25%	1 year quarterly	8,400	a.	b.	c.	d.
7.	1.50%	1 year monthly	5,000	a.	b.	c.	d.
8.	2.50%	1 year daily	1,800	a.	b.	c.	d.

Did You Know?

Investing Abroad

Many Americans have discovered that investing abroad is a smart decision when the U.S. dollar is weak and foreign economies are growing. In a recent 12-month period, international-stock mutual funds had a 29% rate of return, while American-stock funds returned only 19%.

9. Jacob Hernandez invests \$25,000 in a CD for 5 years. The CD earns interest at an annual rate of 5.5% compounded quarterly. What is the annual percentage yield to the nearest hundredth of a percent?

10. Mabel Cousino has \$35,000 to invest in a certificate of deposit for 4 years. The certificate of deposit earns interest at 4.75% compounded daily. What is the annual percentage yield to the nearest thousandth of a percent?

11. Ollie Gibson is considering investing \$10,000 in a certificate of deposit for 4 years at an annual interest rate of 4% compounded daily or 4% compounded monthly. Based on the annual percentage yield, which one is the better investment?

12. May Wattson has \$50,000 to invest in a 4-year certificate of deposit that earns interest at a rate of 3.75% compounded monthly or 3.50% compounded daily. Based on annual yield, which is the better investment?

13. Paul Durant invested \$100,000 at 6% compounded daily for 4 years and \$100,000 at 6% compounded monthly for 1 year. **(a)** What is the interest earned for 1 year on each investment? **(b)** What is the annual percentage yield for each investment?

14. Ben Garison invested \$15,000 at 5% compounded daily in a credit union account that matures in 1 year. He also invested \$20,000 at 5.25% compounded monthly in a Silver Screen account that matures in 4 years. **(a)** What is the interest earned at maturity for both accounts? **(b)** What is the annual percentage yield for each account?

H.O.T. Problems

15. CHALLENGE PROBLEM Ricardo Torres invests \$10,000 at 4% compounded daily for 1 year. At the end of the year, Ricardo reinvests the amount in the account for another year at the same rate. He repeats this process for 2 more years. Compare the amount in the account at the end of 4 years with what he would have had if he had invested the \$10,000 at 4% compounded daily for 4 years.

Spiral Review

Write as a percent. Round answers to the nearest hundredth. (Skill 26)

16. 0.089146 **17.** 1.25642 **18.** 2.0

19. For the first payment, what is **(a)** the interest, **(b)** the payment to principal, and **(c)** the new principal for a mortgage loan of \$76,000 at 6.5%? The monthly payment is \$480.37. (Lesson 10.4)

GET READY for the Next Lesson

PREREQUISITE SKILL **Adding Decimals** (Skill 5)

Find the sum.

20. \$13,478 + \$44.89 **21.** \$2,710 + \$89.91

22. \$5,912 + \$16,703.65 **23.** \$353.19 + \$7,837

24. \$37,891 + \$5,688.90 **25.** \$2,431.46 + \$856

LESSON 12.3

Buying Stocks

Lesson Objective

Calculate the total cost of a stock investment.

Content Vocabulary

- stocks
- stock certificate

GET READY for the Lesson

What does it mean to own stock in a company?

George Barnes recently bought stock in a film animation company. If the company's movies are a hit and the stock increases in value, George could earn a lot of money. He could also lose money if the movies are not successful.

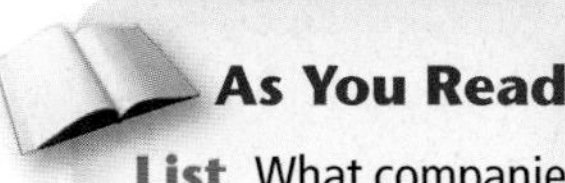

As You Read

List What companies interest you as potential investments?

Total Cost of a Stock Investment You can invest your money in shares of **stocks**. When you purchase a share of stock, you become a part owner of the corporation that issues the stock. Each day you will find the stock prices published in newspapers and on Web sites. Stock prices are usually **quoted** in dollars and cents.

You may receive a **stock certificate** as proof of ownership. The total amount you pay for the stock depends on the cost per share, the number of shares you purchase, and the stockbroker's commission or broker's fee. A *stockbroker* is a consultant who aids investors in the buying and selling of stocks. An online *broker* takes orders and processes them for you and may be available to give advice.

First, you will need to know how to read a stock table. You can find these in the newspaper or online.

Figure 12.1

52 Weeks Hi	52 Weeks Lo	Stock	Sym	Div	Yld. %	PE	Vol. 100s	Hi	Lo	Close	Net Chg.
30.20	21.06	VXIndustry	VX	0.50	1.8	19	160718	27.87	26.25	27.87	+0.50
104.12	66.56	BNovak	BN	1.72	1.9	14	57324	92.53	89.95	92.53	+1.15
47.69	27.46	KenanMills	KMI	0.49	1.3	42	45526	37.64	37.05	37.64	+0.46
46.40	40.70	WestSloan	WS	0.46	1.1	27	47661	42.74	39.90	42.74	+2.02

52 Weeks Hi: Highest price paid for one share of the stock in the past 52 weeks: $30.20.

52 Weeks Lo: Lowest price paid for one share of stock in the past 52 weeks.

Stock: Name of the company.

Sym: Ticker symbol or letters that identify a stock for trading.

Div: Projected annual dividend for next year based on the amount of the firm's last dividend.

Yld. %: Yield percent, or the percent of return based on the dividend and current price of the stock (for VXIndustry $0.50 ÷ $27.87 = 0.0179 = 1.8%).

PE: Price-earnings ratio.

Vol. 100s: Number of shares traded during the day, expressed in hundreds of shares.

Hi: Highest price paid for one share of the stock during the day.

Lo: Lowest price paid for one share of stock during the day.

Close: Price paid in the last transaction of the day.

Net Chg.: Difference between the price paid for the last share traded today and the price paid for the last share traded on the previous day: for VXIndustry $0.50 (in Wall Street terms, VXIndustry "closed up" $0.50 on this day).

When investing in stocks you need these formulas:

Cost of Stock = Number of Shares × Cost per Share

Total Paid = Cost of Stock + Commission

EXAMPLE

Melanie Lambert purchased 100 shares of VXO stock at $106.30 per share. Her online stockbroker charged her a $15.95 commission. What is the total amount that she paid for the stock?

Step 1: Find the cost of the stock.

Number of Shares × Cost per Share

100 × $106.30 = $10,630

Step 2: Find the total paid.

Cost of Stock + Commission

$10,630 + $15.95 = **$10,645.95 total paid**

Reading Math +−÷=

Commission
Learn to recognize the different meanings of the word *commission*. It can mean a group appointed to perform certain duties, or it can mean a fee paid to a person who buys or sells something for you.

Concept CHECK

Complete the problems. Check your answers in the back of the book. Find the total paid.

1. You own 150 shares of TimCo stock, which you purchased at $36.21 per share. You paid a commission of $29.95.
2. You own 400 shares of UnVar stock, which you purchased at $58.80 per share. You paid a commission of $19.95.

Lesson Practice

For Problems 3–6 compute (a) the cost of the stock and (b) the total paid.

	Company	Number of Shares	×	Cost per Share	=	Cost of Stock	+	Commission	=	Total Paid
3.	Nelson Inc.	100	×	$110.50	=	a.	+	$ 9.99	=	b.
4.	Galvin Co.	900	×	$ 45.90	=	a.	+	$50.00	=	b.
5.	Dunkle LTD	500	×	$ 35.60	=	a.	+	$45.50	=	b.
6.	Warncke Co.	2,500	×	$ 62.45	=	a.	+	0.03/share	=	b.

Did You Know?
Bicycle Tires **An important moment in the development of the modern bicycle tire came in 1844, when Charles Goodyear discovered vulcanization, a process that makes rubber flexible in any kind of weather. The first pneumatic (filled with air) tire was introduced in 1887 by John Dunlop, a Scottish veterinarian.**

For Problems 7 and 8, determine (a) the cost of the stock and (b) the total paid.

7. Trudy Fahringer buys 500 shares of Waverson, Inc.
   She pays $32.90 per share.
   The commission is $65.00.
8. David Daly owns 215 shares of Atwood Tire.
   His cost per share is $18.90.
   The online commission is $14.95.
9. Eunice Brudley purchased 3,000 shares of GTI Petroleum at $6.30 per share. The broker's commission was $19.95 for fewer than 1,000 shares, or $0.02 per share for 1,000 or more. **(a)** What was the cost of the stock? **(b)** What was the total paid?
10. Janet and David Scott bought 1,500 shares of Metro Health Care REIT (MHC) at $84.92 per share. The broker's commission was $14.95 for fewer than 1,000 shares or $0.015 per share for 1,000 shares or more. **(a)** What was the cost of the stock? **(b)** What was the total paid?

11. Linda and Martin Sonoma purchased 300 shares of Hampton Publishing at $31.94 per share and 150 shares of Company R at $29.19 per share. The broker charged $19.95 for each transaction. What was the total paid?

Figure 12.2

Broker-Assisted Commissions					
Minimum Charge $39 per Trade					
Transaction Size			Commission		
$ 0	–	$ 2,999	$ 30	+	1.70%
3,000	–	6,999	56	+	0.66%
7,000	–	19,999	76	+	0.34%
20,000	–	49,999	100	+	0.22%
50,000	–		155	+	0.11%

Use Figure 12.2 for Problems 12–14.

12. After consulting with his broker, Dan Hostetler purchased 2,000 shares of Ballon Synergy stock at $4.10 per share. He also purchased 500 shares of Matell Scientific at $26.76 per share. What is the total cost of the stocks, including the commission?

13. Yukiko Nakata, after consulting with her broker, purchased 10,000 shares of McQuire Internet, Inc. at $24.52 per share. She also purchased 5,000 shares of Smithmeyer Capital Group at $45.25 a share. What is the total cost of the stocks, including the commission?

14. CHALLENGE PROBLEM Nickel-n-Dime, Inc. stock is selling at $1.99 per share. Oscar Mellon is thinking of purchasing 1,507 shares. Oscar's friend, who is an experienced stock trader, suggests that he consider purchasing 1,508 shares instead. Why?

Spiral Review

Add. (Skill 5)

15. $55,289 + $39.95 **16.** $5,863 + $19.95 **17.** $980 + $9.95

18. Sandra Ramirez is single and has a health insurance plan with the benefits shown in **Figure 11.1** on page 421. Her recent network health care costs include co-payments for 7 physician visits and 2 specialist visits. She also had 4 co-payments at her local pharmacy, for 3 generic drugs and one brand name drug, and a hospital bill of $2,775. What amount did she pay? (Lesson 11.2)

GET READY for the Next Lesson

PREREQUISITE SKILL **Multiplying Decimals** (Skill 8)

Find the product.

19. 0.19 × 35.7 **20.** 41.55 × 8.4

21. 15.62 × 63.9 **22.** 0.27 × 73.62

23. 19.2 × 55.66 **24.** 10.53 × 88.45

LESSON 12.4

Selling Stocks

Lesson Objective

Calculate the profit or loss from a stock sale.

Content Vocabulary

- profit
- loss

GET READY for the Lesson

Can you think of companies in which you would like to invest?

Colleen Smith bought stock in a small engineering company two years ago. Since she purchased the stock, the company has prospered and grown. If Colleen were to sell her stock today, she would get more than twice what she initially invested.

As You Read

Explain What is profit on a stock?

Selling Stocks When you sell your stocks, the sale can result in either a **profit** or a **loss**. The profit on a stock is the amount of money you make over and above the **initial** money you invested. In business language it means that if the amount you receive for the sale minus the sales commission is greater than the total amount you paid for the stocks, then you made a profit.

A loss on a stock is just the opposite of a profit because you lose some of the money that you invested. If the amount you receive from the sale minus the sales commission is less than the total investment, you lost money on the stock.

In order to compute the profit and loss of stocks, use the following calculations. (Note: Remember that "commission" is the fee charged by the brokerage firm buying and/or selling your stock.)

Net Sale = Amount of Sale − Commission

Profit(Loss) = Net Sale − Investment

In simple terms: if you paid more for the stock than you sell it for, then you lost money.

EXAMPLE

Bill Tennyson paid a total of $3,738.43 for 75 shares of Watson Parcel Service. He sold the stock for $51.50 a share and paid a sales commission of $39.45. What is the profit or loss from the sale?

Step 1: Find the net sale.

Amount of Sale − Commission

($51.50 × 75) − $39.45

$3,862.50 − $39.45 = $3,823.05 net sale

Step 2: Find the profit(loss).

Net Sale − Investment

$3,823.05 − $3,738.43 = **$84.62 profit**

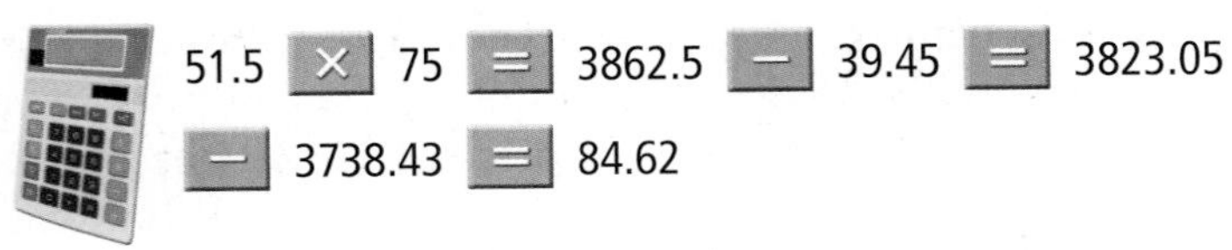

Concept CHECK

Complete the problems to find the profit or loss. Check your answers in the back of the book.

1. You paid $1,829 for 40 shares of JTT stock.
   You sold the stock for $61.50 per share.
   The commission you paid was $35.50.
2. You paid $24,000 for 1,000 shares of EXO stock.
   You sold the stock for $22.50 per share.
   The commission you paid was $49.95.

Reading Math +−÷=

Net

The term *net* refers to an amount after certain deductions have been made. *Net sale* is the amount of the sale after deducting the commission.

Lesson Practice

For Problems 3–8, compute (a) the net sale and (b) the profit or loss.

	Stock	Total Paid	Selling Price per Share	×	Number of Shares	−	Commission	=	Net Sale	Profit or Loss
3.	Sargent Inc.	$ 5,200	$72.00	×	100	−	$30.00	=	a.	b.
4.	Putman Co.	$10,000	$30.00	×	400	−	$50.00	=	a.	b.
5.	Western, Inc.	$ 6,760	$32.50	×	200	−	$20.00	=	a.	b.
6.	St. Clair Land	$ 1,710	$10.50	×	150	−	$15.00	=	a.	b.
7.	MetalCo	$ 4,500	$22.00	×	300	−	$40.00	=	a.	b.
8.	Harmony, Inc.	$ 2,700	$17.50	×	110	−	$15.00	=	a.	b.

For Problems 9–11, determine the profit or loss.

9. Garlan and Kesia Green bought 180 shares of TYV stock.
   They paid a total of $4,512.
   They sold at $30 per share.
   They paid a $40 sales commission.
10. Jasmine and Eric Walton bought 280 shares of WEX stock.
    They paid a total of $9,788.50.
    They sold at $23.00 per share.
    They paid a $60.00 sales commission.
11. Wayne Arnsberg bought 240 shares of TRE stock.
    He paid a total of $28,656.
    He sold at $115.4 per share.
    He paid a $79.95 sales commission.
12. Elean Schenandore purchased 300 shares of CY Energy stock online and paid a total of $8,484.95. She sold the stock at $39.94 per share and paid a $39.95 sales commission. **(a)** What was the net amount of the sale? **(b)** What was the profit or loss from the sale?

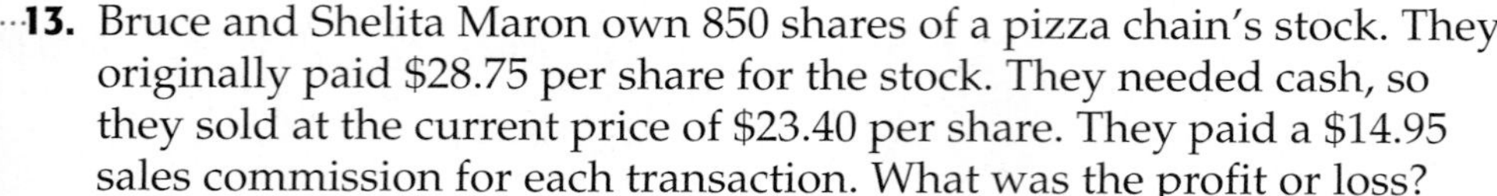

13. Bruce and Shelita Maron own 850 shares of a pizza chain's stock. They originally paid $28.75 per share for the stock. They needed cash, so they sold at the current price of $23.40 per share. They paid a $14.95 sales commission for each transaction. What was the profit or loss?

14. Alfredo Gutierrez bought 2,000 shares of a phone company's stock at $36.50 a share. He sold his stock at $48.25 per share. Each transaction paid a sales commission of $49.95 plus $0.02 per share. **(a)** What was the net amount of the sale? **(b)** What was the profit or loss from the sale?

Did You Know?

1929 Crash **The worst stock-market crash in history began on October 24, 1929, when the Dow Jones Industrial Average lost 9% of its previous day's value. This event began a three-year decline in stock prices. By 1932 stocks had lost nearly 90% of their pre-crash value.**

15. Enrico and Eve Marcucci bought 1,200 shares of a paint store's stock at $28 per share and paid a sales commission of $40 plus $0.02 per share. They sold the stock at $26 per share plus a sales commission of $30 plus $0.03 per share. **(a)** What was the net amount of the sale? **(b)** What was the profit or loss from the sale?

16. Tony Sanchez owned 180 shares of an architecture company's stock, for which he paid $13.50 per share plus a 2% commission on the principal. He sold at $31.50 and paid a 3% sales commission on the principal. What was the profit or loss from the sale?

17. Eddie Watts bought 1,500 shares of a Solar Energy stock at $88 per share and paid a sales commission of $40 plus $0.02 per share. He sold the stock at $96 per share plus a sales commission of $30 plus $0.03 per share. **(a)** What was the net amount of the sale? **(b)** What was the profit or loss from the sale?

18. Tammy Seals owned 280 shares of the Thermo Window Company's stock, for which she paid $83.50 per share plus a 2% commission on the principal. She sold at $81.50 and paid a 3% sales commission on the principal. What was the profit or loss from the sale?

H.O.T. Problems

19. CHALLENGE PROBLEM The Montvilles purchased 150 shares of Allen Pharmaceuticals stock at $34.00. A year later they bought an additional 300 shares at $38.75. They paid a commission of $29.95 on each transaction. A year later they sold the original 150 shares plus 100 shares from the second purchase of 300 shares at $46.71. They paid a sales commission of $40.00 when they sold the stock. What was the profit or loss from the sale of the 250 shares?

Spiral Review

Which number is greater? (Skill 1)

20. 381 or 381.6 **21.** $21.19 or $21.91 **22.** $219.84 or $218.94

23. Digna Cervantes leases a van for family use. She pays $472.10 a month for 48 months. She also pays a deposit of $1,200, a title fee of $99, and a license fee of $225. What is her total lease cost? (Lesson 9.6)

GET READY for the Next Lesson

PREREQUISITE SKILL **Dividing Decimals** (Skill 11)

Find the quotient. Round answers to the nearest hundredth.

24. $34.25 \div 250$ **25.** $88.61 \div 90$ **26.** $18.2 \div 25$

27. $0.672 \div 0.424$ **28.** $25.6 \div 11.2$ **29.** $94.6 \div 48.1$

LESSON 12.5 Stock Dividends

Lesson Objective

Compute the annual dividend and annual yield of a stock investment.

Content Vocabulary

- dividend

GET READY for the Lesson

Do you have to sell a stock to make money from it?

Eduardo Hernandez is happy about a recent investment. Ever since he first bought stock in a local alternative-energy company, its stock price has gone up. He receives money from this investment without having to sell the stock.

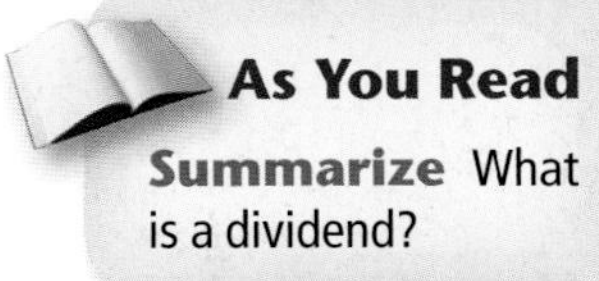

As You Read

Summarize What is a dividend?

Stock Dividends When you own stock, you may receive a **dividend**. A dividend is the money you earn as a shareholder of the company. You may receive an amount specified by the corporation for each share of stock that you own. The annual yield is your annual **proceeds** for holding a stock; it is expressed as a percent of the price. Just like with certificates of deposit, the higher your yield, the greater the return on your investment during the year.

In order to calculate the yield you first need to know the total annual dividend. Use this formula:

$$\text{Total Annual Dividend} = \text{Annual Dividend per Share} \times \text{Number of Shares}$$

The formula for annual yield is:

$$\text{Annual Yield} = \frac{\text{Annual Dividend per Share}}{\text{Cost per Share}}$$

EXAMPLE 1

Susana Valasco owns 100 shares of Wagoneer, Inc. stock. The stock ranged from a low of $37.26 to a high of $52.86 last year. The annual dividend is $1.10. What is the total annual dividend? What is the annual yield based on the high and the low?

Step 1: Find the total annual dividend.

Annual Dividend per Share × Number of Shares

$1.10 × 100 = **$110.00 total annual dividend**

Step 2: Find the annual yield based on the high and the low.

High: $\frac{\text{Annual Dividend per Share}}{\text{Cost per Share}} = \frac{\$1.10}{\$52.86} = 0.02080 = \mathbf{2.08\%\ annual\ yield}$

Low: $\frac{\text{Annual Dividend per Share}}{\text{Cost per Share}} = \frac{\$1.10}{\$37.26} = 0.02952 = \mathbf{2.95\%\ annual\ yield}$

Complete the problem. Check your answers in the back of the book.

1. Joyce Winnetka owns 150 shares of Higginbotham Network Design stock that had a high of $49.88 and a low of $32.64 during the year. The annual dividend was $1.34. What is the **(a)** total annual dividend, **(b)** annual yield based on the low, and **(c)** annual yield based on the high?

Need Help? Go to...

Workshop 36: Problem-Solving Strategy: Using Simple Algebraic Operations, p. 74

EXAMPLE 2 Algebra

Tom and Irene Zach own 400 shares of Bank of America (BAC) stock. After the quarterly dividends are reinvested under their dividend reinvestment program (DRIP), they own 405 shares. BAC is selling at $51.00 a share. Find the annual dividend per share and the annual yield for BAC.

Step 1: Determine the quarterly and annual dividend.

Quarterly dividend in stocks: $405 - 400 = 5$ shares of stock

Value of 5 shares $= 5 \times \$51 = \$255$

Total annual dividend $4 \times \$255 = \$1{,}020$

Step 2: Determine the annual dividend per share

Let $d =$ The annual dividend per share

Total annual dividend $=$ annual dividend per share $\times$ *number of shares*

$$\$1{,}020 = d \times 400$$

$$\$2.55 = d$$

The annual dividend per share for BAC is $2.55

Step 3: Determine the annual yield.

$$\text{Annual Yield} = \frac{\$2.55}{\$51.00} = 0.05 = 5.00\%$$

The annual yield is 5.00%

Study Tip

Yield

Annual yield is expressed as a percent. To convert a decimal to a percent, move the decimal point two places to the right and add a percent sign.

Concept CHECK

Complete the problem. Check your answers in the back of the book.

2. Elena and Arturo Sarmiento own 500 shares of Walgreens (WAG) stock. After the quarterly dividends are reinvested under their dividend reinvestment program (DRIP), they own 501.055 shares. WAG is selling at $45.00 a share. Find **(a)** the annual dividend per share and **(b)** the annual yield for WAG.

Lesson Practice

For Problems 3 and 4, determine the annual yield to the nearest hundredth of a percent.

3. You purchase TEK stock for $15.53 per share. Dividends are $1.48 per share.
4. You purchase CGW stock for $36.91 per share. Dividends are $0.14 per share.

For Problems 5 and 6, determine (a) the total annual dividend and (b) the annual yield to the nearest hundredth of a percent.

5. Christine Gony owns 400 shares of QT Press.
Purchase price was $55.99 a share.
Dividends are $1.52 per share.

6. Ella Franklin owns 325 shares of ITA stock.
Purchase price was $37.85 per share.
Dividends are $1.11 per share.

7. Woody Davenport owns 850 shares of Yoder Mills. High and low prices for the year were $74.46 and $47.50. The dividends are $1.36 per share. **(a)** What are his annual dividends? **(b)** What are the annual yields for the high and low prices?

Did You Know?

Expensive Stock During recent trading a single Class A share of Berkshire Hathaway, the most expensive American stock, sold for $100,100. Warren Buffett, the chairman of the investment holdings company, owned 498,320 Class A shares. The total value of his shares at the high price was approximately $50 billion.

8. Joyce Kronecki buys 350 shares of KOW, Inc. that has a high of $42.50 per share and a low of $23.60. Last year the company paid annual dividends of $0.58 per share. What is the **(a)** total annual dividend, **(b)** annual yield based on the low, and **(c)** annual yield based on the high?

9. Duane Hartley owns 2,000 shares of Heban Oil stock, which he purchased for $28.40 each. Recently he read that the average selling price of his stock was $37.90. The company paid annual dividends of $1.80 per share last year. **(a)** What is the annual yield on his stock? **(b)** For an investor who purchased the stock at $37.90 per share, what is the annual yield?

10. CHALLENGE PROBLEM The Racitis own 300 shares of Clayton Manufacturing, which they purchased at $36.30 per share. They also purchased 200 shares at $22.50 per share. The dividend per share paid by the company is $0.72. **(a)** What is the average price per share? **(b)** What are the Racitis' annual dividends? **(c)** What is the average annual yield?

11. ALGEBRA Adzo and Imamu Cooper own 265.64 shares of Vornado Realty Trust (VNO) stock. After the quarterly dividends are reinvested under their dividend reinvestment program (DRIP), they own 267.85 shares. VNO is selling at $108.00 per share. Find the annual dividend per share and the annual yield for VNO.

Spiral Review

Divide. Round answers to the nearest hundredth. (Skill 11)

12. 24.0 ÷ 200 **13.** 32.61 ÷ 35 **14.** 0.587 ÷ 0.009 **15.** 16.7 ÷ 1.1

16. Find the amount of the down payment and the amount financed on a loan for a kitchen remodeling that cost $9,980 and has a down payment of 20%. (Lesson 8.2)

17. Mohamed Rahim sells real estate at a $7\frac{1}{2}$% straight commission. Last week his sales totaled $580,000. What was his commission? (Lesson 1.6)

GET READY for the Next Lesson

PREREQUISITE SKILL Finding the Percentage (Skill 30)

Find the percent. Round answers to the nearest cent.

18. 12.6% of $855 **19.** 35.85% of $5,000 **20.** 28.5% of $675

21. 0.8% of $90 **22.** 55.2% of $23,630 **23.** 45.75% of $598

LESSON 12.6

Mutual Funds

Lesson Objective

Compute the loading charge, number of shares purchased, and profit or loss when you sell a mutual fund.

Content Vocabulary

- mutual fund
- net asset value (NAV)
- loading charge

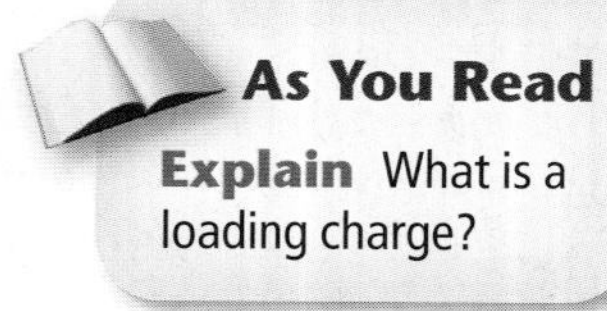

As You Read

Explain What is a loading charge?

GET READY for the Lesson

Who helps people manage their investments?

Teresa Fuentes is a fund manager. She manages money for a group of people and makes investment decisions for everyone in the group. She is skilled at taking reasonable risks and avoiding unreasonable ones.

Mutual Funds Many investors put their money in a **mutual fund**. A mutual fund is offered by an investment company, which **accumulates** the savings of many individuals and invests them in a portfolio of stocks, bonds, or both. The worth of a share of a mutual fund, called the **net asset value** (NAV), is calculated daily by most investment companies. The net asset value per share is determined by dividing the total market value by the number of shares outstanding.

When you buy mutual funds, you might pay a **loading charge** of 0% to 6% of the amount invested. Type "A" mutual funds are front-loaded and make the charge when you buy the fund. Type "B" mutual funds are back-loaded and make the charge when you sell. The percent you are charged is called the loading rate. Most investment professionals today refer to the loading charge as a *load,* and the funds are referred to as a *load* fund, a *no-load* fund, or a *low-load* fund. The mutual fund classification varies, based on what type of loading charge was paid as commission to the investment firm, if any.

The following formulas are used:

Loading Charge = Loading Rate × Amount Invested or Amount of Sale

$$\text{Number of Shares Purchased} = \frac{\text{Amount Invested} - \text{Loading Charge}}{\text{Net Asset Value per Share}}$$

Net Selling Price = (Number of shares × Selling Price per Share) − Loading Charge

Profit(Loss) = Net Selling Price − Investment

EXAMPLE 1

Martin Levy invested $25,000 in the Jennison Dryden Utility Mutual Fund (Type A). The net asset value is $15.58 per share. The fund is front-loaded with a loading rate of 5.50%. What is the loading charge? How many shares did Martin buy?

Step 1: Find the loading charge.

Loading Rate × Amount Invested

5.50% × $25,000 = **$1,375.00 loading charge**

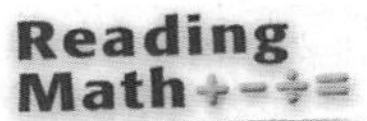

Profit or Loss

The two words in the term "profit (loss)" are opposites. Money you make as a result of an investment is a profit. But your investments can also lose money. Instead of making a "profit," you take a "loss."

Step 2: Find the number of shares purchased.

$$\frac{\text{Amount Invested} - \text{Loading Charge}}{\text{Net Asset Value per Share}}$$

$$\frac{\$25{,}000 - \$1{,}375}{\$15.58} = \textbf{1,516.367 or 1,516.4 shares purchased}$$

Complete the problems. Check your answers in the back of the book.

1. Suki and Taj Majorka invested $12,500 in the Eaton Vance Dividend Builder Fund (Type A). The net asset value is $21.71. The fund is front-loaded with a loading rate of 5.75%. **(a)** What is the loading charge? **(b)** How many shares did they buy?
2. Bayne Grycza invested $30,000 in the Hanson Ryder Mutual Fund (Type A). The net asset value is $16.80 per share. The fund is front-loaded with a loading rate of 3.5%. **(a)** What is the loading charge? **(b)** How many shares did Bayne buy?

EXAMPLE 2

The Washingtons invested $35,200 in the Franklin Templeton "B" Mutual Fund. The net asset value of the fund at the time of purchase was $14.08 and was back-loaded, with a loading rate of 4.25%. When the Washingtons sold their fund shares, the net asset value was $15.75. How many shares did the Washingtons buy? Considering the back-end load, how much profit (loss) did the Washingtons make on their investment?

Step 1: Find the number of shares purchased. ("Back-loaded" means no loading charge at time of purchase)

$$\frac{\text{Amount Invested} - \text{Loading Charge}}{\text{Net Asset Value per Share}}$$

$$\frac{\$35{,}200 - \$0}{\$14.08} = \frac{\$35{,}200}{\$14.08} = \textbf{2,500 shares purchased.}$$

Step 2: Find the back-loading charge.

Loading Rate × Amount of Sale

4.25% × (2,500 × $15.75) = $1,673.44

Step 3: Find the net selling price.

(Number of shares × Selling Price per Share) − Loading Charge

(2,500 × $15.75) − $1,673.44

$39,375.00 − $1,673.44 = $37,701.56 net selling price.

Step 4: Find the profit or loss.

Net Selling Price − Investment

$37,701.56 − 35,200.00 = **$2,501.56 profit**

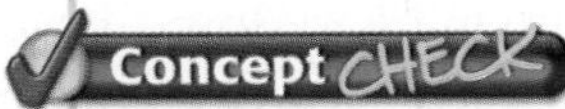

Complete the problem. Check your answer in the back of the book.

3. Diane Kent invested $9,240 in the MFS Utilities "B" Mutual Fund. The net asset value of the fund at the time of purchase was $18.48 and was back-loaded, with a loading rate of 3.0%. When Diane sold her fund shares, the net asset value was $18.25. **(a)** How many shares did Diane buy? **(b)** Considering the back-end load, how much profit (loss) did Diane make on her investment?

Lesson Practice

Complete the table.

	Net Asset Value per Share	Amount Invested	Loading Rate	Loading Charge	Amt. Invested minus Loading Charge	Number of Shares Purchased
4.	$41.00	$ 9,000	———	$ 800	$8,200	a.
5.	$ 5.00	$15,000	8.00%	$1,200	a.	b.
6.	$ 4.95	$75,000	4.00%	a.	b.	c.
7.	$ 3.95	$12,500	3.00%	a.	b.	c.
8.	$ 2.59	$90,000	2.50%	a.	b.	c.
9.	$22.88	$ 7,500	3.80%	a.	b.	c.

Did You Know?

Mutual Funds **Although mutual funds have been available since the 1920s, their popularity is relatively recent. In a recent period, total assets held in mutual funds grew from $1.065 trillion to $6.965 trillion. In a span of 20 years, the number of U.S. households holding mutual funds grew from 10% to 49%.**

10. American Mid-Cap Mutual Fund has a net asset value of $20.00 and is front-loaded at 4%. Tomas Diaz invested $3,400. **(a)** What is the loading charge? **(b)** How many shares did Tomas purchase?

11. Third Avenue Value Fund has a net asset value of $3.95. Bonnie Prince invested $8,250. If the loading rate is 5% front-loaded, how many shares did Bonnie purchase?

12. Artisan Large-Cap Mutual Fund has a net asset value of $20.00. Mike Morgan invests $14,000. The loading rate is 5.5% back-loaded. Mike sold at $21.85 NAV. How much profit (loss) did Mike make?

13. Beta Health Care Mutual Fund has a net asset value of $5.00. Helen Pappas invests $20,000. Helen sold at $5.50 NAV with a loading rate of 4.75% back-loaded. How much profit (loss) did Helen make?

14. Norm Hunter invested $5,000.00 in the Alpha Telecom Mutual Fund. The net asset value is $7.72. The loading rate is 2.6% front-loaded. **(a)** What is the loading charge? **(b)** How many shares did Norm purchase?

15. CHALLENGE PROBLEM Allison Vick started a six month savings program in which she purchased 100 shares of the Alpha-Omega "B" Large Cap Mutual Fund with a NAV of $37.50. Two months later she purchased another 100 shares, this time with a NAV of $38.00. Two months after that she purchased another 100 shares with a NAV of $39.50. The fund was back-loaded, with a loading rate of 4.8%. If Allison sold all 300 shares at a NAV of $40.00, how much profit or loss did she make?

Spiral Review

Find the percentage. (Skill 30)

16. 6.5% of $700 **17.** 93.25% of $15,000 **18.** 0.5% of $40

19. ALGEBRA During a "Doorbuster Sale," which runs from 6 AM to 11 AM on Friday, women's designer jeans are marked down 45%. What is the regular selling price of a pair of jeans that is marked down $29.99? (Lesson 6.6)

GET READY for the Next Lesson

PREREQUISITE SKILL **Finding the Percentage** (Skill 30)

20. $5\frac{1}{2}$% of $400 **21.** 115% of 432 **22.** $12\frac{1}{4}$% of 325

23. 108% of 850 **24.** $98\frac{1}{2}$% of 98 **25.** 105% of $501

LESSON 12.7

Bonds

Lesson Objective

Compute the annual interest and annual yield of a bond investment.

Content Vocabulary

- bonds

GET READY for the Lesson

Can you invest in companies that do not sell stock?

For Janet Woodson's tenth birthday, her grandfather gave her a $10,000 corporate bond with a 15-year maturity date. Janet is 25 now and plans to redeem the bond to help raise money for the down payment on her first home.

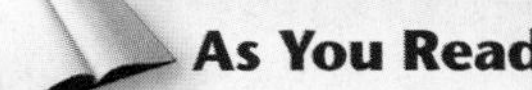

As You Read

Explain What happens when a bond "matures"?

Purchasing Bonds Many corporations and governments raise money by issuing **bonds**. A bond is a written pledge that you will be repaid your specified amount of money plus interest. Unlike stocks, when you invest in a bond, you do not become a part owner of the corporation. Instead, when you buy bonds you are lending money to the corporation or government. In return for the loan, the corporation or government pays you interest.

Eventually a bond "**matures**." This means that you get your money back after a certain amount of time passes. Maturity dates range from 10 to 30 years, and interest is paid every 6 months. Two things influence the value of your bond: (1) how long you keep the bond (despite its maturity date) and (2) when the corporation or government pays interest.

When you redeem your bond, you will receive the face value, which is the amount printed on the bond. The cost of a bond is usually a percent of the value of the bond. A bond price of 90 on a $1,000 bond means that the bond sells for 90% of $1,000, or $900. The interest that you receive from a bond is calculated on its face value. Just as you did for stocks, you can calculate the annual yield for a bond. The following formulas are used:

$$\text{Bond Cost} = \text{Face Value} \times \text{Percent}$$

$$\text{Annual Interest} = \text{Face Value} \times \text{Interest Rate}$$

$$\text{Annual Yield} = \frac{\text{Annual Interest}}{\text{Bond Cost}}$$

EXAMPLE

George Vanderhill purchases a Ford Fund—$1,000 bond at the quoted price of 89.5. The bond pays interest at a rate of 6%. Find **(a)** the interest, **(b)** the cost of the bond, and **(c)** the annual yield.

Step 1: Find the annual interest.

Face Value × Interest Rate

$1,000 × 6% = **$60.00 interest**

Continued on next page

Somos Images/Corbis

Step 2: Find the bond cost.

Face Value ×	Percent	
$1,000 ×	89.5%	= **$895.00 bond cost**

Step 3: Find the annual yield.

$\frac{\text{Annual Interest}}{\text{Bond Cost}} = \frac{\$60}{\$895} =$ **0.067039 or 6.70% annual yield**

Complete the problems. Check your answers in the back of the book.

For the following bonds, find **(a)** the interest, **(b)** the cost of the bond, **(c)** the annual yield.

1. A $1,000 GE Global bond at 80.5 that pays 6% interest.
2. A $10,000 Dallas Municipal bond at 102.5 that pays 5% interest.

GRAPHING CALCULATOR LAB

Compute the Market Value of a Bond

Suppose you obtained a 10-year $10,000 bond. The bond pays 5% per year. On the maturity date, the lender will be paid the maturity value of $10,000. The total amount that the lender receives is the original $10,000 plus $5,000 (10,000 × 0.05 × 10). The market value of a bond is the present value (discounted amount) of the expected payments. To determine the market value of the bond use the TMV solver, twice.

Step 1: From the home screen press

APPS 1 1

Enter: N = 10 (once a year for 10 years)
I% = 5%
PV = Present Value
PMT = 0
FV = −10,000
P/Y = 1 and C/Y = 1

To determine the present value of the bond place your cursor on PMT and press

ALPHA ENTER

The present value of the bond is $6,139.13

Step 2: For the present value of the 10 payments of $500 each, use the TVM solver and input 0 for the FV, and −500 for the PMT.

Calculate the PV (present value) by placing the cursor on PV and press

ALPHA ENTER .

The sum of $4,053.91 and $6,139.13 = $10,000.00

Think and Discuss

1. Describe the display of the first calculator screen.
2. What is the present value of the bond?
3. If the interest rate is changed to 6%, what is the market value of the bond?
4. Suppose you obtain a 10-year $1,000 bond. The bond pays 4% per year. What is the market value of the bond?
5. If the interest rate goes up, what happens to the value of the bond? If the interest rate goes down, what happens to the value of the bond?

Lesson Practice

For Problems 3–6, find (a) the cost of the bond, (b) the interest, and (c) the annual yield.

	Source	Face Value of Bond	Quoted Price	Cost of Bond	Interest Rate	Annual Interest	Annual Yield
3.	GC Inc	$10,000	70.25	a.	3.00%	b.	c.
4.	JFF LLC	$ 1,000	96.00	a.	2.50%	b.	c.
5.	GIT	$10,000	104.00	a.	5.25%	b.	c.
6.	ECE CO.	$ 5,000	104.375	a.	4.75%	b.	c.

For Problems 7–11, determine (a) the cost of the bond, (b) the annual interest, and (c) the annual yield.

7. Celinda Vasquez purchases a McDonald $10,000 bond at 99.2 that pays 4.5% interest.

8. Giuseppe Caviness purchases an Internet, Inc. $100,000 bond at 102.25 that pays 3.5% interest.

9. Sandy and Morry Doran purchase a NYC Municipal $50,000 bond at a quoted price of 94.375. The bond pays annual interest at a rate of 3%.

10. Barry Severes purchased a $25,000 Baltic Ridge School District bond at a quoted price of 105.7. The bond pays annual interest at a rate of 3.7%.

11. Lloyd Zion purchased an ITT $80,000 corporate bond at a quoted price of 96.622. The bond pays annual interest at a rate of 3.65%.

12. CHALLENGE PROBLEM The Sonoma Housing Authority is offering $5,000 bonds that pay 5.2% annual interest. The quoted price of each bond is 92.125. Rollin Kowalski purchases 8 bonds through a broker who charges a 1.75% sales commission. Determine the **(a)** total cost, **(b)** total interest, and **(c)** annual yield of his purchase.

13. CHALLENGE PROBLEM Alex Wosick purchases six $5,000 bonds of ITB Corporation at the closing price for the day of 110.25. The bonds pay 4.2% interest. He had to pay a broker's commission of 2.25%. **(a)** What was the total cost of his purchase? **(b)** What will be his total yearly earnings?

Spiral Review

Divide. Round answers to the nearest hundredth. (Skill 11)

14. 2.22 ÷ 56.80 **15.** 19.4 ÷ 608 **16.** 0.004 ÷ 96.28

17. Ana Andrews bought a game system for $259.95 and a set of extra controllers for $98.99. What is the total sales tax if Ana lives in Austin, Texas, where the state tax is 6.25% and the combined local city and county tax is 2.00%? (Lesson 6.1)

GET READY for the Next Lesson

PREREQUISITE SKILL Dividing Decimals (Skill 11)

Round answers to the nearest hundredth.

18. 23.44 ÷ 2.68 **19.** 11.385 ÷ 0.72 **20.** 58.50 ÷ 14.332

21. 102.53 ÷ 11.111 **22.** 259.6 ÷ 86.78 **23.** 93.603 ÷ 4.55

LESSON 12.8

Real Estate

Lesson Objective

Compute the annual net income, the annual yield, and monthly rent to charge on an investment in real estate rental property.

Content Vocabulary

- rental property
- rent

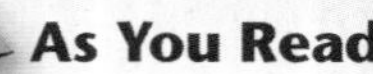

As You Read

Explain How do you find the annual net income on a rental property?

GET READY for the Lesson

What costs are involved in rental property?

When Robert Davies has problems with his apartment, such as a clogged sink or shower, he calls his property manager. The manager arranges and pays for the repairs, because apartment maintenance is included in the cost of rent that Robert pays.

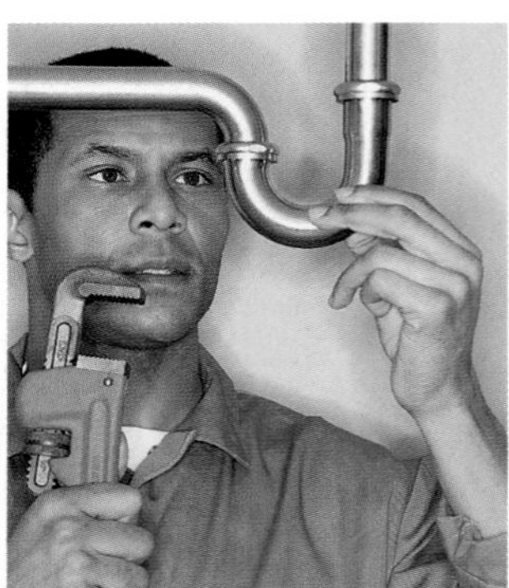

Real Estate Savings accounts, stocks, bonds, and mutual funds are some of the investment opportunities available at financial institutions. Real estate **rental property** is another **alternative**.

The **rent** received from the rental property is comparable to interest and dividends from other investments. Rent is not all profit. You have to consider the annual expenses, which include such things as mortgage interest, taxes, repairs, insurance, and depreciation. These annual expenses are subtracted from the annual rental income to arrive at the annual net income.

Annual Net Income = Annual Rental Income − Annual Expenses

A measure of the quality of an investment is the annual yield. The annual yield is the annual net income expressed as a percent of the cash investment.

$$\text{Annual Yield} = \frac{\text{Annual Net Income}}{\text{Cash Investment}}$$

EXAMPLE 1

Nadine Hobart purchased an older, two-bedroom, one-bath home for \$87,500. She made a \$27,500 down payment and mortgaged the rest. Her annual expenses for mortgage interest, taxes, repairs, insurance, and depreciation totaled \$6,490. Nadine rented the house for \$795 a month. What is the annual net income? What is the annual yield?

Step 1: Find the Annual Net Income.

Annual Rental Income − Annual expenses

= (12 × \$795) − \$6,490 = \$9,540 − \$6,490 = **\$3,050 annual net income**

Step 2: Find the annual yield.

$$\frac{\text{Annual Net Income}}{\text{Cash Investment}} = \frac{\$3,050}{\$27,500} = \mathbf{0.110909 \text{ or } 11.09\% \text{ annual yield}}$$

Tetra Images/SuperStock

Complete the problems and then check your answers in the back of the book. Determine (a) the annual net income and (b) the annual yield.

1. Bev Ray bought a vacation condominium as a real estate rental property for $345,900. After a $100,000 down payment, she mortgaged the rest. Her annual expenses totaled $28,760 and she rented the condo for $3,975 per month.
2. Daryl Mattingly bought a vacation cottage as a real estate rental property for $185,900. After a $40,000 down payment, he mortgaged the rest. His annual expenses totaled $19,850 and he rented the condo for $3,875 per month for 6 months.

Rental Properties Rental properties are purchased for the income the property can produce. To determine what monthly rent to charge, divide the annual rental income by 12. The annual rental income is the desired annual net income plus the annual expenses. The desired annual net income is the desired annual yield multiplied by the cash investment. Market conditions—for example, the typical rent charged in the area for similar rental properties—should be taken into consideration when determining desired annual net income. Formulas:

Desired Annual Net Income = Desired Annual Yield × Cash Investment

$$\text{Monthly Rent} = \frac{\text{Desired Annual Net Income} + \text{Annual Expenses}}{12}$$

EXAMPLE 2

If Nadine in **Example 1** desired a 15% annual yield, rather than the 11.09% she is now getting, what monthly rent would she have to charge?

Step 1: Find the desired annual net income.

Desired Annual Yield × Cash Investment

15% × $27,500 = $4,125

Step 2: Find the monthly rent.

$$\frac{\text{Desired Annual Net Income} + \text{Annual Expenses}}{12}$$

$$\frac{\$4,125 + \$6,490}{12} = \frac{\$10,615}{12} = \mathbf{\$884.58}$$

Nadine would have to charge monthly rent of $884.58 to earn an annual yield of 15%.

Concept CHECK

Complete the problems. Check your answers in the back of the book.

3. If Bev Ray in Problem 1 wanted an annual yield of 25%, what monthly rent would she have to charge?
4. If Bev Ray in Problem 1 wanted an annual yield of 20%, what monthly rent would she have to charge?

Lesson Practice

Complete the table.

	Purchase Price	Cash Invested	Monthly Rent	Annual Expenses	Annual Rental Income	Annual Net Income	Annual Yield
5.	$ 89,700	$ 10,000	$ 450	$ 4,500	$5,400	$900	a.
6.	$ 235,700	$ 40,000	$ 4,000	$ 43,800	a.	b.	c.
7.	$ 515,250	$ 75,000	$ 6,000	$ 67,500	a.	b.	c.
8.	$1,750,000	$350,000	$15,000	$145,000	a.	b.	c.

Did You Know?

Down Payments

Opinions vary about what percent home buyers should put down. Percents range from less than 5% (which may be financially risky) to over 50% (a difficult amount to raise for most households). Financial advisors recommend putting down between 15% and 20%.

For Problems 9 and 10 determine (a) the annual net income and (b) the annual yield, rounded to the nearest hundredth.

9. Mark Shapiro bought a three-bedroom, two-bath house as a rental property. He paid $219,600 with a $50,000 down payment. The annual expenses totaled $26,475. Mark rented the house for $2,500 per month.

10. Chun and Mali Tung bought a house for $135,980. They made a $30,000 down payment. Their annual expenses were mortgage interest of $7,540, depreciation of 2.5% of the purchase price of the house, and taxes, repairs, and insurance of $10,380. They rented the house for $1,850 per month.

11. Sam Clark purchased a four-unit apartment for $845,300. He made a down payment of $95,000 and rented each of the four units for $2,750 per month. His annual expenses were mortgage interest of $46,200, depreciation of 3% of the purchase price, and taxes, repairs, insurance, and miscellaneous totaling $52,425. **(a)** What is the annual net income? **(b)** What is the annual yield? **(c)** What monthly rent should he charge if he desires an annual yield of 10.00%?

12. Clara Teague buys a house for rental purposes for $115,800 with a $25,000 down payment. Her annual expenses total $12,430. What monthly rent should she charge if she desires an annual yield of 8.00%?

13. CHALLENGE PROBLEM Jim Smith invests $2,500,000 in a prime seaside 3-unit strip mall. He has a $500,000 down payment. Kate's Kites and Sandy's Seashells each occupy a 1,200 square foot unit. Seaside Realty occupies the 2,000 square foot unit. The units rent for $8.33 per square foot per month. The annual mortgage interest is $175,000, depreciation is 3.5% of the purchase price, and taxes, insurance, repairs, and upkeep total $125,000. Determine the annual **(a)** net income and **(b)** yield.

Spiral Review

Divide. Round to the nearest hundredth. (Skill 11)

14. 8.5 ÷ 1.25 **15.** 0.3888 ÷ 0.1666 **16.** 4.666 ÷ 1.888

17. ALGEBRA You are guaranteed a minimum salary of $850 per month plus commission of 6.25% of your total sales. What are your total sales for a month in which your gross pay is $1,875? (Lesson 1.6)

GET READY for the Next Lesson

PREREQUISITE SKILL Writing Fractions/Mixed Numbers as Percents (Skill 27)

Write each fraction as a percent. Round to the nearest tenth.

18. $\frac{1}{3}$ **19.** $\frac{4}{5}$ **20.** $\frac{1}{4}$ **21.** $\frac{1}{5}$ **22.** $\frac{3}{8}$ **23.** $\frac{1}{8}$

LESSON 12.9

Retirement Investments

Lesson Objective

Compute the required minimum distribution (RMD) and the penalty for early withdrawal from an individual retirement account (IRA).

Content Vocabulary

- individual retirement account (IRA)
- Roth IRA
- required minimum distribution (RMD)

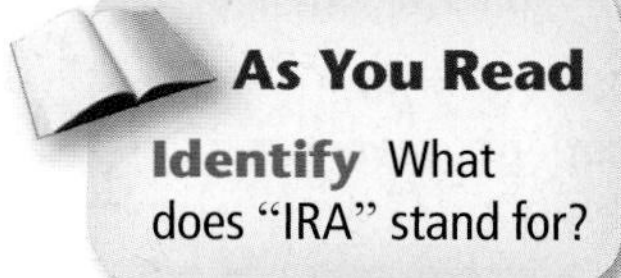

As You Read

Identify What does "IRA" stand for?

GET READY for the Lesson

What are the different retirement investment options?

Each year, Jen Woodson invests part of her savings into a Roth IRA. The interest on her Roth IRA is tax free, and by the time she is ready to retire, she should have enough money saved for a comfortable lifestyle.

Retirement Investments The most common types of retirement investment plans are traditional **individual retirement accounts (IRAs)**, which mature with interest tax deferred, and **Roth IRAs**, which mature with interest tax free.

You must pay a 10% penalty if you withdraw funds from an IRA before $59\frac{1}{2}$ years of age. However, you incur no penalty if the money is used to pay college expenses for you, a spouse, children, or grandchildren or if it is used for a first-time home purchase. Unless funds are withdrawn from your traditional IRA at age $70\frac{1}{2}$, you will pay a penalty equal to 50% of the amount you should have withdrawn. These funds are called your **required minimum distribution (RMD)**. The amount you must begin withdrawing is based on your life expectancy shown in **Figure 12.3** and the fair market value of your IRA. Your life expectancy is considered the **distribution** period for your IRA. There are no required minimum distributions from a Roth IRA.

Figure 12.3

Uniform Life Table			
Age	Life Expectancy Factor	Age	Life Expectancy Factor
70	27.4	76	22.0
71	26.5	77	21.2
72	25.6	78	20.3
73	24.7	79	19.5
74	23.8	80	18.7
75	22.9		

The required minimum distribution is determined using the following formula:

$$\text{Required Minimum Distribution} = \frac{\text{Fair Market Value}}{\text{Life Expectancy Factor}}$$

The penalty for early withdrawal is computed using this formula:

$$\text{Penalty for Early Withdrawal} = 10\% \times \text{Amount of Distribution}$$

The penalty for failure to take a distribution on time is computed using this formula:

$$\text{Penalty for Failure to Take Distribution} = 50\% \times \text{Required Minimum Distribution}$$

EXAMPLE

Bob Bains had saved $2,000.00 per year in his IRA for 35 years. At age 70, the fair market value of his IRA was $256,202.89. Using the uniform lifetime table on page 465, what is his required minimum distribution? What penalty would he pay if he did not take the distribution? If Bob had withdrawn $25,000.00 at age 50 for vacation purposes, what would have been his penalty? What if he had used the $25,000.00 for his children's college expenses?

Step 1: Find the required minimum distribution.

$$\frac{\text{Fair Market Value}}{\text{Life Expectancy Factor}} = \frac{\$256{,}202.89}{27.4} = \$9{,}350.470437$$

Bob's required minimum distribution is $9,350.47

Step 2: Find the penalty for failure to take a distribution.

50% × Required Minimum Distribution

50% × $9,350.47 = **$4,675.24 penalty**

Step 3: Find the penalty for early withdrawal.

10% × Amount of Distribution

10% × $25,000 = **$2,500**

Step 4: Determine the penalty for making an early withdrawal for his children's college expenses.

No penalty for making an early withdrawal for his children's college expenses.

Study Tip

Real Life

Convert the problem into mathematics and use your computation skills to solve it. Then convert your answer back into words that relate to the real-life situation.

Concept CHECK

Complete the problems. Check your answers in the back of the book.

1. May Kawasaki is 72 and has an IRA with a fair market value of $98,000. Use the uniform lifetime table to determine her required minimum distribution. What penalty would she incur if she failed to take the distribution? What penalty would she have paid if she had made an early withdrawal of $10,000 to take a vacation?
2. Amir Bahoud is 70 and has a Roth IRA with a fair market value of $156,800. Use the uniform lifetime table to determine his required minimum distribution. What penalty would he pay if he failed to take the distribution? What penalty would he have incurred if he had made an early withdrawal of $20,000 to pay for his grandchildren's college education?

Lesson Practice

Complete the table.

	IRA Fair Market Value	Amount Withdrawn at Age 55	Penalty for Early Withdrawal	Age	Required Minimum Distribution	Penalty If Not Withdrawn
3.	$260,000	$50,000	$5,000	73	a.	b.
4.	$546,000	$35,000	$3,500	72	a.	b.
5.	$186,400	$10,000	a.	74	b.	c.
6.	$418,680	$35,000	a.	80	b.	c.
7.	$328,840	–0–	a.	77	b.	c.
8.	$284,348	$23,780	a.	71	b.	c.

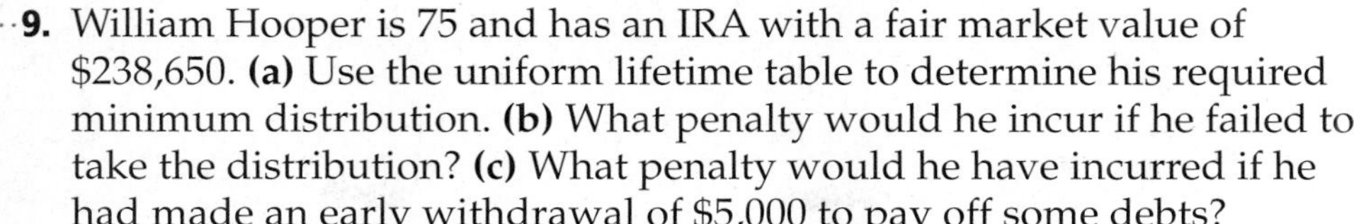

9. William Hooper is 75 and has an IRA with a fair market value of \$238,650. **(a)** Use the uniform lifetime table to determine his required minimum distribution. **(b)** What penalty would he incur if he failed to take the distribution? **(c)** What penalty would he have incurred if he had made an early withdrawal of \$5,000 to pay off some debts?

10. Yvonne Rowley is 75 and has an IRA with a fair market value of \$389,840. **(a)** Use the uniform lifetime table to determine her required minimum distribution. **(b)** What penalty would she incur if she failed to take the distribution? **(c)** What penalty would she have incurred if she had taken an early distribution of \$10,000 to pay off some debts?

11. Nora Beck is 80 and has an IRA with a fair market value of \$350,000. **(a)** Use the uniform lifetime table to determine her required minimum distribution. **(b)** What penalty would she incur if she failed to take the distribution? **(c)** What penalty would she incur if she had made an early withdrawal of \$20,000 to pay for her grandchild's college education?

Did You Know?

China's Retirees The proportion of people aged 60 and over is growing faster in China, the world's most populous nation, than any other country. The United Nations estimates that by 2050, 430 million Chinese, about a third of the total population, will be retirees.

12. Alice McAdams started contributing \$3,000 per year to her IRA at age 25. She earns 6.4% annual interest compounded annually. Her fair market value is now \$717,514.19. **(a)** Using the uniform lifetime table, what is her required minimum distribution now that she is 70 years of age? **(b)** What penalty would she incur if she failed to take the distribution?

H.O.T. Problems

13. CHALLENGE PROBLEM Charles Volt contributes \$5,000 per year to his Roth IRA. He earns 5.8% annual interest compounded annually. He started doing this at age 30 and he is now 80. The fair market value of his Roth IRA is now \$1,358,651.87. **(a)** What is his required minimum distribution? **(b)** What penalty would he incur if he failed to take the distribution? **(c)** What penalty would he have owed if he had withdrawn \$50,000 at age 57 to pay for his grandchildren's college education?

Spiral Review

Write each fraction as a percent. Round to the nearest tenth. (Skill 27)

14. $\frac{13}{30}$ **15.** $\frac{7}{8}$ **16.** $5\frac{3}{8}$

17. On April 10, Brenda Agoyo deposited \$2,125.36 in a savings account that pays 5.5% interest compounded daily. How much interest will the money earn in 31 days? Hint: see **Figure 5.6** on page 232. (Lesson 5.7)

18. ALGEBRA Celia and John Ramirez own 300 shares of a bank stock. After the quarterly dividends are reinvested, they own 305 shares. The stock is selling at \$55.00 a share. Find the annual dividend per share and the annual yield for the stock. (Lesson 12.5)

GET READY for the Next Lesson

PREREQUISITE SKILL Adding Decimals (Skill 5)

Find the sum.

19. \$653.20 + \$21 + \$32.38

20. \$42.63 + \$589 + \$41.35 + \$715

21. \$122.93 + \$73.55 + \$867.24

22. \$94 + \$3.57 + \$738 + \$30.67

23. \$45.86 + \$451 + \$652.09 + \$385

24. \$17.60 + \$23.65 + \$798 + \$8.87 + \$501

CHAPTER 12 Review and Assessment

AFTER YOU READ

Chapter SUMMARY

Wise investing may require a number of different calculations. You can use tables or a formula to compute interest and the annual percentage yield on certificates of deposit. You can calculate the various costs as well as profit or loss associated with buying and selling stocks, bonds, and mutual funds. You can calculate the annual net income, the annual yield, and what monthly rent to charge on an investment in real estate rental property. Lastly, you can compute the required minimum distribution (RMD) and the penalty for early withdrawal from an individual retirement account (IRA).

Vocabulary Check

1. On a sheet of paper, use each of these terms in a sentence.

Content Vocabulary

- certificate of deposit (CD) (p. 441)
- annual percentage yield (APY) (p. 444)
- stocks (p. 447)
- stock certificate (p. 447)
- profit (p. 450)
- loss (p. 450)
- dividend (p. 453)
- mutual fund (p. 456)
- net asset value (NAV) (p. 456)
- loading charge (p. 456)
- bonds (p. 459)
- rental property (p. 462)
- rent (p. 462)
- individual retirement account (IRA) (p. 465)
- Roth IRA (p. 465)
- required minimum distribution (RMD) (p. 465)

Academic Vocabulary

- invest (p. 441)
- compounding (p. 444)
- quoted (p. 447)
- initial (p. 450)
- proceeds (p. 453)
- accumulate (p. 456)
- mature (p. 459)
- alternative (p. 462)
- distribution (p. 465)

Concept Check

2. Name one advantage of investing money in a certificate of deposit.

3. What is annual percentage yield?

4. List two factors that affect the total amount you pay when purchasing stock.

5. List advantages of buying stock from either a stockbroker or an online broker.

6. Differentiate between profit and loss when selling stocks.

7. Give the formula for annual percentage yield.

8. What is a mutual fund?

9. What is a bond?

10. Give the formula for required minimum distribution.

11. CRITICAL THINKING List expenses subtracted from the annual rental income to arrive at the annual net income on a rental property.

Lesson-by-Lesson Review

12.1 Certificates of Deposit (pp. 441–443)

Use tables or a formula to compute interest on certificates of deposit.
Celine Hocking invests $3,500 in a 1-year certificate of deposit that earns interest at an annual rate of 4.5% compounded quarterly. How much interest will she earn at the end of 1 year?

Step 1: Find the amount.

Original Principal × Amount of $1.00
$3,500 × 1.045765 = $3,660.18

Step 2: Find the interest earned.

Amount − Original Principal
$3,660.18 − $3,500.00 = **$160.18 interest earned**

Review Exercises

Use the *Amount of $1.00 Invested—Daily, Monthly, and Quarterly Compounding* table on page A14 to find the amount per $1.00 invested.

	Annual Rate	Interest Period	Original Principal	Amount per $1.00	Amount	Interest Earned
12.	3.00%	1 year; monthly	$ 6,500	a.	b.	c.
13.	3.75%	4 years; daily	$10,000	a.	b.	c.
14.	5.25%	1 year; daily	$ 3,500	a.	b.	c.
15.	4.25%	4 years; monthly	$90,000	a.	b.	c.
16.	4.00%	4 years; quarterly	$35,000	a.	b.	c.

17. **ALGEBRA** Brooke Ruiz invested $15,000 in a 6-month CD paying 5.70% compounded monthly. What is the future value of Brooke's $15,000 in 6 months? How much interest will Brooke earn?

12.2 Annual Percentage Yield (pp. 444–446)

Determine the annual percentage yield.
Andy Eyre invested $3,000 in a CD for 1 year. The certificate earns interest at an annual rate of 5% compounded monthly. What is the annual percentage yield rounded to the nearest thousandth of a percent?

Step 1: Find the amount for 1 year. (Refer to the *Amount of $1.00 Invested—Daily, Monthly, and Quarterly Compounding* table on page A14.)

$3,000 × 1.051162 = $3,153.49

Step 2: Find the compound interest.

Amount − Original Principal
$3,153.49 − $3,000.00 = $153.49 interest for 1 year

Step 3: Find the annual percentage yield.

$$\frac{\text{Interest for 1 Year}}{\text{Principal}}$$

$$\frac{\$153.49}{\$3{,}000.00} = \textbf{0.051163 or 5.116\% annual percentage yield}$$

Lesson-by-Lesson Review (continued)

Review Exercises

Use the *Amount of $1.00 Invested—Daily, Monthly, and Quarterly Compounding* table on page A14 to find the amount per $1.00 invested.

	Annual Rate	Interest Period	Original Principal	Amount per $1.00	Amount	Interest Earned	Annual Percentage Yield
18.	3.50%	1 year; monthly	$ 8,500	a.	b.	c.	d.
19.	5.25%	1 year; quarterly	4,500	a.	b.	c.	d.
20.	2.50%	4 years; daily	15,000	a.	b.	c.	d.
21.	4.75%	4 years; quarterly	25,500	a.	b.	c.	d.
22.	3.25%	1 year; daily	2,300	a.	b.	c.	d.
23.	2.00%	1 year; monthly	10,000	a.	b.	c.	d.

24. Natalia Sanchez can invest $20,000 at either 4.5% compounded daily for 4 years or 5% compounded monthly for 4 years. Based on an annual percentage yield, which is the better investment?

12.3 Buying Stocks (pp. 447–449)

Calculate the total cost of a stock investment.

Derek Abreu purchased 200 shares of stock at $35.11 per share. His full-service stockbroker charged a $50.00 commission for the transaction. What is the total amount he paid for the stock?

Step 1: Find the cost of the stock.

Number of Shares × Cost per Share

200 × $35.11 = $7,022.00

Step 2: Find the total paid.

Cost of Stock + Commission

$7,022.00 + $50.00 = **$7,072.00 total paid**

Review Exercises

	Company	Number of Shares	×	Cost per Share	=	Cost of Stock	+	Commission	=	Total Paid
25.	Forestry Inc.	1,000	×	$59.14	=	a.	+	$ 7.00	=	b.
26.	Safety Lmt.	150	×	$48.79	=	a.	+	$50.00	=	b.
27.	Ross Bank 55	55	×	$53.30	=	a.	+	$12.99	=	b.
28.	Cantwell Co.	2,300	×	$59.09	=	a.	+	$39.50	=	b.
29.	Ott & Assoc.	850	×	$48.77	=	a.	+	$11.50	=	b.
30.	GIS Mapping	2,000	×	$60.01	=	a.	+	$22.00	=	b.

31. Nicholas Renton purchased 2,000 shares of stock at $7.25 per share. The broker's commission was $19.95 for fewer than 1,000 shares, or $0.02 per share for 1,000 or more shares. **(a)** What was the cost of the stock? **(b)** What was the total paid?

Lesson-by-Lesson Review (continued)

12.4 Selling Stocks (pp. 450–452)

Calculate the profit or loss from a stock sale.

Frank Walden paid a total of $3,066.54 for 88 shares of stock. He sold the stock for $57.10 per share and paid a sales commission of $49.50. What is the profit or loss from the sale?

Step 1: Find the net sale: Amount of Sale − Commission

($57.10 × 88) − $49.50 $5,024.80 − $49.50 = $4,975.30

Step 2: Find the profit(loss): Net Sale − Investment

$4,975.30 − $3,066.54 = **$1,908.76 profit**

Review Exercises

	Stock	Total Paid	Selling price per Share	×	Number of Shares	−	Commission	=	Net Sale	Profit or Loss
32.	Tanner Co.	$ 6,787	$26.42	×	150	−	$39.95	=	a.	b.
33.	Maloney Inc.	$ 5,800	$39.01	×	200	−	$45.50	=	a.	b.
34.	Elden Mfg.	$24,000	$42.12	×	600	−	$ 9.99	=	a.	b.
35.	S & R Electric	$ 1,800	$10.52	×	50	−	$12.50	=	a.	b.
36.	PAE Internet	$ 4,800	$58.87	×	100	−	$55.00	=	a.	b.
37.	Aquailla Imp.	$ 3,250	$11.70	×	250	−	$ 7.00	=	a.	b.

38. Carlos and Jade Enrique bought 2,000 shares of stock at $18.80 a share and paid a sales commission of $50.00 plus $0.02 a share. They sold the stock at $21.95 per share plus a sales commission of $45.00 plus $0.03 per share. **(a)** What was the net amount of the sale? **(b)** What was the profit or loss from the sale?

12.5 Stock Dividends (pp. 453–455)

Compute the annual dividend and annual yield of a stock investment.

Patty Slade bought 250 shares of Pine Nursery stock at $32.57 per share. The company paid annual dividends of $1.12 per share. What is the total annual dividend? What is the annual yield to the nearest hundredth of a percent?

Step 1: Find the total annual dividend.

Annual Dividend per Share × Number of Shares

$1.12 × 250 = **$280 total annual dividend**

Step 2: Find the annual yield.

$$\frac{\text{Annual Dividend per Share}}{\text{Cost per Share}} = \frac{\$1.12}{\$32.57} = 0.034387 = \textbf{3.44\% annual yield}$$

Lesson-by-Lesson Review (continued)

Review Exercises

For Problems 39–41, find the annual yield rounded to the nearest hundredth.

	Stock	Annual Dividend per Share	Cost per Share	Annual Yield
39.	Stone Products	$0.60	$38.00	
40.	OFA Education	$1.40	$57.36	
41.	Lazenby, Inc.	$1.36	$34.86	

42. Rose Wallace owns 200 shares of stock. The stock ranged from a low of $44.45 to a high of $54.54 last year. The annual dividend is $2.31 per share. **(a)** What is the total annual dividend? **(b)** What is the annual yield based on the high and the low?

43. **ALGEBRA** Erick and Emilia Sanchez own 200 shares of stock. After the quarterly dividends are reinvested they own 202 shares. The stock is selling at $42.00 a share. Find the **(a)** annual dividend per share and **(b)** annual yield for the stock.

12.6 Mutual Funds (pp. 456–458)

Compute the loading charge, number of shares purchased, and profit or loss when you sell a mutual fund.

Gil Hennesey invested $8,000 in the Adrian Utility Mutual Fund (Type A) which has a net asset value of $19.50. The fund is front-loaded, with a loading rate of 4.50%. What is the loading charge? How many shares did Gil buy?

Step 1: Find the loading charge: Loading Rate × Amount Invested

4.50% × $8,000 = **$360.00 loading charge**

Step 2: Find the number of shares purchased.

$$\frac{\text{Amount Invested} - \text{Loading Charge}}{\text{Net Asset Value Per Share}} = \frac{\$8{,}000 - \$360}{\$19.50} = \frac{\$7{,}640.00}{\$19.50} = \textbf{391.79 or 391.8 shares}$$

Review Exercises

	Net Asset Value per Share	Amount Invested	Loading Rate	Loading Charge	Amt Invested minus Loading Charge	Number of Shares Purchased
44.	$41.00	$ 5,000	—	$800	$4,200	a.
45.	$ 7.67	12,000	6.00%	$720	a.	b.
46.	$ 3.34	65,000	4.00%	a.	b.	c.
47.	$ 2.58	11,500	3.00%	a.	b.	c.

48. A Mid-Cap Fund has a net asset value of $25.00 and is front-loaded at 4%. You invested $4,400. **(a)** What is the loading charge? **(b)** How many shares did you purchase?

49. Samantha Sweigart invested $12,600 in the MFS Utilities "B" Mutual Fund. The net asset value of the fund at the time of purchase was $18.00 and was back-loaded with a loading rate of 3.0%. When she sold her fund shares, the net asset value was $20.25. **(a)** How many shares did Samantha buy? **(b)** Considering the back-end load, how much profit (loss) did Samantha make on her investment?

Lesson-by-Lesson Review (continued)

12.7 Bonds (pp. 459–461)

Compute the annual interest and annual yield of a bond investment.
Graeme Williams purchased a $1,500 bond at the quoted price of 79.75. The bond paid interest at a rate of 5%. What is the annual yield to the nearest hundredth of a percent?

Step 1: Find the annual interest: Face Value × Interest Rate

$1,500 × 5% = $75 annual interest

Step 2: Find the bond cost: Face Value × Percent

$1,500 × 79.75% = $1,196.25 bond cost

Step 3: Find the annual yield: $\frac{\text{Annual Interest}}{\text{Bond Cost}} = \frac{75}{1{,}196.25}$ = **0.06269 = 6.27% annual yield**

Review Exercises

For Problems 50–53 find the bond cost, annual interest, and annual yield.

	Source	Face Value of Bond	Quoted Price	Cost of Bond	Interest Rate	Annual Interest	Annual Yield
50.	Diamond, Co.	$3,000	103.50	a.	4.50%	b.	c.
51.	Gable, Inc.	1,000	82.90	a.	3.25%	b.	c.
52.	Lawns, Inc.	5,000	75.25	a.	2.50%	b.	c.
53.	Bunde Sales	2,000	96.50	a.	5.50%	b.	c.

54. Greg and Lidia Vince purchased one GNMA Mortgage issue bond selling at a premium of 103.27 of its $20,000 face value. The bond pays interest at 7.50%. Find the **(a)** bond cost, **(b)** annual interest, and **(c)** annual yield.

12.8 Real Estate (pp. 462–464)

Compute the annual net income, the annual yield, and monthly rent to charge on an investment in real estate rental property.
Calvin Andre purchased a three-bedroom, one-bath house for $97,500. He made a $37,500 down payment and mortgaged the rest. His annual expenses for mortgage interest, taxes, repairs, insurance, and depreciation totaled $7,490. If Calvin rented the house for $825 a month, what annual net income did he realize? What was Calvin's annual yield?

Step 1: Find the Annual Net Income.

Annual Rental Income − Annual expenses

= (12 × $825) − $7,490 = $9,900 − $7,490 = **$2,410 annual net income**

Step 2: Find the annual yield.

$\frac{\text{Annual Net Income}}{\text{Cash Investment}} = \frac{\$2{,}410}{\$37{,}500}$ = **0.064266 or 6.43% annual yield**

Lesson-by-Lesson Review (continued)

Review Exercises

Complete the table.

	Purchase Price	Cash Invested	Monthly Rent	Annual Expenses	Annual Rental Income	Annual Net Income	Annual Yield
55.	$134,500	$25,000	$1,875	$19,000	$22,500	$3,500	a.
56.	$195,700	$40,000	$4,250	$33,800	a.	b.	c.
57.	$425,250	$75,000	$7,000	$57,500	a.	b.	c.

58. Philippe Isaacs bought a three-bedroom, two-bath house as a rental property. He paid $149,600 with a $75,000 down payment. The annual expenses totaled $8,750. Philippe rented the house for $975 per month. What annual net income did Philippe earn? What was his annual yield?

12.9 Retirement Investments (pp. 465–467)

Compute the required minimum distribution (RMD) and the penalty for early withdrawal from an individual retirement account (IRA).

Sandra Waldo has saved $3,000 per year in her IRA starting at age 35. The fair market value of her IRA at age 70 is $262,992. Use the uniform lifetime table on page 465 to determine her required minimum distribution. What penalty would she pay if she did not take the distribution?

Step 1: Find the required minimum distribution.

$$\frac{\text{Fair Market Value}}{\text{Life Expectancy Factor}} = \frac{262{,}992}{27.4} = 9{,}598.248 = \$9{,}598.25$$

Sandra's required minimum distribution is $9,598.25

Step 2: Find the penalty for failure to take a distribution.

50% × Required minimum distribution

50% × 9,598.25 = **$4,799.13 penalty**

Review Exercises

Determine the penalty for early withdrawal, the required minimum distribution, and the penalty for not withdrawing funds from an IRA.

	IRA Fair Market Value	Amount Withdrawn at Age 55	Penalty for Early Withdrawal	Age	Required Minimum Distribution	Penalty If Not Withdrawn
59.	$106,516	$60,000	$6,000	71	a.	b.
60.	$119,288	$40,000	$4,000	72	a.	b.
61.	$319,712	$20,000	a.	76	b.	c.

62. Oscar Bolden has a traditional IRA with a fair market value of $370,000.00. He is now 75 years of age. Using the uniform lifetime table, what is his required minimum distribution? What penalty would he incur if he failed to take the distribution? What penalty would he incur if he had made an early withdrawal of $20,000.00 to pay for his grandchild's college education?

Practice Test

Record your answers on a sheet of paper.

1. Marcus Nuestro invested $3,450 in a 1-year certificate of deposit, which pays 4.85% compounded daily (365-day year). How much will Marcus have in his account after 1 year?
   A $3,405.65 **B** $3,621.44
   C $5,720.65 **D** $4,350.43

2. Antonio Napoli owned a 1-year $15,000 certificate of deposit that was worth $15,885.60 at maturity. What was the annual percentage yield?
   A 5.904% **B** 0.0590%
   C 5.574% **D** 0.0557

3. Shea Centanni invested $35,600 in a mutual fund that is front-loaded, with a loading rate of 4.75%. What was the loading charge of this fund?
   A $1,861 **B** $4,750
   C $1,420 **D** $1,691

4. Steve Cabrini bought 58 shares of stock that paid annual dividends of $0.23 per share. What was the total annual dividend?
   A $28.48 **B** $14.20
   C $13.34 **D** $26.68

5. Hassan and Clara Metanova paid $1,975 for 50 shares of stock. They sold for $45.60 a share. There was no commission charge. What was their profit?
   A $6.10 **B** $610.00
   C $305.00 **D** $2,280.00

6. Nancy Hansen purchased a house for $102,450. Her annual expenses for mortgage interest, taxes, repairs, and depreciation total $7,105. Nancy rents the house to someone for $975 a month. What is the annual net income of the rental house?
   A $1,985 **B** $3,865
   C $4,595 **D** $11,700

7. Mateo Ernesto is 71 years old. His IRA has a fair market value of $352,850.76. His life expectancy factor is 26.5. What is Mateo's required minimum distribution?
   A $12,877.76 **B** $13,315.12
   C $4,969.30 **D** $1,331.53

8. A stockbroker charges Brent Marsh a $34.50 commission for a stock that sells for $96.57 a share. How much would 75 shares cost Brent?
   A $131.07 **B** $2,587.50
   C $7,242.75 **D** $7,277.25

9. Charo Harrison deposits $6,000 in First Savings' 5-year CD, which pays 5.35% compounded monthly. How much will she have in the account at the end of 5 years?

10. **ALGEBRA** Becky Gullett owns 180 shares of Derby Drone Records (DDR) stock. After the quarterly dividends are reinvested under her dividend reinvestment program, she owns 183.24 shares. DDR is selling for $112.00 per share. Find the annual dividend per share and the annual yield for DDR.

11. Mitur Binderti purchased a $35,000 bond at a quoted price of 88.5. The bond pays annual interest at a rate of 4%. What is the cost of the bond and the annual interest earned?

12. 135% of 786

13. 593.7×0.019

14. $16.4 \div 0.41$

15. $54,787 + $4,791

16. $28.42 \div 2.1$

17. $873.8577 - 541.383$

Standardized Test Practice

Cumulative, Chapters 1–12

PART 1 Multiple Choice

Record your answers on the answer sheet provided by your teacher or on a sheet of paper.

1. Che Mesa's employer pays 80% of his annual health insurance premium. If the annual premium is $5,867, how much does his employer pay?
   A $3,843.60 **B** $5,123.00
   C $4,693.60 **D** $1,173.40

2. Terry Wade's variable costs for his car totaled $1,876.88 last year and his fixed costs totaled $1,685. If he drove 10,846 miles last year, what was his cost per mile? Round to the nearest cent.
   A $0.45 **B** $0.33
   C $0.64 **D** $0.35

3. What is the maturity value of a single-payment loan of $5,650 for 91 days at 13% exact interest?
   A $6,353.44 **B** $5,953.22
   C $5,833.12 **D** $6,103.21

4. Manuel Carmeo paid a total of $4,132.65 for 85 shares of stock. He sold the stock for $49.85 per share with no commission. What was his profit or loss?
   A $228.50 profit **B** $104.60 loss
   C $240.50 loss **D** $104.60 profit

5. If a $1,250 television set is charged on a credit card with a balance of $6,318.97, what is the new balance?
   A $7,568.97 **B** $5,068.97
   C $6,850.97 **D** $6,985.97

TEST-TAKING TIP

Try Easy Questions First Answering easy questions first may jog your memory about useful facts needed for the more difficult questions on the test.

PART 2 Short Response/Griddable

6. Travis Gregg's co-payment for doctor visits is $15. He also pays a $7.50 co-payment for prescriptions. Last month he saw a doctor 4 times and had 5 prescriptions filled. How much did Travis have to pay last month?

7. Brandi Arnett's checking account has a balance of $6,431.67. She is charged a service fee of $0.13 for every check she writes. What is her new balance if she buys an $85.75 pair of shoes, a $13.99 CD, $53.25 of groceries and pays for everything with checks?

PART 3 Extended Response

Show your work.

8. Juan Lapierre's bank granted him a single-payment loan of $8,320 for 91 days at 12% exact interest. What is the maturity value of his loan? What would the maturity value be if it were an ordinary interest loan?

9. Amy Krepp is single and has a health insurance plan with the benefits shown below. Her recent network health care costs include co-payments for 7 physician visits and 5 specialist visits. She had 32 home visits from a nurse at $35 each. She had a stay in the hospital that cost $16,856 with an admission charge of $150. What was the total amount she paid?

Health Care Benefits Schedule

		Network	Non-Network
Annual Deductible	Single	$ 750	$ 950
	Family	$1,450	$2,450
Hospital Charges	(Percent covered by insurance)	90%	70%
Home Health Care	First 50 Visits	Insurance covers 100%	—
Co-payments	Physician Visit	$15	$20
	Specialist Visit	$30	$42

Building Academic Skills

Mathematics

Over the past few years, you have saved $1,000 that you would now like to invest. A friend suggests that you invest in a municipal bond that pays 3.6% interest annually. Municipal-bond income is exempt from federal and state taxes if the municipality is in that state. Another friend recommends a corporate bond that pays 6.3% interest. However, corporate-bond earnings are subject to 15% ordinary capital gains tax and income tax on interest earned. Which bond provides the largest return in the first year, assuming that they have similar risks?

English Language Arts/Writing

Work with a group of students to research investment tips and guidelines for beginning investors. Create a poster display entitled "Top 5 Investment Tips for New Investors." Then share your tips with the class.

Science

How much risk you can tolerate is a mix of how optimistic you are about your future and your current responsibilities. You can find out your tolerance for risk and what that means in terms of investments by answering some questions. Using an Internet search engine, search for "risk tolerance quiz" and take one of the quizzes. Even if some of the questions do not apply to you right now, click on the different choices to see how the answers affect the results. Write a short essay on what you find.

Somos Images/Corbis

Ethics in Action

Covering for the Boss You are employed by a large health care administrator. Your boss Mike has lately been taking two-hour lunches, disappearing for long periods of time, and frequently leaving work early. Sharon, Mike's boss, works in another city and often calls, but Mike has instructed you to say he is "away from his desk." You think Sharon is getting suspicious.

Discuss and Write:

a. Discuss the various reasons why Mike's behavior is unethical. Discuss how you would handle this situation.

b. Write a short memo to Mike expressing your concerns, or work with a partner and role-play talking to Mike about your concerns.

Tech TRENDS

Tracking Stocks on Your PC For people who invest money in stocks, the computer is a powerful tool. Online services allow you to monitor your portfolio automatically, but you can also build and maintain your own "stock watch" system using a basic spreadsheet program. One method is to give one line of the spreadsheet to each stock, while using the columns to track dates.

Activity:

a. Using the Internet, find the stock ticker symbols of five publicly traded companies that interest you.

b. Build a spreadsheet that tracks the five stocks you located. Put each stock name on a different line. Create six columns, one for each of the six previous months. Using the Internet, find each stock's value on the first day of each of those six months and use this information to fill in the spreadsheet.

UNIT 4 Thematic Project

New Investors

In this project you will track the performance of three different stocks over a three-month period.

Your Project Assignment

- ✓ Choose three companies that are located in your community or offer products or services that interest you.
- ✓ Go online to research the performance of each company's stock over the past six months.
- ✓ Determine your potential profit or loss.
- ✓ Use spreadsheet software to keep track of each stock's performance.
- ✓ Create a 3–5 minute presentation.

Greg Hinsdale/Corbis

Skills Preview

Your success in tracking stock performance depends on your skills. Some skills you might use include:

Academic Skills reading, writing, and mathematics

Basic Skills speaking, listening, thinking, problem-solving, and interpersonal skills

Technology Skills word-processing, keyboarding, spreadsheet, presentation, and Internet skills

Project Steps

Step 1 Do Your Research

- Choose three companies that are located in your community or offer products or services that interest you.
- Research the performance of each company's stock over the last three months. Record the stock prices three months ago, two months ago, one month ago, and currently.

Step 2 Explore Your Community

Interview two corporate professionals in your community. Do they keep track of their corporation's stock performance? Do they consider it wise to invest in their own company's stocks or bonds?

Step 3 Determine Your Stock Performance

- If you had invested $500 in each company's stock three months ago, how many shares could you have purchased then?
- With that initial investment, currently what would be your profit or loss for each stock?

Step 4 Develop Your Presentation

Prepare a report of your findings using the following tools, if available:

- Use a word-processing program to write a 1-page report.
  - ✓ Summarize the performance of the three companies' stock prices.
  - ✓ Explain why you chose the companies and if their stock performances surprised you.
  - ✓ Summarize your conversations about investing in one's own employer's stocks.
  - ✓ Share your thoughts on picking stocks yourself as an investment strategy. Why might some investors instead choose to hire a stockbroker?
- With spreadsheet software, create a chart that shows the profit or loss over the past three months had you invested $500 in each company's stock.
- Print your completed report and chart to present to your class.

Academic and Career Portfolio

Add this report to your Academic and Career Portfolio.

Step 5 Evaluate

Go to **connectED.mcgraw-hill.com** to download an evaluation rubric.

UNIT 5

Making Business Decisions

In This Unit

Explore the Photo

Mass Appeal
Whether it is a movie theater or a frozen yogurt franchise, a business only thrives when it reaches new customers. *How are your spending decisions influenced by marketing?*

The Big Picture

Who tallies the votes for Oscar Night?

The accounting firm of PricewaterhouseCoopers counts the ballots and keeps them safe. The table below shows some facts about accounting's role on Oscar Night.

THE BIG PICTURE

PUSHING THE ENVELOPES

1,700	"PERSON-HOURS" IT TAKES PWC TO COUNT AND VERIFY THE BALLOTS BY HAND
420,000	BALLOTS COUNTED BY PWC DURING 73 YEARS ON THE JOB
2,449	WINNERS' ENVELOPES STUFFED BY THE PWC TEAM SINCE 1941

Go to **connectED.mcgraw-hill.com** for the Unit 5 WebQuest activity on the business behind the blockbusters.

Thematic Project Preview

Marketing Healthy Treats

Whether a company sells frozen yogurt or movies, it will not survive and grow without an effective marketing strategy. When a company offers a product that is already well-known—for example, frozen yogurt—it will need to distinguish itself through pricing, promotions, distribution, and style. A health-conscious shopper searching for a snack has many options, and a successful marketing strategy can play a big role in influencing what he or she chooses. After completing this Unit Thematic Project, you will better understand marketing efforts.

Pre-Project Checklist

As you read this unit, use this checklist to prepare for the unit project:

- ✓ Choose a frozen yogurt shop located in your community.
- ✓ Research student opinion on this product and determine its sales potential.
- ✓ Create a marketing presentation for the business owner or CEO.

CHAPTER 13 Personnel

Big Idea

Employing the personnel necessary to operate a business includes many different costs.

Explore the Photo

Employee Benefits Companies must consider many personnel costs. These costs include employee benefits, such as health insurance and vacation days. *What are other employee benefits?*

Ask AN EXPERT

Employee Stock Options

Q: I am considering taking a job that pays slightly less than what I could make elsewhere. However, the company offers its employees stock options. Could these help me earn a higher income?

A: You may end up earning more in the long run, provided stock prices go up. Options are contracts that allow their holders to buy or sell stock at favorable prices. Employers often offer stock options and other incentives to attract quality job applicants. Other incentives may include such benefits as health insurance plans, paid vacations and holidays, sick leave or personal days, flexible schedules, and merit increases.

English Language Arts/Writing Create a list of factors other than salary that would influence your decision on whether or not to take a job.

GET READY for the Chapter

Math Online

To take the Online Readiness Quiz, go to **connectED.mcgraw-hill.com**.

Reading Guide

Before You Read

Identify What expenses are associated with having employees?

Main Idea

When you work for a company, the company is paying more than just your wages or salary. Knowing about employee benefits helps you understand how the company treats its personnel.

Graphic Organizer

Before you read this chapter, draw a diagram like the one below. As you read, keep track of various personnel expenses.

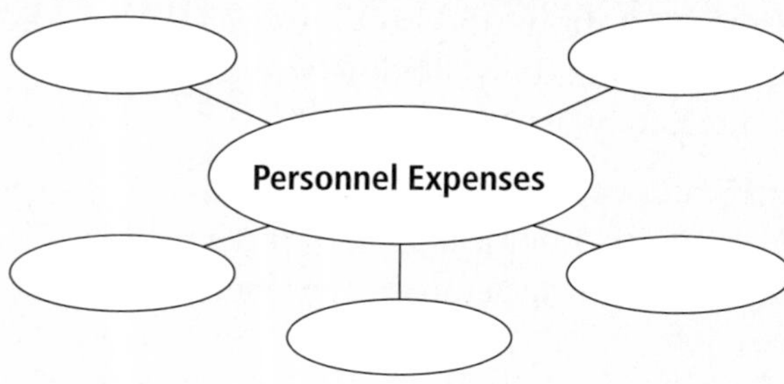

Math Online Go to connectED.mcgraw-hill.com to download this graphic organizer.

Content Vocabulary

You will learn these key terms in this chapter.

- recruiting
- salary scale
- cost-of-living adjustment
- merit increase
- employee benefits
- disability insurance
- workers' compensation insurance
- travel expenses
- release time

Academic Vocabulary

You will see these words in your reading and on your tests.

- sufficient
- estimate
- ratio
- benefits
- exposure
- authorized
- internally

You can find vocabulary definitions in the **Content Vocabulary** Glossary and the **Academic Vocabulary** Glossary in the back of the book.

LESSON 13.1

Hiring New Employees

Lesson Objective
Calculate the cost of recruiting new employees.

Content Vocabulary
- recruiting

GET READY for the Lesson

What are good qualities in a teammate?

When Lila Tucker's science-project team needed one more member, she asked Andrea Kingsley to join. Lila knew Andrea was smart, worked well with her classmates, and had interesting ideas that the team could use.

As You Read
Identify What is recruiting?

Hiring New Employees In order for a business to succeed, it must have a **sufficient** number of personnel to make it run properly. Finding qualified individuals to perform a business's duties is an important function. In order to gain a competitive edge in today's marketplace, a company needs to hire people who will enhance its mission.

To fill openings in your business, you may recruit new employees. **Recruiting** is the act of soliciting qualified people to work for your company. The cost of recruiting includes advertising fees, interviewing expenses (such as travel expenses), and hiring expenses (such as moving expenses). The basic formula is:

$$\text{Total Recruiting Cost} = \text{Advertising Expenses} + \text{Interviewing Expenses} + \text{Hiring Expenses}$$

EXAMPLE 1

Talbot Manufacturing Company is searching for a person to head its production department. The personnel department placed advertisements at a total cost of $6,495 and employed Empire Executive Search Company to locate candidates. Empire recommended Alice Welch, Tomas Valdez, and Cleveland Adams. Talbot paid the candidates' travel expenses (transportation, lodging, and meals) for interviews.

Candidate	Total Travel Expenses
Alice Welch	$ 917
Tomas Valdez	$1,235
Cleveland Adams	$1,135

Continued on next page

Purestock/SuperStock

After the interviews, Talbot hired Cleveland Adams at an annual salary of $154,900. Talbot paid these expenses to hire him:

Moving expenses, $13,600

Real estate broker's fee for sale of home, 6% of $240,000

Empire's finder fee, 25% of Cleveland's first-year salary

What was the total expense of recruiting Cleveland Adams?

Step 1: Find the total Interviewing Expenses

$917 + $1,235 + $1,135 = $3,287

Step 2: Find the total Hiring Expenses

$13,600 + (6% × $240,000) + (25% × $154,900) =

$13,600 + $14,400 + $38,725 = $66,725

Step 3: Find the total Recruiting Cost

Advertising Expenses	+	Interviewing Expenses	+	Hiring Expenses	
$6,495	+	$3,287	+	$66,725	= **$76,507 total cost**

Find the total recruiting cost. Check your answers in the back of the book.

1. Advertising expenses are $1,975. Interviewing expenses are $1,470 and $1,260. Hiring expenses are $475, $8,600, and 6% on the sale of a $190,250 home.
2. Advertising expenses are $2,180. Interviewing expenses are $2,590 and $1,355. Hiring expenses are $575, $7,450, and 6% on a $464,000 home.
3. Advertising expenses are $3,295.50. Interviewing expenses are $1,545.62, $987.31, $365.12, and $2,214.79. Hiring expenses are $1,658.75, $3,254.81, and 4.75% on a $398,880 home.

Need Help? Go to...
Workshop 38: Problem-Solving Strategy: Writing an Equation p. 78

EXAMPLE 2 Algebra

Able Manufacturing Company has a budget of $36,000 for recruiting costs for the position of Chief Engineer. The company has spent $4,500 on advertising expenses and $8,700 on interviewing expenses. Able is willing to pay a 6% commission on selling the selected individual's home. What is the maximum selling price that Able would pay 6% commission on in order to stay at or below $36,000 in total recruiting costs?

Step 1: Let s = the maximum selling price that Able would pay 6% commission on.

Step 2: Write and solve an equation.

	Total Recruiting Cost	=	Advertising Expenses	+	Interviewing Expenses	+	Hiring Expenses
	$36,000	=	$4,500	+	$8,700	+	(6% × s)
Combine like terms →	$36,000	=	$13,200	+	$0.06s$		
Subtract $13,200 from both sides →	$22,800	=	$0.06s$				
Divide both sides by 0.06 →	**$380,000**	=	s				

Able would pay 6% commission on a maximum selling price of $380,000

Complete the problems. Check your answers in the back of the book.

4. Executives at Third Federal Bank are in a national search for a new Director of Human Resources. They have budgeted \$30,000 for the search. They have spent \$8,600 on advertising expenses and \$7,650 on interviewing expenses. They are willing to pay a 5.5% commission on selling the selected individual's home. What is the maximum selling price on which Third Federal would pay 5.5% commission and stay within \$30,000 in total recruiting costs?
5. Atlas Chemical Company wanted to keep their total recruiting cost for the position of Chief Chemist to less than \$100,000. They have spent \$15,500 on advertising expenses and \$32,700 on interviewing expenses. They are willing to pay an 8% commission on selling the selected individual's home. What is the maximum selling price that Atlas would pay 8% commission on and stay under \$100,000 in total recruiting costs?

GRAPHING CALCULATOR LAB

Hiring

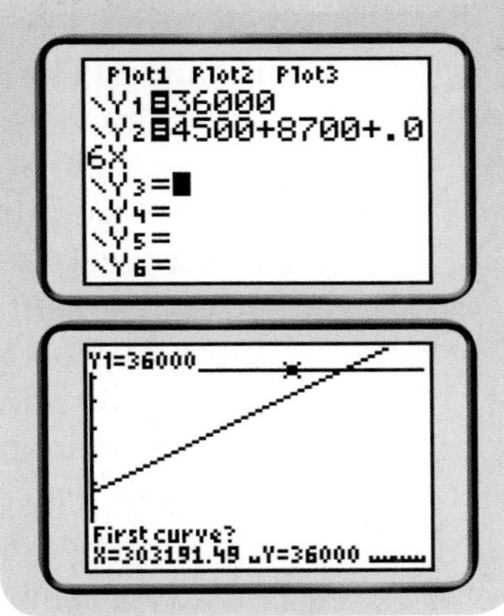

In Example 2, managers at Able Manufacturing Company want to keep their total recruiting cost to less than \$36,000. They have already spent \$4,500 and \$8,700. They are willing to pay a 6% commission on selling the selected individual's home. What can the maximum selling price of the home be to keep under \$36,000 in total recruiting costs?

One way to solve the problem is to write an equation for the problem and then graph each side of the equation to see where the lines intersect. The point of intersection is the maximum selling price. The equation is: $36{,}000 = 4{,}500 + 8{,}700 + 0.06x$

Step 1: Graph. From the home screen press Y=
In Y_1 enter 36000. In Y_2 enter $4500 + 8700 + 0.06x$.

Step 2: Adjust the viewing window. WINDOW
[xmin 0, xmax 500000, xscl 10000; ymin 0, ymax 40000; yscl 5000; xres 1]

Step 3: Intersect is found on the CALCULATE menu.
Follow these keystrokes: 2nd TRACE 5

The graph is displayed with *First curve?* in the bottom-left corner. Press ▲ or ▼, if necessary, to move the cursor to the first function, then press ENTER. *Second curve?* is displayed in the bottom left corner. Press ▲ or ▼, if necessary, to move the cursor to the second function, then press ENTER. Press ENTER again, and the point of intersection is displayed in the bottom-left corner.

Think and Discuss

1. What point is the cursor on in the graph?
2. What is the point of intersection? What is the maximum selling price?
3. If the commission is changed to 8%, what is the maximum selling price?
4. If Able wants to keep total recruiting costs to less than \$30,000 with an 8% commission, what is the maximum selling price?

Teacher
Quality education is important to the future well-being of our country. Dedicated, qualified teachers have the tools to educate young people and help them become successful in life. **Name other careers that involve helping people.**

Lesson Practice

For Problems 6 and 7, determine the total recruiting costs.

6. A tire company recruits a district sales manager. Advertising cost is $917.45; interviewing cost is $694.74; hiring cost is $2,191.47.

7. A manufacturing company recruits a data processing manager. Advertising cost is $1,475.00; interviewing cost is $861.79; hiring cost is $3,791.86.

8. The communications department hired Marilyn Curtis at an annual salary of $154,950. Advertising costs were $2,247.50. Interviewing expenses were: Marilyn Curtis, $1,647.43; Tom Hart, $996.94. The agency fee is 20% of the first year's salary. What was the total cost of hiring Marilyn?

9. A financial services firm interviewed 3 candidates for the position of senior-level investment banker. Expenses were: advertising $12,500, interviewing expenses $3,890, moving expenses $15,000, 6% realtor's fee on the selling price of a $348,000 home, and a 30% finder's fee. The firm decided to hire Jane McNally at a salary of $388,500. What was the total recruiting cost?

10. CHALLENGE PROBLEM Novi Discount Brokers hired Wall Street Search Service to locate candidates for the position of investment bonds manager. The agency's fee is 25% of the first year's salary. Expenses were: advertising $12,816.40, moving expenses of $15,419, real estate broker's fee of 7% on the selling price of a $549,000 home. Novi interviewed three people: Hakeem Golden applied through the agency. His travel costs were $1,948.75. Nancy Cooper answered the advertisement. Her travel costs were $1,516.40. Henry Little applied through the agency. His travel costs were $1,671.80. Henry Little was hired at an annual salary of $254,760 with a $40,000 signing bonus that is not considered a part of his salary. What was the total recruiting cost?

11. ALGEBRA The Consolidated School District budgeted $17,500 for recruiting costs for the new superintendent position. They spent $4,938 on advertising and $3,865 on interviewing expenses. They will pay the real estate broker a 6.5% commission on the sale of the old house. What would the maximum selling price have to be if they wanted to keep the total recruiting costs to $17,500?

Spiral Review

Add. (Skill 3)

12. $1,484 + $815 + $11,650 **13.** $2,241 + $915 + $14,542

14. Ramon Perez worked 37.5 hours at $14.95 per hour and 5 hours of overtime at time and a half. What was his pay for the week? (Lesson 1.2)

GET READY for the Next Lesson

PREREQUISITE SKILL **Finding the Percentage** (Skill 30)

Find the percentage.

15. $18,475 × 4.6% **16.** $23,010 × 6.0% **17.** $6,878 × 13.5%

18. $93,100 × 8.3% **19.** $104,884 × 9.5% **20.** $986,544 × 6.5%

LESSON 13.2

Administering Wages and Salaries

Lesson Objective

Compute the new salary after merit increase and cost-of-living adjustment.

Content Vocabulary

- salary scale
- cost-of-living adjustment
- merit increase

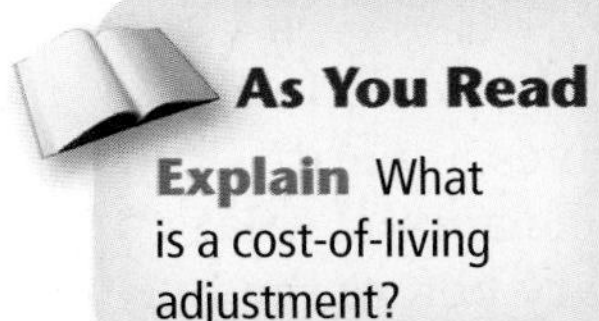

As You Read

Explain What is a cost-of-living adjustment?

GET READY for the Lesson

Have you ever received a raise?

After working one year at Wyco Technology Systems, Dani Navarro met with his manager, Bill Moss, to review his job performance. Mr. Moss praised Dani's work and offered him a 7% pay increase and a reserved parking spot.

Administering Wages and Salaries Many companies have a **salary scale** for most positions. This is a table of wages or salaries used to compare various jobs in a company. The information can be used to compare various jobs or to **estimate** the costs of giving an employee a **cost-of-living adjustment** or a **merit increase**. A cost-of-living adjustment (COLA) is a raise in an employee's salary to help keep up with inflation. A merit increase is a raise in salary to reward an employee for quality work. Compute the new salary using this formula:

New Salary = Present Salary + Cost-of-Living Adjustment + Merit Increase

EXAMPLE 1

Elaine Taylor is a systems analyst (salary level 1 position) for EPD, Inc. The executive board of EPD voted to give all employees a cost-of-living adjustment of 2.8%. In addition, Elaine was awarded a merit increase of 3.5% for excellent work during the year. What will her salary be for the coming year?

Figure 13.1

EPD Inc. Employee Salary Schedule				
Salary Level	Data Entry	Web Designer	Systems Analyst	Project Leader
1	$28,500	$35,000	$40,000	$60,000
2	$30,000	$38,000	$44,000	$65,000
3	$31,500	$41,000	$48,000	$70,000

Step 1: Find the present salary.

The present salary is $40,000.

Step 2: Find the cost-of-living adjustment.

Salary × Cost-of-Living Adjustment Percent

$40,000 × 2.8% = $1,120

Step 3: Find the merit increase.

Salary × Merit Increase Percent

$40,000 × 3.5% = $1,400

Continued on next page

Step 4: Find the new salary.

Present Salary + Cost-of-Living Adjustment + Merit Increase

$40,000 + $1,120 + $1,400 = **$42,520 new salary**

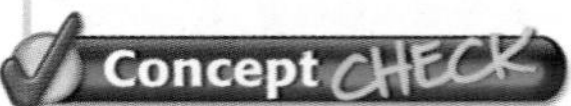

Complete the problems. Check your answers in the back of the book. (Use Figure 13.1 on page 489.)

1. Sam Jordan is a project leader (salary level 1 position) for EPD, Inc. He receives a 2.8% cost-of-living adjustment and a 2% merit increase. Find the new salary.
2. Jeannine Jacoby is a web designer (salary level 3 position) for EPD, Inc. She receives a 3.8% cost-of-living adjustment and a 5.2% merit increase. Find the new salary.

Need Help? Go to...

Workshop 36: Problem-Solving Strategy: Using Simple Algebraic Operations, p. 74

EXAMPLE 2 Algebra

John Baker has a middle-management position with Carbondale Industries, Inc. After his annual performance review, he receives a merit increase of 4.2% and a cost-of-living increase of 2.1%. His annual salary after the increases is $50,492.50. Find John's annual salary before the two increases took effect. Find his merit increase and his cost-of-living increase.

Step 1: Let x = John's annual salary before the two increases took effect

Step 2: Write and solve an equation.

New Salary = Present Salary + Cost-of-Living Adjustment + Merit Increase

$\$50{,}492.50 = x + 2.1\%x + 4.2\%x$

Combine like terms → $\$50{,}492.50 = 1.063x$

Divide both sides by 1.063 → $\$47{,}500 = x$

Step 3: State the solutions.

John's annual salary before the two increases took effect was $47,500

His merit increase is 4.2% × $47,500 = $1,995

His cost-of-living increase is 2.1% × $47,500 = $997.50

Study Tip

Raises

When figuring the effect of two different increases in salary for cost-of-living and merit, use the original salary as the base in both cases. Avoid figuring one increase and adding it to the base before figuring the other increase.

Concept CHECK

Complete the problems. Check your answers in the back of the book.

3. After Enrique Agosto's semi-annual performance review, he received a merit increase of 4.75% and a cost-of-living increase of 3.25%. He is now earning $19.98 per hour with time-and-a-half for all hours over 40 per week. What was his hourly rate before the merit and cost-of-living increases? How much more would he earn now for a 47-hour work week?
4. After Silas Mapes semi-annual performance review, he received a merit increase of 5.75% and a cost-of-living increase of 2.25%. He is now earning $20.52 per hour with time-and-a-half for all hours over 40 per week. What was his hourly rate before the merit and cost-of-living increases? How much more would he earn now in a week in which he worked 44 hours?

Lesson Practice

For Problems 5–9, use Figure 13.1 on page 489 to complete the table.

	Employee	Position	Level	Salary	COLA	Amount	Merit	Amount	New Salary
5.	M. Song	Project Leader	3	**a.**	2.80%	**b.**	3.60%	**c.**	**d.**
6.	B. Apple	Data Entry	3	**a.**	3.20%	**b.**	7.60%	**c.**	**d.**
7.	R. Moore	Systems Analyst	1	**a.**	4.70%	**b.**	4.50%	**c.**	**d.**
8.	R. Tomasi	Web Designer	1	**a.**	4.80%	**b.**	7.40%	**c.**	**d.**
9.	M. Rossi	Data Entry	2	**a.**	3.50%	**b.**	2.50%	**c.**	**d.**

10. John Jacobs earns an annual salary of $150,800. He is paid bi-weekly. **(a)** What is his bi-weekly gross? **(b)** If John receives a 3.8% COLA increase, what will be his new bi-weekly gross?

11. Malik Brooks works 40 hours a week 52 weeks per year for Metro Delivery Company. He earns $9.15 an hour. **(a)** What is his annual gross pay? **(b)** If Malik receives a 4.9% merit increase, what will his new annual gross pay be? **(c)** What will his new hourly rate be?

Did You Know?

UPS Then and Now **A teenager started what is known today as one of the world's biggest delivery services. In 1907, 19-year-old Jim Casey borrowed $100 from a friend to start a Seattle messenger service that eventually became UPS. The corporation's revenues exceed $40 billion each year.**

12. Emily Penn sells for Maumee Electronics. She is paid a base salary of $500 or 7% of all sales, whichever is greater. One week she had sales of $7,280. **(a)** What is Emily's gross pay for that week? **(b)** If she receives a 5% merit increase in her base salary, what would her gross pay be in a week in which she had $7,280 in sales? **(c)** If Emily's rate of commission is increased to 7.5%, but her base remains $500, what would her gross pay be for a week in which she had sales of $7,280?

13. **ALGEBRA** Ruth Maher received a 4.3% merit increase and a 3.25% cost-of-living increase after her quarterly review. Her new weekly salary was $688.32. What was her weekly salary prior to the increases?

Spiral Review

Find the percent. (Skill 30)

14. $17,740 × 4.5% **15.** $21,510 × 8.6% **16.** $15,100 × 3.1%

17. Awan Nakai invests $3,000 in a certificate of deposit for 4 years. The certificate earns interest at an annual rate of 5.25% compounded quarterly. What is the annual percentage yield to the nearest thousandth of a percent? (Lesson 12.2)

GET READY for the Next Lesson

PREREQUISITE SKILL **Finding the Rate** (Skill 31)

Find the rate.

18. Eight thousand two hundred eighty is what percent of 27,600?

19. Six thousand four hundred twenty is what percent of 25,680?

20. Four thousand three hundred is what percent of 21,500?

21. Seven thousand four hundred forty is what percent of 12,400?

22. Two thousand eight hundred twenty is what percent of $3,525?

23. Three thousand six hundred is what percent of $72,000?

LESSON 13.3

Employee Benefits

Lesson Objective
Calculate the rate of employee benefits based on annual gross pay.

Content Vocabulary
- employee benefits

GET READY for the Lesson

What benefits would be important to you as an employee?

Marty Foster just got a public-relations job with the Los Angeles Dodgers baseball team. Marty likes the starting salary and health care benefits, but he especially appreciates the potential for advancement.

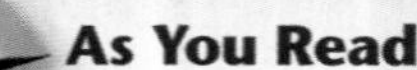

As You Read
Recall Have you ever received employee benefits?

Employee Benefits A business may offer several **employee benefits**. Employers consider employee benefits as part of the cost of employing someone. Benefits vary, but may include the following:

- health insurance
- vision insurance
- dental insurance
- group life insurance
- retirement plans
- Social Security
- Medicare
- stock purchase plans
- paid vacations and holidays
- unemployment insurance
- disability insurance
- sick leave

The **ratio** of the total value of the benefits to the annual gross pay is known as the rate of benefits. The formula is:

$$\text{Rate of Benefits} = \frac{\text{Total Benefits}}{\text{Annual Gross Pay}}$$

Part-Time Employees The benefits offered part-time employees are generally less than the benefits offered full-time employees. Part-time employees normally do not receive benefits such as vacations, holidays, and health insurance. Consequently, the cost of part-time employees is usually less than the cost of full-time employees.

EXAMPLE

The personnel department of Commercial Credit Company is preparing annual reports on employee benefits. Calculate Tamika Rey's rate of benefits.

Tamika Rey   Annual salary: $41,340   Weekly salary: $795

Vacation: 2 weeks @ $795/week	$1,590.00
Holidays: 8 days @ $159/day	1,272.00
Health insurance: 12 months @ $162.50/mo	1,950.00
Sick leave policy: 30 days @ $159/day	4,770.00
Unemployment insurance: 4.6% × $41,340	1,901.64
Social Security (FICA): 6.2% × $41,340	2,563.08
Medicare: 1.45% × $41,340	+ 599.43
Total:	$14,646.15

© D. Hurst / Alamy

Step 1: Determine the weekly and daily salary.

Weekly $= \frac{41{,}340}{52} = \$795$ Daily $= \frac{795}{5} = \$159$

Step 2: Find the total.

See the solutions in the table.

Step 3: Find the rate of benefits.

$$\frac{\text{Total Benefits}}{\text{Annual Gross Pay}} = \frac{14{,}646.15}{41{,}340} = 0.3542 = 35.4\%$$

Rate of benefits = **35.4% of her annual salary**

Concept CHECK

Complete the problem. Check your answers in the back of the book.

1. Complete the table and then calculate the rate of benefits.

Melvin Davis: Annual Salary $21,860	
Find the weekly salary	**a.**
Find the daily salary	**b.**
Vacation: 2 weeks	**c.**
Holidays: 8 days	**d.**
Health insurance: 12 months @ $182.50/mo	**e.**
Sick leave policy: 21 days	**f.**
Unemployment insurance: 4.6% of salary	**g.**
Social Security: 6.2% of salary	**h.**
Medicare: 1.45% of salary	**i.**
Total Benefits	**j.**

Lesson Practice

Study Tip

Needs

When you first read a math word problem, think about *knowns* and *needs*. *Needs* include the answer to the question being asked. In this example, the *need* is the rate of benefits.

Calculate the rate of benefits. Round to the nearest tenth of a percent.

	Total Benefits	÷	Annual Gross Pay	=	Rate of Benefits
2.	$11,870	÷	$ 43,748	=	
3.	15,610	÷	64,600	=	
4.	2,940	÷	14,700	=	
5.	11,392	÷	35,600	=	
6.	39,860	÷	124,650	=	

7. Mary Chambers teaches in Central City Schools. Her annual salary is $43,862. Her benefits include:

State Teachers Retirement System:	$5,921.37
Group life insurance:	$ 647.50
Health insurance:	$ 875.00
Vision and dental insurance:	$ 548.45

(a) What are the total benefits? **(b)** What is the rate of benefits? **(Round to nearest tenth of a percent.)**

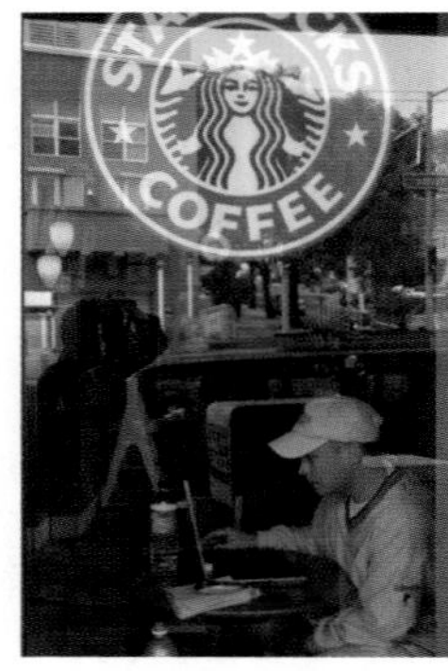

Did You Know?

Largest Coffee Chains
It will probably not surprise you that a recent count of U.S. coffee chain locations found that Starbucks is the largest chain. What may surprise you is the gap between Starbucks and the second-largest U.S. chain, Caribou. Starbucks had approximately 8,000 stores; Caribou had 322.

8. (a) Complete the benefits chart for French Coffee Shoppe's employees. **(Round to the nearest cent.)**

Position	Annual Wage	2-Week Vacation	3.6% Workers Comp.	8-Day Sick Leave	6.2% Social Security	1.45% Medicare	Total Benefits
Manager	$47,580	a.	b.	c.	d.	e.	f.
Counter 1	27,560	a.	b.	c.	d.	e.	f.
Counter 2	22,620	a.	b.	c.	d.	e.	f.
Cleanup	14,560	a.	b.	c.	d.	e.	f.

(b) What is the rate of benefits for each employee? **(Round to the nearest tenth of a percent.)**

9. (a) Complete the benefits chart for Pathology Lab's staff.

Position	Annual Wage	2-Week Vacation	9 Holidays	4.6% Unemp. Ins.	6.2% Social Security	1.45% Medicare	Total Benefits
Lab tech	$51,548	a.	b.	c.	d.	e.	f.
Lab analyst	49,875	a.	b.	c.	d.	e.	f.
Receptionist	20,500	a.	b.	c.	d.	e.	f.

(b) What is the rate of benefits for each employee? **(Round to the nearest tenth of a percent.)**

(c) How much does the lab pay in benefits for the employees?

(d) How much more would it cost the lab to give each employee a 3-week vacation?

(e) How much less would it cost if the lab analyst was a part-time employee and did not receive a 2 week vacation, 9 holidays, nor 4.6% unemployment insurance?

H.O.T. Problems

10. **WRITING IN MATH** Individually or as a class, brainstorm employee benefits. Then make a list of benefits that interest you.

Spiral Review

Find the rate. (Skill 31)

11. Six thousand five hundred is what percent of $32,500?
12. Six thousand seven hundred twenty is what percent of $16,800?
13. A savings account has a previous balance of $1,300; interest, $2.23; deposits of $175.00 and $280.00; withdrawals of $40.00 and $55.00. What is the new balance? (Lesson 5.3)
14. **ALGEBRA** Daisy Sanchez purchased one 40-year Hudson Yards Infrastructure New York Municipal Bond at a discount of 94% of its $10,000 face value. The bonds have an annual yield of 4.62%. Find the bond cost, the annual interest, and the interest rate. (Lesson 12.7)

GET READY for the Next Lesson

PREREQUISITE SKILL Subtracting Whole Numbers (Skill 4)

Solve.

15. 32 + (85 − 22)	**16.** 7 + (44 − 19)	**17.** 91 + (65 − 21)
18. 23 + (58 − 33)	**19.** 19 + (97 − 24)	**20.** 58 + (42 − 18)

LESSON 13.4

Disability Insurance

Lesson Objective

Determine disability benefits under independent retirement systems and under Social Security.

Content Vocabulary

- disability insurance

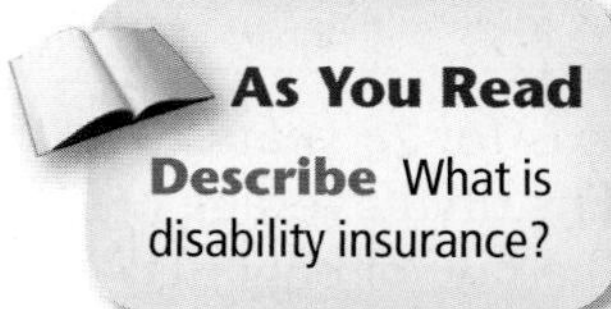

As You Read

Describe What is disability insurance?

GET READY for the Lesson

What happens if you are unable to work because of illness or injury?

Jeanette Brush had an accident and hurt her leg. She will have to stay home from her carpentry job for three weeks. Jeanette is concerned about being able to pay her bills.

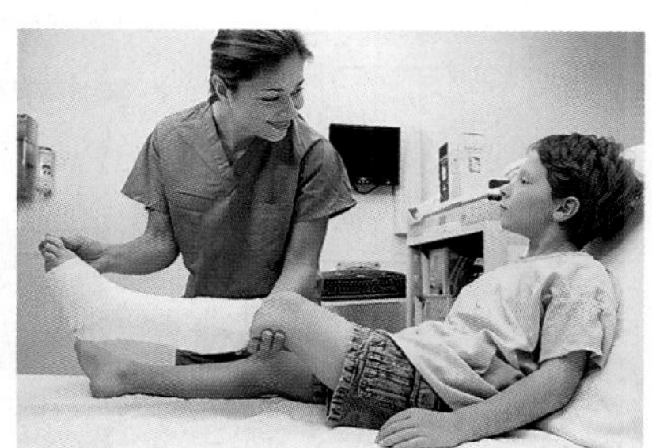

Disability Insurance **Disability insurance** pays **benefits** to individuals who must miss work because of an illness or injury. Short-term disability is covered by an employer's sick leave policy or by a private insurance company. Long-term or permanent disability coverage is provided by Social Security or by an independent retirement system. If you would like an estimate of your disability benefit under Social Security, you can request a statement that displays your earnings record and provides an estimate of your disability benefit.

Most independent retirement systems compute disability benefits based on a percent of the final average salary. The monthly benefit is determined by dividing the annual benefit by 12. The computation of the annual disability benefit uses this formula:

$$\text{Annual Disability Benefit} = \left(\text{Years Worked} + \text{Expected Retirement Age} - \text{Present Age}\right) \times \text{Rate of Benefits} \times \text{Final Average Salary}$$

EXAMPLE

Alicia Walmsley was working at Northern State University as an administrative assistant for 21 years when she became permanently disabled and could not continue to work. She was 52 years old and had planned to retire in 13 years at Northern State's normal retirement age of 65. Her final average salary was $88,740. Northern State's rate of benefits is 2%. What is her monthly disability benefit?

Step 1: Find the annual disability benefit.

$$\left(\text{Years Worked} + \text{Expected Retirement Age} - \text{Present Age}\right) \times \text{Rate of Benefits} \times \text{Final Average Salary}$$

$$(21 + 65 - 52) \times 2\% \times \$88{,}740$$

$= 34 \times 0.02 \times 88{,}740 =$ $60,343.20 annual disability benefit

Step 2: Find the monthly disability benefit.

$$\frac{60{,}343.20}{12} = \mathbf{\$5{,}028.60\ per\ month}$$

Blend Images/SuperStock

Concept CHECK

Complete the problem. Check your answer in the back of the book.

1. Mark Mowler's final average salary is $47,800. He worked for 15 years and will retire in 10 years, when he is 60. The rate of benefits is 1.8%. Find the annual and monthly disability benefits.

Lesson Practice

For Problems 2–4, find the (a) annual and (b) monthly disability benefits.

	(Years Worked	+	Expected Retirement Age	−	Present Age)	×	Rate of Benefits	×	Final Average Salary	=	Annual Disability Benefit	Monthly Disability Benefit
2.	(20	+	65	−	60)	×	2.00%	×	$40,000	=	**a.**	**b.**
3.	(26	+	60	−	54)	×	2.10%	×	56,000	=	**a.**	**b.**
4.	(14	+	62	−	44)	×	1.80%	×	35,700	=	**a.**	**b.**

Did You Know?

Amtrak's Resurgence

More and more American travelers, especially on the East Coast, are choosing to travel by train. Rail service Amtrak reported a 20% increase in new riders in a recent period on its Acela Express route between Boston and Washington, D.C.

5. Paul Thornton had worked for Central Pacific Railroads for 18 years. He suffered a stroke and became disabled at age 49. His final average salary was $36,947.80. Normal retirement age is 65. The rate of benefits is 2.1%. **(a)** What is Paul's annual disability benefit? **(b)** What is his monthly disability benefit?

6. Theresa Cole had worked for Central State University for 13 years when she suffered a heart attack and became disabled. Theresa was 54 years of age and had planned to retire at the normal retirement age of 60. Her final average salary was $41,247.86. Central State's rate of benefits is 2%. What is her monthly disability benefit?

7. Richard Wexler, age 58, was an employee of the state for 16 years when he became permanently disabled. Normal retirement age for the state is 60. The rate of benefits is 2.2%. Wexler's final average salary was $41,870. Find his monthly disability benefit.

H.O.T. Problems

8. **CHALLENGE PROBLEM** Henrietta Jordon, age 54, had been an employee of a State Medical School for 26 years when she became permanently disabled. Normal retirement age is 60. Her final average salary for benefit purposes is based on the average of the last 5 years: $48,960; $51,400; $53,900; $55,500; and $56,100. The rate of benefits is 2.2%. Find her monthly disability benefit.

Spiral Review

Solve. (Skills 3, 4)

9. 17 + (65 − 56) **10.** 9 + (60 − 31) **11.** 23 + (62 − 54)

12. ALGEBRA Tam Ha purchased a new pair of shoes. She gave the clerk a $50 bill and received $8.94 in change. If the sales tax rate was 6%, find the total selling price. (Lesson 6.2)

GET READY for the Next Lesson

PREREQUISITE SKILL Multiplying Decimals (Skill 8)

Multiply.

13. $4.35 × 221 **14.** $7.82 × 635 **15.** $13.58 × 343 **16.** $62.98 × 58

Robert Kaufmann/FEMA

LESSON 13.5

Workers' Compensation Insurance

Lesson Objective

Compute the employer cost for workers' compensation insurance.

Content Vocabulary

- workers' compensation insurance

GET READY for the Lesson

Who pays your bills if you get hurt on the job?

Ed Mendez knows that when a storm knocks out service to electricity customers, he will be asked to help restore service. As a lineman, Ed faces some risks, but he is assured of financial protection in case of work-related injury.

As You Read

Identify Who pays for workers' compensation insurance?

Workers' Compensation Insurance **Workers' compensation insurance** covers employees' medical expenses and lost wages if they are hurt on the job. The premiums for workers' compensation insurance are paid to the state by the employer, not the employee. The premiums vary by state but are based on the total payroll of a company, normally in blocks of \$100, and the type of business.

The state classifies every business according to the frequency and severity of accidents. Roofers, loggers, and coal miners, who have a high **exposure** to injuries, will have a higher premium than office personnel or retail clerks, who have a low exposure to injuries. In most states the premium for workers compensation insurance is computed by multiplying a base rate by the total payroll.

Premium for Workers' Compensation Insurance = Base Rate × Total Payroll

Study Tip

Mental Math
When solving a multi-step problem, you can sometimes do one or more of the steps using mental math. For instance, you can divide any number by 100 by moving the decimal point two places to the left. In this example, divide \$176,800.00 by one hundred as follows: \$176800.00 = \$1768.00 or \$1,768.00.

EXAMPLE

The base rate for workers' compensation insurance for underground coal mining in one state is \$19.89 per \$100 paid to employees. The total monthly payroll for a small underground mine is \$176,800. What is the monthly premium for workers' compensation insurance?

Find the premium for workers' compensation insurance.

$$\text{Base Rate} \times \left(\frac{\text{Total Payroll}}{100}\right) = \$19.89 \times \left(\frac{\$176{,}800}{\$100}\right) = \mathbf{\$35{,}165.52}$$

Concept CHECK

Complete the problem. Check your answer in the back of the book.

1. The owner of McCothche Machine Shop pays the base rate of \$5.52 per \$100 paid in wages. The payroll for September is \$91,780. What is that month's premium for workers' compensation insurance?

MARVIN NAUMAN/FEMA News Photo

Lesson Practice

For Problems 2–5, find the monthly premium for workers' compensation insurance.

	Type of Business	Monthly Payroll	Base Rate per $100	Monthly Premium
2.	Janitorial service	$ 980	$ 4.90	
3.	Window washer service	$3,960	$16.54	
4.	Painting contractor	$7,860	$ 6.10	
5.	Clothing store	$4,650	$ 2.73	

6. The Winston Tree Farm and Nursery has a base rate for the state's workers compensation insurance of $5.93 per $100.00 paid in wages. The monthly payroll for the nursery is $3,560. What is the monthly premium for workers compensation insurance?

7. The base rate for a state's workers' compensation insurance for a service station attendant is $5.12 per $100.00 paid in wages. The payroll for Scott Park Service Station for March is $25,784. What is the monthly premium for workers' compensation insurance?

8. Maria and Enzo Farelli operate a bakery. The base rate for the state's workers' compensation insurance is $2.90 per $100.00 paid in wages. The monthly payroll for the bakers employed by the Farellis is $33,870.00. What is the monthly premium for workers' compensation insurance?

9. CHALLENGE PROBLEM Takis Machine Shop paid a base rate for the state's workers' compensation insurance of $9.40 per $100 paid in wages. Takis has a monthly payroll of $53,896.84. After reevaluating the frequency and severity of accidents at machine shops, the state increased the base rate to $10.52 per $100 paid in wages. Assuming the monthly payroll stays the same, how much more will Takis pay each year for state workers' compensation insurance?

Spiral Review

Multiply. (Skill 8)

10. $3.14 × 320 **11.** $23.85 × 230 **12.** 0.022 × $7,000

13. Italian salad dressing is sold in three sizes. The price of a 16-ounce bottle is $3.29, a 20-ounce bottle is $4.39, and a 36-ounce bottle is $6.09. Based on price alone, which package is the best buy? (Lesson 6.4)

14. ALGEBRA Ricardo Ramirez took out a single-payment loan for $2,500 at 7.8% ordinary interest to pay his federal income tax bill. If the maturity value of the loan was $2,548.75, when would Ricardo have to pay back the loan if he took it out on April 1? (Lesson 8.1)

GET READY for the Next Lesson

PREREQUISITE SKILL Adding Decimals (Skill 5)

Add.

15. $67.12 + $68.76 + $69.01 **16.** $54.44 + $12.12 + $66.35

17. $72.08 + $29.37 + $275.11 **18.** $65.76 + $29.75 + $73.74

LESSON 13.6

Travel Expenses

Lesson Objective
Calculate total business travel expenses.

Content Vocabulary
- travel expenses

GET READY for the Lesson

Why might someone need to travel for work?

When she travels for work, Maria Newquist keeps her receipts. Maria's employer pays for her lodging, mileage, and meals.

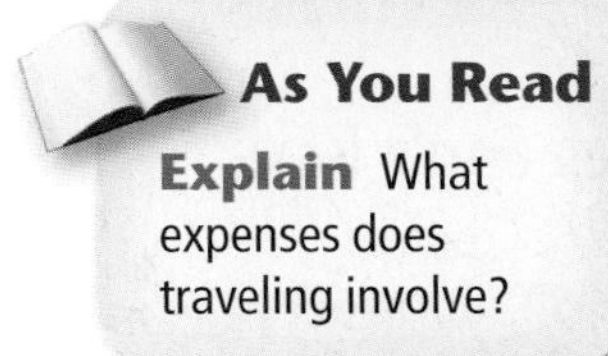

As You Read
Explain What expenses does traveling involve?

Travel Expenses If you travel for your business, you will probably be reimbursed, or paid back, for all **authorized** expenses during your trip. **Travel expenses** usually include transportation, lodging, meals, and additional costs such as conference registration fees. You would be reimbursed the total travel expenses using the formula:

$$\text{Total Travel Expenses} = \text{Cost of Transportation} + \text{Cost of Lodging} + \text{Cost of Meals} + \text{Additional Costs}$$

Business Credit Cards Some companies issue business credit cards. One advantage of a business credit card is that it can be used to manage cash flow. Another key advantage is that employers can monitor employee spending. Employees like business credit cards because they do not have to wait for reimbursement.

Disadvantages include an employee making unauthorized charges or losing the card. Also, keep in mind that money spent on a credit card is debt and must be managed with care.

Reading Math +−÷=

Synonyms
The word *reimburse* means "pay back." Synonyms for this word include *compensate, repay,* and *recompense.*

EXAMPLE 1

Diversified Sales Company will reimburse Roger Martin for attending a 3-day marketing conference. Diversified will pay him $0.55 per mile. Martin's expenses included the following:

Expense Category	Amount
Hotel (9/6)	$274.50
Hotel (9/7)	$274.50
Conference Reg.	$195.00
Meals (9/6)	$ 79.12
Meals (9/7)	$ 98.23
Meals (9/8)	$ 35.62
Mileage	(240 miles round-trip)
Tolls	$ 17.50

What is the total cost of sending Martin to the conference?

Step 1: Find the cost of transportation.

(240 × \$0.55) + \$17.50 = \$132.00 + \$17.50 = \$149.50

Step 2: Find the cost of lodging.

2 × \$274.50 = \$549.00

Step 3: Find the cost of meals.

\$79.12 + \$98.23 + \$35.62 = \$212.97

Step 4: Find the additional costs.

Conference registration = \$195.00

Step 5: Find the total travel expenses.

Cost of Transportation + Cost of Lodging + Cost of Meals + Additional Costs

\$149.50 + \$549.00 + \$212.97 + \$195.00 = **\$1,106.47 total travel expenses**

Concept CHECK

Complete the problems. Check your answers in the back of the book.

1. Cost of transportation to a software conference is \$976. Cost of lodging is \$219 a night for 3 nights. Cost of meals is \$87.52, \$56.90, and \$147.80. Additional costs are \$489 conference registration fee. Find the total travel expenses.
2. Cost of transportation to a nursing conference is \$1,235. Cost of lodging is \$239 a night for 4 nights. Cost of meals is \$67.55, \$42.56, \$68.52, and \$97.87. Additional costs are \$590 conference registration fee. Find the total travel expenses.

EXAMPLE 2 Algebra

Nancy Hoover had total travel expenses of \$438. Her transportation cost \$146, her lodging \$219, and additional costs were \$25. If dinner cost twice as much as lunch, how much was her lunch? How much was her dinner?

Step 1: Let x = The cost of lunch and $2x$ = The cost of dinner

Step 2: Write and then solve an equation.

Total Travel Expenses = Transportation + Lodging + Meals + Additional

$\$438 = \$146 + \$219 + (x + 2x) + \$25$

Combine like terms → $\$438 = \$390 + 3x$

Subtract \$390 from both sides → $\$48 = 3x$

Divide both sides by 3 → $\$16 = x$

Lunch cost \$16 and dinner cost \$32.

Concept CHECK

Complete the problem. Check your answer in the back of the book.

3. Maldo Geronimo conducts two-day training sessions for a respiratory care equipment company at various locations throughout the country. His expenses are: lodging \$235 per night, transportation \$495, breakfast and lunch \$56 per day. He has a budget of \$1,200. What is the maximum he can spend on dinner each of the two nights?

Did You Know?

KVLY-TV Tower **At 2,063 feet tall, North Dakota's KVLY-TV antenna tower is the world's tallest human-made, land-based structure. A baseball dropped from the top of the tower would take nearly 24 seconds to hit the ground.**

Lesson Practice

For Problems 4–9, complete the table for these business trips.

	Name	Miles Traveled	Mileage at $0.62/mile	Meals	Hotel Room	Additional Costs	Total Expenses
4.	T. Willis	48	$29.76	$ 27.80	$ 65.48	$ 145.00	b.
5.	B. Henry	80	a.	$ 46.90	$ 0.00	$ 260.00	b.
6.	M. Diaz	240	a.	$ 71.95	$189.40	$ 410.00	b.
7.	V. Tarski	180	a.	$ 70.40	$210.00	$ 398.00	b.
8.	T. Lanza	417	a.	$238.51	$314.90	$ 980.00	b.
9.	B. Pappas	623	a.	$291.94	$516.85	$1,250.00	b.

10. Kody Landis is a television news reporter. He travels to investigate news stories. This month his travel expenses were airplane fares of $617.60 and $847.80, 156 miles of driving at $0.65 per mile, taxicab fares of $37.25 and $114.50, and meals totaling $776.85. What were his total travel expenses for the month?

11. Cho Wan Sey, a sales representative for Curry Corporation, flew to New York City to make a sales presentation. Airfare was $515. She rented a car for 3 days for $71.40 a day plus $0.32 a mile. She drove a total of 70 miles. Her hotel bill was $184.50 a night for 2 nights. Her meals cost $21.90, $34.85, $69.76, $114.91, $57.80, $19.80, and $214.90. What were Cho's total travel expenses?

H.O.T. Problems

12. ALGEBRA The Payroll Department is sending 2 people to a 2-day training session on a new software program. Expenses per person: registration, $375; supplies, $50; breakfast, $19, lunch, $25, and dinner, $70. Total transportation cost for the 2 people is $60. If the company has budgeted $1,800 for the 2 to attend the training session, what is the most they can each pay for their hotel room per person per night?

Spiral Review

Multiply. (Skill 8)

13. 350 × $0.21 **14.** 540 × $0.20 **15.** 5 × $85.71 **16.** 3 × $93.47

17. The Madison County tax assessor determined the market value of a home to be $595,000. The rate of assessment in Madison County is 40% of market value. The tax rate is 42.73 mills. Calculate the real estate tax. (Lesson 10.5)

18. ALGEBRA Vanesa Vasquez contributes $2,500 per year to her Roth IRA, an ordinary annuity, starting at age 35. If she earns 7.4% annual interest compounded annually, what is the fair market value of her Roth IRA at age 65? How much interest will she have earned? (Lesson 5.8)

GET READY for the Next Lesson

PREREQUISITE SKILL Dividing (Decimal Remainder) (Skill 10)

Divide. Round answers to the nearest cent.

19. $54,860 ÷ 34 **20.** $26,485 ÷ 56 **21.** $38,675 ÷ 27

22. $69,758 ÷ 76 **23.** $16,835 ÷ 210 **24.** $83,093 ÷ 42

LESSON 13.7

Employee Training

Lesson Objective
Compute total employee training costs.

Content Vocabulary
- release time

GET READY for the Lesson

What new things would you like to learn at your first job?

Taylor Field listened attentively to her new manager on her first day at Graphic Design Specialists. Taylor's job is entry level, but she is eager to learn how to use different types of graphic-design software and to be part of a creative team.

As You Read

Recall Have you ever taken part in employee training?

Employee Training Costs Many businesses may pay the expenses involved in training or retraining employees. Employees may be sent to special job-related programs or special training programs may be offered **internally**. Expenses for training during regular work hours include the cost of **release time**. When you are granted release time, you are paid your regular wages or salary while you are away from your job. The person doing the training needs to be paid and additional costs could include training manuals, software packages, travel, and meals. The total training costs are calculated using this formula:

Total Training Costs = Cost of Release Time + Cost of Instruction + Additional Costs

EXAMPLE

Acme Manufacturing Company chose 8 employees to attend a training program in multi-robotic computer assisted manufacturing held within the company. The employees were paid their regular wages while attending the 2-day program. Their combined wages amounted to $1,512 per day. The production control manager, who earns $278 per day, was the course instructor. Refreshments were served twice a day, at a cost of $145.70 per day. Supplies and equipment for the program amounted to $65 per person. What was the total cost for the training program?

Step 1: Find the cost of release time.
2 days × $1,512.00 = $3,024.00 release time

Step 2: Find the cost of instruction.
2 days × $278.00 = $556.00 instruction cost

Step 3: Find the additional costs.
(2 × 145.70) + (8 × 65.00) =
291.40 + $520.00 = $811.40 additional costs

Step 4: Find the total training cost.
Cost of Release Time + Cost of Instruction + Additional Costs
$3,024.00 + $556.00 + $811.40
= **$4,391.40 total training cost**

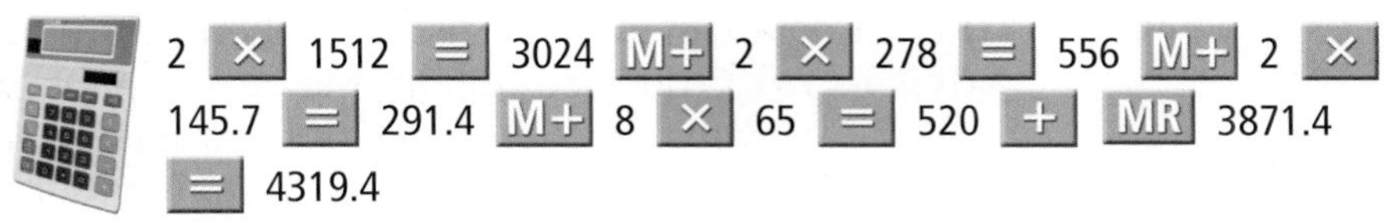

Concept CHECK

Complete the problem. Check your answer in the back of the book.

1. Kyoto Web Design trains 3 employees on new software. Expenses per person are: release time $247; instruction $150; additional costs $56. Find the total training cost.

Lesson Practice

For Problems 2–7, determine the total training cost.

	Number of Days	Daily Cost of Release Time	Daily Cost of Instruction	Daily Cost of Refreshments	Daily Cost of Supplies	Total Training Cost
2.	1	$417	$ 75	$ 45	$ 50	
3.	1	$545	$250	$ 65	$120	
4.	4	$345	$175	$ 96	$100	
5.	3	$716	$200	$132	$ 30	
6.	2	$ 96	$150	$ 58	$ 25	
7.	5	$176	$100	$ 66	$ 15	

For Problems 8 and 9, determine the total training costs.

8. Three nurses attend a 2-day seminar. Expenses per nurse per day are:
   Release time: $280
   Instruction: $675
   Supplies: $425
9. Five salesmen attend a 3-day workshop. Expenses per person per day are:
   Release time: $110
   Instruction: $85
   Meal expense: $99
   Total travel for all 5: $2,285
10. The water department of Metamora Township is sending 2 employees to a 2-day seminar on a new accounting and billing software package. One employee earns $152 per day, while the other earns $168 per day. Registration costs $120 per person. Materials cost $45 per person. What will the 2-day seminar cost Metamora Township?
11. The grafting and pruning department of National Nursery, Inc., is sending 4 technicians to a 2-day local seminar on the new genetic improvments in nursery plant cultivation. Three of the technicians earn $96.40 per day, while the other one earns $116.50 per day. Registration costs $120 per person. Materials cost $85 per person. What will the 2-day seminar cost?

Did You Know?

Solar Energy The world's largest solar power plant is located in California's Mojave Desert. The plant currently supplies 90% of the world's commercially available solar power. The energy output of 1 kilowatt of solar energy is equal to the energy released by burning 170 pounds of coal.

12. The tax department of National Brokerage, Inc., is sending 8 tax advisors to a 2-day seminar on the new Economic Growth and Tax Relief Reconciliation Act. Three of the advisors earn $252 per day, while the other 5 earn $360 per day. Registration costs $350 per person. Materials cost $125 per person. What will the 2-day seminar cost National Brokerage, Inc.?

13. Laser Research, Inc., is sending its 5-person research team to a 3-day conference to learn a new automated lab procedure. One researcher earns $336 daily, 2 earn $360 daily, and 2 earn $390 daily. What will the 3-day conference cost Laser Research, Inc., in lost productivity for the 5 researchers?

14. Six employees of the Solar Energy Company underwent a 5-day machine maintainence training program. Their wage rate averaged $19.65 per hour for an 8-hour day. The trainer, at a daily salary of $246.53, conducted the 5-day session. Total refreshments cost $87.50 per day. Electronic diagnostics kits were provided for each of the 6 employees at a cost of $586.45 each. What was the total cost of the maintainence training program?

15. Adelphia Brokers, a full service brokerage house, brought in W. T. Thomas, a specialist in financial stocks, to meet with their 15 brokers. Mr. Thomas charged a fee of $2,500 for the 4-hour session. The average hourly rate for the 15 brokers was $50.00 per hour. Lunch for the 15 brokers and Mr. Thomas was $24.50 per person. What was the total cost for the 4-hour financial stock training session?

H.O.T. Problems

16. CHALLENGE PROBLEM Forestry Consultants brought in Tom Hollins, an expert on pruning trees, to train 8 summer employees in an 8-hour hands-on training session. Hollins charged a fee of $350.00 plus $0.65 per mile for 165 miles. The summer employees are paid $12.50 an hour. Lunch was $12.50 per person. Each trainee was furnished with a pruning saw that sells for $56.25 each and a hard hat that costs $45.98 each. What is the total cost of the training?

Spiral Review

Divide. Round answers to the nearest cent. (Skill 10)

17. $47,650 ÷ 52 **18.** $34,840 ÷ 52 **19.** $28,645 ÷ 260

20. A pickup truck sticker shows a base price of $35,745.00, with options totaling $3,605.00 and a destination charge of $750.00. *Consumer Reports* shows the dealer's cost as 87.7% of the base price and 90.2% of the options. What is the dealer's cost? (Lesson 9.2)

21. ALGEBRA Marty and Roslyn Seymour purchase a GNMA Mortgage issue bond selling at a premium of 102.7% of its $10,000 face value. The bonds are selling at a premium because they have an annual yield of 8.50%. Find the bond cost, the annual interest, and the interest rate. (Lesson 12.7)

GET READY for the Next Lesson

PREREQUISITE SKILL Rounding Numbers (Skill 2)

Round answers to the nearest tenth of a cent.

22. $0.45398 **23.** $0.93546 **24.** $0.77739

25. $0.54642 **26.** $0.92511 **27.** $0.88609

CHAPTER 13 Review and Assessment

AFTER YOU READ

Chapter SUMMARY

Companies often need to hire and train new employees. Personnel departments calculate the cost of recruiting new employees, new salary after merit increases, cost-of-living adjustments, and the rate of employee benefits on annual gross pay. Additional business expenses include disability benefits under independent retirement systems and under Social Security as well as the employer cost for workers compensation. Other expenses include business travel expenses and the cost of training employees.

Vocabulary Check

1. On a sheet of paper, use each of these terms in a sentence.

Content Vocabulary

- recruiting (p. 485)
- salary scale (p. 489)
- cost-of-living adjustment (p. 489)
- merit increase (p. 489)
- employee benefits (p. 492)
- disability insurance (p. 495)
- workers' compensation insurance (p. 497)
- travel expenses (p. 499)
- release time (p. 502)

Academic Vocabulary

- sufficient (p. 485)
- estimate (p. 489)
- ratio (p. 492)
- benefits (p. 495)
- exposure (p. 497)
- authorized (p. 499)
- internally (p. 502)

Concept Check

2. How do you calculate the total cost of recruiting?
3. Define *merit increase.*
4. List three examples of employee benefits.
5. Give the formula for finding the rate of employee benefits.
6. Provide the formula for finding the annual disability benefit.
7. What does workers compensation insurance cover?
8. What is the formula for calculating total training costs?
9. **CRITICAL THINKING** Make a list of expenses typically associated with a business trip.

Lesson-by-Lesson Review

13.1 Hiring New Employees (pp. 485–488)

Calculate the cost of recruiting new employees.
Goosen Department Store is searching for a person to head its human resources department. Goosen placed advertisements in regional newspapers for a total cost of $5,432.34. Goosen interviewed 3 candidates and paid the travel expenses for each. These expenses totaled $3,245.90. After the interviews, Goosen hired Monica Cain at an annual salary of $85,400 and paid her moving expenses of $14,598. What was the total expense of recruiting Cain?

Find the total recruiting cost.

Advertising Expenses + Interviewing Expenses + Hiring Expenses

$5,432.34 + $3,245.90 + $14,598 = **$23,276.24 total recruiting cost**

Review Exercises

For Problems 10 and 11, find the total recruiting cost.

10. Advertising expenses: $1,456
Interviewing expenses: $1,290 and $1,390
Hiring expenses: $875, $4,500, and 7% on a $234,000 home
11. Advertising expenses: $2,780
Interviewing expenses: $2,211 and $1,745
Hiring expenses: $1,746, $4,500, and 4% on a $375,000 home
12. Webster's Department store hired Van Delgado as its new human resources manager at an annual salary of $123,990. Advertising costs were $3,456.90. Interviewing expenses were: $1,890.23 and $2,132.67. The agency's fee is 20% of the first year's salary. What was the total cost of hiring the human resources manager?
13. A financial services firm searched and found a new corporate fiscal officer. Expenses were: advertising $15,300, interviewing $4,340, moving expenses $22,000, and a 5% realtor's fee on the selling price of a $375,000 home. They hired Jolon Hena at a salary of $475,000 and paid 25% of first year salary as a finder's fee. What was the total recruiting cost?
14. **ALGEBRA** Executives at Second National Bank are searching for a new Director of Human Resources. They have budgeted $40,000 for the search. They have spent $9,800 on advertising expenses and $8,650 on interviewing expenses. What is the maximum selling price of a home on which Second National would pay 5.5% commission and stay within $40,000 in total recruiting costs?

13.2 Administering Wages and Salaries (pp. 489–491)

Compute the new salary after merit increase and cost-of-living adjustment.
Lorena Irwin is a stockbroker for a firm in Topeka, Kansas. Her current salary is $43,260 per year. This year she received a cost-of-living adjustment of 2.8% and a merit increase of 4.7% for excellent work during the year. What will Lorena's salary be for the coming year?

Step 1: Find the present salary.

The present salary is $43,260.00

Step 2: Find the cost-of-living adjustment.

Salary × Cost-of-Living Adjustment Percent

$43,260.00 × 2.8% = $1,211.28

Lesson-by-Lesson Review (continued)

Step 3: Find the merit increase.

Salary × Merit Increase Percent

$43,260.00 × 4.7% = $2,033.22

Step 4: Find the new salary.

Present Salary + Cost-of-Living Adjustment + Merit Increase

$43,260 + $1,211.28 + $2,033.22 = **$46,504.50 new salary**

Review Exercises

For Problems 15–19, use Figure 13.1 on page 489 to complete the table.

	Employee	Position	Level	Salary	COLA	Amount	Merit	Amount	New Salary
15.	C. Delgado	Project Leader	2	a.	3.20%	b.	7.60%	c.	d.
16.	Z. Ruiz	Data Entry	1	a.	2.8 %	b.	3.60%	c.	d.
17.	L. Cata	Systems Analyst	2	a.	4.80%	b.	7.40%	c.	d.
18.	K. Toyama	Web Designer	3	a.	3.50%	b.	6.50%	c.	d.
19.	D. Lee	Data Entry	3	a.	4.70%	b.	3.50%	c.	d.

20. Yom Kwan works 40 hours a week 50 weeks a year for Ishwar Industries. She earns $10.20 per hour. **(a)** What is her annual gross pay? **(b)** If she receives a 5.0% merit increase, what is her new annual gross pay? **(c)** What is her new hourly rate?

21. **ALGEBRA** Felix Harvey has a middle-management position with Kiko Industries, Inc. After his annual performance review, he receives a merit increase of 4.2% and a cost-of-living increase of 3.1%. His annual salary after the increases is $52,742.30. **(a)** Find Felix's annual salary before the two increases took effect. **(b)** Find his merit increase and his cost-of-living increase.

13.3 Employee Benefits (pp. 492–494)

Calculate the rate of employee benefits based on annual gross pay.

Rena Tanaka earns an annual salary of $54,320. Her benefits total $20,694.80. Rena's total annual benefits are what percent of her annual salary?

Find the rate of benefits.

$$\frac{\text{Total Benefits}}{\text{Annual Gross Pay}} = \frac{20{,}694.80}{54{,}320} = \mathbf{38.1\%}$$

Review Exercises

Complete the benefits chart for the OMY Music Store employees.

	Position	Annual Salary	2-Week Vacation	3.6% Workers Comp.	8-Day Sick Leave	6.2% Social Security	1.45% Medi-care	Total Benefits	Rate of Benefits
22.	Manager	$65,300	a.	b.	c.	d.	e.	f.	g.
23.	Technician	32,000	a.	b.	c.	d.	e.	f.	g.
24.	Cashier	22,000	a.	b.	c.	d.	e.	f.	g.
25.	Instructor	31,500	a.	b.	c.	d.	e.	f.	g.

Lesson-by-Lesson Review (continued)

26. Harold Stuckey earns an annual salary of $76,700 as Chief Financial Officer of Enterprise Industries, Inc. His benefits include a 4-week vacation annually, 8 holidays per year, monthly health insurance premium of $225.00, a 30-day sick leave policy, Social Security of 6.2% of salary, and Medicare of 1.45% of salary. Find Harold's rate of benefits.

13.4 Disability Insurance (pp. 495–496)

Determine disability benefits under independent retirement systems and under Social Security.

Bernice Martin had worked at the Pacific Train Station for 19 years when she became permanently disabled and could not continue to work. Bernice was 43 years of age and had planned to work until she was 65. Her final average salary was $31,298. The rate of benefits is 1.9%. What is Bernice's monthly disability benefit?

Step 1: Find the annual disability benefit.

$$\left(\text{Years Worked} + \text{Expected Retirement Age} - \text{Present Age}\right) \times \text{Rate of Benefits} \times \text{Final Average Salary}$$

$$(19 + 65 - 43) \times 1.9\% \times \$31{,}298 = \$24{,}381.14 \text{ annual disability benefit}$$

Step 2: Find the monthly disability benefit

$$\frac{\$24{,}381.14}{12} = \textbf{\$2,031.76 monthly disability benefit}$$

Review Exercises

For Problems 27–32, find the annual and monthly disability benefits.

	(Years Worked	+	Expected Retirement Age	−	Present Age)	×	Rate of Benefits	×	Final Average Salary	=	Annual Disability Benefit	Monthly Disability Benefit
27.	(10	+	65	−	30)	×	2.00%	×	$45,000	=	a.	b.
28.	(15	+	60	−	35)	×	1.80%	×	38,000	=	a.	b.
29.	(18	+	62	−	40)	×	2.10%	×	56,000	=	a.	b.
30.	(24	+	55	−	50)	×	2.20%	×	65,000	=	a.	b.
31.	(29	+	65	−	62)	×	1.75%	×	98,000	=	a.	b.
32.	(13	+	62	−	45)	×	2.10%	×	36,800	=	a.	b.

33. Walter York worked at the Municipal Power Plant for 25 years. He became permanently disabled and could not continue to work. Walter was 45 years of age and had planned to work until he was 65. His final average salary was $46,480. The rate of benefits is 2.1%. What is Walter's monthly disability benefit?

34. Elyssa Thomas worked at the Municipal Water Plant for 21 years. She became permanently disabled and could not continue to work. Elyssa was 47 years of age and had planned to work until she was 65. Her final average salary was $48,228. The rate of benefits is 2.1%. What is Elyssa's monthly disability benefit?

Lesson-by-Lesson Review (continued)

13.5 Workers' Compensation Insurance (pp. 497–498)

Compute the employer cost for workers' compensation insurance.
The base rate for workers' compensation insurance for miners in a certain state is $22.50 per $100 paid to employees. The total monthly payroll for a small underground mine is $125,000. What is the monthly premium for workers' compensation insurance?

Find the premium for workers' compensation insurance.

$$\text{Base Rate} \times \frac{\text{Total Payroll}}{\$100} = \$22.50 \times \frac{\$125{,}000}{\$100} = \textbf{\$28,125 premium}$$

Review Exercises

For Problems 35–38, find the monthly premium for workers' compensation insurance.

	Type of Business	Monthly Payroll	Base Rate per $100	Monthly Premium
35.	Computer manufacturer	$ 8,990	$ 3.35	
36.	Machine shop	6,550	$ 5.52	
37.	Building Construction	11,230	$13.42	

38. The base rate for workers' compensation insurance for construction workers in one state is $21.40 per $100 paid to employees. The total monthly payroll for Candor Construction Co. is $153,850. What is the monthly premium for workers' compensation insurance?

13.6 Travel Expenses (pp. 499–501)

Calculate total business travel expenses.
The network department of Taylor Medical Corporation will reimburse Belinda Smith for attending a 2-day conference. Belinda drove to the conference, so Taylor will pay her $0.62 per mile. Belinda's expenses were: hotel, $89.50 for 1 night; meals, $83.21; and registration, $125. She drove 185 miles round trip. What is the total cost of sending Belinda to the conference?

Find the total cost of travel expenses.

Cost of Transportation + Cost of Lodging + Cost of Meals + Additional Costs

(185 × $0.62) + $89.50 + $83.21 + $125 = **$412.41 total cost of travel expenses**

Review Exercises

For Problems 39–41, complete the table for these business trips.

	Name	Miles Traveled	Mileage at $0.62/mile	Meals	Hotel Room	Additional Costs	Total Expenses
39.	J. Wheaton	58	$35.96	$ 37.80	$ 72.48	$ 155.00	a.
40.	G. Dunn	103	a.	$ 56.90	$ 0.00	$ 280.00	b.
41.	C. Raymer	742	a.	$412.94	$716.85	$1,450.00	b.

Lesson-by-Lesson Review (continued)

42. Marie Vincent had total travel expenses of $638. Her transportation cost $196, her lodging $259, and she had additional costs of $35. If dinner cost 3 times as much as lunch, how much was her lunch? How much was her dinner?

43. Kurt Landry is a network installer for Diversified Software. He travels to various companies to install and test their networks. This month his travel expenses included airplane fares of $717.60 and $927.80, 221 miles of driving at $0.68 per mile, hotel expenses of $212.25 and $414.50, and meals totaling $375.25. What were his total travel expenses for the month?

13.7 Employee Training (pp. 502–504)

Compute total employee training costs.

BR & Associates, a financial services company, plans to train two of its employees on new accounting software. The employees are paid their regular wages while attending the 2-day training. Their combined wages total $623.50 per day. A consultant was hired to conduct the training. She was paid $300.00 per day. The cost of supplies was $39.54 per day. What was the cost for the training program?

Find the total training cost.

Cost of Release Time + Cost of Instruction + Additional Costs

(623.50 × 2) + (300.00 × 2) + (39.54 × 2) = **$1,926.08 total training cost**

Review Exercises

For Problems 44–47, find the total training cost.

	Number of Days	Daily Cost of Release Time	Daily Cost of Instruction	Daily Cost of Refreshments	Daily Cost of Supplies	Total Training Cost
44.	1	$ 850	$500	$55	$50	
45.	2	$1,650	$800	$75	$60	
46.	4	$3,250	$350	$92	$75	
47.	5	$ 325	$100	$62	$30	

48. Longbow & Associates, a solar research company, plans to train two of its employees on new chemical analysis procedures. The employees are paid their regular wages while attending the 3-day training. Their combined wages total $854.50 per day. A consultant was hired to conduct the training. She was paid $600.00 per day. The total cost of supplies was $88.80 per day. What was the cost for the training program?

49. Kang Manufacturing Company chose 8 employees to attend a training program in computer-assisted manufacturing held within the company. The employees were paid their regular wages while attending the 3-day program. Their combined wages amounted to $1,812 per day. The production control manager, who earns $378 per day, was the course instructor. Refreshments were brought in twice a day at a cost of $165.80 per day. Supplies and equipment for the program totaled $85 per person. What was the total cost for the training program?

Practice Test

Record your answers on a sheet of paper.

1. A marketing company spent $1,200.75 on advertising, $765 on interviews, and $2,431 on the hiring when seeking to fill a new position. What was the company's total recruiting cost?
   A $1,200.75 **B** $3,631.75
   C $1,965.75 **D** $4,396.75

2. **ALGEBRA** Ando Matsumuri is a computer operator working for PYT Technologies. After a performance review, he receives a merit increase of 2.8% and a cost-of-living adjustment of 3.2%. His annual salary after the increases is $37,100. What was Ando's salary before the two increases?
   A $33,200 **B** $35,000
   C $35,320 **D** $34,000

3. Marshana Robinson makes an annual salary of $42,680 with benefits totaling $14,550. What is her rate of benefits?
   A 34.1% **B** 34.9%
   C 29.3% **D** 31.9%

4. Mario Pinturo worked for 22 years and retired 3 years early at age 62 due to a disability. His average salary was $41,870 and his benefit rate is 2.1%. What is his annual disability benefit?
   A $19,936.00 **B** $22,582.30
   C $21,981.75 **D** $28,870.00

5. The workers compensation insurance rate for Little Bazoo Racing is $23.75 per $100 paid to employees. The company's total monthly payroll is $112,000. What is their monthly premium for workers compensation?
   A $19,500.75 **B** $29,500.50
   C $11,200.00 **D** $26,600.00

6. **ALGEBRA** Eric Lindell conducts two-day training sessions for a software company. He has a budget of $950. His expenses on one trip are: lodging $175 per night, $360 for transportation, breakfast and lunch $50 per day. What is the maximum he can spend on dinner each of the 2 nights?
   A $70.00 **B** $95.50
   C $64.00 **D** $67.50

7. Brass Key Aviation sent 4 of its employees to a 2-day training seminar. The only cost to the company was the lost wages. If each employee makes $375 a day, what was the total cost to the company of the training seminar?
   A $1,500 **B** $3,000
   C $2,500 **D** $4,000

8. **ALGEBRA** A radio station hired Riley Martin as its new disc jockey. The station spent $8,750 advertising for the position and $2,460 on interviewing expenses. The station pays 2.4% to 5.0% of the first year's salary as a signing bonus for on-air talent. Riley's first year salary was $48,580. If the station spent a total of $13,250.36 in recruiting costs, what percent signing bonus did they give to Riley?

9. The base rate for workers compensation insurance for construction workers in a certain state is $19.96 per $100 paid to employees. A small start-up construction company has a total payroll of $54,625.00 a month. What is the monthly premium for workers compensation insurance?

10. 18.7 + (32.4 − 11.44)

11. $56,821 ÷ $47

12. 73.1% of 84,290

13. 55.986 + 12.4 + 0.32851

14. $801.22 × 51

15. One thousand four hundred twenty is what percent of 7,100?

Standardized Test Practice

Cumulative, Chapters 1–13

PART 1 Multiple Choice

Record your answers on the answer sheet provided by your teacher or on a sheet of paper.

1. Julia Chen purchases an $80,000 life insurance policy. The annual base premium is $15.20 per $1,000. What is her annual premium?
   A $1,216.00 **B** $875.60
   C $1,510.00 **D** $955.20

2. Job Works Incorporated hired Marcus Ghent for a sales position at an annual salary of $34,670. The hiring costs were $420 in advertising, $118 in interview costs, and an agency fee that was 15% of his starting salary. What were the total hiring costs?
   A $6,020.02 **B** $5,658.12
   C $5,738.50 **D** $5,863.33

3. Laura Ballenger's medical insurance has her make a co-pay of $15 for each physician visit, and $12 for each physical therapy visit. She has a $400 deductible. Last year she made 19 doctor's visits and 25 visits to physical therapy. What is the total amount she paid?
   A $400 **B** $455
   C $585 **D** $985

4. Rufus Leekey had worked at Western Reserve Renovations for 20 years when he became permanently disabled. He was 52 and had planned to retire at age 65. His final average salary was $38,575 and WRR's rate of benefits is 2.8%. What is Rufus' annual disability benefit?
   A $34,683.50 **B** $20,095.40
   C $28,170.00 **D** $35,643.30

5. Kelly Gunning paid a total of $5,820 for 60 shares of stock. She sold the stock for $94 a share and paid a brokerage fee of $50. What was her profit or loss on the investment?
   A $130 profit **B** $130 loss
   C $230 loss **D** $290 loss

6. Juan Lapiz works for KT Commodities. The annual premium for his health insurance is $4,205. If his employer pays 65% of the cost, how much does Juan pay?
   A $2,560.75 **B** $1,471.75
   C $1,753.00 **D** $2,733.25

PART 2 Short Response/Griddable

7. Lisa Ferry works for Paisley Industries, earning $33,306 per year. The company provides the following benefits for Lisa:

Vacation	2 weeks
Holidays	8 days
Social Security	6.2%
Medicare	1.45%

   What is the rate of benefits? Round to the nearest tenth of a percent.

PART 3 Extended Response

Show your work.

8. The rate of benefits is one of the things you need to determine the annual disability benefits an employee will receive. What other information do you need to determine disability benefits? Write your answer in the form of the equations you use.

9. Explain the difference between ordinary interest and exact interest.

10. What information is used to determine the cost of recruiting a new employee?

TEST-TAKING TIP

Prepare Analyze your past test results. Each test can prepare you for the next test.

Building Academic Skills

Mathematics

The Tenth National Bank has contracted with Cheryl Malina to provide business writing skills training for its employees. Because she will be giving this training 35 times over the next year at this company, Cheryl has agreed to discount her fee by 7%. She usually charges $85 per hour for classroom time and $55 per hour for preparation time. Each training session will involve 4 hours in the classroom and 3 hours of preparation. How much will Cheryl have invoiced the bank by the end of the year?

English Language Arts/Writing

Supplemental Security Income (SSI, under Social Security) pays benefits only to people who are unable to work because of a disability. Similar private policies can be purchased so you can receive additional money if you are disabled. You also can buy private disability insurance that provides benefits to people who can no longer work at the same professions they worked in before they were disabled. On the Internet, research the costs of these policies. Which kind of policy costs more? Why do you think some people are willing to purchase the more expensive policy? Write a paragraph explaining your choice.

Social Studies/Economics

Companies' salary scales are based on industrial averages, surveys of people in specific fields, and the cost of living where the company is located. Use an Internet search engine or library sources to find the cost of living in various cities in the United States. If you were offered a salary of $35,000 in Columbus, Ohio, what salary would you need to live as well in Chicago, Illinois? In Richmond, Virginia? In San Diego, California? Create a table to compare your results. Pick three cities you think you might like to live in and include them in your chart.

Building Real-World Skills

Career WISE

Human Resources Director Once a company grows to a certain size, it needs a dedicated person whose job is to take care of the needs of all the other employees. This person, the human resources director, is in charge of employee benefits such as insurance and vacation days; he or she is also involved in the hiring (and sometimes firing) of employees.

Research and Share:

- **a.** Locate the Web site of the Society for Human Resource Management. When was the SHRM founded, and how many members does it have?
- **b.** As a class, discuss skills and characteristics that you think would be useful for a Human Resources Manager to have.

21st Century Workplace

Ongoing Training—Right at Your Desk In most careers, training is an ongoing process—you are never finished learning about your role in the company. Training once meant getting everybody together in a classroom. Today, training can be delivered right to the worker's computer, either through the company network or over the Internet.

Research and Write:

- **a.** Imagine you have a job as a graphic designer for a newspaper. What are some ongoing training programs that might benefit you?
- **b.** What are some possible benefits of online training?

Jill Braaten/McGraw-Hill Education

Purchasing and Inventory

Big Idea

This chapter will focus on the trade discounts companies receive when they order supplies and the methods companies use to properly manage inventory.

Explore the Photo

Planning Ahead
Inventory is an important part of many businesses. *Can you think of problems that might arise from having too much or too little of a product in stock?*

Dollar Stores

Q: I buy school supplies at a chain store where almost everything costs one dollar or less. How does this kind of store make a profit with such low prices?

A: Price-point retailers, known as "dollar stores," make money by selling products bought at discount prices well below regular wholesale cost. These low wholesale prices are available for several reasons. Some of the products are generic brands specially made for dollar stores. Other dollar-store products include post-holiday seasonal, or goods made to promote a movie, television show, or event that has passed. Some products actually cost more at dollar stores than at other stores, but customers are willing to pay more because they like paying a single price for everything they buy.

English Language Arts/Writing Make a list of useful products for which you might be able to find an inexpensive generic alternative at a dollar store.

GET READY for the Chapter

Math Online

To take the Online Readiness Quiz, go to **connectED.mcgraw-hill.com**.

Chapter 14 Purchasing and Inventory

Reading Guide

Before You Read

Describe How do you think discounts might be important to companies?

Main Idea

Taking advantage of discounts offered by vendors allows a company to buy for less. Proper management of inventory helps businesses to plan, coordinate, and execute the delivery of goods more efficiently.

Graphic Organizer

Before you read this chapter, draw a diagram like the one below. As you read, keep track of different types of discounts and make notes, such as relevant formulas.

Type of Discount	Notes

Math Online Go to connectED.mcgraw-hill.com to download this graphic organizer.

Content Vocabulary

You will learn these key terms in this chapter.

- list price
- trade discount
- trade-discount rate
- net price
- complement method
- chain discount
- net-price rate
- invoice
- cash discount
- ordinary dating
- end-of-month dating
- inventory
- stock reorder point
- average-cost method
- first in, first out (FIFO)
- last in, first out (LIFO)
- carrying inventory

Academic Vocabulary

You will see these words in your reading and on your tests.

- available
- approach
- convince
- itemize
- granting
- issues
- physical
- adequate

You can find vocabulary definitions in the **Content Vocabulary** Glossary and the **Academic Vocabulary** Glossary in the back of the book.

LESSON 14.1

Trade Discounts

Lesson Objective
Compute the trade discount, the net price, and the trade-discount rate.

Content Vocabulary
- list price
- trade discount
- trade-discount rate
- net price

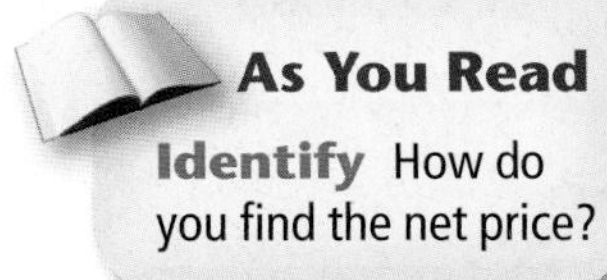
As You Read
Identify How do you find the net price?

GET READY for the Lesson

Where do you like to shop for bargains?

When students in Boston, Massachusetts, want cool fashions at even cooler prices, they take the subway to Filene's Basement. Opened in 1908, Filene's Basement buys clothing and other merchandise from suppliers at a deeply discounted price, then passes the savings along to customers.

Trade Discount Most vendors make **available** a catalog (on the Internet, a paper copy, or both) from which your business can buy merchandise. The catalog includes a description and the **list price** (or catalog price) of each item that the supplier sells. The list price is generally the price at which you may sell the item. You usually purchase the item at a **trade discount**, which is a discount from the list price. The **trade-discount rate** is the amount of the discount expressed as a percent. The **net price** is the price you actually pay for the item. Some wholesalers and manufacturers publish only the list prices and net prices in their catalogs or on Web sites. If you know the net and list prices, you can compute the trade-discount rate. These are the formulas:

$$\text{Trade Discount} = \text{List Price} \times \text{Trade-Discount Rate}$$

$$\text{Net Price} = \text{List Price} - \text{Trade Discount}$$

$$\text{Trade-Discount Rate} = \frac{\text{Trade Discount}}{\text{List Price}}$$

EXAMPLE 1

Johnson Auto Repair Shop is purchasing a cruise-control module for a 6-year old sport coupe. The list price in the wholesaler's catalog is \$845. Johnson receives a 40% trade discount. What is the net price?

Step 1: Find the trade discount: List Price × Trade-Discount Rate

$845.00 × 40% = $338.00 trade discount

Step 2: Find the net price: List Price − Trade Discount

$845.00 − $338.00 = **$507.00 net price**

Concept CHECK

Complete the problems. Check your answers in the back of the book. For Problems 1 and 2, find (a) the trade discount and (b) the net price.

1. List price of paint is \$24.00. Trade-discount rate is 30%.
2. List price of glue is \$34.60. Trade-discount rate is 25%.

EXAMPLE 2

Auto Parts Inc. shows a $156 list price in its catalog for a water pump. The net price to the retailer is $117. What is the trade-discount rate?

Step 1: Find the trade discount.

List Price − Net Price = $156 − $117 = $39 trade discount

Step 2: Find the trade-discount rate.

$$\frac{\text{Trade Discount}}{\text{List Price}} = \frac{\$39}{\$156} = 0.25 = \mathbf{25\%}$$

Reading Math +−÷=

Reread

Understand a sentence before you move on to the next one. Reread sentences as many times as it takes for you to grasp their meaning.

Concept CHECK

Complete the problems. Check your answers in the back of the book. For Problems 3 and 4, find (a) the trade discount and (b) the trade-discount rate.

3. List price for a window is $240. Net price is $168.
4. List price for a lawn mower is $420. Net price is $315.

Lesson Practice

For Problems 5–8, find (a) the trade discount and (b) the net price. Round answers to the nearest cent.

	Item	List Price	Trade-Discount Rate	Trade Discount	Net Price
5.	Vacuum Cleaner	$360.00	15%	a.	b.
6.	Exterior Paint	$174.00	32%	a.	b.
7.	Mobile Phone	$216.80	27%	a.	b.
8.	Binoculars	$150.99	12%	a.	b.

For Problems 9–11, determine the net price.

9. List price for a spark plug is $3.15. Trade-discount rate is 35%.
10. List price for an MP3 player is $219. Trade-discount rate is 32%.
11. List price for computer software is $150. Trade-discount rate is 40%.

For Problems 12–18, find (a) the trade discount and (b) the trade-discount rate. Round the trade-discount rate to the nearest tenth of a percent.

	Item	List Price	Net Price	Trade Discount	Trade-Discount Rate
12.	Office Supplies	$ 75.00	$ 50.00	a.	b.
13.	Dress Shirt	$ 50.00	$ 27.50	a.	b.
14.	Shoes	$ 97.49	$ 68.78	a.	b.
15.	Wireless Card	$ 90.00	$ 63.00	a.	b.

16. List price for shoe dye is $9.00. Net price is $6.00.
17. List price for a computer is $2,560. Net price is $2,100.
18. List price for a door is $184. Net price is $110.

Cost Estimator
Most cost estimators work for the construction or manufacturing industries. Estimators use mathematical and other methods to determine a project's cost before work begins.
What could happen to a business if the costs of expensive projects are not accurately estimated?

19. Harry's Hardware purchases the items shown from the wholesalers. Find the trade discount and net price for each item.

	Item	List	Trade-Discount Rate
a.	Paint thinner	$12.95	35%
b.	Lawn fertilizer	$ 8.99	10%
c.	B&D electric saw	$58.95	15%

20. Beauty Shop Wholesalers offers discounts on most of the items it sells. What is the trade-discount rate for each of the items listed?

	Beauty Shop Wholesalers		
	Item	List	Net
a.	Complexion brushes	$15.79	$11.68
b.	Lighted makeup mirror	$79.99	$44.39
c.	Cleansing brushes	$12.79	$ 9.34
d.	Makeup mirror	$47.49	$33.15

21. Alvin Sales Agency receives a 33% trade-discount rate on farm equipment replacement parts from Land Wholesale Supply. What is the net price for each order?

	Quantity	Stock Item	Description	Unit Price
a.	6	$\frac{3}{4} \times 6$	Heavy bolts	$ 2.95
b.	4	$\frac{3}{4}$	Star-lock washer	$ 0.60
c.	2	24" HOB	Chopper blades	$ 45.45
d.	6	#7271	Tune-up kit	$139.95
e.	4	#5051	PTO Guard	$124.60
f.	12	$\frac{5}{8} \times 24$	Threaded Rod	$ 15.90

22. CHALLENGE PROBLEM A catalytic converter is sold to a jobber for $180.90, then sold to a wholesaler for $241.20, then sold to a retailer for $360.00, who places a retail price of $600.00 on the converter. Find the trade discount and the trade discount rate each time the item is sold.

Spiral Review

Find the percent. (Skill 30) **Round answers to the nearest cent.**

23. $47.80 × 10% **24.** $91.40 × 18% **25.** $416.60 × 20%

26. James Bryan rented a compact car for 3 days at $34.99 per day plus $0.25 a mile over 150 miles. He purchased collision waiver insurance for $8.50 per day. He drove 500 miles and paid $52 for gasoline. **(a)** What was the total cost of renting the car? **(b)** What was the cost per mile? (Lesson 9.7)

GET READY for the Next Lesson

PREREQUISITE SKILL Finding the Percentage (Skill 30)

Round to the nearest cent.

27. $56.70 × 30% **28.** $9.20 × 60% **29.** $110.28 × 25%

30. $1,012.84 × 81% **31.** $689.54 × 38% **32.** $72.06 × 23%

LESSON 14.2

Trade Discounts—Complement Method

Lesson Objective
Calculate the net price using the complement method.

Content Vocabulary
- complement method

GET READY for the Lesson

Do retail stores make the products they sell?

Blake's Music does not actually make drums; it buys them from manufacturers, then resells them to customers. As Blake's buyer, Eric Watson helps the store make a profit while offering top-quality instruments at bargain prices.

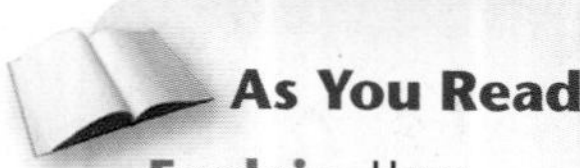

As You Read

Explain How do you find the complement of the trade-discount rate?

Trade Discount–Complement Method The **complement method** is another way of calculating the net price on items that are subject to a trade discount. When you receive a trade discount, you subtract the discount rate from 100%. This gives you the complement of the trade-discount rate, sometimes called the net-price rate or the percent paid. Then you multiply the list price by the complement to find the net price. The formula is:

Net Price = List Price × Complement of Trade-Discount Rate

Percent Paid You can think of the complement of the discount rate as the *percent paid*. It is another **approach** for calculating the net price using the complement method:

Net Price = List Price × Percent Paid

EXAMPLE 1

The list price of a cruise-control module in the wholesaler's catalog is $845. Repair shops receive a 40% trade discount. What is the net price of the module?

Step 1: Find the complement of trade-discount rate.

100% − 40% = 60% complement of trade-discount rate

Step 2: Find the net price.

List Price × Complement of Trade-Discount Rate

$845.00 × 60% = **$507.00 net price**

Concept CHECK

Find the complement and the net price. Check your answers in the back of the book.

1. List price of paint is $24. Trade-discount rate: 30%.
2. List price of glue is $34.50. Trade-discount rate is 25%.

MIXA/Glow Images

Need Help? Go to...

Workshop 38: Problem-Solving Strategy: Writing an Equation, p. 78

EXAMPLE 2 Algebra

Diamond Wholesalers Inc. offers a trade-discount rate that is $\frac{2}{3}$ of the complement of the trade-discount rate. If the list price is $89.97, find the net price and the trade discount.

Step 1: Let r = the complement of the trade-discount rate.

$\frac{2}{3}r$ = the trade-discount rate

Step 2: Write and solve an equation to find the rates.

$$100\% - r = \frac{2}{3}r$$

Multiply both sides by 3 → $300\% - 3r = 2r$

Add $3r$ to both sides → $300\% = 5r$

Divide both sides by 5 → $60\% = r$

The complement of the trade-discount rate is 60%.

The trade-discount rate is (100% − 60%) = 40% or $\frac{2}{3}$ (60%) = 40%

Step 3: Find the net price using the complement.

List Price × Complement of the Trade-Discount Rate

89.97 × 60% = 53.982 = **$53.98 net price**

Step 4: Find the trade discount.

List Price × Trade-Discount Rate

89.97 × 40% = **$35.99 trade discount**

Complete the problems. Check your answers in the back of the book.

3. The Artists' Supply House Inc. offers a trade-discount rate which is 5% less than half the complement of the trade-discount rate. If the list price is $148.50, what is the trade discount? What is the net price?
4. The General Catalog Outlet Co. offers a trade-discount rate that is 3 times its complement. If the net price is $12.40, what is the list price? What is the trade discount?

Did You Know?

Fashion "Knockoffs"

The Council of Fashion Designers of America has asked for legislation giving clothes the same copyright protections as movies, music, and books. "Knockoffs"—near-identical, but less expensive, versions of designer fashions—represent at least 5% of the nearly $200 billion U.S. fashion market.

Lesson Practice

For Problems 5–8, use the complement method to find (a) the complement and (b) the net price. Round to the nearest cent.

	Item	List Price	Trade-Discount Rate	Complement	Net Price
5.	Vacuum Cleaner	$360.00	15%	a.	b.
6.	Exterior Paint	$174.00	32%	a.	b.
7.	Mobile Phone	$216.80	27%	a.	b.
8.	Hand Tools	$ 94.75	9%	a.	b.

For Problems 9 and 10, find the net price.

9. List price for a prom dress is $48.77. Trade-discount rate is 30%.
10. List price for a computer is $2,178.90. Trade-discount rate is 27%.

Reading Math ÷ − ÷ =

Complement
The complement of a percent is the percent that, when added to original percent, will total 100%. For example, the complement of 45% is 55%. 45% added to 55% equals 100%.

11. Andrew's Hardware receives various discounts from its supplier. Find the net price for each amount on the invoice. Round net per item to the nearest cent.

	Stock No.	Description	Quantity	List Price	Discount	Net per Item	Total Net
a.	PT-WG	White paint	36	$18.25	38%		
b.	NA-10	Nails	25	$ 3.69	33%		
c.	HW-132	Paring knife	6	$ 4.95	15%		
d.	HAM-16	Hammer	6	$15.95	20%		
e.	PL-1	Padlock	15	$ 8.50	30%		
f.	LA-22	Ladder	5	$45.00	25%		

12. Gosik Automotive Group receives a 41% trade-discount rate on these auto parts. Determine the total list price and the net price for each part.

	Stock No.	Description	Quantity	List	Total List	Net Price
a.	ED-1	Water pump	2	$155.90		
b.	HL-4	Headlight	4	$ 33.50		
c.	10S	Shock absorber	8	$ 59.95		
d.	PF-91	Sound module	3	$256.50		
e.	SP-15	Speaker	5	$ 35.45		
f.	FB-2	Fan belt	6	$ 28.00		

13. **CHALLENGE PROBLEM** An exhaust system is manufactured and sold to a jobber, who sells it to a wholesaler, who sells it to a retailer. The retailer receives a 40% trade discount from the wholesaler. The wholesaler receives a 33% trade discount from the jobber. The jobber receives a 25% trade discount from the manufacturer. What did each one pay for an exhaust system that retails for $480?

14. **ALGEBRA** The China Company offers a trade-discount rate that is 4 times the complement of the trade-discount rate. If the list price is $58.75, what is the trade discount? What is the net price?

15. **ALGEBRA** Surplus Properties LLC offers a trade-discount rate which is 5% less than twice its complement. If the trade discount is $37.90, what is the list price? What is the net price?

Spiral Review

Solve each proportion. (Skill 23)

16. $\frac{1}{2} = \frac{11}{w}$ **17.** $\frac{m}{6} = \frac{31.5}{42}$ **18.** $\frac{a}{21} = \frac{9}{36}$

19. The replacement value of a home is $175,000. The home is insured for 90% of the replacement value. What is the amount of coverage for personal property? Use **Figure 10.5** on page 391. (Lesson 10.6)

GET READY for the Next Lesson

PREREQUISITE SKILL **Rounding Numbers** (Skill 2)

Round to the nearest cent.

20. $71.8657 **21.** $142.664 **22.** $839.4382

23. $6,591.7221 **24.** $9,889.5656 **25.** $12,436.9948

LESSON 14.3

Chain Discounts

Lesson Objective

Determine the final net price after chain discounts, or a series of trade discounts.

Content Vocabulary

- chain discount
- net-price rate

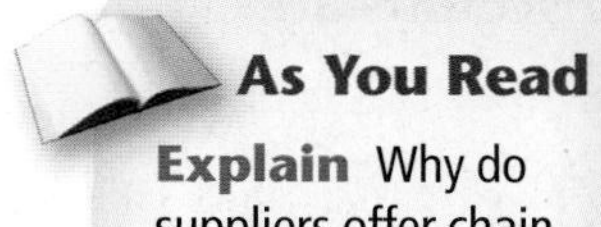

As You Read

Explain Why do suppliers offer chain discounts?

GET READY for the Lesson

How can businesses take advantage of discounts?

Kris Walker purchases sports equipment for Big Sports, a sporting goods retail chain. She buys bathing suits, beach toys, beach blankets and other products at chain discounts to save Big Sports money.

Chain Discounts A chain discount is a series of trade discounts. This is also called a series trade discount. A supplier may offer chain discounts to sell out a discontinued item or to **convince** you to place a larger order. For example:

This does not mean 35% + 20% + 15% off.	**35% less 20% less 15%**	This is often written as 35/20/15.
A 35% discount is deducted from list price to yield first net price.	20% of first net price is deducted from first net price to yield second net price.	15% of second net price is deducted from second net price to yield the final net price.

The complement method applied to trade discounts in Lesson 14.2 can also be applied to chain discounts. First subtract each discount from 100% to find the complements. Then multiply the complements to find the percent that you actually pay. This percent is called the **net-price rate**.

Net-Price Rate = Product of Complements of Chain-Discount Rates

To find the net price, multiply the net-price rate by the list price.

Net Price = List Price × Net-Price Rate

EXAMPLE 1

Lawn Corporation produces a $4\frac{1}{2}$-horsepower lawn mower, which is priced at $695. A new model is ready for production, so the $4\frac{1}{2}$-horsepower model will be discontinued. Lawn Corporation is offering a chain discount of 20% less 10%, also written as 20/10. What is the final net price of the lawn mower?

Step 1: Find the first discount.

List Price × Discount Rate

$695.00 × 20% = $139.00

Continued on next page

Step 2: Find the first net price.

List Price − Discount

$695.00 − $139.00 = $556.00

Step 3: Find the second discount.

$556.00 × 10% = $55.60

Step 4: Find the final net price.

$556.00 − $55.60 = **$500.40 final net price**

695 M+ × 20 % 139 M− RM 556 × 10 %
55.6 M− RM 500.4

Concept CHECK

Complete the problems. Check your answers in the back of the book. The list price of a wool suit is $400. The chain discounts are 30% less 25%.

1. Find the first net price.
2. Find the final net price.

EXAMPLE 2

Calculate the net price of the lawn mower in **Example 1** using the net-price rate.

Step 1: Find the complements.

Complement of 20%: 100% − 20% = 80%

Complement of 10%: 100% − 10% = 90%

Step 2: Find the net-price rate.

Product of Complements of Chain-Discount Rates

80% × 90% = 72% net-price rate or percent paid

Step 3: Find the net price.

List Price × Net-Price Rate

$695 × 72% = **$500.40 net price**

Same answer as found in Example 1.

Concept CHECK

Complete the problem. Check your answers in the back of the book. List price for Model 36XCL motorboat is $2,560. Chain discounts are 30% less 10% less 5%.

3. Find the net-price rate.
4. Find the net price.

SPREADSHEET APPLICATION

Chain Discounts

You can use a spreadsheet to calculate an item's net price after a series of trade discounts. Enter the number ordered, list price, and the trade discounts for each item. The amount, net price and the cost per item are computed automatically.

Math Online Go to **connectED.mcgraw-hill.com** to download a spreadsheet application for this activity.

	A	B	C	D	E	F	G	H	I
1						Trade Discounts			
2	Item	Number Ordered	List Price	Amount	1st	2nd	3rd	Net Price	Cost Per Item
3	Jacket			$0.00				$0.00	$0.00
4	Vest			$0.00				$0.00	$0.00

Jacket, 48, $129.95, 40%, 10%, 5%
Vest, 72, $79.95, 50%, 0%, 0%
Gloves, 72, $15.95, 40%, 15%, 0%
Jeans, 144, $29.95, 40%, 10%, 5%
T-shirt, 36, $8.95, 50%, 5%, 0%

Think and Discuss

1. What is the cost per jacket?
2. What is the cost per T-shirt?
3. What is the total net price for all the items?

Study Tip

Notes
Take notes and write down a summary of the important ideas as you read through new material.

Lesson Practice

	Item	List Price	Chain Discount	First Discount	First Net Price	Second Discount	Final Net Price
5.	Office Supplies	$ 780	25% less 15%	$195.00	$585.00	a.	b.
6.	Fancy Boxes	$1,240	20% less 15%	a.	b.	c.	d.
7.	Garden Shovels	$ 475	40% less 30%	a.	b.	c.	d.
8.	Backpacks	$2,170	40% less 25%	a.	b.	c.	d.

For Problems 9 and 10, determine the net price.

9. A pair of leather shoes has a list price of $74.95. Chain discount is 30/10.

10. A cordless phone has a list price of $125.50. Chain discount is 40/20.

For Problems 11–16, find the (a) net-price rate and (b) net price. Round the trade-discount rate to the nearest tenth of a percent.

	Item	List Price	Chain Discount			Net-Price Rate	Net Price
11.	GPS Map	$ 620.00	30%	20%	—	a.	b.
12.	Camera	$ 140.00	20%	15%	—	a.	b.
13.	Bicycle	$ 436.00	40%	20%	—	a.	b.
14.	Printer	$1,237.00	40%	30%	—	a.	b.
15.	Water Filter	$ 147.80	30%	20%	10%	a.	b.
16.	Wall Paper	$ 96.46	20%	10%	5%	a.	b.

For Problems 17 and 18, determine (a) the net-price rate and (b) the net price.

17. A computer has a list price of $2,150. The chain discount is 15/10.

18. A calculator has a list price of $74.85. The chain discount is 40/15/5.

19. Larson, Inc. offers Mark Stores chain discounts of 30/15. What is the net price for each item?

Item	List Price
Storm door	$197.80
Replacement window	$379.85
Basement window	$185.50
Storm door closer	$ 22.95
Replacement latch	$ 12.50
Weather stripping	$ 10.50

20. General Saw Corporation manufactures tools for concrete construction companies and offers trade discounts and additional discounts to encourage large orders. What is the net price per item if each invoice total is high enough to obtain the additional discount?

Item	List Price	Trade Discount	Additional Discount
Masonry drill	$98.80	50%	5% (if invoice total is over $250)
Ram-tip drill	$76.75	40%	10% (if invoice total is over $500)
Hole saw	$62.53	30%	20% (if invoice total is over $1,000)

H.O.T. Problems

21. CHALLENGE PROBLEM What is the final net price for each of these overstocked items from the Everything Automotive Parts list?

Part Number	Suggested List Price	Chain Discount
B7S	$914.80	40% less 25% less 15%
C37X	$247.50	42% less 22% less 10%
173A	$ 76.67	35% less 15% less 5%
B62Y	$ 8.54	25% less 10% less 7%

Spiral Review

Round to the place value indicated. (Skill 2)

22. $17.71155 (nearest cent)

23. $113.7051 (nearest dollar)

24. 17.98% (nearest tenth of a percent)

25. $8,178.1449 (nearest cent)

26. Sandra Keegan worked 38 hours at $12.95 per hour and 6 hours of overtime at time and a half. What was her pay for the week? (Lesson 1.2)

27. Serena Austin rents a compact car for 2 days for $49.95 a day with unlimited miles. She purchases collision waiver insurance for $21.50 per day. She drives 90 miles each day and pays $28.39 for gasoline. What is the total rental cost? (Lesson 9.7)

GET READY for the Next Lesson

PREREQUISITE SKILL **Subtracting Decimals** (Skill 6)

Subtract.

28. $64.30 − $9.84

29. $86.12 − $31.49

30. $481.93 − $74.15

31. $694.78 − $346.27

32. $8,117.88 − $951.47

33. $54,297.22 − $23,012.10

Cash Discounts—Ordinary Dating

Lesson Objective

Compute the cash price when the discount is based on ordinary dating.

Content Vocabulary

- invoice
- cash discount
- ordinary dating

GET READY for the Lesson

How does the supplier-retailer relationship work?

Matthew Manuel is a supplier for a company that makes educational video games. When retail stores order games from him, he sends with the shipment an invoice showing the amount to be paid. This amount can change depending on how soon the bill is paid.

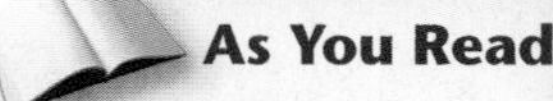

As You Read

Identify Give one reason suppliers might offer a cash discount.

Ordinary Dating You receive an **invoice** for each purchase you make from a supplier. The invoice **itemizes** the quantities and costs of the items purchased. To encourage you to make a prompt payment, the supplier may offer a **cash discount** if the bill is paid within a certain number of days. The exact terms of the discount are stated on the invoice. Many suppliers use **ordinary dating**. You might see suppliers write the ordinary dating one of two ways:

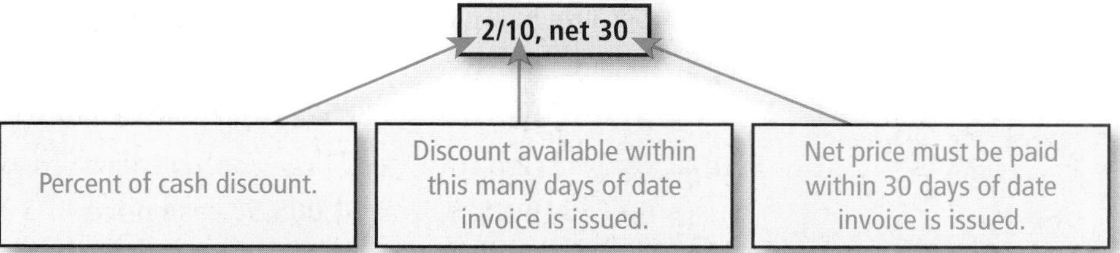

You may also see the ordinary dating written like this: 2/10, n/30. It means the same thing as 2/10, net 30.

The cash discount is a percent of the net price on the invoice and is computed using this formula.

Cash Discount = Net Price × Cash-Discount Rate

The **cash price** is the amount you actually pay the supplier.

Cash Price = Net Price − Cash Discount

Another method to determine the cash price is to use the complement of the cash-discount rate.

Cash Price = Net Price × Complement of Cash-Discount Rate

Note that the invoice must be paid during the cash discount period in order to receive the cash discount.

EXAMPLE

This is part of an invoice that the Lighting Store received for a shipment of lamps. What is the last day the discount can be taken? What is the last day to pay the invoice? What is the cash discount? What is the cash price of the lamps if the bill is paid within ten days? What is the cash price using the complement method?

Oak Hill Lighting

Ship To: The Lighting Store **Invoice No.:** 4-3467
Date: June 5, 20-- **Order No.:** Lh3019 **Terms:** 2/10, Net 30 **Acct. No.:** 712E 4

Style	Color	Qty.	Price	Amount
A9407	BGE	8	$37.25	$ 298.00
A9841	GRN	6	42.15	252.90
J2113	NVY	10	26.40	264.00
J2114	GRN	8	26.40	211.20
			TOTAL	**$1,026.10**

Step 1: Find the last day the discount can be taken.

Date of invoice: June 5; Terms: 2/10, net 30

Discount can be taken until June 15—10 days from date of invoice.

Step 2: Find the last day to pay the invoice.

Terms: 2/10, net 30. The "net 30" means the invoice must be paid by: June 05 + 30 days = June 35 (which does not exist). Obviously you are into July, and because June has 30 days, you subtract 30 days: June 35 – 30 = **July 05**

Step 3: Find the cash discount: Net Price × Cash-Discount Rate = cash discount

$1,026.10 × 2% = **$20.522 or $20.52 cash discount**

Step 4: Find the cash price: Net Price – Cash Discount = cash price

$1,026.10 – $20.52 = **$1,005.58 cash price**

Step 5: Find the cash price using the complement method.

Net Price × Complement of Cash-Discount Rate

1,026.10 × (1.00 – 0.02) =

1,026.10 × 0.98 = 1,005.578 = **$1,005.58 cash price**

1026.1 M+ × 2 % 20.522 M– RM 1005.578

Reading Math +–÷=

Context

When reading numbers, be aware of the context. Sometimes numbers are defined by the context in which they are written. For example, in the context of cash discounts, the expression "3/10" is not a fraction. It represents the terms of a discount.

Concept CHECK

Complete the problems. Check your answers in the back of the book. Date is July 8. Terms are 3/10, n/30. Net price is $640. Determine the following:

1. Last day to take the discount.
2. Last day to pay the invoice.
3. Cash discount.
4. Cash price.
5. Complement of the cash discount.
6. Cash price using the complement method.

Did You Know?

The HP-35 Hewlett-Packard recently celebrated the 35th anniversary of its innovative scientific calculator, the HP-35. Before the HP-35, calculators could only add, subtract, multiply, and divide. The HP-35 could perform trigonometric, logarithmic, and exponential functions.

Lesson Practice

Complete the table.

	Invoice Date	Terms	Last Date to Take Discount	Last Date to Pay Invoice	Date Paid	Net Price	Cash Discount	Cash Price
7.	9-Apr.	2/10, n/30	19-Apr.	9-May	12-Apr.	$ 740.00	$14.80	a.
8.	6-May	3/10, n/30	16-May	5-June	13-May	$ 516.40	a.	b.
9.	3-Sept.	5/15, n/30	a.	b.	23-Sept.	$ 348.64	c.	d.
10.	22-Nov.	7/10, n/30	a.	b.	1-Dec.	$4,178.45	c.	d.

For Problems 11 and 12, determine (a) the last date to take the cash discount; (b) the last date to pay the invoice; (c) the cash discount; (d) the cash price; and (e) the cash price using the complement method.

11. Net price for hardware is $6,715.80. Terms are 4/10, n/30. Date of invoice is October 7. Date paid is October 14.

12. Net price for auto parts is $614.85. Terms are 5/15, net 30. Date of invoice is December 11. Invoice is paid on December 30.

13. An invoice from the Computer Superstore shows a net price of $15,988.32. The terms are 4/15, n/40. The invoice is dated July 18. The invoice is paid August 3. What is the last day to take the discount? What is the last day to pay the invoice? How much is paid on August 3?

14. CHALLENGE PROBLEM An invoice to Sports Corner, Inc. is dated July 12 and carries terms of 3/10, net/30. The net price is $398.50 and the invoice will be paid on July 19. **(a)** Compute the cash price by finding the cash discount and then the cash price. **(b)** Compute the cash price by using the complement method. **(c)** Which answer is correct? **(d)** Explain why the answers are different.

Spiral Review

Subtract. (Skill 6)

15. $916.70 − $27.50 **16.** $3,178.42 − $127.14 **17.** $9,784.52 − $489.21

18. ALGEBRA For a store Grand Opening sale the entire stock of name brand jeans for women is marked down 75% from 6 AM to 10 AM on Wednesday only. The sale price on the jeans during this time is $22.99. What will the regular selling price be after 10 AM? (Lesson 6.7)

GET READY for the Next Lesson

PREREQUISITE SKILL Finding the Percentage (Skill 30)

Find the percentage.

19. $45,860 × 15%

20. $186,933 × 20%

21. $77,462 × 25%

22. $65,500 × 28%

23. $253,750 × 32%

24. $743,920 × 46%

LESSON 14.5

Cash Discounts—EOM Dating

Lesson Objective
Calculate the cash price when the discount is based on end-of-month dating.

Content Vocabulary
- end-of-month dating

GET READY for the Lesson

Do you have any monthly routines?

Bill Demopoulos works a lot of hours as the owner of a tour company in New Orleans, but he puts in a few more hours at the end of each month. It is the time when he pays suppliers' invoices, pays employee wages and salaries, and collects debts from customers.

©Steve Hamblin/Alamy

As You Read
Explain What is your definition of *end-of-month dating*?

End-of-Month Dating Many suppliers and wholesalers use **end-of-month dating** when **granting** cash discounts. With this method of dating, your business receives a cash discount if you pay for your merchandise within a certain number of days after the end of the month. For example:

6/10 EOM

Percent of cash discount.

Discount given if bill paid within this many days after the *end of the month* (EOM) in which the invoice is issued.

Although it is not stated, it is understood that the full amount is due 20 days after the last day for taking the discount. You calculate the discount and cash price as follows:

Cash Discount = Net Price × Cash-Discount Rate

Cash Price = Net Price − Cash Discount

As noted in the previous lesson, the cash price can be calculated using the complement of the cash-discount rate.

EXAMPLE 1

Bob's Drugstore received this invoice from General Wholesalers. What is the last day that Bob's can take advantage of the 4% cash discount? What is the last day to pay the invoice? Find the cash discount, the cash price, and the cash price using the complement method.

Date	Invoice No.	Acct. No.	Store No.	Terms	Vendor No.
July 12	213788-6	208 712	34	4/10 EOM	1207

Salesperson 38L **Via UPS** **Order Reg. No.** 0547-6

Customer Order No.	Style	Quantity	Price	Amount
L3075	02673	10	$17.80	$178.00
L3076	02677	15	24.17	362.55
L3077	02681	25	7.46	186.50
			TOTAL	$727.05

Step 1: Find the last day a discount can be taken.

Date of invoice: July 12 Terms: 4/10 EOM

Discount can be taken until August 10—10 days after the end of July.

Step 2: Find the last day to pay the invoice.

Terms: 4/10 EOM

The full amount is due 20 days after the discount date.

August 10 + 20 = **August 30 last day to pay invoice**

Step 3: Find the cash discount: Net Price × Cash-Discount Rate = cash discount

$727.05 × 4% = **$29.082 or $29.08 cash discount**

Step 4: Find the cash price: Net Price – Cash Discount = cash price

$727.05 – $29.08 = **$697.97 cash price**

Step 5: Find the cash price using the complement method.

Net Price × Complement of Cash Discount Rate

727.05 × (1.00 – 0.04) =

727.05 × 0.96 = 697.968 = **$697.97 cash price**

Study Tip

Start Simple

Try the simpler questions first to help build up your confidence for the harder questions.

Concept CHECK

Complete the problems. Check your answers in the back of the book. An invoice dated November 7 has terms of 2/10 EOM. Net price is $7,100. The invoice is paid December 9. Determine the following:

1. Last day to take the discount.
2. Last day to pay the invoice.
3. Cash discount.
4. Cash price.
5. Complement of the cash discount.
6. Cash price using the complement method.

Extensions When EOM dating is involved, it is common business practice to grant a one-month extension on invoices dated on or after the 26th of the month. An invoice dated June 28 with terms of 3/10 EOM is considered to be dated July 1, and the cash discount may be taken for 10 days after the end of July or until August 10.

EXAMPLE 2

An invoice dated November 27 has terms of 2/10 EOM. Net price is $8,100. The invoice is paid January 9. When is the last day that the 2% cash discount can be taken and the last day to pay the invoice? Find the cash price using the complement method.

Step 1: Find the last day a discount can be taken and the last day to pay the invoice.

Date of invoice: November 27, which is after the 26th. A 1-month extension is granted.

A 1-month extension means **the discount can be taken until January 10—10 days after the end of December.**

The invoice must be paid by January 10 + 20 = January 30.

Step 2: Find the cash price using the complement method.

$8,100 × (100% – 2%) = $8,100 × 0.98 = **$7,938 cash price**

Complete the problems. Check your answers in the back of the book. An invoice dated February 27 has terms of 3/10 EOM. The net price is $2,400.

7. Find the last day to take a discount

8. Find the last day to pay the invoice.

9. Find the cash price using the complement method.

Lesson Practice

	Invoice Date	Terms	Last Date to Take Discount	Last Date to Pay Invoice	Date Paid	Net Price	Cash Discount	Cash Price
10.	Feb. 21	2/10 EOM	Mar. 10	Mar. 30	Mar. 6	$ 615.00	$12.30	a.
11.	April 14	3/15 EOM	May 15	a.	May 12	1,417.80	b.	c.
12.	Sept. 2	4/10 EOM	a.	b.	Oct. 9	7,184.73	c.	d.
13.	Dec. 29	5/10 EOM	a.	b.	Feb. 8	16,517.84	c.	d.

Did You Know?

The Tuxedo Tuxedo Park was an exclusive community built outside of New York City in the 19th century. At Tuxedo Park's 1886 Autumn Ball, a few male guests wore dinner jackets with scarlet, satin lapels, an idea picked up from England's future King Edward VII. This garment became known as the tuxedo.

For Problems 14 and 15, determine (a) the last date to take the cash discount; (b) the last date to pay the invoice; (c) the cash discount; and (d) the cash price.

14. Net price is $916.40.
Terms are 1/10 EOM.
Invoice date is September 20.
Invoice is paid on October 9.

15. Net price is $7,641.60.
Terms are 6/10 EOM, n/30 EOM.
Invoice date is May 29.
Invoice is paid on July 29.

16. An invoice that Gentlemen's Clothiers sent to Champion Tux Rentals shows a net price of $761.87. The terms are 5/15 EOM, n/30 EOM. The invoice is dated August 14. The invoice is paid September 15. What is the last day to take the discount? What is the last day to pay the invoice? How much is paid on September 15?

17. CHALLENGE PROBLEM An invoice from Krio Foods Corporation to Barr Wholesalers carries a net price of $26,715.81. The terms are 7/10 EOM. The invoice is dated Feb. 28. The invoice is paid April 17. What is the last day to take the discount? What is the last day to pay the invoice? What is the cash price?

Spiral Review

Find the percent. (Skill 30)

18. $821.00 × 2% **19.** $12,643.17 × 8% **20.** $8,614.50 × 97%

21. ALGEBRA Adrian Betz earned $110.00 in simple interest in 9 months at an annual interest rate of 8%. How much money did she invest? (Lesson 5.4)

GET READY for the Next Lesson

PREREQUISITE SKILL Subtracting Whole Numbers (Skill 4)

Subtract.

22. 385 – 96 **23.** 86 – 57 **24.** 682 – 272 **25.** 7,935 – 1,012

LESSON 14.6

Inventory

Lesson Objective
Calculate inventory.

Content Vocabulary
- inventory
- stock reorder point

GET READY for the Lesson

Have you been to a store that is sold out of a favorite product?

Allen Foods closes at midnight, but this is when DeMarcus Brown and Patrick Smythe start work. Between midnight and 8 AM they go through the grocery store, recording how much of each product is in stock so popular items can be reordered.

As You Read

Explain Why might keeping an inventory record be important?

Inventory Balances The **inventory** of a business is the items that it has in stock. Records of the items on hand (in stock) may be kept either on a computer or inventory cards. To determine the inventory, you start with the previous inventory. The number of incoming items, called receipts, is added to the previous inventory. The number of outgoing items, called **issues**, is subtracted from the previous inventory. This is frequently done on a computer using Universal Pricing Code (UPC) labels. The basic formula is:

Inventory = Previous Inventory + Receipts − Issues

The inventory record also indicates the **stock reorder point**. This is the minimum level of inventory needed to meet customer demand. When the inventory falls below the stock reorder point, a new order must be placed.

EXAMPLE

The inventory record for Wholesale Paint Supply shows that 80 rolls of masking tape, stock number WL-9, were in inventory on February 1. Each week the inventory record is updated. How many rolls were on hand March 1? When did the inventory fall below the reorder point?

Item: Masking Tape			Stock Number: WL-9	
Week of	Opening Balance	Units Receipts (Qty. In)	Issues (Qty. Out)	Inventory at End of Week
Feb. 1	80	40	62	58
Feb. 8	58	0	25	33
Feb. 15	33	80	28	85
Feb. 22	85	40	37	88
Mar. 1	88		Reorder Point: 80	

Inventory at beginning of week — Number on hand

Step 1: Calculate the inventory on hand.

	Opening Balance	+	Units Receipts (Qty. In)	−	Issues (Qty. Out)	=	Number on Hand
Week of February 1:	80	+	40	−	62	=	58
Week of February 8:	58	+	0	−	25	=	33
Week of February 15:	33	+	80	−	28	=	85
Week of February 22:	85	+	40	−	37	=	**88 on hand March 1**

The inventory fell below the reorder point at the end of the week of February 1 and 8.

Study Tip

Make Time

Block out a period of time each day for studying. Be flexible enough that if something unexpected comes up, you can study at a different time.

Concept CHECK

Complete the problems. Check your answers in the back of the book. The inventory record for the Affiliated Lumber Company shows the status of 4-by-8 sheets of wallboard. Complete the inventory record.

	Month		Opening Balance	Units Receipts (Qty. In)	Issues (Qty. Out)		Number on Hand
1.	January		300	120	150	a.	
2.	February		270	80	140	a.	
3.	March	a.		120	100	b.	
4.	April	a.		0	80	b.	
					Reorder Point: 275		

5. When did the inventory fall below the reorder point?

Lesson Practice

6. The Key Auto Supply Company takes an inventory on a monthly basis. What is the inventory on hand for each item?

Description		Opening Balance	Units Receipts (Qty. In)	Issues (Qty. Out)		Number on Hand
10W-30 oil quarts		147	50	78	a.	
Washer solvent		91	36	45	b.	
5-gal. oil		17	12	23	c.	
Transmission fluid		18	16	28	d.	

7. Complete the inventory card for the dictionaries at the campus bookstore. Use the completed card to determine the stock reorder point.

Last Action Date		Opening Balance	Units Receipts (Qty. In)	Issues (Qty. Out)		Number on Hand
3-Sept.		0	225	0		225
10-Sept.		a.		97	b.	
17-Sept.		a.		54	b.	
24-Sept.		a.		40	b.	
1-Oct.		a.	144	20	b.	
8-Oct.		a.		43	b.	

Did You Know?

Smart Home Hardware chain The Home Depot recently agreed to sponsor an eco-conscious, 6,000 square foot dormitory being built at Duke University in North Carolina. The solar-powered "Smart Home" is designed to be a home and laboratory for engineering students who will test environmental design ideas.

8. Whitewater Supply Company has this inventory record for its inflatable vests. Find the number on hand for each date.

Item History		Date	Units Receipts	Issues		Number on hand
Part No. IV-17		1-June	76			76
Description:		12-June		36	a.	
Inflatable vest		18-June	44		b.	
Location: 24		26-June		58	c.	

9. An inventory record for Wholesale Hardware Supply shows a receipt of 100 chain saws on April 1. Another shipment of 125 arrived on April 15. On May 10, 110 chain saws were shipped out. On June 2, 50 arrived and on June 17, 75 were shipped out. Find the number on hand as of June 17.

10. On January 1 Sport Wholesalers started with an inventory of 175 soccer balls. Shipments of 45, 76, and 25 were sent out on January 13, February 18, and March 11, respectively. Receipts of 36, 144, and 72 were received on January 20, February 25, and March 15, respectively. Find the number on hand as of March 15.

11. **CHALLENGE PROBLEM** The Car Care Company started on August 1 with a balance of 47 cases of car wax. On August 6, 24 cases were shipped out. On August 16, 40 cases were received. On August 27, 36 cases were shipped out, and on August 31, 50 cases were received. Prepare an inventory card showing the balance after each transaction.

12. **CHALLENGE PROBLEM** Sunrise Wholesale Patio Supply began on July 1 with a balance of 74 folding canvas lounge chairs. It received shipments of 30 and 24 chairs on July 20 and September 20, respectively. It made shipments of 24, 40, and 36 chairs on July 17, August 22, and September 30, respectively. Prepare an inventory card showing the number on hand after each transaction.

Spiral Review

Add or Subtract. (Skill 3, 4)

13. 125 + 45 + 25 **14.** 144 − 50 **15.** 7,146 + 5,268 **16.** 14,147 − 9,749

17. ALGEBRA Hector Williams had his annual performance review. He received a merit increase of 3.2% and a cost-of-living increase of 2.3%. His annual salary after the increases is $56,326.50. Find Hector's merit increase, cost-of-living increase, and his annual salary before the two increases took effect. (Lesson 13.2)

GET READY for the Next Lesson

PREREQUISITE SKILL **Dividing Decimals** (Skill 11)

Divide. Round to the nearest tenth.

18. 45.60 ÷ 61.00
19. 7.89 ÷ 9.99
20. 67.59 ÷ 145.35
21. 784.08 ÷ 3,539.50
22. 5.75 ÷ 19.50
23. 1,569.42 ÷ 12,864.94

LESSON 14.7

Valuing Inventory

Lesson Objective

Use the average-cost, FIFO, and LIFO methods to compute inventory value.

Content Vocabulary

- average-cost method
- first in, first out (FIFO)
- last in, first out (LIFO)

GET READY for the Lesson

How do business owners know if they are making money?

Kendra Bailey, owner of Kendra's Garden Center, wants to know how much income the center had during April, a busy month. To find out, she must calculate the value of all the plants, trees, supplies, and other goods that are on hand at the end of the month.

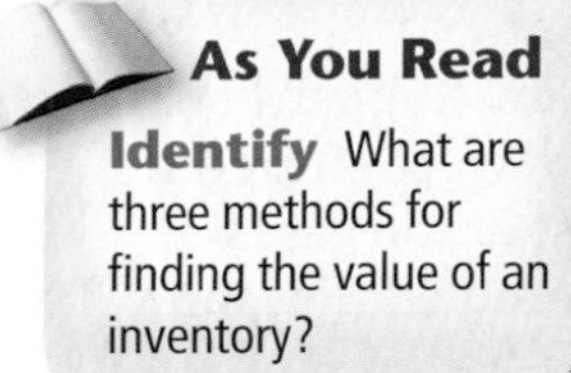

As You Read

Identify What are three methods for finding the value of an inventory?

Inventory Valuation Methods The inventory on hand at the end of a period is the ending inventory. This inventory value is needed when you purchase insurance or compute the worth of your business. The cost of goods sold is the value of the inventory you sold during a period. This value is used to calculate the income your business earned. You must choose a method to value your inventory that best fits the business and use it consistently.

Average-Cost Valuation Method The cost of incoming items (purchases) often varies over time. The **average-cost method** of valuing inventory is based on the average cost of the goods you received. The formula for valuing your inventory is:

Inventory Value = Average Cost per Unit × Number on Hand

EXAMPLE 1

Wholesale Paint Supply is valuing its inventory of masking tape. On February 28, the last day of the month, Wholesale Paint Supply had 88 rolls of masking tape on hand. What is the value of the ending inventory for February?

Item: Latex paint, white		Stock Number: WL-9-gallons	
Week of	Units Received	Unit Cost	Total Cost
Feb. 1	80	$2.15	$172.00
Feb. 8	40	2.25	90.00
Feb. 15	80	2.30	184.00
Feb. 22	40	2.40	96.00
Total	**240**		**$542.00**

Number on hand at beginning of week

Average cost in January

Step 1: Find the average cost per unit.

$$\frac{\text{Total Cost of Units}}{\text{Number Received}} = \frac{\$542}{240} = \$2.283 = \$2.26$$

The average cost per unit is $2.26

Step 2: Find the inventory value.

Average Cost per Unit × Number on Hand

$2.26 × 88 = **$198.88 inventory value**

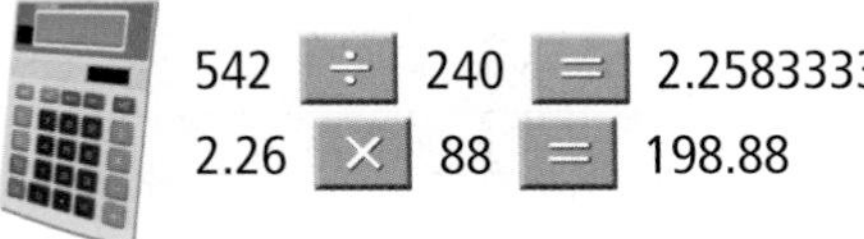

Concept CHECK

Complete the problems. Check your answers in the back of the book. Two items are purchased: 100 packs of felt pens at $4.00 each and 60 packs of felt pens at $3.80 each. (A pack contains 3 felt pens.)

1. Find the average cost per pack.
2. Find the ending inventory value if 50 packs were on hand at the end of the period.

FIFO For most businesses the **physical** flow of inventory is "the first item purchased is the first item sold." The **first in, first out (FIFO)** method assumes that the oldest merchandise is sold first. Therefore, the most recent items purchased remain in inventory. For example, milk sold at the supermarket is stocked as first in, first out. As milk is sold, the most recent purchases of milk are added to the back of the shelves.

EXAMPLE 2

For Wholesale Paint Supply in **Example 1,** use the FIFO method to find the cost of goods sold and the value of the 88 units in ending inventory.

Step 1: Find the cost of goods sold using the FIFO method.

a. Determine the number of units sold.

240 units received (refer to the table in **Example 1**)
− 88 units on hand
152 units sold

b. Assign a value to the units sold. With FIFO, the 152 units sold are assumed to be the earliest units received (first in) as follows:

Week of	Units Received	Unit Cost	Total Cost
Feb. 1 (Beginning Inventory)	80	$2.15	$172.00
Feb. 8	40	2.25	90.00
Feb. 15	32*	2.30	73.60
	152		$335.60

*Of the 80 units received on Feb. 15 (refer to the table in **Example 1**), only 32 were sold. The other 48 (80 − 32) remain in inventory.

c. Add the total cost of the units sold.

$172.00 + $90.00 + $73.60 = **$335.60 cost of goods sold using FIFO**

Step 2: Find the value of the 88 units in ending inventory using FIFO.

a. Assign a value to the ending inventory. The items remaining are assumed to be the most recent units received, as follows:

Continued on next page

Week of	Units Received	Unit Cost	Total Cost
Feb. 15	48**	$2.30	$110.40
Feb. 22	40	2.40	96.00
	88		$206.40

Of the 80 units received on Feb. 15 (refer to the table in **Example 1 on page 536), only 32 were sold. The other 48 (80 − 32) remain in inventory.

b. Add the cost of the ending inventory.
$110.40 + $96.00 = **$206.40 ending inventory value using FIFO**

LIFO Some businesses might use the **last in, first out (LIFO)** method. This method assumes that the most recently purchased merchandise (last in) is sold first. Therefore the oldest units are still on hand at the end of the period. The physical flow of a stone and gravel company is last in, first out. When new gravel is received, it is placed on top of the old gravel. The latest gravel received is the first sold.

EXAMPLE 3

For Wholesale Paint Supply in **Example 1** on page 536, use the LIFO method to find the cost of goods sold and the value of the 88 units in ending inventory.

Step 1: Find the cost of goods sold using the LIFO method.

a. Determine the number of units sold.
240 units received (refer to the table in **Example 1** on page 536)
− 88 units on hand
152 units sold

b. Assign a value to the units sold. With LIFO, the 152 units sold are assumed to be the most recent units received (last in) as follows:

Week of	Units Received	Unit Cost	Total Cost
Feb. 22	40	$2.40	$ 96.00
Feb. 15	80	2.30	184.00
Feb. 8	32*	2.25	72.00
	152		$352.00

*Of the 40 units received on Feb. 8 (refer to the table in **Example 1** on page 536), only 32 were sold. The other 8 (40 − 32) remain in inventory.

c. Add the total cost of the units sold.
$96.00 + 184.00 + 72.00 = **$352.00 cost of goods sold using LIFO**

Step 2: Find the value of the 88 units in ending inventory using LIFO.
(Note: 88 units are on hand—refer to Step 2 in **Example 1** on page 536.)

a. Assign a value to the ending inventory. The items remaining are assumed to be the most recent units received, as follows:

Week of	Units Received	Unit Cost	Total Cost
Feb. 1	80	$2.15	$172.00
Feb. 8	8**	2.25	18.00
	88		$190.00

Of the 40 units received on Feb. 8 (refer to the table in **Example 1 on page 536), only 32 were sold. The other 8 (40 − 32) remain in inventory.

b. Add the total cost of the units sold.

$172.00 + $18.00 = **$190.00 ending inventory value using LIFO**

Concept CHECK

Complete the problems. Check your answers in the back of the book. Assume the 100 packs of felt pens bought at $4.00 each in Problem 1 were purchased first, before the 60 packs of felt pens bought at $3.80 each. 50 packs were on hand at the end of the period.

3. Find the cost of goods sold and the value of the ending inventory using FIFO.

4. Find the cost of goods sold and the value of the ending inventory using LIFO.

Lesson Practice

Reading Math +−÷=

Average
The word *average* means the result obtained by totaling a number of quantities and then dividing by the number of quantities that were totaled.

5. Kitchen World is valuing its inventory of popcorn poppers using the average-cost method. On May 31 Kitchen World had 23 poppers on hand.

(a) What is the average cost per popper?

(b) What is the ending inventory value for May?

Week of	Units Received	Unit Cost	Total Cost
May 1	40	$22.10	$ 884.00
May 8	36	22.15	797.40
May 15	24	22.20	532.80
May 22	36	22.15	797.40
May 29	12	22.25	267.00
Total	**148**	—	**$3,278.60**

6. Granola bars came 16 to the box. Number of boxes on hand on February 8 is 20. Complete the table and then find **(a)** the average cost per unit and **(b)** the value of the inventory using the average-cost method.

Date	Units Received	Unit Cost	Total Cost
12/18	50	$17.99	
01/10	50	19.79	
02/06	40	18.48	
Total		—	

7. Records for Chief Super Market show this opening balance and these receipts for vegetable soup in November. At the end of the month, 31 cans were on hand. What is the value of the ending inventory using the average-cost method?

Date	Units Received	Unit Cost
11/01 (Opening bal.)	94	$1.32
11/10	72	1.30
11/17	36	1.32
11/24	48	1.31

 **Did You Know?**

Swimming Pool Costs and Values **According to recent estimates, the average in-ground, backyard swimming pool costs between $10,000 and $40,000. Above-ground pools cost between $150 and $10,000. Analysts say that pools do not usually add significant property value, but can be a deciding factor for many buyers.**

8. At the end of the month, 79 packages of windshield wipers were on hand. Find the ending inventory value using the average-cost method.

Date	Units Received	Unit Cost
5/01	96	$19.43
5/19	72	19.56
5/31	48	19.63

9. The Leisure Company, a swimming pool supply company, uses the FIFO method of valuing inventory. As of May 31 the Leisure Company had sold 160 of the packets of chlorine.

Date	Units Received	Unit Cost	Total Cost
5/01	100	$9.65	
5/08	65	9.75	
5/19	145	9.90	
Total			

(a) Complete the records for units received of packets of chlorine.

(b) Use the FIFO method to find the cost of the 160 packets sold.

(c) Use the FIFO method to find the value of the 150 packets in ending inventory.

100 at $9.65	=		Of the 65 received on 5/8	5 at $9.75	=	
60 at $9.75	=			145 at $9.90	=	
160 Total				**150 Total**		

10. Suppose that the Leisure Company in Problem 9 used the LIFO method of valuing inventory.

(a) Use the LIFO method to calculate the value of the Leisure Company's 150 packets in ending inventory.

(b) Use the average-cost method to calculate the value of the Leisure Company's 150 packets in ending inventory.

Spiral Review

Multiply or Divide. (Skill 8, 11)

11. 72 × $36.90 **12.** $1,046.25 ÷ 125 **13.** $357.81 ÷ 410

14. **ALGEBRA** Ace Electronics has a budget for total recruiting costs of $28,000. They have spent $2,900 on advertising expenses and $7,200 on interviewing expenses. They are willing to pay an 8% commission on selling the selected individual's home. What is the maximum selling price on which Ace would pay 8% commission and stay within budget? (Lesson 13.1)

GET READY for the Next Lesson

PREREQUISITE SKILL **Finding the Percentage** (Skill 30)

Round to the nearest cent.

15. $681.43 × 54% **16.** $591.00 × 12% **17.** $953.56 × 48%

18. $197.54 × 6% **19.** $720.41 × 90% **20.** $928.45 × 26%

Design Pics/Carson Ganci

LESSON 14.8

Carrying Inventory

Lesson Objective

Calculate the annual cost of carrying inventory.

Content Vocabulary

- carrying inventory

GET READY for the Lesson

Can a business have too much of a supply?

Christine Murphy is an inventory control manager at an auto factory. Her job is to maintain the right amount of items such as door handles on hand—if there are too few, the assembly line might have to stop. If there are too many, the cost of carrying them would be too high.

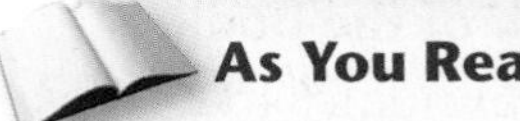

As You Read

List What is included in the annual cost of carrying an inventory?

Carrying Inventory Your business must keep an **adequate** inventory of goods to meet production or sales needs. Based on past records, you may estimate the annual cost of **carrying inventory** (or maintaining) at a certain level for the coming year. The annual cost is often expressed as a percent of the value of the inventory. The annual cost of carrying the inventory includes taxes, insurance, storage fees, and handling charges. The essential formula is:

Annual Cost of Carrying Inventory = Inventory Value × Percent

EXAMPLE 1

Steel Facilitators estimates the annual cost of carrying its inventory to be 25% of the value of the inventory. This year the company plans to maintain inventory totaling $500,000 in value. What amount should be set as the estimated cost of carrying the inventory for the year?

Find the annual cost of carrying inventory.

Inventory Value × Percent

$500,000 × 25% = **$125,000 annual cost of carrying inventory**

Concept CHECK

Complete the problems. Check your answers in the back of the book. Find the annual cost of carrying inventory.

1. Inventory value is $200,000. Estimated annual cost is 30% of value.
2. Inventory value is $85,000. Estimated annual cost is 20% of value.
3. Inventory value is $150,000. Estimated annual cost is 25% of value.

Glow Images

Need Help? Go to...

Workshop 38: Problem-Solving Strategy: Writing an Equation, p. 78

EXAMPLE 2 Algebra

The Takis Stamping Company estimates that it costs \$45,000 annually to carry their inventory of materials. The cost consists of 15% for storage, handling, and storage facilities; 10% for interest; and 5% for taxes and insurance. What is the value of The Takis Stamping Company inventory?

Step 1: Let v = The value of The Takis Stamping Company inventory

Step 2: Substitute into the basic formula:

Annual cost of carrying inventory = Inventory Value × Percent

$\$45{,}000 = v \times (15\% + 10\% + 5\%)$

Combine like terms → $\$45{,}000 = 0.30v$

Divide both sides by 0.30 → $\$150{,}000 = v$

The value of The Takis Stamping Company inventory is \$150,000.

Reading Math +−÷=

Decimal Percents

Use the word "point" to indicate the decimal point in a decimal percent. 1.5% is read "one *point* five percent."

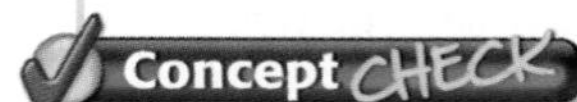

Complete the problems. Check your answers in the back of the book.

4. Uptown Clothiers, Inc. estimates that it costs \$12,500 annually to carry the company's inventory of clothing, shoes, and accessories. The costs are: 15% for storage, 8% for interest, and 2% for taxes and insurance. What is the value of the inventory?
5. Jake's Sports estimates that it costs \$30,000 annually to carry the company's inventory of sporting goods. The costs are: 20% for storage, 6% for interest, and 5% for taxes and insurance. What is the value of the inventory?

Lesson Practice

For Problems 6–11, find the annual cost of carrying inventory.

	Value of Inventory	Percent	Annual Cost of Carrying Inventory
6.	\$ 960	25.00%	
7.	\$ 14,000	35.00%	
8.	\$ 7,800	15.00%	
9.	\$ 41,840	22.00%	
10.	\$134,786	28.50%	
11.	\$514,795	32.50%	

12. Steel Ltd. carries a \$1,564,800 inventory. Steel estimates the annual cost of carrying the inventory at 27% of the inventory value. What is the approximate annual cost of carrying the inventory?
13. Armor Inc. carries an \$850,000 inventory. Armor estimates the annual cost of carrying the inventory at 30% of the inventory value. What is the approximate annual cost of carrying the inventory?
14. A company carries a \$630,000 inventory. The company estimates the annual cost of carrying the inventory at 35% of the inventory value. What is the approximate annual cost of carrying the inventory?

Did You Know?

America's Most Famous Drugstore **South Dakota's Wall Drug is famous for its hundreds of billboards advertising the store throughout all of South Dakota and even in other countries. Some call it a "tourist trap," but approximately one million curious people from around the world visit Wall Drug each year.**

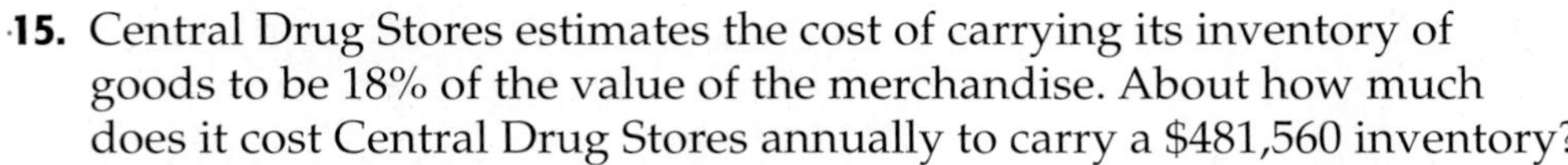

15. Central Drug Stores estimates the cost of carrying its inventory of goods to be 18% of the value of the merchandise. About how much does it cost Central Drug Stores annually to carry a $481,560 inventory?

16. Red Hardware generally carries inventory valued at $380,000. It estimates the annual cost of carrying its inventory at 25% of the value of the inventory. The 25% is broken down as follows:

Type of Expense	Percent
Spoilage and physical deterioration	4.00%
Interest	8.00%
Handling	10.00%
Storage facilities	2.00%
Taxes	0.50%
Insurance	0.50%
Total	**25.00%**

(a) What is the approximate annual cost for each expense of carrying the inventory?

(b) With on-time shipping, Red Hardware was able to reduce its inventory to three-fourths of its original value and still meet customer orders. About how much did Red Hardware save on the total cost of carrying its inventory?

H.O.T. Problems

17. ALGEBRA The Musical Instrument Store estimates costs of $18,750.00 annually to carry inventory of musical instruments and accessories. The costs include 12% for storage, 12% for interest, and 5% for transportation. What is the value of the inventory?

18. ALGEBRA Pearl Mining Supplies, Inc. carries a $150,000.00 inventory. The annual cost of carrying the inventory is 27% of the value of the inventory. It costs 3 times as much for storage as it does for taxes and insurance, and twice as much for interest as it does for taxes and insurance. How much does it cost annually for **(a)** storage, **(b)** interest, **(c)** taxes and insurance?

Spiral Review

Multiply. (Skill 30)

19. $96,400 × 25% **20.** $71,630 × 35% **21.** $347,840 × 28%

22. Gustave and Hanna Rio have obtained an $80,000 mortgage loan on a small retirement condo at an annual interest rate of 7.5% for 30 years. What is the monthly payment using the table? What is the total amount to be paid? Use the Monthly Payment for a $1,000 Loan table on page A13. (Lesson 10.2)

GET READY for the Next Lesson

PREREQUISITE SKILL **Subtracting Decimals** (Skill 6)

Subtract.

23. $68.76 – $49.87 **24.** $591.58 – $21.48

25. $967.28 – $57.70 **26.** $4,689.33 – $759.23

27. $911.45 – $272.56 **28.** $7,395.88 – $489.95

CHAPTER 14

Review and Assessment

AFTER YOU READ

Chapter SUMMARY

Purchasing and inventory are important parts of operating a business. Purchasing may involve computing the trade discount, the net price, and the trade discount rate. You can calculate the net price using the complement method and determine the final net price after a series of trade discounts. If you purchase items, you receive an invoice that may grant a cash discount. You can compute the cash price when the cash discount is based on ordinary dating or on end-of-month dating. You can calculate the total inventory, and value an inventory using the average-cost, FIFO, and LIFO methods. You can also determine the annual cost of carrying inventory.

Vocabulary Check

1. On a sheet of paper, use each of these terms in a sentence.

Content Vocabulary

- list price (p. 517)
- trade discount (p. 517)
- trade-discount rate (p. 517)
- net price (p. 517)
- complement method (p. 520)
- chain discount (p. 523)
- net-price rate (p. 523)
- invoice (p. 527)
- cash discount (p. 527)
- ordinary dating (p. 527)
- end-of-month dating (p. 530)
- inventory (p. 533)
- stock reorder point (p. 533)
- average-cost method (p. 536)
- first in, first out (FIFO) (p. 537)
- last in, first out (LIFO) (p. 538)
- carrying inventory (p. 541)

Academic Vocabulary

- available (p. 517)
- approach (p. 520)
- convince (p. 523)
- itemize (p. 527)
- granting (p. 530)
- issues (p. 533)
- physical (p. 537)
- adequate (p. 541)

Concept Check

2. Differentiate between list price and net price.
3. Give the formula for finding net price using percent paid.
4. Give the formula for finding the cash price after a cash discount.
5. Explain the difference between ordinary dating and end-of-month dating.
6. How do you find the total inventory?
7. Describe how to find inventory value using the average cost method.
8. Provide the formula for annual cost of carrying inventory.
9. **CRITICAL THINKING** Explain differences between the FIFO and LIFO methods of computing inventory value.

Lesson-by-Lesson Review

14.1 Trade Discounts (pp. 517–519)

Compute the trade discount, the net price, and the trade-discount rate.
Professional Home Interiors is purchasing a leather couch for a home it is decorating. The list price in the wholesaler's catalog is $2,950. Professional Home Interiors receives a 45% trade discount. What is the net price of the couch?

Step 1: Find the trade discount.

List Price × Trade-Discount Rate
$2,950.00 × 45% = $1,327.50 trade discount

Step 2: Find the net price.

List Price − Trade Discount
$2,950.00 − $1,327.50 = **$1,622.50 net price**

The wholesale catalog shows a list price of $1,150 and a net price of $644.00 for a leather chair. What is the trade-discount rate?

Step 1: Find the trade discount.

List Price − Net Price
$1,150 − $644 = $506 trade discount

Step 2: Find the trade-discount rate.

$$\frac{\text{Trade Discount}}{\text{List Price}} = \frac{\$506}{\$1,150} = 0.44 = \textbf{44\% trade-discount rate}$$

Review Exercises

Find the (a) trade discount and (b) net price.

	Item	List Price	Trade-Discount Rate		Trade Discount		Net Price
10.	External Hard Drive	$132.00	30%	a.		b.	
11.	Solar Cover	$239.00	15%	a.		b.	
12.	Pool Filter	$395.65	10%	a.		b.	

Round each trade-discount rate to the nearest tenth of a percent.

	Item	List Price	Net Price		Trade Discount		Trade-Discount Rate
13.	Jacket	$ 85.45	$ 56.85	a.		b.	
14.	Coveralls	$ 95.65	$ 48.25	a.		b.	
15.	Necklace	$350.50	$185.50	a.		b.	

16. A stereo unit is sold to a wholesaler for $255, then to a retailer for $360. The retailer sells the stereo unit for $445. Find the trade discount and the trade-discount rate each time the item is sold.

Lesson-by-Lesson Review (continued)

14.2 Trade Discounts–Complement Method (pp. 520–522)

Calculate the net price using the complement method.

Professional Home Interiors is purchasing a leather couch for a home it is decorating. The list price in the wholesaler's catalog is $2,950. Professional Home Interiors receives a 45% trade discount. What is the net price of the couch?

Step 1: Find the complement of trade-discount rate.

100% − 45% = 55% complement of trade-discount rate

Step 2: Find the net price.

List Price × Complement of Trade Discount Rate

$2,950.00 × 55% = **$1,622.50 net price**

Review Exercises

Find the (a) complement and (b) net price.

	Item	List Price	Trade-Discount Rate	Complement	Net Price
17.	Textbook	$115.00	20%	a.	b.
18.	Office Supplies	94.50	37%	a.	b.
19.	Set of Tires	459.22	11%	a.	b.
20.	Digital Camera	650.12	45%	a.	b.
21.	Memory Card	88.45	33.5%	a.	b.
22.	Pen	3.29	75%	a.	b.
23.	Cell Phone	150.00	40%	a.	b.

24. Junior Golf receives a 47% trade discount on these golf accessories. Find the net price for each accessory. Round Net Price per Item to the nearest cent.

	Stock No.	Description	Quantity	List Price	Net Price per Item	Total Net
a.	JG-091	Nine iron club	9	$36.54		
b.	JG-123	Golf bag	30	$95.41		
c.	JG-32A	Golf tees	100	$ 2.99		

25. **ALGEBRA** Toys Inc. offers a trade-discount rate that is 8% less than half the complement of the trade-discount rate. If the list price of an item is $123.90, what is the trade discount? What is the net price?

26. Electronics equipment is manufactured and sold to a wholesaler, who sells it to a retailer. The retailer receives a 35% trade discount from the wholesaler. The wholesaler receives a 25% discount from the manufacturer. What did each one pay for the electronics equipment that retails for $500?

Lesson-by-Lesson Review (continued)

14.3 Chain Discounts (pp. 523–526)

Determine the final net price after chain discounts, or a series of trade discounts. Running Shoe Company produces a low-impact aerobic tennis shoe called Run XX, which is priced at $98.00. Because a new line of shoes will be out shortly, Run XX will be discontinued. Running Shoe Company is offering a chain discount of 30% less 15%. This can also be written as 30/15. What is the final net price of the Run XX shoe?

Step 1: Find the first discount.

List Price × Discount Rate

$98 × 30% = $29.40 first discount

Step 2: Find the first net price.

List Price − Discount

$98.00 − $29.40 = $68.60 first net price

Step 3: Find the second discount.

$68.60 × 15% = $10.29 second discount

Step 4: Find the final net price.

$68.60 − $10.29 = **$58.31 final net price**

The final net price can also be calculated using the net price rate.

Step 1: Find the complements.

Complement of 30%: 100% − 30% = 70%

Complement of 15%: 100% − 15% = 85%

Step 2: Find the net price rate.

Product of Complements of Chain-Discount Rates

70% × 85% = 59.5% net-price rate or percent paid

Step 3: Find the net price.

$98.00 × 59.5% = 58.31 = **$58.31 final net price**

Review Exercises

Complete the tables.

	Item	List Price	Series Discount	First Discount	First Net Price	Second Discount	Final Net Price
27.	Recliner	$ 640	25% less 10%	a.	b.	c.	d.
28.	Garden Shed	$3,250	40% less 25%	a.	b.	c.	d.
29.	Garden Tractor	$3,545	40% less 15%	a.	b.	c.	d.

	Item	List Price	Series Discounts			Net-Price Rate	Net Price
30.	Generator	$1,250.00	40%	20%	—	a.	b.
31.	Counter top	$3,984.00	25%	15%	—	a.	b.
32.	Television	$ 237.60	30%	20%	10%	a.	b.

Lesson-by-Lesson Review (continued)

14.4 Cash Discounts–Ordinary Dating (pp. 527–529)

Compute the cash price when the discount is based on ordinary dating.
This is part of an invoice that The Frame Shop received for a shipment of picture frames. What is the last day the discount can be taken? What is the last day to pay the invoice? What is the cash price of the frames if the bill is paid within 10 days?

Frames Unlimited, Inc.

Ship To: The Frame Shop **Invoice No.:** 3-112AG
Date: May 16, 20-- **Order No.:** F02-44 **Terms:** 2/10, Net 30 **Acct. No.:** 1234565

Style	Color	Qty.	Price	Amount
Futuristic	Silver	15	$18.95	$ 284.25
Traditional	Brown	45	22.50	1,012.50
			TOTAL	$1,296.75

Step 1: Find the last day the discount can be taken.
Date of invoice: May 16
Terms: 2/10, net 30
Discount can be taken until May 26—10 days from date of invoice.

Step 2: Find the last day to pay the invoice.
Terms: 2/10, net 30.
May 16 + 30 days = May 46 (which does not exist). Because you are into June and because May has 31 days, you subtract 31 days.
May 46 – 31 = **June 15**

Step 3: Find the cash discount.
Net Price × Cash-Discount Rate
$1,296.75 × 2% = $25.935 or $25.94 cash discount

Step 4: Find the cash price.
Net Price – Cash Discount
$1,296.75 – $25.94 = **$1,270.81 cash price**

Review Exercises

Complete the table.

	Invoice Date	Terms	Last Date to Take Discount	Last Date to Pay Invoice	Date Paid	Net Price	Cash Discount	Cash Price
33.	May 25	2/10, n/30	June 4	June 24	May 30	$806.50	$16.13	a.
34.	June 27	3/10, n/30	July 7	July 27	July 3	$135.60	a.	b.
35.	Oct. 10	4/10, n/30	a.	b.	Oct. 20	$248.76	c.	d.
36.	March 13	6/10, n/30	a.	b.	March 24	$941.22	c.	d.
37.	April 6	5/15,n/30	a.	b.	April 18	$109.82	c.	d.
38.	May 26	2/15,n/30	a.	b.	June 8	$365.44	c.	d.

Lesson-by-Lesson Review (continued)

39. An invoice from the Computer Store shows a net price of $18,166.40. The terms are 4/10, n/30. The invoice is dated July 12. The invoice is paid July 20. **(a)** What is the last day to take the discount? **(b)** What is the last day to pay the invoice? **(c)** How much is paid on July 20? **(d)** How much would be paid on August 3?

40. An invoice from a sporting goods store shows a net price of $8,110. Terms are 4/15, n/40. The invoice is dated June 1. The invoice is paid on June 9. **(a)** What is the last day to take the discount? **(b)** What is the last day to pay the invoice? **(c)** How much is paid on June 7? **(d)** How much would be paid on July 1?

14.5 Cash Discounts–EOM Dating (pp. 530–532)

Calculate the cash price when the discount is based on end-of-month dating. Kid's Stop received an invoice for $986.50 from General Toy Store. The terms of the sale are 3/10 EOM. The date of the invoice is October 19. What is the last day Kid's Stop can take advantage of the 3% discount? When is the last day to pay the invoice? What is the cash discount? What is the cash price?

Step 1: Find the last day the discount can be taken.

Date of invoice: October 19

Terms: 3/10 EOM

Discount can be taken until November 10—10 days after the end of October.

Step 2: Find the last day to pay the invoice.

The full amount is due 20 days after the discount date.

November 10 + 20 = **November 30**

Step 3: Find the cash discount.

Net Price × Cash-Discount Rate

$986.50 × 3% = **$29.595** or **$29.60 cash discount**

Step 4: Find the cash price.

Net Price − Cash Discount

$986.50 − $29.60 = **$956.90 cash price**

Review Exercises

Complete the table.

	Invoice Date	Terms	Last Date to Take Discount	Last Date to Pay Invoice	Date Paid	Net Price	Cash Discount	Cash Price
41.	Dec. 18	2/10 EOM	a.	b.	Jan. 2	$ 194.50	c.	d.
42.	Feb. 14	3/10 EOM	a.	b.	March 8	$ 365.12	c.	d.
43.	April 15	3/15 EOM	a.	b.	May 6	$ 875.44	c.	d.
44.	July 11	4/10 EOM	a.	b.	Aug. 8	$1,209.81	c.	d.
45.	Sept. 30	5/10 EOM	a.	b.	Oct. 10	$3,291.02	c.	d.
46.	Nov. 20	5/15 EOM	a.	b.	Dec. 7	$ 239.87	c.	d.

Lesson-by-Lesson Review (continued)

47. An invoice from Wholesale Pharmacy Supply to Allied Pharmacy carries a net price of $862.86. The terms are 2/10, n/30 EOM. The invoice is dated March 27 and is paid on May 8. **(a)** What is the last day to take the cash discount? **(b)** What is the last day to pay the invoice? **(c)** What is the cash price?
48. An invoice shows a net price of $1,021.00. The terms are 5/15 EOM, n/30 EOM. The invoice is dated August 14 and is paid September 15. **(a)** What is the last day to take the discount? **(b)** What is the last day to pay the invoice? **(c)** How much is paid on September 15?

14.6 Inventory (pp. 533–535)

Calculate inventory.

Office Store has 135 electric pencil sharpeners in stock on December 1. During December it received 100 and sold 120. How many are on hand on December 31?

Calculate the inventory on hand.

Previous Inventory + Receipts − Issues

135 + 100 − 120 = **115 on hand**

Review Exercises

Find the (a) opening balance and (b) number on hand.

	Month		Opening Balance	Units Receipts (Qty. In)	Issues (Qty. Out)		Number on Hand
49.	April		543	106	50	a.	
50.	May	a.		30	90	b.	
51.	June	a.		100	175	b.	
52.	July	a.		45	75	b.	
53.	August	a.		125	56	b.	
54.	September	a.		39	87	b.	

55. On July 1 the Hat Rack started with an inventory of 370 hats. Shipments of 54, 67, and 52 were sent out on July 12, August 17, and September 12, respectively. Receipts of 63, 114, and 37 were received on July 20, August 25, and September 15, respectively. Find the number on hand as of September 15.
56. The Shoe Depot started on September 1 with a balance of 247 pairs of shoes in stock. On September 7, 124 pairs were shipped out. On September 15, 140 pairs were received. On September 27, 136 pairs were shipped out, and on September 31, 250 pairs were received. Prepare an inventory card showing the balance after each transaction.

Lesson-by-Lesson Review (continued)

14.7 Valuing Inventory (pp. 536–540)

Use the average-cost, FIFO, and LIFO methods to compute inventory value.
On April 30, the discount store had 103 birthday cards on hand. What is the value of the ending inventory for April using the average-cost method?

Date	Units Received	Unit Cost	Total Cost
April 3	52	$0.50	$26.00
April 10	101	0.45	45.45
April 21	35	0.65	22.75
Total	**188**		**$94.20**

Step 1: Find the average cost per unit.

$$\frac{\text{Total Cost of Units}}{\text{Number Received}} = \frac{\$94.20}{188} = 0.50106 = \$0.50 \text{ average cost per unit}$$

Step 2: Find the ending inventory value.

Average Cost per Unit × Number on Hand

$0.50 × 103 = **$51.50 ending inventory value**

To review the FIFO and LIFO methods for valuing inventory, review **Examples 2** and **3** on pages 537–538 before you complete Problem 57 below.

Review Exercises

57. Records for Maxine's Beauty Supply show this opening balance and these units received for Ruby Red fingernail polish in December. At the end of the month, 12 bottles were on hand. What is the value of the ending inventory using the average-cost method?

Date	Units Received	Unit Cost	Total Cost
Dec. 3 (Beginning Inventory)	43	$1.49	$ 64.07
Dec. 10	267	1.43	381.81
Dec. 20	200	1.44	288.00
Total	**510**		**$733.88**

58. Shirley's Bridal Shop's inventory records for short bridal veils show this information. At the end of the month, 15 veils were on hand. Find the value of the ending inventory using the average-cost method.

Date	Units Received	Unit Cost
July 3	36	$45.62
July 15	21	48.99
July 30	75	36.50

Lesson-by-Lesson Review (continued)

59. The Peach Tree, a trendy clothing store, uses the FIFO method of valuing inventory. As of April 30, the Peach Tree has sold 145 belts. Use the FIFO method to calculate the cost of the 145 belts sold. Suppose that instead of FIFO, the Peach Tree uses the LIFO method. Calculate the value of the 15 belts in ending inventory using the LIFO method.

Date	Units Received	Unit Cost
4/02	120	$18.50
4/13	30	19.90
4/22	10	21.50

14.8 Carrying Inventory (pp. 541–543)

Calculate the annual cost of carrying inventory.
Cidermill Games estimates the annual cost of maintaining its inventory to be 28% of the value of the inventory. This year Cidermill plans to maintain inventory totaling $310,000. What amount should be set as the estimated cost of carrying inventory for the year?

Find the annual cost of carrying inventory.

Inventory Value × Percent

$310,000 × 28% = **$86,800 annual cost of carrying inventory**

Review Exercises

Find the annual cost of carrying inventory.

	Value of Inventory	Percent	Annual Cost of Carrying Inventory
60.	$ 1,200	26.0%	
61.	12,300	29.5%	
62.	985	33.0%	
63.	10,500	34.0%	
64.	123,400	34.5%	
65.	595,000	37.5%	

66. Jake's Sporting Goods estimates the cost of carrying its inventory of goods to be 16% of the value of the merchandise. About how much does it cost Jake's Sporting Goods to carry a $608,000 inventory?

67. **ALGEBRA** The Westin Toy Store estimates costs of $78,000 annually to carry the store's inventory of materials. The cost consists of 15% for storage, handling, and storage facilities, 8% for interest, and 7% for taxes and insurance. What is the value of The Westin Toy Store inventory?

Practice Test

Record your answers on a sheet of paper.

1. The list price of a replacement vacuum pump for an airplane is $428.50. Appleton's Flight School receives a 35% trade discount. What is the dollar amount of the discount?
   A $257.00 **B** $116.45
   C $350.00 **D** $149.98

2. TJM Construction Equipment shows a $675.00 list price in its catalog for a gas-powered auger. The net price to a retailer is $519.75. What is the trade-discount rate?
   A 57% **B** 23%
   C 77% **D** 33%

3. **ALGEBRA** Marty-O's Garden Supply sells a seed spreader with a list price of $43.95. The store offers a trade discount rate that is 70% less than its complement. What is the net price?
   A $37.36 **B** $28.95
   C $6.59 **D** $39.75

4. Siam Bonsai lists a Japanese maple at $198.50 in its catalogue. It offers a 19% trade discount to eligible customers. Find the net price.
   A 20% **B** $37.72
   C 81% **D** $160.78

5. Super J's Carpet Barn offers a chain discount of 40/15 on all orders over $500. What is the final net price on an order of $755?
   A $415.25 **B** $339.75
   C $420.55 **D** $385.05

6. Kaitlyn Ameola purchased some parts for her car. The terms on the invoice are 5/10, net 30. The amount of the invoice is $358.50. What is the cash price if the invoice is paid within the discount period?
   A $340.58 **B** $179.25
   C $304.73 **D** $235.58

7. Carey Kowalski received an invoice for office supplies he had purchased. The invoice was dated October 12 and has the terms 4/15 EOM. When is the last day the discount can be taken?
   A October 31 **B** November 15
   C November 30 **D** October 27

8. Boulis Home Furnishings purchased a table with a list price of $1,350. They received a 42% trade discount. What is the net price?
   A $610 **B** $567
   C $760 **D** $783

9. **ALGEBRA** El Mundo Photo Supply estimates an annual cost of $36,000 to carry its inventory of materials. The cost consists of 25% for storage and handling, 12% for interest, and 5% for taxes and insurance. What is the value of El Mundo's inventory?

10. Honroth Industries produces a cordless drill that is priced at $415. Honroth is about to introduce a new model and is offering a chain discount of 30/15 on the old model. What is the final net price of the old drill?

11. On May 1, the discount store had 50 cans of paint on hand. In April they received 80 cans of paint valued at $4.59 per can and 60 cans valued at $4.29 per can. **(a)** What is the average cost per can? **(b)** What is the value of the inventory on May 1?

12. $1,468.57 − $151.78

13. $59.45 × 30%

14. $21,413.88 ÷ $314.91

15. $114,586.76 − $61,303.99

16. $246.86 × 87%

17. $49,106.71 ÷ $650.42

PART 1 Multiple Choice

Record your answers on the answer sheet provided by your teacher or on a sheet of paper.

1. Roberto Iriarte's checking account had a balance of $1,342.09 when he deposited $736.85. What is the new balance?
   A $2,078.94 **B** $605.24
   C $1,989.74 **D** $2,198.04

Amount of $1.00 at 5.5%, Compounded Daily			
Day	Amount	Day	Amount
26	$1.00392	30	$1.00452
27	$1.00407	31	$1.00468
28	$1.00422	32	$1.00483
29	$1.00437	33	$1.00498

2. Bomani Clayton deposited $2,798 into an account that pays 5.5% interest compounded daily. Using the table above, what is the value of his money after being deposited for 31 days?
   A $2,808.97 **B** $2,811.95
   C $2,809.39 **D** $2,811.09

3. **ALGEBRA** Jules Lupica purchased a smoke alarm for her house. The selling price was $35.50. She was charged $2.13 sales tax. What is the sales tax rate where she made the purchase?
   A 4.15% **B** 6.5%
   C 6.0% **D** 5.75%

4. Kaz Zanella purchased a new dog leash for $12.55. He also purchased 4 chew toys for $2.99 each. He had a coupon for $10 off. What is the final price of the items?
   A $24.51 **B** $14.51
   C $5.54 **D** $10.54

TEST-TAKING TIP

Eat Well Studies show that good nutrition boosts your ability to concentrate and your overall performance when taking a test.

5. Naomi Tola's charge account statement shows a previous balance of $856.93, a finance charge of $10.12, new purchases of $230.94, and a $650 payment. What is the new balance?
   A $491.59 **B** $217.05
   C $458.11 **D** $447.99

6. Ralph Querro is buying a new motorcycle for $6,499. He made a down payment of $1,075. How much did Ralph finance?
   A $4,925 **B** $5,424
   C $5,520 **D** $5,499

PART 2 Short Response/Griddable

7. **ALGEBRA** Luke Decapua wanted to buy a new ATV. He found one that was marked down 25%. The sale price of the ATV was $4,205. What was the regular selling price of the ATV?

PART 3 Extended Response

Show your work.

8. What is the definition of *markdown*? What is the difference between a markdown and the markdown rate?

9. Todd Swift took out a single-payment loan of $4,500 for 120 days at 8% ordinary interest. What is the maturity value of the loan?

10. Beau Johnson works at an art store. His hourly wage is $8.75 and he is paid time and a half for overtime. Any hours worked over 40 hours are considered overtime. Last week Beau worked 53.5 hours and was paid $420.65. Was he paid the correct amount? If the answer is no, how much should he have been paid?

11. Explain the unpaid-balance method of computing finance charges used by some companies.

Building Academic Skills

Mathematics

Imagine your employer has asked you to design a cardboard display box for a new line of beauty products. The display needs to hold 4 shampoo bottles and 4 conditioner bottles, each of which is 2 inches by 1 inch at the base. The display also needs to hold 2 bottles of body wash, each of which measures 2 inches by 2 inches at the base. Your employer would like you to present two options for the display. Draw a sketch of your two display box options, including the measurements on all sides.

English Language Arts/Writing

To reduce the cost of delivery, warehousing, and managing inventories, many companies have adopted what is called the just-in-time (JIT) system. Internet communication allows companies to arrange for their suppliers to deliver materials just as they are needed. Use Internet or library sources to find out the industries that use JIT. Write a short article or essay on your findings.

Science

Computer communication has made a number of inventory reduction strategies possible. These strategies often require that different companies share information about their production processes. Years ago, companies protected this sort of data because it could be misused by competitors. Use Internet or library sources to find out more about security issues involved in partnerships for inventory management. Write a short essay describing these issues and how they might affect a company's profits in the long run.

Building Real-World Skills

Career WISE

Disaster Recovery Manager What happens to your company's employees and data when there is a natural or man-made disaster such as a hurricane or terrorist attack? Disaster Recovery Managers plan, coordinate, test, and facilitate a company's disaster recovery plan. These managers are part of the Computer and Information Technology team.

Research and Write:

a. Visit the Web site of the Disaster Recovery Journal and locate the Careers page. Choose three job listings that interest you.

b. Using spreadsheet software or on a sheet of paper, create a table that lists the job title, salary range (if provided), and experience and education level required.

Tech TRENDS

Building a Database Over time, professionals will acquire a lot of contacts—names, phone numbers, and e-mail and Web site addresses. While it is possible to stay organized by filing business cards in a simple file box, many people find it is worthwhile to build a database containing this information so that it is easy to locate. A spreadsheet can be used to accomplish this.

Research and Share:

a. Research and consider different methods of managing contact information, such as a Rolodex, Outlook, and contact management software.

b. As a class, discuss the advantages and disadvantages of the different contact management options.

Getty Images RF

CHAPTER 15 Sales

Big Idea

This chapter focuses on calculating sales factors such as costs, markup and markdown, and determining net profit.

©DreamPictures/Blend Images LLC

Explore the Photo

Selling Price
In order to make money by selling a product, you need to sell it for more than it costs. *How do you determine how much to charge for a product?*

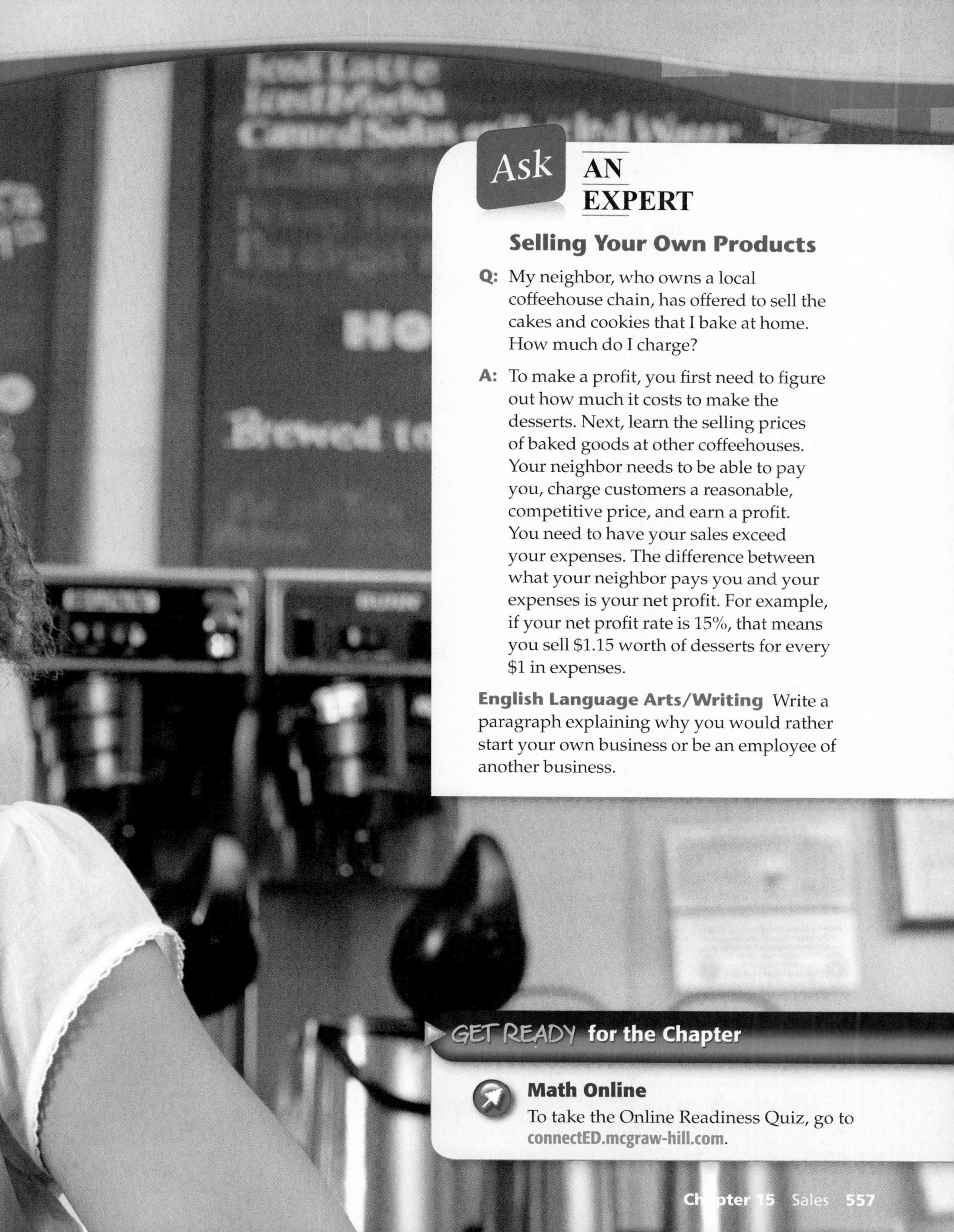

Ask AN EXPERT

Selling Your Own Products

Q: My neighbor, who owns a local coffeehouse chain, has offered to sell the cakes and cookies that I bake at home. How much do I charge?

A: To make a profit, you first need to figure out how much it costs to make the desserts. Next, learn the selling prices of baked goods at other coffeehouses. Your neighbor needs to be able to pay you, charge customers a reasonable, competitive price, and earn a profit. You need to have your sales exceed your expenses. The difference between what your neighbor pays you and your expenses is your net profit. For example, if your net profit rate is 15%, that means you sell $1.15 worth of desserts for every $1 in expenses.

English Language Arts/Writing Write a paragraph explaining why you would rather start your own business or be an employee of another business.

GET READY for the Chapter

Math Online

To take the Online Readiness Quiz, go to **connectED.mcgraw-hill.com**.

Chapter 15 Sales

Reading Guide

Before You Read

Describe How does pricing affect your purchasing decisions?

Main Idea

After your business has purchased merchandise, you must determine the appropriate selling price in order to maximize profits without turning customers away by high prices. The success of a business lies in selling customers what they want to buy at a price they are willing to pay.

Graphic Organizer

Before you read this chapter, draw a diagram like the one below. As you read, note four factors that can affect the selling price of a product.

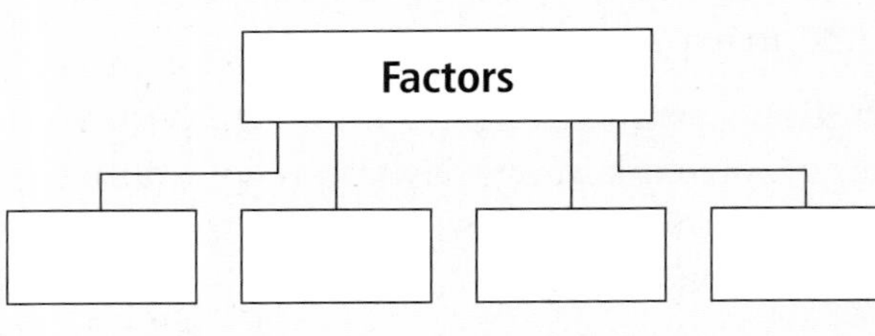

Math Online Go to **connectED.mcgraw-hill.com** to download this graphic organizer.

Content Vocabulary

You will learn these key terms in this chapter.

- cost
- selling price
- markup
- gross profit
- net profit
- markup rate
- operating expenses
- net-profit rate
- markdown
- markdown rate

Academic Vocabulary

You will see these words in your reading and on your tests.

- energy
- generate
- approximate
- consume
- prior
- foundation
- method
- attain

You can find vocabulary definitions in the **Content Vocabulary** Glossary and the **Academic Vocabulary** Glossary in the back of the book.

Markup

Lesson Objective
Compute the markup in dollars.

Content Vocabulary

- cost
- selling price
- markup
- gross profit
- net profit

GET READY for the Lesson

How do you think businesses make money?

Most customers order coffee, juice, or soda at Bill's Diner, and that pleases Bill Davis, the restaurant's owner. A typical drink costs him only a few cents to serve, and the difference between this expense and the price customers pay is profit for Bill.

As You Read
Explain What is net profit?

Markup It is common business practice to sell a product at a higher price than its **cost**, or the amount the business paid for it. The cost includes expenses such as freight charges, operating costs, and **energy** costs. The **selling price**, or retail price, is what a product actually sells for in the store. It is usually higher than the cost of the product. The difference between the cost and the selling price is your **markup**, or **gross profit**. When your markup is greater than your overhead or operating expenses, you make a **net profit**. The basic formula is:

Markup = Selling Price − Cost

EXAMPLE

Discount Electronics purchased HDTV sets for $1,487.83 each. Discount Electronics sells the HDTV sets for $2,299.99 each. What is the markup on each set?

Find the markup.

Selling Price − Cost
$2,299.99 − $1,487.83 = **$812.16 markup**

2299.99 [−] 1487.83 [=] 812.16

Find the markup. Check your answers in the back of the book.

1. A T-shirt sells for $19.49 and costs $12.63.
2. A printer cartridge sells for $29.95 each and a case of 3 costs $47.85.

Urban Planner
Urban planners combine knowledge and imagination to help define the future of their communities. Planners promote the best use of a community's resources for business, residential, and recreational purposes. **What other occupations involve careful planning?**

Lesson Practice

For Problems 3–15, determine the markup.

	Item	Selling Price	–	Cost	=	Markup
3.	Sedan	$20,070.00	–	$18,605.00	=	
4.	Cell phone	$ 149.50	–	$ 97.84	=	
5.	Watch	$ 297.87	–	$ 132.98	=	
6.	Hardcover book	$ 24.97	–	$ 18.43	=	
7.	Chainsaw	$ 297.79	–	$ 235.84	=	
8.	Rosebush	$ 9.97	–	$ 6.68	=	
9.	Bicycle	$ 219.79	–	$ 148.93	=	
10.	Pencil eraser	$ 0.35	–	$ 0.27	=	

11. Walking shoes cost $51.48 and sell for $79.59.

12. A digital camera costs $417.97 and sells for $649.79.

13. Grape jam costs $6.78 for a case of 12 and sells for $0.89 per jar.

14. Bottled water costs $25.68 for a case of 24 and sells for $3.79 per bottle.

15. General Department Stores purchased bedroom curtains from The Linen Company for $6.19. General Department Stores sold the curtains for $9.79.

16. Mostly Kitchens pays $235.80 for a pallet load of paper towels. The pallet holds 36 cases with 12 rolls per case. Mostly Kitchens sells the paper towels for $10.99 a case. **(a)** What is the markup per case? **(b)** What is the markup per roll?

17. Tasty Bakery Company sells chocolate éclairs for $30.96 a dozen. It costs Tasty Bakery $1.48 to produce each éclair. **(a)** What is the markup on a dozen éclairs? **(b)** What is the markup on each éclair?

18. CHALLENGE PROBLEM Theresa Oakley operates a mini-engine repair shop. Recently she bought an older lawn mower for $30.00 at a local auction. She repaired the lawn mower at a cost of $39.17 in parts. She painted and polished the lawn mower at a cost of $36.43. When the lawn mower was finished, Theresa sold it for $155.00. **(a)** What was the markup on the lawn mower? **(b)** If it took 4.5 hours to do all the work, how much did she earn per hour?

Spiral Review

Subtract. (Skill 6)

19. $216.96 – $130.18 **20.** $491.79 – $418.02 **21.** $4,217.83 – $2,319.81

22. John Blakemore's home is located in Columbus, Ohio, where the rate of assessment is 35% of market value. The tax rate is $61.23 per $1,000 of assessed value. His home has a market value of $275,000. **(a)** What is its assessed value? **(b)** What is the property tax? (Lesson 10.5)

GET READY for the Next Lesson

PREREQUISITE SKILL Subtracting Decimals (Skill 6)

23. $54.70 – $17.32 **24.** $84.68 – $22.78 **25.** $71.23 – $42.60

26. $104.59 – $87.54 **27.** $241.60 – $99.34 **28.** $173.10 – $72.06

LESSON 15.2

Markup Rate

Lesson Objective
Calculate the markup as a percent of the selling price.

Content Vocabulary
- markup rate

GET READY for the Lesson

How do fuel prices affect food prices?

Green Grocer store manager DeShawn Prince has had a lot of explaining to do recently about rising food prices. He tells customers that rising gas prices have made transporting food more expensive, thus increasing the store's costs. To still make a profit, the store has to pass those costs along to customers.

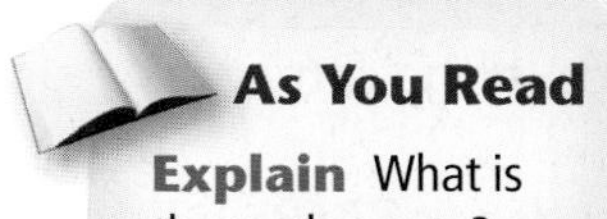

As You Read
Explain What is the markup rate?

Markup Rate Businesses must **generate** a profit or they will not be in business very long. The markup is often expressed as a percent of the selling price. The **markup rate** is determined by finding what percent the markup is of the selling price. The formula is:

$$\text{Markup Rate} = \frac{\text{Markup}}{\text{Selling Price}}$$

EXAMPLE

Roy's Florist buys roses for $15.99 a dozen. It sells them for $37.95 a dozen. What is the markup rate based on the selling price?

Step 1: Find the markup.

Selling Price − Cost
$37.95 − $15.99 = $21.96

Step 2: Find the markup rate based on the selling price.

$$\frac{\text{Markup}}{\text{Selling Price}} = \frac{\$21.96}{\$37.95} = 0.57866 = \textbf{57.9\% markup rate}$$

37.95 M+ − 15.99 = 21.96 ÷ RM 37.95 = 0.5786561

Concept CHECK

Find the (a) markup and (b) markup rate based on the selling price. Round answers to the nearest tenth of a percent. Check your answers in the back of the book.

1. The cost of a vest is $34.85 and the selling price is $49.79.
2. The cost of a shop vacuum is $161.97 and the selling price is $249.19.
3. The selling price for a toy train is $29.95 and the cost is $15.95.
4. The selling price for peanut butter is $3.79 and the cost is $2.84.

Pixtal/AGE Fotostock

Reading Math +−÷=

Multiplication
In a mathematical expression, "of" means "times." 5% of 340 is the same as 5% times 340.

Lesson Practice

Determine the (a) markup and (b) markup rate. Round answers to the nearest tenth of a percent.

	Item	Selling Price	−	Cost	=	Markup	Markup Rate
5.	Sedan	$20,070.00	−	$18,605.00	=	a.	b.
6.	Calculator	$ 149.50	−	$ 97.84	=	a.	b.
7.	Wii	$ 297.87	−	$ 132.98	=	a.	b.
8.	Hardcover book	$ 24.97	−	$ 18.43	=	a.	b.

For Problems 9–13, determine the (a) markup and (b) markup rate based on the selling price. Round answers to the nearest tenth of a percent.

9. Pete Kraemer is a buyer for a mattress store. He purchases twin-size box springs for $146.74 each. The store sells them for $267.49 each.

10. Rodolfo's Fashions buys silk scarves for $18.43. The selling price of each scarf is $42.50.

11. A digital camera costs a store $267.38. The selling price of the camera is $319.99.

12. Office Mate buys a laptop computer for $1,247.68. It sells for $1,699.99.

13. Video Rentals sells used DVDs for $7.95. The cost to Video Rentals is $4.86 per DVD.

14. Convenient Carryout purchases pens for $2.90 a dozen. The selling price of each pen is $0.99. What is the markup rate per pen based on the selling price?

15. CHALLENGE PROBLEM Mostly Kitchens pays $235.80 for a pallet load of paper towels. The pallet holds 36 cases with 12 rolls per case. Mostly Kitchens sells the paper towels for $10.99 a case. **(a)** What is the markup rate per case? **(b)** What is the markup rate per roll?

Spiral Review

Find the rate. Round answers to the nearest tenth of a percent. (Skill 31)

16. $6.13 ÷ $25.45 **17.** $35.79 ÷ $119.29 **18.** $1,309.22 ÷ $1,309.23

19. ALGEBRA In January, The Home Store pays a net price of $12.15 for a queen sheet set after a trade-discount rate of 72%. **(a)** What was the list price? **(b)** What was the trade discount? (Lesson 14.2)

GET READY for the Next Lesson

PREREQUISITE SKILL Finding the Percentage (Skill 30)

Round answers to the nearest cent.

20. $340 × 60%

21. $56.28 × 35%

22. $153.78 × 25%

23. $79.45 × 80%

24. $267.55 × 15%

25. $93.10 × 6%

LESSON 15.3

Net Profit

Lesson Objective

Determine the net profit in dollars.

Content Vocabulary

- operating expenses

GET READY for the Lesson

What unexpected costs might a business encounter?

Jeff Newquist smiled as he greeted customers on the first day at Guapo Comics' new store location. Last year, the landlord at Guapo's old location raised the rent by 75%. Jeff decided the store had to move in order to survive and found an attractive retail space across town.

As You Read

Summarize What is overhead?

Operating Expenses The markup on the products you sell must cover your **operating expenses** or *overhead*. These expenses include wages and salaries of employees, rent, utility charges, and taxes. If you own a small business, you will spend less on wages and salaries, rent, utilities, and other expenses than if you own a firm with thousands of people in several large facilities.

The exact overhead expense on each item sold is difficult to determine accurately. You may **approximate** the overhead expense of each item. For example, if your total overhead expenses are 40% of total sales, you may estimate the overhead expense of each item sold to be 40% of its selling price. When the markup of an item is greater than its overhead expense, you make a net profit on the item. Calculate the overhead expense and net profit using these formulas:

Overhead = Selling Price × Overhead Percent

Net Profit = Markup − Overhead

EXAMPLE 1

Sport Shop purchases life jackets for $44.98 each. It sells the jackets for $89.99 each. The owner estimates the overhead expenses to be 40% of the selling price of the merchandise. What is the net profit on each jacket?

Step 1: Find the markup.

Selling Price − Cost

$89.99 − $44.98 = $45.01

Step 2: Find the overhead.

Selling Price × Overhead Percent

$89.99 × 40% = $35.996 or $36.00

Step 3: Find the net profit.

Markup − Overhead

$45.01 − $36.00 = **$9.01 net profit**

John Flournoy/McGraw-Hill Education

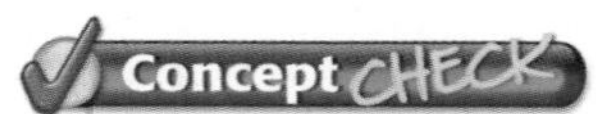

Complete the problems. Find (a) the markup, (b) the overhead, and (c) the net profit. Check your answers in the back of the book.

1. A food processor costs $56 and sells for $140. The overhead is 50% of the selling price.

2. A kitchen range costs $578.40 and sells for $964. The overhead is 35% of the selling price.

Need Help? Go to...
Workshop 39: Problem-Solving Strategy: Linear Combinations, p. 80

EXAMPLE 2 Algebra

Just Diamonds operates on a 35% overhead based on the selling price, which results in an overhead of $62.99 on their signature tennis bracelet. If the bracelet costs Just Diamonds $38.75, find the selling price, the markup, and the net profit.

Let s = The selling price

Overhead = Selling Price × Overhead Percent

$62.99 = s × 35%

Divide both sides by 0.35 → $179.971 = s

The selling price is $179.97

Markup = Selling Price − Cost

Markup = $179.97 − $38.75 = **$141.22**

Net Profit = Markup − Overhead

Net Profit = $141.22 − $62.99 = **$78.23**

Complete the problem. Check your answer in the back of the book.

3. The Corner Deli operates on an overhead percent of 20% of the selling price, which results in an overhead of $1.25 on the company's private-label bags of corn chips. If Corner Deli has a markup of $4.35 on the bags of corn chips, find the **(a)** selling price, **(b)** net profit, and **(c)** cost.

Lesson Practice

Find the (a) markup, (b) overhead, and (c) net profit.

	Item	Selling Price	Cost	Markup	Overhead Percent	Overhead	Net Profit
4.	Shirt	$ 40.00	$ 20.00	a.	30.00%	b.	c.
5.	Ring	$180.00	$ 72.00	a.	40.00%	b.	c.
6.	Bed	$270.00	$189.00	a.	20.00%	b.	c.
7.	Jeans	$ 65.00	$ 30.00	a.	15.00%	b.	c.
8.	Couch	$250.00	$120.00	a.	35.00%	b.	c.
9.	Stereo	$199.00	$135.00	a.	30.00%	b.	c.

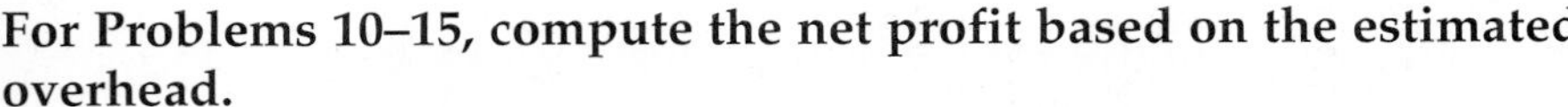

For Problems 10–15, compute the net profit based on the estimated overhead.

10. Hardware Company purchases door hardware sets for $29.86 each. It charges customers $49.99 for the hardware and installation. The labor and other overhead total $11.75 for each set installed.
11. Storm King purchases storm doors at a cost of $41.74 each. The selling price of an installed storm door is $119.50. The overhead for the storm door is estimated to be 40% of the selling price.
12. Mary Callas is a buyer for Classic Shoes. She purchased some sandals at a cost of $13.89 a pair. Her store sells them for $29.99 a pair. Operating expenses are estimated to be 30% of the selling price.
13. Huston Community Market purchases private-label milk at a cost of $3.09 a gallon. The selling price of a gallon is $3.99. The overhead is estimated to be 20% of the selling price.
14. Custom Comp, assemblers of customized professional central processing units, delivered a system to Universal Delivery for a selling price of $1,078,450. The cost of the unit to Custom Comp was $416,785. The system design, programming, installation, and other overhead expenses were estimated to be 38.5% of the selling price.
15. Adams Refrigeration assembles large scale refrigeration units for cold storage warehouses. One system was sold for $556,400. The cost of the unit to Adams Refrigeration was $226,780. The system design, set up, installation, and other overhead expenses were estimated to be 42.8% of the selling price.

Did You Know?

U.S. Energy Consumption
Fewer than 5% of the world's people live in the United States, but the United States uses double the energy of the next-largest consumer, China, which has four times as many people.

H.O.T. Problems

16. **ALGEBRA** Bob's Menswear operates on an overhead percent of 30% of the selling price. On a line of cashmere sweaters, Bob's realizes a net profit of $51.00 after a markup of $90.00. Find the overhead, selling price, and cost.
17. **ALGEBRA** All Sports Inc. uses an overhead percent of 40% of the selling price. On a line of tennis rackets, the overhead is $79.96 on a racket which costs All Sports $58.75. Find the **(a)** selling price, **(b)** markup, and **(c)** net profit.

Spiral Review

Round to the nearest cent. (Skill 2)

18. $1.111
19. $4.545
20. $0.4581
21. Hana Lu is single and has the health insurance benefits shown in **Figure 11.1** on page 421. Her network costs include co-payments for 7 doctor and 2 specialist visits and a hospital bill of $2,775. What amount did she pay? (Lesson 11.2)

GET READY for the Next Lesson

PREREQUISITE SKILL Finding the Rate (Skill 31)

Round answers to the nearest tenth of a percent.

22. $8.45 ÷ $27.80
23. $51.25 ÷ $78.65
24. $4.24 ÷ $10.23
25. $19.93 ÷ $25.25
26. $66.43 ÷ $95.12
27. $84.69 ÷ $102.43

LESSON 15.4

Net-Profit Rate

Lesson Objective

Find the net profit as a percent of the selling price.

Content Vocabulary

- net-profit rate

GET READY for the Lesson

What kinds of deals do you see offered at stores?

While Jane Richards was doing her back-to-school shopping, she found a good sale. One dress shirt cost $24, but if she bought three shirts, the total cost would be $45. The store was willing to accept less profit on each shirt in order to sell more shirts.

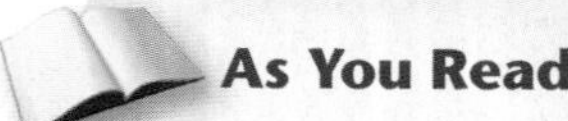

As You Read

List What products do you consume on a regular basis?

Net-Profit Rate Businesses provide us with basic products we **consume**, such as food, clothing, electronic devices, books, and newspapers, as well as other goods and services that make our lives easier. You may want to know the **net-profit rate** of an item your business sells. The net-profit rate is net profit expressed as a percent of the selling price of the item. The formula is:

$$\text{Net-Profit Rate} = \frac{\text{Net Profit}}{\text{Selling Price}}$$

EXAMPLE 1

Giant Discounts sells a mini-vacuum cleaner for $49.99. The cost of the vacuum cleaner to Giant Discounts is $23.74. Giant estimates the overhead expenses on the vacuum to be 30% of the selling price. What is the net-profit rate based on the selling price of the vacuum cleaner?

Step 1: Find the net profit.

Markup	−	Overhead	
($49.99 − $23.74)	−	($49.99 × 30%)	
$26.25	−	$15.00	= $11.25 net profit

Step 2 Find the net-profit rate.

$$\frac{\text{Net Profit}}{\text{Selling Price}} = \frac{\$11.25}{\$49.99} = 0.22504 = \textbf{22.5\% net-profit rate}$$

49.99 [−] 23.74 [=] 26.25 [M+] 49.99 [×] 30 [%]
14.997 [M−] [RM] 11.253 [÷] 49.99 [=] 0.225105

Concept CHECK

Find the (a) markup, (b) overhead, (c) net profit, and (d) net-profit rate. Check your answers in the back of the book.

1. The selling price of a set of bed linens is $119.50. The cost is $44.78. The overhead expense is 40% of the selling price.

Need Help? Go to...

Workshop 38: Problem-Solving Strategy: Writing an Equation, p. 78

EXAMPLE 2 Algebra

The Corner Music Store operates on a net-profit rate of 25% on its DVDs. If the markup is $11.98 and the overhead is $6.33, find the net profit and the selling price.

Step 1: Find the net profit.

Markup − Overhead

11.98 − 6.33 = **$5.65 net profit**

Step 2: Find the selling price using the net-profit rate formula.

Let x = The selling price

$$\text{Net-Profit Rate} = \frac{\text{Net Profit}}{\text{Selling Price}}$$

$$25\% = \frac{5.65}{x}$$

Multiply both sides by x → $0.25x = 5.65$

Divide both sides by 0.25 → $x = \mathbf{22.6}$

The selling price of the DVDs is $22.60.

Concept CHECK

Complete the problem. Check your answer in the back of the book.

2. The General Hardware Store sells general-purpose tools at a net-profit rate of 28%. The markup on a pry-bar is $4.98 and the overhead is $2.07. Find the **(a)** net profit and **(b)** selling price.
3. Oscar's Skate Shop sells skateboarding equipment and apparel at a net-profit rate of 35%. The markup on a skateboard is $11.45 and the overhead is $4.40. Find the **(a)** net profit and **(b)** selling price.

Study Tip

Taking Notes Make sure that you write legibly when taking notes. If you have difficulty reading your own handwriting, it may be wise to type your notes soon after class.

Lesson Practice

Find the (a) overhead, (b) net profit, and (c) net-profit rate. Round answers to the nearest whole percent.

	Item	Markup	Selling Price	Overhead Percent	Overhead	Net Profit	Net-Profit Rate
4.	Basketball	$ 40.00	$ 50.00	30%	a.	b.	c.
5.	Jacket	$ 35.00	$ 70.00	25%	a.	b.	c.
6.	Tent	$ 191.75	$ 449.49	20%	a.	b.	c.
7.	Diamonds	$7,366.90	$8,475.75	40%	a.	b.	c.
8.	Headphones	$ 45.00	$ 99.00	30%	a.	b.	c.
9.	Computer	$ 150.00	$ 895.00	25%	a.	b.	c.
10.	Watch	$ 100.00	$ 165.00	40%	a.	b.	c.

For Problems 11–17, round answers to the nearest tenth of a percent.

11. Court-Time is selling tennis rackets for $64.99. The cost to Court-Time is $37.48 per racket. Overhead is estimated to be 20% of the selling price. What is the net-profit rate?

Did You Know?

The "Discman" **In 1983, no company had yet developed a portable compact disc player. In Japan, a Sony executive displayed a 13.4 cm by 4 cm block of wood and asked his engineers to make a portable player that size. The following year, the "Discman" was introduced to great success.**

12. Value Shop sells sweaters for $87.79 each. The markup on each sweater is $42.85. Overhead is estimated to be 30% of the selling price. What is the net-profit rate?
13. A deli purchases apple butter for $2.03 a jar. It sells the apple butter for $3.59 a jar. The deli estimates the overhead at 25% of the selling price. What is the net-profit rate on each jar of apple butter?
14. Digital Tool Shop sells noise-canceling headphones for $89.99 each. The markup on each set of headphones is $32.85. Overhead is estimated to be 30% of the selling price. What is the net-profit rate?
15. Oak Wood Landscape sells water garden and pond aeration units for $145.56 each. It buys the units for $79.98 each. Oak Wood estimates the overhead at 28% of the selling price. What is the net-profit rate on each unit?
16. The Perryville Pharmacy purchases tooth brushes for $24.80 per case of 48 brushes. The brushes are sold for $0.99 each. Overhead expenses are estimated to be 10.5% of the selling price per brush. What is the net-profit rate per brush?
17. The Sevas Shop purchases steel bars for $29.85 per bar. An automatic machine cuts and forms each bar into 30 steel pins. The 30 pins are packaged individually and marked to sell at $2.19 each. Overhead expenses are estimated to be 12.5% of the selling price per pin. What is the net-profit rate per pin?

18. **ALGEBRA** Clyde's Clothing Store estimates the store overhead expenses to be 18% of the selling price. The overhead on a line of sport coats is $35.73. If the markup on those sport coats is $49.75, find the **(a)** selling price, **(b)** net profit, and **(c)** net-profit rate.
19. **ALGEBRA** An overhead percent of 24% of the selling price results in an overhead of $35.71. If the net-profit rate is 30%, find the **(a)** selling price and **(b)** net profit.

Spiral Review

Find the percentage. Round answers to the nearest cent. (Skill 30)

20. $49.49 × 30% **21.** $9.78 × 20% **22.** $134.49 × 25%

23. The replacement value of Jay and Robin Digna's home is estimated at $178,000. They have insured their home for 80% of its replacement value. According to the guidelines on page 391 and **Figure 10.5**, what is the amount of coverage on Jay and Robin's personal property? (Lesson 10.6)

GET READY for the Next Lesson

PREREQUISITE SKILL Dividing Decimals (Skill 11)

Round answers to the nearest cent.

24. $53.00 ÷ 42%
25. $32.50 ÷ 75%
26. $76.80 ÷ 20%
27. $151.70 ÷ 45%
28. $89.57 ÷ 36%
29. $101.88 ÷ 63%

LESSON 15.5

Selling Price—Markup Based on Selling Price

Lesson Objective

Calculate the selling price of an item based on cost and markup rate based on selling price.

As You Read

Identify What is the relationship between markup rate and profit?

GET READY for the Lesson

What are visible ways companies lower overhead costs?

Nicole Salas works at an office supply retailer. The store is a large, open warehouse-type space with no frills such as carpeting or atmospheric lighting.

Markup Based on Selling Price You can use records of **prior** sales and expenses to plan the markup rate needed to cover overhead expenses and to yield a profit. You can use the cost of an item and the desired markup rate based on the selling price to determine the best selling price. The formula is:

$$\text{Selling Price} = \frac{\text{Cost}}{\text{Complement of Markup Rate}}$$

EXAMPLE

VJ's Sporting Goods Store knows from past expense records (as shown below) that it must aim for a markup that is 40% of the selling price of its merchandise. The store received a shipment of running shoes at a cost of $38.99 per pair. What is the minimum selling price that the store should charge?

Sales for Month: $42,000	Amount	Percent of Total Sales
Cost of goods sold	$25,200	60%
Overhead expenses	$8,400	20%
Profit	$8,400	20%
TOTAL	$42,000	100%

(Note: Markup plus cost equals selling price. If the markup is 40% of the selling price, then the cost must be 60% of the selling price. The complement of 40% is 60%).

Step 1: Find the complement of the markup rate.

100% − 40% = 60% complement of markup rate

Step 2: Find the selling price.

$$\frac{\text{Cost}}{\text{Complement of Markup Rate}} = \frac{\$38.99}{60\%} = \$64.98333 = \$64.98$$

The minimum selling price is $64.98.

Concept CHECK

Find the selling price. Check your answers in the back of the book.

1. A loaf of bread costs $1.40 and the markup is 30% of the selling price.
2. Toothpaste costs $1.49 and the markup is 25% of the selling price.

Study Tip

Review
It is best to review new material right after class when it is still fresh in your memory.

Lesson Practice

Complete the table.

	Item	Cost	Markup Rate	Complement of Markup Rate	Selling Price (Nearest Cent)
3.	Suit	$ 86.74	50.0%	a.	b.
4.	Lawn mower	$420.00	45.0%	a.	b.
5.	Swim wear	$ 47.84	37.5%	a.	b.
6.	Cell phone	$212.60	12.5%	a.	b.

For Problems 7–10, find the selling price.

7. Stapler: $7.48; markup: 60% of the selling price

8. Toolbox: $5.16; markup: 40% of the selling price

9. Runner's Warehouse purchased digital watches for $91.99. Its markup rate is 20% based on the selling price.

10. Paperback Paupers marks up paperback books 35% of the selling price. A paperback book costs Paupers $8.52.

11. Juan Charles prices items at BarBells, Inc. at 53% of the selling price. What selling price does Juan place on these items?

	Item	Cost
a.	Weight set	$ 9.40
b.	Treadmill	$282.00
c.	Pro weight system	$188.00
d.	Cycle	$ 94.00

12. Hillary Lee manages the craft department of Super Craft. What selling price will she place on each of these items?

	Line Item	Code	Description	Unit	Store Cost	Markup Rate
a.	14	63614	Masking tape	Roll	$0.545	55.0%
b.	15	71358	Protractor w/ruler	Each	$0.105	50.0%
c.	16	31615	Cotton twine	Each	$0.302	57.5%

13. CHALLENGE PROBLEM Suppose Hillary Lee in **Problem 12** decided to mark up all the items 55% of the selling price. If you purchase one of each item, how much more or less do you pay for each?

Spiral Review

Divide. Round answers to the nearest cent. (Skill 11)

14. $23.00 ÷ 65% **15.** $48.00 ÷ 80% **16.** $117.40 ÷ 50%

17. ALGEBRA Tammy and Jacob Guimond pay $2,125.86 in annual property taxes. The rate of assessment for their tax district is 35% and their tax rate is 48 mills. What is the market value of their property? (Lesson 10.5)

GET READY for the Next Lesson

PREREQUISITE SKILL Subtracting Decimals (Skill 6)

Subtract.

18. $84.70 − $37.95 **19.** $62.77 − $44.80 **20.** $218.64 − $99.75

LESSON 15.6

Markup Rate Based on Cost

Lesson Objective
Calculate the markup rate based on cost.

GET READY for the Lesson

What might entice you to buy a less popular product or service?

Most of Nathan Haggerty's classmates like to go to the movies on Friday evenings. Nathan prefers Saturday afternoons because the tickets are less expensive due to lower demand.

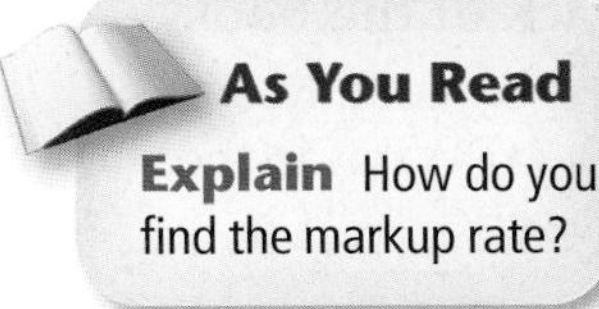

As You Read
Explain How do you find the markup rate?

Markup Rate Based on Cost Your business may use the cost of a product as the **foundation** for the markup rate. The markup rate in supermarkets is relatively low. For example, milk may be marked up 5% of the cost and other dairy products 20% to 30% of the cost. The markup of clothing may be from 80% to 140% of the cost. Items such as watches and jewelry may be marked up 100% or more of the cost. The markup rate formula is:

$$\text{Markup Rate} = \frac{\text{Markup}}{\text{Cost}}$$

EXAMPLE 1

The Table Co. purchases a dinette set for $880 from the manufacturer. It sells the set for $1,188. What is the markup rate based on cost?

Step 1: Find the markup.

Selling Price − Cost
$1,188.00 − $880.00 = $308.00

Step 2: Find the markup rate based on cost.

$\frac{\text{Markup}}{\text{Cost}} = \frac{\$308}{\$880} = 0.35 =$ **35% markup rate based on cost**

1188 [−] 880 [=] 308 [÷] 880 [=] 0.35

Concept CHECK

Complete the problems. Find the markup rate based on cost. Check your answers in the back of the book.

1. Selling price of a jacket is $97.50. Cost is $58.50.
2. Selling price of a tool chest is $148. Cost is $74.

Glow Images

EXAMPLE 2 Algebra

The Main Street store sells 33-gallon trash containers for \$19.99 after a markup rate based on cost of 120%. Find the **(a)** cost and **(b)** markup.

Step 1: Find the cost. Let c = the cost.

	Markup	=	Selling Price	−	Cost
	120%c	=	\$19.99	−	c
Add c to both sides →	2.20c	=	\$19.99		
Divide both sides by 2.20 →	c	=	**\$9.086**		

The cost is \$9.09.

Step 2: Markup = \$19.99 − \$9.09

The markup is \$10.90.

Complete the problem. Check your answer in the back of the book.

3. A can of tennis balls has an 85% markup rate based on cost. Mel's Sporting Goods sells a can of tennis balls for \$3.40. **(a)** What is the cost? **(b)** What is the markup?

GRAPHING CALCULATOR LAB

Markup Rates

You can write a program for the graphing calculator to calculate the different types of discounts and rates. If a florist buys flowers for \$15.99 a dozen and sells them for \$35.99 a dozen, what is the markup rate based on the selling price?

```
PROGRAM: MARKUP
: Disp "COST"
: Input C
: Disp "1SELLPRICE"
: Input S
: S–C → M
: Disp "MARKUP", M
: Disp "RATE", M/S*100
```

The program shown to the right determines the markup and the markup rate based on the selling price. To enter the program into your calculator you need to access PRGM. Create a new program:

PRGM ▶ ▶ 1

In order to name the program, use the ALPHA key and the green letters on the calculator. To enter the **Disp** (Display), follow these keystrokes:

 3

To enter **Input**, follow these keystrokes:

     The → key represents the STO button.

To run the program, from the home screen press PRGM, select the correct program, and enter.

Think and Discuss

1. What is the markup and markup rate for the flowers?
2. In the program, what does $S - C$ determine?
3. Why is the rate multiplied by 100 in the last line of the program?
4. What could you add to the program so that it also figures markup based on cost?
5. A jewelry store buys a watch for \$22.99 and sells it for \$89.99. **(a)** What is the markup rate based on selling price? **(b)** What is the markup rate based on cost?

Lesson Practice

Round markup rates to the nearest tenth of a percent.

	Item	Selling Price	Cost	Markup	Markup Rate Based on Cost
4.	Flower Pot	$ 1.75	$ 1.25	a.	b.
5.	Bib Overalls	$ 50.00	$ 20.00	a.	b.
6.	Kitchen Faucet	$ 85.50	$ 47.50	a.	b.
7.	Scaffold	$791.00	$585.40	a.	b.
8.	Cat Toy	$ 1.04	$ 0.13	a.	b.

Did You Know?

The Tomato **Experts believe the tomato originally came from South America or Mexico. Tomatoes were being grown in Italy and Germany by the mid-1500s. Many early Americans thought the tomato was a poisonous fruit, but today the U.S. produces more than 8 million tons of tomatoes each year.**

For Problems 9–13, determine the markup rate based on the cost to the nearest tenth of a percent.

9. A guitar sells for $226.64. The cost is $141.65.

10. A pair of tomato plants sells for $18.65. The cost is $7.46 each.

11. Jeans, Inc. buys men's carpenter jeans for $28.68 per pair. It marks up each pair $25.31.

12. Quentin Clark, a salesperson at Doolittle's Department Store, sold a pair of golf shoes for $84.95. The shoes cost Doolittle's $27.84 a pair.

13. Trudi Alvarez is a buyer for Small Tots Shoppe. She purchased an assortment of teddy bears for $8.74 each. They were marked to sell for $17.48 each.

14. CHALLENGE PROBLEM Craig Nielson works at his parents' outdoor market. He sells tomatoes for $1.99 a pound. The tomatoes cost $0.89 a pound to grow. **(a)** What is the markup rate based on cost? **(b)** What is the markup rate based on selling price?

15. ALGEBRA A pair of earrings has a 130% markup rate based on cost. The selling price is $98.79. **(a)** What is the cost? **(b)** What is the markup?

16. ALGEBRA Don's Fishing Supply sells fishing lures for $1.82 after marking them up 420% based on cost. Find the **(a)** cost and **(b)** markup.

Spiral Review

Subtract. (Skill 6)

17. $74.80 − $37.40 **18.** $149.49 − $59.80 **19.** $19.19 − $12.38

20. On April 10 Brenda Agoyo deposited $2,125.36 in a savings account that pays 5.5% interest compounded daily. How much interest will the money earn in 31 days? Hint: See **Figure 5.6** on page 232. (Lesson 5.7)

GET READY for the Next Lesson

PREREQUISITE SKILL Adding Decimals (Skill 5)

21. $62.43 + $35.09 **22.** $177.74 + $185.52

23. $568.43 + $329.85 **24.** $958.74 + $474.33

25. $1,310.45 + $333.98 **26.** $946.17 + $1,222.90

LESSON 15.7

Selling Price—Markup Based on Cost

Lesson Objective
Compute the selling price based on cost and markup rate.

Do you usually equate high prices with high quality?

Jordan Leach manages a luxury hotel in Las Vegas, Nevada. He and his staff work hard to create a luxurious atmosphere at the hotel.

As You Read
Discuss Why do you think luxury brands have high markup rates?

Markup Based on Cost Some businesses use the cost of an item and the desired markup rate based on the cost to compute the selling price of an item. One **method** for arriving at the selling price when the markup rate is based on the cost uses these formulas:

Markup = Cost × Markup Rate on Cost

Selling Price = Cost + Markup

EXAMPLE 1

Reinhart Jewelry stores buy silver earrings for $28.45 per pair. The retail price is computed by adding a markup of 160% of the cost. What is the retail selling price?

Step 1: Find the markup.

Cost × Markup Rate on Cost
$28.45 × 160% = $45.52

Step 2: Find the selling price.

Cost + Markup
$28.45 + $45.52 = **$73.97 retail selling price**

28.45 × 160 % 45.52 + 28.45 = 73.97

Concept CHECK

Find the (a) markup and (b) selling price. Check your answers in the back of the book.

1. A boxwood shrub costs $50. The markup is 70% of the cost.
2. An end table costs $140. The markup is 150% of the cost.
3. A pair of shoes cost $89. The markup is 65% of the cost.
4. A set of shelves cost $199. The markup is 80% of the cost.

EXAMPLE 2 Algebra

The Handmade Furniture Store operates on a 215% markup based on the cost. The markup on the store's Adirondack chair is $123.81. Find the **(a)** cost and **(b)** selling price.

Step 1: Let x = the cost

$$215\% = \frac{\$123.81}{x}$$

Multiply both sides by x → $2.15x = \$123.81$

Divide both sides by 2.15 → $x = \mathbf{\$57.586}$

The cost is $57.59

Step 2: Selling price = $57.59 + $123.81

The selling price is $181.40

Concept CHECK

Complete the problems. Find the (a) cost and (b) selling price. Check your answers in the back of the book.

5. The markup based on cost is 95%. The markup is $1.90.

6. The markup based on cost is 425%. The markup is $173.85.

7. The markup based on cost is 80%. The markup is $35.35.

8. The markup based on cost is 125%. The markup is $87.50.

Study Tip

Be Prepared
Being prepared for a test is the best way to reduce test-taking anxiety. Make sure you understand the material well.

Lesson Practice

For Problems 9–14, find the (a) markup and (b) selling price.

	Item	Cost	Markup Rate Based on Cost	Markup	Selling Price
9.	Bracelet	$ 86.40	150.0%	a.	b.
10.	Roses	$ 16.40	225.0%	a.	b.
11.	Refrigerator	$ 751.80	25.5%	a.	b.
12.	Dog Bed	$ 14.24	400.0%	a.	b.
13.	Treadmill	$1,235.00	95.0%	a.	b.
14.	Coffee Table	$ 325.00	120.0%	a.	b.

For Problems 15–21, find the selling price.

15. A hedge trimmer costs $111.87. Markup rate is 60% of cost.

16. A TiVo costs $177.75. Markup rate is 125% of cost.

17. Austin Family Furniture purchases recliners directly from the manufacturer for $240.95 each. The recliners are marked up 195% of cost and sold to customers.

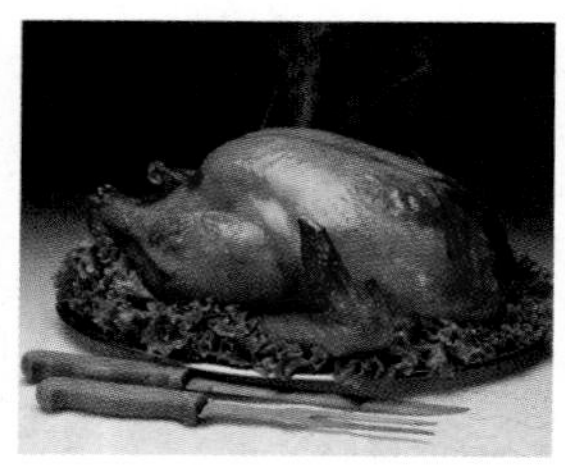

Did You Know?

Medieval Feast The cooks required many ovens to prepare the meat served at a reception in honor of an English archbishop in 1467. Guests at the daylong feast dined on 104 oxen, six wild bulls, 1,000 sheep, 304 calves, 400 swans, 2,000 geese, 2,000 pigs, and 13,500 other birds.

18. The Gourmet Wholesale Company purchases 3.5 lb. ducks directly from the farmer for $10.80 each. The ducks are marked up 210% of cost and sold to retail grocers.

19. The Door Company produces truck-dock door seals. Its 9′ × 10′ seal costs $480 to produce. The markup rate is 75% of cost.

20. Surface Combustion Inc. calculates the cost of manufacturing a particular open-pit furnace as $1,214.78. Surface marks up each furnace 120% based on cost.

21. The Pet Company buys dog collars from a manufacturer for $1.48 each. It marks up each collar 356% of cost.

22. The Glass Company manufactures stem glassware. The cost per gross (144 items) is $132.48. The stemware is sold at a markup of 115% based on cost. **(a)** What is the selling price for one dozen glasses? **(b)** What is the selling price for a single piece of stemware?

23. Cook-n-Serve carries oven mitts that have a selling price of $13.86 a pair. Cook-n-Serve buys the mitts from a wholesaler and receives a 40% trade discount. **(a)** What is the cost? **(b)** What is the markup rate on cost? **(c)** What is the markup rate on selling price?

24. The Gold Co. sells gold bracelets at a markup of 325% based on cost. The markup on one bracelet is $213.60. Find the cost and the selling price.

25. ALGEBRA The Appliance Store sells appliances at a markup of 140% based on cost. The selling price of a new chrome refrigerator is $999.00. Find the **(a)** cost and **(b)** markup.

26. CHALLENGE PROBLEM Alvin Exports buys engine gaskets for $106.56 a dozen from a U.S. manufacturer. Alvin marks up the gaskets 100% based on cost. The overhead is estimated to be 30% of the selling price. **(a)** What is the selling price per gasket? **(b)** What is the markup rate as a percent of the selling price? **(c)** What is the net profit? **(d)** What is the net profit as a percent of the selling price?

Spiral Review

Add. (Skill 5)

27. $85.00 + $44.00 **28.** $144.47 + $185.52 **29.** $1,474.87 + $444.62

30. ALGEBRA Daria Jacobs sells cosmetics for Dagert's Department Store. She is guaranteed a minimum salary of $800 per month plus 6.75% of her total sales. What are her total sales for a month in which her gross pay is $1,075? (Lesson 1.6)

GET READY for the Next Lesson

PREREQUISITE SKILL Finding the Rate (Skill 31)

Round to nearest tenth of a percent.

31. $12.42 ÷ $15.60

32. $3.60 ÷ $12.40

33. $11.46 ÷ $31.11

34. $43.65 ÷ $78.91

35. $89.54 ÷ $133.78

36. $128.34 ÷ $367.21

LESSON 15.8 Markdown

Lesson Objective

Calculate the markdown in dollars and as a percent of the regular selling price.

Content Vocabulary

- markdown
- markdown rate

GET READY for the Lesson

When you are shopping around, what special pricing gets your attention?

Wendy Ballantine, owner of Heavy Lumber, is expecting a large shipment of prime Sitka Spruce boards from Alaska in a few weeks. In order to make room for this in-demand wood, she plans to have a sale on her existing stock of fir and pine boards.

As You Read

Identify Can you think of something you recently bought at a marked down price?

Markdown Your business may sell some merchandise at sale prices to attract customers, to make room for new merchandise, or to **attain** a sales quota. The **markdown**, or discount, is the difference between the regular selling price of an item and its sale price. The **markdown rate** is the markdown expressed as a percent of the regular selling price of the item. The formulas are:

Markdown = Regular Selling Price − Sale Price

$$\text{Markdown Rate} = \frac{\text{Markdown}}{\text{Regular Selling Price}}$$

EXAMPLE 1

Ski's Sport Shop sells cross-country skis at a regular selling price of $298.49. For one week only, Ski's has marked down the price to $168.94. What is the markdown rate?

Step 1: Find the markdown.

Regular Selling Price − Sale Price

$298.49 − $168.94 = $129.55

Step 2: Find the markdown rate.

$$\frac{\text{Markdown}}{\text{Regular Selling Price}} = \frac{\$129.55}{\$298.49} = 0.43401 = 43.4\%$$

The markdown rate is 43.4%

298.49  168.94 = 129.55 ÷ 298.49 = 0.4340178

Design Pics / LJM Photo

Complete the problems. Check your answers in the back of the book. Find the (a) markdown and (b) markdown rate.

1. Regular selling price of a pair of shoes is \$80. Sale price is \$60.
2. Regular selling price of a ceiling fan is \$174.79. Sale price is \$104.87.
3. Regular selling price of a blender is \$125. Sale price is \$89.
4. Regular selling price of a pair of shorts is \$45. Sale price is \$35.

Need Help? Go to...

Workshop 39: Problem-Solving Strategy: Linear Combinations, p. 80

EXAMPLE 2 Algebra

Bender's Auto Supply House has a set of floor mats that are marked down 60% to a sale price of \$32.00. Find the regular selling price and the markdown.

Step 1: Let x = Regular selling price
Let m = Markdown

Step 2: Write the equations

Markdown = Regular Selling Price − Sale Price

$m = x - 32$

$$\text{Markdown Rate} = \frac{\text{Markdown}}{\text{Regular Selling Price}}$$

$$60\% = \frac{m}{x}$$

Step 3: Express one variable in terms of the other. Substitute $x - 32$ for m in the second equation and solve.

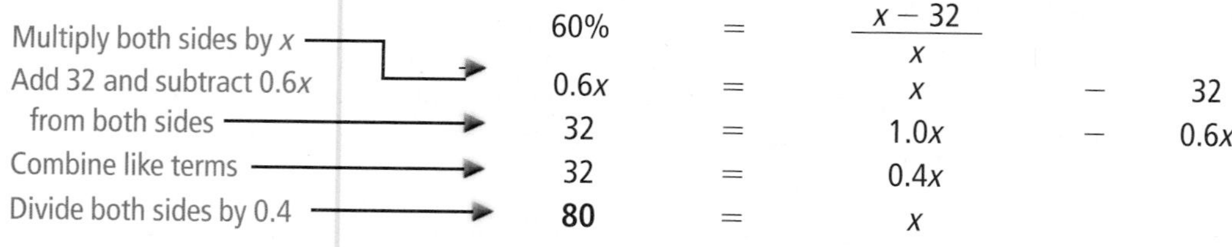

The regular selling price is \$80.00.

Step 4: Find the markdown

$x - 32 = 80 - 32 =$ **\$48 markdown**

Concept CHECK

Complete the problems. Check your answers in the back of the book.

5. Tellas Chocolates has truffles on sale annually for \$19.25 after a markdown of 45%. **(a)** What is the regular selling price? **(b)** What is the markdown?
6. Sarah's Books has tote bags on sale for \$14.65 after a 20% markdown. **(a)** What is the regular selling price? **(b)** What is the markdown?

Study Tip

Compare Notes

Compare your notes with a classmate's to be sure you did not miss any important points.

Did You Know?

Horse-Drawn Vacuums
In 1899, St. Louis entrepreneur John Thurman charged $4 per visit for door-to-door vacuum service. His patented, gasoline-powered device was so large that it was pulled by horses. It sucked dirt from floors and out of the house through hoses that led out a home's windows.

Lesson Practice

Find the (a) markdown and (b) markdown rate. Round answers to the nearest tenth of a percent.

	Item	Regular Price	Sale Price	Markdown	Markdown Rate
7.	Rain gear	$ 25.00	$ 20.00	a.	b.
8.	Fishing rod	$ 99.99	$ 64.99	a.	b.
9.	Recliner rocker	$ 247.87	$ 149.99	a.	b.
10.	Office furniture	$8,674.50	$4,337.25	a.	b.

For problems 11–14, find the markdown rate. Round answers to the nearest tenth of a percent.

11. All Star Foods has a regular price of $1.99 on Spirit Gum. It is on sale for $1.59.

12. ABC has digital cameras at a regular price of $799.99. The sale price is $699.99.

13. Design Center has a vacuum on sale for $179. The regular price is $209.

14. Office Center has marked down a computer from a regular price of $1,179.97 to a sale price of $979.97.

15. At Food Safe a dozen eggs can be purchased for $1.99 with a coupon or for $2.79 without a coupon. What is the markdown rate if the coupon is used?

16. A reciprocating saw is on sale for $99.99, a savings of $30.00 off the regular price. Find the markdown rate.

17. T-Mart is participating in a national promotion of convection ovens. The supreme oven is marked down $9.98 to a sale price of $59.99. The brushed chrome oven is marked down from $139.99 to $129.99. The top-of-the-line ultra oven is marked down $31.02 from the regular price of $329.99. What is the markdown rate for each?

18. **ALGEBRA** After marking down all tennis shoes 65%, All Sports has them on sale for $62.99. Find the **(a)** regular selling price and **(b)** markdown.

19. **ALGEBRA** Designer Furniture Company has all accessory tables marked down 58%. **(a)** What is the regular price of tables on sale for $63.00? **(b)** What is the markdown?

Spiral Review

Subtract. (Skill 6)

20. $74.99 − $14.99 **21.** $7.25 − $2.15 **22.** $126.36 − $87.14

23. The rate of assessment in Arlington, Virginia, is 100%. The tax rate is $8.78 per $1,000 of assessed value. What is the real estate tax on a piece of property that has a market value of $350,000? (Lesson 10.5)

GET READY for the Next Lesson

PREREQUISITE SKILL Finding the Percentage (Skill 30)

Round to the nearest tenth of a percent.

24. 9% of 80 **25.** 30% of 30 **26.** 70% of 20

27. 56% of 82 **28.** 23% of 93 **29.** 45% of 300

CHAPTER 15

Review and Assessment

AFTER YOU READ

Chapter SUMMARY

Business sales may require a number of different calculations. You can compute the markup in dollars and calculate the markup rate as a percent of the selling price. You may also want to compute the net profit in dollars and as a percent of the selling price. You can calculate the selling price of an item based on cost and markup rate. You can also compute the markup rate based on cost and the selling price based on cost and markup rate. Finally, you can calculate the markdown in dollars and as a percent of the regular selling price.

Vocabulary Check

1. On a sheet of paper, use each of these terms in a sentence.

Content Vocabulary

- cost (p. 559)
- selling price (p. 559)
- markup (p. 559)
- gross profit (p. 559)
- net profit (p. 559)
- markup rate (p. 561)
- operating expenses (p. 563)
- net-profit rate (p. 566)
- markdown (p. 577)
- markdown rate (p. 577)

Academic Vocabulary

- energy (p. 559)
- generate (p. 561)
- approximate (p. 563)
- consume (p. 566)
- prior (p. 569)
- foundation (p. 571)
- method (p. 574)
- attain (p. 577)

Concept Check

2. Explain how to compute the markup.
3. List expenses included in an item's cost.
4. Identify the formula for finding the markup rate as a percent of the selling price.
5. List operating expenses.
6. Explain how to determine net profit.
7. Explain how to find the net-profit rate.
8. Identify the formula for calculating the selling price based on cost and markup rate.
9. Explain how to find the markdown in dollars.
10. Identify the formula for finding the markdown rate.
11. **CRITICAL THINKING** Identify the method for finding the selling price when the markup rate is based on cost.

Lesson-by-Lesson Review (continued)

15.1 Markup (pp. 559–560)

Compute the markup in dollars.
Wall-to-Wall purchased throw rugs for $79.95 each. Wall-to-Wall sells the rugs for $129.95 each. What is the markup on each rug?

Find the markup.

Selling Price − Cost
$129.95 − $79.95 = **$50.00**

Review Exercises

Find the markup.

	Item	Selling Price	Cost	Markup
12.	Candy bar	$ 0.79	$ 0.50	
13.	Leather sofa	$1,899.00	$1,095.00	
14.	Tennis shoes	$ 85.50	$ 46.76	
15.	Color printer	$ 299.97	$ 205.00	
16.	Textbook	$ 45.50	$ 21.35	
17.	Router	$ 365.25	$ 210.27	

18. Tom's Nursery buys petunias by the pallet. Each pallet holds 36 petunia plants. The cost of each pallet to Tom's Nursery is $179.64. Tom sells the petunias for $7.99 per plant. **(a)** What is the markup per plant? **(b)** What is the markup per pallet?

15.2 Markup Rate (pp. 561–562)

Calculate the markup as a percent of the selling price.
Lucky Charms buys silver charms for $10.99 each. It sells them for $19.95 each. What is the markup rate based on the selling price?

Step 1: Find the markup.

Selling Price − Cost
$19.95 − $10.99 = $8.96 markup

Step 2: Find the markup rate based on the selling price.

$$\frac{\text{Markup}}{\text{Selling Price}} = \frac{\$8.96}{\$19.95} = 0.44912 = \textbf{44.9\% markup rate based on the selling price}$$

Review Exercises

Find the (a) markup and (b) markup rate to the nearest tenth of a percent.

	Item	Selling Price	Cost	Markup	Markup Rate
19.	Golf shirt	$ 39.95	$ 25.50	a.	b.
20.	Dog collar	12.59	6.45	a.	b.
21.	DVD Player	178.50	95.43	a.	b.
22.	Motorcycle	1,299.97	899.50	a.	b.
23.	Necklace	134.95	65.44	a.	b.

Lesson-by-Lesson Review (continued)

24. Fresh Produce, Inc. buys white button mushrooms for $0.87 a pack. The selling price is $1.50 a pack. What is the markup rate based on the selling price?
25. The Grill Store sells a heavy-duty gas grill for $199.00. The cost is $129.80. What is the markup rate based on the selling price?

15.3 Net Profit (pp. 563–565)

Determine the net profit in dollars.

Carl's Camera Shop purchases digital cameras for $356.98 each. The shop sells the cameras for $629.95. Carl estimates his overhead expenses to be 30% of the selling price of his merchandise. What is the net profit on each camera?

Step 1: Find the markup.

Selling Price − Cost

$629.95 − $356.98 = $272.97 markup

Step 2: Find the overhead.

Selling Price × Overhead Percent

$629.95 × 30% = 188.985 = $188.99 overhead

Step 3: Find the net profit.

Markup − Overhead

$272.97 − $188.99 = **$83.98 net profit**

Review Exercises

Find the (a) markup, (b) overhead, and (c) net profit.

	Item	Selling Price	Cost	Markup	Overhead Percent	Overhead	Net Profit
26.	Scrapbook paper	$ 55.00	$27.00	a.	30%	b.	c.
27.	Office supplies	$198.95	$95.95	a.	25%	b.	c.
28.	Paint	$133.50	$68.00	a.	45%	b.	c.
29.	Kitchen mixer	$147.50	$59.15	a.	22%	b.	c.
30.	Rocking horse	$185.00	$85.00	a.	36%	b.	c.

31. The buyer for Mango Mania purchases Key West-style hats for a cost of $14.50 each. Mango Mania sells them for $29.95 each. Operating expenses are estimated to be 25% of the selling price. What is the net profit per hat?
32. **ALGEBRA** Benny's Clothing operates on an overhead of 25% of the selling price. The overhead on the store's jeans is $18.21. If the jeans cost Benny's Clothing $18.25, find the **(a)** selling price, **(b)** markup, and **(c)** net profit.

Lesson-by-Lesson Review (continued)

15.4 Net-Profit Rate (pp. 566–568)

Find the net profit as a percent of the selling price.

Gina Kamrey is a buyer for a vintage clothing shop. She purchased some vintage handkerchiefs for a cost of $3.28 each. Her store sells them for $9.25 each. Operating expenses are estimated to be 33% of the selling price. What is the net-profit rate based on the selling price of the handkerchief?

Step 1: Find the net profit.

Markup – Overhead

($9.25 – $3.28) – ($9.25 × 33%)

= $5.97 – $3.05 = $2.92 net profit

Step 2: Find the net-profit rate.

$$\frac{\text{Net Profit}}{\text{Selling Price}} = \frac{2.92}{9.25} = 0.3156$$

= **31.6% net-profit rate**

Review Exercises

Determine the (a) overhead, (b) net profit and (c) net-profit rate.

	Item	Markup	Selling Price	Overhead Percent	Overhead	Net Profit	Net-Profit Rate
33.	Lamp	$ 106.00	$ 219.98	40%	a.	b.	c.
34.	Sweater	$ 48.00	$ 73.45	20%	a.	b.	c.
35.	Table saw	$ 132.95	$ 259.95	25%	a.	b.	c.
36.	Hard drive	$ 60.75	$ 109.95	30%	a.	b.	c.
37.	Dishwasher	$ 239.56	$ 446.50	40%	a.	b.	c.
38.	Air conditioner	$1,135.50	$1,950.46	50%	a.	b.	c.
39.	Speakers	$ 89.00	$ 189.00	20%	a.	b.	c.
40.	Pants	$ 45.00	$ 75.00	30%	a.	b.	c.

41. The Fashion Station operates on a net-profit rate of 30% of the selling price of dress shirts. If the markup is $18.50 and the overhead is $9.15, find the **(a)** net profit and **(b)** selling price.

42. The Corner Bakery operates on a net-profit rate of 25% of the selling price of its bread. If the markup is $2.98 and the overhead is $1.25, find the **(a)** net profit and **(b)** selling price.

43. **ALGEBRA** The City Hardware Store operates on a net-profit rate of 25% on their Spray Cans of Paint. The markup is $6.98 and the overhead is $4.44. Find the **(a)** net profit and **(b)** selling price.

Lesson-by-Lesson Review (continued)

15.5 Selling Price – Markup Based on Selling Price (pp. 569–570)

Calculate the selling price of an item based on cost and markup rate based on selling price.

Margie's Gifts purchased some vases for $13.50. Its markup rate is 35% based on the selling price. Find the selling price of the vases.

Step 1: Find the complement of the markup rate.

100% – 35% = 65% complement of the markup rate

Step 2: Find the selling price.

$$\frac{\text{Cost}}{\text{Complement of Markup Rate}} = \frac{\$13.50}{65\%} = \$20.769 = \mathbf{\$20.77\ selling\ price}$$

Review Exercises

Find the (a) complement of markup rate and (b) selling price.

	Item	Cost	Markup Rate	Complement of Markup Rate	Selling Price (Nearest Cent)
44.	Bicycle tire	$ 12.00	35.0%	a.	b.
45.	Child's bike	$ 105.50	22.0%	a.	b.
46.	Rocking chair	$ 129.95	45.0%	a.	b.
47.	Framed picture	$ 83.23	32.0%	a.	b.
48.	Designer jeans	$ 35.91	41.5%	a.	b.
49.	Leather sofa	$1,009.15	18.5%	a.	b.

50. Outdoor World purchased some parkas for $51.79 each. Its markup policy is 40% based on the selling price. What is the selling price?

51. Wauseon Antique Market marks up a drop-leaf table 60% of the selling price. A table is purchased for $185.00. What is the selling price?

15.6 Markup Rate Based on Cost (pp. 571–573)

Calculate the markup rate based on cost.

Boxes, Etc. purchases small wooden jewelry boxes for $31.20 from the manufacturer. Boxes, Etc. sells the boxes for $59.50. What is the markup rate based on cost?

Step 1: Find the markup.

Selling Price – Cost

$59.50 – $31.20 = $28.30 markup

Step 2: Find the markup rate based on cost.

$$\frac{\text{Markup}}{\text{Cost}} = \frac{\$28.30}{\$31.20} = 0.90705 = \mathbf{90.7\%\ markup\ rate\ based\ on\ cost}$$

Lesson-by-Lesson Review (continued)

Review Exercises

Find the (a) markup and (b) markup rate based on cost.

	Item	Selling Price	Cost	Markup	Markup Rate Based on Cost
52.	Flower Pot	$ 2.50	$ 1.75	a.	b.
53.	Video game	29.95	18.53	a.	b.
54.	Wicker basket	38.55	22.45	a.	b.
55.	Book shelf	109.95	79.95	a.	b.
56.	Portable swimming pool	954.33	654.10	a.	b.
57.	Wireless keyboard/mouse	89.75	55.50	a.	b.
58.	Bathroom cabinet	185.45	126.00	a.	b.
59.	Dorm refrigerator	165.50	85.95	a.	b.

60. John's Country Store sells a kitchen set for $125.99 after a markup of $59.50. Find the cost and the markup rate based on cost of the kitchen set.
61. Moore Groceries sells a desk fan for $10.95 after a markup of $4.55. Find the cost and the markup rate based on cost of the fan.
62. Smart Homes sells a blender for $99.00 after a markup of $36.45. Find the cost and the markup rate based on cost of the blender.
63. The Market sells liquid detergent for $18.99 after a markup of $9.26. Find the cost and the markup rate based on cost of the detergent.
64. **ALGEBRA** A diamond pendant has a 240% markup rate based on cost. The selling price is $846.60. **(a)** What is the cost? **(b)** What is the markup?

15.7 Selling Price – Markup Based on Cost (pp. 574–576)

Compute the selling price based on cost and markup rate based on cost.
Wholesale Electronics sells speakers to electronics stores for $18.50 a pair. Wholesale Electronics calculates the suggested retail price and attaches it to each set of speakers. The retail price is computed by marking up the cost to the electronics store by 150%. What is the suggested retail selling price?

Step 1: Find the markup.

Cost × Markup Rate on Cost

$18.50 × 150% = $27.75 markup

Step 2: Find the selling price.

Cost + Markup

$18.50 + $27.75 = **$46.25 selling price**

Lesson-by-Lesson Review (continued)

Review Exercises

Find the markup and the selling price (to the nearest cent).

	Item	Cost	Markup Rate Based on Cost	Markup	Selling Price
65.	Set of sheets	$ 32.00	75.00%	a.	b.
66.	Lamp	$185.50	100.00%	a.	b.
67.	Dishwasher	$229.55	125.00%	a.	b.
68.	Child's playhouse	$ 63.15	200.00%	a.	b.
69.	Shirt	$ 7.66	75.50%	a.	b.
70.	Counter top	$841.02	90.25%	a.	b.
71.	Ceiling fan	$ 85.23	82.00%	a.	b.

72. Regional Jewelry stores buy silver bracelets for $65.40 each. The retail price is computed by adding a markup of 150% of the cost. What is the retail selling price?
73. Winslow Hardware Store buys smoke detectors for $9.85 each. The retail price is computed by adding a markup of 80% of the cost. What is the retail selling price?

15.8 Markdown (pp. 577–579)

Calculate the markdown in dollars and as a percent of the regular selling price. Summer Fun sells a particular jet ski at a regular selling price of $2,995.50. For one week only, Summer Fun has marked down the price to $2,450.00. What is the markdown rate?

Step 1: Find the markdown.

Regular Selling Price − Sale Price

$2,995.50 − $2,450.00 = $545.50 markdown

Step 2: Find the markdown rate.

$$\frac{\text{Markdown}}{\text{Regular Selling Price}} = \frac{\$545.50}{\$2,995.50} = 0.18210 = \textbf{18.2\% markdown rate}$$

Review Exercises

Find the markdown and the markdown rate.

	Item	Regular Price	Sale Price	Markdown	Markdown Rate
74.	Novel	$ 25.00	$ 19.95	a.	b.
75.	Textbook	$ 79.99	$ 65.50	a.	b.
76.	Diamond watch	$1,895.45	$999.95	a.	b.
77.	Beads	$ 1.29	$ 0.79	a.	b.
78.	Small calculator	$ 12.67	$ 5.50	a.	b.
79.	Polo shirt	$ 32.18	$ 26.37	a.	b.

80. **ALGEBRA** At Billiards Supply House, a set of billiard balls is marked down 65% to a sale price of $28.00. Find the regular selling price and the markdown.

Practice Test

Record your answers on a sheet of paper.

1. **ALGEBRA** Murphy's Furnishings operates on an overhead percent of 32%, which results in an overhead of $3.18 on the store's best-selling furniture polish. What is the selling price of the polish?
   A $8.95 **B** $4.29
   C $9.94 **D** $3.95

2. Mellon's Big & Tall clothing store purchases pants for $21.75 each. The selling price for each pair of pants is $58.50. What is the markup rate based on the selling price?
   A 63% **B** 37%
   C 168% **D** 43%

3. Jaykell Photography purchases digital cameras for $385.50 each. The store sells the cameras for $635.25. Jaykell Photography's overhead is 28% of the selling price of its merchandise. What is the net profit on a digital camera?
   A $74.93 **B** $249.75
   C $141.81 **D** $71.88

4. Phaedra Dormus purchases scarves for Loom Inc. at a cost of $5.65 each. Loom sells the scarves with a $4.85 markup. The overhead on each scarf is $2.33. What is the net-profit rate based on the selling price of a scarf?
   A 24% **B** 32%
   C 14% **D** 46%

5. **ALGEBRA** Maltarich's Stationery operates on a net-profit rate of 25% on daily planners. The markup on the planners is $3.85 and the overhead is $1.18. What is the selling price of the planners?
   A $10.68 **B** $5.03
   C $14.57 **D** $8.20

6. Lahoski Shoes purchases a style of running shoes for $48.50 a pair from the manufacturer. The store sells the shoes for $89.99. What is the markup rate based on cost?
   A 48.4% **B** 46.1%
   C 85.5% **D** 89.3%

7. Dixie Bearings sells bearings to auto parts stores for $16.75 each. The suggested retail price is computed by marking up the cost to the auto parts stores by 135%. What is the suggested retail price of a bearing?
   A $22.61 **B** $39.36
   C $18.10 **D** $34.85

8. Paulie's Percussion Paradise sells a certain drum set for $2,150.50. For one week only, Paulie's has marked down the price to $1,750.00. What is the markdown rate?
   A 23.9 **B** 22.8%
   C 81.3% **D** 18.6%

9. S.C. Electronics sells universal remote controls for $19.95 each. The remotes have been marked up $8.96. What is the cost and markup rate based on the cost?

10. Annie's Appliances purchases microwave ovens for $301.98 each. Annie sells the microwaves for $580.89. She estimates her overhead expenses to be 32% of the selling price of her merchandise. What is the net profit on each microwave?

11. Hedo Ilescu is a buyer for a Turkish rug store. He purchased some throw rugs for a cost of $78.95 each. The store sells them for $165 each. Operating expenses for the store are estimated at 35% of the selling price. What is the store's net-profit rate based on the selling price of a rug?

12. $45.32 ÷ $64.50

13. $125.66 + $395.45

14. $21,532.67 − $11,649.05

15. 68% of 344

16. $312.54 ÷ 30%

17. 42% of $8,540.50

Standardized Test Practice

Cumulative, Chapters 1–15

PART 1 Multiple Choice

Record your answers on the answer sheet provided by your teacher or on a sheet of paper.

1. The average daily balance on Oliver McCann's credit card is $187.50. Oliver's previous balance totaled $1,345.89. The credit card company charges a finance charge that is 2% of the average daily balance. What is the dollar amount of the finance charge?
   A $26.92 **B** $3.75
   C $30.67 **D** $23.17

2. **ALGEBRA** Alicia Alexander makes a deposit at an ATM and leaves with $100 in cash. The receipt shows that the total deposit was $912. The checks she deposited totaled 3 times the currency she deposited. How much currency was deposited?
   A $704.00 **B** $812.00
   C $253.00 **D** $203.00

3. **ALGEBRA** Nikos Blackburn invested some money. He earned $216.00 in simple interest for 8 months at an annual interest rate of 4.5%. How much money did Nikos invest?
   A $3,600.00 **B** $4,800.00
   C $7,200.00 **D** $8,225.00

4. A store has a DVD with a price tag that shows a price of $9.99. If the purchase price of this DVD is $10.44, what is the sales tax rate?
   A 9.5% **B** 4.5%
   C 5.0% **D** 3.4

5. Fran Rothermel bought an entertainment center for $3,210.50. If she made a 12% down payment, how much would she be financing?
   A $2,825.24 **B** $1,385.26
   C $2,632.61 **D** $2,728.93

6. Harry's Auto Stores marked up steering wheel covers 60% based on the cost. What is the selling price of a steering wheel cover that cost Harry's $6.24?
   A $10.40 **B** $8.74
   C $9.98 **D** $10.70

PART 2 Short Response/Griddable

7. **ALGEBRA** An electric guitar was marked down 15%. The sale price of the guitar was $523. What was the regular selling price of the guitar?

8. **ALGEBRA** Jodi Meyers owns 200 shares of Caslin Industries (CI) stock. After the quarterly dividend is reinvested, she owns 207.4 shares. CI is selling for $101.20 per share. What is the annual dividend per share and the annual yield for CI?

PART 3 Extended Response

Show your work.

9. Explain a chain discount that reads "40% less 20% less 15%". Using this discount, calculate the final net price of a $614 snow blower.

10. Why would a supplier offer a chain discount?

11. **ALGEBRA** Miko Yachavone is leasing a luxury automobile. The $1,600.00 due at signing includes title and fees. His monthly payment will be $315.63 plus 4% sales tax. The total lease cost is $13,417.19. How many months does the lease last?

TEST-TAKING TIP

Essay Questions Pay close attention to the way the essay or extended response question is phrased. Know what you are being asked before you begin to write.

Building Academic Skills

Mathematics

You want to sell some sports equipment that you no longer use. The equipment originally cost a total of $103.49, but it is a few years old. You estimate that it is probably worth about half of what you paid for it. Before you write a price tag for one-half of the original cost, you determine that you need to add some overhead costs to this amount. After doing research, you add 20% to your estimated value of the equipment. At what price do you sell it? What sort of expenses will the 20% overhead cover?

English Language Arts/Writing

Clothing is often marked up more than 100%. Write a paragraph explaining what this means in terms of the price you pay in the store. Also discuss factors that go into determining the price other than the cost of the clothing before markup.

Social Studies/Economics

You are considering opening a home maintenance and repair business. You realize that your competition will include large plumbing repair companies and electricians, and to a lesser extent, carpenters, painters, roofers, and flooring installers. Use the Internet and library resources to find services similar to yours in your town, to evaluate the competition. Write a list of ways in which you can differentiate yourself from the competition.

Building Real-World Skills

Career WISE

Retail Sales Professional People love to shop—and since more products are available than ever before, helpful retail salespeople are always in demand. Whether it is in a mall clothing store, a local book shop or a luxury auto dealership, friendly retail sales workers who understand their products are beneficial to both the retailer and the customer.

Research and Share:

a. Visit the Web site of the Bureau of Labor Statistics and locate the page on retail salespersons. How many retail salespersons does the BLS say worked in the U.S. at last count? What are the prospects for growth of this job?

b. Make a list of traits that make a person a good retail sales professional. Share your list with the class.

21st Century Workplace

Future Business Leaders of America There are several student organizations that host local and national business math competitions. Participating in competitive events is a great way to challenge yourself, build credentials for your résumé, practice leadership skills, and have fun.

Research and Write:

a. Using the Internet, go to the Web sites of Future Business Leaders of America (FBLA) and of Business Professionals of America (BPA), to research business math and other business competitions. What competitions interest you? Why do students participate in competitive events?

b. Create a flow chart or other graphic organizer that lists three competitions hosted by each organization, or write a paragraph describing the benefits of participating in competitive events.

CHAPTER 16

Marketing

Big Idea

A company's marketing department deals with many factors including surveys, sales potential, market share, sales projections, advertising costs, and pricing.

Explore the Photo

Advertising
Marketing is an important part of almost any business. *What are some of your favorite advertisements?*

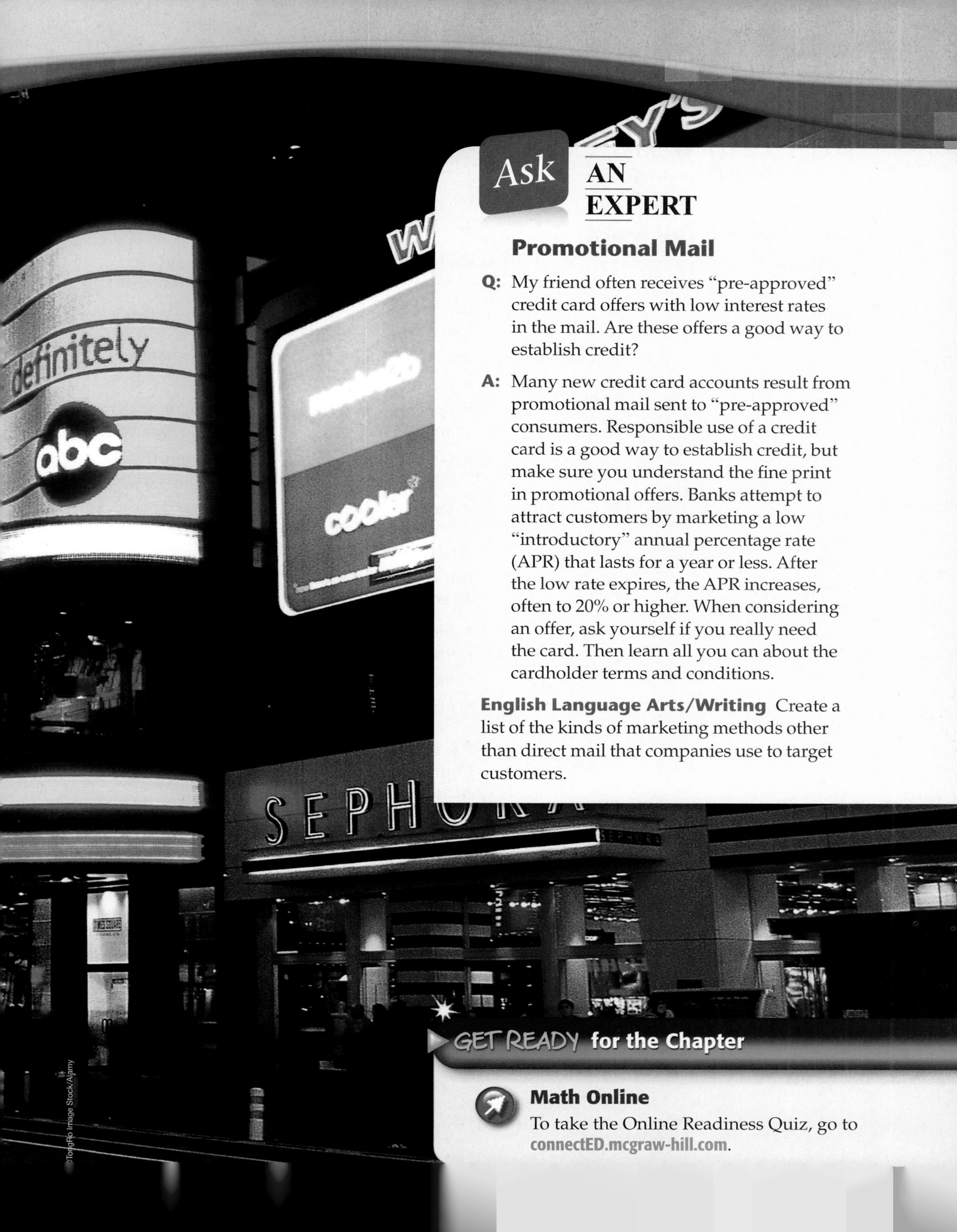

Ask AN EXPERT

Promotional Mail

Q: My friend often receives "pre-approved" credit card offers with low interest rates in the mail. Are these offers a good way to establish credit?

A: Many new credit card accounts result from promotional mail sent to "pre-approved" consumers. Responsible use of a credit card is a good way to establish credit, but make sure you understand the fine print in promotional offers. Banks attempt to attract customers by marketing a low "introductory" annual percentage rate (APR) that lasts for a year or less. After the low rate expires, the APR increases, often to 20% or higher. When considering an offer, ask yourself if you really need the card. Then learn all you can about the cardholder terms and conditions.

English Language Arts/Writing Create a list of the kinds of marketing methods other than direct mail that companies use to target customers.

GET READY for the Chapter

Math Online

To take the Online Readiness Quiz, go to **connectED.mcgraw-hill.com**.

Chapter 16 Marketing

Reading Guide

Before You Read

Describe How do you think marketing affects the purchases you make?

Main Idea

You could create the best product in the world, but if you do not market it properly, you are certain to fail. People need to know about your product or service or you will not sell it.

Graphic Organizer

Before you read this chapter, draw a diagram like the one below. As you read, note various considerations that go into marketing efforts.

Math Online Go to connectED.mcgraw-hill.com to download this graphic organizer.

Content Vocabulary

You will learn these key terms in this chapter.

- product test
- opinion research firm
- opinion survey
- sales potential
- sample
- market
- market share
- sales projection
- factor method
- factor
- pricing

Academic Vocabulary

You will see these words in your reading and on your tests.

- panel
- volume
- indication
- economy
- objective
- generates
- ultimately

You can find vocabulary definitions in the **Content Vocabulary** Glossary and the **Academic Vocabulary** Glossary in the back of the book.

LESSON 16.1

Opinion Surveys

Lesson Objective

Compute the rate of a particular response in an opinion survey.

Content Vocabulary

- product test
- opinion research firm
- opinion survey

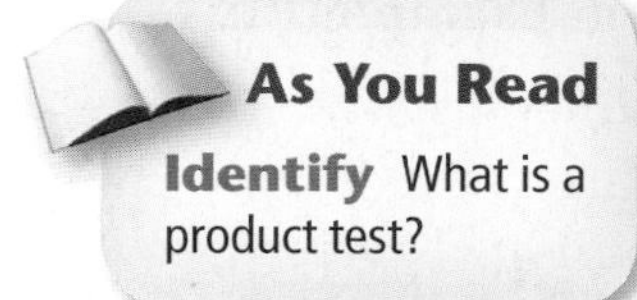

As You Read

Identify What is a product test?

GET READY for the Lesson

Why might a company want to know your opinion about a product or service?

Mika Flores and Dawn McCarthy were walking down the street when a woman offered them passes to watch the taping of a new television talk show. It was an interesting experience—they watched the show, then filled out a card saying what they did and did not like about it.

Opinion Surveys When you develop a new product, you will want to know how likely it is to sell. You may conduct a **product test**. This is when you ask a group of people to try the product. You may hire an **opinion research firm** that specializes in product testing to conduct the test. **Panels** of volunteers try the product and respond to questions in an **opinion survey**. An opinion research firm tabulates the answers to the questions and submits tables of results to you. It is important to note that the use of surveys and statistics in making inferences and valid arguments does have some limitations. You will use this formula when conducting opinion surveys:

$$\text{Percent of Particular Response} = \frac{\text{Number of Times Particular Response Occurs}}{\text{Total Number of Responses}}$$

EXAMPLE 1

Countryside Cereal Company conducted an opinion survey of 2,600 people for its new Good Morning cereal. This table shows the responses of the 2,600 people surveyed.

Opinion	Age Group			
	Under 18	**18 to 40**	**Over 40**	**Total**
Excellent	200	430	1,450	2,080
Good	25	108	215	348
Fair	10	12	99	121
Poor	5	10	36	51
Total	**240**	**560**	**1,800**	**2,600**

Countryside Cereal Company operates on the standard that over 80% of the responses must be "Excellent" or production will be halted. What percent of the total responses rated the cereal "excellent"? What should Countryside do?

Step 1: Compute the rate of the response.

$$\frac{\text{Number of Times Particular Response Occurs}}{\text{Total Number of Responses}} = \frac{2{,}080}{2{,}600} = 0.80 = \mathbf{80\%}$$

The rate of response is 80% "excellent" responses.

Step 2: Technically, Countryside should halt production of their new cereal. Over 80% did not respond "Excellent," exactly 80% responded "Excellent." However, common sense might alter that decision.

When an opinion survey is conducted you may make a prediction (estimate) of the number of responses for a particular question. *Absolute error* is the amount by which a prediction differs from the actual response. *Relative error* is the percent the absolute error is of the actual response.

$$\text{Absolute Error} = \text{Prediction} - \text{Actual Response}$$

$$\text{Relative Error} = \frac{\text{Absolute Error}}{\text{Actual Response}}$$

Concept CHECK

Complete the problems. Check your answers in the back of the book.

Use the Countryside Cereal Company opinion survey in **Example 1** to determine the percent of the total responses that:

1. Rated the cereal "good."
2. Were under 18 years old.
3. Rated the cereal "poor."
4. Were over 40 years old.

Study Tip

Motivate

Help your motivation to study by developing a sense of discovery and taking responsibility for your learning.

EXAMPLE 2

Countryside Cereal Company in **Example 1** had predicted that in the "Under 18" group, 220 would respond "Excellent." Determine the absolute error and the relative error.

Step 1: Determine the absolute error

$$\text{Prediction} - \text{Actual Response} = 220 - 200 = \mathbf{20}$$

The absolute error is 20.

Step 2: Determine the relative error

$$\frac{\text{Absolute Error}}{\text{Actual Response}} = \frac{20}{200} = 0.10 = \mathbf{10\%}$$

The relative error is 10%

Concept CHECK

Complete the problems. Check your answers in the back of the book.

5. Suppose Countryside Cereal Company operates on the standard that over 90% must respond "Excellent" or "Good" or production will be halted. What should they do?
6. Countryside Cereal Company had predicted that 8 in the "18 to 40" group would respond "Poor." Determine the absolute error.
7. Determine the relative error in **Problem 6.**

Aircraft Mechanic
Commercial jets are complicated machines. Advances in computer technology and aircraft operating systems require mechanics to have advanced technical skills and be motivated to learn more. **Can you think of other careers that require ongoing education?**

Lesson Practice

Round answers to the nearest tenth of a percent.

8. Eighteen hundred out of 2,000 people surveyed own computers. What percent of the total people surveyed own computers?

9. Four hundred sixty out of 500 people surveyed "like" the new flavor of Mintie toothpaste. Suppose the manufacturer operates on the standard that over 90% must respond that they "like" the new formula. **(a)** What percent of the total people surveyed like it? **(b)** What should the company do?

10. Fisher Motors conducted a survey on its dealer service. The people surveyed were asked to choose one answer for this question: "If you DO NOT usually go to the dealer from whom you bought your car for service, why not?" The choices and number of responses received for each are shown in the table. What is the percent of each response?

Fisher Motors – Dealer Service Survey			
a. Moved away from vicinity	37	**b.** Disliked quality of service	14
c. Service charges too high	95	**d.** Crowded service department	110
e. Location not convenient	14	**f.** Some other reason	30

11. Suppose Fisher Motors (in Problem 10) decided that 35% must respond that the service charges are too high before they would lower prices. Should they lower the price for service?

12. If Fisher Motors (in Problem 10) had predicted 121 responses to "Crowded service department," determine the absolute error and the relative error.

13. If Fisher Motors (in Problem 10) had predicted 76 responses to "Service charges too high," determine the absolute error and the relative error.

14. The Sleep Well motel chain conducts a follow-up survey of all individuals that have stayed at a Sleep Well motel. The individuals are asked to respond to these questions:

"If the need arises for you to stay at a motel, would you stay at a Sleep Well motel? If not, why not?" The choices and number of responses received for each are shown in the table: What is the percent of each response to the nearest tenth percent?

The Sleep Well Motel survey

(a) I would stay at a Sleep Well again 183

I would not stay at a Sleep Well because

(b) The rooms were not clean 10

(c) The price was too high 20

(d) The check-in process took too long 4

(e) The check-out process took too long 8

(f) Locations are not convenient 25

(g) If 20% or more responded that prices were too high, Sleep Well was going to reduce prices. Will Sleep Well reduce prices?

(h) If Sleep Well had predicted 200 would respond that they would stay at a Sleep Well again, find the absolute error and the relative error.

15. CHALLENGE PROBLEM Before beginning production of its new vacuum cleaner, the Devaney Company conducted an opinion survey of a group of people at the mall. When asked if they would purchase the product, the people gave these responses:

	Age Group				
Response	**Under 25**	**25 to 34**	**35 to 49**	**50 and older**	**Total**
Definitely	53	151	126	75	
Probably	75	184	203	140	
Possibly	87	135	130	99	
No	91	57	54	80	
Total					

(a) Find the total for each response.
(b) Find the total number of people in each age group.
(c) Find the total number of people in the survey.
(d) Find the percent of the total for each response group.
(e) What is the percent of "definitely" responses in each age group?
(f) What age group is most likely to purchase the product?
(g) What is the percent of "no" responses in each age group?
(h) What age group is least likely to purchase the product?
(i) What is the absolute error if Devaney had projected 154 "probably" responses in the "50 and over" age group?
(j) What is the relative error if Devaney had projected 154 "probably" responses in the "50 and over" age group?

Spiral Review

Find the percent. Round to the nearest tenth. (Skill 30)

16. 8% of 70 **17.** 70% of 80 **18.** 30% of 500

19. You have applied for a $90,000 mortgage loan at an annual interest rate of 9.00%. The loan is for a period of 30 years and will be paid in equal monthly payments that include interest. What is the total amount of interest charged? (Lesson 10.2)

20. ALGEBRA Using the compound interest formula [$A = P(1.00 + r)^n$], find the amount of interest on a 5 year CD for $25,000 at 4.24% compounded quarterly.

GET READY for the Next Lesson

PREREQUISITE SKILL Finding the Percentage (Skill 30)

21. 130% of $3,005
22. $2\frac{3}{4}$% of 48
23. 210% of $588
24. $\frac{3}{8}$% of 360
25. 89% of $4,820
26. $8\frac{7}{16}$% of 320

LESSON 16.2 Sales Potential

Lesson Objective
Determine the annual sales potential of a new product.

Content Vocabulary
- sales potential
- sample
- market

GET READY for the Lesson

How do you decide which brand of a product to buy?

Alex Morgan told his mother that he noticed his clean laundry had a different fragrance. Sandra Morgan replied that the family had received a month's supply of a new detergent. In exchange, they would try out the detergent and say whether they liked it enough to buy it in the future.

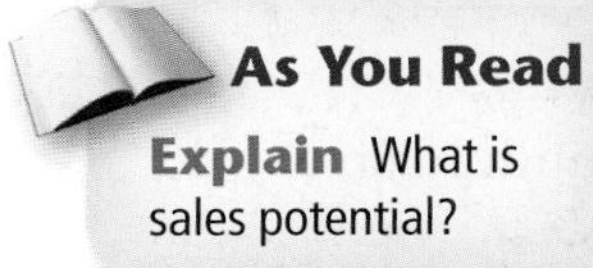

As You Read
Explain What is sales potential?

Sales Potential Before your business produces a new product, you may try to determine the product's **sales potential**. The sales potential is an estimate of the sales **volume** of a product during a specified period of time. You may manufacture a small number of the product for a selected group of people to try. This group is called a **sample**.

The sales potential of your new product is based on: (1) the percent of people in the sample who would purchase your product, (2) an estimate of the size of the **market**, and (3) the average number of times that an individual might purchase this type of product during a specified period of time. The *market* is the total number of people who might purchase the product.

Annual Sales Potential = Estimated Market Size × Individual Rate of Purchase × Percent of Potential Purchasers

EXAMPLE

The Ruston Corporation has developed a suntan cream called Lite Stuff. Ruston chose a sample of teenagers to try the new product. Of the 3,000 teenagers in the sample, 1,200 said they would purchase Lite Stuff. The Ruston Corporation estimates that there are 2,000,000 teenagers who buy suntan cream. Ruston's surveys indicate that each teenager purchases about 3 tubes of suntan cream per year. What is the sales potential for Lite Stuff for one year?

Step 1: Find the percent of potential purchasers.

$\frac{1,200}{3,000} = 0.40 = 40\%$ potential purchasers

Step 2: Find the annual sales potential.

Estimated Market Size	×	Individual Rate of Purchase	×	Percent of Potential Purchasers	
2,000,000	×	3	×	40%	= **2,400,000 annual sales potential**

Find the percent of potential purchasers and the annual sales potential. Check your answers in the back of the book.

1. A new face cream has an estimated market of 1,400,000. Three hundred twenty out of 1,600 would purchase it. The rate of purchase is 2.

Study Tip

Break Time

Take short breaks frequently. Your memory retains the information that you study at the beginning and the end better than what you study in the middle.

Lesson Practice

Complete the table.

	Number in Sample	Number of Potential Customers	Percent of Potential Customers	Estimated Market Size	Individual Rate of Purchase per Year	Annual Sales Potential
2.	400	100	25%	800,000	1 can	a.
3.	500	10	a.	1,800,000	1 once	b.
4.	1,500	300	a.	5,700,000	1 once	b.

For Problems 5 and 6, determine the annual sales potential.

5. A child's car seat was tested by 1,200 people. Three hundred sixty said they would buy it. The estimated market size is 3,000,000. The company estimates that each person would buy the seat once.
6. One thousand people tested dishwashing detergent. Eighty-seven said they would buy it. The estimated market size is 4,500,000. The estimated rate of purchase is 12 times a year.
7. The National Optometrics Company is marketing a new, softer, more pliable disposable contact lens. Out of a sample of 1,200 users, 150 preferred the new lenses. The estimated total market of disposable contact lens users is 1,500,000. The average disposable contact lens wearer purchases 12 lenses per year. What is the sales potential for the new lenses for 1 year?

8. **CHALLENGE PROBLEM** Half the people surveyed said they would buy the new 33-gallon trash bags. If the estimated market is 5.2 million people and it is estimated that each person would buy 4 per month, what is the annual sales potential?

Spiral Review

Find the percentage. Round answers to the nearest hundredth. (Skill 30)

9. $4\frac{1}{4}\%$ of 96 **10.** $\frac{3}{8}$ of 120 **11.** 125% of $4,140

12. Sara McMahon purchased a new car 3 years ago for $24,500.00. The current estimated value is $17,900.00. Annual variable costs this year were $895.60. Insurance was $1,350.00, registration was $132.50, and loan interest totaled $1,080.00. She drove 12,540 miles this year. Compute the cost per mile. (Lesson 9.5)

GET READY for the Next Lesson

PREREQUISITE SKILL **Finding the Rate** (Skill 31)

Find the rate. Round answers to the nearest tenth of a percent.

13. $n\%$ of 56 = 42 **14.** $n\%$ of 50 = 35 **15.** $n\%$ of 340 = 85

LESSON 16.3

Market Share

Lesson Objective

Calculate the market share of a new product.

Content Vocabulary

- market share

How do companies try to earn your business?

Assistant manager Tony Rodriguez smiles as he greets a customer. He knows that customer service is one reason why Les Schwab tires is the top tire seller in the area.

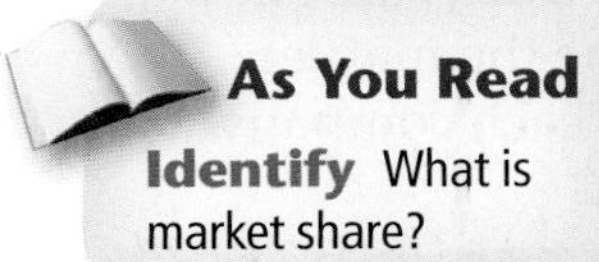

As You Read

Identify What is market share?

Market Share One **indication** of how your product is selling in the marketplace is its **market share**. Market share is the percent of the entire market that purchases your product instead of a competitor's product. You can calculate your percent of the total market share by using either the number of units sold or the dollar value of sales.

$$\text{Market Share} = \frac{\text{Total Product Sales}}{\text{Total Market Sales}}$$

EXAMPLE

Amdex, an air conditioner manufacturer, sold 1,200,000 air conditioners during the year. During the same period, a total of 8,000,000 air conditioners were purchased in the entire U.S. market. What was Amdex's market share for the year?

Find the market share.

$$\frac{\text{Total Product Sales}}{\text{Total Market Sales}} = \frac{1{,}200{,}000}{8{,}000{,}000} = 0.15 = \textbf{15\% market share}$$

Concept CHECK

Find the market share. Check your answers in the back of the book.

1. Units of one brand of toothpaste sold total 2,000,000. Market sales total 20,000,000.
2. Sales of one brand of appliances total $4,000,000. Market sales total $180,000,000.

Lesson Practice

Find the market share. Round to the nearest tenth percent.

	Company	Total Product Sales	Total Market Sales	Market Share
3.	Waida	$8,000,000	$20,000,000	
4.	Simross	700,000	42,000,000	
5.	Hershel	1,400,000	5,000,000	

Mike Kemp / age fotostock

Reading Math +−÷=

Division
Read the line separating the numerator from the denominator in a fraction just like the symbol ÷. Read both $\frac{1}{5}$ and 1 ÷ 5 "one *divided by* 5."

For Problems 6–9, find the market share for the items indicated.

6. A tire company sells approximately 4,000,000 automobile tires per year. There are approximately 44,000,000 automobile tires sold per year in the entire market.

7. A book company sells approximately 9,000,000 paperback books per year. Sales for the entire paperback book market total approximately 30,000,000 books per year.

8. The Grill Company sells about \$3,100,000 in outdoor grills annually. The total annual sales of outdoor grills in the entire market are about \$8,500,000.

9. The Linen Sheet Company has sales totaling approximately \$1,400,000 in fitted sheets. Total sales of fitted sheets by all companies are approximately \$5,350,000.

10. Last month, Internet Survey Inc. collected data on the number of Internet browser software packages sold to 40,000 customers indicated in the table. What market share did each browser have?

Browser Name	Total Market Share	Percent Market Share
MS Internet	31,000	a.
Firefox	6,000	b.
Safari	2,000	c.
Opera	350	d.
Netscape	300	e.
Opera Mini	160	f.
All Others	190	g.
Total	40,000	

11. End-of-year sales data for the number of sales for cars and light trucks are shown. Determine the market share for each company.

	Unit Sales for Cars & Light Trucks	Percent Market Share
General Motors	9,100,000	a.
Toyota	8,520,000	b.
Ford	6,560,000	c.
Chrysler	4,440,000	d.
Honda	3,650,000	e.
Total	32,270,000	

12. CHALLENGE PROBLEM End-of-fiscal-year revenue for all department stores is \$73.5 billion. The larger stores had these sales in billions: Willards, \$7.5; Sally's, \$20.0; Howards, \$27; Right Stuff, \$9; and Bostons, \$3.2. The smaller stores make up the remaining sales. Determine the market share of the smaller stores. Round your answer to the nearest tenth of a percent.

Spiral Review

Find the rate. Round answers to the nearest tenth of a percent. (Skill 31)

13. $n\%$ of 84 = 21 **14.** $n\%$ of 50 = 35 **15.** $n\%$ of 45 = 50

16. ALGEBRA Wapi Hena earned \$225.00 in simple interest in 9 months at an annual interest rate of 7.25%. How much money did he invest? (Lesson 5.4)

GET READY for the Next Lesson

PREREQUISITE SKILL Multiplying Decimals (Skill 8)

Round answers to the nearest thousandth.

17. 389.45 × 100.65 **18.** 631.44 × 6.314 **19.** 0.082 × 900.000

LESSON 16.4 Sales Projections

Lesson Objective
Use the factor method or a graph to determine projected sales.

Content Vocabulary
- sales projection
- factor method
- factor

GET READY for the Lesson

What kind of new business do you think would do well in your community?

Zena Harris was excited about investing in new silkscreening equipment. Her custom t-shirt company did well in its first year of business, but by her calculations she would do even better in the second year. Zena was confident that her revenues would far exceed her costs.

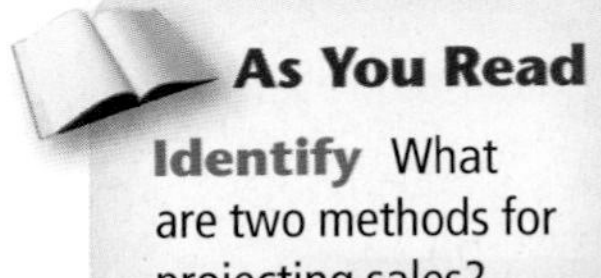

As You Read
Identify What are two methods for projecting sales?

Sales Projections A **sales projection** is an estimate of the dollar volume or unit sales that might occur during a future time period. You may use a sales projection to plan for production or purchasing. A sales projection may be based on past sales. New products or a changing **economy** may result in sales figures that differ from the figures you projected.

One method used to project sales is called the **factor method**. The **factor** is your company's present market share expressed as a percent. Use this formula:

Projected Sales = Projected Market Sales × Market-Share Factor

Another method used to project sales involves a graph of your sales history. You use the graph to project an estimate of future sales:

1. Use points to plot the past sales on a graph. The x-axis is years. The y-axis is sales.
2. Draw a straight line through the approximate middle of the points, so that most of the points are as close as possible to the line. Continue the line to the year for which the projection is being made.
3. Read the sales value at this point on the line.

EXAMPLE 1

Community Food Store has a 6% share of the market for food sales in the Chicago Heights area. Food sales in the area for next year are estimated to be $38,400,000. What is the projected sales figure for Community Food Store in the Chicago Heights area for next year?

Find the projected sales.

Projected Market Sales × Market-Share Factor

38,400,000 × 6% = **$2,304,000 projected sales**

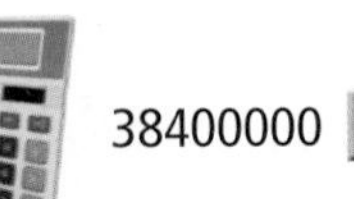

38400000 × 6 % 2304000

PhotoAlto/age fotostock

Complete the problem. Check your answer in the back of the book.

1. Appliance Market has a market-share factor of 8%. The projected market sales are $6,300,000. Find the projected sales.

Reading Math +−÷=

Tables and Charts

Read and understand titles and headings for columns and rows before you analyze the data in a chart or table.

EXAMPLE 2

The marketing department of Stanley Store wants to project sales for the year 2021 using a graph of past sales. The sales are:

Stanley Store's Sales							
Year	2005	2006	2007	2008	2009	2010	2011
Sales (in millions)	$2.50	$2.00	$3.00	$4.30	$3.30	$5.00	$4.50

Using a graph, what sales projection might the marketing department make for 2021?

Step 1: Graph the sales from 2005 through 2011.

Step 2: Draw a straight line through the approximate middle of the points, out to 2021.

Step 3: Read the sales projection for 2021.

Figure 16.1

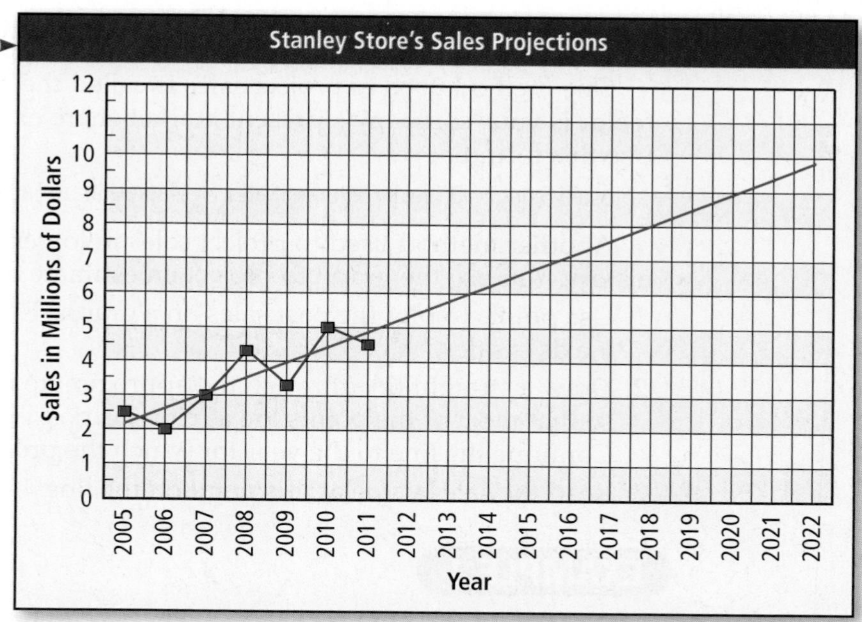

Projected sales for 2021 are approximately $9.25 million.

Concept CHECK

Complete the problems. Check your answers in the back of the book.

2. Refer to **Figure 16.1.** Give the approximate sales projections for: **(a)** 2012, **(b)** 2014, and **(c)** 2016.

SPREADSHEET APPLICATION

Sales Projections

You can use a spreadsheet like the partial one below to project sales using a graph. You will need to enter the past sales. The graph will be automatically constructed for you.

Math Online Go to connectED.mcgraw-hill.com to download the spreadsheet application for this activity.

	A	B	C
1		Year	Sales
2	Year 1	2005	$3.20
3	Year 2	2006	
4	Year 3	2007	

Enter the following sales into the spreadsheet.

Sales Records for Bargin's Sporting Goods (in millions)										
Year	2005	2006	2007	2008	2009	2010	2011	2012	2013	2014
Sales	$3.20	$3.50	$4.00	$4.25	$4.75	$5.10	$5.00	$5.25	$5.35	$5.40

Think and Discuss

1. Change the chart title to "Bargin's Sporting Goods."
2. Add a trendline. Place your cursor on the graphed line, right-click, and select "Add Trend-line." Confirm that the Type is "Linear" and click "OK."
3. What is the approximate sales projection for the year 2018?

Lesson Practice

For Problems 3–5, refer to Figure 16.1 and give the approximate sales projections for:

3. 2017
4. 2018
5. 2019
6. Quick Copy Machines has a market share of 15%. Estimated market sales for next year are $9,100,000. What is Quick Copy's sales projection for next year?
7. Bonaventura Bakery now has 13% of the market for Watson County. The total estimated sales in the county for next year are $4,750,000. What sales volume should Bonaventura Bakery project for next year?
8. Silver Oaks Bowling Lanes has traditionally had 15% of the bowling business in the East Delta area. The total estimated bowling business in this area for next year is $11,900,000. What bowling business can Silver Oaks project for next year?
9. Construct a graph and determine what sales might be projected for 2019 for Target Sporting Goods (in millions) using these data:

Target Sporting Goods' Sales Records										
Year	2005	2006	2007	2008	2009	2010	2011	2012	2013	2014
Sales	$4.40	$4.90	$5.00	$4.50	$5.10	$5.40	$5.00	$5.50	$5.70	$5.00

10. Use **Figure 16.2** for Wilson Inc. to estimate the sales projections for **(a)** 2014, **(b)** 2015, **(c)** 2016, **(d)** 2017, **(e)** 2018, and **(f)** 2019.

Figure 16.2

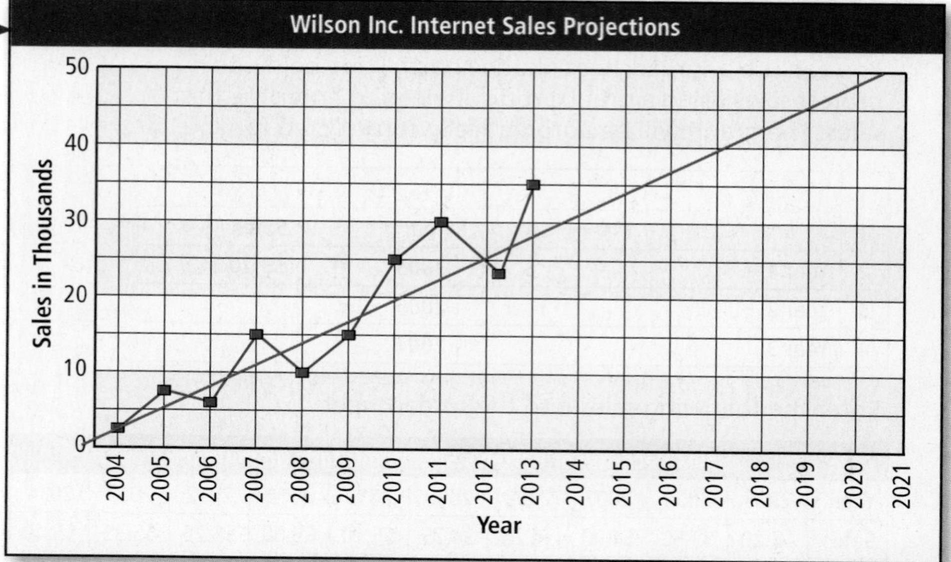

11. Construct a graph of the sales history of Buy-Lo Market. Project sales for: **(a)** 2015, **(b)** 2020, and **(c)** 2025

Buy-Lo Market's Sales Records						
Year	1985	1990	1995	2000	2005	2010
Sales (in millions)	$12	$14	$11	$12	$15	$14

12. **CHALLENGE PROBLEM** Prince Dairy Stores has 4 stores in Leland County that now do 8% of the dairy business there. Estimated dairy product sales for next year are $8,416,000. Prince is adding another store next year and expects to increase its market share by 25%. Project Prince Dairy's sales for next year.

Spiral Review

Multiply. Round answers to the nearest thousandth. (Skill 8)

13. 442.86×0.235

14. $3{,}240.03 \times 1.2564$

15. 0.044×0.587

16. **ALGEBRA** Regina Thomas is interested in a trampoline. It is marked down 28%. Regina could save $150.00 if she buys the trampoline while it is on sale. What is the regular selling price? (Lesson 6.6)

GET READY for the Next Lesson

PREREQUISITE SKILL Finding the Percentage (Skill 30)

Find the percentage. Round answers to the nearest hundredth.

17. 6.4% of 420

18. 8.9% of $2,012

19. 151% of $935

20. 1% of $73,010

21. 0.4% of 6,014

22. 1,500% of $780

LESSON 16.5

Newspaper Advertising Costs

Lesson Objective
Calculate the cost of advertising in a newspaper.

GET READY for the Lesson

Which newspaper advertisements catch your eye?

Elite Electronics gets a lot of business on weekends. Every Friday, a full-page advertisement showing Elite's sale prices appears in the local newspaper's popular weekend entertainment section.

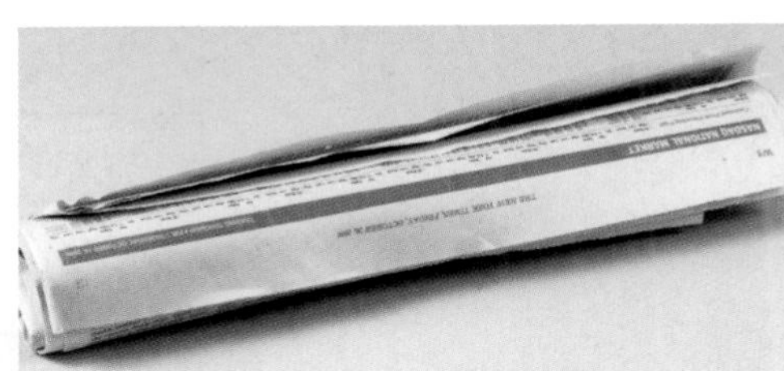

As You Read
List What factors affect the cost of a newspaper advertisement?

Newspaper Advertising Costs To attract customers, you may advertise your products or services in a newspaper. The **objective** is to increase your sales. The cost of the advertisement depends on several factors: the circulation of the newspaper; what day of the week you run the advertisement; whether the advertisement is in color or black and white; and the amount of space it uses. The amount of space is calculated by the page or partial page. Note that advertisements are often called "ads." Use this formula to calculate the cost of the ad:

Cost of Ad = Number of Units × Rate per Unit

EXAMPLE

Northshore Real Estate is placing an ad in the *Daily News* to advertise a new subdivision. The ads will be: five $\frac{1}{2}$ page daily, one full-page Saturday, and one full-page Sunday. What is the cost of the advertisements?

Step 1: Find the rate per $\frac{1}{2}$ page daily ad and the total for 5 days. (See **Figure 16.3,** The *Daily News Advertising Rates* table on page 606.)

The rate per $\frac{1}{2}$ page is \$330

Number of Units × Rate per Unit

5 × \$330 = \$1,650

Step 2: Find the rate per full-page for Saturday and Sunday ads.

Full-page Saturday ad: \$760. Full-page Sunday ad: \$960.

Step 3: Calculate the total cost of the ads.

\$1,650 + \$760 + \$960 = **\$3,370 total advertisement cost**

Concept CHECK

Use the advertising rates in Figure 16.3 on page 606 to find the advertisement cost for The Carpet Store. Check your answer in the back of the book.

1. The ads will be: three $\frac{2}{5}$ page daily, one $\frac{3}{5}$ page on Saturday, and a full page on Sunday.

Figure 16.3

Daily News Advertising Rates			
Units	Daily	Saturday	Sunday
Full page	$660	$760	$960
$\frac{3}{5}$ page	$396	$456	$576
$\frac{1}{2}$ page	$330	$380	$480
$\frac{2}{5}$ page	$264	$304	$384
$\frac{3}{10}$ page	$198	$228	$288
$\frac{1}{5}$ page	$132	$152	$192
$\frac{1}{20}$ page	$ 66	$ 76	$ 96

Lesson Practice

Study Tip

Location
Make sure the place where you study is uncluttered and free from interruptions. It is also important to choose a study space that is always available.

Use Figure 16.3 for the *Daily News* for Problems 2–8.

	Edition	Unit	Number of Units		Rate per Unit		Advertisement Cost
2.	Daily	Full Page	5		$660.00	**a.**	
3.	Daily	$\frac{3}{10}$ page	4	**a.**		**b.**	
4.	Sunday	$\frac{1}{2}$ page	1	**a.**		**b.**	
5.	Saturday	Full Page	1	**a.**		**b.**	

6. The *Daily News* offers a 50% discount on a Monday ad that has already run on a Sunday. The Grey Wolf Ski Lodge contracts for a full page ad to run on a Sunday and a Monday. What is the cost of the ads?

7. The *Daily News* offers a 25% discount on a Saturday ad that also runs on Sunday. The Grey Wolf Ski Lodge contracts for $\frac{1}{2}$ page ads to run every Saturday and Sunday for 15 weeks of the ski season. What is the cost of the ads for the season?

8. CHALLENGE PROBLEM Super Supermarket has an annual contract for the following: One hundred twelve full-page and fifty-two $\frac{1}{2}$ page daily ads. In the Saturday paper Super has fifty-two full-page and twenty-six $\frac{2}{5}$ page ads. What is the annual cost of the contract?

Spiral Review

Multiply. (Skill 8)

9. $50.40 × 40 **10.** $29.27 × 133 **11.** $32.33 × 75

12. A video game has a list price of $29.95. Series discount is 25% less 20%. What is the net price? (Lesson 14.3)

GET READY for the Next Lesson

PREREQUISITE SKILL Multiplying Fractions/Mixed Numbers (Skill 20)

Multiply. Express answers in lowest terms.

13. $\frac{1}{3} \times \frac{5}{8}$ **14.** $\frac{2}{3} \times \frac{3}{4}$ **15.** $\frac{5}{8} \times \frac{4}{9}$ **16.** $\frac{4}{7} \times 1\frac{3}{4}$

LESSON 16.6

Television Advertising Costs

Lesson Objective

Compute the cost of advertising on television.

GET READY for the Lesson

What makes you notice television commercials?

Vasily Zhukov, owner of Euro Classic Furniture, hired a local songwriter to write and record a "jingle"—a brief, catchy tune that would help viewers remember the commercials.

As You Read

Describe Do you have any favorite commercials?

Television Advertising Costs The cost of a television commercial depends on the time of day the ad is shown, the ratings the program **generates**, and the length of the advertisement. Television commercials are generally 10, 30, or 60 seconds long. The cost of a 10-second advertisement is usually one-half (0.5) the cost of a 30-second advertisement. The cost of a 60-second advertisement is usually twice the cost of a 30-second advertisement. The formulas are:

Cost of 10-Second Ad = 0.5 × Cost of 30-Second Ad

Cost of 60-Second Ad = 2 × Cost of 30-Second Ad

EXAMPLE 1

The marketing department of the Zantogo Company plans to advertise new cosmetics on prime-time television during a talent competition. The advertising campaign includes these commercials: four 60-second spots; five 30-second spots, and four 10-second spots. The rates are $700,000 for a 30-second, prime-time commercial. What is the total cost for this advertising campaign?

Step 1: Find the cost of 30-second commercials.

$700,000 × 5 = $3,500,000

Step 2: Find the cost of 10-second commercials.

0.5 × Cost of 30-Second Ad

(0.5 × $700,000) × 4 = $1,400,000

Step 3: Find the cost of 60-second commercials.

2 × Cost of 30-Second Ad

(2 × $700,000) × 4 = $5,600,000

Step 4: Find the total cost.

$3,500,000 + $1,400,000 + $5,600,000 = **$10,500,000 total cost**

700000 × 5 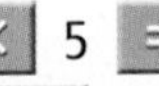 3500000 M+ 0.5 × 700000 × 4  1400000 M+ 2 × 700000 × 4 = 5600000 M+ RM 10500000

Complete the problems. Check your answers in the back of the book.

1. A local 30-second commercial costs $19,000. Find the total cost for four 60-second commercials.
2. A national 30-second commercial costs $350,000. Find the total cost for four 30-second commercials and five 10-second commercials.

Reading Math

Mixed Numbers

A mixed number is a number consisting of an integer and a fraction less than one. The fraction is a proper fraction, with a numerator less than its denominator.

EXAMPLE 2

The marketing department of the Mayberry Company plans to advertise several new snacks on network television. The advertising campaign calls for these commercials: Three 30-second and two ten-second daytime ads; two 30-second and four 60-second prime time ads.

The rates are $60,400 for a 30-second daytime commercial and $250,000 for a 30-second prime-time commercial. What is the total cost for this advertising campaign?

Step 1: Find the cost of 30-second commercials.

Daytime: $ 60,400 × 3 = $181,200

Prime time: $250,000 × 2 = $500,000

Step 2: Find the cost of 10-second commercials.

Daytime: (0.5 × $60,400) × 2 = $60,400

Step 3: Find the cost of 60-second commercials.

2 × Cost of 30-Second Ad

Prime time: (2 × $250,000) × 4 = $2,000,000

Step 4: Find the total cost.

$181,200 + $500,000 + $60,400 + $2,000,000 = **$2,741,600 total cost**

Complete the problems. Check your answers in the back of the book.

What is the cost of the commercials in **Example 2** for:

3. Two 30-second prime-time commercials?
4. Four 10-second daytime and three 60-second prime-time commercials?

Lesson Practice

For Problems 5–8, compute the total cost of the ads.

	Rate per 30-Second Commercial	Number of 10-Second Commercials	Number of 30-Second Commercials	Number of 60-Second Commercials	Total Cost
5.	$ 10,000	4	3	3	
6.	$ 15,000	3	4	0	
7.	$130,000	5	5	2	
8.	$396,500	0	4	3	

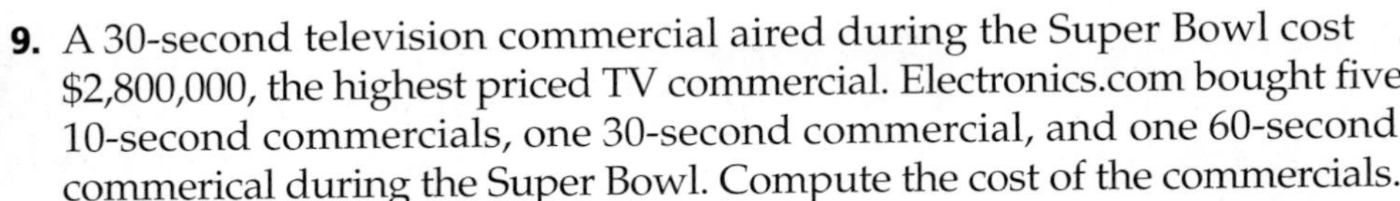

9. A 30-second television commercial aired during the Super Bowl cost $2,800,000, the highest priced TV commercial. Electronics.com bought five 10-second commercials, one 30-second commercial, and one 60-second commerical during the Super Bowl. Compute the cost of the commercials.
10. Pacific New Car Sales is interested in sponsoring the sports coverage on the local television station. The rate per 30-second commercial is $4,475. Pacific New Car Sales has contracts for ten 30-second advertisements, five 10-second advertisements, and five 60-second advertisements. What is the total cost for these advertisements?

Did You Know?

Commercials **According to one study, by age 65 the average American has seen 2 million television commercials.**

11. Alamo Amusement Park has planned a special regional television campaign. It will use a daytime show for twenty 10-second ads and five 30-second ads. It will use a prime-time show for ten 30-second ads and five 60-second ads. The rates are $5,000 per 30-second daytime ad and $80,000 per 30-second prime-time ad. What is the cost of the television campaign?
12. The manufacturers of Amazing Bubble Gum have planned an advertising campaign that includes four 30-second and three 10-second daytime ads, plus five 30-second and six 60-second prime-time ads. The rates are $15,500 for a 30-second daytime commercial and $225,500 for a 30-second prime-time commercial. What is the cost of the advertising campaign?
13. The Delaware City Caps, a minor league baseball team, was planning a TV advertising blitz to announce the beginning of their season. They bought five 10-second, five 30-second, and three 60-second daytime ads, plus ten 30-second and five 60-second prime-time ads. The rates on the local cable station are $17,500 for a daytime 30-second ad and $37,750 for a prime-time 30-second ad. What is the cost of the advertising blitz?

14. **CHALLENGE PROBLEM** Employees in the marketing department of the Nollenberger Basket Company are planning a TV ad campaign to present their new line. They plan on five 60-second ads, three 30-second ads, and six 10-second ads on national daytime. They also plan on two 60-second ads and four 10-second ads on national prime time. Locally they plan on six 60-second ads, five 30-second ads, and ten 10-second ads on local daytime and ten 60-second ads, eight 30-second ads, and five 10-second ads on local prime time. The rates are $65,000 for a 30-second national daytime ad and $325,000 for a 30-second national prime-time ad. The local rates are $12,500 for 30-second local daytime ad and $45,000 for a 30-second local prime-time ad. What is the cost of the advertising campaign?

Spiral Review

Multiply. Express the answers in lowest terms. (Skill 20)

15. $\frac{1}{3} \times \frac{3}{5}$ **16.** $\frac{3}{12} \times \frac{4}{8}$ **17.** $6 \times 7\frac{1}{4}$

18. Digna Cervantes leases a van for family use. She pays $472.10 a month for 48 months. She also pays a deposit of $1,200, a title fee of $99, and a license fee of $225. What is her total lease cost? (Lesson 9.6)

GET READY for the Next Lesson

PREREQUISITE SKILL Subtracting Decimals (Skill 6)

19. $469.4 - 83.2$ **20.** $987.56 - 698.7$ **21.** $16.2 - 2.016$

22. $75 - 34.26$ **23.** $18.094 - 5.6$ **24.** $10.12 - 6.003$

LESSON 16.7 Pricing

Lesson Objective
Calculate the selling price that will result in the highest possible net profit.

Content Vocabulary
- pricing

GET READY for the Lesson

How does pricing affect your purchasing decisions?

When Dana Floyd makes a purchase, she compares the prices of various similar products to decide which is the best deal. She often saves money by avoiding the most popular brands and products.

Onoky/SuperStock

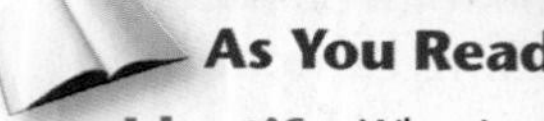

As You Read
Identify What is the formula for finding possible net profit?

Pricing The selling price of your products must be high enough to cover expenses and to make a profit. **Pricing** is the process of assigning a selling price to a good or service. You may determine the selling price of an item by estimating the net profit for each of several possible selling prices and then by choosing the selling price that will result in the highest profit. In manufacturing, the cost per item varies with the number manufactured and **ultimately** sold. Often, the higher the selling price of an item, the fewer the items that will be sold. The formula is:

Possible Net Profit = (Selling Price per Unit − Total Cost per Unit) × Estimated Unit Sales

EXAMPLE 1

Gamma Electronics manufactures preprinted circuit boards. Gamma has a fixed overhead of $120,000. The variable costs to produce the circuit boards are $1.50 per unit. To determine the best selling price, Gamma estimates the number of units that could be sold at various selling prices. What selling price will maximize Gamma's profits?

Selling Price per Unit	Estimated Unit Sales	Fixed Costs	Fixed Costs per Unit	Variable Costs per Unit	Total Cost per Unit
$ 8.00	20,000	$120,000	$ 6.00	$1.50	$ 7.50
$11.00	15,000	120,000	$ 8.00	$1.50	$ 9.50
$15.00	10,000	120,000	$12.00	$1.50	$13.50
$22.00	6,000	120,000	$20.00	$1.50	$21.50

Step 1: Find the possible net profit for each selling price.

(Selling Price per Unit − Total Cost per Unit) × Estimated Unit Sales

($8.00 − $7.50) × 20,000 = $10,000

($11.00 − $9.50) × 15,000 = $22,500

($15.00 − $13.50) × 10,000 = $15,000

($22.00 − $21.50) × 6,000 = $ 3,000

Study Tip

Order of Operations
Use order of operations when solving equations. Remember PEMDAS: perform calculations in Parentheses first, then evaluate Exponents, then perform Multiplication and Division in order from left to right, finally Add and Subtract from left to right.

Step 2: Find the greatest possible profit. **$22,500**

Step 3: Find the best selling price. **$11.00**

Concept CHECK

Complete the problems. Check your answers in the back of the book.

Selling Price per Unit	Estimated Unit Sales	Fixed Costs	Fixed Costs per Unit	Variable Costs per Unit	Total Cost per Unit
$3.00	200,000	$200,000	$1.00	$0.05	$1.05
$4.50	150,000	$200,000	$1.33	$0.05	$1.38

1. Find the possible net profit for each selling price.
2. Which selling price yields the greatest possible profit?

Need Help? Go to... Workshop 38: Problem-Solving Strategy: Writing an Equation, p. 78

EXAMPLE 2 Algebra

General Games LLC would like to realize a possible net profit of $450,000 on its new computer game. The fixed costs for the production are $120,000, while the variable cost per unit is $2.85. The estimated unit sales are 750,000 units. What selling price per unit should General try?

Step 1: Let s = the selling price per unit

Step 2: Substitute into the Net Profit Formula and solve the equation.

$$\text{Possible Net Profit} = \left(\text{Selling Price per Unit} - \text{Total Cost per Unit}\right) \times \text{Estimated Unit Sales}$$

$$\$450{,}000 = \left[s - \left(\frac{\$120{,}000}{750{,}000} + \$2.85\right)\right] \times 750{,}000$$

Divide and combine like terms → $\$450{,}000 = (s - \$3.01) \times 750{,}000$

Apply the distributive property → $\$450{,}000 = 750{,}000s - \$2{,}257{,}500$

Add $2,257,500 to both sides → $\$2{,}707{,}500 = 750{,}000s$

Divide both sides by 750,000 → $\mathbf{\$3.61} = s$

General Games LLC should set a selling price of $3.61 per unit

Concept CHECK

Complete the problems. Check your answers in the back of the book.

3. Creative Crafts Inc. is seeking a possible net profit of $300,000 on its new kitchen utensil. The fixed costs for the production of the new utensil are $364,500 while the variable cost per unit is $1.06. If the estimated unit sales are 1,350,000 units, what selling price per unit should Creative try?
4. Office Innovations LLC is aiming for a net profit of $1,500,000 on its new desk top mini-shredder. The fixed costs for the production are $984,000 while variable costs are $14.50 per unit. The estimated unit sales are 480,000 units. What selling price should the company try?

Lesson Practice

For Problems 5–8, round answers to the nearest cent.

	Selling Price per Unit	Estimated Unit Sales	Fixed Costs	Fixed Costs per Unit	Variable Costs per Unit	Total Cost per Unit	Possible Net Profit
5.	$45.00	10,000	$120,000	$12.00	$21.00	$33.00	a.
6.	$65.00	8,000	$120,000	$15.00	$21.00	$36.00	a.
7.	$75.00	7,000	$120,000	a.	$21.00	b.	c.
8.	$85.00	6,000	$120,000	a.	$21.00	b.	c.

Did You Know?
Organic Products **In a recent four year period, organic produce sales doubled from roughly $3 billion to $6 billion, according to the Organic Trade Association. Sales of organic products are expected to continue to rise.**

For Problems 9 and 10, find the possible net profit:

9. A screwdriver set has a selling price per unit of $24.95, fixed costs of $837,500, variable costs per unit of $3.25, and estimated sales of 50,000.

10. A bottle of organic shampoo has a selling price of $3.95, fixed costs of $9,000, variable costs per unit of $0.75, and estimated sales of 12,000.

11. Complete the table for the Wood Specialties Company. Round answers to the nearest cent. Which selling price yields the greatest possible profit? How many units should be produced?

Selling Price per Unit	Estimated Unit Sales	Fixed Costs	Fixed Costs per Unit	Variable Costs per Unit	Total Cost per Unit	Possible Net Profit
$ 3.75	950,000	$500,000	a.	$1.05	b.	c.
$ 4.50	700,000	$500,000	a.	$1.05	b.	c.
$ 8.50	300,000	$500,000	a.	$1.05	b.	c.
$10.25	250,000	$500,000	a.	$1.05	b.	c.

12. **ALGEBRA** Pool Products Inc. would like a possible net profit of $500,000 on its new pool filter. The fixed costs for the manufacture of the new system are $684,000 and the variable cost per unit is $23.58. If the estimated unit sales are 750,000 units, what selling price per unit should Pool Products try?

Spiral Review

Subtract. (Skill 6)

13. 649.91 − 73.89 **14.** 12.9 − 1.023 **15.** 78 − 32.8

16. Kirsten Ghosh has a mortgage loan of $750,000 at an interest rate of 7%. The monthly payment is $4,987.50. How much of the first monthly payment is for interest? (Lesson 10.4)

GET READY for the Next Lesson

PREREQUISITE SKILL **Dividing (Decimal Remainder)** (Skill 10)

Divide. Round answers to the nearest dollar.

17. $45,850 ÷ 25 **18.** $12,949 ÷ 12

19. $11,427 ÷ 13 **20.** $32,670 ÷ 27

21. $33,852 ÷ 14 **22.** $45,379 ÷ 23

CHAPTER 16 Review and Assessment

Chapter SUMMARY

Marketing involves a number of different factors. You can compute the rate of a particular response in an opinion survey and the annual sales potential and market share of a new product. You may use the factor method or a graph to compute projected sales. You can calculate the cost of advertising in a newspaper and on television. You can also calculate the selling price that will result in the highest possible net profit.

Vocabulary Check

1. On a sheet of paper, use each of these terms in a sentence.

Content Vocabulary

- product test (p. 593)
- opinion research firm (p. 593)
- opinion survey (p. 593)
- sales potential (p. 597)
- sample (p. 597)
- market (p. 597)
- market share (p. 599)
- sales projection (p. 601)
- factor method (p. 601)
- factor (p. 601)
- pricing (p. 610)

Academic Vocabulary

- panel (p. 593)
- volume (p. 597)
- indication (p. 599)
- economy (p. 601)
- objective (p. 605)
- generates (p. 607)
- ultimately (p. 610)

Concept Check

2. Explain how to find the rate of a particular response in an opinion survey.
3. Identify the correct method for determining the annual sales potential of a product.
4. Show the formula for calculating market share of a product.
5. What is a sales projection?
6. Explain how to determine projected sales using the factor method.
7. Identify the formula for calculating the cost of a newspaper ad.
8. List factors that affect the cost of a television commercial.
9. **CRITICAL THINKING** Explain how to find the selling price that will result in the highest possible net profit.

CHAPTER 16 Review and Assessment

Lesson-by-Lesson Review

16.1 Opinion Surveys (pp. 593–596)

Compute the rate of a particular response in an opinion survey.
APP Inc. conducted an opinion survey of 3,000 people for an approval rating of a new Global Positioning System (GPS) unit for vehicles. The following table shows the responses.

	Age Group				
	18 to 25	26 to 35	36 to 45	45 or older	Total
Outstanding	100	200	450	350	1,100
Good	100	300	350	250	1,000
Fair	50	200	310	170	730
Poor	40	70	20	40	170
Total	**290**	**770**	**1,130**	**810**	**3,000**

APP Inc. operates on the standard that over 30% of the responses must be "outstanding" or production will be halted. What percent of the total responses rated the GPS unit "outstanding"? What should APP do? App Inc. predicted in the 18 to 25 age group that 150 would respond "outstanding." Determine the absolute error. Determine the relative error.

Step 1: Compute the rate of the response.

$$\text{Rate of Response} = \frac{\text{Number of Times Particular Response Occurs}}{\text{Total Number of Responses}}$$

$$\frac{1{,}100}{3{,}000} = 0.3666 = \mathbf{36.7\%\ rate\ of\ response}$$

Step 2: APP Inc. should continue with production of the new GPS unit.

Step 3: Determine the absolute error.

Prediction − Actual Response

$150 - 100 =$ **50 absolute error**

Step 4: Determine the relative error.

$$\frac{\text{Absolute Error}}{\text{Actual Response}} = \frac{50}{100} = 0.50 = \mathbf{50\%\ relative\ error}$$

Review Exercises

Round the answers to the nearest tenth of a percent.

For Problems 10–18, use the data table in the above example to answer the following:

10. What percent of the total responses were for "fair"?
11. What percent of the 26 to 35 age group responded "good"?
12. What percent of the 36 to 45 age group responded "outstanding"?
13. What percent of the 45 or older age group responded "outstanding"?
14. What percent of the 18 to 25 age group responded "poor"?
15. What percent of the 45 or older age group responded "good"?
16. What age group is most likely to purchase the product?
17. What is the absolute error if APP had predicted that in the 36 to 45 age group 350 would respond "outstanding"?
18. What is the relative error for 36 to 45 – "outstanding"?

Lesson-by-Lesson Review (continued)

16.2 Sales Potential (pp. 597–598)

Determine the annual sales potential of a new product.
Stamper's Plus has developed a new line of stationery called Pacific Mist. Stamper's chose a sample of women between the ages of 18 and 25 to try the new product. Of the 500 women in the sample, 125 said they would buy the stationery. Stamper's Plus estimates that 1,200,000 women buy stationery. Their surveys indicate that each woman purchases stationery once per year. What is the annual sales potential for Pacific Mist?

Step 1: Find the percent of potential purchasers.

$$\frac{125}{500} = 0.25 = 25\% \text{ potential purchasers}$$

Step 2: Find the annual sales potential.

Estimated Market Size × Individual Rate of Purchase × Percent of Potential Purchasers

1,200,000 × 1 × 25% = **300,000 annual sales potential**

Review Exercises

Complete the table.

	Number in Sample	Number of Potential Customers	Percent of Potential Customers	Estimated Market Size	Individual Rate of Purchase per Year	Annual Sales Potential
19.	400	100	25%	100,000	3 times	a.
20.	600	250	a.	850,000	1 ounce	b.
21.	1,000	500	a.	1,500,000	4 cans	b.
22.	50	10	a.	650,000	10 boxes	b.
23.	350	125	a.	25,000	5 issues	b.
24.	1,500	300	a.	65,000	1 ounce	b.

25. Hand cream was tested by 2,000 people. One thousand two hundred people said they would buy the cream. The estimated market size is 2,500,000. The company estimates that each person would buy 2 tubes of hand cream per year. What is the annual sales potential?

16.3 Market Share (pp. 599–600)

Calculate the market share of a new product.
Alex Irrigation sold 35,000 sprinkler systems during the year. During the same period, 1,650,000 sprinkler systems were purchased in the entire U.S. market. What was Alex's market share for the year?

Find the market share.

$$\frac{\text{Total Product Sales}}{\text{Total Market Sales}} = \frac{35{,}000}{1{,}650{,}000} = 0.02121 = \mathbf{2.1\%\ market\ share}$$

Lesson-by-Lesson Review (continued)

Review Exercises

Find the market share. Round to the nearest tenth percent.

	Company	Total Product Sales	Total Market Sales	Market Share
26.	Online Media	$ 9,500,000	$ 19,000,000	
27.	Computer Surplus	3,200,000	9,000,000	
28.	Office Inc.	900,000	2,500,000	
29.	Printer Specialists	1,200,000	5,000,000	
30.	Electronix	750,000	10,000,000	
31.	New Media	5,400,000	15,400,000	
32.	CB Industry	1,000,000	14,450,000	
33.	South Shore Inc.	2,250,000	11,000,000	

34. A craft company sells approximately 2,500,000 sheets of scrapbook paper per year. Sales for the entire scrapbook market total approximately 25,000,000 sheets per year. What is the market share for the craft company?

16.4 Sales Projections (pp. 601–604)

Use the factor method or a graph to determine projected sales.
Seminole Sun has an 11% market share for sunscreen in the Fort Lauderdale area. Sunscreen sales in the Fort Lauderdale area are estimated to be $3,200,000. What are the projected sales figures for Seminole Sun in the Fort Lauderdale area for next year?

Find the projected sales.

Projected Market Sales × Market-Share Factor

$3,200,000 × 11% = **$352,000 projected sales**

Review Exercises

Use the factor method to find the projected sales.

	Company	Projected Market Sales	Market-Share Factor	Projected Sales
35.	Blake's	$ 13,000,000	12.0%	
36.	ABC Toys	35,300,000	8.5%	
37.	Pencil Pushers	25,400,000	6.6%	
38.	Cathy's Club	50,000,000	11.0%	
39.	Thompson's	41,000,000	7.0%	
40.	Green Thumb	24,500,000	13.0%	

Lesson-by-Lesson Review (continued)

Use a graph to find projected sales.
The marketing department of Central Supply House wants to project sales for the year 2016. The chart below shows Central Supply House's sales history. Use a graph to estimate what sales projection the marketing department might make for Year L.

Central Supply House's Sales						
Year	A	B	C	D	E	F
Sales (in millions)	$3.1	$3.6	$3.7	$3.3	$4.6	$3.4

Step 1: Graph the sales from Year A through Year F.
Step 2: Draw a straight line through the approximate middle of the points to 2016.
Step 3: Read the sales projection for Year L.

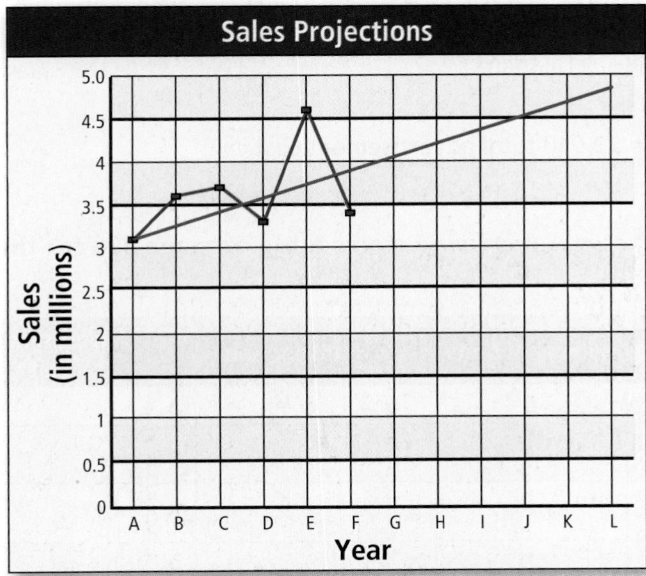

Projected sales for Year L are approximately $4.8 million.

Review Exercises

Use the Central Supply graph above for Problems 41 and 42.

41. What are the sales projections for Year J?

42. What are the sales projections for Year K?

43. Use a graph to determine the projected sales for Year L for a hybrid vehicle.

Sales Projections							
Year	A	B	C	D	E	F	G
Sales (in millions)	$10.0	$11.3	$12.1	$14.0	$12.5	$13.0	$15.0

Lesson-by-Lesson Review (continued)

16.5 Newspaper Advertising Costs (pp. 605–606)

Calculate the cost of advertising in a newspaper.
Southwest Trucking Company contracted with the *Daily News* to advertise a new service in the daily newspaper. The ads will be four $\frac{1}{2}$ page daily, one full-page Saturday, and one full-page Sunday. What is the cost of the advertisement?

Step 1: Find the rate per $\frac{1}{2}$ page daily ad and the total for 4 days. (See **Figure 16.3**, the *Daily News Advertising Rates* table on page 606.)

The rate per $\frac{1}{2}$ page is \$330

Number of Units × Rate per Unit

4 × \$330 = \$1,320

Step 2: Find the rate per full-page for Saturday and Sunday ads.

The rate per full-page Saturday ad is \$760.

The rate per full-page Sunday ad is \$960.

Step 3: Calculate the total cost of the ads.

\$1,320 + \$760 + \$960 = **\$3,040 total advertisement cost**

Review Exercises

Use Figure 16.3, the *Daily News Advertising Rates* table on page 606 for the following problems.

	Edition	Unit	Number of Units		Rate per Unit		Advertisement Cost
44.	Daily	Full page	5		\$660	a.	
45.	Daily	$\frac{3}{10}$ page	4	a.		b.	
46.	Sunday	$\frac{1}{2}$ page	1	a.		b.	
47.	Saturday	Full page	1	a.		b.	
48.	Daily	$\frac{1}{20}$ page	6	a.		b.	
49.	Daily	$\frac{1}{5}$ page	7	a.		b.	

50. The *Daily News* offers a 25% discount on a Monday ad that has already run on a Sunday. The Sundance Amusement Water Park contracts for a half-page ad to run on a Sunday and a Monday. What is the cost of the ads?

51. Suppose the *Daily News* offers a 50% discount on a Saturday ad that also runs on Sunday. The Omega Surf store contracts for $\frac{1}{5}$ page ads to run every Saturday and Sunday for 12 weeks. What is the total cost of the ads?

Lesson-by-Lesson Review (continued)

16.6 Television Advertising Costs (pp. 607–609)

Compute the cost of advertising on television.

Tony's Crab Shack plans to advertise its shrimp and crab platter on local television this weekend. The rates are $1,200 for a 30-second daytime commercial and $2,400 for a 30-second prime-time commercial. If Tony's runs six 10-second daytime ads and five 60-second prime-time ads, what is the total cost of the advertising campaign?

Step 1: Find the cost of the 10-second daytime ads.

0.5 × Cost of 30-Second Ad

(0.5 × $1,200) × 6 = $3,600 cost of the 10-second daytime ads

Step 2: Find the cost of the 60-second prime-time ads.

2 × Cost of 30-Second Ad

(2 × $2,400) × 5 = $24,000 cost of the 60-second prime-time ads

Step 3: Find the total cost.

$3,600 + $24,000 = **$27,600 total cost**

Review Exercises

Find the total cost.

	Rate per 30-Second Commercial	Number of 10-Second Commercials	Number of 30-Second Commercials	Number of 60-Second Commercials	Total Cost
52.	$ 18,000	4	2	2	
53.	$ 25,000	3	4	3	
54.	$1,000,000	10	6	1	
55.	$ 344,000	3	8	2	
56.	$ 224,000	5	1	5	
57.	$ 210,000	6	3	3	

58. The marketing department of Crunchy Snacks plans to advertise several new products on network television. The advertising campaign calls for these commercials: Four 30-second and three ten-second daytime ads; three 30-second and four 60-second prime-time ads. The rates are $58,400 for a 30-second daytime commercial and $260,000 for a 30-second prime time commercial. What is the total cost for this advertising campaign?

16.7 Pricing (pp. 610–612)

Calculate the selling price that will result in the highest possible net profit.

The Yum Yum Shop makes and sells ice cream. Yum Yum has a fixed overhead of $210,000. The variable costs to produce vanilla ice cream are $1.05 per 10-gallon tub. To determine the best selling price, Yum Yum estimates the number of tubs that could be sold at various prices. What selling price will maximize Yum Yum's profits?

Lesson-by-Lesson Review (continued)

Selling Price per Unit	Estimated Unit Sales	Fixed Costs	Fixed Costs per Unit	Variable Costs per Unit	Total Cost per Unit
$10.00	30,000	$210,000	$ 7.00	$1.05	$ 8.05
$12.00	25,000	210,000	$ 8.40	$1.05	$ 9.45
$15.00	20,000	210,000	$10.50	$1.05	$11.55
$18.00	15,000	210,000	$14.00	$1.05	$15.05

Step 1: Find the possible net profit for each selling price.

(Selling Price per Unit − Total Cost per Unit) × Estimated Unit Sales

($10 − $8.05) × 30,000 = $58,500

($12 − $9.45) × 25,000 = $63,750

($15 − $11.55) × 20,000 = $69,000

($18 − $15.05) × 15,000 = $44,250

Step 2: Find the greatest possible profit: $69,000

Step 3: Find the best selling price: **$15.00**

Review Exercises

Complete the table.

	Selling Price per Unit	Estimated Unit Sales	Fixed Costs	Fixed Costs per Unit	Variable Costs per Unit	Total Cost per Unit	Possible Net Profit
59.	$ 54.00	30,000	$240,000	$8.00	$18.00	$26.00	a.
60.	$ 68.00	25,000	$240,000	$9.60	18.00	$27.60	a.
61.	$ 80.00	20,000	$240,000	a.	18.00	b.	c.
62.	$100.00	15,000	$240,000	a.	18.00	b.	c.

Revised data for the Yum Yum Shop is shown below. Use the table to solve Problems 63 and 64.

Selling Price per Unit	Estimated Unit Sales	Fixed Costs	Fixed Costs per Unit	Variable Costs per Unit	Total Cost per Unit
$12.50	25,000	$210,000	$ 8.40	$1.05	$ 9.45
$16.00	20,000	210,000	$10.50	$1.05	$11.55
$22.00	15,000	210,000	$14.00	$1.05	$15.05
$26.00	10,000	210,000	$21.00	$1.05	$22.05

63. Find the possible net profit for each selling price.
64. What selling price will maximize Yum Yum's profits?
65. **ALGEBRA** Webster Games would like to realize a possible net profit of $550,000 on a new family board game. The fixed costs for the production are $110,000 while the variable cost per unit is $4.75. The estimated unit sales are 550,000 units. What selling price per unit should Webster try?

Practice Test

Record your answers on a sheet of paper.

1. Tangy Electronics manufactures circuit boards. The cost to produce the boards is $5.75 per unit and the selling price is $6.50 per unit. What net profit would result from Tangy Electronics selling 25,000 units?
   A $162,500 **B** $6,250
   C $18,750 **D** $12,500

2. Vidmar Used Cars has planned a television advertising campaign. It will use four 10-second ads during daytime shows, and three 30-second ads during prime-time shows. The rates are $6,000 per 30-second daytime ad and $40,000 per 30-second prime-time ad. What is the total cost of the ad campaign?
   A $132,000 **B** $144,000
   C $52,000 **D** $64,000

ParmaPost Advertising Rates			
Units	**Daily**	**Saturday**	**Sunday**
Full page	$660	$760	$960
$\frac{3}{5}$ page	$396	$456	$576
$\frac{1}{2}$ page	$330	$380	$480
$\frac{2}{5}$ page	$264	$304	$384

3. The *ParmaPost* advertising rates are shown in the above table. Herson Cleaning is placing some ads to promote new prices. Herson will place four $\frac{1}{2}$-page ads in the daily edition, and one full-page ad on Sunday. How much will these ads cost?
   A $1,290 **B** $3,210
   C $1,620 **D** $2,280

4. Fred's Frames Inc. did $169,750 in business this past year. The market sales for this past year were $987,875. What was Fred's market share for the past year?
   A 17.2% **B** 5.8%
   C 20.7% **D** 6.3%

5. Blazin' Bill's Ribs conducted a survey of its new barbeque sauce. 1,700 customers completed the survey. 150 said they did not like the sauce, 350 said it was fair, 756 said they liked the new sauce, the rest said they could not tell the difference from the old sauce. To the nearest tenth, what percent of the people surveyed said the sauce was fair?
   A 20.6% **B** 14.0%
   C 8.8% **D** 37.4%

6. Fifteen hundred people tested a new type of sunglasses. One hundred eighty people said they would buy them. The estimated market size is 2,600,000. The average consumer would purchase 1 pair of glasses per year. What is the sales potential for the new type of sunglasses?
   A 14,444 **B** 312,000
   C 260,000 **D** 10,384

7. **ALGEBRA** Gato Electronics Inc. would like to realize a net profit of $730,000 on a new computer mouse it is manufacturing. The fixed costs for the production are $608,000 and the variable cost per unit is $6.75. The estimated unit sales are 810,000 units. What selling price should Gato Inc. try?

8. Sucheski Sporting Goods has a line of snowboards that captured 42% of the local market. Next year's sales are estimated at $1,473,000. Find Sucheski's projected sales for next year.

9. 56.21 × 3.9

10. 35% of $87.40

11. 385.6 ÷ 17.52

12. $392,653.56 − $63,862.93

Standardized Test Practice

Cumulative, Chapters 1–16

PART 1 Multiple Choice

Record your answers on the answer sheet provided by your teacher or on a sheet of paper.

1. The Snelling Company buys ice axes for $46.85. The company sells the axes for $59.99. What is the markup?
   A $106.84 **B** $13.14
   C $14.13 **D** $16.84

2. Strachan Industries manufactures aluminum screen doors. Strachan offers a 35% trade discount to qualified retailers. If the list price of a door were $485.77, how much would a qualified retailer pay?
   A $170.02 **B** $218.60
   C $315.75 **D** $450.77

3. Frankel Farm Equipment purchases seed spreaders for $11.89. The selling price at Frankel is $25.50. The business estimates the overhead for each spreader to be 30% of the selling price. What is the estimated net profit on each spreader?
   A $6.18 **B** $6.16
   C $5.96 **D** $5.98

4. Ichio In-Line purchases in-line skates that have a list price of $149.50. Ichio receives a trade-discount rate of 20%. What is the discount that Ichio In-Line receives for each pair of skates?
   A $119.60 **B** $29.90
   C $19.60 **D** $59.90

5. Debbie Crotteau's group medical coverage costs her $215.35 each month. The company she works for pays 70% of the cost. How much is the annual premium for Debbie's health insurance?
   A $8,614.00 **B** $5,980.00
   C $5,857.55 **D** $2,584.20

6. Jones' Equipment Inc. manufactures an industrial size popcorn maker priced at $985.60. When the company introduced a new model, it offered a chain discount of 20/10 off the old model. What is the final net price on the older model of popcorn maker?
   A $689.92 **B** $873.12
   C $709.63 **D** $295.68

PART 2 Short Response/Griddable

7. **ALGEBRA** Matsura Nurseries pays a net price of $18.50 for a sprinkler after a trade-discount rate of 68%. What is the list price? What is the dollar amount of the discount?

8. Amish Patel's annual salary is $56,380.00. The benefits he receives from his employer have a total value of $14,592.85. To the nearest percent, what is the rate of his benefits?

9. Tammy Russell purchases a thermal beverage jug for $7.99 in Cleveland, Ohio, where the sales tax rate is 7.5%. What is the total purchase price?

PART 3 Extended Response

Show your work.

10. What is market share and how is information about market share used by businesses?

11. Explain how you determine the percent of a particular response given in a survey.

12. Explain the steps involved in using a graph to project future sales.

TEST-TAKING TIP

Pace Yourself Know how much time is allotted for the test and the number of questions it contains. Pace yourself accordingly.

Building Academic Skills

Mathematics

Your class decides to sell candy to raise money for a trip to the state high school volleyball championships. At the planning meeting, you, as the promotion manager, present the following information:

Newspaper Advertising	
School paper	$0
Community Press, 5 half-page ads at $210 each	a.
Direct Mail	
To teachers' mailboxes	$0
To students' homes	$0
Printing on school photocopier	$0
Fulfillment (volunteers)	$0
Postage, 25 cents/piece bulk rate, 1700 pieces	b.
Total cost of advertising	c.
% of total in newspaper advertising	d.
% of total in direct mail advertising	e.

Calculate answers to complete the chart.

English Language Arts/Writing

Based on your calculations above and your knowledge about the people most likely to support your class project, what recommendation about advertising would you make at the planning meeting? Write a paragraph justifying your recommendation. The section about opinion surveys on page 593 may help.

Science

Opinion research is based on the scientific method. Opinion research involves making observations, forming a hypothesis, testing the hypothesis by asking questions, and then reporting results. (In science, you would conduct an experiment to test your hypothesis.) Set up a simple opinion research project that you can run in your class. Decide on a question about students' preferences you would like to research, develop a short questionnaire, conduct the survey, write a few paragraphs explaining your results, and report them to the class. Include whether you expected the results you received or whether they were different from your hypothesis.

Building Real-World Skills

Career WISE

Sales Force Manager Salespeople are crucial to a company, and sales force managers keep these important workers focused, on-task, and motivated. Sales force managers set bonuses and incentives, help locate prospects for new sales, and may help customers.

Research and Write:

a. Visit the Web site of the Bureau of Labor Statistics (BLS) and locate the page on sales worker supervisors.

b. According to the BLS, how many sales worker supervisors were employed in the United States at last count? How many of them were self-employed?

Tech TRENDS

Research Selling Prices Online Use the Internet for pricing research. Web sites such as Amazon and eBay give the average selling price for products and services, information you can use to determine your own prices.

Research and Write:

a. Select five products you would like to sell in your retail store. Using the Internet, find three different companies selling each of those five products.

b. Build a spreadsheet that tracks the five products you have selected.

Marketing Healthy Treats

In this project you will create a marketing presentation for the business owner of a frozen yogurt shop or CEO of the franchise. Based on your market research and analysis, you will make suggestions on how to best market this snack to students.

Your Project Assignment

- ✓ Choose a frozen yogurt store located in your community.
- ✓ Research and then write an opinion survey to be taken by your classmates. Determine this product's sales potential within your entire school.
- ✓ Make recommendations for advertising frozen yogurt to students your age.
- ✓ Create a 3–5 minute marketing presentation for the business owner or CEO of the shop. Summarize your findings and your recommendations.

Skills Preview

Your success in marketing depends on your skills. Some skills you might use include:
Academic Skills reading, writing, and mathematics
Basic Skills speaking, listening, thinking, problem-solving, and interpersonal skills
Technology Skills word-processing, keyboarding, presentation, and Internet skills

Project Steps

Step 1 Do Your Research

- Choose a community frozen yogurt store.
- Research competing healthy treats, and list the three you believe to be the closest competitors to your chosen product.
- Consider the best media outlets for promotion. List the three outlets you would expect to reach the greatest number of students.
- Use the Internet to research opinion surveys. Look for tips on writing effective questions.

Step 2 Explore Your Community

Write a 10-question opinion survey for your classmates, and collect their answers. How often do they purchase your product or its competitors? Which frozen yogurt flavors and toppings do they prefer?

Step 3 Calculate Sales Potential

- Calculate the sales potential for this product among the students in your entire school.
- Analyze the competitiveness of your product.

Step 4 Develop Your Marketing Presentation

Prepare a report of your findings using the following tools, if available:

- Use a word-processing program to write a 2-page report.
  - ✓ Describe the demographics represented in your school's student body.

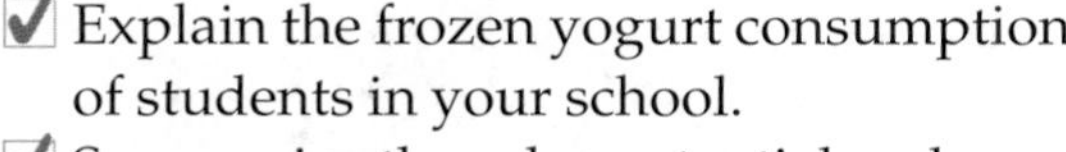

  - ✓ Explain the frozen yogurt consumption of students in your school.
  - ✓ Summarize the sales potential and competitive landscape.
  - ✓ Identify the benefits and features of your product.
  - ✓ Based on the results of the opinion survey, suggest a new flavor, topping, or treat that students would like to see offered at this store.
  - ✓ Make recommendations for promotional activities directed at students at your school.
- With presentation software, create a 5-slide presentation for the business owner of the shop or CEO of the franchise. Include a pie chart or bar graph of the opinion survey results.
- Print your completed report to present to your class or to hand in to your teacher.

Step 5 Evaluate

Go to **connectED.mcgraw-hill.com** to download an evaluation rubric.

Academic and Career Portfolio

Add this report to your Academic and Career Portfolio.

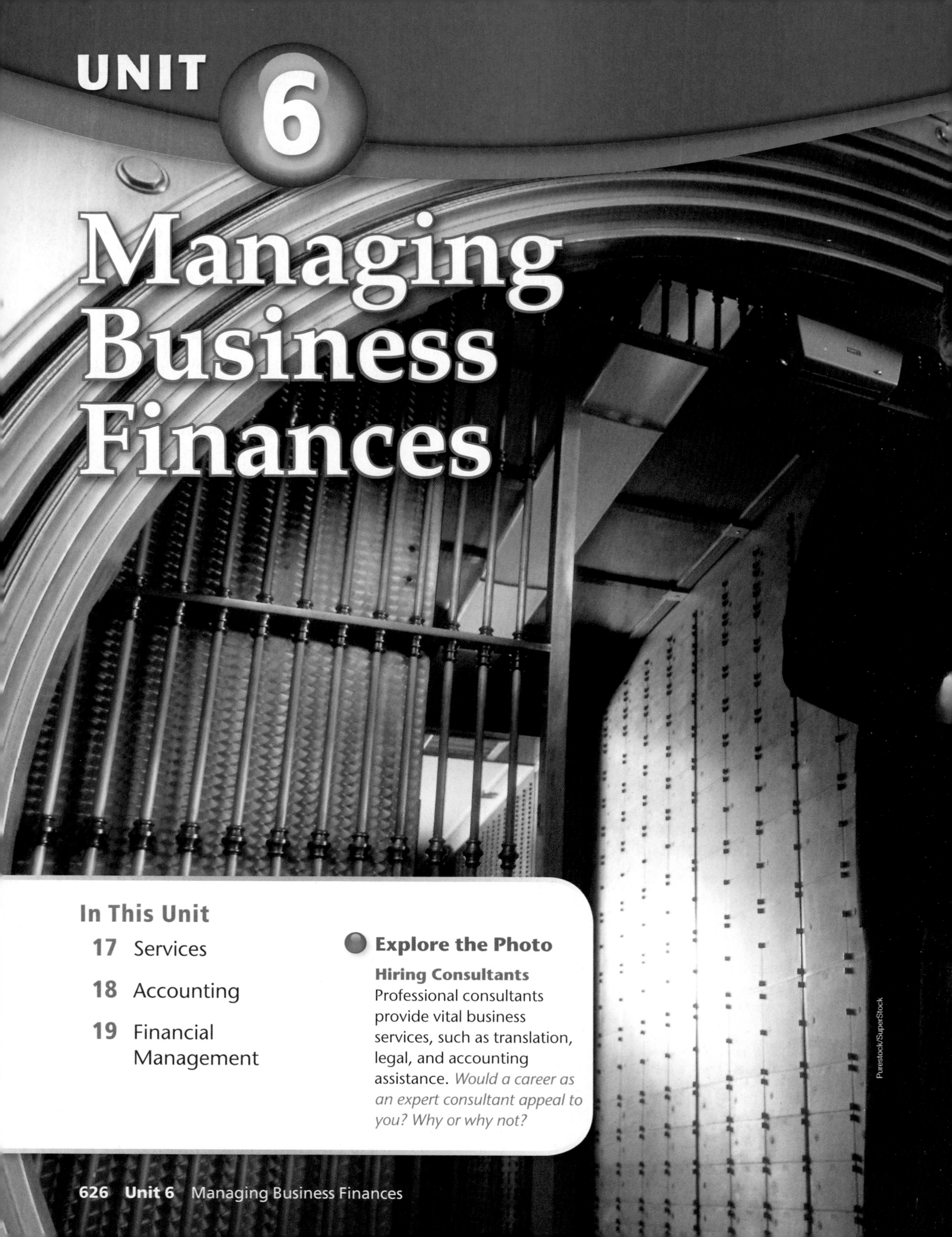

UNIT 6

Managing Business Finances

In This Unit

Explore the Photo

Hiring Consultants
Professional consultants provide vital business services, such as translation, legal, and accounting assistance. *Would a career as an expert consultant appeal to you? Why or why not?*

Purestock/SuperStock

The Big Picture

The table below shows the rising demand for translation services.

Growth in Demand for Translations Into...

Language	Growth	Language	Growth
Latvian	81%	Slovenian	49%
Bulgarian	78%	Chinese*	44%
Estonian	77%	Russian	39%
Romanian	71%	Turkish	36%
Lithuanian	67%	Japanese	28%

* Simplified, written

Data: SDL International Ltd.; data are for the past 12 months

Go to **connected.mcgraw-hill.com** for the Unit 6 WebQuest activity about the many languages of the Internet population.

Thematic Project Preview

Business Services

As a company grows, the costs for professional services, office space, maintenance, and utilities grow, too. Why might fast growth actually be risky for a business? After completing this Unit Thematic Project, you will know how to track a growing business's service costs.

Pre-Project Checklist

As you read this unit, use this checklist to prepare for the unit project:

✓ Think about what service costs increase when a company grows.
✓ Research telephone and electric utilities costs in your area.
✓ Determine total rental costs.

CHAPTER 17 Services

Big Idea

Businesses need to allocate funds for overhead expenses, such as maintenance costs, utilities, and building or office space.

Explore the Photo

Hiring Help

Businesses incur many costs. *Can you think of some advantages of hiring specialized professionals to perform certain tasks?*

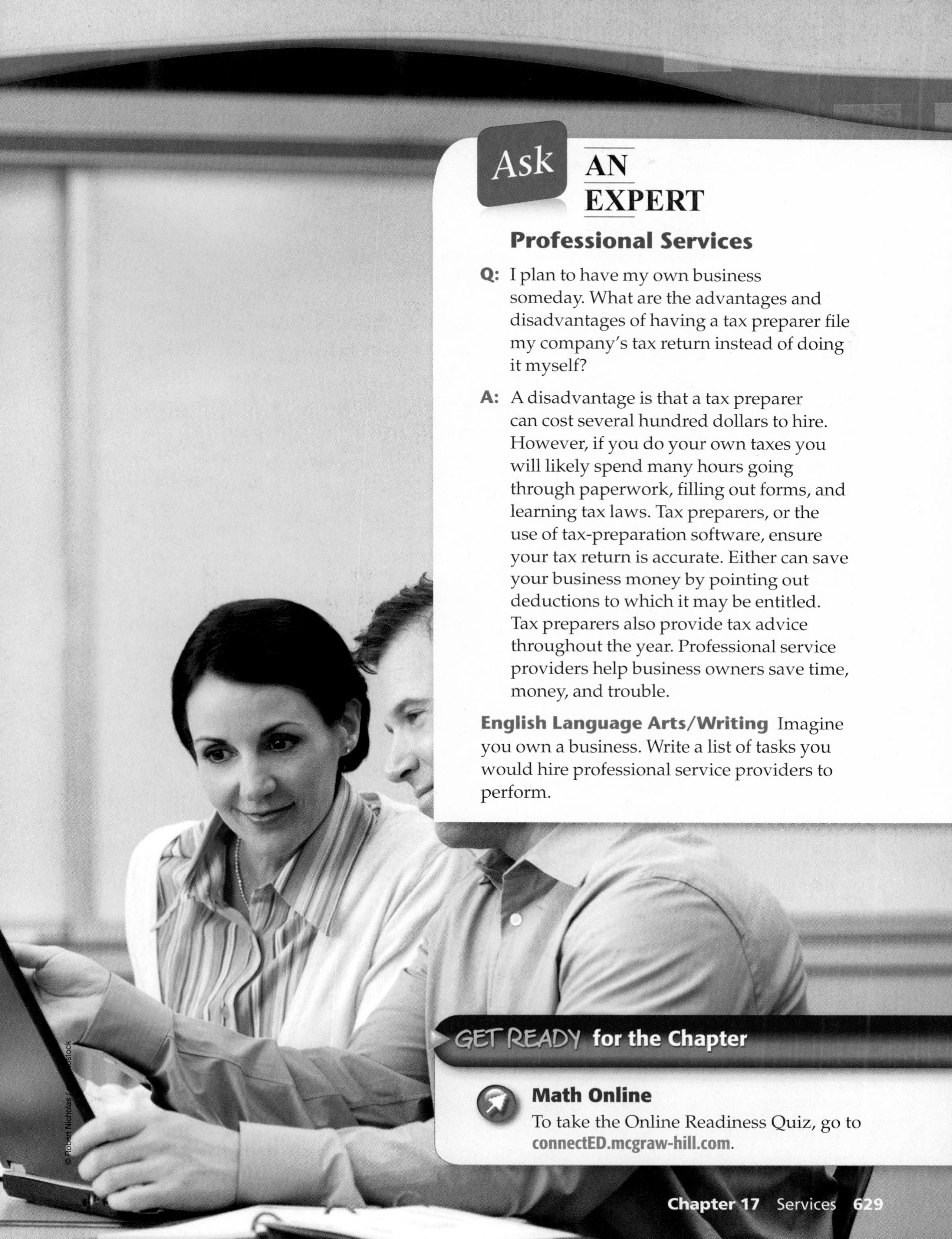

Ask AN EXPERT

Professional Services

Q: I plan to have my own business someday. What are the advantages and disadvantages of having a tax preparer file my company's tax return instead of doing it myself?

A: A disadvantage is that a tax preparer can cost several hundred dollars to hire. However, if you do your own taxes you will likely spend many hours going through paperwork, filling out forms, and learning tax laws. Tax preparers, or the use of tax-preparation software, ensure your tax return is accurate. Either can save your business money by pointing out deductions to which it may be entitled. Tax preparers also provide tax advice throughout the year. Professional service providers help business owners save time, money, and trouble.

English Language Arts/Writing Imagine you own a business. Write a list of tasks you would hire professional service providers to perform.

GET READY for the Chapter

Math Online
To take the Online Readiness Quiz, go to **connectED.mcgraw-hill.com**.

Chapter 17 Services

Reading Guide

Before You Read

Identify What costs are associated with operating a business?

Main Idea

If you manage a business, you will need to budget money for office space, maintenance costs, and costs of utilities.

Graphic Organizer

Before you read this chapter, draw a diagram like the one below. As you read, keep track of different overhead expenses and the formulas to calculate them.

Overhead Expense	Formula

Math Online Go to connectED.mcgraw-hill.com to download this graphic organizer.

Content Vocabulary

You will learn these key terms in this chapter.

- rent
- lease
- labor charge
- equipment rental
- utilities
- monthly service charge
- customer charge
- demand charge
- energy charge
- peak load
- kilowatts
- fuel adjustment charge
- consultant
- consultant's fee

Academic Vocabulary

You will see these words in your reading and on your tests.

- occupy
- structure
- impose
- features
- levy
- project

You can find vocabulary definitions in the **Content Vocabulary** Glossary and the **Academic Vocabulary** Glossary in the back of the book.

LESSON 17.1 Building Rental

Lesson Objective
Compute the monthly rental charge.

Content Vocabulary
- rent
- lease

As You Read

Identify Name one factor involved in setting a monthly rental charge.

GET READY for the Lesson

How do business owners choose where to open their businesses?

Gretchen Merona is considering two different locations for her new bakery, Sweetness. She must consider price, size, and location.

Building Rental Your business may **rent** or **lease** a building or a portion of a building, usually on an annual basis. This is the amount of money you pay to **occupy** the given space. The building owner may charge a certain rate per square foot per year. Your total monthly rental charge depends on the number of square feet that your business occupies. The formula is:

$$\text{Monthly Rental Charge} = \frac{\text{Annual Rate} \times \text{Number of Square Feet}}{12}$$

EXAMPLE 1

Ajax Assemblers rents a portion of a building owned by The Gray Company. The floor space of Ajax's portion of the building measures 80 feet by 60 feet. The Gray Company charges an annual rate of \$10.50 per square foot. To the nearest dollar, what is Ajax's monthly rental charge?

Step 1: Find the number of square feet.

Length $\times$ Width

80 feet $\times$ 60 feet $=$ 4,800 square feet

Step 2: Find the monthly rental charge.

$$\frac{\text{Annual Rate} \times \text{Number of Square Feet}}{12}$$

$$\frac{\$10.50 \times 4{,}800}{12} = \textbf{\$4,200 Monthly Rental Charge}$$

10.50 [×] 80 [×] 60 [=] 50400 [÷] 12 [=] 4200

Concept CHECK

Find the (a) number of square feet and (b) monthly rental charge. Check your answers in the back of the book.

1. The store measures 100 feet × 50 feet at \$8.00 per square foot annually.
2. The office measures 125 feet × 45 feet at \$9.50 per square foot annually.

Need Help? Go to...

Workshop 38: Problem-Solving Strategy: Writing an Equation, p. 78

EXAMPLE 2 Algebra

Polidio Produce Market is expanding to the suburbs. The store's budget allows \$3,800 per month to rent the needed 5,700 square foot space. What is the maximum annual rate per square foot Polidio can pay?

Step 1: Let x = maximum annual rate per square foot

Step 2: Use the Monthly Rental Charge formula and solve for x.

$$\text{Monthly Rental Charge} = \frac{\text{Annual Rate} \times \text{Number of Square Feet}}{12}$$

$$\$3{,}800 = \frac{x \times 5{,}700}{12}$$

Multiply both sides by 12 → $\$45{,}600 = x \times 5{,}700$

Divide both sides by 5,700 → $\$8 = x$

The maximum annual rate is \$8.00 per square foot.

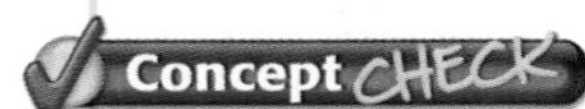

Complete the problem. Check your answer in the back of the book.

3. Paul's Auto Body Shop is planning a second location. The shop needs a service area that is 60 feet by 80 feet. Paul's does not want to spend more than \$4,800 per month in rent. What is the maximum annual rate per square foot that Paul's can pay?

GRAPHING CALCULATOR LAB

Linear Equations

```
Plot1 Plot2 Plot3
\Y1=3800
\Y2=(5700X)/12
\Y3=
\Y4=
\Y5=
\Y6=
\Y7=
```

You can use the graphing calculator to help solve linear equations.
In Example 2 the Polidio Produce Market is expanding to the suburbs. Polidio's budget allows \$3,800 per month to rent the needed 5,700 square foot space. What is the maximum the market can pay per square foot on an annual rate?

Step 1: Write the linear equation.

$$3{,}800 = \frac{x \times 5{,}700}{12}$$

Step 2: Graph each side of the equation and locate the point of intersection.
The x value at the point of intersection is the maximum annual rate.
To access the Y = screen press Y=
Enter the appropriate equations.
To find the point of intersection follow these key strokes.
 and when data appears, press   

Think and Discuss

1. What is the point of intersection? What is the maximum Polidio can pay per square foot?
2. If Polidio's budget is only \$3,000 per month, what is the maximum the market can pay per square foot?
3. Maguire's Movie Rentals has a budget of \$2,500 per month to rent a 4,800 square foot space. What is the maximum Maguire's can pay per square foot on an annual rate?
4. If Maguire's increases the budget by \$400, how much more can the store afford per square foot?

Landscape Architect

Landscape architecture is growing as more developers and business owners seek to combine natural elements with human-made environments. Like building architects, landscape architects use blueprints to design their creations. **How might landscape architects use math in their work?**

Lesson Practice

For Problems 4–9, compute the (a) number of square feet and (b) monthly rental charge to the nearest dollar.

	Annual Rate per Square Foot)	Dimensions		Number of Square Feet	Monthly Rental Charge
		Width	Length		
4.	$ 8.00	20	40	a.	b.
5.	$ 7.50	20	50	a.	b.
6.	$28.00	25	80	a.	b.

7. Dimensions: 45 feet by 50 feet
Annual rental charge: $5.40 per square foot

8. Dimensions: 8 feet by 8 feet
Annual rental charge: $32.75 per square foot

9. The Miller Manufacturing Company is considering the rental of additional manufacturing space at $4.80 per square foot per year. The space Miller wants to rent measures 80 feet by 120 feet.

10. The Flower Shoppe is opening a store in the warehouse district. The rent is $8.75 per square foot per year plus 5% of the store's gross sales. The area of the store is 2,000 square feet. If The Flower Shoppe had $180,000 in gross sales the first year, what monthly rent will it pay?

11. The Luncheonette rents a 30-foot by 50-foot area at the Nottingham Mall. The Luncheonette pays $9.20 per square foot per year plus 2% of gross sales. Last year The Luncheonette had $225,000 in gross sales. What was its monthly rent?

H.O.T. Problems

12. CHALLENGE PROBLEM The C & S Legal Clinic has a 3-year lease for suburban office space at $12.60 per square foot per year. The dimensions of the office are 35 feet by 100 feet. The lease has a 6% rent escalation clause for the second year and a 5% rent escalation clause the third year of the lease. What is the monthly rental charge for each year of the lease?

13. ALGEBRA Ann Petrie wants to rent some space at the City Dock for Annie's Boutique. She would like to have 2,400 square feet but does not want to pay more than $3,000 per month rent. What is the most she can pay per square foot in an annual rate?

Spiral Review

Divide. Round answers to the nearest dollar. (Skill 10)

14. $25,800 ÷ 12 **15.** $14,949 ÷ 12 **16.** $9,070 ÷ 12

17. A 3-year-old sedan has an average retail value of $14,589. Add $443 for a power sunroof, $196 for a satellite radio system, and $85 for remote engine start. Deduct $225 for excessive mileage. What is the average retail price? (Lesson 9.3)

GET READY for the Next Lesson

PREREQUISITE SKILL **Multiplying Decimals** (Skill 8)

Round to the nearest cent.

18. $\$2.68 \times 6 \times 8$ **19.** $\$5.43 \times 2 \times 3$ **20.** $\$9.19 \times 1\frac{3}{4} \times 6$

LESSON 17.2

Maintenance and Improvement

Lesson Objective
Calculate the total building maintenance charge.

Content Vocabulary
- labor charge

GET READY for the Lesson

What types of building and property maintenance have you seen?

Last summer, Henry Simmons made money by washing windows. This summer, his crew expanded its list of clients to include more nearby businesses.

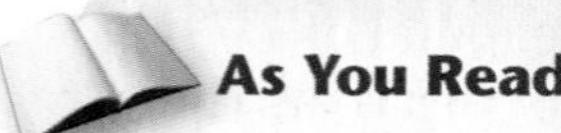

As You Read

List What services might a maintenance department or service firm provide?

Maintenance and Improvement If your business owns a **structure**, you will need people to clean, paint, repair, and maintain the building. You may have your own maintenance department, or you may hire a service firm. The total cost of a maintenance job generally includes a **labor charge**. The labor charge is the cost of paying the people who do the job. It is calculated on an hourly basis for each laborer. In some cases the cleaning and maintenance charge is based on square footage. You will also pay for the materials used. The formula is:

Total Charge = Labor Charge + Materials Charge

EXAMPLE

Central Law Offices hired Commercial Painting Service to paint its offices. Four painters worked 23 hours each to complete the job. The regular hourly rate for each painter is $36.00. All work was done on weekends, so the painters were paid time and a half. The painters used 60 gallons of paint, for which they charged $29.75 per gallon. What was the total charge for painting the offices?

Step 1: Find the labor charge.

($36.00 × 1.5) × 23 hours × 4 = $4,968 labor charge

Step 2: Find the materials charge.

60 × $29.75 = $1,785 materials charge

Step 3: Find the total charge.

Labor Charge + Materials Charge

$4,968 + $1,785 = **$6,753 total charge**

Concept CHECK

Complete the problem. Check your answer in the back of the book.

1. Three painters worked 6 hours each at $35.50 per hour. They used 9 gallons of paint at $29.85 per gallon. Find the total charge.

DreamPictures/Blend Images LLC

Study Tip

Strategize
When you do not immediately know the answer to a quiz or test question, relax. You can skip it and come back to it later.

Lesson Practice

For Problems 2–4, calculate the (a) labor charge and (b) total charge.

		Number of Hours	Number of Employees	Hourly Rate	Labor Charge	Materials Charge	Total
2.	Painter	8	3	$30.30	a.	$ 725.00	b.
3.	Cleaning	3	2	$10.50	a.	$32.00	b.
4.	Carpenter	12	3	$32.20	a.	$2,975.63	b.

5. A janitorial service cleans and maintains an office area measuring 300 feet by 100 feet. The contract calls for a fee of $0.42 per square foot annually. What is the monthly charge?

6. City Cleaners hired 2 carpenters to remodel part of its store. The carpenters earned $28.95 each per hour. Each carpenter worked 36 hours. The materials charge was $2,617.48. Find the total charge.

7. Dr. Alice Desmond is moving to a new office in the same building. It takes 4 people 3 hours to complete the move. The hourly rate per person is $16.80. The rental charge for moving equipment is $268.00. What is the total charge?

8. The National Freight Company used 6 loads of landscape mulch on landscaping around the terminal grounds. The mulch cost $132.75 a load. Ten people were each paid $12.50 an hour to spread the mulch. It took 9 hours. What was the total charge?

9. Scott's Supermarket hired 5 people to refinish tile floors. The job took 8 hours and was done on Sunday. Each worker was paid double the regular rate of $15.25 per hour. Materials cost $571. Scott's rented a floor polishing machine for $85, a pressure washer for $75, and a wet/dry vacuum for $35. Determine the total charge.

10. CHALLENGE PROBLEM City Bank's annual maintenance expenses are: lawn care, $1,655; heat/AC service $324; cleaning 8 fans at $15.50 each; washing windows $750; shampooing lobby carpet 12 times at $148 each. The charge for cleaning the 45-foot by 48-foot interior is $0.0425 per square foot. The interior is cleaned Monday through Saturday minus 12 holidays. What is the monthly charge for maintenance?

Spiral Review

Multiply. (Skill 8)

11. $9.75 × 5 × 3 **12.** $7.43 × 2.5 × 4 **13.** $8.45 × $2\frac{1}{4}$ × 5

14. ALGEBRA Sampsal's Office Supply sells a 12-pack of pens for $5.50 and a 24-pack of pens for $9.75. A combination of 75 of these packages of pens was sold for $578.25. How many of each type was sold? (Lesson 1.4)

GET READY for the Next Lesson

PREREQUISITE SKILL Finding the Percentage (Skill 30)

Find the percentage. Round answers to the nearest cent.

15. 12% of $156 **16.** 5% of $246.30 **17.** 6% of $12.16
18. 30% of $415.05 **19.** 8% of $360.45 **20.** 11% of $121.56

LESSON 17.3

Equipment Rental

Lesson Objective

Determine the total equipment rental cost.

Content Vocabulary

- equipment rental

GET READY for the Lesson

What are some things you would like to be able to rent?

Jessica Woods just started her own business in Los Angeles renting designer handbags. Her clients want to use the high-end accessories when attending social events, but do not want to pay hundreds of dollars each to own them.

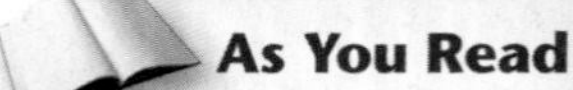

As You Read

Recall Have you ever rented equipment?

Equipment Rental Rather than buying equipment or furniture, some businesses find it is more economical to rent or lease these items. Generally, the total cost of **equipment rental** is determined by the length of time for which you rent the items. Some states **impose** a usage tax on items that are rented. The formula is:

Usage Tax = Rental Charge × Usage Tax Rate

Total Rental Cost = (Rental Charge + Usage Tax) × Time

EXAMPLE

Tax-Aide is renting new furniture and equipment for a small, temporary office. Office Rental Company charges by the month. In addition to the rental charge, there is a 6% usage tax. What is the total cost of renting the furniture and equipment for 5 months?

The items that Tax-Aide is renting are as follows:

Furniture				Equipment			
Item	QTY	Cost/month	Extension	Item	QTY	Cost/month	Extension
Desk	3	$29.50	$88.50	Computer	2	$40.00	$80.00
File cabinet	3	$13.50	$40.50	Copy/Fax/Printer	1	$79.00	$79.00
Swivel chair	2	$18.00	$36.00	Phones	3	$44.50	$133.50
Guest chair	12	$11.00	$132.00	Security System	1	$59.50	$59.50
		Total	$297.00			Total	$352.00

Step 1: Find the total rental charge per month.

Sum of furniture plus equipment = ($297.00 + $352.00) = $649.00

Step 2: Find the usage tax per month.

Rental Charge × Usage Tax Rate = $649 × 6% = $38.94

Step 3: Find the total rental cost.

(Rental Charge + Usage Tax) × Time

($649.00 + $38.94) × 5 = $687.94 × 5 = **$3,439.70**

Jill Braaten/McGraw-Hill Education

Complete the problem. Check your answer in the back of the book.

1. A computer rents for $64 a month. The tax rate is 6%. Four computers are rented for 3 months. Find the total rental cost.

Reading Math +−÷=

Equations
An equation can be read like a sentence, with the equals sign as the verb.

Lesson Practice

Complete the table. All items were rented for 4 months.

	Item	Quantity	Cost per Month	Extension	6% Tax	Total	Total Rental Charge
2.	Phones	4	$28.50	a.	b.	c.	d.
3.	Copy/Fax	1	$39.50	a.	b.	c.	d.
4.	Router	1	$12.00	a.	b.	c.	d.
5.	Total			a.	b.	c.	d.

For Problems 6 and 7, determine the total rental cost.

6. The Watson Wildlife Association is planting 25 acres of wildlife habitat. The group rents a grass seed planter for $15 per acre and a tractor for 2 days at $225 per day. A 5% usage tax is charged.
7. A company plans to rent some equipment for 2 days. The daily rental charges are: concrete power buggy, $75; power trowel, $55, concrete mixer, $65; and laser level, $55. A flat fee of $85.00 for delivery and pickup of the equipment is also subject to the 8% usage tax.

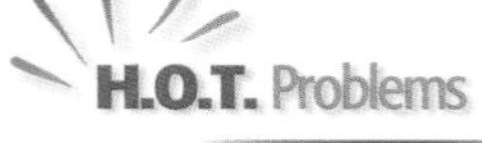

8. **CHALLENGE PROBLEM** Lawrence Painting Company is renting additional equipment for the time indicated in the table below. The various charges are also shown. An 8% usage tax is charged. Determine the most economical way to rent the equipment, then the total charges.

Item	4 Hours	Day	Week	Time Needed
Airless Paint Sprayer	$42.00	$60.00	$240.00	2 weeks
Paint Spray Gun HVLP	$24.50	$35.00	$140.00	8 days
Pressure Washer 2,000 psi	$35.00	$50.00	$180.00	3 hours
Texture Gun and Compressor	$28.00	$40.00	$160.00	2 weeks
Wallpaper Steamer, Electric	$17.50	$25.00	$100.00	3 days

Spiral Review

Find the percentage. Round answers to the nearest hundredth. (Skill 30)

9. 5% of 516 **10.** 6% of 48.40 **11.** 5% of 146.30

12. **ALGEBRA** Tara Sergio took out a single-payment loan for $2,500.00 at 8.75% ordinary interest to pay her federal income tax bill. If the maturity value of the loan was $2,572.92, when would Tara have to pay back the loan if she took it out on April 1? (Lesson 8.1)

GET READY for the Next Lesson

PREREQUISITE SKILL Adding Decimals (Skill 5)

13. $33.89 + ($4,678.00 − $1,303.40)

14. $37.45 + (5% of $450.80)

LESSON 17.4 Utilities Costs—Telephone

Lesson Objective
Calculate the monthly telephone cost.

Content Vocabulary
- utilities
- monthly service charge

GET READY for the Lesson

How do you use the telephone to communicate with your friends and family?

Lisa McMurtry works for a small design company. Many of the people that she works with are located overseas, and she communicates with them primarily via telephone and e-mail.

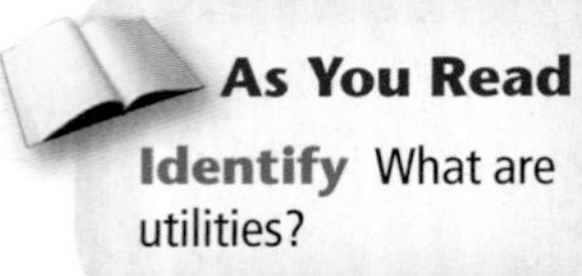

As You Read
Identify What are utilities?

Cost of Utilities To operate your business, you will need several **utilities**. Utilities are public services, such as telephone, electricity, water, and gas. Each utility uses a different cost structure for charging its customers. For example, the **monthly service charge** for your telephone service depends on the total minutes per month, the number of phone lines, the type of equipment, and the type of service and **features** you have. If you use more minutes than the number included in your monthly service charge, you must pay an additional amount per minute. A 3% federal excise tax is also added to your telephone charge each month. The formula is:

Total Cost for the Month = Monthly Service Charge + Cost of Additional Minutes + Cost of Additional Lines + Federal Excise Tax

EXAMPLE 1

Andy's Laundry has 3 telephone lines and uses the $27.00 plan from the Flexible Advantage Calling Plan (see **Figure 17.1**). Andy's uses 1,240 minutes. A 3% federal excise tax is added to the bill. What is the total cost of its telephone service for the month?

Figure 17.1

Flexible Advantage Calling Plan for Two Lines

Monthly Service Plan	Included Minutes	Additional Lines per Month	Overage per Minute Rate
$27.00	up to 1,000	$21.99	$0.06
$52.00	up to 2,000	$21.99	$0.06
$96.00	up to 5,000	$21.99	$0.06

Step 1: Find the cost of additional minutes.
$(1{,}240 - 1{,}000) \times \$0.06 = 240 \times \$0.06 = \$14.40$

Step 2: Find the cost of additional lines.
$(3 - 2) \times \$21.99 = \$21.99$

Step 3: Find the federal excise tax.
$(\$27.00 + \$14.40 + \$21.99) \times 3\% = \$63.39 \times 0.03 = \$1.9017 = \$1.90$

Step 4: Find the total cost for the month.

Monthly Service Charge + Cost of Additional Minutes + Cost of Additional Lines + Federal Excise Tax

$27.00 + $14.40 + $21.99 + $1.90 = **$65.29 total cost for the month**

Study Tip

Active Listening

Listening actively and asking questions helps you retain information and better understand concepts.

Concept CHECK

Find the total cost for the month. The federal tax is 3%. Use Figure 17.1. Check your answers in the back of the book.

1. Monthly phone service plan is $96.
   Six lines and 5,960 minutes are used.
2. Monthly phone service plan is $52.00.
   Four lines and 3,487 minutes are used.
3. Monthly service plan is $27.
   Three lines and 1,488 minutes are used.

Need Help? Go to...
Workshop 38: Problem-Solving Strategy: Writing an Equation, p. 78

EXAMPLE 2 Algebra

The City Realty Company budgets $170 per month for telephone costs which includes the 3% federal excise tax. City Realty uses 1,500 to 2,000 minutes per month, so it signed up for the $52.00 plan in **Figure 17.1.** In order to stay within budget, what is the maximum number of lines per month that City Realty can use?

Step 1: Let x = The maximum number of lines per month that City Realty can use

Step 2: Use the Total Cost for the Month formula and solve for x.

Total Cost for the Month = Monthly Service Charge + Cost of Additional Minutes + Cost of Additional Lines + Federal Excise Tax

Distribute and combine like terms → $170 = [$52.00 + $0 + $21.99($x$ − 2)] + 3%[$52.00 + $0 + $21.99($x$ − 2)]

Subtract $8.2606 from both sides → $170 = 22.6497x$ + $8.2606

Divide both sides by $22.6497 → $161.7394 = 22.6497x$

7.140906 = x

The maximum number of lines that City Realty can use is 7.

Concept CHECK

Complete the problems. Check your answers in the back of the book.

4. Citywide Delivery Inc. budgets $190.00 per month for telephone costs, which include the 3% federal excise tax. Citywide uses approximately 4,000 minutes per month, so the company signed up for the $96.00 plan. What is the maximum number of lines Citywide can sign up for and stay within their budget?
5. Corner Deli uses the $27.00 plan with three lines. If the deli's telephone bill last month was $66.53, including the 3% federal excise tax, how many minutes were used?

Lesson Practice

Use Figure 17.1 on page 638 and a 3% federal tax rate for Problems 6–8.

	Monthly Plan	Minutes Used	Number of Lines	Cost of Additional Minutes	Cost of Additional Lines	Federal Tax	Monthly Cost
6.	$27.00	1,400	2	a.	b.	c.	d.
7.	$52.00	2,250	3	a.	b.	c.	d.
8.	$96.00	6,542	5	a.	b.	c.	d.

For Problems 9–11, use Figure 17.1 on page 638 and a 3% federal excise tax to find the total cost for the month.

9. Spotlight Discount has 2 telephone lines.
Monthly service plan is $52.00.
The company used 3,430 minutes.

10. Public Pharmacy has 3 telephone lines.
Monthly service plan is $96.00.
The pharmacy used 5,894 minutes.

11. The Brown Medical Clinic has 5 telephone lines. The clinic signed up for the $52.00 Flexible Advantage Calling Plan and used 3,530 minutes this past month.

12. Ahmed Young, a broker for stocks and bonds, has 8 telephone lines on the $96.00 Flexible Advantage Calling Plan. Young used 7,176 minutes this past month. He also has call waiting, voice mail, and caller ID for each line at a total of $7.75 per line per month. The federal excise tax rate is 3%. What is the total cost for the month?

Did You Know?

Wasted Time **A recent survey revealed that the average American employee spends about two hours of a normal eight-hour work day doing something other than work, costing employers an estimated $759 billion each year. The number-one reported time waster, according to 44.7% of respondents: personal Internet use.**

H.O.T. Problems

13. ALGEBRA King Pizza uses the $96.00 plan. Its telephone bill this past month, including the 3% federal excise tax, was $250.23. If King Pizza used 5,250 minutes, how many lines does it have?

14. ALGEBRA City Bank Company is trying to decide between the $27.00 plan and the $52.00 plan. The company has 4 lines and uses between 1,000 and 2,000 minutes per month. What criteria should it use to decide?

Spiral Review

Add. (Skill 5, 6, 8, 30)

15. $249.99 + $33.98 + [(3,900 − 3,750) × $0.15] + $9.19

16. $19.99 + (2 × $16.99) + [(68 − 50) × $0.45] + $1.86

17. The Madison County tax assessor determined the market value of a home to be $595,000. The rate of assessment in Madison County is 40% of market value. The tax rate is 42.73 mills. Calculate the real estate tax. (Lesson 10.5)

GET READY for the Next Lesson

PREREQUISITE SKILL **Multiplying Decimals** (Skill 8)

18. 125 × $4.20
19. 100 × $7.22
20. $0.042 × 6,700
21. 1,012 × $0.015
22. 562 × $13.24
23. $45.81 × 300

LESSON 17.5

Utilities Costs—Electricity

Lesson Objective

Compute the monthly cost for electricity.

Content Vocabulary

- customer charge
- demand charge
- energy charge
- peak load
- kilowatts
- fuel adjustment charge

GET READY for the Lesson

When might you increase electricity usage?

Customer comfort is a high priority for businesses in hot-weather cities such as Tucson, Arizona, where the average high temperature in summer is regularly over 100 degrees Fahrenheit.

As You Read

Explain Define *customer charge, demand charge,* and *energy charge.*

Utilities Costs–Electricity The monthly cost of electricity for your business depends on the **customer charge**, the **demand charge**, and the **energy charge**. The customer charge is a basic charge for the electrical service. The demand charge is based on the **peak load** during the month. The peak load is the greatest number of **kilowatts** your business uses at one time during the month. The energy charge is based on the total number of kilowatt hours (kWh) that your business uses during the month. Meters installed at your business record the kilowatt demand and the number of kilowatt hours. The electric company may **levy** a **fuel adjustment charge**, sometimes called an "energy cost adjustment," to your monthly bill to help cover increases in the cost of the fuel needed to produce your electricity. The formula is:

Total Cost for the Month = Customer Charge + Demand Charge + Energy Charge + Fuel Adjustment Charge

EXAMPLE

The Acme Manufacturing Company had a peak demand load of 100 kilowatts of electricity during April. The customer charge is \$20.00. The demand charge is \$6.54 per kilowatt. Acme used a total of 30,000 kilowatt hours of electricity during the month. The energy charge for the first 1,000 kilowatt hours is \$0.076 per kilowatt hour. The cost of the remaining kilowatt hours is \$0.058 per kilowatt hour. The fuel adjustment charge for April is \$0.0155 per kilowatt hour. What is the total cost of the electricity that Acme used in April?

Step 1: Find the demand charge.

100 kW × \$6.54 = \$654.00 demand charge

Step 2: Find the energy charge.

First 1,000 kilowatt hours: 1,000 kWh × 0.076 = \$76.00

Remaining kilowatt hours: (30,000 − 1,000) kWh × \$0.058 = \$1,682.00

\$76.00 + \$1,682.00 = \$1,758.00 energy charge

Continued on next page

erperl/Alamy

Step 3: Find the fuel adjustment charge.

30,000 kWh × \$0.0155 = \$465.00 fuel adjustment charge

Step 4: Find the total cost for the month.

Customer Charge + Demand Charge + Energy Charge + Fuel Adjustment Charge

\$20.00 + \$654.00 + \$1,758.00 + \$465.00 = **\$2,897.00 total cost for the month**

Find the total cost for the month. Check your answer in the back of the book.

1. Central City Deli used 8,700 kilowatt hours of electricity with a peak load of 100 kilowatts in June. The customer charge is \$15.00. The demand charge is \$7.25 per kilowatt. The energy charge is \$0.08 per kilowatt hour for the first 1,000 kilowatt hours and \$0.06 per kilowatt hour for more than 1,000 kilowatt hours. The fuel adjustment charge is \$0.03 per kilowatt hour.

Study Tip

Skimming
To prepare for a lesson, skim and scan the word problems to better understand the questions.

Lesson Practice

For Problems 2–7, determine the total cost of electricity for the month.

	Company	kWh Used	Peak Load (kWh)	Demand Charge per kWh	Energy Charge per kWh	Fuel Adjustment Charge per kWh	Customer Charge	Total Cost for Month
2.	Bax	19,500	100	\$4.50	\$0.076	\$0.017	\$25.00	
3.	Cobra	17,000	120	\$5.80	\$0.110	\$0.008	\$18.00	
4.	Schmitz	25,000	90	\$6.10	\$0.076	\$0.016	\$34.00	
5.	Delta	18,000	80	\$5.60	\$0.080	\$0.017	\$28.00	
6.	P&L	20,000	115	\$5.65	\$0.100	\$0.010	\$20.00	
7.	Edwards	23,000	130	\$6.00	\$0.076	\$0.015	\$30.00	

8. Kigar Wood Shop used 18,400 kilowatt hours of electricity with a peak load of 200 kilowatts in May. The customer charge is \$25.00. The demand charge is \$8.50 per kilowatt. The energy charge is \$0.07 per kilowatt hour for the first 1,000 kilowatt hours and \$0.055 per kilowatt hour for more than 1,000 kilowatt hours. The fuel adjustment charge is \$0.05 per kilowatt hour.
9. The Wilson Spice Company used 33,800 kilowatt hours of electricity last month. The peak load for the month was 220 kilowatts. The customer charge is \$28.00. The demand charge is \$5.91 per kilowatt. The energy charge per kilowatt hour is \$0.0655 for the first 10,000 kilowatt hours and \$0.0555 per kilowatt hour for more than 10,000 kilowatt hours. The fuel adjustment charge is \$0.084 per kilowatt hour.
10. The Pantry Supermarket used 21,400 kilowatt hours of electricity last month. The peak load for the month was 120 kilowatts. The customer charge is \$18.00. The demand charge is \$5.91 per kilowatt. The energy charge per kilowatt hour is \$0.0675 for the first 10,000 kilowatt hours and \$0.0455 per kilowatt hour for more than 10,000 kilowatt hours. The fuel adjustment charge is \$0.015 per kilowatt hour.

11. The Old Home Supply store used 26,000 kilowatt hours of electricity last month. The peak load for the month was 200 kilowatts. The customer charge is $18.00. The demand charge is $5.65 per kilowatt. The energy charge per kilowatt hour is $0.080 for the first 10,000 kilowatt hours and $0.065 per kilowatt hour for more than 10,000 kilowatt hours. The fuel adjustment charge is $0.016 per kilowatt hour.

12. The City Journal used 12,417 kilowatt hours of electricity in August. The peak load during the month was 78 kilowatts. The customer charge is $25.00. The demand charge is $6.96 per kilowatt for the first 45 kilowatts and $6.10 per kilowatt for more than 45 kilowatt hours. The energy charge per kilowatt hour is $0.0872 for the first 3,000 kilowatt hours, $0.0685 per kilowatt hour for the next 7,000 kilowatt hours and $0.0585 for more than 10,000 kilowatt hours. No fuel adjustment charge is levied.

13. **CHALLENGE PROBLEM** City Center Gym used 11,500 kilowatt hours of electricity with a peak load of 100 kilowatts. The customer charge is $20.00. The demand charge is $6.50 per kilowatt hour for the first 50 kilowatt hours and $6.25 per kilowatt hour for more than 50 kilowatt hours. The energy charge for the first 5,000 kilowatt hours is $0.055 per kilowatt hour, $0.05 per kilowatt hour for the next 5,000 kilowatt hours and $0.045 per kilowatt hour for all kilowatt hours over 10,000 hours. The fuel adjustment charge was $0.02 per kilowatt hour but was recently increased by 5%. **(a)** What was the total cost of electricity prior to the increase in the fuel adjustment charge? **(b)** What was the total cost of electricity after the 5% increase in the fuel adjustment charge?

Spiral Review

Multiply. (Skill 8)

14. 1,000 × $0.087
15. 8,700 × $0.063
16. 9,700 × $0.015
17. You deposited $4,000 at 5.5% compounded daily for 35 days. **(a)** Find the amount after 35 days. **(b)** Find the compound interest. (Lesson 5.7)
18. **ALGEBRA** The Honey Bear pays a net price of $12.25 for a gross of ice cream cones after a trade-discount rate of 65%. What was the list price? What was the trade discount? (Lesson 14.2)

GET READY for the Next Lesson

PREREQUISITE SKILL Adding Decimals (Skill 5)

Add.

19. $394.44 + $512.10 + (23 × $3.05)
20. $686.54 + $35.09 + $12.08
21. $31.58 + $515.77 + (3% of $680,000.00)
22. (19 × $4.24) + $341.83 + $7.01 + $86.77
23. $315.23 + $161.04 + (6% of $68,300.00)
24. ($68 × 7.5) + $31.81 + $14,310.12

LESSON 17.6

Professional Services

Lesson Objective
Calculate the total cost of professional services.

Content Vocabulary
- consultant
- consultant's fee

GET READY for the Lesson

What expertise do you have that someone else might need?

Caleb Barrett, a computer science major at the University of Texas, has been a computer whiz kid since he was in the first grade. To make extra money, Caleb works freelance for local businesses, training employees how to use a variety of computer operating systems and software.

PureStock/age fotostock

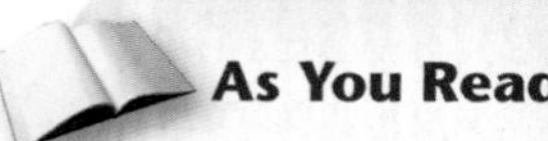

As You Read
List Can you think of projects for which a company might hire a professional consultant?

Professional Services A company may hire professional **consultants** to advise the business on a particular **project**. The method of determining each **consultant's fee** may vary. Some consultants charge a flat fee, some charge a percent of the cost of the project, and some charge by the hour. The formula is:

Total Cost = Sum of Consultant's Fees

EXAMPLE 1

Appleton Wholesale Grocers plans to construct a new building at a cost of $1,375,000. Appleton wants to hire an architect, a systems analyst, and a computer programmer. The architect charges 7% of the total cost of the building. The systems analyst charges a flat fee of $9,000. The computer programmer charges $30 an hour and works 150 hours. What is the total cost of the professional services?

Find the sum of consultant's fees.

Architect: $1,375,000 × 7.00%	$ 96,250
Systems analyst: flat fee	$ 9,000
Computer programmer: $30 × 150	$ 4,500
	$109,750 sum of consultant's fees

Find the total cost. Check your answers in the back of the book.

1. Architect charges 8% of $450,000.
   Lawyer's fee for 20 hours at $120 per hour.
   Surveyor has a $3,500 flat fee.
2. Engineer's fee for 25 hours at $65.50 per hour.
   Computer programmer has a $5,000 flat fee.
   Computer time is a $2,450 flat fee.

EXAMPLE 2 Algebra

Architect Luis Groza does not accept projects for less than a $45,000 fee. He charges $75 per hour plus 6% of the total cost of the project. How many hours would he need to work to generate $45,000 on a project costing $500,000?

Step 1: Let h = The number of hours needed on the project

Step 2: Write an equation for the Consultant's Fee and solve for h.

	Consultant's Fee	=	Hourly Fee	+	Percent of the Cost
	\$45,000	=	\$75h	+	(6% x \$500,000)
Multiply →	\$45,000	=	\$75h	+	\$30,000
Subtract \$30,000 from both sides →	\$15,000	=	\$75h		
Divide both sides by \$75 →	200	=	h		

Luis would need to work 200 hours on the project.

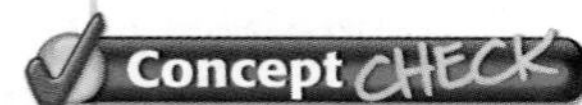

Complete the problem. Check your answer in the back of the book.

3. The Dunbolt Company is going to install a new computer payroll system. The program has two components: hardware cost and installation. The installation budget is $25,000. The systems analyst charges 7% of the cost of the hardware; the programmer charges 5% of the cost of the hardware; and the physical plant designer charges $20.50 per hour for the estimated 30 hours it would take. What is the maximum that Dunbolt can pay for the hardware and stay within its budget?

Reading Math

Decimal Point

When writing out an amount of money, use *and* to indicate the decimal point. $34.50 is read "thirty-four dollars *and* fifty cents."

Lesson Practice

For Problems 4–6, find the total fee.

	Professional Service	Fee Structure	Project Information	Total Fee
4.	Patent attorney	\$125.00 per hour	Worked 20 hours	
5.	Industrial nurse	\$ 41.25 per hour	Worked 40 hours	
6.	Design consultant	\$ 50.00 per hour	Worked 25 hours	

7. Yoko Nagasawa hired an attorney. Attorney fee charges are $150 per hour plus 20% of settlement. The attorney worked 80 hours and the settlement was $200,000. Find the total fee. Find the net paid to Yoko.
8. Sherman Brewer hired an employment consultant to help him find a job. The consultant charges $40 per hour plus 15% of the first year's salary. The consultant works 75 hours and the first year's salary is $80,000. Find the total fee. Find Sherman's net first year salary after paying the consultant.
9. Lakeside Hospital hired an industrial engineering firm, Time Study, to conduct a work sampling on the average nurse's day. Time Study did the work sampling and charged $67.50 per hour. It took Time Study 32 hours to complete the task. What did Time Study's work sampling cost Lakeside Hospital?

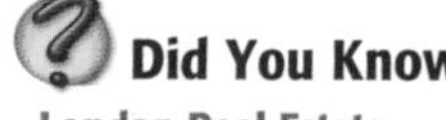

Did You Know?

London Real Estate

Chelsea is one of London, England's most expensive areas. A 77-square-foot Chelsea apartment recently went on sale for about \$335,000, or \$4,350 per square foot. The apartment measures 11 by 7 feet, about the size of a large closet.

10. The June Company hired Maletus Brown, a staff development specialist, to conduct a workshop in London, England, for 83 of its employees. Maletus was paid \$110 per person. What was the total cost of Maletus's services?

11. The Central Farmers Co-op plans to issue \$20,000,000 in bonds to pay for an extensive expansion. One bond broker will sell the bonds for a fee of 3.25 percent of the \$20,000,000 face value of the bonds. What will the broker's services cost Central? What is the net amount to Central?

12. Modern Service Stations plans to sell a large piece of commercial property. The selling price of the property is \$975,000. Marcus Trent will handle the entire transaction for 6.5% of the selling price. What will it cost Modern Service Stations to have Marcus handle the transaction? What is the net amount of the sale?

13. Liberty Bank and Trust plans to build a new branch office. Liberty hired Ed Baker, an architect, to design the new branch office. Ed's fee is 7% of the cost of the project. Liberty hired Tina Pike as project engineer for the new branch. Tina's fee is 4.5% of the cost of the project. Liberty hired attorney Sara Charles to handle the legal aspects of the project. She charges \$175 per hour. It took her 20.5 hours to prepare the legal documents. The cost of the branch office is estimated to be \$4,575,000. What is the total cost for professional services? What is the total cost of the project?

H.O.T. Problems

14. ALGEBRA Attorney Allison Rafi is asked to represent two different clients. Marble Meat Company will pay Allison \$75 per hour plus 20% of the settlement. North Meat, Inc. will pay Allison \$90 per hour plus 18% of the settlement. Allison estimates 30 hours of work for either case. Which criteria should Allison use to decide which case to take, if money is the only consideration?

15. ALGEBRA Jerome Cuentes, JD, does not accept legal cases involving litigation that would result in less than a \$50,000 fee. He charges \$70 per hour plus 30% of the settlement. What is the minimum acceptable settlement on a case on which he spent 200 hours?

Spiral Review

Solve. (Skill 5, 8, 30)

16. (5% of \$1,750,000) + \$14,750

17. (6% of \$3,500,000) + (\$75 × 6.5) + \$1,475

18. Sandra Cole has an annual salary of \$68,225. What is her monthly salary? What is her biweekly salary? (Lesson 1.5)

GET READY for the Next Lesson

PREREQUISITE SKILL Subtracting Decimals (Skill 6)

Subtract.

19. \$956.44 − \$33.33

20. \$59.04 − \$8.47

21. \$2,864.22 − \$904.86

22. \$21,093.71 − \$8,901.60

Chapter 17 Review and Assessment

AFTER YOU READ

Chapter SUMMARY

You have learned that overhead expenses are a necessary part of running a business. You computed the monthly rental charge, the total building maintenance charge, and the total equipment rental cost. You calculated the monthly telephone cost, the monthly cost for electricity, and the total cost of professional services.

Vocabulary Check

1. On a sheet of paper, use each of these terms in a sentence.

Content Vocabulary

- rent (p. 631)
- lease (p. 631)
- labor charge (p. 634)
- equipment rental (p. 636)
- utilities (p. 638)
- monthly service charge (p. 638)
- customer charge (p. 641)
- demand charge (p. 641)
- energy charge (p. 641)
- peak load (p. 641)
- kilowatts (p. 641)
- fuel adjustment charge (p. 641)
- consultant (p. 644)
- consultant's fee (p. 644)

Academic Vocabulary

- occupy (p. 631)
- structure (p. 634)
- impose (p. 636)
- features (p. 638)
- levy (p. 641)
- project (p. 644)

Concept Check

2. Explain how to find the monthly rental charge.
3. Describe how to calculate the total maintenance charge.
4. Identify the formula for total equipment rental cost.
5. List factors that affect the monthly telephone cost.
6. List the charges included in the total monthly cost for electricity.
7. Name three different methods consultants may use when charging fees.
8. **CRITICAL THINKING** List as many overhead expenses as you can think of that a business must consider. How do these compare with expenses in your own life?

Lesson-by-Lesson Review

17.1 Building Rental (pp. 631–633)

Compute the monthly rental charge.
Web Dot Com rents a small office. The floor space measures 12 feet by 20 feet. It pays an annual rate of $11.25 per square foot. Rounding to the nearest dollar, what is Web Dot Com's monthly rental charge?

Step 1: Find the number of square feet.

Length × Width

12 feet × 20 feet = 240 square feet

Step 2: Find the monthly rental charge.

$$\frac{\text{Annual Rate} \times \text{Number of Square Feet}}{12} = \frac{\$11.25 \times 240}{12} = \textbf{\$225 monthly rental charge}$$

Review Exercises

Complete the table.

	Annual Rate per Square Foot	Dimensions			Number of Square Feet		Monthly Rental Charge
		Width	Length				
9.	$ 9.00	10	20	a.		b.	
10.	$ 8.50	30	15	a.		b.	
11.	$10.50	35	25	a.		b.	
12.	$12.75	40	12	a.		b.	
13.	$32.00	30	18	a.		b.	
14.	$11.15	45	22	a.		b.	

15. Red Rambler Coffee House rents a portion of a building owned by The Posadny Company. The floor space measures 50 feet by 110 feet. The annual rent is $12.50 per square foot. To the nearest dollar, what is Red Rambler's monthly rental charge?
16. **ALGEBRA** Posadny Bakery would like to move to a larger space. The budget allows $2,700 per month to rent the needed 4,000 square foot space. What is the maximum the bakery can pay per square foot on an annual rate?

17.2 Maintenance and Improvement (pp. 634–635)

Calculate the total building maintenance charge.
Northern Office Supply hired Universal Roofers to repair the roof on its office building. Two roofers worked 17 hours each to complete the job. The regular hourly rate for each roofer was $28.25. The roofers used $2,653.20 in materials. What was the total charge for fixing the roof?

Step 1: Find the labor charge.

($28.25 × 17) × 2 = $960.50 labor charge

Step 2: Find the materials charge.

$2,653.20 materials charge

Lesson-by-Lesson Review (continued)

Step 3: Find the total charge.

Labor Charge + Materials Charge

$960.50 + $2,653.20 = **$3,613.70 total charge**

Review Exercises

Complete the table.

		Number of Hours	Number of Employees	Hourly Rate		Labor Charge	Materials Charge		Total
17.	Painter	7	3	$27.50	a.		$321.98	b.	
18.	Cleaning	6.5	2	$10.50	a.		$193.58	b.	
19.	Carpenter	4	4	$35.00	a.		$621.90	b.	
20.	Movers	12.2	8	$15.50	a.		$239.66	b.	
21.	Landscapers	3	2	$12.75	a.		$712.90	b.	
22.	Mason	5.5	9	$32.25	a.		$239.76	b.	

23. Dr. Tim Hammond is moving from his present office to another office in the same building. It takes 5 people 6 hours to complete the move. The hourly rate per person is $18.20. The rental charge for moving equipment is $328.00. What is the total charge?

17.3 Equipment Rental (pp. 636–637)

Determine the total equipment rental cost.

Helping Hands is renting new furniture and equipment for a small office. The Rental Company charges by the month. In addition to the rental charge, there is a 7% usage tax. What is the total cost of renting the furniture and equipment for 3 months?

Furniture				Equipment			
Item	Quantity	Cost/month	Extension	Item	Quantity	Cost/month	Extension
Desk	2	$29.50	$ 59.00	Computer	2	$40.00	$ 80.00
File cabinet	2	$13.50	$ 27.00	Copier/Fax/Printer	1	$59.00	$ 59.00
Swivel chair	2	$18.00	$ 36.00	Network Router	1	$15.00	$ 15.00
Guest chair	5	$11.00	$ 55.00	Phones	2	$44.50	$ 89.00
		Total	$177.00			Total	$243.00

Step 1: Find the total rental charge per month.

Sum of furniture plus equipment

($177.00 + $243.00) = $420.00

Step 2: Find the usage tax per month.

$420.00 × 7% = $29.40

Step 3: Find the total rental cost.

(Rental Charge + Usage Tax) × Time

($420.00 + $29.40) × 3 = $449.40 × 3 = **$1,348.20 total rental cost**

Lesson-by-Lesson Review (continued)

Review Exercises

Complete the table. Calculate the total rental charge for 4 months.

	Item	Quantity	Cost per Month		Extension		7% Tax		Total		Total Rental Charge
24.	Computer	3	$48.50	a.		b.		c.		d.	
25.	Phones	3	$27.50	a.		b.		c.		d.	
26.	Copier/Fax	1	$39.50	a.		b.		c.		d.	
27.	Router	1	$10.00	a.		b.		c.		d.	
28.	Printer	2	$75.00	a.		b.		c.		d.	
29.	Total			a.		b.		c.		d.	

30. Lawson Forestry Services is renting a chipper for 2 weeks and a stump grinder for 3 days. The chipper rents for $1,900 per week and the stump grinder rents for $285.60 per day. The usage tax is 5%. Determine the total rental cost.

31. Net Discount Brokers rents an office telecommunications system for 12 months. The monthly rental charge is 12.5% of the list price. The list price of the system is $12,680. There is a 7% usage tax. Determine the total rental cost for the year.

32. Direct Pro rents teleconferencing equipment for 5 months. The rental charge is 12% of the list price. There is a 7.75% usage tax. What is the total rental cost if the list price of the equipment is $10,750?

17.4 Utilities Costs–Telephone (pp. 638–640)

Calculate the monthly telephone cost.

Redwater Video Rental has 3 telephone lines. The owner signs up for the $52.00 plan from the Flexible Advantage Calling Plan (see **Figure 17.1** on page 638). Redwater uses 2,225 minutes. A 3% federal excise tax is added to the bill. What is the total cost of Redwater's telephone service for the month?

Step 1: Find the cost of additional minutes.

(2,225 – 2,000) × $0.06 = $13.50 cost of additional minutes

Step 2: Find the cost of an additional line.

(3 – 2) × $21.99 = $21.99 cost of an additional line

Step 3: Find the federal excise tax.

($52.00 + $13.50 + $21.99) × 3% = $2.62 federal excise tax

Step 4: Find the total cost for the month.

Monthly Service Charge + Cost of Additional Minutes + Cost of Additional Lines + Federal Excise Tax

$52.00 + $13.50 + $21.99 + $2.62 = **$90.11 total cost for the month**

Lesson-by-Lesson Review (continued)

Review Exercises

Use Figure 17.1, *Flexible Advantage Calling Plan,* on page 638 for Problems 33–38.

	Monthly Plan	Minutes Used	Number of Lines		Cost of Additional Minutes		Cost of Additional Lines		Federal Tax		Monthly Cost
33.	$27.00	750	2	a.		b.		c.		d.	
34.	$52.00	1,376	3	a.		b.		c.		d.	
35.	$96.00	1,522	4	a.		b.		c.		d.	
36.	$27.00	1,254	2	a.		b.		c.		d.	
37.	$52.00	2,789	3	a.		b.		c.		d.	
38.	$96.00	5,497	2	a.		b.		c.		d.	

39. Attorney Sienna Albert has 4 telephone lines on the $52.00 Flexible Advantage Calling Plan. Albert used 2,900 minutes last month. A 3% federal excise tax is added to the bill. What is the total cost of her telephone service for the month?

40. **ALGEBRA** Swanton Schools budget $350 per month for telephone costs, which include the 3% federal excise tax. Estimating usage of 4,500 to 5,000 minutes per month, Swanton Schools picks the $96.00 plan. In order to stay within budget, what is the maximum number of lines per month that Swanton Schools can use?

17.5 Utilities Costs–Electricity (pp. 641–643)

Compute the monthly cost for electricity.

Destina Land Company had a peak load of 120 kilowatts of electricity during May. The demand charge is $5.98 per kilowatt. Destina used a total of 35,000 kilowatt hours of electricity during the month. The energy charge for the first 1,000 kilowatt hours is $0.076 per kilowatt hour. The cost of the remaining kilowatt hours is $0.058 per kilowatt hour. The fuel adjustment charge for May is $0.0165 per kilowatt hour. The customer charge is $35.00. What is the total cost of the electricity that Destina Land Company used in May?

Step 1: Find the demand charge.

120 kW × $5.98 = $717.60 demand charge

Step 2: Find the energy charge.

First 1,000 kilowatt hours: 1,000 kWh × $0.076 = $76.00

Remaining kilowatt hours: (35,000 − 1,000) kWh × $0.058 = $1,972

$76 + $1,972 = $2,048 energy charge

Step 3: Find the fuel adjustment charge.

35,000 kWh × $0.0165 = $577.50 fuel adjustment charge

Step 4: Find the total cost for the month.

Customer Charge + Demand Charge + Energy Charge + Fuel Adjustment Charge

$35 + $717.60 + $2,048 + $577.50 = **$3,378.10 total cost for the month**

Lesson-by-Lesson Review (continued)

Review Exercises

Complete the table.

	Company	kWh Used	Peak Load (kWh)	Demand Charge per kWh	Energy Charge per kWh	Fuel Adjustment Charge per kWh	Customer Charge	Total Cost for Month
41.	Amarillo Rentals	18,500	100	$4.50	$0.076	$0.017	$22.00	
42.	Northwest Insurance	21,000	85	$6.10	$0.076	$0.016	$37.00	
43.	Hair Style Inc.	15,000	90	$5.78	$0.080	$0.017	$18.00	
44.	Harry's Boots	30,000	110	$5.05	$0.095	$0.013	$21.00	

45. Midwest Bakery used 18,700 kilowatt hours of electricity with a peak load of 115 kilowatts in June. The demand charge is $7.25 per kilowatt. The energy charge is $0.08 per kilowatt hour for the first 1,000 kilowatt hours and $0.06 per kilowatt hour for more than 1,000 kilowatt hours. The fuel adjustment charge is $0.03 per kilowatt hour and the customer charge is $20. What is the total cost of electricity for Midwest Bakery for June?

17.6 Professional Services (pp. 644–646)

Calculate the total cost of professional services.

A school hired Michele Gaglione to conduct a reading workshop for 25 teachers. Michele was paid $75 per teacher. What was the total cost of her services?

Find the sum of the consultant's fees.

$75 × 25 = **$1,875 consultant's fee**

Review Exercises

Find the total fee.

	Professional Service	Fee Structure	Project Information	Total Fee
46.	Research Consultant	$125.00 per hour	Worked 15 hours	
47.	Private Investigator	$45.00 per hour	Worked 35 hours	
48.	Engineering Services	$75.00 per hour	Worked 12.5 hours	
49.	Landscape Design	6.5% of contract	Sales contract $490,000	
50.	Image Consultant	$150 per hour	Worked 4.25 hours	

51. UP Inc. is building an annex for their data processing system. The cost of the annex is $1,750,000. The architect they hired charges $6\frac{1}{2}$% of the cost of the annex. The systems analyst charges a flat fee of $10,000. The computer programmer charges $45 per hour and will work for 80 hours. What is the total cost of the professional services?

52. **ALGEBRA** Consultant Dennis Schwartz does not accept projects for less than a $35,000 fee. He charges $150 per hour plus 5% of the total cost of the project. How many hours would he need to work to generate $35,000 on a project costing $350,000? Round to the nearest hour.

Practice Test

Record your answers on a sheet of paper.

1. **ALGEBRA** Green Thumb Flowers is expanding its operations and renting more office space. The new office space is 400 square feet. The budget allows $500 per month to rent the new space. What is the maximum amount Green Thumb can pay per square foot on an annual rate?
   A $13.95 **B** $15.00
   C $45.00 **D** $88.83

2. Etling Enterprises is having its offices painted. Two painters worked 15 hours each to complete the job. The painters each earn $19.75 an hour and used $426.58 in supplies. What is the total charge for painting the offices?
   A $887.94 **B** $1,445.66
   C $722.83 **D** $1,019.08

3. Terry's Excavation rents bulldozers. Terry's charges $198.45 per day plus a $65 delivery and pickup charge. How much would it cost to rent the bulldozer for 5 days?
   A $1,057.25 **B** $992.25
   C $1,007.50 **D** $995.20

4. **ALGEBRA** Ciudad Electric budgets $210.00 per month for telephone costs, which include the 3% excise tax. Ciudad uses a $52.00 plan that allows for two lines, and the company never uses more minutes than the plan allows. Each additional line would cost $25 per month. In order to stay within budget, what is the maximum number of lines per month Ciudad can have?
   A 5 **B** 6
   C 7 **D** 8

5. Sirens Restaurant hired Stefan Zweig to conduct a customer service workshop for its 22 servers. Stefan charged the restaurant $48 per server. What was the total cost of the workshop?
   A $1,056 **B** $1,560
   C $986 **D** $1,144

6. Amole Industries had an electricity demand charge of $730 during October. The company used a total of 33,000 kilowatt hours during that month. The energy charge is $0.067 per kilowatt hour and the fuel adjustment charge for October was $0.0165 per kilowatt hour. The customer charge was $25. What is the total cost of the electricity that Amole used in October?
   A $1,030.55 **B** $3,510.50
   C $3,865.00 **D** $2,865.55

7. FeCa Studios rents an office to edit recordings. The floor space measures 20 feet by 28 feet. The company pays an annual rate of $9.50 per square foot. Rounding to the nearest dollar, what is FeCa's monthly rental charge?
   A $453 **B** $443
   C $532 **D** $568

8. **ALGEBRA** Artist Zhenli Ye Gon will not accept a project for less than a $55,000 fee. He charges $85 per hour plus 5% of the total cost. To the nearest hour, how many hours would he need to work in order to generate $55,000 on a project that cost $650,000?

9. Scenic Landscaping used 25,000 kilowatt hours of electricity last month. The energy charge for the first 1,000 kilowatt hours is $0.059 per kilowatt hour. The cost of the remaining kilowatt hours is $0.053 per kilowatt hour. What was Scenic's total energy charge last month?

10. 2.8 × $7,022
11. $9,381 + $2.16 + (5% × $590)
12. ($8,000 − $2,580) × $3.59
13. 8% of $3,762
14. $45.67 − $3.21 − $0.87
15. $73 + $131.89 + $44 + (5% × $42)

PART 1 Multiple Choice

Record your answers on the answer sheet provided by your teacher or on a sheet of paper.

1. Carlson Cleaning shows a $179.00 list price for a vacuum cleaner. The net price to a retailer is $152.15. What is the trade-discount rate?
   A 45% **B** 20%
   C 85% **D** 15%

2. **ALGEBRA** Richard Cana's charge account uses the unpaid-balance method to calculate the monthly finance charge. The periodic rate is 2.3%. If Richard had a finance charge of $12.40, what was his unpaid balance for the month?
   A $539.13 **B** $540.42
   C $460.96 **D** $395.21

3. **ALGEBRA** Charles Harrison took out a single-payment loan for $1,950.00 at 6.5% ordinary interest to pay tuition. If the interest on the loan were $32.04, how long would Charles have to pay back the loan?
   A 90 days **B** 91 days
   C 120 days **D** 121 days

4. Tamika Jones is office manager for The Corner Finance Company. She earns $18.70 per hour and time-and-a-half for all hours over 40 per week. What is Tamika's gross pay for a week in which she worked 52 hours?
   A $972.40 **B** $1,458.60
   C $1,103.30 **D** $1,084.60

5. Nora Harold earns an annual salary of $54,865 with benefits totaling $17,556.80. What is her rate of benefits?
   A 30% **B** 38%
   C 32% **D** 40%

6. **ALGEBRA** The U-Shop convenience store operates on an overhead of 35%, which results in an overhead of $5.95 on a personalized cooler. What is the selling price of the cooler?
   A $17.00 **B** $15.80
   C $25.20 **D** $18.00

PART 2 Short Response/Griddable

7. **ALGEBRA** Chandler Tool offers a trade-discount rate that is 3 times its complement. If the net price of a tool is $21.50, what is the list price?

8. Long's Bookstore sells a certain textbook for $45.85 after a markup of $18.55. What is the markup rate based on cost?

9. Yvonne Herrick borrowed $12,000 for new computers for her office staff. Her bank granted her a single-payment loan of $12,000 for 120 days at 6% ordinary interest. Determine the maturity value of the loan.

10. What is the possible net profit for a notebook cover that has a selling price of $4.95, if the fixed costs are $250,000 and the variable cost per unit $1.50? The possible net profit is based on sales of 125,000 units.

PART 3 Extended Response

Show your work.

11. Explain the factors involved in calculating telephone costs.

12. Explain the purpose of a professional consultant. Include some reasons why a company would hire a consultant.

13. Explain sales potential and on what it is based.

TEST-TAKING TIP

Test Day Bring approved pens, pencils, erasers, and calculators with you to the test.

Building Academic Skills

Mathematics

You are starting your own business as a computer technician for small businesses and home users. You estimate start-up and initial operating costs to be $20,000. You decide to run the business from a home office. You have several choices for financing:

- Bank loan at simple interest of 7.6% for two years
- Use all of your personal savings, currently invested in a mutual fund that is making on average 6.9% annually
- Credit card purchases and cash advances, payable at 11.4% annually

Which alternative do you think is best, based on your calculations of the interest cost to you plus your understanding of the potential needs of the business?

English Language Arts/Writing

The U.S. Small Business Administration provides a great deal of information about business opportunities. Use the Internet to go to the Web site for the SBA. Find out what kinds of businesses the SBA considers "good bets" in the coming years. Also, find out how the SBA is making it easier for financial institutions to work with small business owners to obtain SBA loans (hint: search for SBAExpress). Write a short report on your findings and whether you might be interested in starting a business like those the SBA suggests. Why or why not?

Social Studies/Economics

Assume you are a trained bookkeeper and want to start a business handling bookkeeping and tax preparation. Small companies need someone to do this work only a few times a month, so they often do not have full-time accountants on staff. List the items you need to include in your start-up and operating costs. Assume your office is a room in your home. Then list the items in the start-up and initial operating costs if you were to rent an office.

Building Real-World Skills

21st Century Workplace

Online Video as Marketing Study Tool

Years ago, marketers who wanted to analyze their competition would need to study videotapes of television ads. Today, however, most TV spots can be found online, either at the company's Web site or on video sharing sites such as YouTube. Instant access to the competition's marketing spots can be a powerful tool for marketers.

Research and Write:

a. Imagine you have a job as a marketing executive for a luxury car manufacturer. Using the Internet, find online videos of three of your competitors' TV ads.

b. What are some possible drawbacks to using online video as a research tool?

Ethics in Action

Hiring a Friend Imagine you work for a biotechnology facility. You are authorized to hire another scientist for your alternative fuel research team. A friend from college pressures you to hire her for the position. You know your research team needs someone with more experience than your friend has, but you think you would enjoy working with her and wonder if you should give her a chance.

Discuss and Write:

a. Discuss the definition of *favoritism* and situations in which you have seen examples of it.

b. Write a short essay weighing the benefits of hiring your friend versus the needs of the facility.

CHAPTER 18 Accounting

Big Idea

This chapter focuses on how companies account for their employees, equipment, finances, inventory, and other business expenses.

Explore the Photo

Finances
Accounting plays an important role in any business. *Why do you think it is important for a business to keep track of its expenses?*

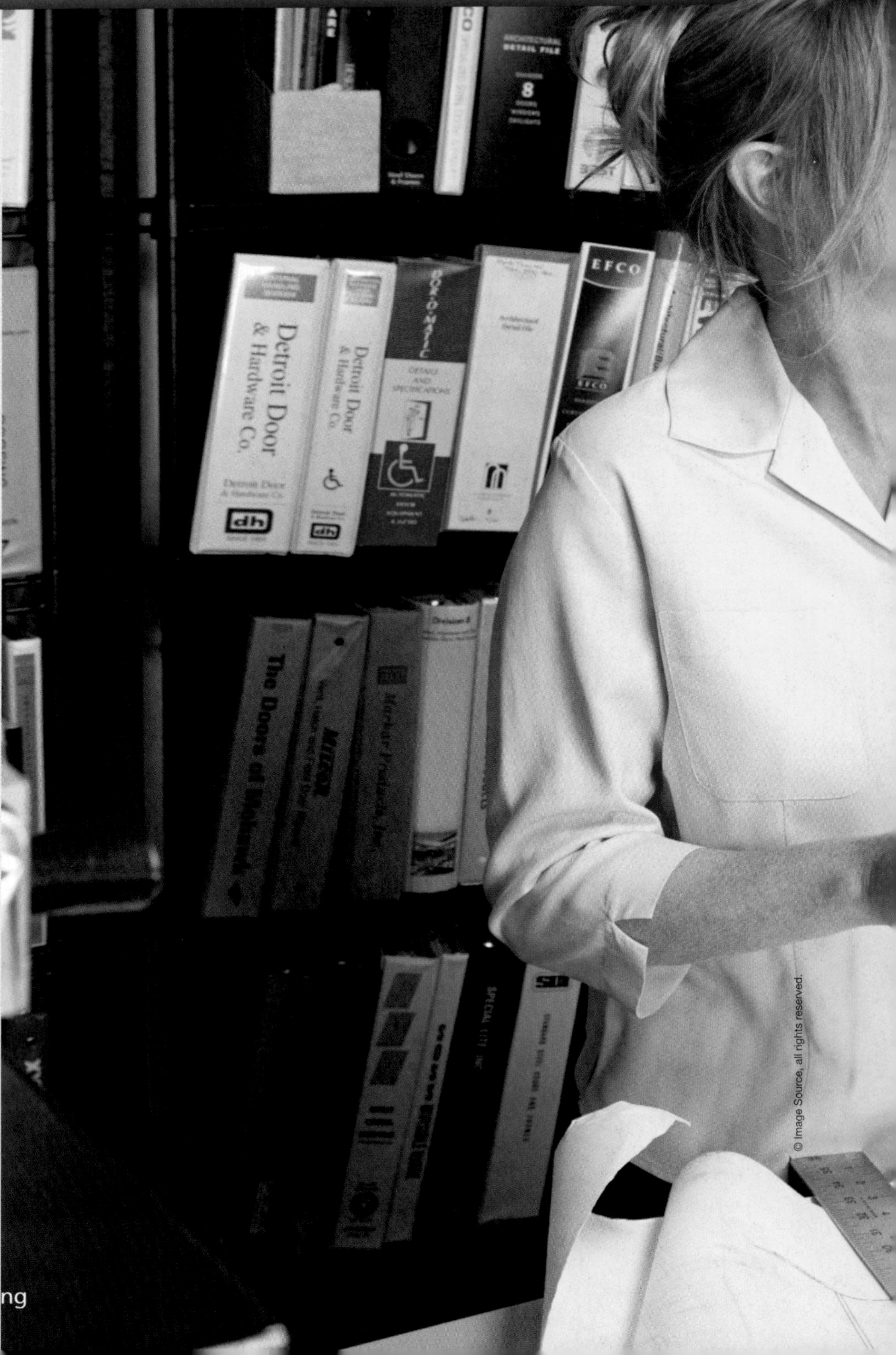

Ask AN EXPERT

Depreciation

Q: The owner of the pizza parlor where I work recently purchased a new, top-of-the-line pizza oven. He said he did not mind paying more because this brand of oven depreciates less quickly. What did he mean?

A: When buying business equipment, business owners consider depreciation, the decrease in value of an item because of age or condition. An oven known for quality loses its value at a lower rate than a cheaply made oven. The low depreciation rate makes the oven a good investment for a pizza-parlor owner. Cheaper equipment may cost less at first but prove to be of lesser value over time because of maintenance costs and lower resale value.

English Language Arts/Writing Write a list of the various items in and around your home that depreciate.

GET READY for the Chapter

Math Online

To take the Online Readiness Quiz, go to **connectED.mcgraw-hill.com**.

Chapter 18 Accounting

Reading Guide

Before You Read

Describe How is managing a company's finances similar to managing your own finances?

Main Idea

Analyzing the finances, personnel, manufacturing capabilities, and inventories of a company is critical to determining the company's strength in the marketplace.

Graphic Organizer

Before you read this chapter, draw a diagram like the one below. As you read, note different accounting formulas.

Accounting Formulas
1.
2.
3.

Math Online Go to **connectED.mcgraw-hill.com** to download this graphic organizer.

Academic Vocabulary

You will see these words in your reading and on your tests.

- register
- precise
- assemble
- primary
- assume
- approximate
- modify
- create
- interpret
- identify
- investigate

Content Vocabulary

You will learn these key terms in this chapter.

- payroll register
- manufacture
- direct material cost
- direct labor cost
- prime costs
- time study
- break-even analysis
- break-even point
- profit
- fixed costs
- variable costs
- depreciation
- estimated life
- straight-line method
- salvage value
- book value
- accumulated depreciation
- modified accelerated cost recovery system (MACRS)
- assets
- liabilities
- owner's equity
- net worth
- capital
- balance sheet
- vertical analysis
- current ratio
- horizontal analysis
- cost of goods sold
- income statement
- profit-and-loss statement
- net income
- net profit

You can find vocabulary definitions in the **Content Vocabulary** Glossary and the **Academic Vocabulary** Glossary in the back of the book.

LESSON 18.1

Payroll Register

Lesson Objective

Complete a payroll register.

Content Vocabulary

- payroll register

Have you wondered how a paycheck is processed?

Maurice Henry, a systems analyst for Kane Tech Solutions, studied his new paycheck carefully to see how much federal tax had been deducted.

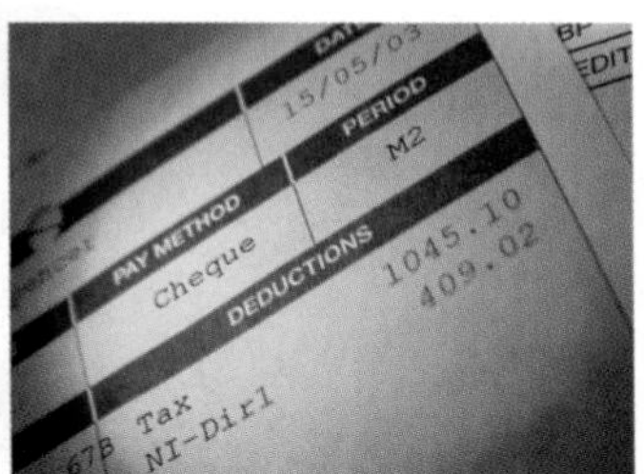

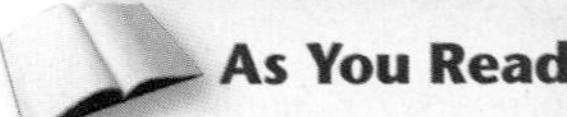

Identify What information is on a payroll register?

Payroll Register Companies keep track of where their money for payroll is going by using a **payroll register**. This is a record of the gross income, deductions, and net income of the company's employees. Most companies use a computer to prepare a payroll register. If the **register** is prepared by hand, the accountant will probably refer to tables to determine the amount of income tax to withhold from each employee's pay. Recall from Lessons 2.4 and 2.6 these two formulas:

Tax Withheld = Gross Pay × Tax Rate

Net Pay = Gross Pay − Total Deductions

Need Help? Go to...

- Skill 2: Rounding Numbers, p. SK3
- Skill 30: Finding the Percentage, p. SK31
- **Application A:** Formulas, p. AP1

EXAMPLE 1

Ajani Samuel is a part-time printer employed by Care Copy. He is single and claims no allowances. Samuel is verifying his paycheck to ensure that the deductions are correct. Determine his net pay for a week when his gross pay was $285. Medicare is 1.45% of gross, Social Security is 6.2% of gross, city tax is 1.5% of gross, and federal income tax is obtained from tables on pages A2–A5.

Step 1: Find the deduction for Medicare, Social Security, and city tax.

Tax Withheld = Gross Pay × Tax Rate

Medicare $285 × 0.0145 = $4.1325 = $4.13

Social Security $285 × 0.062 = $17.67

City Tax $285 × 0.015 = $4.275 = $4.28

Step 2: Find the federal income tax (FIT).

(Use table *Single Persons Weekly Payroll* on pages A2–A3.)

FIT for *At least 280, But less than 290* is $28.00

Step 3: Find the net pay.

Gross Pay − Total Deductions

$285.00 − ($4.13 + $17.67 + $4.28 + $28.00) = $285.00 − $54.08 = **$230.92 net pay**

Powered by Light RF / Alamy

Find the net pay. Check your answer in the back of the book.

1. Dorsey Williams is married and claims 2 allowances. Her weekly gross pay is $735. She has Medicare, Social Security, and federal income tax deductions, and a city tax that is 2% of gross pay.

EXAMPLE 2

Natural Foods Center pays its employees weekly. Mary Clark prepares the payroll register for the center's five employees from the following information. Note that W.K. Fine had $1,800 in sales.

Name	Regular Pay	Overtime Pay	Income Tax Information	Health Insurance Coverage
D.R. Benavides	$ 12.50/hour	Time and a half	Married, 2 allowances	Family
J.A. Babatunde	$ 10.40/hour	Time and a half	Single, 1 allowance	Single
H.L. Chew	$425.00/week	—	Single, 2 allowances	Single
N.J. Nystrand	$535.00/week	—	Married, 3 allowances	Family
W.K. Fine	$360.00/week plus 5% commission	—	Married, 4 allowances	Family

Mary has prepared the payroll register for the week of March 2.

Find the net pay for the week.

Payroll Register for Week of March 2, 20--										
Name	Hours Reg.	Hours OT	Hourly Rate	Gross Pay	FIT	Social Security	Medicare	Hosp Ins	Total Deductions	Net Pay
Benavides	40	3	$12.50	$556.25	$27.00	$34.49	$8.07	$56.50	$126.06	$430.19
Babatunde	40		$10.40	$416.00	$38.00	$25.79	$6.03	$31.00	$100.82	$315.18
Chew	—			$425.00	$29.00	$26.35	$6.16	$31.00	$ 92.51	$332.49
Nystrand	—			$535.00	$19.00	$33.17	$7.76	$56.50	$116.43	$418.57
Fine	—			$450.00	$ 4.00	$27.90	$6.53	$56.50	$ 94.93	$355.07

360 + (5% × 1,800) = 360 + 90 = $450

Concept CHECK

Complete the problem. Check your answer in the back of the book.

2. Use this information to find the net pay: gross weekly pay, $396; FIT, $25; Social Security, $24.55; Medicare, $5.74; health insurance, $42.75.

Lesson Practice

Study Tip

Tables
When looking for information in several tables at once, read the titles and headings carefully to make sure you are using the correct table.

For Problems 3–5, find the total deductions and net pay.

	Employee	Gross Pay	FIT	Social Security	Medicare		Total Ded.		Net Pay
3.	Abbot	$485.00	$48.00	$30.07	$ 7.03		$85.10	a.	
4.	Escobedo	$136.00	$ 9.00	$ 8.43	$ 1.97	a.		b.	
5.	Murakami	$795.00	$81.00	$49.29	$11.53	a.		b.	

Financial Investigator

Financial investigators search accounting records and other documents for evidence of illegal financial activities. Most investigators are certified public accountants.

Have you seen any TV shows about jobs that interest you?

For Problems 6 and 7, find the net pay.

6. Lou's Variety Store's total gross payroll for the week is $416.74, and the total deductions are $97.82.
7. Pre-Fab Company's total gross payroll for the week is $16,478.43, and the total deductions are $3,914.75.

For Problems 8–10, use the tables on pages A2–A5 for federal income tax (FIT), use the Social Security tax rate of 6.2%, and the Medicare tax rate of 1.45%. For the FIT information, (S,1) means "single, one allowance" and (M,3) means "married, 3 allowances."

8. The Goldstone Swimming Complex employs students in the summer. Goldstone pays a standard hourly rate of $12.50. The deductions are federal income tax, Social Security, Medicare, and city income tax (CIT) of 1.5%. Complete the payroll register for the week.

Payroll Register for Goldstone Swimming Complex – Date: June 8, 20--

Employee	FIT Info.	Hours Worked	Gross Pay	FIT	Social Security	Medi-care	CIT	Total Ded.	Net Pay
Banks	S,1	24	a.	b.	c.	d.	e.	f.	g.
Drake	S,0	34	a.	b.	c.	d.	e.	f.	g.
Faust	S,1	36	a.	b.	c.	d.	e.	f.	g.
Harakis	S,0	38	a.	b.	c.	d.	e.	f.	g.
Kendrick	S,0	36	a.	b.	c.	d.	e.	f.	g.
Reese	S,1	38	a.	b.	c.	d.	e.	f.	g.
Segura	S,0	30	a.	b.	c.	d.	e.	f.	g.
Total			a.	b.	c.	d.	e.	f.	g.

9. The Consortium, a general warehouse and distributor of building supplies, pays its employees weekly salaries. Deductions are: federal, 2% state (SIT) and 1.5% city income tax (CIT) as well as Social Security, Medicare and health insurance. Complete the payroll register for the week.

The Consortium

Employee	FIT Info.	Gross Pay	FIT	SIT	CIT	Social Security	Medi-care	Health Ins.	Total Ded.	Net Pay
Calderon	M,3	$600.00	a.	b.	c.	d.	e.	$43.75	f.	g.
Dobbs	M,2	$585.00	a.	b.	c.	d.	e.	$35.00	f.	g.
Haddad	S,1	$415.00	a.	b.	c.	d.	e.	$17.50	f.	g.
Harling	M,2	$564.80	a.	b.	c.	d.	e.	$35.00	f.	g.
Hermey	S,2	$537.50	a.	b.	c.	d.	e.	$26.25	f.	g.
Presser	M,4	$629.20	a.	b.	c.	d.	e.	$52.50	f.	g.
Wilbers	M,0	$612.44	a.	b.	c.	d.	e.	$26.25	f.	g.
Total		a.	b.	c.	d.	e.	f.	g.	h.	i.

Jiang Jin/Purestock/Superstock

H.O.T. Problems

10. CHALLENGE PROBLEM King Sporting Goods pays its employees weekly. Deductions include federal income tax, state income tax of 2.25%, Social Security, Medicare, and 1% for city income tax. Use this information to prepare the payroll register for the week of November 30.

Name	FIT Info	Position	Pay Plan	Total Sales or Hours Worked
Delgado	M,2	Sales	7½% straight commission	$6,740
Lightner	S,1	Sales Manager	7½% straight commission	$7,152
Ramirez	M,3	Sales Manager	$420 + 6% commission	$3,298
Ulrich	S,0	Sales Trainee	5% straight commission	$4,165
Goode	M,1	Maintenance	$16.10 per hour	40 hours

King Sporting Goods Payroll Register Week of: November 30, 20--								
Name	Gross Pay	FIT	Social Security	Medi-care	SIT	CIT	Total Ded.	Net Pay
Delgado	a.	b.	c.	d.	e.	f.	g.	h.
Lightner	a.	b.	c.	d.	e.	f.	g.	h.
Ramirez	a.	b.	c.	d.	e.	f.	g.	h.
Ulrich	a.	b.	c.	d.	e.	f.	g.	h.
Goode	a.	b.	c.	d.	e.	f.	g.	h.
Total	a.	b.	c.	d.	e.	f.	g.	h.

Spiral Review

Add or subtract. (Skill 5, 6)

11. $149.74 + $97.89

12. $412.76 − $26.40

13. $676.83 − $212.91

14. ALGEBRA Tamika Brewster, a certified senior planner, works only with estates in excess of $1 million. She charges $1\frac{1}{2}$% commission on estates worth $1–2 million and $1\frac{1}{4}$% commission on estates worth $2 million or more. What was an estate worth if Tamika earned $34,750? (Lesson 17.6)

GET READY for the Next Lesson

PREREQUISITE SKILL Adding Decimals (Skill 5)

15. $241,750.00 + $13,221.82 + $42,112.37

16. $85,675.28 + $2,319.75 + $5,775.88

17. $4,852.41 + $1,023.46 + $943.68

18. $712,418.65 + $24,004.51 + $11,111.22

19. $8,919.75 + $657.82 + $903.41

20. $564,681.99 + $67,419.01 + $7,394.31

LESSON 18.2

Business Expenses

Lesson Objective

Calculate the percent that a particular business expense is of the total expenses.

What are your biggest expenses?

Fareed Hassan carefully tracks his business expenses every month. As the owner of several product kiosks at Northfield Mall, Fareed knows that without strict control of expenses, his business could lose money.

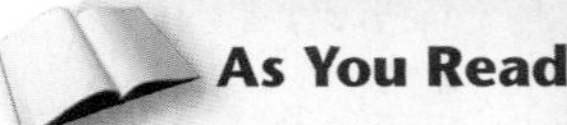

Identify When might records of expenses be useful?

Business Expenses A business must keep **precise** records of all its expenses. The information is useful when preparing income tax forms and when calculating a company's profits. Total expenses may be calculated monthly, quarterly, or annually. To plan for future spending, it is helpful to calculate the percent that a particular business expense is of the total expenses. The formula is:

$$\text{Percent of Total} = \frac{\text{Particular Expense}}{\text{Total Expenses}}$$

Need Help? Go to...

- **Skill 31:** Finding the Rate, p. SK32
- **Application A:** Formulas, p. AP1

EXAMPLE 1

Molded Plastic Products manufactures plastic buckets, containers, and other products. Records of Molded Plastic's expenses for the first quarter of the year are as shown.

Payroll	$422,171.84
Advertising	$ 8,557.65
Raw materials	$122,417.83
Factory/showroom rent	$ 18,500.00
Office supplies	$ 2,216.90
Insurance	$ 8,917.85
Utilities	$ 26,417.93
Total	**$609,200.00**

What percent of total expenses did Molded Plastic spend on advertising during the quarter?

Find the percent of the total.

$$\frac{\text{Particular Expense}}{\text{Total Expenses}} = \frac{\$8{,}557.65}{\$609{,}200.00} = 0.01404 = \textbf{1.40\% spent on advertising}$$

8557.65 ÷ 609200 = 0.014047

Concept CHECK

Use the information in Example 1 to find what percent the following are of the total expenses. Check your answers in the back of the book.

1. Utilities

2. Payroll

Need Help? Go to...

Workshop 36: Problem-Solving Strategy: Using Simple Algebraic Operations, p. 74

EXAMPLE 2 Algebra

The Central School District allocates 85% of its annual budget (total expenses) to employee compensation. The District spends $4,386,000 annually on employee compensation. What is the annual budget of The Central School District?

Step 1: Let x = The annual budget of The Central School District.

Step 2: Substitute in the equation.

$$\text{Percent of Total} = \frac{\text{Particular Expense}}{\text{Total Expenses}}$$

Step 3: Solve the equation.

$$85\% = \frac{\$4{,}386{,}000}{x}$$

Multiply both sides by x → $0.85x = \$4{,}386{,}000$

Divide both sides by 0.85 → $x = \$5{,}160{,}000$

The Central School District's annual budget is $5,160,000.

Study Tip

Rounding

When rounding to the nearest tenth, look at the digit in the hundredths place. If that digit is 5 or greater, add 1 to the digit in the tenths place.

Concept CHECK

Complete the problem. Check your answer in the back of the book.

3. The General Department Store Inc. spends 28% of its annual total expenses on advertising. If The General Department Store Inc. spends $13,125 quarterly on advertising, what are its total annual expenses?

Lesson Practice

For Problems 4 and 5, round to the nearest tenth if necessary.

4. Selected expenses: rent, $300; data processing, $5,200; payroll, $4,500. Rent is what percent of the total?
5. Selected expenses: telephone, $175; electricity, $450; natural gas, $375; water, $200. Water is what percent of the total?

For Problems 6–11, find what percent (to the nearest tenth) each item is of the total.

	Manufacturer's Cost and Profit	
6.	Fabrics and accessories	$ 81.10
7.	Design and factory operations	$ 49.10
8.	Production wages and benefits	$ 68.60
9.	Administrative and sales salaries	$ 39.70
10.	Taxes	$ 9.80
11.	Profit from sale to retailer	$ 9.20
	Total (wholesale price to retailer)	$257.50

12. Trapper Financial Consultants' total expenses are $72,650 for the quarter. The payroll is $48,435. Determine what percent the payroll expense is of the total.
13. Madison Motel has total annual expenses of $514,500. The annual utilities cost $98,400. The utility cost is what percent of the total?

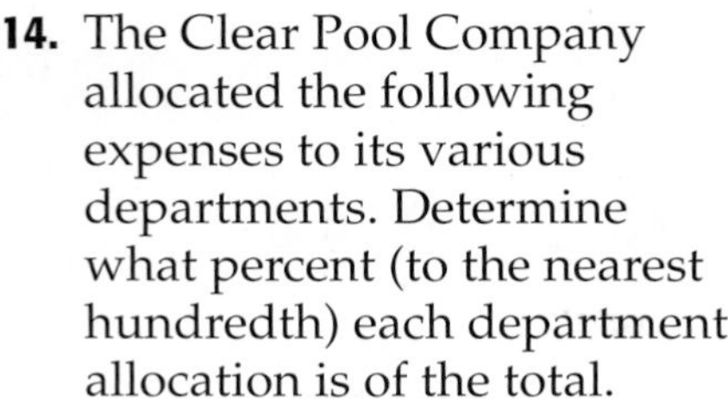

14. The Clear Pool Company allocated the following expenses to its various departments. Determine what percent (to the nearest hundredth) each department allocation is of the total.

	Department	Allocation
a.	Payroll	$144,565
b.	Marketing	$ 6,000
c.	Maintenance	$ 51,496
d.	Physical Resources	$ 67,194
e.	Insurance	$ 12,000
f.	Utilities	$ 6,450
g.	Physical Facilities	$ 14,000
h.	**Total**	

Did You Know?

Too Much Water **A study found that 18% of marathon runners and 29% of Ironman tri-athletes suffered from hyponatremia, or water intoxication. This is caused when excessive water intake dilutes the blood's salt content.**

15. Parson's Traditional Clothiers had these business expenses last month. Determine what percent (nearest hundredth) each item is of the total.

a.	Payroll	$ 9,646
b.	Advertising	$ 8,325
c.	Cost of Goods Sold	$155,525
d.	Rent	$ 7,244
e.	Supplies	$ 4,560
f.	Insurance	$ 6,450
g.	Utilities	$ 14,250
h.	**Total**	

H.O.T. Problems

16. ALGEBRA The Diner spends $23,850 monthly on supplies. If supplies represent $33\frac{1}{3}\%$ of total expenses, what are the annual total expenses?

17. ALGEBRA Aladdin Manufacturing, LLC, allocates 43% of its total expenses for payroll. It increased its total expenses when it spent $250,000 for robotic assemblers. This changes the allocation for payroll to 38% of total expenses. What are the total expenses: **(a)** before purchasing the robotic assemblers, and **(b)** after purchasing the robotic assemblers?

18. ALGEBRA Harbor Wholesale Hardware Supply currently spends 38% of its total expenses on inventory. By introducing a more efficient inventory control system, Harbor was able to reduce inventory costs by $29,730 annually, to only 27% of total expenses. Expenses were reduced by $29,730. Find Harbor's inventory costs and total expenses both before and after the introduction of the more efficient inventory control system.

Spiral Review

Find the rate. Round answers to the nearest tenth of a percent. (Skill 31)

19. What percent of $140,000 is $35,000? **20.** What percent of $1,065 is $212?

21. The Beker Corporation has developed a new cosmetic foundation. Beker chose a sample of 4,000 women. In the sample, 1,200 women said they would purchase the new product once a year. The Corporation estimates that 2,000,000 women buy cosmetic foundations yearly. What is the sales potential for the new cosmetic foundation? (Lesson 16.2)

GET READY for the Next Lesson

PREREQUISITE SKILL Dividing Decimals (Skill 11)

Divide. Round answers to the nearest tenth of a cent.

22. $0.90 ÷ 15 **23.** $0.45 ÷ 38 **24.** $4.36 ÷ 10

25. $5.72 ÷ 9 **26.** $11.56 ÷ 12 **27.** $29.13 ÷ 19

LESSON 18.3

Manufacturing Costs and Time Study

Lesson Objective

Compute the prime cost of manufacturing an item and use time-study results to compute how many units can be produced.

Content Vocabulary

- manufacture
- direct material cost
- direct labor cost
- prime cost
- time study

GET READY for the Lesson

What individual parts make up your favorite products?

Brandon Field is production manager for Perfect Sound, a shop that makes custom guitar and bass amplifiers. Brandon recommended that Perfect Sound raise its prices slightly because of an increase in the cost of the wires and circuits that go into the amplifiers.

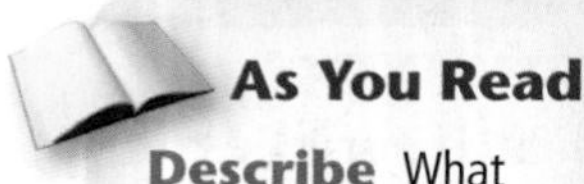

As You Read

Describe What is the role of the production department?

Manufacturing The production department of a business **assembles**, or **manufactures**, and packages the products sold by the business. The cost of manufacturing an item depends, in part, on the **direct material cost** and the **direct labor cost**. The direct material cost is the cost of the goods that are used to produce the item. The direct labor cost includes the wages paid to the employees who make the item. The **prime cost** is the total of the direct material cost and the direct labor cost. The prime cost is frequently expressed on a per-unit basis. The formula is:

Prime Cost per Item = Direct Material Cost per Item + Direct Labor Cost per Item

Need Help? Go to...

Skill 10: Dividing (Decimal Remainder), p. SK11

EXAMPLE 1

Electric Supply produces aluminum circuit housings. The machine operator stamps 20 housings from each strip of aluminum. Each strip costs $1.80. The operator can stamp 720 housings per hour. The direct labor charge is $19.50 per hour. To the nearest tenth of a cent, what is the prime cost of manufacturing the circuit housing?

Step 1: Find the direct material cost per item.

$\frac{\$1.80}{20} = \$0.09$ direct material cost per item

Step 2: Find the direct labor cost per item.

$\frac{\$19.50}{720} = \$0.02708 = \$0.027$ direct labor cost per item

Step 3: Find the prime cost per item.

Direct Material Cost per Item + Direct Labor Cost per Item

$0.09 + $0.027 = **$0.117 cost per housing**

Concept CHECK

Complete the problems. Check your answers in the back of the book.

1. Forty brackets are made from a strip of metal costing $0.80. What is the direct material cost per item?
2. The direct material cost per item is $0.04. The direct labor cost per item is $0.18. Find the prime cost per item.

Time Study Your business may conduct a **time study** to determine how long a particular job should take. A time study involves watching a typical employee complete a job, recording the time required for each task, and calculating the average time for each task. You can use the averages to determine how many units a worker can produce in a fixed period of time.

$$\text{Number of Units} = \frac{\text{Actual Time Worked}}{\text{Average time Required per Unit}}$$

Need Help? Go to...
Workshop 16: Average (Mean), p. 34

EXAMPLE 2

General Lamps did a time study of Beth Peters' job as a carton packer. Her times were recorded. The averages were calculated. If Beth gets a 10-minute break each hour, how many cartons can she fill per hour?

Task	Observations in Seconds					Average Time
	#1	#2	#3	#4	#5	
Pick up carton	3.9	5.4	3.9	4.4	3.9	4.3 sec.
Fill carton	12.0	13.0	14.5	12.5	11.0	12.6 sec.
Apply glue	14.5	12.5	13.0	13.5	13.5	13.4 sec.
Close carton	5.1	4.4	4.6	4.3	5.1	4.7 sec.
Remove filled carton	5.5	5.5	5.5	5.5	5.5	5.5 sec.

$$\frac{\text{Sum of Times}}{\text{Number of Observations}}$$

Step 1: Find the average time required per unit.

$4.3 + 12.6 + 13.4 + 4.7 + 5.5 = 40.5$ seconds

Step 2: Find the actual time worked per hour.

$(60 - 10)$ minutes $\times$ 60 seconds $=$ 3,000 seconds

Step 3: Find the number of units per hour.

$$\frac{\text{Actual Time Worked}}{\text{Average Time Required per Unit}} = \frac{\text{3,000 seconds}}{\text{40.5 seconds per unit}} = 74.07 = \textbf{74 units per hour}$$

Beth can fill 74 cartons per hour.

Study Tip

Nearest Cent
Since one cent is one-hundredth of a dollar, rounding to the nearest cent is like rounding to the nearest hundredth. Rounding to the nearest tenth of a cent is like rounding to the nearest thousandth.

Concept CHECK

Complete the problem. Check your answer in the back of the book.

3. Santana Woods is a circuit board tester for Meta's Electronics. Santana works 8 hours per day less a 10-minute break every 2 hours. He spends 5 minutes per board in the testing process. How many boards per day should Santana be able to test?

Lesson Practice

For Problems 4–9, round answers to the nearest tenth of a cent.

	Cost per Strip	Pieces per Strip		Direct Material Cost per Piece	Labor Cost per Hour	Pieces per Hour		Direct Labor Cost per Piece		Prime Cost
4.	$0.80	10		$0.080	$11.70	1,000		$0.012	a.	
5.	$0.75	25	a.		$13.50	1,200	b.		c.	
6.	$0.70	50	a.		$17.45	80	b.		c.	

7. The Donnely Manufacturing Company manufactures plastic tablecloths. Each roll of printed plastic yields 120 tablecloths. Each roll costs $21.70. The direct labor charge is $19.20 per hour. The machine operator can cut and fold 90 tablecloths per hour. What is the prime cost of manufacturing each tablecloth?
8. A strip of aluminum makes 20 fan blades. The aluminum costs $1.82 per strip. The direct labor cost is $15.65 per hour. One blade is stamped every 5 seconds. What is the prime cost of manufacturing each blade?
9. Eduardo Diaz is a molding machine operator at US Accessories, Inc. He molds 130 tinted license plate holders from one container of molding plastic. Each container costs $5.85. Eduardo is able to mold 1 holder every 3 seconds. The direct labor cost is $18.95 per hour. What is the prime cost of manufacturing 1 tinted license plate holder?

Did You Know?

Inaugural License Plates
The District of Columbia has produced special license plates for use during presidential inaugurations since Franklin Roosevelt's in 1933. The plates measure 6 by 12.5 inches, the standard size used on American cars.

10. American Pump Company prepared a time study of Shirley Monroe's job as an assembler. Find **(a)** the average time per task and **(b)** the average time per unit. **(c)** How many units can she complete in 1 hour if she takes a 10-minute break every hour?

Observations in Seconds						
Task	1	2	3	4	5	Avg.
Move water pump to filter	3.7	4.2	3.9	3.8	3.7	a.
Insert filter coil	5.1	5.2	4.9	5.2	5.1	b.
Affix gasket	4.8	4.4	4.7	4.6	4.8	c.
Hand thread bolts	6.1	6.3	6.3	6.2	6.4	d.
Machine tighten bolts	6.1	6.0	6.2	6.3	6.2	e.

H.O.T. Problems

11. **CHALLENGE PROBLEM** In Problem 10, if American Pump Company permitted Shirley Monroe to power-thread the bolts, she would save 3 seconds per observation. **(a)** How many more units could she complete in 1 hour (with the 10-minute break)? **(b)** If, in addition to power-threading the bolts, her hourly break was reduced to 5 minutes, how many more units could she complete in 1 hour compared to a 10-minute break?

Spiral Review

Divide. Round answers to the nearest tenth of a cent. (Skill 2, 11)

12. $0.90 ÷ 18   13. $17.85 ÷ 470   14. $11.72 ÷ 510

15. Corrine Albright purchases a Ford Fund $5,000 bond at the quoted price of 91.5. The bond pays interest at a rate of 6%. Find the **(a)** interest, **(b)** cost of the bond, and **(c)** annual yield. (Lesson 12.7)

GET READY for the Next Lesson

PREREQUISITE SKILL **Subtracting Decimals** (Skill 6)

Subtract.

16. $18.65 – $9.86   17. $2.74 – $0.86   18. $18.72 – $9.95
19. $106.85 – $89.77   20. $376.19 – $210.12   21. $6,014.08 – $5,230.44

LESSON 18.4

Break-Even Analysis

Lesson Objective

Calculate the break-even point in the number of manufactured units.

Content Vocabulary

- break-even analysis
- break-even point
- profit
- fixed costs
- variable costs

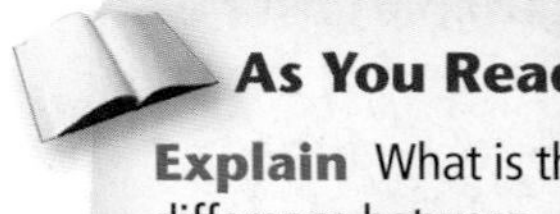

As You Read

Explain What is the difference between a fixed cost and a variable cost?

GET READY for the Lesson

Do you have any ideas for a business?

Shawna Johnson used to earn additional income by making fashion-conscious baby clothes. When Shawna decided to make baby clothes her only job, she realized she needed to create more product in order to cover expenses and make a profit.

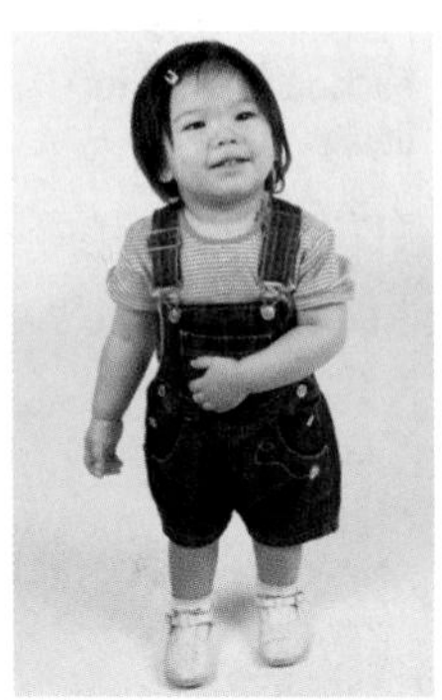

Break-Even Analysis Before you start investing money in a product, you need to know your expenses. Your business can prepare a **break-even analysis**. This determines how many units of a product must be made and sold to cover production expenses. On a break-even analysis chart, you might see the **break-even point**. This shows you the point where income from sales equals the cost of production. Units sold after that point will result in a **profit** for your business. Profit is the **primary** goal for any business (except for not-for-profit organizations).

To calculate the break-even point, you must know the total **fixed costs**, the **variable costs** per unit, and the selling price per unit. Fixed costs include rent, salaries, and other costs that are not changed by the number of units produced. Variable costs include the cost of raw materials, the cost of packaging, and any other costs that vary directly with the number of units produced. Remember that:

$$\text{Break-Even Point in Units} = \frac{\text{Total Fixed Costs}}{\text{Selling Price per Unit} - \text{Variable Costs per Unit}}$$

Need Help? Go to...

Skill 10: Dividing (Decimal Remainder), p. SK11

EXAMPLE

Token Metal Products manufactures can openers. The company plans to manufacture 70,000 hand-held can openers to be sold at \$3.44 each. The fixed costs are estimated to be \$142,570. Variable costs are \$0.99 per unit. How many can openers must be sold for Token Metal Products to break even?

Find the break-even point in units.

$$\frac{\text{Total Fixed Costs}}{\text{Selling Price per Unit} - \text{Variable Costs per Unit}}$$

$$\frac{\$142{,}570}{\$3.44 - \$0.99} = \frac{\$142{,}570}{\$2.45} = 58{,}191.836 = \textbf{58,192 can openers}$$

Concept CHECK

Find the break-even point in units. Check your answers in the back of the book.

1. Sandpaper sells for \$0.79 each. Variable cost per unit is \$0.29. Total fixed costs are \$27,500.00.
2. Floor tile sells for \$1.49 each. Variable cost per unit is \$0.74. Total fixed costs are \$124,500.00.

Reading Math

Main Idea
When reading a math word problem for the first time, look for the main idea. Then go back and reread for details.

Lesson Practice

Complete the table.

	Item	Total Fixed Costs	Selling Price per Unit	Variable Costs per Unit	Break-Even Point in Units
3.	Tomato Juice	$ 95,000	$ 1.79	$ 0.79	
4.	Molding	$ 148,000	$ 0.59	$ 0.34	
5.	PVC Tubing	$ 225,000	$ 2.29	$ 1.79	
6.	Tool Box	$12,476,500	$417.79	$279.81	

7. TenCo junior tennis rackets
Fixed costs: $740,000.00
Selling price per racket: $74.29
Variable cost per racket: $48.76
What is the break-even point in units?

8. Farm Supply rural mailboxes
Fixed costs: $192,800.00
Selling price per mailbox: $39.99
Variable cost per mailbox: $21.43
What is the break-even point in units?

9. Today's Music produces classical CDs. The fixed costs total $2,417,950.00. The selling price per disc is $19.95. The variable cost per disc is $9.48. What is the break-even point in number of discs?

10. True Bounce basketballs are manufactured by General Sports. It has total fixed costs of $3,110,400.00. The variable cost per basketball is $18.47. The selling price per basketball is $24.95. What is the break-even point in number of basketballs?

11. The Alumni Association plans to produce and market monogrammed sweatshirts. It anticipates selling each sweatshirt for $39.95. The variable costs per sweatshirt are $18.19 for supplies and $9.47 per shirt for direct labor. The fixed costs of the operation total $7,450.00. How many monogrammed sweatshirts does The Alumni Association need to sell to break even?

12. CHALLENGE PROBLEM In #11, **(a)** if The Alumni Association increased the selling price per sweatshirt to $44.95, how many fewer sweatshirts would they have to sell to break even? **(b)** If they found a different vendor that charged half of the direct labor cost per shirt, how many fewer sweatshirts would they have to sell to break even at a selling price of $44.95?

Spiral Review

Subtract. (Skill 6)

13. $14.79 − $9.43 **14.** $147.47 − $109.88 **15.** $8,129.00 − $6,417.48

16. ALGEBRA A new printer is marked down 25% if purchased with a desktop computer. The sale price on the printer is $349.00. What is the regular selling price of the printer if purchased alone? (Lesson 6.7)

GET READY for the Next Lesson

PREREQUISITE SKILL Divide (Decimal Remainder) (Skill 10)

Divide.

17. $12,906 ÷ 20 **18.** $9,216.75 ÷ 15 **19.** $7,562.16 ÷ 18

LESSON 18.5

Depreciation—Straight-Line Method

Lesson Objective

Use the straight-line method to compute the annual depreciation of an item.

Content Vocabulary

- depreciation
- estimated life
- straight-line method
- salvage value

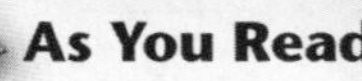

GET READY for the Lesson

What might you be interested in buying used?

When Carissa Springston turned 18, she bought a used coupe. The car was very expensive when it was new, but that was several years ago. Over the years, the value of the car decreased in price.

As You Read

Identify What does the straight-line method assume about the depreciation of an item?

Depreciation—Straight-Line Method In running a business, you may buy items that last longer than a year, such as vehicles or equipment. For tax purposes, the Internal Revenue Service (IRS) allows you to deduct the **depreciation** of these items. Depreciation is spreading the cost of an item over its estimated life. An item's **estimated life** is the number of years it is expected to last before it wears out, is no longer needed, or is outdated.

The **straight-line method** is one way of determining the annual depreciation of an item. This method **assumes** that the depreciation is the same from year to year. To calculate the depreciation, you must know the original cost, the estimated life, and the **salvage value** of the item. The salvage value is the estimated trade-in, resale, or scrap value at the end of the item's expected life. The formula is:

$$\text{Annual Depreciation} = \frac{\text{Original Cost} - \text{Salvage Value}}{\text{Estimated Life}}$$

Need Help? Go to...

- Skill 10: Dividing (Decimal Remainder), p. SK11
- Skill 2: Rounding, p. SK3

EXAMPLE

The law firm of Charles A. Adams purchased a new copier that cost $1,745. The life of the copier is estimated to be 5 years. The total salvage value after 5 years of use is estimated to be $245. Using the straight-line method, find the annual depreciation of the copier.

Find the annual depreciation.

$$\frac{\text{Original Cost} - \text{Salvage Value}}{\text{Estimated Life}} = \frac{(\$1{,}745 - \$245)}{5} = \frac{\$1{,}500}{5} = \$300$$

The annual depreciation is $300.

1745 [−] 245 [=] 1500 [÷] 5 [=] 300

Hannu Liivaar/Alamy

Find the annual depreciation. Check your answers in the back of the book.

1. Original cost: $6,000
   Estimated life: 10 years
   Salvage value: $200

2. Original cost: $185,000
   Estimated life: 3 years
   Salvage value: $35,000

Study Tip

Take Notes
Take notes as you read. Note key terms and define them in your own words.

Lesson Practice

For Problems 3–10, find the annual depreciation. Round to the nearest dollar.

	Item	Original Cost	Salvage Value	Estimated Life in Years	Annual Depreciation
3.	Rental furniture	$ 12,435	$ 435	3	
4.	Taxi	$ 22,186	$ 3,186	5	
5.	Tractor	$ 84,750	$ 2,750	10	
6.	Rental duplex	$195,500	$10,000	27.5	

7. Fiber optic cable: $975,000
   Estimated life of 15 years
   Salvage value estimated at $5,000

8. Car: $46,250
   Estimated life of 5 years
   Salvage value estimated at $7,250

9. Central Dental Clinic recently purchased a new computer system for a total cost of $64,735. The estimated life of the system is 5 years. The trade-in value of the system after 5 years is estimated to be $1,000.

10. Tina Cole is a certified financial advisor. She purchased equipment for her office for $7,843. The trade-in value of the equipment is estimated to be $500 after 7 years of use.

11. Third National Bank recently purchased 6 new laptop computers. Each computer cost $2,245. The estimated life of each computer is 5 years with a trade-in value of $125 at the end of the 5 years. What is the annual depreciation for all 6 computers?

12. **CHALLENGE PROBLEM** Amish-Made Furniture recently purchased a new cut-off saw for $8,325, a new planer for $5,675, and two new sanders at $468 each. The salvage value of the cut-off saw and the planer is expected to be $500 each after 7 years of use. The salvage value of the sanders is expected to be $75 each after 5 years of use. What is the total annual depreciation for the first year?

Spiral Review

Multiply. Round to the nearest cent. (Skill 8)

13. $1,470.00 × 0.055
14. $963.49 × 0.05
15. $1.29 × 0.248

16. **ALGEBRA** Diamond's Men Store is expanding. The store's budget allows $4,100 per month to rent the needed 6,200 square foot space. What is the maximum it can pay per square foot on an annual rate? (Lesson 17.1)

GET READY for the Next Lesson

PREREQUISITE SKILL **Multiplying Decimals** (Skill 8)
Multiply.

17. $65.43 × 25
18. $128.31 × 55
19. $82.36 × 21

LESSON 18.6

Depreciation— Book Value

Lesson Objective

Compute the book value of an item using straight-line depreciation.

Content Vocabulary

- book value
- accumulated depreciation

GET READY for the Lesson

What outdated electronics do you have that you no longer use?

Dr. John Vasquez's clinic leases much of its medical equipment in order to avoid financial loss when the equipment depreciates. The equipment depreciates over time and may become obsolete when new technology is introduced.

As You Read

Identify What is book value?

Depreciation—Book Value **Book value** is the **approximate** value of an item after you have owned it and depreciated it for a period of time. The book value is the original cost minus the **accumulated depreciation**. The accumulated depreciation is the total depreciation to date. At the end of an item's life, its book value and salvage value should be equal. The formulas are:

Accumulated Depreciation = Previous Year's Accumulated Depreciation + Current Year's Depreciation

Book Value at End of Year = Original Cost − Accumulated Depreciation

Need Help? Go to...

- Skill 3: Adding Whole Numbers, p. SK4
- Skill 4: Subtracting Whole Numbers, p. SK5

EXAMPLE

The law firm of Charles A. Adams purchased a new copier for $1,745. The total resale value after 5 years is estimated to be $245. Using the straight-line method, Charles A. Adams determined that the copier would depreciate $300 per year. What is the book value at the end of each year of depreciation?

Step 1: Find the accumulated depreciation.

	Previous Year's Accumulated Depreciation	+	Current Year's Depreciation	=	Accumulated Depreciation
First year:	$ 0	+	$300	=	$ 300
Second year:	300	+	300	=	600
Third year:	600	+	300	=	900
Fourth year:	900	+	300	=	1,200
Fifth year:	1,200	+	300	=	1,500

Step 2: Find the book value.

	Original Cost	−	Accumulated Depreciation	=	Book Value
First year:	$1,745	−	$ 300	=	$1,445
Second year:	1,745	−	600	=	1,145
Third year:	1,745	−	900	=	845
Fourth year:	1,745	−	1,200	=	545
Fifth year:	1,745	−	1,500	=	245

Note: The book value in the last year always equals the salvage value.

Depreciation Schedule for Copier					
End of Year	Original Cost	Annual Depreciation	Accumulated Depreciation	Book Value	
1	$1,745	$300	$ 300	$1,445	← $1,745 – $ 300
2	$1,745	$300	$ 600	$1,145	← $1,745 – $ 600
3	$1,745	$300	$ 900	$ 845	← $1,745 – $ 900
4	$1,745	$300	$1,200	$ 545	← $1,745 – $1,200
5	$1,745	$300	$1,500	$ 245	← $1,745 – $1,500

Note: The book value at the end of the fifth year equals the salvage value.

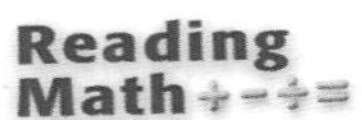

Word Problems
When reading a math word problem, think, "What information am I given? What do I need to find?"

Concept CHECK

Using the table below, calculate the depreciation schedule for a commercial bus that costs $90,000. Its estimated life is 5 years and the salvage value is $10,000. Check your answers in the back of the book.

	End of Year	Original Cost		Annual Depreciation		Accumulated Depreciation		Book Value
	1	$90,000		$16,000		$16,000		$74,000
	2	$90,000		$16,000		$32,000		$58,000
1.	3	$90,000	a.		b.		c.	
2.	4	$90,000	a.		b.		c.	
3.	5	$90,000	a.		b.		c.	

SPREADSHEET APPLICATION

Book Value

You can use a spreadsheet like the partial one below to determine an item's book value. You will enter the original cost, salvage value, and useful life. The annual depreciation, accumulated depreciation, and book value will automatically be calculated for you.

Math Online Go to **connected.mcgraw-hill.com** to download a spreadsheet application for this activity.

Original Cost	
Salvage Value	
Useful Life	

STRAIGHT-LINE DEPRECIATION			
End of Year	Annual Depreciation	Accumulated Depreciation	Book Value
1	$ –	$ –	$0
2	$ –	$ –	$0

Think and Discuss

1. A delivery truck originally cost $60,000. The salvage value is $10,000. The useful life is 5 years. What is the first year's depreciation?
2. Is the depreciation the same every year?
3. When is the truck's book value and salvage value the same?

Lesson Practice

For Problems 4–6, complete the depreciation schedule for new appliances in a residential rental complex. The appliances cost $5,000, have an estimated life of 5 years, and have a salvage value of $1,000.

	End of Year	Original Cost		Annual Depreciation		Accumulated Depreciation		Book Value
	1	$5,000		$ 800		$ 800		$4,200
	2	$5,000		$ 800		$1,600		$3,400
4.	3	$5,000	a.		b.		c.	
5.	4	$5,000	a.		b.		c.	
6.	5	$5,000	a.		b.		c.	

For Problems 7–11, complete the depreciation schedule for new office furniture. The furniture cost $15,000, has an estimated life of 7 years, and has a salvage value of $1,000.

	End of Year	Original Cost		Annual Depreciation		Accumulated Depreciation		Book Value
	1	$15,000		$2,000		$2,000		$13,000
	2	$15,000		$2,000		$4,000		$11,000
7.	3	$15,000	a.		b.		c.	
8.	4	$15,000	a.		b.		c.	
9.	5	$15,000	a.		b.		c.	
10.	6	$15,000	a.		b.		c.	
11.	7	$15,000	a.		b.		c.	

For Problems 12–14, complete the depreciation schedule for Farm Specified–Dairy computer software for Hoffman Dairy LLC. The software cost $22,470, has an estimated life of 3 years, and has no salvage value.

	End of Year		Original Cost		Annual Depreciation		Accumulated Depreciation		Book Value
12.	1	a.		b.		c.		d.	
13.	2	a.		b.		c.		d.	
14.	3	a.		b.		c.		d.	

For Problems 15–17, complete the depreciation schedule for computer software for Marker Graphics. The software cost $12,990, has an estimated life of 3 years, and has no salvage value.

	End of Year	Original Cost		Annual Depreciation		Accumulated Depreciation		Book Value
15.	1	$12,990	a.		b.		c.	
16.	2	$12,990	a.		b.		c.	
17.	3	$12,990	a.		b.		c.	

18. Yolanda Davenport purchased a commercial mixer for her bakery. The mixer cost $1,880, has an estimated life of 7 years, and has a salvage value of $200. Calculate the straight-line depreciation and the book value after each year of use.

End of Year		Original Cost		Annual Depreciation		Accumulated Depreciation		Book Value
1	a.		b.		c.		d.	
2	a.		b.		c.		d.	
3	a.		b.		c.		d.	
4	a.		b.		c.		d.	
5	a.		b.		c.		d.	
6	a.		b.		c.		d.	
7	a.		b.		c.		d.	

19. CHALLENGE PROBLEM Captain Willis Bolger purchased a new tug boat for use on the Mississippi River. The tug cost $195,000. The tug can be depreciated for 10 years and has a salvage value of $28,000. Determine the straight-line depreciation and the book value after each year of use.

End of Year		Original Cost		Annual Depreciation		Accumulated Depreciation		Book Value
1	a.		b.		c.		d.	
2	a.		b.		c.		d.	
3	a.		b.		c.		d.	
4	a.		b.		c.		d.	
5	a.		b.		c.		d.	
6	a.		b.		c.		d.	
7	a.		b.		c.		d.	
8	a.		b.		c.		d.	
9	a.		b.		c.		d.	
10	a.		b.		c.		d.	

Spiral Review

Multiply. (Skill 7, 8)

20. $550.12 × 3 **21.** $1,240.14 × 5 **22.** $17.60 × 4

23. ALGEBRA The Keiser Company estimates a cost of $48,000 annually to carry its inventory of materials. The cost consists of 20% for storage and handling, 10% for interest, and 8% for taxes and insurance. What is the value of The Keiser Company inventory? (Lesson 14.8)

GET READY for the Next Lesson

PREREQUISITE SKILL Finding the Percentage (Skill 30)

Find the percentage. Round answers to the nearest dollar.

24. 6% of $4,580 **25.** 15% of $13,450 **26.** 24% of $5,300

27. 8% of $6,475 **28.** 12% of $16,500 **29.** 34% of $18,250

LESSON 18.7 Modified Accelerated Cost Recovery System (MACRS)

Lesson Objective
Use the modified accelerated cost recovery system to compute the annual depreciation and book value.

Content Vocabulary
- modified accelerated cost recovery system (MACRS)

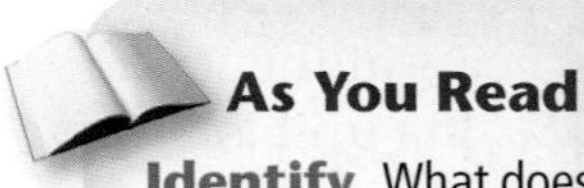

As You Read
Identify What does the MACRS method encourage companies to do?

GET READY for the Lesson

What types of machinery do you see in stores?

Bridge City Coffee Roasters owner Alicia Johnson is shopping for new, industrial-sized coffee roasters. The ones her company has now still work, but a federal tax law allows her to speed up depreciation on the old roasters so she can invest in new ones.

Modified Accelerated Cost Recovery System The **modified accelerated cost recovery system** (MACRS) is another method of computing depreciation. Introduced by the Tax Reform Act of 1986 and further **modified** by the Tax Bill of 1989, MACRS allows businesses to depreciate assets fully over a set period of time. This method encourages businesses to replace equipment earlier than they would if they used other depreciation methods. Under MACRS, assets can be depreciated fully over recovery periods of 4, 6, 8, 11, 16, or 21 years, according to fixed percents. Remember that book value is the approximate value of an item after you have owned it and depreciated it for a period of time. The MACRS depreciation formula is:

Annual MACRS Depreciation = Original Cost × Fixed Percent

EXAMPLE

Prince Pizza purchased a delivery van for $20,000. MACRS allows delivery vans to be depreciated fully in 6 years according to six fixed percents: 20% the first year, 32% the second year, 19.2% the third year, 11.52% the fourth and fifth years, and 5.76% the sixth year. What is the annual depreciation and the book value?

Step 1: Find the annual depreciation.

For year 1, it is $20,000 × 20% = $4,000

For year 2, it is $20,000 × 32% = $6,400

Use the same process for remaining years.

Step 2: Determine the accumulated depreciation.

For year 1, it is $0 + $4,000 = $4,000

For year 2, it is $4,000 + $6,400 = $10,400

Use the same process for remaining years.

Step 3: Determine the book value.

For year 1, it is $20,000 – $4,000 = $16,000

For year 2, it is $20,000 – $10,400 = $9,600

Use the same process for remaining years.

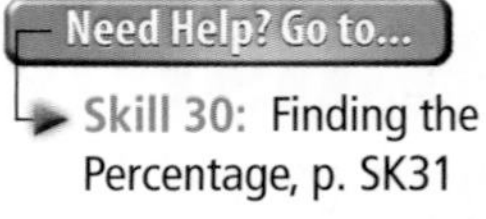

Skill 30: Finding the Percentage, p. SK31

Year	Original Cost	×	Fixed Percent	=	Annual Depreciation	Accumulated Depreciation	Book Value
1	$20,000	×	20.00%	=	$ 4,000	$ 4,000	$16,000
2	$20,000	×	32.00%	=	$ 6,400	$10,400	$ 9,600
3	$20,000	×	19.20%	=	$ 3,840	$14,240	$ 5,760
4	$20,000	×	11.52%	=	$ 2,304	$16,544	$ 3,456
5	$20,000	×	11.52%	=	$ 2,304	$18,848	$ 1,152
6	$20,000	×	5.76%	=	$ 1,152	$20,000	$0
	Total		**100.00%**	=	$20,000		

Study Tip

Multiplying Zeros

Zeros at the end of large numbers can be eliminated when multiplying, as long as you put them back into the product.

Concept CHECK

Complete the problems. Check your answers in the back of the book.

1. MACRS depreciates automobiles in 6 years according to the same six percents used for a delivery van in the **Example**. Find the annual depreciation and the book value for each of the 6 years for an automobile costing $30,000.
2. MACRS depreciates over-the-road tractor units for 4 years at the following percents: 33.33%, 44.45%, 14.81%, and 7.41%. If a unit is purchased for $120,000, what is the depreciation and the book value for each of the 4 years?

Lesson Practice

For Problems 3–9, round answers to the nearest dollar. For Problems 3–6, use the MACRS method to find the annual depreciation.

	Item	Cost	Year 1 20.00%	Year 2 32.00%	Year 3 19.20%	Year 4 11.52%	Year 5 11.52%	Year 6 5.76%
3.	Taxi	$ 16,000	a.	b.	c.	d.	e.	f.
4.	Truck	24,700	a.	b.	c.	d.	e.	f.
5.	Computers	34,800	a.	b.	c.	d.	e.	f.
6.	Furniture	120,000	a.	b.	c.	d.	e.	f.

7. A three-year-old racehorse is purchased for $164,500. It is fully depreciated in 4 years at the following percents: 33.33%, 44.45%, 14.81%, and 7.41%. What is the depreciation and the book value for each of the 4 years?

Year	Percent	Cost	Depreciation	Accumulated Depreciation	Book Value
1	33.33%	a.	b.	c.	d.
2	44.45%	a.	b.	c.	d.
3	14.81%	a.	b.	c.	d.
4	7.41%	a.	b.	c.	d.

 **Did You Know?**

Babylonian Sewers
Between 4,500 and 6,000 years ago in a region of Babylonia (present-day Iraq), well-to-do family homes had pit toilets that led to cesspools made of baked clay. The Babylonians also created one of the earliest known sewer pipes.

8. The Extended Care Center purchased a van for $48,260 to transport residents to and from a shopping center. The van is fully depreciated in 6 years. Fixed percents are 20%, 32%, 19.20%, 11.52%, 11.52%, and 5.76%. Find the depreciation and book value for each year.

Year	Percent	Cost	Depreciation	Accumulated Depreciation	Book Value
1	20.00%	a.	b.	c.	d.
2	32.00%	a.	b.	c.	d.
3	19.20%	a.	b.	c.	d.
4	11.52%	a.	b.	c.	d.
5	11.52%	a.	b.	c.	d.
6	5.76%	a.	b.	c.	d.

H.O.T. Problems

9. CHALLENGE PROBLEM Wastewater treatment plants are depreciated fully in 16 years. Complete the depreciation table for a plant costing $1,400,000.

Year	Percent	Cost	Deprec.	Accum. Deprec.	Book Value	Year	Percent	Cost	Deprec.	Accum. Deprec.	Book Value
1	5.00%	a.	b.	c.	d.	9	5.91%	a.	b.	c.	d.
2	9.50%	a.	b.	c.	d.	10	5.90%	a.	b.	c.	d.
3	8.55%	a.	b.	c.	d.	11	5.91%	a.	b.	c.	d.
4	7.70%	a.	b.	c.	d.	12	5.90%	a.	b.	c.	d.
5	6.93%	a.	b.	c.	d.	13	5.91%	a.	b.	c.	d.
6	6.23%	a.	b.	c.	d.	14	5.90%	a.	b.	c.	d.
7	5.90%	a.	b.	c.	d.	15	5.91%		b.	c.	d.
8	5.90%	a.	b.	c.	d.	16	2.95%		b.	c.	d.

Spiral Review

Find the percentage. Round answers to the nearest dollar. (Skill 30)

10. 38% of $74,555 **11.** 8% of $1,476 **12.** 12% of $840

13. ALGEBRA Miguel Ramirez has a position with Retail Industries. After his annual performance review, he receives a merit increase of 3.5% and a cost-of-living increase of 2.8%. His annual salary after the increases is $60,250. Find Miguel's annual salary before the two increases took effect. Find his merit increase and his cost-of-living increase. (Lesson 13.2)

GET READY for the Next Lesson

PREREQUISITE SKILL Subtracting Decimals (Skill 6)

Subtract.

14. $24,865.00 – $16,785.00

15. $98,743.25 – $24,779.46

16. $101,221.00 – $67,896.12

17. $441,227.50 – $121,885.44

18. $59,642.30 – $36,752.49

19. $5,001.88 – $1,005.99

Assets, Liabilities, and Equity

Lesson Objective

Compute the total assets, liabilities, and owner's equity.

Content Vocabulary

- assets
- liabilities
- owner's equity
- net worth
- capital

GET READY for the Lesson

What would you need in order to start your own business?

Ben and Rudy Trujillo have a plan to buy an old building and convert it to upscale condominiums. They have cash for a down payment and the bank has approved them for a commercial real estate loan.

LIABILITIES AND NET WORTH	
Liabilities	
Auto Note Balance	$14,000
Total Liabilities	$14,000
Net Worth	$26,000
TOTAL LIABILITIES AND NET WORTH	$40,000

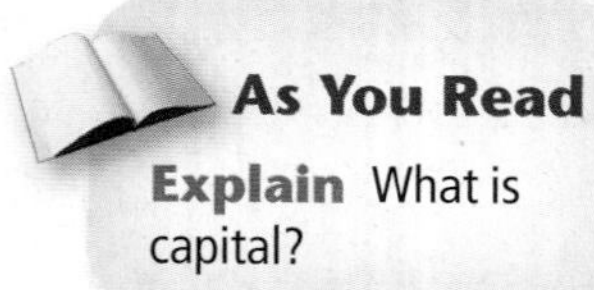

As You Read

Explain What is capital?

Assets, Liabilities, and Equity When you **create** a business, you may need to either buy merchandise to sell or buy materials with which to make your products. You may need to purchase office supplies, equipment, buildings, or land. You must have cash to pay bills and meet other expenses. **Assets** are the total of your cash, the items that you have purchased, and any money that your customers owe you.

You may borrow money to start your business, or you may purchase merchandise on credit. **Liabilities** are the total amount of money that you owe to creditors. **Owner's equity**, **net worth**, or **capital** is the total value of assets that you own minus total liabilities. Owner's equity plus liabilities equal assets. The formulas are:

Assets = Liabilities + Owner's Equity

Owner's Equity = Assets − Liabilities

Liabilities = Assets − Owner's Equity

Need Help? Go to...

- **Skill 3:** Adding Whole Numbers, p. SK4
- **Skill 4:** Subtracting Whole Numbers, p. SK5

EXAMPLE

Tina and John Agee used $60,000 of their own money and took out a bank loan of $25,000 to open a store. The Agees paid $15,000 for merchandise and $10,000 for supplies. This left a cash balance of $60,000. They received another shipment of $8,000 worth of merchandise. They did not pay for this merchandise immediately. What was their owner's equity?

Step 1: Find the assets.

Cash: $85,000 − ($15,000 + $10,000) =	$60,000
Merchandise: $15,000 + $8,000 =	23,000
Supplies	+ 10,000
Total Assets	$93,000

Step 2: Find the liabilities.

Bank loan	$25,000
Unpaid merchandise	+ 8,000
Total Liabilities	$33,000

Step 3: Find the owner's equity. Assets − Liabilities

	$93,000
	− 33,000
Owner's Equity	**$60,000**

Study Tip

Feedback

Do not forget to check your answers as you work through examples and practice problems. Getting feedback is a key to efficient and productive studying.

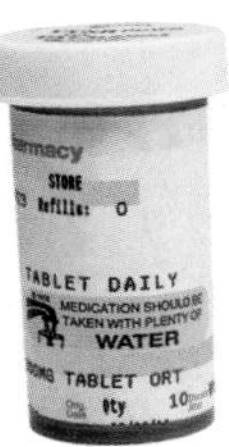

Concept CHECK

Complete the problems. Check your answers in the back of the book.

1. Find the assets
Liabilities: $82,000
Owner's equity: $50,000

2. Find the liabilities
Assets: $18,000 cash, $49,000 merchandise
Owner's equity: $25,000

Did You Know?

Drugstores Until the mid-1900s, pharmacies in the United States made and sold their own medicines. Today, pharmaceutical companies make medicines and drugstore chains Rite-Aid and Revco have more than 28,000 locations combined.

Lesson Practice

Complete the table.

	Liabilities	+	Owner's Equity	=	Assets
3.	$27,000	+	$ 50,000	=	
4.	$14,750	+	$ 37,500	=	
5.	$38,750	+		=	$ 75,000
6.	$54,690	+		=	$143,650
7.		+	$ 25,000	=	$ 42,450
8.		+	$147,470	=	$475,000

9. Family Pharmacy has these assets and liabilities:
Cash, $4,187; Supplies, $7,185; Unpaid merchandise, $11,410
Inventory, $17,450; Building, $125,000; Taxes owed, $847
Equipment, $36,475; Land, $31,500; Real estate loan, $130,000
Calculate the total assets, the total liabilities, and the owner's equity.

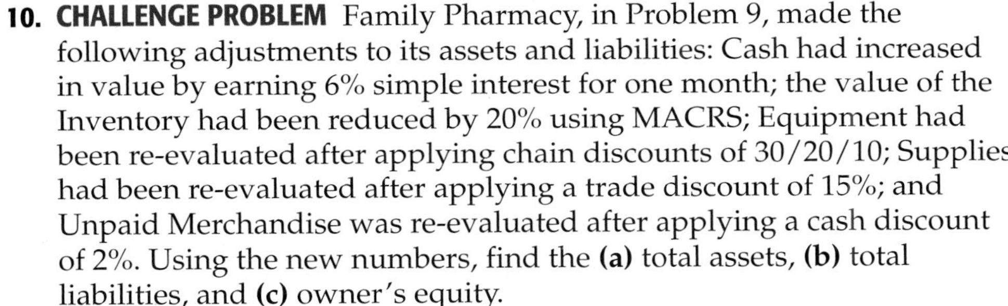

10. CHALLENGE PROBLEM Family Pharmacy, in Problem 9, made the following adjustments to its assets and liabilities: Cash had increased in value by earning 6% simple interest for one month; the value of the Inventory had been reduced by 20% using MACRS; Equipment had been re-evaluated after applying chain discounts of 30/20/10; Supplies had been re-evaluated after applying a trade discount of 15%; and Unpaid Merchandise was re-evaluated after applying a cash discount of 2%. Using the new numbers, find the **(a)** total assets, **(b)** total liabilities, and **(c)** owner's equity.

Spiral Review

Add and subtract. (Skill 5, 6)

11. 31,475.25 + 10,719.50 − 563.85

12. 74,850 − 35,798 + 147,875

13. ALGEBRA Jenna Miller was looking at her account statement. Her new balance was $12,017.54, her previous balance was $9,250.36, she had made a deposit of $2,500, and she had a withdrawal of $300. Find the interest earned on Jenna's savings account. (Lesson 5.3)

GET READY for the Next Lesson

PREREQUISITE SKILL **Adding Whole Numbers** (Skill 3)

Add.

14. $7,856 + $69,265 **15.** $345,675 + $8,347 **16.** $189,966 + $24,305

17. $7,284 + $92,111 **18.** $59,675 + $27,954 **19.** $79,481 + $45,291

LESSON 18.9

Balance Sheet

Lesson Objective

Create a balance sheet.

Content Vocabulary

- balance sheet
- vertical analysis
- current ratio
- horizontal analysis

GET READY for the Lesson

How might business owners find out how their company is performing?

Every three months, accountant Kaitlynn Reisling prepares a report for Buddington & Rose Realtors that shows the company's financial standing. Buddington & Rose's owners use the report to help them make important business decisions.

Buddington & Rose Realtors
Balance Sheet

Assets	
Cash in Bank	$23,868.00
Accounts Receivable	$13,610.00
Office Equipment	$9,825.00
Total Assets	**$47,303.00**

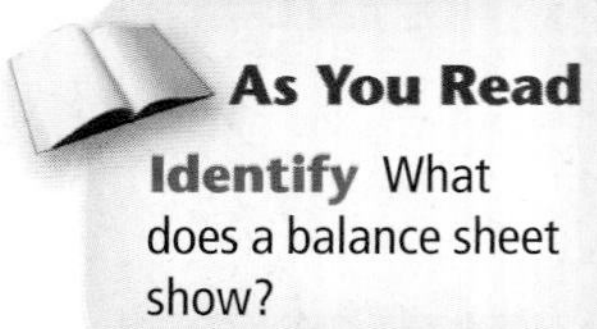

As You Read

Identify What does a balance sheet show?

Balance Sheet A **balance sheet** shows the financial position of your company on a certain date. It is like a snapshot of your company's financial position. You may prepare a balance sheet monthly, quarterly, or annually. The balance sheet shows your total assets, total liabilities, and owner's equity. The balance sheet is designed so that the assets appear on the left. The liabilities and owner's equity appear on the right. The sum of the assets must equal the sum of the liabilities and owner's equity. Recall from Lesson 18.8 this formula:

$$\text{Assets} = \text{Liabilities} + \text{Owner's Equity}$$

Vertical analysis is used to find what percent any item in a financial statement is of the totals in the statement. The **current ratio** is the ratio of the total assests to total liabilities.

$$\text{Current Ratio} = \frac{\text{Total Assets}}{\text{Total Liabilities}}$$

By examining the numbers and percents, you can see what changes have taken place. The balance sheet is an important financial statement, but to make wise decisions you should compare the financial data to a previous balance sheet. **Horizontal analysis** is the calculation of the dollar amount and the percent change from one time period to another.

$$\text{Percent change} = \frac{\text{Amount of Change}}{\text{Original (base) Amount}}$$

The financial statements provide the information, but you must analyze and **interpret** them correctly in order to make accurate recommendations.

EXAMPLE

The Agees (from Lesson 18.8) used $60,000 of their own money plus a $25,000 loan to start their clothing store. They received two shipments of merchandise. They paid cash for the $15,000 shipment. They did not pay immediately for the $8,000 shipment. They bought supplies for $10,000. The Agees have $60,000 left in cash. **(a)** What does their balance sheet show? **(b)** What is the current ratio? **(c)** If the Agees' total liabilities last month were $22,000, what is the percent change in total liabilities?

Step 1: Calculate the balance sheet.

Figure 18.1

Balance Sheet

The Clothing Store		Owed to bank	**May 21**	
Assets		**Liabilities**		
Cash	$60,000	Notes payable	$25,000	
Merchandise inventory	23,000	Accounts payable	8,000	
Supplies	10,000	Total liabilities		$33,000
Shipments valued at $15,000 and $8,000		Owed for merchandise	Cash they invested	
		Owner's Equity		
		Capital		60,000
Total assets	$93,000	Total liabilities and owner's equity		$93,000

Totals must equal. Note double lines under totals.

Reading Math ÷−÷=

Restate

Increase your understanding by finding ways to restate new material. For example, if assets = liabilities + owner's equity, then owner's equity = assets − liabilities.

Step 2: Calculate the current ratio.

$$\text{Current Ratio} = \frac{\text{Total Assets}}{\text{Total Liabilities}} = \frac{\$93{,}000}{\$33{,}000} = 2.818 = 2.8$$

This means that the Agees' total assets are 2.8 times their total liabilities. A current ratio of at least 2 to1 is considered good.

Step 3: Calculate the percent change in total liabilities.

$$\text{Percent Change} = \frac{\text{Amount of Change}}{\text{Original (base) Amount}} = \frac{\$33{,}000 - \$22{,}000}{\$22{,}000} = \frac{\$11{,}000}{\$22{,}000} =$$

$0.50 = 50\%$

This means that the Agees' had a 50% increase in total liabilities.

Concept CHECK

Complete the problems. Check your answers in the back of the book.

Assets		Liabilities	
Cash	$25,000	Notes payable	$10,000
Inventory	30,000	Accounts payable	7,000
Supplies	12,000	Owner's equity	50,000

1. What are the total assets?
2. What are the total liabilities and owner's equity?
3. Calculate the current ratio.
4. If last month the cash was $20,000, what is the percent change?

Lesson Practice

Complete the table.

	Cash	Inventory	Supplies	Total Assets	Bank Loan	Taxes Owed	Total Liabilities	Owner's Equity
5.	$ 18,000	$ 11,500	$ 3,500	a.	$ 10,500	$1,800	b.	c.
6.	45,000	255,700	$11,400	a.	$200,000	$8,800	b.	c.
7.	10,500	41,200	$ 800	a.	b.	$5,000	c.	$ 25,000
8.	125,400	196,700	$12,800	a.	$175,000	b.	c.	$150,000

Did You Know?

Dog Ownership **Statistics confirm that the United States is a nation of dog owners. An estimated 61,080,000 pet dogs live in the U.S., more than twice the number residing in Brazil, the next-ranked country. China, Japan, Russia, South Africa, France, Italy, Poland, and Thailand round out the top 10.**

For problems 9–12, determine the (a) total assets, (b) total liabilities, (c) owner's equity, and (d) the current ratio.

9. Cash: $25,000
Merchandise: $74,800
Owed to bank: $65,000

10. Cash: $8,450
Equipment: $11,170
Owed to bank: $10,000

11. Cash: $15,550
Merchandise: $45,900
Owed to bank: $33,000

12. Cash: $22,500
Equipment: $84,000
Owed to bank: $6,000

13. The balance sheet for Howard's Jewelers is given below. Complete the balance sheet by filling in parts **(a)** to **(d)**. **(e)** Determine the current ratio. **(f)** If the total liabilities last month were $28,000, what is the percent change in total liabilities?

Balance Sheet			
Howard's Jewelers			**June 20 – –**
Assets		**Liabilities**	
Cash on hand	$3,417.00	Bank loan	$12,214.00
Accts. receivable	6,214.00	Accts. Payable	6,470.00
Inventory	13,419.00	Taxes owed	714.85
Supplies	417.50	Wages owed	274.35
Store fixtures	1,250.00	Mortgage loan	31,340.00
Building	35,750.00	Total liabilities	**b.**
Land	20,000.00		
		Owner's Equity	
		Capital	**c.**
Total assets	**a.**	Total liabilities and owner's equity	**d.**

14. Complete the balance sheet for Pet Supplies Inc., then compute the percent change in inventory if the inventory last month was $9,840.

Balance Sheet			
Pet Supplies Inc.			**December 31 – –**
Assets		**Liabilities**	
Cash on hand	$3,128.00	Bank loan	$11,715.00
Accts. receivable	214.85	Accts. Payable	474.84
Inventory	8,426.00	Taxes owed	461.72
Supplies	5,617.40	Wages owed	234.85
Store fixtures	2,405.75	Mortgage loan	54,175.00
Building	43,450.00	Total liabilities	**b.**
Land	24,500.00		
		Owner's Equity	
		Capital	**c.**
Total assets	**a.**	Total liabilities and owner's equity	**d.**

15. Wholesale Grocer Supply Company had these assets and liabilities on December 31:

Balance Sheet

Assets		Liabilities	
Cash	$ 2,417,600	Accounts payable	$84,640,000
Accounts receivable	53,591,500	Notes payable	56,119,400
Inventory	48,478,600	Income taxes	975,450
Property	75,750,000	Other liabilities	864,560
Investments	475,000		
Other assets	18,791,500		

(a) Complete the balance sheet. **(b)** Determine the current ratio. **(c)** Compute the percent change in total assests if the assets a year ago were $189,840,400.

16. Metal Abrasives shows these assets and liabilities as of June 30:

Balance Sheet

Assets (in millions)		Liabilities (in millions)	
Cash	$1.10	Notes payable	$14.90
Accounts receivable	9.8	Accounts payable	4.3
Inventories	11.4	Income taxes	1.2
Property	19.7	Stock	10.3
Foreign Investments	1.3	Other liabilities	4.1
Other assets	4.2		

(a) Complete the balance sheet. **(b)** Determine the current ratio. **(c)** Compute the percent change in accounts receivable if the accounts receivable last quarter were $10.6 million.

17. CHALLENGE PROBLEM (a) Compare (as a multiple), the current ratio if the total assets doubled and the total liabilities were reduced by half to the current ratio in **Problem 16**. **(b)** Compare (as a multiple), the current ratio if the total assets were reduced by half and the total liabilities doubled to the current ratio in Problem 14. **(c)** find the percent change in foreign investments if the foreign investments last quarter were $1,300,000.

Spiral Review

Add. (Skill 3)

18. $14,780 + $13,190

19. $147,560 + $93,480

20. $416,750 + $318,430 + $84,970

21. ALGEBRA Kim Wahn's group medical coverage costs her $112.75 per month. Her employer pays 75% of the cost. How much is the annual premium for Kim's health insurance? (Lesson 2.5)

GET READY for the Next Lesson

PREREQUISITE SKILL Multiplying Decimals (Skill 8)

Multiply.

22. 8 × $6.92 **23.** 16 × $32.97

24. 65 × $24.30 **25.** 78 × $13.76

26. 19 × $78.54 **27.** 24 × $152.93

LESSON 18.10

Cost of Goods Sold

Lesson Objective
Determine the cost of goods sold.

Content Vocabulary
- cost of goods sold

GET READY for the Lesson

Can you think of products that are often out of stock?

Bowers Hardware owner Michael Bowers is happy he decided to stock a new line of push mowers. Customers like the push mowers because they are light, quiet, and non-polluting. Strong sales of the mowers are helping Bowers Hardware turn a profit this year.

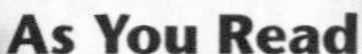

As You Read
List What information do you need in order to determine if your business is making or losing money?

Cost of Goods Sold The balance sheet shows your total assets, total liabilities, and owner's equity at a given point in time. You also need to **identify** whether the company is operating at a profit or loss. To determine if you are making money or losing money, you must know sales figures, expenses, and the **cost of goods sold**. The cost of goods sold is equal to the value of the beginning inventory plus the cost of any goods received (receipts) minus the value of the ending inventory. The formula is:

Cost of Goods Sold = (Beginning Inventory + Receipts) − Ending Inventory

EXAMPLE 1

The Clothing Store began the quarter with an inventory valued at $14,750.00. During the quarter, it received 100 belts that cost $12.49 each, 50 scarves at $15.24 each, 25 sweaters at $29.72 each, and 144 plastic raincoats at $3.50 each. The ending inventory was valued at $12,847.00. What was the cost of goods sold?

Step 1: Find the receipts.

	Number		Cost		
Belts	100	×	$12.49	=	$1,249.00
Scarves	50	×	$15.24	=	$ 762.00
Sweaters	25	×	$29.72	=	$ 743.00
Raincoats	144	×	$ 3.50	=	$ 504.00
Total Receipts					$3,258.00

Step 2: Find the cost of goods sold.

(Beginning Inventory + Receipts) − Ending Inventory

($14,750.00 + $3,258.00) − $12,847.00 = **$5,161.00 cost of goods sold**

100 [×] 12.49 [=] 1249 [M+] 50 [×] 15.24 [=] 762 [M+]
25 [×] 29.72 [=] 743 [M+] 144 [×] 3.5 [=] 504 [M+] [RM]
3258 [+] 14750 [−] 12847 [=] 5161

Study Tip

Connect
Connect new ideas and information to things you already know. You will learn faster and be better able to retain what you learn.

Concept CHECK

Complete the table. Check your answers in the back of the book.

	Beginning Inventory	Receipts	Ending Inventory	Cost of Goods Sold
1.	\$156,470	\$21,960	\$161,510	
2.	\$43,656	\$11,712	\$42,964	

Need Help? Go to...
Workshop 36: Problem-Solving Strategy, Using Simple Algebraic Operations, p. 74

EXAMPLE 2 Algebra

The City Sports Shop had an ending inventory equal to one-fourth (0.25) its beginning inventory. The receipts were half (0.5) the beginning inventory. If the cost of goods sold were \$178,500, find the receipts, the beginning inventory, and the ending inventory.

Step 1: Let x = the beginning inventory.

$0.5x$ = the receipts

$0.25x$ = the ending inventory

Step 2: Use the Cost of Goods Sold formula and solve for x.

Cost of Goods Sold = (Beginning Inventory + Receipts) − Ending Inventory

$\$178,500 = (x + 0.5x) - 0.25x$

Combine like terms → $\$178,500 = 1.25x$

Divide both sides by 1.25 → $\$142,800 = x$

The beginning inventory was \$142,800.

$0.5x = 0.5(\$142,800) =$ **\$71,400 in receipts**

$0.25x = 0.25(\$142,800) =$ **\$35,700 ending inventory**

Concept CHECK

Complete the problem. Check your answer in the back of the book.

3. The Corner Yarn Shoppe had receipts equal to double the beginning inventory. The ending inventory was \$10,000 less than the beginning inventory. If the cost of goods sold equaled \$48,500, find the beginning inventory, the receipts, and the ending inventory.

Lesson Practice

For Problems 4–10 find the cost of the goods sold.

4. Beginning inventory: \$417,600
Receipts: \$75,800
Ending inventory: \$396,800

5. Beginning inventory: \$125,400
Receipts: \$31,200
Ending inventory: \$131,400

6. Beginning inventory: \$75,470
Receipts: \$14,650
Ending inventory: \$72,170

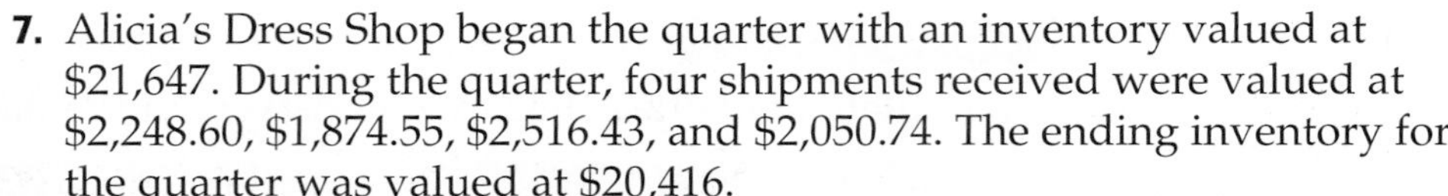

7. Alicia's Dress Shop began the quarter with an inventory valued at $21,647. During the quarter, four shipments received were valued at $2,248.60, $1,874.55, $2,516.43, and $2,050.74. The ending inventory for the quarter was valued at $20,416.
8. Tom's Train Station Inc. began the month with an inventory valued at $34,767.80. During the month, Tom's received 5 shipments valued at $1,274.74, $4,756.44, $983.45, $2,465.39, and $416.93. Tom's month-end inventory was valued at $36,193.48.
9. The Shoehorn Repair Shop started the quarter with an inventory valued at $5,178.43. During the quarter, it received 5 boxes of replacement heels at $10.35 a box, 3 boxes of replacement soles at $26.15 a box, 4 cards of shoelaces at $10.65 a card, 6 spools of nylon thread at $22.13 a spool, and 2 large bottles of industrial-strength adhesive at $39.87 a bottle. The ending inventory for the quarter was valued at $4,241.83. Find the cost of goods sold.
10. Leather Limited started the month with an inventory valued at $18,719.45. During the month, it received 9 men's jackets at $87.53 each, 15 belts at $12.79 each, 4 ladies' long coats at $184.37 each, 5 men's hats at $18.71 each, and 5 ladies' jackets at $138.84 each. The month-end inventory was valued at $16,478.54. Find the cost of goods sold.
11. Battery Market began the quarter with an inventory valued at $12,550. Receipts included: 220 auto batteries at $35 each, 100 marine batteries at $85.50 each, 150 phone batteries at $22 each, and 60 portable tool batteries at $44 each. The ending inventory was valued at $8,400. Determine the total receipts and the cost of goods sold.

Did You Know?

Model Trains **The world's largest model railroad attraction is located in Flemington, New Jersey. It includes eight miles of track, hundreds of bridges (made of millions of tiny pieces of wood), over 4,000 buildings, and half a million trees.**

H.O.T. Problems

12. **ALGEBRA** If the receipts equal the beginning inventory, and the ending inventory is twice the cost of goods sold, find the beginning inventory if the cost of goods sold is $5,000 less than the receipts.
13. **ALGEBRA** Central Auto Parts had a beginning inventory equal to three times its receipts. The ending inventory was twice its receipts. If the cost of goods sold equaled $71,850, find the receipts, the beginning inventory, and the ending inventory.

Spiral Review

Add, subtract or multiply. (Skill 5, 6, 8)

14. $14,178.90 + $2,417.36
15. $16,596.80 − $13,743.34
16. $2,345.23 × 0.245
17. The Billiard Table Co. purchases a billiard table for $1,250 from the manufacturer. It sells the set for $2,675. What is the markup rate based on cost? (Lesson 15.6)

GET READY for the Next Lesson

PREREQUISITE SKILL Adding Decimals (Skill 5)

Add.

18. $78.95 + $6.92
19. $64.75 + $18.44 + $29.75
20. $109.65 + $10.55 + $24.30
21. $7,287.92 + $213.11 + $423.76
22. $115,977.11 + $46,100.43 + $79,543.03
23. $194,429.67 + $37,680.33 + $25,291.76

LESSON 18.11 Income Statement

Lesson Objective
Complete an income statement.

Content Vocabulary
- income statement
- profit-and-loss statement
- net income
- net profit

GET READY for the Lesson

Why should a business owner know his or her income and operating expenses?

Judy Yuse owns The Pottery Corner. She sells ceramic pots for about 35% more than she pays for them, so she makes a good profit.

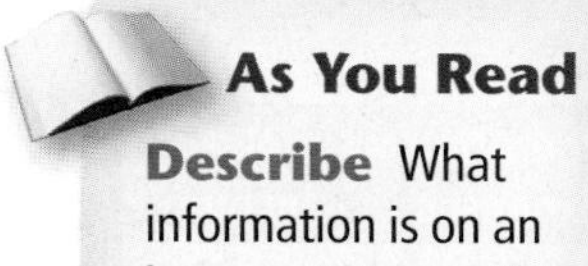

As You Read

Describe What information is on an income statement?

Income Statement At the end of an accounting period, you need to **investigate** how much money your business made or lost. You also want to know how much money you took in from sales and where the money went. The information is reported on your income statement. An **income statement**, or **profit-and-loss statement**, shows in detail your income and operating expenses. If your gross profit is greater than your total operating expenses, your income statement will show a **net income**, or **net profit**. The formulas are:

Gross Profit = Net Sales − Cost of Goods Sold

Net Income = Gross Profit − Total Operating Expenses

Need Help? Go to...
- **Skill 3:** Adding Whole Numbers, p. SK4
- **Skill 4:** Subtracting Whole Numbers, p. SK5

EXAMPLE

Three months after opening The Clothing Store, Tina and John Agee (from Lesson 18.8) prepare an income statement. Sales for the first three months totaled $22,174. Merchandise totaling $173 was returned to them. The Agees' inventory records show that the goods they sold cost them $8,817. Records show that their operating expenses totaled $8,047. What is the net income?

Find the net income.

Income Statement

The Clothing Store			For the Quarter Ended June 30, 20--
Income:	Sales	$22,174	
	Less: Sales returns and allowances	173	
	Net sales		$22,001
Cost of goods sold	Total Sales − Returns		8,817
Gross profit on sales			$13,184
	Net Sales − Cost of Goods Sold		
Operating expenses:	Salaries and wages	$6,400	
	Delivery expenses	142	
	Rent	900	
	Advertising & Supplies	125	
	Utilities	120	
	Depreciation & Insurance	360	
	Total operating expenses		$ 8,047
	Gross Profit − Total Operating Expenses		
Net income			$ 5,137

Study Tip

Do Not Wait
A little studying every day will help you learn new material and perform well on tests. This approach is also less stressful than procrastinating.

For Problems 1 and 2, find (a) the gross profit on sales and (b) the net income. Check your answers in the back of the book.

1. Sales: \$95,000
Returned merchandise: \$3,500
Cost of goods sold: \$30,000
Total operating expenses: \$34,700

2. Sales: \$475,000
Returned merchandise: \$7,500
Cost of goods sold: \$178,500
Total operating expenses: \$105,400

Lesson Practice

Complete the table.

	Total Sales	Returns	Net Sales	Cost of Goods Sold	Gross Profit	Operating Expenses	Net Income
3.	\$ 14,700	\$ 540	\$14,160	\$ 8,750	\$5,410	\$ 725	a.
4.	\$ 38,900	\$4,120	a.	\$ 11,175	b.	\$18,900	c.
5.	\$ 3,750	\$ 75	a.	\$ 1,740	b.	\$ 828	c.
6.	\$174,945	\$ 0	a.	\$ 56,750	b.	\$42,193	c.
7.	\$674,916	\$1,274	a.	\$417,916	b.	\$96,419	c.

8.

Income: Sales		\$47,890
Less: Sales returns and allowances		976
Net sales	**(a)**	\$
Cost of goods sold		21,742
Gross profit on sales	**(b)**	\$
Operating expenses: Salaries and wages		8,500
Taxes		497
Utilities		235
Depreciation		975
Total operating expenses	**(c)**	\$
Net income	**(d)**	\$

9.

Income: Sales		\$463,575
Less: Sales returns and allowances		75,450
Net sales	**(a)**	\$
Cost of goods sold		231,000
Gross profit on sales	**(b)**	\$
Operating expenses: Total operating expenses		71,916
Net income	**(c)**	\$

Did You Know?

Halloween Costumes
Princess is the Halloween costume of choice for 11.8% of kids responding to a recent survey. Other popular choices were witch (5.2%), Spiderman (4.5%) and Darth Vader (3.9%). Among adults, popular choices included witch, vampire, pirate, and zombie.

Prepare an income statement for each business in Problems 10–14.

10. Last month Clarita's Halloween Costume kiosk at the mall had total sales of $8,961. Merchandise totaling $85 was returned. The goods that were sold cost Clarita's $5,617. Operating expenses for the month were $718.

11. Last month Jake's Fishing Supply had total sales of $15,095. Merchandise totaling $1,088 was returned. The goods that were sold cost Jake's $6,010. Operating expenses for the month were $1,100.

12. Advantage Housekeeping Service prepares a monthly income statement. For this past month, it collected $3,150 from homeowners for services provided (sales). It had $70 in allowances for jobs that had to be redone. Operating expenses included salaries and wages of $1,800, supplies of $315 and other expenses of $94.

13. During the past quarter, Henri's Clothes Company had total sales of $27,418 and returns of $220. The cost of goods sold amounted to $9,193. Operating expenses for the quarter included salaries and wages of $2,000, a real estate loan payment of $1,210, advertising at $190, utilities and supplies of $195, a bank loan payment of $350, and other operating expenses of $375.

H.O.T. Problems

14. CHALLENGE PROBLEM Hi-Tech Aluminum Company prepares an annual income statement for distribution to its stockholders. This past year net sales totaled $121.4 million. Cost of goods sold totaled $63.1 million. Operating expenses included wages and salaries of $23.4 million, depreciation and amortization of $3.3 million, general taxes of $1.1 million, interest paid totaling $1.0 million, income taxes of $8.7 million, and miscellaneous operating expenses of $1.2 million. Find the **(a)** gross profit, **(b)** total operating expenses, and **(c)** net income.

Spiral Review

Add and subtract. (Skill 5, 6)

15. 567.56 + 74.92 − 123.74

16. 18,516.50 − 8,743.91 + 191,434.84

17. Daniel Nicholson is making a deposit in his checking account. He has checks for $212.54, $106.78, and $341.58. He has cash consisting of 15 one-dollar bills, 7 five-dollar bills, and 3 ten-dollar bills. What is his total deposit? (Lesson 4.1)

GET READY for the Next Lesson

PREREQUISITE SKILL Finding the Percentage (Skill 30)

Find the percentage. Round answers to the nearest hundredth.

18. 8% of 692

19. 8.66% of 70.48

20. 9.2% of 118

21. 135% of 650

22. 45% of 1,570

23. 67% of 585

CHAPTER 18 Review and Assessment

AFTER YOU READ

Chapter SUMMARY

You may want to complete a payroll register or calculate the percent that a particular expense is of the total expenses. You can compute the prime cost of manufacturing an item and the break-even point in the number of manufactured units. You can calculate the annual depreciation and book value of an item. You can compute the total assets, liabilities, and owner's equity. You may also prepare a balance sheet, determine the cost of goods sold, and complete an income statement.

Vocabulary Check

1. On a sheet of paper, use each of these terms in a written sentence.

Content Vocabulary

- payroll register (p. 659)
- manufacture (p. 666)
- direct material cost (p. 666)
- direct labor cost (p. 666)
- prime cost (p. 666)
- time study (p. 667)
- break-even analysis (p. 669)
- break-even point (p. 669)
- profit (p. 669)
- fixed costs (p. 669)
- variable costs (p. 669)
- depreciation (p. 671)
- estimated life (p. 671)
- straight-line method (p. 671)
- salvage value (p. 671)
- book value (p. 673)
- accumulated depreciation (p. 673)
- modified accelerated cost recovery system (MACRS) (p. 677)
- assets (p. 680)
- liabilities (p. 680)
- owner's equity (p. 680)
- net worth (p. 680)
- capital (p. 680)
- balance sheet (p. 682)
- vertical analysis (p. 682)
- current ratio (p. 682)
- horizontal analysis (p. 682)
- cost of goods sold (p. 686)
- income statement (p. 689)
- profit-and-loss statement (p. 689)
- net income (p. 689)
- net profit (p. 689)

Academic Vocabulary

- register (p. 659)
- precise (p. 663)
- assembles (p. 666)
- primary (p. 669)
- assume (p. 671)
- approximate (p. 673)
- modify (p. 677)
- create (p. 680)
- interpret (p. 682)
- identify (p. 686)
- investigate (p. 689)

Concept Check

2. Describe the purpose of a payroll register.
3. Identify the formula for calculating the percent that each expense is of the total expenses.
4. Explain how to find the prime cost of manufacturing an item.
5. Identify the method for calculating the break-even point.
6. Explain how to find the annual depreciation of an item using the straight-line method.
7. Explain how to find the book value of an item.
8. Differentiate between assets, liabilities, and owner's equity.
9. List the information found on a balance sheet.
10. Identify the formula for determining the cost of goods sold.
11. CRITICAL THINKING Differentiate between gross profit and net income.

Lesson-by-Lesson Review (continued)

18.1 Payroll Register (pp. 659–662)

Complete a payroll register.

Christopher Sampson works part time at Lorenzo's Italian Eatery. He is single and claims no allowances. Christopher is verifying his paycheck to ensure that the deductions are correct. Determine his net pay for a week when his gross pay was $288. Medicare is 1.45% of gross, Social Security is 6.2% of gross, city tax is 1.5% of gross, and federal income tax is obtained from tables on pages A2–A5.

Step 1: Find the deduction for: Medicare, Social Security, city tax.

Tax Withheld = Gross Pay × Tax Rate

Medicare	$288 ×	0.0145	=	$4.176	=	$4.18
Social Security	$288 ×	0.062	=	$17.856	=	$17.86
City tax	$288 ×	0.015	=	$4.32		

Step 2: Find the federal income tax.

(Use table *Single Persons Weekly Payroll* on pages A2–A3.)

FIT for *At least 280, But less than 290* is $28.00

Step 3: Find the net pay

Gross Pay	−	Total Deductions		
$288.00	−	($4.18 + $17.86 + $4.32 + $28.00)	=	
$288.00	−	$54.36	=	**$233.64 net pay**

Review Exercises

12. Harvey's Gym pays a standard hourly rate of $10.75. The deductions are federal income tax (FIT), Social Security (6.2%), Medicare (1.45%), and city income tax (CIT) of 1.5%. Complete the payroll register for the week. For the Payroll Register shown, use the tables on A2–A5 for federal income tax. For the FIT information (S,1) means "single, 1 allowance" and (M,3) means "married, 3 allowances."

Payroll Register for Harvey's Gym—Date: January 8, 20—									
Employee	FIT Info.	Hours Worked	Gross Pay	FIT	Social Security	Medicare	CIT	Total Ded.	Net Pay
Acevedo, R.	S,1	26	a.	b.	c.	d.	e.	f.	g.
Bacci, J.	S,0	36	a.	b.	c.	d.	e.	f.	g.
Cook, P.	S,2	32	a.	b.	c.	d.	e.	f.	g.
Graham, L.	S,0	36	a.	b.	c.	d.	e.	f.	g.
Grajales, W.	S,0	32	a.	b.	c.	d.	e.	f.	g.
Lyons, D.	S,1	39	a.	b.	c.	d.	e.	f.	g.
		Total	a.	b.	c.	d.	e.	f.	g.

13. Jeremy Scharfetter works for Rhodes Electronics and earns $13.50 per hour. He is single and claims 1 allowance. He is paid weekly. Last week, he worked 38 hours. What is his net pay? He has deductions for FIT, Social Security, Medicare, CIT (1.5%) and $12.00 health insurance.

Lesson-by-Lesson Review (continued)

18.2 Business Expenses (pp. 663–665)

Calculate the percent that a particular business expense is of the total expenses.
Osvaldo Electronics manufactures calculators. Its monthly payroll expenses are $9,321 and total monthly expenses are $54,210. Payroll is what percent of the total expenses?

Find the percent of the total.

$$\text{Percent of Total} = \frac{\text{Particular Expense}}{\text{Total Expenses}} = \frac{9{,}321}{54{,}210} = 0.1719 = \mathbf{17.2\%\ of\ total\ expenses}$$

Review Exercises

For Problems 14–19, calculate what percent (to the nearest tenth) each item is of the total.

	Manufacturer's Cost and Profit	
14.	Digital camera from manufacturer	$ 550.00
15.	Advertising, other sales expenses	99.00
16.	Store operations	150.00
17.	Payroll	85.50
18.	Taxes	25.50
19.	Profit from sale to retail customer	140.00
	Total (wholesale price to retailer)	$1,050.00

20. **ALGEBRA** The Toy Shop spends 32% of its annual total expenses on advertising. If The Toy Shop spends $14,125 quarterly on advertising, what are its total annual expenses?

18.3 Manufacturing Costs and Time Study (pp. 666–668)

Compute the prime cost of manufacturing an item and use time-study results to compute how many units can be produced.
Clear Choice produces plastic fishing tackle boxes. The machine operator presses 30 boxes from each piece of plastic. Each piece costs $4.50. The operator can press 250 boxes per hour. The direct labor charge is $20.25 per hour. To the nearest tenth of a cent, what is the prime cost of manufacturing a tackle box?

Step 1: Find the direct material cost per item.

$$\frac{4.50}{30} = \$0.150 \text{ direct material cost per item}$$

Step 2: Find the direct labor cost per item.

$$\frac{20.25}{250} = \$0.081 \text{ direct labor cost per item}$$

Step 3: Find the prime cost per item.

Direct Material Cost per Item + Direct Labor Cost per Item

$0.150 + $0.081 = **$0.231 prime cost per tackle box**

Lesson-by-Lesson Review (continued)

Review Exercises

Round answers to the nearest tenth of a cent.

	Cost per Strip	Pieces per Strip	Direct Material Cost per Piece	Labor Cost per Hour	Pieces per Hour	Direct Labor Cost per Piece	Prime Cost
21.	$0.75	20	$0.038	$12.50	1,000	$0.013	a.
22.	$0.90	50	a.	$15.00	1,200	b.	c.
23.	$0.65	30	a.	$17.95	500	b.	c.
24.	$0.95	25	a.	$20.00	1,800	b.	c.
25.	$1.10	10	a.	$13.25	700	b.	c.
26.	$0.55	15	a.	$15.25	650	b.	c.

27. Tameka Oak's assembly line task is to weld a bracket on support beams for manufactured homes. Tameka works 8.5 hours per day less a 15-minute break at 10:00 AM, a 30-minute lunch break at noon, and a 20-minute break at 3:00 PM. It takes her 12 minutes to weld each bracket. How many brackets per day should Tameka be able to weld?

18.4 Break-Even Analysis (pp. 669–670)

Calculate the break-even point in the number of manufactured units.

Fa Talai manufactures cell phone cases. It plans to manufacture 200,000 cases to be sold at $8.55 each. The fixed costs are estimated to be $300,249. Variable costs are $3.83 per unit. How many cases must be sold for Fa Talai to break even?

Find the break-even point in units.

$$\frac{\text{Total Fixed Costs}}{(\text{Selling Price per Unit} - \text{Variable Costs per Unit})}$$

$$\frac{300{,}249}{(8.55 - 3.83)} = \textbf{63,612.076 or 63,612 cases sold to break even}$$

Review Exercises

	Item	Total Fixed Costs	Selling Price per Unit	Variable Costs per Unit	Break-Even Point in Units
28.	Orange Juice	$ 75,000	$ 1.55	$ 0.55	
29.	Pipe	$ 98,000	$ 0.86	$ 0.29	
30.	IV Tubing	$ 127,000	$ 2.35	$ 1.58	
31.	Beads	$ 456,400	$ 4.59	$ 2.43	
32.	Swimming Pool Pump	$1,230,000	$203.00	$135.56	
33.	Band Saw	$2,987,000	$513.34	$303.50	

34. Bailey Trains manufactures a wooden toy train track. It has total fixed costs of $2,050,000.00. The variable cost per piece of track is $3.58. The selling price per piece of track is $8.95. What is the break-even point in number of pieces of train track?

Lesson-by-Lesson Review (continued)

18.5 Depreciation—Straight-Line Method (pp. 671–672)

Use the straight-line method to compute the annual depreciation of an item.
An advertising agency purchased a color laser printer that cost $4,210. The life of the printer is estimated to be 5 years. The total salvage value after 5 years of use is estimated to be $610. Using the straight-line method, find the annual depreciation of the laser printer.

Find the annual depreciation.

$$\frac{\text{Original Cost} - \text{Salvage Value}}{\text{Estimated Life}} = \frac{(\$4{,}210 - \$610)}{5} = \frac{\$3{,}600}{5} = \$720$$

The annual depreciation is $720.

Review Exercises

Find the annual depreciation. Round to the nearest dollar.

	Item	Original Cost	Salvage Value	Estimated Life in Years	Annual Depreciation
35.	Rental Furniture	$ 8,500	$ 900	3	
36.	Copy machine	$ 25,400	$ 2,800	5	
37.	Tug Boat	$ 1,470,000	$88,000	10	
38.	Carpet	$ 4,310	$ 257	3	
39.	Front end loader	$ 35,000	$ 1,000	7	
40.	Gas Pipeline	$15,418,750	$ 0	15	

41. John Able, CPA, purchased office equipment for $43,800. The trade-in value of the equipment is estimated to be $3,800 after 8 years of use. Find the annual depreciation using the straight-line method.

18.6 Depreciation—Book Value (pp. 673–676)

Compute the book value of an item using straight-line depreciation.
The life of a laser printer that costs $4,210 is estimated to be 4 years. The total salvage value after 4 years of use is estimated to be $610. Using the straight-line method, the printer is estimated to depreciate $900 per year. What is the book value at the end of each year of depreciation?

Step 1: Find the accumulated depreciation.

	Previous Year's Accumulated Depreciation	+	Current Year's Depreciation	=	Accumulated Depreciation
First year:	$ 0	+	$900	=	$ 900
Second year:	900	+	900	=	1,800
Third year:	1,800	+	900	=	2,700
Fourth year:	2,700	+	900	=	3,600

Step 2: Find the book value.

	Original Cost	−	Accumulated Depreciation	=	Book Value
First year:	$4,210	−	$ 900	=	**$3,310**
Second year:	4,210	−	1,800	=	**2,410**
Third year:	4,210	−	2,700	=	**1,510**
Fourth year:	4,210	−	3,600	=	**610**

Lesson-by-Lesson Review (continued)

Review Exercises

Eileen Arthur purchased an underwater camera for her diving students to use. The camera cost $5,290, has an estimated life of 8 years, and has a salvage value of $890. Calculate the **(a)** straight-line depreciation, **(b)** accumulated depreciation, and **(c)** book value after each year of use.

	End of Year	Original Cost	Annual Depreciation	Accumulated Depreciation	Book Value
42.	1	$5,290	a.	b.	c.
43.	2	$5,290	a.	b.	c.
44.	3	$5,290	a.	b.	c.
45.	4	$5,290	a.	b.	c.
46.	5	$5,290	a.	b.	c.
47.	6	$5,290	a.	b.	c.
48.	7	$5,290	a.	b.	c.
49.	8	$5,290	a.	b.	c

18.7 Modified Accelerated Cost Recovery System (MACRS) (pp. 677–679)

Use the MACRS to compute the annual depreciation and book value.

Case Digital Design Company purchased an equipment van for $15,000. MACRS allows equipment vans to be depreciated fully in 6 years according to six fixed percents: 20% the first year, 32% the second year, 19.2% the third year, 11.52% the fourth and fifth years, and 5.76% the sixth year. What is the annual depreciation and book value?

Step 1: Find the annual depreciation.

For year 1, it is $15,000 × 20% = **$3,000**

For year 2, it is $15,000 × 32% = **$4,800** Same process for remaining years.

Step 2: Determine the accumulated depreciation.

For year 1, it is $0 + $3,000 = $3,000

For year 2, it is $3,000 + $4,800 = $7,800 Same process for remaining years.

Step 3: Determine the book value.

For year 1, it is: $15,000 − $3,000 = **$12,000**

For year 2, it is: $15,000 − $7,800 = **$7,200**

Year	Percent		Cost		Depreciation	Accumulated Depreciation	Book Value
1	20.00%	×	$15,000	=	$3,000	$ 3,000	$12,000
2	32.00%	×	$15,000	=	$4,800	$ 7,800	$ 7,200
3	19.20%	×	$15,000	=	$2,880	$10,680	$ 4,320
4	11.52%	×	$15,000	=	$1,728	$12,408	$ 2,592
5	11.52%	×	$15,000	=	$1,728	$14,136	$ 864
6	5.76%	×	$15,000	=	$ 864	$15,000	$ 0

Lesson-by-Lesson Review (continued)

Review Exercises

A laser engraving machine is fully depreciated in 8 years. Complete the depreciation table for a laser engraving machine costing $86,500. Round to the nearest cent.

	Year	Percent	Cost	Depreciation	Accumulated Depreciation	Book Value
50.	1	20.00%	a.	b.	c.	d.
51.	2	16.80%	a.	b.	c.	d.
52.	3	14.20%	a.	b.	c.	d.
53.	4	12.20%	a.	b.	c.	d.
54.	5	9.85%	a.	b.	c.	d.
55.	6	9.15%	a.	b.	c.	d.
56.	7	9.02%	a.	b.	c.	d.
57.	8	8.78%	a.	b.	c.	d.

18.8 Assets, Liabilities, and Equity (pp. 680–681)

Compute the total assets, liabilities, and owner's equity.

Philip Lawson started Yellow Jackets by putting in $30,000 of his own money. Yellow Jackets is a retail outlet for outdoor hunting gear. Lawson obtained a bank loan of $100,000, of which $75,000 was used to purchase inventory. Store fixtures cost $10,000, which he did not pay for immediately. What was Lawson's owner's equity?

Assets:

Cash ($30,000 + $100,000) − $75,000	=	$ 55,000
Inventory	=	75,000
Store Fixtures	=	10,000
Total Assets:	=	**$140,000**

Liabilities:

Bank Loan	=	$ 100,000
Unpaid Fixtures	=	10,000
Total Liabilities	=	**$110,000**

Owner's Equity:

Total Assets – Total Liabilities

$140,000 − $110,000 = **$ 30,000**

Review Exercises

Complete the table.

	Liabilities	+	Owner's Equity	=	Assets
58.	$17,844	+	$ 29,300	=	
59.		+	36,500	=	121,944
60.	9,230	+		=	42,100
61.		+	74,508	=	93,200
62.	32,190	+	64,310	=	
63.	21,390	+		=	25,498

Lesson-by-Lesson Review (continued)

18.9 Balance Sheet (pp. 682–685)

Create a balance sheet.
Prepare a balance sheet for Yellow Jackets based on the information above.

Prepare a balance sheet.

Balance Sheet				
Yellow Jackets				March 15
Assets		Liabilities		
Cash	$ 55,000	Notes payable	$ 10,000	
Inventory	75,000	Bank loan	100,000	
Store fixtures	10,000	Total liabilities		$110,000
		Owner's Equity		
		Capital		30,000
Total assets	$140,000	Total liabilities and owner's equity		$140,000

Review Exercises

Complete the table.

	Cash	Inventory	Supplies	Total Assets	Bank Loan	Taxes Owed	Total Liabilities	Owner's Equity
64.	$ 11,500	$117,000	$ 4,300	a.	$100,000	$13,400	b.	c.
65.	109,864	156,790	21,300	a.	210,600	b.	c.	$ 71,754
66.	78,302	21,400	13,490	a.	b.	11,500	c.	44,802

18.10 Cost of Goods Sold (pp. 686–688)

Determine the cost of goods sold.
The Cat's Meow began the month with an inventory valued at $13,400. During the month it received merchandise valued at $3,200. The ending inventory was valued at $12,300. What was the cost of goods sold?

Find the cost of goods sold.

(Beginning Inventory + Receipts) − Ending Inventory

($13,400 + $3,200) − $12,300 = **$4,300 cost of goods sold**

Review Exercises

Find the cost of goods sold.

	Beginning Inventory	Receipts	Ending Inventory	Cost of Goods Sold
67.	$183,204.00	$ 48,650.00	$ 90,431.00	
68.	104,588.00	132,005.00	100,459.00	
69.	85,430.32	34,509.56	100,231.96	

Lesson-by-Lesson Review (continued)

70. **ALGEBRA** The Craft Lady had an ending inventory equal to one-eighth (0.125) its beginning inventory. The receipts were half (0.5) the beginning inventory. If the cost of goods sold was $268,500, find the receipts, the beginning inventory, and the ending inventory.

18.11 Income Statement (pp. 689–691)

Complete an income statement.

Youssef Weston's music store sales for the year totaled $67,540.32. Merchandise totaling $1,200.00 was returned. The goods he sold cost him $29,304.86. His operating expenses totaled $18,002.29. What is the net income?

Find the net income.

Gross Profit = Net Sales − Cost of Goods Sold

Net Income = Gross Profit − Total Operating Expenses

Income Statement			
Youssef Weston's Music Store		For the Month Ending June 30, 20--	
Income:	Sales	$67,540.32	
	Less: Sales returns and allowances	1,200.00	
	Net sales		$66,340.32
Cost of goods sold			29,304.86
Gross profit on sales			$37,035.46
Operating expenses:	Total operating expenses		$18,002.29
Net income			**$19,033.17**

Review Exercises

Complete the table.

	Total Sales	Returns	Net Sales	Cost of Goods Sold	Gross Profit	Operating Expenses	Net Income
71.	$21,905.00	$1,207.63	$20,697.37	$ 6,509.38	$14,187.99	$12,309.00	a.
72.	39,650.00	$3,400.00	a.	$ 8,540.20	b.	$18,500.00	c.
73.	54,201.11	$8,430.38	a.	$18,409.43	b.	$21,200.00	c.
74.	89,500.32	$5,490.43	a.	$15,900.34	b.	$42,200.00	c.

75. Last month, Sunglass Kiosk had total sales of $9,720. Merchandise totaling $110 was returned. The goods that were sold cost Sunglass Kiosk $4,864. Operating expenses for the month were $1,180. Prepare an income statement for Sunglass Kiosk.

Practice Test

Record your answers on a sheet of paper.

1. **ALGEBRA** Pierce Medical Supplies allocates 80% of its annual budget to employee compensation. Pierce Medical spends $784,950 annually on employee compensation. What is the annual budget of Pierce Medical Supplies?
   A $831,500.00 **B** $1,035,235.80
   C $981,187.50 **D** $1,020,650.40

2. Hooper Manufacturing can produce 720 fasteners from one sheet of stainless steel. Each sheet costs $72.45. The machine operator can produce 4,680 fasteners in one hour. The direct labor charge is $150.75. What is the prime cost per item?
   A $0.133 **B** $0.10
   C $0.032 **D** $0.12

3. DL Music produces hip-hop CDs. The fixed costs total $978,567.00. The selling price of each disc is $12.99. The variable cost per disc is $8.95. What is the break-even point in number of discs? (Round the answer to nearest whole number.)
   A 271,860 **B** 660,341
   C 322,325 **D** 242,220

4. Don Scott Aviation recently purchased a new computer system for a total cost of $83,955. The estimated life of the system is 7 years. The estimated value of the system after 7 years is $875. What is the annual depreciation using the straight-line method?
   A $9,174.17 **B** $11,868.57
   C $11,345.66 **D** $10,056.67

5. Jesus Amezcua's gross weekly pay is $435.00. His FIT is $14. His other deductions are $26.97 for Social Security, $6.31 for Medicare, and $41.54 for health insurance. What is Jesus' net pay?
   A $346.18 **B** $349.50
   C $454.85 **D** $342.55

6. Klubnik's Pharmacy has $93,400 in liabilities. The owner's equity totals $65,000. What are the total assets of the pharmacy?
   A $152,440 **B** $28,400
   C $158,400 **D** $16,878

7. Dupre Marketing purchased a new copier for $1,568. The resale value after 5 years is estimated to be $210. What is the book value of the copier after 3 years, using straight-line depreciation?
   A $938.00 **B** $695.80
   C $1,035.60 **D** $753.20

8. Oskar's Electronics had $120,450 in sales last quarter. Merchandise returned during that time totaled $4,310. Oskar's cost of goods sold was $38,750 and the operating expenses totaled $40,210. What was Oskar's gross profit on sales and its net income?

9. MACRS depreciates automobiles in 6 years according to six fixed percents: 20% the first year, 32% the second year, 19.2% the third year, 11.52% the fourth and fifth years, and 5.76% the sixth year. What is the annual depreciation for each of the 6 years for an automobile costing $28,000?

10. **ALGEBRA** Roberto Hollenbeck is a molding machine operator. He molds 13 rulers out of 1 container of molding plastic. Each container costs $49.50. Roberto can mold 255 rulers in 1 hour. What is the most the company can pay in direct labor costs per hour if they want to hold the prime cost per ruler to $3.90?

11. 81.5% of 875

12. $6,952.74 + $111 + $4.87

13. $85.95 ÷ $5.05

14. 1,618 × 7.22

15. $12,548.79 − $2,310.03 − $721

16. 0.385 × 733.12

Standardized Test Practice

Cumulative, Chapters 1–18

PART 1 Multiple Choice

Record your answers on the answer sheet provided by your teacher or on a sheet of paper.

Exemptions	
Single	$2,000
Married	$4,000
Each Dependent	$2,000

1. **ALGEBRA** Julio Cortez earns $46,750 a year working for a physical therapy provider. He is married and pays $1,923.75 in state income tax each year. What is the tax rate for the state where Julio lives?
   A 5.5% **B** 4.5%
   C 3.5% **D** 2.75%

2. **ALGEBRA** Amala Sinj took out a single-payment loan for $1,800 at 7.2% ordinary interest. The maturity value of the loan is $1,832.40. How many days does Amala have to pay back the loan?
   A 360 days **B** 60 days
   C 90 days **D** 120 days

3. **ALGEBRA** Pitt Security has a recruiting budget of $40,000 for a new position. Pitt spent $6,750 on advertising and $9,500 on interview expenses. Pitt is willing to pay an 8% commission on selling the applicant's home. What is the maximum selling price Pitt would pay the commission on and remain on budget in total recruiting costs?
   A $410,250 **B** $395,675
   C $296,875 **D** $230,750

4. Alterin Manufacturing makes childrens' toys. Of every 1,000 toys Alterin produces, 26 are defective and cannot be sold. Calculate as a percent the number of defective items produced per 1,000.
   A 2.6% **B** 26%
   C 12% **D** 4%

TEST-TAKING TIP

Writing When completing extended response or essay questions, use legible, clear handwriting.

5. **ALGEBRA** Miguel DiMarco is interested in a new HDTV. He finds one that is marked down 35%. He calculates he could save $624.68 if he buys it on sale. What is the regular price of the HDTV?
   A $2,186.38 **B** $1,784.80
   C $1,935.75 **D** $1,052.80

6. **ALGEBRA** Tai-Wah Catering wants to open another location. It needs to have 4,200 square feet and its budget allows $2,625 for monthly rent. What is the maximum Tai-Wah can pay per square foot on an annual rate?
   A $7.50 **B** $15.55
   C $8.50 **D** $2.65

7. Soulfinger Music has a 12% market share for jazz CDs in the Chicago area. Jazz CD sales in the area are estimated at $985,643 annually. What are the projected sales figures for Soulfinger Music for next year?
   A $208,947 **B** $867,365
   C $118,277 **D** $116,429

PART 2 Short Response/Griddable

8. Tanna Roepe bought a new motorcycle for $3,650. After 5 years the salvage value is estimated to be $520. What is the annual depreciation using the straight-line method?

9. **ALGEBRA** Oak Tree Fashions spends $8,244 per month on rent. Oak Tree spends 5% of its monthly budget on rent. What is Oak Tree's monthly budget?

PART 3 Extended Response

Show your work.

10. Explain the average-cost method of calculating inventory value.

11. Explain depreciation and the straight-line method of determining depreciation.

12. What is the MACRS and why is it used?

Building Academic Skills

Mathematics

You can use break-even analysis to find out how much to charge people for an event, so you know you have all your costs covered. The costs for an academic-achievement awards ceremony are:

Food	$13.49/person
Gratuity	20% of food cost
Sales tax	5% of food cost
Room fee	Waived
Dinners for award recipients	6 [$13.49 + (25% × $13.49)]
Dinner for speaker	
AV system rental fee	$50
Program development and printing (200 copies)	$75

What are your total fixed costs and variable costs? If you charge $20 per person, how many tickets do you have to sell to break even?

English Language Arts/Writing

In a short essay, compare and contrast preparing an income statement and balancing a personal checkbook. Share your answers with the class.

Science

In the nineteenth century, Frederick Winslow Taylor pioneered "Scientific Management" in manufacturing. Time and motion studies were done in factories to find the best way to accomplish a task. The purpose was to improve efficiency by eliminating unnecessary steps and actions. This led to today's science of ergonomics. Ergonomics is described as designing tasks and work areas to increase workers' efficiency and work quality. Ergonomics also is involved in sports and leisure, and health and safety. Use Internet or library sources to find out about the kinds of jobs that people involved in ergonomic science do. Write a short essay describing one of those jobs and if you would like to work in this field.

Building Real-World Skills

Career WISE

Accountant Accounting includes the management, measurement and disclosure of financial information about a company and its dealings. Accountants need strong math, analytical, communication, and computer skills.

Research and Share:

a. Visit the Web site of the U.S. Department of Labor's Bureau of Labor Statistics and find the section on "Accountants and Auditors."

b. Find the average annual salary for five different accounting professions, and compile them into a chart.

Tech TRENDS

Supply Chain Management Supply chain management, or SCM, keeps track of products and how they are distributed. Sophisticated computer-based tools allow managers to monitor supply levels in massive warehouses; those managers can also track products as they move from warehouse to supplier to final destination.

Activity:

a. Locate the Web site of the Council of Supply Chain Management Professionals.

b. Research supply chain management software on the Internet. Name three companies that manufacture and sell SCM software.

CHAPTER 19 Financial Management

Big Idea

This chapter focuses on how companies manage their taxes, investments, and loans, and takes into account economic trend indicators.

Explore the Photo

Raising Funds
How a business manages its finances is a key factor in whether or not that business succeeds. *Where do businesses find the money to get started?*

Ask AN EXPERT

Growing a Business

Q: I hope to someday open my own business. If my first shop does well, where do I find enough money to open a second one?

A: Many owners use loans to grow their small business. Banks offer favorable lending rates to successful businesses that appear poised to grow. The U.S. Small Business Administration also offers loans through its Certified Lenders Program. You can also attempt to raise equity capital. This means that you look for individuals who are seeking an investment opportunity with a potential for a high return. The investors take a financial risk by contributing money to help you expand your business. You agree to give the investors a share of future profits.

English Language Arts/Writing Write a list of some of the expenses to consider when expanding a small business.

GET READY for the Chapter

Math Online
To take the Online Readiness Quiz, go to **connectED.mcgraw-hill.com**.

Chapter 19 Financial Management

Reading Guide

Before You Read

Identify What expenses do new business owners have to consider?

Main Idea

A strong financial strategy allows your business to grow. Retail businesses often grow by adding more stores in new locations. Business executives, labor leaders, and other private citizens use the Gross Domestic Product and the Consumer Price Index as guides in making economic decisions.

Graphic Organizer

Before you read this chapter, draw a diagram like the one below. As you read, note three economic factors or measurements relevant to financial management.

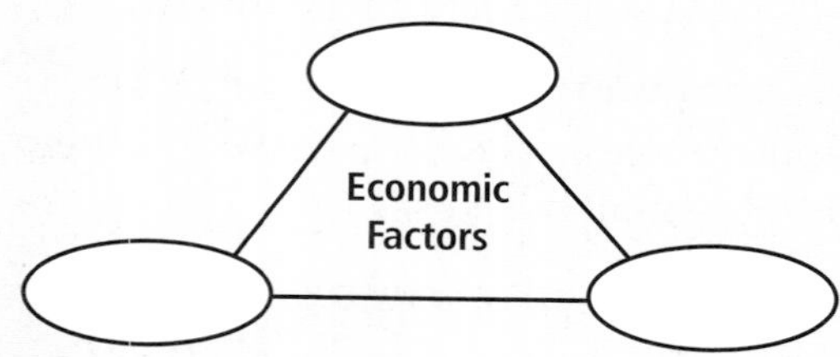

Math Online Go to **connected.mcgraw-hill.com** to download this graphic organizer.

Content Vocabulary

You will learn these key terms in this chapter.

- corporation
- taxable income
- stocks
- bonds
- underwriting commission
- prospectus
- commercial loan
- maturity value
- prime rate
- Treasury bill
- discount
- face value
- yield
- inflation
- deflation
- gross domestic product (GDP)
- real GDP
- per capita GDP
- consumer price index (CPI)

Academic Vocabulary

You will see these words in your reading and on your tests.

- vary
- legal
- chemical
- maximize
- technology
- distortion
- statistical

You can find vocabulary definitions in the **Content Vocabulary** Glossary and the **Academic Vocabulary** Glossary in the back of the book.

Corporate Income Taxes

Lesson Objective
Compute the taxable income and the corporate income tax.

Content Vocabulary
- corporation
- taxable income

GET READY for the Lesson

What are some normal business expenses?

Andrea Davis is a member of the accounting staff at the Lighthouse Theatre Company. At tax time, her job is to organize and add up the company's business expenses. Once Andrea has the total expense amount, the accountants can calculate how much federal tax Lighthouse owes.

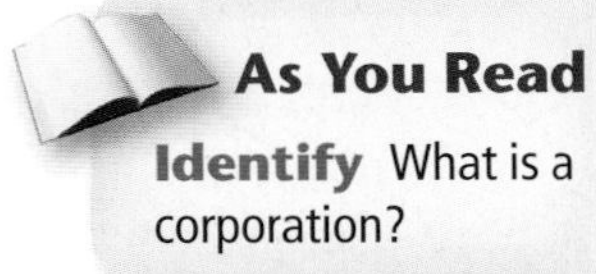

Identify What is a corporation?

Corporate Income Tax Your business must pay federal income taxes. The tax rates **vary** depending on the size and type of your business. **Corporations**, businesses owned by stockholders, are subject to federal tax rates ranging from 15% to 39% of **taxable income**. Taxable income is the portion of your company's gross income that remains after normal business expenses are deducted. Normal business expenses include items such as wages, rent, utilities, interest (paid on loans), property taxes, and depreciation. The structure for federal corporate income taxes is graduated.

Figure 19.1

Federal Corporate Income Tax			
Over—	But not over—	Tax is:	Of the amount over—
$ —	$ 50,000	15%	$ —
50,000	75,000	$ 7,500 + 25%	50,000
75,000	100,000	13,750 + 34%	75,000
100,000	335,000	22,250 + 39%	100,000
335,000	10,000,000	113,900 + 34%	335,000
10,000,000	15,000,000	3,400,000 + 35%	10,000,000
15,000,000	18,333,333	5,150,000 + 38%	15,000,000
18,333,333	—	38%	—

Taxable Income = Annual Gross Income − Deductions

EXAMPLE

Dot-Software had a gross income of $558,145 for the year. It had these business expenses during the year:

Dot-Software Inc.	
Expenses	Amount
Accounting	$ 4,850
Business insurance	$ 5,200
Depreciation	$ 14,720
Interest	$ 9,516
Office supplies	$ 2,200
Rent & Utilities	$ 29,969
Wages & Health Insurance	$398,160
Total	**$464,615**

Management Analyst

Businesses bring in management analysts when they lack the resources to solve a problem. A bookstore might hire an analyst to find the best way to sell books on the Internet.
How do math word problems help you practice finding real-world solutions?

What federal corporate income tax must Dot-Software pay?

Step 1: Find the total deductions (expenses).

Total for the table is $464,615 in deductions.

Step 2: Find the taxable income.

Annual Gross Income – Deductions

$558,145 – $464,615 = $93,530 taxable income

Step 3: Find the federal corporate income tax. (Refer to **Figure 19.1** on page 707.)

$13,750 + 34% of ($93,530 – $75,000) =

$13,750 + (0.34 × $18,530) =

$13,750 + $6,300.20 = **$20,050.20 federal corporate income tax**

Concept CHECK

Use Figure 19.1 on page 707 to find the federal corporate income tax. Check your answers in the back of the book.

1. Wilson Glass Works
   Gross income: $145,000
   Deductions: $60,000
2. Home Painter Inc.
   Gross income: $219,000
   Deductions: $154,000
3. Thomasson Foundry, LLC
   Gross Income: $25,732,680
   Deductions: $8,963,870
4. United Auto Dealers, Inc.
   Gross Income: $762,560
   Deductions: $217,500

Lesson Practice

To complete the table, refer to Figure 19.1 on page 707 for federal corporate income taxes. Round to the nearest dollar.

	Annual Gross Income	–	Deductions	=	Taxable Income	Total Tax
5.	$ 74,918	–	$ 38,172	=	$36,746	a.
6.	$ 95,500	–	$ 59,154	=	a.	b.
7.	$ 121,440	–	$ 78,718	=	a.	b.
8.	$ 180,655	–	$100,120	=	a.	b.
9.	$ 212,971	–	$125,539	=	a.	b.
10.	$ 279,434	–	$214,611	=	a.	b.
11.	$ 720,338	–	$621,913	=	a.	b.
12.	$ 916,418	–	$721,534	=	a.	b.
13.	$1,405,811	–	$990,875	=	a.	b.

Reading Math

Deductions
Angled brackets around numbers, called "wings," are often used on spreadsheets to indicate negative numbers that can represent deductions or a loss. For example, <100> means a deduction or loss of 100.

14. Johnson-Etna Manufacturing Corporation has an annual gross income of $316,921. Deductions total $234,847. What is the federal corporate income tax?

15. The Townnet Company has an annual gross income of $72,173. Deductions total $67,224. What is the federal corporate income tax?

16. The Corner Grill has gross income of $136,896 and deductions of $92,739. What is the federal corporate income tax?

17. Mylo Pharmacy Inc. has an annual gross income of $216,468. Deductions total $98,371. What is the federal corporate income tax?

18. The Law Offices of Jones, Brown, Smith, and Spangler has a gross income of $21,893,765. Deductions total $2,385,986. Find the federal corporate income tax.

19. The Magno-Met Company had these business expenses for the year:

The Magno-Met Company had a gross income of $1,516,749 for the year.

(a) What are the total business expenses?

(b) What is the taxable income?

(c) What is the federal corporate income tax for the year?

Magno-Met Company	
Expenses	**Amount**
Accounting & Insurance	$164,617
Depreciation	$ 26,916
Property taxes	$ 45,495
Interest on a loan	$ 15,465
Office supplies	$ 8,422
Rent & Utilities	$137,197
Wages	$816,147
Total	$

20. CHALLENGE PROBLEM Thomas Brown, CPA, has a gross income of $283,678.50. His deductions equal 22% of his gross income. What does Thomas pay in federal corporate income tax?

Spiral Review

Find the percentage. Round answers to the nearest hundredth. (Skill 30)

21. 7.65% of 80.77

22. 145% of 350

23. 35% of 4,700

24. 34% of 816.9

25. ALGEBRA Juan Ramirez is paid $15.75 an hour for a regular 40-hour week. His overtime pay is $1\frac{1}{2}$ times his regular hourly rate. This past week Juan earned $759.94 in total pay. How many hours of overtime did he work this past week? (Lesson 1.2)

GET READY for the Next Lesson

PREREQUISITE SKILL **Finding the Percentage** (Skill 30)

Find the percentage. Round answers to the nearest hundredth.

26. 4.5% of $2,160,324

27. 6% of $894,371

28. 7.2% of $8,650,000

29. 5% of $548,058

30. 8.2% of $2.5 million

31. 2.8% of $8,470,000

LESSON 19.2

Issuing Stocks and Bonds

Lesson Objective

Calculate the selling expenses and the net proceeds from an issue of stocks or bonds.

Content Vocabulary

- stocks
- bonds
- underwriting commission
- prospectus

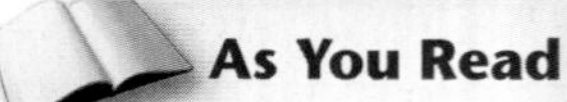

As You Read

List What are expenses associated with issuing stocks or bonds?

GET READY for the Lesson

Have you ever read about stocks and bonds in your local newspaper's business section?

When companies need to raise money for a new building or other major investment, many call on Mario Vargas for help. Mario is an investment banker who specializes in finding buyers for new stocks and bonds.

Glow Images

Issuing Stocks and Bonds Your business may raise money by issuing **stocks** or **bonds**. When you issue stocks, the buyer becomes a part owner of your business. When you issue bonds, the buyer is lending money to your business.

When you issue stocks or bonds, you must pay certain expenses. One expense is an **underwriting commission**. This is a commission to the investment banker who helps you sell the stocks or bonds. Other expenses include accounting costs, **legal** fees, and printing costs. The amount your business actually receives from the sale of the stocks or bonds after paying these expenses is the *net proceeds.* The following formulas are used:

Value of Issue = Price per Share × Number of Shares

Underwriting Commission = Value of Issue × Percent of Underwriting Commission

Net Proceeds = Value of Issue − Total Selling Expenses

Prospectus A **prospectus** is a formal written document that gives the facts about a new offering of securities. The prospectus will indicate the underwriting expenses as cost per share. The formula is:

$$\text{Cost per Share of Underwriting Expenses} = \frac{\text{Total Selling Expenses}}{\text{Total Number of Shares}}$$

EXAMPLE 1

The Landover Company is planning a major expansion program. To finance the program, Landover plans to sell an issue of 4,500,000 shares of stock at $11.50 per share. The underwriting commission will be 6.5% of the value of the stocks. Accounting fees are $550,000, legal fees are $1,650,000, printing costs are $350,000, and other expenses are estimated to be $250,000. Determine the net proceeds and the cost per share of the underwriting expenses.

If all the shares of stock are sold, what net proceeds will Landover Company receive?

Step 1: Find the value of issue.

Price per Share × Number of Shares

$11.50 × 4,500,000 = $51,750,000 value of issue

Step 2a: Find the underwriting commission.

Value of Issue × Percent of Underwriting Commission

$51,750,000 × 6.5% = $3,363,750 underwriting commission

Step 2b: Find the total selling expenses.

Other expenses = $550,000 + $1,650,000 + $350,000 + $250,000 = $2,800,000

Total selling expenses = $3,363,750 + $2,800,000 = $6,163,750

Step 3: Find the net proceeds.

Value of Issue – Total Selling Expenses

$51,750,000 – $6,163,750 = **$45,586,250 net proceeds**

Step 4: Find the cost per share of the underwriting expenses.

$$\frac{\text{Total Selling Expenses}}{\text{Total Number of Shares}} = \frac{\$6{,}163{,}750}{4{,}500{,}000} = \$1.36972 = \mathbf{\$1.37\ cost\ per\ share}$$

Reading Math +−÷=

Decimals

A percent that is a decimal number with only a 0 to the left of the decimal point represents less than 1%. For example 0.5% stands for half of a percent. Its decimal equivalent is 0.005.

Concept CHECK

Find the (a) net proceeds and (b) cost per share of the underwriting expenses. Check your answers in the back of the book.

1. Value of stock: $30,000,000. Underwriting commission: 4.5% of the value of the stock. Other selling expenses: 0.3% of the value of the stock. Sold 1,200,000 shares.

Need Help? Go to...

Workshop 39: Problem-Solving Strategy: Linear Combinations, p. 80

EXAMPLE 2 Algebra

Corporate Investment Bankers earned $420,000 commission for selling 1.4 million shares of The Mitchell Company stock. The commission was 6% of the value of the stock. Find the value of the stock offering and the price of a share of The Mitchell Company stock.

Step 1: Let v = the value of the stock offering.

Let p = the price of a share of the stock.

Step 2: Substitute in the formula.

Underwriting Commission	=	Value of Issue	×	Percent of Underwriting Commission
$420,000	=	v	×	6%
$7,000,000	=	v		

Divide both sides by 6%

The value of the stock offering is $7,000,000.

Step 3: Find the price per share using the formula:

Value of Issue	=	Price per Share	×	Number of Shares
$7,000,000	=	p	×	1,400,000
$5	=	p		

Divide both sides by 1,400,000

The price of a share of the stock is $5.00.

Concept CHECK

Complete the problem. Check your answer in the back of the book.

2. Marble Products Inc. received net proceeds of $2.1 million on the sale of additional shares of their $50.00 stock. If the underwriting commission was 5.4% with additional expenses of $338,788, **(a)** what was the value of the stock offering and **(b)** how many shares of stock were sold?

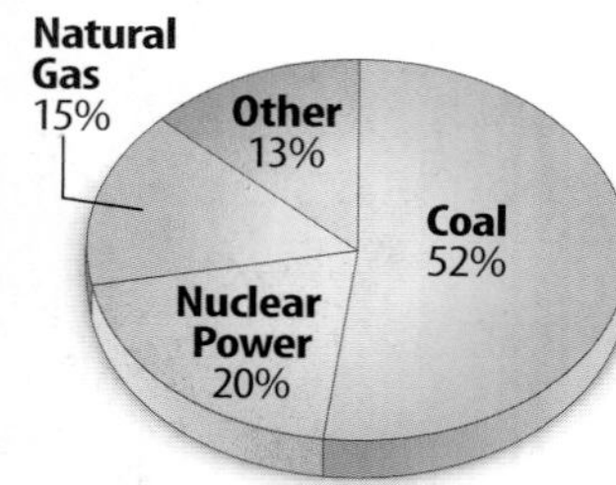

Lesson Practice

Complete the table.

	Value of Issue	Percent	Commission Expenses	Other Expenses	Total Selling Expenses	Net Proceeds	Number of Shares	Selling Cost per Share
3.	$ 6,800,000	6%	a.	$47,500	b.	c.	400,000	d.
4.	$ 950,000	9%	a.	$26,500	b.	c.	40,000	d.
5.	$21,000,000	5%	a.	$54,650	b.	c.	1,000,000	d.
6.	$45,750,000	7%	a.	$94,550	b.	c.	1,500,000	d.

Did You Know?

Electricity Sources Despite technological advances, coal is still by far the biggest source of electricity in the United States. Fifty-two percent of U.S. electricity comes from burning coal, followed by 20% from nuclear power and 15% from natural gas. By contrast, 75% of France's electricity is nuclear-generated.

For Problems 7 and 8, find the (a) net proceeds and (b) cost per share of the underwriting expenses.

7. The value of CoMar stock is $1,750,000. The underwriting commission is 10%. The total of other expenses is $521,640 and 850,000 shares are sold.

8. The value of TruSo bonds is $7,400,000. The underwriting commission is 5.5%. Other expenses total $1,548,650 and 74,000 bonds are sold.

9. Universal Waste Disposal sold 1,350,000 shares of stock at $24.625 per share. The investment banker's commission was 5% of the value of the stock. Accounting fees are $450,000, legal fees are $1,225,000, printing costs are $275,000, and other expenses are estimated to be $350,000. What net proceeds did Universal Waste Disposal receive? What is the selling expense per share?

10. The Mercury Electric Company issued 2,000,000 shares of stock at $62.50 per share. Find the net proceeds and the selling expense per share after these selling expenses are deducted: commissions 4%, legal fees $2,255,500, advertising $450,000, printing costs $324,400, accounting fees $386,600 and miscellaneous expenses of $355,000.

11. ALGEBRA Net proceeds of $34.875 million were realized on the sale of 1 million shares of Worldwide stock. The underwriting commission is 5.5% and other expenses totaled 1.5% of the value of the stock. Find the value of the stock and the price per share.

12. ALGEBRA Certified Underwriters received a commission of $780,000 on 1.2 million shares of Molded Plastics Company stock. Certified Underwriters charges 7.5% commission. Assuming no other expenses, find the value of the stock offering, the price per share of Molded Plastics Company stock, and the net proceeds.

Spiral Review

Find the percentage. (Skill 30)

13. 6.5% of $980,000 **14.** 6% of $743,000 **15.** 5.5% of $1.5 million

16. Find the total program cost: Engineer's fee for 35 hours at $65.50 per hour, computer programmer has a $5,000 flat fee, and computer time is a $2,450 flat fee. (Lesson 17.6)

GET READY for the Next Lesson

PREREQUISITE SKILL Writing Percents as Decimals (Skill 28)

Write the percents as decimals.

17. 4.6% **18.** 580% **19.** 0.73%

20. 1.05% **21.** 110% **22.** $\frac{8}{10}$%

LESSON 19.3 Borrowing

Lesson Objective
Determine the maturity value of a commercial loan.

Content Vocabulary
- commercial loan
- maturity value
- prime rate

As You Read
Identify What is the prime rate on a loan?

GET READY for the Lesson

What type of business might you want to start?

Audrey Coble and Dan Chow are opening a hair salon. They obtained a commercial loan to pay for new equipment and to renovate the retail space.

Borrowing Your business may borrow money to buy raw materials, **chemicals**, products, or equipment. **Commercial loans**, or business loans, are similar to personal loans. The **maturity value** of your loan is the total amount you repay. The maturity value includes both the principal borrowed and the interest owed on the loan.

Prime Rate on a Loan Commercial loans usually have interest rates that are 1% to 2% higher than the **prime rate**. The prime rate is the lowest rate of interest available to commercial customers at a given time.

The interest on commercial loans is usually *ordinary interest at exact time.* That is, the length of time of the loan is calculated by dividing the exact number of days of the loan by 360 days.

Interest = Principal × Rate × Time

Maturity Value = Principal + Interest Owed

EXAMPLE 1

Collins' Drugstore borrowed $80,000 from First National Bank to pay for remodeling. The bank lent the money at 2% above the prime rate of 7%. The loan is ordinary interest for 60 days. What is the maturity value of the loan?

Step 1: Find the interest owed.

Principal × Rate × Time

$\$80{,}000 \times (7\% + 2\%) \times \frac{60}{360} = \frac{\$432{,}000}{360} = \$1{,}200 =$ **$1,200 interest**

Step 2: Find the maturity value.

Principal + Interest Owed

$80,000 + $1,200 = **$81,200 maturity value**

80000 M+ × 9 % × 60 ÷ 360 = 1200 + RM = 81200

ImageSource/age fotostock

The prime rate is 7%. Find the (a) interest and (b) maturity value. Check your answers in the back of the book.

1. Borrowed $100,000 at 3% over prime, ordinary interest for 100 days.
2. Borrowed $150,000 at 2.5% over prime, ordinary interest for 140 days.

Need Help? Go to...
Workshop 38: Problem-Solving Strategy: Writing an Equation, p. 78

EXAMPLE 2 Algebra

The maturity value of a 4-year, 6.5% ordinary interest commercial loan is $1,228,500. Find the principal.

Step 1: Let p = the principal

Step 2: Use the formula for Maturity Value, substituting for Interest, and solve.

Maturity Value = Principal + (Principal × Rate × Time)

$\$1{,}228{,}500 = p + (p \times 6.5\% \times 4)$

Multiply → $\$1{,}228{,}500 = p + 0.26p$

Combine like terms → $\$1{,}228{,}500 = 1.26p$

Divide both sides by 1.26 → $\mathbf{\$975{,}000} = p$

The principal is $975,000.

Concept CHECK

Complete the problem. Check your answer in the back of the book.

3. Pappas Motor Freight Company has a 5-year, 6.0% ordinary interest commercial loan from Second Financial Bank. The maturity value of the loan is $1.625 million. What is the principal of the loan?

Study Tip

Study Partners
Working with a study partner who is good with numbers can help you gain experience and confidence with math.

Lesson Practice

Use ordinary interest at exact time to complete the table.

	Principal	Rate	Time in Days	Interest	Maturity Value
4.	$ 70,000	6.00%	90	a.	b.
5.	$ 95,000	7.50%	100	a.	b.
6.	$ 37,500	12.50%	120	a.	b.
7.	$300,000	10.50%	270	a.	b.

For Problems 8 and 9, find the (a) interest and (b) maturity value of the loan.

8. The amount borrowed for 60 days is $64,000. The interest rate is 3% ordinary interest over prime. The prime rate is 7%.
9. The amount borrowed for 180 days is $37,650. The interest rate is 1.75% ordinary interest over prime. The prime rate is 6.85%.
10. Trust Bank lent $190,000 to Fernandez Home Builders. The term of the loan was 270 days. The interest rate was 3.5% ordinary interest over prime. What was the maturity value of the loan? (The prime rate is 5.25%.)

Did You Know?

Bike-Friendly Cities
***Bicycling* magazine recently named Portland, Oregon, the United States' best overall city for bicycling. For cities with over 1 million residents, San Diego, California, was voted the most bike-friendly, followed by Chicago and New York. Davis, California, took the prize among towns with fewer than 75,000 residents.**

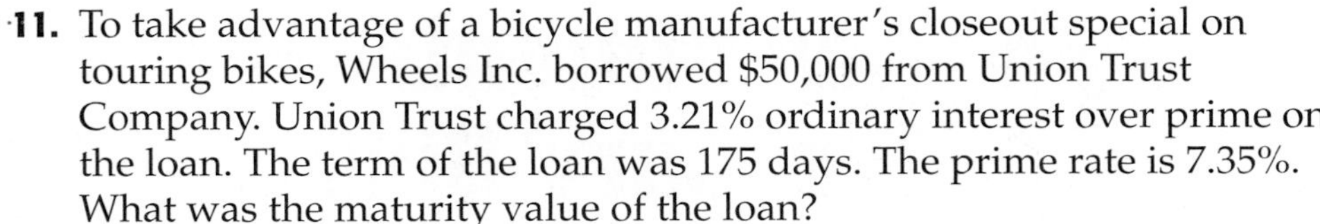

11. To take advantage of a bicycle manufacturer's closeout special on touring bikes, Wheels Inc. borrowed \$50,000 from Union Trust Company. Union Trust charged 3.21% ordinary interest over prime on the loan. The term of the loan was 175 days. The prime rate is 7.35%. What was the maturity value of the loan?

12. The North Company negotiated a \$35 million loan to completely remodel the Southwest Mall. They borrowed the money from Cap City Finance Company for 5 years at 0.8% ordinary interest over prime. What was the maturity value of the loan if the prime rate is 4.6%?

13. The Gibraltar Construction Manufacturing Company was granted a 1-year construction loan of \$650,000 to finance the construction of an apartment complex. Gibraltar borrowed the money from Citizens Trust Company at an interest rate of 0.75% ordinary interest over prime. What was the maturity value of the loan if the prime rate is 9.75%?

14. The Solar Panel Manufacturing Company needs \$1,450,000 for 270 days to help finance the production of an experimental solar hot water heater. The financial manager has arranged financing from three sources. Each loan charges ordinary interest at exact time. The prime is 7.15%.

Lending Institution	Amount of Loan	Time	Interest Rate
Swancreek Trust Company	\$500,000	270 days	2.50% over prime
Universal Investment Company	\$450,000	270 days	2.45% over prime
Investment Bankers, Inc.	\$500,000	270 days	2.25% over prime

(a) Determine the interest for each loan and the total interest.
(b) Determine the maturity value for each loan and the total maturity value.

H.O.T. Problems

15. ALGEBRA The Wonder Works wants to expand its facility. Wonder secures a \$1.2 million loan at 2.00% above prime. The loan is for 3 years. Find the prime rate if the maturity value of the loan is \$1.479 million.

16. ALGEBRA The maturity value of a 6-year, 7.2% ordinary interest commercial loan is \$2,076,400. Find the principal.

Spiral Review

Write the percents as decimals. (Skill 28)

17. 12.7% **18.** 340% **19.** 0.6% **20.** $\frac{7}{10}$%

21. The Mathematics Development House purchased a color laser printer that cost \$9,210. The life of the printer is estimated to be 4 years. The total salvage value after 4 years of use is estimated to be \$825. Using the straight-line method, find the annual depreciation of the laser printer. (Lesson 18.5)

GET READY for the Next Lesson

PREREQUISITE SKILL Dividing Decimals (Skill 10)

Divide. Round to the nearest thousandth.

22. 83 ÷ 9 **23.** 223 ÷ 48 **24.** 6.53 ÷ 100
25. 9.6 ÷ 30 **26.** 850 ÷ 7 **27.** 571.85 ÷ 1,500

LESSON 19.4

Investments—Treasury Bills

Lesson Objective

Determine the cost and yield of a Treasury bill.

Content Vocabulary

- Treasury bill
- discount
- face value
- yield

GET READY for the Lesson

What would you do if your business had excess cash?

Business is good at J&P Electronics. The company is growing and money is in the bank. Owners Jason and Penelope Whitcomb, wanting a safe way to invest some of that extra money, have decided to purchase a few Treasury bills that they can cash in at different times.

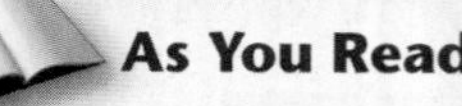

As You Read

Explain What is the face value of a Treasury bill?

Treasury Bills To **maximize** profits, your business may invest surplus cash that is not needed for day-to-day operations. One way to invest your money is to purchase a U.S. **Treasury bill** (or T-bill). You may purchase the bills through a bank or online. When you purchase a Treasury bill, you are actually lending money to the government. In return, you receive interest at the rate that is in effect at the time you purchase the bill. The interest is ordinary interest at exact time. Treasury bills are issued on a **discount** basis. That is, the interest is computed and then subtracted from the **face value** of the bill to determine the cost of the bill. The face value of the Treasury bill is the amount of money you will receive on the maturity date of the bill. Maturity dates for Treasury bills range from 30 days to a year.

You can calculate the **yield** on your Treasury bill by a formula. Yield is the rate of return (usually expressed as a percent) earned by an investor who holds a bond for a certain period of time.

$$\text{Cost of a Treasury Bill} = (\text{Face Value of Bill} - \text{Interest}) + \text{Service Fee}$$

$$\text{Yield} = \frac{\text{Interest}}{\text{Cost} \times \text{Time}}$$

EXAMPLE

The financial manager of the Osinski Manufacturing Company has decided to invest the company's surplus cash in a $100,000 U.S. Treasury bill for 120 days. The interest rate is 6%. The bank charges a service fee of $25 to obtain the Treasury bill. What is the cost of the Treasury bill? What is the yield for the Treasury bill?

Step 1: Find the interest.

$$\text{Principal} \times \text{Rate} \times \text{Time}$$

$$\$100{,}000 \times 6\% \times \frac{120}{360} = \$2{,}000$$

Study Tip

Index
When looking for information on a topic in a book, check the index. Pages on which topics are discussed are listed next to the topic name. Topics covered in the book are listed in alphabetical order.

Step 2: Find the cost of the Treasury bill.

Face Value of Bill − Interest + Service Fee

$100,000 − $2,000 + $25 = **$98,025 cost of the Treasury bill**

Step 3: Find the yield.

$\frac{\text{Interest}}{\text{Cost} \times \text{Time}} = \frac{\$2{,}000}{\$98{,}025 \times \frac{120}{360}} = \frac{\$2{,}000}{\$32{,}675} = 0.061208 =$ **6.121% Treasury bill yield**

Concept CHECK

Use ordinary interest at exact time to find the (a) interest, (b) cost, and (c) yield of the Treasury bill. Check your answers in the back of the book.

1. $120,000 T-bill at 4.00% interest for 30 days. Service fee is $35.
2. $200,000 T-bill at 3.75% interest for 90 days. Service fee is $50.

Lesson Practice

For Problems 3–8, use ordinary interest at exact time to find the (a) interest, (b) cost, and (c) yield of the Treasury bill. Round the yield to the nearest thousandth.

	Face Value of Treasury Bill	Interest Rate	Time in Days		Interest	Bank Service Fee		Cost of Treasury Bill		Yield
3.	$ 70,000	3.74%	30	a.		$25	b.		c.	
4.	$100,000	5.75%	120	a.		$35	b.		c.	
5.	$150,000	2.35%	180	a.		No fee	b.		c.	
6.	$ 85,000	4.23%	91	a.		$30	b.		c.	

7. A company invested its surplus cash in a $60,000 U.S. Treasury bill for 120 days at 3.78%. The bank charges a service fee of $30 to obtain the Treasury bill.

8. **CHALLENGE PROBLEM** The fiscal manager of Lone Star Office Supplies invested the company's extra first-quarter cash in a $200,000 U.S. Treasury bill for 180 days. The interest rate is 4.85%. The bank charges a service fee of 0.02% of the value of the Treasury bill.

Spiral Review

Multiply or divide. Round answers to the nearest thousandth. (Skill 8, 10)

9. 7.475 × 8.1 **10.** 0.57 × 0.41 **11.** 971 ÷ 40

12. ALGEBRA Alisha Reed earns $53,600 per year, is married, and pays $2,728 in state income tax yearly. She claims no other dependents. What is her state's state income tax rate? Hint: She does not pay income tax on her first $4,000. (Lesson 2.2)

GET READY for the Next Lesson

PREREQUISITE SKILL Finding the Rate (Skill 31)

Find the rate. Round answers to the nearest tenth of a percent.

13. $4.85 is what percent of $125.00? **14.** $15.60 is what percent of $98.00?

15. $854 is what percent of $14,600.50? **16.** $6.75 is what percent of $500.50?

LESSON 19.5

Inflation

Lesson Objective
Compute the inflation rate, the current price, and the original price.

Content Vocabulary
- inflation
- deflation

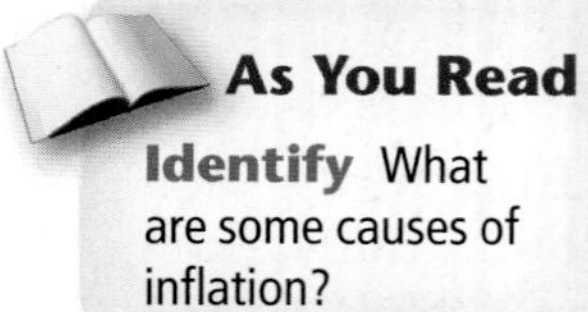
As You Read
Identify What are some causes of inflation?

GET READY for the Lesson

Have you noticed price increases or decreases in goods and services?

Caroline Vinton is a telephone booking agent for a major airline. She knows that because the price of jet fuel has sharply increased, the airlines must raise fares to stay in business.

Inflation Economies go through ups and downs as a result of wars, foreign competition, and changes in **technology**. One way to measure economic activity is by the rate of inflation. **Inflation** is the general increase in the cost of goods and services. At the corporate level, inflation is observed as increases in wholesale prices, cost of utilities, cost of production and shipping, and higher demand for scarce materials. Some of the causes of inflation are heavy spending (resulting in high demand), increased production costs as producers try to maintain profit levels, and lack of competition.

Deflation Rate When the supply of goods is greater than the demand, the result is **deflation**. Deflation occurs when prices decrease over a period of time. Although deflation is the opposite of inflation, the calculations are quite similar. The following formulas are used:

$$\text{Inflation Rate} = \frac{(\text{Current Price} - \text{Original Price})}{\text{Original Price}}$$

[Note: If the current price minus the original is a *negative* number, then you have calculated the rate of deflation. The rate is usually calculated to the nearest tenth of a percent.]

$$\text{Current Price} = \text{Original Price} + (\text{Original Price} \times \text{Inflation Rate})$$

$$\text{Original Price} = \frac{\text{Current Price}}{(1 + \text{Inflation Rate})}$$

EXAMPLE

Liza Turner works in the summer as a junior staff reporter for the local newspaper. Liza was asked to write a story about changes in the economy. One section was on inflation and deflation. She had the following data:

I. A two-door car sold for $18,000 two years ago. The same model, comparably equipped, sells for $18,495 today. Find the inflation rate.

II. The selling price of an air-conditioning unit in Florida last year was \$6,700. The inflation rate for air conditioning units in Florida this year was 5%. Find the current selling price.

III. A single apartment at the local state university rents for \$2,110 per semester this year. This reflects a 5.5% inflation rate increase over the original rent last year. Find the original rent.

IV. A laptop computer sold for \$1,495 last year and is selling for \$1,195 this year. Find the deflation rate.

Step 1: Find the inflation rate for the two-door car.

$$\frac{(\text{Current Price} - \text{Original Price})}{\text{Original Price}}$$

$$\frac{(\$18{,}495 - \$18{,}000)}{\$18{,}000} = \frac{\$495}{\$18{,}000} = 0.0275 = \textbf{2.8\% inflation rate}$$

Step 2: Find the current selling price of an air-conditioning unit in Florida.

Original Price + (Original Price × Inflation Rate)

\$6,700 + (\$6,700 × 5%) =

\$6,700 + \$335 = **\$7,035 current selling price**

Step 3: Find the original rent.

$$\frac{\text{Current Rent}}{(1 + \text{Inflation Rate})} = \frac{2{,}110}{(1.00 + 0.055)} = \textbf{\$2,000 original rent}$$

Step 4: Find the deflation rate for the laptop.

$$\frac{(\text{Current Price} - \text{Original Price})}{\text{Original Price}}$$

$$\frac{(1{,}195 - 1{,}495)}{1{,}495} = \frac{-300}{1{,}495} = -0.20066 = \textbf{−20.1\% deflation rate}$$

[Note: The negative sign indicates deflation.]

Concept CHECK

Complete the problems. Check your answers in the back of the book.

1. Orange juice: original price was \$3.50. Current price is \$3.65. Find the inflation rate.
2. 20-HP tractor: original price was \$12,400. Inflation rate is 6.2%. Find the current price.
3. Theater ticket: current price is \$28.05. Inflation rate is 5.1%. Find the original price.
4. Leather jacket: original price was \$498. Current price is \$458. Find the deflation rate.

Study Tip

Tables

When you look at a table, think about the story it tells. The table on the right says that two factors are considered when determining the current price of some goods: original price and inflation rate.

Lesson Practice

Complete the table. Round to the nearest tenth.

	Item	Inflation Rate	Current Price	Original Price
5.	Groceries	a.	\$ 467.00	\$ 438.98
6.	Office Paper	a.	\$ 79.99	\$ 78.79
7.	Hotel Room	5.0%	a.	\$ 147.00
8.	Compact Car	3.6%	a.	\$17,458.00
9.	Beverage	0.7%	\$ 1.29	a.
10.	Heating Fuel	12.4%	\$8,750.00	a.

11. Work Boots: original price: \$146.95. Current price: \$158.49. Find the inflation rate.
12. Batteries: original price: \$3.50. Inflation rate: 8.4%. Find the current price.
13. Oak Table: current price: \$960. Inflation rate: 6.3%. Find the original price.
14. Flat Screen TV: original price: \$4,378. Current price: \$3,590. Find the deflation rate.
15. The inflation rate over the past year for grocery products has been 5.7%. How much would a cart of groceries cost today if it cost \$172.70 last year?
16. The median cost to heat a small house in New York was \$1,530 last year. This year the median cost to heat the house is \$1,720. Find the rate of inflation.
17. At the grand opening of the Bayview Market in 1938, a 10-ounce box of cereal cost \$0.10. Today the box costs \$4.99. What is the inflation rate for cereal over that time period?
18. At Bayview Market a quart of milk could be purchased for \$0.11 in 1938. The inflation rate for milk since that time has been 1,255%. What does a quart of milk cost today?
19. At Bayview Market 1 pound of coffee costs \$10.99 today. The rate of inflation for coffee since 1938 has been 1,795.2%. What did 1 pound of coffee cost in 1938?

20. **WRITING IN MATH** Last year a new car sold for \$24,950. A comparably equipped car sells this year for \$22,500.
    (a) What can be said about the inflation rate when the current price is less than the original price?
    (b) What is the deflation rate?

Spiral Review

Find the rate. Round answers to the nearest tenth of a percent. (Skill 31)

21. \$12.85 is what percent of \$257.00?
22. \$3.79 is what percent of \$199.99?
23. **ALGEBRA** Michelle Juan had total travel expenses of \$512. Her transportation cost \$237 and her lodging \$219, and she had additional costs, excluding meals, of \$25. If dinner cost twice as much as lunch, how much was her lunch? How much was her dinner? (Lesson 13.6)

GET READY for the Next Lesson

PREREQUISITE SKILL Finding the Percentage (Skill 30)

Find the percentage. Round answers to the nearest cent.

24. \$151,420 × 3.2%
25. \$245,680 × 4.5%
26. \$49,213,659 × 0.6%
27. \$519.8 million × 5.3%
28. \$989,650,131 × 0.09%
29. \$6.3 billion × 1.2%

LESSON 19.6 Gross Domestic Product

Lesson Objective
Explain and compute the gross domestic product.

Content Vocabulary
- gross domestic product (GDP)
- real GDP
- per capita GDP

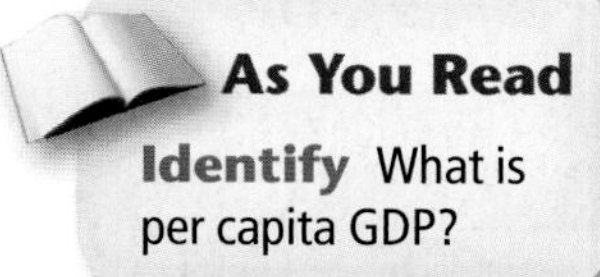

Identify What is per capita GDP?

Reading Math +−÷=

Large Numbers Large numbers can be simplified by rewriting them as decimals. For example, 16,093,400,000 = 16.0934 billion.

Need Help? Go to... Skill 1: Numbers as Decimals, p. SK1

GET READY for the Lesson

How do you contribute to the U.S. economy?

Thompson Construction is known for building luxury homes. Thomson's business is just one of the many thousands driving the U.S. economy today.

Gross Domestic Product An important measure of the country's economic health is its level of *productivity*, or how much it produces. The total value of the goods and services produced in a country in a given year is called its **gross domestic product (GDP)**. Only goods (such as automobiles, machinery, food, and clothing) and services (such as haircuts and appliance repairs) add to the national income. The government uses the GDP to monitor the health of the country's economy.

Real GDP You need to track GDP over a period of time. The effects of inflation and a change in GDP represent increases in production and income. For these reasons, you need to remove the **distortions** of inflation. You can do this by computing **real GDP** (or *adjusted GDP*).

Population and GDP The rate of the population growth influences GDP and economic growth. Labor and size of population are closely linked. Shifts in population can alter economic measures such as GDP. That is why GDP is often measured on a per capita (or per person) basis. The **per capita GDP** indicates the nation's *standard of living*—the amount of goods and services the average citizen can afford to buy. The per capita GDP is the GDP distributed over the population. The following formulas are used:

$$\text{Real GDP} = \text{GDP} - (\text{GDP} \times \text{Inflation Rate})$$

$$\text{Per Capita GDP} = \frac{\text{GDP}}{\text{Population}}$$

EXAMPLE

The United States has an inflation rate of 3.2%, a population of 301,139,947 and a GDP of $12.41 trillion. What is the real GDP? What is the per capita GDP?

Step 1: Find the real GDP.

GDP − (GDP × Inflation Rate)

$12.41 trillion − ($12.41 trillion × 3.2%) = $12.41 trillion − $0.39712 trillion = **$12.01288 trillion**

Continued on next page

Step 2: Find the per capita GDP.

$$\frac{\text{GDP}}{\text{Population}} = \frac{\$12,410,000,000,000}{301,139,947} = \$41,210$$

[Note: The per capita GDP is usually rounded to the nearest dollar.]

Complete the problems. Check your answers in the back of the book.
The island country of Fiji has a GDP of $5,594,000,000, an inflation rate of 7.6%, and a population of 918,675.

1. Calculate the real GDP.
2. Calculate the per capita GDP. (Round to the nearest dollar.)

Lesson Practice

For Problems 3–5, calculate the (a) real GDP and (b) per capita GDP.

	Country	GDP	Inflation Rate	Population	Real GDP	Per Capita GDP
3.	Bahamas	$ 5,696,000,000	1.2%	305,700	a.	b.
4.	Germany	$2,454,000,000,000	2.0%	82,401,000	a.	b.
5.	Ireland	$ 136,900,000,000	2.7%	4,109,000	a.	b.

For Problems 6–9, calculate the (a) real GDP and (b) per capita GDP.

6. Denmark has a GDP of $181.6 billion (or $181,600,000,000). The inflation rate is 2.8%. The population is 5,468,000.
7. Cuba has a GDP of $45,510,000,000. Population is 11,417,000. The inflation rate is 5%.
8. Australia has a population of 20,434,000 and a GDP of $642 billion. The inflation rate is 2.7%.
9. The population of China is 1,321,851,888. China's GDP is $10,170,000,000,000, and the inflation rate is 1.5%.

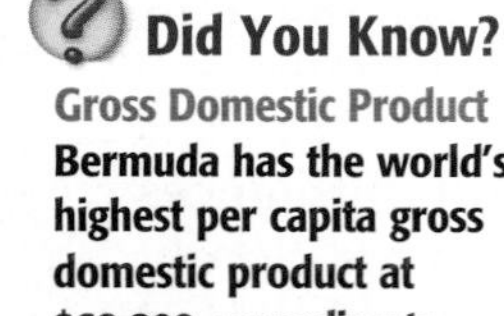

Gross Domestic Product
Bermuda has the world's highest per capita gross domestic product at $69,800, according to recent figures.

10. **CHALLENGE PROBLEM** A few years ago, Argentina had a GDP of $289.1 billion and a reported inflation rate of 3,079%.
    (a) What real GDP do you get using the formula?
    (b) Why is this impossible?

Spiral Review

Multiply. Round answers to the nearest cent. (Skill 8)

11. 234.3 × $45.75 **12.** 156.8 × $378.89 **13.** 112.4 × $7.89

14. ALGEBRA Tia Waspover is an office manager. She earns $15.40 per hour. How many hours per week must she work if she wants to earn approximately $595.00 per week? (Lesson 1.1)

GET READY for the Next Lesson

PREREQUISITE SKILL Multiplying Decimals (Skill 8)

Multiply. Round answers to the nearest cent.

15. 210.3 × $15.31 **16.** 430.7 × $7.67 **17.** 135.2 × $181.29

LESSON 19.7

Consumer Price Index

Lesson Objective

Calculate the consumer price index, the current cost, and the cost of any given commodity.

Content Vocabulary

- consumer price index (CPI)

GET READY for the Lesson

What factors affect what you are willing to pay for goods and services?

While looking through an old magazine for a science project, Brian Torres saw an advertisement for an automobile priced at $11,775. Brian wondered how much the car would have cost in "today's" money.

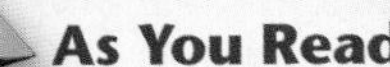

As You Read

Explain What does consumer price index measure?

Consumer Price Index To remove the distortions of inflation, economists construct a **statistical** series to measure changes in prices over time. They start by selecting a base year. This base year serves as a comparison point for all other years. To track inflation, you have to track the price of goods and services at regular intervals and then compare them to the base year. The **consumer price index (CPI)** measures the upward changes for a fixed number of commodities and services, such as housing, electricity, food, and transportation. It is also known as the *cost-of-living index*.

The CPI reports on the price change for about 90,000 items in 364 categories. The Bureau of Labor Statistics measures items in terms of their 1982-84 base-period prices. The CPI for 1983 is set at 100. This is important when computing today's CPI.

$$\text{CPI} = \frac{\text{Current Cost}}{\text{Cost in 1983}} \times 100$$

$$\text{Current Cost} = \frac{\text{Cost in 1983} \times \text{CPI}}{100}$$

$$\text{Cost in Base Year} = \frac{\text{Current Cost}}{\text{CPI}} \times 100$$

EXAMPLE 1

Claudia Smith was asked to write a story about the CPI. She had the following data:

- The current cost of a briefcase is $94.50. The cost in 1983 was $41.27. What is the CPI for the briefcase?
- The cost in 1983 of a good pair of socks was $3.75. The CPI for socks is 131.3. What is the current cost of the socks?
- The current cost of a tire is $124.00. The CPI for tires is 112.3. What was the cost of the tire in 1983?

Step 1: Find the CPI for the briefcase.

$$\frac{\text{Current Cost}}{\text{Cost in 1983}} \times 100 = \frac{\$94.50}{\$41.27} \times 100 = 228.979 = \textbf{229.0 CPI for briefcase}$$

Continued on next page

Step 2: Find the current cost of the sport socks.

$$\frac{\text{Cost in 1983} \times \text{CPI}}{100} = \frac{\$3.75 \times 131.3}{100} = \$4.92375 = \textbf{\$4.92 current cost}$$

Step 3: Find the cost of the tire in 1983.

$$\frac{\text{Current Cost}}{\text{CPI}} \times 100 = \frac{\$124}{112.3} \times 100 = \$110.418 = \textbf{\$110.42 cost of tire}$$

Study Tip

Plan Ahead

Research shows that cramming for a test is not effective. A better strategy is to plan out your studying, study a little each day, and get plenty of sleep before a test.

Concept CHECK

Complete the problem. Check your answer in the back of the book.

1. Using the data from **Example 1**, what was the CPI for the briefcase five years ago if it cost $82.54 at that time?

EXAMPLE 2

Figure 19.2 gives the composite CPI for the years 1983 through 2010. Use it to find:

The cost in 2008 of an auto that sold for $11,980 in 1983.

The cost in 1983 of an apartment that rents for $1,495 in 2005.

The cost in 1995 of a house that sold for $127,500 in 2002.

Figure 19.2

Year	CPI	Year	CPI	Year	CPI	Year	CPI
1983	100.0	1990	130.7	1997	161.3	2004	190.3
1984	103.9	1991	136.2	1998	163.9	2005	196.8
1985	107.6	1992	140.3	1999	168.3	2006	201.8
1986	109.6	1993	145.8	2000	174.0	2007	208.5
1987	113.6	1994	149.7	2001	176.7	2008	213.7
1988	118.3	1995	153.5	2002	180.9	2009	219.1
1989	124.0	1996	158.9	2003	184.3	2010	224.5

Note: 2008-2010 are estimates

Step 1: Find the cost of the auto in 2008.

$$\frac{\text{Cost in 1983} \times \text{CPI}}{100} = \frac{\$11{,}980 \times 213.7}{100} = \textbf{—\$25.601.26 cost of auto}$$

Step 2: Find the cost of the rent in 1983.

$$\frac{\text{Current Cost}}{\text{CPI}} \times 100 = \frac{\$1{,}495}{196.8} \times 100 = \$759.654 = \textbf{\$759.65 cost of rent}$$

Step 3: Find the cost of the house in 1995.

A. First find the cost in 1983.

$$\frac{\text{Current Cost}}{\text{CPI}} \times 100 = \frac{\$127{,}500}{180.9} \times 100 = \$70{,}480.928 = \$70{,}480.93 \text{ 1983 cost of the house}$$

B. Then find the cost in 1995.

$$\frac{\text{Cost in 1983} \times \text{CPI}}{100} = \frac{\$70{,}480.93 \times 153.5}{100} = \$108{,}188.2276 = \textbf{\$108,188.23 1995 cost of the house}$$

Concept CHECK

Complete the problem. Check your answer in the back of the book.

2. The price of a pound of bananas in 1983 was $0.27 a pound. Using the CPI table in **Figure 19.2,** what was the price in 2000?

Lesson Practice

Complete the table. Round answers to the nearest cent.

	Item	CPI	Current Cost	Cost in 1983
3.	Sport coat		$135.29	$ 74.95
4.	Dinner for two		$ 45.75	$ 21.50
5.	Condo Rent	237.1		$325.00
6.	Lawn mower	91.2		$425.50
7.	Pet Food	180.5	$ 15.85	
8.	Newspaper	122.6	$ 1.25	

Did You Know?

Film Production Costs

Due partly to exotic filming locations and star Elizabeth Taylor's life-threatening illness, the 1963 movie "Cleopatra" is famous for being very expensive. Originally budgeted at $2 million, the film ended up costing as much as $44 million to make—about $300 million in today's dollars.

9. Current cost of a movie: $8.20. Cost in 1983: $5.60. Find the CPI.

10. Ice Cream cost $1.22 in 1983. The CPI is 186.1. What is the current cost?

11. The CPI for roasted coffee is 182.3. The current cost is $8.29. Find the cost in 1983.

Use Figure 19.3 of specific CPI indicators for Problems 12–17.

Figure 19.3

Indicators of Specific Items	
Commodity	**CPI**
Fuel oil	261.7
Electricity	177.4
Rent	238.9
Home Insurance	116.6
Groceries	205.8
Handheld calculator	96.5
Computer Software	51.5
Cell phone	37.9

12. In 1983 Lucas Applewhite paid $14,500 annually for electricity. What would he pay today?

13. In 1983 the Johnsons paid $650 for home insurance. What would they pay today?

14. In 1983 the Johnson family paid $94.70 for their weekly groceries. How much could the Johnsons expect to pay for their weekly groceries today?

15. Last month's fuel oil bill for the Crowley family was $256.36. What would the Crowleys have paid for the same amount of fuel oil in 1983?

16. Juan and Maria Ellias spent $187.90 for an accounting computer software program. How much would they have spent in 1983 for similar software?

17. Alice McCarty pays $85 per month for her cell phone. What would McCarty have paid in 1983 for a cell phone?

18. Use **Figure 19.2** to find the cost in 1990 of a house that sold for $858,500 in 2008.

19. WRITING IN MATH The composite CPIs found in **Figure 19.2** have always increased from one year to the next. **(a)** How would you describe the economy for the 28 year span from 1983 to 2010? **(b)** Explain what it would mean if the CPI for 2011 was 220.0.

Spiral Review

Divide. Round answers to the nearest hundredth. (Skill 11)

20. $234.50 ÷ $78.25 **21.** $24.79 ÷ $18.45 **22.** $2.49 ÷ $5.79

23. ALGEBRA Andre Klum earned $112.00 in simple interest in 9 months at an annual interest rate of 4.75%. How much money did he invest? (Lesson 5.4)

CHAPTER 19 Review and Assessment

AFTER YOU READ

Chapter SUMMARY

Companies have to make many calculations to manage their taxes, investments, and loans. You can compute the taxable income and the corporate income tax. You may want to calculate the selling expenses and the net proceeds from an issue of stocks or bonds. You can also calculate the maturity value of a commercial loan and the cost and yield of a Treasury bill. You can compute the inflation rate and the current original price of specific items. You can find the gross domestic product, the consumer price index, the current cost, and the cost of any given commodity.

Vocabulary Check

1. On a sheet of paper, use each of these terms in a sentence.

Content Vocabulary

- corporation (p. 707)
- taxable income (p. 707)
- stocks (p. 710)
- bonds (p. 710)
- underwriting commission (p. 710)
- prospectus (p. 710)
- commercial loan (p. 713)
- maturity value (p. 713)
- prime rate (p. 713)
- Treasury bill (p. 716)
- discount (p. 716)
- face value (p. 716)
- yield (p. 716)
- inflation (p. 718)
- deflation (p. 718)
- gross domestic product (GDP) (p. 721)
- real GDP (p. 721)
- per capita GDP (p. 721)
- consumer price index (CPI) (p. 723)

Academic Vocabulary

- vary (p. 707)
- legal (p. 710)
- chemical (p. 713)
- maximize (p. 716)
- technology (p. 718)
- distortion (p. 721)
- statistical (p. 723)

Concept Check

2. Explain how to find taxable income.
3. Explain how to find the net proceeds from an issue of stocks or bonds.
4. Identify what is included in the maturity value.
5. Identify the formula for determining yield of a Treasury bill.
6. Differentiate between inflation and deflation.
7. Explain how to compute the Consumer Price Index.
8. CRITICAL THINKING Explain the significance of the gross domestic product. How does a government use information about GDP?

Lesson-by-Lesson Review

19.1 Corporate Income Taxes (pp. 707–709)

Compute the taxable income and the corporate income tax.
Use **Figure 19.1** on page 707 to find the federal corporate income tax.

Gross Income: $175,000
Deductions: $38,000

Step 1: Find the taxable income.

Annual Gross Income − Deductions
$175,000 − $38,000 = $137,000 taxable income

Step 2: Find the federal corporate income tax. (Refer to **Figure 19.1** on page 707.)

The tax is $22,250 + 39% of the amount over $100,000.

$22,250 + 39% × ($137,000 − $100,000) =

$22,250 + $14,430 = **$36,680 federal corporate income tax**

Review Exercises

Refer to Figure 19.1 on page 707 for federal corporate income tax. Find the (a) taxable income and (b) total tax. Round to the nearest one dollar.

	Annual Gross Income	Deductions	Taxable Income	Total Tax
9.	$ 230,000	$ 82,371	a.	b.
10.	$ 512,054	$209,732	a.	b.
11.	$ 127,932	$ 85,403	a.	b.
12.	$ 983,210	$356,008	a.	b.
13.	$ 651,287	$410,911	a.	b.
14.	$1,800,529	$432,877	a.	b.
15.	$ 341,900	$ 99,812	a.	b.

16. The Westin Company has an annual gross income of $82,125. Deductions total $57,220. What is the federal corporate income tax?

17. Mark-Towns Manufacturing Corporation has an annual gross income of $406,921. Deductions total $274,821. What is the federal corporate income tax?

18. Campbell's Farm Co. has an annual gross income of $415,486. Deductions total $195,998. What is the federal corporate income tax?

19. McKinsey Equipment has an annual gross income of $1,000,568. Deductions total $701,000. What is the federal corporate income tax?

Lesson-by-Lesson Review (continued)

19.2 Issuing Stocks and Bonds (pp. 710–712)

Calculate the selling expenses and the net proceeds from an issue of stocks or bonds. Find the net proceeds and the cost per share for the following.

Value of stock: $7,000,000 for 500,000 shares
Commission: 4% of the value of the stock
Other selling expenses: 0.3% of the value of the stock

Step 1a: Find the underwriting commission.

Value of Issue × Percent of Underwriting Commission
$7,000,000 × 4% = $280,000 commission

Step 1b: Find the total selling expenses.

Other selling expenses = $7,000,000 × 0.3% = $21,000
Total selling expenses = $280,000 + $21,000 = $301,000

Step 2: Find the net proceeds.

Value of Issue − Total Selling Expenses
$7,000,000 − $301,000 = **$6,699,000 net proceeds**

Step 3: Find the cost per share.

$$\frac{\text{Total Selling Expenses}}{\text{Total Number of Shares}} = \frac{\$301{,}000}{500{,}000} = \$0.602 = \mathbf{\$0.60\ cost\ per\ share}$$

Review Exercises

Complete the table.

	Value of Issue	Percent	Commission Expenses	Other Expenses	Total Selling Expenses	Net Proceeds	Number of Shares	Selling Cost per Share
20.	$ 1,200,000	5%	a.	$ 38,600	b.	c.	35,000	d.
21.	$ 860,000	7%	a.	$ 45,980	b.	c.	27,000	d.
22.	$ 5,750,000	6.5%	a.	$ 73,500	b.	c.	150,000	d.
23.	$ 8,900,000	6%	a.	$120,000	b.	c.	190,000	d.
24.	$32,900,000	8%	a.	$ 98,500	b.	c.	1,150,000	d.
25.	$39,800,000	5.5%	a.	$110,500	b.	c.	1,500,000	d.

26. The McHenry Company issued 3,000,000 shares of stock as an initial public offering (IPO) at $17.50 per share. McHenry paid a 5% commission plus $2,500,000 in legal fees, $750,000 in advertising, $350,000 in printing costs, and $425,000 in accounting costs. Find **(a)** the net proceeds and **(b)** the selling expense per share.

27. **ALGEBRA** Mercil Investments earned $235,000 commission for selling 1.2 million shares of The Callicotte Company stock. The commission was 5% of the value of the stock. Find the value of the stock offering and the price of a share of The Callicotte Company stock.

Lesson-by-Lesson Review (continued)

19.3 Borrowing (pp. 713–715)

Determine the maturity value of a commercial loan.
Tristan's Department Store borrowed $130,000 from the bank to pay for a new line of clothing. The bank lent the money at 7% ordinary interest for 90 days. What was the maturity value of the loan?

Step 1: Find the interest owed.

Principal × Rate × Time

$\$130{,}000 \times 7\% \times \frac{90}{360} = \$2{,}275$ interest owed

Step 2: Find the maturity value.

Principal + Interest Owed

$130,000 + $2,275 = **$132,275 maturity value**

Review Exercises

Complete the table. Determine the ordinary interest and maturity value.

	Principal	Rate	Time in Days	Interest	Maturity Value
28.	$ 65,000	7.5%	90	a.	b.
29.	$110,000	6.0%	120	a.	b.
30.	$ 85,400	8.5%	100	a.	b.
31.	$250,000	7.5%	270	a.	b.
32.	$ 65,400	8.0%	90	a.	b.
33.	$800,500	9.5%	60	a.	b.

34. **ALGEBRA** The maturity value of a 3-year, 7.5% ordinary interest commercial loan is $1,056,562.50. Find the principal.

35. The Taustin Company was granted a 1-year construction loan of $750,000 to finance a construction project. Taustin borrowed the money from a bank at an interest rate of 0.65% ordinary interest over prime. What was the maturity value of the loan if the prime rate is 9.25%?

36. DB Mak & Company negotiated an $18 million dollar loan to build a shopping complex. They borrowed the money from Archen Associates for 5 years at 0.9% ordinary interest over prime. What was the maturity value of the loan if the prime rate is 5.9%?

Lesson-by-Lesson Review (continued)

19.4 Investments–Treasury Bills (pp. 716–717)

Determine the cost and yield of a Treasury bill.

Find the cost and the yield of a Treasury bill with a face value of $150,000 that was purchased at 5.5% ordinary interest for 60 days. The service fee was $40.

Step 1: Find the interest.

$$\text{Principal} \times \text{Rate} \times \text{Time}$$
$$\$150{,}000 \times 5.5\% \times \frac{60}{360} = \$1{,}375$$

Step 2: Find the cost of the Treasury bill.

$$\text{Face Value of Bill} - \text{Interest} + \text{Service Fee}$$
$$\$150{,}000 - \$1{,}375 + \$40 = \mathbf{\$148{,}665\ Treasury\ bill\ cost}$$

Step 3: Find the yield.

$$\frac{\text{Interest}}{\text{Cost} \times \text{Time}} = \frac{\$1{,}375}{\$148{,}665 \times \frac{60}{360}} = \frac{\$1{,}375}{\$24{,}777.50} = 0.055493 = \mathbf{5.549\%\ Treasury\ bill\ yield}$$

Review Exercises

Compute the (a) interest, (b) cost, and (c) yield of the Treasury bill. Round to the nearest thousandth.

	Face Value of Treasury Bill	Interest Rate	Time in Days	Interest	Bank Service Fee	Cost of Treasury Bill	Yield
37.	$ 35,000	5.00%	30	a.	$25	b.	c.
38.	$ 65,000	5.50%	60	a.	$30	b.	c.
39.	$100,000	3.43%	90	a.	$40	b.	c.
40.	$125,000	4.90%	120	a.	$50	b.	c.
41.	$ 75,000	4.80%	180	a.	$35	b.	c.
42.	$ 98,000	2.75%	82	a.	$60	b.	c.

43. The financial manager of Pacific Inc. invested the company's surplus cash in a $70,000 U.S. Treasury bill for 120 days. The interest rate is 4.28%. The bank charges a service fee of $35 to obtain the Treasury bill.

44. The financial manager of the Osaka Balloon Company has decided to invest the company's surplus cash in a $120,000 U.S. Treasury bill for 120 days. The interest rate is 5%. The bank charges a service fee of $25 to obtain the Treasury bill.

45. The financial manager of Hyte Inc. invested the company's surplus cash in a $100,000 U.S. Treasury bill for 120 days. The interest rate is 6%. The bank charges a service fee of $40 to obtain the Treasury bill.

Lesson-by-Lesson Review (continued)

19.5 Inflation (pp. 718–720)

Compute the inflation rate, the current price, and the original price.
The original price of an office chair was $95. The current price is $125. What is the inflation rate?

Find the inflation rate.

$$\text{Inflation Rate} = \frac{(\text{Current Price} - \text{Original Price})}{\text{Original Price}}$$

$$\text{Inflation Rate} = \frac{\$125 - \$95}{\$95} = \textbf{0.3157 or 31.6\% inflation rate}$$

Review Exercises

Complete the table.

	Item	Inflation Rate	Current Price	Original Price
46.	Food	a.	$467.00	$ 438.98
47.	Office Supplies	a.	$ 59.99	$ 58.79
48.	Airline tickets	6.0%	a.	$ 349.00
49.	Tuition	3.0%	a.	$2,676.00
50.	Candy Bar	0.7%	$ 1.59	a.
51.	Rent	2.7%	$850.00	a.

52. A three-bedroom condominium in Florida sold for $989,500 five years ago. The same condominium sold yesterday for $600,000. What is the deflation rate?

53. A new convertible sells today for $34,980. The inflation rate over the past year for this type of automobile was 5.4%. What did the convertible sell for one year ago?

19.6 Gross Domestic Product (pp. 721–722)

Explain and compute the gross domestic product.
Norway has an inflation rate of 2.1% and a GDP of $194.7 billion. The population of Norway is 4,628,000. What is the real GDP? What is the per capita GDP?

Step 1: Find the real GDP.

$$\text{GDP} - (\text{GDP} \times \text{Inflation Rate})$$

$$\$194{,}700{,}000{,}000 - (\$194{,}700{,}000{,}000 \times 2.1\%) =$$

$$\$194{,}700{,}000{,}000 - \$4{,}088{,}700{,}000 = \textbf{\$190,611,300,000 real GDP}$$

Step 2: Find the per capita GDP.

$$\frac{\text{GDP}}{\text{Population}} = \frac{194{,}700{,}000{,}000}{4{,}628{,}000} = \textbf{\$42,070 per capita GDP}$$

Lesson-by-Lesson Review (continued)

Review Exercises

Calculate: (a) the real GDP; (b) the per capita GDP.

	Country	GDP	Inflation Rate	Population	Real GDP	Per Capita GDP
54.	Saudi Arabia	$340,600,000,000	0.4%	27,601,000	a.	b.
55.	Belize	$ 1,778,000,000	3.8%	294,400	a.	b.
56.	Greenland	$ 1,100,000,000	1.6%	56,400	a.	b.
57.	Nigeria	$132,900,000,000	15.6%	135,031,000	a.	b.
58.	Poland	$489,800,000,000	3.5%	38,520,000	a.	b.
59.	Portugal	$196,300,000,000	2.4%	10,643,000	a.	b.

60. Guatemala has an inflation rate of 9.1%, a population of 12,293,545 and a GDP of $56.86 billion. What is the real GDP? What is the per capita GDP?

61. Argentina has an inflation rate of 8.3%, a population of 40,677,348 and a GDP of $483.5 billion. What is the real GDP? What is the per capita GDP?

19.7 Consumer Price Index (pp. 723–725)

Calculate the consumer price index, the current cost, and the cost of any given commodity.

The current cost of a pair of earrings is $36.99. The cost in 1983 was $21.95. What is the CPI?

Find the CPI: $\text{CPI} = \frac{\text{Current Cost}}{\text{Cost in 1983}} \times 100$

$\frac{\$36.99}{\$21.95} \times 100 = \mathbf{168.5\ CPI}$

Review Exercises

Complete the table. Round percents to the nearest tenth.

	Item	CPI	Current Cost	Cost in 1983
62.	Prom dress		$125.75	$ 98.50
63.	Cup of coffee		$ 1.75	$ 1.00
64.	Motorcycle	215.7		$7,495.00
65.	Sunglasses	150.2		$ 6.55
66.	Lipstick	103.6	$ 8.95	
67.	Tennis shoes	124.6	$ 85.65	

68. Using **Figure 19.2** on page 724, find the cost in 2007 of a house that sold for $43,990 in 1983.

69. An automobile that sold for $12,785 in 1989 would sell for how much in 2009? Use the composite CPI in **Figure 19.2** on page 724.

Practice Test

Record your answers on a sheet of paper.

1. Choi Motors had a gross income of $784,082 for the year. It had $669,980 in business expenses during the year. What is Choi Motors' taxable income?
   A $1,445,400 **B** $116,402
   C $1,454,062 **D** $114,102

2. **ALGEBRA** Chandler Investment earned a $385,000 commission for selling 1.1 million shares of stock. If the commission was 8% of the value of the stock, what was the value of the stock?
   A $3,850,000 **B** $4,812,500
   C $588,000 **D** $423,500

3. **ALGEBRA** The maturity value of a 5-year, 5.4% ordinary interest commercial loan is $743,712. What is the principal?
   A $585,600.00 **B** $40,160.45
   C $137,724.44 **D** $614,072.00

4. Amir Gnoska invested $125,000 in a U.S. Treasury bill for 90 days. The interest rate was 4.5% and the service fee was $60. What was the cost of the Treasury bill?
   A $123,593.75 **B** $125,060.00
   C $123,653.75 **D** $119,375.00

5. The median sale price of a home in Colorado last year was $136,800. The current median price is $145,300. What is the annual inflation rate for homes in Colorado?
   A 9.4% **B** 5.3%
   C 8.2% **D** 6.2%

6. A country has a GDP of $120.2 million and an inflation rate of 7.2%. What is the real GDP?
   A $111,545,600 **B** $8,654,400
   C $20,674,400 **D** $235,440,000

7. Melissa McCarty bought a running suit for $39.99 in 1983. The current cost of a comparable suit is $59.99. What is the CPI for the running suit?
   A 66.6 **B** 150.0
   C 20.0 **D** 176.5

8. Clough Tree Farms had a gross income of $142,500 for the year. Its business expenses totaled $58,788. What was Clough Farms' taxable income?
   A $201,288 **B** $125,300
   C $75,882 **D** $83,712

9. **ALGEBRA** Dervic Hardwood Flooring, Inc. received net proceeds of $1.4 million from the sale of additional shares of its $65.00 stock. The underwriting commission was 4.5% with additional expenses of $235,689.62. What was the value of the stock offering?

10. **ALGEBRA** Heidi Cortez borrowed $35,000 from National Bank of Springfield to remodel her store. The maturity value of the loan was $35,656.25. The ordinary interest loan was for 90 days. What was the interest rate of Heidi's loan?

11. Handz Sporting Goods had a gross income of $726,230 for the year. The business expenses for the year totaled $627,707. What is Handz Sporting Goods' taxable income?

12. A country has a GDP of $240.0 billion with a population of 15.6 million. What is the per capita GDP?

13. What percent of $46,780 is $2,947.14?

14. 713 × $5.98

15. 475,690 × 105%

16. $981,692.46 ÷ $44,521.20

17. 38% of $2.8 million

18. 586,419.4937 ÷ 28,972.15

Standardized Test Practice

Cumulative, Chapters 1–19

PART 1 Multiple Choice

Record your answers on the answer sheet provided by your teacher or on a sheet of paper.

1. Abbey Brooks' checking account has a balance of $5,631.84. If she withdrew $994.95, how much would remain in her account?

   A $4,636.89 **B** $6,626.74
   C $4,565.91 **D** $4,986.98

2. **ALGEBRA** Lindsey Koester took out a single-payment loan for $5,200 at 6.2% exact interest to help with her tuition. If the interest on the loan were $80.38, how long would she have to pay back the loan? Round your answer to the nearest whole number.

   A 90 days **B** 120 days
   C 121 days **D** 91 days

3. Holly Mistura owned a 1-year $12,000 certificate of deposit that was worth $12,718.20 at maturity. What was the annual percentage yield?

   A 5.775% **B** 5.565%
   C 5.985% **D** 0.059%

4. Jose Quintero's credit card charges 2.6% of the unpaid balance as a finance charge. If Jose's unpaid balance totaled $580, how much is the finance charge?

   A $16.99 **B** $15.08
   C $13.09 **D** $20.60

5. Franco's Family Fun rents party tents. The charge is $115.50 per day plus a $40 set-up fee. How much would it cost to rent a tent for 3 days?

   A $549.50 **B** $366.70
   C $456.50 **D** $386.50

TEST-TAKING TIP

Confidence On the day of a test, stay relaxed and confident. Remind yourself that you are well-prepared.

6. A bicycle was purchased for $329.99 and a helmet for $42.99. The sales tax rate is 8.25%. What is the total purchase price?

   A $357.21 **B** $372.98
   C $403.75 **D** $404.68

7. Silver Fox Racing receives a 20% trade discount from Lugg's Tires. How much would Silver Fox pay if it purchased a wheel with a list price of $475 from Lugg's?

   A $455 **B** $380
   C $305 **D** $463

PART 2 Short Response/Griddable

8. Janelle Bryant rented a compact car for 3 days at $38.99 per day plus $0.35 a mile over 150 miles. She purchased collision waiver insurance for $8.50 per day. She drove a total of 500 miles and paid $62.50 for gasoline. What was the total cost of renting the car?

9. Robinski Brakes has a 32% share of the brake pad market in the Denver area. Next year market sales are expected to be $776,875. What are Robinski's projected sales for next year?

10. Jencks Dance Studios purchased a new sound system for $1,923. The salvage value in 5 years is estimated to be $213. What is the book value of the system after 2 years (using the straight-line method)?

PART 3 Extended Response

Show your work.

11. Explain "gross domestic product (GDP)" and "real GDP."

12. What does the consumer price index (CPI) measure and on what is it based?

Building Academic Skills

Mathematics

Your company has decided to take out a short-term bank loan to upgrade its computer and communications equipment. To finance the equipment, the company needs $175,000 for 9 months. Because of the company's good credit rating and the short-term nature of the loan, the bank offers an interest rate of 2 points above prime. The current federal funds prime rate is 4.75%. What amount of interest will your company pay, and what will be the total maturity value of this loan?

English Language Arts/Writing

The Great Depression led to the passage of some major federal legislation. The federal Securities and Exchange Commission (SEC) was established to prevent some of the problems that resulted in the stock market crash that brought about the Depression. Use Internet sources, such as the SEC Web site, and library sources to research the purpose of the SEC. Write a brief report on the job of the SEC and give a few examples of some recent specific activities of this agency.

Social Studies/Economics

In a recent period, economists voiced concern about the possibility of a recession. One definition of a recession is a decline in any country's gross domestic product for two or more successive quarters of a year. The concern was that people were spending less on many things because of rising costs of certain essential goods and services, such as gasoline, fuel oil, and medical care. Use Internet or library sources to find out more about the effects of a recession and the reasons for the economists' concerns. Write a short report on your findings.

Building Real-World Skills

Ethics in Action

Using a Toll-Free Number You work in Chicago for a software developer that offers a toll-free number for customers and business associates. While at work you receive a call on your cell phone from a friend in Austin, Texas. You consider asking your friend to call you back, using the toll-free number.

Discuss and Write:

a. Discuss toll-free numbers. Are they actually "free"? Who pays for toll-free calls?

b. Write a list of factors other than the cost of one call that might affect whether you have your friend use the toll-free number.

21st Century Workplace

Coworking Self-employed professionals, frequent business travelers, and telecommuters often feel secluded. An emerging trend is "coworking," where a number of workers from different companies and different businesses get together to share space. They still do their separate work, but they share rent, utilities, and expenses.

Research and Write:

a. Use the Internet to locate and read a *BusinessWeek* article on coworking.

b. Write a brief essay explaining the possible benefits and drawbacks of coworking.

UNIT 6 Thematic Project

Business Services

In this project you will use a spreadsheet application to track and calculate business service costs.

Your Project Assignment

✓ Research a growing company.
✓ Brainstorm the service costs involved in operating a business.
✓ Use spreadsheet software to keep track of total rental costs.
✓ Create a 3–5 minute presentation.

	Commercial Rental Space	Rental Space Dimensions (in Feet)			Total Square Feet	Annual Rent per Sq. Ft.	Annual Rent	Monthly Rent
1	Fashion	100	×	50	5000	$ 6.00	$30,000.00	$2,500.00
2	Pet							
3	Deli							
4	Arcade							
5	Jewelry							
6	Grocery							
7	Video							
8	Shoes							

Skills Preview

Your success in tracking business services depends on your skills. Some skills you might use include:
Academic Skills reading, writing, and mathematics
Basic Skills speaking, listening, thinking, problem-solving, and interpersonal skills
Technology Skills word-processing, keyboarding, spreadsheet, presentation, and Internet skills

Go to **connectED.mcgraw-hill.com** to download a spreadsheet application for this activity.

Ingram Publishing

Project Steps

Step 1 Do Your Research

- Research a company that has grown from a local business to a national—or even international—business operation.
- Search online for an interview with a company executive about the company's growth.

Step 2 Explore Your Community

Interview two entrepreneurs or business owners in your neighborhood. Do they currently rent office space or equipment? What are their plans for their businesses' growth?

Step 3 Determine Service Costs

- Based on your research, what service costs are involved in running this company?
- Would you expect these costs to increase as the company grows, or are they fixed?
- Are telephone and electric costs rising?
- What other rising costs would likely impact this company? Does the business rely on the availability of a specific resource?
- What professional services are important to this company's operations?

Step 4 Spreadsheet Application

- Open the downloadable spreadsheet application for Unit 6. This spreadsheet lists the commercial office space in one neighborhood shopping area.
- Enter the provided information into the appropriate cells.
- Print out your spreadsheet.

Academic and Career Portfolio

Add this report to your Academic and Career Portfolio.

Step 5 Develop Your Presentation

Prepare a report of your findings using the following tools, if available:

- Use a word-processing program to write a 1-page report.
  - ✓ Summarize the growth of the company you researched.
  - ✓ Explain what service costs you believe are most important to its operations.
  - ✓ Share the insights of your interviewees.
  - ✓ Based on the spreadsheet application, when a tenant is required to pay a percentage of gross sales, when might this work in the tenant's favor?
  - ✓ Suggest strategies for companies wishing to reduce office rental space.
- Print your completed report and spreadsheet to present to your class.

Step 6 Evaluate

Go to **connectED.mcgraw-hill.com** to download an evaluation rubric.

Your Reference Files

SKILLS

Thirty-two computational skills, from whole number and decimal operations through rates and percents, provide the basics you will need as a consumer and future business person.

APPLICATIONS

Twenty-eight mathematical applications, covering money, time, measurement, graphs, and more, provide the tools you will need for consumer and business use.

SKILL 1

Numbers

Place Value

In 4,532.869, give the place and value of each digit.

Place:

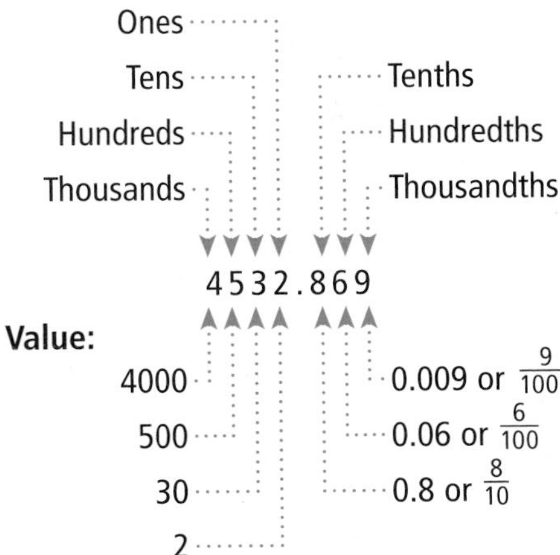

Give the place and value of the underlined digit.

1. 6$\underline{5}$ **2.** 9$\underline{6}$ **3.** 4$\underline{7}$2

4. $\underline{2}$3 **5.** 10$\underline{8}$ **6.** $\underline{5}$36

7. 1,5$\underline{0}$6 **8.** 2,$\underline{8}$21 **9.** 7,$\underline{7}$84

10. $\underline{1}$,492 **11.** 1,00$\underline{9}$ **12.** 1,$\underline{9}$26

13. 0.$\underline{3}$7 **14.** 1.6$\underline{1}$ **15.** 2.73$\underline{9}$

16. $\underline{6}$.3 **17.** 9.4$\underline{2}$ **18.** 4.3$\underline{7}$

19. 2$\underline{4}$.04 **20.** 37.$\underline{3}$29 **21.** 1.8$\underline{2}$4

22. $\underline{4}$93.89 **23.** 90.25$\underline{7}$ **24.** 23.$\underline{5}$72

25. 12.76$\underline{3}$ **26.** 0.$\underline{0}$78 **27.** 5.46$\underline{1}$

Numbers as Words

Write each number in words.

Number	Words
105	*One hundred five*
26	*Twenty-six*
17	*Seventeen*
\$98.09	*Ninety-eight and $\frac{9}{100}$ dollars*
\$33.13	*Thirty-three and $\frac{13}{100}$ dollars*

Write in words.

28. 18 **29.** 34 **30.** 159 **31.** 78 **32.** 103

33. 842 **34.** 207 **35.** 5,012 **36.** 6,005 **37.** 119

38. 72 **39.** 1,240 **40.** 5,102 **41.** 194 **42.** 6,590

43. \$25.00 **44.** \$6.24 **45.** \$17.09 **46.** \$112.35 **47.** \$120.17

48. \$4.37 **49.** \$7,749 **50.** \$65.90 **51.** \$0.50

SKILLS

Numbers as Decimals

Rewrite these large numbers as decimals.

$14,700,000 ····➤ $14.7 million

$245,600 ····➤ $245.6 thousand

Rewrite these decimals as numbers.

$1.2 billion = $1,200,000,000

$43.6 thousand = $43,600

Write in millions.

52. $1,700,000 **53.** $71,640,000 **54.** $618,700,000

Write in thousands.

55. 18,400 **56.** $9,640 **57.** 171,600

Write in billions.

58. $16,450,000,000 **59.** 2,135,000,000 **60.** $171,200,000,000

Write completely in numbers.

61. $3.4 million **62.** 16.2 thousand **63.** $11.2 billion

64. 17.2 million **65.** 7.3 billion **66.** $74.21 thousand

67. 0.4 million **68.** $0.5 thousand **69.** $0.72 billion

Comparing Whole Numbers

Which number is greater: 5,428 or 5,431?

5,428 = 5,000 + 400 + 20 + 8

5,431 = 5,000 + 400 + 30 + 1

Same Same 30 is greater than 20.

So 5,431 is greater than 5,428.

Which number is greater?

70. 23 or 32 **71.** 54 or 45 **72.** 459 or 462

73. 741 or 835 **74.** 810 or 735 **75.** 125 or 211

76. 3,450 or 6,450 **77.** 5,763 or 925 **78.** 1,000 or 999

79. 444 or 4,444 **80.** 3,002 or 4,000 **81.** 1,236 or 820

82. 150 or 149 **83.** 493 or 650 **84.** $2,000 or $1,997

85. $101 or $99 **86.** $482 or $600 **87.** $39 or $93

88. $1,686 or $1,668 **89.** $568 or $742

90. $86,432 or $101,000 **91.** $791,000 or $768,000

Comparing Decimals

Which number is greater 24.93 or 24.86?

24.93 = 20 + 4 + 0.9 + 0.03

24.86 = 20 + 4 + 0.8 + 0.06

Same Same 0.9 is greater than 0.8.

So 24.93 is greater than 24.86.

Which number is greater?

92. 3.1 or 1.3 **93.** 1.2 or 2.0 **94.** 4.50 or 4.05

95. 25.1 or 20.8 **96.** 18.43 or 17.88 **97.** 56.84 or 58

98. 0.4 or 0.6 **99.** 0.01 or 0.1 **100.** 0.82 or 0.28

101. 0.5 or 0.06 **102.** 8.739 or 10 **103.** 0.002 or 0.020

104. $5.99 or $5.00 **105.** $10 or $8.50 **106.** $23.85 or $19.84

107. $11.19 or $19 **108.** $6.98 or $7.50 **109.** $83.59 or $600

110. $4,327.75 or $6,297.86 **111.** $8,391.34 or $9,521.39

112. $4,640.66 or $4,646.40 **113.** $2,000.00 or $1,997.98

SKILL 2

Rounding Numbers

SKILLS

Whole Numbers

Round 7,863 to the nearest hundred.

7,863 — Hundreds place; 5 or more? Yes.

7,900 — Add 1 to hundreds place. Change the digits to the right to zeros.

Round answers to the place value shown.

Nearest ten:

1. 26 **2.** 37 **3.** 68

4. 195 **5.** 217 **6.** 302 **7.** 8,099

Nearest hundred:

8. 119 **9.** 649 **10.** 2,175 **11.** 6,042

Nearest thousand:

12. 7,423 **13.** 15,602 **14.** 22,094 **15.** 750

Decimals

Round 0.6843 to the nearest thousandth.

0.6843 — Thousandths place; 5 or more? No.

0.684 — Do not change. Drop the final digit.

Round answers to the place value shown.

Nearest tenth:

16. 0.63 **17.** 0.091 **18.** 0.407 **19.** 0.452

Nearest hundredth:

20. 0.652 **21.** 0.474 **22.** 0.168 **23.** 0.355

Nearest thousandth:

24. 0.4291 **25.** 0.6007 **26.** 0.0097 **27.** 0.2126

28. 6.3942 **29.** 137.4920 **30.** 9.9999

Mixed Practice

Round answers to the place value shown.

Nearest thousand:

31. 37,874 **32.** 19,266 **33.** 48,092

Nearest hundred:

34. 751 **35.** 919 **36.** 6,771

Nearest ten:

37. 26 **38.** 6,533 **39.** 575

Nearest one:

40. 6.2 **41.** 35.73 **42.** 17.392

Nearest tenth:

43. 189.673 **44.** 10.009 **45.** 0.07

Nearest hundredth:

46. 0.392 **47.** 152.430 **48.** 0.6974

Nearest thousandth:

49. 0.1791 **50.** 16.0005 **51.** 108.4374

SKILL 3

Adding Whole Numbers

Without Carrying

Add.

723 154 + 212	→	723 154 + 212 1,089

1. 65 +41	**2.** 76 +32	**3.** 97 +41	**4.** 32 +25
5. 352 +837	**6.** 361 +834	**7.** 448 +351	**8.** 125 +604
9. 864 + 33	**10.** 721 + 77	**11.** 423 + 65	**12.** 108 + 91
13. 9,037 +1,841	**14.** 9,520 +1,379	**15.** 3,924 +5,063	**16.** 2,840 +1,152

With Carrying

Add.

8,679 + 9,748	→	1 11 8,679 + 9,748 18,427

17. 32 +39	**18.** 54 +48	**19.** 187 + 23	**20.** 49 +86
21. 728 +169	**22.** 527 +284	**23.** 845 +697	**24.** 697 +546
25. 3,046 +1,592	**26.** 7,801 +3,564	**27.** 5,246 +6,978	**28.** 8,347 +1,528
29. 8,448 +3,753	**30.** 108 +7,665	**31.** 9,179 +3,608	**32.** 982 +2,165

Mixed Practice

33. 1,481 +2,317	**34.** 8,495 +1,417	**35.** 5,783 +6,535	**36.** 3,950 +1,615	**37.** 6,259 +1,893
38. 8,347 +1,528	**39.** 6,845 +2,639	**40.** 5,692 +1,204	**41.** 2,642 +4,135	**42.** 7,921 +2,639
43. 7,884 +7,069	**44.** 46,234 +11,325	**45.** 17,694 +15,893	**46.** 37,491 +21,308	**47.** 59,641 +27,840
48. 9,100 536 +2,413	**49.** 7,749 1,240 +6,010	**50.** 6,590 2,408 +5,001	**51.** 5,783 6,535 +2,132	**52.** 6,259 503 +1,893

SKILL 4

Subtracting Whole Numbers

SKILLS

Without Borrowing

Subtract.

9,876
−7,545

↓

9,876
−7,545
2,331

1. 784 −453	**2.** 985 −734	**3.** 693 −542	**4.** 199 −158
5. 7,659 −4,217	**6.** 8,436 −6,223	**7.** 5,792 −2,481	**8.** 4,877 −3,614
9. 6,754 − 5,643	**10.** 1,866 − 853	**11.** 8,191 − 171	**12.** 1,187 − 145
13. 479 −473	**14.** 3,987 −3,085	**15.** 6,358 − 127	**16.** 1,721 − 720

With Borrowing

Subtract.

9,672 −4,136 ↓ (6 12 written above 7 and 2) 9,672 −4,136 = 5,536

8,352 −4,584 ↓ (7 12 14 12 written above 8, 3, 5, 2) 8,352 −4,584 = 3,768

17. 100 − 36	**18.** 512 − 43	**19.** 602 −503	**20.** 250 −162
21. 6,932 −4,674	**22.** 8,724 −2,932	**23.** 4,329 −3,163	**24.** 9,721 −6,842
25. 6,123 −4,214	**26.** 9,231 −6,453	**27.** 7,450 −3,783	**28.** 7,734 −3,935
29. 8,121 −6,846	**30.** 9,000 −7,997	**31.** 9,107 −8,248	**32.** 7,734 −5,935

Mixed Practice

33. 6,140 −3,157	**34.** 8,005 − 6,246	**35.** 7,000 −5,432	**36.** 9,297 −9,286	**37.** 9,811 − 700
38. 9,148 − 954	**39.** 2,625 − 763	**40.** 1,850 − 975	**41.** 7,469 −5,231	**42.** 6,342 −5,793
43. 10,743 − 7,842	**44.** 16,947 −14,523	**45.** 22,493 − 5,967	**46.** 64,654 −57,312	**47.** 79,850 −42,347
48. 172,493 − 67,254	**49.** 249,657 −123,254	**50.** 300,692 −147,593	**51.** 647,593 −546,972	**52.** 800,000 −627,351

SKILLS

SKILL 5

Adding Decimals

Same Number of Places

Add.

```
 658.21            658.21
 292.73  ----->    292.73
+832.08           +832.08
                 1,783.02
```

1. 423.11 + 983.09

2. 987.76 + 998.24

3. 323.35 + 390.04

4. 632.37 + 864.87

5. 456.06 + 443.99

6. 763.88 + 980.21

7. 879.757 + 986.752 + 544.847

8. 57.606 + 443.216 + 463.987

9. 787.332 + 90.887 + 840.783

Different Number of Places

Add.

```
 0.93             0.930
 5.893  ----->    5.893
 8.4              8.400
+81             +81.000
                 96.223
```

Placeholders

10. 34 + 3.4

11. 34.6 + 63.43

12. 27.77 + 95.074

13. 432.32 + 3.644 + 864.876

14. 4.56 + 6.989 + 0.809

15. 63.9 + 0.01 + 980.09

16. 65.65 + 16.82 + 5.452

17. 0.967 + 81.14 + 9.004

18. 7.55 + 0.06 + 0.7

19. 43.73 + 77.8 + 34.724

20. 4.787 + 76.64 + 7.983

21. 3.7 + 9.009 + 7.29

Mixed Practice

22. 23.131 + 93.079

23. 557.766 + 568.264

24. 764.5 + 36.094

25. 998.7 + 84.857

26. 845.876 + 989.19

27. 435.745 + 67.76 + 5.09

28. 76 + 75.879 + 786.87

29. 0.678 + 0.021 + 0.301

30. 0.083 + 0.664 + 0.945

31. 65.4 + 74.042 + 7.978

32. 65.74 + 45.78 + 54.98 + 54.12

33. 654.65 + 65.7 + 56.982 + 9.7

34. 676.974 + 11.743 + 456.999 + 8.7

35. 765.4 + 4.658 + 56.46 + 364.9

36. 765.787 + 6.005 + 98.89 + 789

SKILL 6

Subtracting Decimals

SKILLS

Same Number of Places

Subtract.

$$\begin{array}{r} 597.18 \\ -392.35 \\ \hline \end{array} \longrightarrow \begin{array}{r} 597.\overset{6\,11}{\cancel{1}\cancel{8}} \\ -392.35 \\ \hline 204.83 \end{array}$$

1. $\begin{array}{r} 65.46 \\ -14.31 \\ \hline \end{array}$ 2. $\begin{array}{r} 48.58 \\ -15.47 \\ \hline \end{array}$ 3. $\begin{array}{r} 151.02 \\ -\ 16.13 \\ \hline \end{array}$

4. $\begin{array}{r} 36.25 \\ -13.67 \\ \hline \end{array}$ 5. $\begin{array}{r} 87.56 \\ -82.47 \\ \hline \end{array}$ 6. $\begin{array}{r} 51.634 \\ -27.849 \\ \hline \end{array}$

7. $\begin{array}{r} 69.37 \\ -43.86 \\ \hline \end{array}$ 8. $\begin{array}{r} 89.63 \\ -\ 7.99 \\ \hline \end{array}$ 9. $\begin{array}{r} 109.46 \\ -\ 29.78 \\ \hline \end{array}$

10. $\begin{array}{r} 521.52 \\ -\ 38.56 \\ \hline \end{array}$ 11. $\begin{array}{r} 321.02 \\ -117.18 \\ \hline \end{array}$ 12. $\begin{array}{r} 572.24 \\ -283.35 \\ \hline \end{array}$

Different Number of Places

Subtract.

$$\begin{array}{r} 86.9 \\ -\ 3.84 \\ \hline \end{array} \longrightarrow \begin{array}{r} 86.\overset{8\,10}{\cancel{9}\cancel{0}} \\ -\ 3.84 \\ \hline 83.06 \end{array}$$

Placeholder

13. $\begin{array}{r} 79.6 \\ -\ 8.75 \\ \hline \end{array}$ 14. $\begin{array}{r} 95.1 \\ -\ 9.87 \\ \hline \end{array}$ 15. $\begin{array}{r} 100.1 \\ -\ 15.78 \\ \hline \end{array}$

16. $\begin{array}{r} 16.8 \\ -\ 5.91 \\ \hline \end{array}$ 17. $\begin{array}{r} 36 \\ -16.4 \\ \hline \end{array}$ 18. $\begin{array}{r} 42 \\ -12.94 \\ \hline \end{array}$

19. $\begin{array}{r} 17.9 \\ -\ 9.83 \\ \hline \end{array}$ 20. $\begin{array}{r} 21 \\ -19.7 \\ \hline \end{array}$ 21. $\begin{array}{r} 67.2 \\ -\ 9.76 \\ \hline \end{array}$

22. $\begin{array}{r} 136.1 \\ -\ 69.542 \\ \hline \end{array}$ 23. $\begin{array}{r} 771.9 \\ -394.27 \\ \hline \end{array}$ 24. $\begin{array}{r} 4{,}578 \\ -\ 878.127 \\ \hline \end{array}$

Mixed Practice

25. $\begin{array}{r} 87.56 \\ -82.47 \\ \hline \end{array}$ 26. $\begin{array}{r} 39.27 \\ -18.38 \\ \hline \end{array}$ 27. $\begin{array}{r} 36.1 \\ -16.117 \\ \hline \end{array}$ 28. $\begin{array}{r} 4.546 \\ -2.558 \\ \hline \end{array}$ 29. $\begin{array}{r} 653.05 \\ -327.19 \\ \hline \end{array}$

30. $\begin{array}{r} 198.20 \\ -\ 64.897 \\ \hline \end{array}$ 31. $\begin{array}{r} 854.01 \\ -649.656 \\ \hline \end{array}$ 32. $\begin{array}{r} 316.07 \\ -118.29 \\ \hline \end{array}$ 33. $\begin{array}{r} 800.04 \\ -242.17 \\ \hline \end{array}$ 34. $\begin{array}{r} 985.93 \\ -\ 99.794 \\ \hline \end{array}$

35. $\begin{array}{r} 6{,}194.9 \\ -\ 978.954 \\ \hline \end{array}$ 36. $\begin{array}{r} 719.3 \\ -\ 47.832 \\ \hline \end{array}$ 37. $\begin{array}{r} 5.9871 \\ -4.8693 \\ \hline \end{array}$ 38. $\begin{array}{r} 17.9328 \\ -\ 6.2973 \\ \hline \end{array}$ 39. $\begin{array}{r} 843.002 \\ -\ 64.973 \\ \hline \end{array}$

40. $\begin{array}{r} 87.69 \\ -86.9975 \\ \hline \end{array}$ 41. $\begin{array}{r} 4.97652 \\ -1.37846 \\ \hline \end{array}$ 42. $\begin{array}{r} 3.29131 \\ -2.19378 \\ \hline \end{array}$ 43. $\begin{array}{r} 6.962 \\ -4.21698 \\ \hline \end{array}$ 44. $\begin{array}{r} 9.7 \\ -8.65947 \\ \hline \end{array}$

SKILLS

SKILL 7

Multiplying Whole Numbers

Without Carrying

Multiply.

```
 442          442
×211  ····>  ×211
              442  <····    1 × 442
            4,420  <····   10 × 442
           88,400  <····  200 × 442
           93,262  <····  211 × 442
```

1. 73 × 21 **2.** 42 × 22 **3.** 212 × 412

4. 311 × 232 **5.** 321 × 312 **6.** 223 × 323

7. 232 × 333 **8.** 7,143 × 102 **9.** 8,643 × 111

With Carrying

Multiply.

```
 6,524           6,524
×  273  ····>  ×   273
                19,572  <····    3 × 6,524
               456,680  <····   70 × 6,524
             1,304,800  <····  200 × 6,524
             1,781,052  <····  273 × 6,524
```

10. 61 × 76 **11.** 78 × 36 **12.** 437 × 571

13. 465 × 541 **14.** 542 × 168 **15.** 8,023 × 532

16. 64 × 27 **17.** 37 × 45 **18.** 68 × 71

19. 836 × 372 **20.** 7,501 × 447 **21.** 5,327 × 312

Mixed Practice

22. 480 × 10 **23.** 230 × 300 **24.** 641 × 237 **25.** 231 × 122 **26.** 122 × 40

27. 510 × 700 **28.** 8,233 × 2,584 **29.** 6,010 × 6,000 **30.** 9,000 × 7,011 **31.** 2,973 × 1,504

32. 19,008 × 8,000 **33.** 8,791 × 5,000 **34.** 6,743 × 27 **35.** 4,231 × 253 **36.** 8,427 × 19

37. 13,010 × 13 **38.** 14,231 × 12 **39.** 17,822 × 35 **40.** 22,300 × 15 **41.** 31,942 × 41

42. 27,642 × 321 **43.** 13,231 × 212 **44.** 14,402 × 121 **45.** 49,237 × 321 **46.** 64,159 × 347

SKILL 8

Multiplying Decimals

SKILLS

Decimals Greater Than One

Multiply.

```
 17.45            17.45  ◄····  2 places
× 2.7   ····►   × 2.7   ◄····+1 place
                 47.115 ◄····  3 places
```

1. 2.5×1.8 **2.** 8.3×1.5 **3.** 102×8.61

4. 15.3×5.3 **5.** 25.14×7.5 **6.** 19.36×7.12

7. 27.06×8.53 **8.** 4.367×8.5 **9.** 5.564×7.9

10. 32.63×9.2 **11.** 31.20×9.21 **12.** 6.715×9.03

Decimals Less Than One

Multiply.

```
 0.08            0.08   ◄····  2 places
×0.4   ····►   ×0.4    ◄····+1 place
                0.032  ◄····  3 places
```

13. 0.144×0.7 **14.** 0.86×0.5 **15.** 0.96×0.1

16. 0.56×0.07 **17.** 0.73×0.8 **18.** 0.05×0.9

19. 0.81×0.76 **20.** 0.47×0.84 **21.** 0.63×0.09

22. 0.57×0.03 **23.** 1.23×0.07 **24.** 0.01×0.05

Mixed Practice

25. 41.16×100 **26.** 0.923×0.49 **27.** 0.12×300 **28.** 67.32×10 **29.** 7.243×121

30. 557.4×100 **31.** 327.8×3.7 **32.** 14.923×0.76 **33.** 1.125×100 **34.** $0.009 \times 1{,}000$

35. 2.014×40.7 **36.** 2.854×0.04 **37.** $6{,}243.78 \times 25.9$ **38.** 5.9312×5.62 **39.** 0.534×0.293

40. 16.4591×51.23 **41.** 96.00×0.875 **42.** 0.3172×0.2008 **43.** 0.1543×0.4931 **44.** 0.7984×0.0003

SKILLS

SKILL 9

Dividing (Fractional Remainder)

Two-Digit Divisor

Divide.

46)703

```
     1               15              15 13/46
46)703  ---->  46)703  ---->  46)703
  -46            -46             -46
   24            243             243
                -230            -230
                  13              13
```

1. 27)64
2. 38)89
3. 41)84
4. 46)613
5. 53)754
6. 61)685
7. 21)1,781
8. 55)4,273
9. 43)2,900
10. 73)3,956
11. 23)1,369
12. 34)2,167
13. 81)5,793
14. 78)93

Three-Digit Divisor

Divide.

472)9,463

```
      2                 20 23/472
472)9463           472)9463
   -944               -944
      2                 23
                       - 0
                        23
```

15. 114)1,837
16. 216)5,417
17. 321)4,832
18. 429)9,038
19. 892)7,928
20. 910)11,849
21. 409)9,429
22. 900)7,621
23. 625)8,752
24. 710)15,694
25. 843)17,691
26. 937)22,474

Mixed Practice

27. 19)342
28. 46)782
29. 71)1,136
30. 279)9,778
31. 35)2,520
32. 509)5,089
33. 621)8,716
34. 49)4,959
35. 549)6,937
36. 953)9,597
37. 842)4,975
38. 87)2,139
39. 473)85,642
40. 192)91,845
41. 622)54,641
42. 812)55,692
43. 51)81,603
44. 23)44,364
45. 88)22,222
46. 34)27,945
47. 417)86,902
48. 71)103,205
49. 514)691,507
50. 64)237,605

SKILL 10

Dividing (Decimal Remainder)

SKILLS

Exact Quotient

Divide.

$28\overline{)378}$

```
   13                     13.5
28)378  ···········> 28)378.0
  -28                   -28
   98                    98
  -84                   -84
   14                    140
                        -140
```

1. $8\overline{)89}$
2. $10\overline{)123}$
3. $15\overline{)318}$
4. $16\overline{)264}$
5. $20\overline{)102}$
6. $50\overline{)530}$
7. $12\overline{)237}$
8. $25\overline{)1{,}310}$
9. $32\overline{)1{,}104}$
10. $96\overline{)2{,}988}$

Rounded Quotient

Divide. $39\overline{)818}$

Round to the nearest hundredth.

```
   20                    20.974 <··· Thousandths place
39)818  ···········> 39)818.000
  -78                    78
   38                     380
                          351
                           290
                           273
                            170
                            156
                             14
```

20.974 rounded to the nearest hundredth is 20.97 <···Skill 2

Round answers to the place value shown.

Nearest tenth:

11. $14\overline{)319}$
12. $26\overline{)347}$
13. $23\overline{)371}$
14. $46\overline{)9{,}415}$
15. $47\overline{)9{,}719}$

Nearest hundredth:

16. $19\overline{)427}$
17. $83\overline{)168}$
18. $47\overline{)432}$

Nearest thousandth:

19. $37\overline{)402}$
20. $24\overline{)643}$
21. $21\overline{)452}$

Mixed Practice

Round answers to the nearest hundredth.

22. $28\overline{)1{,}022}$
23. $24\overline{)209}$
24. $72\overline{)1{,}665}$
25. $29\overline{)303}$
26. $85\overline{)1{,}802}$
27. $24\overline{)747}$
28. $67\overline{)701}$
29. $71\overline{)400}$
30. $23\overline{)273}$
31. $36\overline{)630}$
32. $44\overline{)858}$
33. $59\overline{)852}$
34. $37\overline{)673}$
35. $41\overline{)9{,}432}$
36. $73\overline{)1{,}079}$
37. $24\overline{)994}$
38. $27\overline{)3{,}365}$
39. $35\overline{)894}$
40. $42\overline{)5{,}264}$
41. $110\overline{)4{,}345}$

SKILLS

SKILL 11

Dividing Decimals

Divisor Greater Than One

Divide.

$7.2\overline{)16.92}$

$7.2\overline{)16.92}$ → $72\overline{)169.20}$

$$\begin{array}{r} 2.35 \\ 72\overline{)169.20} \\ -144 \\ \hline 252 \\ -216 \\ \hline 360 \\ -360 \\ \hline \end{array}$$

Move 1 decimal place.

Round answers to the nearest hundredth.

1. $2.5\overline{)11.5}$ **2.** $3.8\overline{)4.56}$

3. $3.2\overline{)18.272}$ **4.** $7.5\overline{)27.823}$

5. $3.15\overline{)53.55}$ **6.** $24.12\overline{)369.036}$

7. $4.08\overline{)26.52}$ **8.** $3.02\overline{)10.57}$

9. $4.23\overline{)181.5}$ **10.** $6.67\overline{)25.963}$

Divisor Less Than One

Divide.

$0.032\overline{)14.400}$

$0.032\overline{)14.400}$ → $32\overline{)14400}$

$$\begin{array}{r} 450 \\ 32\overline{)14400} \\ -128 \\ \hline 160 \\ -160 \\ \hline 00 \\ -00 \\ \hline \end{array}$$

Move 3 decimal places.

Round answers to the nearest hundredth.

11. $0.24\overline{)6.24}$ **12.** $0.372\overline{)6.324}$

13. $0.154\overline{)4.774}$ **14.** $0.48\overline{)2.938}$

15. $0.37\overline{)9.62}$ **16.** $0.21\overline{)1.374}$

17. $0.51\overline{)4.569}$ **18.** $0.67\overline{)2.693}$

19. $0.73\overline{)9.641}$ **20.** $0.81\overline{)11.632}$

Mixed Practice

Round answers to the nearest hundredth.

21. $3.12\overline{)4.386}$ **22.** $0.73\overline{)9.48}$ **23.** $0.136\overline{)33.32}$ **24.** $0.21\overline{)130.2}$

25. $6.94\overline{)8.378}$ **26.** $1.23\overline{)0.3813}$ **27.** $0.065\overline{)16.64}$ **28.** $8.34\overline{)7.416}$

29. $0.63\overline{)42.51}$ **30.** $2.91\overline{)5.932}$ **31.** $1.07\overline{)24.153}$ **32.** $1.1\overline{)29.9}$

33. $15.93\overline{)27.931}$ **34.** $12.12\overline{)36.422}$ **35.** $0.05\overline{)1.925}$ **36.** $2.03\overline{)21.249}$

37. $0.007\overline{)0.692}$ **38.** $1.05\overline{)25.421}$ **39.** $0.31\overline{)0.00354}$ **40.** $15.42\overline{)113.005}$

41. $5.02\overline{)86}$ **42.** $0.03\overline{)29}$ **43.** $5.4\overline{)0.062}$ **44.** $0.068\overline{)0.009}$

SKILL 12

Equivalent Fractions

Higher Terms

Complete the equivalent fraction.

$\frac{3}{4} = \frac{?}{20}$

$\frac{3}{4} = \frac{?}{20} \xrightarrow{\times 5} \frac{3}{4} = \frac{15}{20}$

×5

×5

Solve.

1. $\frac{5}{6} = \frac{?}{12}$ **2.** $\frac{4}{9} = \frac{?}{27}$ **3.** $\frac{7}{10} = \frac{35}{?}$

4. $\frac{11}{12} = \frac{22}{?}$ **5.** $\frac{8}{17} = \frac{?}{51}$ **6.** $\frac{15}{17} = \frac{90}{?}$

7. $\frac{11}{18} = \frac{?}{36}$ **8.** $\frac{4}{19} = \frac{12}{?}$ **9.** $\frac{16}{17} = \frac{48}{?}$

10. $\frac{11}{13} = \frac{?}{39}$ **11.** $\frac{3}{4} = \frac{?}{32}$ **12.** $\frac{15}{17} = \frac{60}{?}$

13. $\frac{7}{9} = \frac{?}{45}$ **14.** $\frac{11}{12} = \frac{?}{72}$ **15.** $\frac{5}{8} = \frac{45}{?}$

16. $\frac{11}{8} = \frac{33}{?}$ **17.** $\frac{5}{24} = \frac{?}{96}$ **18.** $\frac{23}{73} = \frac{?}{365}$

Lowest Terms

Reduce $\frac{12}{28}$ to lowest terms.

$\frac{12}{28} = \frac{3}{7} \xrightarrow{\div 4} \frac{12}{28} = \frac{3}{7}$

÷4

÷4

Reduce to lowest terms.

19. $\frac{6}{9}$ **20.** $\frac{4}{16}$ **21.** $\frac{9}{18}$

22. $\frac{20}{22}$ **23.** $\frac{18}{27}$ **24.** $\frac{24}{32}$

25. $\frac{16}{48}$ **26.** $\frac{18}{42}$ **27.** $\frac{55}{66}$

28. $\frac{30}{50}$ **29.** $\frac{20}{54}$ **30.** $\frac{21}{27}$

31. $\frac{8}{14}$ **32.** $\frac{19}{57}$ **33.** $\frac{14}{28}$

34. $\frac{15}{25}$ **35.** $\frac{21}{28}$ **36.** $\frac{200}{365}$

37. $\frac{188}{366}$ **38.** $\frac{150}{365}$ **39.** $\frac{180}{360}$

40. $\frac{225}{365}$ **41.** $\frac{190}{360}$ **42.** $\frac{65}{75}$

43. $\frac{72}{468}$ **44.** $\frac{183}{366}$ **45.** $\frac{232}{1,450}$

46. $\frac{1,792}{5,120}$

SKILLS

SKILL 13

Changing Mixed Numbers/ Improper Fractions

Mixed Numbers to Improper Fractions

Write $3\frac{7}{8}$ as an improper fraction.

$3\frac{7}{8} = \frac{(3 \times 8) + 7}{8}$

$3\frac{7}{8} = \frac{24 + 7}{8}$

$3\frac{7}{8} = \frac{31}{8}$

Write as an improper fraction.

1. $6\frac{1}{4}$
2. $4\frac{3}{4}$
3. $7\frac{3}{8}$
4. $9\frac{1}{2}$
5. $6\frac{2}{3}$
6. $3\frac{5}{6}$
7. $7\frac{4}{5}$
8. $3\frac{1}{8}$
9. $4\frac{3}{10}$
10. $1\frac{1}{16}$
11. $4\frac{7}{32}$
12. $4\frac{1}{5}$
13. $5\frac{1}{3}$
14. $2\frac{1}{6}$
15. $2\frac{9}{10}$
16. $3\frac{1}{10}$
17. $3\frac{5}{16}$
18. $4\frac{9}{16}$
19. $5\frac{5}{32}$
20. $6\frac{3}{5}$
21. $7\frac{2}{11}$
22. $8\frac{5}{6}$
23. $11\frac{2}{5}$
24. $13\frac{1}{3}$

Improper Fractions to Mixed Numbers

Write $\frac{17}{3}$ as a mixed number.

$\frac{17}{3} \rightarrow 3\overline{)17}$ gives $5\frac{2}{3}$ ← Skill 9

-15

2

$\frac{17}{3} = 5\frac{2}{3}$

Write as a mixed number. Reduce any fractional parts to lowest terms.

25. $\frac{13}{2}$
26. $\frac{18}{4}$
27. $\frac{46}{8}$
28. $\frac{19}{4}$
29. $\frac{33}{6}$
30. $\frac{30}{7}$
31. $\frac{21}{9}$
32. $\frac{28}{8}$
33. $\frac{45}{18}$
34. $\frac{49}{21}$
35. $\frac{62}{21}$
36. $\frac{23}{3}$
37. $\frac{35}{6}$
38. $\frac{47}{7}$
39. $\frac{57}{18}$
40. $\frac{37}{9}$
41. $\frac{49}{8}$
42. $\frac{63}{2}$
43. $\frac{45}{7}$
44. $\frac{71}{4}$

SKILL 14

Changing Fractions/Decimals

SKILLS

Fraction to Decimal

Write $\frac{5}{12}$ as a decimal. Round to the nearest hundredth.

$\frac{5}{12} \rightarrow 12\overline{)5.000}$ = 0.416 ← Skill 10

0.416 rounded to the nearest hundredth is 0.42. ← Skill 2

$\frac{5}{12} = 0.42$

Write as a decimal. Round answers to the nearest hundredth.

1. $\frac{4}{5}$
2. $\frac{7}{20}$
3. $1\frac{1}{8}$
4. $\frac{3}{4}$
5. $2\frac{3}{7}$
6. $\frac{7}{12}$
7. $1\frac{11}{30}$
8. $\frac{2}{5}$
9. $\frac{3}{10}$
10. $3\frac{4}{25}$
11. $4\frac{3}{8}$
12. $\frac{7}{10}$
13. $3\frac{1}{12}$
14. $\frac{1}{15}$
15. $\frac{1}{30}$
16. $2\frac{9}{10}$
17. $5\frac{3}{20}$
18. $\frac{9}{20}$
19. $2\frac{3}{25}$
20. $\frac{1}{8}$
21. $7\frac{1}{7}$
22. $2\frac{5}{8}$
23. $\frac{4}{9}$
24. $1\frac{7}{8}$

Decimal to Fraction

Write 0.42 as a fraction in lowest terms.

$0.42 = \frac{42}{100} = \frac{21}{50}$ (Skill 1; ← Skill 12)

$0.42 = \frac{21}{50}$

Write as a fraction in lowest terms.

25. 0.1
26. 3.7
27. 0.30
28. 2.25
29. 0.03
30. 0.09
31. 0.53
32. 1.75
33. 0.003
34. 0.010
35. 0.064
36. 4.206
37. 4.444
38. 0.732
39. 0.469
40. 2.9
41. 7.5
42. 0.32
43. 1.08
44. 0.06
45. 2.83
46. 1.039
47. 0.105
48. 2.422
49. 0.0005
50. 0.2482
51. 1.6432
52. 0.0058
53. 0.0002
54. 6.66

SKILL 15

Adding Fractions, Like Denominators

Fractions

Add.

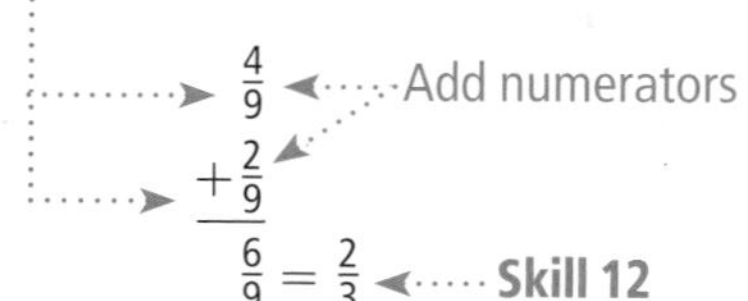

Express answers in lowest terms.

1. $\frac{4}{5} + \frac{3}{5}$

2. $\frac{4}{7} + \frac{2}{7}$

3. $\frac{1}{8} + \frac{5}{8}$

4. $\frac{5}{9} + \frac{7}{9}$

5. $\frac{5}{7} + \frac{6}{7}$

6. $\frac{11}{12} + \frac{7}{12}$

7. $\frac{13}{25} + \frac{16}{25}$

8. $\frac{11}{30} + \frac{19}{30}$

9. $\frac{15}{32} + \frac{27}{32}$

10. $\frac{21}{40} + \frac{31}{40}$

11. $\frac{22}{45} + \frac{31}{45}$

12. $\frac{11}{50} + \frac{19}{50}$

Mixed Numbers

Add.

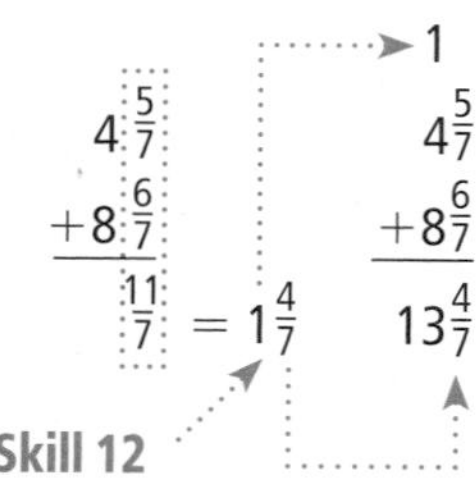

Express answers in lowest terms.

13. $4\frac{1}{3} + 7\frac{1}{3}$

14. $13\frac{4}{5} + 8\frac{3}{5}$

15. $5\frac{4}{7} + 8\frac{5}{7}$

16. $12\frac{3}{8} + 14\frac{1}{8}$

17. $6\frac{11}{12} + 5\frac{5}{12}$

18. $2\frac{12}{13} + 7\frac{2}{13}$

19. $8\frac{9}{16} + 8\frac{11}{16}$

20. $14\frac{5}{24} + 15\frac{7}{24}$

21. $4\frac{13}{32} + 5\frac{15}{32}$

22. $15\frac{19}{45} + 6\frac{28}{45}$

23. $7\frac{8}{35} + 4\frac{6}{35}$

24. $9\frac{5}{32} + 14\frac{7}{32}$

SKILL 16

Adding Fractions, Unlike Denominators

Fractions

Add.

Unlike denominators → Like denominators

$$\begin{array}{r} \frac{5}{8} \\ +\frac{2}{3} \\ \hline \end{array} \rightarrow \begin{array}{r} \frac{15}{24} \\ +\frac{16}{24} \\ \hline \end{array} \rightarrow \begin{array}{r} \frac{15}{24} \\ +\frac{16}{24} \\ \hline \frac{31}{24} \end{array} = 1\frac{7}{24}$$

Skill 12 · Skill 15 · Skill 13

Express answers in lowest terms.

1. $\frac{1}{2} + \frac{3}{5}$
2. $\frac{3}{4} + \frac{1}{6}$
3. $\frac{2}{7} + \frac{2}{3}$
4. $\frac{3}{8} + \frac{1}{5}$
5. $\frac{5}{6} + \frac{1}{3}$
6. $\frac{7}{12} + \frac{3}{7}$
7. $\frac{9}{11} + \frac{3}{10}$
8. $\frac{13}{16} + \frac{9}{8}$
9. $\frac{7}{20} + \frac{19}{30}$
10. $\frac{5}{18} + \frac{19}{24}$
11. $\frac{1}{25} + \frac{13}{30}$
12. $\frac{2}{15} + \frac{29}{30}$

Mixed Numbers

Add.

$$\begin{array}{r} 12\frac{2}{5} \\ +\ 9\frac{3}{4} \\ \hline \end{array} \rightarrow \begin{array}{r} 12\frac{8}{20} \\ +\ 9\frac{15}{20} \\ \hline \frac{23}{20} \end{array} = 1\frac{3}{20} \rightarrow \begin{array}{r} 1 \\ 12\frac{8}{20} \\ +\ 9\frac{15}{20} \\ \hline 22\frac{3}{20} \end{array}$$

Skill 12 · Skill 15

Express answers in lowest terms.

13. $5\frac{1}{2} + 3\frac{2}{3}$
14. $4\frac{3}{8} + 9\frac{3}{4}$
15. $7\frac{5}{6} + 8\frac{1}{2}$
16. $9\frac{7}{8} + 10\frac{7}{16}$
17. $11\frac{2}{13} + 9\frac{15}{26}$
18. $18\frac{2}{3} + 5\frac{7}{11}$
19. $12\frac{4}{7} + 15\frac{7}{9}$
20. $16\frac{5}{6} + 10\frac{6}{7}$
21. $16\frac{5}{8} + 12\frac{1}{7}$
22. $11\frac{4}{9} + 13\frac{3}{8}$
23. $4\frac{2}{3} + 24\frac{7}{16}$
24. $15\frac{5}{8} + 9\frac{4}{7}$

SKILLS

SKILL 17

Subtracting Fractions, Like Denominators

Fractions

Subtract.

Like denominators

$$\begin{array}{r} \frac{11}{12} \\ -\frac{7}{12} \\ \hline \end{array} \quad \cdots\rightarrow \quad \begin{array}{r} \frac{11}{12} \\ -\frac{7}{12} \\ \hline \frac{4}{12} = \frac{1}{3} \end{array}$$

Skill 12

Subtract numerators

Express answers in lowest terms.

1. $\frac{4}{9} - \frac{2}{9}$

2. $\frac{9}{8} - \frac{3}{8}$

3. $\frac{11}{12} - \frac{1}{12}$

4. $\frac{5}{6} - \frac{1}{6}$

5. $\frac{5}{7} - \frac{1}{7}$

6. $\frac{19}{27} - \frac{1}{27}$

7. $\frac{11}{16} - \frac{9}{16}$

8. $\frac{16}{25} - \frac{6}{25}$

9. $\frac{37}{40} - \frac{29}{40}$

10. $\frac{29}{36} - \frac{11}{36}$

11. $\frac{7}{10} - \frac{3}{10}$

12. $\frac{19}{36} - \frac{5}{36}$

13. $\frac{19}{24} - \frac{13}{24}$

14. $\frac{13}{28} - \frac{7}{28}$

15. $\frac{29}{60} - \frac{8}{60}$

Mixed Numbers

Subtract.

$$\begin{array}{r} 8\frac{11}{16} \\ -5\frac{9}{16} \\ \hline \end{array} \quad \cdots\rightarrow \quad \begin{array}{r} 8\frac{11}{16} \\ -5\frac{9}{16} \\ \hline \frac{2}{16} = \frac{1}{8} \end{array} \quad \cdots\rightarrow \quad \begin{array}{r} 8\frac{11}{16} \\ -5\frac{9}{16} \\ \hline 3\frac{1}{8} \end{array}$$

Skill 12

Express answers in lowest terms.

16. $7\frac{3}{4} - 6\frac{1}{4}$

17. $8\frac{6}{7} - 7\frac{5}{7}$

18. $10\frac{4}{5} - 6\frac{1}{5}$

19. $12\frac{5}{8} - 9\frac{3}{8}$

20. $2\frac{16}{21} - 1\frac{5}{21}$

21. $7\frac{11}{24} - 5\frac{7}{24}$

22. $14\frac{17}{20} - 8\frac{9}{20}$

23. $15\frac{15}{32} - 10\frac{9}{32}$

24. $14\frac{7}{8} - 9\frac{3}{8}$

25. $12\frac{11}{13} - 10\frac{4}{13}$

26. $18\frac{17}{20} - 15\frac{9}{20}$

27. $35\frac{39}{40} - 27\frac{19}{40}$

28. $74\frac{41}{75} - 29\frac{16}{75}$

29. $103\frac{11}{35} - 78\frac{1}{35}$

SKILL 18

Subtracting Fractions, Unlike Denominators

SKILLS

Fractions

Subtract. **Express answers in lowest terms.**

Unlike denominators — Like denominators

$$\begin{array}{r} \frac{5}{6} \\ -\frac{3}{10} \\ \hline \end{array} \rightarrow \begin{array}{r} \frac{25}{30} \\ -\frac{9}{30} \\ \hline \end{array} \rightarrow \begin{array}{r} \frac{25}{30} \\ -\frac{9}{30} \\ \hline \frac{16}{30} \end{array} = \frac{8}{15}$$

Skill 12 · Skill 17 · Skill 12

1. $\frac{3}{4} - \frac{3}{8}$
2. $\frac{1}{3} - \frac{2}{9}$
3. $\frac{9}{10} - \frac{3}{4}$
4. $\frac{4}{5} - \frac{2}{3}$
5. $\frac{5}{6} - \frac{7}{9}$
6. $\frac{5}{8} - \frac{5}{12}$
7. $\frac{3}{5} - \frac{8}{15}$
8. $\frac{11}{12} - \frac{3}{4}$
9. $\frac{4}{5} - \frac{13}{20}$
10. $\frac{6}{7} - \frac{10}{21}$
11. $\frac{1}{2} - \frac{2}{5}$
12. $\frac{3}{4} - \frac{11}{16}$

Mixed Numbers

Subtract. **Express answers in lowest terms.**

$$\begin{array}{r} 9\frac{11}{12} \\ -\ 7\frac{3}{8} \\ \hline \end{array} \rightarrow \begin{array}{r} 9\frac{22}{24} \\ -7\frac{9}{24} \\ \hline 2\frac{13}{24} \end{array}$$

Skill 17 · Skill 12

13. $9\frac{3}{4} - 5\frac{1}{2}$
14. $7\frac{5}{6} - 4\frac{2}{3}$
15. $14\frac{4}{9} - 8\frac{1}{6}$
16. $15\frac{3}{7} - 10\frac{1}{3}$
17. $34\frac{11}{12} - 29\frac{4}{5}$
18. $48\frac{4}{7} - 37\frac{5}{9}$
19. $12\frac{5}{8} - 9\frac{1}{2}$
20. $2\frac{16}{21} - 1\frac{2}{3}$
21. $13\frac{3}{4} - 11\frac{3}{5}$
22. $21\frac{5}{6} - 19\frac{5}{8}$
23. $7\frac{11}{24} - 5\frac{1}{3}$
24. $20\frac{15}{38} - 20\frac{1}{19}$

SKILLS

SKILL 19

Subtracting Mixed Numbers, Borrowing

Whole Number and a Mixed Number

Subtract.

$$\begin{array}{r} 8 \\ -4\frac{3}{5} \\ \hline \end{array} \longrightarrow \begin{array}{r} 7\frac{5}{5} \\ -4\frac{3}{5} \\ \hline 3\frac{2}{5} \end{array}$$

Like denominators

Express answers in lowest terms.

1. $3 - 1\frac{1}{2}$ **2.** $4 - 2\frac{3}{4}$

3. $10 - 7\frac{9}{10}$ **4.** $6 - 4\frac{3}{8}$

5. $12 - 9\frac{5}{11}$ **6.** $15 - 12\frac{7}{16}$

Mixed Numbers with Unlike Denominators

Subtract.

Skill 12

$$\begin{array}{r} 6\frac{2}{3} \\ -2\frac{4}{5} \\ \hline \end{array} \longrightarrow \begin{array}{r} 6\frac{10}{15} \\ -2\frac{12}{15} \\ \hline \end{array} \longrightarrow \begin{array}{r} 5\frac{25}{15} \\ -2\frac{12}{15} \\ \hline 3\frac{13}{15} \end{array}$$

Express answers in lowest terms.

7. $5\frac{1}{2} - 2\frac{4}{9}$ **8.** $8\frac{1}{2} - 3\frac{5}{8}$

9. $18\frac{3}{4} - 5\frac{5}{6}$ **10.** $27\frac{2}{7} - 13\frac{3}{4}$

11. $28\frac{3}{7} - 26\frac{9}{10}$ **12.** $40\frac{19}{30} - 39\frac{3}{4}$

13. $6\frac{3}{4} - 3\frac{7}{8}$ **14.** $16\frac{1}{12} - 9\frac{3}{10}$

Mixed Practice

Subtract.

15. $4 - 2\frac{5}{8}$ **16.** $9 - 5\frac{11}{12}$ **17.** $12 - 11\frac{7}{8}$ **18.** $16 - 7\frac{5}{11}$

19. $8\frac{1}{3} - 4\frac{5}{9}$ **20.** $13\frac{1}{2} - 7\frac{3}{5}$ **21.** $14\frac{1}{5} - 13\frac{3}{4}$ **22.** $13 - 6\frac{5}{8}$

23. $27\frac{1}{4} - 15\frac{15}{16}$ **24.** $38\frac{3}{7} - 29\frac{9}{10}$ **25.** $18\frac{1}{12} - 3\frac{11}{36}$ **26.** $17\frac{8}{9} - 5\frac{3}{8}$

27. $19 - 5\frac{2}{7}$ **28.** $16\frac{4}{5} - 6\frac{3}{4}$ **29.** $19\frac{11}{32} - 7\frac{3}{16}$ **30.** $25 - 8\frac{7}{10}$

SKILL 20

Multiplying Fractions/ Mixed Numbers

SKILLS

Fractions

Multiply.

$\frac{5}{8} \times \frac{2}{3} = \frac{5 \times 2}{8 \times 3} = \frac{10}{24} = \frac{5}{12}$

Skill 12

Express answers in lowest terms.

1. $\frac{1}{2} \times \frac{2}{3}$ **2.** $\frac{1}{4} \times \frac{3}{5}$

3. $\frac{5}{6} \times \frac{3}{4}$ **4.** $\frac{8}{9} \times \frac{2}{7}$

5. $\frac{11}{12} \times \frac{5}{11}$ **6.** $\frac{4}{13} \times \frac{8}{9}$

7. $4 \times \frac{1}{2}$ **8.** $17 \times \frac{2}{5}$

9. $21 \times \frac{3}{7}$

Mixed Numbers

Multiply.

$4\frac{1}{3} \times 2\frac{1}{4} = \frac{13}{3} \times \frac{9}{4} = \frac{117}{12} = 9\frac{3}{4}$

Skill 13

Express answers in lowest terms.

10. $1\frac{1}{2} \times 1\frac{1}{3}$ **11.** $3\frac{2}{3} \times 4\frac{2}{5}$

12. $\frac{1}{8} \times 4\frac{4}{5}$ **13.** $7 \times 8\frac{1}{3}$

14. $12\frac{1}{2} \times 1\frac{1}{2}$ **15.** $20\frac{1}{2} \times 2\frac{1}{4}$

Mixed Practice

Express answers in lowest terms.

16. $\frac{2}{5} \times \frac{4}{7}$ **17.** $\frac{3}{8} \times \frac{4}{9}$ **18.** $\frac{2}{3} \times 1\frac{1}{8}$ **19.** $3\frac{2}{3} \times \frac{1}{4}$

20. $6 \times \frac{4}{5}$ **21.** $\frac{3}{4} \times 8$ **22.** $3\frac{1}{3} \times 4\frac{2}{5}$ **23.** $2\frac{1}{4} \times 1\frac{2}{3}$

24. $\frac{3}{4} \times 2\frac{5}{6}$ **25.** $6 \times 3\frac{1}{4}$ **26.** $18\frac{1}{2} \times 2\frac{2}{3}$ **27.** $1\frac{3}{5} \times 5\frac{2}{6}$

28. $5 \times 15\frac{1}{2}$ **29.** $10 \times 6\frac{2}{5}$ **30.** $2\frac{2}{7} \times 1\frac{1}{9}$ **31.** $3\frac{4}{9} \times 7\frac{3}{8}$

32. $\frac{7}{10} \times \frac{5}{9}$ **33.** $11\frac{3}{4} \times 8\frac{1}{3}$ **34.** $\frac{11}{12} \times \frac{4}{33}$ **35.** $6\frac{7}{8} \times 10\frac{1}{3}$

SKILLS

SKILL 21

Dividing Fractions/Mixed Numbers

Fractions

Divide.

$\frac{2}{3} \div \frac{3}{8} = \frac{2}{3} \times \frac{8}{3} = \frac{16}{9} = 1\frac{7}{9}$

Skill 20

Express answers in lowest terms.

1. $\frac{1}{4} \div \frac{1}{8}$
2. $\frac{3}{8} \div \frac{1}{4}$
3. $\frac{3}{4} \div \frac{2}{5}$
4. $5 \div \frac{5}{6}$
5. $7 \div \frac{14}{15}$
6. $8 \div \frac{4}{11}$
7. $\frac{3}{4} \div \frac{1}{8}$
8. $\frac{2}{5} \div \frac{5}{6}$
9. $\frac{4}{7} \div \frac{1}{28}$

Mixed Numbers

Divide.

Skill 13

$$\begin{aligned} 5\tfrac{1}{6} \div 1\tfrac{1}{4} &= \tfrac{31}{6} \div \tfrac{5}{4} \\ &= \tfrac{31}{6} \times \tfrac{4}{5} \\ &= \tfrac{124}{30} \\ &= 4\tfrac{2}{15} \end{aligned}$$

Skill 20

Express answers in lowest terms.

10. $3\frac{2}{3} \div 1\frac{1}{2}$
11. $3\frac{5}{6} \div 1\frac{1}{5}$
12. $2\frac{1}{6} \div 3\frac{1}{3}$
13. $4\frac{2}{3} \div 1\frac{3}{5}$
14. $\frac{3}{4} \div 3\frac{1}{2}$
15. $\frac{5}{8} \div 2\frac{1}{2}$
16. $16 \div 1\frac{1}{8}$
17. $11\frac{1}{3} \div 2\frac{1}{5}$
18. $12 \div 2\frac{12}{17}$
19. $13\frac{1}{17} \div 3\frac{1}{6}$

Mixed Practice

Express answers in lowest terms.

20. $7\frac{1}{2} \div 1\frac{1}{4}$
21. $8\frac{1}{4} \div 5\frac{1}{2}$
22. $\frac{5}{11} \div 2\frac{1}{5}$
23. $\frac{9}{10} \div \frac{3}{5}$
24. $\frac{7}{12} \div \frac{1}{6}$
25. $1\frac{3}{8} \div 2\frac{1}{16}$
26. $13\frac{1}{3} \div \frac{1}{10}$
27. $8\frac{1}{3} \div \frac{5}{9}$
28. $\frac{19}{21} \div 3\frac{1}{2}$
29. $3\frac{5}{7} \div \frac{13}{21}$
30. $8 \div 1\frac{3}{5}$
31. $20 \div \frac{2}{3}$
32. $2\frac{1}{16} \div 11$
33. $5\frac{3}{8} \div 22$
34. $22 \div \frac{3}{5}$
35. $\frac{11}{15} \div 1\frac{12}{13}$
36. $\frac{11}{12} \div \frac{11}{12}$
37. $2\frac{11}{14} \div \frac{3}{7}$
38. $\frac{15}{16} \div \frac{5}{32}$
39. $19\frac{1}{2} \div 19\frac{1}{2}$

SKILL 22

Writing Ratios

SKILLS

Compare Two Numbers

What is the ratio of desks to computers?

Office Inventory		
Computers	Calculators	Desks
12	5	15

Ratio of desks to computers:

15 to 12 or 15:12 or $\frac{15}{12}$

Write the ratio.

Department Sales		
Meat	Produce	Dairy
$1,500	$600	$1,200

1. Ratio of meat to produce
2. Ratio of meat to dairy
3. Ratio of produce to dairy
4. Ratio of dairy to produce
5. Ratio of produce to meat
6. Ratio of dairy to meat

Ratios as Fractions

Write the ratio of tables to chairs as a fraction in lowest terms.

A restaurant has 40 chairs and 16 tables.

Ratio of tables to chairs is $\frac{16}{40}$.

$\frac{16}{40} = \frac{2}{5}$ ◄····· Skill 12

Write the ratio as a fraction in lowest terms.

7. Nurse-to-patient ratio in a hospital is 6 nurses to 30 patients.
8. Teacher-to-student ratio in a school is 8 teachers to 160 students.
9. Door-to-window ratio in a house is 3 doors to 45 windows.
10. Width-to-length ratio of a box is 22 centimeters to 30 centimeters.
11. Room-to-desk ratio in a school is 40 rooms to 1,000 desks.
12. Land area-to-people ratio in a county is 6 square kilometers to 138 people.
13. Car-to-people ratio in a town is 4,000 cars to 10,000 people.
14. Hit-to-strikeout ratio of a batter is 15 hits to 25 strikeouts.

SKILLS

SKILL 23

Proportions

Checking Proportions

Is this proportion true?

$\frac{5}{9} \stackrel{?}{=} \frac{35}{63}$

Cross multiply.

$\frac{5}{9} \stackrel{?}{=} \frac{35}{63} \quad \cdots\cdots\blacktriangleright \quad 5 \times 63 \stackrel{?}{=} 9 \times 35$

$315 = 315$

True. The products are equal.

1. $\frac{1}{3} \stackrel{?}{=} \frac{4}{12}$

2. $\frac{2}{5} \stackrel{?}{=} \frac{4}{10}$

3. $\frac{4}{5} \stackrel{?}{=} \frac{16}{19}$

4. $\frac{5}{6} \stackrel{?}{=} \frac{25}{29}$

5. $\frac{3}{4} \stackrel{?}{=} \frac{6}{9}$

6. $\frac{1}{2} \stackrel{?}{=} \frac{11}{24}$

7. $\frac{3}{8} \stackrel{?}{=} \frac{9}{24}$

8. $\frac{2}{7} \stackrel{?}{=} \frac{14}{49}$

9. $\frac{16}{32} \stackrel{?}{=} \frac{1}{2}$

10. $\frac{13}{23} \stackrel{?}{=} \frac{1}{2}$

11. $\frac{10}{15} \stackrel{?}{=} \frac{5}{8}$

12. $\frac{22}{30} \stackrel{?}{=} \frac{11}{15}$

Solving Proportions

Solve for the number that makes the proportion true.

$\frac{7}{8} = \frac{28}{a}$

Cross multiply.

$\frac{7}{8} = \frac{28}{a} \quad \cdots\cdots\blacktriangleright \quad 7 \times a = 28 \times 8$

$7 \times a = 224$

$a = \frac{224}{7}$

$a = 32$

Solve.

13. $\frac{1}{2} = \frac{9}{h}$

14. $\frac{2}{3} = \frac{12}{y}$

15. $\frac{6}{a} = \frac{9}{11}$

16. $\frac{8}{y} = \frac{12}{15}$

17. $\frac{t}{6} = \frac{1}{11}$

18. $\frac{a}{7} = \frac{2}{19}$

19. $\frac{5}{9} = \frac{n}{10}$

20. $\frac{4}{11} = \frac{x}{33}$

21. $\frac{8}{13} = \frac{y}{20}$

22. $\frac{42}{66} = \frac{y}{11}$

23. $\frac{11}{33} = \frac{c}{60}$

24. $\frac{8}{40} = \frac{5}{n}$

25. $\frac{n}{7} = \frac{15}{21}$

26. $\frac{2}{3} = \frac{18}{n}$

27. $\frac{96}{16} = \frac{n}{4}$

28. $\frac{13}{42} = \frac{65}{c}$

29. $\frac{16}{3} = \frac{t}{12}$

30. $\frac{h}{25} = \frac{15}{125}$

31. $\frac{27}{y} = \frac{81}{45}$

32. $\frac{a}{21} = \frac{9}{27}$

33. $\frac{121}{11} = \frac{550}{h}$

Solving a Rate Problem

Equal Rates as a Proportion

Write the proportion.

Three hundred words keyboarded in 5 minutes.

How many words in 3 minutes?

$$\frac{300 \text{ words}}{5 \text{ minutes}} = \frac{n \text{ words}}{3 \text{ minutes}}$$

$$\frac{300}{5} = \frac{n}{3}$$

Write the proportion.

1. Three oranges cost $1.29. How much does it cost for 7 oranges?
2. A car travels 84 kilometers on 7 liters of gas. How many kilometers can it go on 13 liters of gas?
3. Five centimeters on a map represents 40 kilometers. How many kilometers does 17 centimeters represent?
4. A machine uses 50 kilowatt-hours in 6 hours. How many kilowatt-hours does it use in 45 hours?

Solve a Rate Problem

Find the number of boxes.

5,000 envelopes in 10 boxes.

3,000 envelopes in how many boxes?

$$\frac{5{,}000 \text{ envelopes}}{10 \text{ boxes}} = \frac{3{,}000 \text{ envelopes}}{n \text{ boxes}}$$

$$\frac{5{,}000}{10} = \frac{3{,}000}{n}$$

$n = 6$ ◄····· Skill 23

Solve.

5. Four apples cost $1.29. How much for 22 apples?
6. A machine produces 121 bolts in 3 hours. How many bolts in 15 hours?
7. Thirty-six pages keyboarded in 4 hours. How many pages in 13 hours?
8. A car travels 19 kilometers on 2 liters of gas. How many kilometers on 76 liters of gas?

Mixed Practice

Write the proportion and solve.

9. A machine produces 660 wheels in 4 hours. How many wheels are made in 9 hours?
10. Fuel costs $3.43 for 3 liters. How much would it cost to fill an 84 liter tank?
11. The telephone rate to Poland is $0.67 for 3 minutes. How much for 14 minutes?
12. Carlotta can run 11 kilometers in 60 minutes. How far can she run in 105 minutes?
13. Juan can read 6 pages in 5 minutes. How long will it take him to read 40 pages?

SKILLS

SKILL 25

Comparing Rates

Find the Unit Rate.

Find the number of books.

4,200 books in 200 boxes.

How many books in 1 box?

$$\frac{4{,}200 \text{ books}}{200 \text{ boxes}} = \frac{n \text{ books}}{1 \text{ box}}$$

$n = 21$ ◄····· Skill 24

The unit rate is 21 books per box.

Find the unit rate.

1. There are 3,456 oranges in 12 crates. How many oranges in 1 crate?

2. Ida prints 4,950 words in 9 minutes. How many words in 1 minute?

3. Lou drives 560 kilometers in 7 hours. How many kilometers in 1 hour?

4. You can buy 15 dozen eggs for $28.20. How much for 3 dozen?

5. Sam drives 384 kilometers in 6 hours. How far does he drive in 1 hour? How far in 10 hours?

6. There are 2,500 sheets of bond paper that weigh 100 pounds. How many sheets weigh 1 pound? What will 10,000 sheets weigh?

Compare Unit Rates

Which is faster?

Car A: 280 kilometers in 4 hours

Car B: 455 kilometers in 7 hours

Car A	**Car B**
$\frac{280}{4} = 70$	$\frac{455}{7} = 65$
70 km/h	65 km/h

70 km/h ····► is greater than ····· 65 km/h

Car A is faster.

Compare the unit rates.

7. Which uses less fuel per kilometer?
   Car A: 52 kilometers on 6 liters
   Car B: 59 kilometers on 7 liters

8. Which costs less per kilogram?
   Carton A: $89.25 for 15 kilograms
   Carton B: $117.00 for 20 kilograms

9. Which shipment holds more per crate?
   Shipment A: 1,584 apples in 11 crates
   Shipment B: 1,937 apples in 13 crates

10. Which makes more cogs per hour?
    Machine A: 288 cogs in 4 hours
    Machine B: 414 cogs in 6 hours

11. Which gets more kilometers per liter?
    Car A: 162 kilometers on 18 liters of fuel
    Car B: 220 kilometers on 20 liters of fuel

SKILL 26

Writing Decimals as Percents

SKILLS

Two or More Decimal Places

Write 0.037 as a percent.

0.037 = ?%

0.037 ······➤ 0.037

Move decimal 2 places to the right.

0.037 = 3.7%

Write as a percent.

1. 0.10 **2.** 0.15 **3.** 0.25

4. 0.74 **5.** 0.82 **6.** 0.93

7. 2.13 **8.** 4.212 **9.** 5.753

10. 0.267 **11.** 0.391 **12.** 0.914

13. 12.104 **14.** 0.625 **15.** 10.82

16. 0.007 **17.** 0.106 **18.** 0.008

19. 0.04 **20.** 0.001 **21.** 0.503

Fewer Than Two Decimal Places

Write 0.5 as a percent.

0.5 = ?%

Use zero as a placeholder.

0.5 ······➤ 0.50%

Move decimal 2 places to the right.

0.5 = 50%

Write as a percent.

22. 0.4 **23.** 0.7 **24.** 0.9

25. 7.1 **26.** 9.3 **27.** 10.5

28. 11.0 **29.** 12.6 **30.** 17.1

31. 22.5 **32.** 29.0 **33.** 37.2

34. 0.1 **35.** 7.5 **36.** 1.8

37. 16.3 **38.** 0.3 **39.** 6.2

Mixed Practice

Write as a percent.

40. 0.57 **41.** 3.80 **42.** 0.001 **43.** 0.67 **44.** 20.7

45. 8.8 **46.** 0.2915 **47.** 0.32 **48.** 17.4 **49.** 3.003

50. 139.25 **51.** 0.2187 **52.** 9.1 **53.** 25.00 **54.** 12.004

55. 0.14 **56.** 2.185 **57.** 0.51 **58.** 9.3 **59.** 1.868

60. 8.554 **61.** 0.003 **62.** 3.246 **63.** 0.26 **64.** 0.07

65. 0.0032 **66.** 3.642 **67.** 0.29 **68.** 0.052 **69.** 3.42

70. 0.30 **71.** 2.1 **72.** 0.0001 **73.** 1.67 **74.** 1.0

75. 2.5 **76.** 0.005 **77.** 2.077 **78.** 1.5 **79.** 0.19

SKILL 27

Writing Fractions/Mixed Numbers as Percents

Fractions

Write $\frac{3}{5}$ as a percent.

$\frac{3}{5} = ?\%$

$\frac{3}{5} = 0.6 = 60\%$

Skill 14 Skill 26

Write as a percent.

1. $\frac{1}{4}$
2. $\frac{2}{5}$
3. $\frac{3}{4}$
4. $\frac{7}{10}$
5. $\frac{1}{8}$
6. $\frac{3}{20}$
7. $\frac{7}{20}$
8. $\frac{12}{25}$
9. $\frac{7}{50}$
10. $\frac{7}{40}$
11. $\frac{5}{8}$
12. $\frac{11}{16}$

Mixed Numbers

Write $2\frac{3}{8}$ as a percent.

$2\frac{3}{8} = ?\%$

$2\frac{3}{8} = \frac{19}{8} = 2.375 = 237.5\%$

Skill 13 Skill 14 Skill 26

Write as a percent.

13. $2\frac{3}{4}$
14. $4\frac{5}{8}$
15. $6\frac{2}{3}$
16. $7\frac{1}{6}$
17. $8\frac{5}{9}$
18. $5\frac{4}{15}$
19. $8\frac{7}{40}$
20. $14\frac{3}{16}$
21. $7\frac{11}{50}$

Mixed Practice

Write as a percent.

22. $\frac{3}{5}$
23. $5\frac{3}{8}$
24. $12\frac{5}{6}$
25. $\frac{7}{12}$
26. $\frac{1}{9}$
27. $15\frac{3}{10}$
28. $\frac{9}{40}$
29. $20\frac{4}{5}$
30. $10\frac{6}{25}$
31. $18\frac{5}{8}$
32. $9\frac{3}{40}$
33. $\frac{15}{16}$
34. $8\frac{19}{50}$
35. $11\frac{5}{14}$
36. $16\frac{9}{20}$
37. $\frac{7}{9}$
38. $7\frac{3}{16}$
39. $5\frac{11}{15}$
40. $\frac{11}{30}$
41. $17\frac{7}{20}$

SKILL 28

Writing Percents as Decimals

Percent in Decimal Form

Write 8.75% as a decimal.

Drop % sign.

8.75% ······> 0 08.75

Move 2 places to the left.

8.75% = 0.0875

Write as a decimal.

1. 10.5% **2.** 15.7% **3.** 40%

4. 85% **5.** 120% **6.** 137%

7. 6.7% **8.** 7.1% **9.** 8.9%

10. 95% **11.** 119% **12.** 7.9%

13. 17.2% **14.** 85.6% **15.** 100%

16. 1.35% **17.** 5.3% **18.** 142%

Percent in Fractional Form

Write $\frac{3}{20}$% as a decimal.

$\frac{3}{20}$% = 0.15% ······> 0 00.15

Skill 14

$\frac{3}{20}$% = 0.0015

Write as a decimal.

19. $\frac{7}{10}$% **20.** $\frac{11}{20}$% **21.** $\frac{5}{8}$%

22. $\frac{2}{25}$% **23.** $5\frac{3}{5}$% **24.** $7\frac{1}{10}$%

25. $6\frac{4}{5}$% **26.** $22\frac{3}{4}$% **27.** $30\frac{3}{5}$%

28. $89\frac{13}{20}$% **29.** $57\frac{21}{25}$% **30.** $12\frac{3}{4}$%

Mixed Practice

Write as a decimal.

31. 74.25% **32.** $6\frac{1}{4}$% **33.** $18\frac{4}{5}$% **34.** 0.97% **35.** $14\frac{9}{20}$%

36. $28\frac{3}{40}$% **37.** 0.125% **38.** 6.25% **39.** $\frac{7}{50}$% **40.** 6.63%

41. 8.79% **42.** 100% **43.** $\frac{19}{20}$% **44.** 127% **45.** $\frac{1}{40}$%

46. $20\frac{1}{4}$% **47.** $22\frac{1}{2}$% **48.** 14.6% **49.** $25\frac{1}{5}$% **50.** 18.9%

SKILL 29

Writing Percents as Fractions

Percent in Decimal Form

Write 37.5% as a fraction.

$37.5\% = 0.375 = \frac{3}{8}$

Skill 28 Skill 14

Write as a fraction in lowest terms.

1. 45% **2.** 80% **3.** 175%

4. 200% **5.** 11.7% **6.** 0.1%

7. 0.15% **8.** 67.3% **9.** 10.6%

10. 78.55% **11.** 37.63% **12.** 51.42%

13. 50% **14.** 75% **15.** 10.1%

16. 0.12% **17.** 80.9% **18.** 42.1%

Percent in Fractional Form

Write $16\frac{2}{3}\%$ as a fraction.

$$16\tfrac{2}{3}\% = 16\tfrac{2}{3} \div 100$$
$$= \tfrac{50}{3} \div 100 \quad \text{(Skill 13)}$$
$$= \tfrac{50}{300} \quad \text{(Skill 21)}$$
$$= \tfrac{1}{6} \quad \text{(Skill 12)}$$

Write as a fraction in lowest terms.

19. $6\frac{1}{4}\%$ **20.** $37\frac{1}{2}\%$ **21.** $43\frac{3}{4}\%$

22. $3\frac{1}{2}\%$ **23.** $\frac{1}{4}\%$ **24.** $10\frac{1}{3}\%$

25. $15\frac{1}{2}\%$ **26.** $20\frac{1}{2}\%$ **27.** $25\frac{1}{2}\%$

28. $15\frac{3}{4}\%$ **29.** $16\frac{2}{3}\%$ **30.** $33\frac{1}{3}\%$

Mixed Practice

Write as a fraction in lowest terms.

31. 30% **32.** 57.2% **33.** $31\frac{1}{4}\%$ **34.** 63.5% **35.** $12\frac{1}{2}\%$

36. $13\frac{1}{3}\%$ **37.** $26\frac{2}{3}\%$ **38.** 64.75% **39.** $11\frac{1}{9}\%$ **40.** 78.55%

41. 50% **42.** 75% **43.** $1\frac{1}{4}\%$ **44.** 100% **45.** $12\frac{3}{4}\%$

46. $4\frac{3}{4}\%$ **47.** $5\frac{3}{8}\%$ **48.** 75.91% **49.** $6\frac{2}{3}\%$ **50.** 121%

SKILL 30

Finding the Percentage

SKILLS

Decimal Percents

Find 15.5% of 36.

15.5% of 36 $= n$

Skill 28

$0.155 \times 36 = n$

$5.58 = n$

15.5% of 36 $= 5.58$

Find the percentage.

1. 15% of 60
2. 30% of 72
3. 4% of 96
4. 9% of 122
5. 6.5% of 120
6. 8.3% of 150
7. 17.8% of 80
8. 31.2% of 140
9. 5.81% of 60
10. 7.32% of 45
11. 67.7% of 67
12. 8.92% of 35

Fractional Percents

Find $\frac{3}{4}$% of 1,600.

$\frac{3}{4}$% of 1,600 $= n$

Skill 29

$\frac{3}{400} \times 1{,}600 = n$

$12 = n$

$\frac{3}{4}$% of 1,600 $= 12$

Find the percentage.

13. $2\frac{1}{2}$% of 400
14. $4\frac{1}{2}$% of 200
15. $33\frac{1}{3}$% of 120
16. $3\frac{5}{6}$% of 600
17. $\frac{3}{4}$% of 800
18. $\frac{3}{5}$% of 50
19. $\frac{3}{8}$% of 600
20. $\frac{7}{8}$% of 80

Mixed Practice

Find the percentage.

21. 80% of 160
22. $8\frac{1}{3}$% of 72
23. 9.1% of 90
24. $15\frac{3}{5}$% of 90
25. $16\frac{2}{3}$% of 90
26. 45% of 72
27. $\frac{1}{4}$% of 800
28. 0.75% of 1,000
29. 125% of 64
30. $12\frac{1}{4}$% of 65
31. 7.2% of 127
32. $6\frac{1}{4}$% of 1,600
33. $4\frac{1}{6}$% of 600
34. 16.5% of 84
35. $8\frac{1}{2}$% of 75
36. 24.7% of 80

SKILLS

SKILL 31

Finding the Rate

Percent Less Than Base

What percent of 75 is 60?

$n\%$ of 75 = 60

Write as a proportion and solve.

$$\frac{n}{100} = \frac{60}{75}$$

$$75 \times n = 6{,}000$$

$$n = 80$$ ◄··· Skill 23

80% of 75 = 60

Solve. Round answers to the nearest tenth of a percent.

1. $n\%$ of 40 = 20

2. $n\%$ of 60 = 15

3. $n\%$ of 90 = 18

4. $n\%$ of 60 = 9

5. $n\%$ of 70 = 25

6. $n\%$ of 90 = 65

7. $n\%$ of 65 = 58

8. $n\%$ of 84 = 75

9. $n\%$ of 113 = 79

10. $n\%$ of 410 = 295.5

11. $n\%$ of 94 = 82

12. $n\%$ of 296 = 239.76

Percent Greater Than Base

What percent of 90 is 162?

$n\%$ of 90 = 162

Write as a proportion and solve.

$$\frac{n}{100} = \frac{162}{90}$$

$$90 \times n = 16{,}200$$

$$n = 180$$

180% of 90 = 162

Solve. Round answers to the nearest tenth of a percent.

13. $n\%$ of 20 = 30

14. $n\%$ of 36 = 45

15. $n\%$ of 50 = 60

16. $n\%$ of 70 = 91

17. $n\%$ of 60 = 80

18. $n\%$ of 72 = 96

19. $n\%$ of 24 = 31

20. $n\%$ of 56 = 77

21. $n\%$ of 37 = 148

22. $n\%$ of 60 = 90

23. $n\%$ of 81 = 415.75

24. $n\%$ of 110 = 130

Mixed Practice

Solve. Round answers to the nearest tenth of a percent.

25. $n\%$ of 125 = 100

26. $n\%$ of 100 = 115

27. $n\%$ of 130 = 60

28. $n\%$ of 56 = 96

29. $n\%$ of 89 = 49

30. $n\%$ of 84 = 108

31. $n\%$ of 115 = 92

32. $n\%$ of 42 = 52.5

33. $n\%$ of 64 = 76.8

34. $n\%$ of 64 = 24

35. $n\%$ of 204 = 51

36. $n\%$ of 42 = 6.72

37. $n\%$ of 36 = 50

38. $n\%$ of 173 = 136.25

39. $n\%$ of 18 = 36

40. $n\%$ of 21 = 63

41. $n\%$ of 120 = 80

42. $n\%$ of 15.5 = 62

43. $n\%$ of 90 = 4.5

44. $n\%$ of 125 = 18.75

45. $n\%$ of 75 = 110

SKILL 32

Finding the Base

SKILLS

Decimal Percents

42 is 37.5% of what number?

37.5% of $n = 42$

$0.375 \times n = 42$

$n = 42 \div 0.375$

Skill 28 $n = 112$

37.5% of $112 = 42$

Find the number. Round to the nearest tenth.

1. 12.5% of $n = 9$

2. 62.5% of $n = 55$

3. 8.25% of $n = 664$

4. 7% of $n = 3.5$

5. 5.75% of $n = 92$

6. 9% of $n = 8.2$

7. 11% of $n = 37$

8. 3% of $n = 8.7$

9. 5% of $n = 3$

10. 12.5% of $n = 21$

11. 37.3% of $n = 50$

12. 81% of $n = 14$

Fractional Percents

3 is $6\frac{1}{4}$% of what number?

$6\frac{1}{4}$% of $n = 3$

$\frac{1}{16} n = 3$

$n = 3 \div \frac{1}{16}$

Skill 29 $n = 48$

$6\frac{1}{4}$% of $48 = 3$

Find the number.

13. $2\frac{1}{2}$% of $n = 4$

14. $3\frac{1}{8}$% of $n = 2$

15. $33\frac{1}{3}$% of $n = 20$

16. $\frac{1}{4}$% of $n = 2$

17. $37\frac{1}{2}$% of $n = 34$

18. $\frac{3}{5}$% of $n = 6$

19. $45\frac{1}{2}$% of $n = 25$

20. $\frac{3}{4}$% of $n = 7$

Mixed Practice

Find the number.

21. 80% of $n = 60$

22. 12.5% of $n = 39$

23. 116% of $n = 2.9$

24. 10% of $n = 2.9$

25. 8% of $n = 4.2$

26. 40% of $n = 6.8$

27. $16\frac{2}{3}$% of $n = 13$

28. 145% of $n = 6.38$

29. $66\frac{2}{3}$% of $n = 120$

30. 25% of $n = 36$

31. $2\frac{2}{3}$% of $n = 6$

32. 90% of $n = 72$

33. 6% of $n = 3.3$

34. 7.8% of $n = 9$

35. $16\frac{3}{4}$% of $n = 33$

APPLICATIONS

APPLICATION A

Formulas

Substituting in a Formula

To use a formula to solve a problem, substitute known values in the formula. Then solve. Remember to perform any computations within parentheses first.

► **An airplane travels at a rate of 960 kilometers per hour. How far can the plane travel in 7 hours?**

Formula:	Distance	=	Rate × Time
Substitute:	Distance	=	960 × 7
Solve:	Distance	=	6,720

The plane travels 6,720 kilometers in 7 hours.

Find the distance.

Rate × Time = Distance

	Rate	Time	Distance
1.	100 mi/h	6 h	
2.	55 km/h	4 h	
3.	14 m/s	32 s	
4.	30 mi/h	6 h	
5.	42 m/s	5 s	

Find the area of the triangle.

$\frac{1}{2}$ × Base × Height = Area

	Base	Height	Area
6.	1 m	0.5 m	
7.	64 ft	38 ft	
8.	18 in	5 in	
9.	30 km	24 km	

Find the rate or time.

Rate × Time = Distance

	Rate	Time	Distance
10.	60 mi/h		360 mi
11.		5 h	250 mi
12.	35 m/h		140 mi
13.		7 h	434 mi
14.	72 m/h		468 mi

Find the area of the circle. Round if necessary.

$\pi r^2 = \pi \times r \times r =$ Area

	π	r	Area
15.	3.14	6 feet	
16.	3.14	10 inches	
17.	3.14	15.5 feet	
18.	3.14	20.25 meters	

Find the long-distance telephone charges.

Cost per minute × Minutes = Charge

	Country	Minutes	Cost per Minute	Charges
19.	Australia	15	$0.08	
20.	Bahamas	9	0.15	
21.	Cuba	31	2.20	
22.	Denmark	22	0.49	
23.	Ireland	38	0.80	

APPLICATION B

More Formulas

Multiplying or Dividing to Solve Formulas

To solve some formulas after substituting, you may have to multiply or divide both sides of the equation by the same number.

▶ **An airplane cruising at a rate of 575 kilometers per hour has traveled 2,645 kilometers. How long did it take to make this trip?**

Formula: Distance = Rate × Time

Substitute: 2,645 = 575 × Time

Divide: $\frac{2{,}645}{575} = \frac{575 \times \text{Time}}{575}$

Solve: 4.6 hours = Time

Find the missing amount.

	Rate × Time = Distance		
	Rate	**Time**	**Distance**
1.	88 in/min	3.5 min	
2.	60 km/h		195 km
3.	675 yd/h	13 h	
4.		1.75 h	78.75 km
5.	24 km/h		192 km
6.		$4\frac{1}{2}$ h	$247\frac{1}{2}$ ft
7.	3.2 m/s		96 m

Adding or Subtracting to Solve Formulas

To solve some formulas after substituting, you may have to add the same number to, or subtract it from, both sides of the equation.

▶ **The temperature of a solution is 212°F (degrees Fahrenheit). What is this in degrees Celsius (°C)?**

Formula: °F = (1.8 × °C) + 32

Substitute: 212 = (1.8 × °C) + 32

Subtract: $212 - 32 = (1.8 \times °C) + 32 - 32$; 180 = (1.8 × °C)

Divide: $\frac{180}{1.8} = \frac{(1.8 \times °C)}{1.8}$

Solve: 100 = °C

Find the missing amount.

	(1.8 × °C) + 32 = °F	
	Degrees Celsius	**Degrees Fahrenheit**
8.	50	
9.		86
10.		32
11.	120	
12.		95
13.		68
14.	144	
15.	10	
16.		5

APPLICATIONS

APPLICATION C

Tables and Charts

Reading Tables and Charts

To read a table or chart, find the row containing one of the conditions of the information that you seek. Run down the column containing the other condition until it crosses that row. Read the answer.

▶ **How many sales were made at the Lincoln office?**

The table shows that there were 537 sales made at the Lincoln office.

Imag Corp. Sales Report			
Office	**Agents**	**Sales**	**Income**
Bronx	252	640	$12,000,000
Calgary	204	307	1,800,000
Columbus	92	778	1,200,000
Dallas	50	761	1,300,000
Denver	76	398	1,500,000
Lincoln	35	537	1,500,000
San Diego	128	813	14,300,000
Toronto	710	390	7,900,000

Find the income for each of the following offices:

1. Columbus
2. Denver
3. Toronto
4. Bronx
5. Which offices made more than 500 sales?
6. Which offices have fewer than 200 agents?

Using Tables and Charts

▶ **An order weighing 5 pounds 5 ounces costs $18.50 in shipping charges. How was it delivered?**

The table shows that the order was delivered in the Western U.S. zone and the Standard 3–5 Day Delivery category was used.

Delivery Charges				
	Standard 3–5 Day Delivery		Overnight (By 3:00PM)	
	Zone		Zone	
Weight	Eastern U.S.	Western U.S.	Eastern U.S.	Western U.S.
Minimum Charge	$ 8.00	$ 8.50	$16.00	$17.00
2 lb 1 oz to 4 lb	$13.00	$13.50	$26.00	$27.00
4 lb 1 oz to 8 lb	$19.00	$18.50	$36.00	$37.00
8 lb 1 oz to 14 lb	$22.50	$23.00	$45.00	$46.00
14 lb 1 oz to 20 lb	$26.00	$26.50	$52.00	$53.00

Answer the following. Use the table shown.

7. An order weighing 16 pounds costs $53.00 in shipping charges. How was it delivered?
8. An order weighing 9 pounds 12 ounces costs $22.50 in shipping charges. To what zone was it delivered?
9. An order weighing 10 pounds costs $45.00 in shipping charges. How was it delivered?
10. Find the shipping charges for a 7 pound 4 ounce package sent to the Eastern U.S. zone by the Overnight (By 3:00 PM) method.
11. Find the shipping charges for a 1 pound 9 ounce package sent to the Eastern U.S. zone by the Standard 3–5 Day Delivery method.

APPLICATION D

Making Change

Making Change: Building Up

To make change, build up to the next nickel, dime, quarter, and so on, until the amount presented is reached.

► **Compute the change from $5.00 for a purchase of $3.67.**

CHANGE	
	$3.67
3 pennies ···►	+ .03
	3.70
1 nickel ···►	+ .05
	3.75
1 quarter ···►	+ .25
	4.00
1 dollar ···►	+ 1.00
Amount presented ···►	$5.00

Compute the change from $10 using the fewest coins and bills.

1. $3.75 **2.** $7.78

3. $1.99 **4.** $3.47

5. $5.63 **6.** $9.19

Compute the change using the fewest coins and bills.

7. Amount spent: $15.05
Amount presented: $20

8. Amount spent: $3.37
Amount presented: $20

9. Amount spent: $2.29
Amount presented: $3

Making Change: Loose Coins

The amount presented may contain loose coins so that fewer coins and bills are returned in the change.

► **Compute the change from $5.02 for a purchase of $3.67.**

a. Subtract the loose change.

Amount Presented	Purchase
$5.02	$3.67
− .02	− .02
$5.00	$3.65

b. Now compute the change from $5.00 for a purchase of $3.65.

CHANGE	
	$3.65
1 dime ···►	+ .10
	3.75
1 quarter ···►	+ .25
	4.00
1 dollar ···►	+ 1.00
	$5.00

Compute the change using the fewest coins and bills.

10. Amount spent: $5.26
Amount presented: $6.01

11. Amount spent: $7.79
Amount presented: $10.04

12. Amount spent: $1.07
Amount presented: $5.07

13. Amount spent: $3.92
Amount presented: $10.02

14. Amount spent: $15.21
Amount presented: $20.01

15. Amount spent: $7.81
Amount presented: $10.06

16. Amount spent: $6.03
Amount presented: $21.03

17. Amount spent: $9.62
Amount presented: $21.12

APPLICATION E

Rounding Time: Nearest Quarter Hour

To round to the nearest quarter hour, find the quarter-hour interval that the given time is between. Subtract the earlier quarter from the given time. Subtract the given time from the later quarter. Round to whichever is closer.

▶ **Round 6:19 to the nearest quarter hour.**

```
  6:19          6:30
– 6:15        – 6:19
   4 minutes    11 minutes
```

4 is less than 11; round to 6:15

Round to the nearest quarter hour.

1. 8:39	**2.** 10:40	**3.** 6:55
4. 1:23	**5.** 11:17	**6.** 3:11
7. 12:09	**8.** 4:44	**9.** 3:32
10. 11:11	**11.** 8:51	**12.** 1:50
13. 7:35	**14.** 5:04	**15.** 9:40
16. 10:34	**17.** 12:39	**18.** 6:41
19. 6:01	**20.** 3:49	**21.** 11:36
22. 8:05	**23.** 10:10	**24.** 2:15

APPLICATION F

Elapsed Time (Hours)

APPLICATIONS

Finding Elapsed Time in Hours

To find the elapsed time, subtract the earlier time from the later time. If it is necessary to "borrow," rewrite the later time by subtracting 1 from the hours and by adding 60 to the minutes.

▶ **How much time has elapsed between 11:45 AM and 12:23 PM ?**

```
 12:23 =  11:23 + :60 =  11:83
–11:45 = –11:45       = –11:45
                          38 min
```

Find the elapsed time.

1. From 6:05 PM to 8:51 PM
2. From 4:18 AM to 6:52 AM
3. From 8:30 AM to 11:45 AM
4. From 6:45 PM to 11:59 PM
5. From 10:45 AM to 11:36 AM
6. From 3:45 PM to 5:30 PM

Finding Elapsed Time Spanning 1 O'Clock.

To find the elapsed time when the period spans 1 o'clock, add 12 hours to the later time before subtracting.

▶ **How much time has elapsed between 7:45 PM and 2:52 AM ?**

```
 2:52 =  2:52 + 12:00 =  14:52
–7:45 = – 7:45        = – 7:45
                        7h:7 min
```

Find the elapsed time.

7. From 8:15 AM to 1:30 PM
8. From 4:55 AM to 1:00 PM
9. From 11:30 PM to 7:50 AM
10. From 9:45 PM to 8:00 AM
11. From 3:30 AM to 2:15 PM

APPLICATION G

Elapsed Time (Days)

To find the number of days **between** two dates, or **from** one date **to** the next, use the table on page A10. Find the position of each date in the year. When the date runs from one year to the next year, add 365 to the later date. Then subtract the earlier date from the later. To find the number of days **from** one date through another, find the elapsed time between the dates and add 1 day.

Day No.	Jan.	Feb.	Mar.	Apr.	May	June	July	Aug.	Sept.
1	1	32	60	91	121	152	182	213	244
2	2	33	61	92	122	153	183	214	245
3	3	34	62	93	123	154	184	215	246
4	4	35	63	94	124	155	185	216	247
5	5	36	64	95	125	156	186	217	248
6	6	37	65	96	126	157	187	218	249

▶ **How many days have elapsed between April 4 and January 6?**

Jan. 6: (6 + 365) = 371
Apr. 4: − 94 = − 94
277 days

Find the elapsed time. Use the table on page A10.

1. Between August 10 and December 25
2. From March 21 through September 30
3. Between June 1 and December 30
4. From May 21 to July 2
5. From September 5 through May 20

APPLICATION H

Determining Leap Years

A year is a leap year if it is exactly divisible by 4. Exceptions are years that end in '00' (1900, 2000, and so on); they must be divisible by 400.

▶ **Was 1848 a leap year?**

1848 ÷ 4 = 462; 1848 was a leap year.

Find the leap years.

1. 1949
2. 1980
3. 2000
4. 1912
5. 2100
6. 1954
7. 1992
8. 1951
9. 2400
10. 1882
11. 1920
12. 2004

APPLICATION I

Elapsed Time in a Leap Year

When the dates include February 29 in a leap year, add 1 day to the later date.

▶ **How many days elapsed between January 5, 1980 and September 3, 1980?**

Sept. 3, 1980: (246 + 1) = 247
Jan. 5, 1980: − 5 = − 5
242 days

Find the elapsed time. Use the table on page A10.

1. January 12, 1978, to April 1, 1978
2. July 1, 1979, through March 21, 1980
3. February 5, 1984, to September 23, 1984
4. January 9, 1988, through July 2, 1988
5. February 21, 2000, to September 30, 2000

APPLICATIONS

APPLICATION J

Fractional Parts of a Year

Changing Months into a Part of a Year

To change months into a part of a year, write as a fraction with denominator 12. Express answers in lowest terms.

► **6 months is what part of a year?**

6 months $= \frac{6}{12}$ year $= \frac{1}{2}$ year

Change each term to a part of a year.

1. 9 months
2. 7 months
3. 12 months
4. 20 months
5. 36 months
6. 18 months
7. 21 months
8. 8 months
9. 14 months

Changing Days into a Part of a Year

To change days into a part of a year, write as a fraction with denominator 365 when using the exact year or 360 when using the ordinary year. Express answers in lowest terms.

► **240 days is what part of an exact year?**

240 days $= \frac{240}{365}$ year $= \frac{48}{73}$ year

► **240 days is what part of an ordinary year?**

240 days $= \frac{240}{360}$ year $= \frac{2}{3}$ year

Change each term to a part of a year.

10. 90 days as an exact year
11. 300 days as an ordinary year
12. 120 days as an exact year
13. 175 days as an exact year
14. 146 days as an ordinary year
15. 250 days as an exact year

APPLICATION K

Chronological Expressions

Finding the Number of Occurrences

► **Monthly payments for 30 years. How many payments in all?**

Monthly: 12 times a year

In 30 years: $12 \times 30 = 360$ payments

Common Chronological Expressions (number of occurrences per year)		
	Weekly (52)	Biweekly (26)
Semimonthly (24)	Monthly (12)	Bimonthly (6)
	Quarterly (4)	
Semiannually (2)	Annually (1)	

Find the number of occurrences. Use the table above.

1. Weekly for 1 year
2. Biweekly for 2 years
3. Quarterly for 4 years
4. Semimonthly for 1 year
5. Bimonthly for 2 years
6. Annually for 25 years
7. Monthly for $\frac{1}{2}$ year
8. Weekly for 1.5 years
9. Semimonthly for $2\frac{1}{2}$ years

APPLICATION L

The Complement of a Number

To find the complement of a percent or decimal less than 1, subtract the percent from 100% or the decimal from 1.

▶ **What is the complement of 65%?**

The complement of 65% =

100% − 65% = 35%

▶ **What is the complement of 0.25?**

The complement of 0.25 =

1 − 0.25 = 0.75

Find the complement.

1. 0.15
2. 0.72
3. 0.35
4. 0.50
5. 0.80
6. 0.34
7. 91%
8. 85%
9. 47%
10. 66%
11. 7%
12. 45%
13. 3.5%
14. 56.6%
15. 75.9%

APPLICATION M

Reading Bar Graphs

To read a bar graph, find the bar that represents the information you seek. Trace an imaginary line from the top of the bar to the scale on the left. Read the value represented by the bar from the scale.

▶ **In 1992, what were the average hourly earnings for manufacturing workers?**

The bar graph shows that the average hourly earnings for manufacturing workers were about $11.00 per hour in 1992.

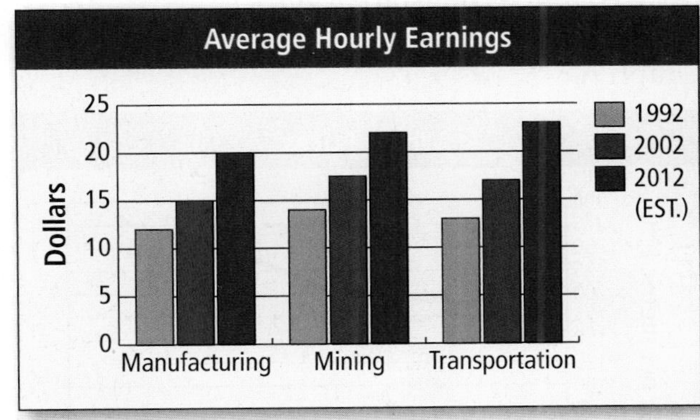

Answer the following. Use the bar graph shown.

1. In 1992, what were the average hourly earnings for mining workers?

2. In 2012, what are the projected average hourly earnings for manufacturing workers?

3. In 1992, what were the average hourly earnings for transportation workers?

4. Did any of the wages decrease over time?

5. Estimate how much wages increased from 1992 to 2002 for the mining workers.

6. How much more would a transportation worker earn in 2012 as compared to 1992?

APPLICATIONS

APPLICATION N

Reading Line Graphs

To read a line graph, find the point that represents the information you seek. Trace an imaginary line from the point to the scale on the left. Read the value represented by the point from the scale.

▶ **What were the predicted and the actual amount of sales for the month of May?**

The line graph shows that the predicted amount of sales was $10,000. The actual amount was $8,000.

Predicted vs. Actual Sales

Sales (in thousands)

Months

Predicted
Actual

Answer the following. Use the line graph shown.

1. What was the predicted amount of sales for the month of August?
2. What was the actual amount of sales for the month of October?
3. Which month(s) actually had the least amount of sales?
4. In which month was the actual amount predicted?

Sometimes data are displayed in a way that persuades you to see things in a certain way. Graphs A & B below show the price of wheat per metric ton by the month. Graph B has a truncated vertical axis. It does not start at zero.

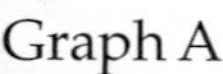

Graph A

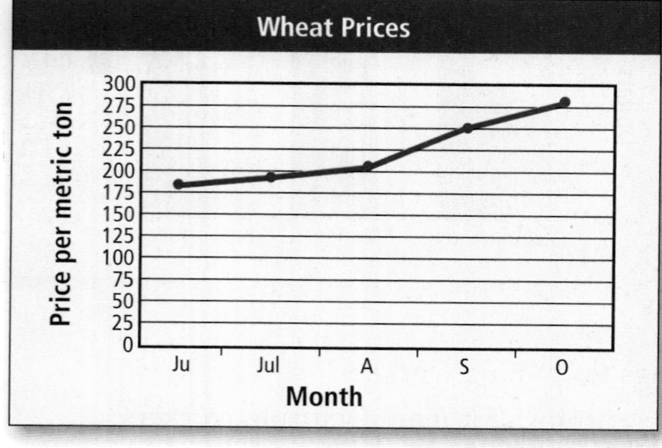

Graph B

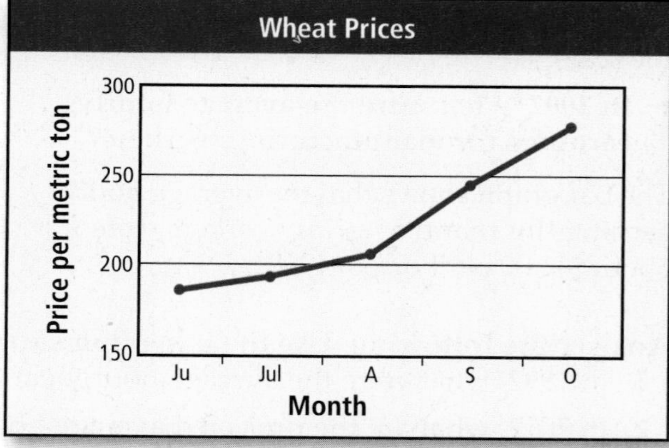

Graph B shows a steeper rise in price than that shown in Graph A, where the increase seems to be more gradual.

Answer the following using Graphs A and B.

5. What is the vertical scale on each graph?
6. How does the difference in the vertical scale affect the appearance of the line graph?
7. Which graph is more likely to persuade you that wheat prices have shown a dramatic increase?
8. Which graph is more likely to persuade you that wheat prices have shown a gradual increase?

APPLICATION O

Reading Pictographs

To read a pictograph, find the scale to see how much each picture represents. Then multiply that amount times the number of pictures on each line to get the total amount.

Hours to Build an Automobile	
🕐 = 5 hours	
General Motors	🕐 🕐 🕐 🕐 🕐 🕐
Ford	🕐 🕐 🕐 🕐 🕐 🕐
Chrysler	🕐 🕐 🕐 🕐 🕐 🕐 ◖
Toyota	🕐 🕐 🕐 🕐 🕐 ◖
Honda	🕐 🕐 🕐 🕐 🕐
Nissan	🕐 🕐 🕐 🕐 🕐

► **How many hours did it take to build a Toyota automobile?**

Each picture represents 5 hours.
The Toyota row has 5.5 pictures
$5.5 \times 5 = 27.5$ hours

Answer the following. Use the pictograph shown.

1. How many hours did it take to build a Chrysler automobile?
2. How many hours did it take to build a Honda automobile?
3. How much longer did it take to build a General Motors automobile than a Toyota?

APPLICATION P

Circle Graphs

Reading Circle Graphs

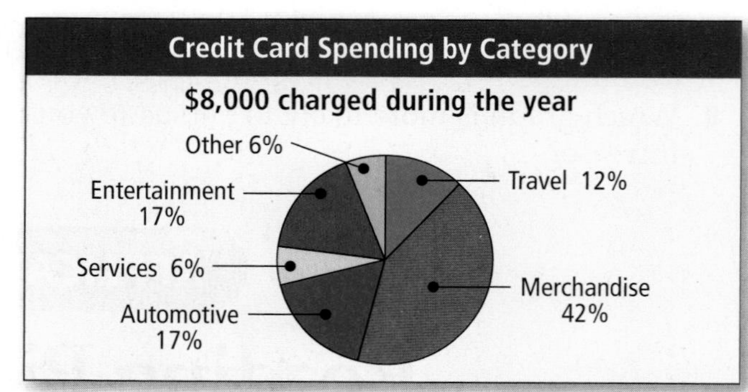

A circle graph is used to compare the parts to the whole. To find what part of the whole each section represents, multiply the amount, or percent, per section times the total amount.

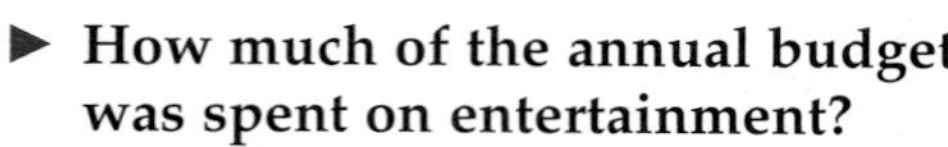

▶ **How much of the annual budget was spent on entertainment?**

Entertainment = 17 percent of the total

$0.17 \times \$8,000 = \$1,360$

Answer the following. Use the circle graph shown.

1. How much was spent on automotive?
2. How much of the credit card spending went for travel?
3. How much was spent on services?
4. Is more spent on merchandise than on all other categories?

Constructing Circle Graphs

To construct a circle graph, find the percent of the total each section represents. Multiply each percent times 360° to find the measure of the angle for each proportion of the circle graph. Use a protractor to draw each portion.

▶ **Construct that portion of a circle graph that represents the Bradford family spending 40 cents out of every dollar for food.**

$\frac{40}{100} = 40\%; 0.40 \times 360° = 144°$

40% for food = 144 degrees

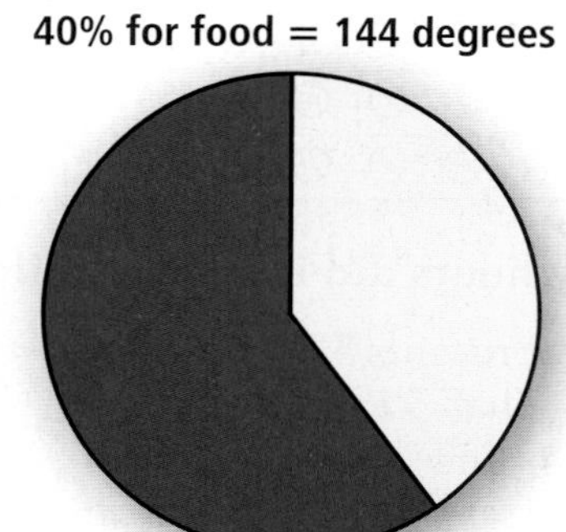

5. Complete the circle graph shown. Use the following information. The Bradford family budgets the rest of each dollar as follows: rent 30 percent; entertainment 15 percent; clothing and personal items 10 percent; and all other expenses 5 percent.
6. Draw a circle graph. Use the following information. A factory budgets each dollar spent as follows: salaries 60 cents; raw materials 20 cents; utilities 10 cents; plant maintenance 5 cents; and research and development 5 cents.

APPLICATION Q

Mean

To find the mean (average) of a group of numbers, find the sum of the group and divide it by the number of items in the group.

► **What is the mean of the following: 454, 376, 416, 472?**

$$\text{Mean} = \frac{(454 + 376 + 416 + 472)}{4}$$
$$= \frac{1{,}718}{4} = 429.5$$

Find the mean for each group.

1. 43, 19, 61, 72, 81, 50
2. 116, 147, 136, 151, 123, 117, 120
3. 4,615, 5,918, 7,437, 8,937
4. 4.0, 3.5, 4.0, 3.0, 3.5, 3.0, 2.0, 0.5, 4.6, 5.0
5. $580,000; $625,000; $105,583; $733,358; $5,750,000; $255,000; $600,000

APPLICATION R

Median

To find the median of a group of numbers, arrange the items in order from smallest to largest. The median is the number in the middle. If there is an even number of items, find the mean of the two middle numbers.

► **What is the median of the following: 454, 376, 416, 472?**

Arrange in order: 376, <u>416</u>, <u>454</u>, 472

$$\text{Median} = \frac{(416 + 454)}{2} = 435$$

Find the median for each group.

1. 141, 136, 191, 187, 149, 148
2. 17, 21, 30, 35, 27, 25, 15
3. 91, 92, 85, 98, 100, 76, 80, 75
4. 4.2, 3.7, 3.1, 4.8, 2.4, 3.0, 2.9
5. 0.07, 0.05, 0.10, 0.12, 0.09, 0.17, 0.01
6. $121,500; $49,750; $72,175; $65,449
7. 2.08, 2.04, 2.00, 2.10, 2.08, 2.24, 1.55, 2.04, 2.13, 2.08, 2.09

APPLICATION S

Mode

To find the mode of a group of numbers, look for the number that appears most often. A group may have no mode, or it may have more than one mode.

► **What is the mode of the following: 92, 98, 76, 84, 92, 1,200?**

The number that appears most often, the mode, is 92.

Find the mode for each group.

1. $51, $13, $24, $62, $55, $57, $24
2. 800, 600, 800, 500, 600, 700
3. 4.1, 4.7, 4.5, 4.3, 4.2, 4.4
4. 3, 3, 5, 3, 4, 2, 3, 2, 4, 4, 4
5. 0.01, 0.1, 0.01, 1.0, 0.01, 0.11, 1.00
6. $45, $63, $27, $91, $65, $8, $43, $90

APPLICATION T

Measures of Dispersion

The range, variance, and the standard deviation are measures of dispersion. That is, how spread the data is and how far the data deviates from the mean. To find the range of a group of numbers, subtract the smallest number from the largest number. To determine the variance and standard deviation do the following.

a. Determine the mean of the numbers. $\overline{X} = \dfrac{\Sigma X}{n}$

Where: ΣX is the sum of the data values

n is the number of values.

b. Subtract the mean from each number and square the result.

c. The variance is the average of the squared differences. $s^2 = \dfrac{\Sigma(X - \overline{X})^2}{n-1}$

d. The standard deviation is the square root of the variance. $s = \sqrt{s^2}$

APPLICATIONS

▶ **Find the mean, variance, standard deviation and the range for the following sample data: 12, 15, 16, 10, and 27**

a. Mean: $\overline{X} = \dfrac{\Sigma X}{n} = \dfrac{12 + 15 + 16 + 10 + 27}{5} = \dfrac{80}{5} = 16$

b. Use the table to show the difference from the mean and the square of the difference.

X	$(X - \overline{X})$			$(X - \overline{X})^2$
10	10–16	=	–6	36
12	12–16	=	–4	16
15	15–16	=	–1	1
16	16–16	=	0	0
27	27–16	=	11	121
80				174

c. Variance: $s^2 = \dfrac{\Sigma(X - \overline{X})^2}{n-1} = \dfrac{174}{5-1} = \dfrac{174}{4} = 43.5$

d. Standard deviation: $s = \sqrt{s^2} = \sqrt{43.5} = 6.595 = 6.6$

e. Range: $27 - 10 = 17$

Determine the (a) mean, (b) variance, (c) standard deviation, and (d) range for the sample data sets. Round answers to the nearest tenth.

1. 16, 17, 20, 21, 23, 35
2. 20, 26, 22, 25, 19, 26
3. 50, 51, 55, 56, 49, 48, 51, 50, 60
4. 10, 0, 15, 7, 9, 5, 3, 1, 0

APPLICATION U

Frequency Distribution

A *frequency distribution* is used to organize data into some meaningful form. The data is grouped into classes showing the number of items in each class. The number of times a data item occurs is the frequency. To create a frequency distribution, determine the number of classes. Determine the class width. Tally the observations into the appropriate classes and count the number of tallies (items) in each class.

▶ **Use the table data to create a frequency distribution.**

The table shows the number of years of employment in a sample of 23 employees. The 23 observations are referred to as data or ungrouped data.

Number of Years of Employment					
1	5	5	8	6	4
3	2	3	8	6	5
9	7	3	4	2	4
4	7	10	6	7	

Number of classes: use five groups or classes of 2 units each.
Class width: use classes "1 up to 3," "3 up to 5," and so on.
Tally: use the Frequency Distribution table to tally the years of employment into the appropriate classes.

Frequency Distribution		
Years of Employment	Tallies	Number of Workers
1 up to 3 years	///	3
3 up to 5 years	~~////~~ //	7
5 up to 7 years	~~////~~ /	6
7 up to 9 years	~~////~~	5
9 up to 11 yrs.	//	2
Total		23

There are 3 workers that worked 1 or 2 years.
There are 7 workers that worked 3 or 4 years.
There are 6 workers that worked 5 or 6 years.
There are 5 workers that worked 7 or 8 years.
There are 2 workers that worked 9 or 10 years.

Continued on next page

A frequency distribution can be portrayed as a frequency polygon. When drawing a frequency polygon, assume that the observations in any group are represented by the mid-point of the group. In the "1 up to 3" group, use 2 as the midpoint. A dot is placed at the class midpoint opposite the number of frequencies in that class. The first plot is over 2 years on the "*x*-axis" and up vertically to 3. The process is repeated for the remaining groups. Normal practice is to extend the lines to the midpoint of the class below the lowest class (0) and to the midpoint of the class above the highest class (12).

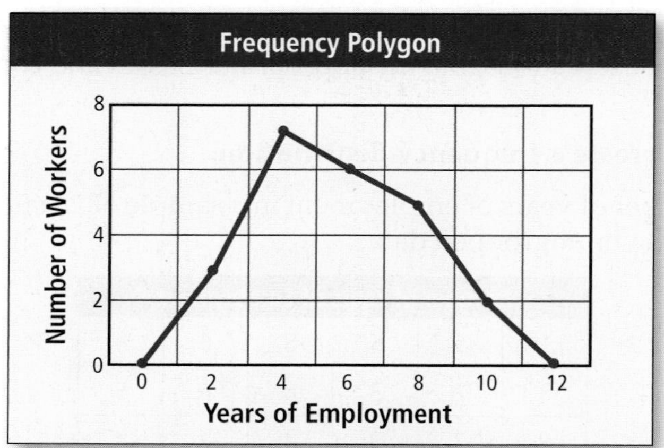

Use the table to complete the following. The table shows the miles per gallon of gasoline for 24 mid-sized cars.

Miles Per Gallon					
16	23	25	30	26	20
20	15	22	29	23	25
32	28	21	21	15	19
26	27	34	24	30	33

1. Complete the frequency distribution.

Frequency Distribution		
Number of mpg	Tallies	Number of Cars
15 up to 19 mpg	///	3
19 up to 23 mpg	~~////~~ /	
Total		

2. Draw a frequency polygon.

APPLICATION V

Metric Length

The common units of length in the metric system are the millimeter, centimeter, meter, and the kilometer.

A millimeter (mm) is about the thickness of a U.S. dime.

A centimeter (cm) is about the thickness of a sugar cube.

A meter (m) is about the length of a baseball bat.

A kilometer (km) is 1,000 m and is used to measure large distances. It is 3,400 kilometers from Toronto to Vancouver.

Name the unit that is most commonly used to measure the object.

1. The length of a tennis court
2. The distance between Detroit and Montreal
3. The thickness of a magazine
4. The length of a standard paper clip
5. The length of your living room
6. The thickness of a soda straw
7. The length of a postage stamp
8. The width of your foot

APPLICATION W

Metric Mass and Volume

The common units of mass and volume in the metric system are the gram, kilogram, metric ton, liter, and kiloliter.

A gram (g) is about the mass of a paper clip.

A kilogram (kg) is about the mass of a hammer.

A metric ton (t) is 1,000 kg and is used to measure very heavy objects.

A liter (L) is about the amount of liquid in a can of motor oil.

A kiloliter (kL) is 1,000 L and is used to measure large volumes, such as that of a railroad tank car.

Name the unit that is most commonly used to measure the object.

1. The mass of your best friend
2. The amount of gas in a car's tank
3. The mass of a nickel
4. The volume of helium in a blimp
5. The mass of an adult blue whale
6. The mass of a baseball
7. The volume of a large fuel tank
8. The mass of a dime
9. The mass of a gumdrop
10. The volume of a milk container

APPLICATION X

Perimeter

The distance around a shape is its perimeter. To find the perimeter of a shape, add the lengths of all its sides.

▶ **What is the perimeter of the triangle at the right?**

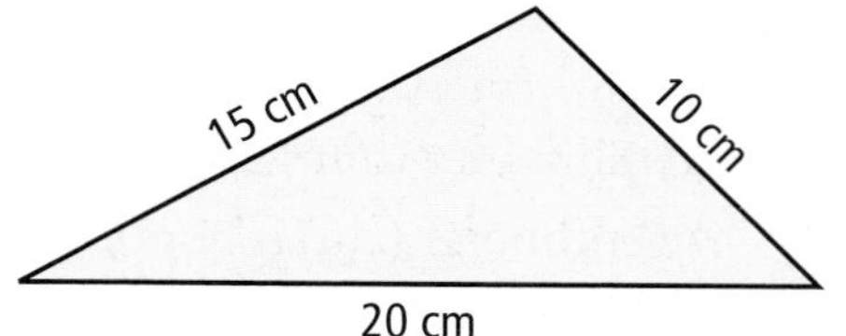

10 cm, 15 cm, 20 cm

Perimeter:

10 cm + 15 cm + 20 cm = 45 cm

Find the perimeter:

1.

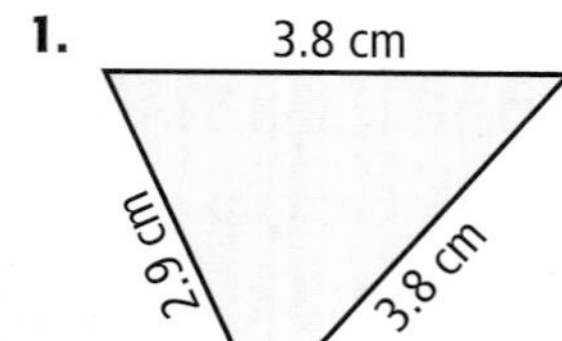

2.

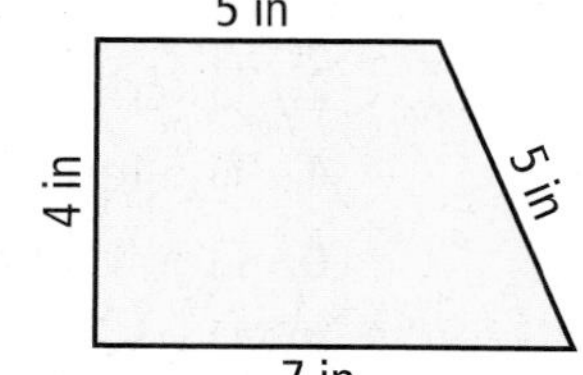

3.

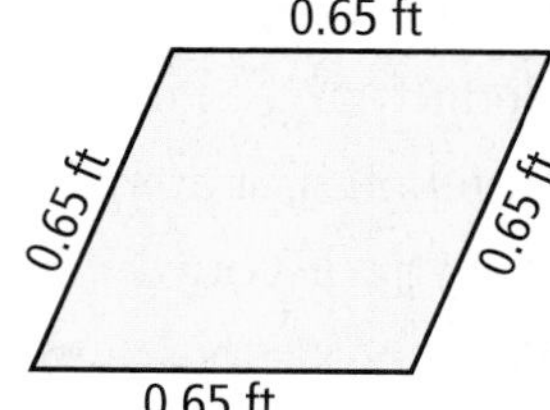

4.

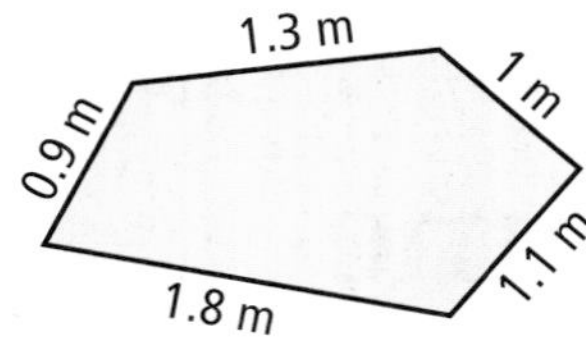

5.

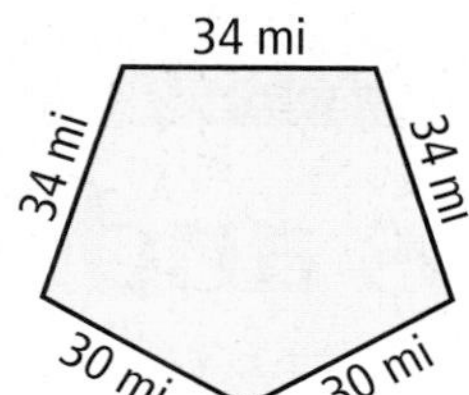

6.

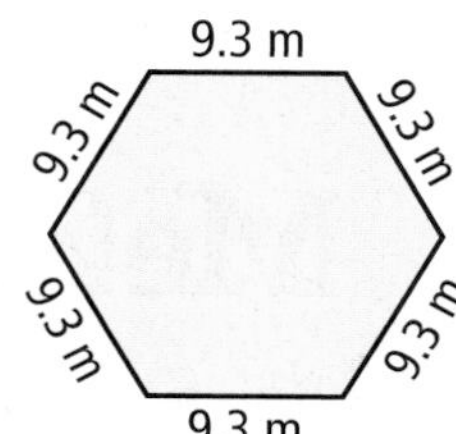

APPLICATION Y

Circumference

The length of a diameter of a circle is twice the length of its radius. The circumference is the distance around a circle. The circumference is estimated by multiplying 3.14 times the length of a diameter.

▶ **The diameter of a circle is 23 mm. What is its circumference?**

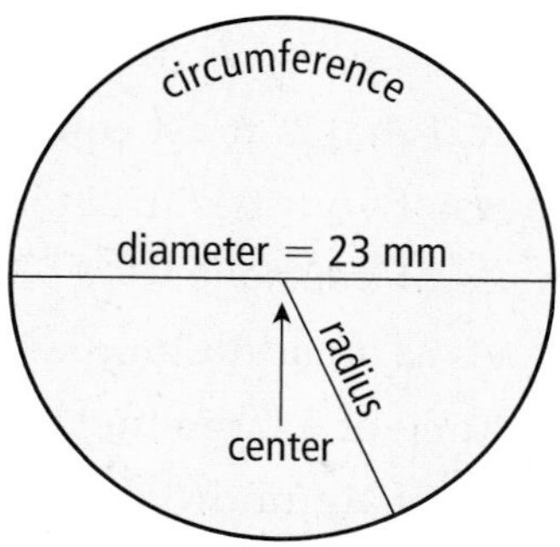

Circumference = 3.14 × Diameter

Circumference = 3.14 × 23 mm

= 72.22 mm

Find the circumference.

1. Diameter: 4 mi
2. Diameter: 3.5 cm
3. Diameter: 0.8 m
4. Radius: 35 mm
5. Radius 0.75 ft
6. Radius: 13 in
7. Diameter: 18 ft
8. Radius: 120 km
9. Diameter: 12.5 mi

APPLICATION Z

Area and Diagonal of a Rectangle or Square

To find the area of a rectangle, multiply length times width. In a square, the length and width are equal. To find the length of a diagonal, take the square root of the sum of the length squared and the width squared.

▶ **What is the area and length of the diagonal of a rectangular board that measures 3 feet by 4 feet?**

Area = length × width or $A = lw$

Area = 3 ft × 4 ft

Area = 12 ft^2

Length of the diagonal.

$d = \sqrt{\text{length}^2 + \text{width}^2}$ or $d = \sqrt{l^2 + w^2}$

$d = \sqrt{4^2 + 3^2}$

$d = \sqrt{16 + 9}$

$d = \sqrt{25} = 5$

The diagonal is 5 feet long.

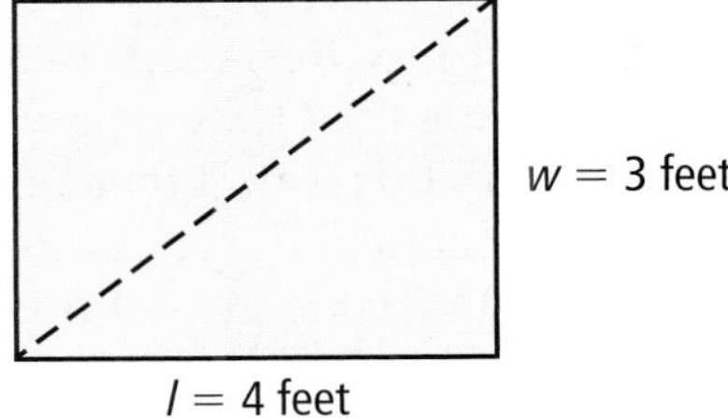

Find the (a) area and (b) length of the diagonal.

1. Rectangle: 12 in long, 5 in wide
2. Rectangle: 6 feet wide, 8 feet long
3. Rectangle: 8 meters long, 5 meters wide
4. Square: 40 cm per side
5. Square: 3.5 yd per side
6. Rectangle: 4.5 feet long, 2.5 feet wide

APPLICATION AA

Area of a Triangle or Circle

To find the area of a triangle or circle, use the formulas below.

Area of Triangle = $\frac{1}{2}$ × Base × Height

Area of Circle = 3.14 × Radius^2

▶ **What is the area of a circle with a radius of 27 m?**

Area of Circle = 3.14 × Radius^2

Area of Circle = 3.14 × 27^2

Area of Circle = 2,289.06 m^2

Find the area.

1. Triangle: base is 3 in, height is 9 in
2. Circle: radius is 5 cm
3. Triangle: base is 16 m, height is 25 m
4. Triangle: base is 132 m, height is 9.6 m
5. Circle: radius is $2\frac{1}{2}$ yd
6. Triangle: base is $9\frac{1}{3}$ ft, height is $3\frac{1}{4}$ ft
7. Circle: radius is 86 mm
8. Bryan is constructing a triangular flower bed. The flower bed will have a base of 8 feet and a height of 6 feet. What is the area of the flower bed?
9. In Problem 8, suppose Bryan doubles the base and height of the flower bed. How does the area of the flower bed change?

APPLICATION AB

Surface Area and Volume of a Rectangular Solid

To find the surface area and volume of a rectangular solid, use these formulas:

Surface Area $SA = 2 \times l \times w + 2 \times l \times h + 2 \times w \times h$

Volume $V = l \times w \times h$

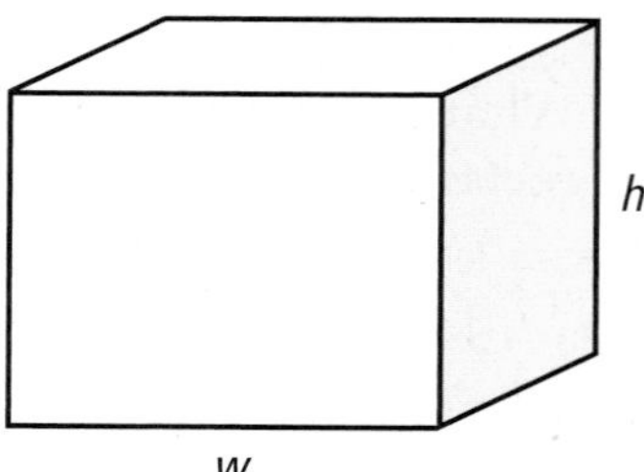

The interior measurements of a rectangular shipping container are: 20 ft. long by 8 ft. wide by 9 ft. high. The shipping container is filled with boxes that measure 5 ft. by 4 ft. by 3 ft. **(a)** What is the surface area of the container? **(b)** What is the surface area of the box? **(c)** What is the volume of the container? **(d)** What is the volume of a box? **(e)** Based on volume, how many boxes will fit in the shipping container?

Surface area is found by: $SA = 2 \times l \times w + 2 \times l \times h + 2 \times w \times h$

a. Container: $SA = 2 \times 20 \times 8 + 2 \times 20 \times 9 + 2 \times 8 \times 9 = 320 + 360 + 144 = 824$ sq ft.

b. Box: $SA = 2 \times 5 \times 4 + 2 \times 5 \times 3 + 2 \times 4 \times 3 = 40 + 30 + 24 = 94$ sq ft.

Volume = Length × Width × Height

c. Volume of container = 20 ft. × 8 ft. × 9 ft. = 1,440 ft^3

d. Volume of the box = 5 ft. × 4 ft. × 3 ft. = 60 ft^3

e. Number that will fit = 1,440 ÷ 60 = 24

Find the (a) surface area and (b) volume.

1. 3 in. long, 4 in. wide, 5 in. high

2. 7.5 ft. long by 3.5 ft. wide by 5.5 high

3. The interior measurements of a rectangular shipping container are: 40 ft. long by 8 ft. wide by 9 ft. high. Based on volume, how many boxes that measure 8 ft. by 4 ft. by 3 ft. will fit in the shipping container?

4. The interior measurements of a shipping carton are 20" by 8" by 10". Based on volume, how many boxes of cereal that measure 5" by 8" by 2" will fit in the carton?

5. Suppose the measurements of the shipping carton in Problem 4 are doubled.

a. What is the new volume? **(b)** How many times greater is it? **(c)** How many of the cereal boxes will fit in the larger carton?

6. Kara is filling rectangular planters with soil. Each planter is 24 inches long, 6 inches wide and 5 inches deep. **(a)** What is the volume of the planter? **(b)** Suppose Kara has another planter that has double the measurements of the first planter. How does this affect the volume of the planter?

Appendix

Table of Contents

SINGLE Persons—**WEEKLY** Payroll Period

If the wages are–		And the number of withholding allowances claimed is—										
At least	But less than	0	1	2	3	4	5	6	7	8	9	10
		The amount of income tax to be withheld is—										
$0	$55	$0	$0	$0	$0	$0	$0	$0	$0	$0	$0	$0
55	60	1	0	0	0	0	0	0	0	0	0	0
60	65	1	0	0	0	0	0	0	0	0	0	0
65	70	2	0	0	0	0	0	0	0	0	0	0
70	75	2	0	0	0	0	0	0	0	0	0	0
75	80	3	0	0	0	0	0	0	0	0	0	0
80	85	3	0	0	0	0	0	0	0	0	0	0
85	90	4	0	0	0	0	0	0	0	0	0	0
90	95	4	0	0	0	0	0	0	0	0	0	0
95	100	5	0	0	0	0	0	0	0	0	0	0
100	105	5	0	0	0	0	0	0	0	0	0	0
105	110	6	0	0	0	0	0	0	0	0	0	0
110	115	6	0	0	0	0	0	0	0	0	0	0
115	120	7	0	0	0	0	0	0	0	0	0	0
120	125	7	1	0	0	0	0	0	0	0	0	0
125	130	8	1	0	0	0	0	0	0	0	0	0
130	135	8	2	0	0	0	0	0	0	0	0	0
135	140	9	2	0	0	0	0	0	0	0	0	0
140	145	9	3	0	0	0	0	0	0	0	0	0
145	150	10	3	0	0	0	0	0	0	0	0	0
150	155	10	4	0	0	0	0	0	0	0	0	0
155	160	11	4	0	0	0	0	0	0	0	0	0
160	165	11	5	0	0	0	0	0	0	0	0	0
165	170	12	5	0	0	0	0	0	0	0	0	0
170	175	12	6	0	0	0	0	0	0	0	0	0
175	180	13	6	0	0	0	0	0	0	0	0	0
180	185	13	7	0	0	0	0	0	0	0	0	0
185	190	14	7	1	0	0	0	0	0	0	0	0
190	195	14	8	1	0	0	0	0	0	0	0	0
195	200	15	8	2	0	0	0	0	0	0	0	0
200	210	16	9	2	0	0	0	0	0	0	0	0
210	220	17	10	3	0	0	0	0	0	0	0	0
220	230	19	11	4	0	0	0	0	0	0	0	0
230	240	20	12	5	0	0	0	0	0	0	0	0
240	250	22	13	6	0	0	0	0	0	0	0	0
250	260	23	14	7	1	0	0	0	0	0	0	0
260	270	25	15	8	2	0	0	0	0	0	0	0
270	280	26	17	9	3	0	0	0	0	0	0	0
280	290	28	18	10	4	0	0	0	0	0	0	0
290	300	29	20	11	5	0	0	0	0	0	0	0
300	310	31	21	12	6	0	0	0	0	0	0	0
310	320	32	23	13	7	0	0	0	0	0	0	0
320	330	34	24	14	8	1	0	0	0	0	0	0
330	340	35	26	16	9	2	0	0	0	0	0	0
340	350	37	27	17	10	3	0	0	0	0	0	0
350	360	38	29	19	11	4	0	0	0	0	0	0
360	370	40	30	20	12	5	0	0	0	0	0	0
370	380	41	32	22	13	6	0	0	0	0	0	0
380	390	43	33	23	14	7	1	0	0	0	0	0
390	400	44	35	25	15	8	2	0	0	0	0	0
400	410	46	36	26	17	9	3	0	0	0	0	0
410	420	47	38	28	18	10	4	0	0	0	0	0
420	430	49	39	29	20	11	5	0	0	0	0	0
430	440	50	41	31	21	12	6	0	0	0	0	0
440	450	52	42	32	23	13	7	0	0	0	0	0
450	460	53	44	34	24	14	8	1	0	0	0	0
460	470	55	45	35	26	16	9	2	0	0	0	0
470	480	56	47	37	27	17	10	3	0	0	0	0
480	490	58	48	38	29	19	11	4	0	0	0	0
490	500	59	50	40	30	20	12	5	0	0	0	0
500	510	61	51	41	32	22	13	6	0	0	0	0
510	520	62	53	43	33	23	14	7	1	0	0	0
520	530	64	54	44	35	25	15	8	2	0	0	0
530	540	65	56	46	36	26	16	9	3	0	0	0
540	550	67	57	47	38	28	18	10	4	0	0	0
550	560	68	59	49	39	29	19	11	5	0	0	0
560	570	70	60	50	41	31	21	12	6	0	0	0
570	580	71	62	52	42	32	22	13	7	0	0	0
580	590	73	63	53	44	34	24	14	8	1	0	0
590	600	74	65	55	45	35	25	16	9	2	0	0

APPENDIX

SINGLE Persons—**WEEKLY** Payroll Period

If the wages are–		And the number of withholding allowances claimed is—										
At least	But less than	0	1	2	3	4	5	6	7	8	9	10
		The amount of income tax to be withheld is—										
$600	**$610**	$76	$66	$56	$47	$37	$27	$17	$10	$3	$0	$0
610	**620**	77	68	58	48	38	28	19	11	4	0	0
620	**630**	79	69	59	50	40	30	20	12	5	0	0
630	**640**	80	71	61	51	41	31	22	13	6	0	0
640	**650**	82	72	62	53	43	33	23	14	7	1	0
650	**660**	84	74	64	54	44	34	25	15	8	2	0
660	**670**	87	75	65	56	46	36	26	16	9	3	0
670	**680**	89	77	67	57	47	37	28	18	10	4	0
680	**690**	92	78	68	59	49	39	29	19	11	5	0
690	**700**	94	80	70	60	50	40	31	21	12	6	0
700	**710**	97	81	71	62	52	42	32	22	13	7	0
710	**720**	99	83	73	63	53	43	34	24	14	8	1
720	**730**	102	86	74	65	55	45	35	25	15	9	2
730	**740**	104	88	76	66	56	46	37	27	17	10	3
740	**750**	107	91	77	68	58	48	38	28	18	11	4
750	**760**	109	93	79	69	59	49	40	30	20	12	5
760	**770**	112	96	80	71	61	51	41	31	21	13	6
770	**780**	114	98	82	72	62	52	43	33	23	14	7
780	**790**	117	101	84	74	64	54	44	34	24	15	8
790	**800**	119	103	87	75	65	55	46	36	26	16	9
800	**810**	122	106	89	77	67	57	47	37	27	18	10
810	**820**	124	108	92	78	68	58	49	39	29	19	11
820	**830**	127	111	94	80	70	60	50	40	30	21	12
830	**840**	129	113	97	81	71	61	52	42	32	22	13
840	**850**	132	116	99	83	73	63	53	43	33	24	14
850	**860**	134	118	102	85	74	64	55	45	35	25	15
860	**870**	137	121	104	88	76	66	56	46	36	27	17
870	**880**	139	123	107	90	77	67	58	48	38	28	18
880	**890**	142	126	109	93	79	69	59	49	39	30	20
890	**900**	144	128	112	95	80	70	61	51	41	31	21
900	**910**	147	131	114	98	82	72	62	52	42	33	23
910	**920**	149	133	117	100	84	73	64	54	44	34	24
920	**930**	152	136	119	103	87	75	65	55	45	36	26
930	**940**	154	138	122	105	89	76	67	57	47	37	27
940	**950**	157	141	124	108	92	78	68	58	48	39	29
950	**960**	159	143	127	110	94	79	70	60	50	40	30
960	**970**	162	146	129	113	97	81	71	61	51	42	32
970	**980**	164	148	132	115	99	83	73	63	53	43	33
980	**990**	167	151	134	118	102	85	74	64	54	45	35
990	**1,000**	169	153	137	120	104	88	76	66	56	46	36
1,000	**1,010**	172	156	139	123	107	90	77	67	57	48	38
1,010	**1,020**	174	158	142	125	109	93	79	69	59	49	39
1,020	**1,030**	177	161	144	128	112	95	80	70	60	51	41
1,030	**1,040**	179	163	147	130	114	98	82	72	62	52	42
1,040	**1,050**	182	166	149	133	117	100	84	73	63	54	44
1,050	**1,060**	184	168	152	135	119	103	86	75	65	55	45
1,060	**1,070**	187	171	154	138	122	105	89	76	66	57	47
1,070	**1,080**	189	173	157	140	124	108	91	78	68	58	48
1,080	**1,090**	192	176	159	143	127	110	94	79	69	60	50
1,090	**1,100**	194	178	162	145	129	113	96	81	71	61	51
1,100	**1,110**	197	181	164	148	132	115	99	83	72	63	53
1,110	**1,120**	199	183	167	150	134	118	101	85	74	64	54
1,120	**1,130**	202	186	169	153	137	120	104	88	75	66	56
1,130	**1,140**	204	188	172	155	139	123	106	90	77	67	57
1,140	**1,150**	207	191	174	158	142	125	109	93	78	69	59
1,150	**1,160**	209	193	177	160	144	128	111	95	80	70	60
1,160	**1,170**	212	196	179	163	147	130	114	98	81	72	62
1,170	**1,180**	214	198	182	165	149	133	116	100	84	73	63
1,180	**1,190**	217	201	184	168	152	135	119	103	86	75	65
1,190	**1,200**	219	203	187	170	154	138	121	105	89	76	66
1,200	**1,210**	222	206	189	173	157	140	124	108	91	78	68
1,210	**1,220**	224	208	192	175	159	143	126	110	94	79	69
1,220	**1,230**	227	211	194	178	162	145	129	113	96	81	71
1,230	**1,240**	229	213	197	180	164	148	131	115	99	82	72
1,240	**1,250**	232	216	199	183	167	150	134	118	101	85	74

MARRIED Persons—**WEEKLY** Payroll Period

If the wages are–		And the number of withholding allowances claimed is—										
At least	But less than	0	1	2	3	4	5	6	7	8	9	10
		The amount of income tax to be withheld is—										
$0	**$125**	$0	$0	$0	$0	$0	$0	$0	$0	$0	$0	$0
125	**130**	0	0	0	0	0	0	0	0	0	0	0
130	**135**	0	0	0	0	0	0	0	0	0	0	0
135	**140**	0	0	0	0	0	0	0	0	0	0	0
140	**145**	0	0	0	0	0	0	0	0	0	0	0
145	**150**	0	0	0	0	0	0	0	0	0	0	0
150	**155**	0	0	0	0	0	0	0	0	0	0	0
155	**160**	0	0	0	0	0	0	0	0	0	0	0
160	**165**	1	0	0	0	0	0	0	0	0	0	0
165	**170**	1	0	0	0	0	0	0	0	0	0	0
170	**175**	2	0	0	0	0	0	0	0	0	0	0
175	**180**	2	0	0	0	0	0	0	0	0	0	0
180	**185**	3	0	0	0	0	0	0	0	0	0	0
185	**190**	3	0	0	0	0	0	0	0	0	0	0
190	**195**	4	0	0	0	0	0	0	0	0	0	0
195	**200**	4	0	0	0	0	0	0	0	0	0	0
200	**210**	5	0	0	0	0	0	0	0	0	0	0
210	**220**	6	0	0	0	0	0	0	0	0	0	0
220	**230**	7	1	0	0	0	0	0	0	0	0	0
230	**240**	8	2	0	0	0	0	0	0	0	0	0
240	**250**	9	3	0	0	0	0	0	0	0	0	0
250	**260**	10	4	0	0	0	0	0	0	0	0	0
260	**270**	11	5	0	0	0	0	0	0	0	0	0
270	**280**	12	6	0	0	0	0	0	0	0	0	0
280	**290**	13	7	0	0	0	0	0	0	0	0	0
290	**300**	14	8	1	0	0	0	0	0	0	0	0
300	**310**	15	9	2	0	0	0	0	0	0	0	0
310	**320**	16	10	3	0	0	0	0	0	0	0	0
320	**330**	17	11	4	0	0	0	0	0	0	0	0
330	**340**	18	12	5	0	0	0	0	0	0	0	0
340	**350**	19	13	6	0	0	0	0	0	0	0	0
350	**360**	20	14	7	1	0	0	0	0	0	0	0
360	**370**	21	15	8	2	0	0	0	0	0	0	0
370	**380**	22	16	9	3	0	0	0	0	0	0	0
380	**390**	23	17	10	4	0	0	0	0	0	0	0
390	**400**	24	18	11	5	0	0	0	0	0	0	0
400	**410**	25	19	12	6	0	0	0	0	0	0	0
410	**420**	26	20	13	7	0	0	0	0	0	0	0
420	**430**	27	21	14	8	1	0	0	0	0	0	0
430	**440**	28	22	15	9	2	0	0	0	0	0	0
440	**450**	29	23	16	10	3	0	0	0	0	0	0
450	**460**	30	24	17	11	4	0	0	0	0	0	0
460	**470**	32	25	18	12	5	0	0	0	0	0	0
470	**480**	33	26	19	13	6	0	0	0	0	0	0
480	**490**	35	27	20	14	7	0	0	0	0	0	0
490	**500**	36	28	21	15	8	1	0	0	0	0	0
500	**510**	38	29	22	16	9	2	0	0	0	0	0
510	**520**	39	30	23	17	10	3	0	0	0	0	0
520	**530**	41	31	24	18	11	4	0	0	0	0	0
530	**540**	42	33	25	19	12	5	0	0	0	0	0
540	**550**	44	34	26	20	13	6	0	0	0	0	0
550	**560**	45	36	27	21	14	7	1	0	0	0	0
560	**570**	47	37	28	22	15	8	2	0	0	0	0
570	**580**	48	39	29	23	16	9	3	0	0	0	0
580	**590**	50	40	30	24	17	10	4	0	0	0	0
590	**600**	51	42	32	25	18	11	5	0	0	0	0
600	**610**	53	43	33	26	19	12	6	0	0	0	0
610	**620**	54	45	35	27	20	13	7	0	0	0	0
620	**630**	56	46	36	28	21	14	8	1	0	0	0
630	**640**	57	48	38	29	22	15	9	2	0	0	0
640	**650**	59	49	39	30	23	16	10	3	0	0	0
650	**660**	60	51	41	31	24	17	11	4	0	0	0
660	**670**	62	52	42	32	25	18	12	5	0	0	0
670	**680**	63	54	44	34	26	19	13	6	0	0	0
680	**690**	65	55	45	35	27	20	14	7	1	0	0
690	**700**	66	57	47	37	28	21	15	8	2	0	0
700	**710**	68	58	48	38	29	22	16	9	3	0	0
710	**720**	69	60	50	40	30	23	17	10	4	0	0
720	**730**	71	61	51	41	32	24	18	11	5	0	0
730	**740**	72	63	53	43	33	25	19	12	6	0	0

MARRIED Persons—**WEEKLY** Payroll Period

If the wages are–		And the number of withholding allowances claimed is—										
At least	But less than	0	1	2	3	4	5	6	7	8	9	10
		The amount of income tax to be withheld is—										
$740	**$750**	$74	$64	$54	$44	$35	$26	$20	$13	$7	$0	$0
750	**760**	75	66	56	46	36	27	21	14	8	1	0
760	**770**	77	67	57	47	38	28	22	15	9	2	0
770	**780**	78	69	59	49	39	29	23	16	10	3	0
780	**790**	80	70	60	50	41	31	24	17	11	4	0
790	**800**	81	72	62	52	42	32	25	18	12	5	0
800	**810**	83	73	63	53	44	34	26	19	13	6	0
810	**820**	84	75	65	55	45	35	27	20	14	7	1
820	**830**	86	76	66	56	47	37	28	21	15	8	2
830	**840**	87	78	68	58	48	38	29	22	16	9	3
840	**850**	89	79	69	59	50	40	30	23	17	10	4
850	**860**	90	81	71	61	51	41	32	24	18	11	5
860	**870**	92	82	72	62	53	43	33	25	19	12	6
870	**880**	93	84	74	64	54	44	35	26	20	13	7
880	**890**	95	85	75	65	56	46	36	27	21	14	8
890	**900**	96	87	77	67	57	47	38	28	22	15	9
900	**910**	98	88	78	68	59	49	39	29	23	16	10
910	**920**	99	90	80	70	60	50	41	31	24	17	11
920	**930**	101	91	81	71	62	52	42	32	25	18	12
930	**940**	102	93	83	73	63	53	44	34	26	19	13
940	**950**	104	94	84	74	65	55	45	35	27	20	14
950	**960**	105	96	86	76	66	56	47	37	28	21	15
960	**970**	107	97	87	77	68	58	48	38	29	22	16
970	**980**	108	99	89	79	69	59	50	40	30	23	17
980	**990**	110	100	90	80	71	61	51	41	31	24	18
990	**1,000**	111	102	92	82	72	62	53	43	33	25	19
1,000	**1,010**	113	103	93	83	74	64	54	44	34	26	20
1,010	**1,020**	114	105	95	85	75	65	56	46	36	27	21
1,020	**1,030**	116	106	96	86	77	67	57	47	37	28	22
1,030	**1,040**	117	108	98	88	78	68	59	49	39	29	23
1,040	**1,050**	119	109	99	89	80	70	60	50	40	31	24
1,050	**1,060**	120	111	101	91	81	71	62	52	42	32	25
1,060	**1,070**	122	112	102	92	83	73	63	53	43	34	26
1,070	**1,080**	123	114	104	94	84	74	65	55	45	35	27
1,080	**1,090**	125	115	105	95	86	76	66	56	46	37	28
1,090	**1,100**	126	117	107	97	87	77	68	58	48	38	29
1,100	**1,110**	128	118	108	98	89	79	69	59	49	40	30
1,110	**1,120**	129	120	110	100	90	80	71	61	51	41	31
1,120	**1,130**	131	121	111	101	92	82	72	62	52	43	33
1,130	**1,140**	132	123	113	103	93	83	74	64	54	44	34
1,140	**1,150**	134	124	114	104	95	85	75	65	55	46	36
1,150	**1,160**	135	126	116	106	96	86	77	67	57	47	37
1,160	**1,170**	137	127	117	107	98	88	78	68	58	49	39
1,170	**1,180**	138	129	119	109	99	89	80	70	60	50	40
1,180	**1,190**	140	130	120	110	101	91	81	71	61	52	42
1,190	**1,200**	141	132	122	112	102	92	83	73	63	53	43
1,200	**1,210**	143	133	123	113	104	94	84	74	64	55	45
1,210	**1,220**	144	135	125	115	105	95	86	76	66	56	46
1,220	**1,230**	146	136	126	116	107	97	87	77	67	58	48
1,230	**1,240**	147	138	128	118	108	98	89	79	69	59	49
1,240	**1,250**	149	139	129	119	110	100	90	80	70	61	51
1,250	**1,260**	150	141	131	121	111	101	92	82	72	62	52
1,260	**1,270**	152	142	132	122	113	103	93	83	73	64	54
1,270	**1,280**	153	144	134	124	114	104	95	85	75	65	55
1,280	**1,290**	155	145	135	125	116	106	96	86	76	67	57
1,290	**1,300**	156	147	137	127	117	107	98	88	78	68	58
1,300	**1,310**	158	148	138	128	119	109	99	89	79	70	60
1,310	**1,320**	159	150	140	130	120	110	101	91	81	71	61
1,320	**1,330**	161	151	141	131	122	112	102	92	82	73	63
1,330	**1,340**	162	153	143	133	123	113	104	94	84	74	64
1,340	**1,350**	164	154	144	134	125	115	105	95	85	76	66
1,350	**1,360**	165	156	146	136	126	116	107	97	87	77	67
1,360	**1,370**	167	157	147	137	128	118	108	98	88	79	69
1,370	**1,380**	170	159	149	139	129	119	110	100	90	80	70
1,380	**1,390**	172	160	150	140	131	121	111	101	91	82	72
1,390	**1,400**	175	162	152	142	132	122	113	103	93	83	73

APPENDIX

Form **1040EZ**

Department of the Treasury—Internal Revenue Service

Income Tax Return for Single and Joint Filers With No Dependents

OMB No. 1545-0074

Label (See page 8.) **Use the IRS label.** Otherwise, please print or type.

LABEL HERE

Your first name and initial	Last name	Your social security number
If a joint return, spouse's first name and initial	Last name	Spouse's social security number
Home address (number and street). If you have a P.O. box, see page 9.	Apt. no.	▲ You **must** enter your SSN(s) above. ▲
City, town or post office, state, and ZIP code. If you have a foreign address, see page 9.		Checking a box below will not change your tax or refund.

Presidential Election Campaign (page 9) ▶ Check here if you, or your spouse if a joint return, want $3 to go to this fund . . . . ▶ ☐ **You** ☐ **Spouse**

Income

Attach Form(s) W-2 here.

Enclose, but do not attach, any payment.

1	Wages, salaries, and tips. This should be shown in box 1 of your Form(s) W-2. Attach your Form(s) W-2.	1
2	Taxable interest. If the total is over $1,500, you cannot use Form 1040EZ.	2
3	Unemployment compensation and Alaska Permanent Fund dividends (see page 10).	3
4	Add lines 1, 2, and 3. This is your **adjusted gross income.**	4
5	If someone can claim you (or your spouse if a joint return) as a dependent, check the applicable box(es) below and enter the amount from the worksheet on back. ☐ **You** ☐ **Spouse** If no one can claim you (or your spouse if a joint return), enter $8,750 if **single;** $17,500 if **married filing jointly.** See back for explanation.	5
6	Subtract line 5 from line 4. If line 5 is larger than line 4, enter -0-. This is your **taxable income.** ▶	6

Payments and tax

7	Federal income tax withheld from box 2 of your Form(s) W-2.	7
8a	**Earned income credit (EIC).**	8a
b	Nontaxable combat pay election. 8b	
9	Add lines 7 and 8a. These are your **total payments.** ▶	9
10	**Tax.** Use the amount on **line 6 above** to find your tax in the tax table on pages 18–26 of the booklet. Then, enter the tax from the table on this line.	10

Refund

Have it directly deposited! See page 15 and fill in 11b, 11c, and 11d or Form 8888.

11a	If line 9 is larger than line 10, subtract line 10 from line 9. This is your **refund.** If Form 8888 is attached, check here ▶ ☐	11a
▶ b	Routing number ☐☐☐☐☐☐☐☐☐ ▶ c Type: ☐ Checking ☐ Savings	
▶ d	Account number ☐☐☐☐☐☐☐☐☐☐☐☐☐☐☐☐☐	

Amount you owe

12	If line 10 is larger than line 9, subtract line 9 from line 10. This is the **amount you owe.** For details on how to pay, see page 16. ▶	12

Third party designee

Do you want to allow another person to discuss this return with the IRS (see page 16)? ☐ **Yes.** Complete the following. ☐ **No**

Designee's name ▶ Phone no. ▶ ( ) Personal identification number (PIN) ▶ ☐☐☐☐☐

Sign here

Joint return? See page 6. Keep a copy for your records.

Under penalties of perjury, I declare that I have examined this return, and to the best of my knowledge and belief, it is true, correct, and accurately lists all amounts and sources of income I received during the tax year. Declaration of preparer (other than the taxpayer) is based on all information of which the preparer has any knowledge.

Your signature	Date	Your occupation	Daytime phone number ( )
Spouse's signature. If a joint return, **both** must sign.	Date	Spouse's occupation	

Paid preparer's use only

Preparer's signature	Date	Check if self-employed ☐	Preparer's SSN or PTIN
Firm's name (or yours if self-employed), address, and ZIP code		EIN	
		Phone no. ( )	

Form **1040EZ**

APPENDIX

IRS forms change; if you wish to complete a 1040EZ form for your own purposes, locate the latest forms online.

Use this form if

- Your filing status is single or married filing jointly. If you are not sure about your filing status, see page 6.
- You (and your spouse if married filing jointly) were under age 65 and not blind at the end of 20--. If you were born on January 1, 1943, you are considered to be age 65 at the end of 20--.
- You do not claim any dependents. For information on dependents, see Pub. 501.
- Your taxable income (line 6) is less than $100,000.
- You do not claim any adjustments to income. For information on adjustments to income, use TeleTax topics 451–453 and 455–458 (see page 30).
- The only tax credit you can claim is the earned income credit. You do not need a qualifying child to claim it. For information on credits, use TeleTax topics 601, 602, 607, 608, and 610 (see page 30).
- You had only wages, salaries, tips, taxable scholarship or fellowship grants, unemployment compensation, or Alaska Permanent Fund dividends, and your taxable interest was not over $1,500. But if you earned tips, including allocated tips, that are not included in box 5 and box 7 of your Form W-2, you may not be able to use Form 1040EZ (see page 9). If you are planning to use Form 1040EZ for a child who received Alaska Permanent Fund dividends, see page 10.
- You did not receive any advance earned income credit payments. If you cannot use this form, use TeleTax topic 352 (see page 30).

Filling in your return

For tips on how to avoid common mistakes, see page 27.

If you received a scholarship or fellowship grant or tax-exempt interest income, such as on municipal bonds, see the booklet before filling in the form. Also, see the booklet if you received a Form 1099-INT showing federal income tax withheld or if federal income tax was withheld from your unemployment compensation or Alaska Permanent Fund dividends.

Remember, you must report all wages, salaries, and tips even if you do not get a Form W-2 from your employer. You must also report all your taxable interest, including interest from banks, savings and loans, credit unions, etc., even if you do not get a Form 1099-INT.

Worksheet for dependents who checked one or both boxes on line 5

(keep a copy for your records)

Use this worksheet to figure the amount to enter on line 5 if someone can claim you (or your spouse if married filing jointly) as a dependent, even if that person chooses not to do so. To find out if someone can claim you as a dependent, see Pub. 501.

A. Amount, if any, from line 1 on front . ________
+ 300.00 Enter total ▶ **A.** ________

B. Minimum standard deduction . . . . **B.** 850.00

C. Enter the **larger** of line A or line B here . . . . **C.** ________

D. Maximum standard deduction. If **single,** enter $5,350; if **married filing jointly,** enter $10,700 . . . . **D.** ________

E. Enter the **smaller** of line C or line D here. This is your standard deduction **E.** ________

F. Exemption amount.
- If single, enter -0-.
- If married filing jointly and—
  - —both you and your spouse can be claimed as dependents, enter -0-.
  - —only one of you can be claimed as a dependent, enter $3,400.

F. ________

G. Add lines E and F. Enter the total here and on line 5 on the front . . . **G.** ________

If you did not check any boxes on line 5, enter on line 5 the amount shown below that applies to you.

- Single, enter $8,750. This is the total of your standard deduction ($5,350) and your exemption ($3,400).
- Married filing jointly, enter $17,500. This is the total of your standard deduction ($10,700), your exemption ($3,400), and your spouse's exemption ($3,400).

Mailing return

Mail your return by **April 15.** Use the envelope that came with your booklet. If you do not have that envelope or if you moved during the year, see the back cover for the address to use.

Form **1040EZ**

APPENDIX

Annual Percentage Rate Table for Monthly Payment Plans

# of Pmts. ▼	Annual Percentage Rate (Finance Charge per $100 of Amount Financed)									
	2.00%	**2.25%**	**2.50%**	**2.75%**	**3.00%**	**3.25%**	**3.50%**	**3.75%**	**4.00%**	**4.25%**
6	$ 0.58	$ 0.66	$ 0.73	$ 0.80	$ 0.88	$ 0.95	$ 1.02	$ 1.10	$ 1.17	$ 1.24
12	1.09	1.22	1.36	1.50	1.63	1.77	1.91	2.04	2.18	2.32
18	1.59	1.79	1.99	2.19	2.39	2.59	2.79	2.99	3.20	3.40
24	2.10	2.36	2.62	2.89	3.15	3.42	3.69	3.95	4.22	4.49
30	2.60	2.93	3.26	3.59	3.92	4.25	4.58	4.92	5.25	5.58
36	3.11	3.51	3.90	4.30	4.69	5.09	5.49	5.89	6.29	6.69
42	3.62	4.08	4.54	5.00	5.47	5.93	6.40	6.86	7.33	7.80
48	4.14	4.66	5.19	5.72	6.24	6.78	7.31	7.84	8.38	8.92
54	4.65	5.24	5.83	6.43	7.03	7.63	8.23	8.83	9.44	10.04
60	5.17	5.82	6.48	7.15	7.81	8.48	9.15	9.82	10.50	11.18
	4.50%	**4.75%**	**5.00%**	**5.25%**	**5.50%**	**5.75%**	**6.00%**	**6.25%**	**6.50%**	**6.75%**
6	$ 1.32	$ 1.39	$ 1.46	$ 1.54	$ 1.61	$ 1.68	$ 1.76	$ 1.83	$ 1.90	$ 1.98
12	2.45	2.59	2.73	2.87	3.00	3.14	3.28	3.42	3.56	3.69
18	3.60	3.80	4.00	4.21	4.41	4.61	4.82	5.02	5.22	5.43
24	4.75	5.02	5.29	5.56	5.83	6.10	6.37	6.64	6.91	7.18
30	5.92	6.25	6.59	6.92	7.26	7.60	7.94	8.28	8.61	8.96
36	7.09	7.49	7.90	8.30	8.71	9.11	9.52	9.93	10.34	10.75
42	8.27	8.74	9.91	9.69	10.16	10.64	11.12	11.60	12.08	12.56
48	9.46	10.00	10.54	11.09	11.63	12.18	12.73	13.28	13.83	14.39
54	10.65	11.26	11.88	12.49	13.11	13.73	14.36	14.98	15.61	16.23
60	11.86	12.54	13.23	13.92	14.61	15.30	16.00	16.70	17.40	18.10
	7.00%	**7.25%**	**7.50%**	**7.75%**	**8.00%**	**8.25%**	**8.50%**	**8.75%**	**9.00%**	**9.25%**
6	$ 2.05	$ 2.13	$ 2.20	$ 2.27	$ 2.35	$ 2.42	$ 2.49	$ 2.57	$ 2.64	$ 2.72
12	3.83	3.97	4.11	4.25	4.39	4.52	4.66	4.80	4.94	5.08
18	5.63	5.84	6.04	6.25	6.45	6.66	6.86	7.07	7.28	7.48
24	7.45	7.73	8.00	8.27	8.55	8.82	9.09	9.37	9.64	9.92
30	9.30	9.64	9.98	10.32	10.66	11.01	11.35	11.70	12.04	12.39
36	11.16	11.57	11.98	12.40	12.81	13.23	13.64	14.06	14.48	14.90
42	13.04	13.52	14.01	14.50	14.98	15.47	15.96	16.45	16.95	17.44
48	14.94	15.50	16.06	16.62	17.18	17.75	18.31	18.88	19.45	20.02
54	16.86	17.50	18.13	18.77	19.41	20.05	20.69	21.34	21.98	22.63
60	18.81	19.52	20.23	20.94	21.66	22.38	23.10	23.82	24.55	25.28
	9.50%	**9.75%**	**10.00%**	**10.25%**	**10.50%**	**10.75%**	**11.00%**	**11.25%**	**11.50%**	**11.75%**
6	$ 2.79	$ 2.86	$ 2.94	$ 3.01	$ 3.08	$ 3.16	$ 3.23	$ 3.31	$ 3.38	$ 3.45
12	5.22	5.36	5.50	5.64	5.78	5.92	6.06	6.20	6.34	6.48
18	7.69	7.90	8.10	8.31	8.52	8.73	8.93	9.14	9.35	9.56
24	10.19	10.47	10.75	11.02	11.30	11.58	11.86	12.14	12.42	12.70
30	12.74	13.09	13.43	13.78	14.13	14.48	14.83	15.19	15.54	15.89
36	15.32	15.74	16.16	16.58	17.01	17.43	17.86	18.29	18.71	19.14
42	17.94	18.43	18.93	19.43	19.93	20.43	20.93	21.44	21.94	22.45
48	20.59	21.16	21.74	22.32	22.90	23.48	24.06	24.64	25.23	25.81
54	23.28	23.94	24.59	25.25	25.91	26.57	27.23	27.90	28.56	29.23
60	26.01	26.75	27.48	28.22	28.96	29.71	30.45	31.20	31.96	32.71

Annual Percentage Rate Table for Monthly Payment Plans

Annual Percentage Rate (Finance Charge per $100 of Amount Financed)

# of Pmts. ▼	12.00%	12.25%	12.50%	12.75%	13.00%	13.25%	13.50%	13.75%	14.00%	14.25%
6	$ 3.53	$ 3.60	$ 3.68	$ 3.75	$ 3.83	$ 3.90	$ 3.97	$ 4.05	$ 4.12	$ 4.20
12	6.62	6.76	6.90	7.04	7.18	7.32	7.46	7.60	7.74	7.89
18	9.77	9.98	10.19	10.40	10.61	10.82	11.03	11.24	11.45	11.66
24	12.98	13.26	13.54	13.82	14.10	14.38	14.66	14.95	15.23	15.51
30	16.24	16.60	16.95	17.31	17.66	18.02	18.38	18.74	19.10	19.45
36	19.57	20.00	20.43	20.87	21.30	21.73	22.17	22.60	23.04	23.48
42	22.96	23.47	23.98	24.49	25.00	25.51	26.03	26.55	27.06	27.58
48	26.40	26.99	27.58	28.18	28.77	29.37	29.97	30.57	31.17	31.77
54	29.91	30.58	31.25	31.93	32.61	33.29	33.98	34.66	35.35	36.04
60	33.47	34.23	34.99	35.75	36.52	37.29	38.06	38.83	39.61	40.39

# of Pmts.	14.50%	14.75%	15.00%	15.25%	15.50%	15.75%	16.00%	16.25%	16.50%	16.75%
6	$ 4.27	$ 4.35	$ 4.42	$ 4.49	$ 4.57	$ 4.64	$ 4.72	$ 4.79	$ 4.87	$ 4.94
12	8.03	8.17	8.31	8.45	8.59	8.74	8.88	9.02	9.16	9.30
18	11.87	12.08	12.29	12.50	12.72	12.93	13.14	13.35	13.57	13.78
24	15.80	16.08	16.37	16.65	16.94	17.22	17.51	17.80	18.09	18.37
30	19.81	20.17	20.54	20.90	21.26	21.62	21.99	22.35	22.72	23.08
36	23.92	24.35	24.80	25.24	25.68	26.12	26.57	27.01	27.46	27.90
42	28.10	28.62	29.15	29.67	30.19	30.72	31.25	31.78	32.31	32.84
48	32.37	32.98	33.59	34.20	34.81	35.42	36.03	36.65	37.27	37.88
54	36.73	37.42	38.12	38.82	39.52	40.22	40.92	41.63	42.33	43.04
60	41.17	41.95	42.74	43.53	44.32	45.11	45.91	46.71	47.51	48.31

# of Pmts.	17.00%	17.25%	17.50%	17.75%	18.00%	18.25%	18.50%	18.75%	19.00%	19.25%	19.50%
6	$ 5.02	$ 5.09	$ 5.17	$ 5.24	$ 5.32	$ 5.39	$ 5.46	$ 5.54	$ 5.61	$ 5.69	$ 5.76
12	9.45	9.59	9.73	9.87	10.02	10.16	10.30	10.44	10.59	10.73	10.87
18	13.99	14.21	14.42	14.64	14.85	15.07	15.28	15.49	15.71	15.93	16.14
24	18.66	18.95	19.24	19.53	19.82	20.11	20.40	20.69	20.98	21.27	21.56
30	23.45	23.81	24.18	24.55	24.92	25.29	25.66	26.03	26.40	26.77	27.14
36	28.35	28.80	29.25	29.70	30.15	30.60	31.05	31.51	31.96	32.42	32.87
42	33.37	33.90	34.44	34.97	35.51	36.05	36.59	37.13	37.67	38.21	38.76
48	38.50	39.13	39.75	40.37	41.00	41.63	42.26	42.89	43.52	44.15	44.79
54	43.75	44.47	45.18	45.90	46.62	47.34	48.06	48.79	49.51	50.24	50.97
60	49.12	49.92	50.73	51.55	52.36	53.18	54.00	54.82	55.64	56.47	57.30

# of Pmts.	19.75%	20.00%	20.25%	20.50%	20.75%	21.00%	21.25%	21.50%	21.75%	22.00%	22.25%
6	$ 5.84	$ 5.91	$ 5.99	$ 6.06	$ 6.14	$ 6.21	$ 6.29	$ 6.36	$ 6.44	$ 6.51	$ 6.59
12	11.02	11.16	11.31	11.45	11.59	11.74	11.88	12.02	12.17	12.31	12.46
18	16.36	16.57	16.79	17.01	17.22	17.44	17.66	17.88	18.09	18.31	18.53
24	21.86	22.15	22.44	22.74	23.03	23.33	23.62	23.92	24.21	24.51	24.80
30	27.52	27.89	28.26	28.64	29.01	29.39	29.77	30.14	30.52	30.90	31.28
36	33.33	33.79	34.25	34.71	35.17	35.63	36.09	36.56	37.02	37.49	37.95
42	39.30	39.85	40.40	40.95	41.50	42.05	42.60	43.15	43.71	44.26	44.82
48	45.43	46.07	46.71	47.35	47.99	48.64	49.28	49.93	50.58	51.23	51.88
54	51.70	52.44	53.17	53.91	54.65	55.39	56.14	56.88	57.63	58.38	59.13
60	58.13	58.96	59.80	60.64	61.48	62.32	63.17	64.01	64.86	65.71	66.57

Amount of $1.00 at 5.5 Percent, Compounded Daily (365-Day Year)

Day	Amount	Day	Amount	Day	Amount	Day	Amount	Day	Amount
1	1.00015	11	1.00165	21	1.00316	31	1.00468	50	1.00755
2	1.00030	12	1.00180	22	1.00331	32	1.00483	60	1.00907
3	1.00045	13	1.00196	23	1.00347	33	1.00498	70	1.01059
4	1.00060	14	1.00211	24	1.00362	34	1.00513	80	1.01212
5	1.00075	15	1.00226	25	1.00377	35	1.00528	90	1.01364
6	1.00090	16	1.00241	26	1.00392	36	1.00543	100	1.01517
7	1.00105	17	1.00256	27	1.00407	37	1.00558	110	1.01670
8	1.00120	18	1.00271	28	1.00422	38	1.00574	120	1.01823
9	1.00135	19	1.00286	29	1.00437	39	1.00589	130	1.01977
10	1.00150	20	1.00301	30	1.00452	40	1.00604	140	1.02131

Elapsed Time Table

The Number of Each Day of the Year

Day No.	Jan.	Feb.	Mar.	Apr.	May	June	July	Aug.	Sept.	Oct.	Nov.	Dec.
1	1	32	60	91	121	152	182	213	244	274	305	335
2	2	33	61	92	122	153	183	214	245	275	306	336
3	3	34	62	93	123	154	184	215	246	276	307	337
4	4	35	63	94	124	155	185	216	247	277	308	338
5	5	36	64	95	125	156	186	217	248	278	309	339
6	6	37	65	96	126	157	187	218	249	279	310	340
7	7	38	66	97	127	158	188	219	250	280	311	341
8	8	39	67	98	128	159	189	220	251	281	312	342
9	9	40	68	99	129	160	190	221	252	282	313	343
10	10	41	69	100	130	161	191	222	253	283	314	344
11	11	42	70	101	131	162	192	223	254	284	315	345
12	12	43	71	102	132	163	193	224	255	285	316	346
13	13	44	72	103	133	164	194	225	256	286	317	347
14	14	45	73	104	134	165	195	226	257	287	318	348
15	15	46	74	105	135	166	196	227	258	288	319	349
16	16	47	75	106	136	167	197	228	259	289	320	350
17	17	48	76	107	137	168	198	229	260	290	321	351
18	18	49	77	108	138	169	199	230	261	291	322	352
19	19	50	78	109	139	170	200	231	262	292	323	353
20	20	51	79	110	140	171	201	232	263	293	324	354
21	21	52	80	111	141	172	202	233	264	294	325	355
22	22	53	81	112	142	173	203	234	265	295	326	356
23	23	54	82	113	143	174	204	235	266	296	327	357
24	24	55	83	114	144	175	205	236	267	297	328	358
25	25	56	84	115	145	176	206	237	268	298	329	359
26	26	57	85	116	146	177	207	238	269	299	330	360
27	27	58	86	117	147	178	208	239	270	300	331	361
28	28	59*	87	118	148	179	209	240	271	301	332	362
29	29		88	119	149	180	210	241	272	302	333	363
30	30		89	120	150	181	211	242	273	303	334	364
31	31		90		151		212	243		304		365

*Add one day for February 29 for leap year. (Leap years are 2004, 2008, and so on.)

Compound Interest—Amount of $1.00

Period "n"	Rate per Period									
	1.000%	1.250%	1.375%	1.500%	2.000%	2.500%	2.750%	2.875%	3.000%	3.125%
1	1.01000	1.01250	1.01375	1.01500	1.02000	1.02500	1.02750	1.02875	1.03000	1.03125
2	1.02010	1.02516	1.02769	1.03023	1.04040	1.05063	1.05576	1.05833	1.06090	1.06348
3	1.03030	1.03797	1.04182	1.04568	1.06121	1.07689	1.08479	1.08875	1.09273	1.09671
4	1.04060	1.05095	1.05614	1.06136	1.08243	1.10381	1.11462	1.12006	1.12551	1.13098
5	1.05101	1.06408	1.07067	1.07728	1.10408	1.13141	1.14527	1.15226	1.15927	1.16633
6	1.06152	1.07738	1.08539	1.09344	1.12616	1.15969	1.17677	1.18538	1.19405	1.20277
7	1.07214	1.09085	1.10031	1.10984	1.14869	1.18869	1.20913	1.21946	1.22987	1.24036
8	1.08286	1.10449	1.11544	1.12649	1.17166	1.21840	1.24238	1.25452	1.26677	1.27912
9	1.09369	1.11829	1.13078	1.14339	1.19509	1.24886	1.27655	1.29059	1.30477	1.31909
10	1.10462	1.13227	1.14633	1.16054	1.21899	1.28008	1.31165	1.32770	1.34392	1.36032
11	1.11567	1.14642	1.16209	1.17795	1.24337	1.31209	1.34772	1.36587	1.38423	1.40283
12	1.12683	1.16075	1.17807	1.19562	1.26824	1.34489	1.38478	1.40514	1.42576	1.44666
13	1.13809	1.17526	1.19427	1.21355	1.29361	1.37851	1.42287	1.44553	1.46853	1.49187
14	1.14947	1.18995	1.21069	1.23176	1.31948	1.41297	1.46199	1.48709	1.51259	1.53849
15	1.16097	1.20483	1.22733	1.25023	1.34587	1.44830	1.50220	1.52985	1.55797	1.58657
16	1.17258	1.21989	1.24421	1.26899	1.37279	1.48451	1.54351	1.57383	1.60471	1.63615
17	1.18430	1.23514	1.26132	1.28802	1.40024	1.52162	1.58596	1.61908	1.65285	1.68728
18	1.19615	1.25058	1.27866	1.30734	1.42825	1.55966	1.62957	1.66563	1.70243	1.74001
19	1.20811	1.26621	1.29624	1.32695	1.45681	1.59865	1.67438	1.71351	1.75351	1.79438
20	1.22019	1.28204	1.31407	1.34686	1.48595	1.63862	1.72043	1.76278	1.80611	1.85046
21	1.23239	1.29806	1.33213	1.36706	1.51567	1.67958	1.76774	1.81346	1.86029	1.90828
22	1.24472	1.31429	1.35045	1.38756	1.54598	1.72157	1.81635	1.86559	1.91610	1.96792
23	1.25716	1.33072	1.36902	1.40838	1.57690	1.76461	1.86630	1.91923	1.97359	2.02942
24	1.26973	1.34735	1.38784	1.42950	1.60844	1.80873	1.91763	1.97441	2.03279	2.09284
25	1.28243	1.36419	1.40693	1.45095	1.64061	1.85394	1.97036	2.03117	2.09378	2.15824
26	1.29526	1.38125	1.42627	1.47271	1.67342	1.90029	2.02455	2.08957	2.15659	2.22568
27	1.30821	1.39851	1.44588	1.49480	1.70689	1.94780	2.08022	2.14964	2.22129	2.29523
28	1.32129	1.41599	1.46576	1.51722	1.74102	1.99650	2.13743	2.21144	2.28793	2.36696
29	1.33450	1.43369	1.48592	1.53998	1.77584	2.04641	2.19621	2.27502	2.35657	2.44093
30	1.34785	1.45161	1.50635	1.56308	1.81136	2.09757	2.25660	2.34043	2.42726	2.51721
31	1.36133	1.46976	1.52706	1.58653	1.84759	2.15001	2.31866	2.40772	2.50008	2.59587
32	1.37494	1.48813	1.54806	1.61032	1.88454	2.20376	2.38242	2.47694	2.57508	2.67699
33	1.38869	1.50673	1.56935	1.63448	1.92223	2.25885	2.44794	2.54815	2.65234	2.76065
34	1.40258	1.52557	1.59092	1.65900	1.96068	2.31532	2.51526	2.62141	2.73191	2.84692
35	1.41660	1.54464	1.61280	1.68388	1.99989	2.37321	2.58443	2.69677	2.81386	2.93588
36	1.43077	1.56394	1.63498	1.70914	2.03989	2.43254	2.65550	2.77431	2.89828	3.02763
37	1.44508	1.58349	1.65746	1.73478	2.08069	2.49335	2.72852	2.85407	2.98523	3.12224
38	1.45953	1.60329	1.68025	1.76080	2.12230	2.55568	2.80356	2.93612	3.07478	3.21981
39	1.47412	1.62333	1.70335	1.78721	2.16474	2.61957	2.88066	3.02054	3.16703	3.32043
40	1.48886	1.64362	1.72677	1.81402	2.20804	2.68506	2.95987	3.10738	3.26204	3.42419
41	1.50375	1.66416	1.75051	1.84123	2.25220	2.75219	3.04127	3.19671	3.35990	3.53120
42	1.51879	1.68497	1.77458	1.86885	2.29724	2.82100	3.12491	3.28862	3.46070	3.64155
43	1.53398	1.70603	1.79898	1.89688	2.34319	2.89152	3.21084	3.38317	3.56452	3.75535
44	1.54932	1.72735	1.82372	1.92533	2.39005	2.96381	3.29914	3.48043	3.67145	3.87270
45	1.56481	1.74895	1.84880	1.95421	2.43785	3.03790	3.38986	3.58050	3.78160	3.99373
46	1.58046	1.77081	1.87422	1.98353	2.48661	3.11385	3.48309	3.68344	3.89504	4.11853
47	1.59626	1.79294	1.89999	2.01328	2.53634	3.19170	3.57887	3.78933	4.01190	4.24723
48	1.61223	1.81535	1.92611	2.04348	2.58707	3.27149	3.67729	3.89828	4.13225	4.37996
49	1.62835	1.83805	1.95260	2.07413	2.63881	3.35328	3.77842	4.01035	4.25622	4.51683
50	1.64463	1.86102	1.97944	2.10524	2.69159	3.43711	3.88232	4.12565	4.38391	4.65798

Future Value of an Ordinary Annuity for $1.00 per Period

Period "n"	Rate per Period									
	0.50%	1.00%	1.50%	2.00%	3.00%	4.00%	5.00%	6.00%	7.00%	8.00%
1	$ 1.00000	$ 1.00000	$ 1.00000	$ 1.00000	$ 1.00000	$ 1.00000	$ 1.00000	$ 1.00000	$ 1.00000	$ 1.00000
2	2.00500	2.01000	2.01500	2.02000	2.03000	2.04000	2.05000	2.06000	2.07000	2.08000
3	3.01502	3.03010	3.04522	3.06040	3.09090	3.12160	3.15250	3.18360	3.21490	3.24640
4	4.03010	4.06040	4.09090	4.12161	4.18363	4.24646	4.31013	4.37462	4.43994	4.50611
5	5.05025	5.10101	5.15227	5.20404	5.30914	5.41632	5.52563	5.63709	5.75074	5.86660
6	6.07550	6.15202	6.22955	6.30812	6.46841	6.63298	6.80191	6.97532	7.15329	7.33593
7	7.10588	7.21354	7.32299	7.43428	7.66246	7.89829	8.14201	8.39384	8.65402	8.92280
8	8.14141	8.28567	8.43284	8.58297	8.89234	9.21423	9.54911	9.89747	10.25980	10.63663
9	9.18212	9.36853	9.55933	9.75463	10.15911	10.58280	11.02656	11.49132	11.97799	12.48756
10	10.22803	10.46221	10.70272	10.94972	11.46388	12.00611	12.57789	13.18079	13.81645	14.48656
11	11.27917	11.56683	11.86326	12.16872	12.80780	13.48635	14.20679	14.97164	15.78360	16.64549
12	12.33556	12.68250	13.04121	13.41209	14.19203	15.02581	15.91713	16.86994	17.88845	18.97713
13	13.39724	13.80933	14.23683	14.68033	15.61779	16.62684	17.71298	18.88214	20.14064	21.49530
14	14.46423	14.94742	15.45038	15.97394	17.08632	18.29191	19.59863	21.01507	22.55049	24.21492
15	15.53655	16.09690	16.68214	17.29342	18.59891	20.02359	21.57856	23.27597	25.12902	27.15211
16	16.61423	17.25786	17.93237	18.63929	20.15688	21.82453	23.65749	25.67253	27.88805	30.32428
17	17.69730	18.43044	19.20136	20.01207	21.76159	23.69751	25.84037	28.21288	30.84022	33.75023
18	18.78579	19.61475	20.48938	21.41231	23.41444	25.64541	28.13238	30.90565	33.99903	37.45024
19	19.87972	20.81090	21.79672	22.84056	25.11687	27.67123	30.53900	33.75999	37.37896	41.44626
20	20.97912	22.01900	23.12367	24.29737	26.87037	29.77808	33.06595	36.78559	40.99549	45.76196
21	22.08401	23.23919	24.47052	25.78332	28.67649	31.96920	35.71925	39.99273	44.86518	50.42292
22	23.19443	24.47159	25.83758	27.29898	30.53678	34.24797	38.50521	43.39229	49.00574	55.45676
23	24.31040	25.71630	27.22514	28.84496	32.45288	36.61789	41.43048	46.99583	53.43614	60.89330
24	25.43196	26.97346	28.63352	30.42186	34.42647	39.08260	44.50200	50.81558	58.17667	66.76476
25	26.55912	28.24320	30.06302	32.03030	36.45926	41.64591	47.72710	54.86451	63.24904	73.10594
26	27.69191	29.52563	31.51397	33.67091	38.55304	44.31174	51.11345	59.15638	68.67647	79.95442
27	28.83037	30.82089	32.98668	35.34432	40.70963	47.08421	54.66913	63.70577	74.48382	87.35077
28	29.97452	32.12910	34.48148	37.05121	42.93092	49.96758	58.40258	68.52811	80.69769	95.33883
29	31.12439	33.45039	35.99870	38.79223	45.21885	52.96629	62.32271	73.63980	87.34653	103.96594
30	32.28002	34.78489	37.53868	40.56808	47.57542	56.08494	66.43885	79.05819	94.46079	113.28321
31	33.44142	36.13274	39.10176	42.37944	50.00268	59.32834	70.76079	84.80168	102.07304	123.34587
32	34.60862	37.49407	40.68829	44.22703	52.50276	62.70147	75.29883	90.88978	110.21815	134.21354
33	35.78167	38.86901	42.29861	46.11157	55.07784	66.20953	80.06377	97.34316	118.93343	145.95062
34	36.96058	40.25770	43.93309	48.03380	57.73018	69.85791	85.06696	104.18375	128.25876	158.62667
35	38.14538	41.66028	45.59209	49.99448	60.46208	73.65222	90.32031	111.43478	138.23688	172.31680
36	39.33610	43.07688	47.27597	51.99437	63.27594	77.59831	95.83632	119.12087	148.91346	187.10215
37	40.53279	44.50765	48.98511	54.03425	66.17422	81.70225	101.62814	127.26812	160.33740	203.07032
38	41.73545	45.95272	50.71989	56.11494	69.15945	85.97034	107.70955	135.90421	172.56102	220.31595
39	42.94413	47.41225	52.48068	58.23724	72.23423	90.40915	114.09502	145.05846	185.64029	238.94122
40	44.15885	48.88637	54.26789	60.40198	75.40126	95.02552	120.79977	154.76197	199.63511	259.05652
41	45.37964	50.37524	56.08191	62.61002	78.66330	99.82654	127.83976	165.04768	214.60957	280.78104
42	46.60654	51.87899	57.92314	64.86222	82.02320	104.81960	135.23175	175.95054	230.63224	304.24352
43	47.83957	53.39778	59.79199	67.15947	85.48389	110.01238	142.99334	187.50758	247.77650	329.58301
44	49.07877	54.93176	61.68887	69.50266	89.04841	115.41288	151.14301	199.75803	266.12085	356.94965
45	50.32416	56.48107	63.61420	71.89271	92.71986	121.02939	159.70016	212.74351	285.74931	386.50562
46	51.57578	58.04589	65.56841	74.33056	96.50146	126.87057	168.68516	226.50812	306.75176	418.42607
47	52.83366	59.62634	67.55194	76.81718	100.39650	132.94539	178.11942	241.09861	329.22439	452.90015
48	54.09783	61.22261	69.56522	79.35352	104.40840	139.26321	188.02539	256.56453	353.27009	490.13216
49	55.36832	62.83483	71.60870	81.94059	108.54065	145.83373	198.42666	272.95840	378.99900	530.34274
50	56.64516	64.46318	73.68283	84.57940	112.79687	152.66708	209.34800	290.33590	406.52893	573.77016

Monthly Payment for a $1,000 Loan

Interest Rate	Length of Loan in Years						
	10	15	20	25	30	35	40
5.00%	$10.61	$ 7.91	$ 6.60	$ 5.85	$ 5.37	$ 5.05	$ 4.82
5.50%	10.85	8.17	6.88	6.14	5.68	5.37	5.16
6.00%	11.10	8.44	7.16	6.44	6.00	5.70	5.50
6.50%	11.35	8.71	7.46	6.75	6.32	6.04	5.85
7.00%	11.61	8.99	7.75	7.07	6.65	6.39	6.21
7.50%	11.87	9.27	8.06	7.39	6.99	6.74	6.58
8.00%	12.13	9.56	8.36	7.72	7.34	7.10	6.95
8.50%	12.40	9.85	8.68	8.05	7.69	7.47	7.33
9.00%	12.67	10.14	9.00	8.39	8.05	7.84	7.71
9.50%	12.94	10.44	9.32	8.74	8.41	8.22	8.10
10.00%	13.22	10.75	9.65	9.09	8.78	8.60	8.49
10.50%	13.49	11.05	9.98	9.44	9.15	8.98	8.89
11.00%	13.78	11.37	10.32	9.80	9.52	9.37	9.28
11.50%	14.06	11.68	10.66	10.16	9.90	9.76	9.68
12.00%	14.35	12.00	11.01	10.53	10.29	10.16	10.08
12.50%	14.64	12.33	11.36	10.90	10.67	10.55	10.49
13.00%	14.93	12.65	11.72	11.28	11.06	10.95	10.90

Monthly Payment on a Simple Interest Installment Loan of $100

Term in Months	Annual Percentage Rate										
	8.00%	9.00%	10.00%	11.00%	12.00%	13.00%	14.00%	15.00%	16.00%	17.00%	18.00%
6	17.06	17.11	17.16	17.21	17.25	17.30	17.35	17.40	17.45	17.50	17.55
12	8.70	8.75	8.79	8.84	8.88	8.93	8.98	9.03	9.07	9.12	9.17
18	5.91	5.96	6.01	6.05	6.10	6.14	6.19	6.24	6.29	6.33	6.38
24	4.52	4.57	4.61	4.66	4.71	4.75	4.80	4.85	4.90	4.94	4.99
30	3.69	3.73	3.78	3.83	3.87	3.92	3.97	4.02	4.07	4.11	4.16
36	3.13	3.18	3.23	3.27	3.32	3.37	3.42	3.47	3.52	3.57	3.62
42	2.74	2.78	2.83	2.88	2.93	2.98	3.03	3.07	3.12	3.18	3.23
48	2.44	2.49	2.54	2.58	2.63	2.68	2.73	2.78	2.83	2.89	2.94
54	2.21	2.26	2.31	2.36	2.41	2.46	2.51	2.56	2.61	2.66	2.72
60	2.03	2.08	2.12	2.17	2.22	2.28	2.33	2.38	2.43	2.49	2.54

Amount of $1.00 Invested—Daily, Monthly, and Quarterly Compounding

Annual Rate	Interest Period—1 Year			Interest Period—4 Years		
	Daily	Monthly	Quarterly	Daily	Monthly	Quarterly
0.50%	1.005012	1.005011	1.005009	1.020201	1.020197	1.020189
0.75%	1.007528	1.007526	1.007521	1.030454	1.030445	1.030426
1.00%	1.010050	1.010046	1.010038	1.040810	1.040793	1.040759
1.25%	1.012578	1.012572	1.012559	1.051270	1.051244	1.051189
1.50%	1.015113	1.015104	1.015085	1.061835	1.061797	1.061717
1.75%	1.017654	1.017641	1.017615	1.072506	1.072453	1.072344
2.00%	1.020201	1.020184	1.020151	1.083285	1.083215	1.083071
2.25%	1.022754	1.022733	1.022691	1.094171	1.094082	1.093898
2.50%	1.025314	1.025288	1.025235	1.105167	1.105056	1.104827
2.75%	1.027881	1.027849	1.027785	1.116273	1.116138	1.115858
3.00%	1.030453	1.030416	1.030339	1.127491	1.127328	1.126992
3.25%	1.033032	1.032989	1.032898	1.138822	1.138628	1.138230
3.50%	1.035618	1.035567	1.035462	1.150266	1.150039	1.149574
3.75%	1.038210	1.038151	1.038031	1.161825	1.161563	1.161023
4.00%	1.040808	1.040742	1.040604	1.173501	1.173199	1.172579
4.25%	1.043413	1.043338	1.043182	1.185293	1.184949	1.184242
4.50%	1.046025	1.045940	1.045765	1.197204	1.196814	1.196015
4.75%	1.048643	1.048548	1.048353	1.209235	1.208796	1.207897
5.00%	1.051267	1.051162	1.050945	1.221386	1.220895	1.219890
5.25%	1.053899	1.053782	1.053543	1.233659	1.233113	1.231994
5.50%	1.056536	1.056408	1.056145	1.246056	1.245451	1.244211
5.75%	1.059180	1.059040	1.058752	1.258577	1.257909	1.256541
6.00%	1.061831	1.061678	1.061364	1.271224	1.270489	1.268986
6.25%	1.064489	1.064322	1.063980	1.283998	1.283193	1.281546
6.50%	1.067153	1.066972	1.066602	1.296900	1.296020	1.294222
6.75%	1.069824	1.069628	1.069228	1.309932	1.308974	1.307017
7.00%	1.072501	1.072290	1.071859	1.323094	1.322054	1.319929
7.25%	1.075185	1.074958	1.074495	1.336389	1.335262	1.332962
7.50%	1.077876	1.077633	1.077136	1.349817	1.348599	1.346114
7.75%	1.080573	1.080313	1.079782	1.363380	1.362067	1.359389
8.00%	1.083278	1.083000	1.082432	1.377079	1.375666	1.372786
8.25%	1.085989	1.085692	1.085088	1.390916	1.389398	1.386306
8.50%	1.088706	1.088391	1.087748	1.404892	1.403265	1.399952
8.75%	1.091431	1.091096	1.090413	1.419008	1.417267	1.413723
9.00%	1.094162	1.093807	1.093083	1.433266	1.431405	1.427621
9.25%	1.096900	1.096524	1.095758	1.447667	1.445682	1.441648
9.50%	1.099645	1.099248	1.098438	1.462212	1.460098	1.455803
9.75%	1.102397	1.101977	1.101123	1.476904	1.474655	1.470089
10.00%	1.105156	1.104713	1.103813	1.491743	1.489354	1.484506
10.25%	1.107921	1.107455	1.106508	1.506731	1.504196	1.499055
10.50%	1.110694	1.110203	1.109207	1.521870	1.519184	1.513738
10.75%	1.113473	1.112958	1.111912	1.537160	1.534317	1.528556
11.00%	1.116260	1.115719	1.114621	1.552604	1.549598	1.543509
11.25%	1.119053	1.118486	1.117336	1.568203	1.565028	1.558600
11.50%	1.121853	1.121259	1.120055	1.583959	1.580608	1.573829
11.75%	1.124660	1.124039	1.122779	1.599873	1.596341	1.589197
12.00%	1.127475	1.126825	1.125509	1.615947	1.612226	1.604706
12.25%	1.130296	1.129617	1.128243	1.632182	1.628266	1.620357
12.50%	1.133124	1.132416	1.130982	1.648580	1.644463	1.636151
12.75%	1.135960	1.135221	1.133727	1.665143	1.660817	1.652089
13.00%	1.138802	1.138032	1.136476	1.681872	1.677330	1.668173
13.25%	1.141652	1.140850	1.139230	1.698769	1.694005	1.684403

Conversion Tables

Time	
60 seconds (s) = 1 minute (min)	52 weeks = 1 year
60 minutes = 1 hour (h)	12 months = 1 year
24 hours = 1 day	100 years = 1 century
7 days = 1 week	

Metric System	
Length	**Volume**
10 millimeters (mm) = 1 centimeter (cm)	1,000 milliliters (mL) = 1 liter (L)
100 centimeters = 1 meter (m)	1,000 cubic centimeters (cm^3) = 1 liter
1,000 meters = 1 kilometer (km)	10 milliliters = 1 centiliter (cL)
	10 deciliters (dL) = 1 liter
Area	**Mass**
100 square millimeters (mm^2) = 1 square centimeter (cm^2)	1,000 milligrams (mg) = 1 gram (g)
10,000 square centimeters = 1 square meter (m^2)	1,000 grams = 1 kilogram (kg)
10,000 square meters = 1 hectare (ha)	1,000 kilograms = 1 metric ton (t)

Customary System	
Length	**Volume**
12 inches (in) = 1 foot (ft)	8 fluid ounces (oz) = 1 cup (c)
3 feet = 1 yard (yd)	2 cups = 1 pint (pt)
5,280 feet = 1 mile (mi)	2 pints = 1 quart (qt)
	4 quarts = 1 gallon (gal)
Area	**Weight**
144 square inches (in^2) = 1 square foot (ft^2)	16 ounces =1 pound
9 square feet = 1 square yard (yd^2)	2,000 pounds = 1 ton (t)
4,837 square yards = 1 acre (A)	

APPENDIX

Selected Answers

Workshop Answers

Workshop 1: *Writing and Reading Numbers* **1.** 24,366 **2.** 436.785 **3.** hundreds; thousandths **4.** Standard form: 5,456.68; Word form: five thousand four hundred fifty-six and sixty-eight hundredths; Point form: five four five six point six eight **5.** Standard form: 56.817; Word form: fifty-six and eight hundred seventeen thousandths; Point form: five six point eight one seven **6.** Word form: eight hundred seventy-five and forty-eight one hundredth dollars or eight hundred seventy-five and $\frac{48}{100}$ dollars or eight hundred seventy-five dollars and forty-eight cents **7.** millions **8.** hundreds **9.** Word form: five hundred forty-three thousand six hundred ninety-eight; Short word form: 543 thousand, 698 **10.** Word form: forty-five million nine hundred eighty-seven thousand one hundred fifty-nine and nine tenths; Short word form: 45 million, 987 thousand, 159 and 9 tenths **11.** Standard form: 654,321; Word form: six hundred fifty-four thousand three hundred twenty-one **12.** Standard form: 56.99; Word form: fifty-six and ninety-nine hundredths **13.** 4,000 + 600 + 70 + 8 **14.** 90,000 + 8,000 + 400 + 30 + 8

Workshop 2: *Rounding Numbers* **1.** 6,000 **2.** 5,693.3 **3.** 5,700 **4.** 5,693 **5.** $21.28 **6.** $967.46 **7.** $138.78 **8.** $647.56 **9.** 16,000,000 **10.** 20,000,000 **11.** 15,749,000 **12.** 15,748,500 **13.** 15,750,000 **14.** 15,700,000 **15. a.** 19,000; 19,000; 18,970 **b.** 26,000; 25,700; 25,690 **c.** 20,000; 20,100; 20,120 **d.** 25,000; 24,600; 24,570 **e.** 19,000; 19,400; 19,420

Workshop 3: *Comparing Numbers* **1.** 8,891 **2.** 7,521 **3.** 284.4 **4.** 0.06 **5.** 29 **6.** 4,210 **7.** 2.65 **8.** 0.696 **9.** 0.4 **10.** 0.9 **11.** 0.03 **12.** 2.244 **13.** 1.36, 1.37, 1.39 **14.** 5.09, 5.10, 5.11 **15.** 7.18, 7.38, 7.58 **16.** 5.81, 5.86, 5.95 **17.** 40.004, 40.04, 40.4 **18.** 121.012, 121.021, 121.210 **19.** 365.15, 365.490, 365.51 **20.** 0.1234, 0.1342, 0.1423 **21. a.** Science: 513.12, 519.03, 532.626, 571.113, 587.41 **b.** Literature: 11.7, 32.615, 34.9, 67.192, 94.79 **c.** Religion: 15.04, 18.7, 26.311, 46.94, 71.21 **d.** Language: 22.5, 38.9, 48.275, 67.21, 93.047 **22. a.** 873.15 and 877.142 **b.** 332.749 and 333.54

Workshop 4: *Adding Decimals* **1.** 70.88 **2.** 178.44 **3.** 222.86 **4.** 183.76 **5.** 365.475 **6.** 1,282.842 **7.** $597.36 **8.** $579.84 **9.** 133.49 **10.** 92.03 **11.** 871.76 **12.** 794.15 **13.** 175.364 **14.** 169.149 **15.** 14.082 **16.** 15.509 **17.** 201.38 **18.** 228.03 **19.** 22.4009 **20.** 155.961 **21.** 601.234 **22.** 288.897 **23.** 649.647 **24.** 190.2 **25.** 1,128.894 **26.** 5,770.453 **27.** 191.968 **28.** 583.4754 **29.** 124.03 **30.** 178.81 **31.** 302.6016 **32.** 31.258 **33.** $123.96 **34.** $428.05 **35.** $289.17 **36.** $84.43

Workshop 5: *Subtracting Decimals* **1.** 53.61 **2.** 38.3 **3.** 610.08 **4.** 68.76 **5.** 63.3 **6.** 10.1 **7.** 11.33 **8.** 5.90 **9.** 39.30 **10.** 83.76 **11.** 4.639 **12.** 58.463 **13.** $67.69 **14.** $47.37 **15.** $665.90 **16.** $262.67 **17.** $264.03 **18.** $189.88 **19.** $16,681.07 **20.** $43,747.81 **21.** 117.5 **22.** 15.6 **23.** 4.50 **24.** $383.23 **25.** $863.15 **26.** $1,666.17 **27. a.** $0.06 **b.** $0.88 **c.** $0.03 **d.** $2.00 **e.** $0.00 **f.** $1.89 **g.** $0.10 **h.** $2.58 **i.** $1.00 **j.** $0.16 **28. a.** $250.33 **b.** $102.60 **c.** $892.85 **d.** $378.72 **e.** $60.33 **f.** $1,020.42 **g.** $500.60

Workshop 6: *Multiplying Decimals* **1.** 8.151 **2.** 89.452 **3.** 0.0858 **4.** 0.0592 **5.** $35.275 = $35.28 **6.** 714 **7.** 4,186.1 **8.** 8.26 **9.** 23.52 **10.** 21.2 **11.** 37.224 **12.** 30.318 **13.** 34.639 **4.** 0.0082 **15.** 0.0592 **16.** 0.0306 **17.** $437.75 **18.** $20.475 = $20.48 **19.** $25.46 **20.** 317 **21.** 57.1 **22.** 3,285 **23.** 4,178.6 **24.** 72,716 **25.** 7,195.6 **26.** 69,178 **27.** 34,287.6

Workshop 7: *Dividing Decimals* **1.** 6.2 **2.** 4.29 **3.** 36 **4.** $1.36 **5.** 0.79 **6.** 1.389 **7.** 9.8628 **8.** 1.8 **9.** 3.5 **10.** 9.3 **11.** 1.83 **12.** 0.905 = 0.91 **13.** 12.002 = 12.00 **14.** 0.93 **15.** 1.442 **16.** 72.681 **17.** 4.298 **18.** 1.3339 **19.** 84.6265 **20.** 5.8969 **21.** 0.32129 **22.** 0.022098 **23.** 6.365218 **24.** 0.387919 **25.** 0.041549

Workshop 8: *Multiplying Fractions*
1. $\frac{3}{4} \times \frac{5}{8} = \frac{3 \times 5}{4 \times 8} = \frac{15}{32}$ **2.** $\frac{7}{8} \times \frac{3}{8} = \frac{7 \times 3}{8 \times 8} = \frac{21}{64}$
3. $\frac{3}{4} \times 600 = \frac{2}{3} \times \frac{600}{1} = \frac{1,200}{3} = 400$
4. $\frac{3}{4} \times \frac{5}{9} = \frac{3 \times 5}{4 \times 9} = \frac{3 \times 5}{2 \times 2 \times 3 \times 3} = \frac{5}{12}$
5. $\frac{2}{15} \times \frac{5}{8} = \frac{2 \times 5}{3 \times 5 \times 2 \times 2 \times 2} = \frac{1}{3 \times 2 \times 2} = \frac{1}{12}$
6. $\frac{5}{6} \times 180 = \frac{5}{6} \times \frac{180}{1} = \frac{5 \times 6 \times 30}{6} = 150$
7. $4\frac{1}{2} \times 8 = \frac{9}{2} \times \frac{8}{1} = \frac{9 \times 2 \times 4}{2} = 36$
8. $3\frac{3}{5} \times 2\frac{2}{9} = \frac{18}{5} \times \frac{20}{9} = \frac{2 \times 9 \times 5 \times 4}{5 \times 9} = \frac{8}{1} = 8$
9. $4\frac{1}{2} \times 3\frac{1}{3} = \frac{9}{2} \times \frac{10}{3} = \frac{3 \times 3 \times 2 \times 5}{2 \times 3} = 15$
10. $\frac{21}{32}$ **11.** $\frac{21}{40}$ **12.** $\frac{21}{22}$ **13.** $\frac{27}{50}$ **14.** 50 **15.** 15 **16.** 180 **17.** 440 **18.** 217 **19.** $1\frac{1}{2}$ **20.** $\frac{3}{20}$ **21.** $\frac{6}{25}$ **22.** 1,656 **23.** $27\frac{5}{8}$ **24.** 18 **25.** $59\frac{3}{8}$ **26.** $110\frac{1}{2}$ **27.** 238

Workshop 9: *Dividing Fractions* **1.** $\frac{3}{5}$ **2.** $\frac{8}{7}$ **3.** $\frac{1}{10}$ **4.** $\frac{2}{5}$ **5.** $\frac{5}{6}$ **6.** $\frac{3}{8}$ **7.** $\frac{2}{5}$ **8.** 5 **9.** $\frac{4}{3}$ **10.** $\frac{8}{5}$ **11.** $\frac{16}{3}$ **12.** $\frac{2}{21}$ **13.** $\frac{10}{1}$ **14.** $\frac{1}{9}$ **15.** $\frac{1}{15}$ **16.** $\frac{1}{7}$ **17.** $\frac{2}{3}$ **18.** $\frac{9}{10}$ **19.** $\frac{7}{24}$ **20.** $2\frac{1}{4}$ **21.** $2\frac{5}{8}$ **22.** 6 **23.** 16 **24.** $\frac{5}{16}$ **25.** $\frac{7}{128}$ **26.** $2\frac{1}{2}$ **27.** 4 **28.** $10\frac{1}{3}$ **29.** $7\frac{12}{13}$ **30.** $12\frac{4}{5}$ servings **31.** 98 bags **32.** 8 pieces of wire **33.** $3\frac{1}{2}$ quarts

Workshop 10: *Adding Fractions* **1.** $\frac{3}{3}$ or 1 **2.** $\frac{23}{18}$ or $1\frac{5}{18}$ **3.** $\frac{14}{7}$ or 2 **4.** $\frac{12}{9}$ or $1\frac{1}{3}$ **5.** $\frac{9}{8}$ or $1\frac{1}{8}$ **6.** $\frac{11}{6}$ or $1\frac{5}{6}$ **7.** $\frac{53}{30}$ or $1\frac{23}{30}$ **8.** $\frac{79}{60}$ or $1\frac{19}{60}$ **9.** $\frac{22}{15}$ or $1\frac{7}{15}$ **10.** $\frac{5}{4}$ or $1\frac{1}{4}$

11. $\frac{19}{18}$ or $1\frac{1}{18}$ **12.** $\frac{13}{12}$ or $1\frac{1}{12}$ **13.** $\frac{65}{42}$ or $1\frac{23}{42}$ **14.** $\frac{95}{72}$ or $1\frac{23}{72}$ **15.** $\frac{65}{44}$ or $1\frac{21}{44}$ **16.** $\frac{49}{40}$ or $1\frac{9}{40}$ **17.** $\frac{59}{63}$ **18.** $\frac{193}{105}$ or $1\frac{88}{105}$ **19.** $\frac{193}{120}$ or $1\frac{73}{120}$ **20.** $\frac{223}{132}$ or $1\frac{91}{132}$ **21.** $\frac{16}{15}$ or $1\frac{1}{15}$ **22.** $\frac{9}{8}$ or $1\frac{1}{8}$ **23.** $\frac{13}{6}$ or $2\frac{1}{6}$ **24.** $\frac{43}{30}$ or $1\frac{13}{30}$ **25.** $\frac{41}{24}$ or $1\frac{17}{24}$ **26.** $\frac{31}{30}$ or $1\frac{1}{30}$ **27.** $\frac{77}{36}$ or $2\frac{5}{36}$ **28.** $\frac{143}{60}$ or $2\frac{23}{60}$ **29.** $\frac{101}{66}$ or $1\frac{35}{66}$ **30.** $\frac{29}{20}$ or $1\frac{9}{20}$ **31.** $\frac{89}{28}$ or $3\frac{5}{28}$ **32.** $\frac{3}{4}$ **33.** 2 **34.** $\frac{15}{16}$ **35.** $\frac{9}{10}$ **36.** $\frac{11}{12}$ **37.** $\frac{59}{60}$ **38.** $\frac{35}{36}$

Workshop 11: *Subtracting Fractions* **1.** $\frac{1}{2}$ **2.** $\frac{2}{3}$ **3.** $\frac{11}{17}$ **4.** $\frac{2}{29}$ **5.** $\frac{1}{4}$ **6.** $\frac{11}{24}$ **7.** $\frac{7}{60}$ **8.** $\frac{29}{60}$ **9.** $3\frac{3}{7}$ **10.** $4\frac{1}{2}$ **11.** $7\frac{5}{8}$ **12.** $\frac{1}{16}$ **13.** $\frac{1}{3}$ **14.** $\frac{5}{9}$ **15.** $\frac{11}{17}$ **16.** $\frac{1}{4}$ **17.** $\frac{5}{24}$ **18.** $\frac{7}{10}$ **19.** $\frac{5}{24}$ **20.** $\frac{11}{20}$ **21.** $\frac{31}{63}$ **22.** $\frac{1}{5}$ **23.** $\frac{13}{30}$ **24.** $\frac{11}{36}$ **25.** $2\frac{5}{12}$ **26.** $5\frac{2}{15}$ **27.** $7\frac{3}{10}$ **28.** $4\frac{13}{15}$ **29.** $\frac{1}{24}$ **30.** $\frac{1}{8}$ **31.** $\frac{1}{12}$ **32.** $\frac{3}{4}$ **33.** $\frac{1}{5}$

Workshop 12: *Comparing Fractions* **1.** $\frac{5}{8} < \frac{7}{8}$ **2.** $\frac{11}{12} > \frac{7}{12}$ **3.** $\frac{2}{3} > \frac{1}{3}$ **4.** $\frac{49}{50} > \frac{41}{50}$ **5.** $\frac{5}{6} < \frac{7}{8}$ **6.** $\frac{7}{12} > \frac{5}{9}$ **7.** $\frac{3}{7} < \frac{7}{15}$ **8.** $\frac{45}{47} > \frac{89}{93}$ **9.** $\frac{8}{11} < \frac{15}{19}$ **10.** $\frac{1}{23} < \frac{2}{45}$ **11.** $\frac{5}{13} > \frac{9}{25}$ **12.** $\frac{147}{347} > \frac{440}{1{,}039}$ **13.** $\frac{4}{5} > \frac{3}{5}$ **14.** $\frac{8}{13} < \frac{10}{13}$ **15.** $\frac{347}{498} > \frac{299}{498}$ **16.** $\frac{1}{4} > \frac{1}{5}$ **17.** $\frac{5}{8} > \frac{11}{18}$ **18.** $\frac{4}{9} < \frac{7}{12}$ **19.** $\frac{43}{45} < \frac{22}{23}$ **20.** $\frac{91}{97} > \frac{45}{49}$ **21.** $\frac{14}{19} > \frac{27}{37}$ **22.** $\frac{7}{15} > \frac{15}{31}$ **23.** $\frac{23}{25} > \frac{45}{49}$ **24.** $\frac{57}{59} < \frac{115}{119}$ **25.** $\frac{3}{11} < \frac{7}{23}$ **26.** $\frac{5}{34} > \frac{9}{67}$ **27.** $\frac{12}{17} > \frac{26}{37}$ **28.** $\frac{132}{235} > \frac{260}{463}$ **29.** Clothing Hut **30.** NASDAQ **31.** Dow Jones Industrials **32.** Bears **33.** Los Angeles

Workshop 13: *Fraction to Decimal, Decimal to Percent* **1.** $0.4285 = 0.429$ **2.** 0.875 **3.** $0.4 = \frac{4}{10} = \frac{2}{5}$ **4.** $7\frac{82}{100} = 7\frac{41}{50}$ **5.** 0.375 **6.** 0.09 **7.** 85% **8.** 7% **9.** 30% **10.** 155% **11.** 0.260 **12.** 0.500 **13.** 0.889 **14.** 0.80 **15.** 0.56 **16.** 0.33 **17.** $\frac{3}{8}$ **18.** $\frac{1}{20}$ **19.** $\frac{287}{20}$ or $14\frac{7}{20}$ **20.** 0.34 **21.** 8.17 **22.** 0.011 **23.** 35% **24.** 1.6% **25.** 412.5%

Workshop 14: *Finding a Percentage* **1.** 28 **2.** 30 **3.** 1.5 **4.** 290 **5.** $24.50 discount **6.** 57 tons **7.** 10.8 **8.** 86.4 **9.** 140.7 **10.** 611.25 **11.** 100.8 **12.** 4 **13.** 3.8 **14.** 2.88 **15.** $3.30 **16.** $4.20 **17.** $2.33 **18.** $27.30 **19.** $12.00 **20.** $19.98 **21.** $6.27 **22.** $1.62 **23.** 243 feet **24.** $138.75

Workshop 15: *Negative Numbers—Adding and Subtracting* **1.** 16 **2.** −12 **3.** −17.5 **4.** $-1\frac{2}{5}$ **5.** 4 **6.** 15 **7.** 4 **8.** −13 **9.** −2.3 **10.** −$30 **11.** −2 **12.** −7 **13.** −9 **14.** 12 **15.** −11 **16.** −5 **17.** −7 **18.** −16 **19.** −30 **20.** 0 **21.** 2 **22.** 3 **23.** −4 **24.** −12 **25.** 7 **26.** −4 **27.** 214°*F* **28.** 15

Workshop 16: *Average (Mean)* **1.** 5 **2.** 5.1 **3.** 130 **4.** $41.33 **5.** 10 **6.** 8 **7.** 80 **8.** 65 **9.** 140 **10.** 326 **11.** 743 **12.** 433 **13.** 4.38 **14.** 4.6 **15.** 3.05 **16.** 5.45 **17.** $14.20 **18.** $62 **19.** 6.7 **20.** 8.0 **21.** 33.9 **22.** 4.69 **23.** 40.04 **24.** $30.46 **25.** 150 **26.** 78 **27.** $2.56 **28.** $150.00 **29.** $425.40 **30.** 93.5 **31.** 85 **32.** 94 **33.** No

Workshop 17: *Elapsed Time* **1.** 2 h:0 min **2.** 3 h:20 min **3.** 7 h:5 min **4.** 8 h:5 min **5.** 3 h:45 min **6.** 7 h:30 min **7.** 1 h:45 min **8.** 9 h:50 min **9.** 8 h:0 min **10.** 8 h:15 min **11.** 8 h:15 min **12.** 8 h:50 min **13.** 7 h:15 min **14.** 5 h:15 min **15.** 5 h:55 min **16.** 2 h:57 min **17.** 8 h:30 min **18.** 9 h:10 min **19.** 3 h:53 min **20.** 8 h:15 min **21.** 4 h:45 min **22.** 7 h:51 min **23.** 8 h:27 min **24.** 5 h:55 min **25.** 3 h:30 min **26.** 35 h:0 min **27.** 4:15 PM

Workshop 18: *Business Data Analysis: Reading Tables and Charts* **1.** $41.00 **2.** $47.00 **3.** $131.05 **4.** $129.20 **5.** Size 38 or 39 **6.** Size 42 **7.** $96.75 **8.** $47.50 **9.** $132.65 **10.** $192.20 **11.** $120.60 **12.** $69.00 **13.** $181.50 **14.** $131.05 **15.** $120.30 **16.** $52.50 **17.** $107.75 **18.** $65.00 **19. a.** 12.0 lb **b.** 3.0 lb **c.** 11.0 lb **d.** 6.0 lb **e.** 13.0 lb **f.** 0.5 lb **20. a.** 37 or 38; 38 **b.** 42; 42 **c.** 46; 46 **d.** 37; 36 **e.** 40; 40 **f.** 39; 38 **21.** Size 36 or 37 **22.** Size 39 or 40

Workshop 19: *Business Data Analysis: Reading Graphs* **1.** Year I **2.** Years D, E, I, and J **3.** Approximately 1,190,000 or just under 1,200,000 **4.** Blackstone Group **5.** Interactive Brokers and OCH-Ziff Capital **6.** $5.4 million **7.** Government **8.** Education **9.** Retail **10.** About 10 million **11.** 2008 **12.** $40 **13.** 2006 **14.** $140 **15.** $100 **16.** $110

Workshop 20: *Business Data Analysis: Constructing Graphs*

1.

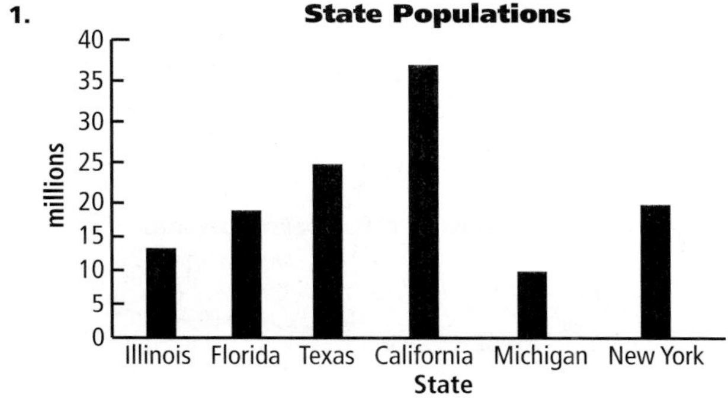

2.

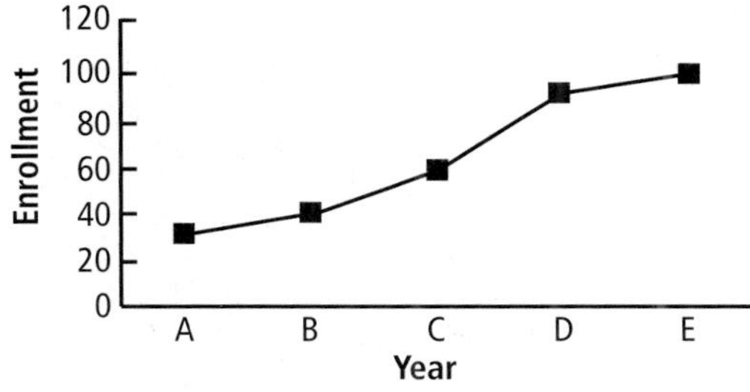

3.

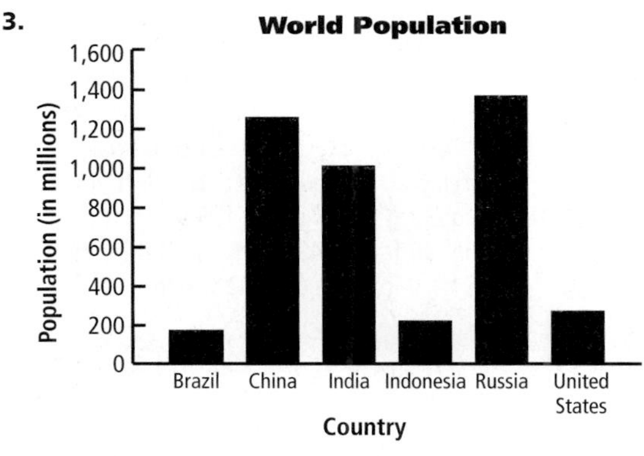

SELECTED ANSWERS

4.

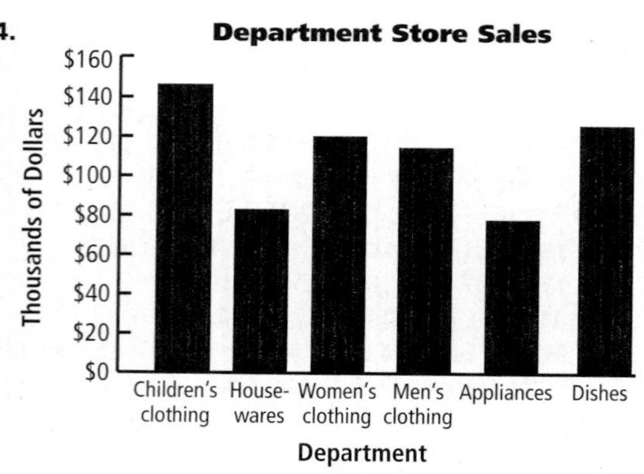

5.

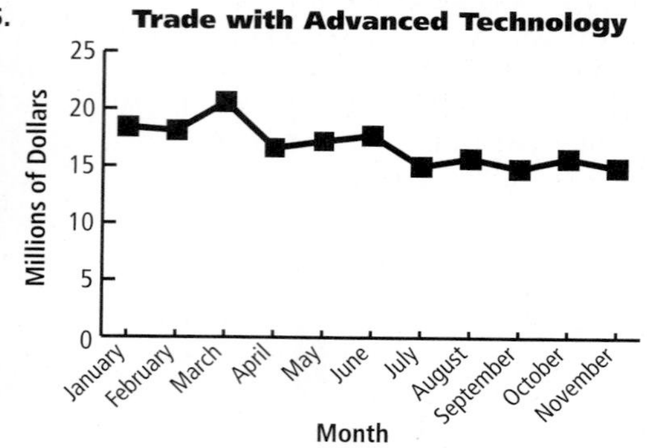

6.

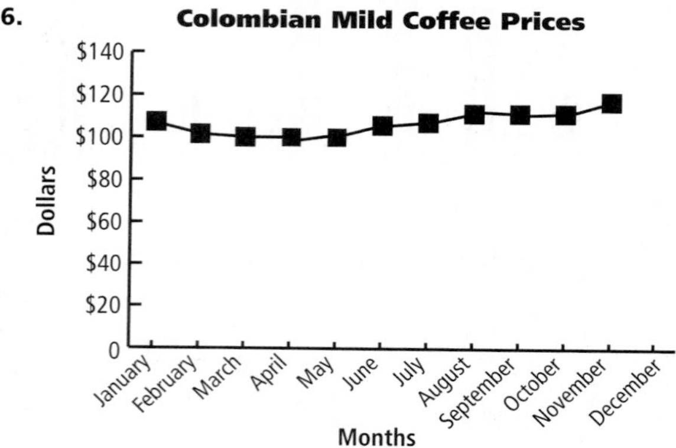

Workshop 21: *Units of Measurement* **1.** 108 in **2.** 150 mL **3.** 8 yd **4.** 3.5 m **5.** 27 ft **6.** 56 qt **7.** 112 oz **8.** 36 in **9.** 96 oz **10.** 4,000 mL **11.** 3,800 m **12.** 32 c **13.** 3,200 g **14.** 2.7 yd **15.** 2.25 gal **16.** 2.625 lb **17.** 3.5 gal **18.** 2.0625 lb **19.** 2 kg **20.** 0.9 m **21.** 3.3 L **22.** 4.5 m **23.** 72,100 g **24.** 3,400 mL **25.** 0.723 kg **26.** 0.011316 L **27.** 180 mm **28.** 3.832 m **29.** 40 in **30.** 50 in **31.** 11 pt **32.** 55 oz **33.** 10 qt **34.** 98 in **35.** 20 qt **36.** 1,000 mL **37.** 8 c **38.** 32 c **39.** 240 in **40.** 3 **41.** 3,900 **42.** 48 gal **43.** 2.13 L **44.** 32 servings **45. a.** 36 ft **b.** 36 ft; 48 ft; 84 ft **c.** 21 ft; 18 ft 8 in; 39 ft 8 in **d.** 22 ft 6 in; 15 ft 4 in; 37 ft 10 in **e.** 22 ft 8 in; 26 ft 4 in; 49 ft **f.** 35 ft 4 in; 25 ft 6 in; 60 ft 10 in **g.** 16 ft 10 in; 15 ft 6 in; 32 ft 4 in **h.** 381 ft 8 in

Workshop 22: *Metric System* **1.** 280 cm **2.** 1.5 dm **3.** 2.61 m **4.** 3.26 km **5.** 2.5 L **6.** 0.098 hm **7.** 3,870 mL **8.** 2,000 g **9. a.** 90 **b.** 900 **c.** 9,000 **d.** 90,000 **e.** 900,000 **f.** 9,000,000 **10. a.** 0.4 **b.** 40 **c.** 400 **d.** 4,000 **e.** 40,000 **f.** 400,000 **11. a.** 0.2 **b.** 2 **c.** 200 **d.** 2,000 **e.** 20,000 **f.** 200,000 **12. a.** 0.5 **b.** 5 **c.** 50 **d.** 500 **e.** 50,000 **f.** 500,000 **13.a.** 0.033 **b.** 0.33 **c.** 3.3 **d.** 33 **e.** 330 **f.** 33,000 **14. a.** 1.2 **b.** 12 **c.** 120 **d.** 1,200 **e.** 12,000 **f.** 120,000 **15.** 200 **16.** 4,000 **17.** 20 **18.** 0.08 **19.** 4 **20.** 3,000 **21.** 0.25 **22.** 600 **23.** 500 **24.** 5,000 **25.** 10 **26.** 8,270 **27.** 38,000 **28.** 18,200 **29.** 0.736 **30.** 600 **31.** 5 **32.** 250 **33.** 8 **34.** 0.004 **35.** 32,000 **36.** 0.8 **37.** 0.0321 **38.** 285.4 **39.** 3,170 g **40.** 0.425 kg **41.** 76,200 mm; 0.304 m **42.** 165.1 mm by 149.2 mm **43.** 2.27 kg

Workshop 23: *Conversion of International Currency—Rates of Exchange* **1.** 188.25 **2.** 49,228.65 **3.** 658.51 **4.** 59,339.95 **5.** 22,869.68 **6.** 1,922.10 **7.** $22,971.62 **8.** $436.45 **9.** 168,132.83 **10.** 676,847.60 **11.** $2,363.25 **12.** 121.74 **13.** $8.72 **14.** 1.06

Workshop 24: *Estimation: Rounding* **1.** 40 − 30 = 10; 16.495 **2.** 42 ÷ 7 = 6; 5.894 **3.** 5 × 5 = 25; $23\frac{11}{12}$ **4.** 64 × 10 = 640; 628.2353 **5.** 6,000 + 2,000 = 8,000; 7,789 **6.** 8 + 2 = 10; 9.942 **7.** 16 – 14 = 2; 2.14 **8.** $73 − $6 = $67; $66.28 **9.** 9 × 8 = 72; 73.9728 **10.** 30 × 5 = 150; $147.68 **11.** 49 ÷ 7 = 7; 7.135 **12.** 60 ÷ 20 = 3; 2.71 **13.** 3 × 2 = 6; $4\frac{1}{8}$ **14.** 13 × 3 = 39; $32\frac{1}{2}$ **15.** $\frac{1}{4}$ × 12 = 3; $3\frac{1}{8}$ **16.** $\frac{1}{3}$ × 18 = 6; 5.58 **17.** $\frac{7}{10}$ × $50 = $35; $34.97 **18.** $\frac{1}{4}$ × 12 = 3; $3.24 **19.** $\frac{1}{2}$ × 160 = 80; 83.2 **20.** $40 + $20 + $30 = $90; $89.53 **21.** 800 ÷ 40 = 20; $18.76 **22.** 20 × 10 = 200; $203\frac{1}{8}$ **23.** $\frac{1}{3}$ × 36 = 12; $11.86

Workshop 25: *Estimation: Front End* **1.** 900; 1,111 **2.** 1,500; 1,631 **3.** 6,000; 7,338 **4.** 800; 871.75 **5.** 1,000 + 200 = 1,200; 1,195 **6.** 800 + 200 = 1,000; 1,006 **7.** 1,700 + 200 = 1,900; 1,900 **8.** 2,300 + 300 = 2,600; 2,582.61 **9.** 15,000; 16,784 **10.** $13.00; $15.01 **11.** 8,000; 8,946 **12.** 16,000; 16,846 **13.** 1,500; 1,505 **14.** $70; $74.96 **15.** $100; $104.26 **16.** $460; $462.81 **17.** 21,000; 21,647 **18.** $23.00; $23.39

Workshop 26: *Estimation: Compatible Numbers* **1.** 640 ÷ 80 = 8; 8.07 **2.** 9,000 ÷ 300 = 30; 7.3 **3.** 50 ÷ 5 = 10; 9.33 **4.** 300 ÷ 6 = 50; 54.99 **5.** $\frac{1}{4}$ × 12 = 3; $3\frac{1}{32}$ **6.** $\frac{1}{2}$ × 30 = 15; $19\frac{1}{8}$ **7.** $\frac{1}{3}$ × $900 = $300; $324.10 **8.** $\frac{1}{4}$ × $800 = $200; $221.40 **9.** 1,000; 1,103 **10.** 700; 697 **11.** 1,200; 1,219 **12.** 110; 107 **13.** 30; 28 **14.** 40; 42.72 **15.** 100; 108.23 **16.** $900; $895.50 **17.** 3; $2\frac{5}{6}$ **18.** 30; $31\frac{11}{14}$ **19.** $215; $215 **20.** $50; $48.75 **21.** 14,000; 14,095.42 **22.** $4,000; $3,958.33 **23.** 7; $6\frac{5}{6}$ **24.** $80; $81.82 **25.** 5,000; 5,500 **26.** $33.00; $32.06 **27.** $3,000; $3,025 **28.** $2,000; $2,050 **29.** $500; $484.62 **30.** $70; $18,200 **31.** $20,000; $17,680 **32.** $600; $554 **33.** $20; $17.88

Workshop 27: *Estimation: Clustering* **1.** 600 × 4 = 2,400; 2,332 **2.** $30 × 4 = $120; $119.09 **3.** (3 × $2) + $1 = $6 + $1 = $7; $6.34 **4.** 800 × 4 = 3,200; 3,127 **5.** 500 × 4 = 2,000; 2,063 **6.** $50 × 4 = $200; $207.86 **7.** $40 × 4 = $160; $161.24 **8.** 90,000 × 4 = 360,000; 362,208 **9.** (8 × 4) + 4 = 32 + 4 = 36; 35.87 **10.** (16 × 4) + 6 = 64 + 6 = 70; 68.5 **11.** ($2 × $4) + $9 = $8 + $9 = $17; 18.28 **12.** ($26 × 3) + ($38 × 2) = $78 + $76 = $154; $154.40 **13.** $7 × 5 = $35; $35.09 **14.** $3 × 6 = $18; $18.60 **15.** ($26 × 3) + ($40 × 2) = $78 + $80 = $158; $157.60 **16.** ($1 × 3) + ($2 × 3) = $3 + $6 = $9.00; $9.40 **17.** ($18 × 4) + $40 = $72 + $40 = $112; $110.05 **18.** 400 × 6 = 2,400; 2,346

19. \$50,000 + (\$90,000 × 3) = \$50,000 + \$270,000 = \$320,000; \$323,610 **20.** (\$6 × 3) + (\$2 × 3) + \$12 = \$18 + \$6 + \$12 = \$36; \$35.56 **21.** \$125; \$122.80 **22. a.** 2,200; Yes **b.** \$40; Yes **c.** 27; No (26.98) **d.** 330; No (331) **e.** 150; Yes **f.** 1,260; Yes **g.** 29; No (28.13) **h.** 63,000; No (63,795)

Workshop 28: *Scientific Notation* **1.** 1,375,000 or One million three hundred seventy-five thousand **2.** 386,420,000 or Three hundred eighty-six million four hundred twenty thousand **3.** 712.3 or Seven hundred twelve and three tenths **4.** 0.00000047945 or Forty-seven thousand nine hundred forty-five hundred billionths **5.** 9.3×10^7 **6.** 3.86×10^{-8} **7.** 7.000216×10^6 **8.** 4.021×10^{-1} **9.** 739,100 or Seven hundred thirty-nine thousand one hundred **10.** 351,096,000 or Three hundred fifty-one million ninety-six thousand **11.** 0.000871 or Eight hundred seventy-one millionths **12.** 62,008,410 or Sixty-two million eight thousand four hundred ten **13.** 292,651,000,000 or Two hundred ninety-two billion six hundred fifty-one million **14.** 0.00000182 or One hundred eighty-two hundred millionths **15.** 1.262038×10^7 **16.** $4.390487285302 \times 10^{12}$ **17.** 2.86×10^{-5} **18.** 1.82×10^{-12} **19.** 4.75×10^6 **20.** 4.75×10^{-6} **21.** 2,600,000,000,000 or Two trillion six hundred billion **22.** 247,000 or Two hundred forty-seven thousand **23.** 10,400,000 or Ten million four hundred thousand **24.** \$0.00145 or One hundred forty-five hundred thousandths of a dollar **25.** 0.000096 or Ninety-six millionths **26.** \$$5.3091 \times 10^7$ **27.** \$$2.0 \times 10^6$

Workshop 29: *Problem-Solving Strategy: Using the Four-Step Method* **1.** \$4,200 **2.** \$12,870 **3.** \$139.88 **4.** \$158.70 **5.** \$11,984 **6.** \$2,421.90 **7.** \$868.50 **8.** 52 weeks **9.** Approximately 1,495 rotations **10.** \$90.69 **11.** 224 miles **12.** \$4.29

Workshop 30: *Problem-Solving Strategy: Identifying Information* **1.** Problem cannot be solved. Need number of payments. **2.** Cannot be solved. Need cost of a lantern. **3.** Cannot be solved. Need relationship between pints and pounds. **4.** Manuel paid \$29 more for the round-trip. **5.** \$74 **6.** \$65.85 **7.** Cannot be solved. Need weight of watermelons. **8.** Cannot be solved. Need to know how many friends. **9.** 5′ 11″ **10.** 2 minutes **11.** Cannot be solved. Need the cost of the tennis balls. **12.** \$1.45 **13.** 19 **14.** \$14.36 **15.** One mile per hour **16.** It is impossible to average 60 miles per hour.

Workshop 31: *Problem-Solving Strategy: Multiple Operations* **1.** \$50.00 − (\$7.95 + \$15.20 + \$12.47) = \$14.38 **2.** 17 **3.** \$418.50 **4.** \$2.68 over **5.** \$29.60 **6.** 117 **7.** \$445.00 **8.** \$20.16 **9.** 28.5 degrees C **10.** 624 miles **11.** 223 **12.** 20 **13.** \$2,250 **14.** 7 **15.** \$4.55 **16.** \$73

Workshop 32: *Problem-Solving Strategy: Using Estimation* **1.** No, he multiplied by 100 instead of 10. Answer is \$39.30. **2. a.** No **b.** He did not change 36 inches to 3 feet; estimate: \$18 **3. a.** Yes **b.** No error **4. a.** No **b.** Used \$40 instead of \$4; estimate: \$20 **5. a.** No **b.** Decimal point; estimate: \$70 **6. a.** Yes **b.** No error **7. a.** Yes **b.** No error **8. a.** No **b.** Decimal point; estimate: \$50 **9. a.** No **b.** Used 10 sq ft instead of 1 sq yd; estimate: \$15 **10. a.** No **b.** Added instead of subtracted; estimate: \$30 **11.** about \$500 **12.** about \$100,000 **13.** about \$1,600 **14. a.** No **b.** Multiplied by 1% not 10%. **15.** about \$200 **16.** about 3 **17. a.** No **b.** He determined total cost rather than the savings. **18.** 4 times **19.** about 25

Workshop 33: *Problem-Solving Strategy: Constructing a Table* **1.** 7 bicycles; 4 unicycles **2.** 9 high school; 5 college **3.** 6 bicycles; 3 tricycles **4.** 11 or more **5.** 20 nickels; 20 quarters **6.** 185 **7.** 25 **8.** 12 **9.** 2 (5 pennies, 15 nickels, 2 dimes or 10 pennies, 6 nickels, 6 dimes) **10.** 4 pennies; 4 dimes; 1 quarter **11.** 28

Workshop 34: *Problem-Solving Strategy: Looking for a Pattern* **1.** 81, 243, 729 **2.** 16, 22, 29 **3.** 34, 40, 46 **4.** 32, 64, 128 **5.** 18, 15, 12 **6.** $\frac{1}{2}, \frac{1}{4}, \frac{1}{8}$ **7.** 25, 36, 49 **8.** 65, 129, 257 **9.** 1,093; 3,280; 9,841 **10.** 21, 34, 55 **11.** 8 dimes; 12 quarters **12.** 112 adult; 73 children **13.** 33 **14.** 512 minutes **15.** 2:30 PM **16.** $\frac{1}{11}$ **17.** 4 × 4; 6 × 3 **18.** \$12.04 **19.** 11 **20.** 36

Workshop 35: *Problem-Solving Strategy: Using Guess and Check* **1.** 7, 8, and 9 **2.** 7 Triads and 15 Tetrads **3.** 15 letters and 6 postcards **4.** 11 hours worked on the weekend **5.** All sums are 12. **6.** Length of 48 m along the existing fence and width of 24 m **7.** The rule is subtraction; 2 **8.** Three ways: 10 3-packs, 0 4-packs; 6 3-packs, 3 4-packs; 2 3-packs, 6 4-packs. 2 3-packs and 6 4-packs would probably be the cheapest. **9.** Green van: 10 years old; white van: 8 years old; blue van: 4 years old **10.** 4, 5, and 6 **11.** Many different ways. Here are two: 888 + 8 + 8 + 8 + 8 + 8 + 8 + 8 + 8 + 8 + 8 + 8 + 8 + 8 + 8 or 888 + 88 + 8 + 8 + 8 **12.** \$15 **13.** 378 bicycles and 108 tricycles

Workshop 36: *Problem-Solving Strategy: Using Simple Algebraic Operations* **1. a.** $m = 5$ **b.** $n = 9$ **c.** $p = 30$ **2.** $r = 7$ **3.** $s = 15$ **4.** $t = 35$ **5.** $u = 9$ **6.** $v = 77$ **7.** $w = 8$ **8.** 8 **9.** \$67.20 **10. a.** 370′ **b.** 375′ **c.** 138,750 square feet **11.** 150 **12.** 193 **13.** 3:00 PM **14.** 19 **15.** 15

Workshop 37: *Problem-Solving Strategy: Working Backward* **1.** 29 days **2.** $3\frac{1}{2}$ miles **3.** 5 cartons **4.** A: 110 L; B: 50 L **5.** \$15,000 **6.** \$60 **7.** 56 dozen **8.** 63 matches **9.** 62 **10.** 20, 35, and 65 **11.** 64 games **12.** 128 games if the champion is undefeated; 129 games if the champion has one loss.

Workshop 38: *Problem-Solving Strategy: Writing an Equation* **1.** 11 **2.** 4.5 hours **3.** Cork: \$0.05; bottle: \$1.05 **4.** 18 m × 9 m **5.** 54 yards **6.** 25 years **7.** \$3,695.33 **8.** \$915.20 **9.** Holstein **10.** 6 years **11.** 7, 9, 11 **12.** 40 **13.** B = 3A − 2; 118 **14.** A = (B + 2) ÷ 3; 85 **15.** Harry = 197; Jerry = 210; Darrel = 192

Workshop 39: *Problem-Solving Strategy: Linear Combinations* **1.** Width = 7 feet; Length = 14 feet; Area = 98 square feet **2.** $c = 7$, $d = 5$ **3.** $g = 8$, $f = 1$ **4.** $m = 20$, $n = 3$ **5.** $p = 4$, $q = 3$ **6.** $r = 11$, $s = 6$ **7.** $v = 53$, $w = 19$ **8.** 31 inhabitants had 3 extremities and 20 inhabitants had 4 extremities **9.** 32 copies of *The New York Times* and 27 copies of *The Washington Post* **10.** 22 girls and 11 boys **11.** Forty-two \$21,500 model and thirty-five \$28,500 model in the first quarter; Twenty-one \$21,500 model and seventy \$28,500 model in the second quarter. **12.** \$0.61 and \$0.86

Workshop 40: *Problem-Solving Strategy: Drawing a Sketch* **1.** 3" + $\frac{1}{4}$" + $\frac{1}{4}$" + 3" + $\frac{1}{4}$" = $6\frac{3}{4}$" **2.** (18 in + 7 in) − 10 in **3.** 2 blocks west and 8 blocks south **4.** 3 miles west and 6 miles north **5.** 20 ft **6.** 8,556.5 sq ft **7.** 16 feet; 19 feet; 25 feet **8.** 18 **9.** 28 minutes **10.** (4L + 7L) − 10L **11.** 3.8 cm **12.** 342.26 sq ft **13.** Cedric or Clare in Canton or Cincinnati; Connie – Cleveland; Charles – Toledo; Carol – Columbus

SELECTED ANSWERS

Workshop 41: *Problem-Solving Strategy: Making a Venn Diagram* **1.** 3 **2. a.** 70 **b.** 59 **c.** 53 **3.** 12 **4. a.** 18 **b.** 7 **5.** none **6. a.** 16 **b.** 11 **c.** 5 **7. a.** 182 **b.** 198

Workshop 42: *Problem-Solving Strategy: Using Simpler Numbers* **1.** 42,390 ÷ 5,280 = 8.028 or 8 miles **2.** (1,595 ÷ 27.5) × \$3.95 = \$229.10 **3.** $25^2 = 625$ **4. a.** $20^2 = 400$ **b.** $15^2 = 225$ **5. a.** 15 **b.** 120 **6. a.** 94 games if champion is undefeated; 95 games if champion has one loss. **b.** The champion may have one loss or may be undefeated.

7. a. $60 \text{ mph} \times 4 \text{ sec} \times \left(\frac{1 \text{ hour}}{3{,}600 \text{ sec}}\right) \times \left(\frac{5{,}280 \text{ ft}}{1 \text{ mile}}\right) = 352 \text{ feet}$

7. b. $60 \text{ mph} \times 50 \text{ sec} \times \left(\frac{1 \text{ hour}}{3{,}600 \text{ sec}}\right) \times \left(\frac{5{,}280 \text{ ft}}{1 \text{ mile}}\right) = 4{,}400 \text{ feet}$

8. a. 31 + 30 + 29 + … + 1 = (31 × 32) ÷ 2 = 496 **b.** (35 × 36) ÷ 2 = 630 **9.** Borrow one horse from neighbor, then $18 \times \frac{1}{2} = 9$ for Rick, $18 \times \frac{1}{3} = 6$ for Mike, and $18 \times \frac{1}{9} = 2$ for Peter, and then return horse to neighbor. **10.** Cyclists will meet in one hour [25 ÷ (15 + 10)], therefore, the bird will fly 40 miles. **11.** 53

Workshop 43: *Business Data Analysis: Probability*

1. P(Random selection of a blue car) $= \frac{9}{50} = 0.18$ or 18%

2. P(green or red) = P(green) + P(red) − P(green and red)

$= \frac{8}{50} + \frac{14}{50} - 0 = \frac{22}{50} = 0.44 = 44\%$

Note: P(green and red) = 0 because the car cannot be both green and red.

3. $P(2) = \frac{4}{52} = \frac{1}{13} = 0.0769$ or 7.7%

4. P(5 or club) = P(5) + P(club) − P(5 and club)

$= \frac{4}{52} + \frac{13}{52} - \frac{1}{52} = \frac{16}{52} = 0.30769$ or 30.8%

5. a) $\frac{12}{60} = \frac{1}{5} = 0.20$ or 20%

b) $\frac{24}{60} + \frac{12}{60} - 0 = \frac{36}{60} = \frac{3}{5} = 0.60$ or 60%

c) Zero – they are mutually exclusive; cannot be both a ginger ale and root beer.

6. a) $\frac{1}{10} = 0.1$ or 10%

b) $\frac{5}{10} = 0.5$ or 50%

c) $\frac{8}{10} = 0.8$ or 80%

7. a) $\frac{2}{11}$ = **0.1818 or 18.2%**

b) $\frac{9}{11} = 0.8181$ or 81.8%

c) $\frac{4}{11} = 0.3636$ or 36.4%

d) $\frac{3}{11} = 0.2727$ or 27.3%

e) $\frac{0}{11} = 0$ or 0%

f) $\frac{11}{11} = 1$ or 100%

8. a) $\frac{310}{355} = 0.8732$ or 87.3%

b) $\frac{125}{135} = 0.9259$ or 92.6%

c) $\frac{25}{260} = 0.0961$ or 9.6%

Chapter 1 Gross Income

Lesson 1.1 *Concept Check* **1.** \$304.00 **2.** \$292.30 **3.** 23.2 hours **4.** 22.75 hours *Lesson Practice* **5.** \$288.00 **7.** \$486.00 **9.** \$452.09 **11.** \$25.00 **13.** 25 **15.** \$255.00 **17.** \$975.00 **19.** \$537.20 **21.** \$107.75 **23.** \$852.00 **25.** 38 hours *Spiral Review* **27.** 0.50 **29.** \$136.13 **31.** \$471.25 **33.** 140 *Get Ready for the Next Lesson* **35.** \$44.54 **37.** \$87.88 **39.** \$461.25

Lesson 1.2 *Concept Check* **1.** \$441.00 **2.** \$534.75 **3.** 8 hours of overtime **4.** \$408.96 straight-time pay *Lesson Practice* **5. a.** \$648.00 **b.** \$194.40 **c.** \$842.40 **7. a.** \$581.00 **b.** \$87.15 **c.** \$668.15 **9. a.** \$408.00 **b.** \$265.20 **c.** \$673.20 **11. a.** \$1,290.00 **b.** \$580.50 **c.** \$1,870.50 **13.** \$846.00 **15.** \$1,034.88 **17.** 4 hours overtime *Spiral Review* **19.** \$441.60 **21.** \$150.00 **23.** \$294.00 *Get Ready for the Next Lesson* **25.** 14 h:15 min **27.** 20 min = $\frac{1}{4}$ hour **29.** 5h:47min = 5h:45min

Lesson 1.3 *Concept Check* **1.** $6\frac{3}{4}$ **2.** $8\frac{1}{4}$ *Lesson Practice* **3.** $7\frac{3}{4}$ **5.** $7\frac{3}{4}$ **7.** $8\frac{1}{2}$ **9.** \$702.94 **11.** \$336.00 **13. a.** \$211.88 **b.** \$510.01 *Spiral Review* **15.** 1 **17.** 8:15 **19.** 12:00 *Get Ready for the Next Lesson* **21.** \$23.40 **23.** \$326.20

Lesson 1.4 *Concept Check* **1.** \$448.00 **2.** \$224.10 **3.** 25 machine fed; 55 hand fed **4.** 25 two-bedroom houses; 33 three-bedroom houses *Lesson Practice* **5.** \$493.00 **7.** \$136.61 **9.** 109 **11.** \$21.50 **13.** \$1,680.00 **15.** \$197.55 **17.** \$183.60 **19.** \$2,313.25 **21.** 74 caps *Spiral Review* **23.** \$264.00 **25.** \$54.36 **27.** \$299.20 *Get Ready for the Next Lesson* **29.** 0.01 **31.** 1.01 **33.** 49.67

Lesson 1.5 *Concept Check* **1.** \$1,650.00 **2.** \$758.33 **3.** 2 hours of overtime *Lesson Practice* **5.** \$1,888.33 **7. a.** \$103,610.00 **b.** \$8,634.17 **9.** \$52,764.00 *Spiral Review* **11.** \$285.80 **13.** 13.01 *Get Ready for the Next Lesson* **15.** 1.35 **17.** 0.005 **19.** 0.00123

Lesson 1.6 *Concept Check* **1.** \$752.00 **2.** \$7,887.00 **3.** \$10,000 total sales **4.** \$14,500 total sales *Lesson Practice* **5.** \$15,840.00 **7.** \$575.88 **9.** \$139.35 **11.** 3% **13. a.** \$1,495.00 **b.** \$1,600.00 **15. a.** \$350.00 **b.** \$850.00 **17.** \$285.00 **19. a.** \$30,315.37 **b.** \$23,244.38 **21.** \$6,545.45 **23.** 6.75 **25.** \$50.00 **27.** \$594.50 **29.** \$8.76 **31. a.** \$58,011.98 **b.** \$4,834.33 **33.** \$345.00 **35.** \$500.00

Lesson 1.7 *Concept Check* **1.** \$2,000.00 **2.** \$559.20 **3.** \$17,680 total sales **4.** \$83,666.67 total sales *Lesson Practice* **5. a.** \$200.00 **b.** 0.00 **c.** 0.00 **d.** \$200.00 **7. a.** \$250.00 **b.** \$800.00 **c.** \$300.00 **d.** \$1,350.00 **9.** \$480.00 **11.** \$1,476.75 **13.** \$87.00 **15.** \$296,780; \$377,094 **17.** Word problems should include two or more commission rates, and rates should increase with higher levels of sales. *Spiral Review* **19.** 0.1025 **21.** \$105.00 **23.** \$542.50 **25.** \$5,082.08; \$1,172.79 *Get Ready for the Next Lesson* **27.** Tens 20 **29.** Thousandths 0.005 or 5/1000 **31.** Hundredths 0.02 or 2/100

Review and Assessment *Lesson-by-Lesson Review* *Lesson 1.1* **15.** \$322.56 **17.** 340.79 **19.** 29.25 hour *Lesson 1.2* **21.** \$458.38 **23.** \$982.40 *Lesson 1.3* **25.** 8.50 **27.** 8.25 **29.** 8.25 **31.** 5:30 PM *Lesson 1.4* **33.** \$202.30 **35.** \$444.65 *Lesson 1.5* **37.** \$941.35 weekly salary **39.** $3,610.83 semimonthly salary **41.** $3,388.58 per month **43.** 2 hours of overtime *Lesson 1.6* **45.** $7,647.50 **47.** $85.60; $250.00 **49.** $4,742.64 *Lesson 1.7* **51.** $925.00 **53.** $1,467.06 **55.** $7,533.33 *Practice Test* **1.** $382.50 **3.** B. 8 hours **5.** D. $96.00 **7.** $23,400 **9.** $471.50 **11.** $12.75 **13.** $1,553.03 **15.** $44.63 *Standardized Test Practice* **1.** D. $11.64 **3.** C. $90.00 **5.** D. $1,675.00 **7.** A. $24,150 **9.** $367.65 **11.** $300

Chapter 2 Net Income

Lesson 2.1 *Concept Check* **1.** $18 **2.** 31 **3.** Allowance amount = $126.92; Taxable wage = $166.31; Tax withheld = $11.53 **4.** Allowance amount = $253.84; Taxable wage = $334.10; Tax withheld = $35.27 *Lesson Practice* **5.** $29.00 **7.** $8.00 **9.** $2.00 **11.** $138.00 **13. a.** $63.46 **b.** $728.56 **c.** $102.79 **15.** Percentage method: $55.10; tax table: $55.00 *Spiral Review* **17.** $173.84 **19.** $438.40 *Get Ready for the Next Lesson* **21.** $1,259.00 **23.** $989.15 **25.** $9,420.01

Lesson 2.2 *Concept Check* **1.** $550.40 **2.** $1,965 **3.** $86,000 **4.** Anton claims an exemption for himself and 3 additional exemptions. *Lesson Practice* **5. a.** $3,000 **b.** $60 **7. a.** $24,000 **b.** $1,200 **9. a.** $133,000 **b.** 3.5% **11. a.** $8,000 **b.** $1,497 **13. a.** $4,000 **b.** $1,817 **15.** $1,128 **17.** $2,891.50 **19.** 4% *Spiral Review* **21.** 26.98 **23.** 30.891 **25.** $10 *Get Ready for the Next Lesson* **27.** 12.04 **29.** 672.79 **31.** 0.27

Lesson 2.3 *Concept Check* **1.** $33.94 **2.** $249.17 *Lesson Practice* **3.** $456 **5.** $211.25 **7.** $462.50 *Spiral Review* **9.** 20.50 **11.** $1,554.00 *Get Ready for the Next Lesson* **13.** 0.7 **15.** 4.65 **17.** 0.567

Lesson 2.4 *Concept Check* **1.** S.S. = $192.20; Med = $44.95; Total deductions = $237.15 **2.** S.S. = $21.70; Med = $5.08; Total deductions = $26.78 *Lesson Practice* **3. a.** $7.75 **b.** $1.81 **c.** $9.56 **5. a.** $14.94 **b.** $3.49 **c.** $18.43 **7. a.** $385.83 **b.** $90.23 **9. a.** Fed = $ 41.00; S.S. = $32.61; Med = $7.63 **b.** Total = $81.24 **11. a.** S.S. = $475.33; Med = $118.42 **b.** Total = $593.75 *Spiral Review* **13.** 620 **15.** $1,537.50 *Get Ready for the Next Lesson* **17.** $1,000 **19.** $0.65 **21.** $13,110.92

Lesson 2.5 *Concept Check* **1.** 30%; $1,971; $164.25 **2.** 20%; $2,400; $46.15 **3.** $3,572.73 **4.** $12,915 *Lesson Practice* **5.** $73.33 **7.** $159.83 **9.** $94.71 **11.** 6,480.00 **13. a.** $13.50 **b.** $40.50 **c.** $162.00 *Spiral Review* **15.** 727.16 **17.** $367.16; $85.87 *Get Ready for the Next Lesson* **19.** 430.85 **21.** $12,561.72 **23.** $408.89

Lesson 2.6 *Concept Check* **1. a.** $24.00 **b.** $19.84 **c.** $4.64 **d.** $4.80 **e.** $26.20 **f.** $25.00 **g.** $104.48; Net pay = $215.52 **2.** $372.37 **3.** $1,460.00 *Lesson Practice* **5. a.** 21.00 **b.** 26.35 **c.** 6.16 **d.** 8.50 **e.** 6.38 **f.** $280.61 **7. a.** $576.92 **b.** 42.00 **c.** 35.77 **d.** 8.37 **e.** 11.54 **f.** 8.65 **g.** 34.50 **h.** 15.00 **i.** 421.09 **9.** $574.16 **11.** FIT = $720.00; SIT = $240.00; Health Ins = $240.00 *Spiral Review* **13.** 61.732 **15.** $189 **17.** $79.20 *Get Ready for the Next Lesson* **19.** 187 **21.** 4.195

Review and Assessment *Lesson-by-Lesson Review Lesson 2.1* **11.** $34 **13.** $39.95 *Lesson 2.2* **15.** $761.54 **17.** $1,590 *Lesson 2.3* **19.** $25.10 **21.** $21.44 *Lesson 2.4* **23. a.** $104.69 **b.** $24.48 **25.** $70.83 **27.** $7,380.34 **29.** $6,106.87.

Practice Test **1.** B. $57 **3.** A. $21,900 **5.** B. 4.7% **7.** D. $660.60 **9.** $1,748 **11.** $3,060 **13.** $217,260

Standardized Test Practice **1.** D. $2,040 **3.** B. $2,240 **5.** C. $43.12 **7.** $42.58

Chapter 3 Recordkeeping

Lesson 3.1 *Concept Check* **1.** $197.22 **2.** $293.31 **3.** $124.04 **4.** You can spend $183.00 for gasoline in June. *Lesson Practice* **5. a.** $3,440.00 **b.** $688.00 **7. a.** $8,802.34 **b.** $1,760.47 **9. a.** $107.91 **b.** $545.45 **11.** $675.00 **13.** $41.00 **15.** Electricity: 400.91; Phone/Internet: 122.99; Water/Sewer: 188.05; Home Repair: 372.13; Home Fuel: 198.31; Averaged over 3 months: $427.46 *Spiral Review* **17.** $1,537.42 **19.** $316.32; $73.98 *Get Ready for the Next Lesson* **21.** $17.90 **23.** $1,023.18 **25.** $38,836.93

Lesson 3.2 *Concept Check* **1.** $1,820 **2.** $1,446.57 *Lesson Practice* **3.** $1,161.50 **5.** $1,742 **7.** $2,306.67 **9.** Any of the fixed expenses—mortgage, insurance, car registration, etc. **11.** Monthly Living Expenses = 44.67%; Fixed Expenses = 38.46%; Share of Monthly Annual Expense = 5.58%. The total of the percents is 88.71% which is less than 100% because the Pender's did not spend more than their net income amount. **13.** $1,642.80 **15.** $547.60 **17.** $61.67 *Get Ready for the Next Lesson* **19.** $11.59 **21.** $885,120.48 **23.** $1,891.71

Lesson 3.3 *Concept Check* **1.** $8.90 less **2.** $24.42 more *Lesson Practice* **3. a.** $12.60 over **b.** $0.65 under **c.** $80.00 under **d.** $0.00 even **e.** $7.20 over **f.** $0.00 even **g.** $16.70 over **h.** $20.00 under **i.** $28.25 under **j.** $10.00 over **k.** $13.75 over **l.** $15.00 over **m.** $33.00 under **n.** $41.80 over **o.** $18.40 over **p.** $0.00 even **q.** $0.00 even **r.** $100 under **s.** $0.00 even **5.** $00.00 less **7.** Credit Payments and Pocket Money **9.** $42.20 over **11.** vacations, visitors, a very hot summer will affect air conditioning bill, etc. **13.** Answers will vary. Yes, everyone should be financially aware of their income and expenditures, therefore they should keep a monthly budget. This may also help reduce the risk of fraudulent activity. *Spiral Review* **15.** $37.19 **17.** $6.84 **19.** $222.84 *Get Ready for the Next Lesson* **21.** $13.69 **23.** $6.84 **25.** $619.969

Review and Assessment *Lesson-by-Lesson Review Lesson 3.1* **11.** $110.55 *Lesson 3.2* **13.** $1,286.30 **15.** $173.90 **17.** No; overspent $105.20 *Lesson 3.3* **19.** They spent less than budgeted by $41.14 **21.** Yes, they spent $5.41 less on car registration than budgeted. **23.** $5.41 less than budgeted due to car registration. **25.** Yes, they spent less on movies than budgeted.

Practice Test **1.** C. rent **3.** D. $29.50 less **5.** A. $79.74 **7.** A. $1,898.33 **9.** D. $650 **11.** $51.22 **13.** $498.33 **15.** $120 **17.** $779.42

Standardized Test Practice **1.** B. $103.75 **3.** B. 2.3% **5.** B. $85.25 **7.** $4,111.93

Chapter 4 Checking Accounts

Lesson 4.1 *Concept Check* **1.** $1,320.30 **2.** $938.66 **3.** He deposited $20 in coin and $120 in checks. **4.** $67.50; $135.00; $202.50 *Lesson Practice* **5.** $289.23 **7.** $1,606.54 **9.** $474.18 **11.** $212.09 **13.** $1,476.71 **15.** $946.00 **17.** $1,556.46 **19.** $6,552.79 **21.** $34.00 **23.** To establish

SELECTED ANSWERS

a money trail. *Spiral Review* **25.** \$579.20 **27.** \$184.92 *Get Ready for the Next Lesson* **29.** 23.10 **31.** Three and $\frac{45}{100}$ dollars **33.** Eighty-six and $\frac{66}{100}$ dollars

Lesson 4.2 *Concept Check* **1.** Twenty-six and $\frac{55}{100}$ dollars **2.** \$30.20 **3.** Harry's Hardware **4.** One hundred sixty-five and $\frac{52}{100}$ dollars **5.** drill press **6.** Manuel Romeo *Lesson Practice* **7.** Forty and $\frac{40}{100}$ dollars **9.** Sixty-three and $\frac{74}{100}$ dollars **11.** One thousand three hundred twenty-seven and $\frac{17}{100}$ dollars **13.** \$221.33 **15.** \$100.01 **17.** As a numeral yes; in words it should be: Two hundred forty-seven and $\frac{25}{100}$ dollars. **19.** No, should be written: Ninety-eight and $\frac{72}{100}$ dollars **21. a.** \$24,545.43 **b.** Twenty-four thousand five hundred forty-five and $\frac{43}{100}$ dollars. *Spiral Review* **23.** \$2,459.68 **25.** \$564.00 *Get Ready for the Next Lesson* **27.** \$17.76 **29.** \$10,291.18 **31.** \$986.54

Lesson 4.3 *Concept Check* **1.** \$1,515.46; \$487.26 **2.** \$680.57; \$819.41 *Lesson Practice* **3.** \$401.43 **5.** \$366.72 **7.** \$269.30 **9. a.** \$103.42 **b.** \$317.22 **c.** \$300.28 **d.** \$225.03 **11.** Need to add \$18.00. *Spiral Review* **13.** \$1,245.96 **15.** \$366.63 **17.** \$2,792.20 *Get Ready for the Next Lesson* **19.** 4.43 **21.** 0.059

Lesson 4.4 *Concept Check* **1.** \$307.55 **2.** \$819.22 **3.** \$27.10 *Lesson Practice* **5.** \$321.63 **7.** \$1,105.52 **9.** \$5,774.37 **11.** \$15,999.77 **13.** \$3.50 **15.** \$360 *Spiral Review* **17.** \$1,066.70 **19.** \$600.82 *Get Ready for the Next Lesson* **21.** \$1.51 **23.** \$13.14 **25.** \$2,099.90

Lesson 4.5 *Concept Check* **1.** \$275.49 **2.** \$916.33 **3. a.** \$1.20 **b.** \$2.86 **c.** \$8,755.99 **d.** \$3,207.64 **e.** \$805.14 **f.** \$8,755.99 *Lesson Practice* **5. a.** \$496.05 **b.** \$496.05 Yes, the register and statement balances agree. *Spiral Review* **7.** \$411.05 **9.** \$93.78 *Get Ready for the Next Lesson* **11.** \$11.54 **13.** \$70.14 **15.** \$11,311.58

Lesson 4.6 *Concept Check* **1.** Total Fees = \$23.45 **2.** Total Fees = \$45.45 **3. a.** \$1,661.57 **b.** \$2,533.35 **c.** \$0.50 **d.** \$2,532.85 **e.** \$38.49 **f.** \$2,494.36 **g.** \$14.07 **h.** \$2,480.29 **i.** \$86.95 **j.** \$2,393.34 *Lesson Practice* **5.** \$45.45 **7. a.** \$6.95 **b.** \$1,568.04 **c.** \$250.00 **d.** \$1,318.04 **e.** \$5,850.00 **f.** \$7,168.04 **g.** \$0.50 **h.** \$7,167.54 **i.** \$0.50 **j.** \$7,167.04 **k.** \$557.86 **l.** \$6,609.18 **m.** \$35.00 **n.** \$6,574.18 **o.** \$85.55 **p.** \$6,488.63 **q.** \$853.39 **r.** \$5,635.24 *Spiral Review* **9.** \$15,359.29 **11.** \$89,650.10 **13.** \$468.75 *Get Ready for the Next Lesson* **15.** \$2.94 **17.** \$335.03 **19.** \$77,756.62

Review and Assessment *Lesson-by-Lesson Review Lesson 4.1* **13.** \$315.75; \$631.50 *Lesson 4.2* **15.** Fifty-four and $\frac{33}{100}$ dollars **17.** Three hundred eighty-seven and $\frac{21}{100}$ dollars *Lesson 4.3* **19.** \$176.52 *Lesson 4.4* **21.** \$891.53 *Lesson 4.5* **23. a.** \$172.21 **b.** \$172.21 balances **25. a.** \$1,252.37 **b.** \$1,252.37 balances *Lesson 4.6* **27.** \$49.15

Practice Test **1.** B. \$684.00 **3.** D. \$326.55 **5.** C. S.S. number **7.** B. \$3,895.90 **9.** \$115.10 **11.** \$986.93 **13.** \$4,335.06 **15.** \$9,752.44 **17.** \$1,953.35

Standardized Test Practice **1.** C. \$148.75 **3.** B. \$30.35 **5.** D. \$65.54 over budget **7.** \$530.40 **9.** \$142.50

Chapter 5 Savings Accounts

Lesson 5.1 *Concept Check* **1.** \$238.10 **2.** \$437.30 **3.** \$32.74 *Lesson Practice* **5.** \$245.90 **7.** \$862.52 **9.** \$2,331.98 **11.** \$319.55 **13.** \$725.70 *Spiral Review* **15.** \$219.72 **17.** \$20.95 *Get Ready for the Next Lesson* **19.** 19.15 **21.** Ninety-eight and $\frac{40}{100}$ dollars **23.** Twenty-nine and $\frac{29}{100}$

Lesson 5.2 *Concept Check* **1.** Sixty and 00/100 dollars **2.** Two hundred eighty and 50/100 dollars **3.** \$98.75 **4.** \$6,586.95 **5. a.** January 10, 20— **b.** 559821 **c.** Yes, One hundred fifty and 00/100 dollars **d.** Tyrone Shumpert *Lesson Practice* **7.** Four hundred six and 00/100 dollars **9.** \$74.10 **11. a.** 81-0-174927 **b.** \$318.29 **c.** Three hundred eighteen and 29/100 dollars **13. a.** 06-029-175 **b.** \$76.70 **c.** Seventy-six and 70/100 dollars **15. a.** 16010368 **b.** \$374.28 **c.** Three hundred seventy-four and 28/100 dollars *Spiral Review* **17.** \$140.70 **19.** \$177.84 **21.** \$218.17 *Get Ready for the Next Lesson* **23.** \$11.90 **25.** \$84,330.68 **27.** \$161.71

Lesson 5.3 *Concept Check* **1.** \$861.50 **2.** \$22480.02 **3.** \$500 *Lesson Practice* **5.** \$411.95 **7.** \$7,442.26 **9.** \$1,947.25 **11. a.** \$235.90 **b.** \$572.02 **c.** \$573.12 **d.** \$575.55 **e.** \$577.92 **f.** \$13.65 *Spiral Review* **13.** \$499.50 **15.** \$4,488.90 **17.** \$712.50 **19.** 0.25 **21.** 0.0124 **23.** 6.03

Lesson 5.4 *Concept Check* **1. a.** \$4960.00 **b.** \$4080,00 **c.** \$4002.63 **2. a.** \$10857.00 **b.** \$6936.42 **c.** \$6591.72 **3.** \$2,000.00 **4.** 6.25% *Lesson Practice* **5. a.** \$216.00 **b.** \$936.00 **7. a.** 0.59 **b.** 720.59 **9. a.** 232.57 **b.** 27,201.01 **11.** \$29.21; \$2,459.21 **13.** \$853,801.17 **15.** \$24.55 *Spiral Review* **17.** 0.25 **19.** 6.25 **21.** \$6,033.33; \$1,392.31 *Get Ready for the Next Lesson* **23.** \$\$811.20 **25.** 308.73 **27.** \$1.77

Lesson 5.5 *Concept Check* **1. a.** \$2,040.00 **b.** \$40.800 **c.** \$40.80 **d.** \$2,080.80 **e.** \$41.616 **f.** \$41.62 **g.** \$2,122.42 **h.** \$42.448 **i.** \$42.45 **j.** \$2,164.87 **2.** \$164.87 *Lesson Practice* **3. a.** \$13.70 **b.** \$927.20 **5. a.** \$2,413.10 **b.** \$54.29 **c.** \$2,467.39 **7. a.** \$2,637.10 **b.** \$30,358.10 **c.** \$2,887.97 **d.** \$33,246.07 **9. a.** \$1236.27 **b.** \$36.27 **11. a.** \$10,152.87, **b.** \$297.87 **13. a.** \$4,957.69, **b.** \$97.69 **15. a.** \$3,799.36, **b.** \$179.36 **17.** \$11,044.80 *Spiral Review* **19.** 0.085 **21.** \$8.75; \$883.75 *Get Ready for the Next Lesson* **23.** 0.01 **25.** 0.0054 **27.** 0.00525 **29.** 0.0189%

Lesson 5.6 *Concept Check* **1.** \$2,230.88; \$230.88 **2.** \$4,776.12; \$276.12 **3.** \$44,344.88 *Lesson Practice* **4.** \$27,288.97 **5. a.** 1.375% **b.** 8 **c.** \$1,003.90 **d.** \$103.90 **7. a.** 1.250% **b.** 12 **c.** \$1,555.41 **d.** \$215.41 **9. a.** 1.000% **b.** 48 **c.** \$,6242.02 **d.** \$2,370.35 **11.** \$144.49 **13.** Rosemont interest is \$969.52, or \$89.96 more than University interest of \$879.56. **15.** \$45,224.91 *Spiral Review* **17.** 0.0175 **19.** 0.00875 **21.** \$51.57 *Get Ready for the Next Lesson* **23.** 133.93 **25.** 4.55 **27.** 3.32

Lesson 5.7 *Concept Check* **1. a.** \$6,022.62 **b.** \$22.62 **2. a.** \$6,028.08, **b.** \$28.08 **3.** \$167.00 *Lesson Practice* **4.** \$364.60 **5. a.** \$80,301.60, **b.** \$301.60 **7. a.** \$15,623.90, **b.** \$302.90 **9.** \$38.57 **11.** \$79.04 **13.** \$2303.05 *Spiral Review* **15.** \$4,085.24 **17.** \$112.38 *Get Ready for the Next Lesson* **19.** 73.106 **21.** 61.6869 **23.** 467.6784

Lesson 5.8 *Concept Check* **1. a.** \$65,206.05 **b.** \$5,206.05 **2. a.** \$66,184.14 **b.** \$6,184.14 **3.** \$78,158.07; \$38,158.07 **4.** \$9.43 *Lesson Practice* **5. a.** 8 **b.** 1.50% **c.** 8.43284 **d.** \$42,164.20 **e.** \$2,164.20 **f.** \$42,796.66 **7. a.** 10 **b.** 4.00% **c.** 12.00611 **d.** \$24,012.22 **e.** \$4,012.22 **f.** \$24,972.71

9. a. $17,784.68 **b.** $1,784.68 **11.** $135,352.95 **13.** $185,711.37; $98,211.37 *Spiral Review* **15.** $15,241.71 **17.** $9,641.82 *Get Ready for the Next Lesson* **19.** 17.1 **21.** $46.08

Review and Assessment *Lesson-by-Lesson Review Lesson 5.1* **13. a.** $335.86 **b.** $284.88 *Lesson 5.2* **15.** Twenty-one and 44/100 dollars. **17. a.** 06029175 **b.** $76.60 **c.** Seventy-six and 60/100 dollars **19. a.** 045-8996 **b.** $985.40 **c.** Nine hundred eighty-five and 40/100 dollars *Lesson 5.3* **21.** $87.00 *Lesson 5.4* **23.** $49.20 **25.** $3.45 **27.** $1,833.33 *Lesson 5.5* **29. a.** $18.00 **b.** $1,218.00 **c.** $18.27 **d.** $1,236.27 **31.** $373.12 *Lesson 5.6* **33. a.** $883.55 **b.** $133.55 **35.** $100.29 *Lesson 5.7* **37. a.** $120,542.40 **b.** $542.40 **39. a.** $1,745.69 **b.** $15.69 *Lesson 5.8* **41. a.** 1% **b.** 8 **c.** $8.28567 **d.** $24,857.01 **43. a.** $126,498.08 **b.** $135,352.95

Practice Test **1.** C. $56.34 **3.** D. $33.09 **5.** A. 10.1649 **7.** B. $12.03 **9.** $3,450.00 **11.** $499.09 **13.** $116.82 **15.** 0.153 **17.** $15,271.20

Standardized Test Practice **1.** B. $297.50 **3.** C. $164.25 **5.** A. $199 **7.** $122.29 **9.** $434.22; $2,535.17

Chapter 6 Cash Purchases

Lesson 6.1 *Concept Check* **1.** $29.40 **2.** $182.70 *Lesson Practice* **3. a.** 3.00% **b.** $2.44 **5. a.** 6.00% **b.** $11.73 **7. a.** 10.63% **b.** $5.30 **9.** $4.52; $90.34 **11.** $155.03 *Spiral Review* **13.** $34.13 **15.** $357.35 **17.** $506.00 *Get Ready for the Next Lesson* **19.** 2.601 **21.** $26.04

Lesson 6.2 *Concept Check* **1.** $365.60 **2.** $21,867.85 **3. a.** 4.00% **b.** $38.00 **c.** $987.99 *Lesson Practice* **5. a.** 6.50% **b.** $12.71 **c.** $208.26 **7. a.** 10.63% **b.** $5.30 **c.** $55.15 **9. a.** $139.68 **b.** $5.59 **c.** $145.27 **11. a.** $76.22 **b.** $5.72 **c.** $81.94 **13. a.** $1139.64 **b.** $72.94 **c.** $1,212.58 **15.** $43,961.86 *Spiral Review* **17.** 142.6152 **19.** $36.27 *Get Ready for the Next Lesson* **21.** 59.87 **23.** $984.1 **25.** $25

Lesson 6.3 *Concept Check* **1.** $1.167 **2.** $0.115 *Lesson Practice* **3.** $0.723 **5.** $1.079 **7.** $0.698 **9.** $84.790 **11.** $0.283 $0.023 $0.188 $1.514 **13.** 6′ = $0.980; 8′ = $1.099; 10′ = $1.068; 12′ = $1.119; 14′ = $1.118; 16′ = $1.118; 18′ = $1.166; 20′ = $1.250 **15.** The amount of both items purchased was less than 1 unit. In division, if the dividend is a number more than zero and the divisor is a decimal or a fraction less than 1, the quotient or result will always be more than the dividend.

$\frac{\text{dividend} > 0 \rightarrow 2.97}{\text{divisor} < 1 \rightarrow ½ \text{ or } 0.5} = 5.94 \leftarrow \text{quotient} > \text{dividend}$

Spiral Review **17.** 4.62 **19.** $281 *Get Ready for the Next Lesson* **21.** $28.44

Lesson 6.4 *Concept Check* **1.** 184-count box **2.** 14-ounce box **3.** 100-pound container = $240.00; 75-pound container = $184.50. *Lesson Practice* **5. a.** 0.4¢ **b.** 0.3¢ better buy **7.** 16-oz: 12.9¢; 48-oz: 8.9¢; 64-oz: 9.0¢; 128-oz: 6.9¢ best buy **9.** 3-pk: 41.7¢; 8-pk: 32.5¢; 28-pk: 27.8¢ best buy **11.** 50-oz: 14.2¢; 100-oz: 10.0¢; 150-oz: 13.5¢; 200-oz: 5.0¢ best buy 26 loads: 27.3¢; 64 loads: 15.6¢ best buy; 96 loads: 21.1¢; 64 loads: 15.6¢ best buy *Spiral Review* **13.** $0.05 **15.** $0.01 *Get Ready for the Next Lesson* **17.** $3.48 **19.** 2.65 **21.** $6.20

Lesson 6.5 *Concept Check* **1.** $4.04 **2.** $2.94 **3.** $6.53 **4.** $7.38 *Lesson Practice* **5.** $3.45 **7.** $54.98 **9.** $24.77 **11.** $221.68 **13.** $100.75 *Spiral Review* **15.** $1.30 **17.** $1.54 *Get Ready for the Next Lesson* **19.** 49.68 **21.** 0.009

Lesson 6.6 *Concept Check* **1.** $13.00 **2.** $88.00 **3.** $666.67 *Lesson Practice* **5.** $5.00 **7.** $99.80 **9.** $80.00 **11.** $39.48 **13. a.** $6.66 **b.** $3.33 **15.** $600.05 **17.** $29.80 **19.** $149.97 **21.** $10.75 *Spiral Review* **23.** 69.776 **25.** $12.59 *Get Ready for the Next Lesson* **27.** 57.3182 **29.** 1.2907 **31.** 3,908.224

Lesson 6.7 *Concept Check* **1.** $30.39 **2.** $230.99 **3.** $32.48 *Lesson Practice* **5. a.** $108.10 **b.** $108.10 **7. a.** $179.99 **b.** $179.99 **9.** $4.17 **11.** $39.96; $4.00; $42.66 **13.** The advertisement is incorrect if a product is marked down from $44.00 to $14.95 **15.** $279.98 *Spiral Review* **17.** 82.806 **19.** 0.0141 **21.** They made 35 of the 22¢ copies and 55 of the 9¢ copies. *Get Ready for the Next Lesson* **23.** $19.37 **25.** 417.395 **27.** $1,926.64

Review and Assessment *Lesson-by-Lesson Review Lesson 6.1* **11.** $32.72 **13.** $0.93 **15.** $10.62 *Lesson 6.2* **17.** $31.07 **19.** $7.55 **21.** $12.06 *Lesson 6.3* **23.** $6.25 per liter **25.** 6.2¢ *Lesson 6.4* **27.** $0.333; $0.313 (better buy) **29.** $0.423; $0.245 (better buy) **31.** $0.109 (best buy); $0.128; $0.143 *Lesson 6.5* **33.** $1.23 **35.** $17.49 **37.** $1381.88 *Lesson 6.6* **39.** $5.30 **41.** $19.01 **43.** $124.75 **45.** $500.00 *Lesson 6.7* **47.** $21,456.75 **49.** $30.38

Practice Test **1.** D. $12.36 **3.** A. $14.50 **5.** D. $2,190.00**7.** B $9.00 **9.** $9.40 **11.** $2,650.54 **13.** $33.46 **15.** $383.61 **17.** $2,324.12 **19.** 12,220.104

Standardized Test Practice **1.** A. 5.2% **3.** C. $526.95 **5.** B. $1.60 **7.** $0.52 9. Selena is correct. Ari may have been confused by the compounding schedule. He may have thought that the rate of 5.5% was semiannual, not annual. They have earned in interest so far: $55.00

Chapter 7 Charge Accounts and Credit Cards

Lesson 7.1 *Concept Check* **1.** $597.50 **2.** $270.78 *Lesson Practice* **3.** $649.00 **5.** $337.65 **7.** $416.34 **9.** $1,809.30 **11.** $182.09 **13. a.** $109.90 **b.** $188.73 **c.** $369.04 *Spiral Review* **15.** $634.10 **17.** $349.63 *Get Ready for the Next Lesson* **19.** 2.88 **21.** 4.68

Lesson 7.2 *Concept Check* **1. a.** $500 **b.** $7.50 **c.** $577.50 **2. a.** $70 **b.** $1.05 **c.** $166.05 **3. a.** $761.67 **b.** $1,111.67 **c.** $1,036.23 **4.** Jordan's monthly periodic rate is 1.90% *Lesson Practice* **5. a.** $275 **b.** $4.13 **c.** $369.13 **7. a.** $380 **b.** $5.70 **c.** $608.20 **9.** $981.90 **11. a.** $409.16 **b.** $5.11 **c.** $435.91 **13. a.** $974.44 **b.** $1,224.44 **c.** $1,368.88 *Spiral Review* **15.** $410.93 *Get Ready for the Next Lesson* **17.** 0.325 **19.** 56.2

Lesson 7.3 *Concept Check* **1. a.** $3,500 **2. a.** $600 **3. a.** $600 **b.** $3,000 **4. a.** $450 **b.** 1 **c.** $450 **5. a.** $450 **b.** 16 **c.** $7,200 **6. a.** 30 **b.** $14,750 **7. a.** $14,750 **b.** 30 **c.** $491.67 **8.** $7.38 **9.** $350.00

10. $457.38 **11.** $1,680.00 *Lesson Practice* **13. a.** 1 day **b.** $740 **15. a.** $620 **b.** 1 day **c.** $620 **17. a.** 30 days **b.** $19,200 **19. a.** $163.90 **b.** $1.97 **c.** $142.91 **21.** 2.6% *Spiral Review* **23.** 1,743.13 **25.** 42.90 *Get Ready for the Next Lesson* **27.** 0.34 **29.** 0.864

Review and Assessment *Lesson-by-Lesson Review* *Lesson 7.1* **9.** $347.84 **11.** $289.74 *Lesson 7.2* **13.** $3.90; $556.06 **15. a.** $486.86 **b.** $661.86 **c.** 771.53 *Lesson 7.3* **17. a.** $261.02 **b.** $5.22 **c.** $301.01

Practice Test **1.** C. 42 **3.** D. 1,082.06 **5.** A. $2,343.98 **7.** B. $702.92 **9.** $2,618.57 **11.** $100.00 **13.** $560.00 **15.** 14.7844

Standardized Test Practice **1.** A. $262.50 **3.** D. $173.44 **5.** D. $88.35 **7.** $385.65 **9.** $500.00 **11.** $248.07

Chapter 8 Loans

Lesson 8.1 *Concept Check* **1. a.** $13.50 **b.** $613.50 **2. a.** $111.62 **b.** $4,961.62 **3.** 370 days *Lesson Practice* **5. a.** $9.67 **b.** $1,969.67 **7. a.** $656.04 **b.** $10,331.04 **9. a.** $403.20 **b.** $8,803.20 **11.** $3,200 **13.** 8.1% *Spiral Review* **15.** $\frac{1}{2}$ **17.** $548.33 *Get Ready for the Next Lesson* **19.** $45.17 **21.** $51.31 **23.** $5,001.01

Lesson 8.2 *Concept Check* **1.** $1,800 **2.** $3,800 **3. a.** $272 **b.** $1,088 **4. a.** $517.50 **b.** $1,207.50 *Lesson Practice* **5. a.** $120 **b.** $520 **7. a.** $1,500 **b.** $8,274 **9. a.** $1,422 **b.** $8,058 **11.** $1,165 **13.** $1,700 **15. a.** $1,255.71 **b.** $7,115.68 **17. a.** $804.04 **b.** $3,216.15 **19. a.** $719.00 b. $2,157.00 **21.** $3,397.74 *Spiral Review* **23.** $49.96 **25.** $414.00 **27.** $32.00 *Get Ready for the Next Lesson* **29.** 42.35 **31.** 3,238.71 **33.** 4,287.19

Lesson 8.3 *Concept Check* **1. a.** $800; **b.** $3,200 **c.** $103.36 **d.** $3,720.96 **e.** $520.96 **2. a.** $662.92 **b.** $47,730.24 **c.** $7,730.24 *Lesson Practice* **3. a.** $17.16 **b.** $171.60 **c.** $1,029.60 **d.** $29.60 **5. a.** $4.52 **b.** $253.12 **c.** $6,074.88 **d.** $474.88 **7. a.** $174.00 **b.** $88.00 **9. a.** $3,000 **b.** $9,000 **c.** $286.20 **d.** $1,303.20 **11. a.** $4,000.00 **b.** $12,000.00 **c.** $553.20 **d.** $1,276.80 **13.** $1,249.28 **15.** $30.68 **17.** Lower finance charge is APR of 8% for 24 months at $156.88 compared to APR of 11% for 18 months at $164.74 **19.** City Loan costs $162.54 less. **21.** $50.00 per payment or $1,800.00 over the life of the loan. **23. a.** $267.93 **b.** $9,645.48 **c.** $1,145.48 *Spiral Review* **25.** 133.20 **27.** $70.00 *Get Ready for the Next Lesson* **29.** 146.25 **31.** 37.20 **33.** 2,759.64

Lesson 8.4 *Concept Check* **1.** $10.03 **2.** $297.05 **3.** $1,207.87 **4. a.** $80 **b.** $32.22 *Lesson Practice* **5. a.** $1,105.44 **7. a.** $54.00 **b.** $275.04 **c.** $6,924.96 **9. a.** $200.75 **b.** $1,035.78 **11. a.** $8.33 **b.** $204.79 **c.** $628.23 **13. a.** $4.21 **b.** $208.91 **c.** $212.48 **15. a.** $214.60 **b.** $2.12 **c.** $212.48 **d.** $0.00 *Spiral Review* **17.** 282.073 **19.** $3,264.71 *Get Ready for the Next Lesson* **21.** 3.2165 **23.** 6,168.69

Lesson 8.5 *Concept Check* **1.** $824.20 **2.** $28.28 *Lesson Practice* **3. a.** $48.00 **b.** $4,848.00 **5. a.** $12.17 **b.** $1,472.97 **7. a.** $29.94 **b.** $3,295.81 **9. a.** $12.24 **b.** $1,847.86 **c.** $31.34 **11. a.** $515.34 **b.** $286.89 **c.** $119.16 *Spiral Review* **13.** 600.38 **15.** $88.57 **17.** 4.73 **19.** 136.88 **21.** 68.15

Lesson 8.6 *Concept Check* **1. a.** $3.08 **b.** 10.50% **2.** 16.19% *Lesson Practice* **3. a.** $3.31 **b.** 11.25% **5. a.** $3.60 **b.** 4.50% **7.** 7.75% **9.** 6.25% **11.** 6.00% **13.** Finance charge for each is $900 − $850 = $50; Adam: 75.36; Betsy: 0.15%; Chris: 7.28%; Darcy: 4.46% *Spiral Review* **15.** 44.17 **17.** 8 oz. unit price = 0.149; 64 oz unit price = 0.092; The 64-ounce size is the better buy. *Get Ready for the Next Lesson* **19.** 4,353.71 **21.** 747.1

Review and Assessment *Lesson-by-Lesson Review* *Lesson 8.1* **11.** $22,006.33 **13.** May 9 *Lesson 8.2* **15. a.** $1,125 **b.** $3,375 **17.** 32% *Lesson 8.3* **19.** Payment = $135.45; Amount Repaid = $4,063.50; Finance Charge = $563.50 **21.** $1,875.00; $5,625.00; Payment = $492.19; Amount Repaid = $5,906.28; Finance Charge = $281.28 *Lesson 8.4* **23. a.** $39.00 **b.** $264.55 **c.** $3,635.45 **25. a.** $8.67 **b.** $96.76 **c.** $1,203.24 **27.** $43.56 **29. a.** Interest = $37.50 **b.** Payment to Principal = $232.95 **c.** New Principal = $4,267.05 *Lesson 8.5* **31. a.** $30.00 **b.** $3,630.00 **33. a.** $48.61 **b.** $4,909.41 **35. a.** $18.24 **b.** $1,842.49 **37. a.** $9.99 **b.** $1509.00 **39.** $12,501.18 **41. a.** $10,389.40 **b.** $1,566.20 *Lesson 8.6* **43. a.** $2.34 **b.** 4.25% **45. a.** $1.80 **b.** 2.25% **47.** APR = 4.37%

Practice Test **1.** B. $671.37 **3.** D. $1,104.58 **5.** C. $440.21 **7.** B. $77.40 **9.** 6.74% **11.** $214.83 **13.** 120 days **15.** 236.80 **17.** $8.56 **19.** 3,569.39

Standardized Test Practice **1.** C. $181.99 **3.** B. $16.89 **5.** D. $29,738.31 **7.** 38% **9.** 7.6% **11.** Find the total amount of yearly expenses and divide by 12 to get the amount that must be set aside each month for the yearly expenses. **13.** When calculating interest owed, the ordinary interest calculation for time is based on 360 days; whereas, the exact interest calculation for time is based on 365 days.

Chapter 9 Vehicle Transportation

Lesson 9.1 *Concept Check* **1.** $27,241 **2.** $27,865 **3.** Power front passenger seat costs $300; Remote keyless entry costs $30 *Lesson Practice* **5.** $23,145 **7.** $54,128 **9.** $36,850 **11.** Upgraded sound system costs $500.00; Navigation system costs $1,000.00 *Spiral Review* **13.** 9,064 **15.** Using the table, $52,164.84. Using the formula, $52,164.85. *Get Ready for the Next Lesson* **17.** 354.12

Lesson 9.2 *Concept Check* **1.** $48,978.90 **2.** $19,168.00 *Lesson Practice* **3.** $24,526.00 **5.** $46,615.85 **7.** $31,275.48 **9. a.** $30,855.00 **b.** $28,487.09 **11.** 24,138.02 **13.** $18,210.00 **13.** $18,210.00 *Spiral Review* **15.** 147 **17.** 2,683.20 **19.** $309.38 *Get Ready for the Next Lesson* **21.** 3,194

Lesson 9.3 *Concept Check* **1.** $16,410 **2.** $12,380 **3.** The V8 from Jacob's friend will cost $265 less. *Lesson Practice* **5. a.** $15,500 **b.** $14,690 **7. a.** $15,500 **b.** $14,800 **9.** $11,545 *Spiral Review* **11.** 7,975 **13.** 1,980 **15.** $377.49 *Get Ready for the Next Lesson* **17.** 62.305 **19.** 7,326.7656 **21.** 8,755.124

Lesson 9.4 *Concept Check* **1. a.** $616 **b.** $924 *Lesson Practice* **3. a.** $709.00 **b.** $1,134.40 **5. a.** $832.00 **b.** $832.00 **7. a.** $845.00 **b.** $2,239.25 **9. a.** $822.00 **b.** $1,767.30 **11. a.** $584 **b.** $1,839.60 **c.** $1,471.68 *Spiral Review* **13.** 99.875 **15.** 264.03 **17.** $11,700 *Get Ready for the Next Lesson* **19.** 7.05 **21.** 18.67 **23.** 0.28

Lesson 9.5 *Concept Check* **1. a.** $4,533.33 **b.** $8,095.83 **c.** $0.67 **2.** $4,382.00 *Lesson Practice*

3. a. $2,250 **b.** $0.38 **5. a.** $3,200 **b.** $0.34 **7. a.** $1,509.33 **b.** $7,345.05 **c.** $0.38 **9.** 12.53 years *Spiral Review* **11.** 21.75 **13.** 0.32 *Get Ready for the Next Lesson* **15.** 311.94 **17.** 224.72

Lesson 9.6 *Concept Check* **1.** $15,756.86 **2.** $19,294.95 **3.** 48 months *Lesson Practice* **5. a.** $14,352.00 **b.** $15,224.00 **7. a.** $20,700.00 **b.** $23,388.00 **9. a.** $16,433.82 **b.** $19,159.82 **11.** $22,325.00 **13.** $199.00 *Spiral Review* **15.** 119.8 **17.** $112.21 *Get Ready for the Next Lesson* **19.** 143.08 **21.** 154.79

Lesson 9.7 *Concept Check* **1. a.** $274.50 **b.** $0.64 **2. a.** $363.85 **b.** $1.84 *Lesson Practice* **3. a.** $188.89 **b.** $0.38 **5. a.** $241.82 **b.** $ 0.58 **7. a.** $141.98 **b.** $ 0.47 **9. a.** $127.29 **b.** $ 0.91 **11. a.** $1,409 **b.** $ 0.57 **c.** $176.13 *Spiral Review* **13.** 23.82 **15.** 1.39 *Get Ready for the Next Lesson* **17.** 52,713 **19.** 52,141

Review and Assessment *Lesson-by-Lesson Review Lesson 9.1* **13.** $25,160 **15.** $36,113 **17. a.** $287.91 **b.** $1,439.55 *Lesson 9.2* **19.** $21,663 **21.** $39,628 *Lesson 9.3* **23.** $15,692 **25.** $17,296 *Lesson 9.4* **27. a.** $702.00 **b.** $2,246.40 **29. a.** $669.00 **b.** $970.05 *Lesson 9.5* **31. a.** $4,587.33 **b.** $0.48 **33. a.** $3,440.33 **b.** $0.24 **35.** $2,140.00 *Lesson 9.6* **37. a.** $12,192.00 **b.** $12,886.00 **39. a.** $13,860.00 **b.** $15,544.00 *Lesson 9.7* **41. a.** $169.74 **b.** $0.47 **43.** $192.23 **b.** $0.26

Practice Test **1.** D. $16,088 **3.** A. $13,388 **5.** D. $0.28 **7.** B. $142.00 **9.** $4,667.89

Standardized Test Practice **1.** A. $9,518.00 **3.** D. 5,532.04 **5.** D. $158.09 **7.** $390.25 **9.** $0.47 **11.** The unit price is determined by total price divided by number of units: $3.99 / 500 = $0.00798 = $0.008 **13.** $19,305.08 **15.** $84,984.12 **17.** $2,459.73

Chapter 10 Housing Costs

Lesson 10.1 *Concept Check* **1. a.** $56,000 **b.** $224,000 **2. a.** $72,750 **b.** $169,750 *Lesson Practice* **3. a.** $37,400 **b.** $149,600 **5. a.** $99,700 **b.** $299,100 **7. a.** $35,480 **b.** $141,920 **9.** $149,200 **11.** Paragraph should reflect an understanding of down payment. *Spiral Review* **13.** 31,600 **15.** 144,000 *Get Ready for the Next Lesson* **17.** 537.6 **19.** 6,168.69 **21.** 3,182.74

Lesson 10.2 *Concept Check* **1. a.** $2574.00 **b.** $617,760 **c.** $227,760 **2. a.** $683.38 **b.** $180,412.32 **c.** $82,412.32 *Lesson Practice* **3. a.** $540.40 **b.** $162,120.00 **c.** $92,120.00 **5. a.** $1,881.00 **b.** $451,440.00 **c.** $226,440.00 **7. a.** $540.00 **b.** $162,000.00 **c.** $82,000.00 **9. a.** $1,289.60 **b.** $309,504 **c.** $149,504 **11.** The 5.5% for 25 years is higher by $15,573.60 **13.** $29,000 **15.** $21,078.60; higher monthly payment by $52.25 *Spiral Review* **17.** 15,523.2 **19.** $27,023.30 *Get Ready for the Next Lesson* **21.** 2,844.45 **23.** 1,340.9 **25.** 85.8272

Lesson 10.3 *Concept Check* **1.** $95,124 *Lesson Practice* **3. a.** $6,144 **b.** $126,144 **5. a.** $16,344 **b.** $436,344 **7.** $91,505 **9.** $175,354.00 *Spiral Review* **11.** 17,640 **13.** 276 **15.** $21.00 *Get Ready for the Next Lesson* **17.** 23,076.96 **19.** 670.977 **21.** 18,812.35

Lesson 10.4 *Concept Check* **1.** $1,865.41 **2.** $189.79 **3.** $279,621.68 **4.** $388.36 **5.** $1,666.84 **6.** $56,587.42 *Lesson Practice* **7. a.** $850.00 **b.** $170.00 **c.** $169,830.00 **9. a.** $650.00 **b.** $395.20 **c.** $119,604.80 **11. a.** $191.67 **b.** $77.43 **c.** $45,922.57 **13. a.** $2,468.58 **b.** $310.60 **c.** $538,289.40 **15. a.** $2,300.00 **b.** $662.40 **c.** $459,337.60 **17. a.** $ 177.90 **b.** $ 1,582.66 **c.** $31,259.65 **d.** $ 169.32 **e.** $ 1,591.24 **f.** $29,668.41 *Spiral Review* **19.** 78,879.02 **21.** $1,014.30 *Get Ready for the Next Lesson* **23.** 1,114.56 **25.** 3,605.7 **27.** 34,609.1742

Lesson 10.5 *Concept Check* **1.** $28,000.00 **2.** 0.0655 **3.** $1,834.00 **4.** $97,670.25 **5. a.** $220,483.64 *Lesson Practice* **7. a.** $63,920 **b.** 0.04623 **c.** $2,955.02 **9.** $1,332.22 **11.** $3,134.10 **13.** City tax = $1,435.07; School tax = $2,307.76; County tax = $430.86; Comm. College tax = $15.94; Total tax = $4,189.63 *Spiral Review* **15.** 2,924.32 **17.** 58.121 *Get Ready for the Next Lesson* **19.** $16.25 **21.** $176.12 **23.** $1,433.32

Lesson 10.6 *Concept Check* **1.** $144,000 **2.** $57,600 **3.** $28,800 *Lesson Practice* **5. a.** $405,000 **b.** $40,500 **c.** $81,000 **d.** $202,500 **7. a.** $291,600 **b.** $29,160 **c.** $58,320 **d.** $145,800 **9.** The difference in the coverage on the home is $32,400, on the garage it is $3,240, on the loss-of-use it is $6,480, and on the personal property it is $16,200. *Spiral Review* **11.** 24,000 **13.** Amber must have annual variable costs of $2,120 or less. *Get Ready for the Next Lesson* **15.** 7,370

Lesson 10.7 *Concept Check* **1. a.** Coverage = $150,000 **b.** Brick, class 11, premium = $944 *Lesson Practice* **3. a.** $300,000 **b.** $1,743 **5. a.** Mortgage = $1,003.20 **b.** Taxes = $225.66 **c.** Insurance = $47.83 **d.** Total = $1,276.69 *Spiral Review* **7.** 7.220 **9.** $122.22 *Get Ready for the Next Lesson* **11.** 115.966

Lesson 10.8 *Concept Check* **1.** $1,382.50; No, the Kwans are not within the guideline. **3.** Yes; monthly expenses of $1,703.40 are less than the maximum $1,785.00 recommended **5.** Yes; monthly expenses of $1,288.96 are less than the maximum $1,316.00 recommended **7.** $2,352.09; no, it was more than the maximum $2,012.50 recommended *Spiral Review* **9.** 2,109.8 **11.** 36 months *Get Ready for the Next Lesson* **13.** $1,806 **15.** $5,907 **17.** $11,194

Lesson 10.9 *Concept Check* **1. a.** $9,840.00 **b.** $480.00 **c.** $528.00 **d.** $720.00 **e.** $1,154.17 **2. a.** $5,760.00 **b.** $636.00 **c.** $528.00 **d.** $96.00 **e.** $715.00 **3. a.** $9,300 **b.** $600 **c.** $660 **d.** $780 **e.** $14,440 **f.** $636 **g.** $528 **h.** $14,839; It costs them $399 less to rent *Lesson Practice* **5. a.** $7,910 **b.** $659.17 **7. a.** $14,376.60 **b.** $1,198.05 **9. a.** $24,564.60 **b.** $2,047.05 **11.** $4,465.42 **13. a.** $15,500.55 **b.** $1,291.71 **15. a.** $9,000 **b.** $600 **c.** $660 **d.** $780 **e.** $14,730 **f.** $636 **g.** $528 **h.** $14,238; It is $492 less expensive to own. *Spiral Review* **17.** $16\frac{3}{4}$ **19.** $25\frac{2}{3}$ **21. a.** $21,800 **b.** $87,200 *Get Ready for the Next Lesson* **23.** 30% **25.** 45% **27.** 42%

Review and Assessment *Lesson-by-Lesson Review Lesson 10.1* **13. a.** $13,125 **b.** $74,375 **15. a.** $24,750 **b.** $173,250 *Lesson 10.2* **17. a.** $463.57 **b.** $139,071.00 **c.** $63,571.00 **19. a.** $836.33 **b.** $250,899.00 **c.** $126,999.00 **21. a.** $901.52 **b.** $324,547.20 **c.** $204,547.20 *Lesson 10.3* **23.** $5,379.00 **25.** $5,056.00

Lesson 10.4 **27. a.** $595.83 **b.** $142.57 **c.** $129,857.43 **29. a.** $666.25 **b.** $192.41 **c.** $159,707.59 *Lesson 10.5* **31. a.** $68,850 **b.** $2,992.22 **33.** $1,330.67 *Lesson 10.6* **35. a.** $112,050 **b.** $56,025 **37. a.** $212,500 **b.** $21,250 *Lesson 10.7* **39. a.** $80,000 **b.** $301 **41. a.** $90,000 **b.** $551 **43. a.** $150,000 **b.** $865 **45. a.** $300,000 **b.** $1,164 **47. a.** $1,766 **b.** $2,021 *Lesson 10.8* **49.** $1,154.30 **51.** 1,923.60 **53. a.** $1,760.88 **b.** No, the average housing costs are not within the 35% recommendation. *Lesson 10.9* **55. a.** $8,100 **b.** $660 **c.** $600 **d.** $780 **e.** $13,202 **f.** $636 **g.** $528 **h.** $13,288; $86 less to rent

Practice Test **1.** C. $114,750 **3.** C. 149,205.60 **5.** A. $38,657.50 **7.** B. 45.6% **9.** B. $1,115.42 **11.** $216.144 **13.** 250.368 **15.** $152.78 **17.** $631,515.70

Standardized Test Practice **1.** B. $262.50 **3.** C. $5,846.01 **5.** A. $1,354.65 **7.** $82,000 **9.** $200.67 **11.** $625.60 **13.** $0.48 per mile **15.** New Balance = Previous Balance + Interest + Deposits − Withdrawals.

Chapter 11 Insurance

Lesson 11.1 *Concept Check* **1. a.** $1,513.75 **b.** $126.15 **2. a.** $3,097.71 **b.** $258.14 *Lesson Practice* **3. a.** 40% **b.** $1,992.00 **c.** $166.00 **5. a.** 25% **b.** $2,666.50 **c.** $222.21 **7. a.** 25% **b.** $3,650.00 **c.** $304.17 **9. a.** $2,776.50 **b.** $53.39 **11. a.** $5,897.50 **b.** $245.73 **13.** $24.88 **15.** $442.50 *Spiral Review* **17.** 40% **19.** 35% *Get Ready for the Next Lesson* **21.** 447 **23.** 13,911 **25.** 639,185

Lesson 11.2 *Concept Check* **1.** $581 **2.** Deductible; Co-payments = 1,460; Hospital = 1,126; Total = $5,586 *Lesson Practice* **3. a.** $250.00 **b.** $2,400.00 **c.** $5,650.00 **5. a.** $520.00 **b.** $2,547.00 **c.** $6,567.00 **7. a.** $300.00 **b.** $6,750.00 **c.** $12,050.00 **9. a.** $350.00 **b.** $7,500.00 **c.** $11,850.00 **11. a.** $1,000 **b.** $1,080 **c.** $2,556 **d.** $4,636 **13.** $3,455.00 **15.** $6,944.00 *Spiral Review* **17.** 10,679 **19.** $6,118.29 *Get Ready for the Next Lesson* **21.** 4.034 **23.** 3.345 **25.** 2.814

Lesson 11.3 *Concept Check* **1.** $138.50 **2.** $325.20 **3.** 32.6% **4.** 50.1% *Lesson Practice* **5. a.** 60 **b.** $2.77 **c.** $166.20 **7. a.** 95 **b.** $2.98 **c.** $283.10 **9.** $180.05 **11.** 27.5% **13.** Edith: $221.60 Peter: $256.80 *Spiral Review* **15.** 544.714 **17.** 3,436.200 **19.** 3.14 hours *Get Ready for the Next Lesson* **21.** 0.46 **23.** 15.79 **25.** 10.19

Lesson 11.4 *Concept Check* **1.** $822.50 **2.** $2,250.00 **3.** $16.00 **4.** $75.00 *Lesson Practice* **5. a.** 50 **b.** $6.25 **c.** $312.50 **d.** $26.56 **7. a.** 200 **b.** $18.00 **c.** $3,600.00 **d.** $306.00 **9. a.** $725 **b.** $366.13 **11.** $950.00; $750.00; $1,700.00 total; $200.00 more *Spiral Review* **13.** 575.00 **15.** 63.26 *Get Ready for the Next Lesson* **17.** 80 **19.** 220

Review and Assessment *Lesson-by-Lesson Review* *Lesson 11.1* **11. a.** 50% **b.** $1,629.50 **c.** $135.79 **13. a.** 10% **b.** $1,560.00 **c.** $130.00 **15. a.** 30% **b.** $4,095.00 **c.** $341.25 **17.** $3,631.75 *Lesson 11.2* **19. a.** $500 **b.** $3,000 **c.** $6,500 **21. a.** $1,120 **b.** $3,600 **c.** $5,720 **23. a.** $700 **b.** $11,000 **c.** $16,700 **25.** $5,979 *Lesson 11.3* **27. a.** 75 **b.** $2.77 **c.** $207.75 **29. a.** 100 **b.** $8.58 **c.** $858.00 **31. a.** 500 **b.** $4.25 **c.** $2,125.00 **33. a.** $447.00 **b.** $596.00 **c.** $49.67 **35.** 47.1% *Lesson 11.4* **37. a.** 125 **b.** $14.50 **c.** $1,812.50 **d.** $154.06 **39. a.** 50 **b.** $46.50 **c.** $2,325.00 **d.** $197.63 **41. a.** 2,100.00 **b.** Sam's policy is $250.00 more than his wife's. **43.** $170

Practice Test **1.** C. $1,370.80 **3.** D. $159.75 **5.** A. $3.21 **7.** B. $1,506.80 **9.** $1,711.25 **11.** $552.50 **13.** 76.955 **15.** $99.61 **17.** 122.12

Standardized Test Practice **1.** A. $3,957.25 **3.** D. $3,105.00 **5.** D. $1,920.00 **7.** $179,000.00 **9.** Multiply the total annual premium by the percent you pay to determine your annual contribution. Divide this amount by 12 to determine how much is deducted from your paycheck. **11.** Taxable wages are calculated by subtracting the exemptions from annual gross pay, $23,875 − $1,800 = $22,075; $22,075 × 0.028 = $618.10 withheld for state tax.

Chapter 12 Investments

Lesson 12.1 *Concept Check* **1.** $948.70; **2.** $1,960.15 **3.** $5,643.77 *Lesson Practice* **5. a.** 1.150266 **b.** $20,704.79 **c.** $2,704.79 **7. a.** 1.043182 **b.** $146,045.48 **c.** $6,045.48 **9. a.** $61,682.95 **b.** $11,682.95 **11. a.** Daily: $11,972.04; Monthly: $11,968.14 **b.** $3.90 greater for daily compounding **13.** The toaster will cost Marsha Johnson $19.50 if she chooses to invest the 4-year CD with Fifth Central. **15. a.** $130,897.40; $30,897.40 **b.** $130,897.38; $30,897.38 **17. a.** $20,870.84 **b.** $1,114.84 *Spiral Review* **19.** 140 **21.** $1,383.75; $115.31 **23.** 8.55% **25.** 107.63% 27. 273.68%

Lesson 12.2 *Concept Check* **1.** Amount = $10,590.40; Interest = $590.40;Yield = 5.904% **2.** Amount = $26,273.63; Interest = $1,273.63;Yield = 5.095% **3.** Daily: $712.36 Yield: 3.562%; Monthly: $763.02 Yield: 3.815%; The better investment is the 3.75% monthly; it yields 3.815% which is greater than the 3.562% yield. **4.** The better investment is the 4.5% quarterly; it yields 4.577% which is greater than the 4.334% yield. *Lesson Practice* **5. a.** 1.035462 **b.** $6,212.77 **c.** $212.77 **d.** 3.546% **7. a.** 1.015104 **b.** $5,075.52 **c.** $75.52 **d.** 1.510% **9.** 5.61% **11.** 4.00% compound daily; it yields 4.081% vs. 4.074% **13. a.** 6% daily: $6,183.10; 6% monthly: $6,167.80 **b.** 6.183% yield; 6.168% yield **15.** $11,734.99 vs. $11,735.01; $0.02 difference. *Spiral Review* **17.** 125.64% **19. a.** Interest: $411.67 **b.** payment to principal: $68.70 **c.** new principal: $75,931.30 *Get Ready for the Next Lesson* **21.** $2,799.91 **23.** $8,190.19 **25.** $3,287.46

Lesson 12.3 *Concept Check* **1.** $5,431.50; $5,461.45 **2.** $23,520; $23,539.95 *Lesson Practice* **3. a.** $11,050.00 **b.** $11,059.99 **5. a.** $17,800.00 **b.** $17,845.50 **7. a.** $16,450.00 **b.** $16,515.00 **9. a.** $18,900.00 **b.** $18,960.00 **11.** $14,000.40 **13.** $472,278.60 based on two transactions OR $472,123.60 based upon one combined stock transaction vs. two individual transactions. *Spiral Review* **15.** $55,328.95 **17.** $989.95 *Get Ready for the Next Lesson* **19.** 6.783 **21.** 998.118 **23.** 1,068.672

Lesson 12.4 *Concept Check* **1.** $595.50 profit **2.** $1,549.95 loss *Lesson Practice* **3. a.** $7,170.00 **b.** $1,970.00 profit **5. a.** $6,480.00 **b.** $280.00 loss **7. a.** $6,560.00 **b.** $2,060.00 profit **9.** $848 profit **11.** $1,039.95 loss **13.** $4,577.40 loss **15. a.** $31,134.00 **b.** $2,530.00 loss **17. a.** $143,925.00 **b.** $11,855.00 **19.** $2,622.57 profit *Spiral Review* **21.** $21.91 **23.** $24,184.80 *Get Ready for the Next Lesson* **25.** 0.98

27. 1.58 **29.** 1.97

Lesson 12.5 *Concept Check* **1. a.** $201.00 **b.** 4.11% **c.** 2.69% **2.** $0.38; 0.84% *Lesson Practice* **3.** 9.53% **5. a.** $608.00 **b.** 2.71% **7. a.** $1,156.00 **b.** high: 1.83%; low: 2.86% **9. a.** 6.34% **b.** 4.75% **11.** $3.59; 3.32% *Spiral Review* **13.** 0.93 **15.** 15.18 **17.** $43,500.00 *Get Ready for the Next Lesson* **19.** $1,792.50 **21.** $0.72 **23.** $273.59

Lesson 12.6 *Concept Check* **1. a.** $718.75 **b.** 542.7 **2. a.** $1,050.00 **b.** 1,723.2 **3. a.** 500 **b.** $388.75 loss *Lesson Practice* **5. a.** $13,800.00 **b.** 2,760 **7. a.** $375.00 **b.** $12,125.00 **c.** 3,069.6 **9. a.** $285.00 **b.** $7,215.00 **c.** 315.3 **11.** 1,984.2 shares **13.** $955.00 profit **15.** Allison lost $76.00 on her investment *Spiral Review* **17.** $13,987.50 **19.** $66.64 *Get Ready for the Next Lesson* **21.** 496.8 **23.** 918 **25.** $526.05

Lesson 12.7 *Concept Check* **1. a.** $60.00 **b.** $805.00 **c.** 7.45% **2. a.** $500.00 **b.** $10,250.00 **c.** 4.88% *Lesson Practice* **3. a.** $7,025 **b.** $300.00 **c.** 4.27% **5. a.** $10,400 **b.** $525.00 **c.** 5.05% **7. a.** $9,920.00 **b.** $450.00 **c.** 4.54% **9. a.** $47,187.50 **b.** $1,500.00 **c.** 3.18% **11. a.** $77,297.60 **b.** $2,920.00 **c.** 3.78% **13. a.** $33,819.19 **b.** $1,260.00 *Spiral Review* **15.** 0.03 **17.** $29.61 *Get Ready for the Next Lesson* **19.** 15.81 **21.** 9.23 **23.** 20.57

Lesson 12.8 *Concept Check* **1. a.** $18,940 **b.** 18.94% **2. a.** $3,400 **b.** 8.5% **3.** $4,480 **4.** $4,063.33 *Lesson Practice* **5. a.** 9.00% **7. a.** $72,000 **b.** $4,500 **c.** 6.00% **9. a.** $3,525 **b.** 7.05% **11. a.** $8,016 **b.** 8.44% **c.** $2,780.92 **13. a.** $52,324 **b.** 10.46% *Spiral Review* **15.** 2.33 **17.** $16,400 *Get Ready for the Next Lesson* **19.** 80.0% **21.** 20.0% **23.** 12.5%

Lesson 12.9 *Concept Check* **1.** Required minimum distribution = $3,846.95; Penalty for failure to take distribution = $1,923.48; Penalty for early distribution = $1,000 **2.** There is no required minimum distribution for a Roth IRA. Therefore, there is no penalty for not taking it. There is no penalty for taking an early distribution for grandchildren's college education. *Lesson Practice* **3. a.** $10,526.32 **b.** $5,263.16 **5. a.** $1,000.00 **b.** $7,831.93 **c.** $3,915.97 **7. a.** -0- **b.** $15,511.32 **c.** $7,755.66 **9.** $10,421.40 RMD; $5,210.70 penalty for not taking the distribution; $500 penalty for taking an early distribution of $5,000.00 **11.** $18,716.58 RMD; $9,358.29 penalty for not taking the distribution; There is no penalty for taking an early distribution for grandchild's college education. **13.** There is no required minimum distribution for a Roth IRA. No penalty. No penalty for withdrawal to pay for his grandchildren's college education. *Spiral Review* **15.** 87.5% **17.** $9.95 *Get Ready for the Next Lesson* **19.** $706.58 **21.** $1,063.72 **23.** $1,533.95

Review and Assessment *Lesson-by-Lesson Review* *Lesson 12.1* **13. a.** 1.161825 **b.** $11,618.25 **c.** $1,618.25 **15. a.** 1.184949 **b.** $106,645.41 **c.** $16,645.41 **17.** $15,432.61; $432.61 *Lesson 12.2* **19. a.** 1.053543 **b.** $4,740.94 **c.** $240.94 **d.** 5.354% **21. a.** 1.048353 **b.** $26,733.00 **c.** $1,233.00 **d.** 4.835% **23. a.** 1.020184 **b.** $10,201.84 **c.** $201.84 **d.** 2.018% *Lesson 12.3* **25. a.** $59,140 **b.** $59,147 **27. a.** $2,931.50 **b.** $2,944.49 **29. a.** $41,454.50 **b.** $41,466 **31. a.** $14,500 **b.** $14,540 *Lesson 12.4* **33. a.** $7,756.50 **b.** $1,956.50 profit **35. a.** $513.50 **b.** $1,286.50 loss **37. a.** $2,918.00 **b.** $332.00 loss *Lesson 12.5* **39.** 1.58% **41.** 3.90% **43. a.** $1.68 **b.** 4.00% *Lesson 12.6* **45. a.** $11,280 **b.** 1,470.7 **47. a.** $345 **b.** $11,155 **c.** 4,323.6 **49. a.** 700 **b.** $1,149.75 profit *Lesson 12.7* **51. a.** $829.00 **b.** $32.50 **c.** 3.92% **53. a.** $1,930.00 **b.** $110 **c.** 5.70% *Lesson 12.8* **55. a.** 14.00% **57. a.** $84,000 **b.** $26,500 **c.** 35.33% *Lesson 12.9* **59. a.** $4,019.47 **b.** $2,009.74 **61. a.** $2,000.00 **b.** $14,532.36 **c.** $7,266.18

Practice Test **1.** B. $3,621.44 **3.** D. $1,691 **5.** C. $305.00 **7.** B. $13,315.12 **9.** $7,835.50 **11.** $30,975.00; $1,400 **13.** 11.2803 **15.** $59,578 **17.** 332.4747

Standardized Test Practice **1.** C. $4,693.60 **3.** C. $5,833.12 **5.** A. $7,568.97 **7.** $6,278.29 **9.** $2,840.60

Chapter 13 Personnel

Lesson 13.1 *Concept Check* **1.** $25,195 **2.** $41,990 **3.** $32,268.70 **4.** $250,000 **5.** $647,500 *Lesson Practice* **7.** $6,128.65 **9.** $168,820 **11.** $133,800 *Spiral Review* **13.** $17,698 *Get Ready for the Next Lesson* **15.** $849.85 **17.** $928.53 **19.** $9,963.98

Lesson 13.2 *Concept Check* **1.** $62,880 **2.** $44,690 **3.** $18.50. He would earn $74.74 more now in a week in which he worked 47 hours. **4.** $19.00. He would earn $69.92 more now in a week in which he worked 44 hours. *Lesson Practice* **5. a.** $70,000 **b.** $1,960 **c.** $2,520 **d.** $74,480 **7. a.** $40,000 **b.** $1,880 **c.** $1,800 **d.** $43,680 **9. a.** $30,000 **b.** $1,050 **c.** $750 **d.** $31,800 **11. a.** $19,032.00 **b.** $19,964.57 **c.** $9.60 **13.** $640.00 *Spiral Review* **15.** $1,849.86 **17.** 5.354% *Get Ready for the Next Lesson* **19.** 25% **21.** 60% **23.** 5%

Lesson 13.3 *Concept Check* **1. a.** 420.38 **b.** 84.08 **c.** $840.76 **d.** $672.64 **e.** $2,190.00 **f.** $1,765.68 **g.** $1,005.56 **h.** $1,355.32 **i.** $316.97 **j.** $8,146.93 *Lesson Practice* **3.** 24.2 **5.** 32.0% **7. a.** $7,992.32 **b.** 18.2% **9.** **(Lab tech)** **a.** $1,982.62 **b.** $1,784.35 **c.** $2,371.21 **d.** $3,195.98 **e.** $747.45 **f.** $10,081.61; **(Lab analyst)** **a.** $1,918.27 **b.** $1,726.44 **c.** $2,294.25 **d.** $3,092.25 **e.** $723.19 **f.** $9,754.40; **(Receptionist)** **a.** $788.46 **b.** $709.62 **c.** $943.00 **d.** $1,271.00 **e.** $297.25 **f.** $4,009.33 **9. b.** 19.6% **c.** $23,845.34 **d.** $2,344.67 **e.** $5,938.96 *Spiral Review* **11.** 20% **13.** $1,662.23 *Get Ready for the Next Lesson* **15.** 95 **17.** 135 **19.** 92

Lesson 13.4 *Concept Check* **1.** Annual = $21,510; Monthly = $1,792.50 *Lesson Practice* **3. a.** $37,632.00 **b.** $3,136.00 **5. a.** $26,380.73 **b.** $2,198.39 **7.** $1,381.71 *Spiral Review* **9.** 26 **11.** 31 *Get Ready for the Next Lesson* **13.** $961.35 **15.** $4,657.94

Lesson 13.5 *Concept Check* **1.** $5,066.26 *Lesson Practice* **3.** $654.98 **5.** $126.95 **7.** $1,320.14 **9.** $7,243.74 *Spiral Review* **11.** $5,485.50 **13.** 36 ounce bottle *Get Ready for the Next Lesson* **15.** $204.89 **17.** $376.56

Lesson 13.6 *Concept Check* **1.** $2,414.22 **2.** $3,057.50 **3.** $61.50 *Lesson Practice* **5. a.** $49.60 **b.** $356.50 **7. a.** $111.60 **b.** $790.00 **9. a.** $386.26 **b.** $2,445.05 **11.** $1,654.52 *Spiral Review* **13.** $73.50 **15.** $428.55 **17.** $10,169.74 *Get Ready for the Next Lesson* **19.** $1,613.53 **21.** $1,432.41 **23.** $80.17

Lesson 13.7 *Concept Check* **1.** $1,359 *Lesson Practice* **3.** $980 **5.** $3,234 **7.** $1,785 **9.** $6,695 **11.** $1,631.40 **13.** $5,508 **15.** $5,892 *Spiral Review* **17.** $916.35 **19.** $110.17 **21.** $10,270; $872.95; 8.73% *Get Ready for the Next Lesson* **23.** $0.935 **25.** $0.546 **27.** $0.886

Review and Assessment *Lesson-by-Lesson Review Lesson 13.1* **11.** $27,982.00 **13.** $179,140.00 *Lesson 13.2* **15. a.** 65,000.00 **b.** 2,080.00 **c.** 4,940.00 **d.** 72,020.00 **17. a.** 44,000.00 **b.** 2,112.00 **c.** 3,256.00 **d.** 49,368.00 **19. a.** 31,500.00 **b.** 1,480.50 **c.** 1,102.50 **d.** 34,083.00 **21. a.** $49,154.05 **b.** $2,064.47; $1,523.78 *Lesson 13.3* **23. a.** $1,230.77 **b.** $1,152.00 **c.** $984.62 **d.** $1,984.00 **e.** $464.00 **f.** $5,815.39 **g.** 18.2% **25. a.** $1,211.54 **b.** $1,134.00 **c.** $969.23 **d.** $1,953.00 **e.** $456.75 **f.** $5,724.52 **g.** 18.2% *Lesson 13.4* **27. a.** 40,500.00 **b.** 3,375.00 **29. a.** 47,040.00 **b.** 3,920.00 **31. a.** 54,880.00 **b.** 4,573.33 **33.** $3,660.30 *Lesson 13.5* **35.** $301.17 **37.** $1,507.07 *Lesson 13.6* **39. a.** $301.24 **41. a.** 460.04 **b.** $3,039.83 **43.** $2,797.68 *Lesson 13.7* **45.** $5,170 **47.** $2,585 **49.** $7,747.40

Practice Test **1.** D. $4,396.75 **3.** A. 34.1% **5.** D. $26,600.00 **7.** B. $3,000 **9.** $10,903.15 **11.** $1,208.96 **13.** 68.71451 **15.** 20%

Standardized Test Practice **1.** A. $1,216.00 **3.** D. $985 **5.** C. $230 loss **7.** 0.14573 or 14.6% **9.** Ordinary interest is calculated by basing the time of the loan on a 360-day year. Exact interest is based on a 365-day year.

Chapter 14 Purchasing and Inventory

Lesson 14.1 *Concept Check* **1.** Trade discount = $7.20; Net price = $16.80 **2.** Trade discount = $8.65; Net price = $25.95 **3.** Trade discount = $72.00; Rate = 30% **4.** Trade discount = $105.00; Rate = 25% *Lesson Practice* **5. a.** $54.00 **b.** $306.00 **7. a.** $58.54 **b.** $158.26 **9.** $2.05 **11.** $90.00 **13. a.** $22.50 **b.** 45.0% **15. a.** $27.00 **b.** 30% **17. a.** $460 **b.** 18.0% **19. a.** $4.53; $8.42 **b.** $0.90; $8.09 **c.** $8.84; $50.11 **21. a.** $11.86 **b.** $1.61 **c.** $60.90 **d.** $562.60 **e.** $333.93 **f.** $127.84 **23.** $4.78 **25.** $83.32 *Get Ready for the Next Lesson* **27.** $17.01 **29.** $27.57 **31.** $262.03

Lesson 14.2 *Concept Check* **1.** Complement = 70%; Net price = $16.80 **2.** Complement = 75%; Net price = $25.88 **3.** The complement of the trade-discount rate is 70%; The trade-discount rate is 30%; Trade Discount = $44.55; Net Price = $103.95 **4.** The complement of the trade-discount rate is 25%. The trade-discount rate is 75%. $49.60 = List Price. The trade discount is $37.20 *Lesson Practice* **5. a.** 85% **b.** $306.00 **7. a.** 73% **b.** $158.26 **9.** $34.14 **11. a.** $11.32; $407.52 **b.** $2.47; $61.75 **c.** $4.21; $25.26 **d.** $12.76; $76.56 **e.** $5.95; $89.25 **f.** $33.75; 168.75 **13.** Retailer pays 60% of $480 = $288.00; Wholesaler pays 67% of $288 = $192.96; Jobber pays 75% of $192.96 = $144.72 **15.** $58.31; $20.41 *Spiral Review* **17.** 4.5 **19.** $78,750 *Get Ready for the Next Lesson* **21.** $142.66 **23.** $6,591.72 **25.** $12,436.99

Lesson 14.3 *Concept Check* **1.** $280 **2.** $210 **3.** 59.85% **4.** $1,532.16 *Lesson Practice* **5. a.** $87.75 **b.** $497.25 **7. a.** $190.00 **b.** $285.00 **c.** $85.50 **d.** $ 199.50 **9.** $47.22 **11. a.** 56% **b.** $347.20 **13. a.** 48% **b.** $209.28 **15. a.** 50.4% **b.** $74.49 **17. a.** 76.5% **b.** $1,644.75 **19.** Storm door $117.69; Replacement window $226.01; Basement window $110.37; Storm door closer $13.66; Replacement latch $7.44; Weather stripping $6.25 **21.** B7S $349.91; C37X $100.77; 173A $40.24; B62Y $5.36 *Spiral Review* **23.** $114 **25.** $8,178.14 **27.** $171.29 *Get Ready for the Next Lesson* **29.** $54.63 **31.** $348.51 **33.** $31,285.12

Lesson 14.4 *Concept Check* **1.** July 18 **2.** August 7 **3.** $19.20 **4.** $620.80 **5.** 97% **6.** $620.80 *Lesson Practice* **7. a.** $725.20 **9. a.** 18-Sep **b.** 3-Oct **c.** $0.00 **d.** $348.64 **11. a.** 17-Oct **b.** 6-Nov **c.** $268.63 **d.** $6,447.17 **e.** $6,447.17 **13.** August 2; August 27; $15,988.32 paid too late to get discount *Spiral Review* **15.** $889.20 **17.** $9,295.31 *Get Ready for the Next Lesson* **19.** $6,879 **21.** $19,365.50 **23.** $81,200

Lesson 14.5 *Concept Check* **1.** 10 days into December **2.** 12/30. **3.** $142 **4.** 6,958 **5.** 98% **6.** Cash price using the complement method = $6,958 **7.** Last day to take a discount with a 1 month extension is 10 days into April or April 10 **8.** April 30 **9.** $2,328 *Lesson Practice* **11. a.** 4-June **b.** $42.53 **c.** $1,375.27 **13. a.** 10-Feb **b.** 1-Mar or 2-Mar **c.** $825.89 **d.** $15,691.95 **15. a.** 10-July **b.** 30-July **c.** $0.00 **d.** $7,641.60 **17.** 10-April; 30-April; $26,715.81 *Spiral Review* **19.** $1,011.45 **21.** $1,833.33 *Get Ready for the Next Lesson* **23.** 29 **25.** 6,923

Lesson 14.6 *Concept Check* **1. a.** 270 **2. a.** 210 **3. a.** March = 210 from end of February **b.** 230 **4. a.** April = 230 from the end March **b.** 150 **5.** Every month. *Lesson Practice* **7.** (10-Sep) **a.** 225 **b.** 128; (17-Sep) **a.** 128 **b.** 74; (24-Sep) **a.** 74 **b.** 34; (1-Oct) **a.** 34 **b.** 158; (8-Oct) **a.** 158 **b.** 115; The stock reorder number is probably 34, because a new order was received the next week. **9.** 90

11.

Date	Receipts	Shipments	Balance
Aug. 1			47
Aug. 6		24	23
Aug. 16	40		63
Aug. 27		36	27
Aug. 31	50		77

Spiral Review **13.** 195 **15.** 12,414 **17.** $1,708.48; $1,227.97; $53,390.05 *Get Ready for the Next Lesson* **19.** 0.8 **21.** 0.2 **23.** 0.1

Lesson 14.7 *Concept Check* **1.** $3.93 **2.** $196.50 **3.** 110 packs sold; cost of goods sold = $438; Ending inventory value = $190.00 **4.** 110 packs sold; cost of goods sold = $428; Ending inventory value = $200.00 *Lesson Practice* **5. a.** $22.15 **b.** $509.45 **7.** $40.61

9.

Date	Units Received	Unit Cost	Total Cost
5/01	100	$9.65	$ 965.00
5/08	65	9.75	$ 633.75
5/19	145	9.90	$1435.50
Total	310		$3034.25

b. $1,550.00 **c.** $1484.25 *Spiral Review* **11.** $2,656.8 **13.** $0.87 *Get Ready for the Next Lesson* **15.** $367.97 **17.** $457.71 **19.** $648.37

Lesson 14.8 *Concept Check* **1.** $60,000 **2.** $17,000 **3.** $37,500 **4.** $50,000. **5.** $96,774.19 *Lesson Practice* **7.** $4,900.00 **9.** $9,204.80 **11.** $167,308.38 **13.** $255,000.00 **15.** $86,680.80 **17.** $64,655.17 *Spiral Review* **19.** $24,100 **21.** $97,395.20 *Get Ready for the Next Lesson* **23.** $18.89 **25.** $909.58 **27.** $638.89

Review and Assessment *Lesson-by-Lesson Review Lesson 14.1* **11. a.** $35.85 **b.** $203.15 **13. a.** $28.60 **b.** 33.5% **15. a.** $165.00 **b.** 47.1% *Lesson 14.2* **17. a.** 80% **b.** $92.00 **19. a.** 89% **b.** $408.71 **21. a.** 66.5% **b.** $58.82 **23. a.** 60% b. $90.00 **25.** $34.69; $89.21 *Lesson 14.3* **27. a.** $160.00 **b.** $480.00 **c.** $48.00 **d.** $432.00 **29. a.** $1,418.00 **b.** $2,127.00 **c.** $319.05 **d.** $1,807.95 **31. a.** 63.75% **b.** $2,539.80 *Lesson 14.4* **33. a.** $790.37 **35. a.** 20-Oct **b.** 9-Nov **c.** 9.95 **d.** $238.81 **37. a.** 21-Apr **b.** 6-May **c.** 5.49 **d.** $104.33 **39. a.** July, 22 **b.** August, 11 **c.** $17,439.74 **d.** $18,166.40 *Lesson 14.5* **41. a.** Jan. 10 **b.** Jan. 30 **c.** $3.89 **d.** $190.61 **43. a.** May 15 **b.** June 4 **c.** $26.26 **d.** $849.18 **45. a.** Nov. 10 **b.** Nov. 30 **c.** $164.55 **d.** $3,126.47 **47. a.** May 10 **b.** May 30 **c.** $845.60 *Lesson 14.6* **49. a.** 599 **51. a.** 539 **b.** 464 **53. a.** 434 **b.** 503 **55.** 411 *Lesson 14.7* **57.** $17.28 **59.** FIFO cost of the 145 belts sold: $2,717.50; LIFO value of the 15 belts in ending inventory: $277.50 *Lesson 14.8* **61.** $3,628.50 **63.** $3,570.00 **65.** $223,125.00 **67.** $260,000

Practice Test **1.** D. $149.98 **3.** A. $37.36 **5.** D. $385.05 **7.** B. November 15 **9.** $85,714.29 **11.** a. $4.46 **b.** $223.00 **13.** $17.84 **15.** $53,282.77 **17.** $75.50

Standardized Test Practice **1.** A. $2,078.94 **3.** C. 6.0% **5.** D. $447.99 **7.** $5,606.67 **9.** $4620 **11.** The unpaid-balance method is used to compute finance charges. The finance charge is based on the portion of the previous bill that has not been paid.

Chapter 15 Sales

Lesson 15.1 *Concept Check* **1.** $6.86 **2.** $14.00 *Lesson Practice* **3.** $1,465.00 **5.** $164.89 **7.** $61.95 **9.** $70.86 **11.** $28.11 **13.** $0.325 **15.** $3.60 **17. a.** $13.20 **b.** $1.10 *Spiral Review* **19.** $86.78 **21.** $1,898.02 *Get Ready for the Next Lesson* **23.** $37.38 **25.** $28.63 **27.** $142.26

Lesson 15.2 *Concept Check* **1. a.** $14.94 **b.** 30.0% **2. a.** $87.22 **b.** 35.0% **3. a.** $14.00 **b.** 46.7% **4. a.** $0.95 **b.** 25.1% *Lesson Practice* **5. a.** $1,465.00 **b.** 7.3% **7. a.** $164.89 **b.** 55.4% **9. a.** $120.75 **b.** 45.1% **11. a.** $52.61 **b.** 16.4% **13. a.** $3.09 **b.** 38.9% **15. a.** 40.4% **b.** 40.4% *Spiral Review* **17.** 30.0% **19.** $43.39; $31.24 *Get Ready for the Next Lesson* **21.** $19.70 **23.** $63.56 **25.** $5.59

Lesson 15.3 *Concept Check* **1. a.** $84 **b.** $70 **c.** $14 **2. a.** $385.60 **b.** $337.40 **c.** $48.20 **3. a.** $6.25 **b.** $3.10 **c.** $1.90 *Lesson Practice* **5. a.** $108.00 **b.** $72.00 **c.** $36.00 **7. a.** $35.00 **b.** $9.75 **c.** $25.25 **9. a.** $64.00 **b.** $59.70 **c.** $4.30 **11.** $29.96 **13.** $0.10 **15.** $91,480.80 **17.** $199.90; $141.15; $61.19 *Spiral Review* **19.** $4.55 **21.** $1,477.50 *Get Ready for the Next Lesson* **23.** 65.2% **25.** 78.9% **27.** 82.7%

Lesson 15.4 *Concept Check* **1. a.** $74.72 **b.** $47.80 **c.** $26.92 **d.** 22.5% **2. a.** $2.91 **b.** $10.39 **3. a.** $7.05 **b.** 20.14 *Lesson Practice* **5. a.** $17.50 **b.** $17.50 **c.** 25% **7. a.** $3,390.30 **b.** $3,976.60 **c.** 47% **9. a.** $223.75 **b.** −$73.75 **c.** −8% **11.** 22.3% **13.** 18.4% **15.** 17.1% **17.** 42.2% **19.** $148.79; $44.64 *Spiral Review* **21.** $1.96 **23.** $71,200 *Get Ready for the Next Lesson* **25.** $43.33 **27.** $337.11 **29.** $161.71

Lesson 15.5 *Concept Check* **1.** 70%; $2.00 **2.** 75%; $1.99 *Lesson Practice* **3. a.** 50.0% **b.** $173.48 **5. a.** 62.5% **b.** $76.54 **7.** $18.70 **9.** $114.99 **11. a.** $20.00 **b.** $600.00 **c.** $400.00 **d.** $200.00 **13. a.** SP $1.21; $0.00 same **b.** SP $0.23; $0.02 more **c.** SP $0.67; $0.04 less *Spiral Review* **15.** $60.00 **17.** $126,539.29 *Get Ready for the Next Lesson* **19.** $17.97

Lesson 15.6 *Concept Check* **1.** 66.7% **2.** 100% **3. a.** $1.84 **b.** $1.56 *Lesson Practice* **5. a.** $30.00 **b.** 150.0% **7. a.** $205.60 **b.** 35.1% **9.** 60.0% **11.** 88.2% **13.** 100.0% **15.** $42.95; $55.84 *Spiral Review* **17.** $37.40 **19.** $6.81 *Get Ready for the Next Lesson* **21.** $97.52 **23.** $898.28 **25.** $1,644.43

Lesson 15.7 *Concept Check* **1. a.** $35 **b.** $85 **2. a.** $210 **b.** $350 **3. a.** $57.85 **b.** $146.85 **4. a.** $159.20 **b.** $358.20 **5. a.** $2.00 **b.** $3.90 **6. a.** $40.91 **b.** $214.76 **7. a.** $44.19 **b.** $79.54 **8. a.** $70.00 **b.** $157.50 *Lesson Practice* **9. a.** $129.60 **b.** $216.00 **11. a.** $191.71 **b.** $943.51 **13. a.** $1,173.25 **b.** $2,408.25 **15.** $178.99 **17.** $710.80 **19.** $840.00 **21.** $6.75 **23. a.** $8.32 **b.** 66.6% **c.** 40.0% **25. a.** $416.25 **b.** $582.75 *Spiral Review* **27.** $129.00 **29.** $1,919.49 *Get Ready for the Next Lesson* **31.** 79.6% **33.** 36.8% **35.** 66.9%

Lesson 15.8 *Concept Check* **1. a.** $20 **b.** 25% **2. a.** $69.92 **b.** 40% **3. a.** $36.00 **b.** 28.8% **4. a.** $10.00 **b.** 22.2% **5. a.** $35.00 **b.** $15.75 **6. a.** $18.31 **b.** $3.66 *Lesson Practice* **7. a.** $5.00 **b.** 20.0% **9. a.** $97.88 **b.** 39.5% **11.** 20.1% **13.** 14.4% **15.** 28.7% **17.** 14.3%; 7.1%; 9.4% **19. a.** $150.00 **b.** $87 .00 *Spiral Review* **21.** $5.10 **23.** $3,073 *Get Ready for the Next Lesson* **25.** 9.0 **27.** 45.9 **29.** 135.0

Review and Assessment *Lesson-by-Lesson Review Lesson 15.1* **13.** $804.00 **15.** $94.97 **17.** $154.98 *Lesson 15.2* **19. a.** $14.45 **b.** 36.2% **21. a.** $83.07 **b.** 46.5% **23. a.** $69.51 **b.** 51.5% **25.** 34.8% *Lesson 15.3* **27. a.** $103.00 **b.** $49.74 **c.** $53.26 **29. a.** $88.35 **b.** $32.45 **c.** $55.90 **31.** $7.96 *Lesson 15.4* **33. a.** $87.99 **b.** $18.01 **c.** 8.2% **35. a.** $64.99 **b.** $67.96 **c.** 26.1% **37. a.** $178.60 **b.** $60.96 **c.** 13.7% **39. a.** $37.80 **b.** $51.20 **c.** 27.1% **41. a.** $9.35 **b.** $31.17 **43. a.** $2.54 **b.** $10.16 *Lesson 15.5* **45. a.** 78% **b.** $135.26 **47. a.** 68% **b.** $122.40 **49. a.** 81.5% **b.** $1,238.22 **51.** $462.50 *Lesson 15.6* **53. a.** $11.42 **b.** 61.6% **55. a.** $30.00 **b.** 37.5% **57. a.** $34.25 **b.** 61.7% **59. a.** $79.55 **b.** 92.5% **61. a.** $6.40 **b.** 71.1% **63. a.** $9.73 **b.** 95.2% *Lesson 15.7* **65. a.** $24.00 **b.** $56.00 **67. a.** $286.94 **b.** $516.49 **69. a.** $5.78 **b.** $13.44 **71. a.** $69.89 **b.** $155.12 **73.** $17.73 *Lesson 15.8* **75. a.** $14.49 **b.** 18.1% **77. a.** $0.50 **b.** 38.8% **79. a.** $5.81 **b.** 18.1%

Practice Test **1.** C. $9.94 **3.** D. $71.88 **5.** A. $10.68 **7.** B. $39.36 **9.** $10.99; 81.5% **11.** 17.2% **13.** $521.11 **15.** 233.92 **17.** $3,587.01

Standardized Test Practice **1.** B. $3.75 **3.** C. $7,200.00 **5.** A. $2,825.24 **7.** $615.29 **9.** 40% deducted from list price to yield first net price; 20% is deducted to yield 2nd cash price; 15% is deducted to yield final price. $250.51 **11.** 36 months

Chapter 16 Marketing

Lesson 16.1 *Concept Check* **1.** 13.4% **2.** 9.2% **3.** 2.0% **4.** 69.2% **5.** 93.4% This is within the standard of over 90%, so production should continue. **6.** 2 **7.** 20% *Lesson Practice* **9.** 92.0%; the company should continue making the Mintie toothpaste since over 90% like the new formula. **11.** No, they should not lower the prices since 95/300 = 31.67% **13.** Absolute Error = 76 − 95 = 19; Relative Error = 19 / 95 = .2 = 20% **15. a.** Definitely 405; Probably 602; Possibly 451; No 282 **b.** Under 25 306; 25 to 34 527; 35 to 49 513; 50 and older 394 **c.** 1,740 **d.** Definitely 23.3%; Probably 34.6%; Possibly 25.9%; No 16.2% **e.** Under 25 13.1%; 25 to 34 37.3%; 35 to 49 31.1%; 50 and older 18.5% **f.** Age Group "25 to 34." **g.** Under 25 32.3%; 25 to 34 20.2%; 35 to 49 19.1%; 50 and older 28.4% **h.** Age Group "Under 25." **i.** Absolute Error is 14 **j.** Relative Error is 10% **17.** 56.0 **19.** $170,820 *Get Ready for the Next Lesson* **21.** $3,906.50 **23.** $1,234.80 **25.** $4,289.80

Lesson 16.2 *Concept Check* **1.** 560,000 *Lesson Practice* **3. a.** 2.00% **b.** 36,000 **5.** 900,000 **7.** 2,250,000 *Spiral Review* **9.** 4.08 **11.** $5,175 *Get Ready for the Next Lesson* **13.** 75.0 **15.** 25.0

Lesson 16.3 *Concept Check* **1.** 10% **2.** 2.2% *Lesson Practice* **3.** 40.0% **5.** 28.0% **7.** 30.0% **9.** 26.2% **11. a.** 28.2% **b.** 26.4% **c.** 20.3% **d.** 13.8% **e.** 11.3% *Spiral Review* **13.** 25.0% **15.** 111.1% *Get Ready for the Next Lesson* **17.** 39,198.143 **19.** 73.800

Lesson 16.4 *Concept Check* **1.** $504,000 **2. a.** approximately $5.3 million **b.** approximately $6.2 million **c.** approximately $7.0 million *Lesson Practice* **3.** approximately 7.5 million **5.** approximately 8.5 million **7.** $617,500 **9.** $5.9 million

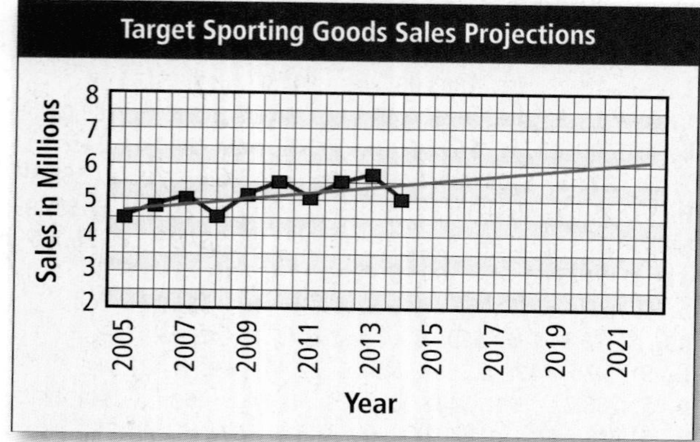

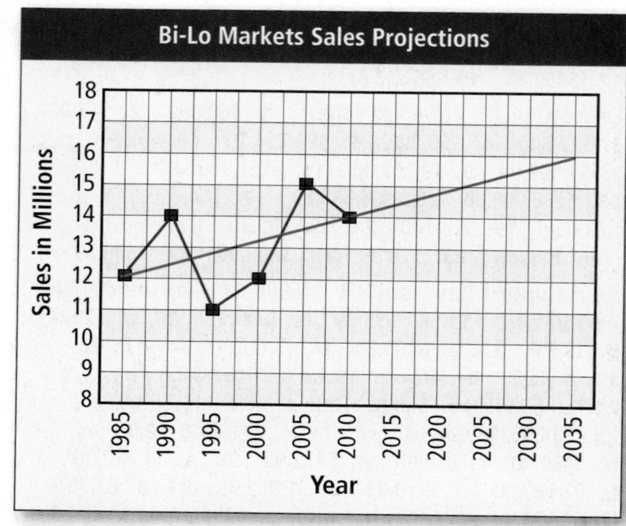

11. a. approximately $14.5 million **b.** approximately $14.8 **c.** approximately $15.2 *Spiral Review* **13.** 104.072 **15.** 0.026 *Get Ready for the Next Lesson* **17.** 26.88 **19.** $1,411.85 **21.** 24.06

Lesson 16.5 *Concept Check* **1.** $2,208 *Lesson Practice* **3. a.** $198.00 **b.** $792.00 **5. a.** $760.00 **b.** $760.00 **7.** $11,475 *Spiral Review* **9.** $2,016 **11.** $2,424.75 *Get Ready for the Next Lesson* **13.** 5/24 **15.** 5/18

Lesson 16.6 *Concept Check* **1.** $152,000 **2.** $2,275,000 **3.** $500,000 **4.** $1,620,800 *Lesson Practice* **5.** $110,000 **7.** $1,495,000 **9.** $15,400,000 **11.** $1,675,000 **13.** $991,250.00 *Spiral Review* **15.** 1/5 **17.** 43 1/2 *Get Ready for the Next Lesson* **19.** 386.2 **21.** 14.184 **23.** 12.494

Lesson 16.7 *Concept Check* **1.** $390,000; $468,000 **2.** A $4.50 selling price yields the greatest possible profit. **3.** $1.55. **4.** $19.68 *Lesson Practice* **5. a.** $120,000 **7. a.** $17.14 **b.** $38.14 **c.** $258,020 **9.** $247,500 **11.** (SP $3.75) **a.** $0.53 **b.** $1.58 **c.** $2,061,500; (SP $4.50) **a.** $0.71 **b.** $1.76 **c.** $1,918,000; (SP $8.50) **a.** $1.67 **b.** $2.72 **c.** $1,734,000; (SP $10.25) **a.** $2.00 **b.** $3.05 **c.** $1,800,000; Selling price of $3.75 yields the greatest profit. They should produce 950,000 units. *Spiral Review* **13.** 576.02 **15.** 45.2 *Get Ready for the Next Lesson* **17.** $1,834 **19.** $879 **21.** $2,418

Review and Assessment *Lesson-by-Lesson Review* *Lesson 16.1* **11.** 39.0% **13.** 43.2% **15.** 30.9% **17.** 100 *Lesson 16.2* **19. a.** 75,000 **21. a.** 50.0% **b.** 3,000,000 **23. a.** 35.7% **b.** 44,625 **25.** 3,000,000 *Lesson 16.3* **27.** 35.6% **29.** 24.0% **31.** 35.1% **33.** 20.5% *Lesson 16.4* **35.** $1,560,000 **37.** $1,676,400 **39.** $2,870,000 **41.** about $4.5 million **43.** about $18.0 million

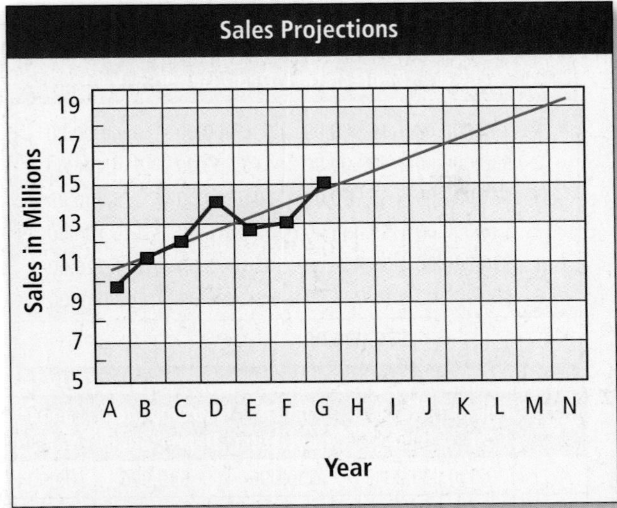

Lesson 16.5 **45. a.** $198.00 **b.** $792.00 **47. a.** $760.00 **b.** $760.00 **49. a.** $132.00 **b.** $924.00 **51.** $3,216.50 *Lesson 16.6* **53.** $287,500 **55.** $4,644,000 **57.** $2,520,000 *Lesson 16.7* **59. a.** $840,000.00 **61. a.** $12.00 **b.** $30.00 **c.** $1,000,000.00 **63.** $76,250; $89,000; $104,250; $39,500 **65.** $5.95

Practice Test **1.** C. $18,750 **3.** D. $2,280 **5.** A. 20.6% **7.** $8.40 **9.** 219.219 **11.** 22.009

Standardized Test Practice **1.** B. $13.14 **3.** C. $5.96 **5.** A. $8,614.00 **7.** $57.81; $39.31 **9.** $8.59 **11.** The percent of a particular given response in a survey is determined by dividing the number of particular responses by the number of total responses.

Chapter 17 Services

Lesson 17.1 *Concept Check* **1. a.** 5,000 Sq. Ft. **b.** $3,333.33 **2. a.** 5,625 Sq. Ft. **b.** $4,453.13 **3.** $12.00 per square foot *Lesson Practice* **5. a.** 1,000 **b.** $625 **7. a.** 2,250 **b.** $1,013 **9. a.** 9,600 **b.** $3,840 **11.** $1,525.00 **13.** $15.00 *Spiral Review* **15.** $1,246 **17.** $15,088 *Get Ready for the Next Lesson* **19.** $32.58

Lesson 17.2 *Concept Check* **1.** $907.65 *Lesson Practice* **3. a.** $63.00 **b.** $95.00 **5.** $1,050 **7.** $469.60 **9.** $1,986.00 *Spiral Review* **11.** $146.25 **13.** $95.06 *Get Ready for the Next Lesson* **15.** $18.72 **17.** $0.73 **19.** $28.84

Lesson 17.3 *Concept Check* **1.** $814.08 *Lesson Practice* **3. a.** $39.50 **b.** $2.37 **c.** $41.87 **d.** $167.48 **5. a.** $165.50 **b.** $9.93 **c.** $175.43 **d.** $701.72 **7.** $631.80 *Spiral Review* **9.** 25.80 **11.** 7.32 *Get Ready for the Next Lesson* **13.** $3,408.49

Lesson 17.4 *Concept Check* **1.** $248.81 **2.** $190.76 **3.** $80.62 **4.** 6 lines **5.** 1,260 minutes *Lesson Practice* **7. a.** $15.00 **b.** $21.99 **c.** $2.67 **d.** $91.66 **9.** $141.93 **11.** $216.06 **13.** 8 lines *Spiral Review* **15.** $315.66 **17.** $10,169.74 real estate tax *Get Ready for the Next Lesson* **19.** $722.00 **21.** $15.18 **23.** $13,743.00

Lesson 17.5 *Concept Check* **1.** $1,543.00 *Lesson Practice* **3.** $2,720.00 **5.** $2,222.00 **7.** $2,903.00 **9.** $6,143.30 **11.** $3,404.00 **13. a.** $1,480.00 **b.** $1,491.50 *Spiral Review* **15.** $548.10 **17. a.** $4,021.12 **b.** $21.12 *Get Ready for the Next Lesson* **19.** $976.69 **21.** $20,947.35 **23.** $4,574.27

Lesson 17.6 *Concept Check* **1.** $41,900 **2.** $9,087.50 **3.** $203,208.33 *Lesson Practice* **5.** $1,650.00 **7.** $52,000; $148,000 **9.** $2,160.00 **11. a.** $650,000.00 **b.** $19,350,000.00 **13.** $529,712.50 for services; $5,104,712.50 total cost of project **15.** $120,000 *Spiral Review* **17.** $211,962.50 *Get Ready for the Next Lesson* **19.** $923.11 **21.** $1,959.36

Review and Assessment *Lesson-by-Lesson Review* *Lesson 17.1* **9. a.** 200 **b.** $150.00 **11. a.** 875 **b.** $765.63 **13. a.** 540 **b.** $1,440.00 **15.** $5,729 *Lesson 17.2* **17. a.** $577.50 **b.** $899.48 **19. a.** $560.00 **b.** $1,181.90 **21. a.** $76.50 **b.** $789.40 **23.** $874.00 *Lesson 17.3* **25. a.** $82.50 **b.** $5.78 **c.** $88.28 **d.** $353.12 **27. a.** $10.00 **b.** $0.70 **c.** $10.70 **d.** $42.80 **29. a.** $427.50 **b.** $29.94 **c.** $457.44 **d.** $1,829.76 **31.** $20,351.40 *Lesson 17.4* **33. a.** $0.00 **b.** $0.00 **c.** $0.81 **d.** $27.81 **35. a.** $0.00 **b.** $43.98 **c.** $4.20 **d.** $144.18 **37. a.** $47.34 **b.** $21.99 **c.** $3.64 **d.** $124.97 **39.** $154.48 *Lesson 17.5* **41.** $2,192.50 **43.** $1,993.20 **45.** $2,556.75 *Lesson 17.6* **47.** $1,575.00 **49.** $31,850.00 **51.** $127,350.00

Practice Test **1.** B. $15.00 **3.** A. $1,057.25 **5.** A. $1,056 **7.** B. $443 Note: the answer to this problem when divided is 443.33 but the multiple choice option is 443. **9.** $1,331.00 **11.** $9,412.66 **13.** $300.96 **15.** $250.99

Standardized Test Practice **1.** D. 15% **3.** B. 91 days **5.** C. 32% **7.** $86.00 **9.** $12,240 **11.** The total telephone cost = monthly service charge + cost of additional minutes + cost of additional lines + federal excise tax; the monthly service charge is the cost of having phone service and will vary depending on the provider. The cost of additional minutes and lines is dependent on how many lines and minutes your service provides. The federal excise tax is added to your monthly charge. **13.** The sales potential is an estimate of the sales volume of a product during a specified period of time. The sales potential of a product is based on a sample group of people who try the product. The potential depends on the number of people in the sample that would purchase the product, the estimated size of the market, and the number of times a person would purchase the product during a specified period of time.

Chapter 18 Accounting

Lesson 18.1 *Concept Check* **1.** $611.07 **2.** $297.96 *Lesson Practice* **3. a.** $399.90 **5. a.** $141.82 **b.** $653.18 **7.** $12,563.68 **9. a.** $3,943.94

Employee	FIT	SIT	CIT	Social Security	Medicare	Hosp. Ins.	Total Ded.	Net Pay
Calderon	a. $26	b. $12.00	c. $ 9.00	d. $ 37.20	e. $ 8.70	$43.75	f. $136.65	g. $463.35
Dobbs	a. $30	b. $11.70	c. $ 8.78	d. $ 36.27	e. $ 8.48	$35.00	f. $130.23	g. $454.77
Haddad	a. $38	b. $ 8.30	c. $ 6.23	d. $ 25.73	e. $ 6.02	$17.50	f. $101.78	g. $313.22
Harling	a. $28	b. $11.30	c. $ 8.47	d. $ 35.02	e. $ 8.19	$35.00	f. $125.98	g. $438.82
Hermey	a. $46	b. $10.75	c. $ 8.06	d. $ 33.33	e. $ 7.79	$26.25	f. $132.18	g. $405.32
Presser	a. $21	b. $12.58	c. $ 9.44	d. $ 39.01	e. $ 9.12	$52.50	f. $143.65	g. $485.55
Wilbers	a. $54	b. $12.25	c. $ 9.19	d. $ 37.97	e. $ 8.88	$26.25	f. $148.54	g. $463.90
Total	b. $243	c. $78.88	d. $59.17	e. $244.53	e. $57.18	g. $236.25	h. $919.01	i. $3,024.93

Spiral Review **11.** $247.63 **13.** $463.92 *Get Ready for the Next Lesson* **15.** $297,084.19 **17.** $6,819.55 **19.** $10,480.98

Lesson 18.2 *Concept Check* **1.** 4.34% **2.** 69.3% **3.** $187,500 *Lesson Practice* **5.** 16.7% **7.** 19.1% **9.** 15.4% **11.** 3.6% **13.** 19.13% **15. a.** 4.68% **b.** 4.04% **c.** 75.50% **d.** 3.52% **e.** 2.21% **f.** 3.13% **g.** 6.92% **h.** $206,000; 100.00% **17. a.** $1,900,000 **b.** $2,150,000 *Spiral Review* **19.** 25.0% **21.** $600,000 annual sales potential *Get Ready for the Next Lesson* **23.** $0.012 **25.** $0.636 **27.** $1.533

Lesson 18.3 *Concept Check* **1.** $0.02 **2.** $0.22 **3.** 88 units *Lesson Practice* **5. a.** $0.030 **b.** $0.011 **c.** $0.041 **7.** $0.394 **9.** $0.061 **11. a.** she could complete 15 more units per hour **b.** she could complete 13 more per units hour *Spiral Review* **13.** $0.038 **15. a.** $300.00 **b.** $4,575 **c.** 6.56% *Get Ready for the Next Lesson* **17.** $1.88 **19.** $17.08 **21.** $783.64

Lesson 18.4 *Concept Check* **1.** 55,000 **2.** 166,000 *Lesson Practice* **3.** 95,000 **5.** 450,000 **7.** 28,986 **9.** 230,941 **11.** 606 *Spiral Review* **13.** $5.36 **15.** $1,711.52 *Get Ready for the Next* **17.** $645.30 **19.** $420.12

Lesson 18.5 *Concept Check* **1.** $580.00 **2.** $50,000 *Lesson Practice* **3.** $4,000 **5.** $8,200 **7.** $64,667 **9.** $12,747 **11.** $2,544 *Spiral Review* **13.** $80.85 **15.** $0.32 *Get Ready for the Next Lesson* **17.** $1,635.75 **19.** $1,729.56

Lesson 18.6 *Concept Check* **1. a.** $16,000 **b.** $48,000 **c.** $42,000 **2. a.** $16,000 **b.** $64,000 **c.** $26,000 **3. a.** $16,000 **b.** $80,000 **c.** $10,000 *Lesson Practice* **5. a.** $800 **b.** $3,200 **c.** $1,800 **7. a.** $2,000 **b.** $6,000 **c.** $9,000 **9. a.** $2,000 **b.** $10,000 **c.** $5,000 **11. a.** $2,000 **b.** $14,000 **c.** $1,000 **13. a.** $22,470 **b.** $7,490 **c.** $14,980 **d.** $7,490 **15. a.** $4,330 **b.** $4,330 **c.** $8,660 **17. a.** $4,330 **b.** $12,990 **c.** $0.00

19.

End of Year	Original Cost	Annual Depreciation	Accumulated Depreciation	Book Value
1	a. $195,000	b. $16,700	c. $ 16,700	d. $178,300
2	a. $195,000	b. $16,700	c. $ 33,400	d. $161,600
3	a. $195,000	b. $16,700	c. $ 50,100	d. $144,900
4	a. $195,000	b. $16,700	c. $ 66,800	d. $128,200
5	a. $195,000	b. $16,700	c. $ 83,500	d. $111,500
6	a. $195,000	b. $16,700	c. $100,200	d. $ 94,800
7	a. $195,000	b. $16,700	c. $116,900	d. $ 78,100
8	a. $195,000	b. $16,700	c. $133,600	d. $ 61,400
9	a. $195,000	b. $16,700	c. $150,300	d. $ 44,700
10	a. $195,000	b. $16,700	c. $167,000	d. $ 28,000

Spiral Review **21.** $6,200.70 **23.** $126,315.79 *Get Ready for the Next Lesson* **25.** $2,018 **27.** $518 **29.** $6,205

Lesson 18.7 *Concept Check*

1.

Year	Original Cost	Annual Depreciation	Accumulated Depreciation	Book Value
1	$30,000.00	$6,000.00	$ 6,000.00	$24,000.00
2	$30,000.00	$9,600.00	$15,600.00	$14,400.00
3	$30,000.00	$5,760.00	$21,360.00	$ 8,640.00
4	$30,000.00	$3,456.00	$24,816.00	$ 5,184.00
5	$30,000.00	$3,456.00	$28,272.00	$ 1,728.00
6	$30,000.00	$1,728.00	$30,000.00	0.00
		$30,000.00		

2.

Year	Original Cost	Fixed %	Annual Depreciation	Accumulated Depreciation	Book Value
1	$120,000	33.33%	$39,996	$39,996	$80,004
2	$120,000	44.45%	$53,340	$93,336	$26,664
3	$120,000	14.81%	$17,772	$111,108	$8,892
4	$120,000	7.41%	$8,892	$120,000	$0.00
		100%	$120,000		

Lesson Practice

	1	2	3	4	5	6
	20.00%	32.00%	19.20%	11.52%	11.52%	5.76%
3.	a. $3,200	b. $ 5,120	c. $3,072	d. $1,843	e. $1,843	f. $ 922
5.	a. $6,960	b. $11,136	c. $6,682	d. $4,009	e. $4,009	f. $2,004

7.

Year	Percent	Cost	Depreciation	Accumulated Depreciation	Book Value
1	33.33%	a. $164,500	b. $54,828	c. $ 54,828	d. $109,672
2	44.45%	a. $164,500	b. $73,120	c. $127,948	d. $ 36,552
3	14.81%	a. $164,500	b. $24,362	c. $152,310	d. $ 12,190
4	7.41%	a. $164,500	b. $12,189	c. $164,499	d. $ 1

8.

Year	Percent	Cost	Depreciation	Accumulated Depreciation	Book Value
1	20.00%	a. $48,260	b. $ 9,652	c. $ 9,652	d. $38,608
2	32.00%	a. $48,260	b. $15,443	c. $25,095	d. $23,165
3	19.20%	a. $48,260	b. $ 9,266	c. $34,361	d. $13,899
4	11.52%	a. $48,260	b. $ 5,560	c. $39,921	d. $ 8,339
5	11.52%	a. $48,260	b. $ 5,560	c. $45,481	d. $ 2,779
6	5.76%	a. $48,260	b. $ 2,780	c. $48,261	d. ($1)

9.

Year	Percent	Cost	Depreciation	Accumulated Depreciation	Book Value
1	5.00%	a. $1,400,000	b. $ 70,000	c. $ 70,000	d. $1,330,000
2	9.50%	a. $1,400,000	b. $133,000	c. $ 203,000	d. $1,197,000
3	8.55%	a. $1,400,000	b. $119,700	c. $ 322,700	d. $1,077,300
4	7.70%	a. $1,400,000	b. $107,800	c. $ 430,500	d. $ 969,500
5	6.93%	a. $1,400,000	b. $ 97,020	c. $ 527,520	d. $ 872,480
6	6.23%	a. $1,400,000	b. $ 87,220	c. $ 614,740	d. $ 785,260
7	5.90%	a. $1,400,000	b. $ 82,600	c. $ 697,340	d. $ 702,660
8	5.90%	a. $1,400,000	b. $ 82,600	c. $ 779,940	d. $ 620,060
9	5.91%	a. $1,400,000	b. $ 82,740	c. $ 862,680	d. $ 537,320
10	5.90%	a. $1,400,000	b. $ 82,600	c. $ 945,280	d. $ 454,720
11	5.91%	a. $1,400,000	b. $ 82,740	c. $1,028,020	d. $ 371,980
12	5.90%	a. $1,400,000	b. $ 82,600	c. $1,110,620	d. $ 289,380
13	5.91%	a. $1,400,000	b. $ 82,740	c. $1,193,360	d. $ 206,640
14	5.90%	a. $1,400,000	b. $ 82,600	c. $1,275,960	d. $ 124,040
15	5.91%	a. $1,400,000	b. $ 82,740	c. $1,358,700	d. $ 41,300
16	2.95%	a. $1,400,000	b. $ 41,300	c. $1,400,000	d. $0

Spiral Review **11.** $118 **13.** $56,679.21 *Get Ready for the Next Lesson* **15.** $73,963.79 **17.** $319,342.06 **19.** $3,995.89

Lesson 18.8 *Concept Check* **1.** $132,000 **2.** $42,000 *Lesson Practice* **3.** $77,000 **5.** $36,250 **7.** $17,450 **9.** Assets: $221,797; Liabilities: $142,257; Owners Equity: $79,540 *Spiral Review* **11.** 41,630.90 **13.** $567.18 *Get Ready for the Next Lesson* **15.** $354,022 **17.** $99,395 **19.** $124,772

Lesson 18.9 *Concept Check* **1.** $67,000 **2.** $67,000 **3.** 3.9 **4.** 25% *Lesson Practice* **5. a.** $33,000 **b.** $12,300 **c.** $20,700 **7. a.** $52,500 **b.** $22,500 **c.** $27,500 **9. a.** $99,800 **b.** $65,000 **c.** $34,800 **d.** 1.5 **11. a.** $61,450 **b.** $33,000 **c.** $28,450 **d.** 1.9 **13. a.** $80,467.50 **b.** $51,013.20 **c.** $29,454.30 **d.** $80,467.50 **e.** 1.6 **f.** 82% increase **15. a.** Total assets = $199,504,200; Total Liabilities = $142,599,410; Owner's Equity = $56,904,790; Total liabilities and owner's equity = $199,504,200 **b.** 1.4 **c.** 5% increase **17. a.** If total assets doubled and total liabilities were reduced to half, the current ratio would be 5.5 ($95 million / $17.4 million) **b.** The current ratio would be .34 ($23.75 million / $69.6 million) **c.** 0% (both amounts are $1.3 million) *Spiral Review* **19.** $241,040 **21.** $5,412 *Get Ready for the Next Lesson* **23.** $527.52 **25.** $1,073.28 **27.** $3,670.32

Lesson 18.10 *Concept Check* **1.** $16,920 **2.** $12,404 **3.** The beginning inventory = $19,250; The receipts = $38,500; The ending inventory = $9,250 *Lesson Practice* **5.** $25,200 **7.** $9,921.32 **9.** $1,321.92 **11.** $22,190; $26,340 **13.** $35,925; $107,775; $71,850 *Spiral Review* **15.** $2,853.46 **17.** 114% *Get Ready for the Next Lesson* **19.** $112.94 **21.** $7,924.79 **23.** $257,401.76

Lesson 18.11 *Concept Check* **1. a.** $61,500 **b.** $26,800 **2. a.** $289,000 **b.** $183,600 *Lesson Practice* **3. a.** $4,685 **5. a.** $3,675 **b.** $1,935 **c.** $1,107 **7. a.** $673,642 **b.** $255,726 **c.** $159,307 **9. a.** $388,125 **b.** $157,125 **c.** $85,209 **11.** Net Sales $14,007; Gross Profit $7,997; Net Income $6,897 **13.** Net Sales $27,198; Gross Profit $18,005; Net Income $13,685 *Spiral Review* **15.** 518.74 **17.** $740.90 *Get Ready for the Next Lesson* **19.** 6.10 **21.** 877.50 **23.** 391.95

Review and Assessment *Lesson-by-Lesson Review* *Lesson 18.1* **13.** FIT: $53; Social Security: $31.81; Medicare: $7.44; CIT: $7.70; Health Ins. $12.00; $401.05 net pay *Lesson 18.2* **15.** 9.4% **17.** 8.1% **19.** 13.3% *Lesson 18.3* **21. a.** $0.051 **23. a.** $0.022 **b.** $0.036 **c.** $0.058 **25. a.** $0.110 **b.** $0.019 **c.** $0.129 **27.** 37 per hour *Lesson 18.4* **29.** 171,930 **31.** 211,296 **33.** 14,235 *Lesson 18.5* **35.** $2,533 **37.** $138,200 **39.** $4,857 **41.** $5,000 *Lesson 18.6* **43. a.** $550 **b.** $1,100 **c.** $4,190 **45. a.** $550 **b.** $2200 **c.** $3,090 **47. a.** $550 **b.** $3300 **c.** $1,990 **49. a.** $550 **b.** $4400 **c.** $890 *Lesson 18.7* **51. a.** 86,500.00 **b.** 14,532.00 **c.** 31,832.00 **d.** 54,668.00 **53. a.** 86,500.00 **b.** 10,553.00 **c.** 54,668.00 **d.** 31,832.00 **55. a.** 86,500.00 **b.** 7,914.75 **c.** 71,103.00 **d.** 15,397.00 **57. a.** 86,500.00 **b.** 7,594.70 **c.** 86,500.00 **d.** 0.00 *Lesson 18.8* **59.** $85,444 **61.** $18,692 **63.** $4,108 *Lesson 18.9* **65. a.** $287,954 **b.** $5,600 **c.** 216,200 *Lesson 18.10* **67.** $141,423 **69.** $19,707.92 *Lesson 18.11* **71. a.** $1,878.99 **73. a.** $45,770.73 **b.** $27,361.30 **c.** $6,161.30 **75. a.** Net sales $9,610; Gross profit $4,746; Net income $3,566

Practice Test **1.** C. $981,187.50 **3.** D. 242,220 **5.** A. $346.18 **7.** D. $753.20 **9.** $5,600.00 the first year; $8,960.00 the second year; $5,376.00 the third year; $3,225.60 the fourth year; $3,225.60 the fifth year; $1,612.80 the sixth year **11.** 713.125 **13.** $17.0198 **15.** $9,517.76

Standardized Test Practice **1.** B. 45% **3.** C. $296,875 **5.** B. $1,784.80 **7.** C. $118,277 **9.** $164,880 **11.** Depreciation is spreading the cost of an item over its estimated life. The straight-line method assumes that the depreciation is the same from year to year. To calculate straight-line depreciation subtract the salvage value from the original cost and divide by the estimated life of the item.

Chapter 19 Financial Management

Lesson 19.1 *Concept Check* **1.** Taxable income = $85,000; Tax = $17,150 **2.** Taxable income = $65,000; Tax = $11,250 **3.** $5,822,147.80 **4.** $185,320.40 *Lesson Practice* **5. a.** $5,512 **7. a.** $42,722 **b.** $6,408 **9. a.** $87,432 **b.** $17,977 **11. a.** $98,425 **b.** $21,715 **13. a.** $414,936 **b.** 141,078 **15.** $742 **17.** $29,308 **19. a.** $1,214,259 **b.** $302,490 **c.** $101,221 *Spiral Review* **21.** 6.18 **23.** 1,645.00 **25.** 5.5 hours *Get Ready for the Next Lesson* **27.** $53,662.26 **29.** $27,402.90 **31.** $237,160.00

Lesson 19.2 *Concept Check* **1. a.** $28,560,000 **b.** $120 **2. a.** $2,578,000 **b.** 51,560 shares *Lesson Practice* **3. a.** $408,000 **b.** $455,500 **c.** $6,344,500 **d.** $1.14 **5. a.** $1,050,000 **b.** $1,104,650 **c.** $19,895,350 **d.** $1.10 **7. a.** $1,053,360 **b.** $0.82 **9. a.** $29,281,563 **b.** $2.93 **11.** $37,500,000; $37.50 *Spiral Review* **13.** $63,700 **15.** $82,500 *Get Ready for the Next Lesson* **17.** 0.046 **19.** 0.0073 **21.** 1.10

Lesson 19.3 *Concept Check* **1. a.** $2,777.78 **b.** $102,777.78 **2. a.** $5,541.67 **b.** $155,541.67 **3.** $1,250,000 *Lesson Practice* **5. a.** $1,979.17 **b.** $96,979.17 **7. a.** $23,625.00 **b.** $323,625.00 **9. a.** $1,618.95 **b.** $39,268.95 **11.** $52,566.67 **13.** $718,250.00 **15.** 5.75% *Spiral Review* **17.** 0.127 **19.** 0.006 **21.** $2,096.25 *Get Ready for the Next Lesson* **23.** 4.646 **25.** 0.320 **27.** 0.381

Lesson 19.4 *Concept Check* **1. a.** $400 **b.** $119,635 **c.** 4.012% **2. a.** $1,875 **b.** $198,175 **c.** 3.785% *Lesson Practice* **3. a.** $218.17 **b.** $69,806.83 **c.** 3.750% **5. a.** $1,762.50 **b.** $148,237.50 **c.** 2.378% **7. a.** $756.00 **b.** $59,274.00 **c.** 3.826% *Spiral Review* **9.** 60.548 **11.** 24.275 *Get Ready for the Next Lesson* **13.** 3.9% **15.** 5.8%

Lesson 19.5 *Concept Check* **1.** 4.3% **2.** $13,168.80 **3.** $26.69 **4.** −8.0% *Lesson Practice* **5. a.** 6.4% **7. a.** $154.35 **9. a.** $1.28 **11.** 7.9% **13.** $903.10 **15.** $182.54 **17.** 4890.0% **19.** $0.58 *Spiral Review* **21.** 5.0% **23.** $10.33; $20.66 *Get Ready for the Next Lesson* **25.** $11,055.60 **27.** $27,549,400.00 **29.** $75,600,000.00

Lesson 19.6 *Concept Check* **1.** $5,168,856,000 **2.** $6,089 *Lesson Practice* **3. a.** $5,627,648,000 **b.** $18,633 **5. a.** $133,203,700,000 **b.** $33,317 **7. a.** $43,234,500,000 **b.** $3,986 **9. a.** $10,017,450,000,000 **b.** $7,694 *Spiral Review* **11.** $10,719.23 **13.** $886.84 *Get Ready for the Next Lesson* **15.** $3,219.69 **17.** $24,510.41

Lesson 19.7 *Concept Check* **1.** 200.0 **2.** $0.47 *Lesson Practice* **3.** 180.5 **5.** $770.58 **7.** $8.78 **9.** 146.4 **11.** $4.55 **13.** $757.90 **15.** $97.96 **17.** $224.27 **19. a.** The economy has always been increasing. In the composite, prices have always gone up. **b.** If the composite CPI goes down from one year to the next, it means that prices, in the composite, have decreased. *Spiral Review* **21.** 1.34 **23.** $3,143.86

Review and Assessment *Lesson-by-Lesson Review Lesson 19.1* **9. a.** $147,629 **b.** $40,825 **11. a.** $42,529 **b.** $6,379 **13. a.** $240,376 **b.** $76,997 **15. a.** $242,088 **b.** $77,664 **17.** $34,769 **19.** $100,082 *Lesson 19.2* **21. a.** $60,200 **b.** $106,180 **c.** $753,820 **d.** $3.93 **23. a.** $534,000 **b.** $654,000 **c.** $8,246,000 **d.** $3.44 **25. a.** $2,189,000 **b.** $2,299,500 **c.** $37,500,500 **d.** $1.53 **27.** $4,700,000; $3.92 *Lesson 19.3* **29. a.** $2,200.00 **b.** $112,200.00 **31. a.** $14,062.50 **b.** $264,062.50 **33. a.** $12,674.58 **b.** $813,174.58 **35.** $824,250 *Lesson 19.4* **37. a.** $145.83 **b.** $34,879.17 **c.** 5.017% **39. a.** $857.50 **b.** $99,182.50 **c.** 3.458% **41. a.** $1,800.00 **b.** $73,235.00 **c.** 4.916% **43. a.** $998.67 **b.** $69,036.33 **c.** 4.340% **45. a.** $2000.00 **b.** $98,040.00 **c.** 6.120% *Lesson 19.5* **47. a.** 2.0% **49. a.** $2,756.28 **51. a.** $827.65 **53.** $33,187.86 *Lesson 19.6* **55. a.** $1,710,436,000 **b.** $6,039 **57. a.** $112,167,600,000 **b.** $984 **59. a.** $191,588,800,000 **b.** $18,444 **61.** $443.37 billion; $11,886.20 *Lesson 19.7* **63.** 175.0 **65.** $9.84 **67.** $68.74 **69.** $22,590.27

Practice Test **1.** D. $114,102 **3.** A. $585,600.00 **5.** D. 6.2% **7.** B. 150.0 **9.** $1,712,764 **11.** $98,523 **13.** 6.3% **15.** 499,474.5 **17.** $1,064,000

Standardized Test Practice **1.** A. $4,636.89 **3.** C. 5.985% **5.** D. $386.50 **7.** B. $380.00 **9.** $248,600 **11.** The GDP is the total value of goods and services produced in a country in a given year. A country's government uses the GDP to monitor the country's economy. The real GDP is also known as the adjusted GDP and is calculated with the distortion of inflation removed.

Skills Answers

Skill 1

Numbers **1.** Ones; 5 **3.** Tens; 70 **5.** Ones; 8 **7.** Tens; 0 **9.** Hundreds; 700 **11.** Ones; 9 **13.** Tenths; 0.3 **15.** Thousandths; 0.009 **17.** Hundredths; 0.02 **19.** Ones; 4 **21.** Hundredths; 0.02 **23.** Thousandths; 0.007 **25.** Thousandths; 0.003 **27.** Thousandths; 0.001 **29.** Thirty-four **31.** Seventy-eight **33.** Eight hundred forty-two **35.** Five thousand twelve **37.** One hundred nineteen **39.** One thousand two hundred forty **41.** One hundred ninety-four **43.** Twenty-five and $\frac{00}{100}$ dollars **45.** Seventeen and $\frac{9}{100}$ dollars **47.** One hundred twenty and $\frac{17}{100}$ dollars **49.** Seven thousand seven hundred forty-nine dollars **51.** $\frac{50}{100}$ dollars or fifty cents **53.** $71.64 million **55.** 18.4 thousand **57.** 171.6 thousand **59.** 2.135 billion **61.** $3,400,000 **63.** $11,200,000,000 **65.** 7,300,000,000 **67.** 400,000 **69.** $720,000,000 **71.** 54 **73.** 835 **75.** 211 **77.** 5,763 **79.** 4,444 **81.** 1,236 **83.** 650 **85.** $101 **87.** $93 **89.** $742 **91.** $791,000 **93.** 2.0 **95.** 25.1 **97.** 58 **99.** 0.1 **101.** 0.5 **103.** 0.020 **105.** $10 **107.** $19 **109.** $600 **111.** $9,521.39 **113.** $2,000.00

Skill 2

Rounding Numbers **1.** 30 **3.** 70 **5.** 220 **7.** 8,100 **9.** 600 **11.** 6,000 **13.** 16,000 **15.** 1,000 **17.** 0.1 **19.** 0.5 **21.** 0.47 **23.** 0.36 **25.** 0.601 **27.** 0.213 **29.** 137.492 **31.** 38,000 **33.** 48,000 **35.** 900 **37.** 30 **39.** 580 **41.** 36 **43.** 189.7 **45.** 0.1 **47.** 152.43 **49.** 0.179 **51.** 108.437

Skill 3

Adding Whole Numbers **1.** 106 **3.** 138 **5.** 1,189 **7.** 799 **9.** 897 **11.** 488 **13.** 10,878 **15.** 8,987 **17.** 71 **19.** 210 **21.** 897 **23.** 1,542 **25.** 4,638 **27.** 12,224 **29.** 12,201 **31.** 12,787 **33.** 3,798 **35.** 12,318 **37.** 8,152 **39.** 9,484 **41.** 6,777 **43.** 14,953 **45.** 33,587 **47.** 87,481 **49.** 14,999 **51.** 14,450

Skill 4

Subtracting Whole Numbers **1.** 331 **3.** 151 **5.** 3,442 **7.** 3,311 **9.** 1,111 **11.** 8,020 **13.** 6 **15.** 6,231 **17.** 64 **19.** 99 **21.** 2,258 **23.** 1,166 **25.** 1,909 **27.** 3,667 **29.** 1,275 **31.** 859 **33.** 2,983 **35.** 1,568 **37.** 9,111 **39.** 1,862 **41.** 2,238 **43.** 2,901 **45.** 16,526 **47.** 37,503 **49.** 126,403 **51.** 100,621

Skill 5

Adding Decimals **1.** 1,406.20 **3.** 713.39 **5.** 900.05 **7.** 2,411.356 **9.** 1,719.002 **11.** 98.03 **13.** 1,300.840 **15.** 1,044.00 **17.** 91.111 **19.** 156.254 **21.** 19.999 **23.** 1,126.030 **25.** 1,083.557 **27.** 508.595 **29.** 1.000 **31.** 147.420 **33.** 787.032 **35.** 1,191.418

Skill 6

Subtracting Decimals **1.** 51.15 **3.** 134.89 **5.** 5.09 **7.** 25.51 **9.** 79.68 **11.** 203.84 **13.** 70.85 **15.** 84.32 **17.** 19.6 **19.** 8.07 **21.** 57.44 **23.** 377.63 **25.** 5.09 **27.** 19.983 **29.** 325.86 **31.** 204.354 **33.** 557.87 **35.** 5,215.946 **37.** 1.1178 **39.** 778.029 **41.** 3.59806 **43.** 2.74502

SELECTED ANSWERS

Skill 7

Multiplying Whole Numbers **1.** 1,533 **3.** 87,344 **5.** 100,152 **7.** 77,256 **9.** 959,373 **11.** 2,808 **13.** 251,565 **15.** 4,268,236 **17.** 1,665 **19.** 310,992 **21.** 1,662,024 **23.** 69,000 **25.** 28,182 **27.** 357,000 **29.** 36,060,000 **31.** 4,471,392 **33.** 43,955,000 **35.** 1,070,443 **37.** 169,130 **39.** 623,770 **41.** 1,309,622 **43.** 2,804,972 **45.** 15,805,077

Skill 8

Multiplying Decimals **1.** 4.5 **3.** 878.22 **5.** 188.55 **7.** 230.8218 **9.** 43.9556 **11.** 287.352 **13.** 0.1008 **15.** 0.096 **17.** 0.584 **19.** 0.6156 **21.** 0.0567 **23.** 0.0861 **25.** 4,116 **27.** 36 **29.** 876.403 **31.** 1,212.86 **33.** 112.5 **35.** 81.9698 **37.** 161,713.902 **39.** 0.156462 **41.** 84 **43.** 0.07608533

Skill 9

Dividing (Fractional Remainder) **1.** $2\frac{10}{27}$ **3.** $2\frac{2}{41}$ **5.** $14\frac{12}{53}$ **7.** $84\frac{17}{21}$ **9.** $67\frac{19}{43}$ **11.** $59\frac{12}{23}$ **13.** $71\frac{42}{81}$ **15.** $16\frac{13}{114}$ **17.** $15\frac{17}{321}$ **19.** $8\frac{792}{892}$ **21.** $23\frac{22}{409}$ **23.** $14\frac{2}{625}$ **25.** $20\frac{831}{843}$ **27.** 18 **29.** 16 **31.** 72 **33.** $14\frac{22}{621}$ **35.** $12\frac{349}{549}$ **37.** $5\frac{765}{842}$ **39.** $181\frac{29}{473}$ **41.** $87\frac{527}{622}$ **43.** $1{,}600\frac{3}{51}$ **45.** $252\frac{46}{88}$ **47.** $208\frac{166}{417}$ **49.** $1{,}345\frac{177}{514}$

Skill 10

Dividing (Decimal Remainder) **1.** 11.125 **3.** 21.2 **5.** 5.1 **7.** 19.75 **9.** 34.5 **11.** 22.8 **13.** 16.1 **15.** 206.8 **17.** 2.02 **19.** 10.865 **21.** 21.524 **23.** 8.71 **25.** 10.45 **27.** 31.13 **29.** 5.63 **31.** 17.50 **33.** 14.44 **35.** 230.05 **37.** 41.42 **39.** 25.54 **41.** 39.50

Skill 11

Dividing Decimals **1.** 4.60 **3.** 5.71 **5.** 17.00 **7.** 6.50 **9.** 42.91 **11.** 26.00 **13.** 31.00 **15.** 26.00 **17.** 8.96 **19.** 13.21 **21.** 1.41 **23.** 245.00 **25.** 1.21 **27.** 256.00 **29.** 67.48 **31.** 22.57 **33.** 1.75 **35.** 38.50 **37.** 98.86 **39.** 0.01 **41.** 17.13 **43.** 0.01

Skill 12

Equivalent Fractions **1.** 10 **3.** 50 **5.** 24 **7.** 22 **9.** 51 **11.** 24 **13.** 35 **15.** 72 **17.** 20 **19.** $\frac{2}{3}$ **21.** $\frac{1}{2}$ **23.** $\frac{2}{3}$ **25.** $\frac{1}{3}$ **27.** $\frac{5}{6}$ **29.** $\frac{10}{27}$ **31.** $\frac{4}{7}$ **33.** $\frac{1}{2}$ **35.** $\frac{3}{4}$ **37.** $\frac{94}{183}$ **39.** $\frac{1}{2}$ **41.** $\frac{19}{36}$ **43.** $\frac{2}{13}$ **45.** $\frac{4}{25}$

Skill 13

Changing Mixed Numbers/Improper Fractions

1. $\frac{25}{4}$ **3.** $\frac{59}{8}$ **5.** $\frac{20}{3}$ **7.** $\frac{39}{5}$ **9.** $\frac{43}{10}$ **11.** $\frac{135}{32}$ **13.** $\frac{16}{3}$ **15.** $\frac{29}{10}$ **17.** $\frac{53}{16}$ **19.** $\frac{165}{32}$ **21.** $\frac{79}{11}$ **23.** $\frac{57}{5}$ **25.** $6\frac{1}{2}$ **27.** $5\frac{3}{4}$ **29.** $5\frac{1}{2}$ **31.** $2\frac{1}{3}$ **33.** $2\frac{1}{2}$ **35.** $2\frac{20}{21}$ **37.** $5\frac{5}{6}$ **39.** $3\frac{1}{6}$ **41.** $6\frac{1}{8}$ **43.** $6\frac{3}{7}$

Skill 14

Changing Fractions/Decimals **1.** 0.80 **3.** 1.13 **5.** 2.43 **7.** 1.37 **9.** 0.30 **11.** 4.38 **13.** 3.08 **15.** 0.03 **17.** 5.15 **19.** 2.12 **21.** 7.14 **23.** 0.44 **25.** $\frac{1}{10}$ **27.** $\frac{3}{10}$ **29.** $\frac{3}{100}$ **31.** $\frac{53}{100}$ **33.** $\frac{3}{1{,}000}$ **35.** $\frac{8}{125}$ **37.** $4\frac{111}{250}$ **39.** $\frac{469}{1{,}000}$ **41.** $7\frac{1}{2}$ **43.** $1\frac{2}{25}$ **45.** $2\frac{83}{100}$ **47.** $\frac{21}{200}$ **49.** $\frac{1}{2{,}000}$ **51.** $1\frac{402}{625}$ **53.** $\frac{1}{5{,}000}$

Skill 15

Adding Fractions, Like Denominators

1. $1\frac{2}{5}$ **3.** $\frac{3}{4}$ **5.** $1\frac{4}{7}$ **7.** $1\frac{4}{25}$ **9.** $1\frac{5}{16}$ **11.** $1\frac{8}{45}$ **13.** $11\frac{2}{3}$ **15.** $14\frac{2}{7}$ **17.** $12\frac{1}{3}$ **19.** $17\frac{1}{4}$ **21.** $9\frac{7}{8}$ **23.** $11\frac{2}{5}$

Skill 16

Adding Fractions, Unlike Denominators

1. $1\frac{1}{10}$ **3.** $\frac{20}{21}$ **5.** $1\frac{1}{6}$ **7.** $1\frac{13}{110}$ **9.** $\frac{59}{60}$ **11.** $\frac{71}{150}$ **13.** $9\frac{1}{6}$ **15.** $16\frac{1}{3}$ **17.** $20\frac{19}{26}$ **19.** $28\frac{22}{63}$ **21.** $28\frac{43}{56}$ **23.** $29\frac{5}{48}$

Skill 17

Subtracting Fractions, Like Denominators

1. $\frac{2}{9}$ **3.** $\frac{5}{6}$ **5.** $\frac{4}{7}$ **7.** $\frac{1}{8}$ **9.** $\frac{1}{5}$ **11.** $\frac{2}{5}$ **13.** $\frac{1}{4}$ **15.** $\frac{7}{20}$ **17.** $1\frac{1}{7}$ **19.** $3\frac{1}{4}$ **21.** $2\frac{1}{6}$ **23.** $5\frac{3}{16}$ **25.** $2\frac{7}{13}$ **27.** $8\frac{1}{2}$ **29.** $25\frac{2}{7}$

Skill 18

Subtracting Fractions, Unlike Denominators

1. $\frac{3}{8}$ **3.** $\frac{3}{20}$ **5.** $\frac{1}{18}$ **7.** $\frac{1}{15}$ **9.** $\frac{3}{20}$ **11.** $\frac{1}{10}$ **13.** $4\frac{1}{4}$ **15.** $6\frac{5}{18}$ **17.** $5\frac{7}{60}$ **19.** $3\frac{1}{8}$ **21.** $2\frac{3}{20}$ **23.** $2\frac{1}{8}$

Skill 19

Subtracting Mixed Numbers, Borrowing **1.** $1\frac{1}{2}$ **3.** $2\frac{1}{10}$ **5.** $2\frac{6}{11}$ **7.** $3\frac{1}{18}$ **9.** $12\frac{11}{12}$ **11.** $1\frac{37}{70}$ **13.** $2\frac{7}{8}$ **15.** $1\frac{3}{8}$ **17.** $\frac{1}{8}$ **19.** $3\frac{7}{9}$ **21.** $\frac{9}{20}$ **23.** $11\frac{5}{16}$ **25.** $14\frac{7}{9}$ **27.** $13\frac{5}{7}$ **29.** $12\frac{5}{32}$

Skill 20

Multiplying Fractions/Mixed Numbers

1. $\frac{1}{3}$ **3.** $\frac{5}{8}$ **5.** $\frac{5}{12}$ **7.** 2 **9.** 9 **11.** $16\frac{2}{15}$ **13.** $58\frac{1}{3}$ **15.** $46\frac{1}{8}$ **17.** $\frac{1}{6}$ **19.** $\frac{11}{12}$ **21.** 6 **23.** $3\frac{3}{4}$ **25.** $19\frac{1}{2}$ **27.** $8\frac{8}{15}$ **29.** 64 **31.** $25\frac{29}{72}$ **33.** $97\frac{11}{12}$ **35.** $71\frac{1}{24}$

Skill 21

Dividing Fractions/Mixed Numbers **1.** 2 **3.** $1\frac{7}{8}$ **5.** $7\frac{1}{2}$ **7.** 6 **9.** 16 **11.** $3\frac{7}{36}$ **13.** $2\frac{11}{12}$ **15.** $\frac{1}{4}$ **17.** $5\frac{5}{33}$ **19.** $4\frac{40}{323}$ **21.** $1\frac{1}{2}$ **23.** $1\frac{1}{2}$ **25.** $\frac{2}{3}$ **27.** 15 **29.** 6 **31.** 30 **33.** $\frac{43}{176}$ **35.** $\frac{143}{375}$ **37.** $6\frac{1}{2}$ **39.** 1

Skill 22

Writing Ratios **1.** 1,500:600 **3.** 600:1,200 **5.** 600:1,500 **7.** $\frac{1}{5}$ **9.** $\frac{1}{15}$ **11.** $\frac{1}{25}$ **13.** $\frac{2}{5}$

Skill 23

Proportions **1.** T **3.** F **5.** F **7.** T **9.** T **11.** F **13.** 18 **15.** $7\frac{1}{3}$ **17.** $\frac{6}{11}$ **19.** $5\frac{5}{9}$ **21.** $12\frac{4}{13}$ **23.** 20 **25.** 5 **27.** 24 **29.** 64 **31.** 15 **33.** 50

Skill 24

Solving a Rate Problem

1. $\frac{3 \text{ oranges}}{\$1.29} = \frac{7 \text{ oranges}}{n}$ **3.** $\frac{5 \text{ cm}}{40 \text{ kilometers}} = \frac{17 \text{ cm}}{n}$ **5.** \$7.10 **7.** 117 pp. **9.** $\frac{660 \text{ wheels}}{4 \text{ hours}} = \frac{n}{9 \text{ hours}}$; 1,485 wheels **11.** $\frac{\$0.67 \text{ wheels}}{3 \text{ min.}} = \frac{n}{14 \text{ min.}}$; \$3.13 **13.** $\frac{6\text{pp.}}{5 \text{ min.}} = \frac{40\text{pp.}}{n}$; $33\frac{1}{3}$ minutes

Skill 25

Comparing Rates **1.** 288 **3.** 80 km **5.** 64 km; 640 km **7.** A **9.** B **11.** B

Skill 26

Writing Decimals as Percents **1.** 10% **3.** 25% **5.** 82% **7.** 213% **9.** 575.3% **11.** 39.1% **13.** 1,210.4% **15.** 1,082% **17.** 10.6% **19.** 4% **21.** 50.3% **23.** 70% **25.** 710% **27.** 1,050% **29.** 1,260% **31.** 2,250% **33.** 3,720% **35.** 750% **37.** 1,630% **39.** 620% **41.** 380% **43.** 67% **45.** 880% **47.** 32% **49.** 300.3% **51.** 21.87% **53.** 2,500% **55.** 14% **57.** 51% **59.** 186.8% **61.** 0.3% **63.** 26% **65.** 0.32% **67.** 29% **69.** 342% **71.** 210% **73.** 167% **75.** 250% **77.** 207.7% **79.** 19%

Skill 27

Writing Fractions/Mixed Numbers as Percents **1.** 25% **3.** 75% **5.** 12.5% **7.** 35% **9.** 14% **11.** 62.5% **13.** 275% **15.** 666.7% **17.** 855.6% **19.** 817.5% **21.** 722% **23.** 537.5% **25.** 58.3% **27.** 1,530% **29.** 2,080% **31.** 1,862.5% **33.** 93.8% **35.** 1,135.7% **37.** 77.8% **39.** 573.3% **41.** 1,735%

Skill 28

Writing Percents as Decimals **1.** 0.105 **3.** 0.40 **5.** 1.20 **7.** 0.067 **9.** 0.089 **11.** 1.19 **13.** 0.172 **15.** 1.00 **17.** 0.053 **19.** 0.007 **21.** 0.00625 **23.** 0.056 **25.** 0.068 **27.** 0.306 **29.** 0.5784 **31.** 0.7425 **33.** 0.1880 **35.** 0.1445 **37.** 0.00125 **39.** 0.0014 **41.** 0.0879 **43.** 0.0095 **45.** 0.00025 **47.** 0.225 **49.** 0.252

Skill 29

Writing Percents as Fractions **1.** $\frac{9}{20}$ **3.** $1\frac{3}{4}$ **5.** $\frac{117}{1,000}$ **7.** $\frac{3}{2,000}$ **9.** $\frac{53}{500}$ **11.** $\frac{3,763}{10,000}$ **13.** $\frac{1}{2}$ **15.** $\frac{101}{1,000}$ **17.** $\frac{809}{1,000}$ **19.** $\frac{1}{16}$ **21.** $\frac{7}{16}$ **23.** $\frac{1}{400}$ **25.** $\frac{31}{200}$ **27.** $\frac{51}{200}$ **29.** $\frac{1}{6}$ **31.** $\frac{3}{10}$ **33.** $\frac{5}{16}$ **35.** $\frac{1}{8}$ **37.** $\frac{4}{15}$ **39.** $\frac{1}{9}$ **41.** $\frac{1}{2}$ **43.** $\frac{1}{80}$ **45.** $\frac{51}{400}$ **47.** $\frac{43}{800}$ **49.** $\frac{1}{15}$

Skill 30

Finding the Percentage **1.** 9 **3.** 3.84 **5.** 7.8 **7.** 14.24 **9.** 3.486 **11.** 45.359 **13.** 10 **15.** 40 **17.** 6 **19.** 2.25 **21.** 128 **23.** 8.19 **25.** 15 **27.** 2 **29.** 80 **31.** 9.144 **33.** 25 **35.** 6.375

Skill 31

Finding the Rate **1.** 50% **3.** 20% **5.** 35.7% **7.** 89.2% **9.** 69.9% **11.** 87.2% **13.** 150% **15.** 120% **17.** 133.3% **19.** 129.2% **21.** 400% **23.** 513.3% **25.** 80% **27.** 46.2% **29.** 55.1% **31.** 80% **33.** 120% **35.** 25% **37.** 138.9% **39.** 200% **41.** 66.7% **43.** 5% **45.** 146.7%

Skill 32

Finding the Base **1.** 72 **3.** 8,048.5 **5.** 1,600 **7.** 336.4 **9.** 60 **11.** 134 **13.** 160 **15.** 60 **17.** $90\frac{2}{3}$ **19.** $54\frac{86}{91}$ **21.** 75 **23.** 2.5 **25.** 52.5 **27.** 78 **29.** 180 **31.** 225 **33.** 55 **35.** $197\frac{1}{67}$

Applications Answers

Application A Answers **1.** 600 mi **3.** 448 m **5.** 210 m **7.** 1,216 sq ft **9.** 360 sq km **11.** 50 mi/h **13.** 62 mi/h **15.** 113.04 square feet **17.** 754.39 square feet **19.** $1.20 **21.** $68.20 **23.** $30.40

Application B Answers **1.** 308 in **3.** 8,775 yd **5.** 8 h **7.** 30 s **9.** 30 **11.** 248 **13.** 20 **15.** 50

Application C Answers **1.** $1,200,000 **3.** $7,900,000 **5.** Bronx, Columbus, Dallas, Lincoln, San Diego **7.** Western US zone and Overnight (By 3:00 PM) **9.** Eastern U.S. zone and Overnight (By 3:00 PM) **11.** $8.00

Application D Answers **1.** 1 quarter, 1 dollar, 1 $5 bill **3.** 1 penny, 3 dollars, 1 $5 bill **5.** 2 pennies, 1 dime, 1 quarter, 4 dollars **7.** 2 dimes, 3 quarters, 4 dollars **9.** 1 penny, 2 dimes, 2 quarters **11.** 1 quarter, 2 dollars **13.** 1 dime, 1 dollar, 1 $5 bill **15.** 1 quarter, 2 dollars **17.** 2 quarters, 1 dollar, 1 $10 bill

Application E Answers **1.** 8:45 **3.** 7:00 **5.** 11:15 **7.** 12:15 **9.** 3:30 **11.** 8:45 **13.** 7:30 **15.** 9:45 **17.** 12:45 **19.** 6:00 **21.** 11:30 **23.** 10:15

Application F Answers **1.** 2 h:46 min **3.** 3 h:15 min **5.** 51 min **7.** 5 h:15 min **9.** 8 h:20 min **11.** 10 h:45 min

Application G Answers **1.** 137 days **3.** 212 days **5.** 257 days

Application H Answers **1.** No **3.** Yes **5.** No **7.** Yes **9.** Yes **11.** Yes

Application I Answers **1.** 79 days **3.** 231 days **5.** 222 days

Application J Answers **1.** $\frac{3}{4}$ yr **3.** 1 yr **5.** 3 yr **7.** $1\frac{3}{4}$ yr **9.** $1\frac{1}{6}$ yr **11.** $\frac{5}{6}$ yr **13.** $\frac{35}{73}$ yr **15.** $\frac{50}{73}$ yr

Application K Answers **1.** 52 **3.** 16 **5.** 12 **7.** 6 **9.** 60

Application L Answers **1.** 0.85 **3.** 0.65 **5.** 0.20 **7.** 9% **9.** 53% **11.** 93% **13.** 96.5% **15.** 24.1%

Application M Answers **1.** $14.00 **3.** $13.00 **5.** About $4.00

Application N Answers **1.** $8,000 **3.** October and November **5.** Graph A is from 0 to 300; Graph B is from 150 to 300. **7.** Graph B

Application O Answers **1.** 32.5 hours **3.** 2.5 hours

Application P Answers **1.** $1,360 **3.** $480

5.

	Percent	Degrees
Food	40%	144
Rent	30%	108
Entertainment	15%	54
Clothing etc.	10%	36
Other	5%	18
	100%	360

Application Q Answers **1.** 54.3 **3.** 6,726.75 **5.** $1,235,563

Application R Answers **1.** 148.5 **3.** 88 **5.** 0.09 **7.** 2.08

Application S Answers **1.** \$24 **3.** None **5.** 0.01

Application T Answers **1. a.** 22.0 **b.** 47.2 **c.** 6.9 **d.** 19.0 **3. a.** 52.2 **b.** 15.4 **c.** 3.9 **d.** 12.0

Application U Answers

1.

Frequency Distribution		
Number of mpg	Tallies	Number of Cars
15 up to 19 mpg	///	3
19 up to 23 mpg	~~////~~ /	6
23 up to 27 mpg	~~////~~ //	7
27 up to 31 mpg	~~////~~	5
31 up to 35 mpg	///	3
Total		24

Application V Answers **1.** meter **3.** millimeter **5.** meter **7.** centimeter

Application W Answers **1.** kilogram **3.** gram **5.** metric ton **7.** kiloliter **9.** gram

Application X Answers **1.** 10.5 cm **3.** 2.6 ft **5.** 162 mi

Application Y Answers **1.** 12.56 mi **3.** 2.512 m **5.** 4.71 ft **7.** 56.52 ft **9.** 39.25 mi

Application Z Answers **1. a.** 60 in^2 **b.** 13 in **3. a.** 40 m^2 **b.** 9.4 m **5. a.** 12.25 yd^2 **b.** 4.9 yd

Application AA Answers **1.** 13.5 in^2 **3.** 200 m^2 **5.** 19.625 yd^2 **7.** 23,223.44 mm^2 **9.** The area increases to 96 square feet. It is four times the area of problem 8.

Application AB Answers **1. a.** 94 in^2 **b.** 60 in^3 **3.** 30 boxes **5. a.** 12,800 in^3 **b.** 8 **c.** 160

SELECTED ANSWERS

Glossary

A

account statement A bank statement that shows the status of your account, including all deposits to, withdrawals from, and interest earned and credited to your account.
accumulated depreciation The total depreciation of an item to date.
amount financed The portion of the cash price owed after making the down payment.
annual expense Expenses which occur only once a year, such as real estate taxes.
annual interest rate The percent of the principal earned as interest in one year.
annual percentage rate An index showing the cost of borrowing money on a yearly basis, expressed as a percent.
annual percentage yield (APY) The rate of return on your investment for a one-year period.
annual premium The amount you pay each year for insurance coverage.
annuity An account into which someone deposits an equal amount of money at equal periods or equal intervals of time.
annuity due An account in which equal deposits are made at the beginning of the interest period and start earning interest immediately.
assessed value The dollar value a tax assessor assigns to a property for taxation purposes.
assets The total of cash, items purchased, and any money that customers owe a business.
automated teller machine (ATM) Performs basic banking functions, such as handling check deposits or issuing cash withdrawals.
average-cost method A way of valuing inventory based on the average cost of goods received by a business.
average-daily-balance method Computing the finance charge on a credit account based on the average balance at the end of each day of the billing period.

B

balance The amount of money you have in an account.
balance sheet A statement that shows a company's total assets, total liabilities, and owner's equity on a given date.
bank statement From your bank, lists all activity in your account.
base price The price of the engine, chassis, and any other standard equipment for a particular model, referred to as the manufacturer's suggested retail price.
beneficiary The person who receives money from a life insurance policy if the insured dies.
bonds A written pledge from a business or government that indicates the holder has lent the issuer money and will be repaid, with interest, after a certain amount of time.
book value The approximate value of an item after it has been owned and depreciated for a period of time.
break-even analysis Determining how many units of a product must be made and sold to cover production expenses.
break-even point The point at which income from sales of a product equals the cost of producing the item.
budget A plan for using money in a way that meets your wants and needs.
budget sheet A record of monthly expenses.

C

capital The amount of owner's equity.
carrying inventory Maintaining adequate goods to meet production or sales needs.
cash discount A discount granted by a supplier if a bill is paid within a certain number of days, used to encourage prompt payment.
cash value The amount of money you will receive if you cancel your whole life insurance policy.
certificate of deposit A kind of savings account that requires a specific amount deposited for a specified period of time, and which earns a higher interest rate than a regular savings account.
chain discounts A sequence of trade discounts offered by a supplier, often to sell out a discontinued item or to encourage a customer to place a large order.
charge account An existing line of credit at the business that issued it.
check A paper document directing a bank to deduct money from your checking account and make a payment to the person named on the check.

check register A record of checking account deposits, withdrawals, and electronic transfers.

checking account A deposit account held at a bank that gives you convenient access to your money.

closed-end lease A contract that allows you the use of property, such as a vehicle, for a set time period by making a specified number of payments.

closing costs Costs associated with the transfer of property from the seller to the buyer, which may include fees for the property survey, loan application, document preparation, and points.

co-insurance Requires you to pay either a set amount or a certain percent of medical expenses.

collision insurance Pays for damage to the insured vehicle caused by a collision with another motor vehicle or an object such as a telephone pole.

commercial loans Loans made to businesses rather than individuals, also known as business loans.

commission An amount of money paid for selling a product or service.

commission rate A specified amount of money paid for each sale or a percent of the total value of sales.

comparison shopping Comparing prices to find the best value.

complement method A way of calculating the net price on items that are subject to a trade discount by subtracting the discount rate from 100 percent.

compound interest Interest earned not only on the original principal but also on the interest earned during previous interest periods, earning interest on interest.

compound interest table A tool to calculate compound interest quickly.

comprehensive insurance Pays for damage to the insured vehicle from losses due to fire, vandalism, theft, and just about any cause other than a collision.

consultant Professional adviser hired by a business to advise on a particular project.

consultant's fee Payment to a consultant for professional services, sometimes charged as a flat fee, a percent of the cost of the project, or by an hourly rate.

consumer price index Measures the upward changes on a fixed number of commodities and services, such as housing, electricity, food, and transportation, also known as the cost-of-living index.

co-payment A predetermined flat fee you pay for health care services.

corporation Businesses owned by stockholders.

cost The actual amount paid for a product, which can include freight charges, operating costs, and energy costs.

cost of goods sold The value of the beginning inventory plus the cost of any goods received, minus the value of the ending inventory.

cost-of-living adjustment A raise in an employee's salary to help keep up with inflation.

coupons Discounts offered by manufacturers, stores, and service establishments in the form of tickets that are redeemed at the time of purchase.

credit card A card authorizing purchases on credit.

current ratio The ratio of the total assets to total liabilities.

customer charge The basic monthly charge for electrical service.

D

daily compounding Interest that is computed each day and added to the account balance.

dealer's cost The price the dealer actually pays for a vehicle, usually expressed as a percent of the base price, plus a percept of the options price, plus the destination charge.

deductible The amount of money you must pay each year before your insurance company starts paying.

deductible clause A clause in an insurance policy that requires the insured to pay a certain amount before the insurance company pays.

deflation A decrease in the cost of goods and services over time, when the supply of goods is greater than the demand for them.

demand charge Part of the total cost for electrical service, based on a business's peak load each month.

deposit Checks, currency, or coins put into a banking account, savings and loan, credit union, or brokerage firm.

depreciation The decrease in the value of your vehicle from one year to the next because of its age and condition.

depreciation Spreading the cost of an item over its estimated life.

destination charge The cost of shipping a vehicle from the factory to the dealer.

direct deposit A deposit electronically transferred from your employer's checking account to your checking account.

direct labor cost The cost of labor used to make a product, including wages paid to employees.

direct material cost The cost of the goods or materials that are used to produce an item.

disability insurance Pays benefits to individuals who must miss work because of an injury or illness.

discount The difference between the face value and the maturity value of a bond or Treasury bill.

dividend Money earned as a shareholder of a corporation.

double time An overtime pay rate of twice the regular hourly rate.

down payment A portion of the cash price of an item you are purchasing which you pay before financing the rest on credit, usually required when purchasing an item with an installment loan.

E

emergency fund Extra money set aside to be used for unpredictable expenses, such as medical bills and vehicle repairs.

employee benefits Services offered by businesses to employees beyond salary or wages, such as health insurance, paid vacation, and a retirement plan.

end-of-month dating Terms of payment on an invoice from a supplier which grants a cash discount if a bill is paid within a certain number of days after the end of the month when the invoice is issued.

energy charge Part of the total cost for electrical service, based on the total number of kilowatt hours a business uses during the month.

equipment rental Renting or leasing office equipment or furniture, rather than buying the items.

estimated life The length of time, usually in years, an item is expected to last.

exact interest Interest on a loan calculated by basing the loan's time period on a 365-day year.

exemption Withholding allowances, which allow for supporting yourself, your spouse, and others in your family who are your dependents.

expenditures Items you spend money on.

expense summary A monthly report that compares the amounts that you have spent to the amounts that you have budgeted.

F

face value The amount of money you will receive on the maturity date of a bond or Treasury bill.

factor A company's present market share expressed as a percent.

factor method A method used to project a company's sales by multiplying the company's present market share by the projected sales for the entire market for the coming year.

federal income tax Money withheld by an employer from an employee's paycheck to pay federal government taxes.

final payment Payment on a simple interest loan that consists of the previous balance plus the current month's interest.

finance charge Interest charged by a credit card or charge account company for not paying the total amount owed by the due date.

financial literacy The ability to read, analyze, manage, and communicate about the personal financial conditions that affect a person's material well-being.

fire protection class A number assigned by an insurance company to a building that reflects how fire resistant it is and how close it is to a water source.

first in, first out (FIFO) A method for managing physical flow of inventory that assumes that the oldest inventory is sold first.

fixed costs Production or vehicle costs which remain about the same regardless of how much you produce or drive, such as building rent or vehicle registration.

fixed expenses Regular expenses which do not vary from one month to the next, such as rent.

fuel adjustment charge A charge added to an electricity bill to help cover increases in the cost of the fuel needed to produce electricity, sometimes called an energy cost adjustment.

G

graduated commission Pay based on a different rate of commission for each of several levels of sales.

graduated income tax A system that increases the tax rate at different levels of income.

gross domestic product (GDP) The total value of the goods and services produced in a country in a given year, used to monitor the health of a country's economy.

gross income The total amount paid during a pay period.

gross profit The difference between the cost of a product and the selling price when the selling price is higher, also known as the markup.

group insurance Health insurance offered by many businesses to employees, paid in part by the business and in part by the employee.

H

health insurance Provides financial protection against overwhelming medical expenses.

health maintenance organization (HMO) A prepaid health plan in which care providers contract with (or are) employees of the HMO to provide you with services.

homeowners insurance Provides financial protection for homeowners against various losses.
horizontal analysis Comparing two or more income statements for different periods by calculating the dollar amount and the percent change from one time period to another.
hourly rate A fixed amount of money paid for each hour of work.

I

income statement A statement that shows in detail a business's income and operating expenses, also called a profit-and-loss statement.
inflation A general increase in the cost of goods and services.
installment loan A loan you repay in equal payments over a specified period of time.
interest The amount of money paid for the use of a lender's money.
inventory The items that a business has in stock.
invoice An itemized list of the quantities and costs of items purchased.

K

kilowatts A unit of electrical power equal to 1,000 watts, used by power companies to measure energy use.

L

labor charge The cost of paying people to do a job, usually calculated on an hourly basis for each service person.
last in, first out (LIFO) A method for managing physical flow of inventory that assumes that the most recently purchased merchandise is the first to be sold.
lease An agreement for the use of property, such as a building or vehicle, usually on an annual basis.
liabilities The total amount of money owed to creditors.
liability insurance Provides financial protection to the policyholder against claims for bodily injury and property damage as a result of an accident.
life insurance Financial protection for a family in case the main source of income dies.
limited payment policy A whole life insurance policy that is paid up after a specified number of years, or until the insured reaches a certain age, but offers lifetime protection.
list price The price at which a business generally sells an item, also called the catalog price.
living expenses Routine expenses, including amounts for food, utility bills, and pocket expenses.
loading charge A fee paid to an investment company either when purchasing shares of a mutual fund or when selling shares, based on a percent of the amount invested.
loss When the amount of money received from the sale of a product or stock is less than the amount initially invested.
loss-of-use coverage Pays for the expenses for living away from home while your damaged home is being repaired.

M

manufactures Makes, or produces, a product.
markdown The difference between the regular selling price of an item and its sale price, also known as a discount.
markdown rate The markdown expressed as a percent of the regular selling price of the item.
market The total number of people who might purchase a product.
market share The percent of the entire market that purchases a product instead of a competing product.
market value The price at which a property can be bought or sold.
markup The difference between the cost of a product and the selling price when the selling price is higher, also known as the gross profit.
markup rate The markup on an item expressed as a percent of its selling price.
maturity value The total amount you must repay for a loan.
medical coverage Pays for medical expenses for nonfamily members accidentally injured on your property.
Medicare A federal government program to provide medical insurance.
merit increase A raise in salary to reward an employee for the quality of the work.
modified accelerated cost recovery system (MACRS) A method of computing depreciation by which assets can be depreciated fully over recovery periods of 4, 6, 8, 11, 16, or 21 years, according to fixed percents.
monthly service charge The base amount charged monthly by a utility, such as a phone company, to its customers for use of its services.
mortgage loan A long-term loan extended to someone to buy property.
mutual fund A kind of investment offered by an investment company, which accumulates the saving of many individuals and invests them in a portfolio of stocks, bonds, or both.

N

net asset value (NAV) The worth of a share of a mutual fund, determined by dividing the total market value by the number of shares outstanding.

net income Any money left over after expenses have been deducted from gross profits, also called net profit.

net pay The amount of money you have left after your employer subtracts all tax withholdings and personal deductions from your gross pay, also called net income or take-home pay.

net price The price actually paid for a discounted item.

net profit Any money left over after expenses have been deducted from gross profits, also called net income.

net worth The amount by which assets exceed liabilities.

net-price rate The percent of the price paid for an item, found by multiplying the complements of the chain discounts.

net-profit rate The net profit on an item expressed as a percent of the selling price.

O

online banking Internet banking allows you to view your account, pay bills, and transfer money any time.

open-end lease A contract allowing you the use of property, such as a vehicle, for a set time period by making a specified number of payments. At lease end, you can purchase the item for its residual value.

operating expenses Also known as overhead, the costs of running a business, such as wages and salaries of employees, rent, utility charges, and taxes.

opinion research firm A business that specializes in product testing and opinion surveys.

opinion survey A series of questions about a new product submitted to a panel of volunteers to find out how well the product will sell.

options Extra equipment on a vehicle for convenience, safety, or appearance, such as a sunroof, air conditioning, and tinted glass, which is not included in the base price.

ordinary annuity An account in which equal deposits are made at the end of each interest period.

ordinary dating Terms of payment on an invoice from a supplier which grants a cash discount if a bill is paid within a certain number of days.

ordinary interest Interest on a loan calculated by basing the loan's time period on a 360-day year.

overtime pay Extra pay for hours worked beyond the regular number of hours.

owner's equity Total assets owned minus total liabilities.

P

payroll register A record of the gross income, deductions, and net income of a company's employees.

peak load The greatest number of kilowatts a business uses at one time during a month, used to determine the demand charge.

per capita GDP The gross domestic product of a country distributed over the population, or the GDP per person, which indicates a nation's standard of living.

personal identification number (PIN) A personal number for an ATM card that gives you access to your bank account electronically.

personal liability coverage Provides financial protection for homeowners if someone alleges that their negligence caused him or her bodily injury or property damage while on the insured's property.

piecework A worker receives a specified amount of money for each item of work completed.

population and real gross domestic product The rate of population growth influences GDP and economic growth, as labor and size of population are closely linked.

preferred provider organization (PPO) A group of selected health care providers who offer comprehensive services at preset reimbursement levels.

premium The amount paid to an insurance company for insurance coverage.

pricing The process of assigning a selling price to a good or service.

prime costs The total of the direct material cost and the direct labor cost to make a product.

prime rate The lowest rate of interest available to commercial customers at a given time.

principal The amount of money earning interest.

product test Asking a group of people to try a new product, in order to learn their opinions and gauge how likely the product will sell.

profit The amount of money made on a product or an investment over and above the initial amount invested.

profit-and-loss statement A statement that shows in detail the income and operating expenses of a business, also called an income statement.

promissory note A written promise to pay a certain sum of money on a specific date in the future.
property damage coverage Provides financial protection against damage to one's home and personal property from fire, windstorm, rain, lightening, and other unpredictable events.
prospectus A formal written document that gives the facts about a new offering of securities.

R

rate of assessment The percent of a property's market value that is taxed.
real estate taxes Taxes collected by the city or county from homeowners to pay for roads, parks, schools, government offices, and other services.
real GDP The gross domestic product adjusted to include the effects of inflation.
rebates Discounts given by manufacturers, stores, and service establishments in the form of a refund.
reconcile To compare your check register with your bank statement to make sure they agree.
recordkeeping Keeping track of items you spend money on during a period of time, to help you manage your money.
recruiting The act of soliciting qualified people to work for a company.
release time Time an employee spends away from the job for which a business will still pay a regular salary, such as for a training program.
rent Agreeing to pay a set fee for the use of property, such as a vehicle or building, often on a daily, weekly, or monthly basis.
rental property Real estate available for or being rented and an alternative to investment opportunities available at financial institutions.
repayment schedule Shows the distribution of interest and principal over the life of a loan.
replacement value The amount required to reconstruct a home if it is destroyed.
required minimum distribution (RMD) The amount you are required to withdraw from a traditional IRA once you reach retirement age, based on life expectancy.
Roth IRA Individual retirement accounts, which mature with interest being tax free.

S

salary A fixed amount of money earned on a regular basis.
salary scale A table of wages or salaries that compares various jobs in a company, used to estimate the costs of giving an employee a cost-of-living adjustment or a merit increase.
sale price The regular selling price of an item minus the discount or markdown on the price.
sales potential An estimate of the sales volume of a product during a specified period of time.
sales projection An estimate of the dollar volume or unit sales of a product that might occur during a future time period.
sales receipt A proof of purchase that shows the selling price of each item or service purchased, the total selling price of all items purchased, any sales tax, and the total purchase amount.
sales tax A state or local tax on the selling price of an item or service you purchase, usually expressed as a percent.
salvage value The estimated trade-in, resale, or scrap value at the end of an item's expected life.
sample A selected group of people (who are representative of a much larger group) who try out a new product to find out how well the product will sell.
savings account A specific kind of savings account that earns interest.
security deposit Made when signing a lease, it is a one-time payment that may be used to pay for cleaning the apartment at termination of the rental agreement, to change the locks, or to repair damage to the rental unit.
selling price What a product sells for in a store, also known as retail price.
service charge Charges by a bank, for services rendered, to your account.
simple interest Interest paid only on the original principal.
simple interest installment loan The loan's monthly interest rate is applied to the unpaid balance of the loan, and if you wish to pay the loan off early, you pay the unpaid balance plus the interest on the unpaid balance up to the payoff date.
single-payment loan A loan you repay with one payment after a specified period of time.
Social Security A federal government program to pay for retirement and disability benefits.
sticker price The total cost of a new vehicle, including base price, options, and destination charge.
stock certificate Proof of ownership in a corporation.
stock reorder point The minimum level of inventory a business needs in order to meet customers' demands.
stocks Share of ownership in a corporation.
straight commission Pay that consists only of money earned from sales.

straight-line method A method of determining the annual depreciation of an item which assumes that the depreciation is the same from year to year.

straight-time pay The total amount of money earned for a pay period at the regular hourly rate.

T

tax rate The percent of income, sales, or property value collected in taxes. The tax rate on property is sometimes expressed in mills per dollar of the property's assessed value.

taxable income The portion of a company's gross income that remains after normal business expenses are deducted, upon which taxes are based.

term The amount of time for which a loan is granted.

term life insurance Life insurance for a specified term, such as five years, or to a specified age.

time and a half An overtime pay rate of $1\frac{1}{2}$ times the regular hourly rate.

total purchase price The total selling price plus the sales tax.

trade discount A discount from the list price.

trade-discount rate The amount of the discount of an item expressed as a percent of the list price.

traditional IRA Individual retirement accounts, which mature with interest being tax deferred.

traditional plan Offers health care coverage where the health care provider is paid a predetermined dollar amount for the service given.

travel expenses Costs required for business travel, such as transportation, lodging, and meals, which are often reimbursed by a company.

Treasury bill A bill that can be purchased from the federal government in various amounts and that pays interest. It is a loan to the government, also known as "T-bill."

U

underwriting commission An amount of money paid to an investment banker who a business hires to distribute stocks or bonds.

unit pricing A technique that allows shoppers to compare the prices of various items.

universal life insurance A combination of a life insurance policy and a savings account. It covers the insured for his or her lifetime, and any amount the insured pays over the minimum premium goes into an investment account that earns interest.

unpaid-balance method Computing the finance charge on a credit account based on the portion of the previous monthly balance you have not paid.

used-vehicle guide Guides published monthly that give the average prices for used vehicles that were purchased from dealers during the previous month.

utilities Public services, such as telephone, electricity, water, and gas.

utility costs The costs of services such as electricity, gas, water, telephone, cell phone, cable TV, Internet service, and heating fuel.

V

variable costs Costs of producing a product that vary directly with the number of units produced, such as raw materials and packaging. Also, vehicle costs that increase the more you drive, such as gasoline and tires.

vertical analysis Used to find what percent any item in a financial statement is of the totals in the statement.

W

weekly time card A daily record of the time you report to work and the time you depart.

whole life insurance Also known as permanent life insurance, offers financial protection for your entire life.

withdrawal Money taken out of a bank account.

withholding allowance The number of people an employee supports, which helps employers know how much money to withhold for federal income tax.

workers compensation insurance Covers employees' medical expenses and lost wages if they are hurt on the job.

Y

yield The rate of return, usually expressed as a percent, on a stock, bond, Treasury bill, or savings account earned by an investor after a certain period of time.

Glosario

A

account statement/estado de cuenta Un estado bancario que muestra el estatus de su cuenta, incluyendo todos los depósitos a, extracciones de e intereses devengados y acreditados a su cuenta.

accumulated depreciation/depreciación acumulada La depreciación total de un artículo hasta la fecha.

amount financed/monto financiado La parte del precio en efectivo adeudada después del pago inicial.

annual expense/gastos anuales Gastos que ocurren una vez al año, tales como los impuestos inmobiliarios.

annual interest rate/tasa de interés anual El porcentaje del principal percibido en un año en forma de interés.

annual percentage rate/tasa de porcentaje anual Un índice que muestra el costo anual de un préstamo de dinero, expresado como porcentaje.

annual percentage yield (APY)/porcentaje anual de rendimiento (APY, por sus siglas en inglés) La tasa a la cual el dinero devenga un interés simple en un año; también denominado rendimiento anual efectivo.

annual premium/prima anual El monto que usted paga cada año para cobertura de seguro.

annuity/anualidad Una cuenta en la cual una persona deposita la misma cantidad de dinero en períodos o intervalos iguales de tiempo.

annuity due/anualidad vencida Una cuenta en la cual se realizan depósitos iguales al comienzo del período de interés y comienza a devengar interés inmediatamente.

assessed value/valor evaluado El valor en dólares que un tasador asigna a un bien con fines impositivos.

assets/activos El total de efectivo, bienes comprados, y dinero que los clientes le deben a un negocio.

automated teller machine (ATM)/cajero automático (ATM, por sus siglas en inglés) Realiza funciones bancarias básicas, tales como aceptar depósitos de cheques o emitir extracciones de dinero en efectivo.

average-cost method/método del costo promedio Una forma de evaluar el inventario en base al costo promedio de la mercadería recibida por un negocio.

average-daily-balance method/método del saldo promedio diario El cálculo de los costos financieros de una cuenta de crédito en base al saldo promedio al final de cada día del período de facturación.

B

balance/saldo El monto de dinero que tiene en una cuenta.

balance sheet/balance general Un estado de cuenta que muestra el total de activos y pasivos de una empresa, y el capital del propietario, en cualquier fecha.

bank statement/estado de cuenta bancario Proviene de su banco, e incluye toda la actividad registrada en su cuenta.

base price/precio base El precio del motor, chasis y cualquier otro equipo estándar de un modelo en particular, al que se conoce como precio de venta recomendado por el fabricante.

beneficiary/beneficiario La persona que recibe dinero de una póliza de seguro de vida si el asegurado muere.

bonds/bonos Una garantía por escrito de un negocio o gobierno que indica que el tenedor ha prestado dinero al emisor, el cual le será devuelto con intereses después de una cierta cantidad de tiempo.

book value/valor contable El valor aproximado de un artículo después de haber pertenecido a alguien y haberse depreciado por un período de tiempo.

break-even analysis/análisis de equilibrio Determinar cuántas unidades de un producto se deben fabricar y vender para cubrir los gastos de producción.

break-even point/punto de equilibrio El punto en el que los ingresos de las ventas de un producto equiparán el costo de la fabricación del mismo.

budget/presupuesto Un plan para usar dinero de manera que satisfaga sus deseos y necesidades.

budget sheet/planilla de presupuesto Un registro de los gastos mensuales.

C

capital/capital La cantidad de recursos propios de los propietarios.

carrying inventory/inventario continuo o perpetuo Mantener la cantidad adecuada de mercadería para satisfacer las necesidades de producción o ventas.

cash discount/descuento en efectivo Un descuento otorgado por un proveedor cuando la factura se abona dentro de un cierto número de días; se utiliza para incentivar el "pronto pago."

cash value/valor en efectivo El monto de dinero que recibirá si cancela su póliza de seguro de vida entera.

certificate of deposit/certificado de depósito Un tipo de cuenta de ahorro que requiere depositar un monto específico de dinero por un período de tiempo específico, y devenga una tasa de interés superior que una cuenta de ahorros común.

chain discounts/descuentos en cadena Una secuencia de descuentos comerciales ofrecidos por un proveedor, la mayoría de las veces para agotar todas las existencias de un artículo fuera de fabricación o para incentivar al cliente a hacer grandes volúmenes de pedidos.

charge acount/cuenta de crédito Una línea de crédito existente con el negocio que la emitió.

check/cheque Un documento impreso que autoriza a un banco a deducir dinero de su cuenta corriente y efectuar un pago a la persona indicada en el cheque.

check register/registro de cheques Un registro de los depósitos, extracciones y transferencias electrónicas de una cuenta corriente.

checking account/cuenta corriente Una cuenta de depósito mantenida en un banco que le da acceso conveniente a su dinero.

closed-end lease/arrendamiento cerrado Un contrato que le permite usar un bien, tal como un vehículo, durante un período de tiempo fijo, efectuando una cantidad determinada de pagos.

closing costs/costos de cierre Costos correspondientes a la transferencia de un bien inmueble del vendedor al comprador, puede incluir cargos por la inspección de la propiedad, la solicitud del préstamo, la preparación de la documentación y los puntos.

co-insurance/coseguro Le exige pagar ya sea un monto especificado o un determinado porcentaje de los gastos médicos.

collision insurance/seguro de colisión Paga por los daños al vehículo asegurado como consecuencia de un choque con otro vehículo automotor o con un objeto, tal como un poste telefónico.

commercial loans/préstamos comerciales Préstamos hechos a un negocio, en lugar de a una persona; también denominados préstamos empresariales.

commission/comisión Monto de dinero abonado por la venta de un producto o servicio.

commission rate/tasa de comisión Un monto específico de dinero pagado por cada venta o un porcentaje del valor total de las ventas.

comparison shopping/comparación de precios Comparar los precios para encontrar el mejor valor.

complement method/método complementario Una forma de calcular el precio neto de los artículos sujetos a un descuento comercial, restando la tasa de descuento del 100 por ciento.

compound interest/interés compuesto Interés devengado no sólo sobre el capital original sino también sobre el interés devengado durante los períodos de interés anteriores; ganar intereses sobre intereses.

compound interest table/tabla de interés compuesto Una herramienta para calcular rápidamente el interés compuesto.

comprehensive insurance/seguro contra todo riesgo Pago por los daños que el vehículo asegurado haya sufrido como consecuencia de incendio, vandalismo, robo y prácticamente toda otra causa, excepto un choque.

consultant/consultor(a) Asesor(a) profesional contratado(a) por un negocio para prestar servicios de consultoría sobre un proyecto en particular.

consultant's fee/tarifa por servicios de consultoría Pago a un(a) consultor(a) en concepto de servicios profesionales, ya sea mediante una tarifa fija, un porcentaje del costo del proyecto o por hora.

consumer price index/índice de precios de consumo Mide los cambios ascendentes de un número fijo de bienes de consumo y servicios, tales como vivienda, electricidad, alimentación y transporte, conocido también como "índice del costo de vida."

co-payment/copago Una tarifa fija, predeterminada, que se paga para obtener servicios médicos.

corporation/corporación Empresa que es propiedad de los accionistas.

cost/costo El monto real pagado por un producto, que puede incluir cargos operativos, de flete y de energía.

cost of goods sold/costo de ventas El valor del inventario inicial más el costo de toda mercadería recibida, menos el valor del inventario final.

GLOSARIO

cost-of-living adjustment/ajuste del costo de vida Un aumento en el salario de un empleado para mantenerse al día con la inflación.

coupons/cupones Descuentos ofrecidos por los fabricantes, comercios y establecimientos de servicios bajo la forma de boletos que se canjean al momento de la compra.

credit card/tarjeta de crédito Una tarjeta que permite efectuar compras a crédito.

current ratio/coeficiente de solvencia El índice del total de activos frente al total de pasivos.

customer charge/cargo al cliente El cargo mensual básico por servicios eléctricos.

D

daily compounding/interés compuesto diario Interés que se calcula cada día y se agrega al saldo de la cuenta.

dealer's cost/costo del comerciante El precio real que el concesionario paga por un vehículo, generalmente expresado como un porcentaje del precio base, más un porcentaje del precio de las opciones, más el cargo de envío.

deductible/deducible El monto de dinero que debe pagar cada año antes de que su seguro comience a realizar los pagos.

deductible clause/cláusula de deducible Una cláusula en una póliza de seguro que requiere que el asegurado pague un determinado monto antes de que la compañía de seguro efectúe el pago.

deflation/deflación Una disminución del costo de la mercadería y servicios a lo largo del tiempo, cuando el suministro de los productos supera la demanda de los mismos.

demand charge/cobro por demanda Parte del costo total en concepto de servicios eléctricos, basado en la carga máxima mensual de un negocio.

deposit/depósito Cheques, divisas o monedas colocadas en una cuenta bancaria, asociación de ahorros y préstamos, uniones de crédito o empresas de corretaje.

depreciation/depreciación La disminución del valor de su vehículo de un año a otro como consecuencia de su antigüedad o estado.

depreciation/depreciación Distribuir el costo de un artículo a lo largo de su estimada vida útil.

destination charge/cargo de destino El costo de enviar un vehículo desde la fábrica al concesionario.

direct deposit/depósito directo Un depósito transferido electrónicamente desde la cuenta corriente del empleador a la cuenta corriente del empleado.

direct labor cost/costo de mano de obra directa El costo de la mano de obra utilizada para fabricar un producto, incluyendo los salarios pagados a los empleados.

direct material cost/costo de material directo El costo de las mercaderías o materiales que se usan para producir un artículo.

disability insurance/seguro de discapacidad Paga beneficios a personas que tienen que faltar al trabajo como consecuencia de una lesión o enfermedad.

discount/descuento La diferencia entre el valor nominal y el valor de vencimiento de un bono o letra del Tesoro.

dividend/dividendo Dinero ganado como accionista de una corporación.

double time/tiempo doble Una tasa de pago de tiempo extra equivalente al doble de la tasa de pago regular por hora.

down payment/pago inicial Una parte del precio en efectivo de un artículo que está comprando y que se paga antes de la financiación a crédito del resto; generalmente se requiere cuando se compra un artículo con un préstamo a plazos.

E

emergency fund/fondo para emergencias Dinero extra separado que es usado para gastos imprevistos, tales como gastos médicos y reparación de vehículos.

employee benefits/beneficios del empleado Servicios ofrecidos por negocios a los empleados, además del salario o sueldo, tales como seguro médico, vacaciones pagadas y un plan de jubilación.

end-of-month dating/fecha de fin de mes Términos de pago de la factura de un proveedor que otorgan un descuento en efectivo si la factura se paga dentro de un cierto número de días después del final del mes en el que se emitió la factura.

energy charge/cargo por electricidad Parte del costo total del servicio eléctrico, en base al número total de kilovatios-hora que un negocio consume durante el mes.

equipment rental/alquiler de equipos Alquilar o arrendar equipo o mobiliario de oficina en lugar de comprarlo.

estimated life/vida útil estimada La duración de tiempo, generalmente en años, que se anticipa durará un artículo.

exact interest/interés exacto Interés sobre un préstamo, calculado basando el período de tiempo del préstamo en un año de 365 días.

exemption/exención Retención de deducciones que le permiten mantenerse a usted mismo, a su cónyuge y a otros miembros de su familia que estén a su cargo.

expenditures/gastos Artículos en los que gasta dinero.

expense summary/resumen de gastos Un informe mensual que compara los montos que ha gastado con los que ha presupuestado.

F

face value/valor nominal El monto de dinero que recibirá en la fecha de vencimiento de un bono o letra del Tesoro.

factor/factor La participación de mercado actual de una empresa expresada como porcentaje.

factor method/método de factores Método utilizado para proyectar las ventas de una empresa multiplicando la participación de mercado actual por las ventas proyectadas para todo el mercado durante el año siguiente.

federal income tax/impuesto federal sobre la renta Dinero que un empleador retiene del cheque de un empleado para pagar los impuestos del gobierno federal.

final payment/pago final Pago de un préstamo con interés simple que consiste en el saldo anterior más los intereses del mes en curso.

finance charge/cargo por financiamiento Interés cobrado por una empresa de tarjetas de crédito o cuenta corriente por no pagar el monto total adeudado en la fecha de vencimiento.

financial literacy/conocimientos financieros La capacidad de poder leer, analizar, administrar y comunicar las condiciones financieras personales que afectan al bienestar material de una persona.

fire protection class/clase asignada a la protección contra incendios Un número asignado por una compañía de seguros a un edificio, que refleja su nivel de resistencia a incendios y su proximidad a una boca de incendio.

first in, first out (FIFO)/método de primeras entradas, primeras salidas (FIFO, por sus siglas en inglés) Método para administrar el flujo físico del inventario que supone que el inventario más antiguo es el primero en venderse.

fixed costs/costos fijos Costos de producción o vehículos que permanecen más o menos igual, independientemente de su producción o uso, tales como alquiler de vivienda o registro de vehículos.

fixed expenses/gastos fijos Gastos regulares que no varían de un mes al siguiente, tales como el alquiler.

fuel adjustment charge/cargo por ajuste de combustible Cargo agregado a la factura de electricidad para ayudar a cubrir los aumentos en el costo del combustible necesario para producir electricidad; a veces denominado ajuste del costo de la energía.

G

graduated commission/comisión escalonada Pago basado en un porcentaje de comisión diferente de acuerdo con cada uno de los diferentes niveles de ventas.

graduated income tax/impuesto escalonado sobre la renta Un sistema que aumenta la tasa tributaria según los diferentes niveles de ingresos.

gross domestic product (GDP)/producto bruto interno (PBI) El valor total de la mercadería y servicios producidos en un país en un año dado; utilizado para controlar el estado de la economía de un país.

gross income/ingresos brutos El monto total pagado durante un período de pago.

gross profit/ganancia bruta La diferencia entre el costo de un producto y el precio de venta cuando este último es mayor; también denominado margen de ganancias.

group insurance/seguro de grupo Seguro médico ofrecido por muchos negocios a sus empleados, pagado en parte por el negocio y en parte por el empleado.

H

health insurance/seguro médico Proporciona protección financiera contra gastos médicos que son demasiado altos.

health maintenance organization (HMO)/ Organización para el Mantenimiento de la Salud (HMO, por sus siglas en inglés) Un plan médico prepagado en el cual los proveedores médicos tienen un contrato con la HMO (o son empleados de la misma) para proporcionarle servicios a usted.

horizontal analysis/análisis horizontal Comparación de dos o más estados de resultados de diferentes períodos mediante el cálculo del monto en dólares y el cambio porcentual de un período de tiempo a otro.

hourly rate/tarifa horaria o por hora Un monto fijo de dinero pagado por cada hora de trabajo.

I

income statement/estado de resultados Un estado que muestra en detalle los ingresos y gastos operativos de un negocio; también denominado estado de ganancias y pérdidas.

inflation/inflación Aumento general en el costo de la mercadería y servicios.

installment loan/préstamo a plazos Un préstamo que se debe saldar en pagos iguales a lo largo de un período de tiempo específico.

interest/interés El monto de dinero pagado por el uso del dinero del prestamista.

inventory/inventario Los artículos que un negocio tiene en existencias.

invoice/factura Una lista detallada de las cantidades y los costos de los artículos comprados.

K

kilowatts/kilovatios Unidad de potencia eléctrica equivalente a 1,000 vatios, utilizada por las empresas eléctricas para medir el uso de la energía eléctrica.

L

labor charge/costo de mano de obra El costo de pagarle a las personas por el trabajo que hacen; generalmente calculado por hora para cada persona que presta el servicio.

last in, first out (LIFO)/método de últimas entradas, primeras salidas (LIFO, por sus siglas en inglés) Método para administrar el flujo físico del inventario, que supone que la mercadería comprada más recientemente es la primera en venderse.

lease/arrendamiento Un acuerdo para el uso de un bien, tal como un edificio o vehículo, generalmente durante un año.

liabilities/pasivos El monto total de dinero adeudado a los acreedores.

liability insurance/seguro de responsabilidad civil Proporciona protección financiera al titular de la póliza contra reclamos por lesiones corporales y daños a la propiedad como resultado de un accidente.

life insurance/seguro de vida Protección financiera para una familia en caso de muerte de la persona que es la fuente principal de ingresos.

limited payment policy/póliza de pagos limitados Una póliza de seguro de vida entera que se paga después de una cantidad de años específica o hasta que el asegurado llega a cierta edad, pero que ofrece protección vitalicia.

list price/precio de lista El precio al que, generalmente, un negocio vende un artículo; también denominado precio de catálogo.

living expenses/gastos de subsistencia Gastos habituales, incluyendo los gastos de alimentos, servicios públicos y gastos de bolsillo.

loading charge/gastos de gestión Una tarifa pagada a una compañía inversionista ya sea cuando se compren o se vendan acciones de un fondo mutuo, en base a un porcentaje del monto invertido.

loss/pérdida Cuando el monto de dinero recibido de la venta de un producto o una acción es inferior al monto invertido inicialmente.

loss-of-use coverage/cobertura por privación de uso Paga por los gastos incurridos por vivir fuera de casa mientras su vivienda dañada está siendo reparada.

M

manufactures/fabricantes Fabrican o producen un producto.

markdown/rebaja La diferencia entre el precio de venta regular de un artículo y su precio de oferta; también denominado descuento.

markdown rate/índice de rebaja La rebaja expresada como un porcentaje del precio de venta regular de un artículo.

market/mercado El número total de personas que podrían comprar un producto.

market share/participación de mercado El porcentaje del mercado total que compra un producto, en lugar de comprar un producto de la competencia.

market value/valor de mercado El precio al cual se puede comprar o vender un bien.

markup/margen de ganancia La diferencia entre el costo de un producto y el precio de venta cuando este último es mayor; también denominado ganancia bruta.

markup rate/tasa de margen de ganancia El margen de ganancia de un artículo expresado como un porcentaje de su precio de venta.

maturity value/valor de vencimiento El monto total que debe pagar por un préstamo.

medical coverage/cobertura médica Paga los gastos médicos de personas que no sean sus familiares y que se hayan lesionado accidentalmente en su propiedad.

Medicare/Medicare Un programa del gobierno federal que proporciona seguro médico.

merit increase/aumento salarial por mérito Un aumento en el salario para recompensar a un empleado por la calidad de su trabajo.

modified accelerated cost recovery system (MACRS)/sistema modificado de recuperación acelerada de costo (MACRS, por sus siglas en inglés) Método de cálculo de la depreciación mediante el cual se pueden depreciar completamente los activos a lo largo de períodos de recuperación de 4, 6, 8, 11, 16 ó 21 años, según porcentajes fijos.

monthly service charge/cargo mensual por servicios El monto base que una empresa de servicios públicos—por ejemplo, una empresa telefónica—cobra mensualmente a sus clientes por el uso de sus servicios.

mortgage loan/préstamo hipotecario Un préstamo para bienes inmuebles que otorga al prestamista, generalmente un banco, una asociación de ahorro y préstamos, una cooperativa de crédito o una compañía hipotecaria, el derecho de recuperar y vender la propiedad si el prestatario no efectúa los pagos del préstamo.

mutual fund/fondo mutuo Tipo de inversión ofrecida por una empresa inversionista que acumula los ahorros de muchas personas y los invierte en una cartera de acciones, bonos o ambos.

N

net asset value (NAV)/valor neto de los activos (NAV, por sus siglas en inglés) El valor de la acción de un fondo mutuo; se determina dividiendo el valor total de mercado por el número de acciones en circulación.

net income/ingreso neto Todo el dinero restante una vez deducidos los gastos de las ganancias brutas; también denominado beneficio neto.

net pay/pago neto La cantidad de dinero que le queda después de que su empleador resta las retenciones fiscales y deducciones personales de su pago bruto; también denominado ingreso neto o sueldo neto.

net price/precio neto El precio real pagado por un artículo en oferta.

net profit/beneficio neto Todo el dinero que queda una vez deducidos los gastos de las ganancias brutas; también denominado ingreso neto.

net worth/capital neto El monto por el cual los activos superan a los pasivos.

net-price rate/tasa de precio neto El porcentaje del precio pagado por un artículo, determinado multiplicando los complementos de los descuentos en cadena.

net-profit rate/tasa de beneficio neto El beneficio neto de un artículo expresado como un porcentaje del precio de venta.

O

open-end lease/arrendamiento abierto Un contrato que le permite usar un bien, tal como un vehículo, durante un período de tiempo fijo, efectuando una cantidad determinada de pagos. Al final del arrendamiento, puede comprar el artículo por su valor residual.

operating expenses/gastos operativos También denominados gastos generales; los costos de administrar un negocio, tales como sueldos y salarios de los empleados, alquiler, cargos por servicios públicos e impuestos.

opinion research firm/empresa de investigación de mercado Compañía especializada en la prueba de productos y encuestas de opinión.

opinion survey/encuesta de opinión Una serie de preguntas sobre un nuevo producto presentada a un panel de voluntarios para determinar cuán exitosa será la venta del producto.

options/opciones Equipamiento adicional en un vehículo con fines de conveniencia, seguridad o estética, tales como techo corredizo, aire acondicionado y vidrios polarizados, que no está incluido en el precio base.

ordinary annuity/anualidad ordinaria Una cuenta en la cual se efectúan depósitos iguales al final de cada período de interés.

ordinary dating/fecha ordinaria Términos de pago de una factura de un proveedor que otorga un descuento en efectivo si la factura se abona dentro de un determinado número de días.

ordinary interest/interés ordinario Interés sobre un préstamo calculado basando el período de tiempo del préstamo en un año de 360 días.

overtime pay/pago de horas extras Pago adicional por horas trabajadas fuera del número de horas regulares.

owner's equity/recursos propios del propietario Total de activos menos el total de pasivos.

P

payroll register/registro de nómina Registro de los ingresos brutos, deducciones e ingresos netos de los empleados de una empresa.

peak load/carga máxima El mayor número de kilovatios que un negocio utiliza en un determinado momento durante un mes; se usa para determinar el cobro por demanda.

per capita GDP/PBI (producto bruto interno) per cápita El producto bruto interno de un país distribuido entre toda la población o el PBI por persona, lo cual indica el nivel de vida del país.

personal identification number (PIN)/ número de identificación personal (PIN, por sus siglas en inglés) Un número personal en una tarjeta de cajero automático que le da acceso electrónico a su cuenta bancaria.

personal liability coverage/seguro de responsabilidad personal Proporciona protección financiera al propietario de una vivienda en caso de que alguien alegue haber sufrido lesiones corporales o daños a la propiedad mientras estaba en la propiedad del asegurado, por negligencia del propietario.

piecework/trabajo a destajo Un trabajador recibe una cantidad específica de dinero por cada pieza de trabajo completada.

population and real gross domestic product/población y producto bruto interno real El índice de crecimiento de la población ejerce influencia sobre el PBI y el desarrollo económico, dado que la mano de obra y el número de habitantes están estrechamente relacionados.

preferred provider organization (PPO)/ Organización de Proveedores Preferidos (PPO, por sus siglas en inglés) Un grupo selecto de proveedores de servicios médicos que ofrecen servicios integrales a niveles de reembolso preestablecidos.

premium/prima El monto de dinero que se paga a una compañía de seguros en concepto de cobertura de seguro.

pricing/aplicación de precio El proceso de asignar un precio a un bien o un servicio.

prime costs/costos primarios El total del costo directo de materiales y de mano de obra necesarios para fabricar un producto.

prime rate/tasa preferencial El tipo de interés más bajo disponible para los clientes comerciales en un momento dado.

principal/principal El monto de dinero que devenga intereses.

product test/prueba de productos Pedir a un grupo de personas que prueben un producto nuevo para conocer su opinión y medir las probabilidades de venta del producto.

profit/ganancia El monto de dinero obtenido con un producto o una inversión por sobre el monto inicial invertido.

profit-and-loss statement/estado de ganancias y pérdidas Un estado que muestra en detalle los ingresos y gastos operativos de un negocio; también denominado estado de resultados.

promissory note/pagaré Una promesa por escrito de pagar una determinada suma de dinero en una fecha futura específica.

property damage coverage/cobertura contra daños a la propiedad Proporciona protección financiera contra los daños a la vivienda y bienes personales como consecuencia de incendio, tormentas de viento, lluvia, rayos y demás acontecimientos imprevisibles.

prospectus/folleto informativo Un documento formal por escrito que proporciona información sobre una nueva oferta de valores.

R

rate of assessment/tipo de tasación El porcentaje del valor de mercado de una propiedad sujeto a impuestos.

real estate taxes/impuestos inmobiliarios Impuestos cobrados por la ciudad o el condado a los propietarios de vivienda para pagar por los trabajos viales, escuelas, oficinas gubernamentales y otros servicios.

real GDP/PBI real El producto bruto interno ajustado para incluir los efectos de la inflación.

rebates/reembolsos Descuentos otorgados por los fabricantes, negocios y establecimientos de servicios bajo la forma de un reintegro de dinero.

reconcile/conciliar Comparar su chequera con el estado de cuenta bancario para verificar que ambos coinciden.

recordkeeping/gestión de registros Llevar un seguimiento de los artículos en los que gasta dinero durante un período de tiempo, para ayudarle a administrar su dinero.

recruiting/reclutamiento Ofrecer trabajo en una empresa a personas que reúnan las condiciones necesarias.

release time/tiempo de capacitación con goce de sueldo El tiempo que un empleado pasa fuera del trabajo, pero por el cual la empresa sigue pagando el salario regular, tal como para programas de capacitación.

rent/alquiler o renta Aceptar pagar una tarifa establecida por el uso de un bien, tal como un vehículo o una propiedad, a menudo en forma diaria, semanal o mensual.

rental property/propiedad de alquiler o renta Bien inmueble disponible para su alquiler/ renta o en alquiler/renta, como alternativa a oportunidades de inversión disponibles en instituciones financieras.

repayment schedule/plan de amortización Muestra la distribución de interés y principal durante toda la vida de un préstamo.

replacement value/valor de reemplazo El monto requerido para reconstruir una vivienda destruida.

required minimum distribution (RMD)/ distribución mínima requerida (RMD, por sus siglas en inglés) El monto que debe retirar de una cuenta IRA tradicional una vez alcanzada la edad de jubilación, basándose en la expectativa de vida.

Roth IRA/cuenta individual de jubilación Roth (IRA, por sus siglas en inglés) Cuentas individuales de jubilación a cuyo vencimiento los intereses no están sujetos al pago de impuestos.

S

salary/salario Un monto fijo de dinero ganado en forma regular.

salary schedule/escala salarial Una tabla de sueldos y salarios que compara varios puestos en una empresa y se usa para calcular los costos de otorgarle a un empleado un ajuste del costo de vida o un aumento salarial por mérito.

sale price/precio de oferta El precio de venta regular de un artículo menos el descuento o rebaja sobre dicho precio.

sales potential/potencial de ventas Un estimado del volumen de ventas de un producto durante un período de tiempo especificado.

sales projection/proyección de ventas Un cálculo del volumen, en dólares o las unidades de venta, de un producto que podría ocurrir durante un período de tiempo futuro.

sales receipt/recibo de venta Un comprobante de venta que muestra el precio de venta de cada artículo o servicio comprado, el precio de venta total de todos los artículos comprados, el impuesto total sobre las ventas y la cantidad total comprada.

sales tax/impuesto sobre las ventas Impuesto estatal o local sobre el precio de venta de un artículo o servicio que usted compra, generalmente expresado en cifras porcentuales.

salvage value/valor residual El valor estimado de canje, reventa o desecho al final de la vida útil de un artículo.

sample/muestra Un grupo selecto de personas (representativo de un grupo mucho más amplio) que prueban un producto nuevo para determinar el nivel de ventas que tendrá dicho producto.

savings account/cuenta de ahorros Un tipo específico de cuenta de ahorros que devenga intereses.

security deposit/depósito de garantía Se efectúa al firmar un contrato de alquiler/ renta o arrendamiento; es un pago que se hace por única vez y puede ser utilizado para pagar por la limpieza del apartamento al término del contrato de alquiler/renta, para cambiar las cerraduras o para reparar los daños de la unidad en alquiler/renta.

selling price/precio de venta El precio al cual se vende un producto en un negocio; también denominado precio de venta al público.

service charge/cobro por servicios Los cobros del banco a su cuenta por los servicios proporcionados.

simple interest/interés simple Interés pagado solamente sobre el principal original.

simple interest installment loan/préstamo a plazos con interés simple El tipo de interés mensual del préstamo se aplica al saldo adeudado de un préstamo, y si desea pagar el préstamo por adelantado, debe pagar el saldo adeudado más los intereses del mismo hasta la fecha de cancelación del pago.

single-payment loan/préstamo de pago único Un préstamo que se paga mediante un solo pago después de un período de tiempo específico.

Social Security/Seguro Social Un programa del gobierno federal que paga beneficios de jubilación y discapacidad.

sticker price/precio de venta al público El costo total de un vehículo nuevo, incluido el precio base, las opciones y el cobro de envío.

stock certificate/certificado de acciones Prueba de propiedad de las acciones de una corporación.

stock reorder point/nivel de pedido de inventario El nivel mínimo de inventario que un negocio necesita para satisfacer la demanda de los clientes.

stocks/acciones Participación de propiedad en una corporación.

straight commission/comisión directa Pago que se realiza solamente en base al dinero obtenido de las ventas.

straight-line method/método de amortización lineal Método para determinar la depreciación anual de un artículo que supone que la depreciación es la misma de un año a otro.

straight-time pay/salario básico El monto total de dinero ganado en un período de pago a la tarifa horaria regular.

T

tax rate/tasa impositiva El porcentaje de los ingresos, ventas o valor de un bien inmueble cobrado en impuestos. En ocasiones, la tasa impositiva sobre los bienes inmuebles se expresa en milésimas de dólar del valor del inmueble tasado.

taxable income/ingresos imponibles La parte que queda de los ingresos brutos de una empresa una vez deducidos los gastos comerciales, sobre la cual se basan los impuestos.

term/término La cantidad de tiempo por la cual se otorga un préstamo.

term life insurance/seguro de vida a plazo fijo Seguro de vida por un término específico, por ejemplo, 5 años, o hasta una edad específica.

time and a half/tiempo y medio Una tarifa de pago de tiempo extra de 1 ½ veces la tarifa regular por hora.

total purchase price/precio de compra total El precio de venta total más el impuesto sobre las ventas.

trade discount/descuento comercial Un descuento sobre el precio de lista.

trade-discount rate/índice de descuento comercial El monto de descuento de un artículo expresado como un porcentaje del precio de lista.

traditional IRA/cuenta individual de jubilación tradicional (IRA, por sus siglas en inglés) Cuentas individuales de jubilación con impuestos diferidos.

traditional plan/plan tradicional Ofrece cobertura médica en la que el proveedor de servicios médicos recibe un pago predeterminado por los servicios prestados.

travel expenses/gastos de viaje Costos necesarios para viajes de negocios, tales como transporte, alojamiento y comida, que a menudo son reembolsados por la empresa.

Treasury bill/letra del Tesoro Una letra que se le puede comprar al gobierno federal por diferentes montos y que devenga intereses. Es un préstamo al gobierno, también denominado en inglés "T-bill."

U

underwriting commission/comisión garantizada Un monto de dinero pagado a un inversionista profesional contratado por un negocio para distribuir acciones o bonos.

unit pricing/precio por unidad Una técnica que permite a los consumidores comparar los precios de varios artículos.

universal life insurance/seguro de vida universal Una combinación de una póliza de seguro de vida y una cuenta de ahorros. Cubre al asegurado durante toda su vida y todo monto que el asegurado paga superior a la prima mínima es transferido a una cuenta de inversión que devenga intereses.

unpaid-balance method/método de saldo adeudado Cálculo de los cargos por financiamiento de una cuenta de crédito basado en la parte del saldo del mes anterior que no se ha pagado.

used-vehicle guide/guía de vehículos usados Guías publicadas mensualmente que dan los precios promedio para los vehículos usados que fueron comprados por los concesionarios durante el mes anterior.

utilities/servicios públicos Servicios tales como teléfono, electricidad, agua y gas.

utility costs/costos de servicios públicos El costo de servicios tales como electricidad, gas, agua, teléfono, teléfono móvil, TV por cable, servicio de Internet y calefacción.

V

variable costs/costos variables Los costos de producción de un producto, que varían en relación directa con el número de unidades producidas, tales como materia prima y embalaje. También, costos de los vehículos que aumentan cuanto más se conduce; por ejemplo, gasolina y neumáticos.

vertical analysis/análisis vertical Se utiliza para determinar qué porcentaje representa un artículo en un estado financiero con respecto al total de dicho estado.

W

weekly time card/tarjeta horaria semanal Un registro diario de la hora en que ingresa al trabajo y la hora en que sale del mismo.

whole life insurance/seguro de vida entera También denominado seguro de vida permanente, ofrece protección financiera para toda la vida.

withdrawal/extracción o retiro Dinero retirado de su cuenta bancaria.

withholding allowances/retención de deducciones El número de personas que están a cargo de un empleado; ayuda a los empleadores a saber cuánto dinero retener a efectos del impuesto federal sobre la renta.

workers' compensation insurance/seguro de compensación laboral Cubre los gastos médicos y pérdida de salario de los empleados si resultan lesionados en su trabajo.

Y

yield/rendimiento La tasa de rentabilidad, generalmente expresada como porcentaje, de una acción, un bono, una letra del Tesoro o una cuenta de ahorros obtenida por un inversionista después de cierto período de tiempo.

ACADEMIC GLOSSARY

Academic Glossary

A

access Freedom or ability to obtain or make use of.

accumulate To increase gradually in quantity or number.

acquire To get as one's own.

adequate Sufficient for a specific requirement.

affect To produce a material influence upon or alteration in.

allocate To set apart or earmark.

alternative Offering or expressing a choice.

annual An event that occurs yearly.

approach The taking of preliminary steps toward a particular purpose.

approximate To come near or be close to in position, value, or characteristics.

assembles To fit together the parts of.

assess To determine the rate or amount of.

assume To take as granted or true.

attain To reach as an end.

authorized To establish by or as if by authority.

available Present or ready for immediate use.

B

benefit A payment or service provided for under an annuity, pension plan, or insurance policy.

C

calculate To determine by mathematical process.

candidate One likely or suited to undergo or to be chosen for something specified.

capable Having general efficiency and ability.

chemical A substance obtained by a chemical process or used for producing a chemical effect.

claim To assert to be rightfully one's own.

classic A typical or perfect example.

coincide To be in accord or agreement.

community A group linked by a common policy.

compound To pay interest on both the accrued interest and the principal.

comprehensive Covering completely or broadly.

compute To determine especially by mathematical means.

consume To utilize economic goods.

consumer One that utilizes economic goods.

convince Demonstrate, prove.

create To produce through imaginative skill.

currency Something (as coins, treasury notes, and banknotes) that is in circulation as a medium of exchange; paper money in circulation.

D

device Something devised or contrived as a plan procedure, or technique.

display A setting or presentation of something in open view.

distortions To twist out of a natural, normal, original shape or condition.

distribution The act or process of distributing, to divide among several or many.

document An original or official paper relied on as the basis, proof, or support of something.

duration The time during which something exists or lasts.

E

economy The structure of economic life in a country, area or period. A social science concerned chiefly with description and analysis of the production, distribution, and consumption of goods and services.

energy Usable power.

estimate To produce a statement of the approximate cost of.

exposure The condition of being unprotected.

F

factor A quantity by which a given quantity is multiplied or divided in order to indicate a difference in measurement.

features Something offered to the public or advertised as particularly attractive.

fee A sum paid or charged for a service.

finance To raise or provide funds or capital.

fixed Not subject to change or fluctuation.

fluctuate To ebb and flow in waves.

formula A general fact, rule, or principle expressed in usual mathematical symbols.

foundation A basis on which something stands.

G

generate To bring into existence.

granting To permit as a right, privilege, or favor.

I

identify To practice psychological determination.

impose To establish or imply by authority.

incentive Something that incites or has a tendency to incite to determination or action.

income A gain or recurrent benefit usually measured in money that derives from capital or labor.

index A number (as a ratio) derived from a series of observations and used as an indicator or measure.

indication To point out or point to.

injury An act that damages or hurts.

initial Of or relating to the beginning.

internally Of, relating to, or occurring within the confines of an organized structure.

interpret To explain or tell the meaning of.

intervals A space of time between events or states.

invest To commit money in order to earn a financial return.

investigate To observe or study by close examination.

issues The action of going, coming, or flowing out.

itemizes To set down in detail or by particulars.

L

legal Of, relating to, or having the characteristics of the profession of law or one of its members.

levy To impose or collect by legal authority.

license To give permission or consent to.

M

mature Having completed natural growth and development.

maximize To make the most of.

media A medium of cultivation, conveyance, or expression.

medical Of, relating to, or concerned with physicians or the practice of medicine.

method A way, technique, or process of or for doing something.

modify To make minor changes in.

monitor To watch, keep track of, or check, usually for a special purpose.

motive Moving or tending to move to action.

O

objective Something toward which effort is directed.

obtain To gain or attain usually by planned action or effort.

occupy To reside in as an owner or tenant.

P

panel A group of persons who discuss a topic of public interest before an audience.

percent Reckoned on the basis of a whole divided into one hundred parts.

period The interval of time required for a cyclic motion or phenomenon to complete a cycle and begin to repeat itself.

physical Having a material existence.

policy A writing whereby a contract of insurance is made.

portion An often limited part set off or abstracted from a whole.

potential Something that can develop or become actual.

precise Exactly or sharply defined or stated.

previous Going before in time or order.

primary First in order of time or development.

principal A capital sum placed at interest, due as a debt, or used as a fund.

prior Earlier in time or in order.

proceeds To come forth from a source.

project A planned undertaking.

promote To present (merchandise) for buyer acceptance through advertising, publicity, or discounting.

published To make public announcement of.

purchase Something obtained especially for a price in money or its equivalent.

Q

quote To state the current price.

R

rate A charge, payment or price fixed according to a ratio, scale, or standard.

ratio The relationship in quantity, amount, or size between two or more things.

recover To make up for.

register A written record containing regular entries of items or details.

require To claim or ask for by right and authority.

S

secure To give pledge of payment to a creditor or of an obligation.

service Useful labor that does not produce a tangible commodity.

specific Sharing or being those properties of something that allow it to be referred to a particular category.

specify To name or state explicitly in detail.

statistical A quantity (as the mean of a sample) that is computed from a sample.

status State of affairs.

structure Something (as a building) that is constructed.

sufficient Enough to meet the needs of a situation or a proposed end.

sustain To carry or withstand.

T

technique A methodology of accomplishing a desired aim.

technology A capability given by the practical application of knowledge.

termination The end in time or existence.

transfer To cause to pass from one to another.

U

ultimately In the end, finally, fundamentally, eventually.

utilize To make use of.

V

vary To exhibit or undergo change.

vehicle A means of carrying or transporting something.

volume Involving large quantities.

Index

C

INDEX

INDEX

INDEX

T

U

V

W

Y

Z